SELECTED STATUTES AND REGULATIONS

CONSUMER TRANSACTIONS

FIFTH EDITION

by

MICHAEL M. GREENFIELD
George Alexander Madill Professor of
Contracts and Commercial Law
Washington University in St. Louis

FOUNDATION PRESS

2009

© 1983, 1991, 1999, 2003 FOUNDATION PRESS
© 2009 By THOMSON REUTERS/FOUNDATION PRESS

195 Broadway, 9th Floort
New York, NY 10007
Phone Toll Free 1–877–888–1330
Fax (212) 367–6799
foundation–press.com

Printed in the United States of America

ISBN 978–1–59941–368–6

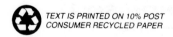

TEXT IS PRINTED ON 10% POST CONSUMER RECYCLED PAPER

PREFACE

This supplement contains the statutory and regulatory materials referred to in CONSUMER TRANSACTIONS (5th ed.). The federal materials appear first, roughly in the order in which they appear in the casebook. State materials follow, again roughly in the order in which they appear in the casebook.

Omissions are numerous. The table of sections that precedes each lengthy statute indicates which sections of the statute are omitted in their entirety. When only a portion of a section is omitted, an ellipsis appears at the point of the omission. Most of the official commentary to the uniform acts is omitted without any indication of the omission.

MICHAEL M. GREENFIELD

*

TABLE OF CONTENTS

PART TWO.   STATE STATUTES

ALPHABETICAL LISTING

Page

SELECTED STATUTES AND REGULATIONS

CONSUMER TRANSACTIONS

*

PART ONE. FEDERAL STATUTES AND REGULATIONS

ODOMETER REGULATION

SUBTITLE VI—MOTOR VEHICLE AND DRIVER PROGRAMS

CHAPTER 327—ODOMETERS

49 U.S.C. §§ 32701–32711

Table of Sections

---

§ 32701. Findings and purposes

(a) Findings.—Congress finds that—

(1) buyers of motor vehicles rely heavily on the odometer reading as an index of the condition and value of a vehicle;

(2) buyers are entitled to rely on the odometer reading as an accurate indication of the mileage of the vehicle;

(3) an accurate indication of the mileage assists a buyer in deciding on the safety and reliability of the vehicle; and

(4) motor vehicles move in, or affect, interstate and foreign commerce.

(b) Purposes.—The purposes of this chapter are—

(1) to prohibit tampering with motor vehicle odometers; and

(2) to provide safeguards to protect purchasers in the sale of motor vehicles with altered or reset odometers.

§ 32702. Definitions

In this chapter—

(1) "auction company" means a person taking possession of a motor vehicle owned by another to sell at an auction.

(2) "dealer" means a person that sold at least 5 motor vehicles during the prior 12 months to buyers that in good faith bought the vehicles other than for resale.

(3) "distributor" means a person that sold at least 5 motor vehicles during the prior 12 months for resale.

(4) "leased motor vehicle" means a motor vehicle leased to a person for at least 4 months by a lessor that leased at least 5 vehicles during the prior 12 months.

(5) "odometer" means an instrument for measuring and recording the distance a motor vehicle is driven, but does not include an auxiliary instrument designed to be reset by the operator of the vehicle to record mileage of a trip.

(6) "repair" and "replace" mean to restore to a sound working condition by replacing any part of an odometer or by correcting any inoperative part of an odometer.

(7) "title" means the certificate of title or other document issued by the State indicating ownership.

(8) "transfer" means to change ownership by sale, gift, or any other means.

§ 32703. Preventing tampering

A person may not—

(1) advertise for sale, sell, use, install, or have installed, a device that makes an odometer of a motor vehicle register a mileage different from the mileage the vehicle was driven, as registered by the odometer within the designed tolerance of the manufacturer of the odometer;

(2) disconnect, reset, alter, or have disconnected, reset, or altered, an odometer of a motor vehicle intending to change the mileage registered by the odometer;

(3) with intent to defraud, operate a motor vehicle on a street, road, or highway if the person knows that the odometer of the vehicle is disconnected or not operating; or

(4) conspire to violate this section or section 32704 or 32705 of this title.

§ 32704. Service, repair, and replacement

(a) **Adjusting mileage.**—A person may service, repair, or replace an odometer of a motor vehicle if the mileage registered by the odometer remains the same as before the service, repair, or replacement. If the mileage cannot remain the same—

(1) the person shall adjust the odometer to read zero; and

(2) the owner of the vehicle or agent of the owner shall attach a written notice to the left door frame of the vehicle specifying the mileage before the service, repair, or replacement and the date of the service, repair, or replacement.

(b) Removing or altering notice.—A person may not, with intent to defraud, remove or alter a notice attached to a motor vehicle as required by this section.

§ 32705. Disclosure requirements on transfer of motor vehicles

(a)(1) Disclosure requirements.—Under regulations prescribed by the Secretary of Transportation that include the way in which information is disclosed and retained under this section, a person transferring ownership of a motor vehicle shall give the transferee the following written disclosure:

(A) Disclosure of the cumulative mileage registered on the odometer.

(B) Disclosure that the actual mileage is unknown, if the transferor knows that the odometer reading is different from the number of miles the vehicle has actually traveled.

(2) A person transferring ownership of a motor vehicle may not violate a regulation prescribed under this section or give a false statement to the transferee in making the disclosure required by such a regulation.

(3) A person acquiring a motor vehicle for resale may not accept a written disclosure under this section unless it is complete.

(4)(A) This subsection shall apply to all transfers of motor vehicles (unless otherwise exempted by the Secretary by regulation), except in the case of transfers of new motor vehicles from a vehicle manufacturer jointly to a dealer and a person engaged in the business of renting or leasing vehicles for a period of 30 days or less.

(B) For purposes of subparagraph (A), the term "new motor vehicle" means any motor vehicle driven with no more than the limited use necessary in moving, transporting, or road testing such vehicle prior to delivery from the vehicle manufacturer to a dealer, but in no event shall the odometer reading of such vehicle exceed 300 miles.

(5) The Secretary may exempt such classes or categories of vehicles as the Secretary deems appropriate from these requirements. Until such time as the Secretary amends or modifies the regulations set forth in 49 CFR 580.6, such regulations shall have full force and effect.

(b) Mileage statement requirement for licensing.—(1) A motor vehicle the ownership of which is transferred may not be licensed for use in a State unless the transferee, in submitting an application to a State for the title on which the license will be issued, includes with the application the transferor's title and, if that title contains the space referred to in paragraph (3)(A)(iii) of this subsection, a statement, signed and dated by the

3

transferor, of the mileage disclosure required under subsection (a) of this section. This paragraph does not apply to a transfer of ownership of a motor vehicle that has not been licensed before the transfer.

(2)(A) Under regulations prescribed by the Secretary, if the title to a motor vehicle issued to a transferor by a State is in the possession of a lienholder when the transferor transfers ownership of the vehicle, the transferor may use a written power of attorney (if allowed by State law) in making the mileage disclosure required under subsection (a) of this section. Regulations prescribed under this paragraph—

(i) shall prescribe the form of the power of attorney;

(ii) shall provide that the form be printed by means of a secure printing process (or other secure process);

(iii) shall provide that the State issue the form to the transferee;

(iv) shall provide that the person exercising the power of attorney retain a copy and submit the original to the State with a copy of the title showing the restatement of the mileage;

(v) may require that the State retain the power of attorney and the copy of the title for an appropriate period or that the State adopt alternative measures consistent with section 32701(b) of this title, after considering the costs to the State;

(vi) shall ensure that the mileage at the time of transfer be disclosed on the power of attorney document;

(vii) shall ensure that the mileage be restated exactly by the person exercising the power of attorney in the space referred to in paragraph (3)(A)(iii) of this subsection;

(viii) may not require that a motor vehicle be titled in the State in which the power of attorney was issued;

(ix) shall consider the need to facilitate normal commercial transactions in the sale or exchange of motor vehicles; and

(x) shall provide other conditions the Secretary considers appropriate.

(B) Section 32709(a) and (b) applies to a person granting or granted a power of attorney under this paragraph.

(3)(A) A motor vehicle the ownership of which is transferred may not be licensed for use in a State unless the title issued by the State to the transferee—

(i) is produced by means of a secure printing process (or other secure process);

(ii) indicates the mileage disclosure required to be made under subsection (a) of this section; and

(iii) contains a space for the transferee to disclose the mileage at the time of a future transfer and to sign and date the disclosure.

(B) Subparagraph (A) of this paragraph does not require a State to verify, or preclude a State from verifying, the mileage information contained in the title.

(c) Leased motor vehicles.—(1) For a leased motor vehicle, the regulations prescribed under subsection (a) of this section shall require written disclosure about mileage to be made by the lessee to the lessor when the lessor transfers ownership of that vehicle.

(2) Under those regulations, the lessor shall provide written notice to the lessee of—

(A) the lessee's mileage disclosure requirements under paragraph (1) of this subsection; and

(B) the penalties for failure to comply with those requirements.

(3) The lessor shall retain the disclosures made by a lessee under paragraph (1) of this subsection for at least 4 years following the date the lessor transfers the leased motor vehicle.

(4) If the lessor transfers ownership of a leased motor vehicle without obtaining possession of the vehicle, the lessor, in making the disclosure required by subsection (a) of this section, may indicate on the title the mileage disclosed by the lessee under paragraph (1) of this subsection unless the lessor has reason to believe that the disclosure by the lessee does not reflect the actual mileage of the vehicle.

(d) State alternate vehicle mileage disclosure requirements.—The requirements of subsections (b) and (c)(1) of this section on the disclosure of motor vehicle mileage when motor vehicles are transferred or leased apply in a State unless the State has in effect alternate motor vehicle mileage disclosure requirements approved by the Secretary. The Secretary shall approve alternate motor vehicle mileage disclosure requirements submitted by a State unless the Secretary decides that the requirements are not consistent with the purpose of the disclosure required by subsection (b) or (c), as the case may be.

(e) Auction sales.—If a motor vehicle is sold at an auction, the auction company conducting the auction shall maintain the following records for at least 4 years after the date of the sale:

(1) the name of the most recent owner of the motor vehicle (except the auction company) and the name of the buyer of the motor vehicle.

(2) the vehicle identification number required under chapter 301 or 331 of this title.

(3) the odometer reading on the date the auction company took possession of the motor vehicle.

(f) Application and revision of State law.—(1) Except as provided in paragraph (2) of this subsection, subsections (b)–(e) of this section apply to the transfer of a motor vehicle after April 28, 1989.

(2) If a State requests, the Secretary shall assist the State in revising its laws to comply with subsection (b) of this section. If a State requires time beyond April 28, 1989, to revise its laws to achieve compliance, the Secretary, on request of the State, may grant additional time that the Secretary considers reasonable by publishing a notice in the Federal Register. The notice shall include the reasons for granting the additional time. In granting additional time, the Secretary shall ensure that the State is making reasonable efforts to achieve compliance.

§ 32706. Inspections, investigations, and records

(a) **Authority to inspect and investigate.**—Subject to section 32707 of this title, the Secretary of Transportation may conduct an inspection or investigation necessary to carry out this chapter or a regulation prescribed or order issued under this chapter. The Secretary shall cooperate with State and local officials to the greatest extent possible in conducting an inspection or investigation. The Secretary may give the Attorney General information about a violation of this chapter or a regulation prescribed or order issued under this chapter.

(b) **Entry, inspection, and impoundment.**—(1) In carrying out subsection (a) of this section, an officer or employee designated by the Secretary, on display of proper credentials and written notice to the owner, operator, or agent in charge, may—

(A) enter and inspect commercial premises in which a motor vehicle or motor vehicle equipment is manufactured, held for shipment or sale, maintained, or repaired;

(B) enter and inspect noncommercial premises in which the Secretary reasonably believes there is a motor vehicle or motor vehicle equipment that is an object of a violation of this chapter;

(C) inspect that motor vehicle or motor vehicle equipment; and

(D) impound for not more than 72 hours for inspection a motor vehicle or motor vehicle equipment that the Secretary reasonably believes is an object of a violation of this chapter.

(2) An inspection or impoundment under this subsection shall be conducted at a reasonable time, in a reasonable way, and with reasonable promptness. The written notice may consist of a warrant issued under section 32707 of this title.

(c) **Reasonable compensation.**—When the Secretary impounds for inspection a motor vehicle (except a vehicle subject to subchapter I of chapter 135 of this title) or motor vehicle equipment under subsection (b)(1)(D) of this section, the Secretary shall pay reasonable compensation to the owner of the vehicle or equipment if the inspection or impoundment results in denial of use, or reduction in value, of the vehicle or equipment.

(d) **Records and information requirements.**—(1) To enable the Secretary to decide whether a dealer or distributor is complying with this chapter and regulations prescribed and orders issued under this chapter, the Secretary may require the dealer or distributor—

(A) to keep records;

(B) to provide information from those records if the Secretary states the purpose for requiring the information and identifies the information to the fullest extent practicable; and

(C) to allow an officer or employee designated by the Secretary to inspect relevant records of the dealer or distributor.

(2) This subsection and subsection (e)(1)(B) of this section do not authorize the Secretary to require a dealer or distributor to provide information on a regular periodic basis.

(e) Administrative authority and civil actions to enforce.—(1) In carrying out this chapter, the Secretary may—

(A) inspect and copy records of any person at reasonable times;

(B) order a person to file written reports or answers to specific questions, including reports or answers under oath; and

(C) conduct hearings, administer oaths, take testimony, and require (by subpena or otherwise) the appearance and testimony of witnesses and the production of records the Secretary considers advisable.

(2) A witness summoned under this subsection is entitled to the same fee and mileage the witness would have been paid in a court of the United States.

(3) A civil action to enforce a subpena or order of the Secretary under this subsection may be brought in the United States district court for any judicial district in which the proceeding by the Secretary is conducted. The court may punish a failure to obey an order of the court to comply with the subpena or order of the Secretary as a contempt of court.

(f) Prohibitions.—A person may not fail to keep records, refuse access to or copying of records, fail to make reports or provide information, fail to allow entry or inspection, or fail to permit impoundment, as required under this section.

§ 32707. Administrative warrants

(a) Definition.—In this section, "probable cause" means a valid public interest in the effective enforcement of this chapter or a regulation prescribed under this chapter sufficient to justify the inspection or impoundment in the circumstances stated in an application for a warrant under this section.

(b) Warrant requirement and issuance.—(1) Except as provided in paragraph (4) of this subsection, an inspection or impoundment under section 32706 of this title may be carried out only after a warrant is obtained.

(2) A judge of a court of the United States or a State court of record or a United States magistrate may issue a warrant for an inspection or impoundment under section 32706 of this title within the territorial jurisdiction of the court or magistrate. The warrant must be based on an affidavit that—

(A) establishes probable cause to issue the warrant; and

(B) is sworn to before the judge or magistrate by an officer or employee who knows the facts alleged in the affidavit.

(3) The judge or magistrate shall issue the warrant when the judge or magistrate decides there is a reasonable basis for believing that probable cause exists to issue the warrant. The warrant must—

(A) identify the premises, property, or motor vehicle to be inspected and the items or type of property to be impounded;

(B) state the purpose of the inspection, the basis for issuing the warrant, and the name of the affiant;

(C) direct an individual authorized under section 32706 of this title to inspect the premises, property, or vehicle for the purpose stated in the warrant and, when appropriate, to impound the property specified in the warrant;

(D) direct that the warrant be served during the hours specified in the warrant; and

(E) name the judge or magistrate with whom proof of service is to be filed.

(4) A warrant under this section is not required when—

(A) the owner, operator, or agent in charge of the premises consents;

(B) it is reasonable to believe that the mobility of the motor vehicle to be inspected makes it impractical to obtain a warrant;

(C) an application for a warrant cannot be made because of an emergency;

(D) records are to be inspected and copied under section 32706(e)(1)(A) of this title; or

(E) a warrant is not constitutionally required.

(c) Service and impoundment of property.—(1) A warrant issued under this section must be served and proof of service filed not later than 10 days after its issuance date. The judge or magistrate may allow additional time in the warrant if the Secretary of Transportation demonstrates a need for additional time. Proof of service must be filed promptly with a written inventory of the property impounded under the warrant. The inventory shall be made in the presence of the individual serving the warrant and the individual from whose possession or premises the property was impounded, or if that individual is not present, a credible individual except the individual making the inventory. The individual serving the warrant shall verify the inventory. On request, the judge or magistrate shall send a copy of the inventory to the individual from whose possession or premises the property was impounded and to the applicant for the warrant.

(2) When property is impounded under a warrant, the individual serving the warrant shall—

    (A) give the person from whose possession or premises the property was impounded a copy of the warrant and a receipt for the property; or

    (B) leave the copy and receipt at the place from which the property was impounded.

(3) The judge or magistrate shall file the warrant, proof of service, and all documents filed about the warrant with the clerk of the United States district court for the judicial district in which the inspection is made.

§ 32708. Confidentiality of information

(a) General.—Information obtained by the Secretary of Transportation under this chapter related to a confidential matter referred to in section 1905 of title 18 may be disclosed only—

(1) to another officer or employee of the United States Government for use in carrying out this chapter; or

(2) in a proceeding under this chapter.

(b) Withholding information from Congress.—This section does not authorize information to be withheld from a committee of Congress authorized to have the information.

§ 32709. Penalties and enforcement

(a) Civil penalty.—(1) A person that violates this chapter or a regulation prescribed or order issued under this chapter is liable to the United States Government for a civil penalty of not more than $2,000 for each violation. A separate violation occurs for each motor vehicle or device involved in the violation. The maximum penalty under this subsection for a related series of violations is $100,000.

(2) The Secretary of Transportation shall impose a civil penalty under this subsection. The Attorney General shall bring a civil action to collect the penalty. Before referring a penalty claim to the Attorney General, the Secretary may compromise the amount of the penalty. Before compromising the amount of the penalty, the Secretary shall give the person charged with a violation an opportunity to establish that the violation did not occur.

(3) In determining the amount of a civil penalty under this subsection, the Secretary shall consider—

    (A) the nature, circumstances, extent, and gravity of the violation;

(B) with respect to the violator, the degree of culpability, any history of prior violations, the ability to pay, and any effect on the ability to continue doing business; and

(C) other matters that justice requires.

(b) Criminal penalty.—A person that knowingly and willfully violates this chapter or a regulation prescribed or order issued under this chapter shall be fined under title 18, imprisoned for not more than 3 years, or both. If the person is a corporation, the penalties of this subsection also apply to a director, officer, or individual agent of a corporation who knowingly and willfully authorizes, orders, or performs an act in violation of this chapter or a regulation prescribed or order issued under this chapter without regard to penalties imposed on the corporation.

(c) Civil actions by Attorney General.—The Attorney General may bring a civil action to enjoin a violation of this chapter or a regulation prescribed or order issued under this chapter. The action may be brought in the United States district court for the judicial district in which the violation occurred or the defendant is found, resides, or does business. Process in the action may be served in any other judicial district in which the defendant resides or is found. A subpena for a witness in the action may be served in any judicial district.

(d) Civil actions by States.—(1) When a person violates this chapter or a regulation prescribed or order issued under this chapter, the chief law enforcement officer of the State in which the violation occurs may bring a civil action—

(A) to enjoin the violation; or

(B) to recover amounts for which the person is liable under section 32710 of this title for each person on whose behalf the action is brought.

(2) An action under this subsection may be brought in an appropriate United States district court or in a State court of competent jurisdiction. The action must be brought not later than 2 years after the claim accrues.

§ 32710. Civil actions by private persons

(a) Violation and amount of damages.—A person that violates this chapter or a regulation prescribed or order issued under this chapter, with intent to defraud, is liable for 3 times the actual damages or $1,500, whichever is greater.

(b) Civil actions.—A person may bring a civil action to enforce a claim under this section in an appropriate United States district court or in another court of competent jurisdiction. The action must be brought not later than 2 years after the claim accrues. The court shall award costs and a reasonable attorney's fee to the person when a judgment is entered for that person.

§ 32711. Relationship to State law

Except to the extent that State law is inconsistent with this chapter, this chapter does not—

(1) affect a State law on disconnecting, altering, or tampering with an odometer with intent to defraud; or

(2) exempt a person from complying with that law.

NATIONAL HIGHWAY TRAFFIC SAFETY ADMINISTRATION, DEPARTMENT OF TRANSPORTATION

ODOMETER DISCLOSURE REQUIREMENTS

49 C.F.R. Part 580

Table of Sections

---

§ 580.3 Definitions

All terms defined in sections 2 and 402 of the Motor Vehicle Information and Cost Savings Act are used in their statutory meaning. Other terms used in this part are defined as follows:

Lessee means any person, or the agent for any person, to whom a motor vehicle has been leased for a term of at least 4 months.

Lessor means any person, or the agent for any person, who has leased 5 or more motor vehicles in the past 12 months.

Mileage means actual distance that a vehicle has traveled.

Original power of attorney means, for single copy forms, the document set forth by secure process which is issued by the State, and, for multicopy forms, any and all copies set forth by secure process which are issued by the State.

Secure printing process or other secure process means any process which deters and detects counterfeiting and/or unauthorized reproduction and allows alterations to be visible to the naked eye.

Transferee means any person to whom ownership of a motor vehicle is transferred, by purchase, gift, or any means other than by the creation of a security interest, and any person who, as agent, signs an odometer disclosure statement for the transferee.

Transferor means any person who transfers his ownership of a motor vehicle by sale, gift, or any means other than by the creation of a security interest, and any person who, as agent, signs an odometer disclosure statement for the transferor.

§ 580.4   Security of title documents and power of attorney forms

Each title shall be set forth by means of a secure printing process or other secure process. In addition, power of attorney forms issued pursuant to §§ 580.13 and 580.14 and documents which are used to reassign the title shall be issued by the State and shall be set forth by a secure process.

§ 580.5   Disclosure of odometer information

(a) Each title, at the time it is issued to the transferee, must contain the mileage disclosed by the transferor when ownership of the vehicle was transferred and contain a space for the information required to be disclosed under paragraphs (c), (d), (e) and (f) of this section at the time of future transfer.

(b) Any documents which are used to reassign a title shall contain a space for the information required to be disclosed under paragraphs (c), (d), (e) and (f) of this section at the time of transfer of ownership.

(c) In connection with the transfer of ownership of a motor vehicle, each transferor shall disclose the mileage to the transferee in writing on the title or, except as noted below, on the document being used to reassign the title. In the case of a transferor in whose name the vehicle is titled, the transferor shall disclose the mileage on the title, and not on a reassignment document. This written disclosure must be signed by the transferor, including the printed name. In connection with the transfer of ownership of a motor vehicle in which more than one person is a transferor, only one transferor need sign the written disclosure. In addition to the signature and printed name of the transferor, the written disclosure must contain the following information:

(1) The odometer reading at the time of transfer (not to include tenths of miles);

(2) The date of transfer;

(3) The transferor's name and current address;

(4) The transferee's name and current address; and

(5) The identity of the vehicle, including its make, model, year, and body type, and its vehicle identification number.

(d) In addition to the information provided under paragraph (c) of this section, the statement shall refer to the Federal law and shall state that failure to complete or providing false information may result in fines and/or imprisonment. Reference may also be made to applicable State law.

(e) In addition to the information provided under paragraphs (c) and (d) of this section,

(1) The transferor shall certify that to the best of his knowledge the odometer reading reflects the actual mileage, or;

(2) If the transferor knows that the odometer reading reflects the amount of mileage in excess of the designed mechanical odometer limit, he shall include a statement to that effect; or

(3) If the transferor knows that the odometer reading differs from the mileage and that the difference is greater than that caused by odometer calibration error, he shall include a statement that the odometer reading does not reflect the actual mileage, and should not be relied upon. This statement shall also include a warning notice to alert the transferee that a discrepancy exists between the odometer reading and the actual mileage.

(f) The transferee shall sign the disclosure statement, print his name, and return a copy to his transferor.

(g) If the vehicle has not been titled or if the title does not contain a space for the information required, the written disclosure shall be executed as a separate document.

(h) No person shall sign an odometer disclosure statement as both the transferor and transferee in the same transaction, unless permitted by §§ 580.13 or 580.14.

§ 580.6   [Reserved]

§ 580.7   Disclosure of odometer information for leased motor vehicles

(a) Before executing any transfer of ownership document, each lessor of a leased motor vehicle shall notify the lessee in writing that the lessee is required to provide a written disclosure to the lessor regarding the mileage. This notice shall contain a reference to the federal law and shall state that failure to complete or providing false information may result in fines and/or imprisonment. Reference may also be made to applicable State law.

(b) In connection with the transfer of ownership of the leased motor vehicle, the lessee shall furnish to the lessor a written statement regarding the mileage of the vehicle. This statement must be signed by the lessee and, in addition to the information required by paragraph (a) of this section, shall contain the following information:

(1) The printed name of the person making the disclosure;

(2) The current odometer reading (not to include tenths of miles);

(3) The date of the statement;

(4) The lessee's name and current address;

(5) The lessor's name and current address;

(6) The identity of the vehicle, including its make, model, year, and body type, and its vehicle identification number;

(7) The date that the lessor notified the lessee of disclosure requirements;

(8) The date that the completed disclosure statement was received by the lessor; and

(9) The signature of the lessor.

(c) In addition to the information provided under paragraphs (a) and (b) of this section,

(1) The lessee shall certify that to the best of his knowledge the odometer reading reflects the actual mileage; or

(2) If the lessee knows that the odometer reading reflects the amount of mileage in excess of the designed mechanical odometer limit, he shall include a statement to that effect; or

(3) If the lessee knows that the odometer reading differs from the mileage and that the difference is greater than that caused by odometer calibration error, he shall include a statement that the odometer reading is not the actual mileage and should not be relied upon.

(d) If the lessor transfers the leased vehicle without obtaining possession of it, the lessor may indicate on the title the mileage disclosed by the lessee under paragraph (b) and (c) of this section, unless the lessor has reason to believe that the disclosure by the lessee does not reflect the actual mileage of the vehicle.

§ 580.8   Odometer disclosure statement retention

(a) Dealers and distributors of motor vehicles who are required by this part to execute an odometer disclosure statement shall retain for five years a photostat, carbon or other facsimile copy of each odometer mileage statement which they issue and receive. They shall retain all odometer disclosure statements at their primary place of business in an order that is appropriate to business requirements and that permits systematic retrieval.

(b) Lessors shall retain, for five years following the date they transfer ownership of the leased vehicle, each odometer disclosure statement which they receive from a lessee. They shall retain all odometer disclosure statements at their primary place of business in an order that is appropriate to business requirements and that permits systematic retrieval.

(c) Dealers and distributors of motor vehicles who are granted a power of attorney by their transferor pursuant to § 580.13, or by their transferee pursuant to § 580.14, shall retain for five years a photostat, carbon, or other facsimile copy of each power of attorney that they receive. They shall retain all powers of attorney at their primary place of business in an order that is appropriate to business requirements and that permits systematic retrieval.

§ 580.9　Odometer record retention for auction companies

Each auction company shall establish and retain at its primary place of business in an order that is appropriate to business requirements and that permits systematic retrieval, for five years following the date of sale of each motor vehicle, the following records:

(a) The name of the most recent owner (other than the auction company);

(b) The name of the buyer;

(c) The vehicle identification number; and

(d) The odometer reading on the date which the auction company took possession of the motor vehicle.

§ 580.13　Disclosure of odometer information by power of attorney

(a) If the transferor's title is physically held by a lienholder, or if the transferor to whom the title was issued by the State has lost his title and the transferee obtains a duplicate title on behalf of the transferor, and if otherwise permitted by State law, the transferor may give a power of attorney to his transferee for the purpose of mileage disclosure. The power of attorney shall be on a form issued by the State to the transferee that is set forth by means of a secure printing process or other secure process, and shall contain, in part A, a space for the information required to be disclosed under paragraphs (b), (c), (d), and (e) of this section. If a State permits the use of a power of attorney in the situation described in § 580.14(a), the form must also contain, in part B, a space for the information required to be disclosed under § 580.14, and, in part C, a space for the certification required to be made under § 580.15.

(b) In connection with the transfer of ownership of a motor vehicle, each transferor to whom a title was issued by the State whose title is physically held by a lienholder or whose title has been lost, and who elects to give his transferee a power of attorney for the purpose of mileage disclosure, must appoint the transferee his attorney-in-fact for the purpose of mileage disclosure and disclose the mileage on the power of attorney form issued by the State. This written disclosure must be signed by the transferor, including the printed name, and contain the following information:

    (1) The odometer reading at the time of transfer (not to include tenths of miles);

    (2) The date of transfer;

    (3) The transferor's name and current address;

    (4) The transferee's name and current address; and

    (5) The identity of the vehicle, including its make, model year, body type and vehicle identification number.

(c) In addition to the information provided under paragraph (b) of this section, the power of attorney form shall refer to the Federal odometer law and state that providing false information or the failure of the person granted the power of attorney to submit the form to the State may result in fines and/or imprisonment. Reference may also be made to applicable State law.

(d) In addition to the information provided under paragraphs (b) and (c) of this section:

    (1) The transferor shall certify that to the best of his knowledge the odometer reading reflects the actual mileage; or

    (2) If the transferor knows that the odometer reading reflects mileage in excess of the designed mechanical odometer limit, he shall include a statement to that effect; or

    (3) If the transferor knows that the odometer reading differs from the mileage and the difference is greater than that caused by a calibration error, he shall include a statement that the odometer reading does not reflect the actual mileage and should not be relied upon. This statement shall also include a warning notice to alert the transferee that a discrepancy exists between the odometer reading and the actual mileage.

(e) The transferee shall sign the power of attorney form, print his name, and return a copy of the power of attorney form to the transferor.

(f) Upon receipt of the transferor's title, the transferee shall complete the space for mileage disclosure on the title exactly as the mileage was disclosed by the transferor on the power of attorney form. The transferee shall submit the original power of attorney form to the State that issued it, with a copy of the transferor's title or with the actual title when the transferee submits a new title application at the same time. The State shall retain the power of attorney form and title for three years or a period equal to the State titling record retention period, whichever is shorter. If the mileage disclosed on the power of attorney form is lower than the mileage appearing on the title, the power of attorney is void and the dealer shall not complete the mileage disclosure on the title.

§ 580.14 Power of attorney to review title documents and acknowledge disclosure

(a) In circumstances where part A of a secure power of attorney form has been used pursuant to § 580.13 of this part, and if otherwise permitted by State law, a transferee may give a power of attorney to his transferor to review the title and any reassignment documents for mileage discrepancies, and if no discrepancies are found, to acknowledge disclosure on the title. The power of attorney shall be on part B of the form referred to in § 580.13(a), which shall contain a space for the information required to be disclosed under paragraphs (b), (c), (d), and (e) of this section and, in part C, a space for the certification required to be made under § 580.15.

(b) The power of attorney must include a mileage disclosure from the transferor to the transferee and must be signed by the transferor, including the printed name, and contain the following information:

(1) The odometer reading at the time of transfer (not to include tenths of miles);

(2) The date of transfer;

(3) The transferor's name and current address;

(4) The transferee's name and current address; and

(5) The identity of the vehicle, including its make, model year, body type and vehicle identification number.

(c) In addition to the information provided under paragraph (b) of this section, the power of attorney form shall refer to the Federal odometer law and state that providing false information or the failure of the person granted the power of attorney to submit the form to the State may result in fines and/or imprisonment. Reference may also be made to applicable State law.

(d) In addition to the information provided under paragraphs (b) and (c) of this section:

(1) The transferor shall certify that to the best of his knowledge the odometer reading reflects the actual mileage;

(2) If the transferor knows that the odometer reading reflects mileage in excess of the designed mechanical odometer limit, he shall include a statement to that effect; or

(3) If the transferor knows that the odometer reading differs from the mileage and the difference is greater than that caused by a calibration error, he shall include a statement that the odometer reading does not reflect the actual mileage and should not be relied upon. This statement shall also include a warning notice to alert the transferee that a discrepancy exists between the odometer reading and the actual mileage.

(e) The transferee shall sign the power of attorney form, and print his name.

(f) The transferor shall give a copy of the power of attorney form to his transferee.

§ 580.15   Certification by person exercising powers of attorney

(a) A person who exercises a power of attorney under both §§ 580.13 and 580.14 must complete a certification that he has disclosed on the title document the mileage as it was provided to him on the power of attorney form, and that upon examination of the title and any reassignment documents, the mileage disclosure he has made on the title pursuant to the power of attorney is greater than that previously stated on the title and reassignment documents. This certification shall be under part C of the same form as the powers of attorney executed under §§ 580.13 and 580.14 and shall include:

(1) The signature and printed name of the person exercising the power of attorney;

(2) The address of the person exercising the power of attorney; and

(3) The date of the certification.

(b) If the mileage reflected by the transferor on the power of attorney is less than that previously stated on the title and any reassignment documents, the power of attorney shall be void.

§ 580.16   Access of transferee to prior title and power of attorney documents

(a) In circumstances in which a power of attorney has been used pursuant to § 580.13 of this part, if a subsequent transferee elects to return to his transferor to sign the disclosure on the title when the transferor obtains the title and does not give his transferor a power of attorney to review the title and reassignment documents, upon the transferee's request, the transferor shall show to the transferee a copy of the power of attorney that he received from his transferor.

(b) Upon request of a purchaser, a transferor who was granted a power of attorney by his transferor and who holds the title to the vehicle in his own name, must show to the purchaser the copy of the previous owner's title and the power of attorney form.

§ 580.17   Exemptions

Notwithstanding the requirements of §§ 580.5 and 580.7:

(a) A transferor or a lessee of any of the following motor vehicles need not disclose the vehicle's odometer mileage:

(1) A vehicle having a Gross Vehicle Weight Rating, as defined in § 571.3 of this title, of more than 16,000 pounds;

(2) A vehicle that is not self-propelled;

19

(3) A vehicle that was manufactured in a model year beginning at least ten years before January 1 of the calendar year in which the transfer occurs; or

Example to paragraph (a)(3): For vehicle transfers occurring during calendar year 1998, model year 1988 or older vehicles are exempt.

(4) A vehicle sold directly by the manufacturer to any agency of the United States in conformity with contractual specifications.

(b) A transferor of a new vehicle prior to its first transfer for purposes other than resale need not disclose the vehicle's odometer mileage.

(c) A lessor of any of the vehicles listed in paragraph (a) of this section need not notify the lessee of any of these vehicles of the disclosure requirements of § 580.7.

APPENDIX B TO PART 580—DISCLOSURE FORM FOR TITLE

ODOMETER DISCLOSURE STATEMENT

Federal law (and State law, if applicable) requires that you state the mileage in connection with the transfer of ownership. Failure to complete or providing a false statement may result in fines and/or imprisonment.

I state that the odometer now reads _____ (no tenths) miles and to the best of my knowledge that it reflects the actual mileage of the vehicle described herein, unless one of the following statements is checked.

___ (1) I hereby certify that to the best of my knowledge the odometer reading reflects the amount of mileage in excess of its mechanical limits.

___ (2) I hereby certify that the odometer reading is NOT the actual mileage. WARNING—ODOMETER DISCREPANCY.

(Transferor's Signature)

(Transferee's Signature)

(Printed name)

(Printed name)

Date of Statement _____
Transferee's Name _____
Transferee's Address _____

(Street)

(City)   (State)   (ZIP Code)

APPENDIX C TO PART 580—SEPARATE DISCLOSURE FORM

ODOMETER DISCLOSURE STATEMENT

Federal law (and State law, if applicable) requires that you state the mileage upon transfer of ownership. Failure to complete or providing a false statement may result in fines and/or imprisonment.

I, _____ (transferor's name, Print) state that the odometer now reads _____ (no tenths) miles and to the best of my knowledge that it reflects the actual mileage of the vehicle described below, unless one of the following statements is checked.

___ (1) I hereby certify that to the best of my knowledge the odometer reading reflects the amount of mileage in excess of its mechanical limits.

___ (2) I hereby certify that the odometer reading is NOT the actual mileage. WARNING—ODOMETER DISCREPANCY.

Make _____ - _____

Model _____

Body Type _____

Vehicle Identification Number _____

Year _____

_____
(Transferor's Signature)

_____
(Printed name)

Transferor's Address _____
(Street)

_____
(City)   (State)   (ZIP Code)

Date of Statement _____

_____
(Transferee's Signature)

_____
(Printed name)

Transferee's Name _____

Transferee's Address _____
(Street)

_____
(City)   (State)   (ZIP Code)

APPENDIX D TO PART 580—DISCLOSURE FORM FOR LEASED VEHICLE

ODOMETER DISCLOSURE STATEMENT (LEASED VEHICLE)

Federal law (and State law, if applicable) requires that the lessee disclose the mileage to the lessor in connection with the transfer of ownership. Failure to complete or making a false statement may result in fines and/or imprisonment. Complete disclosure form below and return to lessor.

I, _____ (name of person making disclosure, Print) state that the odometer now reads _____ (no tenths) miles and to the best of my knowledge that it reflects the actual mileage of the vehicle described below, unless one of the following statements is checked.

___ (1) I hereby certify that to the best of my knowledge the odometer reading reflects the amount of mileage in excess of its mechanical limits.

___ (2) I hereby certify that the odometer reading is NOT the actual mileage.

Make _____

Model _____

Body Type _____   _____

Vehicle Identification Number _____

Year _____

Lessee's Name _____

Lessee's Address _____
                                            (Street)

_____
          (City)   (State)   (ZIP Code)

Lessee's Signature _____

Date of Statement _____

Lessor's Name _____

Lessor's Address _____
                                            (Street)

_____
          (City)   (State)   (ZIP Code)

Date Disclosure Form Sent to Lessee _____

Date Completed Disclosure Form Received from Lessee _____

Lessor's Signature _____

FEDERAL TRADE COMMISSION ACT

15 U.S.C. §§ 41–58

Table of Sections

---

§ 1. Federal Trade Commission Established; Membership; Vacancies; Seal [15 U.S.C. § 41]

A commission is created and established, to be known as the Federal Trade Commission (hereinafter referred to as the Commission), which shall be composed of five Commissioners, who shall be appointed by the President, by and with the advice and consent of the Senate. Not more than three of the Commissioners shall be members of the same political party. . . .

§ 4. Definitions [15 U.S.C. § 44]

The words defined in this section shall have the following meaning when found in this subchapter, to wit:

"Commerce" means commerce among the several States or with foreign nations, or in any Territory of the United States or in the District of Columbia, or between any such Territory and another, or between any such Territory and any State or foreign nation, or between the District of Columbia and any State or Territory or foreign nation.

.   .   .

§ 5. Unfair Methods of Competition Unlawful; Prevention by Commission [15 U.S.C. § 45]

(a) Declaration of unlawfulness; power to prohibit unfair practices; inapplicability to foreign trade

(1) Unfair methods of competition in or affecting commerce, and unfair or deceptive acts or practices in or affecting commerce, are declared unlawful.

(2) The Commission is empowered and directed to prevent persons, partnerships, or corporations, except banks, savings and loan institutions described in section 18(f)(3), Federal credit unions described in section 18f(4), common carriers subject to the Acts to regulate commerce, air carriers and foreign air carriers subject to the Federal Aviation Act of 1958, and persons, partnerships, or corporations insofar as they are subject to the Packers and Stockyards Act, 1921, except as provided in section 406(b) of said Act, from using unfair methods of competition in or affecting commerce and unfair or deceptive acts or practices in or affecting commerce.

.   .   .

(b) Proceeding by Commission; modifying and setting aside orders

Whenever the Commission shall have reason to believe that any such person, partnership, or corporation has been or is using any unfair method of competition or unfair or deceptive act or practice in or affecting commerce, and if it shall appear to the Commission that a proceeding by it in respect thereof would be to the interest of the public, it shall issue and serve upon such person, partnership, or corporation a complaint stating its charges in that respect and containing a notice of a hearing upon a day and at a place therein fixed at least thirty days after the service of said complaint. The person, partnership, or corporation so complained of shall have the right to appear at the place and time so fixed and show cause why an order should not be entered by the Commission requiring such person, partnership, or corporation to cease and desist from the violation of the law so charged in said complaint. Any person, partnership, or corporation may make application, and upon good cause shown may be allowed by the Commission to intervene and appear in said proceeding by counsel or in person. The testimony in any such proceeding shall be reduced to writing and filed in the office of the Commission. If upon such hearing the Commission shall be of the opinion that the method of competition or the act or practice in question is prohibited by this Act, it shall make a report in writing in which it shall state its findings as to the facts and shall issue and cause to be served on such person, partnership, or corporation an order requiring such person, partnership, or corporation to cease and desist from using such method of competition or such act or practice. Until the expiration of the time allowed for filing a petition for review, if no such petition has been duly filed within such time, or, if a petition for review has been filed within such time then until the record in the proceeding has been filed in a court of appeals of the United States, as hereinafter provided, the Commission may at any time, upon such notice and in such manner as it shall deem proper, modify or set aside, in whole or in part, any report or any order made or issued by it under this section. After the expiration of the time allowed for filing a petition for review, if no such petition has been duly filed within such time, the Commission may at any time, after notice and opportunity for hearing, reopen and alter, modify, or set aside, in whole or in part any report or order made or issued by it under this section, whenever in the opinion of the Commission conditions of fact or of law have so changed as to require such action or if the public interest shall so require, except that (1) the said person, partnership, or corporation may, within sixty days after service upon him or it of said report or order entered after such a reopening, obtain a review thereof in the appropriate court of appeals of the United States, in the manner provided in subsection (c) of this section; and (2) in the case of an order, the Commission shall reopen any such order to consider whether such order (including any affirmative relief provision contained in such order) should be altered, modified, or set aside, in whole or in part, if the person, partnership, or corporation involved files a request with the Commission which makes a satisfactory showing that changed conditions of law or fact require such order to be altered, modified, or set aside, in whole or in part. The Commission shall determine whether to alter, modify, or set aside any order of the Commission in response to a request made by a person, partnership, or corporation under paragraph (2) not later than 120 days after the date of the filing of such request.

(c) Review of order; rehearing

Any person, partnership, or corporation required by an order of the Commission to cease and desist from using any method of competition or act or practice may obtain a review of such order in the court of appeals of the United States, within any circuit where the method of competition or the act or practice in question was used or where such person, partnership, or corporation resides or carries on business, by filing in the court, within sixty days from the date of the service of such order, a written petition praying that the order of the Commission be set aside. A copy of such petition shall be forthwith transmitted by the clerk of the court to the Commission, and thereupon the Commission shall file in the court the record in the proceeding, as provided in section 2112 of title 28. Upon such filing of the petition the court shall have jurisdiction of the proceeding and of the question determined therein concurrently with the Commission until the filing of the record and shall have power to make and enter a decree affirming, modifying, or setting aside the order of the Commission, and enforcing the same to the extent that such order is affirmed and to issue such writs as are ancillary to its jurisdiction or are necessary in its judgment to prevent injury to the public or to competitors pendente lite. The findings of the Commission as to the facts, if supported by evidence, shall be conclusive. To the extent that the order of the Commission is affirmed, the court shall thereupon issue its own order commanding obedience to the terms of such order of the Commission. If either party shall apply to the court for leave to adduce additional evidence, and shall show to the satisfaction of the court that such additional evidence is material and that there were reasonable grounds for the failure to adduce such evidence in the proceeding before the Commission, the court may order such additional evidence to be taken before the Commission and to be adduced upon the hearing in such manner and upon such terms and conditions as to the court may seem proper. The Commission may modify its findings as to the facts, or make new findings, by reason of the additional evidence so taken, and it shall file such modified or new findings, which, if supported by evidence, shall be conclusive, and its recommendation, if any, for the modification or setting aside of its original order, with the return of such additional evidence. The judgment and decree of the court shall be final, except that the same shall be subject to review by the Supreme Court upon certiorari, as provided in section 1254 of title 28.

(d) Jurisdiction of court

Upon the filing of the record with it the jurisdiction of the court of appeals of the United States to affirm, enforce, modify, or set aside orders of the Commission shall be exclusive. . . .

(l) Penalty for violation of order; injunctions and other appropriate equitable relief

Any person, partnership, or corporation who violates an order of the Commission after it has become final, and while such order is in effect, shall forfeit and pay to the United States a civil penalty of not more than $10,000 for each violation, which shall accrue to the United States and may be recovered in a civil action brought by the Attorney General of the United States. Each separate violation of such an order shall be a separate offense, except that in a case of a violation through continuing failure to obey or neglect to obey a final order of the Commission, each day of continuance of such failure or neglect shall be deemed a separate offense. In such actions, the United States district courts are empowered to grant mandatory injunctions and such other and further equitable relief as they deem appropriate in the enforcement of such final orders of the Commission.

(m) Civil actions for recovery of penalties for knowing violations of rules and cease and desist orders respecting unfair or deceptive acts or practices; jurisdiction; maximum amount of penalties; continuing violations; de novo determinations; compromise or settlement procedure

(1)(A) The Commission may commence a civil action to recover a civil penalty in a district court of the United States against any person, partnership, or corporation which violates any rule under this Act respecting unfair or deceptive acts or practices (other than an interpretive rule or a rule violation of which the Commission has provided is not an unfair or deceptive act or practice in violation of subsection (a)(1) of this section) with actual knowledge or knowledge fairly implied on the basis of objective circumstances that such act is unfair or deceptive and is prohibited by such rule. In such action, such person, partnership, or corporation shall be liable for a civil penalty of not more than $10,000 for each violation.

(B) If the Commission determines in a proceeding under subsection (b) of this section that any act or practice is unfair or deceptive, and issues a final cease and desist order, other than a consent order, with respect to such act or practice, then the Commission may commence a civil action to obtain a civil penalty in a district court of the United States against any person, partnership, or corporation which engages in such act or practice—

(1) after such cease and desist order becomes final (whether or not such person, partnership, or corporation was subject to such cease and desist order), and

(2) with actual knowledge that such act or practice is unfair or deceptive and is unlawful under subsection (a)(1) of this section.

In such action, such person, partnership, or corporation shall be liable for a civil penalty of not more than $10,000 for each violation.

(C) In the case of a violation through continuing failure to comply with a rule or with subsection (a)(1) of this section, each day of continuance of such failure shall be treated as a separate violation, for purposes of subparagraphs (A) and (B). In determining the amount of such a civil penalty, the court shall take into account the degree of culpability, any history of prior such conduct, ability to pay, effect on ability to continue to do business, and such other matters as justice may require.

(2) If the cease and desist order establishing that the act or practice is unfair or deceptive was not issued against the defendant in a civil penalty action under paragraph (1)(B) the issues of fact in such action against such defendant shall be tried de novo. Upon request of any party to such an action against such defendant, the court shall also review the determination of law made by the Commission in the proceeding under subsection (b) of this section, that the act or practice which was the subject of such proceeding constituted an unfair deceptive act or practice in violation of subsection (a) of this section.

(3) The Commission may compromise or settle any action for a civil penalty if such compromise or settlement is accompanied by a public statement of its reasons and is approved by the court.

(n) Standard of proof; public policy considerations

The Commission shall have no authority under this section or section 18 to declare unlawful an act or practice on the grounds that such act or practice is unfair unless the act or practice causes or is likely to cause substantial injury to consumers which is not reasonably avoidable by consumers themselves and not outweighed by countervailing benefits to consumers or to competition. In determining whether an act or practice is unfair, the Commission may consider established public policies as evidence to be considered with all other evidence. Such public policy considerations may not serve as a primary basis for such determination.

[§ 5a.]   Labels on Products [15 U.S.C. § 45a]

To the extent any person introduces, delivers for introduction, sells, advertises, or offers for sale in commerce a product with a "Made in the U.S.A." or "Made in America" label, or the equivalent thereof, in order to represent that such product was in whole or substantial part of domestic origin, such label shall be consistent with decisions and orders of the Federal Trade Commission issued pursuant to section 5. This section only applies to such labels. Nothing in this section shall preclude the application of other provisions of law relating to labeling. The Commission may periodically consider an appropriate percentage of imported components which may be included in the product and still be reasonably consistent with such decisions and orders. Nothing in this section shall preclude use of such labels for products that contain imported components under the label when the label also discloses such information in a clear and conspicuous manner. The Commission shall administer this section pursuant to section 5 and may from time to time issue rules pursuant to section 553 of Title 5 for such purpose. If a rule is issued, such violation shall be treated by the Commission as a violation of a rule under section 18 regarding unfair or deceptive acts or practices. This section shall be effective upon publication in the Federal Register of a Notice of the provisions of this section. The Commission shall publish such notice within six months after September 13, 1994.

§ 6.   Additional Powers of Commission [15 U.S.C. § 46]

The Commission shall also have power—

(a) Investigation of persons, partnerships, or corporations

To gather and compile information concerning, and to investigate from time to time the organization, business, conduct, practices, and management of any person, partnership, or corporation engaged in or whose business affects commerce, excepting banks, savings and loan institutions described in section 18(f)(3), and common carriers subject to the Act to regulate commerce, and its relation to other persons, partnerships, and corporations.

(b) Reports of persons, partnerships, and corporations

To require, by general or special orders, persons, partnerships, and corporations, engaged in or whose business affects commerce, excepting banks, savings and loan institutions described in section 18(f)(3), Federal credit unions described in section 18(f)(4), and common carriers subject to the Act to regulate commerce, or any class of them, or any of them, respectively, to file with the Commission in such form as the Commission may prescribe annual or special, or both annual and special, reports or answers in writing to specific questions, furnishing to the Commission such information as it may require as to the organization, business, conduct, practices, management, and relation to other corporations, partnerships, and individuals of the respective persons, partnerships, and corporations filing such reports or answers in writing. Such reports and answers shall be made under oath, or otherwise, as the Commission may prescribe, and shall be filed with the Commission within such reasonable period as the Commission may prescribe, unless additional time be granted in any case by the Commission.

. . .

(f) Publication of information; reports

To make public from time to time such portions of the information obtained by it hereunder as are in the public interest; and to make annual and special reports to the Congress and to submit therewith recommendations for additional legislation; and to provide for the publication of its reports and decisions in such form and manner as may be best adapted for public information and use: *Provided,* That the Commission shall not have any authority to make public any trade secret or any commercial or financial information which is obtained from any person and which is privileged or confidential, ...

(g) Classification of corporations; regulations

From time to time classify corporations and (except as provided in section 18(a)(2)) to make rules and regulations for the purpose of carrying out the provisions of this Act.

. . .

Provided, That the exception of "banks, savings and loan institutions described in section 18(f)(3), and common carriers subject to the Act to regulate commerce" from the Commission's powers defined in clauses (a) and (b) of this section, shall not be construed to limit the Commission's authority to gather and compile information, to investigate, or to require reports or answers from, any person, partnership, or corporation to the extent that such action is necessary to the investigation of any person, partnership, or corporation, group of persons, partnerships, or corporations, or industry which is not engaged or is engaged only incidentally in banking, in business as a savings and loan institution, or in business as a common carrier subject to the Act to regulate commerce.

The Commission shall establish a plan designed to substantially reduce burdens imposed upon small businesses as a result of requirements established by the Commission under clause (b) relating to the filing of quarterly financial reports. Such plan shall (1) be established after consultation with small businesses and persons who use the information contained in such quarterly financial reports; (2) provide for a reduction of the number of small businesses required to file such quarterly financial reports; and (3) make revisions in the forms used for such quarterly financial reports for the purpose of reducing the complexity of such forms. . . .

Nothing in this section (other than the provisions of clause (c) and clause (d)) shall apply to the business of insurance, except that the Commission shall have authority to conduct studies and prepare reports relating to the business of insurance. The Commission may exercise such authority only upon receiving a request which is agreed to by a majority of the members of the Committee on Commerce, Science, and Transportation of the Senate or the Committee on Energy and Commerce of the House of Representatives. The authority to conduct any such study shall expire at the end of the Congress during which the request for such study was made.

§ 8. Information and Assistance from Departments [15 U.S.C. § 48]

The several departments and bureaus of the Government when directed by the President shall furnish the Commission, upon its request, all records, papers, and information in their possession relating to any corporation subject to any of the provisions of this Act, and shall detail from time to time such officials and employees to the Commission as he may direct.

§ 9. Documentary Evidence; Depositions; Witnesses [15 U.S.C. § 49]

For the purposes of this Act the Commission, or its duly authorized agent or agents, shall at all reasonable times have access to, for the purpose of examination, and the right to copy any documentary evidence of any person, partnership, or corporation being investigated or proceeded against; and the Commission shall have power to require by subpoena the attendance and testimony of witnesses and the production of all such documentary evidence relating to any matter under investigation. Any member of the Commission may sign subpoenas, and members and examiners of the Commission may administer oaths and affirmations, examine witnesses, and receive evidence.

Such attendance of witnesses, and the production of such documentary evidence, may be required from any place in the United States, at any designated place of hearing. And in case of disobedience to a subpoena the Commission may invoke the aid of any court of the United States in requiring the attendance and testimony of witnesses and the production of documentary evidence.

Any of the district courts of the United States within the jurisdiction of which such inquiry is carried on may, in case of contumacy or refusal to obey a subpoena issued to any person, partnership, or corporation issue an order requiring such person, partnership, or corporation to appear before the Commission, or to produce documentary evidence if so ordered, or to give evidence touching the matter in question; and any failure to obey such order of the court may be punished by such court as a contempt thereof.

Upon the application of the Attorney General of the United States, at the request of the Commission, the district courts of the United States shall have jurisdiction to issue writs of mandamus commanding any person, partnership, or corporation to comply with the provisions of this Act or any order of the Commission made in pursuance thereof.

The Commission may order testimony to be taken by deposition in any proceeding or investigation pending under this Act at any stage of such proceeding or investigation. Such depositions may be taken before any person designated by the Commission and having power to administer oaths. Such testimony shall be reduced to writing by the person taking the deposition, or under his direction, and shall then be subscribed by the deponent. Any person may be compelled to appear and depose and to produce documentary evidence in the same manner as witnesses may be compelled to appear and testify and produce documentary evidence before the Commission as hereinbefore provided.

Witnesses summoned before the Commission shall be paid the same fees and mileage that are paid witnesses in the courts of the United States and witnesses whose depositions are taken and the persons taking the same shall severally be entitled to the same fees as are paid for like services in the courts of the United States.

§ 10.   Offenses and Penalties [15 U.S.C. § 50]

Any person who shall neglect or refuse to attend and testify, or to answer any lawful inquiry or to produce any documentary evidence, if in his power to do so, in obedience to an order of a district court of the United States directing compliance with the subpoena or lawful requirement of the Commission, shall be guilty of an offense and upon conviction thereof by a court of competent jurisdiction shall be punished by a fine of not less than $1,000 nor more than $5,000, or by imprisonment for not more than one year, or by both such fine and imprisonment.

Any person who shall willfully make, or cause to be made, any false entry or statement of fact in any report required to be made under this Act, or who shall willfully make, or cause to be made, any false entry in any account, record, or memorandum kept by any person, partnership, or corporation subject to this Act, or who shall willfully neglect or fail to make, or to cause to be made, full, true, and correct entries in such accounts, records, or memoranda of all facts and transactions appertaining to the business of such person, partnership, or corporation, or who shall willfully remove out of the jurisdiction of the United States, or willfully mutilate, alter, or by any other means falsify any documentary evidence of such person, partnership, or corporation, or who shall willfully refuse to submit to the Commission or to any of its authorized agents, for the purpose of inspection and taking copies, any documentary evidence of such person, partnership, or corporation in his possession or within his control, shall be deemed guilty of an offense against the United States, and shall be subject, upon conviction in any court of the United States of competent jurisdiction, to a fine of not less than $1,000 nor more than $5,000, or to imprisonment for a term of not more than three years, or to both such fine and imprisonment.

.   .   .

§ 11. Effect on Other Statutory Provisions [15 U.S.C. § 51]

Nothing contained in this Act shall be construed to prevent or interfere with the enforcement of the provisions of the antitrust Acts or the Acts to regulate commerce, nor shall anything contained in this Act be construed to alter, modify, or repeal the said antitrust Acts or the Acts to regulate commerce or any part or parts thereof.

§ 12. Dissemination of False Advertisements [15 U.S.C. § 52]

(a) Unlawfulness

It shall be unlawful for any person, partnership, or corporation to disseminate, or cause to be disseminated, any false advertisement—

(1) By United States mails, or in or having an effect upon commerce, by any means, for the purpose of inducing, or which is likely to induce, directly or indirectly the purchase of food, drugs, devices, services, or cosmetics; or

(2) By any means, for the purpose of inducing, or which is likely to induce, directly or indirectly, the purchase in or having an effect upon commerce, of food, drugs, devices, services, or cosmetics.

(b) Unfair or Deceptive Act or Practice

The dissemination or the causing to be disseminated of any false advertisement within the provisions of subsection (a) of this section shall be an unfair or deceptive act or practice in or affecting commerce within the meaning of section 5.

§ 13. False Advertisements; Injunctions and Restraining Orders [15 U.S.C. § 53]

(a) Power of Commission; jurisdiction of courts

Whenever the Commission has reason to believe—

(1) that any person, partnership, or corporation is engaged in, or is about to engage in, the dissemination or the causing of the dissemination of any advertisement in violation of section 12, and

(2) that the enjoining thereof pending the issuance of a complaint by the Commission under section 5, and until such complaint is dismissed by the Commission or set aside by the court on review, or the order of the Commission to cease and desist made thereon has become final within the meaning of section 5, would be to the interest of the public,

the Commission by any of its attorneys designated by it for such purpose may bring suit in a district court of the United States or in the United States court of any Territory, to enjoin the dissemination or the causing of the dissemination of such advertisement. Upon proper showing a temporary injunction or restraining order shall be granted without bond. Any such suit may be brought where such person, partnership, or corporation resides or transacts business, or wherever venue is proper under section 1391 of Title 28.   . . .

(b) Temporary restraining orders; preliminary injunctions

Whenever the Commission has reason to believe—

(1) that any person, partnership, or corporation is violating, or is about to violate, any provision of law enforced by the Federal Trade Commission, and

(2) that the enjoining thereof pending the issuance of a complaint by the Commission and until such complaint is dismissed by the Commission or set aside by the court on review, or until the order of the Commission made thereon has become final, would be in the interest of the public—

the Commission by any of its attorneys designated by it for such purpose may bring suit in a district court of the United States to enjoin any such act or practice. Upon a proper showing that, weighing the equities and considering the Commission's likelihood of ultimate success, such action would be in the public interest, and after notice to the defendant, a temporary restraining order or a preliminary injunction may be granted without bond: *Provided, however,* That if a complaint is not filed within such period (not exceeding 20 days) as may be specified by the court after issuance of the temporary restraining order or preliminary injunction, the order or injunction shall be dissolved by the court and be of no further force and effect: *Provided further,* That in proper cases the Commission may seek, and after proper proof, the court may issue, a permanent injunction. Any such suit may be brought where such person, partnership, or corporation resides or transacts business, or wherever venue is proper under section 1391 of Title 28.   . . .

(d) Exception of periodical publications

Whenever it appears to the satisfaction of the court in the case of a newspaper, magazine, periodical, or other publication, published at regular intervals—

(1) that restraining the dissemination of a false advertisement in any particular issue of such publication would delay the delivery of such issue after the regular time therefor, and

(2) that such delay would be due to the method by which the manufacture and distribution of such publication is customarily conducted by the publisher in accordance with sound business practice, and not to any method or device adopted for the evasion of this section or to prevent or delay the issuance of an injunction or restraining order with respect to such false advertisement or any other advertisement,

the court shall exclude such issue from the operation of the restraining order or injunction.

§ 14.   False Advertisements; Penalties [15 U.S.C. § 54]

(a) Imposition of penalties

Any person, partnership, or corporation who violates any provision of section 12(a) shall, if the use of the commodity advertised may be injurious to health because of results from such use under the conditions prescribed in the advertisement thereof, or under such conditions as are customary or usual, or if such violation is with intent to defraud or mislead, be guilty of a misdemeanor, and upon conviction shall be punished by a fine of not more than $5,000 or by imprisonment for not more than six months, or by both such fine and imprisonment; except that if the conviction is for a violation committed after a first conviction of such person, partnership, or corporation, for any violation of such section, punishment shall be by a fine of not more than $10,000 or by imprisonment for not more than one year, or by both such fine and imprisonment: *Provided,* That for the purposes of this section meats and meat food products duly inspected, marked, and labeled in accordance with rules and regulations issued under the Meat Inspection Act shall be conclusively presumed not injurious to health at the time the same leave official "establishments."

(b) Exception of advertising medium or agency

No publisher, radio-broadcast licensee, or agency or medium for the dissemination of advertising, except the manufacturer, packer, distributor, or seller of the commodity to which the false advertisement relates, shall be liable under this section by reason of the dissemination by him of any false advertisement, unless he has refused, on the request of the Commission, to furnish the Commission the name and post-office address of the manufacturer, packer, distributor, seller, or advertising agency, residing in the United States, who caused him to disseminate such advertisement. No advertising agency shall be liable under this section by reason of the causing by it of the dissemination of any false advertisement, unless it has refused, on the request of the Commission, to furnish the Commission the name and post-office address of the manufacturer, packer, distributor, or seller, residing in the United States, who caused it to cause the dissemination of such advertisement.

§ 15. Additional Definitions [15 U.S.C. § 55]

For the purposes of sections 12, 13, and 14—

(a) False advertisement

(1) The term "false advertisement" means an advertisement, other than labeling, which is misleading in a material respect; and in determining whether any advertisement is misleading, there shall be taken into account (among other things) not only representations made or suggested by statement, word, design, device, sound, or any combination thereof, but also the extent to which the advertisement fails to reveal facts material in the light of such representations or material with respect to consequences which may result from the use of the commodity to which the advertisement relates under the conditions prescribed in said advertisement, or under such conditions as are customary or usual. No advertisement of a drug shall be deemed to be false if it is disseminated only to members of the medical profession, contains no false representation of a material fact, and includes, or is accompanied in each instance by truthful disclosure of, the formula showing quantitatively each ingredient of such drug.

(2) In the case of oleomargarine or margarine an advertisement shall be deemed misleading in a material respect if in such advertisement representations are made or suggested by statement, word, grade designation, design, device, symbol, sound, or any combination thereof, that such oleomargarine or margarine is a dairy product, except that nothing contained herein shall prevent a truthful, accurate, and full statement in any such advertisement of all the ingredients contained in such oleomargarine or margarine.

(b) Food

The term "food" means (1) articles used for food or drink for man or other animals, (2) chewing gum, and (3) articles used for components of any such article.

(c) Drug

The term "drug" means (1) articles recognized in the official United States Pharmacopoeia, official Homoeopathic Pharmacopoeia of the United States, or official National Formulary, or any supplement to any of them; and (2) articles intended for use in the diagnosis, cure, mitigation, treatment, or prevention of disease in man or other animals; and (3) articles (other than food) intended to affect the structure or any function of the body of man or other animals; and (4) articles intended for use as a component of any article specified in clause (1), (2), or (3); but does not include devices or their components, parts, or accessories.

(d) Device

The term "device" (except when used in subsection (a) of this section) means an instrument, apparatus, implement, machine, contrivance, implant, in vitro reagent, or other similar or related article, including any component, part, or accessory, which is—

(1) recognized in the official National Formulary, or the United States Pharmacopeia, or any supplement to them,

(2) intended for use in the diagnosis of disease or other conditions, or in the cure, mitigation, treatment, or prevention of disease, in man or other animals, or

(3) intended to affect the structure or any function of the body of man or other animals, and

which does not achieve any of its principal intended purposes through chemical action within or on the body of man or other animals and which is not dependent upon being metabolized for the achievement of any of its principal intended purposes.

(e) Cosmetic

The term "cosmetic" means (1) articles to be rubbed, poured, sprinkled, or sprayed on, introduced into, or otherwise applied to the human body or any part thereof intended for cleansing, beautifying, promoting attractiveness, or altering the appearance, and (2) articles intended for use as a component of any such article; except that such term shall not include soap.

(f) Oleomargarine or margarine

For the purposes of this section and section 407 of the Food, Drug, and Cosmetic Act, the term "oleomargarine" or "margarine" includes—

(1) all substances, mixtures, and compounds known as oleomargarine or margarine;

(2) all substances, mixtures, and compounds which have a consistence similar to that of butter and which contain any edible oils or fats other than milk fat if made in imitation or semblance of butter.

§ 16. Commencement, Defense, Intervention and Supervision of Litigation and Appeal by Commission or Attorney General [15 U.S.C. § 56]

(a) Procedure for exercise of authority to litigate or appeal

(1) Except as otherwise provided in paragraph (2) or (3), if—

(A) before commencing, defending, or intervening in, any civil action involving this Act (including an action to collect a civil penalty) which the Commission, or the Attorney General on behalf of the Commission, is authorized to commence, defend, or intervene in, the Commission gives written notification and undertakes to consult with the Attorney General with respect to such action; and

(B) the Attorney General fails within 45 days after receipt of such notification to commence, defend, or intervene in, such action;

the Commission may commence, defend, or intervene in, and supervise the litigation or, such action and any appeal of such action in its own name by any of its attorneys designated by it for such purpose.

(2) Except as otherwise provided in paragraph (3), in any civil action—

   (A) under section 13 (relating to injunctive relief);

   (B) under section 19 (relating to consumer redress);

   (C) to obtain judicial review of a rule prescribed by the Commission, or a cease and desist order issued under section 5; or

   (D) under the second paragraph of section 9 (relating to enforcement of a subpena) and under the fourth paragraph of such section (relating to compliance with section 6);

the Commission shall have exclusive authority to commence or defend, and supervise the litigation of, such action and any appeal of such action in its own name by any of its attorneys designated by it for such purpose, unless the Commission authorizes the Attorney General to do so. The Commission shall inform the Attorney General of the exercise of such authority and such exercise shall not preclude the Attorney General from intervening on behalf of the United States in such action and any appeal of such action as may be otherwise provided by law.

(3)(A) If the Commission makes a written request to the Attorney General, within the 10–day period which begins on the date of the entry of the judgment in any civil action in which the Commission represented itself pursuant to paragraph (1) or (2), to represent itself through any of its attorneys designated by it for such purpose before the Supreme Court in such action, it may do so, if—

   (i) the Attorney General concurs with such request; or

   (ii) the Attorney General, within the 60–day period which begins on the date of the entry of such judgment—

      (a) refuses to appeal or file a petition for writ of certiorari with respect to such civil action, in which case he shall give written notification to the Commission of the reasons for such refusal within such 60–day period; or

      (b) the Attorney General fails to take any action with respect to the Commission's request.

(B) In any case where the Attorney General represents the Commission before the Supreme Court in any civil action in which the Commission represented itself pursuant to paragraph (1) or (2), the Attorney General may not agree to any settlement, compromise, or dismissal of such action, or confess error in the Supreme Court with respect to such action, unless the Commission concurs.

(C) For purposes of this paragraph (with respect to representation before the Supreme Court), the term "Attorney General" includes the Solicitor General.

(4) If, prior to the expiration of the 45–day period specified in paragraph (1) of this section or a 60–day period specified in paragraph (3), any right of the Commission to commence, defend, or intervene in, any such

action or appeal may be extinguished due to any procedural requirement of any court with respect to the time in which any pleadings, notice of appeal, or other acts pertaining to such action or appeal may be taken, the Attorney General shall have one-half of the time required to comply with any such procedural requirement of the court (including any extension of such time granted by the court) for the purpose of commencing, defending, or intervening in the civil action pursuant to paragraph (1) or for the purpose of refusing to appeal or file a petition for writ of certiorari and the written notification or failing to take any action pursuant to paragraph 3(A)(ii).

(5) The provisions of this subsection shall apply notwithstanding chapter 31 of title 28, or any other provision of law.

(b) Certification by Commission to Attorney General for criminal proceedings

Whenever the Commission has reason to believe that any person, partnership, or corporation is liable for a criminal penalty under this Act, the Commission shall certify the facts to the Attorney General, whose duty it shall be to cause appropriate criminal proceedings to be brought.

§ 17. Separability Clause [15 U.S.C. § 57]

If any provision of this Act, or the application thereof to any person, partnership, or corporation, or circumstance, is held invalid, the remainder of this Act, and the application of such provisions to any other person, partnership, corporation, or circumstance, shall not be affected thereby.

§ 18. Unfair or Deceptive Acts or Practices Rulemaking Proceedings [15 U.S.C. § 57a]

(a) Authority of Commission to prescribe rules and general statements of policy

(1) Except as provided in subsection (h) of this section, the Commission may prescribe—

(A) interpretive rules and general statements of policy with respect to unfair or deceptive acts or practices in or affecting commerce (within the meaning of section 5(a)(1)), and

(B) rules which define with specificity acts or practices which are unfair or deceptive acts or practices in or affecting commerce (within the meaning of section 5(a)(1)), except that the Commission shall not develop or promulgate any trade rule or regulation with regard to the regulation of the development and utilization of the standards and certification activities pursuant to this section. Rules under this subparagraph may include requirements prescribed for the purpose of preventing such acts or practices.

(2) The Commission shall have no authority under this Act, other than its authority under this section, to prescribe any rule with respect to unfair

or deceptive acts or practices in or affecting commerce (within the meaning of section 5(a)(1)). The preceding sentence shall not affect any authority of the Commission to prescribe rules (including interpretive rules), and general statements of policy, with respect to unfair methods of competition in or affecting commerce.

(b) Procedures applicable

(1) When prescribing a rule under subsection (a)(1)(B) of this section, the Commission shall proceed in accordance with section 553 of title 5 (without regard to any reference in such section to sections 556 and 557 of such title), and shall also (A) publish a notice of proposed rulemaking stating with particularity the text of the rule, including any alternatives, which the Commission proposes to promulgate, and the reason for the proposed rule; (B) allow interested persons to submit written data, views, and arguments, and make all such submissions publicly available; (C) provide an opportunity for an informal hearing in accordance with subsection (c) of this section; and (D) promulgate, if appropriate, a final rule based on the matter in the rulemaking record (as defined in subsection (e)(1)(B) of this section), together with a statement of basis and purpose.

(2)(A) Prior to the publication of any notice of proposed rulemaking pursuant to paragraph (1)(A), the Commission shall publish an advance notice of proposed rulemaking in the Federal Register. Such advance notice shall—

(i) contain a brief description of the area of inquiry under consideration, the objectives which the Commission seeks to achieve, and possible regulatory alternatives under consideration by the Commission; and

(ii) invite the response of interested parties with respect to such proposed rulemaking, including any suggestions or alternative methods for achieving such objectives.

(B) The Commission shall submit such advance notice of proposed rulemaking to the Committee on Commerce, Science, and Transportation of the Senate and to the Committee on Energy and Commerce of the House of Representatives. The Commission may use such additional mechanisms as the Commission considers useful to obtain suggestions regarding the content of the area of inquiry before the publication of a general notice of proposed rulemaking under paragraph (1)(A).

(C) The Commission shall, 30 days before the publication of a notice of proposed rulemaking pursuant to paragraph (1)(A), submit such notice to the Committee on Commerce, Science, and Transportation of the Senate and to the Committee on Energy and Commerce of the House of Representatives.

(3) The Commission shall issue a notice of proposed rulemaking pursuant to paragraph (1)(A) only where it has reason to believe that the unfair or deceptive acts or practices which are the subject of the proposed rulemaking are prevalent. The Commission shall make a determination

that unfair or deceptive acts or practices are prevalent under this paragraph only if—

(A) it has issued cease and desist orders regarding such acts or practices, or

(B) any other information available to the Commission indicates a widespread pattern of unfair or deceptive acts or practices.

(c) Informal hearing procedure

The Commission shall conduct any informal hearings required by subsection (b)(1)(C) of this section in accordance with the following procedure:

(1)(A) The Commission shall provide for the conduct of proceedings under this subsection by hearing officers who shall perform their functions in accordance with the requirements of this subsection.

(B) The officer who presides over the rulemaking proceedings shall be responsible to a chief presiding officer who shall not be responsible to any other officer or employee of the Commission. The officer who presides over the rulemaking proceeding shall make a recommended decision based upon the findings and conclusions of such officer as to all relevant and material evidence, except that such recommended decision may be made by another officer if the officer who presided over the proceeding is no longer available to the Commission.

(C) Except as required for the disposition of ex parte matters as authorized by law, no presiding officer shall consult any person or party with respect to any fact in issue unless such officer gives notice and opportunity for all parties to participate.

(2) Subject to paragraph (3) of this subsection, an interested person is entitled—

(A) to present his position orally or by documentary submission (or both), and

(B) if the Commission determines that there are disputed issues of material fact it is necessary to resolve, to present such rebuttal submissions and to conduct (or have conducted under paragraph (3)(B)) such cross-examination of persons as the Commission determines (i) to be appropriate, and (ii) to be required for a full and true disclosure with respect to such issues.

(3) The Commission may prescribe such rules and make such rulings concerning proceedings in such hearings as may tend to avoid unnecessary costs or delay. Such rules or rulings may include (A) imposition of reasonable time limits on each interested person's oral presentations, and (B) requirements that any cross-examination to which a person may be entitled under paragraph (2) be conducted by the Commission on behalf of that person in such manner as the Commission determines (i) to be appropriate, and (ii) to be required for a full and true disclosure with respect to disputed issues of material fact.

(4)(A) Except as provided in subparagraph (B), if a group of persons each of whom under paragraphs (2) and (3) would be entitled to conduct (or have conducted) cross-examination and who are determined by the Commission to have the same or similar interests in the proceeding cannot agree upon a single representative of such interests for purposes of cross-examination, the Commission may make rules and rulings (i) limiting the representation of such interest, for such purposes, and (ii) governing the manner in which such cross-examination shall be limited.

(B) When any person who is a member of a group with respect to which the Commission has made a determination under subparagraph (A) is unable to agree upon group representation with the other members of the group, then such person shall not be denied under the authority of subparagraph (A) the opportunity to conduct (or have conducted) cross-examination as to issues affecting his particular interests if (i) he satisfies the Commission that he has made a reasonable and good faith effort to reach agreement upon group representation with the other members of the group and (ii) the Commission determines that there are substantial and relevant issues which are not adequately presented by the group representative.

(5) A verbatim transcript shall be taken of any oral presentation, and cross-examination, in an informal hearing to which this subsection applies. Such transcript shall be available to the public.

(d) Statement of basis and purpose accompanying rule; "Commission" defined; judicial review of amendment or repeal of rule; violation of rule

(1) The Commission's statement of basis and purpose to accompany a rule promulgated under subsection (a)(1)(B) of this section shall include (A) a statement as to the prevalence of the acts or practices treated by the rule; (B) a statement as to the manner and context in which such acts or practices are unfair or deceptive; and (C) a statement as to the economic effect of the rule, taking into account the effect on small business and consumers.

(2)(A) The term "Commission" as used in this subsection and subsections (b) and (c) of this section includes any person authorized to act in behalf of the Commission in any part of the rulemaking proceeding.

(B) A substantive amendment to, or repeal of, a rule promulgated under subsection (a)(1)(B) of this section shall be prescribed, and subject to judicial review, in the same manner as a rule prescribed under such subsection. An exemption under subsection (g) of this section shall not be treated as an amendment or repeal of a rule.

(3) When any rule under subsection (a)(1)(B) of this section takes effect a subsequent violation thereof shall constitute an unfair or deceptive act or practice in violation of section 5(a)(1), unless the Commission otherwise expressly provides in such rule.

(e) Judicial review; petition; jurisdiction and venue; rule-making record; additional submissions and presentations; scope of review and relief; review by Supreme Court; additional remedies

(1)(A) Not later than 60 days after a rule is promulgated under subsection (a)(1)(B) of this section by the Commission, any interested person (including a consumer or consumer organization) may file a petition, in the United States Court of Appeals for the District of Columbia circuit or for the circuit in which such person resides or has his principal place of business, for judicial review of such rule. Copies of the petition shall be forthwith transmitted by the clerk of the court to the Commission or other officer designated by it for that purpose. The provisions of section 2112 of title 28 shall apply to the filing of the rulemaking record of proceedings on which the Commission based its rule and to the transfer of proceedings in the courts of appeals.

(B) For purposes of this section, the term "rulemaking record" means the rule, its statement of basis and purpose, the transcript required by subsection (c)(5) of this section, any written submissions, and any other information which the Commission considers relevant to such rule.

.   .   .

(5) .   .   . The contents and adequacy of any statement required by subsection (b)(1)(D) of this section shall not be subject to judicial review in any respect.

(f) Unfair or deceptive acts or practices by banks, savings and loan institutions, or Federal credit unions; promulgation of regulations by Board of Governors of Federal Reserve System, Federal Home Loan Bank Board, and National Credit Union Administration Board; agency enforcement and compliance proceedings; violations; power of other Federal agencies unaffected; reporting requirements

(1) In order to prevent unfair or deceptive acts or practices in or affecting commerce (including acts or practices which are unfair or deceptive to consumers) by banks or savings and loan institutions described in paragraph (3), each agency specified in paragraph (2) or (3) of this subsection shall establish a separate division of consumer affairs which shall receive and take appropriate action upon complaints with respect to such acts or practices by banks or savings and loan institutions described in paragraph (3) subject to its jurisdiction. The Board of Governors of the Federal Reserve System (with respect to banks) and the Federal Home Loan Bank Board (with respect to savings and loan institutions described in paragraph (3)) and the National Credit Union Administration Board (with respect to Federal credit unions described in paragraph (4)) shall prescribe regulations to carry out the purposes of this section, including regulations defining with specificity such unfair or deceptive acts or practices, and containing requirements prescribed for the purpose of preventing

such acts or practices. Whenever the Commission prescribes a rule under subsection (a)(1)(B) of this section, then within 60 days after such rule takes effect each such Board shall promulgate substantially similar regulations prohibiting acts or practices of banks or savings and loan institutions described in paragraph (3), or Federal credit unions described in paragraph (4), as the case may be, which are substantially similar to those prohibited by rules of the Commission and which impose substantially similar requirements, unless (A) any such Board finds that such acts or practices of banks or savings and loan institutions described in paragraph (3), or Federal credit unions described in paragraph (4), as the case may be, are not unfair or deceptive, or (B) the Board of Governors of the Federal Reserve System finds that implementation of similar regulations with respect to banks, savings and loan institutions, or Federal credit unions would seriously conflict with essential monetary and payments systems policies of such Board, and publishes any such finding, and the reasons therefor, in the Federal Register.

(2) Compliance with regulations prescribed under this subsection shall be enforced under section 1818 of Title 12, in the case of—

(A) national banks, banks operating under the code of law for the District of Columbia, and Federal branches and Federal agencies of foreign banks, by the division of consumer affairs established by the Comptroller of the Currency;

(B) member banks of the Federal Reserve System [with certain exceptions], by the division of consumer affairs established by the Board of Governors of the Federal Reserve System; and

(C) banks insured by the Federal Deposit Insurance Corporation (other than banks referred to in subparagraph (A) or (B)) and insured State branches of foreign banks, by the division of consumer affairs established by the Board of Directors of the Federal Deposit Insurance Corporation.

(3) Compliance with regulations prescribed under this subsection shall be enforced under section 1818 of Title 12 with respect to savings associations as defined in section 1813 of Title 12.

(4) Compliance with regulations prescribed under this subsection shall be enforced with respect to Federal credit unions under sections 1766 and 1786.

(5) For the purpose of the exercise by any agency referred to in paragraph (2) of its powers under any Act referred to in that paragraph, a violation of any regulation prescribed under this subsection shall be deemed to be a violation of a requirement imposed under that Act. In addition to its powers under any provision of law specifically referred to in paragraph (2), each of the agencies referred to in that paragraph may exercise, for the purpose of enforcing compliance with any regulation prescribed under this subsection, any other authority conferred on it by law.

(6) The authority of the Board of Governors of the Federal Reserve System to issue regulations under this subsection does not impair the authority of any other agency designated in this subsection to make rules respecting its own procedures in enforcing compliance with regulations prescribed under this subsection.

(7) Each agency exercising authority under this subsection shall transmit to the Congress each year a detailed report on its activities under this paragraph during the preceding calendar year.

The terms used in this paragraph that are not defined in section 1813(s) of Title 12 shall have the meaning given to them in section 3101 of Title 12.

(g) Exemptions and stays from application of rules; procedures

(1) Any person to whom a rule under subsection (a)(1)(B) of this section applies may petition the Commission for an exemption from such rule.

(2) If, on its own motion or on the basis of a petition under paragraph (1), the Commission finds that the application of a rule prescribed under subsection (a)(1)(B) of this section to any person or class of persons is not necessary to prevent the unfair or deceptive act or practice to which the rule relates, the Commission may exempt such person or class from all or part of such rule. Section 553 of title 5 shall apply to action under this paragraph.

(3) Neither the pendency of a proceeding under this subsection respecting an exemption from a rule, nor the pendency of judicial proceedings to review the Commission's action or failure to act under this subsection, shall stay the applicability of such rule under subsection (a)(1)(B) of this section.

(h) Restriction on rulemaking authority of Commission respecting children's advertising proceedings pending on May 28, 1980

The Commission shall not have any authority to promulgate any rule in the children's advertising proceeding pending on May 28, 1980, or in any substantially similar proceeding on the basis of a determination by the Commission that such advertising constitutes an unfair act or practice in or affecting commerce.

(*i*) Meetings with outside parties

(1) For purposes of this subsection, the term "outside party" means any person other than (A) a Commissioner; (B) an officer or employee of the Commission; or (C) any person who has entered into a contract or any other agreement or arrangement with the Commission to provide any goods or services (including consulting services) to the Commission.

(2) Not later than 60 days after May 28, 1980, the Commission shall publish a proposed rule, and not later than 180 days after May 28, 1980, the Commission shall promulgate a final rule, which shall authorize the

Commission or any Commissioner to meet with any outside party concerning any rulemaking proceeding of the Commission. Such rule shall provide that—

> (A) notice of any such meeting shall be included in any weekly calendar prepared by the Commission; and

> (B) a verbatim record or a summary of any such meeting, or of any communication relating to any such meeting, shall be kept, made available to the public, and included in the rulemaking record.

(j) Communications by investigative personnel with staff of Commission concerning matters outside rulemaking record prohibited

Not later than 60 days after May 28, 1980, the Commission shall publish a proposed rule, and not later than 180 days after May 28, 1980, the Commission shall promulgate a final rule, which shall prohibit any officer, employee, or agent of the Commission with any investigative responsibility or other responsibility relating to any rulemaking proceeding within any operating bureau of the Commission, from communicating or causing to be communicated to any Commissioner or to the personal staff of any Commissioner any fact which is relevant to the merits of such proceeding and which is not on the rulemaking record of such proceeding, unless such communication is made available to the public and is included in the rulemaking record. The provisions of this subsection shall not apply to any communication to the extent such communication is required for the disposition of ex parte matters as authorized by law.

§ 19. Civil Actions for Violations of Rules and Cease and Desist Orders Respecting Unfair or Deceptive Acts or Practices [15 U.S.C. § 57b]

(a) Suits by Commission against persons, partnerships, or corporations; jurisdiction; relief for dishonest or fraudulent acts

(1) If any person, partnership, or corporation violates any rule under this Act respecting unfair or deceptive acts or practices (other than an interpretive rule, or a rule violation of which the Commission has provided is not an unfair or deceptive act or practice in violation of section 5(a)), then the Commission may commence a civil action against such person, partnership, or corporation for relief under subsection (b) of this section in a United States district court or in any court of competent jurisdiction of a State.

(2) If any person, partnership, or corporation engages in any unfair or deceptive act or practice (within the meaning of section 5(a)(1)) with respect to which the Commission has issued a final cease and desist order which is applicable to such person, partnership, or corporation, then the Commission may commence a civil action against such person, partnership, or corporation in a United States district court or in any court of competent jurisdiction of a State. If the Commission satisfies the court that the act or

practice to which the cease and desist order relates is one which a reasonable man would have known under the circumstances was dishonest or fraudulent, the court may grant relief under subsection (b) of this section.

(b) Nature of relief available

The court in an action under subsection (a) of this section shall have jurisdiction to grant such relief as the court finds necessary to redress injury to consumers or other persons, partnerships, and corporations resulting from the rule violation or the unfair or deceptive act or practice, as the case may be. Such relief may include, but shall not be limited to, rescission or reformation of contracts, the refund of money or return of property, the payment of damages, and public notification respecting the rule violation or the unfair or deceptive act or practice, as the case may be; except that nothing in this subsection is intended to authorize the imposition of any exemplary or punitive damages.

(c) Conclusiveness of findings of Commission in cease and desist proceedings; notice of judicial proceedings to injured persons, etc.

(1) If (A) a cease and desist order issued under section 5(b) has become final under section 5(g) with respect to any person's, partnership's, or corporation's rule violation or unfair or deceptive act or practice, and (B) an action under this section is brought with respect to such person's, partnership's, or corporation's rule violation or act or practice, then the findings of the Commission as to the material facts in the proceeding under section 5(b) with respect to such person's, partnership's, or corporation's rule violation or act or practice, shall be conclusive unless (i) the terms of such cease and desist order expressly provide that the Commission's findings shall not be conclusive, or (ii) the order became final by reason of section 5(g)(1), in which case such finding shall be conclusive if supported by evidence.

(2) The court shall cause notice of an action under this section to be given in a manner which is reasonably calculated, under all of the circumstances, to apprise the persons, partnerships, and corporations allegedly injured by the defendant's rule violation or act or practice of the pendency of such action. Such notice may, in the discretion of the court, be given by publication.

(d) Time for bringing of actions

No action may be brought by the Commission under this section more than 3 years after the rule violation to which an action under subsection (a)(1) of this section relates, or the unfair or deceptive act or practice to which an action under subsection (a)(2) of this section relates; except that if a cease and desist order with respect to any person's, partnership's, or corporation's rule violation or unfair or deceptive act or practice has become final and such order was issued in a proceeding under section 5(b) which was commenced not later than 3 years after the rule violation or act or practice occurred, a civil action may be commenced under this section against such person, partnership, or corporation at any time before the expiration of one year after such order becomes final.

(e) Availability of additional Federal or State remedies; other authority of Commission unaffected

Remedies provided in this section are in addition to, and not in lieu of, any other remedy or right of action provided by State or Federal law. Nothing in this section shall be construed to affect any authority of the Commission under any other provision of law.

§ 20. Civil Investigative Demands [15 U.S.C. § 57b–1]

(a) Definitions

For purposes of this section:

(1) The terms "civil investigative demand" and "demand" mean any demand issued by the Commission under subsection (c)(1) of this section.

(2) The term "Commission investigation" means any inquiry conducted by a Commission investigator for the purpose of ascertaining whether any person is or has been engaged in any unfair or deceptive acts or practices in or affecting commerce (within the meaning of section 5(a)(1)) or in any antitrust violations.

(3) The term "Commission investigator" means any attorney or investigator employed by the Commission who is charged with the duty of enforcing or carrying into effect any provisions relating to unfair or deceptive acts or practices in or affecting commerce (within the meaning of section 5(a)(1)) or any provisions relating to antitrust violations.

(4) The term "custodian" means the custodian or any deputy custodian designated under section 21(b)(2)(A).

(5) The term "documentary material" includes the original or any copy of any book, record, report, memorandum, paper, communication, tabulation, chart, or other document.

(6) The term "person" means any natural person, partnership, corporation, association, or other legal entity, including any person acting under color or authority of State law.

(7) The term "violation" means any act or omission constituting an unfair or deceptive act or practice in or affecting commerce (within the meaning of section 5(a)(1)) or any antitrust violation.

(8) The term "antitrust violation" means—

(A) any unfair method of competition (within the meaning of section 5(a)(1));

(B) any violation of the Clayton Act [15 U.S.C. § 12 et seq.] or of any Federal statute that prohibits, or makes available to the Commission a civil remedy with respect to, any restraint upon or monopolization of interstate or foreign trade or commerce;

(C) with respect to the International Antitrust Enforcement Assistance Act of 1994 [15 U.S.C. § 6201 et seq.], any violation of any of the foreign antitrust laws (as defined in section 12 of such Act [15 U.S.C. § 6211]) with respect to which a request is made under section 3 of such Act [15 U.S.C. § 6202]; or

(D) any activity in preparation for a merger, acquisition, joint venture, or similar transaction, which if consummated, may result in any such unfair method of competition or in any such violation.

(b) Actions conducted by Commission respecting unfair or deceptive acts or practices in or affecting commerce

For the purpose of investigations performed pursuant to this section with respect to unfair or deceptive acts or practices in or affecting commerce (within the meaning of section 5(a)(1)); all actions of the Commission taken under section 6 and section 9 shall be conducted pursuant to subsection (c) of this section.

(c) Issuance of demand; contents; service; verified return; sworn certificates; answers; taking of oral testimony

(1) Whenever the Commission has reason to believe that any person may be in possession, custody, or control of any documentary material or tangible things, or may have any information, relevant to unfair or deceptive acts or practices in or affecting commerce (within the meaning of section 5(a)(1)) or to antitrust violations, the Commission may, before the institution of any proceedings under this Act, issue in writing, and cause to be served upon such person, a civil investigative demand requiring such person to produce such documentary material for inspection and copying or reproduction, to submit such tangible things, to file written reports or answers to questions, to give oral testimony concerning documentary material or other information, or to furnish any combination of such material, answers, or testimony.

(2) Each civil investigative demand shall state the nature of the conduct constituting the alleged violation which is under investigation and the provision of law applicable to such violation.

(3) Each civil investigative demand for the production of documentary material shall—

(A) describe each class of documentary material to be produced under the demand with such definiteness and certainty as to permit such material to be fairly identified;

(B) prescribe a return date or dates which will provide a reasonable period of time within which the material so demanded may be assembled and made available for inspection and copying or reproduction; and

(C) identify the custodian to whom such material shall be made available.

(4) Each civil investigative demand for the submission of tangible things shall—

(A) describe each class of tangible things to be submitted under the demand with such definiteness and certainty as to permit such things to be fairly identified;

(B) prescribe a return date or dates which will provide a reasonable period of time within which the things so demanded may be assembled and submitted; and

(C) identify the custodian to whom such things shall be submitted.

(5) Each civil investigative demand for written reports or answers to questions shall—

(A) propound with definiteness and certainty the reports to be produced or the questions to be answered;

(B) prescribe a date or dates at which time written reports or answers to questions shall be submitted; and

(C) identify the custodian to whom such reports or answers shall be submitted.

. . .

(d) Procedures for demand material

Materials received as a result of a civil investigative demand shall be subject to the procedures established in section 21.

(e) Petition for enforcement

Whenever any person fails to comply with any civil investigative demand duly served upon him under this section, or whenever satisfactory copying or reproduction of material requested pursuant to the demand cannot be accomplished and such person refuses to surrender such material, the Commission, through such officers or attorneys as it may designate, may file, in the district court of the United States for any judicial district in which such person resides, is found, or transacts business, and serve upon such person, a petition for an order of such court for the enforcement of this section. All process of any court to which application may be made as provided in this subsection may be served in any judicial district.

. . .

(h) Jurisdiction of court

Whenever any petition is filed in any district court of the United States under this section, such court shall have jurisdiction to hear and determine the matter so presented, and to enter such order or orders as may be required to carry into effect the provisions of this section. Any final order so entered shall be subject to appeal pursuant to section 1291 of title 28. Any disobedience of any final order entered under this section by any court shall be punished as a contempt of such court.

(*i*) Commission authority to issue subpoenas or make demand for information

Notwithstanding any other provision of law, the Commission shall have no authority to issue a subpoena or make a demand for information, under authority of this Act or any other provision of law, unless such subpoena or demand for information is signed by a Commissioner acting pursuant to a Commission resolution. The Commission shall not delegate the power conferred by this section to sign subpoenas or demands for information to any other person.

(j) Applicability of this section

The provisions of this section shall not—

(1) apply to any proceeding under section 5(b), any proceeding under section 11(b) of the Clayton Act, or any adjudicative proceeding under any other provision of law; or

(2) apply to or affect the jurisdiction, duties, or powers of any agency of the Federal Government, other than the Commission, regardless of whether such jurisdiction, duties, or powers are derived in whole or in part, by reference to this Act.

§ 21.   Confidentiality [15 U.S.C. § 57b–2]

(a) Definitions

For purposes of this section:

(1) The term "material" means documentary material, tangible things, written reports or answers to questions, and transcripts of oral testimony.

(2) The term "Federal agency" has the meaning given it in section 552(e) of title 5.

(b) Procedures respecting documents, tangible things, or transcripts of oral testimony received pursuant to compulsory process or investigation

(1) With respect to any document or transcript of oral testimony received by the Commission pursuant to compulsory process in an investigation, a purpose of which is to determine whether any person may have violated any provision of the laws administered by the Commission, the procedures established in paragraph (2) through paragraph (7) shall apply.

(2)(A) The Commission shall designate a duly authorized agent to serve as custodian of documentary material, tangible things, or written reports or answers to questions, and transcripts of oral testimony, and such additional duly authorized agents as the Commission shall determine from time to time to be necessary to serve as deputies to the custodian.

. . .

(3)(A) The custodian to whom any documentary material, tangible things, written reports or answers to questions, and transcripts of oral testimony are delivered shall take physical possession of such material, reports or answers, and transcripts, and shall be responsible for the use made of such material, reports or answers, and transcripts, and for the return of material, pursuant to the requirements of this section.

. . .

(C) Except as otherwise provided in this section, while in the possession of the custodian, no documentary material, tangible things, reports or answers to questions, and transcripts of oral testimony shall be available for examination by any individual other than a duly authorized officer or employee of the Commission without the consent of the person who produced the material or transcripts. Nothing in this section is intended to prevent disclosure to either House of the Congress or to any committee or subcommittee of the Congress, except that the Commission immediately shall notify the owner or provider of any such information of a request for information designated as confidential by the owner or provider.

. . .

(4) Whenever the Commission has instituted a proceeding against a person, partnership, or corporation, the custodian may deliver to any officer or employee of the Commission documentary material, tangible things, written reports or answers to questions, and transcripts of oral testimony for official use in connection with such proceeding. Upon the completion of the proceeding, the officer or employee shall return to the custodian any such material so delivered which has not been received into the record of the proceeding.

(5) If any documentary material, tangible things, written reports or answers to questions, and transcripts of oral testimony have been produced in the course of any investigation by any person pursuant to compulsory process and—

    (A) any proceeding arising out of the investigation has been completed; or

    (B) no proceeding in which the material may be used has been commenced within a reasonable time after completion of the examination and analysis of all such material and other information assembled in the course of the investigation;

then the custodian shall, upon written request of the person who produced the material, return to the person any such material which has not been received into the record of any such proceeding (other than copies of such material made by the custodian pursuant to paragraph (3)(B)).

(6) The custodian of any documentary material, written reports or answers to questions, and transcripts of oral testimony may deliver to any officers or employees of appropriate Federal law enforcement agencies, in response to a written request, copies of such material for use in connection with an investigation or proceeding under the jurisdiction of any such agency. The custodian of any tangible things may make such things available for inspection to such persons on the same basis. Such materials

shall not be made available to any such agency until the custodian received certification of any officer of such agency that such information will be maintained in confidence and will be used only for official law enforcement purposes. Such documentary material, results of inspections of tangible things, written reports or answers to questions, and transcripts of oral testimony may be used by any officer or employee of such agency only in such manner and subject to such conditions as apply to the Commission under this section. The custodian may make such materials available to any State law enforcement agency upon the prior certification of any officer of such agency that such information will be maintained in confidence and will be used only for official law enforcement purposes.

. . .

(d) Particular disclosures allowed

(1) The provisions of subsection (c) of this section shall not be construed to prohibit—

(A) the disclosure of information to either House of the Congress or to any committee or subcommittee of the Congress, except that the Commission immediately shall notify the owner or provider of any such information of a request for information designated as confidential by the owner or provider;

(B) the disclosure of the results of any investigation or study carried out or prepared by the Commission, except that no information shall be identified nor shall information be disclosed in such a manner as to disclose a trade secret of any person supplying the trade secret, or to disclose any commercial or financial information which is obtained from any person and which is privileged or confidential;

(C) the disclosure of relevant and material information in Commission adjudicative proceedings or in judicial proceedings to which the Commission is a party; or

(D) the disclosure to a Federal agency of disaggregated information obtained in accordance with section 3512 of title 44, except that the recipient agency shall use such disaggregated information for economic, statistical, or policymaking purposes only, and shall not disclose such information in an individually identifiable form.

(2) Any disclosure of relevant and material information in Commission adjudicative proceedings or in judicial proceedings to which the Commission is a party shall be governed by the rules of the Commission for adjudicative proceedings or by court rules or orders, except that the rules of the Commission shall not be amended in a manner inconsistent with the purposes of this section.

(e) Effect on other statutory provisions limiting disclosure

Nothing in this section shall supersede any statutory provision which expressly prohibits or limits particular disclosures by the Commission, or which authorizes disclosures to any other Federal agency.

(f) Exemption from disclosure

Any material which is received by the Commission in any investigation, a purpose of which is to determine whether any person may have violated any provision of the laws administered by the Commission, and which is provided pursuant to any compulsory process under this subchapter or which is provided voluntarily in place of such compulsory process shall be exempt from disclosure under section 552 of title 5.

§ 22. Rulemaking Process [15 U.S.C. § 57b–3]

(a) Definitions

For purposes of this section:

(1) The term "rule" means any rule promulgated by the Commission under section 6 or section 18, except that such term does not include interpretive rules, rules involving Commission management or personnel, general statements of policy, or rules relating to Commission organization, procedure, or practice. Such term does not include any amendment to a rule unless the Commission—

(A) estimates that such amendment will have an annual effect on the national economy of $100,000,000 or more;

(B) estimates that such amendment will cause a substantial change in the cost or price of goods or services which are used extensively by particular industries, which are supplied extensively in particular geographic regions, or which are required in significant quantities by the Federal Government, or by State or local governments; or

(C) otherwise determines that such amendment will have a significant impact upon persons subject to regulation under such amendment and upon consumers.

(2) The term "rulemaking" means any Commission process for formulating or amending a rule.

(b) Notice of proposed rulemaking; regulatory analysis; contents; issuance

(1) In any case in which the Commission publishes notice of a proposed rulemaking, the Commission shall issue a preliminary regulatory analysis relating to the proposed rule involved. Each preliminary regulatory analysis shall contain—

(A) a concise statement of the need for, and the objectives of, the proposed rule;

(B) a description of any reasonable alternatives to the proposed rule which may accomplish the stated objective of the rule in a manner consistent with applicable law; and

(C) for the proposed rule, and for each of the alternatives described in the analysis, a preliminary analysis of the projected benefits and any adverse economic effects and any other effects, and of the effectiveness of the proposed rule and each alternative in meeting the stated objectives of the proposed rule.

(2) In any case in which the Commission promulgates a final rule, the Commission shall issue a final regulatory analysis relating to the final rule. Each final regulatory analysis shall contain—

(A) a concise statement of the need for, and the objectives of, the final rule;

(B) a description of any alternatives to the final rule which were considered by the Commission;

(C) an analysis of the projected benefits and any adverse economic effects and any other effects of the final rule;

(D) an explanation of the reasons for the determination of the Commission that the final rule will attain its objectives in a manner consistent with applicable law and the reasons the particular alternative was chosen; and

(E) a summary of any significant issues raised by the comments submitted during the public comment period in response to the preliminary regulatory analysis, and a summary of the assessment by the Commission of such issues.

(3)(A) In order to avoid duplication or waste, the Commission is authorized to—

(i) consider a series of closely related rules as one rule for purposes of this subsection; and

(ii) whenever appropriate, incorporate any data or analysis contained in a regulatory analysis issued under this subsection in the statement of basis and purpose to accompany any rule promulgated under section 18(a)(1)(B), and incorporate by reference in any preliminary or final regulatory analysis information contained in a notice of proposed rulemaking or a statement of basis and purpose.

(B) The Commission shall include, in each notice of proposed rulemaking and in each publication of a final rule, a statement of the manner in which the public may obtain copies of the preliminary and final regulatory analyses. The Commission may charge a reasonable fee for the copying and mailing of regulatory analyses. The regulatory analyses shall be furnished without charge or at a reduced charge if the Commission determines that waiver or reduction of the fee is in the public interest because furnishing the information primarily benefits the general public.

(4) The Commission is authorized to delay the completion of any of the requirements established in this subsection by publishing in the Federal Register, not later than the date of publication of the final rule involved, a finding that the final rule is being promulgated in response to an emergency which makes timely compliance with the provisions of this subsection impracticable. Such publication shall include a statement of the reasons for such finding.

(5) The requirements of this subsection shall not be construed to alter in any manner the substantive standards applicable to any action by the Commission, or the procedural standards otherwise applicable to such action.

(c) Judicial review

(1) The contents and adequacy of any regulatory analysis prepared or issued by the Commission under this section, including the adequacy of any procedure involved in such preparation or issuance, shall not be subject to any judicial review in any court, except that a court, upon review of a rule pursuant to section 18(e) may set aside such rule if the Commission has failed entirely to prepare a regulatory analysis.

(2) Except as specified in paragraph (1), no Commission action may be invalidated, remanded, or otherwise affected by any court on account of any failure to comply with the requirements of this section.

(3) The provisions of this subsection do not alter the substantive or procedural standards otherwise applicable to judicial review of any action by the Commission.

(d) Regulatory agenda; contents; publication dates in Federal Register

(1) The Commission shall publish at least semiannually a regulatory agenda. Each regulatory agenda shall contain a list of rules which the Commission intends to propose or promulgate during the 12–month period following the publication of the agenda. On the first Monday in October of each year, the Commission shall publish in the Federal Register a schedule showing the dates during the current fiscal year on which the semiannual regulatory agenda of the Commission will be published.

(2) For each rule listed in a regulatory agenda, the Commission shall—

   (A) describe the rule;

   (B) state the objectives of and the legal basis for the rule; and

   (C) specify any dates established or anticipated by the Commission for taking action, including dates for advance notice of proposed rulemaking, notices of proposed rulemaking, and final action by the Commission.

(3) Each regulatory agenda shall state the name, office address, and office telephone number of the Commission officer or employee responsible for responding to any inquiry relating to each rule instead.

(4) The Commission shall not propose or promulgate a rule which was not listed on a regulatory agenda unless the Commission publishes with the rule an explanation of the reasons the rule was omitted from such agenda.

§ 23. Good Faith Reliance on Actions of Board of Governors [15 U.S.C. § 57b–4]

(a) "Board of Governors" defined

For purposes of this section, the term "Board of Governors" means the Board of Governors of the Federal Reserve System.

(b) Use as defense

Notwithstanding any other provision of law, if—

(1) any person, partnership, or corporation engages in any conduct or practice which allegedly constitutes a violation of any Federal law with respect to which the Board of Governors of the Federal Reserve System has rulemaking authority; and

(2) such person, partnership, or corporation engaged in such conduct or practice in good faith reliance upon, and in conformity with, any rule, regulation, statement of interpretation, or statement of approval prescribed or issued by the Board of Governors under such Federal law;

then such good faith reliance shall constitute a defense in any administrative or judicial proceeding commenced against such person, partnership, or corporation by the Commission under this Act or in any administrative or judicial proceeding commenced against such person, partnership, or corporation by the Attorney General of the United States, upon request made by the Commission, under any provision of law.

(c) Applicability of subsection (b)

The provisions of subsection (b) of this section shall apply regardless of whether any rule, regulation, statement of interpretation, or statement of approval prescribed or issued by the Board of Governors is amended, rescinded, or held to be invalid by judicial authority or any other authority after a person, partnership, or corporation has engaged in any conduct or practice in good faith reliance upon, and in conformity with, such rule, regulation, statement of interpretation, or statement of approval.

(d) Request for issuance of statement or interpretation concerning conduct or practice

If, in any case in which—

(1) the Board of Governors has rulemaking authority with respect to any Federal law; and

(2) the Commission is authorized to enforce the requirements of such Federal law;

any person, partnership, or corporation submits a request to the Board of Governors for the issuance of any statement of interpretation or statement of approval relating to any conduct or practice of such person, partnership, or corporation which may be subject to the requirements of such Federal law, then the Board of Governors shall dispose of such request as soon as practicable after the receipt of such request.

§ 26. Short Title [15 U.S.C. § 58]

This Act may be cited as the "Federal Trade Commission Act."

FTC REGULATIONS

COOLING–OFF PERIOD FOR DOOR–TO–DOOR SALES

16 C.F.R. Part 429

Table of Sections

---

§ 429.0   Definitions

For the purposes of this part the following definitions shall apply:

(a) *Door-to-Door Sale*—A sale, lease, or rental of consumer goods or services with a purchase price of $25 or more, whether under single or multiple contracts, in which the seller or his representative personally solicits the sale, including those in response to or following an invitation by the buyer, and the buyer's agreement or offer to purchase is made at a place other than the place of business of the seller (e.g., sales at the buyer's residence or at facilities rented on a temporary or short-term basis, such as hotel or motel rooms, convention centers, fairgrounds and restaurants, or sales at the buyer's workplace or in dormitory lounges). The term *door-to-door* sale does not include a transaction:

(1) Made pursuant to prior negotiations in the course of a visit by the buyer to a retail business establishment having a fixed permanent location where the goods are exhibited or the services are offered for sale on a continuing basis; or

(2) In which the consumer is accorded the right of rescission by the provisions of the Consumer Credit Protection Act (15 U.S.C. § 1635) or regulations issued pursuant thereto; or

(3) In which the buyer has initiated the contact and the goods or services are needed to meet a bona fide immediate personal emergency of the buyer, and the buyer furnishes the seller with a separate dated and signed personal statement in the buyer's handwriting describing the situation requiring immediate remedy and expressly acknowledging and waiving the right to cancel the sale within 3 business days; or

(4) Conducted and consummated entirely by mail or telephone; and without any other contact between the buyer and the seller or its representative prior to delivery of the goods or performance of the services; or

(5) In which the buyer has initiated the contact and specifically requested the seller to visit the buyer's home for the purpose of repairing or performing maintenance upon the buyer's personal property. If, in the course of such a visit, the seller sells the buyer the right to receive additional services or goods other than replacement parts necessarily used in performing the maintenance or in making the repairs, the sale of those additional goods or services would not fall within this exclusion; or

(6) Pertaining to the sale or rental of real property, to the sale of insurance, or to the sale of securities or commodities by a broker-dealer registered with the Securities and Exchange Commission.

(b) *Consumer Goods or Services*—Goods or services purchased, leased, or rented primarily for personal, family, or household purposes, including courses of instruction or training regardless of the purpose for which they are taken.

(c) *Seller*—Any person, partnership, corporation, or association engaged in the door-to-door sale of consumer goods or services.

(d) *Place of Business*—The main or permanent branch office or local address of a seller.

(e) *Purchase Price*—The total price paid or to be paid for the consumer goods or services, including all interest and service charges.

(f) *Business Day*—Any calendar day except Sunday or any federal holiday (e.g., New Year's Day, Presidents' Day, Martin Luther King's Birthday, Memorial Day, Independence Day, Labor Day, Columbus Day, Veterans' Day, Thanksgiving Day, and Christmas Day.)

§ 429.1   The Rule

In connection with any door-to-door sale, it constitutes an unfair and deceptive act or practice for any seller to:

(a) Fail to furnish the buyer with a fully completed receipt or copy of any contract pertaining to such sale at the time of its execution, which is in the same language, e.g., Spanish, as that principally used in the oral sales presentation and which shows the date of the transaction and contains the name and address of the seller, and in immediate proximity to the space reserved in the contract for the signature of the buyer or on the front page of the receipt if a contract is not used and in bold face type of a minimum size of 10 points, a statement in substantially the following form:

> "You, the buyer, may cancel this transaction at any time prior to midnight of the third business day after the date of this transaction. See the attached notice of cancellation form for an explanation of this right."

The seller may select the method of providing the buyer with the duplicate notice of cancellation form set forth in paragraph (b) of this section, provided however, that in the event of cancellation the buyer must be able to retain a complete copy of the contract or receipt. Furthermore, if both forms are not attached to the contract or receipt, the seller is required to alter the last sentence in the statement above to conform to the actual location of the forms.

(b) Fail to furnish each buyer, at the time the buyer signs the door-to-door sales contract or otherwise agrees to buy consumer goods or services from the seller, a completed form in duplicate, captioned either "NOTICE OF RIGHT TO CANCEL" or "NOTICE OF CANCELLATION," which shall (where applicable) contain in ten point bold face type the following information and statements in the same language, e.g., Spanish, as that used in the contract.

Notice of Cancellation

[enter date of transaction]

_____

(Date)

You may CANCEL this transaction, without any Penalty or Obligation, within THREE BUSINESS DAYS from the above date.

If you cancel, any property traded in, any payments made by you under the contract or sale, and any negotiable instrument executed by you will be returned within TEN BUSINESS DAYS following receipt by the seller of your cancellation notice, and any security interest arising out of the transaction will be cancelled.

If you cancel, you must make available to the seller at your residence, in substantially as good condition as when received, any goods delivered to you under this contract or sale, or you may, if you wish, comply with the instructions of the seller regarding the return shipment of the goods at the seller's expense and risk.

If you do make the goods available to the seller and the seller does not pick them up within 20 days of the date of your Notice of Cancellation, you may retain or dispose of the goods without any further obligation. If you fail to make the goods available to the seller, or if you agree to return the goods to the seller and fail to do so, then you remain liable for performance of all obligations under the contract.

To cancel this transaction, mail or deliver a signed and dated copy of this Cancellation Notice or any other written notice, or send a telegram, to [Name of seller], at [address of seller's place of business] NOT LATER THAN MIDNIGHT OF [date].

I HEREBY CANCEL THIS TRANSACTION.

(Date) _____

(Buyer's signature) _____

(c) Fail, before furnishing copies of the "Notice of Cancellation" to the buyer, to complete both copies by entering the name of the seller, the address of the seller's place of business, the date of the transaction, and the date, not earlier than the third business day following the date of the transaction, by which the buyer may give notice of cancellation.

(d) Include in any door-to-door contract or receipt any confession of judgment or any waiver of any of the rights to which the buyer is entitled under this section including specifically the buyer's right to cancel the sale in accordance with the provisions of this section.

(e) Fail to inform each buyer orally, at the time the buyer signs the contract or purchases the goods or services, of the buyer's right to cancel.

(f) Misrepresent in any manner the buyer's right to cancel.

(g) Fail or refuse to honor any valid notice of cancellation by a buyer and within 10 business days after the receipt of such notice, to: (i) Refund all payments made under the contract or sale; (ii) return any goods or property traded in, in substantially as good condition as when received by the seller; (iii) cancel and return any negotiable instrument executed by the buyer in connection with the contract or sale and take any action necessary or appropriate to terminate promptly any security interest created in the transaction.

(h) Negotiate, transfer, sell, or assign any note or other evidence of indebtedness to a finance company or other third party prior to midnight of the fifth business day following the day the contract was signed or the goods or services were purchased.

(*i*) Fail, within 10 business days of receipt of the buyer's notice of cancellation, to notify the buyer whether the seller intends to repossess or to abandon any shipped or delivered goods.

§ 429.2   Effect on State Laws and Municipal Ordinances

(a) The Commission is cognizant of the significant burden imposed upon door-to-door sellers by the various and often inconsistent State laws that provide the buyer the right to cancel a door-to-door sales transaction. However, it does not believe that this constitutes sufficient justification for preempting all of the provisions of such laws and the ordinances of the political subdivisions of the various States. The rulemaking record in this proceeding supports the view that the joint and coordinated efforts of both the Commission and State and local officials are required to insure that consumers who have purchased from a door-to-door seller something they do not want, do not need, or cannot afford, be accorded a unilateral right to rescind, without penalty, their agreements to purchase those goods or services.

(b) This part will not be construed to annul, or exempt any seller from complying with, the laws of any State or the ordinances of a political subdivision thereof that regulate door-to-door sales, except to the extent that such laws or ordinances, if they permit door-to-door selling, are directly inconsistent with the provisions of this part. Such laws or ordinances which do not accord the buyer, with respect to the particular transaction, a right to cancel a door-to-door sale that is substantially the same or greater than that provided in this part, which permit the imposition of any fee or penalty on the buyer for the exercise of such right, or which do not provide for giving the buyer a notice of the right to cancel the transaction in substantially the same form and manner provided for in this part, are among those which will be considered directly inconsistent.

§ 429.3 Exemptions

(a) The requirements of this part do not apply for sellers of automobiles, vans, trucks or other motor vehicles sold at auctions, tent sales or other temporary places of business, provided that the seller is a seller of vehicles with a permanent place of business.

(b) The requirements of this part do not apply for sellers of arts or crafts sold at fairs or similar places.

PRESERVATION OF CONSUMERS' CLAIMS AND DEFENSES

16 C.F.R. Part 433

Table of Sections

---

§ 433.1 Definitions

(a) *Person.* An individual, corporation, or any other business organization.

(b) *Consumer.* A natural person who seeks or acquires goods or services for personal, family, or household use.

(c) *Creditor.* A person who, in the ordinary course of business, lends purchase money or finances the sale of goods or services to consumers on a deferred payment basis; *Provided,* such person is not acting, for the purposes of a particular transaction, in the capacity of a credit card issuer.

(d) *Purchase Money Loan.* A cash advance which is received by a consumer in return for a "Finance Charge" within the meaning of the Truth in Lending Act and Regulation Z, which is applied, in whole or substantial part, to a purchase of goods or services from a seller who (1) refers consumers to the creditor or (2) is affiliated with the creditor by common control, contract, or business arrangement.

(e) *Financing a Sale.* Extending credit to a consumer in connection with a "Credit Sale" within the meaning of the Truth in Lending Act and Regulation Z.

(f) *Contract.* Any oral or written agreement, formal or informal, between a creditor and a seller, which contemplates or provides for cooperative or concerted activity in connection with the sale of goods or services to consumers or the financing thereof.

(g) *Business Arrangement.* Any understanding, procedure, course of dealing, or arrangement, formal or informal, between a creditor and a seller, in connection with the sale of goods or services to consumers or the financing thereof.

(h) *Credit Card Issuer.* A person who extends to cardholders the right to use a credit card in connection with purchases of goods or services.

(*i*) *Consumer Credit Contract.* Any instrument which evidences or embodies a debt arising from a "Purchase Money Loan" transaction or a "financed sale" as defined in paragraphs (d) and (e).

(*j*) *Seller.* A person who, in the ordinary course of business, sells or leases goods or services to consumers.

§ 433.2 Preservation of Consumers' Claims and Defenses, Unfair or Deceptive Acts or Practices

In connection with any sale or lease of goods or services to consumers, in or affecting commerce as "commerce" is defined in the Federal Trade Commission Act, it is an unfair or deceptive act or practice within the meaning of Section 5 of that Act for a seller, directly or indirectly, to:

(a) Take or receive a consumer credit contract which fails to contain the following provision in at least ten point, bold face, type:

NOTICE

ANY HOLDER OF THIS CONSUMER CREDIT CONTRACT IS SUBJECT TO ALL CLAIMS AND DEFENSES WHICH THE DEBTOR COULD ASSERT AGAINST THE SELLER OF GOODS OR SERVICES OBTAINED PURSUANT HERETO OR WITH THE PROCEEDS HEREOF. RECOVERY HEREUNDER BY THE DEBTOR SHALL NOT EXCEED AMOUNTS PAID BY THE DEBTOR HEREUNDER.

or,

(b) Accept, as full or partial payment for such sale or lease, the proceeds of any purchase money loan (as purchase money loan is defined herein), unless any consumer credit contract made in connection with such purchase money loan contains the following provision in at least ten point, bold face, type:

NOTICE

ANY HOLDER OF THIS CONSUMER CREDIT CONTRACT IS SUBJECT TO ALL CLAIMS AND DEFENSES WHICH THE DEBTOR COULD ASSERT AGAINST THE SELLER OF GOODS OR SERVICES OBTAINED WITH THE PROCEEDS HEREOF. RECOVERY HEREUNDER BY THE DEBTOR SHALL NOT EXCEED AMOUNTS PAID BY THE DEBTOR HEREUNDER.

§ 433.3 Exemption of Sellers Taking or Receiving Open End Consumer Credit Contracts Before November 1, 1977, from Requirements of § 433.2(a)

(a) Any seller who has taken or received an open end consumer credit contract before November 1, 1977, shall be exempt from the requirements of 16 CFR Part 433 with respect to such contract provided the contract does not cut off consumers' claims and defenses.

(b) *Definitions.* The following definitions apply to this exemption:

63

(1) All pertinent definitions contained in 16 CFR 433.1.

(2) Open end consumer credit contract: a consumer credit contract pursuant to which "open end credit" is extended.

(3) "Open end credit": Consumer credit extended on an account pursuant to a plan under which a creditor may permit an applicant to make purchases or make loans from time to time directly from the creditor or indirectly by use of a credit card, check or other device as the plan may provide. The term does not include negotiated advances under an open-end real estate mortgage or a letter of credit.

(4) Contract which does not cut off consumers' claims and defenses: a consumer credit contract which does not constitute or contain a negotiable instrument, or contain any waiver, limitation, term, or condition which has the effect of limiting a consumer's right to assert against any holder of the contract all legally sufficient claims and defenses which the consumer could assert against the seller of goods or services purchased pursuant to the contract.

CREDIT PRACTICES

16 C.F.R. Part 444

Table of Sections

---

§ 444.1   Definitions

(a) *Lender.*   A person who engages in the business of lending money to consumers within the jurisdiction of the Federal Trade Commission.

(b) *Retail Installment Seller.*   A person who sells goods or services to consumers on a deferred payment basis or pursuant to a lease-purchase arrangement within the jurisdiction of the Federal Trade Commission.

(c) *Person.*   An individual, corporation, or other business organization.

(d) *Consumer.*   A natural person who seeks or acquires goods, services, or money for personal, family, or household use.

(e) *Obligation.*   An agreement between a consumer and a lender or retail installment seller.

(f) *Creditor.*   A lender or a retail installment seller.

(g) *Debt.*   Money that is due or alleged to be due from one to another.

(h) *Earnings.*   Compensation paid or payable to an individual or for his or her account for personal services rendered or to be rendered by him or her, whether denominated as wages, salary, commission, bonus, or otherwise, including periodic payments pursuant to a pension, retirement, or disability program.

(i) *Household Goods.*   Clothing, furniture, appliances, one radio and one television, linens, china, crockery, kitchenware, and personal effects (including wedding rings) of the consumer and his or her dependents, provided that the following are not included within the scope of the term "household goods":

(1) Works of art;

(2) Electronic entertainment equipment (except one television and one radio);

(3) Items acquired as antiques; and

(4) Jewelry (except wedding rings).

65

(j) *Antique.* Any item over one hundred years of age, including such items that have been repaired or renovated without changing their original form or character.

(k) *Cosigner.* A natural person who renders himself or herself liable for the obligation of another person without compensation. The term shall include any person whose signature is requested as a condition to granting credit to another person, or as a condition for forbearance on collection of another person's obligation that is in default. The term shall not include a spouse whose signature is required on a credit obligation to perfect a security interest pursuant to State law. A person who does not receive goods, services, or money in return for a credit obligation does not receive compensation within the meaning of this definition. A person is a cosigner within the meaning of this definition whether or not he or she is designated as such on a credit obligation.

§ 444.2 Unfair Credit Practices

(a) In connection with the extension of credit to consumers in or affecting commerce, as commerce is defined in the Federal Trade Commission Act, it is an unfair act or practice within the meaning of section 5 of that Act for a lender or retail installment seller directly or indirectly to take or receive from a consumer an obligation that:

(1) Constitutes or contains a cognovit or confession of judgment (for purposes other than executory process in the State of Louisiana), warrant of attorney, or other waiver of the right to notice and the opportunity to be heard in the event of suit or process thereon.

(2) Constitutes or contains an executory waiver or a limitation of exemption from attachment, execution, or other process on real or personal property held, owned by, or due to the consumer, unless the waiver applies solely to property subject to a security interest executed in connection with the obligation.

(3) Constitutes or contains an assignment of wages or other earnings unless:

(i) The assignment by its terms is revocable at the will of the debtor, or

(ii) The assignment is a payroll deduction plan or preauthorized payment plan, commencing at the time of the transaction, in which the consumer authorizes a series of wage deductions as a method of making each payment, or

(iii) The assignment applies only to wages or other earnings already earned at the time of the assignment.

(4) Constitutes or contains a non-possessory security interest in household goods other than a purchase money security interest.

§ 444.3   Unfair or Deceptive Cosigner Practices

(a) In connection with the extension of credit to consumers in or affecting commerce, as commerce is defined in the Federal Trade Commission Act, it is:

(1) A deceptive act or practice within the meaning of section 5 of that Act for a lender or retail installment seller, directly or indirectly, to misrepresent the nature or extent of cosigner liability to any person.

(2) An unfair act or practice within the meaning of section 5 of that Act for a lender or retail installment seller, directly or indirectly, to obligate a cosigner unless the cosigner is informed prior to becoming obligated, which in the case of open end credit shall mean prior to the time that the agreement creating the cosigner's liability for future charges is executed, of the nature of his or her liability as cosigner.

(b) Any lender or retail installment seller who complies with the preventive requirements in paragraph (c) of this section does not violate paragraph (a) of this section.

(c) To prevent these unfair or deceptive acts or practices, a disclosure, consisting of a separate document that shall contain the following statement and no other, shall be given to the cosigner prior to becoming obligated, which in the case of open end credit shall mean prior to the time that the agreement creating the cosigner's liability for future charges is executed:

NOTICE TO COSIGNER

You are being asked to guarantee this debt. Think carefully before you do. If the borrower doesn't pay the debt, you will have to. Be sure you can afford to pay if you have to, and that you want to accept this responsibility.

You may have to pay up to the full amount of the debt if the borrower does not pay. You may also have to pay late fees or collection costs, which increase this amount.

The creditor can collect this debt from you without first trying to collect from the borrower. The creditor can use the same collection methods against you that can be used against the borrower, such as suing you, garnishing your wages, etc. If this debt is ever in default, that fact may become a part of *your* credit record.

This notice is not the contract that makes you liable for the debt.

§ 444.4   Late Charges

(a) In connection with collecting a debt arising out of an extension of credit to a consumer in or affecting commerce, as commerce is defined in the Federal Trade Commission Act, it is an unfair act or practice within the meaning of section 5 of that Act for a creditor, directly or indirectly, to levy or collect any delinquency charge on a payment, which payment is otherwise a full payment for the applicable period and is paid on its due date or within an applicable grace period, when the only delinquency is attributable to late fee(s) or delinquency charge(s) assessed on earlier installment(s).

(b) For purposes of this section, "collecting a debt" means any activity other than the use of judicial process that is intended to bring about or does bring about repayment of all or part of a consumer debt.

§ 444.5   State Exemptions

(a) If, upon application to the Federal Trade Commission by an appropriate State agency, the Federal Trade Commission determines that:

(1) There is a State requirement or prohibition in effect that applies to any transaction to which a provision of this rule applies; and

(2) The State requirement or prohibition affords a level of protection to consumers that is substantially equivalent to, or greater than, the protection afforded by this rule;

Then that provision of the rule will not be in effect in that State to the extent specified by the Federal Trade Commission in its determination for as long as the State administers and enforces the State requirement or prohibition effectively.

USED MOTOR VEHICLES

16 C.F.R. Part 455

Table of Sections

---

§ 455.1 General Duties of a Used Vehicle Dealer; Definitions

(a) It is a deceptive act or practice for any used vehicle dealer, when that dealer sells or offers for sale a used vehicle in or affecting commerce as "commerce" is defined in the Federal Trade Commission Act:

(1) To misrepresent the mechanical condition of a used vehicle;

(2) To misrepresent the terms of any warranty offered in connection with the sale of a used vehicle; and

(3) To represent that a used vehicle is sold with a warranty when the vehicle is sold without any warranty.

(b) It is an unfair act or practice for any used vehicle dealer, when that dealer sells or offers for sale a used vehicle in or affecting commerce as "commerce" is defined in the Federal Trade Commission Act:

(1) To fail to disclose, prior to sale, that a used vehicle is sold without any warranty; and

(2) To fail to make available, prior to sale, the terms of any written warranty offered in connection with the sale of a used vehicle.

(c) The Commission has adopted this Rule in order to prevent the unfair and deceptive acts or practices defined in paragraphs (a) and (b). It is a violation of this Rule for any used vehicle dealer to fail to comply with the requirements set forth in §§ 455.2 through 455.5 of this part. If a used vehicle dealer complies with the requirements of §§ 455.2 through 455.5 of this part, the dealer does not violate this Rule.

(d) The following definitions shall apply for purposes of this part:

(1) "Vehicle" means any motorized vehicle, other than a motorcycle, with a gross vehicle weight rating (GVWR) of less than 8500 lbs., a curb weight of less than 6,000 lbs., and a frontal area of less than 46 sq. ft.

69

(2) "Used vehicle" means any vehicle driven more than the limited use necessary in moving or road testing a new vehicle prior to delivery to a consumer, but does not include any vehicle sold only for scrap or parts (title documents surrendered to the State and a salvage certificate issued).

(3) "Dealer" means any person or business which sells or offers for sale a used vehicle after selling or offering for sale five (5) or more used vehicles in the previous twelve months, but does not include a bank or financial institution, a business selling a used vehicle to an employee of that business, or a lessor selling a leased vehicle by or to that vehicle's lessee or to an employee of the lessee.

(4) "Consumer" means any person who is not a used vehicle dealer.

(5) "Warranty" means any undertaking in writing, in connection with the sale by a dealer of a used vehicle, to refund, repair, replace, maintain or take other action with respect to such used vehicle and provided at no extra charge beyond the price of the used vehicle.

(6) "Implied warranty" means an implied warranty arising under State law (as modified by the Magnuson–Moss Act) in connection with the sale by a dealer of a used vehicle.

(7) "Service contract" means a contract in writing for any period of time or any specific mileage to refund, repair, replace, or maintain a used vehicle and provided at an extra charge beyond the price of the used vehicle, provided that such contract is not regulated in your State as the business of insurance.

(8) "You" means any dealer, or any agent or employee of a dealer, except where the term appears on the window form required by § 455.2(a).

§ 455.2 Consumer Sales—Window Form

(a) *General duty.* Before you offer a used vehicle for sale to a consumer, you must prepare, fill in as applicable and display on that vehicle a "Buyers Guide" as required by this Rule.

(1) The Buyers Guide shall be displayed prominently and conspicuously in any location on a vehicle and in such fashion that both sides are readily readable. You may remove the form temporarily from the vehicle during any test drive, but you must return it as soon as the test drive is over.

(2) The capitalization, punctuation and wording of all items, headings, and text on the form must be exactly as required by this Rule. The entire form must be printed in 100% black ink on a white stock no smaller than 11 inches high by 7¼ inches wide in the type styles, sizes and format indicated.

BUYERS GUIDE

IMPORTANT: Spoken promises are difficult to enforce. Ask the dealer to put all promises in writing. Keep this form.

_____ _____ _____ _____
VEHICLE MAKE   MODEL   YEAR   VIN NUMBER

_____
DEALER STOCK NUMBER (Optional)

WARRANTIES FOR THIS VEHICLE:

☐ **AS IS - NO WARRANTY**

YOU WILL PAY ALL COSTS FOR ANY REPAIRS. The dealer assumes no responsibility for any repairs regardless of any oral statements about the vehicle.

☐ **WARRANTY**

☐ FULL ☐ LIMITED WARRANTY. The dealer will pay _____% of the labor and _____% of the parts for the covered systems that fail during the warranty period. Ask the dealer for a copy of the warranty document for a full explanation of warranty coverage, exclusions, and the dealer's repair obligations. Under state law, "implied warranties" may give you even more rights.

SYSTEMS COVERED: **DURATION:**

☐ SERVICE CONTRACT. A service contract is available at an extra charge on this vehicle. Ask for details as to coverage, deductable, price, and exclusions. If you buy a service contract within 90 days of the time of sale, state law "implied warranties" may give you additional rights.

PRE PURCHASE INSPECTION: ASK THE DEALER IF YOU MAY HAVE THIS VEHICLE INSPECTED BY YOUR MECHANIC EITHER ON OR OFF THE LOT.

SEE THE BACK OF THIS FORM for important additional information, including a list of some major defects that may occur in used motor vehicles.

Annotations (right margin, printer's specifications):

28 pt Triumvirate Bold caps

2 pt Rule

10/12 Triumvirate Bold c & lc flush left ragged right maximum line 42 picas

10 pt Baseline Rule
6 pt Triumvirate Bold caps

10 pt Baseline Rule
6 pt Triumvirate Bold caps

10 pt Triumvirate Bold caps

2 pt Rule

54 pt Box
42 pt Triumvirate Bold caps

10/10 Triumvirate Bold c & lc flush left ragged right maximum line 42 picas

1 pt Rule

54 pt Box
42 pt Triumvirate Bold caps

10/10 Triumvirate Bold c & lo 4½ picas indent on 2nd line

10 pt Triumvirate Bold caps

10 pt Baseline Rule

10/10 Triumvirate Bold c & lc maximum line 42 picas

10/10 Triumvirate Bold caps flush left ragged right maximum line 42 picas

10/10 Triumvirate Bold c & lc flush left ragged right maximum line 42 picas

12 pt Triumvirate Bold lc
flush left ragged right
maximum line 42 picas

2 pt Rule

Below is a list of some major defects that may occur in used motor vehicles.

8/9 Triumvirate Bold c & lc
flush left ragged right
maximum line 20 picas
1 em indent on 2nd line

Frame & Body
Frame-cracks, corrective welds, or rusted through
Dogtracks—bent or twisted frame

Engine
Oil leakage, excluding normal seepage
Cracked block or head
Belts missing or inoperable
Knocks or misses related to camshaft lifters and
    push rods
Abnormal exhaust discharge

Transmission & Drive Shaft
Improper fluid level or leakage, excluding normal
    seepage
Cracked or damaged case which is visible
Abnormal noise or vibration caused by faulty
    transmission or drive shaft
Improper shifting or functioning in any gear
Manual clutch slips or chatters

Differential
Improper fluid level or leakage excluding normal
    seepage
Cracked or damaged housing which is visible
Abnormal noise or vibration caused by faulty
    differential

Cooling System
Leakage including radiator
Improperly functioning water pump

Electrical System
Battery leakage
Improperly functioning alternator, generator,
    battery, or starter

Fuel System
Visible leakage

Inoperable Accessories
Gauges or warning devices
Air conditioner
Heater & Defroster

Brake System
Failure warning light broken
Pedal not firm under pressure (DOT spec.)
Not enough pedal reserve (DOT spec.)
Does not stop vehicle in straight (DOT spec.)
Hoses damaged
Drum or rotor too thin (Mfgr. Specs)
Lining or pad thickness less than 1/32 inch
Power unit not operating or leaking
Structural or mechanical parts damaged

Steering System
Too much free play at steering wheel (DOT specs.)
Free play in linkage more than 1/4 inch
Steering gear binds or jams
Front wheels aligned improperly (DOT specs.)
Power unit belts cracked or slipping
Power unit fluid level improper

Suspension System
Ball joint seals damaged
Structural parts bent or damaged
Stabilizer bar disconnected
Spring broken
Shock absorber mounting loose
Rubber bushings damaged or missing
Radius rod damaged or missing
Shock absorber leaking or functioning improperly

Tires
Tread depth less than 2/32 inch
Sizes mismatched
Visible damage

Wheels
Visible cracks, damage or repairs
Mounting bolts loose or missing

Exhaust System
Leakage

2 pt Rule

10 pt Baseline Rule
6 pt Triumvirate Bold caps

DEALER

ADDRESS

SEE FOR COMPLAINTS

2 pt Rule

IMPORTANT: The information on this form is part of any contract to buy this vehicle. Removal of this label before consumer purchase (except for purpose of test-driving) is a violation of federal law (16 C.F.R. 455).

10/12 Triumvirate Bold c & lc
maximum line 42 picas

When filling out the form, follow the directions in (b) through (e) of this section and § 455.4 of this part.

(b) *Warranties—(1) No Implied Warranty—"As Is"/No Warranty.* (i) If you offer the vehicle without any implied warranty, *i.e.,* "as is," mark the box provided. If you offer the vehicle with implied warranties only, substitute the disclosure specified below, and mark the box provided. If you first offer the vehicle "as is" or with implied warranties only but then sell it with a warranty, cross out the "As Is—No Warranty" or "Implied Warranties Only" disclosure, and fill in the warranty terms in accordance with paragraph (b)(2) of this section.

(ii) If your State law limits or prohibits "as is" sales of vehicles, that State law overrides this part and this rule does not give you the right to sell "as is." In such States, the heading "As Is—No Warranty" and the paragraph immediately accompanying that phrase must be deleted from the form, and the following heading and paragraph must be substituted. If you sell vehicles in States that permit "as is" sales, but you choose to offer implied warranties only, you must also use the following disclosure instead of "As Is—No Warranty."[1]

Implied Warranties Only

This means that the dealer does not make any specific promises to fix things that need repair when you buy the vehicle or after the time of sale. But, State law "implied warranties" may give you some rights to have the dealer take care of serious problems that were not apparent when you bought the vehicle.

(2) *Full/Limited Warranty.* If you offer the vehicle with a warranty, briefly describe the warranty terms in the space provided. This description must include the following warranty information:

(i) Whether the warranty offered is "Full" or "Limited."[2] Mark the box next to the appropriate designation.

(ii) Which of the specific systems are covered (for example, "engine, transmission, differential"). You cannot use shorthand, such as "drive train" or "power train" for covered systems.

(iii) The duration (for example, "30 days or 1,000 miles, whichever occurs first").

(iv) The percentage of the repair cost paid by you (for example, "The dealer will pay 100% of the labor and 100% of the parts").

(v) If the vehicle is still under the manufacturer's original warranty, you may add the following paragraph below the "Full/Limited Warranty" disclosure: MANUFACTURER'S WARRANTY STILL APPLIES. The manufacturer's original warranty has not expired on the vehicle. Consult the manufacturer's warranty booklet for details as to warranty coverage, service location, etc.

If, following negotiations, you and the buyer agree to changes in the warranty coverage, mark the changes on the form, as appropriate. If you first offer the vehicle with a warranty, but then sell it without one, cross out the offered warranty and mark either the "As Is—No Warranty" box or the "Implied Warranties Only" box, as appropriate.

(3) *Service contracts.* If you make a service contract (other than a contract that is regulated in your State as the business of insurance)

---

1. *See* § 455.5 n. 4 for the Spanish version of this disclosure.

2. A "Full" warranty is defined by the Federal Minimum Standards for Warranty set forth in 104 of the Magnuson–Moss Warranty Act, 15 U.S.C. 2304 (1975). The Mag-

nuson–Moss Warranty Act does not apply to vehicles manufactured before July 4, 1975. Therefore, if you choose not to designate "Full" or "Limited" for such cars, cross out both designations, leaving only "Warranty."

available on the vehicle, you must add the following heading and paragraph below the "Full/Limited Warranty" disclosure and mark the box provided.[3]

☐ Service Contract

A service contract is available at an extra charge on this vehicle. If you buy a service contract within 90 days of the time of sale, State law "implied warranties" may give you additional rights.

(c) *Name and Address.*   Put the name and address of your dealership in the space provided.   If you do not have a dealership, use the name and address of your place of business (for example, your service station) or your own name and home address.

(d) *Make, Model, Model Year, VIN.*   Put the vehicle's name (for example, "Chevrolet"), model (for example, "Vega"), model year, and Vehicle Identification Number (VIN) in the spaces provided.   You may write the dealer stock number in the space provided or you may leave this space blank.

(e) *Complaints.*   In the space provided, put the name and telephone number of the person who should be contacted if any complaints arise after sale.

(f) *Optional Signature Line.* In the space provided for the name of the individual to be contacted in the event of complaints after sale, you may include a signature line for a buyer's signature. If you opt to include a signature line, you must include a disclosure in immediate proximity to the signature line stating: "I hereby acknowledge receipt of the Buyers Guide at the closing of this sale." You may pre-print this language on the form if you choose.

§ 455.3   Window Form

(a) *Form given to buyer.*   Give the buyer of a used vehicle sold by you the window form displayed under § 455.2 containing all of the disclosures required by the Rule and reflecting the warranty coverage agreed upon.   If you prefer, you may give the buyer a copy of the original, so long as that copy accurately reflects all of the disclosures required by the Rule and the warranty coverage agreed upon.

(b) *Incorporated into contract.*   The information on the final version of the window form is incorporated into the contract of sale for each used vehicle you sell to a consumer.   Information on the window form overrides any contrary provisions in the contract of sale.   To inform the consumer of these facts, include the following language conspicuously in each consumer contract of sale:

The information you see on the window form for this vehicle is part of this contract.   Information on the window form overrides any contrary provisions in the contract of sale.

---

3. *See* § 455.5 n. 4 for the Spanish version of this disclosure.

§ 455.4   Contrary Statements

You may not make any statements, oral or written, or take other actions which alter or contradict the disclosures required by §§ 455.2 and 455.3.   You may negotiate over warranty coverage, as provided in § 455.2(b) of this part, as long as the final warranty terms are identified in the contract of sale and summarized on the copy of the window form you give to the buyer.

§ 455.5   Spanish Language Sales

If you conduct a sale in Spanish, the window form required by § 455.2 and the contract disclosures required by § 455.3 must be in that language. You may display on a vehicle both an English language window form and a Spanish language translation of that form.   Use the following translation and layout for Spanish language sales: [4]

4. Use the following language for the "Implied Warranties Only" disclosure when required by § 455.2(b)(1):

Garantias implicitas solamente

Este término significa que el vendedor no hace promesas especificas de arreglar lo que requiera reparación cuando usted compra el vehiculo o después del momento de la venta.   Pero, las "garantias implicitas" de la ley estatal pueden darle a usted algunos derechos y hacer que el vendedor resuelva problemas graves que no fueron evidentes cuando usted compró el vehiculo.

Use the following language for the "Service Contract" disclosure required by § 455.2(b)(3):

CONTRATO DE SERVICIO.   Este vehiculo tiene disponible un contrato de servicio a un precio adicional.   Pida los detalles en cuanto a cobertura, deducible, precio y exclusiones.   Si adquiere usted un contrato de servicio dentro de los 90 dias del momento de la venta, las "garantias implicitas" de acuerdo a la ley del estado pueden concederle derechos adicionales.

GUÍA DEL COMPRADOR

IMPORTANTE: Las promesas verbales son difíciles de hacer cumplir. Solicite al vendedor que ponga todas las promesas por escrito. Conserve este formulario.

MARCA DEL VEHÍCULO   MODELO   AÑO   NÚMERO DE IDENTIFICACIÓN

NÚMERO DE ABASTO DEL DISTRIBUIDOR (Opcional)

GARANTÍAS PARA ESTE VEHÍCULO:

☐ COMO ESTÁ—SIN GARANTÍA

USTED PAGARA TODOS LOS GASTOS DE CUALQUIER REPARACIÓN QUE SEA NECESARIA. El vendedor no asume ninguna responsabilidad por cualquier reparación, sean cuales sean las declaraciones verbales que haya hecho acerca del vehículo.

☐ GARANTÍA

☐ **COMPLETA**   ☐ **LIMITADA. El vendedor pagará el _____ % de la mano de obra y el _____ % de los repuestos de los sistemas cubiertos que dejen de funcionar durante el período de garantía. Pida al vendedor una copia del documento de garantía donde se explican detalladamente la cobertura de le garantía, exclusiones y las obligaciones que tiene el vendedor de realizar reparaciones. Conforme a la ley estatal, las "garantías implícitas" pueden darle a usted incluso más derechos.**

SISTEMAS CUBIERTOS POR LA GARANTÍA: **DURACIÓN:**

_____   _____
_____   _____
_____   _____
_____   _____
_____   _____
_____   _____
_____   _____
_____   _____

CONTRATO DE SERVICIO. Este vehículo tiene disponible un contrato de servicio a un precio adicional. Pida los detalles en cuanto a cobertura, deducible, precio y exclusiones. Si adquiere usted un contrato de servicio dentro de los 90 días del momento de la venta, las 'garantías implícitas' de acuerdo a la ley del estado pueden concederle derechos adicionales.

INSPECCION PREVIA A LA COMPRA: PREGUNTE AL VENDEDOR SI PUEDE USTED TRAER UN MECANICO PARA QUE INSPECCIONE EL AUTOMOVIL O LLEVAR EL AUTOMÓVIL PARA QUE ESTE LO INSPECCIONE EN SU TALLER.

VEASE EL DORSO DE ESTE FORMULARIO donde se proporciona información adicional importante, incluyendo una lista de algunos de los principales defectos que pueden ocurrir en vehículos usados.

Margin annotations (typographic specifications):
- 28 pt Triumvirate Bold caps
- 2 pt Rule
- 10/10 Triumvirate Bold c & lc / maximum line 38 picas
- Hairline Rule
- 6/6 pt Triumvirate Bold caps
- Hairline Rule
- 6/6 pt Triumvirate Bold caps
- 10 pt Triumvirate Bold caps
- 2 pt Rule
- 28 pt Box
- 24 pt Triumvirate Bold c & lc
- 10/10 Triumvirate Bold c & lc / maximum line 38 picas
- 1 pt Rule
- 28 pt Box
- 24 pt Triumvirate Bold c & lc
- 10/10 Triumvirate Bold c & lc / 7½ picas indent on runovers
- 10/10 Triumvirate Bold caps
- 10/12 Hairline Rule
- 10/10 Triumvirate Bold c & lc / maximum line 38 picas
- 10/10 Triumvirate Bold caps / maximum line 38 picas
- 10/10 Triumvirate Bold c & lc / maximum line 38 picas

A continuación presentamos una lista de algunos de los principales defectos que pueden ocurrir en vehiculos usados.

Chasis y carrocería
Chasis-grietas, soldaduras correctivas u oxidado
Chasis doblado o torcido

Motor
Fuga de aceite, excluyendo el escape normal
Bloque o tapa de recamara agrietados
Correas que faltan o no funcionan
Fallo o pistoneo
Emisión excesiva de humo por el sistema de escape

Transmisión y eje de cardan
Nivel di liquido inadecuado o fuga, excluyendo filtración normal
Vibración o ruido anormal ocasión do por una transmisión o eje de cardan defectuoso
Cambio de marchas o funcionmiento inadecuado en cualquier marcha
Embrague manual patina o vibra

Diferencial
Nivel de liquido inadecuado o fuga excluyendo filtración normal
Cubierta agrietada o dañada visible
Ruido o vibración anormal ocasionado por diferencial defectuoso

Sistema de refrigeración
Fuga, incluido el radiador
Bomba de agua defectuosa

Sistema electrico
Fuga en las baterías
Alternador generador, batería, o motor de arranque defectuosos

Sistema de combustible
Escape visible de combustible

Accesorios averiados
Indicadores o medidores del cuadro de instrumentos
Acondicionador de aire
Calefactor y descarchador

Sistema de frenos
Luz de advertencia de falla dañada
Pedal no firma bajo presión (Especif. del Dpto de Transp.)
Juego insuficiente en el pedal (Especif. del Dpto de Transp.)
No detiene el vehículo en linea recta (Especif. del Dpto de Transp.)
Conductos dañados
Tambor o disco muy delgados (Especif. del fabricante)
Grosor de las bandas de los frenos menor de 1/32 de pulgada
Sistema de servofreno dañado o con escape
Partes estructurales o mecánicas dañadas

Sistema de dirección
Juego excesivo en el volante (Especif. Dpto de Transp.)
Juego en el varillaje en exceso de 1/4 pulgada
Engranaje del volante de dirección se agarrota
Ruedas delanteras mal alineadas (Especif. del Dpto de Transp.)
Correas del sistema de servodirección agrietadas o flojas
Nivel del liquido del sistema de serviodirección inadecuado

Sistema de suspensión
Sellos de conexión de rodamentos defectuosos
Piezas estructurales dobladas o dañadas
Barra de estabilización desconectada
Resorte roto
Montura del amortiguador floja
Bujes de goma dañadas o ausentes
Estabilizador para curvas dañadas o ausente
Amortiguador tiene fuga o funciona defectuosamente

Llantas
Profundidad de la banda de rodamiento menor de 2/32 de pulgada
Diferentes tamaños de llanta
Daños visibles

Ruedas
Grietas visibles, danos o reparaciones
Pernos de montaje sueltos o ausentes

Sistema de Escape
Fuga

VENDEDOR

DIRECCION

VEASE PARA RECLAMACIONES

IMPORTANTE: La informacion contenida en este formulario forma parte de todo contrato de compra de este vehiculo. Constituye una contravencion de la ley federal (16 C.F.R. 455) quitar este rotulo antes de la compra del vehiculo por el consumidor (salvo para conducir el automovil en calidad de prueba).

12 pt Triumvirate Bold lc
flush left ragged right
maximum line 42 picas

2 pt Rule

8/9 Triumvirate Bold c & lc
flush left ragged right
maximum line 20 picas
1 em indent on 2nd line

2 pt Rule

10 pt Baseline Rule

6 pt Triumvirate Bold caps

2 pt Rule

10/12 Triumvirate Bold c & lc
maximum line 42 picas

§ 455.6 State Exemptions

(a) If, upon application to the Commission by an appropriate State agency, the Commission determines, that—

(1) There is a State requirement in effect which applies to any transaction to which this rule applies; and

(2) That State requirement affords an overall level of protection to consumers which is as great as, or greater than, the protection afforded by this Rule; then the Commission's Rule will not be in effect in that State to the extent specified by the Commission in its determination, for as long as the State administers and enforces effectively the State requirement.

(b) Applications for exemption under subsection (a) should be directed to the Secretary of the Commission. When appropriate, proceedings will be commenced in order to make a determination described in paragraph (a) of this section, and will be conducted in accordance with Subpart C of Part 1 of the Commission's Rules of Practice.

§ 455.7 Severability

The provisions of this part are separate and severable from one another. If any provision is determined to be invalid, it is the Commission's intention that the remaining provisions shall continue in effect.

POLICY STATEMENT REGARDING ADVERTISING SUBSTANTIATION PROGRAM

49 Fed. Reg. 30999 (Aug. 2, 1984)

Introduction

On March 11, 1983, the Commission published a notice requesting comments on its advertising substantiation program. To facilitate analysis of the program, the notice posed a number of questions concerning the program's procedures, standards, benefits, and costs, and solicited suggestions for making the program more effective. Based on the public comments and the staff's review, the Commission has drawn certain conclusions about how the program is being implemented and how it might be refined to serve better the objective of maintaining a marketplace free of unfair and deceptive acts or practices. This statement articulates the Commission's policy with respect to advertising substantiation.

The Reasonable Basis Requirement

First, we reaffirm our commitment to the underlying legal requirement of advertising substantiation—that advertisers and ad agencies have a reasonable basis for advertising claims before they are disseminated.

The Commission intends to continue vigorous enforcement of this existing legal requirement that advertisers substantiate express and implied claims, however conveyed, that make objective assertions about the item or service advertised. Objective claims for products or services represent explicitly or by implication that the advertiser has a reasonable basis supporting these claims. These representations of substantiation are material to consumers. That is, consumers would be less likely to rely on claims for products and services if they knew the advertiser did not have a reasonable basis for believing them to be true. Therefore, a firm's failure to possess and rely upon a reasonable basis for objective claims constitutes an unfair and deceptive act or practice in violation of section 5 of the Federal Trade Commission Act.

Standards for Prior Substantiation

Many ads contain express or implied statements regarding the amount of support the advertiser has for the product claim. When the substantiation claim is express (e.g., "tests prove," "doctors recommend," and "studies show"), the Commission expects the firm to have at least the advertised level of substantiation. Of course, an ad may imply more substantiation than it expressly claims or may imply to consumers that the firm has a certain type of support; in such cases, the advertiser must possess the amount and type of substantiation the ad actually communicates to consumers.

79

Absent an express or implied reference to a certain level of support, and absent other evidence indicating what consumer expectations would be, the Commission assumes that consumers expect a "reasonable basis" for claims. The Commission's determination of what constitutes a reasonable basis depends, as it does in an unfairness analysis, on a number of factors relevant to the benefits and costs of substantiating a particular claim. These factors include: the type of claim, the product, the consequences of a false claim, the benefits of a truthful claim, the cost of developing substantiation for the claim, and the amount of substantiation experts in the field believe is reasonable. Extrinsic evidence, such as expert testimony or consumer surveys, is useful to determine what level of substantiation consumers expect to support a particular product claim and the adequacy of evidence an advertiser possesses.

One issue the Commission examined was substantiation for implied claims. Although firms are unlikely to possess substantiation for implied claims they do not believe the ad makes, they should generally be aware of reasonable interpretations and will be expected to have prior substantiation for such claims. The Commission will take care to assure that it only challenges reasonable interpretations of advertising claims.

Procedures for Obtaining Substantiation

In the past, the Commission has sought substantiation from firms in two different ways: Through industry-wide "rounds" that involved publicized inquiries with identical or substantially similar demands to a number of firms within a targeted industry or to firms in different industries making the same type of claim; and on a case-by-case basis, by sending specific requests to individual companies under investigation. The Commission's review indicates that "rounds" have been costly to both the recipient and to the agency and have produced little or no law enforcement benefit over a case-by-case approach.

The Commission's traditional investigatory procedures allows the staff to investigate a number of firms within an industry at the same time, to develop necessary expertise within the area of investigation, and to announce our activities publicly in circumstances where public notice or comment is desirable. The Commission intends to continue undertaking such law enforcement efforts when appropriate. However, since substantiation is principally a law enforcement tool and the Commission's concern in such investigations is with the substantiation in the advertiser's possession, there is little, if any, information that the public could contribute in such investigations. Therefore, the Commission anticipates that substantiation investigations will rarely be made public before they are completed.

Accordingly, the Commission has determined that in the future it will rely on nonpublic requests for substantiation directed to individual companies via an informal access letter or, if necessary, a formal civil investigative demand. The Commission believes that tailored, firm-specific requests, whether directed to one firm or to several firms within the same industry, are a more efficient law enforcement technique. The Commission cannot presently foresee circumstances under which the past approach of industry-wide rounds would be appropriate in the ad substantiation area.

Relevance of Post–Claim Evidence in Substantiation Cases

The reasonable basis doctrine requires that firms have substantiation before disseminating a claim. The Commission has on occasion exercised its discretion, however, to consider supporting materials developed after dissemination. The Commission has not previously identified in one document the circumstances in which it may, in its discretion, consider post-claim evidence in substantiation cases. Such guidance can serve to clarify the program's actual operation as well as focus consideration of post-claim evidence on cases in which it is appropriate.

The Commission emphasizes that as a matter of law, firms lacking a reasonable basis before an ad is disseminated violate section 5 of the FTC Act and are subject to prosecution. The goal of the advertising substantiation requirement is to assure that advertising is truthful, however, and the truth of falsity of a claim is always relevant to the Commission's deliberations. Therefore, it is important that the agency retain the discretion and flexibility to consider additional substantiating evidence, not as a substitute for an advertiser's prior substantiation, but rather in the following circumstances:

- When deciding, before issuance of a complaint, whether there is a public interest in proceeding against a firm;

- When assessing the adequacy of the substantiation an advertiser possessed before a claim was made; and

- When deciding the need for or appropriate scope of an order to enter against a firm that lacked a reasonable basis prior to disseminating an advertisement.

First, using post-claim evidence to evaluate the truth of a claim, or otherwise using such evidence in deciding whether there is a public interest in continuing an investigation or issuing a complaint, is appropriate policy. This does not mean that the Commission will postpone action while firms create post-claim substantiation to prove the truthfulness of claims, nor does it mean that subsequent evidence of truthfulness absolves a firm of liability for failing to possess prior substantiation for a claim. The Commission focuses instead on whether existing evidence that claims are true should lead us in the exercise of our prosecutorial discretion to decline to initiate a law enforcement proceeding. If available post-claim evidence proves that the claim is true, issuing a complaint against a firm that may have violated the prior substantiation requirement is often inappropriate, particularly in light of competing demands on the Commission's resources.

Second, post-claim evidence may indicate that apparent deficiencies in the pre-claim substantiation materials have no practical significance. In evaluating the adequacy of prior substantiation, the Commission will consider only post-claim substantiation that sheds light on pre-existing substantiation. Thus, advertisers will not be allowed to create entirely new substantiation simply because their prior substantiation was inadequate.

Finally, the Commission may use post-claim evidence in determining the need for or appropriate scope of an order to be entered against a firm that lacked a reasonable basis. Thus, when additional evidence offered for the first time at trial suggests that the claim is true, the Commission may frame a narrower order than if there had been no post-claim evidence.

The Commission remains committed to the prior substantiation requirement and further believes that these discretionary factors will provide necessary flexibility. The Commission will consider post-claim evidence only in the circumstances listed above. But, whether it will do so in any particular case remains within its discretion.

Self–Regulation Groups and Government Agencies

The Commission traditionally has enjoyed a close working relationship with self-regulation groups and government agencies whose regulatory policies have some bearing on our law enforcement initiatives. The Commission will not necessarily defer, however, to a finding by a self-regulation group. An imprimatur from a self-regulation group will not automatically shield a firm from Commission prosecution, and an unfavorable determination will not mean the Commission will automatically take issue, or find liability if it does. Rather the Commission will make its judgment independently, evaluating each case on its merits. We intend to continue our useful relationships with self-regulation groups and to rely on the expertise and findings of other government agencies in our proceedings to the greatest extent possible.

TELEMARKETING REGULATION

TELEPHONE CONSUMER PROTECTION ACT

47 U.S.C. § 227

§ 227. Restrictions on the Use of Telephone Equipment

(a) Definitions

As used in this section—

(1) The term "automatic telephone dialing system" means equipment which has the capacity—

    (A) to store or produce telephone numbers to be called, using a random or sequential number generator; and

    (B) to dial such numbers.

(2) The term "established business relationship," for purposes only of subsection (b)(1)(C)(i) of this section, shall have the meaning given the term in section 64.1200 of title 47, Code of Federal Regulations, as in effect on January 1, 2003, except that—

    (A) such term shall include a relationship between a person or entity and a business subscriber subject to the same terms applicable under such section to a relationship between a person or entity and a residential subscriber; and

    (B) an established business relationship shall be subject to any time limitation established pursuant to paragraph (2)(G).

(3) The term "telephone facsimile machine" means equipment which has the capacity (A) to transcribe text or images, or both, from paper into an electronic signal and to transmit that signal over a regular telephone line, or (B) to transcribe text or images (or both) from an electronic signal received over a regular telephone line onto paper.

(4) The term "telephone solicitation" means the initiation of a telephone call or message for the purpose of encouraging the purchase or rental of, or investment in, property, goods, or services, which is transmitted to any person, but such term does not include a call or message (A) to any person with that person's prior express invitation or permission, (B) to any person with whom the caller has an established business relationship, or (C) by a tax exempt nonprofit organization.

(5) The term "unsolicited advertisement" means any material advertising the commercial availability or quality of any property, goods, or services which is transmitted to any person without that person's prior express invitation or permission, in writing or otherwise.

(b) Restrictions on the Use of Automated Telephone Equipment

(1) Prohibitions

It shall be unlawful for any person within the United States, or any person outside the United States if the recipient is within the United States—

(A) to make any call (other than a call made for emergency purposes or made with the prior express consent of the called party) using any automatic telephone dialing system or an artificial or prerecorded voice—

> (i) to any emergency telephone line (including any "911" line and any emergency line of a hospital, medical physician or service office, health care facility, poison control center, or fire protection or law enforcement agency);

> (ii) to the telephone line of any guest room or patient room of a hospital, health care facility, elderly home, or similar establishment; or

> (iii) to any telephone number assigned to a paging service, cellular telephone service, specialized mobile radio service, or other radio common carrier service, or any service for which the called party is charged for the call;

(B) to initiate any telephone call to any residential telephone line using an artificial or prerecorded voice to deliver a message without the prior express consent of the called party, unless the call is initiated for emergency purposes or is exempted by rule or order by the Commission under paragraph (2)(B);

(C) to use any telephone facsimile machine, computer, or other device to send, to a telephone facsimile machine, an unsolicited advertisement, unless—

> (i) the unsolicited advertisement is from a sender with an established business relationship with the recipient;

> (ii) the sender obtained the number of the telephone facsimile machine through—

>> (I) the voluntary communication of such number, within the context of such established business relationship, from the recipient of the unsolicited advertisement, or

>> (II) a directory, advertisement, or site on the Internet to which the recipient voluntarily agreed to make available its facsimile number for public distribution,

except that this clause shall not apply in the case of an unsolicited advertisement that is sent based on an established business relationship with the recipient that was in existence before July 9, 2005, if the sender possessed the facsimile machine number of the recipient before such date of enactment; and

> (iii) the unsolicited advertisement contains a notice meeting the requirements under paragraph (2)(D),

except that the exception under clauses (i) and (ii) shall not apply with respect to an unsolicited advertisement sent to a telephone facsimile machine by a sender to whom a request has been made not to send future unsolicited advertisements to such telephone facsimile machine that complies with the requirements under paragraph (2)(E); or

(D) to use an automatic telephone dialing system in such a way that two or more telephone lines of a multi-line business are engaged simultaneously.

(2) Regulations; Exemptions and Other Provisions

The Commission shall prescribe regulations to implement the requirements of this subsection. In implementing the requirements of this subsection, the Commission—

(A) shall consider prescribing regulations to allow businesses to avoid receiving calls made using an artificial or prerecorded voice to which they have not given their prior express consent;

(B) may, by rule or order, exempt from the requirements of paragraph (1)(B) of this subsection, subject to such conditions as the Commission may prescribe—

(i) calls that are not made for a commercial purpose; and

(ii) such classes or categories of calls made for commercial purposes as the Commission determines—

(I) will not adversely affect the privacy rights that this section is intended to protect; and

(II) do not include the transmission of any unsolicited advertisement;

(C) may, by rule or order, exempt from the requirements of paragraph (1)(A)(iii) of this subsection calls to a telephone number assigned to a cellular telephone service that are not charged to the called party, subject to such conditions as the Commission may prescribe as necessary in the interest of the privacy rights this section is intended to protect;

(D) shall provide that a notice contained in an unsolicited advertisement complies with the requirements under this subparagraph only if—

(i) the notice is clear and conspicuous and on the first page of the unsolicited advertisement;

(ii) the notice states that the recipient may make a request to the sender of the unsolicited advertisement not to send any future unsolicited advertisements to a telephone facsimile machine or machines and that failure to comply, within the shortest reasonable time, as determined by the Commission, with such a request meeting the requirements under subparagraph (E) is unlawful;

(iii) the notice sets forth the requirements for a request under subparagraph (E);

(iv) the notice includes—

(I) a domestic contact telephone and facsimile machine number for the recipient to transmit such a request to the sender; and

(II) a cost-free mechanism for a recipient to transmit a request pursuant to such notice to the sender of the unsolicited advertisement; the Commission shall by rule require the sender to provide such a mechanism and may, in the discretion of the Commission and subject to such conditions as the Commission may prescribe, exempt certain classes of small business senders, but only if the Commission determines that the costs to such class are unduly burdensome given the revenues generated by such small businesses;

(v) the telephone and facsimile machine numbers and the cost-free mechanism set forth pursuant to clause (iv) permit an individual or business to make such a request at any time on any day of the week; and

(vi) the notice complies with the requirements of subsection (d) of this section;

(E) shall provide, by rule, that a request not to send future unsolicited advertisements to a telephone facsimile machine complies with the requirements under this subparagraph only if—

(i) the request identifies the telephone number or numbers of the telephone facsimile machine or machines to which the request relates;

(ii) the request is made to the telephone or facsimile number of the sender of such an unsolicited advertisement provided pursuant to subparagraph (D)(iv) or by any other method of communication as determined by the Commission; and

(iii) the person making the request has not, subsequent to such request, provided express invitation or permission to the sender, in writing or otherwise, to send such advertisements to such person at such telephone facsimile machine;

(F) may, in the discretion of the Commission and subject to such conditions as the Commission may prescribe, allow professional or trade associations that are tax-exempt nonprofit organizations to send unsolicited advertisements to their members in furtherance of the association's tax-exempt purpose that do not contain the notice required by paragraph (1)(C)(iii), except that the Commission may take action under this subparagraph only—

(i) by regulation issued after public notice and opportunity for public comment; and

(ii) if the Commission determines that such notice required by paragraph (1)(C)(iii) is not necessary to protect the ability of the members of such associations to stop such associations from sending any future unsolicited advertisements; and

(G)(i) may, consistent with clause (ii), limit the duration of the existence of an established business relationship, however, before establishing any such limits, the Commission shall—

(I) determine whether the existence of the exception under paragraph (1)(C) relating to an established business relationship has resulted in a significant number of complaints to the Commission regarding the sending of unsolicited advertisements to telephone facsimile machines;

(II) determine whether a significant number of any such complaints involve unsolicited advertisements that were sent on the basis of an established business relationship that was longer in duration than the Commission believes is consistent with the reasonable expectations of consumers;

(III) evaluate the costs to senders of demonstrating the existence of an established business relationship within a specified period of time and the benefits to recipients of establishing a limitation on such established business relationship; and

(IV) determine whether with respect to small businesses, the costs would not be unduly burdensome; and

(ii) may not commence a proceeding to determine whether to limit the duration of the existence of an established business relationship before the expiration of the 3–month period that begins on July 9, 2005.

(3) Private Right of Action

A person or entity may, if otherwise permitted by the laws or rules of court of a State, bring in an appropriate court of that State—

(A) an action based on a violation of this subsection or the regulations prescribed under this subsection to enjoin such violation,

(B) an action to recover for actual monetary loss from such a violation, or to receive $500 in damages for each such violation, whichever is greater, or

(C) both such actions.

If the court finds that the defendant willfully or knowingly violated this subsection or the regulations prescribed under this subsection, the court may, in its discretion, increase the amount of the award to an amount equal to not more than 3 times the amount available under subparagraph (B) of this paragraph.

(c) Protection of Subscriber Privacy Rights

(1) Rulemaking Proceeding Required

Within 120 days after December 20, 1991, the Commission shall initiate a rulemaking proceeding concerning the need to protect residential telephone subscribers' privacy rights to avoid receiving telephone solicitations to which they object. The proceeding shall—

(A) compare and evaluate alternative methods and procedures (including the use of electronic databases, telephone network technologies, special directory markings, industry-based or company-specific "do not call" systems, and any other alternatives, individually or in combination) for their effectiveness in protecting such privacy rights, and in terms of their cost and other advantages and disadvantages;

(B) evaluate the categories of public and private entities that would have the capacity to establish and administer such methods and procedures;

(C) consider whether different methods and procedures may apply for local telephone solicitations, such as local telephone solicitations of small businesses or holders of second class mail permits;

(D) consider whether there is a need for additional Commission authority to further restrict telephone solicitations, including those calls exempted under subsection (a)(3) of this section, and, if such a finding is made and supported by the record, propose specific restrictions to the Congress; and

(E) develop proposed regulations to implement the methods and procedures that the Commission determines are most effective and efficient to accomplish the purposes of this section.

(2) Regulations

Not later than 9 months after December 20, 1991, the Commission shall conclude the rulemaking proceeding initiated under paragraph (1) and shall prescribe regulations to implement methods and procedures for protecting the privacy rights described in such paragraph in an efficient, effective, and economic manner and without the imposition of any additional charge to telephone subscribers.

(3) Use of Database Permitted

The regulations required by paragraph (2) may require the establishment and operation of a single national database to compile a list of telephone numbers of residential subscribers who object to receiving telephone solicitations, and to make that compiled list and parts thereof available for purchase. If the Commission determines to require such a database, such regulations shall—

(A) specify a method by which the Commission will select an entity to administer such database;

(B) require each common carrier providing telephone exchange service, in accordance with regulations prescribed by the Commission, to inform subscribers for telephone exchange service of the opportunity to provide notification, in accordance with regulations established under this paragraph, that such subscriber objects to receiving telephone solicitations;

(C) specify the methods by which each telephone subscriber shall be informed, by the common carrier that provides local exchange service to that subscriber, of (i) the subscriber's right to give or revoke a notification of an objection under subparagraph (A), and (ii) the methods by which such right may be exercised by the subscriber;

(D) specify the methods by which such objections shall be collected and added to the database;

(E) prohibit any residential subscriber from being charged for giving or revoking such notification or for being included in a database compiled under this section;

(F) prohibit any person from making or transmitting a telephone solicitation to the telephone number of any subscriber included in such database;

(G) specify (i) the methods by which any person desiring to make or transmit telephone solicitations will obtain access to the database, by area code or local exchange prefix, as required to avoid calling the telephone numbers of subscribers included in such database; and (ii) the costs to be recovered from such persons;

(H) specify the methods for recovering, from persons accessing such database, the costs involved in identifying, collecting, updating, disseminating, and selling, and other activities relating to, the operations of the database that are incurred by the entities carrying out those activities;

(I) specify the frequency with which such database will be updated and specify the method by which such updating will take effect for purposes of compliance with the regulations prescribed under this subsection;

(J) be designed to enable States to use the database mechanism selected by the Commission for purposes of administering or enforcing State law;

(K) prohibit the use of such database for any purpose other than compliance with the requirements of this section and any such State law and specify methods for protection of the privacy rights of persons whose numbers are included in such database; and

(L) require each common carrier providing services to any person for the purpose of making telephone solicitations to notify such person of the requirements of this section and the regulations thereunder.

(4) Considerations Required for Use of Database Method

If the Commission determines to require the database mechanism described in paragraph (3), the Commission shall—

(A) in developing procedures for gaining access to the database, consider the different needs of telemarketers conducting business on a national, regional, State, or local level;

(B) develop a fee schedule or price structure for recouping the cost of such database that recognizes such differences and—

(i) reflect the relative costs of providing a national, regional, State, or local list of phone numbers of subscribers who object to receiving telephone solicitations;

(ii) reflect the relative costs of providing such lists on paper or electronic media; and

(iii) not place an unreasonable financial burden on small businesses; and

(C) consider (i) whether the needs of telemarketers operating on a local basis could be met through special markings of area white pages directories, and (ii) if such directories are needed as an adjunct to database lists prepared by area code and local exchange prefix.

(5) Private Right of Action

A person who has received more than one telephone call within any 12-month period by or on behalf of the same entity in violation of the regulations prescribed under this subsection may, if otherwise permitted by the laws or rules of court of a State bring in an appropriate court of that State—

(A) an action based on a violation of the regulations prescribed under this subsection to enjoin such violation,

(B) an action to recover for actual monetary loss from such a violation, or to receive up to $500 in damages for each such violation, whichever is greater, or

(C) both such actions.

It shall be an affirmative defense in any action brought under this paragraph that the defendant has established and implemented, with due care, reasonable practices and procedures to effectively prevent telephone solicitations in violation of the regulations prescribed under this subsection. If the court finds that the defendant willfully or knowingly violated the regulations prescribed under this subsection, the court may, in its discretion, increase the amount of the award to an amount equal to not more than 3 times the amount available under subparagraph (B) of this paragraph.

(6) Relation to Subsection (B)

The provisions of this subsection shall not be construed to permit a communication prohibited by subsection (b) of this section.

(d) Technical and Procedural Standards

(1) Prohibition

It shall be unlawful for any person within the United States—

(A) to initiate any communication using a telephone facsimile machine, or to make any telephone call using any automatic telephone dialing system, that does not comply with the technical and procedural standards prescribed under this subsection, or to use any telephone facsimile machine or automatic telephone dialing system in a manner that does not comply with such standards; or

(B) to use a computer or other electronic device to send any message via a telephone facsimile machine unless such person clearly marks, in a margin at the top or bottom of each transmitted page of the message or on the first page of the transmission, the date and time it is sent and an identification of the business, other entity, or individual sending the message and the telephone number of the sending machine or of such business, other entity, or individual.

(2) Telephone Facsimile Machines

The Commission shall revise the regulations setting technical and procedural standards for telephone facsimile machines to require that any such machine which is manufactured after one year after December 20, 1991, clearly marks, in a margin at the top or bottom of each transmitted page or on the first page of each transmission, the date and time sent, an identification of the business, other entity, or individual sending the message, and the telephone number of the sending machine or of such business, other entity, or individual.

(3) Artificial or Prerecorded Voice Systems

The Commission shall prescribe technical and procedural standards for systems that are used to transmit any artificial or prerecorded voice message via telephone. Such standards shall require that—

(A) all artificial or prerecorded telephone messages (i) shall, at the beginning of the message, state clearly the identity of the business, individual, or other entity initiating the call, and (ii) shall, during or after the message, state clearly the telephone number or address of such business, other entity, or individual; and

(B) any such system will automatically release the called party's line within 5 seconds of the time notification is transmitted to the system that the called party has hung up, to allow the called party's line to be used to make or receive other calls.

(e) Effect on State Law

(1) State Law Not Preempted

Except for the standards prescribed under subsection (d) of this section and subject to paragraph (2) of this subsection, nothing in this section or in the regulations prescribed under this section shall preempt any State law that imposes more restrictive intrastate requirements or regulations on, or which prohibits—

(A) the use of telephone facsimile machines or other electronic devices to send unsolicited advertisements;

(B) the use of automatic telephone dialing systems;

(C) the use of artificial or prerecorded voice messages; or

(D) the making of telephone solicitations.

(2) State Use of Databases

If, pursuant to subsection (c)(3) of this section, the Commission requires the establishment of a single national database of telephone numbers of subscribers who object to receiving telephone solicitations, a State or local authority may not, in its regulation of telephone solicitations, require the use of any database, list, or listing system that does not include the part of such single national database that relates to such State.

(f) Actions by States

(1) Authority of States

Whenever the attorney general of a State, or an official or agency designated by a State, has reason to believe that any person has engaged or is engaging in a pattern or practice of telephone calls or other transmissions to residents of that State in violation of this section or the regulations prescribed under this section, the State may bring a civil action on behalf of its residents to enjoin such calls, an action to recover for actual monetary loss or receive $500 in damages for each violation, or both such actions. If the court finds the defendant willfully or knowingly violated such regulations, the court may, in its discretion, increase the amount of the award to an amount equal to not more than 3 times the amount available under the preceding sentence.

(2) Exclusive Jurisdiction of Federal Courts

The district courts of the United States, the United States courts of any territory, and the District Court of the United States for the District of Columbia shall have exclusive jurisdiction over all civil actions brought under this subsection. Upon proper application, such courts shall also have jurisdiction to issue writs of mandamus, or orders affording like relief, commanding the defendant to comply with the provisions of this section or regulations prescribed under this section, including the requirement that the defendant take such action as is necessary to remove the danger of such violation. Upon a proper showing, a permanent or temporary injunction or restraining order shall be granted without bond.

(3) Rights of Commission

The State shall serve prior written notice of any such civil action upon the Commission and provide the Commission with a copy of its complaint, except in any case where such prior notice is not feasible, in which case the State shall serve such notice immediately upon instituting such action. The Commission shall have the right (A) to intervene in the action, (B) upon so intervening, to be heard on all matters arising therein, and (C) to file petitions for appeal.

(4) Venue; Service of Process

Any civil action brought under this subsection in a district court of the United States may be brought in the district wherein the defendant is found or is an inhabitant or transacts business or wherein the violation occurred or is occurring, and process in such cases may be served in any district in which the defendant is an inhabitant or where the defendant may be found.

(5) Investigatory Powers

For purposes of bringing any civil action under this subsection, nothing in this section shall prevent the attorney general of a State, or an official or agency designated by a State, from exercising the powers conferred on the attorney general or such official by the laws of such State to conduct investigations or to administer oaths or affirmations or to compel the attendance of witnesses or the production of documentary and other evidence.

(6) Effect on State Court Proceedings

Nothing contained in this subsection shall be construed to prohibit an authorized State official from proceeding in State court on the basis of an alleged violation of any general civil or criminal statute of such State.

(7) Limitation

Whenever the Commission has instituted a civil action for violation of regulations prescribed under this section, no State may, during the pendency of such action instituted by the Commission, subsequently institute a civil action against any defendant named in the Commission's complaint for any violation as alleged in the Commission's complaint.

(8) Definition

As used in this subsection, the term "attorney general" means the chief legal officer of a State.

(g) Junk Fax Enforcement Report

The Commission shall submit an annual report to Congress regarding the enforcement during the past year of the provisions of this section relating to sending of unsolicited advertisements to telephone facsimile machines, which report shall include—

(1) the number of complaints received by the Commission during such year alleging that a consumer received an unsolicited advertisement via telephone facsimile machine in violation of the Commission's rules;

(2) the number of citations issued by the Commission pursuant to section 503 of this title during the year to enforce any law, regulation, or policy relating to sending of unsolicited advertisements to telephone facsimile machines;

(3) the number of notices of apparent liability issued by the Commission pursuant to section 503 of this title during the year to enforce any law, regulation, or policy relating to sending of unsolicited advertisements to telephone facsimile machines;

(4) for each notice referred to in paragraph (3)—

(A) the amount of the proposed forfeiture penalty involved;

(B) the person to whom the notice was issued;

(C) the length of time between the date on which the complaint was filed and the date on which the notice was issued; and

(D) the status of the proceeding;

(5) the number of final orders imposing forfeiture penalties issued pursuant to section 503 of this title during the year to enforce any law, regulation, or policy relating to sending of unsolicited advertisements to telephone facsimile machines;

(6) for each forfeiture order referred to in paragraph (5)—

(A) the amount of the penalty imposed by the order;

(B) the person to whom the order was issued;

(C) whether the forfeiture penalty has been paid; and

(D) the amount paid;

(7) for each case in which a person has failed to pay a forfeiture penalty imposed by such a final order, whether the Commission referred such matter for recovery of the penalty; and

(8) for each case in which the Commission referred such an order for recovery—

(A) the number of days from the date the Commission issued such order to the date of such referral;

(B) whether an action has been commenced to recover the penalty, and if so, the number of days from the date the Commission referred such order for recovery to the date of such commencement; and

(C) whether the recovery action resulted in collection of any amount, and if so, the amount collected.

TELEPHONE DISCLOSURE AND DISPUTE RESOLUTION ACT

---

§ 1. Short title; findings [15 U.S.C. § 5701]

(a) Short Title

This chapter may be cited as the "Telephone Disclosure and Dispute Resolution Act."

(b) Findings

The Congress finds the following:

(1) The use of pay-per-call services, most commonly through the use of 900 telephone numbers, has grown exponentially in the past few years into a national, billion-dollar industry as a result of recent technological innovations. Such services are convenient to consumers, cost-effective to vendors, and profitable to communications common carriers.

(2) Many pay-per-call businesses provide valuable information, increase consumer choices, and stimulate innovative and responsive services that benefit the public.

(3) The interstate nature of the pay-per-call industry means that its activities are beyond the reach of individual States and therefore requires Federal regulatory treatment to protect the public interest.

(4) The lack of nationally uniform regulatory guidelines has led to confusion for callers, subscribers, industry participants, and regulatory agencies as to the rights of callers and the oversight responsibilities of regulatory authorities, and has allowed some pay-per-call businesses to engage in practices that abuse the rights of consumers.

(5) Some interstate pay-per-call businesses have engaged in practices which are misleading to the consumer, harmful to the public interest, or contrary to accepted standards of business practices and thus cause harm to the many reputable businesses that are serving the public.

(6) Because the consumer most often incurs a financial obligation as soon as a pay-per-call transaction is completed, the accuracy and descriptiveness of vendor advertisements become crucial in avoiding consumer abuse. The obligation for accuracy should include price-per-call and duration-of-call information, odds disclosure for lotteries, games, and sweepstakes, and obligations for obtaining parental consent from callers under 18.

(7) The continued growth of the legitimate pay-per-call industry is dependent upon consumer confidence that unfair and deceptive behavior will be effectively curtailed and that consumers will have adequate rights of redress.

(8) Vendors of telephone-billed goods and services must also feel confident in their rights and obligations for resolving billing disputes if they are to use this new marketplace for the sale of products of more than nominal value.

TITLE I.   CARRIER OBLIGATIONS AND CONSUMER RIGHTS CONCERNING PAY–PER–CALL TRANSACTIONS

§ 101.   Regulation of carrier offering of pay-per-call services [47 U.S.C. § 228]

(a) Purpose

It is the purpose of this section—

(1) to put into effect a system of national regulation and review that will oversee interstate pay-per-call services; and

(2) to recognize the Commission's authority to prescribe regulations and enforcement procedures and conduct oversight to afford reasonable protection to consumers of pay-per-call services and to assure that violations of Federal law do not occur.

(b) General Authority for Regulations

The Commission by regulation shall, within 270 days after October 28, 1992, establish a system for oversight and regulation of pay-per-call services in order to provide for the protection of consumers in accordance with this chapter and other applicable Federal statutes and regulations. The Commission's final rules shall—

(1) include measures that provide a consumer of pay-per-call services with adequate and clear descriptions of the rights of the caller;

(2) define the obligations of common carriers with respect to the provision of pay-per-call services;

(3) include requirements on such carriers to protect against abusive practices by providers of pay-per-call services;

(4) identify procedures by which common carriers and providers of pay-per-call services may take affirmative steps to protect against nonpayment of legitimate charges; and

(5) require that any service described in subparagraphs (A) and (B) of subsection (i)(1) of this section be offered only through the use of certain telephone number prefixes and area codes.

(c) Common Carrier Obligations

Within 270 days after October 28, 1992, the Commission shall, by regulation, establish the following requirements for common carriers:

(1) Contractual Obligations to Comply

Any common carrier assigning to a provider of pay-per-call services a telephone number with a prefix or area code designated by the Commission in accordance with subsection (b)(5) of this section shall require by contract or tariff that such provider comply with the provisions of titles II and III of the Telephone Disclosure and Dispute Resolution Act and the regulations prescribed by the Federal Trade Commission pursuant to those titles.

(2) Information Availability

A common carrier that by tariff or contract assigns a telephone number with a prefix or area code designated by the Commission in accordance with subsection (b)(5) of this section to a provider of a pay-per-call service shall make readily available on request to Federal and State agencies and other interested persons—

(A) a list of the telephone numbers for each of the pay-per-call services it carries;

(B) a short description of each such service;

(C) a statement of the total cost or the cost per minute and any other fees for each such service;

(D) a statement of the pay-per-call service's name, business address, and business telephone; and

(E) such other information as the Commission considers necessary for the enforcement of this section and other applicable Federal statutes and regulations.

(3) Compliance Procedures

A common carrier that by contract or tariff assigns a telephone number with a prefix or area code designated by the Commission in accordance with subsection (b)(5) of this section to a provider of pay-per-call services shall terminate, in accordance with procedures specified in such regulations, the offering of a pay-per-call service of a provider if the carrier knows or reasonably should know that such service is not provided in compliance with title II or III of the Telephone Disclosure and Dispute Resolution Act or the regulations prescribed by the Federal Trade Commission pursuant to such titles.

(4) Subscriber Disconnection Prohibited

A common carrier shall not disconnect or interrupt a subscriber's local exchange telephone service or long distance telephone service because of nonpayment of charges for any pay-per-call service.

(5) Blocking and Presubscription

A common carrier that provides local exchange service shall—

(A) offer telephone subscribers (where technically feasible) the option of blocking access from their telephone number to all, or to certain specific, prefixes or area codes used by pay-per-call services, which option—

(i) shall be offered at no charge (I) to all subscribers for a period of 60 days after the issuance of the regulations under subsection (b) of this section, and (II) to any subscriber who subscribes to a new telephone number until 60 days after the time the new telephone number is effective; and

(ii) shall otherwise be offered at a reasonable fee; and

(B) offer telephone subscribers (where the Commission determines it is technically and economically feasible), in combination with the blocking option described under subparagraph (A), the option of presubscribing to or blocking only specific pay-per-call services for a reasonable one-time charge.

The regulations prescribed under subparagraph (A)(i) of this paragraph may permit the costs of such blocking to be recovered by contract or tariff, but such costs may not be recovered from local or long-distance ratepayers. Nothing in this subsection precludes a common carrier from filing its rates and regulations regarding blocking and presubscription in its interstate tariffs.

(6) Verification of Charitable Status

A common carrier that assigns by contract or tariff a telephone number with a prefix or area code designated by the Commission in accordance with subsection (b)(5) of this section to a provider of pay-per-call services that the carrier knows or reasonably should know is engaged in soliciting charitable contributions shall obtain from such provider proof of the tax exempt status of any person or organization for which contributions are solicited.

(7) Billing for 800 Calls

A common carrier shall prohibit by tariff or contract the use of any 800 telephone number, or other telephone number advertised or widely understood to be toll free, in a manner that would result in—

(A) the calling party being assessed, by virtue of completing the call, a charge for the call;

(B) the calling party being connected to a pay-per-call service;

(C) the calling party being charged for information conveyed during the call unless—

   (i) the calling party has a written agreement (including an agreement transmitted through electronic medium) that meets the requirements of paragraph (8); or

   (ii) the calling party is charged for the information in accordance with paragraph (9);

(D) the calling party being called back collect for the provision of audio information services or simultaneous voice conversation services; or

(E) the calling party being assessed, by virtue of being asked to connect or otherwise transfer to a pay-per-call service, a charge for the call.

(8) Subscription Agreements for Billing for Information Provided Via Toll-free Calls

(A) In General

For purposes of paragraph (7)(C)(i), a written subscription does not meet the requirements of this paragraph unless the agreement specifies the material terms and conditions under which the information is offered and includes—

   (i) the rate at which charges are assessed for the information;

   (ii) the information provider's name;

   (iii) the information provider's business address;

   (iv) the information provider's regular business telephone number;

   (v) the information provider's agreement to notify the subscriber at least one billing cycle in advance of all future changes in the rates charged for the information; and

   (vi) the subscriber's choice of payment method, which may be by direct remit, debit, prepaid account, phone bill, or credit or calling card.

(B) Billing Arrangements

If a subscriber elects, pursuant to subparagraph (A)(vi), to pay by means of a phone bill—

(i) the agreement shall clearly explain that the subscriber will be assessed for calls made to the information service from the subscriber's phone line;

(ii) the phone bill shall include, in prominent type, the following disclaimer:

"Common carriers may not disconnect local or long distance telephone service for failure to pay disputed charges for information services."; and

(iii) the phone bill shall clearly list the 800 number dialed.

(C) Use of PINS to Prevent Unauthorized Use

A written agreement does not meet the requirements of this paragraph unless it—

(i) includes a unique personal identification number or other subscriber-specific identifier and requires a subscriber to use this number or identifier to obtain access to the information provided and includes instructions on its use; and

(ii) assures that any charges for services accessed by use of the subscriber's personal identification number or subscriber-specific identifier be assessed to subscriber's source of payment elected pursuant to subparagraph (A)(vi).

(D) Exceptions

Notwithstanding paragraph (7)(C), a written agreement that meets the requirements of this paragraph is not required—

(i) for calls utilizing telecommunications devices for the deaf;

(ii) for directory services provided by a common carrier or its affiliate or by a local exchange carrier or its affiliate; or

(iii) for any purchase of goods or of services that are not information services.

(E) Termination of Service

On receipt by a common carrier of a complaint by any person that an information provider is in violation of the provisions of this section, a carrier shall—

(i) promptly investigate the complaint; and

(ii) if the carrier reasonably determines that the complaint is valid, it may terminate the provision of service to an information provider unless the provider supplies evidence of a written agreement that meets the requirements of this section.

(F) Treatment of Remedies

The remedies provided in this paragraph are in addition to any other remedies that are available under title V of this chapter.

(9) Charges by credit, prepaid, debit, charge, or calling card in absence of agreement

For purposes of paragraph (7)(C)(ii), a calling party is not charged in accordance with this paragraph unless the calling party is charged by means of a credit, prepaid, debit, charge, or calling card and the information service provider includes in response to each call an introductory disclosure message that—

(A) clearly states that there is a charge for the call;

(B) clearly states the service's total cost per minute and any other fees for the service or for any service to which the caller may be transferred;

(C) explains that the charges must be billed on either a credit, prepaid, debit, charge, or calling card;

(D) asks the caller for the card number;

(E) clearly states that charges for the call begin at the end of the introductory message; and

(F) clearly states that the caller can hang up at or before the end of the introductory message without incurring any charge whatsoever.

(10) Bypass of Introductory Disclosure Message

The requirements of paragraph (9) shall not apply to calls from repeat callers using a bypass mechanism to avoid listening to the introductory message: *Provided*, That information providers shall disable such a bypass mechanism after the institution of any price increase and for a period of time determined to be sufficient by the Federal Trade Commission to give callers adequate and sufficient notice of a price increase.

(11) Definition of Calling Card

As used in this subsection, the term "calling card" means an identifying number or code unique to the individual, that is issued to the individual by a common carrier and enables the individual to be charged by means of a phone bill for charges incurred independent of where the call originates.

(d) Billing and Collection Practices

The regulations required by this section shall require that any common carrier that by tariff or contract assigns a telephone number with a prefix or area code designated by the Commission in accordance with subsection (b)(5) of this section to a provider of a pay-per-call service and that offers billing and collection services to such provider—

(1) ensure that a subscriber is not billed—

(A) for pay-per-call services that such carrier knows or reasonably should know was provided in violation of the regulations issued pursuant to title II of the Telephone Disclosure and Dispute Resolution Act; or

(B) under such other circumstances as the Commission determines necessary in order to protect subscribers from abusive practices;

(2) establish a local or a toll-free telephone number to answer questions and provide information on subscribers' rights and obligations with regard to their use of pay-per-call services and to provide to callers the name and mailing address of any provider of pay-per-call services offered by the common carrier;

(3) within 60 days after the issuance of final regulations pursuant to subsection (b) of this section, provide, either directly or through contract with any local exchange carrier that provides billing or collection services to the common carrier, to all of such common carrier's telephone subscribers, to all new subscribers, and to all subscribers requesting service at a new location, a disclosure statement that sets forth all rights and obligations of the subscriber and the carrier with respect to the use and payment for pay-per-call services, including the right of a subscriber not to be billed and the applicable blocking option; and

(4) in any billing to telephone subscribers that includes charges for any pay-per-call service—

(A) display any charges for pay-per-call services in a part of the subscriber's bill that is identified as not being related to local and long distance telephone charges;

(B) for each charge so displayed, specify, at a minimum, the type of service, the amount of the charge, and the date, time, and duration of the call; and

(C) identify the toll-free number established pursuant to paragraph (2).

(e) Liability

(1) Common Carriers Not Liable for Transmission or Billing

No common carrier shall be liable for a criminal or civil sanction or penalty solely because the carrier provided transmission or billing and collection for a pay-per-call service unless the carrier knew or reasonably should have known that such service was provided in violation of a provision of, or regulation prescribed pursuant to, title II or III of the Telephone Disclosure and Dispute Resolution Act or any other Federal law. This paragraph shall not prevent the Commission from imposing a sanction or penalty on a common carrier for a violation by that carrier of a regulation prescribed under this section.

(2) Civil Liability

No cause of action may be brought in any court or administrative agency against any common carrier or any of its affiliates on account of any act of the carrier or affiliate to terminate any pay-per-call service in order to comply with the regulations prescribed under this section, title II or III of the Telephone Disclosure and Dispute Resolution Act, or any other Federal law unless the complainant demonstrates that the carrier or affiliate did not act in good faith.

(f) Special Provisions

(1) Consumer Refund Requirements

The regulations required by subsection (d) of this section shall establish procedures, consistent with the provisions of titles II and III of the Telephone Disclosure and Dispute Resolution Act, to ensure that carriers and other parties providing billing and collection services with respect to pay-per-call services provide appropriate refunds to subscribers who have been billed for pay-per-call services pursuant to programs that have been found to have violated this section or such regulations, any provision of, or regulations prescribed pursuant to, title II or III of the Telephone Disclosure and Dispute Resolution Act, or any other Federal law.

(2) Recovery of Costs

The regulations prescribed by the Commission under this section shall permit a common carrier to recover its cost of complying with such regulations from providers of pay-per-call services, but shall not permit such costs to be recovered from local or long distance ratepayers.

(3) Recommendations on Data Pay-per-call

The Commission, within one year after October 28, 1992, shall submit to the Congress the Commission's recommendations with respect to the extension of regulations under this section to persons that provide, for a per-call charge, data services that are not pay-per-call services.

(g) Effect on Other Law

(1) No Preemption of Election Law

Nothing in this section shall relieve any provider of pay-per-call services, common carrier, local exchange carrier, or any other person from the obligation to comply with Federal, State, and local election statutes and regulations.

(2) Consumer Protection Laws

Nothing in this section shall relieve any provider of pay-per-call services, common carrier, local exchange carrier, or any other person from the obligation to comply with any Federal, State, or local statute or regulation relating to consumer protection or unfair trade.

(3) Gambling Laws

Nothing in this section shall preclude any State from enforcing its statutes and regulations with regard to lotteries, wagering, betting, and other gambling activities.

(4) State Authority

Nothing in this section shall preclude any State from enacting and enforcing additional and complementary oversight and regulatory systems or procedures, or both, so long as such systems and procedures govern intrastate services and do not significantly impede the enforcement of this section or other Federal statutes.

(5) Enforcement of Existing Regulations

Nothing in this section shall be construed to prohibit the Commission from enforcing regulations prescribed prior to October 28, 1992 in fulfilling the requirements of this section to the extent that such regulations are consistent with the provisions of this section.

(h) Effect on Dial-a-porn Prohibitions

Nothing in this section shall affect the provisions of section 223 of this title.

(i) Definition of Pay-per-call Services

For purposes of this section—

(1) The term "pay-per-call services" means any service—

   (A) in which any person provides or purports to provide—

      (i) audio information or audio entertainment produced or packaged by such person;

      (ii) access to simultaneous voice conversation services; or

      (iii) any service, including the provision of a product, the charges for which are assessed on the basis of the completion of the call;

   (B) for which the caller pays a per-call or per-time-interval charge that is greater than, or in addition to, the charge for transmission of the call; and

   (C) which is accessed through use of a 900 telephone number or other prefix or area code designated by the Commission in accordance with subsection (b)(5) of this section.

(2) Such term does not include directory services provided by a common carrier or its affiliate or by a local exchange carrier or its affiliate, or any service for which users are assessed charges only after entering into a presubscription or comparable arrangement with the provider of such service.

TITLE II. REGULATION OF UNFAIR AND DECEPTIVE ACTS AND PRACTICES IN CONNECTION WITH PAY-PER-CALL SERVICES

§ 201. Federal Trade Commission regulations [15 U.S.C. § 5711]

(a) In General

(1) Advertising Regulations

The Commission shall prescribe rules in accordance with this subsection to prohibit unfair and deceptive acts and practices in any advertisement for pay-per-call services. Such rules shall require that the person offering such pay-per-call services—

(A) clearly and conspicuously disclose in any advertising the cost of the use of such telephone number, including the total cost or the cost per minute and any other fees for that service and for any other pay-per-call service to which the caller may be transferred;

(B) in the case of an advertisement which offers a prize or award or a service or product at no cost or for a reduced cost, clearly and conspicuously disclose the odds of being able to receive such prize, award, service, or product at no cost or reduced cost, or, if such odds are not calculable in advance, disclose the factors determining such odds;

(C) in the case of an advertisement that promotes a service that is not operated or expressly authorized by a Federal agency but that provides information on a Federal program, include at the beginning of such advertisement a clear disclosure that the service is not authorized, endorsed, or approved by any Federal agency;

(D) shall not direct such advertisement at children under the age of 12, unless such service is a bona fide educational service;

(E) in the case of advertising directed primarily to individuals under the age of 18, clearly and conspicuously state in such advertising that such individual must have the consent of such individual's parent or legal guardian for the use of such services;

(F) be prohibited from using advertisements that emit electronic tones which can automatically dial a pay-per-call telephone number;

(G) ensure that, whenever the number to be called is shown in television and print media advertisements, the charges for the call are clear and conspicuous and (when shown in television advertisements) displayed for the same duration as that number is displayed;

(H) in delivering any telephone message soliciting calls to a pay-per-call service, specify clearly, and at no less than the audible volume of the solicitation, the total cost and the cost per minute and any other fees for that service and for any other pay-per-call service to which the caller may be transferred; and

(I) not advertise an 800 telephone number, or any other telephone number advertised or widely understood to be toll free, from which callers are connected to an access number for a pay-per-call service.

(2) Pay-per-call Service Standards

The Commission shall prescribe rules to require that each provider of pay-per-call services—

(A) include in each pay-per-call message an introductory disclosure message that—

(i) describes the service being provided;

(ii) specifies clearly and at a reasonably understandable volume the total cost or the cost per minute and any other fees for that service and for any other pay-per-call service to which the caller may be transferred;

(iii) informs the caller that charges for the call begin at the end of the introductory message;

(iv) informs the caller that parental consent is required for calls made by children; and

(v) in the case of a pay-per-call service that is not operated or expressly authorized by a Federal agency but that provides information on any Federal program, a statement that clearly states that the service is not authorized, endorsed, or approved by any Federal agency;

(B) enable the caller to hang up at or before the end of the introductory message without incurring any charge whatsoever;

(C) not direct such services at children under the age of 12, unless such service is a bona fide educational service;

(D) stop the assessment of time-based charges immediately upon disconnection by the caller;

(E) disable any bypass mechanism which allows frequent callers to avoid listening to the disclosure message described in subparagraph (A) after the institution of any price increase and for a period of time sufficient to give such frequent callers adequate and sufficient notice of the price change;

(F) be prohibited from providing pay-per-call services through an 800 number or other telephone number advertised or widely understood to be toll free;

(G) be prohibited from billing consumers in excess of the amounts described in the introductory message and from billing for services provided in violation of the rules prescribed by the Commission pursuant to this section;

(H) ensure that any billing statement for such provider's charges shall—

(i) display any charges for pay-per-call services in a part of the consumer's bill that is identified as not being related to local and long distance telephone charges; and

(ii) for each charge so displayed, specify, at a minimum, the type of service, the amount of the charge, and the date, time, and duration of the call;

(I) be liable for refunds to consumers who have been billed for pay-per-call services pursuant to programs that have been found to have violated the regulations prescribed pursuant to this section or subchapter II of this chapter or any other Federal law; and

(J) comply with such additional standards as the Commission may prescribe to prevent abusive practices.

(3) Access to Information

The Commission shall by rule require a common carrier that provides telephone services to a provider of pay-per-call services to make available to the Commission any records and financial information maintained by such carrier relating to the arrangements (other than for the provision of local exchange service) between such carrier and any provider of pay-per-call services.

(4) Evasions

The rules issued by the Commission under this section shall include provisions to prohibit unfair or deceptive acts or practices that evade such rules or undermine the rights provided to customers under this title, including through the use of alternative billing or other procedures.

(5) Exemptions

The regulations prescribed by the Commission pursuant to paragraph (2)(A) may exempt from the requirements of such paragraph—

(A) calls from frequent callers or regular subscribers using a bypass mechanism to avoid listening to the disclosure message required by such regulations, subject to the requirements of paragraph (2)(E); or

(B) pay-per-call services provided at nominal charges, as defined by the Commission in such regulations.

(6) Consideration of Other Rules Required

In conducting a proceeding under this section, the Commission shall consider requiring, by rule or regulation, that providers of pay-per-call services—

(A) automatically disconnect a call after one full cycle of the program; and

(B) include a beep tone or other appropriate and clear signal during a live interactive group program so that callers will be alerted to the passage of time.

(7) Special Rule for Infrequent Publications

The rules prescribed by the Commission under subparagraphs (A) and (G) of paragraph (1) may permit, in the case of publications that are widely distributed, that are printed annually or less frequently, and that have an established policy of not publishing specific prices, advertising that in lieu of the cost disclosures required by such subparagraphs, clearly and conspicuously disclose that use of the telephone number may result in a substantial charge.

(8) Treatment of Rules

A rule issued under this subsection shall be treated as a rule issued under section 18(a)(1)(B) of [the Federal Trade Commission Act].

(b) Rulemaking

The Commission shall prescribe the rules under subsection (a) of this section within 270 days after October 28, 1992. Such rules shall be prescribed in accordance with section 553 of Title 5.

(c) Enforcement

Any violation of any rule prescribed under subsection (a) of this section shall be treated as a violation of a rule respecting unfair or deceptive acts or practices under section 5 of [the Federal Trade Commission Act]. Notwithstanding section 5(a)(2) of [the Federal Trade Commission Act], communications common carriers shall be subject to the jurisdiction of the Commission for purposes of this subchapter.

§ 202.   Actions by States [15 U.S.C. § 5712]

(a) In General

Whenever an attorney general of any State has reason to believe that the interests of the residents of that State have been or are being threatened or adversely affected because any person has engaged or is engaging in a pattern or practice which violates any rule of the Commission under section 201(a) of this Act, the State may bring a civil action on behalf of its residents in an appropriate district court of the United States to enjoin such pattern or practice, to enforce compliance with such rule of the Commission, to obtain damages on behalf of their residents, or to obtain such further and other relief as the court may deem appropriate.

(b) Notice

The State shall serve prior written notice of any civil action under subsection (a) of this section upon the Commission and provide the Commission with a copy of its complaint, except that if it is not feasible for the State to provide such prior notice, the State shall serve such notice immediately upon instituting such action. Upon receiving a notice respecting a civil action, the Commission shall have the right (1) to intervene in such action, (2) upon so intervening, to be heard on all matters arising therein, and (3) to file petitions for appeal.

(c) Venue

Any civil action brought under this section in a district court of the United States may be brought in the district wherein the defendant is found or is an inhabitant or transacts business or wherein the violation occurred or is occurring, and process in such cases may be served in any district in which the defendant is an inhabitant or wherever the defendant may be found.

(d) Investigatory Powers

For purposes of bringing any civil action under this section, nothing in this Act shall prevent the attorney general from exercising the powers conferred on the attorney general by the laws of such State to conduct investigations or to administer oaths or affirmations or to compel the attendance of witnesses or the production of documentary and other evidence.

(e) Effect on State Court Proceedings

Nothing contained in this section shall prohibit an authorized State official from proceeding in State court on the basis of an alleged violation of any general civil or criminal antifraud statute of such State.

(f) Limitation

Whenever the Commission has instituted a civil action for violation of any rule or regulation under this Act, no State may, during the pendency of such action instituted by the Commission, subsequently institute a civil action against any defendant named in the Commission's complaint for violation of any rule as alleged in the Commission's complaint.

(g) Actions by Other State Officials

(1) Nothing contained in this section shall prohibit an authorized State official from proceeding in State court on the basis of an alleged violation of any general civil or criminal statute of such State.

(2) In addition to actions brought by an attorney general of a State under subsection (a) of this section, such an action may be brought by officers of such State who are authorized by the State to bring actions in such State for protection of consumers and who are designated by the Commission to bring an action under subsection (a) of this section against persons that the Commission has determined have or are engaged in a pattern or practice which violates a rule of the Commission under section 201(a) of this Act.

§ 203. Administration and applicability of title [15 U.S.C. § 5713]

(a) In General

Except as otherwise provided in section 202 of this Act, this title shall be enforced by the Commission under the Federal Trade Commission Act

(15 U.S.C. 41 et seq.). Consequently, no activity which is outside the jurisdiction of that Act shall be affected by this Act, except for purposes of this title.

(b) Actions by Commission

The Commission shall prevent any person from violating a rule of the Commission under section 201 of this Act in the same manner, by the same means, and with the same jurisdiction, powers, and duties as though all applicable terms and provisions of the Federal Trade Commission Act (15 U.S.C. 41 et seq.) were incorporated into and made a part of this title. Any person who violates such rule shall be subject to the penalties and entitled to the privileges and immunities provided in the Federal Trade Commission Act in the same manner, by the same means, and with the same jurisdiction, power, and duties as though all applicable terms and provisions of the Federal Trade Commission Act were incorporated into and made a part of this title.

§ 204.   Definitions [15 U.S.C. § 5714]

For purposes of this title:

(1) The term "pay-per-call services" has the meaning provided in section 228(i) of Title 47, except that the Commission by rule may, notwithstanding subparagraphs (B) and (C) of section 228(i)(1) of Title 47, extend such definition to other similar services providing audio information or audio entertainment if the Commission determines that such services are susceptible to the unfair and deceptive practices that are prohibited by the rules prescribed pursuant to section 201(a) of this Act.

(2) The term "attorney general" means the chief legal officer of a State.

(3) The term "State" means any State of the United States, the District of Columbia, Puerto Rico, the Northern Mariana Islands, and any territory or possession of the United States.

(4) The term "Commission" means the Federal Trade Commission.

TITLE III.   BILLING AND COLLECTION

§ 301.   Regulations [15 U.S.C. § 5721]

(a) in General

(1) Rules Required

The Commission shall, in accordance with the requirements of this section, prescribe rules establishing procedures for the correction of billing errors with respect to telephone-billed purchases. The rules prescribed by the Commission shall also include provisions to prohibit unfair or deceptive acts or practices that evade such rules or undermine the rights provided to customers under this title.

(2) Substantial Similarity to Credit Billing

The Commission shall promulgate rules under this section that impose requirements that are substantially similar to the requirements imposed, with respect to the resolution of credit disputes, under the Truth in Lending and Fair Credit Billing Acts.

(3) Treatment of Rule

A rule issued under paragraph (1) shall be treated as a rule issued under section [18(a)(1)(B) of the Federal Trade Commission Act].

(b) Rulemaking Schedule and Procedure

The Commission shall prescribe the rules under subsection (a) of this section within 270 days after October 28, 1992. Such rules shall be prescribed in accordance with section 553 of Title 5.

(c) Enforcement

Any violation of any rule prescribed under subsection (a) of this section shall be treated as a violation of a rule under section 5 of [the Federal Trade Commission Act] regarding unfair or deceptive acts or practices. Notwithstanding section 5(a)(2) of [the Federal Trade Commission Act], communications common carriers shall be subject to the jurisdiction of the Commission for purposes of this title.

(d) Correction of Billing Errors and Correction of Credit Reports

In prescribing rules under this section, the Commission shall consider, with respect to telephone-billed purchases, the following:

(1) The initiation of a billing review by a customer.

(2) Responses by billing entities and providing carriers to the initiation of a billing review.

(3) Investigations concerning delivery of telephone-billed purchases.

(4) Limitations upon providing carrier responsibilities, including limitations on a carrier's responsibility to verify delivery of audio information or entertainment.

(5) Requirements on actions by billing entities to set aside charges from a customer's billing statement.

(6) Limitations on collection actions by billing entities and vendors.

(7) The regulation of credit reports on billing disputes.

(8) The prompt notification of credit to an account.

(9) Rights of customers and telephone common carriers regarding claims and defenses.

(10) The extent to which the regulations should diverge from requirements under the Truth in Lending and Fair Credit Billing Acts in order to protect customers, and in order to be cost effective to billing entities.

§ 302. Relation to State laws [15 U.S.C. § 5722]

(a) State Law Applicable Unless Inconsistent

This title does not annul, alter, or affect, or exempt any person subject to the provisions of this title from complying with, the laws of any State with respect to telephone billing practices, except to the extent that those laws are inconsistent with any provision of this title, and then only to the extent of the inconsistency. The Commission is authorized to determine whether such inconsistencies exist. The Commission may not determine that any State law is inconsistent with any provision of this title if the Commission determines that such law gives greater protection to the consumer.

(b) Regulatory Exemptions

The Commission shall by regulation exempt from the requirements of this title any class of telephone-billed purchase transactions within any State if it determines that under the law of that State that class of transactions is subject to requirements substantially similar to those imposed under this title or that such law gives greater protection to the consumer, and that there is adequate provision for enforcement.

§ 303. Enforcement [15 U.S.C. § 5723]

The Commission shall enforce the requirements of this title. For the purpose of the exercise by the Commission of its functions and powers under the Federal Trade Commission Act, a violation of any requirement imposed under this title shall be deemed a violation of a requirement imposed under that Act. All the functions and powers of the Commission under that Act are available to the Commission to enforce compliance by any person with the requirements imposed under this title, irrespective of whether that person is engaged in commerce or meets any other jurisdictional tests in that Act. The Commission may prescribe such regulations as are necessary or appropriate to implement the provisions of this title.

§ 304. Definitions [15 U.S.C. § 5724]

As used in this title—

(1) The term "telephone-billed purchase" means any purchase that is completed solely as a consequence of the completion of the call or a subsequent dialing, touch tone entry, or comparable action of the caller. Such term does not include—

(A) a purchase by a caller pursuant to a preexisting agreement with the vendor;

(B) local exchange telephone services or interexchange telephone services or any service that the Federal Communications Commission determines, by rule—

(i) is closely related to the provision of local exchange telephone services or interexchange telephone services; and

(ii) is subject to billing dispute resolution procedures required by Federal or State statute or regulation; or

(C) the purchase of goods or services which is otherwise subject to billing dispute resolution procedures required by Federal statute or regulation.

(2) A "billing error" consists of any of the following:

(A) A reflection on a billing statement for a telephone-billed purchase which was not made by the customer or, if made, was not in the amount reflected on such statement.

(B) A reflection on a billing statement of a telephone-billed purchase for which the customer requests additional clarification, including documentary evidence thereof.

(C) A reflection on a billing statement of a telephone-billed purchase that was not accepted by the customer or not provided to the customer in accordance with the stated terms of the transaction.

(D) A reflection on a billing statement of a telephone-billed purchase for a call made to an 800 or other toll free telephone number.

(E) The failure to reflect properly on a billing statement a payment made by the customer or a credit issued to the customer with respect to a telephone-billed purchase.

(F) A computation error or similar error of an accounting nature on a statement.

(G) Failure to transmit the billing statement to the last known address of the customer, unless that address was furnished less than twenty days before the end of the billing cycle for which the statement is required.

(H) Any other error described in regulations prescribed by the Commission pursuant to section 553 of Title 5.

(3) The term "Commission" means the Federal Trade Commission.

(4) The term "providing carrier" means a local exchange or interexchange common carrier providing telephone services (other than local exchange services) to a vendor for a telephone-billed purchase that is the subject of a billing error complaint.

(5) The term "vendor" means any person who, through the use of the telephone, offers goods or services for a telephone-billed purchase.

(6) The term "customer" means any person who acquires or attempts to acquire goods or services in a telephone-billed purchase.

TELEMARKETING AND CONSUMER FRAUD AND ABUSE PREVENTION ACT

(15 U.S.C. §§ 6101–6108)

Table of Sections

---

§ 1. Short title

This Act may be cited as the Telemarketing and Consumer Fraud and Abuse Prevention Act.

§ 2. Findings [15 U.S.C. § 6101]

The Congress makes the following findings:

(1) Telemarketing differs from other sales activities in that it can be carried out by sellers across State lines without direct contact with the consumer. Telemarketers also can be very mobile, easily moving from State to State.

(2) Interstate telemarketing fraud has become a problem of such magnitude that the resources of the Federal Trade Commission are not sufficient to ensure adequate consumer protection from such fraud.

(3) Consumers and others are estimated to lose $40 billion a year in telemarketing fraud.

(4) Consumers are victimized by other forms of telemarketing deception and abuse.

(5) Consequently, Congress should enact legislation that will offer consumers necessary protection from telemarketing deception and abuse.

§ 3. Telemarketing rules [15 U.S.C. § 6102]

(a) In General

(1) The Commission shall prescribe rules prohibiting deceptive telemarketing acts or practices and other abusive telemarketing acts or practices.

(2) The Commission shall include in such rules respecting deceptive telemarketing acts or practices a definition of deceptive telemarketing acts or practices which shall include fraudulent charitable solicitations, and which may include acts or practices of entities or individuals that assist or facilitate deceptive telemarketing, including credit card laundering.

(3) The Commission shall include in such rules respecting other abusive telemarketing acts or practices—

(A) a requirement that telemarketers may not undertake a pattern of unsolicited telephone calls which the reasonable consumer would consider coercive or abusive of such consumer's right to privacy,

(B) restrictions on the hours of the day and night when unsolicited telephone calls can be made to consumers,

(C) a requirement that any person engaged in telemarketing for the sale of goods or services shall promptly and clearly disclose to the person receiving the call that the purpose of the call is to sell goods or services and make such other disclosures as the Commission deems appropriate, including the nature and price of the goods and services, and

(D) a requirement that any person engaged in telemarketing for the solicitation of charitable contributions, donations, or gifts of money or any other thing of value, shall promptly and clearly disclose to the person receiving the call that the purpose of the call is to solicit charitable contributions, donations, or gifts, and make such other disclosures as the Commission considers appropriate, including the name and mailing address of the charitable organization on behalf of which the solicitation is made.

In prescribing the rules described in this paragraph, the Commission shall also consider recordkeeping requirements.

(b) Rulemaking

The Commission shall prescribe the rules under subsection (a) of this section within 365 days after August 16, 1994. Such rules shall be prescribed in accordance with section 553 of Title 5.

(c) Enforcement

Any violation of any rule prescribed under subsection (a) of this section shall be treated as a violation of a rule under section [18 of the Federal Trade Commission Act, 15 U.S.C. § 57a] regarding unfair or deceptive acts or practices.

(d) Securities and Exchange Commission Rules

(1) Promulgation

(A) In General

Except as provided in subparagraph (B), not later than 6 months after the effective date of rules promulgated by the Federal Trade Commission under subsection (a) of this section, the Securities and Exchange Commission shall promulgate, or require any national securities exchange or registered securities association to promulgate, rules substantially similar to such rules to prohibit deceptive and other abusive telemarketing acts or practices by persons described in paragraph (2).

(B) Exception

The Securities and Exchange Commission is not required to promulgate a rule under subparagraph (A) if it determines that—

(i) Federal securities laws or rules adopted by the Securities and Exchange Commission thereunder provide protection from deceptive and other abusive telemarketing by persons described in paragraph (2) substantially similar to that provided by rules promulgated by the Federal Trade Commission under subsection (a) of this section; or

(ii) such a rule promulgated by the Securities and Exchange Commission is not necessary or appropriate in the public interest, or for the protection of investors, or would be inconsistent with the maintenance of fair and orderly markets.

If the Securities and Exchange Commission determines that an exception described in clause (i) or (ii) applies, the Securities and Exchange Commission shall publish in the Federal Register its determination with the reasons for it.

(2) Application

(A) In General

The rules promulgated by the Securities and Exchange Commission under paragraph (1)(A) shall apply to a broker, dealer, transfer agent, municipal securities dealer, municipal securities broker, government securities broker, government securities dealer, investment adviser or investment company, or any individual associated with a broker, dealer, transfer agent, municipal securities dealer, municipal securities broker, government securities broker, government securities dealer, investment adviser or investment company. The rules promulgated by the Federal Trade Commission under subsection (a) of this section shall not apply to persons described in the preceding sentence.

(B) Definitions

For purposes of subparagraph (A)—

(i) the terms "broker," "dealer," "transfer agent," "municipal securities dealer," "municipal securities broker," "government securities broker," and "government securities dealer" have the meanings given such terms by paragraphs (4), (5), (25), (30), (31), (43), and (44) of section 78c(a) of Title 15;

(ii) the term "investment adviser" has the meaning given such term by section 80b–2(a)(11) of Title 15; and

(iii) the term "investment company" has the meaning given such term by section 80a–3(a) of Title 15.

(e) Commodity Futures Trading Commission Rules

(1) Application

The rules promulgated by the Federal Trade Commission under subsection (a) of this section shall not apply to persons described in section 9b(1) of Title 7. . . .

§ 4. Actions by States [15 U.S.C. § 6103]

(a) In General

Whenever an attorney general of any State has reason to believe that the interests of the residents of that State have been or are being threatened or adversely affected because any person has engaged or is engaging in a pattern or practice of telemarketing which violates any rule of the Commission under section 3 of this Act, the State, as parens patriae, may bring a civil action on behalf of its residents in an appropriate district court of the United States to enjoin such telemarketing, to enforce compliance with such rule of the Commission, to obtain damages, restitution, or other compensation on behalf of residents of such State, or to obtain such further and other relief as the court may deem appropriate.

(b) Notice

The State shall serve prior written notice of any civil action under subsection (a) or (f)(2) of this section upon the Commission and provide the Commission with a copy of its complaint, except that if it is not feasible for the State to provide such prior notice, the State shall serve such notice immediately upon instituting such action. Upon receiving a notice respecting a civil action, the Commission shall have the right (1) to intervene in such action, (2) upon so intervening, to be heard on all matters arising therein, and (3) to file petitions for appeal.

(c) Construction

For purposes of bringing any civil action under subsection (a) of this section, nothing in this chapter shall prevent an attorney general from exercising the powers conferred on the attorney general by the laws of such State to conduct investigations or to administer oaths or affirmations or to compel the attendance of witnesses or the production of documentary and other evidence.

(d) Actions by Commission

Whenever a civil action has been instituted by or on behalf of the Commission for violation of any rule prescribed under section 3 of this Act, no State may, during the pendency of such action instituted by or on behalf of the Commission, institute a civil action under subsection (a) or (f)(2) of this section against any defendant named in the complaint in such action for violation of any rule as alleged in such complaint.

(e) Venue; Service of Process

Any civil action brought under subsection (a) of this section in a district court of the United States may be brought in the district in which the defendant is found, is an inhabitant, or transacts business or wherever venue is proper under section 1391 of Title 28. Process in such an action may be served in any district in which the defendant is an inhabitant or in which the defendant may be found.

(f) Actions by Other State Officials

(1) Nothing contained in this section shall prohibit an authorized State official from proceeding in State court on the basis of an alleged violation of any civil or criminal statute of such State.

(2) In addition to actions brought by an attorney general of a State under subsection (a) of this section, such an action may be brought by officers of such State who are authorized by the State to bring actions in such State on behalf of its residents.

§ 5.   Actions by private persons [15 U.S.C. § 6104]

(a) In General

Any person adversely affected by any pattern or practice of telemarketing which violates any rule of the Commission under section 3 of this Act, or an authorized person acting on such person's behalf, may, within 3 years after discovery of the violation, bring a civil action in an appropriate district court of the United States against a person who has engaged or is engaging in such pattern or practice of telemarketing if the amount in controversy exceeds the sum or value of $50,000 in actual damages for each person adversely affected by such telemarketing. Such an action may be brought to enjoin such telemarketing, to enforce compliance with any rule of the Commission under section 3 of this Act, to obtain damages, or to obtain such further and other relief as the court may deem appropriate.

(b) Notice

The plaintiff shall serve prior written notice of the action upon the Commission and provide the Commission with a copy of its complaint, except in any case where such prior notice is not feasible, in which case the person shall serve such notice immediately upon instituting such action. The Commission shall have the right (A) to intervene in the action, (B) upon so intervening, to be heard on all matters arising therein, and (C) to file petitions for appeal.

(c) Action by Commission

Whenever a civil action has been instituted by or on behalf of the Commission for violation of any rule prescribed under section 3 of this Act, no person may, during the pendency of such action instituted by or on behalf of the Commission, institute a civil action against any defendant named in the complaint in such action for violation of any rule as alleged in such complaint.

(d) Cost and Fees

The court, in issuing any final order in any action brought under subsection (a) of this section, may award costs of suit and reasonable fees for attorneys and expert witnesses to the prevailing party.

(e) Construction

Nothing in this section shall restrict any right which any person may have under any statute or common law.

(f) Venue; Service of Process

Any civil action brought under subsection (a) of this section in a district court of the United States may be brought in the district in which the defendant is found, is an inhabitant, or transacts business or wherever venue is proper under section 1391 of Title 28. Process in such an action may be served in any district in which the defendant is an inhabitant or in which the defendant may be found.

§ 6. Administration and applicability of chapter [15 U.S.C. § 6105]

(a) In General

Except as otherwise provided in sections 3(d), 3(e), 4, and 5 of this Act, this Act shall be enforced by the Commission under the Federal Trade Commission Act (15 U.S.C. § 41 et seq.). Consequently, no activity which is outside the jurisdiction of that Act shall be affected by this chapter.

(b) Actions by Commission

The Commission shall prevent any person from violating a rule of the Commission under section 3 of this Act in the same manner, by the same means, and with the same jurisdiction, powers, and duties as though all applicable terms and provisions of the Federal Trade Commission Act (15 U.S.C. § 41 et seq.) were incorporated into and made a part of this chapter. Any person who violates such rule shall be subject to the penalties and entitled to the privileges and immunities provided in the Federal Trade Commission Act in the same manner, by the same means, and with the same jurisdiction, power, and duties as though all applicable terms and provisions of the Federal Trade Commission Act were incorporated into and made a part of this chapter.

(c) Effect on Other Laws

Nothing contained in this chapter shall be construed to limit the authority of the Commission under any other provision of law.

§ 7.   Definitions [15 U.S.C. § 6106]

For purposes of this chapter:

(1) The term "attorney general" means the chief legal officer of a State.

(2) The term "Commission" means the Federal Trade Commission.

(3) The term "State" means any State of the United States, the District of Columbia, Puerto Rico, the Northern Mariana Islands, and any territory or possession of the United States.

(4) The term "telemarketing" means a plan, program, or campaign which is conducted to induce purchases of goods or services, or a charitable contribution, donation, or gift of money or any other thing of value, by use of one or more telephones and which involves more than one interstate telephone call. The term does not include the solicitation of sales through the mailing of a catalog which—

(A) contains a written description, or illustration of the goods or services offered for sale,

(B) includes the business address of the seller,

(C) includes multiple pages of written material or illustrations, and

(D) has been issued not less frequently than once a year,

where the person making the solicitation does not solicit customers by telephone but only receives calls initiated by customers in response to the catalog and during those calls takes orders only without further solicitation.

§ 8.   Enforcement of orders [15 U.S.C. § 6107]

(a) General Authority

Subject to subsections (b) and (c) of this section, the Federal Trade Commission may bring a criminal contempt action for violations of orders of the Commission obtained in cases brought under section [13(b) of the Federal Trade Commission Act, 15 U.S.C. § 53(b)].

(b) Appointment

An action authorized by subsection (a) of this section may be brought by the Federal Trade Commission only after, and pursuant to, the appointment by the Attorney General of an attorney employed by the Commission, as a special assistant United States Attorney.

(c) Request for Appointment

(1) Appointment Upon Request or Motion

A special assistant United States Attorney may be appointed under subsection (b) of this section upon the request of the Federal Trade

Commission or the court which has entered the order for which contempt is sought or upon the Attorney General's own motion.

(2) Timing

The Attorney General shall act upon any request made under paragraph (1) within 45 days of the receipt of the request.

(d) Termination of Authority

The authority of the Federal Trade Commission to bring a criminal contempt action under subsection (a) of this section expires 2 years after the date of the first promulgation of rules under section 3 of this Act. The expiration of such authority shall have no effect on an action brought before the expiration date.

§ 9. Review [15 U.S.C. § 6108]

Upon the expiration of 5 years following the date of the first promulgation of rules under section 3 of this Act, the Commission shall review the implementation of this chapter and its effect on deceptive telemarketing acts or practices and report the results of the review to the Congress.

FEDERAL COMMUNICATIONS COMMISSION REGULATION

RESTRICTIONS ON TELEPHONE SOLICITATION

47 C.F.R. Part 64.1200

Table of Sections

---

§ 64.1200   Delivery restrictions

(a) No person or entity may:

(1) Initiate any telephone call (other than a call made for emergency purposes or made with the prior express consent of the called party) using an automatic telephone dialing system or an artificial or prerecorded voice;

(i) To any emergency telephone line, including any 911 line and any emergency line of a hospital, medical physician or service office, health care facility, poison control center, or fire protection or law enforcement agency;

(ii) To the telephone line of any guest room or patient room of a hospital, health care facility, elderly home, or similar establishment; or

(iii) To any telephone number assigned to a paging service, cellular telephone service, specialized mobile radio service, or other radio common carrier service, or any service for which the called party is charged for the call.

(iv) A person will not be liable for violating the prohibition in paragraph (a)(1)(iii) of this section when the call is placed to a wireless number that has been ported from wireline service and such call is a voice call; not knowingly made to a wireless number; and made within 15 days of the porting of the number from wireline to wireless service, provided the number is not already on the national do-not-call registry or caller's company-specific do-not-call list.

(2) Initiate any telephone call to any residential line using an artificial or prerecorded voice to deliver a message without the prior express consent of the called party, unless the call;

(i) Is made for emergency purposes;

(ii) Is not made for a commercial purpose;

(iii) Is made for a commercial purpose but does not include or introduce an unsolicited advertisement or constitute a telephone solicitation;

(iv) Is made to any person with whom the caller has an established business relationship at the time the call is made; or

(v) Is made by or on behalf of a tax-exempt nonprofit organization.

(3) Use a telephone facsimile machine, computer, or other device to send an unsolicited advertisement to a telephone facsimile machine, unless—

(i) The unsolicited advertisement is from a sender with an established business relationship, as defined in paragraph (f)(5) of this section, with the recipient; and

(ii) The sender obtained the number of the telephone facsimile machine through—

(A) The voluntary communication of such number by the recipient directly to the sender, within the context of such established business relationship; or

(B) A directory, advertisement, or site on the Internet to which the recipient voluntarily agreed to make available its facsimile number for public distribution. If a sender obtains the facsimile number from the recipient's own directory, advertisement, or Internet site, it will be presumed that the number was voluntarily made available for public distribution, unless such materials explicitly note that unsolicited advertisements are not accepted at the specified facsimile number. If a sender obtains the facsimile number from other sources, the sender must take reasonable steps to verify that the recipient agreed to make the number available for public distribution.

(C) This clause shall not apply in the case of an unsolicited advertisement that is sent based on an established business relationship with the recipient that was in existence before July 9, 2005 if the sender also possessed the facsimile machine number of the recipient before July 9, 2005. There shall be a rebuttable presumption that if a valid established business relationship was formed prior to July 9, 2005, the sender possessed the facsimile number prior to such date as well; and

(iii) The advertisement contains a notice that informs the recipient of the ability and means to avoid future unsolicited advertisements. A notice contained in an advertisement complies with the requirements under this paragraph only if—

(A) The notice is clear and conspicuous and on the first page of the advertisement;

(B) The notice states that the recipient may make a request to the sender of the advertisement not to send any future advertisements to a telephone facsimile machine or machines and that failure to comply, within 30 days, with such a request meeting the requirements under paragraph (a)(3)(v) of this section is unlawful;

(C) The notice sets forth the requirements for an opt-out request under paragraph (a)(3)(v) of this section;

(D) The notice includes—

(1) A domestic contact telephone number and facsimile machine number for the recipient to transmit such a request to the sender; and

(2) If neither the required telephone number nor facsimile machine number is a toll-free number, a separate cost-free mechanism including a Web site address or e-mail address, for a recipient to transmit a request pursuant to such notice to the sender of the advertisement. A local telephone number also shall constitute a cost-free mechanism so long as recipients are local and will not incur any long distance or other separate charges for calls made to such number; and

(E) The telephone and facsimile numbers and cost-free mechanism identified in the notice must permit an individual or business to make an opt-out request 24 hours a day, 7 days a week.

(iv) A facsimile advertisement that is sent to a recipient that has provided prior express invitation or permission to the sender must include an opt-out notice that complies with the requirements in paragraph (a)(3)(iii) of this section.

(v) A request not to send future unsolicited advertisements to a telephone facsimile machine complies with the requirements under this subparagraph only if—

(A) The request identifies the telephone number or numbers of the telephone facsimile machine or machines to which the request relates;

(B) The request is made to the telephone number, facsimile number, Web site address or e-mail address identified in the sender's facsimile advertisement; and

(C) The person making the request has not, subsequent to such request, provided express invitation or permission to the sender, in writing or otherwise, to send such advertisements to such person at such telephone facsimile machine.

(vi) A sender that receives a request not to send future unsolicited advertisements that complies with paragraph (a)(3)(v) of this section must honor that request within the shortest reasonable time from the date of such request, not to exceed 30 days, and is prohibited from sending unsolicited advertisements to the recipient unless the recipient subsequently provides prior express invitation or permission to the sender. The recipient's opt-out request terminates the established business relationship exemption for purposes of sending future unsolicited advertisements. If such requests are recorded or maintained by a party other than the sender on whose behalf the unsolicited advertisement is sent, the sender will be liable for any failures to honor the opt-out request.

(vii) A facsimile broadcaster will be liable for violations of paragraph (a)(3) of this section, including the inclusion of opt-out notices on unsolicited advertisements, if it demonstrates a high degree of involvement in, or actual notice of, the unlawful activity and fails to take steps to prevent such facsimile transmissions.

(4) Use an automatic telephone dialing system in such a way that two or more telephone lines of a multi-line business are engaged simultaneously.

(5) Disconnect an unanswered telemarketing call prior to at least 15 seconds or four (4) rings.

(6) Abandon more than three percent of all telemarketing calls that are answered live by a person, or measured over a 30–day period. A call is "abandoned" if it is not connected to a live sales representative within two (2) seconds of the called person's completed greeting. Whenever a sales representative is not available to speak with the person answering the call, that person must receive, within two (2) seconds after the called person's completed greeting, a prerecorded identification message that states only the name and telephone number of the business, entity, or individual on whose behalf the call was placed, and that the call was for "telemarketing purposes." The telephone number so provided must permit any individual to make a do-not-call request during regular business hours for the duration of the telemarketing campaign. The telephone number may not be a 900 number or any other number for which charges exceed local or long distance transmission charges. The seller or telemarketer must maintain records establishing compliance with paragraph (a)(6) of this section.

(i) A call for telemarketing purposes that delivers an artificial or prerecorded voice message to a residential telephone line that is assigned to a person who either has granted prior express consent for the call to be made or has an established business relationship with the caller shall not be considered an abandoned call if the message begins within two (2) seconds of the called person's completed greeting.

(ii) Calls made by or on behalf of tax-exempt nonprofit organizations are not covered by paragraph (a)(6) of this section.

(7) Use any technology to dial any telephone number for the purpose of determining whether the line is a facsimile or voice line.

(b) All artificial or prerecorded telephone messages shall:

(1) At the beginning of the message, state clearly the identity of the business, individual, or other entity that is responsible for initiating the call. If a business is responsible for initiating the call, the name under which the entity is registered to conduct business with the State Corporation Commission (or comparable regulatory authority) must be stated, and

(2) During or after the message, state clearly the telephone number (other than that of the autodialer or prerecorded message player that placed the call) of such business, other entity, or individual. The telephone number provided may not be a 900 number or any other number for which charges exceed local or long distance transmission charges. For telemarketing messages to residential telephone subscribers, such telephone number must permit any individual to make a do-not-call request during regular business hours for the duration of the telemarketing campaign.

(c) No person or entity shall initiate any telephone solicitation, as defined in paragraph (f)(12) of this section, to:

(1) Any residential telephone subscriber before the hour of 8 a.m. or after 9 p.m. (local time at the called party's location), or

(2) A residential telephone subscriber who has registered his or her telephone number on the national do-not-call registry of persons who do not wish to receive telephone solicitations that is maintained by the Federal Government. Such do-not-call registrations must be honored indefinitely, or until the registration is cancelled by the consumer or the telephone number is removed by the database administrator. Any person or entity making telephone solicitations (or on whose behalf telephone solicitations are made) will not be liable for violating this requirement if:

(i) It can demonstrate that the violation is the result of error and that as part of its routine business practice, it meets the following standards:

(A) *Written procedures.* It has established and implemented written procedures to comply with the national do-not-call rules;

(B) *Training of personnel.* It has trained its personnel, and any entity assisting in its compliance, in procedures established pursuant to the national do-not-call rules;

(C) *Recording.* It has maintained and recorded a list of telephone numbers that the seller may not contact;

(D) *Accessing the national do-not-call database.* It uses a process to prevent telephone solicitations to any telephone number on any list established pursuant to the do-not-call rules, employing a version of the national do-not-call registry obtained from the administrator of the registry no more than 31 days prior to the date any call is made, and maintains records documenting this process.

Note to paragraph(c)(2)(i)(D): The requirement in paragraph 64.1200(c)(2)(i)(D) for persons or entities to employ a version of the national do-not-call registry obtained from the administrator no more than 31 days prior to the date any call is made is effective January 1, 2005. Until January 1, 2005, persons or entities must continue to employ a version of the registry obtained from the administrator of the registry no more than three months prior to the date any call is made.

(E) *Purchasing the national do-not-call database.* It uses a process to ensure that it does not sell, rent, lease, purchase or use the national do-not-call database, or any part thereof, for any purpose except compliance with this section and any such state or federal law to prevent telephone solicitations to telephone numbers registered on the national database. It purchases access to the relevant do-not-call data from the administrator of the national database and does not participate in any arrangement to share the cost of accessing the national database, including any arrangement with telemarketers who may not divide the costs to access the national database among various client sellers; or

(ii) It has obtained the subscriber's prior express invitation or permission. Such permission must be evidenced by a signed, written agreement between the consumer and seller which states that the consumer agrees to be contacted by this seller and includes the telephone number to which the calls may be placed; or

(iii) The telemarketer making the call has a personal relationship with the recipient of the call.

(d) No person or entity shall initiate any call for telemarketing purposes to a residential telephone subscriber unless such person or entity has instituted procedures for maintaining a list of persons who request not to receive telemarketing calls made by or on behalf of that person or entity. The procedures instituted must meet the following minimum standards:

(1) *Written policy.* Persons or entities making calls for telemarketing purposes must have a written policy, available upon demand, for maintaining a do-not-call list.

(2) *Training of personnel engaged in telemarketing.* Personnel engaged in any aspect of telemarketing must be informed and trained in the existence and use of the do-not-call list.

(3) *Recording, disclosure of do-not-call requests.* If a person or entity making a call for telemarketing purposes (or on whose behalf such a call is made) receives a request from a residential telephone subscriber not to receive calls from that person or entity, the person or entity must record the request and place the subscriber's name, if provided, and telephone number on the do-not-call list at the time the request is made. Persons or entities making calls for telemarketing purposes (or on whose behalf such calls are made) must honor a residential subscriber's do-not-call request within a reasonable time from the date such request is made. This period may not exceed thirty days from the date of such request. If such requests are recorded or

maintained by a party other than the person or entity on whose behalf the telemarketing call is made, the person or entity on whose behalf the telemarketing call is made will be liable for any failures to honor the do-not-call request. A person or entity making a call for telemarketing purposes must obtain a consumer's prior express permission to share or forward the consumer's request not to be called to a party other than the person or entity on whose behalf a telemarketing call is made or an affiliated entity.

(4) *Identification of sellers and telemarketers.* A person or entity making a call for telemarketing purposes must provide the called party with the name of the individual caller, the name of the person or entity on whose behalf the call is being made, and a telephone number or address at which the person or entity may be contacted. The telephone number provided may not be a 900 number or any other number for which charges exceed local or long distance transmission charges.

(5) *Affiliated persons or entities.* In the absence of a specific request by the subscriber to the contrary, a residential subscriber's do-not-call request shall apply to the particular business entity making the call (or on whose behalf a call is made), and will not apply to affiliated entities unless the consumer reasonably would expect them to be included given the identification of the caller and the product being advertised.

(6) *Maintenance of do-not-call lists.* A person or entity making calls for telemarketing purposes must maintain a record of a consumer's request not to receive further telemarketing calls. A do-not-call request must be honored for 5 years from the time the request is made.

(7) Tax-exempt nonprofit organizations are not required to comply with 64.1200(d).

(e) The rules set forth in paragraph (c) and (d) of this section are applicable to any person or entity making telephone solicitations or telemarketing calls to wireless telephone numbers to the extent described in the Commission's Report and Order, CG Docket No. 02–278, FCC 03–153, "Rules and Regulations Implementing the Telephone Consumer Protection Act of 1991."

(f) As used in this section:

(1) The terms *automatic telephone dialing system* and *autodialer* mean equipment which has the capacity to store or produce telephone numbers to be called using a random or sequential number generator and to dial such numbers.

(2) The term *clear and conspicuous* for purposes of paragraph (a)(3)(iii)(A) of this section means a notice that would be apparent to the reasonable consumer, separate and distinguishable from the advertising copy or other disclosures, and placed at either the top or bottom of the facsimile.

(3) The term *emergency purposes* means calls made necessary in any situation affecting the health and safety of consumers.

(4) The term *established business relationship* for purposes of telephone solicitations means a prior or existing relationship formed by a voluntary two-way communication between a person or entity and a residential subscriber with or without an exchange of consideration, on the basis of the subscriber's purchase or transaction with the entity within the eighteen (18) months immediately preceding the date of the telephone call or on the basis of the subscriber's inquiry or application regarding products or services offered by the entity within the three months immediately preceding the date of the call, which relationship has not been previously terminated by either party.

(i) The subscriber's seller-specific do-not-call request, as set forth in paragraph (d)(3) of this section, terminates an established business relationship for purposes of telemarketing and telephone solicitation even if the subscriber continues to do business with the seller.

(ii) The subscriber's established business relationship with a particular business entity does not extend to affiliated entities unless the subscriber would reasonably expect them to be included given the nature and type of goods or services offered by the affiliate and the identity of the affiliate.

(5) The term *established business relationship* for purposes of paragraph (a)(3) of this section on the sending of facsimile advertisements means a prior or existing relationship formed by a voluntary two-way communication between a person or entity and a business or residential subscriber with or without an exchange of consideration, on the basis of an inquiry, application, purchase or transaction by the business or residential subscriber regarding products or services offered by such person or entity, which relationship has not been previously terminated by either party.

(6) The term *facsimile broadcaster* means a person or entity that transmits messages to telephone facsimile machines on behalf of another person or entity for a fee.

(7) The term *seller* means the person or entity on whose behalf a telephone call or message is initiated for the purpose of encouraging the purchase or rental of, or investment in, property, goods, or services, which is transmitted to any person.

(8) The term *sender* for purposes of paragraph (a)(3) of this section means the person or entity on whose behalf a facsimile unsolicited advertisement is sent or whose goods or services are advertised or promoted in the unsolicited advertisement.

(9) The term *telemarketer* means the person or entity that initiates a telephone call or message for the purpose of encouraging the

purchase or rental of, or investment in, property, goods, or services, which is transmitted to any person.

(10) The term *telemarketing* means the initiation of a telephone call or message for the purpose of encouraging the purchase or rental of, or investment in, property, goods, or services, which is transmitted to any person.

(11) The term *telephone facsimile machine* means equipment which has the capacity to transcribe text or images, or both, from paper into an electronic signal and to transmit that signal over a regular telephone line, or to transcribe text or images (or both) from an electronic signal received over a regular telephone line onto paper.

(12) The term *telephone solicitation* means the initiation of a telephone call or message for the purpose of encouraging the purchase or rental of, or investment in, property, goods, or services, which is transmitted to any person, but such term does not include a call or message:

    (i) To any person with that person's prior express invitation or permission;

    (ii) To any person with whom the caller has an established business relationship; or

    (iii) By or on behalf of a tax-exempt nonprofit organization.

(13) The term *unsolicited advertisement* means any material advertising the commercial availability or quality of any property, goods, or services which is transmitted to any person without that person's prior express invitation or permission, in writing or otherwise.

(14) The term *personal relationship* means any family member, friend, or acquaintance of the telemarketer making the call.

(g) Beginning January 1, 2004, common carriers shall:

(1) When providing local exchange service, provide an annual notice, via an insert in the subscriber's bill, of the right to give or revoke a notification of an objection to receiving telephone solicitations pursuant to the national do-not-call database maintained by the federal government and the methods by which such rights may be exercised by the subscriber. The notice must be clear and conspicuous and include, at a minimum, the Internet address and toll-free number that residential telephone subscribers may use to register on the national database.

(2) When providing service to any person or entity for the purpose of making telephone solicitations, make a one-time notification to such person or entity of the national do-not-call requirements, including, at a minimum, citation to 47 CFR 64.1200 and 16 CFR 310. Failure to receive such notification will not serve as a defense to any person or entity making telephone solicitations from violations of this section.

(h) The administrator of the national do-not-call registry that is maintained by the federal government shall make the telephone numbers in the database available to the States so that a State may use the telephone numbers that relate to such State as part of any database, list or listing system maintained by such State for the regulation of telephone solicitations.

§ 64.1201   Restrictions on billing name and address disclosure

(a) As used in this section:

(1) The term *billing name and address* means the name and address provided to a local exchange company by each of its local exchange customers to which the local exchange company directs bills for its services.

(2) The term *telecommunications service provider* means interexchange carriers, operator service providers, enhanced service providers, and any other provider of interstate telecommunications services.

(3) The term *authorized billing agent* means a third party hired by a telecommunications service provider to perform billing and collection services for the telecommunications service provider.

(4) The term *bulk basis* means billing name and address information for all the local exchange service subscribers of a local exchange carrier.

(5) The term *LEC joint use card* means a calling card bearing an account number assigned by a local exchange carrier, used for the services of the local exchange carrier and a designated interexchange carrier, and validated by access to data maintained by the local exchange carrier.

(b) No local exchange carrier providing billing name and address shall disclose billing name and address information to any party other than a telecommunications service provider or an authorized billing and collection agent of a telecommunications service provider.

(c)(1) No telecommunications service provider or authorized billing and collection agent of a telecommunications service provider shall use billing name and address information for any purpose other than the following:

(i) Billing customers for using telecommunications services of that service provider and collecting amounts due;

(ii) Any purpose associated with the "equal access" requirement of *United States v. AT&T,* 552 F.Supp. 131 (D.D.C. 1982); and

(iii) Verification of service orders of new customers, identification of customers who have moved to a new address, fraud prevention, and similar nonmarketing purposes.

(2) In no case shall any telecommunications service provider or authorized billing and collection agent of a telecommunications service provider disclose the billing name and address information of any subscriber to any third party, except that a telecommunications service provider may disclose

billing name and address information to its authorized billing and collection agent.

(d) [Reserved]

(e)(1) All local exchange carriers providing billing name and address information shall notify their subscribers that:

(i) The subscriber's billing name and address will be disclosed, pursuant to Policies and Rules Concerning Local Exchange Carrier Validation and Billing Information for Joint Use Calling Cards, CC Docket No. 91–115, FCC 93–254, adopted May 13, 1993, whenever the subscriber uses a LEC joint use card to pay for services obtained from the telecommunications service provider, and

(ii) The subscriber's billing name and address will be disclosed, pursuant to Policies and Rules Concerning Local Exchange Carrier Validation and Billing Information for Joint Use Calling Cards, CC Docket No. 91–115, FCC 93–254, adopted May 13, 1993, whenever the subscriber accepts a third party or collect call to a telephone station provided by the LEC to the subscriber.

(2) In addition to the notification specified in paragraph (e)(1) of this section, all local exchange carriers providing billing name and address information shall notify their subscribers with unlisted or nonpublished telephone numbers that:

(i) Customers have a right to request that their BNA not be disclosed, and that customers may prevent BNA disclosure for third party and collect calls as well as calling card calls;

(ii) LECs will presume that unlisted and nonpublished end users consent to disclosure and use of their BNA if customers do not affirmatively request that their BNA not be disclosed; and

(iii) The presumption in favor of consent for disclosure will begin 30 days after customers receive notice.

(3) No local exchange carrier shall disclose the billing name and address information associated with any calling card call made by any subscriber who has affirmatively withheld consent for disclosure of BNA information, or for any third party or collect call charged to any subscriber who has affirmatively withheld consent for disclosure of BNA information.

FEDERAL COMMUNICATIONS COMMISSION REGULATION

INTERSTATE PAY–PER–CALL AND OTHER INFORMATION SERVICES

47 C.F.R. Part 64.1500

Table of Sections

---

§ 64.1501 Definitions

For purposes of this subpart, the following definitions shall apply:

(a) *Pay-per-call service* means any service:

(1) In which any person provides or purports to provide:

(i) Audio information or audio entertainment produced or packaged by such person;

(ii) Access to simultaneous voice conversation services; or

(iii) Any service, including the provision of a product, the charges for which are assessed on the basis of the completion of the call;

(2) For which the caller pays a per-call or per-time-interval charge that is greater than, or in addition to, the charge for transmission of the call; and

(3) Which is accessed through use of a 900 number;

(4) Provided, however, such term does not include directory services provided by a common carrier or its affiliate or by a local exchange carrier or its affiliate, or any service for which users are assessed charges only

133

after entering into a presubscription or comparable arrangement with the provider of such service.

(b) *Presubscription or comparable arrangement* means a contractual agreement in which:

(1) The service provider clearly and conspicuously discloses to the consumer all material terms and conditions associated with the use of the service, including the service provider's name and address, a business telephone number which the consumer may use to obtain additional information or to register a complaint, and the rates for the service;

(2) The service provider agrees to notify the consumer of any future rate changes;

(3) The consumer agrees to use the service on the terms and conditions disclosed by the service provider; and

(4) The service provider requires the use of an identification number or other means to prevent unauthorized access to the service by nonsubscribers;

(5) Provided, however, that disclosure of a credit, prepaid account, debit, charge, or calling card number, along with authorization to bill that number, made during the course of a call to an information service shall constitute a presubscription or comparable arrangement if an introductory message containing the information specified in § 64.1504(c)(2) is provided prior to, and independent of, assessment of any charges. No other action taken by a consumer during the course of a call to an information service, for which charges are assessed, can create a presubscription or comparable arrangement.

(6) Provided, that a presubscription arrangement to obtain information services provided by means of a toll-free number shall conform to the requirements of § 64.1504(c).

(c) *Calling card* means an identifying number or code unique to the individual, that is issued to the individual by a common carrier and enables the individual to be charged by means of a phone bill for charges incurred independent of where the call originates.

§ 64.1502   Limitations on the provision of pay-per-call services

Any common carrier assigning a telephone number to a provider of interstate pay-per-call service shall require, by contract or tariff, that such provider comply with the provisions of this subpart and of titles II and III of the Telephone Disclosure and Dispute Resolution Act (TDDRA) and the regulations prescribed by the Federal Trade Commission pursuant to those titles.

§ 64.1503   Termination of pay-per-call and other information programs

(a) Any common carrier assigning a telephone number to a provider of interstate pay-per-call service shall specify by contract or tariff that pay-per-call programs not in compliance with § 64.1502 shall be terminated following written notice to the information provider. The information provider shall be afforded a period of no less than seven and no more than 14 days during which a program may be brought into compliance. Programs not in compliance at the expiration of such period shall be terminated immediately.

(b) Any common carrier providing transmission or billing and collection services to a provider of interstate information service through any 800 telephone number, or other telephone number advertised or widely understood to be toll-free, shall promptly investigate any complaint that such service is not provided in accordance with § 64.1504 or § 64.1510(c), and, if the carrier reasonably determines that the complaint is valid, may terminate the provision of service to an information provider unless the provider supplies evidence of a written agreement that meets the requirements of this § 64.1504(c)(1).

§ 64.1504 Restrictions on the use of toll-free numbers

A common carrier shall prohibit by tariff or contract the use of any 800 telephone number, or other telephone number advertised or widely understood to be toll-free, in a manner that would result in:

(a) The calling party or the subscriber to the originating line being assessed, by virtue of completing the call, a charge for a call;

(b) The calling party being connected to a pay-per-call service;

(c) The calling party being charged for information conveyed during the call unless:

(1) The calling party has a written agreement (including an agreement transmitted through electronic medium) that specifies the material terms and conditions under which the information is offered and includes:

(i) The rate at which charges are assessed for the information;

(ii) The information provider's name;

(iii) The information provider's business address;

(iv) The information provider's regular business telephone number;

(v) The information provider's agreement to notify the subscriber at least one billing cycle in advance of all future changes in the rates charged for the information;

(vi) The subscriber's choice of payment method, which may be by direct remit, debit, prepaid account, phone bill, or credit or calling card and, if a subscriber elects to pay by means of phone bill, a clear explanation that the subscriber will be assessed for calls made to the information service from the subscriber's phone line;

(vii) A unique personal identification number or other subscriber-specific identifier that must be used to obtain access to the information

135

service and instructions on its use, and, in addition, assures that any charges for services accessed by use of the subscriber's personal identification number or subscriber-specific identifier be assessed to subscriber's source of payment elected pursuant to paragraph (c)(1)(vi) of this section; or

(2) The calling party is charged for the information by means of a credit, prepaid, debit, charge, or calling card and the information service provider includes in response to each call an introductory message that:

    (i) Clearly states that there is a charge for the call;

    (ii) Clearly states the service's total cost per minute and any other fees for the service or for any service to which the caller may be transferred;

    (iii) Explains that the charges must be billed on either a credit, prepaid, debit, charge, or calling card;

    (iv) Asks the caller for the card number;

    (v) Clearly states that charges for the call begin at the end of the introductory message; and

    (vi) Clearly states that the caller can hang at or before the end of the introductory message without incurring any charge whatsoever.

(d) The calling party being called back collect for the provision of audio or data information services, simultaneous voice conversation services, or products; and

(e) The calling party being assessed by virtue of the caller being asked to connect or otherwise transfer to a pay-per-call service, a charge for the call.

(f) Provided, however, that:

(1) Notwithstanding paragraph (c)(1) of this section, a written agreement that meets the requirements of that paragraph is not required for:

    (i) Calls utilizing telecommunications devices for the deaf;

    (ii) Directory services provided by a common carrier or its affiliate or by a local exchange carrier or its affiliate; or

    (iii) Any purchase of goods or of services that are not information services.

(2) The requirements of paragraph (c)(2) of this section shall not apply to calls from repeat callers using a bypass mechanism to avoid listening to the introductory message: *Provided,* That information providers shall disable such a bypass mechanism after the institution of any price increase for a period of time determined to be sufficient by the Federal Trade Commission to give callers adequate and sufficient notice of a price increase.

§ 64.1505   Restrictions on collect telephone calls

(a) No common carrier shall provide interstate transmission or billing and collection services to an entity offering any service within the scope of § 64.1501(a)(1) that is billed to a subscriber on a collect basis at a per-call or per-time-interval charge that is greater than, or in addition to, the charge for transmission of the call.

(b) No common carrier shall provide interstate transmission services for any collect information services billed to a subscriber at a tariffed rate unless the called party has taken affirmative action clearly indicating that it accepts the charges for the collect service.

§ 64.1506   Number designation

Any interstate service described in § 64.1501(a)(1)–(2), and not subject to the exclusions contained in § 64.1501(a)(4), shall be offered only through telephone numbers beginning with a 900 service access code.

§ 64.1507   Prohibition on disconnection or interruption of service for failure to remit pay-per-call or similar service charges

No common carrier shall disconnect or interrupt in any manner, or order the disconnection or interruption of, a telephone subscriber's local exchange or long distance telephone service as a result of that subscriber's failure to pay:

(a) Charges for interstate pay-per-call service;

(b) Charges for interstate information services provided pursuant to a presubscription or comparable arrangement; or

(c) Charges for interstate information services provided on a collect basis which have been disputed by the subscriber.

§ 64.1508   Blocking access to 900 service

(a) Local exchange carriers must offer to their subscribers, where technically feasible, an option to block access to services offered on the 900 service access code. Blocking is to be offered at no charge, on a one-time basis, to:

(1) All telephone subscribers during the period from November 1, 1993 through December 31, 1993; and

(2) Any subscriber who subscribes to a new telephone number for a period of 60 days after the new number is effective.

(b) For blocking requests not within the one-time option or outside the time frames specified in paragraph (a) of this section, and for unblocking requests, local exchange carriers may charge a reasonable one-time fee. Requests by subscribers to remove 900 services blocking must be in writing.

(c) The terms and conditions under which subscribers may obtain 900 services blocking are to be included in tariffs filed with this Commission.

§ 64.1509 Disclosure and dissemination of pay-per-call information

(a) Any common carrier assigning a telephone number to a provider of interstate pay-per-call services shall make readily available, at no charge, to Federal and State agencies and all other interested persons:

(1) A list of the telephone numbers for each of the pay-per-call services it carries;

(2) A short description of each such service;

(3) A statement of the total cost or the cost per minute and any other fees for each such service; and

(4) A statement of the pay-per-call service provider's name, business address, and business telephone number.

(b) Any common carrier assigning a telephone number to a provider of interstate pay-per-call services and offering billing and collection services to such provider shall:

(1) Establish a local or toll-free telephone number to answer questions and provide information on subscribers' rights and obligations with regard to their use of pay-per-call services and to provide to callers the name and mailing address of any provider of pay-per-call services offered by that carrier; and

(2) Provide to all its telephone subscribers, either directly or through contract with any local exchange carrier providing billing and collection services to that carrier, a disclosure statement setting forth all rights and obligations of the subscriber and the carrier with respect to the use and payment of pay-per-call services. Such statement must include the prohibition against disconnection of basic communications services for failure to pay pay-per-call charges established by § 64.1507, the right of a subscriber to obtain blocking in accordance with § 64.1508, the right of a subscriber not to be billed for pay-per-call services not offered in compliance with federal laws and regulations established by § 64.1510(a)(1), and the possibility that a subscriber's access to 900 services may be involuntarily blocked pursuant to § 64.1512 for failure to pay legitimate pay-per-call charges. Disclosure statements must be forwarded to:

(i) All telephone subscribers no later than 60 days after these regulations take effect;

(ii) All new telephone subscribers no later than 60 days after service is established;

(iii) All telephone subscribers requesting service at a new location no later than 60 days after service is established; and

(iv) Thereafter, to all subscribers at least once per calendar year, at intervals of not less than 6 months nor more than 18 months.

§ 64.1510   Billing and collection of pay-per-call and similar service charges

(a) Any common carrier assigning a telephone number to a provider of interstate pay-per-call services and offering billing and collection services to such provider shall:

(1) Ensure that a subscriber is not billed for interstate pay-per-call services that such carrier knows or reasonably should know were provided in violation of the regulations set forth in this subpart or prescribed by the Federal Trade Commission pursuant to titles II or III of the TDDRA or any other federal law;

(2) In any billing to telephone subscribers that includes charges for any interstate pay-per-call service:

(i) Include a statement indicating that:

(A) Such charges are for non-communications services;

(B) Neither local nor long distances services can be disconnected for non-payment although an information provider may employ private entities to seek to collect such charges;

(C) 900 number blocking is available upon request; and

(D) Access to pay-per-call services may be involuntarily blocked for failure to pay legitimate charges;

(ii) Display any charges for pay-per-call services in a part of the bill that is identified as not being related to local and long distance telephone charges;

(iii) Specify, for each pay-per-call charge made, the type of service, the amount of the charge, and the date, time, and, for calls billed on a time-sensitive basis, the duration of the call; and

(iv) Identify the local or toll-free number established in accordance with § 64.1509(b)(1).

(b) Any common carrier offering billing and collection services to an entity providing interstate information services on a collect basis shall, to the extent possible, display the billing information in the manner described in paragraphs (a)(2)(i), (A), (B), (D) and (a)(2)(ii) of this section.

(c) If a subscriber elects, pursuant to § 64.1504(c)(1)(vi), to pay by means of a phone bill for any information service provided by through any 800 telephone number, or other telephone number advertised or widely understood to be toll-free, the phone bill shall:

(1) Include, in prominent type, the following disclaimer: "Common carriers may not disconnect local or long distance telephone service for failure to pay disputed charges for information services;" and

(2) Clearly list the 800 or other toll-free number dialed.

§ 64.1511   Forgiveness of charges and refunds

(a) Any carrier assigning a telephone number to a provider of interstate pay-per-call services or providing transmission for interstate information services provided pursuant to a presubscription or comparable arrangement or on a collect basis, and providing billing and collection for such services, shall establish procedures for the handling of subscriber complaints regarding charges for those services. A billing carrier is afforded discretion to set standards for determining when a subscriber's complaint warrants forgiveness, refund or credit of interstate pay-per-call or information services charges provided that such charges must be forgiven, refunded, or credited when a subscriber has complained about such charges and either this Commission, the Federal Trade Commission, or a court of competent jurisdiction has found or the carrier has determined, upon investigation, that the service has been offered in violation of federal law or the regulations that are either set forth in this subpart or prescribed by the Federal Trade Commission pursuant to titles II or III of the TDDRA. Carriers shall observe the record retention requirements set forth in § 42.6 of this chapter except that relevant records shall be retained by carriers beyond the requirements of part 42 of this chapter when a complaint is pending at the time the specified retention period expires.

(b) Any carrier assigning a telephone number to a provider of interstate pay-per-call services but not providing billing and collection services for such services, shall, by tariff or contract, require that the provider and/or its billing and collection agents have in place procedures whereby, upon complaint, pay-per-call charges may be forgiven, refunded, or credited, provided that such charges must be forgiven, refunded, or credited when a subscriber has complained about such charges and either this Commission, the Federal Trade Commission, or a court of competent jurisdiction has found or the carrier has determined, upon investigation, that the service has been offered in violation of federal law or the regulations that are either set forth in this subpart or prescribed by the Federal Trade Commission pursuant to titles II of III of the TDDRA.

§ 64.1512   Involuntary blocking of pay-per-call services

Nothing in this subpart shall preclude a common carrier or information provider from blocking or ordering the blocking of its interstate pay-per-call programs from numbers assigned to subscribers who have incurred, but not paid, legitimate pay-per-call charges, except that a subscriber who has filed a complaint regarding a particular pay-per-call program pursuant to procedures established by the Federal Trade Commission under title III of the TDDRA shall not be involuntarily blocked from access to that program while such a complaint is pending. This restriction is not intended to preclude involuntary blocking when a carrier or IP has decided in one instance to sustain charges against a subscriber but that subscriber files additional separate complaints.

§ 64.1513   Verification of charitable status

Any common carrier assigning a telephone number to a provider of interstate pay-per-call services that the carrier knows or reasonably should know is engaged in soliciting charitable contributions shall obtain verification that the entity or individual for whom contributions are solicited has been granted tax exempt status by the Internal Revenue Service.

§ 64.1514   Generation of signalling tones

No common carrier shall assign a telephone number for any pay-per-call service that employs broadcast advertising which generates the audible tones necessary to complete a call to a pay-per-call service.

§ 64.1515   Recovery of costs

No common carrier shall recover its cost of complying with the provisions of this subpart from local or long distance ratepayers.

FEDERAL TRADE COMMISSION REGULATION

TRADE REGULATION RULE PURSUANT TO THE TELEPHONE DISCLOSURE AND DISPUTE RESOLUTION ACT OF 1992

16 C.F.R. Part 308

Table of Sections

---

§ 308.1   Scope of regulations in this part

This rule implements titles II and III of the Telephone Disclosure and Dispute Resolution Act of 1992   .   .   .   .

§ 308.2   Definitions

(a) *Bona fide educational service* means any pay-per-call service dedicated to providing information or instruction relating to education, subjects of academic study, or other related areas of school study.

(b) *Commission* means the Federal Trade Commission.

(c) *Pay-per-call service* has the meaning provided in section 228 of the Communications Act of 1934, 47 U.S.C. § 228.

(d) *Person* means any individual, partnership, corporation, association, government or governmental subdivision or agency, or other entity.

(e)(1) *Presubscription or comparable arrangement* means a contractual agreement in which

    (i) The service provider clearly and conspicuously discloses to the consumer all material terms and conditions associated with the use of the service, including the service provider's name and address, a business telephone number which the consumer may use to obtain additional information or to register a complaint, and the rates for the service;

(ii) The service provider agrees to notify the consumer of any future rate changes;

(iii) The consumer agrees to utilize the service on the terms and conditions disclosed by the service provider; and

(iv) The service provider requires the use of an identification number or other means to prevent unauthorized access to the service by nonsubscribers.

(2) Disclosure of a credit card or charge card number, along with authorization to bill that number, made during the course of a call to a pay-per-call service shall constitute a presubscription or comparable arrangement if the credit or charge card is subject to the dispute resolution requirements of the Fair Credit Billing Act and the Truth in Lending Act, as amended. No other action taken by the consumer during the course of a call to a pay-per-call service can be construed as creating a presubscription or comparable arrangement.

(f) *Program-length commercial* means any commercial or other advertisement fifteen (15) minutes in length or longer or intended to fill a television or radio broadcasting or cablecasting time slot of fifteen (15) minutes in length or longer.

(g) *Provider of pay-per-call* services means any person who sells or offers to sell a pay-per-call service. A person who provides only transmission services or billing and collection services shall not be considered a provider of pay-per-call services.

(h) *Reasonably understandable volume* means at an audible level that renders the message intelligible to the receiving audience, and, in any event, at least the same audible level as that principally used in the advertisement or the pay-per-call service.

(*i*) *Service bureau* means any person, other than a common carrier, who provides, among other things, access to telephone service and voice storage to pay-per-call service providers.

(j) *Slow and deliberate manner* means at a rate that renders the message intelligible to the receiving audience, and, in any event, at a cadence or rate no faster than that principally used in the advertisement or the pay-per-call service.

(k) *Sweepstakes*, including games of chance, means a game or promotional mechanism that involves the elements of a prize and chance and does not require consideration.

§ 308.3   Advertising of pay-per-call services

(a) *General requirements*. The following requirements apply to disclosures required in advertisements under §§ 308.3(b)–(d), and (f):

(1) The disclosures shall be made in the same language as that principally used in the advertisement.

(2) Television video and print disclosures shall be of a color or shade that readily contrasts with the background of the advertisement.

(3) In print advertisements, disclosures shall be parallel with the base of the advertisement.

(4) Audio disclosures, whether in television or radio, shall be delivered in a slow and deliberate manner and in a reasonably understandable volume.

(5) Nothing contrary to, inconsistent with, or in mitigation of, the required disclosures shall be used in any advertisement in any medium; nor shall any audio, video or print technique be used that is likely to detract significantly from the communication of the disclosures.

(6) In any program-length commercial, required disclosures shall be made at least three times (unless more frequent disclosure is otherwise required) near the beginning, middle and end of the commercial.

(b) *Cost of the call.* (1) The provider of pay-per-call services shall clearly and conspicuously disclose the cost of the call, in Arabic numerals, in any advertisement for the pay-per-call service, as follows:

(i) If there is a flat fee for the call, the advertisement shall state the total cost of the call.

(ii) If the call is billed on a time-sensitive basis, the advertisement shall state the cost per minute and any minimum charges. If the length of the program can be determined in advance, the advertisement shall also state the maximum charge that could be incurred if the caller listens to the complete program.

(iii) If the call is billed on a variable rate basis, the advertisement shall state, in accordance with §§ 308.3(b)(1)(i) and (ii), the cost of the initial portion of the call, any minimum charges, and the range of rates that may be charged depending on the options chosen by the caller.

(iv) The advertisement shall disclose any other fees that will be charged for the service.

(v) if the caller may be transferred to another pay-per-call service, the advertisement shall disclose the cost of the other call, in accordance with §§ 308.3(b)(1)(i), (ii), (iii), and (iv).

(2) For purposes of § 308.3(b), disclosures shall be made "clearly and conspicuously" as set forth in § 308.3(a) and as follows:

(i) In a television or videotape advertisement, the video disclosure shall appear adjacent to each video presentation of the pay-per-call number. However, in an advertisement displaying more than one pay-per-call number with the same cost, the video disclosure need only appear adjacent to the largest presentation of the pay-per-call number. Each letter or numeral of the video disclosure shall be, at a minimum, one-half the size of each letter or numeral of the pay-per-call number to which the disclosure is adjacent. In addition, the video disclosure shall appear on the screen for the duration of the presentation of the pay-per-call number. An audio disclosure shall be made at least once, simultaneously with a video presentation of the disclosure. However, no audio presentation of the disclosure is required in: (A) An advertisement fifteen (15) seconds or less in length in which the pay-per-call number is not presented in the audio portion, or (B) an advertisement in which there is no audio presentation of information regarding the pay-per-call service, including the pay-per-call number. In an advertisement in which the pay-per-call number is presented only in the audio portion, the cost of the call shall be delivered immediately following the first and last delivery of the pay-per-call number, except that in a program-length commercial, the disclosure shall be delivered immediately following each delivery of the pay-per-call number.

(ii) In a print advertisement, the disclosure shall be placed adjacent to each presentation of the pay-per-call number. However, in an advertisement displaying more than one pay-per-call number with the same cost, the disclosure need only appear adjacent to the largest presentation of the pay-per-call number. Each letter or numeral of the disclosure shall be, at a minimum, one-half the size of each letter or numeral of the pay-per-call number to which the disclosure is adjacent.

(iii) In a radio advertisement, the disclosure shall be made at least once, and shall be delivered immediately following the first delivery of the pay-per-call number. In a program-length commercial, the disclosure shall be delivered immediately following each delivery of the pay-per-call number.

(c) *Sweepstakes; games of chance.* (1) The provider of pay-per-call services that advertises a prize or award or a service or product at no cost or for a reduced cost, to be awarded to the winner of any sweepstakes, including games of chance, shall clearly and conspicuously disclose in the advertisement the odds of being able to receive the prize, award, service, or product at no cost or reduced cost. If the odds are not calculable in advance, the advertisement shall disclose the factors used in calculating the odds. Either the advertisement or the preamble required by § 308.5(a) for such service shall clearly and conspicuously disclose that no call to the pay-per-call service is required to participate, and shall also disclose the existence of a free alternative method of entry, and either instructions on how to enter, or a local or toll-free telephone number or address to which consumers may call or write for information on how to enter the sweepstakes. Any description or characterization of the prize, award, service, or product that is being offered at no cost or reduced cost shall be truthful and accurate.

(2) For purposes of § 308.3(c), disclosures shall be made "clearly and conspicuously" as set forth in § 308.3(a) and as follows:

(i) In a television or videotape advertisement, the disclosures may be made in either the audio or video portion of the advertisement. If the disclosures are made in the video portion, they shall appear on the screen in sufficient size and for sufficient time to allow consumers to read and comprehend the disclosures.

(ii) In a print advertisement, the disclosures shall appear in a sufficient size and prominence and such location to be readily noticeable, readable and comprehensible.

(d) *Federal programs.* (1) The provider of pay-per-call services that advertises a pay-per-call service that is not operated or expressly authorized by a Federal agency, but that provides information on a Federal program, shall clearly and conspicuously disclose in the advertisement that the pay-per-call service is not authorized, endorsed, or approved by any Federal agency. Advertisements providing information on a Federal program shall include, but not be limited to, advertisements that contain a seal, insignia, trade or brand name, or any other term or symbol that reasonably could be interpreted or construed as implying any Federal government connection, approval, or endorsement.

(2) For purposes of § 308.3(d), disclosures shall be made "clearly and conspicuously" as set forth in § 308.3(a) and as follows:

(i) In a television or videotape advertisement, the disclosure may be made in either the audio or video portion of the advertisement. If the disclosure is made in the video portion, it shall appear on the screen in sufficient size and for sufficient time to allow consumers to read and comprehend the disclosure. The disclosure shall begin within the first fifteen (15) seconds of the advertisement.

(ii) In a print advertisement, the disclosure shall appear in a sufficient size and prominence and such location to be readily noticeable, readable and comprehensible. The disclosure shall appear in the top one-third of the advertisement.

(iii) In a radio advertisement, the disclosure shall begin within the first fifteen (15) seconds of the advertisement.

(e) *Prohibition on advertising to children.* (1) The provider of pay-per-call services shall not direct advertisements for such pay-per-call services to children under the age of 12, unless the service is a bona fide educational service.

(2) For the purposes of this regulation, advertisements directed to children under 12 shall include: any pay-per-call advertisement appearing during or immediately adjacent to programming for which competent and reliable audience composition data demonstrate that more than 50% of the audience is composed of children under 12, and any pay-per-call advertisement appearing in a periodical for which competent and reliable readership data demonstrate that more than 50% of the readership is composed of children under 12.

(3) For the purposes of this regulation, if competent and reliable audience composition or readership data does not demonstrate that more than 50% of the audience or readership is composed of children under 12,

then the Commission shall consider the following criteria in determining whether an advertisement is directed to children under 12:

(i) Whether the advertisement appears in a publication directed to children under 12, including, but not limited to, books, magazines and comic books;

(ii) Whether the advertisement appears during or immediately adjacent to television programs directed to children under 12, including, but not limited to, children's programming as defined by the Federal Communications Commission, animated programs, and after-school programs;

(iii) Whether the advertisement appears on a television station or channel directed to children under 12;

(iv) Whether the advertisement is broadcast during or immediately adjacent to radio programs directed to children under 12, or broadcast on a radio station directed to children under 12;

(v) Whether the advertisement appears on the same video as a commercially-prepared video directed to children under 12, or preceding a movie directed to children under 12 shown in a movie theater;

(vi) Whether the advertisement or promotion appears on product packaging directed to children under 12; and

(vii) Whether the advertisement, regardless of when or where it appears, is directed to children under 12 in light of its subject matter, visual content, age of models, language, characters, tone, message, or the like.

(f) *Advertising to individuals under the age of 18.* (1) The provider of pay-per-call services shall ensure that any pay-per-call advertisement directed primarily to individuals under the age of 18 shall contain a clear and conspicuous disclosure that all individuals under the age of 18 must have the permission of such individual's parent or legal guardian prior to calling such pay-per-call service.

(2) For purposes of § 308.3(f), disclosures shall be made "clearly and conspicuously" as set forth in § 308.3(a) and as follows:

(i) In a television or videotape advertisement, each letter or numeral of the video disclosure shall be, at a minimum, one-half the size of each letter or numeral of the largest presentation of the pay-per-call number. The video disclosure shall appear on the screen for sufficient time to allow consumers to read and comprehend the disclosure. An audio disclosure shall be made at least once, simultaneously with a video presentation of the disclosure. However, no audio presentation of the disclosure is required in: (A) An advertisement fifteen (15) seconds or less in length in which the pay-per-call number is not presented in the audio portion, or (B) an advertisement in which there is no audio presentation of information regarding the pay-per-call service, including the pay-per-call number.

147

(ii) In a print advertisement, each letter or numeral of the disclosure shall be, at a minimum, one-half the size of each letter or numeral of the largest presentation of the pay-per-call number.

(3) For the purposes of this regulation, advertisements directed primarily to individuals under 18 shall include: Any pay-per-call advertisement appearing during or immediately adjacent to programming for which competent and reliable audience composition data demonstrate that more than 50% of the audience is composed of individuals under 18, and any pay-per-call advertisement appearing in a periodical for which competent and reliable readership data demonstrate that more than 50% of the readership is composed of individuals under 18.

(4) For the purposes of this regulation, if competent and reliable audience composition or readership data does not demonstrate that more than 50% of the audience or readership is composed of individuals under 18, then the Commission shall consider the following criteria in determining whether an advertisement is directed primarily to individuals under 18:

(i) Whether the advertisement appears in publications directed primarily to individuals under 18, including, but not limited to, books, magazines and comic books;

(ii) Whether the advertisement appears during or immediately adjacent to television programs directed primarily to individuals under 18, including, but not limited to, mid-afternoon weekday television shows;

(iii) Whether the advertisement is broadcast on radio stations that are directed primarily to individuals under 18;

(iv) Whether the advertisement appears on a cable or broadcast television station directed primarily to individuals under 18;

(v) Whether the advertisement appears on the same video as a commercially-prepared video directed primarily to individuals under 18, or preceding a movie directed primarily to individuals under 18 shown in a movie theater; and

(vi) Whether the advertisement, regardless of when or where it appears, is directed primarily to individuals under 18 in light of its subject matter, visual content, age of models, language, characters, tone, massage, or the like.

(g) *Electronic tones in advertisements.* The provider of pay-per-call services is prohibited from using advertisements that emit electronic tones that can automatically dial a pay-per-call service.

(h) *Telephone solicitations.* The provider of pay-per-call services shall ensure that any telephone message that solicits calls to the pay-per-call service discloses the cost of the call in a slow and deliberate manner and in a reasonably understandable volume, in accordance with §§ 308.3(b)(1)(i)–(v).

(*i*) *Referral to toll-free telephone numbers.* The provider of pay-per-call services is prohibited from referring in advertisements to an 800 telephone number, or any other telephone number advertised as or widely understood to be toll-free, if that number violates the prohibition concerning toll-free numbers set forth in § 308.5(i).

§ 308.4 Special rule for infrequent publications

(a) The provider of any pay-per-call service that advertises a pay-per-call service in a publication that meets the requirements set forth in § 308.4(c) may include in such advertisement, in lieu of the cost disclosures required by § 308.3(b), a clear and conspicuous disclosure that a call to the advertised pay-per-call service may result in a substantial charge.

(b) The provider of any pay-per-call service that places an alphabetical listing in a publication that meets the requirements set forth in § 308.4(c) is not required to make any of the disclosures required by §§ 308.3(b), (c), (d) and (f) in the alphabetical listing, provided that such listing does not contain any information except the name, address and telephone number of the pay-per-call provider.

(c) The publication referred to in § 308.4(a) and (b) must be:

(1) Widely distributed;

(2) Printed annually or less frequently; and

(3) One that has an established policy of not publishing specific prices in advertisements.

§ 308.5 Pay-per-call service standards

(a) *Preamble message.* The provider of pay-per-call services shall include, in each pay-per-call message, an introductory disclosure message ("preamble") in the same language as that principally used in the pay-per-call message, that clearly, in a slow and deliberate manner and in a reasonably understandable volume:

(1) Identifies the name of the provider of the pay-per-call service and describes the service being provided;

(2) Specifies the cost of the service as follows:

(i) If there is a flat fee for the call, the preamble shall state the total cost of the call;

(ii) If the call is billed on a time-sensitive basis, the preamble shall state the cost per minute and any minimum charges; if the length of the program can be determined in advance, the preamble shall also state the maximum charge that could be incurred if the caller listens to the complete program;

(iii) If the call is billed on a variable rate basis, the preamble shall state, in accordance with §§ 308.5(a)(2)(i) and (ii), the cost of the initial portion of the call, any minimum charges, and the range of rates that may be charged depending on the options chosen by the caller;

(iv) Any other fees that will be charged for the service shall be disclosed, as well as fees for any other pay-per-call service to which the caller may be transferred;

(3) Informs the caller that charges for the call begin, and that to avoid charges the call must be terminated, three seconds after a clearly discernible signal or tone indicating the end of the preamble;

(4) Informs the caller that anyone under the age of 18 must have the permission of parent or legal guardian in order to complete the call; and

(5) Informs the caller, in the case of a pay-per-call service that is not operated or expressly authorized by a Federal agency but that provides information on a Federal program, or that uses a trade or brand name or any other term that reasonably could be interpreted or construed as implying any Federal government connection, approval or endorsement, that the pay-per-call service is not authorized, endorsed, or approved by any Federal agency.

(b) *No charge to caller for preamble message*. The provider of pay-per-call services is prohibited from charging a caller any amount whatsoever for such a service if the caller hangs up at any time prior to three seconds after the signal or tone indicating the end of the preamble described in § 308.5(a). However, the three-second delay, and the message concerning such delay described in § 308.5(a)(3), is not required if the provider of pay-per-call services offers the caller an affirmative means (such as pressing a key on a telephone keypad) of indicating a decision to incur the charges.

(c) *Nominal cost calls*. The preamble described in § 308.5(a) is not required when the entire cost of the pay-per-call service, whether billed as a flat rate or on a time sensitive basis, is $2.00 or less.

(d) *Data service calls*. The preamble described in § 308.5(a) is not required when the entire call consists of the non-verbal transmission of information.

(e) *Bypass mechanism*. The provider of pay-per-call services that offers to frequent callers or regular subscribers to such services the option of activating a bypass mechanism to avoid listening to the preamble during subsequent calls shall not be deemed to be in violation of § 308.5(a), *provided* that any such bypass mechanism shall be disabled for a period of no less than 30 days immediately after the institution of an increase in the price for the service or a change in the nature of the service offered.

(f) *Billing limitations*. The provider of pay-per-call services is prohibited from billing consumers in excess of the amount described in the preamble for those services and from billing for any services provided in violation of any section of this rule.

(g) *Stopping the assessment of time-based charges.* The provider of pay-per-call services shall stop the assessment of time-based charges immediately upon disconnection by the caller.

(h) *Prohibition on services to children.* The provider of pay-per-call services shall not direct such services to children under the age of 12, unless such service is a bona fide educational service. The Commission shall consider the following criteria in determining whether a pay-per-call service is directed to children under 12:

(1) Whether the pay-per-call service is advertised in the manner set forth in §§ 308.3(e)(2) and (3); and

(2) Whether the pay-per-call service, regardless of when or where it is advertised, is directed to children under 12, in light of its subject matter, content, language, featured personality, characters, tone, message, or the like.

(*i*) *Prohibition concerning toll-free numbers.* Any person is prohibited from using an 800 number or other telephone number advertised as or widely understood to be toll-free in a manner that would result in:

(1) The calling party being assessed, by virtue of completing the call, a charge for the call;

(2) The calling party being connected to an access number for, or otherwise transferred to, a pay-per-call service;

(3) The calling party being charged for information conveyed during the call unless the calling party has a presubscription or comparable arrangement to be charged for the information; or

(4) The calling party being called back collect for the provision of audio or data information services, simultaneous voice conversation services, or products.

(j) *Disclosure requirements for billing statements.* The provider of pay-per-call services shall ensure that any billing statement for such provider's charges shall:

(1) Display any charges for pay-per-call services in a portion of the consumer's bill that is identified as not being related to local and long distance telephone charges;

(2) For each charge so displayed, specify the type of service, the amount of the charge, and the date, time, and, for calls billed on a time-sensitive basis, the duration of the call; and

(3) Display the local or toll-free telephone number where consumers can obtain answers to their questions and information on their rights and obligations with regard to their use of pay-per-call services, and can obtain the name and mailing address of the provider of pay-per-call services.

(k) *Refunds to consumers.* The provider of pay-per-call services shall be liable for refunds or credits to consumers who have been billed for pay-per-call services, and who have paid the charges for such services, pursuant to pay-per-call programs that have been found to have violated any provision of this rule or any other Federal rule or law.

(*l*) *Service bureau liability.* A service bureau shall be liable for violations of the rule by pay-per-call services using its call processing facilities where it knew or should have known of the violation.

§ 308.6　Access to information

Any common carrier that provides telecommunication services to any provider of pay-per-call services shall make available to the Commission, upon written request, any records and financial information maintained by such carrier relating to the arrangements (other than for the provision of local exchange service) between such carrier and any provider of pay-per-call services.

§ 308.7　Billing and collection for pay-per-call services

(a) *Definitions.* For the purposes of this section, the following definitions shall apply:

(1) *Billing entity* means any person who transmits a billing statement to a customer for a telephone-billed purchase, or any person who assumes responsibility for receiving and responding to billing error complaints or inquiries.

(2) *Billing error* means any of the following:

(i) A reflection on a billing statement of a telephone-billed purchase that was not made by the customer nor made from the telephone of the customer who was billed for the purchase or, if made, was not in the amount reflected on such statement.

(ii) A reflection on a billing statement of a telephone-billed purchase for which the customer requests additional clarification, including documentary evidence thereof.

(iii) A reflection on a billing statement of a telephone-billed purchase that was not accepted by the customer or not provided to the customer in accordance with the stated terms of the transaction.

(iv) A reflection on a billing statement of a telephone-billed purchase for a call made to an 800 or other toll free telephone number.

(v) The failure to reflect properly on a billing statement a payment made by the customer or a credit issued to the customer with respect to a telephone-billed purchase.

(vi) A computation error or similar error of an accounting nature on a billing statement of a telephone-billed purchase.

(vii) Failure to transmit a billing statement for a telephone-billed purchase to a customer's last known address if that address was furnished by the customer at least twenty days before the end of the billing cycle for which the statement was required.

(viii) A reflection on a billing statement of a telephone-billed purchase that is not identified in accordance with the requirements of § 308.5(j).

(3) *Customer* means any person who acquires or attempts to acquire goods or services in a telephone-billed purchase, or who receives a billing statement for a telephone-billed purchase charged to a telephone number assigned to that person by a providing carrier.

(4) *Preexisting agreement* means a "presubscription or comparable arrangement," as that term is defined in § 308.2(e).

(5) *Providing carrier* means a local exchange or interexchange common carrier providing telephone services (other than local exchange services) to a vendor for a telephone-billed purchase that is the subject of a billing error complaint or inquiry.

(6) *Telephone-billed purchase* means any purchase that is completed solely as a consequence of the completion of the call or a subsequent dialing, touch tone entry, or comparable action of the caller. Such term does not include:

(i) A purchase by a caller pursuant to a preexisting agreement with a vendor;

(ii) Local exchange telephone services or interexchange telephone services or any service that the Federal Communications Commission determines by rule—

(A) Is closely related to the provision of local exchange telephone services or interexchange telephone services; and

(B) Is subject to billing dispute resolution procedures required by Federal or state statute or regulation; or

(iii) The purchase of goods or services that is otherwise subject to billing dispute resolution procedures required by Federal statute or regulation.

(7) *Vendor* means any person who, through the use of the telephone, offers goods or services for a telephone-billed purchase.

(b) *Initiation of billing review*. A customer may initiate a billing review with respect to a telephone-billed purchase by providing the billing entity with notice of a billing error no later than 60 days after the billing entity transmitted the first billing statement that contains a charge for such telephone-billed purchase. If the billing error is the reflection on a billing statement of a telephone-billed purchase not provided to the customer in accordance with the stated terms of the transaction, the 60–day period shall begin to run from the date the goods or services are delivered or, if not delivered, should have been delivered, if such date is later than the date the billing statement was transmitted. A billing error notice shall:

(1) Set forth or otherwise enable the billing entity to identify the customer's name and the telephone number to which the charge was billed;

(2) Indicate the customer's belief that the statement contains a billing error and the type, date, and amount of such; and

(3) Set forth the reasons for the customer's belief, to the extent possible, that the statement contains a billing error.

(c) *Disclosure of method of providing notice; presumption if oral notice is permitted.* A billing entity shall clearly and conspicuously[2] disclose on each billing statement or on other material accompanying the billing statement the method (oral or written) by which the customer may provide notice to initiate review of a billing error in the manner set forth in § 308.7(b). If oral notice is permitted, any customer who orally communicates an allegation of a billing error to a billing entity shall be presumed to have properly initiated a billing review in accordance with the requirements of § 308.7(b).

(d) *Response to customer notice.* A billing entity that receives notice of a billing error as described in § 308.7(b) shall:

(1) Send a written acknowledgement to the customer including a statement that any disputed amount need not be paid pending investigation of the billing error. This shall be done no later than forty (40) days after receiving the notice, unless the action required by § 308.7(d)(2) is taken within such 40-day period; and

(2)(i) Correct the billing error and credit the customer's account for any disputed amount and any related charges, and notify the customer of the correction. The billing entity also shall disclose to the customer that collection efforts may occur despite the credit, and shall provide the names, mailing addresses, and business telephone numbers of the vendor and providing carrier, as applicable, that are the subject of the telephone-billed purchase, or provide the customer with a local or toll-free telephone number that the customer may call to obtain this information directly. However, the billing entity is not required to make the disclosure concerning collection efforts if the vendor, its agent, or the providing carrier, as applicable, will not collect or attempt to collect the disputed charge; or

(ii) Transmit an explanation to the customer, after conducting a reasonable investigation (including, where appropriate, contacting the vendor or providing carrier),[3] setting forth the reasons why it has

---

2. The standard for "clear and conspicuous" as used in this section shall be the standard enunciated by the Board of Governors of the Federal Reserve System in its Official Staff Commentary on Regulation Z, which requires simply that the disclosures be in a reasonably understandable form. See 12 CFR part 226, Supplement I, Comment 226.5(a)(1)–1.

3. If a customer submits a billing error notice alleging either the nondelivery of goods or services or that information appearing on a billing statement has been re-ported incorrectly to the billing entity, the billing entity shall not deny the assertion unless it conducts a reasonable investigation and determines that the goods or services were actually delivered as agreed or that the information was correct. There shall be a rebuttable presumption that goods or services were actually delivered to the extent that a vendor or providing carrier produces documents prepared and maintained in the ordinary course of business showing the date on, and the place to, which the goods or services were transmitted or delivered.

determined that no billing error occurred or that a different billing error occurred from that asserted, make any appropriate adjustments to the customer's account, and, if the customer so requests, provide a written explanation and copies of documentary evidence of the customer's indebtedness.

(3) The action required by § 308.7(d)(2) shall be taken no later than two complete billing cycles of the billing entity (in no event later than ninety (90) days) after receiving the notice of the billing error and before taking any action to collect the disputed amount, or any part thereof. After complying with § 308.7(d)(2), the billing entity shall:

(i) If it is determined that any disputed amount is in error, promptly notify the appropriate providing carrier or vendor, as applicable, of its disposition of the customer's billing error and the reasons therefor; and

(ii) Promptly notify the customer in writing of the time when payment is due of any portion of the disputed amount determined not to be in error, which time shall be the longer of ten (10) days or the number of days the customer is ordinarily allowed (whether by custom, contract or state law) to pay undisputed amounts, and that failure to pay such amount may be reported to a credit reporting agency or subject the customer to a collection action, if that in fact may happen.

(e) *Withdrawal of billing error notice.* A billing entity need not comply with the requirements of § 308.7(d) if the customer has, after giving notice of a billing error and before the expiration of the time limits specified therein, agreed that the billing statement was correct or agreed to withdraw voluntarily the billing error notice.

(f) *Limitation on responsibility for billing error.* After complying with the provisions of § 308.7(d), a billing entity has no further responsibility under that section if the customer continues to make substantially the same allegation with respect to a billing error.

(g) *Customer's right to withhold disputed amount; limitation on collection action.* Once the customer has submitted notice of a billing error to a billing entity, the customer need not pay, and the billing entity, providing carrier, or vendor may not try to collect, any portion of any required payment that the customer reasonably believes is related to the disputed amount until the billing entity receiving the notice has complied with the requirements of § 308.7(d). The billing entity, providing carrier, or vendor are not prohibited from taking any action to collect any undisputed portion of the bill, or from reflecting a disputed amount and related charges on a billing statement, provided that the billing statement clearly states that payment of any disputed amount or related charges is not required pending the billing entity's compliance with § 308.7(d).

(h) *Prohibition on charges for initiating billing review.* A billing entity, providing carrier, or vendor may not impose on the customer any charge related to the billing review, including charges for documentation or investigation.

(i) *Restrictions on credit reporting*—(1) *Adverse credit reports prohibited.* Once the customer has submitted notice of a billing error to a billing entity, a billing entity, providing carrier, vendor, or other agent may not report or threaten directly or indirectly to report adverse information to any person because of the customer's withholding payment of the disputed amount or related charges, until the billing entity has met the requirements of § 308.7(d) and allowed the customer as many days thereafter to make payment as prescribed by § 308.7(d)(3)(ii).

(2) *Reports on continuing disputes.* If a billing entity receives further notice from a customer within the time allowed for payment under § 308.7(i)(1) that any portion of the billing error is still in dispute, a billing entity, providing carrier, vendor, or other agent may not report to any person that the customer's account is delinquent because of the customer's failure to pay that disputed amount unless the billing entity, providing carrier, vendor, or other agent also reports that the amount is in dispute and notifies the customer in writing of the name and address of each person to whom the vendor, billing entity, providing carrier, or other agent has reported the account as delinquent.

(3) *Reporting of dispute resolutions required.* A billing entity, providing carrier, vendor, or other agent shall report in writing any subsequent resolution of any matter reported pursuant to § 308.7(i)(2) to all persons to whom such matter was initially reported.

(j) *Forfeiture of right to collect disputed amount.* Any billing entity, providing carrier, vendor, or other agent who fails to comply with the requirements of §§ 308.7(c), (d), (g), (h), or (i) forfeits any right to collect from the customer the amount indicated by the customer, under § 308.7(b)(2), to be in error, and any late charges or other related charges thereon, up to $50 per transaction.

(k) *Prompt notification of returns and crediting of refunds.* When a vendor other than the billing entity accepts the return of property or forgives a debt for services in connection with a telephone-billed purchase, the vendor shall, within seven (7) business days from accepting the return or forgiving the debt, either:

(1) Mail or deliver a cash refund directly to the customer's address, and notify the appropriate billing entity that the customer has been given a refund, or

(2) Transmit a credit statement to the billing entity through the vendor's normal channels for billing telephone-billed purchases. The billing entity shall, within seven (7) business days after receiving a credit statement, credit the customer's account with the amount of the refund.

(*l*) *Right of customer to assert claims or defenses.* Any billing entity or providing carrier who seeks to collect charges from a customer for a telephone-billed purchase that is the subject of a dispute between the customer and the vendor shall be subject to all claims (other than tort claims) and defenses arising out of the transaction and relating to the failure to resolve the dispute that the customer could assert against the vendor, if the customer has made a good faith attempt to resolve the dispute with the vendor or providing carrier (other than the billing entity). The billing entity or providing carrier shall not be liable under this paragraph for any amount greater than the amount billed to the customer for the purchase (including any related charges).

(m) *Retaliatory actions prohibited.* A billing entity, providing carrier, vendor, or other agent may not accelerate any part of the customer's indebtedness or restrict or terminate the customer's access to pay-per-call services solely because the customer has exercised in good faith rights provided by this section.

(n) *Notice of billing error rights*—(1) *Annual statement.* (i) A billing entity shall mail or deliver to each customer, with the first billing statement for a telephone-billed purchase mailed or delivered after the effective date of these regulations, a statement of the customer's billing rights with respect to telephone-billed purchases. Thereafter the billing entity shall mail or deliver the billing rights statement at least once per calendar year to each customer to whom it has mailed or delivered a billing statement for a telephone-billed purchase during the previous twelve months. The billing rights statement shall disclose that the rights and obligations of the customer and the billing entity, set forth therein, are provided under the federal Telephone Disclosure and Dispute Resolution Act. The statement shall describe the procedure that the customer must follow to notify the billing entity of a billing error and the steps that the billing entity must take in response to the customer's notice. If the customer is permitted to provide oral notice of a billing error, the statement shall disclose that a customer who orally communicates an allegation of a billing error is presumed to have provided sufficient notice to initiate a billing review. The statement shall also disclose the customer's right to withhold payment of any disputed amount, and that any action to collect any disputed amount will be suspended, pending completion of the billing review. The statement shall further disclose the customer's rights and obligations if the billing entity determines that no billing error occurred, including what action the billing entity may take if the customer continues to withhold payment of the disputed amount. Additionally, the statement shall inform the customer of the billing entity's obligation to forfeit any disputed amount (up to $50 per transaction) if the billing entity fails to follow the billing and collection procedures prescribed by § 308.7 of this rule.

(ii) A billing entity that is a common carrier may comply with § 308.7(n)(1)(i) by, within 60 days after the effective date of these regulations, mailing or delivering the billing rights statement to all of its customers and, thereafter, mailing or delivering the billing rights statement at least once per calendar year, at intervals of not less than 6 months nor more than 18 months, to all of its customers.

(2) *Alternative summary statement.* As an alternative to § 308.7(n)(1), a billing entity may mail or deliver, on or with each billing statement, a statement that sets forth the procedure that a customer must follow to notify the billing entity of a billing error. The statement shall also disclose the customer's right to withhold payment of any disputed amount, and that any action to collect any disputed amount will be suspended, pending completion of the billing review.

(3) *General disclosure requirements.* (i) The disclosures required by § 308.7(n)(1) shall be made clearly and conspicuously on a separate statement that the customer may keep.

(ii) The disclosures required by § 308.7(n)(2) shall be made clearly and conspicuously and may be made on a separate statement or on the customer's billing statement. If any of the disclosures are provided on the back of the billing statement, the billing entity shall include a reference to those disclosures on the front of the statement.

(iii) At the billing entity's option, additional information or explanations may be supplied with the disclosures required by § 308.7(n), but none shall be stated, utilized, or placed so as to mislead or confuse the customer or contradict, obscure, or detract attention from the information required to be disclosed. The disclosures required by § 308.7(n) shall appear separately and above any other disclosures.

(o) *Multiple billing entities.* If a telephone-billed purchase involves more than one billing entity, only one set of disclosures need by given, and the billing entities shall agree among themselves which billing entity must comply with the requirements that this regulation imposes on any or all of them. The billing entity designated to receive and respond to billing errors shall remain the only billing entity responsible for complying with the terms of § 308.7(d). If a billing entity other than the one designated to receive and respond to billing errors receives notice of a billing error as described in § 308.7(b), that billing entity shall either: (1) Promptly transmit to the customer the name, mailing address, and business telephone number of the billing entity designated to receive and respond to billing errors; or (2) transmit the billing error notice within fifteen (15) days to the billing entity designated to receive and respond to billing errors. The time requirements in § 308.7(d) shall not begin to run until the billing entity designated to receive and respond to billing errors receives notice of the billing error, either from the customer or from the billing entity to whom the customer transmitted the notice.

(p) *Multiple customers.* If there is more than one customer involved in a telephone-billed purchase, the disclosures may be made to any customer who is primarily liable on the account.

§ 308.8   Severability

The provisions of this rule are separate and severable from one another. If any provision is stayed or determined to be invalid, it is the Commission's intention that the remaining provisions shall continue in effect.

§ 308.9   Rulemaking review

No later than four years after the effective date of this Rule, the Commission shall initiate a rulemaking review proceeding to evaluate the operation of the rule.

FEDERAL TRADE COMMISSION REGULATION
TELEMARKETING SALES RULE
16 C.F.R. Part 310

Table of Sections

----

§ 310.1 Scope of regulations in this part

This part implements the Telemarketing and Consumer Fraud and Abuse Prevention Act, 15 U.S.C. §§ 6101–6108, as amended.

§ 310.2 Definitions

(a) *Acquirer* means a business organization, financial institution, or an agent of a business organization or financial institution that has authority from an organization that operates or licenses a credit card system to authorize merchants to accept, transmit, or process payment by credit card through the credit card system for money, goods or services, or anything else of value.

(b) *Attorney General* means the chief legal officer of a state.

(c) *Billing information* means any data that enables any person to access a customer's or donor's account, such as a credit card, checking, savings, share or similar account, utility bill, mortgage loan account, or debit card.

(d) *Caller identification service* means a service that allows a telephone subscriber to have the telephone number, and, where available, name of the calling party transmitted contemporaneously with the telephone call, and displayed on a device in or connected to the subscriber's telephone.

(e) *Cardholder* means a person to whom a credit card is issued or who is authorized to use a credit card on behalf of or in addition to the person to whom the credit card is issued.

(f) *Charitable contribution* means any donation or gift of money or any other thing of value.

160

(g) *Commission* means the Federal Trade Commission.

(h) *Credit* means the right granted by, a creditor to a debtor to defer payment of debt or to incur debt and defer its payment.

(i) *Credit card* means any card, plate, coupon book, or other credit device existing for the purpose of obtaining money, property, labor, or services on credit.

(j) *Credit card sales draft* means any record or evidence of a credit card transaction.

(k) *Credit card system* means any method or procedure used to process credit card transactions involving credit cards issued or licensed by the operator of that system.

(l) *Customer* means any person who is or may be required to pay for goods or services offered through telemarketing.

(m) *Donor* means any person solicited to make a charitable contribution.

(n) *Established business relationship* means a relationship between a seller and a consumer based on:

(1) the consumer's purchase, rental, or lease of the seller's goods or services or a financial transaction between the consumer and seller, within the eighteen (18) months immediately preceding the date of a telemarketing call; or

(2) the consumer's inquiry or application regarding a product or service offered by the seller, within the three (3) months immediately preceding the date of a telemarketing call.

(o) *Free-to-pay conversion* means, in an offer or agreement to sell or provide any goods or services, a provision under which a customer receives a product or service for free for an initial period and will incur an obligation to pay for the product or service if he or she does not take affirmative action to cancel before the end of that period.

(p) *Investment opportunity* means anything, tangible or intangible, that is offered, offered for sale, sold, or traded based wholly or in part on representations, either express or implied, about past, present, or future income, profit, or appreciation.

(q) *Material* means likely to affect a person's choice of, or conduct regarding, goods or services or a charitable contribution.

(r) *Merchant* means a person who is authorized under a written contract with an acquirer to honor or accept credit cards, or to transmit or process for payment credit card payments, for the purchase of goods or services or a charitable contribution.

(s) *Merchant agreement* means a written contract between a merchant and an acquirer to honor or accept credit cards, or to transmit or process for payment credit card payments, for the purchase of goods or services or a charitable contribution.

(t) *Negative option feature* means, in an offer or agreement to sell or provide any goods or services, a provision under which the customer's silence or failure to take an affirmative action to reject goods or services or to cancel the agreement is interpreted by the seller as acceptance of the offer.

(u) *Outbound telephone call* means a telephone call initiated by a telemarketer to induce the purchase of goods or services or to solicit a charitable contribution.

(v) *Person* means any individual, group, unincorporated association, limited or general partnership, corporation, or other business entity.

(w) *Preacquired account information* means any information that enables a seller or telemarketer to cause a charge to be placed against a customer's or donor's account without obtaining the account number directly from the customer or donor during the telemarketing transaction pursuant to which the account will be charged.

(x) *Prize* means anything offered, or purportedly offered, and given, or purportedly given, to a person by chance. For purposes of this definition, chance exists if a person is guaranteed to receive an item and, at the time of the offer or purported offer, the telemarketer does not identify the specific item that the person will receive.

(y) *Prize promotion* means:

(1) A sweepstakes or other game of chance; or

(2) An oral or written express or implied representation that a person has won, has been selected to receive, or may be eligible to receive a prize or purported prize.

(z) *Seller* means any person who, in connection with a telemarketing transaction, provides, offers to provide, or arranges for others to provide goods or services to the customer in exchange for consideration.

(aa) *State* means any state of the United States, the District of Columbia, Puerto Rico, the Northern Mariana Islands, and any territory or possession of the United States.

(bb) *Telemarketer* means any person who, in connection with telemarketing, initiates or receives telephone calls to or from a customer or donor.

(cc) *Telemarketing* means a plan, program, or campaign which is conducted to induce the purchase of goods or services or a charitable contribution, by use of one or more telephones and which involves more than one interstate telephone call. The term does not include the solicitation of sales through the mailing of a catalog which: contains a written description or illustration of the goods or services offered for sale; includes the business address of the seller; includes multiple pages of written material or illustrations; and has been issued not less frequently than once a year, when the person making the solicitation does not solicit customers by telephone but only receives calls initiated by customers in response to the catalog and during those calls takes orders only without further solicitation. For purposes of the previous sentence, the term "further solicitation" does not include providing the customer with information about, or attempting to sell, any other item included in the same catalog which prompted the customer's call or in a substantially similar catalog.

(dd) *Upselling* means soliciting the purchase of goods or services following an initial transaction during a single telephone call. The upsell is a separate telemarketing transaction, not a continuation of the initial transaction. An "external upsell" is a solicitation made by or on behalf of a seller different from the seller in the initial transaction, regardless of whether the initial transaction and the subsequent solicitation are made by the same telemarketer. An "internal upsell" is a solicitation made by or on behalf of the same seller as in the initial transaction, regardless of whether the initial transaction and subsequent solicitation are made by the same telemarketer.

§ 310.3 Deceptive telemarketing acts or practices

(a) *Prohibited deceptive telemarketing acts or practices*. It is a deceptive telemarketing act or practice and a violation of this Rule for any seller or telemarketer to engage in the following conduct:

(1) Before a customer pays[1] for goods or services offered, failing to disclose truthfully, in a clear and conspicuous manner, the following material information:

(i) The total costs to purchase, receive, or use, and the quantity of, any goods or services that are the subject of the sales offer;[2]

(ii) All material restrictions, limitations, or conditions to purchase, receive, or use the goods or services that are the subject of the sales offer;

(iii) If the seller has a policy of not making refunds, cancellations, exchanges, or repurchases, a statement informing the customer that this is the seller's policy; or, if the seller or telemarketer makes a representation about a refund, cancellation, exchange, or repurchase policy, a statement of all material terms and conditions of such policy;

(iv) In any prize promotion, the odds of being able to receive the prize, and, if the odds are not calculable in advance, the factors used in calculating the odds; that no purchase or payment is required to win a prize or to participate in a prize promotion and that any purchase or

---

1. When a seller or telemarketer uses, or directs a customer to use, a courier to transport payment, the seller or telemarketer must make the disclosures required by § 310.3(a)(1) before sending a courier to pick up payment or authorization for payment, or directing a customer to have a courier pick up payment or authorization for payment.

2. For offers of consumer credit products subject to the Truth in Lending Act, 15 U.S.C. § 1601 *et seq.*, and Regulation Z, 12 CFR part 226, compliance with the disclosure requirements under the Truth in Lending Act and Regulation Z shall constitute compliance with § 310.3(a)(*l*)(i) of this Rule.

payment will not increase the person's chances of winning; and the no-purchase/no-payment method of participating in the prize promotion with either instructions on how to participate or an address or local or toll-free telephone number to which customers may write or call for information on how to participate;

(v) All material costs, or conditions to receive or redeem a prize that is the subject of the prize promotion;

(vi) In the sale of any goods or services represented to protect, insure, or otherwise limit a customer's liability in the event of unauthorized use of the customer's credit card, the limits on a cardholder's liability for unauthorized use of a credit card pursuant to 15 U.S.C. § 1643; and

(vii) If the offer includes a negative option feature, all material terms and conditions of the negative option feature, including, but not limited to, the fact that the customer's account will be charged unless the customer takes an affirmative action to avoid the charge(s), the date(s) the charge(s) will be submitted for payment, and the specific steps the customer must take to avoid the charge(s).

(2) Misrepresenting, directly or by implication, in the sale of goods or services any of the following material information:

(i) The total costs to purchase, receive, or use, and the quantity of, any goods or services that are the subject of a sales offer;

(ii) Any material restriction, limitation, or condition to purchase, receive, or use goods or services that are the subject of a sales offer;

(iii) Any material aspect of the performance, efficacy, nature, or central characteristics of goods or services that are the subject of a sales offer;

(iv) Any material aspect of the nature or terms of the seller's refund, cancellation, exchange, or repurchase policies;

(v) Any material aspect of a prize promotion including, but not limited to, the odds of being able to receive a prize, the nature or value of a prize, or that a purchase or payment is required to win a prize or to participate in a prize promotion;

(vi) Any material aspect of an investment opportunity including, but not limited to, risk, liquidity, earnings potential, or profitability;

(vii) A seller's or telemarketer's affiliation with, or endorsement or sponsorship by, any person or government entity;

(viii) That any customer needs offered goods or services to provide protections a customer already has pursuant to 15 U.S.C. § 1643; or

(ix) Any material aspect of a negative option feature including, but not limited to, the fact that the customer's account will be charged unless the customer takes an affirmative action to avoid the charge(s), the date(s) the charge(s) will be submitted for payment, and the specific steps the customer must take to avoid the charge(s).

(3) Causing billing information to be submitted for payment, or collecting or attempting to collect payment for goods or services or a charitable contribution, directly or indirectly, without the customer's or donor's express verifiable authorization, except when the method of payment used is a credit card subject to protections of the Truth in Lending Act and Regulation Z,[3] or a debit card subject to the protections of the Electronic Fund Transfer Act and Regulation E.[4] Such authorization shall be deemed verifiable if any of the following means is employed:

(i) Express written authorization by the customer or donor, which includes the customer's or donor's signature;[5]

(ii) Express oral authorization which is audio-recorded and made available upon request to the customer or donor, and the customer's or donor's bank or other billing entity, and which evidences clearly both the customer's or donor's authorization of payment for the goods or services or charitable contribution that are the subject of the telemarketing transaction and the customer's or donor's receipt of all of the following information:

(A) The number of debits, charges, or payments (if more than one);

(B) The date(s) the debit(s), charge(s), or payment(s) will be submitted for payment;

(C) The amount(s) of the debit(s), charge(s), or payment(s);

(D) The customer's or donor's name;

(E) The customer's or donor's billing information, identified with sufficient specificity such that the customer or donor understands what account will be used to collect payment for the goods or services or charitable contribution that are the subject of the telemarketing transaction;

(F) A telephone number for customer or donor inquiry that is answered during normal business hours; and

(G) The date of the customer's or donor's oral authorization; or

(iii) Written confirmation of the transaction, identified in a clear and conspicuous manner as such on the outside of the envelope, sent to the customer or donor via first class mail prior to the submission for

---

3. Truth in Lending Act, 15 U.S.C. § 1601 *et seq.*, and Regulation Z, 12 CFR part 226.

4. Electronic Fund Transfer Act, 15 U.S.C. § 1693 *et seq.*, and Regulation E, 12 CFR part 205.

5. For purposes of this Rule, the term "signature" shall include an electronic or digital form of signature, to the extent that such form of signature is recognized as a valid signature under applicable federal law or state contract law.

payment of the customer's or donor's billing information, and that includes all of the information contained in §§ 310.3(a)(3)(ii)(A)–(G) and a clear and conspicuous statement of the procedures by which the customer or donor can obtain a refund from the seller or telemarketer or charitable organization in the event the confirmation is inaccurate; *provided*, however, that this means of authorization shall not be deemed verifiable in instances in which goods or services are offered in a transaction involving a free-to-pay conversion and preacquired account information.

(4) Making a false or misleading statement to induce any person to pay for goods or services or to induce a charitable contribution.

(b) *Assisting and facilitating.* It is a deceptive telemarketing act or practice and a violation of this Rule for a person to provide substantial assistance or support to any seller or telemarketer when that person knows or consciously avoids knowing that the seller or telemarketer is engaged in any act or practice that violates §§ 310.3(a), (c) or (d), or § 310.4 of this Rule.

(c) *Credit card laundering.* Except as expressly permitted by the applicable credit card system, it is a deceptive telemarketing act or practice and a violation of this Rule for:

(1) A merchant to present to or deposit into, or cause another to present to or deposit into, the credit card system for payment, a credit card sales draft generated by a telemarketing transaction that is not the result of a telemarketing credit card transaction between the cardholder and the merchant;

(2) Any person to employ, solicit, or otherwise cause a merchant, or an employee, representative, or agent of the merchant, to present to or deposit into the credit card system for payment, a credit card sales draft generated by a telemarketing transaction that is not the result of a telemarketing credit card transaction between the cardholder and the merchant; or

(3) Any person to obtain access to the credit card system through the use of a business relationship or an affiliation with a merchant, when such access is not authorized by the merchant agreement or the applicable credit card system.

(d) *Prohibited deceptive acts or practices in the solicitation of charitable contributions.* It is a fraudulent charitable solicitation, a deceptive telemarketing act or practice, and a violation of this Rule for any telemarketer soliciting charitable contributions to misrepresent, directly or by implication, any of the following material information:

(1) The nature, purpose, or mission of any entity on behalf of which a charitable contribution is being requested;

(2) That any charitable contribution is tax deductible in whole or in part;

(3) The purpose for which any charitable contribution will be used;

(4) The percentage or amount of any charitable contribution that will go to a charitable organization or to any particular charitable program;

(5) Any material aspect of a prize promotion including, but not limited to: the odds of being able to receive a prize; the nature or value of a prize; or that a charitable contribution is required to win a prize or to participate in a prize promotion; or

(6) A charitable organization's or telemarketer's affiliation with, or endorsement or sponsorship by, any person or government entity.

§ 310.4 Abusive telemarketing acts or practices

(a) *Abusive conduct generally*. It is an abusive telemarketing act or practice and a violation of this Rule for any seller or telemarketer to engage in the following conduct:

(1) Threats, intimidation, or the use of profane or obscene language;

(2) Requesting or receiving payment of any fee or consideration for goods or services represented to remove derogatory information from, or improve, a person's credit history, credit record, or credit rating until:

(i) The time frame in which the seller has represented all of the goods or services will be provided to that person has expired; and

(ii) The seller has provided the person with documentation in the form of a consumer report from a consumer reporting agency demonstrating that the promised results have been achieved, such report having been issued more than six months after the results were achieved. Nothing in this Rule should be construed to affect the requirement in the Fair Credit Reporting Act, 15 U.S.C. § 1681, that a consumer report may only be obtained for a specified permissible purpose;

(3) Requesting or receiving payment of any fee or consideration from a person for goods or services represented to recover or otherwise assist in the return of money or any other item of value paid for by, or promised to, that person in a previous telemarketing transaction, until seven (7) business days after such money or other item is delivered to that person. This provision shall not apply to goods or services provided to a person by a licensed attorney;

(4) Requesting or receiving payment of any fee or consideration in advance of obtaining a loan or other extension of credit when the seller or telemarketer has guaranteed or represented a high likelihood of success in obtaining or arranging a loan or other extension of credit for a person;

(5) Disclosing or receiving, for consideration, unencrypted consumer account numbers for use in telemarketing; *provided*, however, that this paragraph shall not apply to the disclosure or receipt of a customer's or donor's billing information to process a payment for goods or services or a charitable contribution pursuant to a transaction;

(6) Causing billing information to be submitted for payment, directly or indirectly, without the express informed consent of the customer or donor. In any telemarketing transaction, the seller or telemarketer must obtain the express informed consent of the customer or donor to be charged for the goods or services or charitable contribution and to be charged using the identified account. In any telemarketing transaction involving preacquired account information, the requirements immediately below must be met to evidence express informed consent.

(i) In any telemarketing transaction involving preacquired account information and a free-to-pay conversion feature, the seller or telemarketer must:

(A) obtain from the customer, at a minimum, the last four (4) digits of the account number to be charged;

(B) obtain from the customer his or her express agreement to be charged for the goods or services and to be charged using the account number pursuant to subsection (A) of this section; and,

(C) make and maintain an audio recording of the entire telemarketing transaction.

(ii) In any other telemarketing transaction involving preacquired account information not described in section (i) above, the seller or telemarketer must:

(A) at a minimum, identify the account to be charged with sufficient specificity for the customer or donor to understand what account will be charged; and

(B) obtain from the customer or donor his or her express agreement to be charged for the goods or services and to be charged using the account number identified pursuant to subsection (A) of this section; or

(7) Failing to transmit or cause to be transmitted the telephone number, and, when made available by the telemarketer's carrier, the name of the telemarketer, to any caller identification service in use by a recipient of a telemarketing call; *provided* that it shall not be a violation to substitute (for the name and phone number used in, or billed for, making the call) the name of the seller or charitable organization on behalf of which a telemarketing call is placed, and the seller's or charitable organization's customer or donor service telephone number, which is answered during regular business hours.

(b) *Pattern of calls.*

(1) It is an abusive telemarketing act or practice and a violation of this Rule for a telemarketer to engage in, or for a seller to cause a telemarketer to engage in, the following conduct:

(i) Causing any telephone to ring, or engaging any person in telephone conversation, repeatedly or continuously with intent to annoy, abuse, or harass any person at the called number;

(ii) Denying or interfering in any way, directly or indirectly, with a person's right to be placed on any registry of names and/or telephone numbers of persons who do not wish to receive outbound telephone calls established to comply with § 310.4(b)(1)(iii);

(iii) Initiating any outbound telephone call to a person when:

(A) that person previously has stated that he or she does not wish to receive an outbound telephone call made by or on behalf of the seller whose goods or services are being offered or made on behalf of the charitable organization for which a charitable contribution is being solicited; or

(B) that person's telephone number is on the "do-not-call" registry, maintained by the Commission, of persons who do not wish to receive outbound telephone calls to induce the purchase of goods or services unless the seller

(i) has obtained the express agreement, in writing, of such person to place calls to that person. Such written agreement shall clearly evidence such person's authorization that calls made by or on behalf of a specific party may be placed to that person, and shall include the telephone number to which the calls may be placed and the signature[6] of that person; or

(ii) has an established business relationship with such person, and that person has not stated that he or she does not wish to receive outbound telephone calls under subsection (A) immediately above; or

(iv) Abandoning any outbound telephone call. An outbound telephone call is "abandoned" under this section if a person answers it and the telemarketer does not connect the call to a sales representative within two (2) seconds of the person's completed greeting.

(v) Initiating any outbound telephone call that delivers a prerecorded message, other than a prerecorded message permitted for compliance with the call abandonment safe harbor in § 310.4(b)(4)(iii), unless:

(A) in any such call to induce the purchase of any good or service, the seller has obtained from the recipient of the call an express agreement, in writing, that:

(i) the seller obtained only after a clear and conspicuous disclosure that the purpose of the agreement is to authorize the seller to place prerecorded calls to such person;

(ii) the seller obtained without requiring, directly or indirectly, that the agreement be executed as a condition of purchasing any good or service;

---

6. For purposes of this Rule, the term "signature" shall include an electronic or digital form of signature, to the extent that such form of signature is recognized as a valid signature under applicable federal law or state contract law.

(iii) evidences the willingness of the recipient of the call to receive calls that deliver prerecorded messages by or on behalf of a specific seller; and

(iv) includes such person's telephone number and signature;[7] and

(B) in any such call to induce the purchase of any good or service, or to induce a charitable contribution from a member of, or previous donor to, a non-profit charitable organization on whose behalf the call is made, the seller or telemarketer:

(i) allows the telephone to ring for at least fifteen (15) seconds or four (4) rings before disconnecting an unanswered call; and

(ii) within two (2) seconds after the completed greeting of the person called, plays a prerecorded message that promptly provides the disclosures required by § 310.4(d) or (e), followed immediately by a disclosure of one or both of the following:

(A) in the case of a call that could be answered in person by a consumer, that the person called can use an automated interactive voice and/or keypress-activated opt-out mechanism to assert a Do Not Call request pursuant to § 310.4(b)(1)(iii)(A) at any time during the message. The mechanism must:

(1) automatically add the number called to the seller's entity-specific Do Not Call list;

(2) once invoked, immediately disconnect the call; and

(3) be available for use at any time during the message; and

(B) in the case of a call that could be answered by an answering machine or voicemail service, that the person called can use a toll-free telephone number to assert a Do Not Call request pursuant to § 310.4(b)(1)(iii)(A). The number provided must connect directly to an automated interactive voice or keypress-activated opt-out mechanism that:

(1) automatically adds the number called to the seller's entity-specific Do Not Call list;

(2) immediately thereafter disconnects the call; and

---

7. For purposes of this Rule, the term "signature" shall include an electronic or digital form of signature, to the extent that such form of signature is recognized as a valid signature under applicable federal law or state contract law.

(3) is accessible at any time throughout the duration of the telemarketing campaign; and

(iii) Complies with all other requirements of this Part and other applicable federal and state laws.

(C) Any call that complies with all applicable requirements of this paragraph (v) shall not be deemed to violate § 310.4(b)(1)(iv) of this Part.

(D) This paragraph (v) shall not apply to any outbound telephone call that delivers a prerecorded healthcare message made by, or on behalf of, a covered entity or its business associate, as those terms are defined in the HIPAA Privacy Rule, 45 CFR 160.103.

(2) It is an abusive telemarketing act or practice and a violation of this Rule for any person to sell, rent, lease, purchase, or use any list established to comply with § 310.4(b)(1)(iii)(A) or maintained by the Commission pursuant to § 310.4(b)(1)(iii)(B) for any purpose except compliance with the provisions of this Rule or otherwise to prevent telephone calls to telephone numbers on such lists.

(3) A seller or telemarketer will not be liable for violating § 310.4(b)(1)(ii) and (iii) if it can demonstrate that, as part of the seller's or telemarketer's routine business practice:

(i) It has established and implemented written procedures to comply with § 310.4(b)(1)(ii) and (iii);

(ii) It has trained its personnel, and any entity assisting in its compliance, in the procedures established pursuant to § 310.4(b)(3)(i);

(iii) The seller, or a telemarketer or another person acting on behalf of the seller or charitable organization, has maintained and recorded a list of telephone numbers the seller or charitable organization may not contact, in compliance with § 310.4(b)(1)(iii)(A);

(iv) The seller or a telemarketer uses a process to prevent telemarketing to any telephone number on any list established pursuant to §§ 310.4(b)(3)(iii) or 310.4(b)(1)(iii)(B), employing a version of the "do-not-call" registry obtained from the Commission no more than three (3) months prior to the date any call is made, and maintains records documenting this process;

(v) The seller or a telemarketer or another person acting on behalf of the seller or charitable organization, monitors and enforces compliance with the procedures established pursuant to § 310.4(b)(3)(i); and

(vi) Any subsequent call otherwise violating § 310.4(b)(1)(ii) or (iii) is the result of error.

(4) A seller or telemarketer will not be liable for violating § 310.4(b)(1)(iv) if:

(i) The seller or telemarketer employs technology that ensures abandonment of no more than three (3) percent of all calls answered by a person, measured over the duration of a single calling campaign, if less than 30 days, or separately over each successive 30–day period or portion thereof that the campaign continues;

(ii) The seller or telemarketer, for each telemarketing call placed, allows the telephone to ring for at least fifteen (15) seconds or four (4) rings before disconnecting an unanswered call;

(iii) Whenever a sales representative is not available to speak with the person answering the call within two (2) seconds after the person's completed greeting, the seller or telemarketer promptly plays a recorded message that states the name and telephone number of the seller on whose behalf the call was placed[8]; and

(iv) The seller or telemarketer, in accordance with § 310.5(b)–(d), retains records establishing compliance with § 310.4(b)(4)(i)–(iii).

(c) *Calling time restrictions.* Without the prior consent of a person, it is an abusive telemarketing act or practice and a violation of this Rule for a telemarketer to engage in outbound telephone calls to a person's residence at any time other than between 8:00 a.m. and 9:00 p.m. local time at the called person's location.

(d) *Required oral disclosures in the sale of goods or services.* It is an abusive telemarketing act or practice and a violation of this Rule for a telemarketer in an outbound telephone call or internal or external upsell to induce the purchase of goods or services to fail to disclose truthfully, promptly, and in a clear and conspicuous manner to the person receiving the call, the following information:

(1) The identity of the seller;

(2) That the purpose of the call is to sell goods or services;

(3) The nature of the goods or services; and

(4) That no purchase or payment is necessary to be able to win a prize or participate in a prize promotion if a prize promotion is offered and that any purchase or payment will not increase the person's chances of winning. This disclosure must be made before or in conjunction with the description of the prize to the person called. If requested by that person, the telemarketer must disclose the no-purchase/no-payment entry method for the prize promotion; *provided,* however, that, in any internal upsell for the sale of goods or services, the seller or telemarketer must provide the disclosures listed in this section only to the extent that the information in the upsell differs from the disclosures provided in the initial telemarketing transaction.

---

8. This provision does not affect any seller's or telemarketer's obligation to comply with relevant state and federal laws, including but not limited to the TCPA, 47 U.S.C. § 227, and 47 CFR part 64.1200.

(e) *Required oral disclosures in charitable solicitations.* It is an abusive telemarketing act or practice and a violation of this Rule for a telemarketer, in an outbound telephone call to induce a charitable contribution, to fail to disclose truthfully, promptly, and in a clear and conspicuous manner to the person receiving the call, the following information:

(1) The identity of the charitable organization on behalf of which the request is being made; and

(2) That the purpose of the call is to solicit a charitable contribution.

§ 310.5 Recordkeeping requirements

(a) Any seller or telemarketer shall keep, for a period of 24 months from the date the record is produced, the following records relating to its telemarketing activities:

(1) All substantially different advertising, brochures, telemarketing scripts, and promotional materials;

(2) The name and last known address of each prize recipient and the prize awarded for prizes that are represented, directly or by implication, to have a value of $25.00 or more;

(3) The name and last known address of each customer, the goods or services purchased, the date such goods or services were shipped or provided, and the amount paid by the customer for the goods or services;[9]

(4) The name, any fictitious name used, the last known home address and telephone number, and the job title(s) for all current and former employees directly involved in telephone sales or solicitations; *provided,* however, that if the seller or telemarketer permits fictitious names to be used by employees, each fictitious name must be traceable to only one specific employee; and

(5) All verifiable authorizations or records of express informed consent or express agreement required to be provided or received under this Rule.

(b) A seller or telemarketer may keep the records required by § 310.5(a) in any form, and in the same manner, format, or place as they keep such records in the ordinary course of business. Failure to keep all records required by § 310.5(a) shall be a violation of this Rule.

(c) The seller and the telemarketer calling on behalf of the seller may, by written agreement, allocate responsibility between themselves for the recordkeeping required by this Section. When a seller and telemarketer have entered into such an agreement, the terms of that agreement shall govern, and the seller or telemarketer, as the case may be, need not keep records that duplicate those of the other. If the agreement is unclear as to who must maintain any required record(s), or if no such agreement exists,

---

9. For offers of consumer credit products subject to the Truth in Lending Act, 15 U.S.C. § 1601 *et seq.*, and Regulation Z, 12 CFR part 226, compliance with the recordkeeping requirements under the Truth in Lending Act, and Regulation Z, shall constitute compliance with § 310.5(a)(3) of this Rule.

the seller shall be responsible for complying with §§ 310.5(a)(1)–(3) and (5); the telemarketer shall be responsible for complying with § 310.5(a)(4).

(d) In the event of any dissolution or termination of the seller's or telemarketer's business, the principal of that seller or telemarketer shall maintain all records as required under this Section. In the event of any sale, assignment, or other change in ownership of the seller's or telemarketer's business, the successor business shall maintain all records required under this Section.

§ 310.6 Exemptions

(a) Solicitations to induce charitable contributions via outbound telephone calls are not covered by § 310.4(b)(1)(iii)(B) of this Rule.

(b) The following acts or practices are exempt from this Rule:

(1) The sale of pay-per-call services subject to the Commission's Rule entitled "Trade Regulation Rule Pursuant to the Telephone Disclosure and Dispute Resolution Act of 1992," 16 CFR Part 308, *provided*, however, that this exemption does not apply to the requirements of §§ 310.4(a)(1), (a)(7), (b), and (c);

(2) The sale of franchises subject to the Commission's Rule entitled "Disclosure Requirements and Prohibitions Concerning Franchising and Business Opportunity Ventures," ("Franchise Rule") 16 CFR Part 436, *provided*, however, that this exemption does not apply to the requirements of §§ 310.4(a)(1), (a)(7), (b), and (c);

(3) Telephone calls in which the sale of goods or services or charitable solicitation is not completed, and payment or authorization of payment is not required, until after a face-to-face sales or donation presentation by the seller or charitable organization, *provided*, however, that this exemption does not apply to the requirements of §§ 310.4(a)(1), (a)(7), (b), and (c);

(4) Telephone calls initiated by a customer or donor that are not the result of any solicitation by a seller, charitable organization, or telemarketer, *provided*, however, that this exemption does not apply to any instances of upselling included in such telephone calls;

(5) Telephone calls initiated by a customer or donor in response to an advertisement through any medium, other than direct mail solicitation, *provided*, however, that this exemption does not apply to calls initiated by a customer or donor in response to an advertisement relating to investment opportunities, business opportunities other than business arrangements covered by the Franchise Rule, or advertisements involving goods or services described in §§ 310.3(a)(1)(vi) or 310.4(a)(2)–(4); or to any instances of upselling included in such telephone calls;

(6) Telephone calls initiated by a customer or donor in response to a direct mail solicitation, including solicitations via the U.S. Postal Service, facsimile transmission, electronic mail, and other similar

methods of delivery in which a solicitation is directed to specific address(es) or person(s), that clearly, conspicuously, and truthfully discloses all material information listed in § 310.3(a)(1) of this Rule, for any goods or services offered in the direct mail solicitation, and that contains no material misrepresentation regarding any item contained in § 310.3(d) of this Rule for any requested charitable contribution; *provided*, however, that this exemption does not apply to calls initiated by a customer in response to a direct mail solicitation relating to prize promotions, investment opportunities, business opportunities other than business arrangements covered by the Franchise Rule, or goods or services described in §§ 310.4(a)(2)–(4); or to any instances of upselling included in such telephone calls; and

(7) Telephone calls between a telemarketer and any business, except calls to induce the retail sale of nondurable office or cleaning supplies; *provided*, however, that § 310.4(b)(1)(iii)(B) and § 310.5 of this Rule shall not apply to sellers or telemarketers of nondurable office or cleaning supplies.

§ 310.7 Actions by states and private persons

(a) Any attorney general or other officer of a state authorized by the state to bring an action under the Telemarketing and Consumer Fraud and Abuse Prevention Act, and any private person who brings an action under that Act, shall serve written notice of its action on the Commission, if feasible, prior to its initiating an action under this Rule. The notice shall be sent to the Office of the Director, Bureau of Consumer Protection, Federal Trade Commission, Washington, D.C. 20580, and shall include a copy of the state's or private person's complaint and any other pleadings to be filed with the court. If prior notice is not feasible, the state or private person shall serve the Commission with the required notice immediately upon instituting its action.

(b) Nothing contained in this Section shall prohibit any attorney general or other authorized state official from proceeding in state court on the basis of an alleged violation of any civil or criminal statute of such state.

§ 310.8 Fee for access to "do-not-call" registry

(a) It is a violation of this Rule for any seller to initiate, or cause any telemarketer to initiate, an outbound telephone call to any person whose telephone number is within a given area code unless such seller, either directly or through another person, first has paid the annual fee, required by § 310.8(c), for access to telephone numbers within that area code that are included in the National Do Not Call Registry maintained by the Commission under § 310.4(b)(1)(iii)(B); provided, however, that such payment is not necessary if the seller initiates, or causes a telemarketer to initiate, calls solely to persons pursuant to §§ 310.4(b)(1)(iii)(B)(*i*) or (*ii*), and the seller does not access the National Do Not Call Registry for any other purpose.

(b) It is a violation of this Rule for any telemarketer, on behalf of any seller, to initiate an outbound telephone call to any person whose telephone number is within a given area code unless that seller, either directly or through another person, first has paid the annual fee, required by § 310.8(c), for access to the telephone numbers within that area code that are included in the National Do Not Call Registry; provided, however, that such payment is not necessary if the seller initiates, or causes a telemarketer to initiate, calls solely to persons pursuant to §§ 310.4(b)(1)(iii)(B)*(i)* or *(ii)*, and the seller does not access the National Do Not Call Registry for any other purpose.

(c) The annual fee, which must be paid by any person prior to obtaining access to the National Do Not Call Registry, is $54 for each area code of data accessed, up to a maximum of $14,850; provided, however, that there shall be no charge to any person for accessing the first five area codes of data, and provided further, that there shall be no charge to any person engaging in or causing others to engage in outbound telephone calls to consumers and who is accessing area codes of data in the National Do Not Call Registry if the person is permitted to access, but is not required to access, the National Do Not Call Registry under this Rule, 47 CFR 64.1200, or any other Federal regulation or law. Any person accessing the National Do Not Call Registry may not participate in any arrangement to share the cost of accessing the registry, including any arrangement with any telemarketer or service provider to divide the costs to access the registry among various clients of that telemarketer or service provider.

. . .

(e) Access to the National Do Not Call Registry is limited to telemarketers, sellers, others engaged in or causing others to engage in telephone calls to consumers, service providers acting on behalf of such persons, and any government agency that has law enforcement authority. Prior to accessing the National Do Not Call Registry, a person must provide the identifying information required by the operator of the registry to collect the fee, and must certify, under penalty of law, that the person is accessing the registry solely to comply with the provisions of this Rule or to otherwise prevent telephone calls to telephone numbers on the registry. If the person is accessing the registry on behalf of sellers, that person also must identify each of the sellers on whose behalf it is accessing the registry, must provide each seller's unique account number for access to the national registry, and must certify, under penalty of law, that the sellers will be using the information gathered from the registry solely to comply with the provisions of this Rule or otherwise to prevent telephone calls to telephone numbers on the registry.

§ 310.9   Severability

The provisions of this Rule are separate and severable from one another. If any provision is stayed or determined to be invalid, it is the Commission's intention that the remaining provisions shall continue in effect.

CONSUMER CREDIT PROTECTION ACT

(15 U.S.C. §§ 1601–1693r)

SUBCHAPTER I.   CONSUMER CREDIT COST DISCLOSURE (TRUTH–IN–LENDING ACT)

(15 U.S.C. §§ 1601–1667f)

Table of Sections

PART A. GENERAL PROVISIONS

PART B. CREDIT TRANSACTIONS

PART A.   GENERAL PROVISIONS

§ 101.   Short title

This subchapter may be cited as the Truth in Lending Act.

§ 102.   Congressional findings and declaration of purpose [15 U.S.C. § 1601]

(a) Informed use of credit

The Congress finds that economic stabilization would be enhanced and the competition among the various financial institutions and other firms engaged in the extension of consumer credit would be strengthened by the informed use of credit. The informed use of credit results from an awareness of the cost thereof by consumers. It is the purpose of this subchapter to assure a meaningful disclosure of credit terms so that the consumer will be able to compare more readily the various credit terms available to him and avoid the uninformed use of credit, and to protect the consumer against inaccurate and unfair credit billing and credit card practices.

(b) Terms of personal property leases

The Congress also finds that there has been a recent trend toward leasing automobiles and other durable goods for consumer use as an alternative to installment credit sales and that these leases have been offered without adequate cost disclosures. It is the purpose of this subchapter to assure a meaningful disclosure of the terms of leases of personal property for personal, family, or household purposes so as to enable the lessee to compare more readily the various lease terms available to him, limit balloon payments in consumer leasing, enable comparison of lease terms with credit terms where appropriate, and to assure meaningful and accurate disclosures of lease terms in advertisements.

§ 103.   Definitions and rules of construction [15 U.S.C. § 1602]

(a) The definitions and rules of construction set forth in this section are applicable for the purposes of this subchapter.

(b) The term "Board" refers to the Board of Governors of the Federal Reserve System.

(c) The term "organization" means a corporation, government or governmental subdivision or agency, trust, estate, partnership, cooperative, or association.

(d) The term "person" means a natural person or an organization.

(e) The term "credit" means the right granted by a creditor to a debtor to defer payment of debt or to incur debt and defer its payment.

(f) The term "creditor" refers only to a person who both (1) regularly extends, whether in connection with loans, sales of property or services, or otherwise, consumer credit which is payable by agreement in more than four installments or for which the payment of a finance charge is or may be required, and (2) is the person to whom the debt arising from the consumer credit transaction is initially payable on the face of the evidence of indebtedness or, if there is no such evidence of indebtedness, by agreement. Notwithstanding the preceding sentence, in the case of an open-end credit plan involving a credit card, the card issuer and any person who honors the credit card and offers a discount which is a finance charge are creditors. For the purpose of the requirements imposed under part D of this subchapter and sections 127(a)(5), 127(a)(6), 127(a)(7), 127(b)(1), 127(b)(2), 127(b)(3), 127(b)(8), and 127(b)(10), the term "creditor" shall also include card issuers whether or not the amount due is payable by agreement in more than four installments or the payment of a finance charge is or may be required, and the Board shall, by regulation, apply these requirements to such card issuers, to the extent appropriate, even though the requirements are by their terms applicable only to creditors offering open-end credit plans. Any person who originates 2 or more mortgages referred to in subsection (aa) of this section in any 12–month period or any person who originates 1 or more such mortgages through a mortgage broker shall be considered to be a creditor for purposes of this subchapter.

(g) The term "credit sale" refers to any sale in which the seller is a creditor. The term includes any contract in the form of a bailment or lease if the bailee or lessee contracts to pay as compensation for use a sum substantially equivalent to or in excess of the aggregate value of the property and services involved and it is agreed that the bailee or lessee will become, or for no other or a nominal consideration has the option to become, the owner of the property upon full compliance with his obligations under the contract.

(h) The adjective "consumer," used with reference to a credit transaction, characterizes the transaction as one in which the party to whom credit is offered or extended is a natural person, and the money, property, or services which are the subject of the transaction are primarily for personal, family, or household purposes.

(i) The term "open end credit plan" means a plan under which the creditor reasonably contemplates repeated transactions, which prescribes the terms of such transactions, and which provides for a finance charge which may be computed from time to time on the outstanding unpaid balance. A credit plan which is an open end credit plan within the meaning of the preceding sentence is an open end credit plan even if credit information is verified from time to time.

(j) The term "adequate notice," as used in section 133, means a printed notice to a cardholder which sets forth the pertinent facts clearly and conspicuously so that a person against whom it is to operate could reasonably be expected to have noticed it and understood its meaning. Such notice may be given to a cardholder by printing the notice on any credit card, or on each periodic statement of account, issued to the cardholder, or by any other means reasonably assuring the receipt thereof by the cardholder.

(k) The term "credit card" means any card, plate, coupon book or other credit device existing for the purpose of obtaining money, property, labor, or services on credit.

(l) The term "accepted credit card" means any credit card which the cardholder has requested and received or has signed or has used, or authorized another to use, for the purpose of obtaining money, property, labor, or services on credit.

(m) The term "cardholder" means any person to whom a credit card is issued or any person who has agreed with the card issuer to pay obligations arising from the issuance of a credit card to another person.

(n) The term "card issuer" means any person who issues a credit card, or the agent of such person with respect to such card.

(o) The term "unauthorized use," as used in section 133, means a use of a credit card by a person other than the cardholder who does not have actual, implied, or apparent authority for such use and from which the cardholder receives no benefit.

(p) The term "discount" as used in section 167 means a reduction made from the regular price. The term "discount" as used in section 167 shall not mean a surcharge.

(q) The term "surcharge" as used in this section and section 167 means any means of increasing the regular price to a cardholder which is not imposed upon customers paying by cash, check, or similar means.

(r) The term "State" refers to any State, the Commonwealth of Puerto Rico, the District of Columbia, and any territory or possession of the United States.

(s) The term "agricultural purposes" includes the production, harvest, exhibition, marketing, transportation, processing, or manufacture of agricultural products by a natural person who cultivates, plants, propagates, or nurtures those agricultural products, including but not limited to the acquisition of farmland, real property with a farm residence, and personal property and services used primarily in farming.

(t) The term "agricultural products" includes agricultural, horticultural, viticultural, and dairy products, livestock, wildlife, poultry, bees, forest products, fish and shellfish, and any products thereof, including processed and manufactured products, and any and all products raised or produced on farms and any processed or manufactured products thereof.

(u) The term "material disclosures" means the disclosure, as required by this subchapter, of the annual percentage rate, the method of determining the finance charge and the balance upon which a finance charge will be imposed, the amount of the finance charge, the amount to be financed, the total of payments, the number and amount of payments, the due dates or periods of payments scheduled to repay the indebtedness, and the disclosures required by section 129(a).

(v) The term "dwelling" means a residential structure or mobile home which contains one to four family housing units, or individual units of condominiums or cooperatives.

(w) The term "residential mortgage transaction" means a transaction in which a mortgage, deed of trust, purchase money security interest arising under an installment sales contract, or equivalent consensual security interest is created or retained against the consumer's dwelling to finance the acquisition or initial construction of such dwelling.

(x) As used in this section and section 167, the term "regular price" means the tag or posted price charged for the property or service if a single price is tagged or posted, or the price charged for the property or service when payment is made by use of an open-end credit plan or a credit card if either (1) no price is tagged or posted, or (2) two prices are tagged or posted, one of which is charged when payment is made by use of an open-end credit plan or a credit card and the other when payment is made by use of cash, check, or similar means. For purposes of this definition, payment by check, draft, or other negotiable instrument which may result in the debiting of an open-end credit plan or a credit cardholder's open-end account shall not be considered payment made by use of the plan or the account.

(y) Any reference to any requirement imposed under this subchapter or any provision thereof includes reference to the regulations of the Board under this subchapter or the provision thereof in question.

(z) The disclosure of an amount or percentage which is greater than the amount or percentage required to be disclosed under this subchapter does not in itself constitute a violation of this subchapter.

(aa)(1) A mortgage referred to in this subsection means a consumer credit transaction that is secured by the consumer's principal dwelling, other than a residential mortgage transaction, a reverse mortgage transaction, or a transaction under an open end credit plan, if—

(A) the annual percentage rate at consummation of the transaction will exceed by more than 10 percentage points the yield on Treasury securities having comparable periods of maturity on the fifteenth day of the month immediately preceding the month in which the application for the extension of credit is received by the creditor; or

(B) the total points and fees payable by the consumer at or before closing will exceed the greater of—

(i) 8 percent of the total loan amount; or

(ii) $400.

(2)(A) After the 2–year period beginning on the effective date of the regulations promulgated under section 155 of the Riegle Community Development and Regulatory Improvement Act of 1994, and no more frequently than biennially after the first increase or decrease under this subparagraph, the Board may by regulation increase or decrease the number of percentage points specified in paragraph (1)(A), if the Board determines that the increase or decrease is—

(i) consistent with the consumer protections against abusive lending provided by the amendments made by subtitle B of title I of the Riegle Community Development and Regulatory Improvement Act of 1994; and

(ii) warranted by the need for credit.

(B) An increase or decrease under subparagraph (A) may not result in the number of percentage points referred to in subparagraph (A) being—

(i) less than 8 percentage points; or

(ii) greater than 12 percentage points.

(C) In determining whether to increase or decrease the number of percentage points referred to in subparagraph (A), the Board shall consult with representatives of consumers, including low-income consumers, and lenders.

(3) The amount specified in paragraph (1)(B)(ii) shall be adjusted annually on January 1 by the annual percentage change in the Consumer Price Index, as reported on June 1 of the year preceding such adjustment.

(4) For purposes of paragraph (1)(B), points and fees shall include—

(A) all items included in the finance charge, except interest or the time-price differential;

(B) all compensation paid to mortgage brokers;

(C) each of the charges listed in section 106(e) (except an escrow for future payment of taxes), unless—

(i) the charge is reasonable;

(ii) the creditor receives no direct or indirect compensation; and

(iii) the charge is paid to a third party unaffiliated with the creditor; and

(D) such other charges as the Board determines to be appropriate.

(5) This subsection shall not be construed to limit the rate of interest or the finance charge that a person may charge a consumer for any extension of credit.

(bb) The term "reverse mortgage transaction" means a nonrecourse transaction in which a mortgage, deed of trust, or equivalent consensual security interest is created against the consumer's principal dwelling—

(1) securing one or more advances; and

(2) with respect to which the payment of any principal, interest, and shared appreciation or equity is due and payable (other than in the case of default) only after—

(A) the transfer of the dwelling;

(B) the consumer ceases to occupy the dwelling as a principal dwelling; or

(C) the death of the consumer.

§ 104.　Exempted transactions [15 U.S.C. § 1603]

This subchapter does not apply to the following:

(1) Credit transactions involving extensions of credit primarily for business, commercial, or agricultural purposes, or to government or governmental agencies or instrumentalities, or to organizations.

(2) Transactions in securities or commodities accounts by a broker-dealer registered with the Securities and Exchange Commission.

(3) Credit transactions, other than those in which a security interest is or will be acquired in real property, or in personal property used or expected to be used as the principal dwelling of the consumer, in which the total amount financed exceeds $25,000.

(4) Transactions under public utility tariffs, if the Board determines that a State regulatory body regulates the charges for the public utility services involved, the charges for delayed payment, and any discount allowed for early payment.

(5) Transactions for which the Board, by rule, determines that coverage under this subchapter is not necessary to carry out the purposes of this subchapter.

(6) Repealed. Pub.L. 96–221, Title VI, § 603(c)(3), Mar. 31, 1980, 94 Stat. 169.

(7) Loans made, insured, or guaranteed pursuant to a program authorized by Title IV of the Higher Education Act of 1965 (20 U.S.C. § 1070 et seq.).

§ 105. Disclosure guidelines [15 U.S.C. § 1604]

(a) Promulgation, contents, etc., of regulations

The Board shall prescribe regulations to carry out the purposes of this subchapter. Except in the case of a mortgage referred to in section 103(aa), these regulations may contain such classifications, differentiations, or other provisions, and may provide for such adjustments and exceptions for any class of transactions, as in the judgment of the Board are necessary or proper to effectuate the purposes of this subchapter, to prevent circumvention or evasion thereof, or to facilitate compliance therewith.

(b) Model disclosure forms and clauses; publication, criteria, compliance, etc.

The Board shall publish model disclosure forms and clauses for common transactions to facilitate compliance with the disclosure requirements of this subchapter and to aid the borrower or lessee in understanding the transaction by utilizing readily understandable language to simplify the technical nature of the disclosures. In devising such forms, the Board shall consider the use by creditors or lessors of data processing or similar automated equipment. Nothing in this subchapter may be construed to require a creditor or lessor to use any such model form or clause prescribed by the Board under this section. A creditor or lessor shall be deemed to be in compliance with the disclosure provisions of this subchapter with respect to other than numerical disclosures if the creditor or lessor (1) uses any appropriate model form or clause as published by the Board, or (2) uses any such model form or clause and changes it by (A) deleting any information which is not required by this subchapter, or (B) rearranging the format, if in making such deletion or rearranging the format, the creditor or lessor does not affect the substance, clarity, or meaningful sequence of the disclosure.

(c) Procedures applicable for adoption of model forms and clauses

Model disclosure forms and clauses shall be adopted by the Board after notice duly given in the Federal Register and an opportunity for public comment in accordance with section 553 of Title 5.

(d) Effective dates of regulations containing new disclosure requirements

Any regulation of the Board, or any amendment or interpretation thereof, requiring any disclosure which differs from the disclosures previously required by this part, part D, or part E of this subchapter, or by any regulation of the Board promulgated thereunder shall have an effective date of that October 1 which follows by at least six months the date of promulgation, except that the Board may at its discretion take interim action by regulation, amendment, or interpretation to lengthen the period of time permitted for creditors or lessors to adjust their forms to accommodate new requirements or shorten the length of time for creditors or lessors to make such adjustments when it makes a specific finding that such action is necessary to comply with the findings of a court or to prevent unfair or deceptive disclosure practices. Notwithstanding the previous sentence, any creditor or lessor may comply with any such newly promulgated disclosure requirements prior to the effective date of the requirements.

(f) Exemption authority

(1) In general

The Board may exempt, by regulation, from all or part of this subchapter any class of transactions, other than transactions involving any mortgage described in section 103(aa), for which, in the determination of the Board, coverage under all or part of this subchapter does not provide a meaningful benefit to consumers in the form of useful information or protection.

(2) Factors for consideration

In determining which classes of transactions to exempt in whole or in part under paragraph (1), the Board shall consider the following factors and publish its rationale at the time a proposed exemption is published for comment:

(A) The amount of the loan and whether the disclosures, right of rescission, and other provisions provide a benefit to the consumers who are parties to such transactions, as determined by the Board.

(B) The extent to which the requirements of this subchapter complicate, hinder, or make more expensive the credit process for the class of transactions.

(C) The status of the borrower, including—

(i) any related financial arrangements of the borrower, as determined by the Board;

(ii) the financial sophistication of the borrower relative to the type of transaction; and

(iii) the importance to the borrower of the credit, related supporting property, and coverage under this subchapter, as determined by the Board;

(D) Whether the loan is secured by the principal residence of the consumer; and

(E) Whether the goal of consumer protection would be undermined by such an exemption.

(g) Waiver for certain borrowers

(1) In general

The Board, by regulation, may exempt from the requirements of this subchapter certain credit transactions if—

(A) the transaction involves a consumer—

(i) with an annual earned income of more than $200,000; or

(ii) having net assets in excess of $1,000,000 at the time of the transaction; and

(B) a waiver that is handwritten, signed, and dated by the consumer is first obtained from the consumer.

(2) Adjustments by the Board

The Board, at its discretion, may adjust the annual earned income and net asset requirements of paragraph (1) for inflation.

§ 106. Determination of finance charge [15 U.S.C. § 1605]

(a) "Finance charge" defined

Except as otherwise provided in this section, the amount of the finance charge in connection with any consumer credit transaction shall be determined as the sum of all charges, payable directly or indirectly by the person to whom the credit is extended, and imposed directly or indirectly by the creditor as an incident to the extension of credit. The finance charge does not include charges of a type payable in a comparable cash transaction. The finance charge shall not include fees and amounts imposed by third party closing agents (including settlement agents, attorneys, and escrow and title companies) if the creditor does not require the imposition of the charges or the services provided and does not retain the charges. Examples of charges which are included in the finance charge include any of the following types of charges which are applicable:

(1) Interest, time price differential, and any amount payable under a point, discount, or other system of additional charges.

(2) Service or carrying charge.

(3) Loan fee, finder's fee, or similar charge.

(4) Fee for an investigation or credit report.

(5) Premium or other charge for any guarantee or insurance protecting the creditor against the obligor's default or other credit loss.

(6) Borrower-paid mortgage broker fees, including fees paid directly to the broker or the lender (for delivery to the broker) whether such fees are paid in cash or financed.

(b) Life, accident, or health insurance premiums included in finance charge

Charges or premiums for credit life, accident, or health insurance written in connection with any consumer credit transaction shall be included in the finance charge unless

(1) the coverage of the debtor by the insurance is not a factor in the approval by the creditor of the extension of credit, and this fact is clearly disclosed in writing to the person applying for or obtaining the extension of credit; and

(2) in order to obtain the insurance in connection with the extension of credit, the person to whom the credit is extended must give specific affirmative written indication of his desire to do so after written disclosure to him of the cost thereof.

(c) Property damage and liability insurance premiums included in finance charge

Charges or premiums for insurance, written in connection with any consumer credit transaction, against loss of or damage to property or against liability arising out of the ownership or use of property, shall be included in the finance charge unless a clear and specific statement in writing is furnished by the creditor to the person to whom the credit is extended, setting forth the cost of the insurance if obtained from or through the creditor, and stating that the person to whom the credit is extended may choose the person through which the insurance is to be obtained.

(d) Items exempted from computation of finance charge in all credit transactions

If any of the following items is itemized and disclosed in accordance with the regulations of the Board in connection with any transaction, then the creditor need not include that item in the computation of the finance charge with respect to that transaction:

(1) Fees and charges prescribed by law which actually are or will be paid to public officials for determining the existence of or for perfecting or releasing or satisfying any security related to the credit transaction.

(2) The premium payable for any insurance in lieu of perfecting any security interest otherwise required by the creditor in connection with the transaction, if the premium does not exceed the fees and charges described in paragraph (1) which would otherwise be payable.

(3) Any tax levied on security instruments or on documents evidencing indebtedness if the payment of such taxes is a precondition for recording the instrument securing the evidence of indebtedness.

(e) Items exempted from computation of finance charge in extensions of credit secured by an interest in real property

The following items, when charged in connection with any extension of credit secured by an interest in real property, shall not be included in the computation of the finance charge with respect to that transaction:

(1) Fees or premiums for title examination, title insurance, or similar purposes.

(2) Fees for preparation of loan-related documents.

(3) Escrows for future payments of taxes and insurance.

(4) Fees for notarizing deeds and other documents.

(5) Appraisal fees, including fees related to any pest infestation or flood hazard inspections conducted prior to closing.

(6) Credit reports.

(f) Tolerances for accuracy

In connection with credit transactions not under an open end credit plan that are secured by real property or a dwelling, the disclosure of the finance charge and other disclosures affected by any finance charge—

(1) shall be treated as being accurate for purposes of this subchapter if the amount disclosed as the finance charge—

(A) does not vary from the actual finance charge by more than $100; or

(B) is greater than the amount required to be disclosed under this subchapter; and

(2) shall be treated as being accurate for purposes of section 125 if—

(A) except as provided in subparagraph (B), the amount disclosed as the finance charge does not vary from the actual finance charge by more than an amount equal to one-half of one percent of the total amount of credit extended; or

(B) in the case of a transaction, other than a mortgage referred to in section 103(aa), which—

(i) is a refinancing of the principal balance then due and any accrued and unpaid finance charges of a residential mortgage transaction as defined in section 103(w), or is any subsequent refinancing of such a transaction; and

(ii) does not provide any new consolidation or new advance;

if the amount disclosed as the finance charge does not vary from the actual finance charge by more than an amount equal to one percent of the total amount of credit extended.

§ 107. Determination of annual percentage rate [15 U.S.C. § 1606]

(a) "Annual percentage rate" defined

The annual percentage rate applicable to any extension of consumer credit shall be determined, in accordance with the regulations of the Board,

(1) in the case of any extension of credit other than under an open end credit plan, as

(A) that nominal annual percentage rate which will yield a sum equal to the amount of the finance charge when it is applied to the unpaid balances of the amount financed, calculated according to the actuarial method of allocating payments made on a debt between the amount financed and the amount of the finance charge, pursuant to which a payment is applied first to the accumulated finance charge and the balance is applied to the unpaid amount financed; or

(B) the rate determined by any method prescribed by the Board as a method which materially simplifies computation while retaining reasonable accuracy as compared with the rate determined under subparagraph (A).

(2) in the case of any extension of credit under an open end credit plan, as the quotient (expressed as a percentage) of the total finance charge for the period to which it relates divided by the amount upon which the finance charge for that period is based, multiplied by the number of such periods in a year.

(b) Computation of rate of finance charges for balances within a specified range

Where a creditor imposes the same finance charge for balances within a specified range, the annual percentage rate shall be computed on the median balance within the range, except that if the Board determines that a rate so computed would not be meaningful, or would be materially misleading, the annual percentage rate shall be computed on such other basis as the Board may by regulation require.

(c) Allowable tolerances for purposes of compliance with disclosure requirements

The disclosure of an annual percentage rate is accurate for the purpose of this subchapter if the rate disclosed is within a tolerance not greater than one-eighth of 1 per centum more or less than the actual rate or rounded to the nearest one-fourth of 1 per centum. The Board may allow a greater tolerance to simplify compliance where irregular payments are involved.

(d) Use of rate tables or charts having allowable variance from determined rates

The Board may authorize the use of rate tables or charts which may provide for the disclosure of annual percentage rates which vary from the rate determined in accordance with subsection (a)(1)(A) of this section by not more than such tolerances as the Board may allow. The Board may not allow a tolerance greater than 8 per centum of that rate except to simplify compliance where irregular payments are involved.

(e) Authorization of tolerances in determining annual percentage rates

In the case of creditors determining the annual percentage rate in a manner other than as described in subsection (d) of this section, the Board may authorize other reasonable tolerances.

§ 108.   Administrative enforcement [15 U.S.C. § 1607]

(a) Enforcing agencies

Compliance with the requirements imposed under this subchapter shall be enforced under

(1) section 8 of the Federal Deposit Insurance Act, in the case of—

(A) national banks, and Federal branches and Federal agencies of foreign banks, by the Office of the Comptroller of the Currency;

(B) member banks of the Federal Reserve System (other than national banks), branches and agencies of foreign banks (other than Federal branches, Federal agencies, and insured State branches of foreign banks), commercial lending companies owned or controlled by foreign banks, and organizations operating under section 25 or 25(a) of the Federal Reserve Act, by the Board; and

(C) banks insured by the Federal Deposit Insurance Corporation (other than members of the Federal Reserve System) and insured State branches of foreign banks, by the Board of Directors of the Federal Deposit Insurance Corporation;

(2) section 8 of the Federal Deposit Insurance Act, by the Director of the Office of Thrift Supervision, in the case of a savings association the deposits of which are insured by the Federal Deposit Insurance Corporation.

(3) the Federal Credit Union Act, by the National Credit Union Administration Board with respect to any Federal credit union.

(4) part A of subtitle VII of title 49, by the Secretary of Transportation with respect to any air carrier or foreign air carrier subject to that part.

(5) the Packers and Stockyards Act, 1921 (except as provided in section 406 of that Act), by the Secretary of Agriculture with respect to any activities subject to that Act.

(6) the Farm Credit Act of 1971 by the Farm Credit Administration with respect to any Federal land bank, Federal land bank association, Federal intermediate credit bank, or production credit association.

The terms used in paragraph (1) that are not defined in this subchapter or otherwise defined in section 3(s) of the Federal Deposit Insurance Act (12 U.S.C. § 1813(s)) shall have the meaning given to them in section 1(b) of the International Banking Act of 1978 (12 U.S.C. § 3101).

(b) Violations of this subchapter deemed violations of pre-existing statutory requirements; additional agency powers

For the purpose of the exercise by any agency referred to in subsection (a) of this section of its powers under any Act referred to in that subsection, a violation of any requirement imposed under this subchapter shall be deemed to be a violation of a requirement imposed under that Act. In addition to its powers under any provision of law specifically referred to in subsection (a) of this section, each of the agencies referred to in that subsection may exercise, for the purpose of enforcing compliance with any requirement imposed under this subchapter, any other authority conferred on it by law.

(c) Federal Trade Commission as overall enforcing agency

Except to the extent that enforcement of the requirements imposed under this subchapter is specifically committed to some other Government agency under subsection (a) of this section, the Federal Trade Commission shall enforce such requirements. For the purpose of the exercise by the Federal Trade Commission of its functions and powers under the Federal Trade Commission Act, a violation of any requirement imposed under this subchapter shall be deemed a violation of a requirement imposed under that Act. All of the functions and powers of the Federal Trade Commission under the Federal Trade Commission Act are available to the Commission to enforce compliance by any person with the requirements imposed under this subchapter, irrespective of whether that person is engaged in commerce or meets any other jurisdictional tests in the Federal Trade Commission Act.

(d) Rules and regulations

The authority of the Board to issue regulations under this subchapter does not impair the authority of any other agency designated in this section to make rules respecting its own procedures in enforcing compliance with requirements imposed under this subchapter.

(e) Adjustment of finance charges; procedures applicable, coverage criteria, etc.

(1) In carrying out its enforcement activities under this section, each agency referred to in subsection (a) or (c) of this section, in cases where an annual percentage rate or finance charge was inaccurately disclosed, shall notify the creditor of such disclosure error and is authorized in accordance with the provisions of this subsection to require the creditor to make an adjustment to the account of the person to whom credit was extended, to assure that such person will not be required to pay a finance charge in excess of the finance charge actually disclosed or the dollar equivalent of the annual percentage rate actually disclosed, whichever is lower. For the purposes of this subsection, except where such disclosure error resulted from a willful violation which was intended to mislead the person to whom credit was extended, in determining whether a disclosure error has occurred and in calculating any adjustment, (A) each agency shall apply (i) with respect to the annual percentage rate, a tolerance of one-quarter of 1 percent more or less than the actual rate, determined without regard to section 107(c), and (ii) with respect to the finance charge, a corresponding numerical tolerance as generated by the tolerance provided under this subsection for the annual percentage rate; except that (B) with respect to transactions consummated after two years following March 31, 1980, each agency shall apply (i) for transactions that have a scheduled amortization of ten years or less, with respect to the annual percentage rate, a tolerance not to exceed one-quarter of 1 percent more or less than the actual rate, determined without regard to section 107(c), but in no event a tolerance of less than the tolerances allowed under section 107(c), (ii) for transactions that have a scheduled amortization of more than ten years, with respect to

the annual percentage rate, only such tolerances as are allowed under section 107(c), and (iii) for all transactions, with respect to the finance charge, a corresponding numerical tolerance as generated by the tolerances provided under this subsection for the annual percentage rate.

(2) Each agency shall require such an adjustment when it determines that such disclosure error resulted from (A) a clear and consistent pattern or practice of violations, (B) gross negligence, or (C) a willful violation which was intended to mislead the person to whom the credit was extended. Notwithstanding the preceding sentence, except where such disclosure error resulted from a willful violation which was intended to mislead the person to whom credit was extended, an agency need not require such an adjustment if it determines that such disclosure error—

(A) resulted from an error involving the disclosure of a fee or charge that would otherwise be excludable in computing the finance charge, including but not limited to violations involving the disclosures described in sections 106(b), (c) and (d), in which event the agency may require such remedial action as it determines to be equitable, except that for transactions consummated after two years after March 31, 1980, such an adjustment shall be ordered for violations of section 106(b);

(B) involved a disclosed amount which was 10 per centum or less of the amount that should have been disclosed and (i) in cases where the error involved a disclosed finance charge, the annual percentage rate was disclosed correctly, and (ii) in cases where the error involved a disclosed annual percentage rate, the finance charge was disclosed correctly; in which event the agency may require such adjustment as it determines to be equitable;

(C) involved a total failure to disclose either the annual percentage rate or the finance charge, in which event the agency may require such adjustment as it determines to be equitable; or

(D) resulted from any other unique circumstance involving clearly technical and nonsubstantive disclosure violations that do not adversely affect information provided to the consumer and that have not misled or otherwise deceived the consumer.

In the case of other such disclosure errors, each agency may require such an adjustment.

(3) Notwithstanding paragraph (2), no adjustment shall be ordered—

(A) if it would have a significantly adverse impact upon the safety or soundness of the creditor, but in any such case, the agency may—

(i) require a partial adjustment in an amount which does not have such an impact; or

(ii) require the full adjustment, but permit the creditor to make the required adjustment in partial payments over an extended period of time which the agency considers to be reasonable, if (in the case of an agency referred to in paragraph (1), (2), or (3) of subsection (a) of this section), the agency determines that a partial adjustment or making partial payments over an extended period is necessary to avoid causing the creditor to become undercapitalized pursuant to section 1831o of Title 12.

(B) the amount of the adjustment would be less than $1, except that if more than one year has elapsed since the date of the violation, the agency may require that such amount be paid into the Treasury of the United States, or

(C) except where such disclosure error resulted from a willful violation which was intended to mislead the person to whom credit was extended, in the case of an open-end credit plan, more than two years after the violation, or in the case of any other extension of credit, as follows:

(i) with respect to creditors that are subject to examination by the agencies referred to in paragraphs (1) through (3) of subsection (a) of this section, except in connection with violations arising from practices identified in the current examination and only in connection with transactions that are consummated after the date of the immediately preceding examination, except that where practices giving rise to violations identified in earlier examinations have not been corrected, adjustments for those violations shall be required in connection with transactions consummated after the date of the examination in which such practices were first identified;

(ii) with respect to creditors that are not subject to examination by such agencies, except in connection with transactions that are consummated after May 10, 1978; and

(iii) in no event after the later of (I) the expiration of the life of the credit extension, or (II) two years after the agreement to extend credit was consummated.

(4)(A) Notwithstanding any other provision of this section, an adjustment under this subsection may be required by an agency referred to in subsection (a) or (c) of this section only by an order issued in accordance with cease and desist procedures provided by the provision of law referred to in such subsections.

(B) In case of an agency which is not authorized to conduct cease and desist proceedings, such an order may be issued after an agency hearing on the record conducted at least thirty but not more than sixty days after notice of the alleged violation is served on the creditor. Such a hearing shall be deemed to be a hearing which is subject to the provisions of section 8(h) of the Federal Deposit Insurance Act and shall be subject to judicial review as provided therein.

(5) Except as otherwise specifically provided in this subsection and notwithstanding any provision of law referred to in subsection (a) or (c) of

this section, no agency referred to in subsection (a) or (c) of this section may require a creditor to make dollar adjustments for errors in any requirements under this subchapter, except with regard to the requirements of section 165.

(6) A creditor shall not be subject to an order to make an adjustment, if within sixty days after discovering a disclosure error, whether pursuant to a final written examination report or through the creditor's own procedures, the creditor notifies the person concerned of the error and adjusts the account so as to assure that such person will not be required to pay a finance charge in excess of the finance charge actually disclosed or the dollar equivalent of the annual percentage rate actually disclosed, whichever is lower.

(7) Notwithstanding the second sentence of subsection (e)(1), subsection (e)(3)(C)(i), and subsection (e)(3)(C)(ii) of this section, each agency referred to in subsection (a) or (c) of this section shall require an adjustment for an annual percentage rate disclosure error that exceeds a tolerance of one quarter of one percent less than the actual rate, determined without regard to section 107(c), with respect to any transaction consummated between January 1, 1977, and March 31, 1980.

§ 109.   Views of other agencies [15 U.S.C. § 1608]

In the exercise of its functions under this subchapter, the Board may obtain upon request the views of any other Federal agency which, in the judgment of the Board, exercises regulatory or supervisory functions with respect to any class of creditors subject to this subchapter.

§ 111.   Effect on other laws [15 U.S.C. § 1610]

(a) Inconsistent provisions; procedures applicable for determination

(1) Except as provided in subsection (e) of this section, this part and parts B and C of this subchapter do not annul, alter, or affect the laws of any State relating to the disclosure of information in connection with credit transactions, except to the extent that those laws are inconsistent with the provisions of this subchapter and then only to the extent of the inconsistency. Upon its own motion or upon the request of any creditor, State or other interested party which is submitted in accordance with procedures prescribed in regulations of the Board, the Board shall determine whether any such inconsistency exists. If the Board determines that a State-required disclosure is inconsistent, creditors located in that State may not make disclosures using the inconsistent term or form, and shall incur no liability under the law of that State for failure to use such term or form, notwithstanding that such determination is subsequently amended, rescinded, or determined by judicial or other authority to be invalid for any reason.

(2) Upon its own motion or upon the request of any creditor, State, or other interested party which is submitted in accordance with procedures

prescribed in regulations of the Board, the Board shall determine whether any disclosure required under the law of any State is substantially the same in meaning as a disclosure required under this subchapter. If the Board determines that a State-required disclosure is substantially the same in meaning as a disclosure required by this subchapter, then creditors located in that State may make such disclosure in compliance with such State law in lieu of the disclosure required by this subchapter, except that the annual percentage rate and finance charge shall be disclosed as required by section 122, and such State-required disclosure may not be made in lieu of the disclosures applicable to certain mortgages under section 129.

(b) State credit charge statutes

Except as provided in section 129, this subchapter does not otherwise annul, alter or affect in any manner the meaning, scope or applicability of the laws of any State, including, but not limited to, laws relating to the types, amounts or rates of charges, or any element or elements of charges, permissible under such laws in connection with the extension or use of credit, nor does this subchapter extend the applicability of those laws to any class of persons or transactions to which they would not otherwise apply. The provisions of section 129 do not annul, alter, or affect the applicability of the laws of any State or exempt any person subject to the provisions of section 129 from complying with the laws of any State, with respect to the requirements for mortgages referred to in section 103(aa), except to the extent that those State laws are inconsistent with any provisions of section 129, and then only to the extent of the inconsistency.

(c) Disclosure as evidence

In any action or proceeding in any court involving a consumer credit sale, the disclosure of the annual percentage rate as required under this subchapter in connection with that sale may not be received as evidence that the sale was a loan or any type of transaction other than a credit sale.

(d) Contract or other obligations under State or Federal law

Except as specified in sections 125, 130, and 166, this subchapter and the regulations issued thereunder do not affect the validity or enforceability of any contract or obligation under State or Federal law.

(e) Certain credit and charge card application and solicitation disclosure provisions

The provisions of subsection (c) of section 122 and subsections (c), (d), (e), and (f) of section 127 shall supersede any provision of the law of any State relating to the disclosure of information in any credit or charge card application or solicitation which is subject to the requirements of section 127(c) or any renewal notice which is subject to the requirements of section 127(d), except that any State may employ or establish State laws for the purpose of enforcing the requirements of such sections.

§ 112. Criminal liability for willful and knowing violation [15 U.S.C. § 1611]

Whoever willfully and knowingly

(1) gives false or inaccurate information or fails to provide information which he is required to disclose under the provisions of this subchapter or any regulation issued thereunder,

(2) uses any chart or table authorized by the Board under section 107 in such a manner as to consistently understate the annual percentage rate determined under section 107(a)(1)(A), or

(3) otherwise fails to comply with any requirement imposed under this subchapter,

shall be fined not more than $5,000 or imprisoned not more than one year, or both.

§ 113. Effect on government agencies [15 U.S.C. § 1612]

(a) Consultation requirements respecting compliance of credit instruments issued to participating creditor

Any department or agency of the United States which administers a credit program in which it extends, insures, or guarantees consumer credit and in which it provides instruments to a creditor which contain any disclosures required by this subchapter shall, prior to the issuance or continued use of such instruments, consult with the Board to assure that such instruments comply with this subchapter.

(b) Inapplicability of Federal civil or criminal penalties to Federal, state, and local agencies

No civil or criminal penalty provided under this subchapter for any violation thereof may be imposed upon the United States or any department or agency thereof, or upon any State or political subdivision thereof, or any agency of any State or political subdivision.

(c) Inapplicability of Federal civil or criminal penalties to participating creditor where violating instrument issued by United States

A creditor participating in a credit program administered, insured, or guaranteed by any department or agency of the United States shall not be held liable for a civil or criminal penalty under this subchapter in any case in which the violation results from the use of an instrument required by any such department or agency.

(d) Applicability of State penalties to violations by participating creditor

A creditor participating in a credit program administered, insured, or guaranteed by any department or agency of the United States shall not be held liable for a civil or criminal penalty under the laws of any State (other than laws determined under section 111 to be inconsistent with this subchapter) for any technical or procedural failure, such as a failure to use a specific form, to make information available at a specific place on an instrument, or to use a specific typeface, as required by State law, which is caused by the use of an instrument required to be used by such department or agency.

§ 114. Annual reports to Congress by Board [15 U.S.C. § 1613]

Each year the Board shall make a report to the Congress concerning the administration of its functions under this subchapter, including such recommendations as the Board deems necessary or appropriate. In addition, each report of the Board shall include its assessment of the extent to which compliance with the requirements imposed under this subchapter is being achieved.

[§ 116.]   Prohibition on use of "Rule of 78's" in connection with mortgage refinancings and other consumer loans [15 U.S.C. § 1615]

(a) Prompt refund of unearned interest required

(1) In general

If a consumer prepays in full the financed amount under any consumer credit transaction, the creditor shall promptly refund any unearned portion of the interest charge to the consumer.

(2) Exception for refund of de minimis amount

No refund shall be required under paragraph (1) with respect to the prepayment of any consumer credit transaction if the total amount of the refund would be less than $1.

(3) Applicability to refinanced transactions and acceleration by the creditor

This subsection shall apply with respect to any prepayment of a consumer credit transaction described in paragraph (1) without regard to the manner or the reason for the prepayment, including—

(A) any prepayment made in connection with the refinancing, consolidation, or restructuring of the transaction; and

(B) any prepayment made as a result of the acceleration of the obligation to repay the amount due with respect to the transaction.

(b) Use of "Rule of 78's" prohibited

For the purpose of calculating any refund of interest required under subsection (a) of this section for any precomputed consumer credit transaction of a term exceeding 61 months which is consummated after September 30, 1993, the creditor shall compute the refund based on a method which is at least as favorable to the consumer as the actuarial method.

(c) Statement of prepayment amount

(1) In general

Before the end of the 5–day period beginning on the date an oral or written request is received by a creditor from a consumer for the disclosure of the amount due on any precomputed consumer credit account, the creditor or assignee shall provide the consumer with a statement of—

> (A) the amount necessary to prepay the account in full; and

> (B) if the amount disclosed pursuant to subparagraph (A) includes an amount which is required to be refunded under this section with respect to such prepayment, the amount of such refund.

(2) Written statement required if request is in writing

If the customer's request is in writing, the statement under paragraph (1) shall be in writing.

(3) 1 free annual statement

A consumer shall be entitled to obtain 1 statement under paragraph (1) each year without charge.

(4) Additional statements subject to reasonable fees

Any creditor may impose a reasonable fee to cover the cost of providing any statement under paragraph (1) to any consumer in addition to the 1 free annual statement required under paragraph (3) if the amount of the charge for such additional statement is disclosed to the consumer before furnishing such statement.

(d) Definitions

For the purpose of this section—

(1) Actuarial method

The term "actuarial method" means the method of allocating payments made on a debt between the amount financed and the finance charge pursuant to which a payment is applied first to the accumulated finance charge and any remainder is subtracted from, or any deficiency is added to, the unpaid balance of the amount financed.

(2) Consumer, credit

The terms "consumer" and "creditor" have the meanings given to such terms in section 103.

(3) Creditor

The term "creditor"—

> (A) has the meaning given to such term in section 103; and

> (B) includes any assignee of any creditor with respect to credit extended in connection with any consumer credit transaction and any subsequent assignee with respect to such credit.

PART B.   CREDIT TRANSACTIONS

§ 121.   Disclosure requirements [15 U.S.C. § 1631]

(a) Duty of creditor or lessor respecting one or more than one obligor

Subject to subsection (b) of this section, a creditor or lessor shall disclose to the person who is obligated on a consumer lease or a consumer credit transaction the information required under this subchapter. In a transaction involving more than one obligor, a creditor or lessor, except in a transaction under section 125, need not disclose to more than one of such obligors if the obligor given disclosure is a primary obligor.

(b) Creditor or lessor required to make disclosure

If a transaction involves one creditor as defined in section 103(f), or one lessor as defined in section 181(3), such creditor or lessor shall make the disclosures. If a transaction involves more than one creditor or lessor, only one creditor or lessor shall be required to make the disclosures. The Board shall by regulation specify which creditor or lessor shall make the disclosures.

(c) Estimates as satisfying statutory requirements; basis of disclosure for per diem interest.

The Board may provide by regulation that any portion of the information required to be disclosed by this subchapter may be given in the form of estimates where the provider of such information is not in a position to know exact information. In the case of any consumer credit transaction a portion of the interest on which is determined on a per diem basis and is to be collected upon the consummation of such transaction, any disclosure with respect to such portion of interest shall be deemed to be accurate for purposes of this subchapter if the disclosure is based on information actually known to the creditor at the time that the disclosure documents are being prepared for the consummation of the transaction.

(d) Tolerances for numerical disclosures

The Board shall determine whether tolerances for numerical disclosures other than the annual percentage rate are necessary to facilitate compliance with this subchapter, and if it determines that such tolerances are necessary to facilitate compliance, it shall by regulation permit disclosures within such tolerances. The Board shall exercise its authority to permit tolerances for numerical disclosures other than the annual percentage rate so that such tolerances are narrow enough to prevent such tolerances from resulting in misleading disclosures or disclosures that circumvent the purposes of this subchapter.

§ 122. Form of disclosure; additional information [15 U.S.C. § 1632]

(a) Information clearly and conspicuously disclosed; "annual percentage rate" and "finance charge"; order of disclosures and use of different terminology

Information required by this subchapter shall be disclosed clearly and conspicuously, in accordance with regulations of the Board. The terms "annual percentage rate" and "finance charge" shall be disclosed more conspicuously than other terms, data, or information provided in connection with a transaction, except information relating to the identity of the creditor. Except as provided in subsection (c) of this section, regulations of the Board need not require that disclosures pursuant to this subchapter be made in the order set forth in this subchapter and, except as otherwise provided, may permit the use of terminology different from that employed in this subchapter if it conveys substantially the same meaning.

(b) Optional information by creditor or lessor

Any creditor or lessor may supply additional information or explanation with any disclosures required under parts D and E of this subchapter and, except as provided in sections 127A(b)(3) and 128(b)(1), under this part.

(c) Tabular format required for certain disclosures under section 127(c)

(1) In general

The information described in paragraphs (1)(A), (3)(B)(i)(I), (4)(A), and (4)(C)(i)(I) of section 127(c) shall be—

(A) disclosed in the form and manner which the Board shall prescribe by regulations; and

(B) placed in a conspicuous and prominent location on or with any written application, solicitation, or other document or paper with respect to which such disclosure is required.

(2) Tabular format

(A) Form of table to be prescribed

In the regulations prescribed under paragraph (1)(A) of this subsection, the Board shall require that the disclosure of such information shall, to the extent the Board determines to be practicable and appropriate, be in the form of a table which—

(i) contains clear and concise headings for each item of such information; and

(ii) provides a clear and concise form for stating each item of information required to be disclosed under each such heading.

(B) Board discretion in prescribing order and wording of table

In prescribing the form of the table under subparagraph (A), the Board may—

    (i) list the items required to be included in the table in a different order than the order in which such items are set forth in paragraph (1)(A) or (4)(A) of section 127(c); and

    (ii) subject to subparagraph (C), employ terminology which is different than the terminology which is employed in section 127(c) if such terminology conveys substantially the same meaning.

(C) Grace period

Either the heading or the statement under the heading which relates to the time period referred to in section 127(c)(1)(A)(iii) shall contain the term "grace period."

§ 123. Exemption for State-regulated transactions [15 U.S.C. § 1633]

The Board shall by regulation exempt from the requirements of this part any class of credit transactions within any State if it determines that under the law of that State that class of transactions is subject to requirements substantially similar to those imposed under this part, and that there is adequate provision for enforcement.

§ 124. Effect of subsequent occurrence [15 U.S.C. § 1634]

If information disclosed in accordance with this part is subsequently rendered inaccurate as the result of any act, occurrence, or agreement subsequent to the delivery of the required disclosures, the inaccuracy resulting therefrom does not constitute a violation of this part.

§ 125. Right of rescission as to certain transactions [15 U.S.C. § 1635]

(a) Disclosure of obligor's right to rescind

Except as otherwise provided in this section, in the case of any consumer credit transaction (including opening or increasing the credit limit for an open end credit plan) in which a security interest, including any such interest arising by operation of law, is or will be retained or acquired in any property which is used as the principal dwelling of the person to whom credit is extended, the obligor shall have the right to rescind the transaction until midnight of the third business day following the consummation of the transaction or the delivery of the information and rescission forms required under this section together with a statement containing the material disclosures required under this subchapter, whichever is later, by notifying the creditor, in accordance with regulations of the Board, of his intention to do so. The creditor shall clearly and conspicuously disclose, in accordance with regulations of the Board, to any obligor in a transaction subject to this section the rights of the obligor under this section. The creditor shall also provide, in accordance with regulations of the Board, appropriate forms for the obligor to exercise his right to rescind any transaction subject to this section.

(b) Return of money or property following rescission

When an obligor exercises his right to rescind under subsection (a) of this section, he is not liable for any finance or other charge, and any security interest given by the obligor, including any such interest arising by operation of law, becomes void upon such a rescission. Within 20 days after receipt of a notice of rescission, the creditor shall return to the obligor any money or property given as earnest money, downpayment, or otherwise, and shall take any action necessary or appropriate to reflect the termination of any security interest created under the transaction. If the creditor has delivered any property to the obligor, the obligor may retain possession of it. Upon the performance of the creditor's obligations under this section, the obligor shall tender the property to the creditor, except that if return of the property in kind would be impracticable or inequitable, the obligor shall tender its reasonable value. Tender shall be made at the location of the property or at the residence of the obligor, at the option of the obligor. If the creditor does not take possession of the property within 20 days after tender by the obligor, ownership of the property vests in the obligor without obligation on his part to pay for it. The procedures prescribed by this subsection shall apply except when otherwise ordered by a court.

(c) Rebuttable presumption of delivery of required disclosures

Notwithstanding any rule of evidence, written acknowledgment of receipt of any disclosures required under this subchapter by a person to whom information, forms, and a statement is required to be given pursuant to this section does no more than create a rebuttable presumption of delivery thereof.

(d) Modification and waiver of rights

The Board may, if it finds that such action is necessary in order to permit homeowners to meet bona fide personal financial emergencies, prescribe regulations authorizing the modification or waiver of any rights created under this section to the extent and under the circumstances set forth in those regulations.

(e) Exempted transactions; reapplication of provisions

This section does not apply to—

(1) a residential mortgage transaction as defined in section 103(w);

(2) a transaction which constitutes a refinancing or consolidation (with no new advances) of the principal balance then due and any accrued and unpaid finance charges of an existing extension of credit by the same creditor secured by an interest in the same property;

(3) a transaction in which an agency of a State is the creditor; or

(4) advances under a preexisting open end credit plan if a security interest has already been retained or acquired and such advances are in accordance with a previously established credit limit for such plan.

(f) Time limit for exercise of right

An obligor's right of rescission shall expire three years after the date of consummation of the transaction or upon the sale of the property, whichever occurs first, notwithstanding the fact that the information and forms required under this section or any other disclosures required under this part have not been delivered to the obligor, except that if (1) any agency empowered to enforce the provisions of this subchapter institutes a proceeding to enforce the provisions of this section within three years after the date of consummation of the transaction, (2) such agency finds a violation of this section, and (3) the obligor's right to rescind is based in whole or in part on any matter involved in such proceeding, then the obligor's right of rescission shall expire three years after the date of consummation of the transaction or upon the earlier sale of the property, or upon the expiration of one year following the conclusion of the proceeding, or any judicial review or period for judicial review thereof, whichever is later.

(g) Additional relief

In any action in which it is determined that a creditor has violated this section, in addition to rescission the court may award relief under section 130 for violations of this subchapter not relating to the right to rescind.

(h) Limitation on rescission

An obligor shall have no rescission rights arising solely from the form of written notice used by the creditor to inform the obligor of the rights of the obligor under this section, if the creditor provided the obligor the appropriate form of written notice published and adopted by the Board, or a comparable written notice of the rights of the obligor, that was properly completed by the creditor, and otherwise complied with all other requirements of this section regarding notice.

(*i*) Rescission rights in foreclosure

(1) In general

Notwithstanding section 139, and subject to the time period provided in subsection (f) of this section, in addition to any other right of rescission available under this section for a transaction, after the initiation of any judicial or nonjudicial foreclosure process on the primary dwelling of an obligor securing an extension of credit, the obligor shall have a right to rescind the transaction equivalent to other rescission rights provided by this section, if—

(A) a mortgage broker fee is not included in the finance charge in accordance with the laws and regulations in effect at the time the consumer credit transaction was consummated; or

(B) the form of notice of rescission for the transaction is not the appropriate form of written notice published and adopted by the Board or a comparable written notice, and otherwise complied with all the requirements of this section regarding notice.

(2) Tolerance for disclosures

Notwithstanding section 106(f), and subject to the time period provided in subsection (f) of this section, for the purposes of exercising any rescission rights after the initiation of any judicial or nonjudicial foreclosure process on the principal dwelling of the obligor securing an extension of credit, the disclosure of the finance charge and other disclosures affected by any finance charge shall be treated as being accurate for purposes of this section if the amount disclosed as the finance charge does not vary from the actual finance charge by more than $35 or is greater than the amount required to be disclosed under this subchapter.

(3) Right of recoupment under State law

Nothing in this subsection affects a consumer's right of rescission in recoupment under State law.

(4) Applicability

This subsection shall apply to all consumer credit transactions in existence or consummated on or after September 30, 1995.

§ 127. Open end consumer credit plans [15 U.S.C. § 1637]

(a) Required disclosures by creditor

Before opening any account under an open end consumer credit plan, the creditor shall disclose to the person to whom credit is to be extended each of the following items, to the extent applicable:

(1) The conditions under which a finance charge may be imposed, including the time period (if any) within which any credit extended may be repaid without incurring a finance charge, except that the creditor may, at his election and without disclosure, impose no such finance charge if payment is received after the termination of such time period. If no such time period is provided, the creditor shall disclose such fact.

(2) The method of determining the balance upon which a finance charge will be imposed.

(3) The method of determining the amount of the finance charge, including any minimum or fixed amount imposed as a finance charge.

(4) Where one or more periodic rates may be used to compute the finance charge, each such rate, the range of balances to which it is applicable, and the corresponding nominal annual percentage rate determined by multiplying the periodic rate by the number of periods in a year.

(5) Identification of other charges which may be imposed as part of the plan, and their method of computation, in accordance with regulations of the Board.

(6) In cases where the credit is or will be secured, a statement that a security interest has been or will be taken in (A) the property purchased as

part of the credit transaction, or (B) property not purchased as part of the credit transaction identified by item or type.

(7) A statement, in a form prescribed by regulations of the Board of the protection provided by sections 161 and 170 to an obligor and the creditor's responsibilities under sections 162 and 170. With respect to one billing cycle per calendar year, at intervals of not less than six months or more than eighteen months, the creditor shall transmit such statement to each obligor to whom the creditor is required to transmit a statement pursuant to subsection (b) of this section for such billing cycle.

(8) In the case of any account under an open end consumer credit plan which provides for any extension of credit which is secured by the consumer's principal dwelling, any information which—

(A) is required to be disclosed under section 127A(a); and

(B) the Board determines is not described in any other paragraph of this subsection.

(b) Statement required with each billing cycle

The creditor of any account under an open end consumer credit plan shall transmit to the obligor, for each billing cycle at the end of which there is an outstanding balance in that account or with respect to which a finance charge is imposed, a statement setting forth each of the following items to the extent applicable:

(1) The outstanding balance in the account at the beginning of the statement period.

(2) The amount and date of each extension of credit during the period, and a brief identification, on or accompanying the statement of each extension of credit in a form prescribed by the Board sufficient to enable the obligor either to identify the transaction or to relate it to copies of sales vouchers or similar instruments previously furnished, except that a creditor's failure to disclose such information in accordance with this paragraph shall not be deemed a failure to comply with this part or this subchapter if (A) the creditor maintains procedures reasonably adapted to procure and provide such information, and (B) the creditor responds to and treats any inquiry for clarification or documentation as a billing error and an erroneously billed amount under section 161. In lieu of complying with the requirements of the previous sentence, in the case of any transaction in which the creditor and seller are the same person, as defined by the Board, and such person's open end credit plan has fewer than 15,000 accounts, the creditor may elect to provide only the amount and date of each extension of credit during the period and the seller's name and location where the transaction took place if (A) a brief identification of the transaction has been previously furnished, and (B) the creditor responds to and treats any inquiry for clarification or documentation as a billing error and an erroneously billed amount under section 161.

(3) The total amount credited to the account during the period.

(4) The amount of any finance charge added to the account during the period, itemized to show the amounts, if any, due to the application of percentage rates and the amount, if any, imposed as a minimum or fixed charge.

(5) Where one or more periodic rates may be used to compute the finance charge, each such rate, the range of balances to which it is applicable, and, unless the annual percentage rate (determined under section 107(a)(2)) is required to be disclosed pursuant to paragraph (6), the corresponding nominal annual percentage rate determined by multiplying the periodic rate by the number of periods in a year.

(6) Where the total finance charge exceeds 50 cents for a monthly or longer billing cycle, or the pro rata part of 50 cents for a billing cycle shorter than monthly, the total finance charge expressed as an annual percentage rate (determined under section 107(a)(2)), except that if the finance charge is the sum of two or more products of a rate times a portion of the balance, the creditor may, in lieu of disclosing a single rate for the total charge, disclose each such rate expressed as an annual percentage rate, and the part of the balance to which it is applicable.

(7) The balance on which the finance charge was computed and a statement of how the balance was determined. If the balance is determined without first deducting all credits during the period, that fact and the amount of such payments shall also be disclosed.

(8) The outstanding balance in the account at the end of the period.

(9) The date by which or the period (if any) within which, payment must be made to avoid additional finance charges, except that the creditor may, at his election and without disclosure, impose no such additional finance charge if payment is received after such date or the termination of such period.

(10) The address to be used by the creditor for the purpose of receiving billing inquiries from the obligor.

(11)(A) In the case of an open end credit plan that requires a minimum monthly payment of not more than 4 percent of the balance on which finance charges are accruing, the following statement, located on the front of the billing statement, disclosed clearly and conspicuously: "Minimum Payment Warning: Making only the minimum payment will increase the interest you pay and the time it takes to repay your balance. For example, making only the typical 2% minimum monthly payment on a balance of $1,000 at an interest rate of 17% would take 88 months to repay the balance in full. For an estimate of the time it would take to repay your balance, making only minimum payments, call this toll-free number: _____." (the blank space to be filled in by the creditor).

(B) In the case of an open end credit plan that requires a minimum monthly payment of more than 4 percent of the balance on which finance charges are accruing, the following statement, in a prominent location on the front of the billing statement, disclosed clearly and conspicuously:

"Minimum Payment Warning: Making only the required minimum payment will increase the interest you pay and the time it takes to repay your balance. Making a typical 5% minimum monthly payment on a balance of $300 at an interest rate of 17% would take 24 months to repay the balance in full. For an estimate of the time it would take to repay your balance, making only minimum monthly payments, call this toll-free number: _____." (the blank space to be filled in by the creditor).

(C) Notwithstanding subparagraphs (A) and (B), in the case of a creditor with respect to which compliance with this title is enforced by the Federal Trade Commission, the following statement, in a prominent location on the front of the billing statement, disclosed clearly and conspicuously: "Minimum Payment Warning: Making only the required minimum payment will increase the interest you pay and the time it takes to repay your balance. For example, making only the typical 5% minimum monthly payment on a balance of $300 at an interest rate of 17% would take 24 months to repay the balance in full. For an estimate of the time it would take to repay your balance, making only minimum monthly payments, call the Federal Trade Commission at this toll-free number: _____." (the blank space to be filled in by the creditor). A creditor who is subject to this subparagraph shall not be subject to subparagraph (A) or (B).

(D) Notwithstanding subparagraph (A), (B), or (C), in complying with any such subparagraph, a creditor may substitute an example based on an interest rate that is greater than 17 percent. Any creditor that is subject to subparagraph (B) may elect to provide the disclosure required under subparagraph (A) in lieu of the disclosure required under subparagraph (B).

(E) The Board shall, by rule, periodically recalculate, as necessary, the interest rate and repayment period under subparagraphs (A), (B), and (C).

(F)(i) The toll-free telephone number disclosed by a creditor or the Federal Trade Commission under subparagraph (A), (B), or (G), as appropriate, may be a toll-free telephone number established and maintained by the creditor or the Federal Trade Commission, as appropriate, or may be a toll-free telephone number established and maintained by a third party for use by the creditor or multiple creditors or the Federal Trade Commission, as appropriate. The toll-free telephone number may connect consumers to an automated device through which consumers may obtain information described in subparagraph (A), (B), or (C), by inputting information using a touch-tone telephone or similar device, if consumers whose telephones are not equipped to use such automated device are provided the opportunity to be connected to an individual from whom the information described in subparagraph (A), (B), or (C), as applicable, may be obtained. A person that receives a request for information described in subparagraph (A), (B), or (C) from an obligor through the toll-free telephone number disclosed under subparagraph (A), (B), or (C), as applicable, shall disclose in response to such request only the information set forth in the table promulgated by the Board under subparagraph (H)(i).

(ii)(I) The Board shall establish and maintain for a period not to exceed 24 months following the effective date of the Bankruptcy Abuse Prevention and Consumer Protection Act of 2005, a toll-free telephone number, or provide a toll-free telephone number established and maintained by a third party, for use by creditors that are depository institutions (as defined in section 1813 of Title 12), including a Federal credit union or State credit union (as defined in section 1752 of Title 12), with total assets not exceeding $250,000,000. The toll-free telephone number may connect consumers to an automated device through which consumers may obtain information described in subparagraph (A) or (B), as applicable, by inputting information using a touch-tone telephone or similar device, if consumers whose telephones are not equipped to use such automated device are provided the opportunity to be connected to an individual from whom the information described in subparagraph (A) or (B), as applicable, may be obtained. A person that receives a request for information described in subparagraph (A) or (B) from an obligor through the toll-free telephone number disclosed under subparagraph (A) or (B), as applicable, shall disclose in response to such request only the information set forth in the table promulgated by the Board under subparagraph (H)(i). The dollar amount contained in this subclause shall be adjusted according to an indexing mechanism established by the Board.

(II) Not later than 6 months prior to the expiration of the 24–month period referenced in subclause (I), the Board shall submit to the Committee on Banking, Housing, and Urban Affairs of the Senate and the Committee on Financial Services of the House of Representatives a report on the program described in subclause (I).

(G) The Federal Trade Commission shall establish and maintain a toll-free number for the purpose of providing to consumers the information required to be disclosed under subparagraph (C).

(H) The Board shall—

(i) establish a detailed table illustrating the approximate number of months that it would take to repay an outstanding balance if a consumer pays only the required minimum monthly payments and if no other advances are made, which table shall clearly present standardized information to be used to disclose the information required to be disclosed under subparagraph (A), (B), or (C), as applicable;

(ii) establish the table required under clause (i) by assuming—

(I) a significant number of different annual percentage rates;

(II) a significant number of different account balances;

(III) a significant number of different minimum payment amounts; and

(IV) that only minimum monthly payments are made and no additional extensions of credit are obtained; and

(iii) promulgate regulations that provide instructional guidance regarding the manner in which the information contained in the table established under clause (i) should be used in responding to the request of an obligor for any information required to be disclosed under subparagraph (A), (B), or (C).

(I) The disclosure requirements of this paragraph do not apply to any charge card account, the primary purpose of which is to require payment of charges in full each month.

(J) A creditor that maintains a toll-free telephone number for the purpose of providing customers with the actual number of months that it will take to repay the customer's outstanding balance is not subject to the requirements of subparagraph (A) or (B).

(K) A creditor that maintains a toll-free telephone number for the purpose of providing customers with the actual number of months that it will take to repay an outstanding balance shall include the following statement on each billing statement: "Making only the minimum payment will increase the interest you pay and the time it takes to repay your balance. For more information, call this toll-free number: _____." (the blank space to be filled in by the creditor).

(12) If a late payment fee is to be imposed due to the failure of the obligor to make payment on or before a required payment due date, the following shall be stated clearly and conspicuously on the billing statement:

(A) The date on which that payment is due or, if different, the earliest date on which a late payment fee may be charged.

(B) The amount of the late payment fee to be imposed if payment is made after such date.

(c) Disclosure in credit and charge card applications and solicitations

(1) Direct mail applications and solicitations

(A) Information in tabular format

Any application to open a credit card account for any person under an open end consumer credit plan, or a solicitation to open such an account without requiring an application, that is mailed to consumers shall disclose the following information, subject to subsection (e) of this section and section 122(c):

(i) Annual percentage rates

(I) Each annual percentage rate applicable to extensions of credit under such credit plan.

(II) Where an extension of credit is subject to a variable rate, the fact that the rate is variable, the annual percentage rate in effect at the time of the mailing, and how the rate is determined.

(III) Where more than one rate applies, the range of balances to which each rate applies.

(ii) Annual and other fees

(I) Any annual fee, other periodic fee, or membership fee imposed for the issuance or availability of a credit card, including any account maintenance fee or other charge imposed based on activity or inactivity for the account during the billing cycle.

(II) Any minimum finance charge imposed for each period during which any extension of credit which is subject to a finance charge is outstanding.

(III) Any transaction charge imposed in connection with use of the card to purchase goods or services.

(iii) Grace period

(I) The date by which or the period within which any credit extended under such credit plan for purchases of goods or services must be repaid to avoid incurring a finance charge, and, if no such period is offered, such fact shall be clearly stated.

(II) If the length of such "grace period" varies, the card issuer may disclose the range of days in the grace period, the minimum number of days in the grace period, or the average number of days in the grace period, if the disclosure is identified as such.

(iv) Balance calculation method

(I) The name of the balance calculation method used in determining the balance on which the finance charge is computed if the method used has been defined by the Board, or a detailed explanation of the balance calculation method used if the method has not been so defined.

(II) In prescribing regulations to carry out this clause, the Board shall define and name not more than the 5 balance calculation methods determined by the Board to be the most commonly used methods.

(B) Other information

In addition to the information required to be disclosed under subparagraph (A), each application or solicitation to which such subparagraph applies shall disclose clearly and conspicuously the following information, subject to subsections (e) and (f) of this section:

(i) Cash advance fee

Any fee imposed for an extension of credit in the form of cash.

(ii) Late fee

Any fee imposed for a late payment.

(iii) Over-the-limit fee

Any fee imposed in connection with an extension of credit in excess of the amount of credit authorized to be extended with respect to such account.

(2) Telephone solicitations

(A) In general

In any telephone solicitation to open a credit card account for any person under an open end consumer credit plan, the person making the solicitation shall orally disclose the information described in paragraph (1)(A).

(B) Exception

Subparagraph (A) shall not apply to any telephone solicitation if—

(i) the credit card issuer—

(I) does not impose any fee described in paragraph (1)(A)(ii)(I); or

(II) does not impose any fee in connection with telephone solicitations unless the consumer signifies acceptance by using the card;

(ii) the card issuer discloses clearly and conspicuously in writing the information described in paragraph (1) within 30 days after the consumer requests the card, but in no event later than the date of delivery of the card; and

(iii) the card issuer discloses clearly and conspicuously that the consumer is not obligated to accept the card or account and the consumer will not be obligated to pay any of the fees or charges disclosed unless the consumer elects to accept the card or account by using the card.

(3) Applications and solicitations by other means

(A) In general

Any application to open a credit card account for any person under an open end consumer credit plan, and any solicitation to open such an account without requiring an application, that is made available to the public or contained in catalogs, magazines, or other publications shall meet the disclosure requirements of subparagraph (B), (C), or (D).

(B) Specific information

An application or solicitation described in subparagraph (A) meets the requirement of this subparagraph if such application or solicitation contains—

(i) the information—

(I) described in paragraph (1)(A) in the form required under section 122(c), subject to subsection (e) of this section, and

(II) described in paragraph (1)(B) in a clear and conspicuous form, subject to subsections (e) and (f) of this section;

(ii) a statement, in a conspicuous and prominent location on the application or solicitation, that—

(I) the information is accurate as of the date the application or solicitation was printed;

(II) the information contained in the application or solicitation is subject to change after such date; and

(III) the applicant should contact the creditor for information on any change in the information contained in the application or solicitation since it was printed;

(iii) a clear and conspicuous disclosure of the date the application or solicitation was printed; and

(iv) a disclosure, in a conspicuous and prominent location on the application or solicitation, of a toll free telephone number or a mailing address at which the applicant may contact the creditor to obtain any change in the information provided in the application or solicitation since it was printed.

(C) General information without any specific term

An application or solicitation described in subparagraph (A) meets the requirement of this subparagraph if such application or solicitation—

(i) contains a statement, in a conspicuous and prominent location on the application or solicitation, that—

(I) there are costs associated with the use of credit cards; and

(II) the applicant may contact the creditor to request disclosure of specific information of such costs by calling a toll free telephone number or by writing to an address, specified in the application;

(ii) contains a disclosure, in a conspicuous and prominent location on the application or solicitation, of a toll free telephone number and a mailing address at which the applicant may contact the creditor to obtain such information; and

(iii) does not contain any of the items described in paragraph (1).

(D) Applications or solicitations containing subsection (a) disclosures

An application or solicitation meets the requirement of this subparagraph if it contains, or is accompanied by—

(i) the disclosures required by paragraphs (1) through (6) of subsection (a) of this section;

(ii) the disclosures required by subparagraphs (A) and (B) of paragraph (1) of this subsection included clearly and conspicuously (except that the provisions of section 122(c) shall not apply); and

(iii) a toll free telephone number or a mailing address at which the applicant may contact the creditor to obtain any change in the information provided.

(E) Prompt response to information requests

Upon receipt of a request for any of the information referred to in subparagraph (B), (C), or (D), the card issuer or the agent of such issuer shall promptly disclose all of the information described in paragraph (1).

(4) Charge card applications and solicitations

(A) In general

Any application or solicitation to open a charge card account shall disclose clearly and conspicuously the following information in the form required by section 122(c), subject to subsection (e) of this section:

(i) Any annual fee, other periodic fee, or membership fee imposed for the issuance or availability of the charge card, including any account maintenance fee or other charge imposed based on activity or inactivity for the account during the billing cycle.

(ii) Any transaction charge imposed in connection with use of the card to purchase goods or services.

(iii) A statement that charges incurred by use of the charge card are due and payable upon receipt of a periodic statement rendered for such charge card account.

(B) Other information

In addition to the information required to be disclosed under subparagraph (A), each written application or solicitation to which such subparagraph applies shall disclose clearly and conspicuously the following information, subject to subsections (e) and (f) of this section:

(i) Cash advance fee

Any fee imposed for an extension of credit in the form of cash.

(ii) Late fee

Any fee imposed for a late payment.

(iii) Over-the-limit fee

Any fee imposed in connection with an extension of credit in excess of the amount of credit authorized to be extended with respect to such account.

(C) Applications and solicitations by other means

Any application to open a charge card account, and any solicitation to open such an account without requiring an application, that is made available to the public or contained in catalogs, magazines, or other publications shall contain—

    (i) the information—

        (I) described in subparagraph (A) in the form required under section 122(c), subject to subsection (e) of this section, and

        (II) described in subparagraph (B) in a clear and conspicuous form, subject to subsections (e) and (f) of this section;

    (ii) a statement, in a conspicuous and prominent location on the application or solicitation, that—

        (I) the information is accurate as of the date the application or solicitation was printed;

        (II) the information contained in the application or solicitation is subject to change after such date; and

        (III) the applicant should contact the creditor for information on any change in the information contained in the application or solicitation since it was printed;

    (iii) a clear and conspicuous disclosure of the date the application or solicitation was printed; and

    (iv) a disclosure, in a conspicuous and prominent location on the application or solicitation, of a toll free telephone number or a mailing address at which the applicant may contact the creditor to obtain any change in the information provided in the application or solicitation since it was printed.

(D) Issuers of charge cards which provide access to open end consumer credit plans

If a charge card permits the card holder to receive an extension of credit under an open end consumer credit plan, which is not maintained by the charge card issuer, the charge card issuer may provide the information described in subparagraphs (A) and (B) in the form required by such subparagraphs in lieu of the information required to be provided under paragraph (1), (2), or (3) with respect to any credit extended under such plan, if the charge card issuer discloses clearly and conspicuously to the consumer in the application or solicitation that—

    (i) the charge card issuer will make an independent decision as to whether to issue the card;

    (ii) the charge card may arrive before the decision is made with respect to an extension of credit under an open end consumer credit plan; and

    (iii) approval by the charge card issuer does not constitute approval by the issuer of the extension of credit.

The information required to be disclosed under paragraph (1) shall be provided to the charge card holder by the creditor which maintains such open end consumer credit plan before the first extension of credit under such plan.

(E) "Charge card" defined

For the purposes of this subsection, the term "charge card" means a card, plate, or other single credit device that may be used from time to time to obtain credit which is not subject to a finance charge.

(5) Regulatory authority of the Board

The Board may, by regulation, require the disclosure of information in addition to that otherwise required by this subsection or subsection (d) of this section, and modify any disclosure of information required by this subsection or subsection (d) of this section, in any application to open a credit card account for any person under an open end consumer credit plan or any application to open a charge card account for any person, or a solicitation to open any such account without requiring an application, if the Board determines that such action is necessary to carry out the purposes of, or prevent evasions of, any paragraph of this subsection.

(6) Additional notice concerning "introductory rates"

(A) In general

Except as provided in subparagraph (B), an application or solicitation to open a credit card account and all promotional materials accompanying such application or solicitation for which a disclosure is required under paragraph (1), and that offers a temporary annual percentage rate of interest, shall—

(i) use the term "introductory" in immediate proximity to each listing of the temporary annual percentage rate applicable to such account, which term shall appear clearly and conspicuously;

(ii) if the annual percentage rate of interest that will apply after the end of the temporary rate period will be a fixed rate, state in a clear and conspicuous manner in a prominent location closely proximate to the first listing of the temporary annual percentage rate (other than a listing of the temporary annual percentage rate in the tabular format described in section 1632(c) of this title), the time period in which the introductory period will end and the annual percentage rate that will apply after the end of the introductory period; and

(iii) if the annual percentage rate that will apply after the end of the temporary rate period will vary in accordance with an index, state in a clear and conspicuous manner in a prominent location closely proximate to the first listing of the temporary annual percentage rate (other than a listing in the tabular format prescribed by section 1632(c) of this title), the time period in which the introductory period will end and the rate that will apply after that, based on an annual percentage rate that was in effect within 60 days before the date of mailing the application or solicitation.

(B) Exception

Clauses (ii) and (iii) of subparagraph (A) do not apply with respect to any listing of a temporary annual percentage rate on an envelope or other enclosure in which an application or solicitation to open a credit card account is mailed.

(C) Conditions for introductory rates

An application or solicitation to open a credit card account for which a disclosure is required under paragraph (1), and that offers a temporary annual percentage rate of interest shall, if that rate of interest is revocable under any circumstance or upon any event, clearly and conspicuously disclose, in a prominent manner on or with such application or solicitation—

(i) a general description of the circumstances that may result in the revocation of the temporary annual percentage rate; and

(ii) if the annual percentage rate that will apply upon the revocation of the temporary annual percentage rate—

(I) will be a fixed rate, the annual percentage rate that will apply upon the revocation of the temporary annual percentage rate; or

(II) will vary in accordance with an index, the rate that will apply after the temporary rate, based on an annual percentage rate that was in effect within 60 days before the date of mailing the application or solicitation.

(D) Definitions

In this paragraph—

(i) the terms "temporary annual percentage rate of interest" and "temporary annual percentage rate" mean any rate of interest applicable to a credit card account for an introductory period of less than 1 year, if that rate is less than an annual percentage rate that was in effect within 60 days before the date of mailing the application or solicitation; and

(ii) the term "introductory period" means the maximum time period for which the temporary annual percentage rate may be applicable.

(E) Relation to other disclosure requirements

Nothing in this paragraph may be construed to supersede subsection (a) of section 1632 of this title, or any disclosure required by paragraph (1) or any other provision of this subsection.

(7) Internet-based solicitations

(A) In general

In any solicitation to open a credit card account for any person under an open end consumer credit plan using the Internet or other interactive computer service, the person making the solicitation shall clearly and conspicuously disclose—

> (i) the information described in subparagraphs (A) and (B) of paragraph (1); and

> (ii) the information described in paragraph (6).

(B) Form of disclosure

The disclosures required by subparagraph (A) shall be—

> (i) readily accessible to consumers in close proximity to the solicitation to open a credit card account; and

> (ii) updated regularly to reflect the current policies, terms, and fee amounts applicable to the credit card account.

(C) Definitions

For purposes of this paragraph—

> (i) the term "Internet" means the international computer network of both Federal and non-Federal interoperable packet switched data networks; and

> (ii) the term "interactive computer service" means any information service, system, or access software provider that provides or enables computer access by multiple users to a computer server, including specifically a service or system that provides access to the Internet and such systems operated or services offered by libraries or educational institutions.

(d) Disclosure prior to renewal

(1) In general

Except as provided in paragraph (2), a card issuer that imposes any fee described in subsection (c)(1)(A)(ii)(I) or (c)(4)(A)(i) of this section shall transmit to a consumer at least 30 days prior to the scheduled renewal date of the consumer's credit or charge card account a clear and conspicuous disclosure of—

> (A) the date by which, the month by which, or the billing period at the close of which, the account will expire if not renewed;

> (B) the information described in subsection (c)(1)(A) or (c)(4)(A) of this section that would apply if the account were renewed, subject to subsection (e) of this section; and

> (C) the method by which the consumer may terminate continued credit availability under the account.

(2) Special rule for certain disclosures

(A) In general

The disclosures required by this subsection may be provided—

> (i) prior to posting a fee described in subsection (c)(1)(A)(ii)(I) or (c)(4)(A)(i) of this section to the account, or

(ii) with the periodic billing statement first disclosing that the fee has been posted to the account.

(B) Limitation on use of special rule

Disclosures may be provided under subparagraph (A) only if—

(i) the consumer is given a 30–day period to avoid payment of the fee or to have the fee recredited to the account in any case where the consumer does not wish to continue the availability of the credit; and

(ii) the consumer is permitted to use the card during such period without incurring an obligation to pay such fee.

(3) Short-term renewals

The Board may by regulation provide for fewer disclosures than are required by paragraph (1) in the case of an account which is renewable for a period of less than 6 months.

(e) Other rules for disclosures under subsections (c) and (d)

(1) Fees determined on the basis of a percentage

If the amount of any fee required to be disclosed under subsection (c) or (d) of this section is determined on the basis of a percentage of another amount, the percentage used in making such determination and the identification of the amount against which such percentage is applied shall be disclosed in lieu of the amount of such fee.

(2) Disclosure only of fees actually imposed

If a credit or charge card issuer does not impose any fee required to be disclosed under any provision of subsection (c) or (d) of this section, such provision shall not apply with respect to such issuer.

(f) Disclosure of range of certain fees which vary by State allowed

If the amount of any fee required to be disclosed by a credit or charge card issuer under paragraph (1)(B), (3)(B)(i)(II), (4)(B), or (4)(C)(i)(II) of subsection (c) of this section varies from State to State, the card issuer may disclose the range of such fees for purposes of subsection (c) of this section in lieu of the amount for each applicable State, if such disclosure includes a statement that the amount of such fee varies from State to State.

(g) Insurance in connection with certain open end credit card plans

(1) Change in insurance carrier

Whenever a card issuer that offers any guarantee or insurance for repayment of all or part of the outstanding balance of an open end credit card plan proposes to change the person providing that guarantee or insurance, the card issuer shall send each insured consumer written notice of the proposed change not less than 30 days prior to the change, including notice of any increase in the rate or substantial decrease in coverage or service which will result from such change. Such notice may be included on or with the monthly statement provided to the consumer prior to the month in which the proposed change would take effect.

(2) Notice of new insurance coverage

In any case in which a proposed change described in paragraph (1) occurs, the insured consumer shall be given the name and address of the new guarantor or insurer and a copy of the policy or group certificate containing the basic terms and conditions, including the premium rate to be charged.

(3) Right to discontinue guarantee or insurance

The notices required under paragraphs (1) and (2) shall each include a statement that the consumer has the option to discontinue the insurance or guarantee.

(4) No preemption of State law

No provision of this subsection shall be construed as superseding any provision of State law which is applicable to the regulation of insurance.

(5) Board definition of substantial decrease in coverage or service

The Board shall define, in regulations, what constitutes a "substantial decrease in coverage or service" for purposes of paragraph (1).

(h) Prohibition on certain actions for failure to incur finance charges

A creditor of an account under an open end consumer credit plan may not terminate an account prior to its expiration date solely because the consumer has not incurred finance charges on the account. Nothing in this subsection shall prohibit a creditor from terminating an account for inactivity in 3 or more consecutive months.

§ 127A. Disclosure requirements for open end consumer credit plans secured by the consumer's principal dwelling [15 U.S.C. § 1637a]

(a) Application disclosures

In the case of any open end consumer credit plan which provides for any extension of credit which is secured by the consumer's principal dwelling, the creditor shall make the following disclosures in accordance with subsection (b) of this section:

(1) Fixed annual percentage rate

Each annual percentage rate imposed in connection with extensions of credit under the plan and a statement that such rate does not include costs other than interest.

(2) Variable percentage rate

In the case of a plan which provides for variable rates of interest on credit extended under the plan—

(A) a description of the manner in which such rate will be computed and a statement that such rate does not include costs other than interest;

(B) a description of the manner in which any changes in the annual percentage rate will be made, including—

(i) any negative amortization and interest rate carryover;

(ii) the timing of any such changes;

(iii) any index or margin to which such changes in the rate are related; and

(iv) a source of information about any such index;

(C) if an initial annual percentage rate is offered which is not based on an index—

(i) a statement of such rate and the period of time such initial rate will be in effect; and

(ii) a statement that such rate does not include costs other than interest;

(D) a statement that the consumer should ask about the current index value and interest rate;

(E) a statement of the maximum amount by which the annual percentage rate may change in any 1–year period or a statement that no such limit exists;

(F) a statement of the maximum annual percentage rate that may be imposed at any time under the plan;

(G) subject to subsection (b)(3) of this section, a table, based on a $10,000 extension of credit, showing how the annual percentage rate and the minimum periodic payment amount under each repayment option of the plan would have been affected during the preceding 15–year period by changes in any index used to compute such rate;

(H) a statement of—

(i) the maximum annual percentage rate which may be imposed under each repayment option of the plan;

(ii) the minimum amount of any periodic payment which may be required, based on a $10,000 outstanding balance, under each such option when such maximum annual percentage rate is in effect; and

(iii) the earliest date by which such maximum annual interest rate may be imposed; and

(I) a statement that interest rate information will be provided on or with each periodic statement.

(3) Other fees imposed by the creditor

An itemization of any fees imposed by the creditor in connection with the availability or use of credit under such plan, including annual fees, application fees, transaction fees, and closing costs (including costs commonly described as "points"), and the time when such fees are payable.

(4) Estimates of fees which may be imposed by third parties

(A) Aggregate amount

An estimate, based on the creditor's experience with such plans and stated as a single amount or as a reasonable range, of the aggregate amount of additional fees that may be imposed by third parties (such as governmental authorities, appraisers, and attorneys) in connection with opening an account under the plan.

(B) Statement of availability

A statement that the consumer may ask the creditor for a good faith estimate by the creditor of the fees that may be imposed by third parties.

(5) Statement of risk of loss of dwelling

A statement that—

(A) any extension of credit under the plan is secured by the consumer's dwelling; and

(B) in the event of any default, the consumer risks the loss of the dwelling.

(6) Conditions to which disclosed terms are subject

(A) Period during which such terms are available

A clear and conspicuous statement—

(i) of the time by which an application must be submitted to obtain the terms disclosed; or

(ii) if applicable, that the terms are subject to change.

(B) Right of refusal if certain terms change

A statement that—

(i) the consumer may elect not to enter into an agreement to open an account under the plan if any term changes (other than a change contemplated by a variable feature of the plan) before any such agreement is final; and

(ii) if the consumer makes an election described in clause (i), the consumer is entitled to a refund of all fees paid in connection with the application.

(C) Retention of information

A statement that the consumer should make or otherwise retain a copy of information disclosed under this subparagraph.

(7) Rights of creditor with respect to extensions of credit

A statement that—

(A) under certain conditions, the creditor may terminate any account under the plan and require immediate repayment of any outstanding balance, prohibit any additional extension of credit to the account, or reduce the credit limit applicable to the account; and

(B) the consumer may receive, upon request, more specific information about the conditions under which the creditor may take any action described in subparagraph (A).

(8) Repayment options and minimum periodic payments

The repayment options under the plan, including—

(A) if applicable, any differences in repayment options with regard to—

(i) any period during which additional extensions of credit may be obtained; and

(ii) any period during which repayment is required to be made and no additional extensions of credit may be obtained;

(B) the length of any repayment period, including any differences in the length of any repayment period with regard to the periods described in clauses (i) and (ii) of subparagraph (A); and

(C) an explanation of how the amount of any minimum monthly or periodic payment will be determined under each such option, including any differences in the determination of any such amount with regard to the periods described in clauses (i) and (ii) of subparagraph (A).

(9) Example of minimum payments and maximum repayment period

An example, based on a $10,000 outstanding balance and the interest rate (other than a rate not based on the index under the plan) which is, or was recently, in effect under such plan, showing the minimum monthly or periodic payment, and the time it would take to repay the entire $10,000 if the consumer paid only the minimum periodic payments and obtained no additional extensions of credit.

(10) Statement concerning balloon payments

If, under any repayment option of the plan, the payment of not more than the minimum periodic payments required under such option over the length of the repayment period—

(A) would not repay any of the principal balance; or

(B) would repay less than the outstanding balance by the end of such period, as the case may be, a statement of such fact, including an explicit statement that at the end of such repayment period a balloon payment (as defined in section 147(f)) would result which would be required to be paid in full at that time.

(11) Negative amortization

If applicable, a statement that—

(A) any limitation in the plan on the amount of any increase in the minimum payments may result in negative amortization;

(B) negative amortization increases the outstanding principal balance of the account; and

(C) negative amortization reduces the consumer's equity in the consumer's dwelling.

(12) Limitations and minimum amount requirements on extensions of credit

(A) Number and dollar amount limitations

Any limitation contained in the plan on the number of extensions of credit and the amount of credit which may be obtained during any month or other defined time period.

(B) Minimum balance and other transaction amount requirements

Any requirement which establishes a minimum amount for—

(i) the initial extension of credit to an account under the plan;

(ii) any subsequent extension of credit to an account under the plan; or

(iii) any outstanding balance of an account under the plan.

(13) Statement regarding tax deductibility

A statement that—

(A) the consumer should consult a tax advisor regarding the deductibility of interest and charges under the plan; and

(B) in any case in which the extension of credit exceeds the fair market value (as defined under Title 26) of the dwelling, the interest on the portion of the credit extension that is greater than the fair market value of the dwelling is not tax deductible for Federal income tax purposes.

(14) Disclosure requirements established by Board

Any other term which the Board requires, in regulations, to be disclosed.

(b) Time and form of disclosures

(1) Time of disclosure

(A) In general

The disclosures required under subsection (a) of this section with respect to any open end consumer credit plan which provides for any extension of credit which is secured by the consumer's principal dwelling and the pamphlet required under subsection (e) of this section shall be provided to any consumer at the time the creditor distributes an application to establish an account under such plan to such consumer.

(B) Telephone, publications, and third party applications

In the case of telephone applications, applications contained in magazines or other publications, or applications provided by a third party, the disclosures required under subsection (a) of this section and the pamphlet required under subsection (e) of this section shall be provided by the creditor before the end of the 3–day period beginning on the date the creditor receives a completed application from a consumer.

(2) Form

(A) In general

Except as provided in paragraph (1)(B), the disclosures required under subsection (a) of this section shall be provided on or with any application to establish an account under an open end consumer credit plan which provides for any extension of credit which is secured by the consumer's principal dwelling.

(B) Segregation of required disclosures from other information

The disclosures required under subsection (a) of this section shall be conspicuously segregated from all other terms, data, or additional information provided in connection with the application, either by grouping the disclosures separately on the application form or by providing the disclosures on a separate form, in accordance with regulations of the Board.

(C) Precedence of certain information

The disclosures required by paragraphs (5), (6), and (7) of subsection (a) of this section shall precede all of the other required disclosures.

(D) Special provision relating to variable interest rate information

Whether or not the disclosures required under subsection (a) of this section are provided on the application form, the variable rate information described in subsection (a)(2) of this section may be provided separately from the other information required to be disclosed.

(3) Requirement for historical table

In preparing the table required under subsection (a)(2)(G) of this section, the creditor shall consistently select one rate of interest for each year and the manner of selecting the rate from year to year shall be consistent with the plan.

(c) Third party applications

In the case of an application to open an account under any open end consumer credit plan described in subsection (a) of this section which is provided to a consumer by any person other than the creditor—

(1) such person shall provide such consumer with—

(A) the disclosures required under subsection (a) of this section with respect to such plan, in accordance with subsection (b) of this section; and

(B) the pamphlet required under subsection (e) of this section; or

(2) if such person cannot provide specific terms about the plan because specific information about the plan terms is not available, no nonrefundable fee may be imposed in connection with such application before the end of the 3–day period beginning on the date the consumer receives the disclosures required under subsection (a) of this section with respect to the application.

(d) "Principal dwelling" defined

For purposes of this section and sections 137 and 147, the term "principal dwelling" includes any second or vacation home of the consumer.

(e) Pamphlet

In addition to the disclosures required under subsection (a) of this section with respect to an application to open an account under any open end consumer credit plan described in such subsection, the creditor or other person providing such disclosures to the consumer shall provide—

(1) a pamphlet published by the Board pursuant to section 4 of the Home Equity Consumer Protection Act of 1988; or

(2) any pamphlet which provides substantially similar information to the information described in such section, as determined by the Board.

§ 128. Transactions other than under open end credit plan [15 U.S.C. § 1638]

(a) Required disclosures by creditor

For each consumer credit transaction other than under an open end credit plan, the creditor shall disclose each of the following items, to the extent applicable:

(1) The identity of the creditor required to make disclosure.

(2)(A) The "amount financed," using that term, which shall be the amount of credit of which the consumer has actual use. This amount shall be computed as follows, but the computations need not be disclosed and shall not be disclosed with the disclosures conspicuously segregated in accordance with subsection (b)(1) of this section:

(i) take the principal amount of the loan or the cash price less downpayment and trade-in;

(ii) add any charges which are not part of the finance charge or of the principal amount of the loan and which are financed by the consumer, including the cost of any items excluded from the finance charge pursuant to section 106; and

(iii) subtract any charges which are part of the finance charge but which will be paid by the consumer before or at the time of the consummation of the transaction, or have been withheld from the proceeds of the credit.

(B) In conjunction with the disclosure of the amount financed, a creditor shall provide a statement of the consumer's right to obtain, upon a written request, a written itemization of the amount financed. The statement shall include spaces for a "yes" and "no" indication to be initialed by the consumer to indicate whether the consumer wants a written itemization of the amount financed. Upon receiving an affirmative indication, the creditor shall provide, at the time other disclosures are required to be furnished, a written itemization of the amount financed. For the purposes of this subparagraph, "itemization of the amount financed" means a disclosure of the following items, to the extent applicable:

(i) the amount that is or will be paid directly to the consumer;

(ii) the amount that is or will be credited to the consumer's account to discharge obligations owed to the creditor;

(iii) each amount that is or will be paid to third persons by the creditor on the consumer's behalf, together with an identification of or reference to the third person; and

(iv) the total amount of any charges described in the preceding subparagraph (A)(iii).

(3) The "finance charge," not itemized, using that term.

(4) The finance charge expressed as an "annual percentage rate," using that term. This shall not be required if the amount financed does not exceed $75 and the finance charge does not exceed $5, or if the amount financed exceeds $75 and the finance charge does not exceed $7.50.

(5) The sum of the amount financed and the finance charge, which shall be termed the "total of payments."

(6) The number, amount, and due dates or period of payments scheduled to repay the total of payments.

(7) In a sale of property or services in which the seller is the creditor required to disclose pursuant to section 121(b), the "total sale price," using that term, which shall be the total of the cash price of the property or services, additional charges, and the finance charge.

(8) Descriptive explanations of the terms "amount financed," "finance charge," "annual percentage rate," "total of payments," and "total sale price" as specified by the Board. The descriptive explanation of "total sale price" shall include reference to the amount of the downpayment.

(9) Where the credit is secured, a statement that a security interest has been taken in (A) the property which is purchased as part of the credit

transaction, or (B) property not purchased as part of the credit transaction identified by item or type.

(10) Any dollar charge or percentage amount which may be imposed by a creditor solely on account of a late payment, other than a deferral or extension charge.

(11) A statement indicating whether or not the consumer is entitled to a rebate of any finance charge upon refinancing or prepayment in full pursuant to acceleration or otherwise, if the obligation involves a precomputed finance charge. A statement indicating whether or not a penalty will be imposed in those same circumstances if the obligation involves a finance charge computed from time to time by application of a rate to the unpaid principal balance.

(12) A statement that the consumer should refer to the appropriate contract document for any information such document provides about nonpayment, default, the right to accelerate the maturity of the debt, and prepayment rebates and penalties.

(13) In any residential mortgage transaction, a statement indicating whether a subsequent purchaser or assignee of the consumer may assume the debt obligation on its original terms and conditions.

(14) In the case of any variable interest rate residential mortgage transaction, in disclosures provided at application as prescribed by the Board for a variable rate transaction secured by the consumer's principal dwelling, at the option of the creditor, a statement that the periodic payments may increase or decrease substantially, and the maximum interest rate and payment for a $10,000 loan originated at a recent interest rate, as determined by the Board, assuming the maximum periodic increases in rates and payments under the program, or a historical example illustrating the effects of interest rate changes implemented according to the loan program.

(15) In the case of a consumer credit transaction that is secured by the principal dwelling of the consumer, in which the extension of credit may exceed the fair market value of the dwelling, a clear and conspicuous statement that—

(A) the interest on the portion of the credit extension that is greater than the fair market value of the dwelling is not tax deductible for Federal income tax purposes; and

(B) the consumer should consult a tax adviser for further information regarding the deductibility of interest and charges.

(b) Form and timing of disclosures; residential mortgage transaction requirements

(1) Except as otherwise provided in this part, the disclosures required under subsection (a) of this section shall be made before the credit is extended. Except for the disclosures required by subsection (a)(1) of this section, all disclosures required under subsection (a) of this section and any

disclosure provided for in subsection (b), (c), or (d) of section 106 shall be conspicuously segregated from all other terms, data, or information provided in connection with a transaction, including any computations or itemization.

(2)(A) In the case of any extension of credit that is secured by the dwelling of a consumer which is also subject to the Real Estate Settlement Procedures Act, good faith estimates of the disclosures required under subsection (a) of this section shall be made in accordance with regulations of the Board under section 121(c) and shall be delivered or placed in the mail not later than three business days after the creditor receives the consumer's written application, which shall be at least 7 business days before consummation of the transaction.

(B) In the case of an extension of credit that is secured by the dwelling of a consumer, the disclosures provided under subparagraph (A), shall be in addition to the other disclosures required by subsection (a), and shall—

(i) state in conspicuous type size and format, the following: "You are not required to complete this agreement merely because you have received these disclosures or signed a loan application."; and

(ii) be provided in the form of final disclosures at the time of consummation of the transaction, in the form and manner prescribed by this section.

(C) In the case of an extension of credit that is secured by the dwelling of a consumer, under which the annual rate of interest is variable, or with respect to which the regular payments may otherwise be variable, in addition to the other disclosures required by subsection (a), the disclosures provided under this subsection shall do the following:

(i) Label the payment schedule as follows: "Payment Schedule: Payments Will Vary Based on Interest Rate Changes."

(ii) State in conspicuous type size and format examples of adjustments to the regular required payment on the extension of credit based on the change in the interest rates specified by the contract for such extension of credit. Among the examples required to be provided under this clause is an example that reflects the maximum payment amount of the regular required payments on the extension of credit, based on the maximum interest rate allowed under the contract, in accordance with the rules of the Board. Prior to issuing any rules pursuant to this clause, the Board shall conduct consumer testing to determine the appropriate format for providing the disclosures required under this subparagraph to consumers so that such disclosures can be easily understood, including the fact that the initial regular payments are for a specific time period that will end on a certain date, that payments will adjust afterwards potentially to a higher amount, and that there is no guarantee that the borrower will be able to refinance to a lower amount.

(D) In any case in which the disclosure statement under subparagraph (A) contains an annual percentage rate of interest that is no longer accurate, as determined under section 107(c) of this subchapter, the creditor shall furnish an additional, corrected statement to the borrower, not later than 3 business days before the date of consummation of the transaction.

(E) The consumer shall receive the disclosures required under this paragraph before paying any fee to the creditor or other person in connection with the consumer's application for an extension of credit that is secured by the dwelling of a consumer. If the disclosures are mailed to the consumer, the consumer is considered to have received them 3 business days after they are mailed. A creditor or other person may impose a fee for obtaining the consumer's credit report before the consumer has received the disclosures under this paragraph, provided the fee is bona fide and reasonable in amount.

(F) Waiver of timeliness of disclosures

To expedite consummation of a transaction, if the consumer determines that the extension of credit is needed to meet a bona fide personal financial emergency, the consumer may waive or modify the timing requirements for disclosures under subparagraph (A), provided that—

(i) the term "bona fide personal emergency" may be further defined in regulations issued by the Board;

(ii) the consumer provides to the creditor a dated, written statement describing the emergency and specifically waiving or modifying those timing requirements, which statement shall bear the signature of all consumers entitled to receive the disclosures required by this paragraph; and

(iii) the creditor provides to the consumers at or before the time of such waiver or modification, the final disclosures required by paragraph (1).

(G) The requirements of subparagraphs (B), (C), (D) and (E) shall not apply to extensions of credit relating to plans described in section 101(53D) of Title 11.

(3) In the case of a credit transaction described in paragraph (15) of subsection (a) of this section, disclosures required by that paragraph shall be made to the consumer at the time of application for such extension of credit.

(c) Timing of disclosures on unsolicited mailed or telephone purchase orders or loan requests

(1) If a creditor receives a purchase order by mail or telephone without personal solicitation, and the cash price and the total sale price and the terms of financing, including the annual percentage rate, are set forth in the creditor's catalog or other printed material distributed to the public,

then the disclosures required under subsection (a) of this section may be made at any time not later than the date the first payment is due.

(2) If a creditor receives a request for a loan by mail or telephone without personal solicitation and the terms of financing, including the annual percentage rate for representative amounts of credit, are set forth in the creditor's printed material distributed to the public, or in the contract of loan or other printed material delivered to the obligor, then the disclosures required under subsection (a) of this section may be made at any time not later than the date the first payment is due.

(d) Timing of disclosure in cases of an addition of a deferred payment price to an existing outstanding balance

If a consumer credit sale is one of a series of consumer credit sales transactions made pursuant to an agreement providing for the addition of the deferred payment price of that sale to an existing outstanding balance, and the person to whom the credit is extended has approved in writing both the annual percentage rate or rates and the method of computing the finance charge or charges, and the creditor retains no security interest in any property as to which he has received payments aggregating the amount of the sales price including any finance charges attributable thereto, then the disclosure required under subsection (a) of this section for the particular sale may be made at any time not later than the date the first payment for that sale is due. For the purposes of this subsection, in the case of items purchased on different dates, the first purchased shall be deemed first paid for, and in the case of items purchased on the same date, the lowest priced shall be deemed first paid for.

§ 129. Requirements for certain mortgages [15 U.S.C. § 1639]

(a) Disclosures

(1) Specific disclosures

In addition to other disclosures required under this subchapter, for each mortgage referred to in section 103(aa), the creditor shall provide the following disclosures in conspicuous type size:

(A) "You are not required to complete this agreement merely because you have received these disclosures or have signed a loan application."

(B) "If you obtain this loan, the lender will have a mortgage on your home. You could lose your home, and any money you have put into it, if you do not meet your obligations under the loan."

(2) Annual percentage rate

In addition to the disclosures required under paragraph (1), the creditor shall disclose—

(A) in the case of a credit transaction with a fixed rate of interest, the annual percentage rate and the amount of the regular monthly payment; or

(B) in the case of any other credit transaction, the annual percentage rate of the loan, the amount of the regular monthly payment, a statement that the interest rate and monthly payment may increase, and the amount of the maximum monthly payment, based on the maximum interest rate allowed pursuant to section 3806 of Title 12.

(b) Time of disclosures

(1) In general

The disclosures required by this section shall be given not less than 3 business days prior to consummation of the transaction.

(2) New disclosures required

(A) In general

After providing the disclosures required by this section, a creditor may not change the terms of the extension of credit if such changes make the disclosures inaccurate, unless new disclosures are provided that meet the requirements of this section.

(B) Telephone disclosure

A creditor may provide new disclosures pursuant to subparagraph (A) by telephone, if—

(i) the change is initiated by the consumer; and

(ii) at the consummation of the transaction under which the credit is extended—

(I) the creditor provides to the consumer the new disclosures, in writing; and

(II) the creditor and consumer certify in writing that the new disclosures were provided by telephone, by not later than 3 days prior to the date of consummation of the transaction.

(3) Modifications

The Board may, if it finds that such action is necessary to permit homeowners to meet bona fide personal financial emergencies, prescribe regulations authorizing the modification or waiver of rights created under this subsection, to the extent and under the circumstances set forth in those regulations.

(c) No prepayment penalty

(1) In general

(A) Limitation on terms

A mortgage referred to in section 103(aa) may not contain terms under which a consumer must pay a prepayment penalty for paying all or part of the principal before the date on which the principal is due.

(B) Construction

For purposes of this subsection, any method of computing a refund of unearned scheduled interest is a prepayment penalty if it is less favorable to the consumer than the actuarial method (as that term is defined in section 116(d)).

(2) Exception

Notwithstanding paragraph (1), a mortgage referred to in section 103(aa) may contain a prepayment penalty (including terms calculating a refund by a method that is not prohibited under section 116(b) for the transaction in question) if—

    (A) at the time the mortgage is consummated—

        (i) the consumer is not liable for an amount of monthly indebtedness payments (including the amount of credit extended or to be extended under the transaction) that is greater than 50 percent of the monthly gross income of the consumer; and

        (ii) the income and expenses of the consumer are verified by a financial statement signed by the consumer, by a credit report, and in the case of employment income, by payment records or by verification from the employer of the consumer (which verification may be in the form of a copy of a pay stub or other payment record supplied by the consumer);

    (B) the penalty applies only to a prepayment made with amounts obtained by the consumer by means other than a refinancing by the creditor under the mortgage, or an affiliate of that creditor;

    (C) the penalty does not apply after the end of the 5–year period beginning on the date on which the mortgage is consummated; and

    (D) the penalty is not prohibited under other applicable law.

(d) Limitations after default

A mortgage referred to in section 103(aa) may not provide for an interest rate applicable after default that is higher than the interest rate that applies before default. If the date of maturity of a mortgage referred to in subsection 103(aa) is accelerated due to default and the consumer is entitled to a rebate of interest, that rebate shall be computed by any method that is not less favorable than the actuarial method (as that term is defined in section 116(d)).

(e) No balloon payments

A mortgage referred to in section 103(aa) having a term of less than 5 years may not include terms under which the aggregate amount of the regular periodic payments would not fully amortize the outstanding principal balance.

(f) No negative amortization

A mortgage referred to in section 103(aa) may not include terms under which the outstanding principal balance will increase at any time over the course of the loan because the regular periodic payments do not cover the full amount of interest due.

(g) No prepaid payments

A mortgage referred to in section 103(aa) may not include terms under which more than 2 periodic payments required under the loan are consolidated and paid in advance from the loan proceeds provided to the consumer.

(h) Prohibition on extending credit without regard to payment ability of consumer

A creditor shall not engage in a pattern or practice of extending credit to consumers under mortgages referred to in section 103(aa) based on the consumers' collateral without regard to the consumers' repayment ability, including the consumers' current and expected income, current obligations, and employment.

(i) Requirements for payments under home improvement contracts

A creditor shall not make a payment to a contractor under a home improvement contract from amounts extended as credit under a mortgage referred to in section 103(aa), other than—

(1) in the form of an instrument that is payable to the consumer or jointly to the consumer and the contractor; or

(2) at the election of the consumer, by a third party escrow agent in accordance with terms established in a written agreement signed by the consumer, the creditor, and the contractor before the date of payment.

(j) Consequence of failure to comply

Any mortgage that contains a provision prohibited by this section shall be deemed a failure to deliver the material disclosures required under this subchapter, for the purpose of section 125.

(k) "Affiliate" defined

For purposes of this section, the term "affiliate" has the same meaning as in section 1841(k) of Title 12.

(l) Discretionary regulatory authority of Board

(1) Exemptions

The Board may, by regulation or order, exempt specific mortgage products or categories of mortgages from any or all of the prohibitions specified in subsections (c) through (i) of this section, if the Board finds that the exemption—

(A) is in the interest of the borrowing public; and

(B) will apply only to products that maintain and strengthen home ownership and equity protection.

(2) Prohibitions

The Board, by regulation or order, shall prohibit acts or practices in connection with—

(A) mortgage loans that the Board finds to be unfair, deceptive, or designed to evade the provisions of this section; and

(B) refinancing of mortgage loans that the Board finds to be associated with abusive lending practices, or that are otherwise not in the interest of the borrower.

§ 129A. Fiduciary duty of servicers of pooled residential mortgage [15 U.S.C. § 1639a]

(a) In general

Except as may be established in any investment contract between a servicer of pooled residential mortgages and an investor, a servicer of pooled residential mortgages—

(1) owes any duty to maximize the net present value of the pooled mortgages in an investment to all investors and parties having a direct or indirect interest in such investment, not to any individual party or group of parties; and

(2) shall be deemed to act in the best interests of all such investors and parties if the servicer agrees to or implements a modification or workout plan, including any modification or refinancing undertaken pursuant to the HOPE for Homeowners Act of 2008, for a residential mortgage or a class of residential mortgages that constitute a part or all of the pooled mortgages in such investment, provided that any mortgage so modified meets the following criteria:

(A) Default on the payment of such mortgage has occurred or is reasonably foreseeable.

(B) The property securing such mortgage is occupied by the mortgagor of such mortgage.

(C) The anticipated recovery on the principal outstanding obligation of the mortgage under the modification or workout plan exceeds, on a net present value basis, the anticipated recovery on the principal outstanding obligation of the mortgage through foreclosure.

(b) Definition

As used in this section, the term "servicer" means the person responsible for servicing of a loan (including the person who makes or holds a loan if such person also services the loan).

§ 130. Civil liability [15 U.S.C. § 1640]

(a) Individual or class action for damages; amount of award; factors determining amount of award

Except as otherwise provided in this section, any creditor who fails to comply with any requirement imposed under this part, including any requirement under section 125, or part D or E of this subchapter with respect to any person is liable to such person in an amount equal to the sum of—

(1) any actual damage sustained by such person as a result of the failure;

(2)(A)(i) in the case of an individual action twice the amount of any finance charge in connection with the transaction, (ii) in the case of an individual action relating to a consumer lease under part E of this subchapter, 25 per centum of the total amount of monthly payments under the lease, except that the liability under this subparagraph shall not be less than $100 nor greater than $1,000, or (iii) in the case of an individual action relating to a credit transaction not under an open end credit plan that is secured by real property or a dwelling, not less than $400 or greater than $4,000; or

(B) in the case of a class action, such amount as the court may allow, except that as to each member of the class no minimum recovery shall be applicable, and the total recovery under this subparagraph in any class action or series of class actions arising out of the same failure to comply by the same creditor shall not be more than the lesser of $500,000 or 1 per centum of the net worth of the creditor;

(3) in the case of any successful action to enforce the foregoing liability or in any action in which a person is determined to have a right of rescission under section 125, the costs of the action, together with a reasonable attorney's fee as determined by the court; and

(4) in the case of a failure to comply with any requirement under section 129, an amount equal to the sum of all finance charges and fees paid by the consumer, unless the creditor demonstrates that the failure to comply is not material.

In determining the amount of award in any class action, the court shall consider, among other relevant factors, the amount of any actual damages awarded, the frequency and persistence of failures of compliance by the creditor, the resources of the creditor, the number of persons adversely affected, and the extent to which the creditor's failure of compliance was intentional. In connection with the disclosures referred to in subsections (a) and (b) of section 127, a creditor shall have a liability determined under paragraph (2) only for failing to comply with the requirements of section 125, section 127(a), or of paragraph (4), (5), (6), (7), (8), (9), or (10) of section 127(b) or for failing to comply with disclosure requirements under State law for any term or item which the Board has determined to be substantially the same in meaning under section 111(a)(2) as any of the terms or items referred to in section 127(a) or any of those paragraphs of section 127(b). In connection with the disclosures referred to in subsection (c) or (d) of section 127, a card issuer shall have a liability under this section only to a cardholder who pays a fee described in section 127(c)(1)(A)(ii)(I) or section 127(c)(4)(A)(i) or who uses the credit card or charge card. In connection with the disclosures referred to in section 128, a creditor shall have a liability determined under paragraph (2) only for failing to comply with the requirements of section 125 or of paragraph (2) (insofar as it requires a disclosure of the "amount financed"), (3), (4), (5), (6), or (9) of section 128(a), or section 128(b)(2)(C)(ii), or for failing to comply with disclosure requirements under State law for any term which the Board has determined to be substantially the same in meaning under section 111(a)(2) as any of the terms referred to in any of those paragraphs of section 128(a) or section 128(b)(2)(C)(ii). With respect to any failure to make disclosures required under this part or part D or E of this subchapter, liability shall be imposed only upon the creditor required to make disclosure, except as provided in section 131.

(b) Correction of errors

A creditor or assignee has no liability under this section or section 108 or section 112 for any failure to comply with any requirement imposed under this part or part E of this subchapter, if within sixty days after discovering an error, whether pursuant to a final written examination report or notice issued under section 108(e)(1) or through the creditor's or assignee's own procedures, and prior to the institution of an action under this section or the receipt of written notice of the error from the obligor, the creditor or assignee notifies the person concerned of the error and makes whatever adjustments in the appropriate account are necessary to assure that the person will not be required to pay an amount in excess of the charge actually disclosed, or the dollar equivalent of the annual percentage rate actually disclosed, whichever is lower.

(c) Unintentional violations; bona fide errors

A creditor or assignee may not be held liable in any action brought under this section or section 125 for a violation of this subchapter if the creditor or assignee shows by a preponderance of evidence that the violation was not intentional and resulted from a bona fide error notwithstanding the maintenance of procedures reasonably adapted to avoid any such error. Examples of a bona fide error include, but are not limited to, clerical, calculation, computer malfunction and programing, and printing errors, except that an error of legal judgment with respect to a person's obligations under this subchapter is not a bona fide error.

(d) Liability in transaction or lease involving multiple obligors

When there are multiple obligors in a consumer credit transaction or consumer lease, there shall be no more than one recovery of damages under subsection (a)(2) of this section for a violation of this subchapter.

(e) Jurisdiction of courts; limitations on actions; State attorney general enforcement

Any action under this section may be brought in any United States district court, or in any other court of competent jurisdiction, within one year from the date of the occurrence of the violation. This subsection does not bar a person from asserting a violation of this subchapter in an action to collect the debt which was brought more than one year from the date of the occurrence of the violation as a matter of defense by recoupment or set-off in such action, except as otherwise provided by State law. An action to enforce a violation of section 129 may also be brought by the appropriate State attorney general in any appropriate United States district court, or any other court of competent jurisdiction, not later than 3 years after the date on which the violation occurs. The State attorney general shall provide prior written notice of any such civil action to the Federal agency responsible for enforcement under section 108 and shall provide the agency with a copy of the complaint. If prior notice is not feasible, the State attorney general shall provide notice to such agency immediately upon instituting the action. The Federal agency may—

(1) intervene in the action;

(2) upon intervening—

(A) remove the action to the appropriate United States district court, if it was not originally brought there; and

(B) be heard on all matters arising in the action; and

(3) file a petition for appeal.

(f) Good faith compliance with rule, regulation, or interpretation of Board or with interpretation or approval of duly authorized official or employee of Federal Reserve System

No provision of this section, section 108(b), section 108(c), section 108(e), or section 112 imposing any liability shall apply to any act done or omitted in good faith in conformity with any rule, regulation, or interpretation thereof by the Board or in conformity with any interpretation or approval by an official or employee of the Federal Reserve System duly authorized by the Board to issue such interpretations or approvals under such procedures as the Board may prescribe therefor, notwithstanding that after such act or omission has occurred, such rule, regulation, interpretation, or approval is amended, rescinded, or determined by judicial or other authority to be invalid for any reason.

(g) Recovery for multiple failures to disclose

The multiple failure to disclose to any person any information required under this part or part D or E of this subchapter to be disclosed in connection with a single account under an open end consumer credit plan, other single consumer credit sale, consumer loan, consumer lease, or other extension of consumer credit, shall entitle the person to a single recovery under this section but continued failure to disclose after a recovery has been granted shall give rise to rights to additional recoveries. This subsection does not bar any remedy permitted by section 125.

(h) Offset from amount owed to creditor or assignee; rights of defaulting consumer

A person may not take any action to offset any amount for which a creditor or assignee is potentially liable to such person under subsection (a)(2) of this section against any amount owed by such person, unless the amount of the creditor's or assignee's liability under this subchapter has been determined by judgment of a court of competent jurisdiction in an action of which such person was a party. This subsection does not bar a consumer then in default on the obligation from asserting a violation of this subchapter as an original action, or as a defense or counterclaim to an action to collect amounts owed by the consumer brought by a person liable under this subchapter.

(*i*) Class action moratorium

(1) In general

During the period beginning on May 18, 1995, and ending on October 1, 1995, no court may enter any order certifying any class in any action under this subchapter—

(A) which is brought in connection with any credit transaction not under an open end credit plan which is secured by a first lien on real property or a dwelling and constitutes a refinancing or consolidation of an existing extension of credit; and

(B) which is based on the alleged failure of a creditor—

(i) to include a charge actually incurred (in connection with the transaction) in the finance charge disclosed pursuant to section 128 of this title;

(ii) to properly make any other disclosure required under section 128 as a result of the failure described in clause (i); or

(iii) to provide proper notice of rescission rights under section 125(a) due to the selection by the creditor of the incorrect form from among the model forms prescribed by the Board or from among forms based on such model forms.

(2) Exceptions for certain alleged violations

Paragraph (1) shall not apply with respect to any action—

(A) described in clause (i) or (ii) of paragraph (1)(B), if the amount disclosed as the finance charge results in an annual percentage rate that exceeds the tolerance provided in section 107(c); or

(B) described in paragraph (1)(B)(iii), if—

(i) no notice relating to rescission rights under section 125(a) was provided in any form; or

(ii) proper notice was not provided for any reason other than the reason described in such paragraph.

§ 131. Liability of assignees [15 U.S.C. § 1641]

(a) Prerequisites

Except as otherwise specifically provided in this subchapter, any civil action for a violation of this subchapter or proceeding under section 108 which may be brought against a creditor may be maintained against any assignee of such creditor only if the violation for which such action or proceeding is brought is apparent on the face of the disclosure statement, except where the assignment was involuntary. For the purpose of this section, a violation apparent on the face of the disclosure statement includes, but is not limited to (1) a disclosure which can be determined to be incomplete or inaccurate from the face of the disclosure statement or other documents assigned, or (2) a disclosure which does not use the terms required to be used by this subchapter.

(b) Proof of compliance with statutory provisions

Except as provided in section 125(c), in any action or proceeding by or against any subsequent assignee of the original creditor without knowledge to the contrary by the assignee when he acquires the obligation, written acknowledgement of receipt by a person to whom a statement is required to be given pursuant to this subchapter shall be conclusive proof of the delivery thereof and, except as provided in subsection (a) of this section, of compliance with this part. This section does not affect the rights of the obligor in any action against the original creditor.

(c) Right of rescission by consumer unaffected

Any consumer who has the right to rescind a transaction under section 125 may rescind the transaction as against any assignee of the obligation.

(d) Rights upon assignment of certain mortgages

(1) In general

Any person who purchases or is otherwise assigned a mortgage referred to in section 103(aa) shall be subject to all claims and defenses with respect to that mortgage that the consumer could assert against the creditor of the mortgage, unless the purchaser or assignee demonstrates, by a preponderance of the evidence, that a reasonable person exercising ordinary due diligence, could not determine, based on the documentation required by this subchapter, the itemization of the amount financed, and other disclosure of disbursements that the mortgage was a mortgage referred to in section 103(aa). The preceding sentence does not affect rights of a consumer under subsection (a), (b), or (c) of this section or any other provision of this subchapter.

(2) Limitation on damages

Notwithstanding any other provision of law, relief provided as a result of any action made permissible by paragraph (1) may not exceed—

(A) with respect to actions based upon a violation of this subchapter, the amount specified in section 130; and

(B) with respect to all other causes of action, the sum of—

(i) the amount of all remaining indebtedness; and

(ii) the total amount paid by the consumer in connection with the transaction.

(3) Offset

The amount of damages that may be awarded under paragraph (2)(B) shall be reduced by the amount of any damages awarded under paragraph (2)(A).

(4) Notice

Any person who sells or otherwise assigns a mortgage referred to in section 103(aa) shall include a prominent notice of the potential liability under this subsection as determined by the Board.

(e) Liability of assignee for consumer credit transactions secured by real property

(1) In general

Except as otherwise specifically provided in this subchapter, any civil action against a creditor for a violation of this subchapter, and any proceeding under section 108 against a creditor, with respect to a consumer credit transaction secured by real property may be maintained against any assignee of such creditor only if—

(A) the violation for which such action or proceeding is brought is apparent on the face of the disclosure statement provided in connection with such transaction pursuant to this subchapter; and

(B) the assignment to the assignee was voluntary.

(2) Violation apparent on the face of the disclosure described

For the purpose of this section, a violation is apparent on the face of the disclosure statement if—

(A) the disclosure can be determined to be incomplete or inaccurate by a comparison among the disclosure statement, any itemization of the amount financed, the note, or any other disclosure of disbursement; or

(B) the disclosure statement does not use the terms or format required to be used by this subchapter.

(f) Treatment of servicer

(1) In general

A servicer of a consumer obligation arising from a consumer credit transaction shall not be treated as an assignee of such obligation for purposes of this section unless the servicer is or was the owner of the obligation.

(2) Servicer not treated as owner on basis of assignment for administrative convenience

A servicer of a consumer obligation arising from a consumer credit transaction shall not be treated as the owner of the obligation for purposes of this section on the basis of an assignment of the obligation from the creditor or another assignee to the servicer solely for the administrative convenience of the servicer in servicing the obligation. Upon written request by the obligor, the servicer shall provide the obligor, to the best knowledge of the servicer, with the name, address, and telephone number of the owner of the obligation or the master servicer of the obligation.

(3) Servicer defined

For purposes of this subsection, the term "servicer" has the same meaning as in section 2605(i)(2) of Title 12.

(4) Applicability

This subsection shall apply to all consumer credit transactions in existence or consummated on or after September 30, 1995.

§ 132. Issuance of credit cards [15 U.S.C. § 1642]

No credit card shall be issued except in response to a request or application therefor. This prohibition does not apply to the issuance of a credit card in renewal of, or in substitution for, an accepted credit card.

§ 133. Liability of holder of credit card [15 U.S.C. § 1643]

(a) Limits on liability

(1) A cardholder shall be liable for the unauthorized use of a credit card only if—

    (A) the card is an accepted credit card;

    (B) the liability is not in excess of $50;

    (C) the card issuer gives adequate notice to the cardholder of the potential liability;

    (D) the card issuer has provided the cardholder with a description of a means by which the card issuer may be notified of loss or theft of the card, which description may be provided on the face or reverse side of the statement required by section 127(b) or on a separate notice accompanying such statement;

    (E) the unauthorized use occurs before the card issuer has been notified that an unauthorized use of the credit card has occurred or may occur as the result of loss, theft, or otherwise; and

    (F) the card issuer has provided a method whereby the user of such card can be identified as the person authorized to use it.

(2) For purposes of this section, a card issuer has been notified when such steps as may be reasonably required in the ordinary course of business to provide the card issuer with the pertinent information have been taken, whether or not any particular officer, employee, or agent of the card issuer does in fact receive such information.

(b) Burden of proof

In any action by a card issuer to enforce liability for the use of a credit card, the burden of proof is upon the card issuer to show that the use was authorized or, if the use was unauthorized, then the burden of proof is upon the card issuer to show that the conditions of liability for the unauthorized use of a credit card, as set forth in subsection (a) of this section, have been met.

(c) Liability imposed by other laws or by agreement with issuer

Nothing in this section imposes liability upon a cardholder for the unauthorized use of a credit card in excess of his liability for such use under other applicable law or under any agreement with the card issuer.

(d) Exclusiveness of liability

Except as provided in this section, a cardholder incurs no liability from the unauthorized use of a credit card.

§ 134. Fraudulent use of credit cards; penalties [15 U.S.C. § 1644]

(a) Use, attempt or conspiracy to use card in transaction affecting interstate or foreign commerce

Whoever knowingly in a transaction affecting interstate or foreign commerce, uses or attempts or conspires to use any counterfeit, fictitious, altered, forged, lost, stolen, or fraudulently obtained credit card to obtain money, goods, services, or anything else of value which within any one-year period has a value aggregating $1,000 or more; or

(b) Transporting, attempting or conspiring to transport card in interstate commerce

Whoever, with unlawful or fraudulent intent, transports or attempts or conspires to transport in interstate or foreign commerce a counterfeit, fictitious, altered, forged, lost, stolen, or fraudulently obtained credit card knowing the same to be counterfeit, fictitious, altered, forged, lost, stolen, or fraudulently obtained; or

(c) Use of interstate commerce to sell or transport card

Whoever, with unlawful or fraudulent intent, uses any instrumentality of interstate or foreign commerce to sell or transport a counterfeit, fictitious, altered, forged, lost, stolen, or fraudulently obtained credit card knowing the same to be counterfeit, fictitious, altered, forged, lost, stolen, or fraudulently obtained; or

(d) Receipt, concealment, etc., of goods obtained by use of card

Whoever knowingly receives, conceals, uses, or transports money, goods, services, or anything else of value (except tickets for interstate or foreign transportation) which (1) within any one-year period has a value aggregating $1,000 or more, (2) has moved in or is part of, or which constitutes interstate or foreign commerce, and (3) has been obtained with a counterfeit, fictitious, altered, forged, lost, stolen, or fraudulently obtained credit card; or

(e) Receipt, concealment, etc., of tickets for interstate or foreign transportation obtained by use of card

Whoever knowingly receives, conceals, uses, sells, or transports in interstate or foreign commerce one or more tickets for interstate or foreign transportation, which (1) within any one-year period have a value aggregating $500 or more, and (2) have been purchased or obtained with one or more counterfeit, fictitious, altered, forged, lost, stolen, or fraudulently obtained credit cards; or

(f) Furnishing of money, etc., through use of card

Whoever in a transaction affecting interstate or foreign commerce furnishes money, property, services, or anything else of value, which within any one-year period has a value aggregating $1,000 or more, through the use of any counterfeit, fictitious, altered, forged, lost, stolen, or fraudulently obtained credit card knowing the same to be counterfeit, fictitious, altered, forged, lost, stolen, or fraudulently obtained shall be fined not more than $10,000 or imprisoned not more than ten years, or both.

§ 135. Business credit cards; limits on liability of employees [15 U.S.C. § 1645]

The exemption provided by section 104(1) does not apply to the provisions of sections 132, 133, and 134, except that a card issuer and a business or other organization which provides credit cards issued by the same card issuer to ten or more of its employees may by contract agree as to liability of the business or other organization with respect to unauthorized use of such credit cards without regard to the provisions of section 133, but in no case may such business or other organization or card issuer impose liability upon any employee with respect to unauthorized use of such a credit card except in accordance with and subject to the limitations of section 133.

§ 136. Dissemination of annual percentage rates; implementation, etc. [15 U.S.C. § 1646]

(a) Annual percentage rates

The Board shall collect, publish, and disseminate to the public, on a demonstration basis in a number of standard metropolitan statistical areas to be determined by the Board, the annual percentage rates charged for representative types of nonsale credit by creditors in such areas. For the purpose of this section, the Board is authorized to require creditors in such areas to furnish information necessary for the Board to collect, publish, and disseminate such information.

(b) Credit card price and availability information

(1) Collection required

The Board shall collect, on a semiannual basis, credit card price and availability information, including the information required to be disclosed under section 127(c), from a broad sample of financial institutions which offer credit card services.

(2) Sample requirements

The broad sample of financial institutions required under paragraph (1) shall include—

(A) the 25 largest issuers of credit cards; and

(B) not less than 125 additional financial institutions selected by the Board in a manner that ensures—

(i) an equitable geographical distribution within the sample; and

(ii) the representation of a wide spectrum of institutions within the sample.

(3) Report of information from sample

Each financial institution in the broad sample established pursuant to paragraph (2) shall report the information to the Board in accordance with such regulations or orders as the Board may prescribe.

(4) Public availability of collected information; report to Congress

The Board shall—

(A) make the information collected pursuant to this subsection available to the public upon request; and

(B) report such information semiannually to Congress.

(c) Implementation

The Board is authorized to enter into contracts or other arrangements with appropriate persons, organizations, or State agencies to carry out its functions under subsections (a) and (b) of this section and to furnish financial assistance in support thereof.

§ 137. Home equity plans [15 U.S.C. § 1647]

(a) Index requirement

In the case of extensions of credit under an open end consumer credit plan which are subject to a variable rate and are secured by a consumer's principal dwelling, the index or other rate of interest to which changes in the annual percentage rate are related shall be based on an index or rate of interest which is publicly available and is not under the control of the creditor.

(b) Grounds for acceleration of outstanding balance

A creditor may not unilaterally terminate any account under an open end consumer credit plan under which extensions of credit are secured by a consumer's principal dwelling and require the immediate repayment of any outstanding balance at such time, except in the case of—

(1) fraud or material misrepresentation on the part of the consumer in connection with the account;

(2) failure by the consumer to meet the repayment terms of the agreement for any outstanding balance; or

(3) any other action or failure to act by the consumer which adversely affects the creditor's security for the account or any right of the creditor in such security.

This subsection does not apply to reverse mortgage transactions.

(c) Change in terms

(1) In general

No open end consumer credit plan under which extensions of credit are secured by a consumer's principal dwelling may contain a provision which permits a creditor to change unilaterally any term required to be disclosed under section 127A(a) or any other term, except a change in insignificant terms such as the address of the creditor for billing purposes.

(2) Certain changes not precluded

Notwithstanding the provisions of subsection (1), a creditor may make any of the following changes:

(A) Change the index and margin applicable to extensions of credit under such plan if the index used by the creditor is no longer available and the substitute index and margin would result in a substantially similar interest rate.

(B) Prohibit additional extensions of credit or reduce the credit limit applicable to an account under the plan during any period in which the value of the consumer's principal dwelling which secures any outstanding balance is significantly less than the original appraisal value of the dwelling.

(C) Prohibit additional extensions of credit or reduce the credit limit applicable to the account during any period in which the creditor has reason to believe that the consumer will be unable to comply with the repayment requirements of the account due to a material change in the consumer's financial circumstances.

(D) Prohibit additional extensions of credit or reduce the credit limit applicable to the account during any period in which the consumer is in default with respect to any material obligation of the consumer under the agreement.

(E) Prohibit additional extensions of credit or reduce the credit limit applicable to the account during any period in which—

(i) the creditor is precluded by government action from imposing the annual percentage rate provided for in the account agreement; or

(ii) any government action is in effect which adversely affects the priority of the creditor's security interest in the account to the extent that the value of the creditor's secured interest in the property is less than 120 percent of the amount of the credit limit applicable to the account.

(F) Any change that will benefit the consumer.

(3) Material obligations

Upon the request of the consumer and at the time an agreement is entered into by a consumer to open an account under an open end consumer credit plan under which extensions of credit are secured by the consumer's principal dwelling, the consumer shall be given a list of the categories of contract obligations which are deemed by the creditor to be material obligations of the consumer under the agreement for purposes of paragraph (2)(D).

(4) Consumer benefit

(A) In general

For purposes of paragraph (2)(F), a change shall be deemed to benefit the consumer if the change is unequivocally beneficial to the borrower and the change is beneficial through the entire term of the agreement.

(B) Board categorization

The Board may, by regulation, determine categories of changes that benefit the consumer.

(d) Terms changed after application

If any term or condition described in section 127A(a) which is disclosed to a consumer in connection with an application to open an account under an open end consumer credit plan described in such section (other than a variable feature of the plan) changes before the account is opened, and if, as a result of such change, the consumer elects not to enter into the plan agreement, the creditor shall refund all fees paid by the consumer in connection with such application.

(e) Additional requirements relating to refunds and imposition of nonrefundable fees

(1) In general

No nonrefundable fee may be imposed by a creditor or any other person in connection with any application by a consumer to establish an account under any open end consumer credit plan which provides for extensions of credit which are secured by a consumer's principal dwelling before the end of the 3–day period beginning on the date such consumer receives the disclosure required under section 127A(a) and the pamphlet required under section 127A(e) with respect to such application.

(2) Constructive receipt

For purposes of determining when a nonrefundable fee may be imposed in accordance with this subsection if the disclosures and pamphlet referred to in paragraph (1) are mailed to the consumer, the date of the receipt of the disclosures by such consumer shall be deemed to be 3 business days after the date of mailing by the creditor.

§ 138. Reverse mortgages [15 U.S.C. § 1648]

(a) In general

In addition to the disclosures required under this subchapter, for each reverse mortgage, the creditor shall, not less than 3 days prior to consummation of the transaction, disclose to the consumer in conspicuous type a good faith estimate of the projected total cost of the mortgage to the consumer expressed as a table of annual interest rates. Each annual interest rate shall be based on a projected total future credit extension balance under a projected appreciation rate for the dwelling and a term for the mortgage. The disclosure shall include—

(1) statements of the annual interest rates for not less than 3 projected appreciation rates and not less than 3 credit transaction periods, as determined by the Board, including—

(A) a short-term reverse mortgage;

(B) a term equaling the actuarial life expectancy of the consumer; and

(C) such longer term as the Board deems appropriate; and

(2) a statement that the consumer is not obligated to complete the reverse mortgage transaction merely because the consumer has received the disclosure required under this section or has signed an application for the reverse mortgage.

(b) Projected total cost

In determining the projected total cost of the mortgage to be disclosed to the consumer under subsection (a) of this section, the creditor shall take into account—

(1) any shared appreciation or equity that the lender will, by contract, be entitled to receive;

(2) all costs and charges to the consumer, including the costs of any associated annuity that the consumer elects or is required to purchase as part of the reverse mortgage transaction;

(3) all payments to and for the benefit of the consumer, including, in the case in which an associated annuity is purchased (whether or not required by the lender as a condition of making the reverse mortgage), the annuity payments received by the consumer and financed from the proceeds of the loan, instead of the proceeds used to finance the annuity; and

(4) any limitation on the liability of the consumer under reverse mortgage transactions (such as nonrecourse limits and equity conservation agreements).

§ 139. Certain limitations on liability [15 U.S.C. § 1649]

(a) Limitations on liability

For any closed end consumer credit transaction that is secured by real property or a dwelling, that is subject to this subchapter, and that is consummated before September 30, 1995, a creditor or any assignee of a creditor shall have no civil, administrative, or criminal liability under this subchapter for, and a consumer shall have no extended rescission rights under section 125(f) with respect to—

(1) the creditor's treatment, for disclosure purposes, of—

(A) taxes described in section 106(d)(3);

(B) fees described in section 106(e)(2) and (5);

(C) fees and amounts referred to in the 3rd sentence of section 106(a); or

(D) borrower-paid mortgage broker fees referred to in section 106(a)(6);

(2) the form of written notice used by the creditor to inform the obligor of the rights of the obligor under section 125 if the creditor provided the obligor with a properly dated form of written notice published and adopted by the Board or a comparable written notice, and otherwise complied with all the requirements of this section regarding notice; or

(3) any disclosure relating to the finance charge imposed with respect to the transaction if the amount or percentage actually disclosed—

(A) may be treated as accurate for purposes of this subchapter if the amount disclosed as the finance charge does not vary from the actual finance charge by more than $200;

(B) may, under section 106(f)(2), be treated as accurate for purposes of section 125; or

(C) is greater than the amount or percentage required to be disclosed under this subchapter.

(b) Exceptions

Subsection (a) of this section shall not apply to—

(1) any individual action or counterclaim brought under this subchapter which was filed before June 1, 1995;

(2) any class action brought under this subchapter for which a final order certifying a class was entered before January 1, 1995;

(3) the named individual plaintiffs in any class action brought under this subchapter which was filed before June 1, 1995; or

(4) any consumer credit transaction with respect to which a timely notice of rescission was sent to the creditor before June 1, 1995.

PART C.   CREDIT ADVERTISING

§ 141. Catalogs and multiple-page advertisements [15 U.S.C. § 1661]

For the purposes of this part, a catalog or other multiple-page advertisement shall be considered a single advertisement if it clearly and conspicuously displays a credit terms table on which the information required to be stated under this part is clearly set forth.

§ 142. Advertising of downpayments and installments [15 U.S.C. § 1662]

No advertisement to aid, promote, or assist directly or indirectly any extension of consumer credit may state

(1) that a specific periodic consumer credit amount or installment amount can be arranged, unless the creditor usually and customarily arranges credit payments or installments for that period and in that amount.

(2) that a specified downpayment is required in connection with any extension of consumer credit, unless the creditor usually and customarily arranges downpayments in that amount.

§ 143. Advertising of open end credit plans [15 U.S.C. § 1663]

No advertisement to aid, promote, or assist directly or indirectly the extension of consumer credit under an open end credit plan may set forth any of the specific terms of that plan unless it also clearly and conspicuously sets forth all of the following items:

(1) Any minimum or fixed amount which could be imposed.

(2) In any case in which periodic rates may be used to compute the finance charge, the periodic rates expressed as annual percentage rates.

(3) Any other term that the Board may by regulation require to be disclosed.

§ 144. Advertising of credit other than open end plans [15 U.S.C. § 1664]

(a) Exclusion of open end credit plans

Except as provided in subsection (b) of this section, this section applies to any advertisement to aid, promote, or assist directly or indirectly any consumer credit sale, loan, or other extension of credit subject to the provisions of this subchapter, other than an open end credit plan.

(b) Advertisements of residential real estate

The provisions of this section do not apply to advertisements of residential real estate except to the extent that the Board may by regulation require.

(c) Rate of finance charge expressed as annual percentage rate

If any advertisement to which this section applies states the rate of a finance charge, the advertisement shall state the rate of that charge expressed as an annual percentage rate.

(d) Requisite disclosures in advertisement

If any advertisement to which this section applies states the amount of the downpayment, if any, the amount of any installment payment, the dollar amount of any finance charge, or the number of installments or the period of repayment, then the advertisement shall state all of the following items:

(1) The downpayment, if any.

(2) The terms of repayment.

(3) The rate of the finance charge expressed as an annual percentage rate.

(e) Credit transaction secured by principal dwelling of consumer

Each advertisement to which this section applies that relates to a consumer credit transaction that is secured by the principal dwelling of a consumer in which the extension of credit may exceed the fair market value of the dwelling, and which advertisement is disseminated in paper form to the public or through the internet, as opposed to by radio or television, shall clearly and conspicuously state that—

(1) the interest on the portion of the credit extension that is greater than the fair market value of the dwelling is not tax deductible for Federal income tax purposes; and

(2) the consumer should consult a tax adviser for further information regarding the deductibility of interest and charges.

§ 145. Nonliability of advertising media [15 U.S.C. § 1665]

There is no liability under this part on the part of any owner or personnel, as such, of any medium in which an advertisement appears or through which it is disseminated.

§ 146. Use of annual percentage rate in oral disclosures; exceptions [15 U.S.C. § 1665a]

In responding orally to any inquiry about the cost of credit, a creditor, regardless of the method used to compute finance charges, shall state rates only in terms of the annual percentage rate, except that in the case of an open end credit plan, the periodic rate also may be stated and, in the case of an other than open end credit plan where a major component of the finance charge consists of interest computed at a simple annual rate, the simple annual rate also may be stated. The Board may, by regulation, modify the requirements of this section or provide an exception from this section for a transaction or class of transactions for which the creditor cannot determine in advance the applicable annual percentage rate.

§ 147.   Advertising of open end consumer credit plans secured by consumer's principal dwelling [15 U.S.C. § 1665b]

(a) In general

If any advertisement to aid, promote, or assist, directly or indirectly, the extension of consumer credit through an open end consumer credit plan under which extensions of credit are secured by the consumer's principal dwelling states, affirmatively or negatively, any of the specific terms of the plan, including any periodic payment amount required under such plan, such advertisement shall also clearly and conspicuously set forth the following information, in such form and manner as the Board may require:

(1) Loan fees and opening cost estimates

Any loan fee the amount of which is determined as a percentage of the credit limit applicable to an account under the plan and an estimate of the aggregate amount of other fees for opening the account, based on the creditor's experience with the plan and stated as a single amount or as a reasonable range.

(2) Periodic rates

In any case in which periodic rates may be used to compute the finance charge, the periodic rates expressed as an annual percentage rate.

(3) Highest annual percentage rate

The highest annual percentage rate which may be imposed under the plan.

(4) Other information

Any other information the Board may by regulation require.

(b) Tax deductibility

(1) In general

If any advertisement described in subsection (a) of this section contains a statement that any interest expense incurred with respect to the plan is or may be tax deductible, the advertisement shall not be misleading with respect to such deductibility.

(2) Credit in excess of fair market value

Each advertisement described in subsection (a) of this section that relates to an extension of credit that may exceed the fair market value of the dwelling, and which advertisement is disseminated in paper form to the public or through the Internet, as opposed to by radio or television, shall include a clear and conspicuous statement that—

> (A) the interest on the portion of the credit extension that is greater than the fair market value of the dwelling is not tax deductible for Federal income tax purposes; and

> (B) the consumer should consult a tax adviser for further information regarding the deductibility of interest and charges.

(c) Certain terms prohibited

No advertisement described in subsection (a) of this section with respect to any home equity account may refer to such loan as "free money" or use other terms determined by the Board by regulation to be misleading.

(d) Discounted initial rate

(1) In general

If any advertisement described in subsection (a) of this section includes an initial annual percentage rate that is not determined by the index or formula used to make later interest rate adjustments, the advertisement shall also state with equal prominence the current annual percentage rate that would have been applied using the index or formula if such initial rate had not been offered.

(2) Quoted rate must be reasonably current

The annual percentage rate required to be disclosed under the paragraph (1) rate must be current as of a reasonable time given the media involved.

(3) Period during which initial rate is in effect

Any advertisement to which paragraph (1) applies shall also state the period of time during which the initial annual percentage rate referred to in such paragraph will be in effect.

(e) Balloon payment

If any advertisement described in subsection (a) of this section contains a statement regarding the minimum monthly payment under the plan, the advertisement shall also disclose, if applicable, the fact that the plan includes a balloon payment.

(f) "Balloon payment" defined

For purposes of this section and section 127A, the term "balloon payment" means, with respect to any open end consumer credit plan under which extensions of credit are secured by the consumer's principal dwelling, any repayment option under which—

> (1) the account holder is required to repay the entire amount of any outstanding balance as of a specified date or at the end of a specified period of time, as determined in accordance with the terms of the agreement pursuant to which such credit is extended; and

(2) the aggregate amount of the minimum periodic payments required would not fully amortize such outstanding balance by such date or at the end of such period.

PART D.   CREDIT BILLING

§ 161.   Correction of billing errors [15 U.S.C. § 1666]

(a) Written notice by obligor to creditor; time for and contents of notice; procedure upon receipt of notice by creditor

If a creditor, within sixty days after having transmitted to an obligor a statement of the obligor's account in connection with an extension of consumer credit, receives at the address disclosed under section 127(b)(10) a written notice (other than notice on a payment stub or other payment medium supplied by the creditor if the creditor so stipulates with the disclosure required under section 127(a)(7)) from the obligor in which the obligor—

(1) sets forth or otherwise enables the creditor to identify the name and account number (if any) of the obligor,

(2) indicates the obligor's belief that the statement contains a billing error and the amount of such billing error, and

(3) sets forth the reasons for the obligor's belief (to the extent applicable) that the statement contains a billing error,

the creditor shall, unless the obligor has, after giving such written notice and before the expiration of the time limits herein specified, agreed that the statement was correct—

(A) not later than thirty days after the receipt of the notice, send a written acknowledgment thereof to the obligor, unless the action required in subparagraph (B) is taken within such thirty-day period, and

(B) not later than two complete billing cycles of the creditor (in no event later than ninety days) after the receipt of the notice and prior to taking any action to collect the amount, or any part thereof, indicated by the obligor under paragraph (2) either—

(i) make appropriate corrections in the account of the obligor, including the crediting of any finance charges on amounts erroneously billed, and transmit to the obligor a notification of such corrections and the creditor's explanation of any change in the amount indicated by the obligor under paragraph (2) and, if any such change is made and the obligor so requests, copies of documentary evidence of the obligor's indebtedness; or

(ii) send a written explanation or clarification to the obligor, after having conducted an investigation, setting forth to the extent applicable the reasons why the creditor believes the account of the obligor was correctly shown in the statement and, upon request of the obligor, provide copies of documentary evidence of the obligor's indebtedness. In the case of a billing error where the obligor alleges that the creditor's billing statement reflects goods not delivered to the obligor or his designee in accordance with the agreement made at the time of the transaction, a creditor may not construe such amount to be correctly shown unless he determines that such goods were actually delivered, mailed, or otherwise sent to the obligor and provides the obligor with a statement of such determination.

After complying with the provisions of this subsection with respect to an alleged billing error, a creditor has no further responsibility under this section if the obligor continues to make substantially the same allegation with respect to such error.

(b) Billing error

For the purpose of this section, a "billing error" consists of any of the following:

(1) A reflection on a statement of an extension of credit which was not made to the obligor or, if made, was not in the amount reflected on such statement.

(2) A reflection on a statement of an extension of credit for which the obligor requests additional clarification including documentary evidence thereof.

(3) A reflection on a statement of goods or services not accepted by the obligor or his designee or not delivered to the obligor or his designee in accordance with the agreement made at the time of a transaction.

(4) The creditor's failure to reflect properly on a statement a payment made by the obligor or a credit issued to the obligor.

(5) A computation error or similar error of an accounting nature of the creditor on a statement.

(6) Failure to transmit the statement required under section 127(b) to the last address of the obligor which has been disclosed to the creditor, unless that address was furnished less than twenty days before the end of the billing cycle for which the statement is required.

(7) Any other error described in regulations of the Board.

(c) Action by creditor to collect amount or any part thereof regarded by obligor to be a billing error

For the purposes of this section, "action to collect the amount, or any part thereof, indicated by an obligor under paragraph (2)" does not include the sending of statements of account, which may include finance charges on amounts in dispute, to the obligor following written notice from the obligor as specified under subsection (a) of this section, if—

(1) the obligor's account is not restricted or closed because of the failure of the obligor to pay the amount indicated under paragraph (2) of subsection (a) of this section, and

(2) the creditor indicates the payment of such amount is not required pending the creditor's compliance with this section.

Nothing in this section shall be construed to prohibit any action by a creditor to collect any amount which has not been indicated by the obligor to contain a billing error.

(d) Restricting or closing by creditor of account regarded by obligor to contain a billing error

Pursuant to regulations of the Board, a creditor operating an open end consumer credit plan may not, prior to the sending of the written explanation or clarification required under paragraph (B)(ii), restrict or close an account with respect to which the obligor has indicated pursuant to subsection (a) of this section that he believes such account to contain a billing error solely because of the obligor's failure to pay the amount indicated to be in error. Nothing in this subsection shall be deemed to prohibit a creditor from applying against the credit limit on the obligor's account the amount indicated to be in error.

(e) Effect of noncompliance with requirements by creditor

Any creditor who fails to comply with the requirements of this section or section 162 forfeits any right to collect from the obligor the amount indicated by the obligor under paragraph (2) of subsection (a) of this section, and any finance charges thereon, except that the amount required to be forfeited under this subsection may not exceed $50.

§ 162. Regulation of credit reports [15 U.S.C. § 1666a]

(a) Reports by creditor on obligor's failure to pay amount regarded as billing error

After receiving a notice from an obligor as provided in section 161(a), a creditor or his agent may not directly or indirectly threaten to report to any person adversely on the obligor's credit rating or credit standing because of the obligor's failure to pay the amount indicated by the obligor under section 161(a)(2), and such amount may not be reported as delinquent to any third party until the creditor has met the requirements of section 161 and has allowed the obligor the same number of days (not less than ten) thereafter to make payment as is provided under the credit agreement with the obligor for the payment of undisputed amounts.

(b) Reports by creditor on delinquent amounts in dispute; notification of obligor of parties notified of delinquency

If a creditor receives a further written notice from an obligor that an amount is still in dispute within the time allowed for payment under subsection (a) of this section, a creditor may not report to any third party that the amount of the obligor is delinquent because the obligor has failed to pay an amount which he has indicated under section 161(a)(2), unless the creditor also reports that the amount is in dispute and, at the same time, notifies the obligor of the name and address of each party to whom the creditor is reporting information concerning the delinquency.

(c) Reports by creditor of subsequent resolution of delinquent amounts

A creditor shall report any subsequent resolution of any delinquencies reported pursuant to subsection (b) of this section to the parties to whom such delinquencies were initially reported.

§ 163. Length of billing period in credit statement for imposition of finance charge; effect of failure of timely mailing or delivery of statement [15 U.S.C. § 1666b]

(a) Additional finance charge

If an open end consumer credit plan provides a time period within which an obligor may repay any portion of the credit extended without incurring an additional finance charge, such additional finance charge may not be imposed with respect to such portion of the credit extended for the billing cycle of which such period is a part unless a statement which includes the amount upon which the finance charge for that period is based was mailed at least fourteen days prior to the date specified in the statement by which payment must be made in order to avoid imposition of that finance charge.

(b) Excusable cause

Subsection (a) of this section does not apply in any case where a creditor has been prevented, delayed, or hindered in making timely mailing or delivery of such periodic statement within the time period specified in such subsection because of an act of God, war, natural disaster, strike, or other excusable or justifiable cause, as determined under regulations of the Board.

§ 164. Prompt crediting of payments; imposition of finance charge [15 U.S.C. § 1666c]

Payments received from an obligor under an open end consumer credit plan by the creditor shall be posted promptly to the obligor's account as specified in regulations of the Board. Such regulations shall prevent a finance charge from being imposed on any obligor if the creditor has received the obligor's payment in readily identifiable form in the amount, manner, location, and time indicated by the creditor to avoid the imposition thereof.

§ 165. Treatment of credit balances [15 U.S.C. § 1666d]

Whenever a credit balance in excess of $1 is created in connection with a consumer credit transaction through (1) transmittal of funds to a creditor in excess of the total balance due on an account, (2) rebates of unearned finance charges or insurance premiums, or (3) amounts otherwise owed to or held for the benefit of an obligor, the creditor shall—

    (A) credit the amount of the credit balance to the consumer's account;

    (B) refund any part of the amount of the remaining credit balance, upon request of the consumer; and

    (C) make a good faith effort to refund to the consumer by cash, check, or money order any part of the amount of the credit balance remaining in the account for more than six months, except that no further action is required in any case in which the consumer's current location is not known by the creditor and cannot be traced through the consumer's last known address or telephone number.

§ 166. Notification of credit card issuer by seller of return of goods, etc., by obligor; credit for account of obligor [15 U.S.C. § 1666e]

With respect to any sales transaction where a credit card has been used to obtain credit, where the seller is a person other than the card issuer, and where the seller accepts or allows a return of the goods or forgiveness of a debit for services which were the subject of such sale, the seller shall promptly transmit to the credit card issuer, a credit statement with respect thereto and the credit card issuer shall credit the account of the obligor for the amount of the transaction.

§ 167. Inducements to cardholders by sellers of cash discounts for payments by cash, check or similar means; credit card surcharge prohibition; finance charge for sales transactions involving cash discounts [15 U.S.C. § 1666f]

(a) Cash discounts

With respect to credit card which may be used for extensions of credit in sales transactions in which the seller is a person other than the card issuer, the card issuer may not, by contract, or otherwise, prohibit any such seller from offering a discount to a cardholder to induce the cardholder to pay by cash, check, or similar means rather than use a credit card.

(b) Finance charge

With respect to any sales transaction, any discount from the regular price offered by the seller for the purpose of inducing payment by cash, checks, or other means not involving the use of an open-end credit plan or a credit card shall not constitute a finance charge as determined under section 106 if such discount is offered to all prospective buyers and its availability is disclosed clearly and conspicuously.

§ 168. Tie-in services prohibited for issuance of credit card [15 U.S.C. § 1666g]

Notwithstanding any agreement to the contrary, a card issuer may not require a seller, as a condition to participating in a credit card plan, to open an account with or procure any other service from the card issuer or its subsidiary or agent.

§ 169. Offset of cardholder's indebtedness by issuer of credit card with funds deposited with issuer by cardholder; remedies of creditors under State law not affected [15 U.S.C. § 1666h]

(a) Offset against consumer's funds

A card issuer may not take any action to offset a cardholder's indebtedness arising in connection with a consumer credit transaction under the relevant credit card plan against funds of the cardholder held on deposit with the card issuer unless—

(1) such action was previously authorized in writing by the cardholder in accordance with a credit plan whereby the cardholder agrees periodically to pay debts incurred in his open end credit account by permitting the card issuer periodically to deduct all or a portion of such debt from the cardholder's deposit account, and

(2) such action with respect to any outstanding disputed amount not be taken by the card issuer upon request of the cardholder.

In the case of any credit card account in existence on the effective date of this section, the previous written authorization referred to in clause (1) shall not be required until the date (after such effective date) when such account is renewed, but in no case later than one year after such effective date. Such written authorization shall be deemed to exist if the card issuer has previously notified the cardholder that the use of his credit card account will subject any funds which the card issuer holds in deposit accounts of such cardholder to offset against any amounts due and payable on his credit card account which have not been paid in accordance with the terms of the agreement between the card issuer and the cardholder.

(b) Attachments and levies

This section does not alter or affect the right under State law of a card issuer to attach or otherwise levy upon funds of a cardholder held on deposit with the card issuer if that remedy is constitutionally available to creditors generally.

§ 170. Assertion by cardholder against card issuer of claims and defenses arising out of credit card transaction; prerequisites; limitation on amount of claims or defenses [15 U.S.C. § 1666i]

(a) Claims and defenses assertible

Subject to the limitation contained in subsection (b) of this section, a card issuer who has issued a credit card to a cardholder pursuant to an open end consumer credit plan shall be subject to all claims (other than tort claims) and defenses arising out of any transaction in which the credit card is used as a method of payment or extension of credit if (1) the obligor has made a good faith attempt to obtain satisfactory resolution of a disagreement or problem relative to the transaction from the person honoring the credit card; (2) the amount of the initial transaction exceeds $50; and (3) the place where the initial transaction occurred was in the same State as the mailing address previously provided by the cardholder or was within 100 miles from such address, except that the limitations set forth in clauses (2) and (3) with respect to an obligor's right to assert claims and defenses against a card issuer shall not be applicable to any transaction in which the person honoring the credit card (A) is the same person as the card issuer, (B) is controlled by the card issuer, (C) is under direct or indirect common control with the card issuer, (D) is a franchised dealer in the card issuer's products or services, or (E) has obtained the order for such transaction through a mail solicitation made by or participated in by the card issuer in which the cardholder is solicited to enter into such transaction by using the credit card issued by the card issuer.

(b) Amount of claims and defenses assertible

The amount of claims or defenses asserted by the cardholder may not exceed the amount of credit outstanding with respect to such transaction at the time the cardholder first notifies the card issuer or the person honoring the credit card of such claim or defense. For the purpose of determining the amount of credit outstanding in the preceding sentence, payments and credits to the cardholder's account are deemed to have been applied, in the order indicated, to the payment of: (1) late charges in the order of their entry to the account; (2) finance charges in order of their entry to the account; and (3) debits to the account other than those set forth above, in the order in which each debit entry to the account was made.

§ 171. Applicability of State laws [15 U.S.C. § 1666j]

(a) Consistency of provisions

This part does not annul, alter, or affect, or exempt any person subject to the provisions of this part from complying with, the laws of any State with respect to credit billing practices, except to the extent that those laws are inconsistent with any provision of this part, and then only to the extent of the inconsistency. The Board is authorized to determine whether such inconsistencies exist. The Board may not determine that any State law is inconsistent with any provision of this part if the Board determines that such law gives greater protection to the consumer.

(b) Exemptions by Board from credit billing requirements

The Board shall by regulation exempt from the requirements of this part any class of credit transactions within any State if it determines that under the law of that State that class of transactions is subject to requirements substantially similar to those imposed under this part or that such law gives greater protection to the consumer, and that there is adequate provision for enforcement.

(c) Finance charge or other charge for credit for sales transactions involving cash discounts

Notwithstanding any other provisions of this subchapter, any discount offered under section 167(b) shall not be considered a finance charge or other charge for credit under the usury laws of any State or under the laws of any State relating to disclosure of information in connection with credit transactions, or relating to the types, amounts or rates of charges, or to any element or elements of charges permissible under such laws in connection with the extension or use of credit.

PART E.   CONSUMER LEASES

§ 181.   Definitions [15 U.S.C. § 1667]

For purposes of this part—

(1) The term "consumer lease" means a contract in the form of a lease or bailment for the use of personal property by a natural person for a period of time exceeding four months, and for a total contractual obligation not exceeding $25,000, primarily for personal, family, or household purposes, whether or not the lessee has the option to purchase or otherwise become the owner of the property at the expiration of the lease, except that such term shall not include any credit sale as defined in section 103(g). Such term does not include a lease for agricultural, business, or commercial purposes, or to a government or governmental agency or instrumentality, or to an organization.

(2) The term "lessee" means a natural person who leases or is offered a consumer lease.

(3) The term "lessor" means a person who is regularly engaged in leasing, offering to lease, or arranging to lease under a consumer lease.

(4) The term "personal property" means any property which is not real property under the laws of the State where situated at the time offered or otherwise made available for lease.

(5) The terms "security" and "security interest" mean any interest in property which secures payment or performance of an obligation.

§ 182.   Consumer lease disclosures [15 U.S.C. § 1667a]

Each lessor shall give a lessee prior to the consummation of the lease a dated written statement on which the lessor and lessee are identified setting out accurately and in a clear and conspicuous manner the following information with respect to that lease, as applicable:

(1) A brief description or identification of the leased property;

(2) The amount of any payment by the lessee required at the inception of the lease;

(3) The amount paid or payable by the lessee for official fees, registration, certificate of title, or license fees or taxes;

(4) The amount of other charges payable by the lessee not included in the periodic payments, a description of the charges and that the lessee shall be liable for the differential, if any, between the anticipated fair market value of the leased property and its appraised actual value at the termination of the lease, if the lessee has such liability;

(5) A statement of the amount or method of determining the amount of any liabilities the lease imposes upon the lessee at the end of the term and whether or not the lessee has the option to purchase the leased property and at what price and time;

(6) A statement identifying all express warranties and guarantees made by the manufacturer or lessor with respect to the leased property, and identifying the party responsible for maintaining or servicing the leased property together with a description of the responsibility;

(7) A brief description of insurance provided or paid for by the lessor or required of the lessee, including the types and amounts of the coverages and costs;

(8) A description of any security interest held or to be retained by the lessor in connection with the lease and a clear identification of the property to which the security interest relates;

(9) The number, amount, and due dates or periods of payments under the lease and the total amount of such periodic payments;

(10) Where the lease provides that the lessee shall be liable for the anticipated fair market value of the property on expiration of the lease, the fair market value of the property at the inception of the lease, the aggregate cost of the lease on expiration, and the differential between them; and

(11) A statement of the conditions under which the lessee or lessor may terminate the lease prior to the end of the term and the amount or method of determining any penalty or other charge for delinquency, default, late payments, or early termination.

The disclosures required under this section may be made in the lease contract to be signed by the lessee. The Board may provide by regulation that any portion of the information required to be disclosed under this section may be given in the form of estimates where the lessor is not in a position to know exact information.

§ 183.   Lessee's liability on expiration or termination of lease [15 U.S.C. § 1667b]

(a) Estimated residual value of property as basis; presumptions; action by lessor for excess liability; mutually agreeable final adjustment

Where the lessee's liability on expiration of a consumer lease is based on the estimated residual value of the property such estimated residual value shall be a reasonable approximation of the anticipated actual fair market value of the property on lease expiration. There shall be a rebuttable presumption that the estimated residual value is unreasonable to the extent that the estimated residual value exceeds the actual residual value by more than three times the average payment allocable to a monthly period under the lease. In addition, where the lessee has such liability on expiration of a consumer lease there shall be a rebuttable presumption that the lessor's estimated residual value is not in good faith to the extent that the estimated residual value exceeds the actual residual value by more than three times the average payment allocable to a monthly period under the lease and such lessor shall not collect from the lessee the amount of such excess liability on expiration of a consumer lease unless the lessor brings a successful action with respect to such excess liability. In all actions, the lessor shall pay the lessee's reasonable attorney's fees. The presumptions stated in this section shall not apply to the extent the excess of estimated over actual residual value is due to physical damage to the property beyond reasonable wear and use, or to excessive use, and the lease may set standards for such wear and use if such standards are not unreasonable. Nothing in this subsection shall preclude the right of a willing lessee to make any mutually agreeable final adjustment with respect to such excess residual liability, provided such an agreement is reached after termination of the lease.

(b) Penalties and charges for delinquency, default, or early termination

Penalties or other charges for delinquency, default, or early termination may be specified in the lease but only at an amount which is reasonable in the light of the anticipated or actual harm caused by the delinquency, default, or early termination, the difficulties of proof of loss, and the inconvenience or nonfeasibility of otherwise obtaining an adequate remedy.

(c) Independent professional appraisal of residual value of property at termination of lease; finality

If a lease has a residual value provision at the termination of the lease, the lessee may obtain at his expense, a professional appraisal of the leased property by an independent third party agreed to by both parties. Such appraisal shall be final and binding on the parties.

§ 184. Consumer lease advertising; liability of advertising media [15 U.S.C. § 1667c]

(a) In general

If an advertisement for a consumer lease includes a statement of the amount of any payment or a statement that any or no initial payment is required, the advertisement shall clearly and conspicuously state, as applicable—

(1) the transaction advertised is a lease;

(2) the total amount of any initial payments required on or before consummation of the lease or delivery of the property, whichever is later;

(3) that a security deposit is required;

(4) the number, amount, and timing of scheduled payments; and

(5) with respect to a lease in which the liability of the consumer at the end of the lease term is based on the anticipated residual value of the property, that an extra charge may be imposed at the end of the lease term.

(b) Advertising medium not liable

No owner or employee of any entity that serves as a medium in which an advertisement appears or through which an advertisement is disseminated, shall be liable under this section.

(c) Radio advertisements

(1) In general

An advertisement by radio broadcast to aid, promote, or assist, directly or indirectly, any consumer lease shall be deemed to be in compliance with the requirements of subsection (a) of this section if such advertisement clearly and conspicuously—

(A) states the information required by paragraphs (1) and (2) of subsection (a) of this section;

(B) states the number, amounts, due dates or periods of scheduled payments, and the total of such payments under the lease;

(C) includes—

(i) a referral to—

(I) a toll-free telephone number established in accordance with paragraph (2) that may be used by consumers to obtain the information required under subsection (a) of this section; or

(II) a written advertisement that—

(aa) appears in a publication in general circulation in the community served by the radio station on which such advertisement is broadcast during the period beginning 3 days before any such broadcast and ending 10 days after such broadcast; and

(bb) includes the information required to be disclosed under subsection (a) of this section; and

(ii) the name and dates of any publication referred to in clause (i)(II); and

(D) includes any other information which the Board determines necessary to carry out this part.

(2) Establishment of toll-free number

(A) In general

In the case of a radio broadcast advertisement described in paragraph (1) that includes a referral to a toll-free telephone number, the lessor who offers the consumer lease shall—

    (i) establish such a toll-free telephone number not later than the date on which the advertisement including the referral is broadcast;

    (ii) maintain such telephone number for a period of not less than 10 days, beginning on the date of any such broadcast; and

    (iii) provide the information required under subsection (a) of this section with respect to the lease to any person who calls such number.

(B) Form of information

The information required to be provided under subparagraph (A)(iii) shall be provided verbally or, if requested by the consumer, in written form.

(3) No effect on other law

Nothing in this subsection shall affect the requirements of Federal law as such requirements apply to advertisement by any medium other than radio broadcast.

§ 185. Civil liability of lessors [15 U.S.C. § 1667d]

(a) Grounds for maintenance of action

Any lessor who fails to comply with any requirement imposed under section 182 or 183 with respect to any person is liable to such person as provided in section 130.

(b) Additional grounds for maintenance of action; "creditor" defined

Any lessor who fails to comply with any requirement imposed under section 184 with respect to any person who suffers actual damage from the violation is liable to such person as provided in section 130. For the purposes of this section, the term "creditor" as used in sections 130 and 131 shall include a lessor as defined in this part.

(c) Jurisdiction of courts; time limitation

Notwithstanding section 130(e), any action under this section may be brought in any United States district court or in any other court of competent jurisdiction. Such actions alleging a failure to disclose or otherwise comply with the requirements of this part shall be brought within one year of the termination of the lease agreement.

§ 186. Applicability of State laws; exemptions by Board from leasing requirements [15 U.S.C. § 1667e]

(a) This part does not annul, alter, or affect, or exempt any person subject to the provisions of this part from complying with, the laws of any State with respect to consumer leases, except to the extent that those laws are inconsistent with any provision of this part, and then only to the extent of the inconsistency. The Board is authorized to determine whether such inconsistencies exist. The Board may not determine that any State law is inconsistent with any provision of this part if the Board determines that such law gives greater protection and benefit to the consumer.

(b) The Board shall by regulation exempt from the requirements of this part any class of lease transactions within any State if it determines that under the law of that State that class of transactions is subject to requirements substantially similar to those imposed under this part or that such law gives greater protection and benefit to the consumer, and that there is adequate provision for enforcement.

§ 187. Regulations [15 U.S.C. § 1667f]

(a) Regulations authorized

(1) In general

The Board shall prescribe regulations to update and clarify the requirements and definitions applicable to lease disclosures and contracts, and any other issues specifically related to consumer leasing, to the extent that the Board determines such action to be necessary—

(A) to carry out this part;

(B) to prevent any circumvention of this part; or

(C) to facilitate compliance with the requirements of the part.

(2) Classifications, adjustments

Any regulations prescribed under paragraph (1) may contain classifications and differentiations, and may provide for adjustments and exceptions for any class of transactions, as the Board considers appropriate.

(b) Model disclosure

(1) Publication

The Board shall establish and publish model disclosure forms to facilitate compliance with the disclosure requirements of this part and to aid the consumer in understanding the transaction to which the subject disclosure form relates.

(2) Use of automated equipment

In establishing model forms under this subsection, the Board shall consider the use by lessors of data processing or similar automated equipment.

(3) Use optional

A lessor may utilize a model disclosure form established by the Board under this subsection for purposes of compliance with this part, at the discretion of the lessor.

(4) Effect of use

Any lessor who properly uses the material aspects of any model disclosure form established by the Board under this subsection shall be deemed to be in compliance with the disclosure requirements to which the form relates.

SUBCHAPTER III. RESTRICTION ON GARNISHMENT

(15 U.S.C. §§ 1671–1677)

Table of Sections

---

§ 301. Congressional findings and declaration of purpose [15 U.S.C. § 1671]

(a) Disadvantages of garnishment

The Congress finds:

(1) The unrestricted garnishment of compensation due for personal services encourages the making of predatory extensions of credit. Such extensions of credit divert money into excessive credit payments and thereby hinder the production and flow of goods in interstate commerce.

(2) The application of garnishment as a creditors' remedy frequently results in loss of employment by the debtor, and the resulting disruption of employment, production, and consumption constitutes a substantial burden on interstate commerce.

(3) The great disparities among the laws of the several States relating to garnishment have, in effect, destroyed the uniformity of the bankruptcy laws and frustrated the purposes thereof in many areas of the country.

(b) Necessity for regulation

On the basis of the findings stated in subsection (a) of this section, the Congress determines that the provisions of this subchapter are necessary and proper for the purpose of carrying into execution the powers of the Congress to regulate commerce and to establish uniform bankruptcy laws.

§ 302. Definitions [15 U.S.C. § 1672]

For the purposes of this subchapter:

(a) The term "earnings" means compensation paid or payable for personal services, whether denominated as wages, salary, commission, bonus, or otherwise, and includes periodic payments pursuant to a pension or retirement program.

(b) The term "disposable earnings" means that part of the earnings of any individual remaining after the deduction from those earnings of any amounts required by law to be withheld.

(c) The term "garnishment" means any legal or equitable procedure through which the earnings of any individual are required to be withheld for payment of any debt.

§ 303. Restriction on garnishment [15 U.S.C. § 1673]

(a) Maximum allowable garnishment

Except as provided in subsection (b) of this section and in section 305, the maximum part of the aggregate disposable earnings of an individual for any workweek which is subjected to garnishment may not exceed

(1) 25 per centum of his disposable earnings for that week, or

(2) the amount by which his disposable earnings for that week exceed thirty times the Federal minimum hourly wage prescribed by section 206(a)(1) of Title 29 in effect at the time the earnings are payable,

whichever is less. In the case of earnings for any pay period other than a week, the Secretary of Labor shall by regulation prescribe a multiple of the Federal minimum hourly wage equivalent in effect to that set forth in paragraph (2).

(b) Exceptions

(1) The restrictions of subsection (a) of this section do not apply in the case of

(A) any order for the support of any person issued by a court of competent jurisdiction or in accordance with an administrative procedure, which is established by State law, which affords substantial due process, and which is subject to judicial review.

(B) any order of any court of the United States having jurisdiction over cases under chapter 13 of Title 11.

(C) any debt due for any State or Federal tax.

(2) The maximum part of the aggregate disposable earnings of an individual for any workweek which is subject to garnishment to enforce any order for the support of any person shall not exceed—

(A) where such individual is supporting his spouse or dependent child (other than a spouse or child with respect to whose support such order is used), 50 per centum of such individual's disposable earnings for that week; and

(B) where such individual is not supporting such a spouse or dependent child described in clause (A), 60 per centum of such individual's disposable earnings for that week;

except that, with respect to the disposable earnings of any individual for any workweek, the 50 per centum specified in clause (A) shall be deemed to be 55 per centum and the 60 per centum specified in clause (B) shall be deemed to be 65 per centum, if and to the extent that such earnings are subject to garnishment to enforce a support order with respect to a period which is prior to the twelve-week period which ends with the beginning of such workweek.

(c) Execution or enforcement of garnishment order or process prohibited

No court of the United States or any State, and no State (or officer or agency thereof), may make, execute, or enforce any order or process in violation of this section.

§ 304. Restriction on discharge from employment by reason of garnishment [15 U.S.C. § 1674]

(a) Termination of employment

No employer may discharge any employee by reason of the fact that his earnings have been subjected to garnishment for any one indebtedness.

(b) Penalties

Whoever willfully violates subsection (a) of this section shall be fined not more than $1,000, or imprisoned not more than one year, or both.

§ 305. Exemption for State-regulated garnishments [15 U.S.C. § 1675]

The Secretary of Labor may by regulation exempt from the provisions of section 303(a) and (b)(2) garnishments issued under the laws of any State if he determines that the laws of that State provide restrictions on garnishment which are substantially similar to those provided in section 303(a) and (b)(2).

§ 306. Enforcement by Secretary of Labor [15 U.S.C. § 1676]

The Secretary of Labor, acting through the Wage and Hour Division of the Department of Labor, shall enforce the provisions of this subchapter.

§ 307. Effect on State laws [15 U.S.C. § 1677]

This subchapter does not annul, alter, or affect, or exempt any person from complying with, the laws of any State

(1) prohibiting garnishments or providing for more limited garnishment than are allowed under this subchapter, or

(2) prohibiting the discharge of any employee by reason of the fact that his earnings have been subjected to garnishment for more than one indebtedness.

SUBCHAPTER IV.   CREDIT REPAIR ORGANIZATIONS ACT

Table of Sections

---

§ 401.   Short title

This subchapter may be cited as the "Credit Repair Organizations Act."

§ 402.   Findings and purposes [15 U.S.C. § 1679]

(a) Findings

The Congress makes the following findings:

(1) Consumers have a vital interest in establishing and maintaining their credit worthiness and credit standing in order to obtain and use credit. As a result, consumers who have experienced credit problems may seek assistance from credit repair organizations which offer to improve the credit standing of such consumers.

(2) Certain advertising and business practices of some companies engaged in the business of credit repair services have worked a financial hardship upon consumers, particularly those of limited economic means and who are inexperienced in credit matters.

(b) Purposes

The purposes of this subchapter are—

(1) to ensure that prospective buyers of the services of credit repair organizations are provided with the information necessary to make an informed decision regarding the purchase of such services; and

(2) to protect the public from unfair or deceptive advertising and business practices by credit repair organizations.

§ 403. Definitions [15 U.S.C. § 1679a]

For purposes of this subchapter, the following definitions apply:

(1) Consumer

The term "consumer" means an individual.

(2) Consumer credit transaction

The term "consumer credit transaction" means any transaction in which credit is offered or extended to an individual for personal, family, or household purposes.

(3) Credit repair organization

The term "credit repair organization"—

(A) means any person who uses any instrumentality of interstate commerce or the mails to sell, provide, or perform (or represent that such person can or will sell, provide, or perform) any service, in return for the payment of money or other valuable consideration, for the express or implied purpose of—

> (i) improving any consumer's credit record, credit history, or credit rating; or

> (ii) providing advice or assistance to any consumer with regard to any activity or service described in clause (i); and

(B) does not include—

> (i) any nonprofit organization which is exempt from taxation under section 501(c)(3) of Title 26;

> (ii) any creditor (as defined in section 103 of the Truth in Lending Act), with respect to any consumer, to the extent the creditor is assisting the consumer to restructure any debt owed by the consumer to the creditor; or

> (iii) any depository institution (as that term is defined in section 1813 of Title 12) or any Federal or State credit union (as those terms are defined in section 1752 of Title 12), or any affiliate or subsidiary of such a depository institution or credit union.

(4) Credit

The term "credit" has the meaning given to such term in section 103 of the Truth in Lending Act.

§ 404. Prohibited practices [15 U.S.C. § 1679b]

(a) In general

No person may—

(1) make any statement, or counsel or advise any consumer to make any statement, which is untrue or misleading (or which, upon the exercise of reasonable care, should be known by the credit repair organization, officer, employee, agent, or other person to be untrue or misleading) with

respect to any consumer's credit worthiness, credit standing, or credit capacity to—

(A) any consumer reporting agency (as defined in section 603(f) of the Fair Credit Reporting Act); or

(B) any person—

(i) who has extended credit to the consumer; or

(ii) to whom the consumer has applied or is applying for an extension of credit;

(2) make any statement, or counsel or advise any consumer to make any statement, the intended effect of which is to alter the consumer's identification to prevent the display of the consumer's credit record, history, or rating for the purpose of concealing adverse information that is accurate and not obsolete to—

(A) any consumer reporting agency;

(B) any person—

(i) who has extended credit to the consumer; or

(ii) to whom the consumer has applied or is applying for an extension of credit;

(3) make or use any untrue or misleading representation of the services of the credit repair organization; or

(4) engage, directly or indirectly, in any act, practice, or course of business that constitutes or results in the commission of, or an attempt to commit, a fraud or deception on any person in connection with the offer or sale of the services of the credit repair organization.

(b) Payment in advance

No credit repair organization may charge or receive any money or other valuable consideration for the performance of any service which the credit repair organization has agreed to perform for any consumer before such service is fully performed.

§ 405. Disclosures [15 U.S.C. § 1679c]

(a) Disclosure required

Any credit repair organization shall provide any consumer with the following written statement before any contract or agreement between the consumer and the credit repair organization is executed:

"Consumer Credit File Rights Under State and Federal Law

"You have a right to dispute inaccurate information in your credit report by contacting the credit bureau directly. However, neither you nor any 'credit repair' company or credit repair organization has the right to have accurate, current, and verifiable information removed from your credit report. The credit bureau must remove accurate, negative information from your report only if it is over 7 years old. Bankruptcy information can be reported for 10 years.

"You have a right to obtain a copy of your credit report from a credit bureau. You may be charged a reasonable fee. There is no fee, however, if you have been turned down for credit, employment, insurance, or a rental dwelling because of information in your credit report within the preceding 60 days. The credit bureau must provide someone to help you interpret the information in your credit file. You are entitled to receive a free copy of your credit report if you are unemployed and intend to apply for employment in the next 60 days, if you are a recipient of public welfare assistance, or if you have reason to believe that there is inaccurate information in your credit report due to fraud.

"You have a right to sue a credit repair organization that violates the Credit Repair Organization Act. This law prohibits deceptive practices by credit repair organizations.

"You have the right to cancel your contract with any credit repair organization for any reason within 3 business days from the date you signed it.

"Credit bureaus are required to follow reasonable procedures to ensure that the information they report is accurate. However, mistakes may occur.

"You may, on your own, notify a credit bureau in writing that you dispute the accuracy of information in your credit file. The credit bureau must then reinvestigate and modify or remove inaccurate or incomplete information. The credit bureau may not charge any fee for this service. Any pertinent information and copies of all documents you have concerning an error should be given to the credit bureau.

"If the credit bureau's reinvestigation does not resolve the dispute to your satisfaction, you may send a brief statement to the credit bureau, to be kept in your file, explaining why you think the record is inaccurate. The credit bureau must include a summary of your statement about disputed information with any report it issues about you.

"The Federal Trade Commission regulates credit bureaus and credit repair organizations. For more information contact:

"The Public Reference Branch

"Federal Trade Commission

"Washington, D.C. 20580."

(b) Separate statement requirement

The written statement required under this section shall be provided as a document which is separate from any written contract or other agreement between the credit repair organization and the consumer or any other written material provided to the consumer.

(c) Retention of compliance records

(1) In general

The credit repair organization shall maintain a copy of the statement signed by the consumer acknowledging receipt of the statement.

(2) Maintenance for 2 years

The copy of any consumer's statement shall be maintained in the organization's files for 2 years after the date on which the statement is signed by the consumer.

§ 406. Credit repair organizations contracts [15 U.S.C. § 1679d]

(a) Written contracts required

No services may be provided by any credit repair organization for any consumer—

(1) unless a written and dated contract (for the purchase of such services) which meets the requirements of subsection (b) of this section has been signed by the consumer; or

(2) before the end of the 3-business-day period beginning on the date the contract is signed.

(b) Terms and conditions of contract

No contract referred to in subsection (a) of this section meets the requirements of this subsection unless such contract includes (in writing)—

(1) the terms and conditions of payment, including the total amount of all payments to be made by the consumer to the credit repair organization or to any other person;

(2) a full and detailed description of the services to be performed by the credit repair organization for the consumer, including—

(A) all guarantees of performance; and

(B) an estimate of—

(i) the date by which the performance of the services (to be performed by the credit repair organization or any other person) will be complete; or

(ii) the length of the period necessary to perform such services;

(3) the credit repair organization's name and principal business address; and

(4) a conspicuous statement in bold face type, in immediate proximity to the space reserved for the consumer's signature on the contract, which reads as follows: "You may cancel this contract without penalty or obligation at any time before midnight of the 3rd business day after the date on which you signed the contract. See the attached notice of cancellation form for an explanation of this right."

§ 407. Right to cancel contract [15 U.S.C. § 1679e]

(a) In general

Any consumer may cancel any contract with any credit repair organization without penalty or obligation by notifying the credit repair organization of the consumer's intention to do so at any time before midnight of the 3rd business day which begins after the date on which the contract or agreement between the consumer and the credit repair organization is executed or would, but for this subsection, become enforceable against the parties.

(b) Cancellation form and other information

Each contract shall be accompanied by a form, in duplicate, which has the heading "Notice of Cancellation" and contains in bold face type the following statement:

"You may cancel this contract, without any penalty or obligation, at any time before midnight of the 3rd day which begins after the date the contract is signed by you.

"To cancel this contract, mail or deliver a signed, dated copy of this cancellation notice, or any other written notice to [name of credit repair organization] at [address of credit repair organization] before midnight on [date]

"I hereby cancel this transaction,

[date]

[purchaser's signature].".

(c) Consumer copy of contract required

Any consumer who enters into any contract with any credit repair organization shall be given, by the organization—

(1) a copy of the completed contract and the disclosure statement required under section 405; and

(2) a copy of any other document the credit repair organization requires the consumer to sign,

at the time the contract or the other document is signed.

§ 408. Noncompliance with this subchapter [15 U.S.C. § 1679f]

(a) Consumer waivers invalid

Any waiver by any consumer of any protection provided by or any right of the consumer under this subchapter—

(1) shall be treated as void; and

(2) may not be enforced by any Federal or State court or any other person.

(b) Attempt to obtain waiver

Any attempt by any person to obtain a waiver from any consumer of any protection provided by or any right of the consumer under this subchapter shall be treated as a violation of this subchapter.

(c) Contracts not in compliance

Any contract for services which does not comply with the applicable provisions of this subchapter—

(1) shall be treated as void; and

(2) may not be enforced by any Federal or State court or any other person.

§ 409. Civil liability [15 U.S.C. § 1679g]

(a) Liability established

Any person who fails to comply with any provision of this subchapter with respect to any other person shall be liable to such person in an amount equal to the sum of the amounts determined under each of the following paragraphs:

(1) Actual damages

The greater of—

(A) the amount of any actual damage sustained by such person as a result of such failure; or

(B) any amount paid by the person to the credit repair organization.

(2) Punitive damages

(A) Individual actions

In the case of any action by an individual, such additional amount as the court may allow.

(B) Class actions

In the case of a class action, the sum of—

(i) the aggregate of the amount which the court may allow for each named plaintiff; and

(ii) the aggregate of the amount which the court may allow for each other class member, without regard to any minimum individual recovery.

(3) Attorneys' fees

In the case of any successful action to enforce any liability under paragraph (1) or (2), the costs of the action, together with reasonable attorneys' fees.

(b) Factors to be considered in awarding punitive damages

In determining the amount of any liability of any credit repair organization under subsection (a)(2) of this section, the court shall consider, among other relevant factors—

(1) the frequency and persistence of noncompliance by the credit repair organization;

(2) the nature of the noncompliance;

(3) the extent to which such noncompliance was intentional; and

(4) in the case of any class action, the number of consumers adversely affected.

§ 410. Administrative enforcement [15 U.S.C. § 1679h]

(a) In general

Compliance with the requirements imposed under this subchapter with respect to credit repair organizations shall be enforced under the Federal Trade Commission Act [15 U.S.C. § 41 et seq.] by the Federal Trade Commission.

(b) Violations of this subchapter treated as violations of Federal Trade Commission Act

(1) In general

For the purpose of the exercise by the Federal Trade Commission of the Commission's functions and powers under the Federal Trade Commission Act, any violation of any requirement or prohibition imposed under this subchapter with respect to credit repair organizations shall constitute an unfair or deceptive act or practice in commerce in violation of section 5(a) of the Federal Trade Commission Act.

(2) Enforcement authority under other law

All functions and powers of the Federal Trade Commission under the Federal Trade Commission Act shall be available to the Commission to enforce compliance with this subchapter by any person subject to enforcement by the Federal Trade Commission pursuant to this subsection, including the power to enforce the provisions of this subchapter in the same manner as if the violation had been a violation of any Federal Trade Commission trade regulation rule, without regard to whether the credit repair organization—

(A) is engaged in commerce; or

(B) meets any other jurisdictional tests in the Federal Trade Commission Act.

(c) State action for violations

(1) Authority of States

In addition to such other remedies as are provided under State law, whenever the chief law enforcement officer of a State, or an official or agency designated by a State, has reason to believe that any person has violated or is violating this subchapter, the State—

(A) may bring an action to enjoin such violation;

(B) may bring an action on behalf of its residents to recover damages for which the person is liable to such residents under section 1679g of this title as a result of the violation; and

(C) in the case of any successful action under subparagraph (A) or (B), shall be awarded the costs of the action and reasonable attorney fees as determined by the court.

(2) Rights of Commission

(A) Notice to Commission

The State shall serve prior written notice of any civil action under paragraph (1) upon the Federal Trade Commission and provide the Commission with a copy of its complaint, except in any case where such prior notice is not feasible, in which case the State shall serve such notice immediately upon instituting such action.

(B) Intervention

The Commission shall have the right—

(i) to intervene in any action referred to in subparagraph (A);

(ii) upon so intervening, to be heard on all matters arising in the action; and

(iii) to file petitions for appeal.

(3) Investigatory powers

For purposes of bringing any action under this subsection, nothing in this subsection shall prevent the chief law enforcement officer, or an official or agency designated by a State, from exercising the powers conferred on the chief law enforcement officer or such official by the laws of such State to conduct investigations or to administer oaths or affirmations or to compel the attendance of witnesses or the production of documentary and other evidence.

(4) Limitation

Whenever the Federal Trade Commission has instituted a civil action for violation of this subchapter, no State may, during the pendency of such action, bring an action under this section against any defendant named in the complaint of the Commission for any violation of this subchapter that is alleged in that complaint.

§ 411. Statute of limitations [15 U.S.C. § 1679i]

Any action to enforce any liability under this subchapter may be brought before the later of—

(1) the end of the 5-year period beginning on the date of the occurrence of the violation involved; or

(2) in any case in which any credit repair organization has materially and willfully misrepresented any information which—

(A) the credit repair organization is required, by any provision of this subchapter, to disclose to any consumer; and

(B) is material to the establishment of the credit repair organization's liability to the consumer under this subchapter,

the end of the 5-year period beginning on the date of the discovery by the consumer of the misrepresentation.

§ 412. Relation to State law [15 U.S.C. § 1679j]

This subchapter shall not annul, alter, affect, or exempt any person subject to the provisions of this subchapter from complying with any law of any State except to the extent that such law is inconsistent with any provision of this subchapter, and then only to the extent of the inconsistency.

SUBCHAPTER VI.   FAIR CREDIT REPORTING ACT

(15 U.S.C. §§ 1681–1681u)

Table of Sections

---

§ 602.   Congressional findings and statement of purpose [15 U.S.C. § 1681]

(a) Accuracy and fairness of credit reporting

The Congress makes the following findings:

(1) The banking system is dependent upon fair and accurate credit reporting. Inaccurate credit reports directly impair the efficiency of the banking system, and unfair credit reporting methods undermine the public confidence which is essential to the continued functioning of the banking system.

(2) An elaborate mechanism has been developed for investigating and evaluating the credit worthiness, credit standing, credit capacity, character, and general reputation of consumers.

(3) Consumer reporting agencies have assumed a vital role in assembling and evaluating consumer credit and other information on consumers.

(4) There is a need to insure that consumer reporting agencies exercise their grave responsibilities with fairness, impartiality, and a respect for the consumer's right to privacy.

(b) Reasonable procedures

It is the purpose of this subchapter to require that consumer reporting agencies adopt reasonable procedures for meeting the needs of commerce for consumer credit, personnel, insurance, and other information in a manner which is fair and equitable to the consumer, with regard to the confidentiality, accuracy, relevancy, and proper utilization of such information in accordance with the requirements of this subchapter.

§ 603. Definitions; rules of construction [15 U.S.C. § 1681a]

(a) Definitions and rules of construction set forth in this section are applicable for the purposes of this subchapter.

(b) The term "person" means any individual, partnership, corporation, trust, estate, cooperative, association, government or governmental subdivision or agency, or other entity.

(c) The term "consumer" means an individual.

(d) Consumer report.—

(1) In general.—The term "consumer report" means any written, oral, or other communication of any information by a consumer reporting agency bearing on a consumer's credit worthiness, credit standing, credit capacity, character, general reputation, personal characteristics, or mode of living which is used or expected to be used or collected in whole or in part for the purpose of serving as a factor in establishing the consumer's eligibility for—

(A) credit or insurance to be used primarily for personal, family, or household purposes;

(B) employment purposes; or

(C) any other purpose authorized under section 604.

(2) Exclusions.—Except as provided in paragraph (3), the term "consumer report" does not include—

(A) subject to section 624, any—

(i) report containing information solely as to transactions or experiences between the consumer and the person making the report;

(ii) communication of that information among persons related by common ownership or affiliated by corporate control; or

(iii) communication of other information among persons related by common ownership or affiliated by corporate control, if it is clearly and conspicuously disclosed to the consumer that the information may be communicated among such persons and the consumer is given the opportunity, before the time that the information is initially communicated, to direct that such information not be communicated among such persons;

(B) any authorization or approval of a specific extension of credit directly or indirectly by the issuer of a credit card or similar device;

(C) any report in which a person who has been requested by a third party to make a specific extension of credit directly or indirectly to a consumer conveys his or her decision with respect to such request, if the third party advises the consumer of the name and address of the person to whom the request was made, and such person makes the disclosures to the consumer required under section 615; or

(D) a communication described in subsection (*o*) or (x) of this section.

(3) Restriction on sharing of medical information

Except for information or any communication of information disclosed as provided in section 604(g)(3) of this title, the exclusions in paragraph (2) shall not apply with respect to information disclosed to any person related by common ownership or affiliated by corporate control, if the information is—

(A) medical information;

(B) an individualized list or description based on the payment transactions of the consumer for medical products or services; or

(C) an aggregate list of identified consumers based on payment transactions for medical products or services.

(e) The term "investigative consumer report" means a consumer report or portion thereof in which information on a consumer's character, general reputation, personal characteristics, or mode of living is obtained through personal interviews with neighbors, friends, or associates of the consumer reported on or with others with whom he is acquainted or who may have knowledge concerning any such items of information. However, such information shall not include specific factual information on a consumer's credit record obtained directly from a creditor of the consumer or from a consumer reporting agency when such information was obtained directly from a creditor of the consumer or from the consumer.

(f) The term "consumer reporting agency" means any person which, for monetary fees, dues, or on a cooperative nonprofit basis, regularly engages in whole or in part in the practice of assembling or evaluating consumer credit information or other information on consumers for the purpose of furnishing consumer reports to third parties, and which uses any means or facility of interstate commerce for the purpose of preparing or furnishing consumer reports.

(g) The term "file," when used in connection with information on any consumer, means all of the information on that consumer recorded and retained by a consumer reporting agency regardless of how the information is stored.

(h) The term "employment purposes" when used in connection with a consumer report means a report used for the purpose of evaluating a consumer for employment, promotion, reassignment or retention as an employee.

(*i*) Medical information

The term "medical information"—

(1) means information or data, whether oral or recorded, in any form or medium, created by or derived from a health care provider or the consumer, that relates to—

(A) the past, present, or future physical, mental, or behavioral health or condition of an individual;

(B) the provision of health care to an individual; or

(C) the payment for the provision of health care to an individual; and

(2) does not include the age or gender of a consumer, demographic information about the consumer, including a consumer's residence address or e-mail address, or any other information about a consumer that does not relate to the physical, mental, or behavioral health or condition of a consumer, including the existence or value of any insurance policy.

(j) Definitions relating to child support obligations.—

(1) Overdue support.—The term "overdue support" has the meaning given to such term in section 666(e) of Title 42.

(2) State or local child support enforcement agency.—The term "State or local child support enforcement agency" means a State or local agency which administers a State or local program for establishing and enforcing child support obligations.

(k) Adverse action.—

(1) Actions included.—The term "adverse action"—

(A) has the same meaning as in section 701(d)(6) of the Equal Credit Opportunity Act, and

(B) means—

(i) a denial or cancellation of, an increase in any charge for, or a reduction or other adverse or unfavorable change in the terms of coverage or amount of, any insurance, existing or applied for, in connection with the underwriting of insurance;

(ii) a denial of employment or any other decision for employment purposes that adversely affects any current or prospective employee;

(iii) a denial or cancellation of, an increase in any charge for, or any other adverse or unfavorable change in the terms of, any license or benefit described in section 604(a)(3)(D); and

(iv) an action taken or determination that is—

(I) made in connection with an application that was made by, or a transaction that was initiated by, any consumer, or in connection with a review of an account under section 604(a)(3)(F)(ii); and

(II) adverse to the interests of the consumer.

(2) Applicable findings, decisions, commentary, and orders.— For purposes of any determination of whether an action is an adverse action under paragraph (1)(A), all appropriate final findings, decisions, commentary, and orders issued under section 701(d)(6) of the Equal Credit Opportunity Act by the Board of Governors of the Federal Reserve System or any court shall apply.

(l) Firm offer of credit or insurance.—The term "firm offer of credit or insurance" means any offer of credit or insurance to a consumer that will be honored if the consumer is determined, based on information in a consumer report on the consumer, to meet the specific criteria used to select the consumer for the offer, except that the offer may be further conditioned on one or more of the following:

(1) The consumer being determined, based on information in the consumer's application for the credit or insurance, to meet specific criteria bearing on credit worthiness or insurability, as applicable, that are established—

(A) before selection of the consumer for the offer; and

(B) for the purpose of determining whether to extend credit or insurance pursuant to the offer.

(2) Verification—

(A) that the consumer continues to meet the specific criteria used to select the consumer for the offer, by using information in a consumer report on the consumer, information in the consumer's application for the credit or insurance, or other information bearing on the credit worthiness or insurability of the consumer; or

(B) of the information in the consumer's application for the credit or insurance, to determine that the consumer meets the specific criteria bearing on credit worthiness or insurability.

(3) The consumer furnishing any collateral that is a requirement for the extension of the credit or insurance that was—

(A) established before selection of the consumer for the offer of credit or insurance; and

(B) disclosed to the consumer in the offer of credit or insurance.

(m) Credit or insurance transaction that is not initiated by the consumer.—The term "credit or insurance transaction that is not initiated by the consumer" does not include the use of a consumer report by a person with which the consumer has an account or insurance policy, for purposes of—

(1) reviewing the account or insurance policy; or

(2) collecting the account.

(n) State.—The term "State" means any State, the Commonwealth of Puerto Rico, the District of Columbia, and any territory or possession of the United States.

(o) Excluded communications.—A communication is described in this subsection if it is a communication—

(1) that, but for subsection (d)(2)(D) of this section, would be an investigative consumer report;

(2) that is made to a prospective employer for the purpose of—

(A) procuring an employee for the employer; or

(B) procuring an opportunity for a natural person to work for the employer;

(3) that is made by a person who regularly performs such procurement;

(4) that is not used by any person for any purpose other than a purpose described in subparagraph (A) or (B) of paragraph (2); and

(5) with respect to which—

(A) the consumer who is the subject of the communication—

(i) consents orally or in writing to the nature and scope of the communication, before the collection of any information for the purpose of making the communication;

(ii) consents orally or in writing to the making of the communication to a prospective employer, before the making of the communication; and

(iii) in the case of consent under clause (i) or (ii) given orally, is provided written confirmation of that consent by the person making the communication, not later than 3 business days after the receipt of the consent by that person;

(B) the person who makes the communication does not, for the purpose of making the communication, make any inquiry that if made by a prospective employer of the consumer who is the subject of the communication would violate any applicable Federal or State equal employment opportunity law or regulation; and

(C) the person who makes the communication—

(i) discloses in writing to the consumer who is the subject of the communication, not later than 5 business days after receiving any request from the consumer for such disclosure, the nature and substance of all information in the consumer's file at the time of the request, except that the sources of any information that is acquired solely for use in making the communication and is actually used for no other purpose, need not be disclosed other than under appropriate discovery procedures in any court of competent jurisdiction in which an action is brought; and

(ii) notifies the consumer who is the subject of the communication, in writing, of the consumer's right to request the information described in clause (i).

(p) Consumer reporting agency that compiles and maintains files on consumers on a nationwide basis.—The term "consumer reporting agency that compiles and maintains files on consumers on a nationwide basis" means a consumer reporting agency that regularly engages in the practice of assembling or evaluating, and maintaining, for the purpose of furnishing consumer reports to third parties bearing on a consumer's credit worthiness, credit standing, or credit capacity, each of the following regarding consumers residing nationwide:

(1) Public record information.

(2) Credit account information from persons who furnish that information regularly and in the ordinary course of business.

(q) Definitions relating to fraud alerts

(1) Active duty military consumer

The term "active duty military consumer" means a consumer in military service who—

(A) is on active duty (as defined in section 101(d)(1) of Title 10) or is a reservist performing duty under a call or order to active duty under a provision of law referred to in section 101(a)(13) of Title 10; and

(B) is assigned to service away from the usual duty station of the consumer.

(2) Fraud alert; active duty alert

The terms "fraud alert" and "active duty alert" mean a statement in the file of a consumer that—

(A) notifies all prospective users of a consumer report relating to the consumer that the consumer may be a victim of fraud, including identity theft, or is an active duty military consumer, as applicable; and

(B) is presented in a manner that facilitates a clear and conspicuous view of the statement described in subparagraph (A) by any person requesting such consumer report.

(3) Identity theft

The term "identity theft" means a fraud committed using the identifying information of another person, subject to such further definition as the Commission may prescribe, by regulation.

(4) Identity theft report

The term "identity theft report" has the meaning given that term by rule of the Commission, and means, at a minimum, a report—

(A) that alleges an identity theft;

(B) that is a copy of an official, valid report filed by a consumer with an appropriate Federal, State, or local law enforcement agency, including the United States Postal Inspection Service, or such other government agency deemed appropriate by the Commission; and

(C) the filing of which subjects the person filing the report to criminal penalties relating to the filing of false information if, in fact, the information in the report is false.

(5) New credit plan

The term "new credit plan" means a new account under an open end credit plan (as defined in section 103 of the Truth-in-Lending Act) or a new credit transaction not under an open end credit plan.

(r) Credit and debit related terms

(1) Card issuer

The term "card issuer" means—

(A) a credit card issuer, in the case of a credit card; and

(B) a debit card issuer, in the case of a debit card.

(2) Credit card

The term "credit card" has the same meaning as in section 103 of the Truth-in-Lending Act.

(3) Debit card

The term "debit card" means any card issued by a financial institution to a consumer for use in initiating an electronic fund transfer from the account of the consumer at such financial institution, for the purpose of transferring money between accounts or obtaining money, property, labor, or services.

(4) Account and electronic fund transfer

The terms "account" and "electronic fund transfer" have the same meanings as in section 903 of the Electronic Funds Transfer Act.

(5) Credit and creditor

The terms "credit" and "creditor" have the same meanings as in section 702 of the Equal Credit Opportunity Act.

(s) Federal banking agency

The term "Federal banking agency" has the same meaning as in section 1813 of Title 12.

(t) Financial institution

The term "financial institution" means a State or National bank, a State or Federal savings and loan association, a mutual savings bank, a State or Federal credit union, or any other person that, directly or indirectly, holds a transaction account (as defined in section 461(b) of Title 12) belonging to a consumer.

(u) Reseller

The term "reseller" means a consumer reporting agency that—

(1) assembles and merges information contained in the database of another consumer reporting agency or multiple consumer reporting agencies concerning any consumer for purposes of furnishing such information to any third party, to the extent of such activities; and

(2) does not maintain a database of the assembled or merged information from which new consumer reports are produced.

(v) Commission

The term "Commission" means the Federal Trade Commission.

(w) Nationwide specialty consumer reporting agency

The term "nationwide specialty consumer reporting agency" means a consumer reporting agency that compiles and maintains files on consumers on a nationwide basis relating to—

(1) medical records or payments;

(2) residential or tenant history;

(3) check writing history;

(4) employment history; or

(5) insurance claims.

(x) Exclusion of certain communications for employee investigations

(1) Communications described in this subsection

A communication is described in this subsection if—

(A) but for subsection (d)(2)(D) of this section, the communication would be a consumer report;

(B) the communication is made to an employer in connection with an investigation of—

(i) suspected misconduct relating to employment; or

(ii) compliance with Federal, State, or local laws and regulations, the rules of a self-regulatory organization, or any preexisting written policies of the employer;

(C) the communication is not made for the purpose of investigating a consumer's credit worthiness, credit standing, or credit capacity; and

(D) the communication is not provided to any person except—

(i) to the employer or an agent of the employer;

(ii) to any Federal or State officer, agency, or department, or any officer, agency, or department of a unit of general local government;

(iii) to any self-regulatory organization with regulatory authority over the activities of the employer or employee;

(iv) as otherwise required by law; or

(v) pursuant to section 608.

(2) Subsequent disclosure

After taking any adverse action based in whole or in part on a communication described in paragraph (1), the employer shall disclose to the consumer a summary containing the nature and substance of the communication upon which the adverse action is based, except that the sources of information acquired solely for use in preparing what would be but for subsection (d)(2)(D) of this section an investigative consumer report need not be disclosed.

(3) Self-regulatory organization defined

For purposes of this subsection, the term "self-regulatory organization" includes any self-regulatory organization (as defined in section 78c(a)(26) of this title), any entity established under title I of the Sarbanes–Oxley Act of 2002, any board of trade designated by the Commodity Futures Trading Commission, and any futures association registered with such Commission.

§ 604. Permissible purposes of consumer reports [15 U.S.C. § 1681b]

(a) **In general**.—Subject to subsection (c) of this section, any consumer reporting agency may furnish a consumer report under the following circumstances and no other:

(1) In response to the order of a court having jurisdiction to issue such an order, or a subpoena issued in connection with proceedings before a Federal grand jury.

(2) In accordance with the written instructions of the consumer to whom it relates.

(3) To a person which it has reason to believe—

(A) intends to use the information in connection with a credit transaction involving the consumer on whom the information is to be furnished and involving the extension of credit to, or review or collection of an account of, the consumer; or

(B) intends to use the information for employment purposes; or

(C) intends to use the information in connection with the underwriting of insurance involving the consumer; or

(D) intends to use the information in connection with a determination of the consumer's eligibility for a license or other benefit granted by a governmental instrumentality required by law to consider an applicant's financial responsibility or status; or

(E) intends to use the information, as a potential investor or servicer, or current insurer, in connection with a valuation of, or an assessment of the credit or prepayment risks associated with, an existing credit obligation; or

(F) otherwise has a legitimate business need for the information—

(i) in connection with a business transaction that is initiated by the consumer; or

(ii) to review an account to determine whether the consumer continues to meet the terms of the account.

(G) executive departments and agencies in connection with the issuance of government-sponsored individually-billed travel charge cards.

(4) In response to a request by the head of a State or local child support enforcement agency (or a State or local government official authorized by the head of such an agency), if the person making the request certifies to the consumer reporting agency that—

(A) the consumer report is needed for the purpose of establishing an individual's capacity to make child support payments or determining the appropriate level of such payments;

(B) the paternity of the consumer for the child to which the obligation relates has been established or acknowledged by the consumer in accordance with State laws under which the obligation arises (if required by those laws);

(C) the person has provided at least 10 days' prior notice to the consumer whose report is requested, by certified or registered mail to the last known address of the consumer, that the report will be requested; and

(D) the consumer report will be kept confidential, will be used solely for a purpose described in subparagraph (A), and will not be used in connection with any other civil, administrative, or criminal proceeding, or for any other purpose.

(5) To an agency administering a State plan under section 654 of Title 42 for use to set an initial or modified child support award.

(6) To the Federal Deposit Insurance Corporation or the National Credit Union Administration as part of its preparation for its appointment or as part of its exercise of powers, as conservator, receiver, or liquidating agent for an insured depository institution or insured credit union under the Federal Deposit Insurance Act or the Federal Credit Union Act, or other applicable Federal or State law, or in connection with the resolution or liquidation of a failed or failing insured depository institution or insured credit union, as applicable.

(b) Conditions for furnishing and using consumer reports for employment purposes.—

(1) Certification from user.—A consumer reporting agency may furnish a consumer report for employment purposes only if—

(A) the person who obtains such report from the agency certifies to the agency that—

(i) the person has complied with paragraph (2) with respect to the consumer report, and the person will comply with paragraph (3) with respect to the consumer report if paragraph (3) becomes applicable; and

(ii) information from the consumer report will not be used in violation of any applicable Federal or State equal employment opportunity law or regulation; and

(B) the consumer reporting agency provides with the report, or has previously provided, a summary of the consumer's rights under this subchapter, as prescribed by the Federal Trade Commission under section 609(c)(3).

(2) Disclosure to consumer.—

(A) In general.—Except as provided in subparagraph (B), a person may not procure a consumer report, or cause a consumer report to be procured, for employment purposes with respect to any consumer, unless—

(i) a clear and conspicuous disclosure has been made in writing to the consumer at any time before the report is procured or caused to be procured, in a document that consists solely of the disclosure, that a consumer report may be obtained for employment purposes; and

(ii) the consumer has authorized in writing (which authorization may be made on the document referred to in clause (i)) the procurement of the report by that person.

(B) Application by mail, telephone, computer, or other similar means.—If a consumer described in subparagraph (C) applies for employment by mail, telephone, computer, or other similar means, at any time before a consumer report is procured or caused to be procured in connection with that application—

(i) the person who procures the consumer report on the consumer for employment purposes shall provide to the consumer, by oral, written, or electronic means, notice that a consumer's report may be obtained for employment purposes, and a summary of the consumer's rights under section 615(a)(3); and

(ii) the consumer shall have consented, orally, in writing, or electronically to the procurement of the report by that person.

(C) Scope.—Subparagraph (B) shall apply to a person procuring a consumer report on a consumer in connection with the consumer's application for employment only if—

(i) the consumer is applying for a position over which the Secretary of Transportation has the power to establish qualifications and maximum hours of service pursuant to the provisions of section 31502 of title 49, or a position subject to safety regulation by a State transportation agency; and

(ii) as of the time at which the person procures the report or causes the report to be procured the only interaction between the consumer and the person in connection with that employment application has been by mail, telephone, computer, or other similar means.

(3) Conditions on use for adverse actions.—

(A) In general.—Except as provided in subparagraph (B), in using a consumer report for employment purposes, before taking any adverse action based in whole or in part on the report, the person intending to take such action shall provide to the consumer to whom the report relates—

(i) a copy of the report; and

(ii) a description in writing of the rights of the consumer under this title, as prescribed by the Federal Trade Commission under section 609(c)(3).

(B) Application by mail, telephone, computer, or other similar means.—

(i) If a consumer described in subparagraph (C) applies for employment by mail, telephone, computer, or other similar means, and if a person who has procured a consumer report on the consumer for employment purposes takes adverse action on the employment application based in whole or in part on the report, then the person must provide to the consumer to whom the report relates, in lieu of the notices required under subparagraph (A) of this section and under section 615(a), within 3 business days of taking such action, an oral, written or electronic notification—

(I) that adverse action has been taken based in whole or in part on a consumer report received from a consumer reporting agency;

(II) of the name, address and telephone number of the consumer reporting agency that furnished the consumer report (including a toll-free telephone number established by the agency if the agency complies and maintains files on consumers on a nationwide basis);

(III) that the consumer reporting agency did not make the decision to take the adverse action and is unable to provide to the consumer the specific reasons why the adverse action was taken; and

(IV) that the consumer may, upon providing proper identification, request a free copy of a report and may dispute with the consumer reporting agency the accuracy or completeness of any information in a report.

(ii) If, under clause (B)(i)(IV), the consumer requests a copy of a consumer report from the person who procured the report, then, within 3 business days of receiving the consumer's request, together with proper identification, the person must send or provide to the consumer a copy of a report and a copy of the consumer's rights as prescribed by the Federal Trade Commission under section 609(c)(3).

(C) Scope.—Subparagraph (B) shall apply to a person procuring a consumer report on a consumer in connection with the consumer's application for employment only if—

(i) the consumer is applying for a position over which the Secretary of Transportation has the power to establish qualifications and maximum hours of service pursuant to the provisions of section 31502 title 49, or a position subject to safety regulation by a State transportation agency; and

(ii) as of the time at which the person procures the report or causes the report to be procured the only interaction between the consumer and the person in connection with that employment application has been by mail, telephone, computer, or other similar means.

(4) Exception for national security investigations.—

(A) In general.—In the case of an agency or department of the United States Government which seeks to obtain and use a consumer report for employment purposes, paragraph (3) shall not apply to any adverse action by such agency or department which is based in part on such consumer report, if the head of such agency or department makes a written finding that—

(i) the consumer report is relevant to a national security investigation of such agency or department;

(ii) the investigation is within the jurisdiction of such agency or department;

(iii) there is reason to believe that compliance with paragraph (3) will—

(I) endanger the life or physical safety of any person;

(II) result in flight from prosecution;

(III) result in the destruction of, or tampering with, evidence relevant to the investigation;

(IV) result in the intimidation of a potential witness relevant to the investigation;

(V) result in the compromise of classified information; or

(VI) otherwise seriously jeopardize or unduly delay the investigation or another official proceeding.

(B) Notification of consumer upon conclusion of investigation.—Upon the conclusion of a national security investigation described in subparagraph (A), or upon the determination that the exception under subparagraph (A) is no longer required for the reasons set forth in such subparagraph, the official exercising the authority in such subparagraph shall provide to the consumer who is the subject of the consumer report with regard to which such finding was made—

(i) a copy of such consumer report with any classified information redacted as necessary;

(ii) notice of any adverse action which is based, in part, on the consumer report; and

(iii) the identification with reasonable specificity of the nature of the investigation for which the consumer report was sought.

(C) Delegation by head of agency or department.—For purposes of subparagraphs (A) and (B), the head of any agency or department of the United States Government may delegate his or her authorities under this paragraph to an official of such agency or department who has personnel security responsibilities and is a member of the Senior Executive Service or equivalent civilian or military rank.

(D) Definitions.—For purposes of this paragraph, the following definitions shall apply:

(i) Classified information.—The term "classified information" means information that is protected from unauthorized disclosure under Executive Order No. 12958 or successor orders.

(ii) National security investigation.—The term "national security investigation" means any official inquiry by an agency or department of the United States Government to determine the eligibility of a consumer to receive access or continued access to classified information or to determine whether classified information has been lost or compromised.

(c) Furnishing reports in connection with credit or insurance transactions that are not initiated by the consumer.—

(1) In general.—A consumer reporting agency may furnish a consumer report relating to any consumer pursuant to subparagraph (A) or (C) of subsection (a)(3) of this section in connection with any credit or insurance transaction that is not initiated by the consumer only if—

(A) the consumer authorizes the agency to provide such report to such person; or

(B)(i) the transaction consists of a firm offer of credit or insurance;

(ii) the consumer reporting agency has complied with subsection (e) of this section; and

(iii) there is not in effect an election by the consumer, made in accordance with subsection (e) of this section, to have the consumer's name and address excluded from lists of names provided by the agency pursuant to this paragraph.

(2) Limits on information received under paragraph (1)(B).—A person may receive pursuant to paragraph (1)(B) only—

(A) the name and address of a consumer;

(B) an identifier that is not unique to the consumer and that is used by the person solely for the purpose of verifying the identity of the consumer; and

(C) other information pertaining to a consumer that does not identify the relationship or experience of the consumer with respect to a particular creditor or other entity.

(3) Information regarding inquiries.—Except as provided in section 609(a)(5), a consumer reporting agency shall not furnish to any person a record of inquiries in connection with a credit or insurance transaction that is not initiated by a consumer.

(d) Reserved

(e) Election of consumer to be excluded from lists.—

(1) In general.—A consumer may elect to have the consumer's name and address excluded from any list provided by a consumer reporting agency under subsection (c)(1)(B) of this section in connection with a credit or insurance transaction that is not initiated by the consumer, by notifying the agency in accordance with paragraph (2) that the consumer does not consent to any use of a consumer report relating to the consumer in connection with any credit or insurance transaction that is not initiated by the consumer.

(2) Manner of notification.—A consumer shall notify a consumer reporting agency under paragraph (1)—

(A) through the notification system maintained by the agency under paragraph (5); or

(B) by submitting to the agency a signed notice of election form issued by the agency for purposes of this subparagraph.

(3) Response of agency after notification through system.— Upon receipt of notification of the election of a consumer under paragraph (1) through the notification system maintained by the agency under paragraph (5), a consumer reporting agency shall—

(A) inform the consumer that the election is effective only for the 5–year period following the election if the consumer does not submit to the agency a signed notice of election form issued by the agency for purposes of paragraph (2)(B); and

(B) provide to the consumer a notice of election form, if requested by the consumer, not later than 5 business days after receipt of the notification of the election through the system established under paragraph (5), in the case of a request made at the time the consumer provides notification through the system.

(4) Effectiveness of election.—An election of a consumer under paragraph (1)—

(A) shall be effective with respect to a consumer reporting agency beginning 5 business days after the date on which the consumer notifies the agency in accordance with paragraph (2);

(B) shall be effective with respect to a consumer reporting agency—

(i) subject to subparagraph (C), during the 5–year period beginning 5 business days after the date on which the consumer notifies the agency of the election, in the case of an election for which a consumer notifies the agency only in accordance with paragraph (2)(A); or

(ii) until the consumer notifies the agency under subparagraph (C), in the case of an election for which a consumer notifies the agency in accordance with paragraph (2)(B);

(C) shall not be effective after the date on which the consumer notifies the agency, through the notification system established by the agency under paragraph (5), that the election is no longer effective; and

(D) shall be effective with respect to each affiliate of the agency.

(5) Notification system.—

(A) In general.—Each consumer reporting agency that, under subsection (c)(1)(B) of this section, furnishes a consumer report in connection with a credit or insurance transaction that is not initiated by a consumer, shall—

(i) establish and maintain a notification system, including a toll-free telephone number, which permits any consumer whose consumer report is maintained by the agency to notify the agency, with appropriate identification, of the consumer's election to have the consumer's name and address excluded from any such list of names and addresses provided by the agency for such a transaction; and

(ii) publish by not later than 365 days after September 30, 1996, and not less than annually thereafter, in a publication of general circulation in the area served by the agency—

(I) a notification that information in consumer files maintained by the agency may be used in connection with such transactions; and

(II) the address and toll-free telephone number for consumers to use to notify the agency of the consumer's election under clause (i).

(B) Establishment and maintenance as compliance.—Establishment and maintenance of a notification system (including a toll-free telephone number) and publication by a consumer reporting agency on the agency's own behalf and on behalf of any of its affiliates in accordance with this paragraph is deemed to be compliance with this paragraph by each of those affiliates.

(6) Notification system by agencies that operate nationwide.—Each consumer reporting agency that compiles and maintains files on consumers on a nationwide basis shall establish and maintain a notification system for purposes of paragraph (5) jointly with other such consumer reporting agencies.

(f) Certain use or obtaining of information prohibited.—A person shall not use or obtain a consumer report for any purpose unless—

(1) the consumer report is obtained for a purpose for which the consumer report is authorized to be furnished under this section; and

(2) the purpose is certified in accordance with section 607 by a prospective user of the report through a general or specific certification.

(g) Protection of medical information

(1) Limitation on consumer reporting agencies

A consumer reporting agency shall not furnish for employment purposes, or in connection with a credit or insurance transaction, a consumer report that contains medical information (other than medical contact information treated in the manner required under section 605(a)(6) of this title) about a consumer, unless—

(A) if furnished in connection with an insurance transaction, the consumer affirmatively consents to the furnishing of the report;

(B) if furnished for employment purposes or in connection with a credit transaction—

(i) the information to be furnished is relevant to process or effect the employment or credit transaction; and

(ii) the consumer provides specific written consent for the furnishing of the report that describes in clear and conspicuous language the use for which the information will be furnished; or

(C) the information to be furnished pertains solely to transactions, accounts, or balances relating to debts arising from the receipt of medical services, products, or devises, where such information, other than account status or amounts, is restricted or reported using codes that do not identify, or do not provide information sufficient to infer, the specific provider or the nature of such services, products, or devices, as provided in section 605(a)(6).

(2) Limitation on creditors

Except as permitted pursuant to paragraph (3)(C) or regulations prescribed under paragraph (5)(A), a creditor shall not obtain or use medical information (other than medical information treated in the manner required under section 605(a)(6)) pertaining to a consumer in connection with any determination of the consumer's eligibility, or continued eligibility, for credit.

§ 605. Requirements relating to information contained in consumer reports [15 U.S.C. § 1681c]

(a) Information excluded from consumer reports.—Prohibited items

Except as authorized under subsection (b) of this section, no consumer reporting agency may make any consumer report containing any of the following items of information:

(1) Cases under Title 11 or under the Bankruptcy Act that, from the date of entry of the order for relief or the date of adjudication, as the case may be, antedate the report by more than 10 years.

(2) Civil suits, civil judgments, and records of arrest that, from date of entry, antedate the report by more than seven years or until the governing statute of limitations has expired, whichever is the longer period.

(3) Paid tax liens which, from date of payment, antedate the report by more than seven years.

(4) Accounts placed for collection or charged to profit and loss which antedate the report by more than seven years.

(5) Any other adverse item of information; other than records of convictions of crimes, which antedates the report by more than seven years.

(6) The name, address, and telephone number of any medical information furnisher that has notified the agency of its status, unless—

    (A) such name, address, and telephone number are restricted or reported using codes that do not identify, or provide information sufficient to infer, the specific provider or the nature of such services, products, or devices to a person other than the consumer; or

    (B) the report is being provided to an insurance company for a purpose relating to engaging in the business of insurance other than property and casualty insurance.

(b) Exempted cases

The provisions of paragraphs (1) through (5) of subsection (a) of this section are not applicable in the case of any consumer credit report to be used in connection with—

(1) a credit transaction involving, or which may reasonably be expected to involve, a principal amount of $150,000 or more;

(2) the underwriting of life insurance involving, or which may reasonably be expected to involve, a face amount of $150,000 or more; or

(3) the employment of any individual at an annual salary which equals, or which may reasonably be expected to equal 75,000, or more.

(c) Running of reporting period

(1) In general.—The 7–year period referred to in paragraphs (4) and (5) of subsection (a) of this section shall begin, with respect to any delinquent account that is placed for collection (internally or by referral to a third party, whichever is earlier), charged to profit and loss, or subjected to any similar action, upon the expiration of the 180–day period beginning on the date of the commencement of the delinquency which immediately preceded the collection activity, charge to profit and loss, or similar action.

(2) Effective date.—Paragraph (1) shall apply only to items of information added to the file of a consumer on or after the date that is 455 days after September 30, 1996.

(d) Information required to be disclosed

(1) Title 11 information

Any consumer reporting agency that furnishes a consumer report that contains information regarding any case involving the consumer that arises under Title 11, shall include in the report an identification of the chapter of such Title 11 under which such case arises if provided by the source of the information. If any case arising or filed under Title 11, is withdrawn by the consumer before a final judgment, the consumer reporting agency shall include in the report that such case or filing was withdrawn upon receipt of documentation certifying such withdrawal.

(2) Key factor in credit score information

Any consumer reporting agency that furnishes a consumer report that contains any credit score or any other risk score or predictor on any consumer shall include in the report a clear and conspicuous statement that a key factor (as defined in section 609(f)(2)(B)) that adversely affected such score or predictor was the number of enquiries, if such a predictor was in fact a key factor that adversely affected such score. This paragraph shall not apply to a check services company, acting as such, which issues authorizations for the purpose of approving or processing negotiable instruments, electronic fund transfers, or similar methods of payments, but only to the extent that such company is engaged in such activities.

(e) Indication of closure of account by consumer

If a consumer reporting agency is notified pursuant to section 623(a)(4) that a credit account of a consumer was voluntarily closed by the consumer, the agency shall indicate that fact in any consumer report that includes information related to the account.

(f) Indication of dispute by consumer

If a consumer reporting agency is notified pursuant to section 623(a)(3) that information regarding a consumer who was furnished to the agency is disputed by the consumer, the agency shall indicate that fact in each consumer report that includes the disputed information.

(g) Truncation of credit card and debit card numbers

(1) In general

Except as otherwise provided in this subsection, no person that accepts credit cards or debit cards for the transaction of business shall print more than the last 5 digits of the card number or the expiration date upon any receipt provided to the cardholder at the point of the sale or transaction.

(2) Limitation

This subsection shall apply only to receipts that are electronically printed, and shall not apply to transactions in which the sole means of recording a credit card or debit card account number is by handwriting or by an imprint or copy of the card.

(3) Effective date

This subsection shall become effective—

(A) 3 years after December 4, 2003, with respect to any cash register or other machine or device that electronically prints receipts for credit card or debit card transactions that is in use before January 1, 2005; and

(B) 1 year after December 4, 2003, with respect to any cash register or other machine or device that electronically prints receipts for credit card or debit card transactions that is first put into use on or after January 1, 2005.

(h) Notice of discrepancy in address

(1) In general

If a person has requested a consumer report relating to a consumer from a consumer reporting agency described in section 603(p), the request includes an address for the consumer that substantially differs from the addresses in the file of the consumer, and the agency provides a consumer report in response to the request, the consumer reporting agency shall notify the requester of the existence of the discrepancy.

(2) Regulations

(A) Regulations required

The Federal banking agencies, the National Credit Union Administration, and the Commission shall jointly, with respect to the entities that are subject to their respective enforcement authority under section 621, prescribe regulations providing guidance regarding reasonable policies and procedures that a user of a consumer report should employ when such user has received a notice of discrepancy under paragraph (1).

(B) Policies and procedures to be included

The regulations prescribed under subparagraph (A) shall describe reasonable policies and procedures for use by a user of a consumer report—

(i) to form a reasonable belief that the user knows the identity of the person to whom the consumer report pertains; and

(ii) if the user establishes a continuing relationship with the consumer, and the user regularly and in the ordinary course of business furnishes information to the consumer reporting agency from which the notice of discrepancy pertaining to the consumer was obtained, to reconcile the address of the consumer with the consumer reporting agency by furnishing such address to such consumer reporting agency as part of information regularly furnished by the user for the period in which the relationship is established.

§ 605A. Identity theft prevention; fraud alerts and active duty alerts [15 U.S.C. § 1681c–1]

(a) One-call fraud alerts

(1) Initial alerts

Upon the direct request of a consumer, or an individual acting on behalf of or as a personal representative of a consumer, who asserts in good faith a suspicion that the consumer has been or is about to become a victim of fraud or related crime, including identity theft, a consumer reporting agency described in section 603(p) that maintains a file on the consumer and has received appropriate proof of the identity of the requester shall—

(A) include a fraud alert in the file of that consumer, and also provide that alert along with any credit score generated in using that file, for a period of not less than 90 days, beginning on the date of such request, unless the consumer or such representative requests that such fraud alert be removed before the end of such period, and the agency has received appropriate proof of the identity of the requester for such purpose; and

(B) refer the information regarding the fraud alert under this paragraph to each of the other consumer reporting agencies described in section 603(p), in accordance with procedures developed under section 621(f).

(2) Access to free reports

In any case in which a consumer reporting agency includes a fraud alert in the file of a consumer pursuant to this subsection, the consumer reporting agency shall—

(A) disclose to the consumer that the consumer may request a free copy of the file of the consumer pursuant to section 612(d); and

(B) provide to the consumer all disclosures required to be made under section 603, without charge to the consumer, not later than 3 business days after any request described in subparagraph (A).

(b) Extended alerts

(1) In general

Upon the direct request of a consumer, or an individual acting on behalf of or as a personal representative of a consumer, who submits an identity theft report to a consumer reporting agency described in section 603(p) of this title that maintains a file on the consumer, if the agency has received appropriate proof of the identity of the requester, the agency shall—

(A) include a fraud alert in the file of that consumer, and also provide that alert along with any credit score generated in using that file, during the 7–year period beginning on the date of such request, unless the consumer or such representative requests that such fraud alert be removed before the end of such period and the agency has received appropriate proof of the identity of the requester for such purpose;

(B) during the 5–year period beginning on the date of such request, exclude the consumer from any list of consumers prepared by the consumer reporting agency and provided to any third party to offer credit or insurance to the consumer as part of a transaction that was not initiated by the consumer, unless the consumer or such representative requests that such exclusion be rescinded before the end of such period; and

(C) refer the information regarding the extended fraud alert under this paragraph to each of the other consumer reporting agencies described in section 603(p), in accordance with procedures developed under section 621(f).

(2) Access to free reports

In any case in which a consumer reporting agency includes a fraud alert in the file of a consumer pursuant to this subsection, the consumer reporting agency shall—

(A) disclose to the consumer that the consumer may request 2 free copies of the file of the consumer pursuant to section 612(d) of this title during the 12–month period beginning on the date on which the fraud alert was included in the file; and

(B) provide to the consumer all disclosures required to be made under section 609, without charge to the consumer, not later than 3 business days after any request described in subparagraph (A).

(c) Active duty alerts

Upon the direct request of an active duty military consumer, or an individual acting on behalf of or as a personal representative of an active duty military consumer, a consumer reporting agency described in section 603(p) that maintains a file on the active duty military consumer and has received appropriate proof of the identity of the requester shall—

(1) include an active duty alert in the file of that active duty military consumer, and also provide that alert along with any credit score generated in using that file, during a period of not less than 12 months, or such longer period as the Commission shall determine, by regulation, beginning on the date of the request, unless the active duty military consumer or such representative requests that such fraud alert be removed before the end of such period, and the agency has received appropriate proof of the identity of the requester for such purpose;

(2) during the 2–year period beginning on the date of such request, exclude the active duty military consumer from any list of consumers prepared by the consumer reporting agency and provided to any third party to offer credit or insurance to the consumer as part of a transaction that was not initiated by the consumer, unless the consumer requests that such exclusion be rescinded before the end of such period; and

(3) refer the information regarding the active duty alert to each of the other consumer reporting agencies described in section 603(p), in accordance with procedures developed under section 621(f).

(d) Procedures

Each consumer reporting agency described in section 603(p) shall establish policies and procedures to comply with this section, including procedures that inform consumers of the availability of initial, extended, and active duty alerts and procedures that allow consumers and active duty military consumers to request initial, extended, or active duty alerts (as applicable) in a simple and easy manner, including by telephone.

303

(e) Referrals of alerts

Each consumer reporting agency described in section 603(p) of this title that receives a referral of a fraud alert or active duty alert from another consumer reporting agency pursuant to this section shall, as though the agency received the request from the consumer directly, follow the procedures required under—

(1) paragraphs (1)(A) and (2) of subsection (a) of this section, in the case of a referral under subsection (a)(1)(B) of this section;

(2) paragraphs (1)(A), (1)(B), and (2) of subsection (b) of this section, in the case of a referral under subsection (b)(1)(C) of this section; and

(3) paragraphs (1) and (2) of subsection (c) of this section, in the case of a referral under subsection (c)(3) of this section.

(f) Duty of reseller to reconvey alert

A reseller shall include in its report any fraud alert or active duty alert placed in the file of a consumer pursuant to this section by another consumer reporting agency.

(g) Duty of other consumer reporting agencies to provide contact information

If a consumer contacts any consumer reporting agency that is not described in section 603(p) to communicate a suspicion that the consumer has been or is about to become a victim of fraud or related crime, including identity theft, the agency shall provide information to the consumer on how to contact the Commission and the consumer reporting agencies described in section 603(p) to obtain more detailed information and request alerts under this section.

(h) Limitations on use of information for credit extensions

(1) Requirements for initial and active duty alerts

(A) Notification

Each initial fraud alert and active duty alert under this section shall include information that notifies all prospective users of a consumer report on the consumer to which the alert relates that the consumer does not authorize the establishment of any new credit plan or extension of credit, other than under an open-end credit plan (as defined in section 103(i) of the Truth-in-Lending Act), in the name of the consumer, or issuance of an additional card on an existing credit account requested by a consumer, or any increase in credit limit on an existing credit account requested by a consumer, except in accordance with subparagraph (B).

(B) Limitation on users

(i) In general

No prospective user of a consumer report that includes an initial fraud alert or an active duty alert in accordance with this section may establish a new credit plan or extension of credit, other than under an open-end credit plan (as defined in section 103(i) of the Truth-in-Lending Act), in the name of the consumer, or issue an additional card on an existing credit account requested by a consumer, or grant any increase in credit limit on an existing credit account requested by a consumer, unless the user utilizes reasonable policies and procedures to form a reasonable belief that the user knows the identity of the person making the request.

(ii) Verification

If a consumer requesting the alert has specified a telephone number to be used for identity verification purposes, before authorizing any new credit plan or extension described in clause (i) in the name of such consumer, a user of such consumer report shall contact the consumer using that telephone number or take reasonable steps to verify the consumer's identity and confirm that the application for a new credit plan is not the result of identity theft.

(2) Requirements for extended alerts

(A) Notification

Each extended alert under this section shall include information that provides all prospective users of a consumer report relating to a consumer with—

(i) notification that the consumer does not authorize the establishment of any new credit plan or extension of credit described in clause (i), other than under an open-end credit plan (as defined in section 103(i) of the Truth-in-Lending Act), in the name of the consumer, or issuance of an additional card on an existing credit account requested by a consumer, or any increase in credit limit on an existing credit account requested by a consumer, except in accordance with subparagraph (B); and

(ii) a telephone number or other reasonable contact method designated by the consumer.

(B) Limitation on users

No prospective user of a consumer report or of a credit score generated using the information in the file of a consumer that includes an extended fraud alert in accordance with this section may establish a new credit plan or extension of credit, other than under an open-end credit plan (as defined in section 103(i) of the Truth-in-Lending Act), in the name of the consumer, or issue an additional card on an existing credit account requested by a consumer, or any increase in credit limit on an existing credit account requested by a consumer, unless the user contacts the consumer in person or using the contact method described in subparagraph (A)(ii) to confirm that the application for a new credit plan or increase in credit limit, or request for an additional card is not the result of identity theft.

§ 605B. Block of information resulting from identity theft [15 U.S.C. § 1681c–2]

(a) Block

Except as otherwise provided in this section, a consumer reporting agency shall block the reporting of any information in the file of a consumer that the consumer identifies as information that resulted from an alleged identity theft, not later than 4 business days after the date of receipt by such agency of—

(1) appropriate proof of the identity of the consumer;

(2) a copy of an identity theft report;

(3) the identification of such information by the consumer; and

(4) a statement by the consumer that the information is not information relating to any transaction by the consumer.

(b) Notification

A consumer reporting agency shall promptly notify the furnisher of information identified by the consumer under subsection (a) of this section—

(1) that the information may be a result of identity theft;

(2) that an identity theft report has been filed;

(3) that a block has been requested under this section; and

(4) of the effective dates of the block.

(c) Authority to decline or rescind

(1) In general

A consumer reporting agency may decline to block, or may rescind any block, of information relating to a consumer under this section, if the consumer reporting agency reasonably determines that—

(A) the information was blocked in error or a block was requested by the consumer in error;

(B) the information was blocked, or a block was requested by the consumer, on the basis of a material misrepresentation of fact by the consumer relevant to the request to block; or

(C) the consumer obtained possession of goods, services, or money as a result of the blocked transaction or transactions.

(2) Notification to consumer

If a block of information is declined or rescinded under this subsection, the affected consumer shall be notified promptly, in the same manner as consumers are notified of the reinsertion of information under section 611(a)(5)(B).

(3) Significance of block

For purposes of this subsection, if a consumer reporting agency rescinds a block, the presence of information in the file of a consumer prior to the blocking of such information is not evidence of whether the consumer knew or should have known that the consumer obtained possession of any goods, services, or money as a result of the block.

(d) Exception for resellers

(1) No reseller file

This section shall not apply to a consumer reporting agency, if the consumer reporting agency—

(A) is a reseller;

(B) is not, at the time of the request of the consumer under subsection (a) of this section, otherwise furnishing or reselling a consumer report concerning the information identified by the consumer; and

(C) informs the consumer, by any means, that the consumer may report the identity theft to the Commission to obtain consumer information regarding identity theft.

(2) Reseller with file

The sole obligation of the consumer reporting agency under this section, with regard to any request of a consumer under this section, shall be to block the consumer report maintained by the consumer reporting agency from any subsequent use, if—

(A) the consumer, in accordance with the provisions of subsection (a) of this section, identifies, to a consumer reporting agency, information in the file of the consumer that resulted from identity theft; and

(B) the consumer reporting agency is a reseller of the identified information.

(3) Notice

In carrying out its obligation under paragraph (2), the reseller shall promptly provide a notice to the consumer of the decision to block the file. Such notice shall contain the name, address, and telephone number of each consumer reporting agency from which the consumer information was obtained for resale.

(e) Exception for verification companies

The provisions of this section do not apply to a check services company, acting as such, which issues authorizations for the purpose of approving or processing negotiable instruments, electronic fund transfers, or similar methods of payments, except that, beginning 4 business days after receipt of information described in paragraphs (1) through (3) of subsection (a) of this section, a check services company shall not report to a national consumer reporting agency described in section 603(p) of this title, any information identified in the subject identity theft report as resulting from identity theft.

(f) Access to blocked information by law enforcement agencies

No provision of this section shall be construed as requiring a consumer reporting agency to prevent a Federal, State, or local law enforcement agency from accessing blocked information in a consumer file to which the agency could otherwise obtain access under this title.

§ 606. Disclosure of investigative consumer reports [15 U.S.C. § 1681d]

(a) Disclosure of fact of preparation

A person may not procure or cause to be prepared an investigative consumer report on any consumer unless—

(1) it is clearly and accurately disclosed to the consumer that an investigative consumer report including information as to his character, general reputation, personal characteristics, and mode of living, whichever are applicable, may be made, and such disclosure (A) is made in a writing mailed, or otherwise delivered, to the consumer, not later than three days after the date on which the report was first requested, and (B) includes a statement informing the consumer of his right to request the additional disclosures provided for under subsection (b) of this section and the written summary of the rights of the consumer prepared pursuant to section 609(c); and

(2) the person certifies or has certified to the consumer reporting agency that—

    (A) the person has made the disclosures to the consumer required by paragraph (1); and

    (B) the person will comply with subsection (b) of this section.

(b) Disclosure on request of nature and scope of investigation

Any person who procures or causes to be prepared an investigative consumer report on any consumer shall, upon written request made by the consumer within a reasonable period of time after the receipt by him of the disclosure required by subsection (a)(1) of this section, make a complete and accurate disclosure of the nature and scope of the investigation requested. This disclosure shall be made in a writing mailed, or otherwise delivered, to the consumer not later than five days after the date on which the request for such disclosure was received from the consumer or such report was first requested, whichever is the later.

(c) Limitation on liability upon showing of reasonable procedures for compliance with provisions

No person may be held liable for any violation of subsection (a) or (b) of this section if he shows by a preponderance of the evidence that at the time of the violation he maintained reasonable procedures to assure compliance with subsection (a) or (b) of this section.

(d) Prohibitions

(1) Certification.—A consumer reporting agency shall not prepare or furnish an investigative consumer report unless the agency has received a certification under subsection (a)(2) of this section from the person who requested the report.

(2) Inquiries.—A consumer reporting agency shall not make an inquiry for the purpose of preparing an investigative consumer report on a consumer for employment purposes if the making of the inquiry by an employer or prospective employer of the consumer would violate any applicable Federal or State equal employment opportunity law or regulation.

(3) Certain public record information.—Except as otherwise provided in section 613, a consumer reporting agency shall not furnish an investigative consumer report that includes information that is a matter of public record and that relates to an arrest, indictment, conviction, civil judicial action, tax lien, or outstanding judgment, unless the agency has verified the accuracy of the information during the 30–day period ending on the date on which the report is furnished.

(4) Certain adverse information.—A consumer reporting agency shall not prepare or furnish an investigative consumer report on a consumer that contains information that is adverse to the interest of the consumer and that is obtained through a personal interview with a neighbor, friend, or associate of the consumer or with another person with whom the consumer is acquainted or who has knowledge of such item of information, unless—

(A) the agency has followed reasonable procedures to obtain confirmation of the information, from an additional source that has independent and direct knowledge of the information; or

(B) the person interviewed is the best possible source of the information.

§ 607. Compliance procedures [15 U.S.C. § 1681e]

(a) Identity and purposes of credit users

Every consumer reporting agency shall maintain reasonable procedures designed to avoid violations of section 605 and to limit the furnishing of consumer reports to the purposes listed under section 604. These procedures shall require that prospective users of the information identify themselves, certify the purposes for which the information is sought, and certify that the information will be used for no other purpose. Every consumer reporting agency shall make a reasonable effort to verify the identity of a new prospective user and the uses certified by such prospective user prior to furnishing such user a consumer report. No consumer reporting agency may furnish a consumer report to any person if it has reasonable grounds for believing that the consumer report will not be used for a purpose listed in section 604.

(b) Accuracy of report

Whenever a consumer reporting agency prepares a consumer report it shall follow reasonable procedures to assure maximum possible accuracy of the information concerning the individual about whom the report relates.

(c) Disclosure of consumer reports by users allowed

A consumer reporting agency may not prohibit a user of a consumer report furnished by the agency on a consumer from disclosing the contents of the report to the consumer, if adverse action against the consumer has been taken by the user based in whole or in part on the report.

(d) Notice to users and furnishers of information

(1) Notice requirement.—A consumer reporting agency shall provide to any person—

> (A) who regularly and in the ordinary course of business furnishes information to the agency with respect to any consumer; or

> (B) to whom a consumer report is provided by the agency;

a notice of such person's responsibilities under this subchapter.

(2) Content of notice.—The Federal Trade Commission shall prescribe the content of notices under paragraph (1), and a consumer reporting agency shall be in compliance with this subsection if it provides a notice under paragraph (1) that is substantially similar to the Federal Trade Commission prescription under this paragraph.

(e) Procurement of consumer report for resale

(1) Disclosure.—A person may not procure a consumer report for purposes of reselling the report (or any information in the report) unless the person discloses to the consumer reporting agency that originally furnishes the report—

> (A) the identity of the end-user of the report (or information); and

> (B) each permissible purpose under section 604 for which the report is furnished to the end-user of the report (or information).

(2) Responsibilities of procurers for resale.—A person who procures a consumer report for purposes of reselling the report (or any information in the report) shall—

> (A) establish and comply with reasonable procedures designed to ensure that the report (or information) is resold by the person only for a purpose for which the report may be furnished under section 604, including by requiring that each person to which the report (or information) is resold and that resells or provides the report (or information) to any other person—

(i) identifies each end user of the resold report (or information);

(ii) certifies each purpose for which the report (or information) will be used; and

(iii) certifies that the report (or information) will be used for no other purpose; and

(B) before reselling the report, make reasonable efforts to verify the identifications and certifications made under subparagraph (A).

(3) Resale of consumer report to a federal agency or department.— Notwithstanding paragraph (1) or (2), a person who procures a consumer report for purposes of reselling the report (or any information in the report) shall not disclose the identity of the end-user of the report under paragraph (1) or (2) if—

(A) the end user is an agency or department of the United States Government which procures the report from the person for purposes of determining the eligibility of the consumer concerned to receive access or continued access to classified information (as defined in section 604(b)(4)(E)(i)); and

(B) the agency or department certifies in writing to the person reselling the report that nondisclosure is necessary to protect classified information or the safety of persons employed by or contracting with, or undergoing investigation for work or contracting with the agency or department.

§ 608. Disclosures to governmental agencies [15 U.S.C. § 1681f]

Notwithstanding the provisions of section 604, a consumer reporting agency may furnish identifying information respecting any consumer, limited to his name, address, former addresses, places of employment, or former places of employment, to a governmental agency.

§ 609. Disclosures to consumers [15 U.S.C. § 1681g]

(a) Information on file; sources; report recipients

Every consumer reporting agency shall, upon request, and subject to section 610(a)(1), clearly and accurately disclose to the consumer:

(1) All information in the consumer's file at the time of the request, except that—

(A) if the consumer to whom the file relates requests that the first 5 digits of the social security number (or similar identification number) of the consumer not be included in the disclosure and the consumer reporting agency has received appropriate proof of the identity of the requester, the consumer reporting agency shall so truncate such number in such disclosure; and

(B) nothing in this paragraph shall be construed to require a consumer reporting agency to disclose to a consumer any information concerning credit scores or any other risk scores or predictors relating to the consumer.

(2) The sources of the information; except that the sources of information acquired solely for use in preparing an investigative consumer report and actually used for no other purpose need not be disclosed: *Provided,* That in the event an action is brought under this subchapter, such sources shall be available to the plaintiff under appropriate discovery procedures in the court in which the action is brought.

(3)(A) Identification of each person (including each end-user identified under section 607(e)(1)) that procured a consumer report—

(i) for employment purposes, during the 2–year period preceding the date on which the request is made; or

(ii) for any other purpose, during the 1–year period preceding the date on which the request is made.

(B) An identification of a person under subparagraph (A) shall include—

(i) the name of the person or, if applicable, the trade name (written in full) under which such person conducts business; and

(ii) upon request of the consumer, the address and telephone number of the person.

(C) Subparagraph (A) does not apply if—

(i) the end user is an agency or department of the United States Government that procures the report from the person for purposes of determining the eligibility of the consumer to whom the report relates to receive access or continued access to classified information (as defined in section 604(b)(4)(E)(i)); and

(ii) the head of the agency or department makes a written finding as prescribed under section 604(b)(4)(A).

(4) The dates, original payees, and amounts of any checks upon which is based any adverse characterization of the consumer, included in the file at the time of the disclosure.

(5) A record of all inquiries received by the agency during the 1–year period preceding the request that identified the consumer in connection with a credit or insurance transaction that was not initiated by the consumer.

(6) If the consumer requests the credit file and not the credit score, a statement that the consumer may request and obtain a credit score.

(b) Exempt information

The requirements of subsection (a) of this section respecting the disclosure of sources of information and the recipients of consumer reports do not apply to information received or consumer reports furnished prior to the effective date of this subchapter except to the extent that the matter involved is contained in the files of the consumer reporting agency on that date.

(c) Summary of rights to obtain and dispute information in consumer reports and to obtain credit scores

(1) Commission summary of rights required

(A) In general

The Commission shall prepare a model summary of the rights of consumers under this subchapter.

(B) Content of summary

The summary of rights prepared under subparagraph (A) shall include a description of—

(i) the right of a consumer to obtain a copy of a consumer report under subsection (a) of this section from each consumer reporting agency;

(ii) the frequency and circumstances under which a consumer is entitled to receive a consumer report without charge under section 612;

(iii) the right of a consumer to dispute information in the file of the consumer under section 611;

(iv) the right of a consumer to obtain a credit score from a consumer reporting agency, and a description of how to obtain a credit score;

(v) the method by which a consumer can contact, and obtain a consumer report from, a consumer reporting agency without charge, as provided in the regulations of the Commission prescribed under section 211(c) of the Fair and Accurate Credit Transactions Act of 2003; and

(vi) the method by which a consumer can contact, and obtain a consumer report from, a consumer reporting agency described in section 603(w) of this title, as provided in the regulations of the Commission prescribed under section 612(a)(1)(C) of this title.

(C) Availability of summary of rights

The Commission shall—

(i) actively publicize the availability of the summary of rights prepared under this paragraph;

(ii) conspicuously post on its Internet website the availability of such summary of rights; and

(iii) promptly make such summary of rights available to consumers, on request.

(2) Summary of rights required to be included with agency disclosures

A consumer reporting agency shall provide to a consumer, with each written disclosure by the agency to the consumer under this section—

(A) the summary of rights prepared by the Commission under paragraph (1);

(B) in the case of a consumer reporting agency described in section 603(p), a toll-free telephone number established by the agency, at which personnel are accessible to consumers during normal business hours;

(C) a list of all Federal agencies responsible for enforcing any provision of this subchapter, and the address and any appropriate phone number of each such agency, in a form that will assist the consumer in selecting the appropriate agency;

(D) a statement that the consumer may have additional rights under State law, and that the consumer may wish to contact a State or local consumer protection agency or a State attorney general (or the equivalent thereof) to learn of those rights; and

(E) a statement that a consumer reporting agency is not required to remove accurate derogatory information from the file of a consumer, unless the information is outdated under section 605 of this title or cannot be verified.

(d) Summary of rights of identity theft victims

(1) In general

The Commission, in consultation with the Federal banking agencies and the National Credit Union Administration, shall prepare a model summary of the rights of consumers under this subchapter with respect to the procedures for remedying the effects of fraud or identity theft involving credit, an electronic fund transfer, or an account or transaction at or with a financial institution or other creditor.

(2) Summary of rights and contact information

Beginning 60 days after the date on which the model summary of rights is prescribed in final form by the Commission pursuant to paragraph (1), if any consumer contacts a consumer reporting agency and expresses a belief that the consumer is a victim of fraud or identity theft involving credit, an electronic fund transfer, or an account or transaction at or with a financial institution or other creditor, the consumer reporting agency shall, in addition to any other action that the agency may take, provide the consumer with a summary of rights that contains all of the information required by the Commission under paragraph (1), and information on how to contact the Commission to obtain more detailed information.

(e) Information available to victims

(1) In general

For the purpose of documenting fraudulent transactions resulting from identity theft, not later than 30 days after the date of receipt of a request from a victim in accordance with paragraph (3), and subject to verification of the identity of the victim and the claim of identity theft in accordance with paragraph (2), a business entity that has provided credit to, provided for consideration products, goods, or services to, accepted payment from, or otherwise entered into a commercial transaction for consideration with, a person who has allegedly made unauthorized use of the means of identification of the victim, shall provide a copy of application and business transaction records in the control of the business entity, whether maintained by the business entity or by another person on behalf of the business entity, evidencing any transaction alleged to be a result of identity theft to—

(A) the victim;

(B) any Federal, State, or local government law enforcement agency or officer specified by the victim in such a request; or

(C) any law enforcement agency investigating the identity theft and authorized by the victim to take receipt of records provided under this subsection.

(2) Verification of identity and claim

Before a business entity provides any information under paragraph (1), unless the business entity, at its discretion, otherwise has a high degree of confidence that it knows the identity of the victim making a request under paragraph (1), the victim shall provide to the business entity—

(A) as proof of positive identification of the victim, at the election of the business entity—

(i) the presentation of a government-issued identification card;

(ii) personally identifying information of the same type as was provided to the business entity by the unauthorized person; or

(iii) personally identifying information that the business entity typically requests from new applicants or for new transactions, at the time of the victim's request for information, including any documentation described in clauses (i) and (ii); and

(B) as proof of a claim of identity theft, at the election of the business entity—

(i) a copy of a police report evidencing the claim of the victim of identity theft; and

(ii) a properly completed—

(I) copy of a standardized affidavit of identity theft developed and made available by the Commission; or

(II) affidavit of fact that is acceptable to the business entity for that purpose.

(3) Procedures

The request of a victim under paragraph (1) shall—

(A) be in writing;

(B) be mailed to an address specified by the business entity, if any; and

(C) if asked by the business entity, include relevant information about any transaction alleged to be a result of identity theft to facilitate compliance with this section including—

(i) if known by the victim (or if readily obtainable by the victim), the date of the application or transaction; and

(ii) if known by the victim (or if readily obtainable by the victim), any other identifying information such as an account or transaction number.

(4) No charge to victim

Information required to be provided under paragraph (1) shall be so provided without charge.

(5) Authority to decline to provide information

A business entity may decline to provide information under paragraph (1) if, in the exercise of good faith, the business entity determines that—

(A) this subsection does not require disclosure of the information;

(B) after reviewing the information provided pursuant to paragraph (2), the business entity does not have a high degree of confidence in knowing the true identity of the individual requesting the information;

(C) the request for the information is based on a misrepresentation of fact by the individual requesting the information relevant to the request for information; or

(D) the information requested is Internet navigational data or similar information about a person's visit to a website or online service.

(6) Limitation on liability

Except as provided in section 621, sections 616 and 617 do not apply to any violation of this subsection.

(7) Limitation on civil liability

No business entity may be held civilly liable under any provision of Federal, State, or other law for disclosure, made in good faith pursuant to this subsection.

(8) No new recordkeeping obligation

Nothing in this subsection creates an obligation on the part of a business entity to obtain, retain, or maintain information or records that are not otherwise required to be obtained, retained, or maintained in the ordinary course of its business or under other applicable law.

(9) Rule of construction

(A) In general

No provision of [the Financial Services Modernization Act of 1999], subtitle A of title V of Public Law 106–102, prohibiting the disclosure of financial information by a business entity to third parties shall be used to deny disclosure of information to the victim under this subsection.

(B) Limitation

Except as provided in subparagraph (A), nothing in this subsection permits a business entity to disclose information, including information to law enforcement under subparagraphs (B) and (C) of paragraph (1), that the business entity is otherwise prohibited from disclosing under any other applicable provision of Federal or State law.

(10) Affirmative defense

In any civil action brought to enforce this subsection, it is an affirmative defense (which the defendant must establish by a preponderance of the evidence) for a business entity to file an affidavit or answer stating that—

(A) the business entity has made a reasonably diligent search of its available business records; and

(B) the records requested under this subsection do not exist or are not reasonably available.

(11) Definition of victim

For purposes of this subsection, the term "victim" means a consumer whose means of identification or financial information has been used or transferred (or has been alleged to have been used or transferred) without the authority of that consumer, with the intent to commit, or to aid or abet, an identity theft or a similar crime.

(12) Effective date

This subsection shall become effective 180 days after December 4, 2003.

(13) Effectiveness study

Not later than 18 months after December 4, 2003, the Comptroller General of the United States shall submit a report to Congress assessing the effectiveness of this provision.

(f) Disclosure of credit scores

(1) In general

Upon the request of a consumer for a credit score, a consumer reporting agency shall supply to the consumer a statement indicating that the information and credit scoring model may be different than the credit score that may be used by the lender, and a notice which shall include—

(A) the current credit score of the consumer or the most recent credit score of the consumer that was previously calculated by the credit reporting agency for a purpose related to the extension of credit;

(B) the range of possible credit scores under the model used;

(C) all of the key factors that adversely affected the credit score of the consumer in the model used, the total number of which shall not exceed 4, subject to paragraph (9);

(D) the date on which the credit score was created; and

(E) the name of the person or entity that provided the credit score or credit file upon which the credit score was created.

(2) Definitions

For purposes of this subsection, the following definitions shall apply:

(A) Credit score

The term "credit score"—

(i) means a numerical value or a categorization derived from a statistical tool or modeling system used by a person who makes or arranges a loan to predict the likelihood of certain credit behaviors, including default (and the numerical value or the categorization derived from such analysis may also be referred to as a "risk predictor" or "risk score"); and

(ii) does not include—

(I) any mortgage score or rating of an automated underwriting system that considers one or more factors in addition to credit information, including the loan to value ratio, the amount of down payment, or the financial assets of a consumer; or

(II) any other elements of the underwriting process or underwriting decision.

(B) Key factors

The term "key factors" means all relevant elements or reasons adversely affecting the credit score for the particular individual, listed in the order of their importance based on their effect on the credit score.

(3) Timeframe and manner of disclosure

The information required by this subsection shall be provided in the same timeframe and manner as the information described in subsection (a) of this section.

(4) Applicability to certain uses

This subsection shall not be construed so as to compel a consumer reporting agency to develop or disclose a score if the agency does not—

(A) distribute scores that are used in connection with residential real property loans; or

(B) develop scores that assist credit providers in understanding the general credit behavior of a consumer and predicting the future credit behavior of the consumer.

(5) Applicability to credit scores developed by another person

(A) In general

This subsection shall not be construed to require a consumer reporting agency that distributes credit scores developed by another person or entity to provide a further explanation of them, or to process a dispute arising pursuant to section 1681i of this title, except that the consumer reporting agency shall provide the consumer with the name and address and website for contacting the person or entity who developed the score or developed the methodology of the score.

(B) Exception

This paragraph shall not apply to a consumer reporting agency that develops or modifies scores that are developed by another person or entity.

(6) Maintenance of credit scores not required

This subsection shall not be construed to require a consumer reporting agency to maintain credit scores in its files.

(7) Compliance in certain cases

In complying with this subsection, a consumer reporting agency shall—

(A) supply the consumer with a credit score that is derived from a credit scoring model that is widely distributed to users by that consumer reporting agency in connection with residential real property loans or with a credit score that assists the consumer in understanding the credit scoring assessment of the credit behavior of the consumer and predictions about the future credit behavior of the consumer; and

(B) a statement indicating that the information and credit scoring model may be different than that used by the lender.

(8) Fair and reasonable fee

A consumer reporting agency may charge a fair and reasonable fee, as determined by the Commission, for providing the information required under this subsection.

(9) Use of enquiries as a key factor

If a key factor that adversely affects the credit score of a consumer consists of the number of enquiries made with respect to a consumer report, that factor shall be included in the disclosure pursuant to paragraph (1)(C) without regard to the numerical limitation in such paragraph.

(g) Disclosure of credit scores by certain mortgage lenders

(1) In general

Any person who makes or arranges loans and who uses a consumer credit score, as defined in subsection (f) of this section, in connection with an application initiated or sought by a consumer for a closed end loan or the establishment of an open end loan for a consumer purpose that is secured by 1 to 4 units of residential real property (hereafter in this subsection referred to as the "lender") shall provide the following to the consumer as soon as reasonably practicable:

(A) Information required under subsection (f)—

(i) In general

A copy of the information identified in subsection (f) of this section that was obtained from a consumer reporting agency or was developed and used by the user of the information.

(ii) Notice under subparagraph (D)

In addition to the information provided to it by a third party that provided the credit score or scores, a lender is only required to provide the notice contained in subparagraph (D).

(B) Disclosures in case of automated underwriting system

(i) In general

If a person that is subject to this subsection uses an automated underwriting system to underwrite a loan, that person may satisfy the obligation to provide a credit score by disclosing a credit score and associated key factors supplied by a consumer reporting agency.

(ii) Numerical credit score

However, if a numerical credit score is generated by an automated underwriting system used by an enterprise, and that score is disclosed to the person, the score shall be disclosed to the consumer consistent with subparagraph (C).

(iii) Enterprise defined

For purposes of this subparagraph, the term "enterprise" has the same meaning as in paragraph (6) of section 4502 of Title 12.

(C) Disclosures of credit scores not obtained from a consumer reporting agency

A person that is subject to the provisions of this subsection and that uses a credit score, other than a credit score provided by a consumer reporting agency, may satisfy the obligation to provide a credit score by disclosing a credit score and associated key factors supplied by a consumer reporting agency.

(D) Notice to home loan applicants

A copy of the following notice, which shall include the name, address, and telephone number of each consumer reporting agency providing a credit score that was used:

NOTICE TO THE HOME LOAN APPLICANT

In connection with your application for a home loan, the lender must disclose to you the score that a consumer reporting agency distributed to users and the lender used in connection with your home loan, and the key factors affecting your credit scores.

The credit score is a computer generated summary calculated at the time of the request and based on information that a consumer reporting agency or lender has on file. The scores are based on data about your credit history and payment patterns. Credit scores are important because they are used to assist the lender in determining whether you will obtain a loan. They may also be used to determine what interest rate you may be offered on the mortgage. Credit scores can change over time, depending on your conduct, how your credit history and payment patterns change, and how credit scoring technologies change.

Because the score is based on information in your credit history, it is very important that you review the credit-related information that is being furnished to make sure it is accurate. Credit records may vary from one company to another.

If you have questions about your credit score or the credit information that is furnished to you, contact the consumer reporting agency at the address and telephone number provided with this notice, or contact the lender, if the lender developed or generated the credit score. The consumer reporting agency plays no part in the decision to take any action on the loan application and is unable to provide you with specific reasons for the decision on a loan application.

If you have questions concerning the terms of the loan, contact the lender.

(E) Actions not required under this subsection

This subsection shall not require any person to—

(i) explain the information provided pursuant to subsection (f) of this section;

(ii) disclose any information other than a credit score or key factors, as defined in subsection (f) of this section;

(iii) disclose any credit score or related information obtained by the user after a loan has closed;

(iv) provide more than 1 disclosure per loan transaction; or

(v) provide the disclosure required by this subsection when another person has made the disclosure to the consumer for that loan transaction.

(F) No obligation for content

(i) In general

The obligation of any person pursuant to this subsection shall be limited solely to providing a copy of the information that was received from the consumer reporting agency.

(ii) Limit on liability

No person has liability under this subsection for the content of that information or for the omission of any information within the report provided by the consumer reporting agency.

(G) Person defined as excluding enterprise

As used in this subsection, the term "person" does not include an enterprise (as defined in paragraph (6) of section 4502 of Title 12).

(2) Prohibition on disclosure clauses null and void

(A) In general

Any provision in a contract that prohibits the disclosure of a credit score by a person who makes or arranges loans or a consumer reporting agency is void.

(B) No liability for disclosure under this subsection

A lender shall not have liability under any contractual provision for disclosure of a credit score pursuant to this subsection.

§ 610.   Conditions and form of disclosure to consumers [15 U.S.C. § 1681h]

(a) In general

(1) Proper identification.—A consumer reporting agency shall require, as a condition of making the disclosures required under section 609, that the consumer furnish proper identification.

(2) Disclosure in writing.—Except as provided in subsection (b) of this section, the disclosures required to be made under section 602(g) shall be provided under that section in writing.

(b) Other forms of disclosure

(1) In general.—If authorized by a consumer, a consumer reporting agency may make the disclosures required under 609—

(A) other than in writing; and

(B) in such form as may be—

(i) specified by the consumer in accordance with paragraph (2); and

(ii) available from the agency.

(2) Form.—A consumer may specify pursuant to paragraph (1) that disclosures under section 609 shall be made—

(A) in person, upon the appearance of the consumer at the place of business of the consumer reporting agency where disclosures are regularly provided, during normal business hours, and on reasonable notice;

(B) by telephone, if the consumer has made a written request for disclosure by telephone;

(C) by electronic means, if available from the agency; or

(D) by any other reasonable means that is available from the agency.

(c) Trained personnel

Any consumer reporting agency shall provide trained personnel to explain to the consumer any information furnished to him pursuant to section 609.

(d) Persons accompanying consumer

The consumer shall be permitted to be accompanied by one other person of his choosing, who shall furnish reasonable identification. A consumer reporting agency may require the consumer to furnish a written statement granting permission to the consumer reporting agency to discuss the consumer's file in such person's presence.

(e) Limitation of liability

Except as provided in sections 616 and 617, no consumer may bring any action or proceeding in the nature of defamation, invasion of privacy, or negligence with respect to the reporting of information against any consumer reporting agency, any user of information, or any person who furnishes information to a consumer reporting agency, based on information disclosed pursuant to section 609, 610, or 615, or based on information disclosed by a user of a consumer report to or for a consumer against whom the user has taken adverse action, based in whole or in part on the report except as to false information furnished with malice or willful intent to injure such consumer.

§ 611. Procedure in case of disputed accuracy [15 U.S.C. § 1681*i*]

(a) Reinvestigations of disputed information

(1) Reinvestigation required.—

(A) In general.—Subject to subsection (f), if the completeness or accuracy of any item of information contained in a consumer's file at a consumer reporting agency is disputed by the consumer and the consumer notifies the agency directly, or indirectly through a reseller, of such dispute, the agency shall, free of charge, conduct a reasonable reinvestigation to determine whether the disputed information is inaccurate and record the current status of the disputed information, or delete the item from the file in accordance with paragraph (5), before the end of the 30–day period beginning on the date on which the agency receives the notice of the dispute from the consumer or reseller.

(B) Extension of period to reinvestigate.—Except as provided in subparagraph (C), the 30–day period described in subparagraph (A) may be extended for not more than 15 additional days if the consumer reporting agency receives information from the consumer during that 30–day period that is relevant to the reinvestigation.

(C) Limitations on extension of period to reinvestigate.—Subparagraph (B) shall not apply to any reinvestigation in which, during the 30–day period described in subparagraph (A), the information that is the subject of the reinvestigation is found to be inaccurate or incomplete or the consumer reporting agency determines that the information cannot be verified.

(2) Prompt notice of dispute to furnisher of information.—

(A) In general.—Before the expiration of the 5–business-day period beginning on the date on which a consumer reporting agency receives notice of a dispute from any consumer or a reseller in accordance with paragraph (1), the agency shall provide notification of the dispute to any person who provided any item of information in dispute, at the address and in the manner established with the person. The notice shall include all relevant information regarding the dispute that the agency has received from the consumer or reseller.

(B) Provision of other information.—The consumer reporting agency shall promptly provide to the person who provided the information in dispute all relevant information regarding the dispute that is received by the agency from the consumer or the reseller after the period referred to in subparagraph (A) and before the end of the period referred to in paragraph (1)(A).

(3) Determination that dispute is frivolous or irrelevant.—

(A) In general.—Notwithstanding paragraph (1), a consumer reporting agency may terminate a reinvestigation of information disputed by a consumer under that paragraph if the agency reasonably determines that the dispute by the consumer is frivolous or irrelevant, including by reason of a failure by a consumer to provide sufficient information to investigate the disputed information.

(B) Notice of determination.—Upon making any determination in accordance with subparagraph (A) that a dispute is frivolous or irrelevant, a consumer reporting agency shall notify the consumer of such determination not later than 5 business days after making such determination, by mail or, if authorized by the consumer for that purpose, by any other means available to the agency.

(C) Contents of notice.—A notice under subparagraph (B) shall include—

(i) the reasons for the determination under subparagraph (A); and

(ii) identification of any information required to investigate the disputed information, which may consist of a standardized form describing the general nature of such information.

(4) Consideration of consumer information.—In conducting any reinvestigation under paragraph (1) with respect to disputed information in the file of any consumer, the consumer reporting agency shall review and consider all relevant information submitted by the consumer in the period described in paragraph (1)(A) with respect to such disputed information.

(5) Treatment of inaccurate or unverifiable information.—

(A) In general.—If, after any reinvestigation under paragraph (1) of any information disputed by a consumer, an item of the information is found to be inaccurate or incomplete or cannot be verified, the consumer reporting agency shall—

(i) promptly delete that item of information from the file of the consumer, or modify that item of information, as appropriate, based on the results of the reinvestigation; and

(ii) promptly notify the furnisher of that information that the information has been modified or deleted from the file of the consumer.

(B) Requirements relating to reinsertion of previously deleted material.—

(i) **Certification of accuracy of information**.—If any information is deleted from a consumer's file pursuant to subparagraph (A), the information may not be reinserted in the file by the consumer reporting agency unless the person who furnishes the information certifies that the information is complete and accurate.

(ii) **Notice to consumer**.—If any information that has been deleted from a consumer's file pursuant to subparagraph (A) is reinserted in the file, the consumer reporting agency shall notify the consumer of the reinsertion in writing not later than 5 business days after the reinsertion or, if authorized by the consumer for that purpose, by any other means available to the agency.

(iii) **Additional information**.—As part of, or in addition to, the notice under clause (ii), a consumer reporting agency shall provide to a consumer in writing not later than 5 business days after the date of the reinsertion—

(I) a statement that the disputed information has been reinserted;

(II) the business name and address of any furnisher of information contacted and the telephone number of such furnisher, if reasonably available, or of any furnisher of information that contacted the consumer reporting agency, in connection with the reinsertion of such information; and

(III) a notice that the consumer has the right to add a statement to the consumer's file disputing the accuracy or completeness of the disputed information.

(C) Procedures to prevent reappearance.—A consumer reporting agency shall maintain reasonable procedures designed to prevent the reappearance in a consumer's file, and in consumer reports on the consumer, of information that is deleted pursuant to this paragraph (other than information that is reinserted in accordance with subparagraph (B)(i)).

(D) Automated reinvestigation system.—Any consumer reporting agency that compiles and maintains files on consumers on a nationwide basis shall implement an automated system through which furnishers of information to that consumer reporting agency may report the results of a reinvestigation that finds incomplete or inaccurate information in a consumer's file to other such consumer reporting agencies.

(6) Notice of results of reinvestigation.—

(A) In general.—A consumer reporting agency shall provide written notice to a consumer of the results of a reinvestigation under this subsection not later than 5 business days after the completion of the reinvestigation, by mail or, if authorized by the consumer for that purpose, by other means available to the agency.

(B) Contents.—As part of, or in addition to, the notice under subparagraph (A), a consumer reporting agency shall provide to a consumer in writing before the expiration of the 5–day period referred to in subparagraph (A)—

(i) a statement that the reinvestigation is completed;

(ii) a consumer report that is based upon the consumer's file as that file is revised as a result of the reinvestigation;

(iii) a notice that, if requested by the consumer, a description of the procedure used to determine the accuracy and completeness of the information shall be provided to the consumer by the agency, including the business name and address of any furnisher of information contacted in connection with such information and the telephone number of such furnisher, if reasonably available;

(iv) a notice that the consumer has the right to add a statement to the consumer's file disputing the accuracy or completeness of the information; and

(v) a notice that the consumer has the right to request under subsection (d) of this section that the consumer reporting agency furnish notifications under that subsection.

(7) Description of reinvestigation procedure.—A consumer reporting agency shall provide to a consumer a description referred to in paragraph (6)(B)(iii) by not later than 15 days after receiving a request from the consumer for that description.

(8) Expedited dispute resolution.—If a dispute regarding an item of information in a consumer's file at a consumer reporting agency is resolved in accordance with paragraph (5)(A) by the deletion of the disputed information by not later than 3 business days after the date on which the agency receives notice of the dispute from the consumer in accordance with paragraph (1)(A), then the agency shall not be required to comply with paragraphs (2), (6), and (7) with respect to that dispute if the agency—

   (A) provides prompt notice of the deletion to the consumer by telephone;

   (B) includes in that notice, or in a written notice that accompanies a confirmation and consumer report provided in accordance with subparagraph (C), a statement of the consumer's right to request under subsection (d) of this section that the agency furnish notifications under that subsection; and

   (C) provides written confirmation of the deletion and a copy of a consumer report on the consumer that is based on the consumer's file after the deletion, not later than 5 business days after making the deletion.

(b) Statement of dispute

If the reinvestigation does not resolve the dispute, the consumer may file a brief statement setting forth the nature of the dispute. The consumer reporting agency may limit such statements to not more than one hundred words if it provides the consumer with assistance in writing a clear summary of the dispute.

(c) Notification of consumer dispute in subsequent consumer reports

Whenever a statement of a dispute is filed, unless there is reasonable grounds to believe that it is frivolous or irrelevant, the consumer reporting agency shall, in any subsequent consumer report containing the information in question, clearly note that it is disputed by the consumer and provide either the consumer's statement or a clear and accurate codification or summary thereof.

(d) Notification of deletion of disputed information

Following any deletion of information which is found to be inaccurate or whose accuracy can no longer be verified or any notation as to disputed information, the consumer reporting agency shall, at the request of the consumer, furnish notification that the item has been deleted or the statement, codification or summary pursuant to subsection (b) or (c) of this section to any person specifically designated by the consumer who has within two years prior thereto received a consumer report for employment purposes, or within six months prior thereto received a consumer report for any other purpose, which contained the deleted or disputed information.

(e) Treatment of complaints and report to Congress

(1) In general

The Commission shall—

(A) compile all complaints that it receives that a file of a consumer that is maintained by a consumer reporting agency described in section 603(p) contains incomplete or inaccurate information, with respect to which, the consumer appears to have disputed the completeness or accuracy with the consumer reporting agency or otherwise utilized the procedures provided by subsection (a) of this section; and

(B) transmit each such complaint to each consumer reporting agency involved.

(2) Exclusion

Complaints received or obtained by the Commission pursuant to its investigative authority under the Federal Trade Commission Act shall not be subject to paragraph (1).

(3) Agency responsibilities

Each consumer reporting agency described in section 603(p) that receives a complaint transmitted by the Commission pursuant to paragraph (1) shall—

(A) review each such complaint to determine whether all legal obligations imposed on the consumer reporting agency under this subchapter (including any obligation imposed by an applicable court or administrative order) have been met with respect to the subject matter of the complaint;

(B) provide reports on a regular basis to the Commission regarding the determinations of and actions taken by the consumer reporting agency, if any, in connection with its review of such complaints; and

(C) maintain, for a reasonable time period, records regarding the disposition of each such complaint that is sufficient to demonstrate compliance with this subsection.

(4) Rulemaking authority

The Commission may prescribe regulations, as appropriate to implement this subsection.

(5) Annual report

The Commission shall submit to the Committee on Banking, Housing, and Urban Affairs of the Senate and the Committee on Financial Services of the House of Representatives an annual report regarding information gathered by the Commission under this subsection.

(f) Reinvestigation requirement applicable to resellers

(1) Exemption from general reinvestigation requirement

Except as provided in paragraph (2), a reseller shall be exempt from the requirements of this section.

(2) Action required upon receiving notice of a dispute

If a reseller receives a notice from a consumer of a dispute concerning the completeness or accuracy of any item of information contained in a consumer report on such consumer produced by the reseller, the reseller shall, within 5 business days of receiving the notice, and free of charge—

(A) determine whether the item of information is incomplete or inaccurate as a result of an act or omission of the reseller; and

(B) if—

(i) the reseller determines that the item of information is incomplete or inaccurate as a result of an act or omission of the reseller, not later than 20 days after receiving the notice, correct the information in the consumer report or delete it; or

(ii) if the reseller determines that the item of information is not incomplete or inaccurate as a result of an act or omission of the reseller, convey the notice of the dispute, together with all relevant information provided by the consumer, to each consumer reporting agency that provided the reseller with the information that is the subject of the dispute, using an address or a notification mechanism specified by the consumer reporting agency for such notices.

(3) Responsibility of consumer reporting agency to notify consumer through reseller

Upon the completion of a reinvestigation under this section of a dispute concerning the completeness or accuracy of any information in the file of a consumer by a consumer reporting agency that received notice of the dispute from a reseller under paragraph (2)—

(A) the notice by the consumer reporting agency under paragraph (6), (7), or (8) of subsection (a) of this section shall be provided to the reseller in lieu of the consumer; and

(B) the reseller shall immediately reconvey such notice to the consumer, including any notice of a deletion by telephone in the manner required under paragraph (8)(A).

(4) Reseller reinvestigations

No provision of this subsection shall be construed as prohibiting a reseller from conducting a reinvestigation of a consumer dispute directly.

§ 612. Charges for certain disclosures [15 U.S.C. § 1681j]

(a) Free annual disclosure

(1) Nationwide consumer reporting agencies

(A) In general

All consumer reporting agencies described in subsections (p) and (w) of section 603 shall make all disclosures pursuant to section 609 once during any 12–month period upon request of the consumer and without charge to the consumer.

(B) Centralized source

Subparagraph (A) shall apply with respect to a consumer reporting agency described in section 603(p) only if the request from the consumer is made using the centralized source established for such purpose in accordance with section 211(c) of the Fair and Accurate Credit Transactions Act of 2003.

(C) Nationwide specialty consumer reporting agency

(i) In general

The Commission shall prescribe regulations applicable to each consumer reporting agency described in section 603 to require the establishment of a streamlined process for consumers to request consumer reports under subparagraph (A), which shall include, at a minimum, the establishment by each such agency of a toll-free telephone number for such requests.

(ii) Considerations

In prescribing regulations under clause (i), the Commission shall consider—

(I) the significant demands that may be placed on consumer reporting agencies in providing such consumer reports;

(II) appropriate means to ensure that consumer reporting agencies can satisfactorily meet those demands, including the efficacy of a system of staggering the availability to consumers of such consumer reports; and

(III) the ease by which consumers should be able to contact consumer reporting agencies with respect to access to such consumer reports.

(iii) Date of issuance

The Commission shall issue the regulations required by this subparagraph in final form not later than 6 months after December 4, 2003.

(iv) Consideration of ability to comply

The regulations of the Commission under this subparagraph shall establish an effective date by which each nationwide specialty consumer reporting agency (as defined in section 603) shall be required to comply with subsection (a) of this section, which effective date—

(I) shall be established after consideration of the ability of each nationwide specialty consumer reporting agency to comply with subsection (a) of this section; and

(II) shall be not later than 6 months after the date on which such regulations are issued in final form (or such additional period not to exceed 3 months, as the Commission determines appropriate).

(2) Timing

A consumer reporting agency shall provide a consumer report under paragraph (1) not later than 15 days after the date on which the request is received under paragraph (1).

(3) Reinvestigations

Notwithstanding the time periods specified in section 611(a)(1), a reinvestigation under that section by a consumer reporting agency upon a request of a consumer that is made after receiving a consumer report under this subsection shall be completed not later than 45 days after the date on which the request is received.

(4) Exception for first 12 months of operation

This subsection shall not apply to a consumer reporting agency that has not been furnishing consumer reports to third parties on a continuing basis during the 12–month period preceding a request under paragraph (1), with respect to consumers residing nationwide.

(b) Free disclosure after adverse notice to consumer

Each consumer reporting agency that maintains a file on a consumer shall make all disclosures pursuant to section 609 without charge to the consumer if, not later than 60 days after receipt by such consumer of a notification pursuant to section 615, or of a notification from a debt collection agency affiliated with that consumer reporting agency stating that the consumer's credit rating may be or has been adversely affected, the consumer makes a request under section 609.

(c) Free disclosure under certain other circumstances

Upon the request of the consumer, a consumer reporting agency shall make all disclosures pursuant to section 609 once during any 12–month period without charge to that consumer if the consumer certifies in writing that the consumer—

(1) is unemployed and intends to apply for employment in the 60–day period beginning on the date on which the certification is made;

(2) is a recipient of public welfare assistance; or

(3) has reason to believe that the file on the consumer at the agency contains inaccurate information due to fraud.

(d) Free disclosures in connection with fraud alerts

Upon the request of a consumer, a consumer reporting agency described in section 603(p) shall make all disclosures pursuant to section 609 without charge to the consumer, as provided in subsections (a)(2) and (b)(2) of section 605A, as applicable.

(e) Other charges prohibited

A consumer reporting agency shall not impose any charge on a consumer for providing any notification required by this subchapter or making any disclosure required by this subchapter, except as authorized by subsection (f) of this section.

(f) Reasonable charges allowed for certain disclosures

(1) In general.—In the case of a request from a consumer other than a request that is covered by any of subsections (a) through (d) of this section, a consumer reporting agency may impose a reasonable charge on a consumer—

> (A) for making a disclosure to the consumer pursuant to section 609, which charge—
>
>> (i) shall not exceed $8; and
>>
>> (ii) shall be indicated to the consumer before making the disclosure; and
>
> (B) for furnishing, pursuant to section 611(d), following a reinvestigation under section 611(a), a statement, codification, or summary to a person designated by the consumer under that section after the 30–day period beginning on the date of notification of the consumer under paragraph (6) or (8) of section 611(a) with respect to the reinvestigation, which charge—
>
>> (i) shall not exceed the charge that the agency would impose on each designated recipient for a consumer report; and
>>
>> (ii) shall be indicated to the consumer before furnishing such information.

(2) Modification of amount.—The Federal Trade Commission shall increase the amount referred to in paragraph (1)(A)(i) on January 1 of each year, based proportionally on changes in the Consumer Price Index, with fractional changes rounded to the nearest fifty cents.

§ 613. Public record information for employment purposes [15 U.S.C. § 1681k]

(a) In general

A consumer reporting agency which furnishes a consumer report for employment purposes and which for that purpose compiles and reports items of information on consumers which are matters of public record and are likely to have an adverse effect upon a consumer's ability to obtain employment shall—

> (1) at the time such public record information is reported to the user of such consumer report, notify the consumer of the fact that public record information is being reported by the consumer reporting agency, together with the name and address of the person to whom such information is being reported; or

(2) maintain strict procedures designed to insure that whenever public record information which is likely to have an adverse effect on a consumer's ability to obtain employment is reported it is complete and up to date. For purposes of this paragraph, items of public record relating to arrests, indictments, convictions, suits, tax liens, and outstanding judgments shall be considered up to date if the current public record status of the item at the time of the report is reported.

(b) Exemption for national security investigations.—Subsection (a) does not apply in the case of an agency or department of the United States Government that seeks to obtain and use a consumer report for employment purposes, if the head of the agency or department makes a written finding as prescribed under section 604(b)(4)(A).

§ 614. Restrictions on investigative consumer reports [15 U.S.C. § 1681*l*]

Whenever a consumer reporting agency prepares an investigative consumer report, no adverse information in the consumer report (other than information which is a matter of public record) may be included in a subsequent consumer report unless such adverse information has been verified in the process of making such subsequent consumer report, or the adverse information was received within the three-month period preceding the date the subsequent report is furnished.

§ 615. Requirements on users of consumer reports [15 U.S.C. § 1681m]

(a) Duties of users taking adverse actions on the basis of information contained in consumer reports

If any person takes any adverse action with respect to any consumer that is based in whole or in part on any information contained in a consumer report, the person shall—

(1) provide oral, written, or electronic notice of the adverse action to the consumer;

(2) provide to the consumer orally, in writing, or electronically—

(A) the name, address, and telephone number of the consumer reporting agency (including a toll-free telephone number established by the agency if the agency compiles and maintains files on consumers on a nationwide basis) that furnished the report to the person; and

(B) a statement that the consumer reporting agency did not make the decision to take the adverse action and is unable to provide the consumer the specific reasons why the adverse action was taken; and

(3) provide to the consumer an oral, written, or electronic notice of the consumer's right—

(A) to obtain, under section 612, a free copy of a consumer report on the consumer from the consumer reporting agency referred to in paragraph (2), which notice shall include an indication of the 60–day period under that section for obtaining such a copy; and

(B) to dispute, under section 611, with a consumer reporting agency the accuracy or completeness of any information in a consumer report furnished by the agency.

(b) Adverse action based on information obtained from third parties other than consumer reporting agencies

(1) In general.—Whenever credit for personal, family, or household purposes involving a consumer is denied or the charge for such credit is increased either wholly or partly because of information obtained from a person other than a consumer reporting agency bearing upon the consumer's credit worthiness, credit standing, credit capacity, character, general reputation, personal characteristics, or mode of living, the user of such information shall, within a reasonable period of time, upon the consumer's written request for the reasons for such adverse action received within sixty days after learning of such adverse action, disclose the nature of the information to the consumer. The user of such information shall clearly and accurately disclose to the consumer his right to make such written request at the time such adverse action is communicated to the consumer.

(2) Duties of person taking certain actions based on information provided by affiliate.—

(A) Duties, generally.—If a person takes an action described in subparagraph (B) with respect to a consumer, based in whole or in part on information described in subparagraph (C), the person shall—

(i) notify the consumer of the action, including a statement that the consumer may obtain the information in accordance with clause (ii); and

(ii) upon a written request from the consumer received within 60 days after transmittal of the notice required by clause (i), disclose to the consumer the nature of the information upon which the action is based by not later than 30 days after receipt of the request.

(B) Action described.—An action referred to in subparagraph (A) is an adverse action described in section 603(k)(1)(A), taken in connection with a transaction initiated by the consumer, or any adverse action described in clause (i) or (ii) of section 602(k)(1)(B).

(C) Information described.—Information referred to in subparagraph (A)—

(i) except as provided in clause (ii), is information that—

(I) is furnished to the person taking the action by a person related by common ownership or affiliated by common corporate control to the person taking the action; and

(II) bears on the credit worthiness, credit standing, credit capacity, character, general reputation, personal characteristics, or mode of living of the consumer; and

(ii) does not include—

(I) information solely as to transactions or experiences between the consumer and the person furnishing the information; or

(II) information in a consumer report.

(c) Reasonable procedures to assure compliance

No person shall be held liable for any violation of this section if he shows by a preponderance of the evidence that at the time of the alleged violation he maintained reasonable procedures to assure compliance with the provisions of this section.

(d) Duties of users making written credit or insurance solicitations on the basis of information contained in consumer files

(1) In general.—Any person who uses a consumer report on any consumer in connection with any credit or insurance transaction that is not initiated by the consumer, that is provided to that person under section 604(c)(1)(B), shall provide with each written solicitation made to the consumer regarding the transaction a clear and conspicuous statement that—

(A) information contained in the consumer's consumer report was used in connection with the transaction;

(B) the consumer received the offer of credit or insurance because the consumer satisfied the criteria for credit worthiness or insurability under which the consumer was selected for the offer;

(C) if applicable, the credit or insurance may not be extended if, after the consumer responds to the offer, the consumer does not meet the criteria used to select the consumer for the offer or any applicable criteria bearing on credit worthiness or insurability or does not furnish any required collateral;

(D) the consumer has a right to prohibit information contained in the consumer's file with any consumer reporting agency from being used in connection with any credit or insurance transaction that is not initiated by the consumer; and

(E) the consumer may exercise the right referred to in subparagraph (D) by notifying a notification system established under section 604(e).

(2) Disclosure of address and telephone number; format

A statement under paragraph (1) shall—

(A) include the address and toll-free telephone number of the appropriate notification system established under section 604(e) of this title; and

(B) be presented in such format and in such type size and manner as to be simple and easy to understand, as established by the Commission, by rule, in consultation with the Federal banking agencies and the National Credit Union Administration.

(3) Maintaining criteria on file.—A person who makes an offer of credit or insurance to a consumer under a credit or insurance transaction described in paragraph (1) shall maintain on file the criteria used to select the consumer to receive the offer, all criteria bearing on credit worthiness or insurability, as applicable, that are the basis for determining whether or not to extend credit or insurance pursuant to the offer, and any requirement for the furnishing of collateral as a condition of the extension of credit or insurance, until the expiration of the 3–year period beginning on the date on which the offer is made to the consumer.

(4) Authority of Federal agencies regarding unfair or deceptive acts or practices not affected.—This section is not intended to affect the authority of any Federal or State agency to enforce a prohibition against unfair or deceptive acts or practices, including the making of false or misleading statements in connection with a credit or insurance transaction that is not initiated by the consumer.

(e) Red flag guidelines and regulations required

(1) Guidelines

The Federal banking agencies, the National Credit Union Administration, and the Commission shall jointly, with respect to the entities that are subject to their respective enforcement authority under section 621—

(A) establish and maintain guidelines for use by each financial institution and each creditor regarding identity theft with respect to account holders at, or customers of, such entities, and update such guidelines as often as necessary;

(B) prescribe regulations requiring each financial institution and each creditor to establish reasonable policies and procedures for implementing the guidelines established pursuant to subparagraph (A), to identify possible risks to account holders or customers or to the safety and soundness of the institution or customers; and

(C) prescribe regulations applicable to card issuers to ensure that, if a card issuer receives notification of a change of address for an existing account, and within a short period of time (during at least the first 30 days after such notification is received) receives a request for an additional or replacement card for the same account, the card issuer may not issue the additional or replacement card, unless the card issuer, in accordance with reasonable policies and procedures—

(i) notifies the cardholder of the request at the former address of the cardholder and provides to the cardholder a means of promptly reporting incorrect address changes;

(ii) notifies the cardholder of the request by such other means of communication as the cardholder and the card issuer previously agreed to; or

(iii) uses other means of assessing the validity of the change of address, in accordance with reasonable policies and procedures established by the card issuer in accordance with the regulations prescribed under subparagraph (B).

(2) Criteria

(A) In general

In developing the guidelines required by paragraph (1)(A), the agencies described in paragraph (1) shall identify patterns, practices, and specific forms of activity that indicate the possible existence of identity theft.

(B) Inactive accounts

In developing the guidelines required by paragraph (1)(A), the agencies described in paragraph (1) shall consider including reasonable guidelines providing that when a transaction occurs with respect to a credit or deposit account that has been inactive for more than 2 years, the creditor or financial institution shall follow reasonable policies and procedures that provide for notice to be given to a consumer in a manner reasonably designed to reduce the likelihood of identity theft with respect to such account.

(3) Consistency with verification requirements

Guidelines established pursuant to paragraph (1) shall not be inconsistent with the policies and procedures required under section 5318(1) of Title 31.

(f) Prohibition on sale or transfer of debt caused by identity theft

(1) In general

No person shall sell, transfer for consideration, or place for collection a debt that such person has been notified under section 605B has resulted from identity theft.

(2) Applicability

The prohibitions of this subsection shall apply to all persons collecting a debt described in paragraph (1) after the date of a notification under paragraph (1).

(3) Rule of construction

Nothing in this subsection shall be construed to prohibit—

(A) the repurchase of a debt in any case in which the assignee of the debt requires such repurchase because the debt has resulted from identity theft;

(B) the securitization of a debt or the pledging of a portfolio of debt as collateral in connection with a borrowing; or

(C) the transfer of debt as a result of a merger, acquisition, purchase and assumption transaction, or transfer of substantially all of the assets of an entity.

(g) Debt collector communications concerning identity theft

If a person acting as a debt collector (as that term is defined in the Fair Debt Collection Practices Act) on behalf of a third party that is a creditor or other user of a consumer report is notified that any information relating to a debt that the person is attempting to collect may be fraudulent or may be the result of identity theft, that person shall—

(1) notify the third party that the information may be fraudulent or may be the result of identity theft; and

(2) upon request of the consumer to whom the debt purportedly relates, provide to the consumer all information to which the consumer would otherwise be entitled if the consumer were not a victim of identity theft, but wished to dispute the debt under provisions of law applicable to that person.

(h) Duties of users in certain credit transactions

(1) In general

Subject to rules prescribed as provided in paragraph (6), if any person uses a consumer report in connection with an application for, or a grant, extension, or other provision of, credit on material terms that are materially less favorable than the most favorable terms available to a substantial proportion of consumers from or through that person, based in whole or in part on a consumer report, the person shall provide an oral, written, or electronic notice to the consumer in the form and manner required by regulations prescribed in accordance with this subsection.

(2) Timing

The notice required under paragraph (1) may be provided at the time of an application for, or a grant, extension, or other provision of, credit or the time of communication of an approval of an application for, or grant, extension, or other provision of, credit, except as provided in the regulations prescribed under paragraph (6).

(3) Exceptions

No notice shall be required from a person under this subsection if—

(A) the consumer applied for specific material terms and was granted those terms, unless those terms were initially specified by the person after the transaction was initiated by the consumer and after the person obtained a consumer report; or

(B) the person has provided or will provide a notice to the consumer under subsection (a) of this section in connection with the transaction.

(4) Other notice not sufficient

A person that is required to provide a notice under subsection (a) of this section cannot meet that requirement by providing a notice under this subsection.

(5) Content and delivery of notice

A notice under this subsection shall, at a minimum—

(A) include a statement informing the consumer that the terms offered to the consumer are set based on information from a consumer report;

(B) identify the consumer reporting agency furnishing the report;

(C) include a statement informing the consumer that the consumer may obtain a copy of a consumer report from that consumer reporting agency without charge; and

(D) include the contact information specified by that consumer reporting agency for obtaining such consumer reports (including a toll-free telephone number established by the agency in the case of a consumer reporting agency described in section 603(p)).

(6) Rulemaking

(A) Rules required

The Commission and the Board shall jointly prescribe rules.

(B) Content

Rules required by subparagraph (A) shall address, but are not limited to—

(i) the form, content, time, and manner of delivery of any notice under this subsection;

(ii) clarification of the meaning of terms used in this subsection, including what credit terms are material, and when credit terms are materially less favorable;

(iii) exceptions to the notice requirement under this subsection for classes of persons or transactions regarding which the agencies determine that notice would not significantly benefit consumers;

(iv) a model notice that may be used to comply with this subsection; and

(v) the timing of the notice required under paragraph (1), including the circumstances under which the notice must be provided after the terms offered to the consumer were set based on information from a consumer report.

(7) Compliance

A person shall not be liable for failure to perform the duties required by this section if, at the time of the failure, the person maintained reasonable policies and procedures to comply with this section.

(8) Enforcement

(A) No civil actions

Sections 616 and 617 shall not apply to any failure by any person to comply with this section.

(B) Administrative enforcement

This section shall be enforced exclusively under section 621 by the Federal agencies and officials identified in that section.

§ 616. Civil liability for willful noncompliance [15 U.S.C. § 1681n]

(a) In general

Any person who willfully fails to comply with any requirement imposed under this subchapter with respect to any consumer is liable to that consumer in an amount equal to the sum of—

(1)(A) any actual damages sustained by the consumer as a result of the failure or damages of not less than $100 and not more than $1,000; or

(B) in the case of liability of a natural person for obtaining a consumer report under false pretenses or knowingly without a permissible purpose, actual damages sustained by the consumer as a result of the failure or $1,000, whichever is greater;

(2) such amount of punitive damages as the court may allow; and

(3) in the case of any successful action to enforce any liability under this section, the costs of the action together with reasonable attorney's fees as determined by the court.

(b) Civil liability for knowing noncompliance

Any person who obtains a consumer report from a consumer reporting agency under false pretenses or knowingly without a permissible purpose shall be liable to the consumer reporting agency for actual damages sustained by the consumer reporting agency or $1,000, whichever is greater.

(c) Attorney's fees

Upon a finding by the court that an unsuccessful pleading, motion, or other paper filed in connection with an action under this section was filed in bad faith or for purposes of harassment, the court shall award to the prevailing party attorney's fees reasonable in relation to the work expended in responding to the pleading, motion, or other paper.

(d) Clarification of willful noncompliance

For the purposes of this section, any person who printed an expiration date on any receipt provided to a consumer cardholder at a point of sale or transaction between December 4, 2004, and June 3, 2008, but otherwise complied with the requirements of section 605(g) for such receipt shall not be in willful noncompliance with section 605(g) by reason of printing such expiration date on the receipt.

§ 617. Civil liability for negligent noncompliance [15 U.S.C. § 1681*o*]

(a) In general

Any person who is negligent in failing to comply with any requirement imposed under this subchapter with respect to any consumer is liable to that consumer in an amount equal to the sum of—

(1) any actual damages sustained by the consumer as a result of the failure; and

(2) in the case of any successful action to enforce any liability under this section, the costs of the action together with reasonable attorney's fees as determined by the court.

(b) Attorney's fees

On a finding by the court that an unsuccessful pleading, motion, or other paper filed in connection with an action under this section was filed in bad faith or for purposes of harassment, the court shall award to the prevailing party attorney's fees reasonable in relation to the work expended in responding to the pleading, motion, or other paper.

§ 618. Jurisdiction of courts; limitation of actions [15 U.S.C. § 1681p]

An action to enforce any liability created under this subchapter may be brought in any appropriate United States district court, without regard to the amount in controversy, or in any other court of competent jurisdiction, not later than the earlier of—

(1) 2 years after the date of discovery by the plaintiff of the violation that is the basis for such liability; or

(2) 5 years after the date on which the violation that is the basis for such liability occurs.

§ 619. Obtaining information under false pretenses [15 U.S.C. § 1681q]

Any person who knowingly and willfully obtains information on a consumer from a consumer reporting agency under false pretenses shall be fined under Title 18, imprisoned for not more than 2 years, or both.

§ 620. Unauthorized disclosures by officers or employees [15 U.S.C. § 1681r]

Any officer or employee of a consumer reporting agency who knowingly and willfully provides information concerning an individual from the agency's files to a person not authorized to receive that information shall be fined under Title 18, imprisoned for not more than 2 years, or both.

§ 621. Administrative enforcement [15 U.S.C. § 1681s]

(a) Federal Trade Commission; powers

(1) Enforcement by Federal Trade Commission. Compliance with the requirements imposed under this subchapter shall be enforced under the Federal Trade Commission Act by the Federal Trade Commission with respect to consumer reporting agencies and all other persons subject thereto, except to the extent that enforcement of the requirements imposed under this subchapter is specifically committed to some other government agency under subsection (b) hereof. For the purpose of the exercise by the Federal Trade Commission of its functions and powers under the Federal Trade Commission Act, a violation of any requirement or prohibition imposed under this subchapter shall constitute an unfair or deceptive act or practice in commerce in violation of section 5(a) of the Federal Trade Commission Act and shall be subject to enforcement by the Federal Trade Commission under section 5(b) thereof with respect to any consumer reporting agency or person subject to enforcement by the Federal Trade Commission pursuant to this subsection, irrespective of whether that person is engaged in commerce or meets any other jurisdictional tests in the Federal Trade Commission Act. The Federal Trade Commission shall have such procedural, investigative, and enforcement powers, including the power to issue procedural rules in enforcing compliance with the requirements imposed under this subchapter and to require the filing of reports, the production of documents, and the appearance of witnesses as though the applicable terms and conditions of the Federal Trade Commission Act were part of this subchapter. Any person violating any of the provisions of this subchapter shall be subject to the penalties and entitled to the privileges and immunities provided in the Federal Trade Commission Act as though the applicable terms and provisions thereof were part of this subchapter.

(2)(A) In the event of a knowing violation, which constitutes a pattern or practice of violations of this subchapter, the Commission may commence a civil action to recover a civil penalty in a district court of the United States against any person that violates this subchapter. In such action, such person shall be liable for a civil penalty of not more than $2,500 per violation.

(B) In determining the amount of a civil penalty under subparagraph (A), the court shall take into account the degree of culpability, any history of prior such conduct, ability to pay, effect on ability to continue to do business, and such other matters as justice may require.

(3) Notwithstanding paragraph (2), a court may not impose any civil penalty on a person for a violation of section 623(a)(1) unless the person has been enjoined from committing the violation, or ordered not to commit the violation, in an action or proceeding brought by or on behalf of the Federal Trade Commission, and has violated the injunction or order, and the court may not impose any civil penalty for any violation occurring before the date of the violation of the injunction or order.

(b) Enforcement by other agencies

Compliance with the requirements imposed under this subchapter with respect to consumer reporting agencies, persons who use consumer reports from such agencies, persons who furnish information to such agencies, and users of information that are subject to subsection (d) of section 615 shall be enforced under—

(1) section 8 of the Federal Deposit Insurance Act, in the case of—

(A) national banks, and Federal branches and Federal agencies of foreign banks, by the Office of the Comptroller of the Currency;

(B) member banks of the Federal Reserve System (other than national banks), branches and agencies of foreign banks (other than Federal branches, Federal agencies, and insured State branches of foreign banks), commercial lending companies owned or controlled by foreign banks, and organizations operating under section 25 or 25A of the Federal Reserve Act, by the Board of Governors of the Federal Reserve System; and

(C) banks insured by the Federal Deposit Insurance Corporation (other than members of the Federal Reserve System) and insured State branches of foreign banks, by the Board of Directors of the Federal Deposit Insurance Corporation;

(2) Section 8 of the Federal Deposit Insurance Act, by the Director of the Office of Thrift Supervision, in the case of a savings association the deposits of which are insured by the Federal Deposit Insurance Corporation.

(3) the Federal Credit Union Act, by the Administrator of the National Credit Union Administration with respect to any Federal credit union;

(4) subtitle IV of Title 49, by the Secretary of Transportation, with respect to all carriers subject to the jurisdiction of the Surface Transportation Board;

(5) part A of subtitle VII of title 49, by the Secretary of Transportation with respect to any air carrier or foreign air carrier subject to that part; and

(6) the Packers and Stockyards Act, 1921 (except as provided in section 406 of that Act), by the Secretary of Agriculture with respect to any activities subject to that Act.

The terms used in paragraph (1) that are not defined in this subchapter or otherwise defined in section 3(s) of the Federal Deposit Insurance Act (12 U.S.C. 1813(s)) shall have the meaning given to them in section 1(b) of the International Banking Act of 1978 (12 U.S.C. 3101).

(c) State action for violations

(1) Authority of States.—In addition to such other remedies as are provided under State law, if the chief law enforcement officer of a State, or an official or agency designated by a State, has reason to believe that any person has violated or is violating this subchapter, the State—

(A) may bring an action to enjoin such violation in any appropriate United States district court or in any other court of competent jurisdiction;

(B) subject to paragraph (5), may bring an action on behalf of the residents of the State to recover—

(i) damages for which the person is liable to such residents under sections 616 and 617 as a result of the violation;

(ii) in the case of a violation described in any of paragraphs (1) through (3) of section 623(c), damages for which the person would, but for section 623(c), be liable to such residents as a result of the violation; or

(iii) damages of not more than $1,000 for each willful or negligent violation; and

(C) in the case of any successful action under subparagraph (A) or (B), shall be awarded the costs of the action and reasonable attorney fees as determined by the court.

(2) Rights of Federal regulators.—The State shall serve prior written notice of any action under paragraph (1) upon the Federal Trade Commission or the appropriate Federal regulator determined under subsection (b) of this section and provide the Commission or appropriate Federal regulator with a copy of its complaint, except in any case in which such prior notice is not feasible, in which case the State shall serve such notice immediately upon instituting such action. The Federal Trade Commission or appropriate Federal regulator shall have the right—

(A) to intervene in the action;

(B) upon so intervening, to be heard on all matters arising therein;

(C) to remove the action to the appropriate United States district court; and

(D) to file petitions for appeal.

(3) Investigatory powers.—For purposes of bringing any action under this subsection, nothing in this subsection shall prevent the chief law enforcement officer, or an official or agency designated by a State, from exercising the powers conferred on the chief law enforcement officer or such official by the laws of such State to conduct investigations or to administer oaths or affirmations or to compel the attendance of witnesses or the production of documentary and other evidence.

(4) Limitation on State action while Federal action pending.—If the Federal Trade Commission or the appropriate Federal regulator has instituted a civil action or an administrative action under section 1818 of Title 12 for a violation of this subchapter, no State may, during the pendency of such action, bring an action under this section against any defendant named in the complaint of the Commission or the appropriate Federal regulator for any violation of this subchapter that is alleged in that complaint.

(5) Limitations on State actions for certain violations.—

(A) Violation of injunction required.—A State may not bring an action against a person under paragraph (1)(B) for a violation described in any of paragraphs (1) through (3) of section 623(c), unless—

(i) the person has been enjoined from committing the violation, in an action brought by the State under paragraph (1)(A); and

(ii) the person has violated the injunction.

(B) Limitation on damages recoverable.—In an action against a person under paragraph (1)(B) for a violation described in any of paragraphs (1) through (3) of section 623(c), a State may not recover any damages incurred before the date of the violation of an injunction on which the action is based.

(d) Enforcement under other authority

For the purpose of the exercise by any agency referred to in subsection (b) of this section of its powers under any Act referred to in that subsection, a violation of any requirement imposed under this subchapter shall be deemed to be a violation of a requirement imposed under that Act. In addition to its powers under any provision of law specifically referred to in subsection (b) of this section, each of the agencies referred to in that subsection may exercise, for the purpose of enforcing compliance with any requirement imposed under this subchapter any other authority conferred on it by law.

(e) Interpretive authority

(1) The Federal banking agencies referred to in paragraphs (1) and (2) of subsection (b) shall jointly prescribe such regulations as necessary to carry out the purposes of this Act with respect to any persons identified under paragraphs (1) and (2) of subsection (b), and the Board of Governors of the Federal Reserve System shall have authority to prescribe regulations consistent with such joint regulations with respect to bank holding companies and affiliates (other than depository institutions and consumer reporting agencies) of such holding companies.

(2) The Board of the National Credit Union Administration shall prescribe such regulations as necessary to carry out the purposes of this Act with respect to any persons identified under paragraph (3) of subsection (b).

(f) Coordination of consumer complaint investigations

(1) In general

Each consumer reporting agency described in section 603(p) shall develop and maintain procedures for the referral to each other such agency of any consumer complaint received by the agency alleging identity theft, or requesting a fraud alert under section 605A or a block under section 605B.

(2) Model form and procedure for reporting identity theft

The Commission, in consultation with the Federal banking agencies and the National Credit Union Administration, shall develop a model form and model procedures to be used by consumers who are victims of identity theft for contacting and informing creditors and consumer reporting agencies of the fraud.

(3) Annual summary reports

Each consumer reporting agency described in section 603(p) shall submit an annual summary report to the Commission on consumer complaints received by the agency on identity theft or fraud alerts.

(g) FTC regulation of coding of trade names

If the Commission determines that a person described in paragraph (9) of section 623(a) has not met the requirements of such paragraph, the Commission shall take action to ensure the person's compliance with such paragraph, which may include issuing model guidance or prescribing reasonable policies and procedures, as necessary to ensure that such person complies with such paragraph.

§ 622. Information on overdue child support obligations [15 U.S.C. § 1681s–1]

Notwithstanding any other provision of this subchapter, a consumer reporting agency shall include in any consumer report furnished by the agency in accordance with section 604, any information on the failure of the consumer to pay overdue support which—

(1) is provided—

(A) to the consumer reporting agency by a State or local child support enforcement agency; or

(B) to the consumer reporting agency and verified by any local, State, or Federal Government agency; and

(2) antedates the report by 7 years or less.

§ 623. Responsibilities of furnishers of information to consumer reporting agencies [15 U.S.C. § 1681s–2]

(a) Duty of furnishers of information to provide accurate information

(1) Prohibition

(A) Reporting information with actual knowledge of errors

A person shall not furnish any information relating to a consumer to any consumer reporting agency if the person knows or has reasonable cause to believe that the information is inaccurate.

(B) Reporting information after notice and confirmation of errors

A person shall not furnish information relating to a consumer to any consumer reporting agency if—

    (i) the person has been notified by the consumer, at the address specified by the person for such notices, that specific information is inaccurate; and

    (ii) the information is, in fact, inaccurate.

(C) No address requirement

A person who clearly and conspicuously specifies to the consumer an address for notices referred to in subparagraph (B) shall not be subject to subparagraph (A); however, nothing in subparagraph (B) shall require a person to specify such an address.

(D) Definition

For purposes of subparagraph (A), the term "reasonable cause to believe that the information is inaccurate" means having specific knowledge, other than solely allegations by the consumer, that would cause a reasonable person to have substantial doubts about the accuracy of the information.

(2) Duty to correct and update information

A person who—

    (A) regularly and in the ordinary course of business furnishes information to one or more consumer reporting agencies about the person's transactions or experiences with any consumer; and

    (B) has furnished to a consumer reporting agency information that the person determines is not complete or accurate,

shall promptly notify the consumer reporting agency of that determination and provide to the agency any corrections to that information, or any additional information, that is necessary to make the information provided by the person to the agency complete and accurate, and shall not thereafter furnish to the agency any of the information that remains not complete or accurate.

(3) Duty to provide notice of dispute

If the completeness or accuracy of any information furnished by any person to any consumer reporting agency is disputed to such person by a consumer, the person may not furnish the information to any consumer reporting agency without notice that such information is disputed by the consumer.

(4) Duty to provide notice of closed accounts

A person who regularly and in the ordinary course of business furnishes information to a consumer reporting agency regarding a consumer who has a credit account with that person shall notify the agency of the voluntary closure of the account by the consumer, in information regularly furnished for the period in which the account is closed.

(5) Duty to provide notice of delinquency of accounts

(A) In general

A person who furnishes information to a consumer reporting agency regarding a delinquent account being placed for collection, charged to profit or loss, or subjected to any similar action shall, not later than 90 days after furnishing the information, notify the agency of the date of delinquency on the account, which shall be the month and year of the commencement of the delinquency on the account that immediately preceded the action.

(B) Rule of construction

For purposes of this paragraph only, and provided that the consumer does not dispute the information, a person that furnishes information on a delinquent account that is placed for collection, charged for profit or loss, or subjected to any similar action, complies with this paragraph, if—

(i) the person reports the same date of delinquency as that provided by the creditor to which the account was owed at the time at which the commencement of the delinquency occurred, if the creditor previously reported that date of delinquency to a consumer reporting agency;

(ii) the creditor did not previously report the date of delinquency to a consumer reporting agency, and the person establishes and follows reasonable procedures to obtain the date of delinquency from the creditor or another reliable source and reports that date to a consumer reporting agency as the date of delinquency; or

(iii) the creditor did not previously report the date of delinquency to a consumer reporting agency and the date of delinquency cannot be reasonably obtained as provided in clause (ii), the person establishes and follows reasonable procedures to ensure the date reported as the date of delinquency precedes the date on which the account is placed for collection, charged to profit or loss, or subjected to any similar action, and reports such date to the credit reporting agency.

(6) Duties of furnishers upon notice of identity theft-related information

(A) Reasonable procedures

A person that furnishes information to any consumer reporting agency shall have in place reasonable procedures to respond to any notification that it receives from a consumer reporting agency under section 605B relating to information resulting from identity theft, to prevent that person from refurnishing such blocked information.

(B) Information alleged to result from identity theft

If a consumer submits an identity theft report to a person who furnishes information to a consumer reporting agency at the address specified by that person for receiving such reports stating that information maintained by such person that purports to relate to the consumer resulted from identity theft, the person may not furnish such information that purports to relate to the consumer to any consumer reporting agency, unless the person subsequently knows or is informed by the consumer that the information is correct.

(7) Negative information

(A) Notice to consumer required

(i) In general

If any financial institution that extends credit and regularly and in the ordinary course of business furnishes information to a consumer reporting agency described in section 603(p) furnishes negative information to such an agency regarding credit extended to a customer, the financial institution shall provide a notice of such furnishing of negative information, in writing, to the customer.

(ii) Notice effective for subsequent submissions

After providing such notice, the financial institution may submit additional negative information to a consumer reporting agency described in section 603(p) with respect to the same transaction, extension of credit, account, or customer without providing additional notice to the customer.

(B) Time of notice

(i) In general

The notice required under subparagraph (A) shall be provided to the customer prior to, or no later than 30 days after, furnishing the negative information to a consumer reporting agency described in section 603(p).

(ii) Coordination with new account disclosures

If the notice is provided to the customer prior to furnishing the negative information to a consumer reporting agency, the notice may not be included in the initial disclosures provided under section 127(a) of the Truth-in-Lending Act.

(C) Coordination with other disclosures

The notice required under subparagraph (A)—

(i) may be included on or with any notice of default, any billing statement, or any other materials provided to the customer; and

(ii) must be clear and conspicuous.

(D) Model disclosure

(i) Duty of board to prepare

The Board shall prescribe a brief model disclosure a financial institution may use to comply with subparagraph (A), which shall not exceed 30 words.

(ii) Use of model not required

No provision of this paragraph shall be construed as requiring a financial institution to use any such model form prescribed by the Board.

(iii) Compliance using model

A financial institution shall be deemed to be in compliance with subparagraph (A) if the financial institution uses any such model form prescribed by the Board, or the financial institution uses any such model form and rearranges its format.

(E) Use of notice without submitting negative information

No provision of this paragraph shall be construed as requiring a financial institution that has provided a customer with a notice described in subparagraph (A) to furnish negative information about the customer to a consumer reporting agency.

(F) Safe harbor

A financial institution shall not be liable for failure to perform the duties required by this paragraph if, at the time of the failure, the financial institution maintained reasonable policies and procedures to comply with this paragraph or the financial institution reasonably believed that the institution is prohibited, by law, from contacting the consumer.

(G) Definitions

For purposes of this paragraph, the following definitions shall apply:

(i) Negative information

The term "negative information" means information concerning a customer's delinquencies, late payments, insolvency, or any form of default.

(ii) Customer; financial institution

The terms "customer" and "financial institution" have the same meanings as in section 6809 of Title 15.

(8) Ability of consumer to dispute information directly with furnisher

(A) In general

The Federal banking agencies, the National Credit Union Administration, and the Commission shall jointly prescribe regulations that shall identify the circumstances under which a furnisher shall be required to reinvestigate a dispute concerning the accuracy of information contained in a consumer report on the consumer, based on a direct request of a consumer.

(B) Considerations

In prescribing regulations under subparagraph (A), the agencies shall weigh—

(i) the benefits to consumers with the costs on furnishers and the credit reporting system;

(ii) the impact on the overall accuracy and integrity of consumer reports of any such requirements;

(iii) whether direct contact by the consumer with the furnisher would likely result in the most expeditious resolution of any such dispute; and

(iv) the potential impact on the credit reporting process if credit repair organizations, as defined in section 403(a)(3) of the Credit Repair Organizations Act, including entities that would be a credit repair organization, but for section 403(3)(B)(i) of Credit Repair Organizations Act, are able to circumvent the prohibition in subparagraph (G).

(C) Applicability

Subparagraphs (D) through (G) shall apply in any circumstance identified under the regulations promulgated under subparagraph (A).

(D) Submitting a notice of dispute

A consumer who seeks to dispute the accuracy of information shall provide a dispute notice directly to such person at the address specified by the person for such notices that—

(i) identifies the specific information that is being disputed;

(ii) explains the basis for the dispute; and

(iii) includes all supporting documentation required by the furnisher to substantiate the basis of the dispute.

(E) Duty of person after receiving notice of dispute

After receiving a notice of dispute from a consumer pursuant to subparagraph (D), the person that provided the information in dispute to a consumer reporting agency shall—

(i) conduct an investigation with respect to the disputed information;

(ii) review all relevant information provided by the consumer with the notice;

(iii) complete such person's investigation of the dispute and report the results of the investigation to the consumer before the

351

expiration of the period under section 611(a)(1) within which a consumer reporting agency would be required to complete its action if the consumer had elected to dispute the information under that section; and

(iv) if the investigation finds that the information reported was inaccurate, promptly notify each consumer reporting agency to which the person furnished the inaccurate information of that determination and provide to the agency any correction to that information that is necessary to make the information provided by the person accurate.

(F) Frivolous or irrelevant dispute

(i) In general

This paragraph shall not apply if the person receiving a notice of a dispute from a consumer reasonably determines that the dispute is frivolous or irrelevant, including—

(I) by reason of the failure of a consumer to provide sufficient information to investigate the disputed information; or

(II) the submission by a consumer of a dispute that is substantially the same as a dispute previously submitted by or for the consumer, either directly to the person or through a consumer reporting agency under subsection (b) of this section, with respect to which the person has already performed the person's duties under this paragraph or subsection (b), as applicable.

(ii) Notice of determination

Upon making any determination under clause (i) that a dispute is frivolous or irrelevant, the person shall notify the consumer of such determination not later than 5 business days after making such determination, by mail or, if authorized by the consumer for that purpose, by any other means available to the person.

(iii) Contents of notice

A notice under clause (ii) shall include—

(I) the reasons for the determination under clause (i); and

(II) identification of any information required to investigate the disputed information, which may consist of a standardized form describing the general nature of such information.

(G) Exclusion of credit repair organizations

This paragraph shall not apply if the notice of the dispute is submitted by, is prepared on behalf of the consumer by, or is submitted on a form supplied to the consumer by, a credit repair organization, as defined in section 403(3) of the Credit Repair Organizations Act, or an entity that would be a credit repair organization, but for section 403(3)(B)(i) of the Credit Repair Organizations Act.

(9) Duty to provide notice of status as medical information furnisher

A person whose primary business is providing medical services, products, or devices, or the person's agent or assignee, who furnishes information to a consumer reporting agency on a consumer shall be considered a medical information furnisher for purposes of this subchapter, and shall notify the agency of such status.

(b) Duties of furnishers of information upon notice of dispute

(1) In general

After receiving notice pursuant to section 611(a)(2) of a dispute with regard to the completeness or accuracy of any information provided by a person to a consumer reporting agency, the person shall—

(A) conduct an investigation with respect to the disputed information;

(B) review all relevant information provided by the consumer reporting agency pursuant to section 611(a)(2);

(C) report the results of the investigation to the consumer reporting agency;

(D) if the investigation finds that the information is incomplete or inaccurate, report those results to all other consumer reporting agencies to which the person furnished the information and that compile and maintain files on consumers on a nationwide basis; and

(E) if an item of information disputed by a consumer is found to be inaccurate or incomplete or cannot be verified after any reinvestigation under paragraph (1), for purposes of reporting to a consumer reporting agency only, as appropriate, based on the results of the reinvestigation promptly—

(i) modify that item of information;

(ii) delete that item of information; or

(iii) permanently block the reporting of that item of information.

(2) Deadline

A person shall complete all investigations, reviews, and reports required under paragraph (1) regarding information provided by the person to a consumer reporting agency, before the expiration of the period under section 611(a)(1) within which the consumer reporting agency is required to complete actions required by that section regarding that information.

(c) Limitation on liability

Except as provided in section 621(c)(1)(B) of this title, sections 616 and 617 do not apply to any violation of—

> (1) subsection (a) of this section, including any regulations issued thereunder;

> (2) subsection (e) of this section, except that nothing in this paragraph shall limit, expand, or otherwise affect liability under section 616 or 617, as applicable, for violations of subsection (b) of this section; or

> (3) subsection (e) of section 615.

(d) Limitation on enforcement

The provisions of law described in paragraphs (1) through (3) of subsection (c) of this section (other than with respect to the exception described in paragraph (2) of subsection (c) of this section) shall be enforced exclusively as provided under section 621 by the Federal agencies and officials and the State officials identified in section 621 of this title.

(e) Accuracy guidelines and regulations required

(1) Guidelines

The Federal banking agencies, the National Credit Union Administration, and the Commission shall, with respect to the entities that are subject to their respective enforcement authority under section 1681m of this title, and in coordination as described in paragraph (2)—

> (A) establish and maintain guidelines for use by each person that furnishes information to a consumer reporting agency regarding the accuracy and integrity of the information relating to consumers that such entities furnish to consumer reporting agencies, and update such guidelines as often as necessary; and

> (B) prescribe regulations requiring each person that furnishes information to a consumer reporting agency to establish reasonable policies and procedures for implementing the guidelines established pursuant to subparagraph (A).

(2) Coordination

Each agency required to prescribe regulations under paragraph (1) shall consult and coordinate with each other such agency so that, to the extent possible, the regulations prescribed by each such entity are consistent and comparable with the regulations prescribed by each other such agency.

(3) Criteria

In developing the guidelines required by paragraph (1)(A), the agencies described in paragraph (1) shall—

> (A) identify patterns, practices, and specific forms of activity that can compromise the accuracy and integrity of information furnished to consumer reporting agencies;

(B) review the methods (including technological means) used to furnish information relating to consumers to consumer reporting agencies;

(C) determine whether persons that furnish information to consumer reporting agencies maintain and enforce policies to assure the accuracy and integrity of information furnished to consumer reporting agencies; and

(D) examine the policies and processes that persons that furnish information to consumer reporting agencies employ to conduct reinvestigations and correct inaccurate information relating to consumers that has been furnished to consumer reporting agencies.

§ 624. Affiliate sharing [15 U.S.C. § 1681s–3]

(a) Special rule for solicitation for purposes of marketing

(1) Notice

Any person that receives from another person related to it by common ownership or affiliated by corporate control a communication of information that would be a consumer report, but for clauses (i), (ii), and (iii) of section 603(d)(2)(A), may not use the information to make a solicitation for marketing purposes to a consumer about its products or services, unless—

(A) it is clearly and conspicuously disclosed to the consumer that the information may be communicated among such persons for purposes of making such solicitations to the consumer; and

(B) the consumer is provided an opportunity and a simple method to prohibit the making of such solicitations to the consumer by such person.

(2) Consumer choice

(A) In general

The notice required under paragraph (1) shall allow the consumer the opportunity to prohibit all solicitations referred to in such paragraph, and may allow the consumer to choose from different options when electing to prohibit the sending of such solicitations, including options regarding the types of entities and information covered, and which methods of delivering solicitations the consumer elects to prohibit.

(B) Format

Notwithstanding subparagraph (A), the notice required under paragraph (1) shall be clear, conspicuous, and concise, and any method provided under paragraph (1)(B) shall be simple. The regulations prescribed to implement this section shall provide specific guidance regarding how to comply with such standards.

(3) Duration

(A) In general

The election of a consumer pursuant to paragraph (1)(B) to prohibit the making of solicitations shall be effective for at least 5 years, beginning on the date on which the person receives the election of the consumer, unless the consumer requests that such election be revoked.

(B) Notice upon expiration of effective period

At such time as the election of a consumer pursuant to paragraph (1)(B) is no longer effective, a person may not use information that the person receives in the manner described in paragraph (1) to make any solicitation for marketing purposes to the consumer, unless the consumer receives a notice and an opportunity, using a simple method, to extend the opt-out for another period of at least 5 years, pursuant to the procedures described in paragraph (1).

(4) Scope

This section shall not apply to a person—

(A) using information to make a solicitation for marketing purposes to a consumer with whom the person has a pre-existing business relationship;

(B) using information to facilitate communications to an individual for whose benefit the person provides employee benefit or other services pursuant to a contract with an employer related to and arising out of the current employment relationship or status of the individual as a participant or beneficiary of an employee benefit plan;

(C) using information to perform services on behalf of another person related by common ownership or affiliated by corporate control, except that this subparagraph shall not be construed as permitting a person to send solicitations on behalf of another person, if such other person would not be permitted to send the solicitation on its own behalf as a result of the election of the consumer to prohibit solicitations under paragraph (1)(B);

(D) using information in response to a communication initiated by the consumer;

(E) using information in response to solicitations authorized or requested by the consumer; or

(F) if compliance with this section by that person would prevent compliance by that person with any provision of State insurance laws pertaining to unfair discrimination in any State in which the person is lawfully doing business.

(5) No retroactivity

This subsection shall not prohibit the use of information to send a solicitation to a consumer if such information was received prior to the date on which persons are required to comply with regulations implementing this subsection.

(b) Notice for other purposes permissible

A notice or other disclosure under this section may be coordinated and consolidated with any other notice required to be issued under any other provision of law by a person that is subject to this section, and a notice or other disclosure that is equivalent to the notice required by subsection (a) of this section, and that is provided by a person described in subsection (a) of this section to a consumer together with disclosures required by any other provision of law, shall satisfy the requirements of subsection (a) of this section.

(c) User requirements

Requirements with respect to the use by a person of information received from another person related to it by common ownership or affiliated by corporate control, such as the requirements of this section, constitute requirements with respect to the exchange of information among persons affiliated by common ownership or common corporate control, within the meaning of section 625(b)(2).

(d) Definitions

For purposes of this section, the following definitions shall apply:

(1) Pre-existing business relationship

The term "pre-existing business relationship" means a relationship between a person, or a person's licensed agent, and a consumer, based on—

> (A) a financial contract between a person and a consumer which is in force;

> (B) the purchase, rental, or lease by the consumer of that person's goods or services, or a financial transaction (including holding an active account or a policy in force or having another continuing relationship) between the consumer and that person during the 18–month period immediately preceding the date on which the consumer is sent a solicitation covered by this section;

> (C) an inquiry or application by the consumer regarding a product or service offered by that person, during the 3–month period immediately preceding the date on which the consumer is sent a solicitation covered by this section; or

> (D) any other pre-existing customer relationship defined in the regulations implementing this section.

(2) Solicitation

The term "solicitation" means the marketing of a product or service initiated by a person to a particular consumer that is based on an exchange of information described in subsection (a) of this section, and is intended to encourage the consumer to purchase such product or service, but does not include communications that are directed at the general public or determined not to be a solicitation by the regulations prescribed under this section.

§ 625. Relation to State laws [15 U.S.C. § 1681t]

(a) In general

Except as provided in subsections (b) and (c) of this section, this subchapter does not annul, alter, affect, or exempt any person subject to the provisions of this subchapter from complying with the laws of any State with respect to the collection, distribution, or use of any information on consumers, or for the prevention or mitigation of identify theft, except to the extent that those laws are inconsistent with any provision of this subchapter, and then only to the extent of the inconsistency.

(b) General exceptions

No requirement or prohibition may be imposed under the laws of any State—

(1) with respect to any subject matter regulated under—

(A) subsection (c) or (e) of section 604, relating to the prescreening of consumer reports;

(B) section 611, relating to the time by which a consumer reporting agency must take any action, including the provision of notification to a consumer or other person, in any procedure related to the disputed accuracy of information in a consumer's file, except that this subparagraph shall not apply to any State law in effect on September 30, 1996;

(C) subsections (a) and (b) of section 615, relating to the duties of a person who takes any adverse action with respect to a consumer;

(D) section 615(d), relating to the duties of persons who use a consumer report of a consumer in connection with any credit or insurance transaction that is not initiated by the consumer and that consists of a firm offer of credit or insurance;

(E) section 605, relating to information contained in consumer reports, except that this subparagraph shall not apply to any State law in effect on September 30, 1996;

(F) section 623, relating to the responsibilities of persons who furnish information to consumer reporting agencies, except that this paragraph shall not apply—

(i) with respect to section 54A(a) of chapter 93 of the Massachusetts Annotated Laws (as in effect on September 30, 1996); or

(ii) with respect to section 1785.25(a) of the California Civil Code (as in effect on September 30, 1996);

(G) section 609(e), relating to information available to victims under section 609(e);

(H) section 624, relating to the exchange and use of information to make a solicitation for marketing purposes; or

(I) section 615(h), relating to the duties of users of consumer reports to provide notice with respect to terms in certain credit transactions;

(2) with respect to the exchange of information among persons affiliated by common ownership or common corporate control, except that this paragraph shall not apply with respect to subsection (a) or (c)(1) of section 2480e of title 9, Vermont Statutes Annotated (as in effect on September 30, 1996); or

(3) with respect to the disclosures required to be made under subsection (c), (d), (e), or (g) of section 609, or subsection (f) of section 609 of this title relating to the disclosure of credit scores for credit granting purposes, except that this paragraph—

(A) shall not apply with respect to sections 1785.10, 1785.16, and 1785.20.2 of the California Civil Code (as in effect on December 4, 2003) and section 1785.15 through section 1785.15.2 of such Code (as in effect on such date);

(B) shall not apply with respect to sections 5–3–106(2) and 212–14.3–104.3 of the Colorado Revised Statutes (as in effect on December 4, 2003); and

(C) shall not be construed as limiting, annulling, affecting, or superseding any provision of the laws of any State regulating the use in an insurance activity, or regulating disclosures concerning such use, of a credit-based insurance score of a consumer by any person engaged in the business of insurance;

(4) with respect to the frequency of any disclosure under section 612(a), except that this paragraph shall not apply—

(A) with respect to section 12–14.3–105(1)(d) of the Colorado Revised Statutes (as in effect on December 4, 2003);

(B) with respect to section 10–1–393(29)(C) of the Georgia Code (as in effect on December 4, 2003);

(C) with respect to section 1316.2 of title 10 of the Maine Revised Statutes (as in effect on December 4, 2003);

(D) with respect to sections 14–1209(a)(1) and 14–1209(b)(1)(i) of the Commercial Law Article of the Code of Maryland (as in effect on December 4, 2003);

(E) with respect to section 59(d) and section 59(e) of chapter 93 of the General Laws of Massachusetts (as in effect December 4, 2003);

(F) with respect to section 56:11–37.10(a)(1) of the New Jersey Revised Statutes (as in effect on December 4, 2003); or

(G) with respect to section 2480c(a)(1) of title 9 of the Vermont Statutes Annotated (as in effect on December 4, 2003); or

(5) with respect to the conduct required by the specific provisions of—

     (A) section 603(g);

     (B) section 605A;

     (C) section 605B;

     (D) section 609(a)(1)(A);

     (E) section 612(a);

     (F) subsections (e), (f), and (g) of section 615;

     (G) section 621(f);

     (H) section 623(a)(6); or

     (I) section 628.

(c) Definition of firm offer of credit or insurance

Notwithstanding any definition of the term "firm offer of credit or insurance" (or any equivalent term) under the laws of any State, the definition of that term contained in section 603(l) shall be construed to apply in the enforcement and interpretation of the laws of any State governing consumer reports.

(d) Limitations

Subsections (b) and (c) of this section do not affect any settlement, agreement, or consent judgment between any State Attorney General and any consumer reporting agency in effect on September 30, 1996.

§ 626. Disclosures to FBI for counterintelligence purposes [15 U.S.C. § 1681u]

(a) Identity of financial institutions

Notwithstanding section 604 or any other provision of this subchapter, a consumer reporting agency shall furnish to the Federal Bureau of Investigation the names and addresses of all financial institutions (as that term is defined in section 3401 of Title 12) at which a consumer maintains or has maintained an account, to the extent that information is in the files of the agency, when presented with a written request for that information, signed by the Director of the Federal Bureau of Investigation, or the Director's designee in a position not lower than Deputy Assistant Director at Bureau headquarters or a Special Agent in Charge of a Bureau field office designated by the Director, which certifies compliance with this section. The Director or the Director's designee may make such a certification only if the Director or the Director's designee has determined in writing that such information is sought for the conduct of an authorized investigation to protect against international terrorism or clandestine intelligence activities, provided that such an investigation of a United States person is not conducted solely upon the basis of activities protected by the first amendment to the Constitution of the United States.

(b) Identifying information

Notwithstanding the provisions of section 604 or any other provision of this subchapter, a consumer reporting agency shall furnish identifying information respecting a consumer, limited to name, address, former addresses, places of employment, or former places of employment, to the Federal Bureau of Investigation when presented with a written request, signed by the Director or the Director's designee in a position not lower than Deputy Assistant Director at Bureau headquarters or a Special Agent in Charge of a Bureau field office designated by the Director, which certifies compliance with this subsection. The Director or the Director's designee may make such a certification only if the Director or the Director's designee has determined in writing that such information is sought for the conduct of an authorized investigation to protect against international terrorism or clandestine intelligence activities, provided that such an investigation of a United States person is not conducted solely upon the basis of activities protected by the first amendment to the Constitution of the United States.

(c) Court order for disclosure of consumer reports

Notwithstanding section 604 or any other provision of this subchapter, if requested in writing by the Director of the Federal Bureau of Investigation, or a designee of the Director in a position not lower than Deputy Assistant Director at Bureau headquarters or a Special Agent in Charge in a Bureau field office designated by the Director, a court may issue an order ex parte directing a consumer reporting agency to furnish a consumer report to the Federal Bureau of Investigation, upon a showing in camera that the consumer report is sought for the conduct of an authorized investigation to protect against international terrorism or clandestine intelligence activities, provided that such an investigation of a United States person is not conducted solely upon the basis of activities protected by the first amendment to the Constitution of the United States. The terms of an order issued under this subsection shall not disclose that the order is issued for purposes of a counterintelligence investigation.

(d) Confidentiality

(1) If the Director of the Federal Bureau of Investigation, or his designee in a position not lower than Deputy Assistant Director at Bureau headquarters or a Special Agent in Charge in a Bureau field office designated by the Director, certifies that otherwise there may result a danger to the national security of the United States, interference with a criminal, counterterrorism, or counterintelligence investigation, interference with diplomatic relations, or danger to the life or physical safety of any person, no consumer reporting agency or officer, employee, or agent of a consumer reporting agency shall disclose to any person (other than those to whom such disclosure is necessary to comply with the request or an attorney to

obtain legal advice or legal assistance with respect to the request) that the Federal Bureau of Investigation has sought or obtained the identity of financial institutions or a consumer report respecting any consumer under subsection (a), (b), or (c) of this section, and no consumer reporting agency or officer, employee, or agent of a consumer reporting agency shall include in any consumer report any information that would indicate that the Federal Bureau of Investigation has sought or obtained such information on a consumer report.

(2) The request shall notify the person or entity to whom the request is directed of the nondisclosure requirement under paragraph (1).

(3) Any recipient disclosing to those persons necessary to comply with the request or to an attorney to obtain legal advice or legal assistance with respect to the request shall inform such persons of any applicable nondisclosure requirement. Any person who receives a disclosure under this subsection shall be subject to the same prohibitions on disclosure under paragraph (1).

(4) At the request of the Director of the Federal Bureau of Investigation or the designee of the Director, any person making or intending to make a disclosure under this section shall identify to the Director or such designee the person to whom such disclosure will be made or to whom such disclosure was made prior to the request, except that nothing in this section shall require a person to inform the Director or such designee of the identity of an attorney to whom disclosure was made or will be made to obtain legal advice or legal assistance with respect to the request for the identity of financial institutions or a consumer report respecting any consumer under this section.

(e) Payment of fees

The Federal Bureau of Investigation shall, subject to the availability of appropriations, pay to the consumer reporting agency assembling or providing report or information in accordance with procedures established under this section a fee for reimbursement for such costs as are reasonably necessary and which have been directly incurred in searching, reproducing, or transporting books, papers, records, or other data required or requested to be produced under this section.

(f) Limit on dissemination

The Federal Bureau of Investigation may not disseminate information obtained pursuant to this section outside of the Federal Bureau of Investigation, except to other Federal agencies as may be necessary for the approval or conduct of a foreign counterintelligence investigation, or, where the information concerns a person subject to the Uniform Code of Military Justice, to appropriate investigative authorities within the military department concerned as may be necessary for the conduct of a joint foreign counterintelligence investigation.

(g) Rules of construction

Nothing in this section shall be construed to prohibit information from being furnished by the Federal Bureau of Investigation pursuant to a subpoena or court order, in connection with a judicial or administrative proceeding to enforce the provisions of this subchapter. Nothing in this section shall be construed to authorize or permit the withholding of information from the Congress.

(h) Reports to Congress

(1) On a semiannual basis, the Attorney General shall fully inform the Permanent Select Committee on Intelligence and the Committee on Banking, Finance and Urban Affairs of the House of Representatives, and the Select Committee on Intelligence and the Committee on Banking, Housing, and Urban Affairs of the Senate concerning all requests made pursuant to subsections (a), (b), and (c) of this section.

(2) In the case of the semiannual reports required to be submitted under paragraph (1) to the Permanent Select Committee on Intelligence of the House of Representatives and the Select Committee on Intelligence of the Senate, the submittal dates for such reports shall be as provided in section 507 of the National Security Act of 1947.

(*i*) Damages

Any agency or department of the United States obtaining or disclosing any consumer reports, records, or information contained therein in violation of this section is liable to the consumer to whom such consumer reports, records, or information relate in an amount equal to the sum of—

(1) $100, without regard to the volume of consumer reports, records, or information involved;

(2) any actual damages sustained by the consumer as a result of the disclosure;

(3) if the violation is found to have been willful or intentional, such punitive damages as a court may allow; and

(4) in the case of any successful action to enforce liability under this subsection, the costs of the action, together with reasonable attorney fees, as determined by the court.

(j) Disciplinary actions for violations

If a court determines that any agency or department of the United States has violated any provision of this section and the court finds that the circumstances surrounding the violation raise questions of whether or not an officer or employee of the agency or department acted willfully or intentionally with respect to the violation, the agency or department shall promptly initiate a proceeding to determine whether or not disciplinary action is warranted against the officer or employee who was responsible for the violation.

(k) Good-faith exception

Notwithstanding any other provision of this subchapter, any consumer reporting agency or agent or employee thereof making disclosure of consumer reports or identifying information pursuant to this subsection in good-faith reliance upon a certification of the Federal Bureau of Investigation pursuant to provisions of this section shall not be liable to any person for such disclosure under this subchapter, the constitution of any State, or any law or regulation of any State or any political subdivision of any State.

(*l*) Limitation of remedies

Notwithstanding any other provision of this subchapter, the remedies and sanctions set forth in this section shall be the only judicial remedies and sanctions for violation of this section.

(m) Injunctive relief

In addition to any other remedy contained in this section, injunctive relief shall be available to require compliance with the procedures of this section. In the event of any successful action under this subsection, costs together with reasonable attorney fees, as determined by the court, may be recovered.

§ 627. Disclosures to governmental agencies for counterterrorism purposes [15 U.S.C. § 1681v]

(a) Disclosure

Notwithstanding section 604 or any other provision of this subchapter, a consumer reporting agency shall furnish a consumer report of a consumer and all other information in a consumer's file to a government agency authorized to conduct investigations of, or intelligence or counterintelligence activities or analysis related to, international terrorism when presented with a written certification by such government agency that such information is necessary for the agency's conduct or such investigation, activity or analysis.

(b) Form of certification

The certification described in subsection (a) shall be signed by a supervisory official designated by the head of a Federal agency or an officer of a Federal agency whose appointment to office is required to be made by the President, by and with the advice and consent of the Senate.

(c) Confidentiality

(1) If the head of a government agency authorized to conduct investigations of intelligence or counterintelligence activities or analysis related to international terrorism, or his designee, certifies that otherwise there may result a danger to the national security of the United States, interference with a criminal, counterterrorism, or counterintelligence investigation, interference with diplomatic relations, or danger to the life or physical safety of any person, no consumer reporting agency or officer, employee, or agent of such consumer reporting agency, shall disclose to any person

(other than those to whom such disclosure is necessary to comply with the request or an attorney to obtain legal advice or legal assistance with respect to the request), or specify in any consumer report, that a government agency has sought or obtained access to information under subsection (a) of this section.

(2) The request shall notify the person or entity to whom the request is directed of the nondisclosure requirement under paragraph (1).

(3) Any recipient disclosing to those persons necessary to comply with the request or to any attorney to obtain legal advice or legal assistance with respect to the request shall inform such persons of any applicable nondisclosure requirement. Any person who receives a disclosure under this subsection shall be subject to the same prohibitions on disclosure under paragraph (1).

(4) At the request of the authorized government agency, any person making or intending to make a disclosure under this section shall identify to the requesting official of the authorized government agency the person to whom such disclosure will be made or to whom such disclosure was made prior to the request, except that nothing in this section shall require a person to inform the requesting official of the identity of an attorney to whom disclosure was made or will be made to obtain legal advice or legal assistance with respect to the request for information under subsection (a) of this section.

(d) Rule of construction

Nothing in section 626 shall be construed to limit the authority of the Director of the Federal Bureau of Investigation under this section.

(e) Safe harbor

Notwithstanding any other provision of this subchapter, any consumer reporting agency or agent or employee thereof making disclosure of consumer reports or other information pursuant to this section in good-faith reliance upon a certification of a government agency pursuant to the provisions of this section shall not be liable to any person for such disclosure under this subchapter, the constitution of any State, or any law or regulation of any State or any political subdivision of any State.

(f) Reports to Congress

(1) On a semi-annual basis, the Attorney General shall fully inform the Committee on the Judiciary, the Committee on Financial Services, and the Permanent Select Committee on Intelligence of the House of Representatives and the Committee on the Judiciary, the Committee on Banking, Housing, and Urban Affairs, and the Select Committee on Intelligence of the Senate concerning all requests made pursuant to subsection (a) of this section.

(2) In the case of the semiannual reports required to be submitted under paragraph (1) to the Permanent Select Committee on Intelligence of the House of Representatives and the Select Committee on Intelligence of

the Senate, the submittal dates for such reports shall be as provided in section 415b of Title 50.

§ 628.   Disposal of records [15 U.S.C. § 1681w]

(a) Regulations

(1) In general

Not later than 1 year after December 4, 2003, the Federal banking agencies, the National Credit Union Administration, and the Commission with respect to the entities that are subject to their respective enforcement authority under section 1681s of this title, and the Securities and Exchange Commission, and in coordination as described in paragraph (2), shall issue final regulations requiring any person that maintains or otherwise possesses consumer information, or any compilation of consumer information, derived from consumer reports for a business purpose to properly dispose of any such information or compilation.

(2) Coordination

Each agency required to prescribe regulations under paragraph (1) shall—

(A) consult and coordinate with each other such agency so that, to the extent possible, the regulations prescribed by each such agency are consistent and comparable with the regulations by each such other agency; and

(B) ensure that such regulations are consistent with the requirements and regulations issued pursuant to Public Law 106–102 and other provisions of Federal law.

(3) Exemption authority

In issuing regulations under this section, the Federal banking agencies, the National Credit Union Administration, the Commission, and the Securities and Exchange Commission may exempt any person or class of persons from application of those regulations, as such agency deems appropriate to carry out the purpose of this section.

(b) Rule of construction

Nothing in this section shall be construed—

(1) to require a person to maintain or destroy any record pertaining to a consumer that is not imposed under other law; or

(2) to alter or affect any requirement imposed under any other provision of law to maintain or destroy such a record.

§ 629.   Corporate and technological circumvention prohibited [15 U.S.C. § 1681x]

The Commission shall prescribe regulations, to become effective not later than 90 days after December 4, 2003, to prevent a consumer reporting agency from circumventing or evading treatment as a consumer reporting agency described in section 603(p) for purposes of this subchapter, including—

(1) by means of a corporate reorganization or restructuring, including a merger, acquisition, dissolution, divestiture, or asset sale of a consumer reporting agency; or

(2) by maintaining or merging public record and credit account information in a manner that is substantially equivalent to that described in paragraphs (1) and (2) of section 603(p), in the manner described in section 603(p).

SUBCHAPTER VII. EQUAL CREDIT OPPORTUNITY ACT

(15 U.S.C. §§ 1691–1691f)

Table of Sections

----

§ 701. Scope of prohibition [15 U.S.C. § 1691]

(a) Activities constituting discrimination

It shall be unlawful for any creditor to discriminate against any applicant, with respect to any aspect of a credit transaction—

(1) on the basis of race, color, religion, national origin, sex or marital status, or age (provided the applicant has the capacity to contract);

(2) because all or part of the applicant's income derives from any public assistance program; or

(3) because the applicant has in good faith exercised any right under the Consumer Credit Protection Act.

(b) Activities not constituting discrimination

It shall not constitute discrimination for purposes of this subchapter for a creditor—

(1) to make an inquiry of marital status if such inquiry is for the purpose of ascertaining the creditor's rights and remedies applicable to the particular extension of credit and not to discriminate in a determination of credit-worthiness;

(2) to make an inquiry of the applicant's age or of whether the applicant's income derives from any public assistance program if such inquiry is for the purpose of determining the amount and probable continuance of income levels, credit history, or other pertinent element of credit-worthiness as provided in regulations of the Board;

(3) to use any empirically derived credit system which considers age if such system is demonstrably and statistically sound in accordance with

regulations of the Board, except that in the operation of such system the age of an elderly applicant may not be assigned a negative factor or value; or

(4) to make an inquiry or to consider the age of an elderly applicant when the age of such applicant is to be used by the creditor in the extension of credit in favor of such applicant.

(c) Additional activities not constituting discrimination

It is not a violation of this section for a creditor to refuse to extend credit offered pursuant to—

(1) any credit assistance program expressly authorized by law for an economically disadvantaged class of persons;

(2) any credit assistance program administered by a nonprofit organization for its members or an economically disadvantaged class of persons; or

(3) any special purpose credit program offered by a profit-making organization to meet special social needs which meets standards prescribed in regulations by the Board; if such refusal is required by or made pursuant to such program.

(d) Reason for adverse action; procedure applicable; "adverse action" defined

(1) Within thirty days (or such longer reasonable time as specified in regulations of the Board for any class of credit transaction) after receipt of a completed application for credit, a creditor shall notify the applicant of its action on the application.

(2) Each applicant against whom adverse action is taken shall be entitled to a statement of reasons for such action from the creditor. A creditor satisfies this obligation by—

(A) providing statements of reasons in writing as a matter of course to applicants against whom adverse action is taken; or

(B) giving written notification of adverse action which discloses (i) the applicant's right to a statement of reasons within thirty days after receipt by the creditor of a request made within sixty days after such notification, and (ii) the identity of the person or office from which such statement may be obtained. Such statement may be given orally if the written notification advises the applicant of his right to have the statement of reasons confirmed in writing on written request.

(3) A statement of reasons meets the requirements of this section only if it contains the specific reasons for the adverse action taken.

(4) Where a creditor has been requested by a third party to make a specific extension of credit directly or indirectly to an applicant, the notification and statement of reasons required by this subsection may be made directly by such creditor, or indirectly through the third party, provided in either case that the identity of the creditor is disclosed.

(5) The requirements of paragraph (2), (3), or (4) may be satisfied by verbal statements or notifications in the case of any creditor who did not act on more than one hundred and fifty applications during the calendar year preceding the calendar year in which the adverse action is taken, as determined under regulations of the Board.

(6) For purposes of this subsection, the term "adverse action" means a denial or revocation of credit, a change in the terms of an existing credit arrangement, or a refusal to grant credit in substantially the amount or on substantially the terms requested. Such term does not include a refusal to extend additional credit under an existing credit arrangement where the applicant is delinquent or otherwise in default, or where such additional credit would exceed a previously established credit limit.

(e) Appraisals; copies of reports to applicants; costs

Each creditor shall promptly furnish an applicant, upon written request by the applicant made within a reasonable period of time of the application, a copy of the appraisal report used in connection with the applicant's application for a loan that is or would have been secured by a lien on residential real property. The creditor may require the applicant to reimburse the creditor for the cost of the appraisal.

§ 702. Definitions; rules of construction [15 U.S.C. § 1691a]

(a) The definitions and rules of construction set forth in this section are applicable for the purposes of this subchapter.

(b) The term "applicant" means any person who applies to a creditor directly for an extension, renewal, or continuation of credit, or applies to a creditor indirectly by use of an existing credit plan for an amount exceeding a previously established credit limit.

(c) The term "Board" refers to the Board of Governors of the Federal Reserve System.

(d) The term "credit" means the right granted by a creditor to a debtor to defer payment of debt or to incur debts and defer its payment or to purchase property or services and defer payment therefor.

(e) The term "creditor" means any person who regularly extends, renews, or continues credit; any person who regularly arranges for the extension, renewal, or continuation of credit; or any assignee of an original creditor who participates in the decision to extend, renew, or continue credit.

(f) The term "person" means a natural person, a corporation, government or governmental subdivision or agency, trust, estate, partnership, cooperative, or association.

(g) Any reference to any requirement imposed under this subchapter or any provision thereof includes reference to the regulations of the Board under this subchapter or the provision thereof in question.

§ 703. Promulgation of regulations by Board; establishment of Consumer Advisory Council by Board; duties, membership, etc., of Council [15 U.S.C. § 1691b]

(a) Regulations

(1) The Board shall prescribe regulations to carry out the purposes of this subchapter. These regulations may contain but are not limited to such classifications, differentiation, or other provision, and may provide for such adjustments and exceptions for any class of transactions, as in the judgment of the Board are necessary or proper to effectuate the purposes of this subchapter, to prevent circumvention or evasion thereof, or to facilitate or substantiate compliance therewith.

(2) Such regulations may exempt from the provisions of this subchapter any class of transactions that are not primarily for personal, family, or household purposes, or business or commercial loans made available by a financial institution, except that a particular type within a class of such transactions may be exempted if the Board determines, after making an express finding that the application of this subchapter or of any provision of this subchapter of such transaction would not contribute substantially to effecting the purposes of this subchapter.

(3) An exemption granted pursuant to paragraph (2) shall be for no longer than five years and shall be extended only if the Board makes a subsequent determination, in the manner described by such paragraph, that such exemption remains appropriate.

(4) Pursuant to Board regulations, entities making business or commercial loans shall maintain such records or other data relating to such loans as may be necessary to evidence compliance with this subsection or enforce any action pursuant to the authority of this chapter. In no event shall such records or data be maintained for a period of less than one year. The Board shall promulgate regulations to implement this paragraph in the manner prescribed by chapter 5 of Title 5.

(5) The Board shall provide in regulations that an applicant for a business or commercial loan shall be provided a written notice of such applicant's right to receive a written statement of the reasons for the denial of such loan.

(b) Consumer Advisory Council

The Board shall establish a Consumer Advisory Council to advise and consult with it in the exercise of its functions under this chapter and to advise and consult with it concerning other consumer related matters it may place before the Council. In appointing the members of the Council, the Board shall seek to achieve a fair representation of the interests of creditors and consumers. The Council shall meet from time to time at the call of the Board. Members of the Council who are not regular full-time employees of the United States shall, while attending meetings of such Council, be entitled to receive compensation at a rate fixed by the Board, but not exceeding $100 per day, including travel time. Such members may be allowed travel expenses, including transportation and subsistence, while away from their homes or regular place of business.

§ 704. Administrative enforcement [15 U.S.C. § 1691c]

(a) Enforcing agencies

Compliance with the requirements imposed under this subchapter shall be enforced under:

(1) section 8 of the Federal Deposit Insurance Act, in the case of—

(A) national banks, and Federal branches and Federal agencies of foreign banks, by the Office of the Comptroller of the Currency;

(B) member banks of the Federal Reserve System (other than national banks), branches and agencies of foreign banks (other than Federal branches, Federal agencies, and insured State branches of foreign banks), commercial lending companies owned or controlled by foreign banks, and organizations operating under section 25 or 25(a) of the Federal Reserve Act, by the Board; and

(C) banks insured by the Federal Deposit Insurance Corporation (other than members of the Federal Reserve System) and insured State branches of foreign banks, by the Board of Directors of the Federal Deposit Insurance Corporation;

(2) Section 8 of the Federal Deposit Insurance Act, by the Director of the Office of Thrift Supervision, in the case of a savings association the deposits of which are insured by the Federal Deposit Insurance Corporation.

(3) The Federal Credit Union Act, by the Administrator of the National Credit Union Administration with respect to any Federal Credit Union.

(4) Subtitle IV of Title 49, by the Secretary of Transportation, with respect to all carriers subject to the jurisdiction of the Surface Transportation Board.

(5) Part A of subtitle VII of title 49, by the Secretary of Transportation with respect to any air carrier or foreign air carrier subject to that part.

(6) The Packers and Stockyards Act, 1921 (except as provided in section 406 of that Act), by the Secretary of Agriculture with respect to any activities subject to that Act.

(7) The Farm Credit Act of 1971, by the Farm Credit Administration with respect to any Federal land bank, Federal land bank association, Federal intermediate credit bank, and production credit association;

(8) The Securities Exchange Act of 1934, by the Securities and Exchange Commission with respect to brokers and dealers; and

(9) The Small Business Investment Act of 1958, by the Small Business Administration, with respect to small business investment companies.

The terms used in paragraph (1) that are not defined in this subchapter or otherwise defined in section 3(s) of the Federal Deposit Insurance Act (12 U.S.C. 1813(s)) shall have the meaning given to them in section 1(b) of the International Banking Act of 1978 (12 U.S.C. 3101).

(b) Violations of subchapter deemed violations of preexisting statutory requirements; additional agency powers

For the purpose of the exercise by any agency referred to in subsection (a) of this section of its powers under any Act referred to in that subsection, a violation of any requirement imposed under this subchapter shall be deemed to be a violation of a requirement imposed under that Act. In addition to its powers under any provision of law specifically referred to in subsection (a) of this section, each of the agencies referred to in that subsection may exercise for the purpose of enforcing compliance with any requirement imposed under this subchapter, any other authority conferred on it by law. The exercise of the authorities of any of the agencies referred to in subsection (a) of this section for the purpose of enforcing compliance with any requirement imposed under this subchapter shall in no way preclude the exercise of such authorities for the purpose of enforcing compliance with any other provision of law not relating to the prohibition of discrimination on the basis of sex or marital status with respect to any aspect of a credit transaction.

(c) Overall enforcement authority of Federal Trade Commission

Except to the extent that enforcement of the requirements imposed under this subchapter is specifically committed to some other Government agency under subsection (a) of this section, the Federal Trade Commission shall enforce such requirements. For the purpose of the exercise by the Federal Trade Commission of its functions and powers under the Federal Trade Commission Act, a violation of any requirement imposed under this subchapter shall be deemed a violation of a requirement imposed under that Act. All of the functions and powers of the Federal Trade Commission under the Federal Trade Commission Act are available to the Commission to enforce compliance by any person with the requirements imposed under this subchapter, irrespective of whether that person is engaged in commerce or meets any other jurisdictional tests in the Federal Trade Commission Act, including the power to enforce any Federal Reserve Board regulation promulgated under this subchapter in the same manner as if the violation had been a violation of a Federal Trade Commission trade regulation rule.

(d) Rules and regulations by enforcing agencies

The authority of the Board to issue regulations under this subchapter does not impair the authority of any other agency designated in this section to make rules respecting its own procedures in enforcing compliance with requirements imposed under this subchapter.

§ 705. Incentives for self-testing and self-correction [15 U.S.C. § 1691c–1]

(a) Privileged information

(1) Conditions for privilege

A report or result of a self-test (as that term is defined by regulations of the Board) shall be considered to be privileged under paragraph (2) if a creditor—

（A）conducts, or authorizes an independent third party to conduct, a self-test of any aspect of a credit transaction by a creditor, in order to determine the level or effectiveness of compliance with this subchapter by the creditor; and

（B）has identified any possible violation of this subchapter by the creditor and has taken, or is taking, appropriate corrective action to address any such possible violation.

(2) Privileged self-test

If a creditor meets the conditions specified in subparagraphs (A) and (B) of paragraph (1) with respect to a self-test described in that paragraph, any report or results of that self-test—

（A）shall be privileged; and

（B）may not be obtained or used by any applicant, department, or agency in any—

（i）proceeding or civil action in which one or more violations of this subchapter are alleged; or

（ii）examination or investigation relating to compliance with this subchapter.

(b) Results of self-testing

(1) In general

No provision of this section may be construed to prevent an applicant, department, or agency from obtaining or using a report or results of any self-test in any proceeding or civil action in which a violation of this subchapter is alleged, or in any examination or investigation of compliance with this subchapter if—

（A）the creditor or any person with lawful access to the report or results—

（i）voluntarily releases or discloses all, or any part of, the report or results to the applicant, department, or agency, or to the general public; or

（ii）refers to or describes the report or results as a defense to charges of violations of this subchapter against the creditor to whom the self-test relates; or

(B) the report or results are sought in conjunction with an adjudication or admission of a violation of this subchapter for the sole purpose of determining an appropriate penalty or remedy.

(2) Disclosure for determination of penalty or remedy

Any report or results of a self-test that are disclosed for the purpose specified in paragraph (1)(B)—

(A) shall be used only for the particular proceeding in which the adjudication or admission referred to in paragraph (1)(B) is made; and

(B) may not be used in any other action or proceeding.

(c) Adjudication

An applicant, department, or agency that challenges a privilege asserted under this section may seek a determination of the existence and application of that privilege in—

(1) a court of competent jurisdiction; or

(2) an administrative law proceeding with appropriate jurisdiction.

§ 706. Applicability of other laws [15 U.S.C. § 1691d]

(a) Requests for signature of husband and wife for creation of valid lien, etc.

A request for the signature of both parties to a marriage for the purpose of creating a valid lien, passing clear title, waiving inchoate rights to property, or assigning earnings, shall not constitute discrimination under this subchapter: *Provided, however,* That this provision shall not be construed to permit a creditor to take sex or marital status into account in connection with the evaluation of creditworthiness of any applicant.

(b) State property laws affecting creditworthiness

Consideration or application of State property laws directly or indirectly affecting creditworthiness shall not constitute discrimination for purposes of this subchapter.

(c) State laws prohibiting separate extension of consumer credit to husband and wife

Any provision of State law which prohibits the separate extension of consumer credit to each party to a marriage shall not apply in any case where each party to a marriage voluntarily applies for separate credit from the same creditor: *Provided,* That in any case where such a State law is so preempted, each party to the marriage shall be solely responsible for the debt so contracted.

(d) Combining credit accounts of husband and wife with same creditor to determine permissible finance charges or loan ceilings under Federal or State laws

When each party to a marriage separately and voluntarily applies for and obtains separate credit accounts with the same creditor, those accounts shall not be aggregated or otherwise combined for purposes of determining permissible finance charges or permissible loan ceilings under the laws of any State or of the United States.

(e) Election of remedies under subchapter or State law; nature of relief determining applicability

Where the same act or omission constitutes a violation of this subchapter and of applicable State law, a person aggrieved by such conduct may bring a legal action to recover monetary damages either under this subchapter or under such State law, but not both. This election of remedies shall not apply to court actions in which the relief sought does not include monetary damages or to administrative actions.

(f) Compliance with inconsistent State laws; determination of inconsistency

This subchapter does not annul, alter, or affect, or exempt any person subject to the provisions of this subchapter from complying with, the laws of any State with respect to credit discrimination, except to the extent that those laws are inconsistent with any provision of this subchapter, and then only to the extent of the inconsistency. The Board is authorized to determine whether such inconsistencies exist. The Board may not determine that any State law is inconsistent with any provision of this subchapter if the Board determines that such law gives greater protection to the applicant.

(g) Exemption by regulation of credit transactions covered by State law; failure to comply with State law

The Board shall by regulation exempt from the requirements of sections 701 and 702 any class of credit transactions within any State if it determines that under the law of that State that class of transactions is subject to requirements substantially similar to those imposed under this subchapter or that such law gives greater protection to the applicant, and that there is adequate provision for enforcement. Failure to comply with any requirement of such State law in any transaction so exempted shall constitute a violation of this subchapter for the purposes of section 707.

§ 707. Civil liability [15 U.S.C. § 1691e]

(a) Individual or class action for actual damages

Any creditor who fails to comply with any requirement imposed under this subchapter shall be liable to the aggrieved applicant for any actual damages sustained by such applicant acting either in an individual capacity or as a member of a class.

(b) Recovery of punitive damages in individual and class actions for actual damages; exemptions; maximum amount of punitive damages in individual actions; limitation on total recovery in class actions; factors determining amount of award

Any creditor, other than a government or governmental subdivision or agency, who fails to comply with any requirement imposed under this subchapter shall be liable to the aggrieved applicant for punitive damages in an amount not greater than $10,000, in addition to any actual damages provided in subsection (a) of this section, except that in the case of a class action the total recovery under this subsection shall not exceed the lesser of $500,000 or 1 per centum of the net worth of the creditor. In determining the amount of such damages in any action, the court shall consider, among other relevant factors, the amount of any actual damages awarded, the frequency and persistence of failures of compliance by the creditor, the resources of the creditor, the number of persons adversely affected, and the extent to which the creditor's failure of compliance was intentional.

(c) Action for equitable and declaratory relief

Upon application by an aggrieved applicant, the appropriate United States district court or any other court of competent jurisdiction may grant such equitable and declaratory relief as is necessary to enforce the requirements imposed under this subchapter.

(d) Recovery of costs and attorney fees

In the case of any successful action under subsection (a), (b), or (c) of this section, the costs of the action, together with a reasonable attorney's fee as determined by the court, shall be added to any damages awarded by the court under such subsection.

(e) Good faith compliance with rule, regulation, or interpretation of Board or interpretation or approval by an official or employee of Federal Reserve System duly authorized by Board

No provision of this subchapter imposing liability shall apply to any act done or omitted in good faith in conformity with any official rule, regulation, or interpretation thereof by the Board or in conformity with any interpretation or approval by an official or employee of the Federal Reserve System duly authorized by the Board to issue such interpretations or approvals under such procedures as the Board may prescribe therefor, notwithstanding that after such act or omission has occurred, such rule, regulation, interpretation, or approval is amended, rescinded, or determined by judicial or other authority to be invalid for any reason.

(f) Jurisdiction of courts; time for maintenance of action; exceptions

Any action under this section may be brought in the appropriate United States district court without regard to the amount in controversy, or in any other court of competent jurisdiction. No such action shall be brought later than two years from the date of the occurrence of the violation, except that—

(1) whenever any agency having responsibility for administrative enforcement under section 704 commences an enforcement proceeding within two years from the date of the occurrence of the violation,

(2) whenever the Attorney General commences a civil action under this section within two years from the date of the occurrence of the violation,

then any applicant who has been a victim of the discrimination which is the subject of such proceeding or civil action may bring an action under this section not later than one year after the commencement of that proceeding or action.

(g) Request by responsible enforcement agency to Attorney General for civil action

The agencies having responsibility for administrative enforcement under section 704, if unable to obtain compliance with section 701, are authorized to refer the matter to the Attorney General with a recommendation that an appropriate civil action be instituted. Each agency referred to in paragraphs (1), (2), and (3) of section 704(a) shall refer the matter to the Attorney General whenever the agency has reason to believe that 1 or more creditors has engaged in a pattern or practice of discouraging or denying applications for credit in violation of section 701(a). Each such agency may refer the matter to the Attorney General whenever the agency has reason to believe that 1 or more creditors has violated section 701(a).

(h) Authority for Attorney General to bring civil action; jurisdiction

When a matter is referred to the Attorney General pursuant to subsection (g) of this section, or whenever he has reason to believe that one or more creditors are engaged in a pattern or practice in violation of this subchapter, the Attorney General may bring a civil action in any appropriate United States district court for such relief as may be appropriate, including actual and punitive damages and injunctive relief.

(i) Recovery under both subchapter and fair housing enforcement provisions prohibited for violation based on same transaction

No person aggrieved by a violation of this subchapter and by a violation of section 3605 of Title 42 shall recover under this subchapter and section 3612 of Title 42, if such violation is based on the same transaction.

(j) Discovery of creditor's granting standards

Nothing in this subchapter shall be construed to prohibit the discovery of a creditor's credit granting standards under appropriate discovery procedures in the court or agency in which an action or proceeding is brought.

(k) Notice to HUD of violations

Whenever an agency referred to in paragraph (1), (2), or (3) of section 704(a)—

(1) has reason to believe, as a result of receiving a consumer complaint, conducting a consumer compliance examination, or otherwise, that a violation of this subchapter has occurred;

(2) has reason to believe that the alleged violation would be a violation of the Fair Housing Act; and

(3) does not refer the matter to the Attorney General pursuant to subsection (g) of this section,

the agency shall notify the Secretary of Housing and Urban Development of the violation, and shall notify the applicant that the Secretary of Housing and Urban Development has been notified of the alleged violation and that remedies for the violation may be available under the Fair Housing Act.

§ 708. Annual reports to Congress; contents [15 U.S.C. § 1691f]

Each year, the Board and the Attorney General shall, respectively, make reports to the Congress concerning the administration of their functions under this subchapter, including such recommendations as the Board and the Attorney General, respectively, deem necessary or appropriate. In addition, each report of the Board shall include its assessment of the extent to which compliance with the requirements of this subchapter is being achieved, and a summary of the enforcement actions taken by each of the agencies assigned administrative enforcement responsibilities under section 704.

SUBCHAPTER VIII. FAIR DEBT COLLECTION PRACTICES ACT

(15 U.S.C. §§ 1692–1692m)

Table of Sections

---

§ 801. Short title

This title may be cited as the "Fair Debt Collection Practices Act."

§ 802. Congressional findings and declaration of purpose [15 U.S.C. § 1692]

(a) Abusive practices

There is abundant evidence of the use of abusive, deceptive, and unfair debt collection practices by many debt collectors. Abusive debt collection practices contribute to the number of personal bankruptcies, to marital instability, to the loss of jobs, and to invasions of individual privacy.

(b) Inadequacy of laws

Existing laws and procedures for redressing these injuries are inadequate to protect consumers.

(c) Available non-abusive collection methods

Means other than misrepresentation or other abusive debt collection practices are available for the effective collection of debts.

(d) Interstate commerce

Abusive debt collection practices are carried on to a substantial extent in interstate commerce and through means and instrumentalities of such commerce. Even where abusive debt collection practices are purely intrastate in character, they nevertheless directly affect interstate commerce.

(e) Purposes

It is the purpose of this title to eliminate abusive debt collection practices by debt collectors, to insure that those debt collectors who refrain from using abusive debt collection practices are not competitively disadvantaged, and to promote consistent State action to protect consumers against debt collection abuses.

§ 803. Definitions [15 U.S.C. § 1692a]

As used in this title—

(1) The term "Commission" means the Federal Trade Commission.

(2) The term "communication" means the conveying of information regarding a debt directly or indirectly to any person through any medium.

(3) The term "consumer" means any natural person obligated or allegedly obligated to pay any debt.

(4) The term "creditor" means any person who offers or extends credit creating a debt or to whom a debt is owed, but such term does not include any person to the extent that he receives an assignment or transfer of a debt in default solely for the purpose of facilitating collection of such debt for another.

(5) The term "debt" means any obligation or alleged obligation of a consumer to pay money arising out of a transaction in which the money, property, insurance, or services which are the subject of the transaction are primarily for personal, family, or household purposes, whether or not such obligation has been reduced to judgment.

(6) The term "debt collector" means any person who uses any instrumentality of interstate commerce or the mails in any business the principal purpose of which is the collection of any debts, or who regularly collects or attempts to collect, directly or indirectly, debts owed or due or asserted to be owed or due another. Notwithstanding the exclusion provided by clause (F) of the last sentence of this paragraph, the term includes any creditor who, in the process of collecting his own debts, uses any name other than his own which would indicate that a third person is collecting or attempting to collect such debts. For the purpose of section 808(6), such term also includes any person who uses any instrumentality of interstate commerce or the mails in any business the principal purpose of which is the enforcement of security interests. The term does not include—

(A) any officer or employee of a creditor while, in the name of the creditor, collecting debts for such creditor;

(B) any person while acting as a debt collector for another person, both of whom are related by common ownership or affiliated by corporate control, if the person acting as a debt collector does so only for persons to whom it is so related or affiliated and if the principal business of such person is not the collection of debts;

(C) any officer or employee of the United States or any State to the extent that collecting or attempting to collect any debt is in the performance of his official duties;

(D) any person while serving or attempting to serve legal process on any other person in connection with the judicial enforcement of any debt;

(E) any nonprofit organization which, at the request of consumers, performs bona fide consumer credit counseling and assists consumers in the liquidation of their debts by receiving payments from such consumers and distributing such amounts to creditors; and

(F) any person collecting or attempting to collect any debt owed or due or asserted to be owed or due another to the extent such activity (i) is incidental to a bona fide fiduciary obligation or a bona fide escrow arrangement; (ii) concerns a debt which was originated by such person; (iii) concerns a debt which was not in default at the time it was obtained by such person; or (iv) concerns a debt obtained by such person as a secured party in a commercial credit transaction involving the creditor.

(7) The term "location information" means a consumer's place of abode and his telephone number at such place, or his place of employment.

(8) The term "State" means any State, territory, or possession of the United States, the District of Columbia, the Commonwealth of Puerto Rico, or any political subdivision of any of the foregoing.

§ 804. Acquisition of location information [15 U.S.C. § 1692b]

Any debt collector communicating with any person other than the consumer for the purpose of acquiring location information about the consumer shall—

(1) identify himself, state that he is confirming or correcting location information concerning the consumer, and, only if expressly requested, identify his employer;

(2) not state that such consumer owes any debt;

(3) not communicate with any such person more than once unless requested to do so by such person or unless the debt collector reasonably believes that the earlier response of such person is erroneous or incomplete and that such person now has correct or complete location information;

(4) not communicate by post card;

(5) not use any language or symbol on any envelope or in the contents of any communication effected by the mails or telegram that indicates that

the debt collector is in the debt collection business or that the communication relates to the collection of a debt; and

(6) after the debt collector knows the consumer is represented by an attorney with regard to the subject debt and has knowledge of, or can readily ascertain, such attorney's name and address, not communicate with any person other than that attorney, unless the attorney fails to respond within a reasonable period of time to communication from the debt collector.

§ 805. Communication in connection with debt collection [15 U.S.C. § 1692c]

(a) Communication with the consumer generally

Without the prior consent of the consumer given directly to the debt collector or the express permission of a court of competent jurisdiction, a debt collector may not communicate with a consumer in connection with the collection of any debt—

(1) at any unusual time or place or a time or place known or which should be known to be inconvenient to the consumer. In the absence of knowledge of circumstances to the contrary, a debt collector shall assume that the convenient time for communicating with a consumer is after 8 o'clock antemeridian and before 9 o'clock postmeridian, local time at the consumer's location;

(2) if the debt collector knows the consumer is represented by an attorney with respect to such debt and has knowledge of, or can readily ascertain, such attorney's name and address, unless the attorney fails to respond within a reasonable period of time to a communication from the debt collector or unless the attorney consents to direct communication with the consumer; or

(3) at the consumer's place of employment if the debt collector knows or has reason to know that the consumer's employer prohibits the consumer from receiving such communication.

(b) Communication with third parties

Except as provided in section 804, without the prior consent of the consumer given directly to the debt collector, or the express permission of a court of competent jurisdiction, or as reasonably necessary to effectuate a postjudgment judicial remedy, a debt collector may not communicate, in connection with the collection of any debt, with any person other than the consumer, his attorney, a consumer reporting agency if otherwise permitted by law, the creditor, the attorney of the creditor, or the attorney of the debt collector.

(c) Ceasing communication

If a consumer notifies a debt collector in writing that the consumer refuses to pay a debt or that the consumer wishes the debt collector to cease further communication with the consumer, the debt collector shall not communicate further with the consumer with respect to such debt, except—

> (1) to advise the consumer that the debt collector's further efforts are being terminated;

> (2) to notify the consumer that the debt collector or creditor may invoke specified remedies which are ordinarily invoked by such debt collector or creditor; or

> (3) where applicable, to notify the consumer that the debt collector or creditor intends to invoke a specified remedy.

If such notice from the consumer is made by mail, notification shall be complete upon receipt.

(d) "Consumer" defined

For the purpose of this section, the term "consumer" includes the consumer's spouse, parent (if the consumer is a minor), guardian, executor, or administrator.

§ 806.   Harassment or abuse [15 U.S.C. § 1692d]

A debt collector may not engage in any conduct the natural consequence of which is to harass, oppress, or abuse any person in connection with the collection of a debt. Without limiting the general application of the foregoing, the following conduct is a violation of this section:

(1) The use or threat of use of violence or other criminal means to harm the physical person, reputation, or property of any person.

(2) The use of obscene or profane language or language the natural consequence of which is to abuse the hearer or reader.

(3) The publication of a list of consumers who allegedly refuse to pay debts, except to a consumer reporting agency or to persons meeting the requirements of section 603(f) or 604(3) of this Act.

(4) The advertisement for sale of any debt to coerce payment of the debt.

(5) Causing a telephone to ring or engaging any person in telephone conversation repeatedly or continuously with intent to annoy, abuse, or harass any person at the called number.

(6) Except as provided in section 804, the placement of telephone calls without meaningful disclosure of the caller's identity.

§ 807.   False or misleading representations [15 U.S.C. § 1692e]

A debt collector may not use any false, deceptive, or misleading representation or means in connection with the collection of any debt. Without limiting the general application of the foregoing, the following conduct is a violation of this section:

(1) The false representation or implication that the debt collector is vouched for, bonded by, or affiliated with the United States or any State, including the use of any badge, uniform, or facsimile thereof.

(2) The false representation of—

(A) the character, amount, or legal status of any debt; or

(B) any services rendered or compensation which may be lawfully received by any debt collector for the collection of a debt.

(3) The false representation or implication that any individual is an attorney or that any communication is from an attorney.

(4) The representation or implication that nonpayment of any debt will result in the arrest or imprisonment of any person or the seizure, garnishment, attachment, or sale of any property or wages of any person unless such action is lawful and the debt collector or creditor intends to take such action.

(5) The threat to take any action that cannot legally be taken or that is not intended to be taken.

(6) The false representation or implication that a sale, referral, or other transfer of any interest in a debt shall cause the consumer to—

(A) lose any claim or defense to payment of the debt; or

(B) become subject to any practice prohibited by this subchapter.

(7) The false representation or implication that the consumer committed any crime or other conduct in order to disgrace the consumer.

(8) Communicating or threatening to communicate to any person credit information which is known or which should be known to be false, including the failure to communicate that a disputed debt is disputed.

(9) The use or distribution of any written communication which simulates or is falsely represented to be a document authorized, issued, or approved by any court, official, or agency of the United States or any State, or which creates a false impression as to its source, authorization or approval.

(10) The use of any false representation or deceptive means to collect or attempt to collect any debt or to obtain information concerning a consumer.

(11) The failure to disclose in the initial written communication with the consumer and, in addition, if the initial communication with the consumer is oral, in that initial oral communication, that the debt collector is attempting to collect a debt and any information obtained will be used for that purpose, and the failure to disclose in subsequent communications that the communication is from a debt collector, except that this paragraph shall not apply to a formal pleading made in connection with a legal action.

(12) The false representation or implication that accounts have been turned over to innocent purchasers for value.

(13) The false representation or implication that documents are legal process.

(14) The use of any business, company, or organization name other than the true name of the debt collector's business, company, or organization.

(15) The false representation or implication that documents are not legal process forms or do not require action by the consumer.

(16) The false representation or implication that a debt collector operates or is employed by a consumer reporting agency as defined by section 603(f) of this Act.

§ 808.   Unfair practices [15 U.S.C. § 1692f]

A debt collector may not use unfair or unconscionable means to collect or attempt to collect any debt. Without limiting the general application of the foregoing, the following conduct is a violation of this section:

(1) The collection of any amount (including any interest, fee, charge, or expense incidental to the principal obligation) unless such amount is expressly authorized by the agreement creating the debt or permitted by law.

(2) The acceptance by a debt collector from any person of a check or other payment instrument postdated by more than five days unless such person is notified in writing of the debt collector's intent to deposit such check or instrument not more than ten nor less than three business days prior to such deposit.

(3) The solicitation by a debt collector of any postdated check or other postdated payment instrument for the purpose of threatening or instituting criminal prosecution.

(4) Depositing or threatening to deposit any postdated check or other postdated payment instrument prior to the date on such check or instrument.

(5) Causing charges to be made to any person for communications by concealment of the true purpose of the communication. Such charges include, but are not limited to, collect telephone calls and telegram fees.

(6) Taking or threatening to take any nonjudicial action to effect dispossession or disablement of property if—

(A) there is no present right to possession of the property claimed as collateral through an enforceable security interest;

(B) there is no present intention to take possession of the property; or

(C) the property is exempt by law from such dispossession or disablement.

(7) Communicating with a consumer regarding a debt by post card.

(8) Using any language or symbol, other than the debt collector's address, on any envelope when communicating with a consumer by use of the mails or by telegram, except that a debt collector may use his business name if such name does not indicate that he is in the debt collection business.

§ 809. Validation of debts [15 U.S.C. § 1692g]

(a) Notice of debt; contents

Within five days after the initial communication with a consumer in connection with the collection of any debt, a debt collector shall, unless the following information is contained in the initial communication or the consumer has paid the debt, send the consumer a written notice containing—

(1) the amount of the debt;

(2) the name of the creditor to whom the debt is owed;

(3) a statement that unless the consumer, within thirty days after receipt of the notice, disputes the validity of the debt, or any portion thereof, the debt will be assumed to be valid by the debt collector;

(4) a statement that if the consumer notifies the debt collector in writing within the thirty-day period that the debt, or any portion thereof, is disputed, the debt collector will obtain verification of the debt or a copy of a judgment against the consumer and a copy of such verification or judgment will be mailed to the consumer by the debt collector; and

(5) a statement that, upon the consumer's written request within the thirty-day period, the debt collector will provide the consumer with the name and address of the original creditor, if different from the current creditor.

(b) Disputed debts

If the consumer notifies the debt collector in writing within the thirty-day period described in subsection (a) of this section that the debt, or any portion thereof, is disputed, or that the consumer requests the name and address of the original creditor, the debt collector shall cease collection of the debt, or any disputed portion thereof, until the debt collector obtains verification of the debt or a copy of a judgment, or the name and address of the original creditor, and a copy of such verification or judgment, or name and address of the original creditor, is mailed to the consumer by the debt collector.

Collection activities and communications that do not otherwise violate this subchapter may continue during the 30–day period referred to in subsection (a) of this section unless the consumer has notified the debt collector in writing that the debt, or any portion of the debt, is disputed or that the consumer requests the name and address of the original creditor. Any collection activities and communication during the 30–day period may not overshadow or be inconsistent with the disclosure of the consumer's right to dispute the debt or request the name and address of the original creditor.

(c) Admission of liability

The failure of a consumer to dispute the validity of a debt under this section may not be construed by any court as an admission of liability by the consumer.

(d) Legal pleadings

A communication in the form of a formal pleading in a civil action shall not be treated as an initial communication for purposes of subsection (a) of this section.

(e) Notice provisions

The sending or delivery of any form or notice which does not relate to the collection of a debt and is expressly required by the Internal Revenue Code of 1986, chapter 94 of this title [15 U.S.C. § 6801 et seq.], or any provision of Federal or State law relating to notice of data security breach or privacy, or any regulation prescribed under any such provision of law, shall not be treated as an initial communication in connection with debt collection for purposes of this section.

§ 810. Multiple debts [15 U.S.C. § 1692h]

If any consumer owes multiple debts and makes any single payment to any debt collector with respect to such debts, such debt collector may not apply such payment to any debt which is disputed by the consumer and, where applicable, shall apply such payment in accordance with the consumer's directions.

§ 811. Legal actions by debt collectors [15 U.S.C. § 1692i]

(a) Venue

Any debt collector who brings any legal action on a debt against any consumer shall—

(1) in the case of an action to enforce an interest in real property securing the consumer's obligation, bring such action only in a judicial district or similar legal entity in which such real property is located; or

(2) in the case of an action not described in paragraph (1), bring such action only in the judicial district or similar legal entity—

(A) in which such consumer signed the contract sued upon; or

(B) in which such consumer resides at the commencement of the action.

(b) Authorization of actions

Nothing in this subchapter shall be construed to authorize the bringing of legal actions by debt collectors.

§ 812. Furnishing certain deceptive forms [15 U.S.C. § 1692j]

(a) It is unlawful to design, compile, and furnish any form knowing that such form would be used to create the false belief in a consumer that a person other than the creditor of such consumer is participating in the collection of or in an attempt to collect a debt such consumer allegedly owes such creditor, when in fact such person is not so participating.

(b) Any person who violates this section shall be liable to the same extent and in the same manner as a debt collector is liable under section 813 for failure to comply with a provision of this subchapter.

§ 813. Civil liability [15 U.S.C. § 1692k]

(a) Amount of damages

Except as otherwise provided by this section, any debt collector who fails to comply with any provision of this subchapter with respect to any person is liable to such person in an amount equal to the sum of—

(1) any actual damage sustained by such person as a result of such failure;

(2)(A) in the case of any action by an individual, such additional damages as the court may allow, but not exceeding $1,000; or

(B) in the case of a class action, (i) such amount for each named plaintiff as could be recovered under subparagraph (A), and (ii) such amount as the court may allow for all other class members, without regard to a minimum individual recovery, not to exceed the lesser of $500,000 or 1 per centum of the net worth of the debt collector; and

(3) in the case of any successful action to enforce the foregoing liability, the costs of the action, together with a reasonable attorney's fee as determined by the court. On a finding by the court that an action under this section was brought in bad faith and for the purpose of harassment, the court may award to the defendant attorney's fees reasonable in relation to the work expended and costs.

(b) Factors considered by court

In determining the amount of liability in any action under subsection (a) of this section, the court shall consider, among other relevant factors—

(1) in any individual action under subsection (a)(2)(A) of this section, the frequency and persistence of noncompliance by the debt collector, the nature of such noncompliance, and the extent to which such noncompliance was intentional; or

(2) in any class action under subsection (a)(2)(B) of this section, the frequency and persistence of noncompliance by the debt collector, the nature of such noncompliance, the resources of the debt collector, the number of persons adversely affected, and the extent to which the debt collector's noncompliance was intentional.

(c) Intent

A debt collector may not be held liable in any action brought under this subchapter if the debt collector shows by a preponderance of evidence that the violation was not intentional and resulted from a bona fide error notwithstanding the maintenance of procedures reasonably adapted to avoid any such error.

(d) Jurisdiction

An action to enforce any liability created by this subchapter may be brought in any appropriate United States district court without regard to the amount in controversy, or in any other court of competent jurisdiction, within one year from the date on which the violation occurs.

(e) Advisory opinions of Commission

No provision of this section imposing any liability shall apply to any act done or omitted in good faith in conformity with any advisory opinion of the Commission, notwithstanding that after such act or omission has occurred, such opinion is amended, rescinded, or determined by judicial or other authority to be invalid for any reason.

§ 814.   Administrative enforcement [15 U.S.C. § 1692*l*]

(a) Federal Trade Commission

Compliance with this subchapter shall be enforced by the Commission, except to the extent that enforcement of the requirements imposed under this subchapter is specifically committed to another agency under subsection (b) of this section. For purpose of the exercise by the Commission of its functions and powers under the Federal Trade Commission Act, a violation of this subchapter shall be deemed an unfair or deceptive act or practice in violation of that Act. All of the functions and powers of the Commission under the Federal Trade Commission Act are available to the Commission to enforce compliance by any person with this subchapter, irrespective of whether that person is engaged in commerce or meets any other jurisdictional tests in the Federal Trade Commission Act, including the power to enforce the provisions of this subchapter in the same manner as if the violation had been a violation of a Federal Trade Commission trade regulation rule.

(b) Applicable provisions of law

Compliance with any requirements imposed under this subchapter shall be enforced under—

(1) section 8 of Federal Deposit Insurance Act, in the case of—

(A) national banks and Federal branches and Federal agencies of foreign banks, by the Comptroller of the Currency;

(B) member banks of the Federal Reserve System [with specified exceptions], by the Board of Governors of the Federal Reserve System; and

(C) banks insured by the Federal Deposit Insurance Corporation (other than members of the Federal Reserve System) and insured State branches of foreign banks, by the Board of Directors of the Federal Deposit Insurance Corporation;

(2) section 8 of the Federal Deposit Insurance Act, by the Director of the Office of Thrift Supervision, in the case of a savings association the deposits of which are insured by the Federal Deposit Insurance Corporation;

(3) the Federal Credit Union Act, by the National Credit Union Administration Board with respect to any Federal credit union;

(4) subtitle IV of Title 49, by the Secretary of Transportation, with respect to all carriers subject to the jurisdiction of the Surface Transportation Board;

(5) the Federal Aviation Act of 1958, by the Secretary of Transportation with respect to any air carrier or any foreign air carrier subject to that Act; and

(6) the Packers and Stockyards Act, 1921 (except as provided in section 406 of that Act), by the Secretary of Agriculture with respect to any activities subject to that Act.

The terms used in paragraph (1) that are not defined in this Act or otherwise defined in section 3(s) of the Federal Deposit Insurance Act (12 U.S.C. § 1813(s)) shall have the meaning given to them in section 1(b) of the International Banking Act of 1978 (12 U.S.C. § 1301).

(c) Agency powers

For the purpose of the exercise by any agency referred to in subsection (b) of this section of its powers under any Act referred to in that subsection, a violation of any requirement imposed under this subchapter shall be deemed to be a violation of a requirement imposed under that Act. In addition to its powers under any provision of law specifically referred to in subsection (b) of this section, each of the agencies referred to in that subsection may exercise, for the purpose of enforcing compliance with any requirement imposed under this subchapter any other authority conferred on it by law, except as provided in subsection (d) of this section.

(d) Rules and regulations

Neither the Commission nor any other agency referred to in subsection (b) of this section may promulgate trade regulation rules or other regulations with respect to the collection of debts by debt collectors as defined in this subchapter.

§ 815. Reports to Congress by the Commission; views of other Federal agencies [15 U.S.C. § 1692m]

(a) Not later than one year after the effective date of this subchapter and at one-year intervals thereafter, the Commission shall make reports to the Congress concerning the administration of its functions under this subchapter, including such recommendations as the Commission deems necessary or appropriate. In addition, each report of the Commission shall include its assessment of the extent to which compliance with this subchapter is being achieved and a summary of the enforcement actions taken by the Commission under section 814.

(b) In the exercise of its functions under this subchapter, the Commission may obtain upon request the views of any other Federal agency which exercises enforcement functions under section 814.

§ 816. Relation to State laws [15 U.S.C. § 1692n]

This title does not annul, alter, or affect, or exempt any person subject to the provisions of this subchapter from complying with the laws of any State with respect to debt collection practices, except to the extent that those laws are inconsistent with any provision of this subchapter, and then only to the extent of the inconsistency. For purposes of this section, a State law is not inconsistent with this subchapter if the protection such law affords any consumer is greater than the protection provided by this title.

§ 817. Exemption for State regulation [15 U.S.C. § 1692o]

The Commission shall by regulation exempt from the requirements of this subchapter any class of debt collection practices within any State if the Commission determines that under the law of that State that class of debt collection practices is subject to requirements substantially similar to those imposed by this subchapter, and that there is adequate provision for enforcement.

§ 818. Exception for certain bad check enforcement programs operated by private entities [15 U.S.C. § 1692p]

(a) In general

(1) Treatment of certain private entities

Subject to paragraph (2), a private entity shall be excluded from the definition of a debt collector, pursuant to the exception provided in section 803(6), with respect to the operation by the entity of a program described in paragraph (2)(A) under a contract described in paragraph (2)(B).

(2) Conditions of applicability

Paragraph (1) shall apply if—

(A) a State or district attorney establishes, within the jurisdiction of such State or district attorney and with respect to alleged bad check violations that do not involve a check described in subsection (b) of this section, a pretrial diversion program for alleged bad check offenders who agree to participate voluntarily in such program to avoid criminal prosecution;

(B) a private entity, that is subject to an administrative support services contract with a State or district attorney and operates under the direction, supervision, and control of such State or district attorney, operates the pretrial diversion program described in subparagraph (A); and

(C) in the course of performing duties delegated to it by a State or district attorney under the contract, the private entity referred to in subparagraph (B)—

(i) complies with the penal laws of the State;

(ii) conforms with the terms of the contract and directives of the State or district attorney;

(iii) does not exercise independent prosecutorial discretion;

(iv) contacts any alleged offender referred to in subparagraph (A) for purposes of participating in a program referred to in such paragraph—

(I) only as a result of any determination by the State or district attorney that probable cause of a bad check violation under State penal law exists, and that contact with the alleged offender for purposes of participation in the program is appropriate; and

(II) the alleged offender has failed to pay the bad check after demand for payment, pursuant to State law, is made for payment of the check amount;

(v) includes as part of an initial written communication with an alleged offender a clear and conspicuous statement that—

(I) the alleged offender may dispute the validity of any alleged bad check violation;

(II) where the alleged offender knows, or has reasonable cause to believe, that the alleged bad check violation is the result of theft or forgery of the check, identity theft, or other fraud that is not the result of the conduct of the alleged offender, the alleged offender may file a crime report with the appropriate law enforcement agency; and

(III) if the alleged offender notifies the private entity or the district attorney in writing, not later than 30 days after being contacted for the first time pursuant to clause (iv), that there is a dispute pursuant to this subsection, before further restitution efforts are pursued, the district attorney or an employee of the district attorney authorized to make such a determination makes a determination that there is probable cause to believe that a crime has been committed; and

(vi) charges only fees in connection with services under the contract that have been authorized by the contract with the State or district attorney.

(b) Certain checks excluded

A check is described in this subsection if the check involves, or is subsequently found to involve—

(1) a postdated check presented in connection with a payday loan, or other similar transaction, where the payee of the check knew that the issuer had insufficient funds at the time the check was made, drawn, or delivered;

(2) a stop payment order where the issuer acted in good faith and with reasonable cause in stopping payment on the check;

(3) a check dishonored because of an adjustment to the issuer's account by the financial institution holding such account without providing notice to the person at the time the check was made, drawn, or delivered;

(4) a check for partial payment of a debt where the payee had previously accepted partial payment for such debt;

(5) a check issued by a person who was not competent, or was not of legal age, to enter into a legal contractual obligation at the time the check was made, drawn, or delivered; or

(6) a check issued to pay an obligation arising from a transaction that was illegal in the jurisdiction of the State or district attorney at the time the check was made, drawn, or delivered.

(c) Definitions

For purposes of this section, the following definitions shall apply:

(1) State or district attorney

The term "State or district attorney" means the chief elected or appointed prosecuting attorney in a district, county (as defined in section 2 of title 1, United States Code), municipality, or comparable jurisdiction, including State attorneys general who act as chief elected or appointed prosecuting attorneys in a district, county (as so defined), municipality or comparable jurisdiction, who may be referred to by a variety of titles such as district attorneys, prosecuting attorneys, commonwealth's attorneys, solicitors, county attorneys, and state's attorneys, and who are responsible for the prosecution of State crimes and violations of jurisdiction-specific local ordinances.

(2) Check

The term "check" has the same meaning as in section 5002(6) of Title 12.

(3) Bad check violation

The term "bad check violation" means a violation of the applicable State criminal law relating to the writing of dishonored checks.

SUBCHAPTER IX. ELECTRONIC FUND TRANSFER ACT

(15 U.S.C. §§ 1693–1693r)

Table of Sections

---

§ 901. Short title

This Act may be cited as the "Electronic Fund Transfer Act."

§ 902. Congressional findings and declaration of purpose [15 U.S.C. § 1693]

(a) Rights and liabilities undefined

The Congress finds that the use of electronic systems to transfer funds provides the potential for substantial benefits to consumers. However, due to the unique characteristics of such systems, the application of existing consumer protection legislation is unclear, leaving the rights and liabilities of consumers, financial institutions, and intermediaries in electronic fund transfers undefined.

(b) Purpose

It is the purpose of this subchapter to provide a basic framework establishing the rights, liabilities, and responsibilities of participants in electronic fund transfer systems. The primary objective of this subchapter, however, is the provision of individual consumer rights.

§ 903. Definitions [15 U.S.C. § 1693a]

As used in this subchapter—

(1) the term "accepted card or other means of access" means a card, code, or other means of access to a consumer's account for the purpose of initiating electronic fund transfers when the person to whom such card or other means of access was issued has requested and received or has signed or has used, or authorized another to use, such card or other means of access for the purpose of transferring money between accounts or obtaining money, property, labor, or services;

(2) the term "account" means a demand deposit, savings deposit, or other asset account (other than an occasional or incidental credit balance in an open end credit plan as defined in section 103(i) of this Act), as described in regulations of the Board, established primarily for personal, family, or household purposes, but such term does not include an account held by a financial institution pursuant to a bona fide trust agreement;

(3) the term "Board" means the Board of Governors of the Federal Reserve System;

(4) the term "business day" means any day on which the offices of the consumer's financial institution involved in an electronic fund transfer are open to the public for carrying on substantially all of its business functions;

(5) the term "consumer" means a natural person;

(6) the term "electronic fund transfer" means any transfer of funds, other than a transaction originated by check, draft, or similar paper instrument, which is initiated through an electronic terminal, telephonic instrument, or computer or magnetic tape so as to order, instruct, or authorize a financial institution to debit or credit an account. Such term includes, but is not limited to, point-of-sale transfers, automated teller machine transactions, direct deposits or withdrawals of funds, and transfers initiated by telephone. Such term does not include—

(A) any check guarantee or authorization service which does not directly result in a debit or credit to a consumer's account;

(B) any transfer of funds, other than those processed by automated clearinghouse, made by a financial institution on behalf of a consumer by means of a service that transfers funds held at either Federal Reserve banks or other depository institutions and which is not designed primarily to transfer funds on behalf of a consumer;

(C) any transaction the primary purpose of which is the purchase or sale of securities or commodities through a broker-dealer registered with or regulated by the Securities and Exchange Commission;

(D) any automatic transfer from a savings account to a demand deposit account pursuant to an agreement between a consumer and a financial institution for the purpose of covering an overdraft or maintaining an agreed upon minimum balance in the consumer's demand deposit account; or

(E) any transfer of funds which is initiated by a telephone conversation between a consumer and an officer or employee of a financial institution which is not pursuant to a prearranged plan and under which periodic or recurring transfers are not contemplated;

as determined under regulations of the Board;

(7) the term "electronic terminal" means an electronic device, other than a telephone operated by a consumer, through which a consumer may initiate an electronic fund transfer. Such term includes, but is not limited to, point-of-sale terminals, automated teller machines, and cash dispensing machines;

(8) the term "financial institution" means a State or National bank, a State or Federal savings and loan association, a mutual savings bank, a State or Federal credit union, or any other person who, directly or indirectly, holds an account belonging to a consumer;

(9) the term "preauthorized electronic fund transfer" means an electronic fund transfer authorized in advance to recur at substantially regular intervals;

(10) the term "State" means any State, territory, or possession of the United States, the District of Columbia, the Commonwealth of Puerto Rico, or any political subdivision of any of the foregoing; and

(11) the term "unauthorized electronic fund transfer" means an electronic fund transfer from a consumer's account initiated by a person other than the consumer without actual authority to initiate such transfer and from which the consumer receives no benefit, but the term does not include any electronic fund transfer (A) initiated by a person other than the consumer who was furnished with the card, code, or other means of access to such consumer's account by such consumer, unless the consumer has notified the financial institution involved that transfers by such other person are no longer authorized, (B) initiated with fraudulent intent by the consumer or any person acting in concert with the consumer, or (C) which constitutes an error committed by a financial institution.

§ 904. Regulations [15 U.S.C. § 1693b]

(a) Prescription by Board

The Board shall prescribe regulations to carry out the purposes of this subchapter. In prescribing such regulations, the Board shall:

(1) consult with the other agencies referred to in section 917 and take into account, and allow for, the continuing evolution of electronic banking services and the technology utilized in such services,

(2) prepare an analysis of economic impact which considers the costs and benefits to financial institutions, consumers, and other users of elec-

tronic fund transfers, including the extent to which additional documentation, reports, records, or other paper work would be required, and the effects upon competition in the provision of electronic banking services among large and small financial institutions and the availability of such services to different classes of consumers, particularly low income consumers,

(3) to the extent practicable, the Board shall demonstrate that the consumer protections of the proposed regulations outweigh the compliance costs imposed upon consumers and financial institutions, and

(4) any proposed regulations and accompanying analyses shall be sent promptly to Congress by the Board.

(b) Issuance of model clauses

The Board shall issue model clauses for optional use by financial institutions to facilitate compliance with the disclosure requirements of section 905 and to aid consumers in understanding the rights and responsibilities of participants in electronic fund transfers by utilizing readily understandable language. Such model clauses shall be adopted after notice duly given in the Federal Register and opportunity for public comment in accordance with section 553 of Title 5. With respect to the disclosures required by section 905(a)(3) and (4), the Board shall take account of variations in the services and charges under different electronic fund transfer systems and, as appropriate, shall issue alternative model clauses for disclosure of these differing account terms.

(c) Criteria; modification of requirements

Regulations prescribed hereunder may contain such classifications, differentiations, or other provisions, and may provide for such adjustments and exceptions for any class of electronic fund transfers, as in the judgment of the Board are necessary or proper to effectuate the purposes of this subchapter, to prevent circumvention or evasion thereof, or to facilitate compliance therewith. The Board shall by regulation modify the requirements imposed by this subchapter on small financial institutions if the Board determines that such modifications are necessary to alleviate any undue compliance burden on small financial institutions and such modifications are consistent with the purpose and objective of this subchapter.

(d) Applicability to service providers other than certain financial institutions

(1) In general

If electronic fund transfer services are made available to consumers by a person other than a financial institution holding a consumer's account, the Board shall by regulation assure that the disclosures, protections, responsibilities, and remedies created by this subchapter are made applicable to such persons and services.

(2) State and local government electronic benefit transfer systems

(A) Definition of electronic benefit transfer system

In this paragraph, the term "electronic benefit transfer system"—

(i) means a system under which a government agency distributes needs-tested benefits by establishing accounts that may be accessed by recipients electronically, such as through automated teller machines or point-of-sale terminals; and

(ii) does not include employment-related payments, including salaries and pension, retirement, or unemployment benefits established by a Federal, State, or local government agency.

(B) Exemption generally

The disclosures, protections, responsibilities, and remedies established under this subchapter, and any regulation prescribed or order issued by the Board in accordance with this subchapter, shall not apply to any electronic benefit transfer system established under State or local law or administered by a State or local government.

(C) Exception for direct deposit into recipient's account

Subparagraph (b) shall not apply with respect to any electronic funds transfer under an electronic benefit transfer system for a deposit directly into a consumer account held by the recipient of the benefit.

(D) Rule of Construction

No provision of this paragraph—

(i) affects or alters the protections otherwise applicable with respect to benefits established by any other provision Federal, State, or local law; or

(ii) otherwise supersedes the application of any State or local law.

(3) Fee disclosures at automated teller machines

(A) In general

The regulations prescribed under paragraph (1) shall require any automated teller machine operator who imposes a fee on any consumer for providing host transfer services to such consumer to provide notice in accordance with subparagraph (B) to the consumer (at the time the service is provided) of—

(i) the fact that a fee is imposed by such operator for providing the service; and

(ii) the amount of any such fee.

(B) Notice requirements

(i) On the machine. The notice required under clause (i) of subparagraph (A) with respect to any fee described in such subparagraph shall be posted in a prominent and conspicuous location on or at the automated teller machine at which the electronic fund transfer is initiated by the consumer.

(ii) On the screen. The notice required under clauses (i) and (ii) of subparagraph (A) with respect to any fee described in such subparagraph shall appear on the screen of the automated teller machine, or on a paper notice issued from such machine, after the transaction is initiated and before the consumer is irrevocably committed to completing the transaction, except that during the period beginning on the date of the enactment of the Gramm–Leach–Bliley Act and ending on December 31, 2004, this clause shall not apply to any automated teller machine that lacks the technical capability to disclose the notice on the screen or to issue a paper notice after the transaction is initiated and before the consumer is irrevocably committed to completing the transaction.

(C) Prohibition on fees not properly disclosed and explicitly assumed by consumer

No fee may be imposed by any automated teller machine operator in connection with any electronic fund transfer initiated by a consumer for which a notice is required under subparagraph (A), unless—

(i) the consumer receives such notice in accordance with subparagraph (B); and

(ii) the consumer elects to continue in the manner necessary to effect the transaction after receiving such notice.

(D) Definitions

For purposes of this paragraph, the following definitions shall apply:

(i) *Automated teller machine operator.* The term "automated teller machine operator" means any person who—

(I) operates an automated teller machine at which consumers initiate electronic fund transfers; and

(II) is not the financial institution that holds the account of such consumer from which the transfer is made.

(ii) *Electronic fund transfer.* The term "electronic fund transfer" includes a transaction that involves a balance inquiry initiated by a consumer in the same manner as an electronic fund transfer, whether or not the consumer initiates a transfer of funds in the course of the transaction.

(iii) *Host transfer services.* The term "host transfer services" means any electronic fund transfer made by an automated teller machine operator in connection with a transaction initiated by a consumer at an automated teller machine operated by such operator.

§ 905. Terms and conditions of transfers [15 U.S.C. § 1693c]

(a) Disclosures; time; form; contents

The terms and conditions of electronic fund transfers involving a consumer's account shall be disclosed at the time the consumer contracts for an electronic fund transfer service, in accordance with regulations of the Board. Such disclosures shall be in readily understandable language and shall include, to the extent applicable—

(1) the consumer's liability for unauthorized electronic fund transfers and, at the financial institution's option, notice of the advisability of prompt reporting of any loss, theft, or unauthorized use of a card, code, or other means of access;

(2) the telephone number and address of the person or office to be notified in the event the consumer believes that an unauthorized electronic fund transfer has been or may be effected;

(3) the type and nature of electronic fund transfers which the consumer may initiate, including any limitations on the frequency or dollar amount of such transfers, except that the details of such limitations need not be disclosed if their confidentiality is necessary to maintain the security of an electronic fund transfer system, as determined by the Board;

(4) any charges for electronic fund transfers or for the right to make such transfers;

(5) the consumer's right to stop payment of a preauthorized electronic fund transfer and the procedure to initiate such a stop payment order;

(6) the consumer's right to receive documentation of electronic fund transfers under section 906;

(7) a summary, in a form prescribed by regulations of the Board, of the error resolution provisions of section 908 and the consumer's rights thereunder. The financial institution shall thereafter transmit such summary at least once per calendar year;

(8) the financial institution's liability to the consumer under section 910; and

(9) under what circumstances the financial institution will in the ordinary course of business disclose information concerning the consumer's account to third persons.

(10) a notice to the consumer that a fee may be imposed by—

(A) an automated teller machine operator (as defined in section 904(d)(3)(D)(i)) if the consumer initiates a transfer from an automated teller machine that is not operated by the person issuing the card or other means of access; and

(B) any national, regional, or local network utilized to effect the transaction.

(b) Notification of changes to consumer

A financial institution shall notify a consumer in writing at least twenty-one days prior to the effective date of any change in any term or condition of the consumer's account required to be disclosed under subsection (a) of this section if such change would result in greater cost or liability for such consumer or decreased access to the consumer's account. A financial institution may, however, implement a change in the terms or conditions of an account without prior notice when such change is immediately necessary to maintain or restore the security of an electronic fund transfer system or a consumer's account. Subject to subsection (a)(3) of this section, the Board shall require subsequent notification if such a change is made permanent.

(c) Time for disclosures respecting accounts accessible prior to effective date of this subchapter

For any account of a consumer made accessible to electronic fund transfers prior to the effective date of this subchapter, the information required to be disclosed to the consumer under subsection (a) of this section shall be disclosed not later than the earlier of—

(1) the first periodic statement required by section 906(c) after the effective date of this title; or

(2) thirty days after the effective date of this title.

§ 906. Documentation of transfers [15 U.S.C. § 1693d]

(a) Availability of written documentation to consumer; contents

For each electronic fund transfer initiated by a consumer from an electronic terminal, the financial institution holding such consumer's account shall, directly or indirectly, at the time the transfer is initiated, make available to the consumer written documentation of such transfer. The documentation shall clearly set forth to the extent applicable—

(1) the amount involved and date the transfer is initiated;

(2) the type of transfer;

(3) the identity of the consumer's account with the financial institution from which or to which funds are transferred;

(4) the identity of any third party to whom or from whom funds are transferred; and

(5) the location or identification of the electronic terminal involved.

(b) Notice of credit to consumer

For a consumer's account which is scheduled to be credited by a preauthorized electronic fund transfer from the same payor at least once in each successive sixty-day period, except where the payor provides positive notice of the transfer to the consumer, the financial institution shall elect to provide promptly either positive notice to the consumer when the credit is made as scheduled, or negative notice to the consumer when the credit is not made as scheduled, in accordance with regulations of the Board. The means of notice elected shall be disclosed to the consumer in accordance with section 905.

(c) Periodic statement; contents

A financial institution shall provide each consumer with a periodic statement for each account of such consumer that may be accessed by means of an electronic fund transfer. Except as provided in subsections (d) and (e) of this section, such statement shall be provided at least monthly for each monthly or shorter cycle in which an electronic fund transfer affecting the account has occurred, or every three months, whichever is more frequent. The statement, which may include information regarding transactions other than electronic fund transfers, shall clearly set forth—

(1) with regard to each electronic fund transfer during the period, the information described in subsection (a) of this section, which may be provided on an accompanying document;

(2) the amount of any fee or charge assessed by the financial institution during the period for electronic fund transfers or for account maintenance;

(3) the balances in the consumer's account at the beginning of the period and at the close of the period; and

(4) the address and telephone number to be used by the financial institution for the purpose of receiving any statement inquiry or notice of account error from the consumer. Such address and telephone number shall be preceded by the caption "Direct Inquiries To:" or other similar language indicating that the address and number are to be used for such inquiries or notices.

(d) Consumer passbook accounts

In the case of a consumer's passbook account which may not be accessed by electronic fund transfers other than preauthorized electronic fund transfers crediting the account, a financial institution may, in lieu of complying with the requirements of subsection (c) of this section, upon presentation of the passbook provide the consumer in writing with the amount and date of each such transfer involving the account since the passbook was last presented.

(e) Accounts other than passbook accounts

In the case of a consumer's account, other than a passbook account, which may not be accessed by electronic fund transfers other than preauthorized electronic fund transfers crediting the account, the financial institution may provide a periodic statement on a quarterly basis which otherwise complies with the requirements of subsection (c) of this section.

(f) Documentation as evidence

In any action involving a consumer, any documentation required by this section to be given to the consumer which indicates that an electronic fund transfer was made to another person shall be admissible as evidence of such transfer and shall constitute prima facie proof that such transfer was made.

§ 907.　Preauthorized transfers [15 U.S.C. § 1693e]

(a) A preauthorized electronic fund transfer from a consumer's account may be authorized by the consumer only in writing, and a copy of such authorization shall be provided to the consumer when made. A consumer may stop payment of a preauthorized electronic fund transfer by notifying the financial institution orally or in writing at any time up to three business days preceding the scheduled date of such transfer. The financial institution may require written confirmation to be provided to it within fourteen days of an oral notification if, when the oral notification is made, the consumer is advised of such requirement and the address to which such confirmation should be sent.

(b) In the case of preauthorized transfers from a consumer's account to the same person which may vary in amount, the financial institution or designated payee shall, prior to each transfer, provide reasonable advance notice to the consumer, in accordance with regulations of the Board, of the amount to be transferred and the scheduled date of the transfer.

§ 908.　Error resolution [15 U.S.C. § 1693f]

(a) Notification to financial institution of error

If a financial institution, within sixty days after having transmitted to a consumer documentation pursuant to section 906(a), (c), or (d) or notification pursuant to section 906(b), receives oral or written notice in which the consumer—

(1) sets forth or otherwise enables the financial institution to identify the name and account number of the consumer;

(2) indicates the consumer's belief that the documentation, or, in the case of notification pursuant to section 906(b), the consumer's account, contains an error and the amount of such error; and

(3) sets forth the reasons for the consumer's belief (where applicable) that an error has occurred,

the financial institution shall investigate the alleged error, determine whether an error has occurred, and report or mail the results of such investigation and determination to the consumer within ten business days. The financial institution may require written confirmation to be provided to it within ten business days of an oral notification of error if, when the oral notification is made, the consumer is advised of such requirement and the address to which such confirmation should be sent. A financial institution which requires written confirmation in accordance with the previous sentence need not provisionally recredit a consumer's account in accordance with subsection (c) of this section, nor shall the financial institution be liable under subsection (e) of this section if the written confirmation is not received within the ten-day period referred to in the previous sentence.

(b) Correction of error; interest

If the financial institution determines that an error did occur, it shall promptly, but in no event more than one business day after such determination, correct the error, subject to section 909, including the crediting of interest where applicable.

(c) Provisional recredit of consumer's account

If a financial institution receives notice of an error in the manner and within the time period specified in subsection (a) of this section, it may, in lieu of the requirements of subsections (a) and (b) of this section, within ten business days after receiving such notice provisionally recredit the consumer's account for the amount alleged to be in error, subject to section 909, including interest where applicable, pending the conclusion of its investigation and its determination of whether an error has occurred. Such investigation shall be concluded not later than forty-five days after receipt of notice of the error. During the pendency of the investigation, the consumer shall have full use of the funds provisionally recredited.

(d) Absence of error; finding; explanation

If the financial institution determines after its investigation pursuant to subsection (a) or (c) of this section that an error did not occur, it shall deliver or mail to the consumer an explanation of its findings within 3 business days after the conclusion of its investigation, and upon request of the consumer promptly deliver or mail to the consumer reproductions of all documents which the financial institution relied on to conclude that such error did not occur. The financial institution shall include notice of the right to request reproductions with the explanation of its findings.

(e) Treble damages

If in any action under section 915, the court finds that—

> (1) the financial institution did not provisionally recredit a consumer's account within the ten-day period specified in subsection (c) of this section, and the financial institution (A) did not make a good faith investigation of the alleged error, or (B) did not have a reasonable basis for believing that the consumer's account was not in error; or

> (2) the financial institution knowingly and willfully concluded that the consumer's account was not in error when such conclusion could not reasonably have been drawn from the evidence available to the financial institution at the time of its investigation,

then the consumer shall be entitled to treble damages determined under section 915(a)(1).

(f) Acts constituting error

For the purpose of this section, an error consists of—

(1) an unauthorized electronic fund transfer;

(2) an incorrect electronic fund transfer from or to the consumer's account;

(3) the omission from a periodic statement of an electronic fund transfer affecting the consumer's account which should have been included;

(4) a computational error by the financial institution;

(5) the consumer's receipt of an incorrect amount of money from an electronic terminal;

(6) a consumer's request for additional information or clarification concerning an electronic fund transfer or any documentation required by this title; or

(7) any other error described in regulations of the Board.

§ 909.   Consumer liability [15 U.S.C. § 1693g]

(a) Unauthorized electronic fund transfers; limit

A consumer shall be liable for any unauthorized electronic fund transfer involving the account of such consumer only if the card or other means of access utilized for such transfer was an accepted card or other means of access and if the issuer of such card, code, or other means of access has provided a means whereby the user of such card, code, or other means of access can be identified as the person authorized to use it, such as by signature, photograph, or fingerprint or by electronic or mechanical confirmation. In no event, however, shall a consumer's liability for an unauthorized transfer exceed the lesser of—

(1) $50; or

(2) the amount of money or value of property or services obtained in such unauthorized electronic fund transfer prior to the time the financial institution is notified of, or otherwise becomes aware of, circumstances which lead to the reasonable belief that an unauthorized electronic fund transfer involving the consumer's account has been or may be effected. Notice under this paragraph is sufficient when such steps have been taken as may be reasonably required in the ordinary course of business to provide the financial institution with the pertinent information, whether or not any particular officer, employee, or agent of the financial institution does in fact receive such information.

Notwithstanding the foregoing, reimbursement need not be made to the consumer for losses the financial institution establishes would not have occurred but for the failure of the consumer to report within sixty days of transmittal of the statement (or in extenuating circumstances such as extended travel or hospitalization, within a reasonable time under the circumstances) any unauthorized electronic fund transfer or account error which appears on the periodic statement provided to the consumer under section 906. In addition, reimbursement need not be made to the consumer for losses which the financial institution establishes would not have occurred but for the failure of the consumer to report any loss or theft of a card or other means of access within two business days after the consumer learns of the loss or theft (or in extenuating circumstances such as extended travel or hospitalization, within a longer period which is reasonable under the circumstances), but the consumer's liability under this subsection in any such case may not exceed a total of $500, or the amount of unauthorized electronic fund transfers which occur following the close of two business days (or such longer period) after the consumer learns of the loss or theft but prior to notice to the financial institution under this subsection, whichever is less.

(b) Burden of proof

In any action which involves a consumer's liability for an unauthorized electronic fund transfer, the burden of proof is upon the financial institution to show that the electronic fund transfer was authorized or, if the electronic fund transfer was unauthorized, then the burden of proof is upon the financial institution to establish that the conditions of liability set forth in subsection (a) of this section have been met, and, if the transfer was initiated after the effective date of section 905, that the disclosures required to be made to the consumer under section 905(a)(1) and (2) were in fact made in accordance with such section.

(c) Determination of limitation on liability

In the event of a transaction which involves both an unauthorized electronic fund transfer and an extension of credit as defined in section 103(e) of this Act pursuant to an agreement between the consumer and the financial institution to extend such credit to the consumer in the event the consumer's account is overdrawn, the limitation on the consumer's liability for such transaction shall be determined solely in accordance with this section.

(d) Restriction on liability

Nothing in this section imposes liability upon a consumer for an unauthorized electronic fund transfer in excess of his liability for such a transfer under other applicable law or under any agreement with the consumer's financial institution.

(e) Scope of liability

Except as provided in this section, a consumer incurs no liability from an unauthorized electronic fund transfer.

§ 910. Liability of financial institutions [15 U.S.C. § 1693h]

(a) Action or failure to act proximately causing damages

Subject to subsections (b) and (c) of this section, a financial institution shall be liable to a consumer for all damages proximately caused by—

(1) the financial institution's failure to make an electronic fund transfer, in accordance with the terms and conditions of an account, in the correct amount or in a timely manner when properly instructed to do so by the consumer, except where—

(A) the consumer's account has insufficient funds;

(B) the funds are subject to legal process or other encumbrance restricting such transfer;

(C) such transfer would exceed an established credit limit;

(D) an electronic terminal has insufficient cash to complete the transaction; or

(E) as otherwise provided in regulations of the Board;

(2) the financial institution's failure to make an electronic fund transfer due to insufficient funds when the financial institution failed to credit, in accordance with the terms and conditions of an account, a deposit of funds to the consumer's account which would have provided sufficient funds to make the transfer, and

(3) the financial institution's failure to stop payment of a preauthorized transfer from a consumer's account when instructed to do so in accordance with the terms and conditions of the account.

(b) Acts of God and technical malfunctions

A financial institution shall not be liable under subsection (a)(1) or (2) of this section if the financial institution shows by a preponderance of the evidence that its action or failure to act resulted from—

(1) an act of God or other circumstance beyond its control, that it exercised reasonable care to prevent such an occurrence, and that it exercised such diligence as the circumstances required; or

(2) a technical malfunction which was known to the consumer at the time he attempted to initiate an electronic fund transfer or, in the case of a preauthorized transfer, at the time such transfer should have occurred.

(c) Intent

In the case of a failure described in subsection (a) of this section which was not intentional and which resulted from a bona fide error, notwithstanding the maintenance of procedures reasonably adapted to avoid any such error, the financial institution shall be liable for actual damages proved.

(d) Exception for damaged notices

If the notice required to be posted pursuant to section 904(d)(3)(B)(i) by an automated teller machine operator has been posted by such operator in compliance with such section and the notice is subsequently removed, damaged, or altered by any person other than the operator of the automated teller machine, the operator shall have no liability under this section for failure to comply with section 904(d)(3)(B)(i).

§ 911. Issuance of cards or other means of access [15 U.S.C. § 1693*i*]

(a) Prohibition; proper issuance

No person may issue to a consumer any card, code, or other means of access to such consumer's account for the purpose of initiating an electronic fund transfer other than—

(1) in response to a request or application therefor; or

(2) as a renewal of, or in substitution for, an accepted card, code, or other means of access, whether issued by the initial issuer or a successor.

(b) Exceptions

Notwithstanding the provisions of subsection (a) of this section, a person may distribute to a consumer on an unsolicited basis a card, code, or other means of access for use in initiating an electronic fund transfer from such consumer's account, if—

(1) such card, code, or other means of access is not validated;

(2) such distribution is accompanied by a complete disclosure, in accordance with section 905, of the consumer's rights and liabilities which will apply if such card, code, or other means of access is validated;

(3) such distribution is accompanied by a clear explanation, in accordance with regulations of the Board, that such card, code, or other means of access is not validated and how the consumer may dispose of such code, card, or other means of access if validation is not desired; and

(4) such card, code, or other means of access is validated only in response to a request or application from the consumer, upon verification of the consumer's identity.

(c) Validation

For the purpose of subsection (b) of this section, a card, code, or other means of access is validated when it may be used to initiate an electronic fund transfer.

§ 912. Suspension of obligations [15 U.S.C. § 1693j]

If a system malfunction prevents the effectuation of an electronic fund transfer initiated by a consumer to another person, and such other person has agreed to accept payment by such means, the consumer's obligation to the other person shall be suspended until the malfunction is corrected and the electronic fund transfer may be completed, unless such other person has subsequently, by written request, demanded payment by means other than an electronic fund transfer.

§ 913. Compulsory use of electronic fund transfers [15 U.S.C. § 1693k]

No person may—

(1) condition the extension of credit to a consumer on such consumer's repayment by means of preauthorized electronic fund transfers; or

(2) require a consumer to establish an account for receipt of electronic fund transfers with a particular financial institution as a condition of employment or receipt of a government benefit.

§ 914. Waiver of rights [15 U.S.C. § 1693*l*]

No writing or other agreement between a consumer and any other person may contain any provision which constitutes a waiver of any right conferred or cause of action created by this subchapter. Nothing in this section prohibits, however, any writing or other agreement which grants to a consumer a more extensive right or remedy or greater protection than contained in this title or a waiver given in settlement of a dispute or action.

§ 915. Civil liability [15 U.S.C. § 1693m]

(a) Individual or class action for damages; amount of award

Except as otherwise provided by this section and section 910, any person who fails to comply with any provision of this subchapter with respect to any consumer, except for an error resolved in accordance with section 908, is liable to such consumer in an amount equal to the sum of—

(1) any actual damage sustained by such consumer as a result of such failure;

(2)(A) in the case of an individual action, an amount not less than $100 nor greater than $1,000; or

(B) in the case of a class action, such amount as the court may allow, except that (i) as to each member of the class no minimum recovery shall be applicable, and (ii) the total recovery under this subparagraph in any class action or series of class actions arising out of the same failure to comply by the same person shall not be more than the lesser of $500,000 or 1 per centum of the net worth of the defendant; and

(3) in the case of any successful action to enforce the foregoing liability, the costs of the action, together with a reasonable attorney's fee as determined by the court.

(b) Factors determining amount of award

In determining the amount of liability in any action under subsection (a) of this section, the court shall consider, among other relevant factors—

(1) in any individual action under subsection (a)(2)(A) of this section, the frequency and persistence of noncompliance, the nature of such noncompliance, and the extent to which the noncompliance was intentional; or

(2) in any class action under subsection (a)(2)(B) of this section, the frequency and persistence of noncompliance, the nature of such noncompliance, the resources of the defendant, the number of persons adversely affected, and the extent to which the noncompliance was intentional.

(c) Unintentional violations; bona fide error

Except as provided in section 910, a person may not be held liable in any action brought under this section for a violation of this subchapter if the person shows by a preponderance of evidence that the violation was not intentional and resulted from a bona fide error notwithstanding the maintenance of procedures reasonably adapted to avoid any such error.

(d) Good faith compliance with rule, regulation, or interpretation of Board or approval of duly authorized official or employee of Federal Reserve System

No provision of this section or section 916 imposing any liability shall apply to—

(1) any act done or omitted in good faith in conformity with any rule, regulation, or interpretation thereof by the Board or in conformity with any interpretation or approval by an official or employee of the Federal Reserve System duly authorized by the Board to issue such interpretations or approvals under such procedures as the Board may prescribe therefor; or

(2) any failure to make disclosure in proper form if a financial institution utilized an appropriate model clause issued by the Board,

notwithstanding that after such act, omission, or failure has occurred, such rule, regulation, approval, or model clause is amended, rescinded, or determined by judicial or other authority to be invalid for any reason.

(e) Notification to consumer prior to action; adjustment of consumer's account

A person has no liability under this section for any failure to comply with any requirement under this subchapter if, prior to the institution of an action under this section, the person notifies the consumer concerned of the failure, complies with the requirements of this subchapter, and makes an appropriate adjustment to the consumer's account and pays actual damages or, where applicable, damages in accordance with section 910.

(f) Action in bad faith or for harassment; attorney's fees

On a finding by the court that an unsuccessful action under this section was brought in bad faith or for purposes of harassment, the court shall award to the defendant attorney's fees reasonable in relation to the work expended and costs.

(g) Jurisdiction of courts; time for maintenance of action

Without regard to the amount in controversy, any action under this section may be brought in any United States district court, or in any other court of competent jurisdiction, within one year from the date of the occurrence of the violation.

§ 916. Criminal liability [15 U.S.C. § 1693n]

(a) Violations respecting giving of false or inaccurate information, failure to provide information, and failure to comply with provisions of this subchapter

Whoever knowingly and willfully—

(1) gives false or inaccurate information or fails to provide information which he is required to disclose by this subchapter or any regulation issued thereunder; or

(2) otherwise fails to comply with any provision of this subchapter;

shall be fined not more than $5,000 or imprisoned not more than one year, or both.

(b) Violations affecting interstate or foreign commerce

Whoever—

(1) knowingly, in a transaction affecting interstate or foreign commerce, uses or attempts or conspires to use any counterfeit, fictitious, altered, forged, lost, stolen, or fraudulently obtained debit instrument to obtain money, goods, services, or anything else of value which within any one-year period has a value aggregating $1,000 or more; or

(2) with unlawful or fraudulent intent, transports or attempts or conspires to transport in interstate or foreign commerce a counterfeit, fictitious, altered, forged, lost, stolen, or fraudulently obtained debit instrument knowing the same to be counterfeit, fictitious, altered, forged, lost, stolen, or fraudulently obtained; or

(3) with unlawful or fraudulent intent, uses any instrumentality of interstate or foreign commerce to sell or transport a counterfeit, fictitious, altered, forged, lost, stolen, or fraudulently obtained debit instrument knowing the same to be counterfeit, fictitious, altered, forged, lost, stolen, or fraudulently obtained; or

(4) knowingly receives, conceals, uses, or transports money, goods, services, or anything else of value (except tickets for interstate or foreign transportation) which (A) within any one-year period has a value aggregating $1,000 or more, (B) has moved in or is part of, or which constitutes interstate or foreign commerce, and (C) has been obtained with a counterfeit, fictitious, altered, forged, lost, stolen, or fraudulently obtained debit instrument; or

(5) knowingly receives, conceals, uses, sells, or transports in interstate or foreign commerce one or more tickets for interstate or foreign transportation, which (A) within any one-year period have a value aggregating $500 or more, and (B) have been purchased or obtained with one or more counterfeit, fictitious, altered, forged, lost, stolen, or fraudulently obtained debit instrument; or

(6) in a transaction affecting interstate or foreign commerce, furnishes money, property, services, or anything else of value, which within any one-year period has a value aggregating $1,000 or more, through the use of any counterfeit, fictitious, altered, forged, lost, stolen, or fraudulently obtained debit instrument knowing the same to be counterfeit, fictitious, altered, forged, lost, stolen, or fraudulently obtained—

shall be fined not more than $10,000 or imprisoned not more than ten years, or both.

(c) "Debit instrument" defined

As used in this section, the term "debit instrument" means a card, code, or other device, other than a check, draft, or similar paper instrument, by the use of which a person may initiate an electronic fund transfer.

§ 917. Administrative enforcement [15 U.S.C. § 1693o]

(a) Enforcing agencies

Compliance with the requirements imposed under this subchapter shall be enforced under—

(1) section 8 of the Federal Deposit Insurance Act, in the case of—

(A) national banks and Federal branches and Federal agencies of foreign banks, by the Comptroller of the Currency;

(B) member banks of the Federal Reserve System (other than national banks), branches and agencies of foreign banks (other than Federal branches, Federal agencies, and insured State branches of foreign banks), commercial lending companies owned or controlled by foreign banks, and organizations operating under section 25 or 25(a) of the Federal Reserve Act, by the Board; and

(C) banks insured by the Federal Deposit Insurance Corporation (other than members of the Federal Reserve System) and insured State branches of foreign banks, by the Board of Directors of the Federal Deposit Insurance Corporation;

(2) section 8 of the Federal Deposit Insurance Act, by the Director of the Office of Thrift Supervision, in the case of a savings association the deposits of which are insured by the Federal Deposit Insurance Corporation;

(3) the Federal Credit Union Act, by the Administrator of the National Credit Union Administration with respect to any Federal credit union;

(4) the Federal Aviation Act of 1958, by the Secretary of Transportation, with respect to any air carrier or foreign air carrier subject to that Act; and

(5) the Securities Exchange Act of 1934, by the Securities and Exchange Commission, with respect to any broker or dealer subject to that Act.

The terms used in paragraph (1) that are not defined in this title or otherwise defined in section 3(s) of the Federal Deposit Insurance Act (12 U.S.C. § 1813(s)) shall have the meaning given to them in section 1(b) of the International Banking Act of 1978 (12 U.S.C. § 1301).

(b) Violations of subchapter deemed violations of pre-existing statutory requirements; additional powers

For the purpose of the exercise by any agency referred to in subsection (a) of this section of its powers under any Act referred to in that subsection, a violation of any requirement imposed under this subchapter shall be deemed to be a violation of a requirement imposed under that Act. In addition to its powers under any provision of law specifically referred to in subsection (a) of this section, each of the agencies referred to in that subsection may exercise, for the purpose of enforcing compliance with any requirement imposed under this subchapter, any other authority conferred on it by law.

(c) Overall enforcement authority of Federal Trade Commission

Except to the extent that enforcement of the requirements imposed under this subchapter is specifically committed to some other Government agency under subsection (a) of this section, the Federal Trade Commission shall enforce such requirements. For the purpose of the exercise by the Federal Trade Commission of its functions and powers under the Federal Trade Commission Act, a violation of any requirement imposed under this subchapter shall be deemed a violation of a requirement imposed under that Act. All of the functions and powers of the Federal Trade Commission under the Federal Trade Commission Act are available to the Commission to enforce compliance by any person subject to the jurisdiction of the Commission with the requirements imposed under this subchapter, irrespective of whether that person is engaged in commerce or meets any other jurisdictional tests in the Federal Trade Commission Act.

§ 918.   Reports to Congress [15 U.S.C. § 1693p]

(a) Not later than twelve months after the effective date of this subchapter and at one-year intervals thereafter, the Board shall make reports to the Congress concerning the administration of its functions under this subchapter, including such recommendations as the Board deems necessary and appropriate. In addition, each report of the Board shall include its assessment of the extent to which compliance with this subchapter is being achieved, and a summary of the enforcement actions taken under section 917. In such report, the Board shall particularly address the effects of this subchapter on the costs and benefits to financial institutions and consumers, on competition, on the introduction of new technology, on the operations of financial institutions, and on the adequacy of consumer protection.

(b) In the exercise of its functions under this subchapter, the Board may obtain upon request the views of any other Federal agency which, in the judgment of the Board, exercises regulatory or supervisory functions with respect to any class of persons subject to this subchapter.

§ 919. Relation to State laws [15 U.S.C. § 1693q]

This subchapter does not annul, alter, or affect the laws of any State relating to electronic fund transfers, except to the extent that those laws are inconsistent with the provisions of this subchapter, and then only to the extent of the inconsistency. A State law is not inconsistent with this subchapter if the protection such law affords any consumer is greater than the protection afforded by this subchapter. The Board shall, upon its own motion or upon the request of any financial institution, State, or other interested party, submitted in accordance with procedures prescribed in regulations of the Board, determine whether a State requirement is inconsistent or affords greater protection. If the Board determines that a State requirement is inconsistent, financial institutions shall incur no liability under the law of that State for a good faith failure to comply with that law, notwithstanding that such determination is subsequently amended, rescinded, or determined by judicial or other authority to be invalid for any reason. This subchapter does not extend the applicability of any such law to any class of persons or transactions to which it would not otherwise apply.

§ 920. Exemption for State regulation [15 U.S.C. § 1693r]

The Board shall by regulation exempt from the requirements of this subchapter any class of electronic fund transfers within any State if the Board determines that under the law of that State that class of electronic fund transfers is subject to requirements substantially similar to those imposed by this subchapter, and that there is adequate provision for enforcement.

FEDERAL RESERVE BOARD, REGULATION Z, TRUTH–IN–LENDING

12 C.F.R. Part 226

Table of Sections

Subpart A.   General

Subpart B. Open–End Credit

Subpart C. Closed–End Credit

Subpart D. Miscellaneous

Sec.

Subpart E. Special Rules for Certain Home Mortgage Transactions

---

SUBPART A.   GENERAL

§ 226.1   Authority, purpose, coverage, organization, enforcement and liability

(a) *Authority.* This regulation, known as Regulation Z, is issued by the Board of Governors of the Federal Reserve System to implement the Federal Truth in Lending Act, which is contained in Title I of the Consumer Credit Protection Act, as amended (15 U.S.C. 1601 et seq.). This regulation also implements title XII, section 1204 of the Competitive Equality Banking Act of 1987 (Pub.L. 100–86, 101 Stat. 552). Information-collection requirements contained in this regulation have been approved by the Office of Management and Budget under the provisions of 44 U.S.C. 3501 et seq. and have been assigned OMB No. 7100–0199.

(b) *Purpose.* The purpose of this regulation is to promote the informed use of consumer credit by requiring disclosures about its terms and cost. The regulation also gives consumers the right to cancel certain credit transactions that involve a lien on a consumer's principal dwelling, regulates certain credit card practices, and provides a means for fair and timely resolution of credit billing disputes. The regulation does not govern charges for consumer credit. The regulation requires a maximum interest rate to be stated in variable-rate contracts secured by the consumer's dwelling. It also imposes limitations on home equity plans that are subject to the requirements of § 226.5b and mortgages that are subject to the requirements of § 226.32. The regulation prohibits certain acts or practices in connection with credit secured by a consumer's principal dwelling.

(c) *Coverage.* (1) In general, this regulation applies to each individual or business that offers or extends credit when four conditions are met: (i) the credit is offered or extended to consumers; (ii) the offering or extension of credit is done regularly;[1] (iii) the credit is subject to a finance charge or is payable by a written agreement in more than 4 installments; and (iv) the credit is primarily for personal, family, or household purposes.

(2) If a credit card is involved, however, certain provisions apply even if the credit is not subject to a finance charge, or is not payable by a written agreement in more than 4 installments, or if the credit card is to be used for business purposes.

(3) In addition, certain requirements of § 226.5b apply to persons who are not creditors but who provide applications for home equity plans to consumers.

(d) *Organization.* The regulation is divided into subparts and appendices as follows:

(1) Subpart A contains general information. It sets forth: (i) the authority, purpose, coverage, and organization of the regulation; (ii) the definitions of basic terms; (iii) the transactions that are exempt from coverage; and (iv) the method of determining the finance charge.

(2) Subpart B contains the rules for open-end credit. It requires that initial disclosures and periodic statements be provided, as well as additional disclosures for credit and charge card applications and solicitations and for home equity plans subject to the requirements of §§ 226.5a and 226.5b, respectively.

(3) Subpart C relates to closed-end credit. It contains rules on disclosures, treatment of credit balances, annual percentage rate calculations, rescission requirements, and advertising.

(4) Subpart D contains rules on oral disclosures, Spanish language disclosure in Puerto Rico, record retention, effect on state laws, state exemptions, and rate limitations.

(5) Subpart E contains special rules for mortgage transactions. Section 226.32 requires certain disclosures and provides limitations for loans that have rates and fees above specified amounts. Section 226.33 requires disclosures, including the total annual loan cost rate, for reverse mortgage

---

1. The meaning of "regularly" is explained in the definition of "creditor" in § 226.2(a).

transactions. Section 226.34 prohibits specific acts and practices in connection with mortgage transactions.

(6) Several appendices contain information such as the procedures for determinations about state laws, state exemptions and issuance of staff interpretations, special rules for certain kinds of credit plans, a list of enforcement agencies, and the rules for computing annual percentage rates in closed-end credit transactions and total annual loan cost rates for reverse mortgage transactions.

(e) *Enforcement and liability.* Section 108 of the act contains the administrative enforcement provisions. Sections 112, 113, 130, 131, and 134 contain provisions relating to liability for failure to comply with the requirements of the act and the regulation. Section 1204(c) of Title XII of the Competitive Equality Banking Act of 1987, Pub.L. No. 100–86, 101 Stat. 552, incorporates by reference administrative enforcement and civil liability provisions of sections 108 and 130 of the act.

§ 226.2   Definitions and rules of construction

(a) *Definitions.* For purposes of this regulation, the following definitions apply:

(1) Act means the Truth in Lending Act (15 U.S.C. 1601 et seq.).

(2) Advertisement means a commercial message in any medium that promotes, directly or indirectly, a credit transaction.

(3) [Reserved][2]

(4) *Billing cycle* or *cycle* means the interval between the days or dates of regular periodic statements. These intervals shall be equal and no longer than a quarter of a year. An interval will be considered equal if the number of days in the cycle does not vary more than 4 days from the regular day or date of the periodic statement.

(5) *Board* means the Board of Governors of the Federal Reserve System.

(6) *Business day* means a day on which the creditor's offices are open to the public for carrying on substantially all of its business functions. However, for purposes of rescission under §§ 226.15 and 226.23, and for purposes of § 226.19(a)(1)(ii) and § 226.31, the term means all calendar days except Sundays and the legal public holidays specified in 5 U.S.C. 6103(a), such as New Year's Day, the Birthday of Martin Luther King, Jr., Washington's Birthday, Memorial Day, Independence Day, Labor Day, Columbus Day, Veterans Day, Thanksgiving Day, and Christmas Day.

(7) *Card issuer* means a person that issues a credit card or that person's agent with respect to the card.

(8) *Cardholder* means a natural person to whom a credit card is issued for consumer credit purposes, or a natural person who has agreed with the

2. [Reserved]

card issuer to pay consumer credit obligations arising from the issuance of a credit card to another natural person. For purposes of § 226.12(a) and (b), the term includes any person to whom a credit card is issued for any purpose, including business, commercial, or agricultural use, or a person who has agreed with the card issuer to pay obligations arising from the issuance of such a credit card to another person.

(9) *Cash price* means the price at which a creditor, in the ordinary course of business, offers to sell for cash the property or service that is the subject of the transaction. At the creditor's option, the term may include the price of accessories, services related to the sale, service contracts and taxes and fees for license, title, and registration. The term does not include any finance charge.

(10) *Closed-end credit* means consumer credit other than open-end credit as defined in this section.

(11) *Consumer* means a cardholder or a natural person to whom consumer credit is offered or extended. However, for purposes of rescission under §§ 226.15 and 226.23, the term also includes a natural person in whose principal dwelling a security interest is or will be retained or acquired, if that person's ownership interest in the dwelling is or will be subject to the security interest.

(12) *Consumer credit* means credit offered or extended to a consumer primarily for personal, family, or household purposes.

(13) *Consummation* means the time that a consumer becomes contractually obligated on a credit transaction.

(14) *Credit* means the right to defer payment of debt or to incur debt and defer its payment.

(15) *Credit card* means any card, plate, coupon book, or other single credit device that may be used from time to time to obtain credit. Charge card means a credit card on an account for which no periodic rate is used to compute a finance charge.

(16) *Credit sale* means a sale in which the seller is a creditor. The term includes a bailment or lease (unless terminable without penalty at any time by the consumer) under which the consumer:

(i) Agrees to pay as compensation for use a sum substantially equivalent to, or in excess of, the total value of the property and services involved; and

(ii) Will become (or has the option to become), for no additional consideration or for nominal consideration, the owner of the property upon compliance with the agreement.

(17) *Creditor* means:

(i) A person (A) who regularly extends consumer credit[3] that is subject to a finance charge or is payable by written agreement in more

---

3. A person regularly extends consumer credit only if it extended credit (other than credit subject to the requirements of § 226.32) more than 25 times (or more than

than 4 installments (not including a downpayment), and (B) to whom the obligation is initially payable, either on the face of the note or contract, or by agreement when there is no note or contract.

(ii) For purposes of § 226.4(c)(8) (discounts), § 226.9(d) (Finance charge imposed at time of transaction), and § 226.12(e) (Prompt notification of returns and crediting of refunds), a person that honors a credit card.

(iii) For purposes of Subpart B, any card issuer that extends either open-end credit or credit that is not subject to a finance charge and is not payable by written agreement in more than 4 installments.

(iv) For purposes of Subpart B (except for the credit and charge card disclosures contained in §§ 226.5a and 226.9(e) and (f), the finance charge disclosures contained in §§ 226.6(a) and 226.7(d) through (g), and the right of rescission set forth in § 226.15) and Subpart C, any card issuer that extends closed-end credit that is subject to a finance charge or is payable by written agreement in more than four installments.

(18) *Down payment* means an amount, including the value of any property used as a trade-in, paid to a seller to reduce the cash price of goods or services purchased in a credit sale transaction. A deferred portion of a downpayment may be treated as part of the downpayment if it is payable not later than the due date of the second otherwise regularly scheduled payment and is not subject to a finance charge.

(19) *Dwelling* means a residential structure that contains 1 to 4 units, whether or not that structure is attached to real property. The term includes an individual condominium unit, cooperative unit, mobile home, and trailer, if it is used as a residence.

(20) *Open-end credit* means consumer credit extended by a creditor under a plan in which:

(i) The creditor reasonably contemplates repeated transactions;

(ii) The creditor may impose a finance charge from time to time on an outstanding unpaid balance; and

(iii) The amount of credit that may be extended to the consumer during the term of the plan (up to any limit set by the creditor) is generally made available to the extent that any outstanding balance is repaid.

5 times for transaction secured by a dwelling) in the preceding calendar year. If a person did not meet these numerical standards in the preceding calendar year, the numerical standards shall be applied to the current calendar year. A person regularly extends consumer credit if, in any 12–month period, the person originates more than one credit extension that is subject to the requirements of § 226.32 or one or more such credit extensions through a mortgage broker.

(21) *Periodic rate* means a rate of finance charge that is or may be imposed by a creditor on a balance for a day, week, month, or other subdivision of a year.

(22) *Person* means a natural person or an organization, including a corporation, partnership, proprietorship, association, cooperative, estate, trust, or government unit.

(23) *Prepaid finance charge* means any finance charge paid separately in cash or by check before or at consummation of a transaction, or withheld from the proceeds of the credit at any time.

(24) *Residential mortgage transaction* means a transaction in which a mortgage, deed of trust, purchase money security interest arising under an installment sales contract, or equivalent consensual security interest is created or retained in the consumer's principal dwelling to finance the acquisition or initial construction of that dwelling.

(25) *Security interest* means an interest in property that secures performance of a consumer credit obligation and that is recognized by state or federal law. It does not include incidental interests such as interests in proceeds, accessions, additions, fixtures, insurance proceeds (whether or not the creditor is a loss payee or beneficiary), premium rebates, or interests in after-acquired property. For purposes of disclosure under §§ 226.6 and 226.18, the term does not include an interest that arises solely by operation of law. However, for purposes of the right of rescission under §§ 226.15 and 226.23, the term does include interests that arise solely by operation of law.

(26) *State* means any state, the District of Columbia, the Commonwealth of Puerto Rico, and any territory or possession of the United States.

(b) *Rules of construction.* For purposes of this regulation, the following rules of construction apply:

(1) Where appropriate, the singular form of a word includes the plural form and plural includes singular.

(2) Where the words *obligation* and *transaction* are used in this regulation, they refer to a consumer *credit obligation* or transaction, depending upon the context. Where the word *credit* is used in this regulation, it means *consumer credit* unless the context clearly indicates otherwise.

(3) Unless defined in this regulation, the words used have the meanings given to them by state law or contract.

(4) Footnotes have the same legal effect as the text of the regulation.

(5) Where the word "amount" is used in this regulation to describe disclosure requirements, it refers to a numerical amount.

§ 226.3 Exempt transactions

This regulation does not apply to the following:[4]

(a) *Business, commercial, agricultural, or organizational credit.* (1) An extension of credit primarily for a business, commercial or agricultural purpose.

(2) An extension of credit to other than a natural person, including credit to government agencies or instrumentalities.

(b) *Credit over $25,000 not secured by real property or a dwelling.* An extension of credit not secured by real property, or by personal property used or expected to be used as the principal dwelling of the consumer, in which the amount financed exceeds $25,000 or in which there is an express written commitment to extend credit in excess of $25,000.

(c) *Public utility credit.* An extension of credit that involves public utility services provided through pipe, wire, other connected facilities, or radio or similar transmission (including extensions of such facilities) if the charges for service, delayed payment, or any discounts for prompt payment are filed with or regulated by any government unit. The financing of durable goods or home improvements by a public utility is not exempt.

(d) *Securities or commodities accounts.* Transactions in securities or commodities accounts in which credit is extended by a broker-dealer registered with the Securities and Exchange Commission or the Commodity Futures Trading Commission.

(e) *Home fuel budget plans.* An installment agreement for the purchase of home fuels in which no finance charge is imposed.

(f) *Student loan programs.* Loans made, insured, or guaranteed pursuant to a program authorized by Title IV of the Higher Education Act of 1965 (20 U.S.C. 1070 et seq.).

§ 226.4 Finance charge

(a) *Definition.* The finance charge is the cost of consumer credit as a dollar amount. It includes any charge payable directly or indirectly by the consumer and imposed directly or indirectly by the creditor as an incident to or a condition of the extension of credit. It does not include any charge of a type payable in a comparable cash transaction.

(1) *Charges by third parties.* The finance charge includes fees and amounts charged by someone other than the creditor, unless otherwise excluded under this section, if the creditor:

---

4. The provisions in § 226.12(a) and (b) governing the issuance of credit cards and the liability for their unauthorized use apply to all credit cards, even if the credit cards are issued for use in connection with extensions of credit that otherwise are exempt under this section.

(i) requires the use of a third party as a condition of or an incident to the extension of credit, even if the consumer can choose the third party; or

(ii) retains a portion of the third-party charge, to the extent of the portion retained.

(2) *Special rule; closing agent charges.* Fees charged by a third party that conducts the loan closing (such as a settlement agent, attorney, or escrow or title company) are finance charges only if the creditor:

(i) Requires the particular services for which the consumer is charged;

(ii) Requires the imposition of the charge; or

(iii) Retains a portion of the third-party charge, to the extent of the portion retained.

(3) *Special rule; mortgage broker fees.* Fees charged by a mortgage broker (including fees paid by the consumer directly to the broker or to the creditor for delivery to the broker) are finance charges even if the creditor does not require the consumer to use a mortgage broker and even if the creditor does not retain any portion of the charge.

(b) *Example of finance charge.* The finance charge includes the following types of charges, except for charges specifically excluded by paragraphs (c) through (e) of this section:

(1) Interest, time price differential, and any amount payable under an add-on or discount system of additional charges.

(2) Service, transaction, activity, and carrying charges, including any charge imposed on a checking or other transaction account to the extent that the charge exceeds the charge for a similar account without a credit feature.

(3) Points, loan fees, assumption fees, finder's fees, and similar charges.

(4) Appraisal, investigation, and credit report fees.

(5) Premiums or other charges for any guarantee or insurance protecting the creditor against the consumer's default or other credit loss.

(6) Charges imposed on a creditor by another person for purchasing or accepting a consumer's obligation, if the consumer is required to pay the charges in cash, as an addition to the obligation, or as a deduction from the proceeds of the obligation.

(7) Premiums or other charges for credit life, accident, health, or loss-of-income insurance, written in connection with a credit transaction.

(8) Premiums or other charges for insurance against loss of or damage to property, or against liability arising out of the ownership or use of property, written in connection with a credit transaction.

(9) Discounts for the purpose of inducing payment by a means other than the use of credit.

(10) *Debt cancellation fees.* Charges or premiums paid for debt cancellation coverage written in connection with a credit transaction, whether or not the debt cancellation coverage is insurance under applicable law.

(c) *Charges excluded from the finance charge.* The following charges are not finance charges:

(1) Application fees charged to all applicants for credit, whether or not credit is actually extended.

(2) Charges for actual unanticipated late payment, for exceeding a credit limit, or for delinquency, default, or a similar occurrence.

(3) Charges imposed by a financial institution for paying items that overdraw an account, unless the payment of such items and the imposition of the charge were previously agreed upon in writing.

(4) Fees charged for participation in a credit plan, whether assessed on an annual or other periodic basis.

(5) Seller's points.

(6) Interest forfeited as a result of an interest reduction required by law on a time deposit used as security for an extension of credit.

(7) *Real-estate related fees.* The following fees in a transaction secured by real property or in a residential mortgage transaction, if the fees are bona fide and reasonable in amount:

(i) Fees for title examination, abstract of title, title insurance, property survey, and similar purposes.

(ii) Fees for preparing loan-related documents, such as deeds, mortgages, and reconveyance or settlement documents.

(iii) Notary and credit report fees.

(iv) Property appraisal fees or fees for inspections to assess the value or condition of the property if the service is performed prior to closing, including fees related to pest infestation or flood hazard determinations.

(v) Amounts required to be paid into escrow or trustee accounts if the amounts would not otherwise be included in the finance charge.

(8) Discounts offered to induce payment for a purchase by cash, check, or other means, as provided in § 167(b) of the act.

(d) *Insurance and debt cancellation coverage.*—(1) Voluntary credit insurance premiums. Premiums for credit life, accident, health or loss-of-income insurance may be excluded from the finance charge if the following conditions are met:

(i) The insurance coverage is not required by the creditor, and this fact is disclosed in writing.

(ii) The premium for the initial term of insurance coverage is disclosed. If the term of insurance is less than the term of the transaction, the term of insurance also shall be disclosed. The premium may be disclosed on a unit-cost basis only in open-end credit transactions, closed-end credit transactions by mail or telephone under § 226.17(g), and certain closed-end credit transactions involving an insurance plan that limits the total amount of indebtedness subject to coverage.

(iii) The consumer signs or initials an affirmative written request for the insurance after receiving the disclosures specified in this paragraph. Any consumer in the transaction may sign or initial the request.

(2) Premiums for insurance against loss of or damage to property, or against liability arising out of the ownership or use of property,[5] may be excluded from the finance charge if the following conditions are met:

(i) The insurance coverage may be obtained from a person of the consumer's choice[6], and this fact is disclosed.

(ii) If the coverage is obtained from or through the creditor, the premium for the initial term of insurance coverage shall be disclosed. If the term of insurance is less than the term of the transaction, the term of insurance shall also be disclosed. The premium may be disclosed on a unit-cost basis only in open-end credit transactions, closed-end transactions by mail or telephone under 226.17(g), and certain closed-end credit transactions involving an insurance plan that limits the total amount of indebtedness subject to coverage.

(3) *Voluntary debt cancellation fees.* (i) Charges or premiums paid for debt cancellation coverage of the type specified in paragraph (d)(3)(ii) of this section may be excluded from the finance charge, whether or not the coverage is insurance, if the following conditions are met:

(A) The debt cancellation agreement or coverage is not required by the creditor, and this fact is disclosed in writing;

(B) The fee or premium for the initial term of coverage is disclosed. If the term of coverage is less than the term of the credit transaction, the term of coverage also shall be disclosed. The fee or premium may be disclosed on a unit-cost basis only in open-end credit transactions, closed-end credit transactions by mail or telephone under § 226.17(g), and certain closed-end credit transactions involving a debt cancellation agreement that limits the total amount of indebtedness subject to coverage;

5. This includes single interest insurance if the insurer waives all right of subrogation against the consumer.

6. A creditor may reserve the right to refuse to accept, for reasonable cause, an insurer offered by the consumer.

(C) The consumer signs or initials an affirmative written request for coverage after receiving the disclosures specified in this paragraph. Any consumer in the transaction may sign or initial the request.

(ii) Paragraph (d)(3)(i) of this section applies to fees paid for debt cancellation coverage that provides for cancellation of all or part of the debtor's liability for amounts exceeding the value of the collateral securing the obligation, or in the event of the loss of life, health, or income or in case of accident.

(e) *Certain security interest charges.* If itemized and disclosed, the following charges may be excluded from the finance charge:

(1) Taxes and fees prescribed by law that actually are or will be paid to public officials for determining the existence of or for perfecting, releasing, or satisfying a security interest.

(2) The premium for insurance in lieu of perfecting a security interest to the extent that the premium does not exceed the fees described in paragraph (e)(1) of this section that otherwise would be payable.

(3) *Taxes on security instruments.* Any tax levied on security instruments or on documents evidencing indebtedness if the payment of such taxes is a requirement for recording the instrument securing the evidence of indebtedness.

(f) *Prohibited offsets.* Interest, dividends, or other income received or to be received by the consumer on deposits or investments shall not be deducted in computing the finance charge.

SUBPART B. OPEN–END CREDIT

§ 226.5 General disclosure requirements

(a) *Form of disclosures.* (1) The creditor shall make the disclosures required by this subpart clearly and conspicuously in writing,[7] in a form that the consumer may keep.[8] The disclosures required by this subpart may be provided to the consumer in electronic form, subject to compliance with the consumer consent and other applicable provisions of the Electronic Signatures in Global and National Commerce Act (E–Sign Act) (15 U.S.C. § 7001 et seq.). The disclosures required by §§ 226.5a, 22.5b, and 226.16 may be provided to the consumer in electronic form without regard to the consumer consent or other provisions of the E–Sign Act in the circumstances set forth in those sections.

---

7. The disclosure required by section 226.9(d) when a finance charge is imposed at the time of a transaction need not be written.

8. The disclosures required under § 226.5a for credit and charge card applications and solicitations, the home equity disclosures required under § 226.5b(d), the al-ternative summary billing rights statement provided for in § 226.9(a)(2), the credit and charge card renewal disclosures required under § 226.9(e), and the disclosures made under § 226.10(b) about payment requirements need not be in a form that the consumer can keep.

(2) The terms *finance charge* and *annual percentage rate*, when required to be disclosed with a corresponding amount or percentage rate, shall be more conspicuous than any other required disclosure.[9]

(3) Certain disclosures required under § 226.5a for credit and charge card applications and solicitations must be provided in a tabular format or in a prominent location in accordance with the requirements of that section.

(4) For rules governing the form of disclosures for home equity plans, see § 226.5b(a).

(b) *Time of disclosures.* (1) Initial disclosures. The creditor shall furnish the initial disclosure statement required by § 226.6 before the first transaction is made under the plan.

(2) *Periodic statements.* (i) The creditor shall mail or deliver a periodic statement as required by § 226.7 for each billing cycle at the end of which an account has a debit or credit balance of more than $1 or on which a finance charge has been imposed. A periodic statement need not be sent for an account if the creditor deems it uncollectible, or if delinquency collection proceedings have been instituted, or if furnishing the statement would violate federal law.

   (ii) The creditor shall mail or deliver the periodic statement at least 14 days prior to any date or the end of any time period required to be disclosed under § 226.7(j) in order for the consumer to avoid an additional finance or other charge.[10] A creditor that fails to meet this requirement shall not collect any finance or other charge imposed as a result of such failure.

(3) *Credit and charge card application and solicitation disclosures.* The card issuer shall furnish the disclosures for credit and charge card applications and solicitations in accordance with the timing requirements of § 226.5a.

(4) *Home equity plans.* Disclosures for home equity plans shall be made in accordance with the timing requirements of § 226.5b(b).

(c) *Basis of disclosures and use of estimates.* Disclosures shall reflect the terms of the legal obligation between the parties. If any information necessary for accurate disclosure is unknown to the creditor, it shall make the disclosure based on the best information reasonably available and shall state clearly that the disclosure is an estimate.

---

9. The terms need not be more conspicuous when used under § 226.5a generally for credit and charge card applications and solicitations under § 226.7(d) on periodic statements, under § 226.9(e) in credit and charge card renewal disclosures, and under § 226.16 in advertisements. (But see special rule for annual percentage rate for purchases, § 226.5a(b)(1).)

10. This timing requirement does not apply if the creditor is unable to meet the requirement because of an act of God, war, civil disorder, natural disaster, or strike.

(d) *Multiple creditors; multiple consumers.* If the credit plan involves more than one creditor, only one set of disclosures shall be given, and the creditors shall agree among themselves which creditor must comply with the requirements that this regulation imposes on any or all of them. If there is more than one consumer, the disclosures may be made to any consumer who is primarily liable on the account. If the right of rescission under § 226.15 is applicable, however, the disclosures required by §§ 226.6 and 226.15(b) shall be made to each consumer having the right to rescind.

(e) *Effect of subsequent events.* If a disclosure becomes inaccurate because of an event that occurs after the creditor mails or delivers the disclosures, the resulting inaccuracy is not a violation of this regulation, although new disclosures may be required under § 226.9(c).

§ 226.5a   Credit and charge card applications and solicitations

(a) *General rules.* The card issuer shall provide the disclosures required under this section on or with a solicitation or an application to open a credit or charge card account.

(1) *Definition of solicitation.* For purposes of this section, the term "solicitation" means an offer by the card issuer to open a credit or charge card account that does not require the consumer to complete an application.

(2) *Form of disclosures.* (i) The disclosures in paragraph (b)(1) through (7) of this section shall be provided in a prominent location on or with an application or a solicitation, or other applicable document, and in the form of a table with headings, content, and format substantially similar to any of the applicable tables found in Appendix G.

(ii) The disclosures in paragraphs (b)(8) through (11) of this section shall be provided either in the table containing the disclosures in paragraphs (b)(1) through (7), or clearly and conspicuously elsewhere on or with the application or solicitation.

(iii) The disclosure required under paragraph (b)(5) of this section shall contain the term *grace period.*

(iv) The terminology in the disclosures under paragraph (b) of this section shall be consistent with that to be used in the disclosures under §§ 226.6 and 226.7.

(v) For an application or a solicitation that is accessed by the consumer in electronic form, the disclosures required under this section may be provided to the consumer in electronic form on or with the application or solicitation.

(3) Exceptions. This section does not apply to home-equity plans accessible by a credit or charge card that are of the type subject to the requirements of § 226.5b; overdraft lines of credit tied to asset accounts accessed by check-guarantee cards or by debit cards; or lines of credit

accessed by check-guarantee cards or by debit cards that can be used only at automated teller machines.

(4) *Fees based on a percentage.* If the amount of any fee required to be disclosed under this section is determined on the basis of a percentage of another amount, the percentage used and the identification of the amount against which the percentage is applied may be disclosed instead of the amount of the fee.

(5) *Certain fees that vary by state.* If the amount of any fee referred to in paragraph (b)(8) through (10) of this section varies from state to state, the card issuer may disclose the range of the fees instead of the amount for each state, if the disclosure includes a statement that the amount of the fee varies from state to state.

(b) *Required disclosures.* The card issuer shall disclose the items in this paragraph on or with an application or a solicitation in accordance with the requirements of paragraphs (c), (d), or (e) of this section. A credit card issuer shall disclose all applicable items in this paragraph except for paragraph (b)(7) of this section. A charge card issuer shall disclose the applicable items in paragraphs (b)(2), (4), and (7) through (11) of this section.

(1) *Annual percentage rate.* Each periodic rate that may be used to compute the finance charge on an outstanding balance for purchases, a cash advance, or a balance transfer, expressed as an annual percentage rate (as determined by § 226.14(b)). When more than one rate applies for a category of transactions, the range of balances to which each rate is applicable shall also be disclosed. The annual percentage rate for purchases disclosed pursuant to this paragraph shall be in at least 18–point type, except for the following: a temporary initial rate that is lower than the rate that will apply after the temporary rate expires, and a penalty rate that will apply upon the occurrence of one or more specific events.

(i) If the account has a variable rate, the card issuer shall also disclose the fact that the rate may vary and how the rate is determined.

(ii) When variable rate disclosures are provided under paragraph (c) of this section, an annual percentage rate disclosure is accurate if the rate was in effect within 60 days before mailing the disclosures. When variable rate disclosures are provided under paragraph (e) of this section, an annual percentage rate disclosure is accurate if the rate was in effect within 30 days before printing the disclosures. Disclosures provided by electronic communication are subject to paragraph (b)(1)(iii) of this section.

(iii) When variable rate disclosures are provided by electronic communication, an annual percentage rate disclosure is accurate if the rate was in effect within 30 days before mailing the disclosures to a consumer's electronic mail address. If disclosures are made available at another location such as the card issuer's Internet web site, the annual percentage rate must be one in effect within the last 30 days.

(2) *Fees for issuance or availability.* Any annual or other periodic fee, expressed as an annualized amount, or any other fee that may be imposed for the issuance or availability of a credit or charge card, including any fee based on account activity or inactivity.

(3) *Minimum finance charge.* Any minimum or fixed finance charge that could be imposed during a billing cycle.

(4) *Transaction charges.* Any transaction charge imposed for the use of the card for purchases.

(5) *Grace period.* The date by which or the period within which any credit extended for purchases may be repaid without incurring a finance charge. If no grace period is provided, that fact must be disclosed. If the length of the grace period varies, the card issuer may disclose the range of days, the minimum number of days, or the average number of days in the grace period, if the disclosure is identified as a range, minimum, or average.

(6) *Balance computation method.* The name of the balance computation method listed in paragraph (g) of this section that is used to determine the balance for purchases on which the finance charge is computed, or an explanation of the method used if it is not listed. The explanation may appear outside the table if the table contains a reference to the explanation. In determining which balance computation method to disclose, the card issuer shall assume that credit extended for purchases will not be repaid within the grace period, if any.

(7) *Statement on charge card payments.* A statement that charges incurred by use of the charge card are due when the periodic statement is received.

(8) *Cash advance fee.* Any fee imposed for an extension of credit in the form of cash.

(9) *Late payment fee.* Any fee imposed for a late payment.

(10) *Over-the-limit fee.* Any fee imposed for exceeding a credit limit.

(11) *Balance transfer fee.* Any fee imposed to transfer an outstanding balance.

(c) *Direct mail applications and solicitations.* The card issuer shall disclose the applicable items in paragraph (b) of this section on or with an application or solicitation that is mailed to consumers or provided by electronic communication.

(d) *Telephone applications and solicitations—*(1) *Oral disclosure.* The card issuer shall orally disclose the information in paragraph (b)(1) through (7) of this section, to the extent applicable, in a telephone application or solicitation initiated by the card issuer.

(2) *Alternative disclosure.* The oral disclosure under paragraph (d)(1) of this section need not be given if the card issuer either does not impose a

fee described in paragraph (b)(2) of this section or does not impose such a fee unless the consumer uses the card, and the card issuer discloses in writing within 30 days after the consumer requests the card (but in no event later than the delivery of the card) the following:

(i) The applicable information in paragraph (b) of this section; and

(ii) The fact that the consumer need not accept the card or pay any fee disclosed unless the consumer uses the card.

(e) *Applications and solicitations made available to general public.* The card issuer shall provide disclosures, to the extent applicable, on or with an application or solicitation that is made available to the general public, including one contained in a catalog, magazine, or other generally available publication. The disclosures shall be provided in accordance with paragraph (e)(1), (2) or (3) of this section.

(1) *Disclosure of required credit information.* The card issuer may disclose in a prominent location on the application or solicitation the following:

(i) The applicable information in paragraph (b) of this section;

(ii) The date the required information was printed, including a statement that the required information was accurate as of that date and is subject to change after that date; and

(iii) A statement that the consumer should contact the card issuer for any change in the required information since it was printed, and a toll-free telephone number or a mailing address for that purpose.

(2) *Inclusion of certain initial disclosures.* The card issuer may disclose on or with the application or solicitation the following:

(i) The disclosures required under § 226.6(a) through (c); and

(ii) A statement that the consumer should contact the card issuer for any change in the required information, and a toll-free telephone number or a mailing address for that purpose.

(3) *No disclosure of credit information.* If none of the items in paragraph (b) of this section is provided on or with the application or solicitation, the card issuer may state in a prominent location on the application or solicitation the following:

(i) There are costs associated with the use of the card; and

(ii) The consumer may contact the card issuer to request specific information about the costs, along with a toll-free telephone number and a mailing address for that purpose.

(4) *Prompt response to requests for information.* Upon receiving a request for any of the information referred to in this paragraph, the card issuer shall promptly and fully disclose the information requested.

(f) *Special charge card rule—card issuer and person extending credit not the same person.* If a cardholder may by use of a charge card access an open-end credit plan that is not maintained by the charge card issuer, the card issuer need not provide the disclosures in paragraphs (c), (d) or (e) of this section for the open-end credit plan if the card issuer states on or with an application or a solicitation the following:

(1) The card issuer will make an independent decision whether to issue the card;

(2) The charge card may arrive before the decision is made about extending credit under the open-end credit plan; and

(3) Approval for the charge card does not constitute approval for the open-end credit plan.

(g) *Balance computation methods defined.* The following methods may be described by name. Methods that differ due to variations such as the allocation of payments, whether the finance charge begins to accrue on the transaction date or the date of posting the transaction, the existence or length of a grace period, and whether the balance is adjusted by charges such as late fees, annual fees and unpaid finance charges do not constitute separate balance computation methods.

(1)(i) *Average daily balance (including new purchases).* This balance is figured by adding the outstanding balance (including new purchases and deducting payments and credits) for each day in the billing cycle, and then dividing by the number of days in the billing cycle.

(ii) *Average daily balance (excluding new purchases).* This balance is figured by adding the outstanding balance (excluding new purchases and deducting payments and credits) for each day in the billing cycle, and then dividing by the number of days in the billing cycle.

(2)(i) *Two-cycle average daily balance (including new purchases).* This balance is the sum of the average daily balances for two billing cycles. The first balance is for the current billing cycle, and is figured by adding the outstanding balance (including new purchases and deducting payments and credits) for each day in the billing cycle, and then dividing by the number of days in the billing cycle. The second balance is for the preceding billing cycle.

(ii) *Two-cycle average daily balance (excluding new purchases).* This balance is the sum of the average daily balances for two billing cycles. The first balance is for the current billing cycle, and is figured by adding the outstanding balance (excluding new purchases and deducting payments and credits) for each day in the billing cycle, and then dividing by the number of days in the billing cycle. The second balance is for the preceding billing cycle.

(3) *Adjusted balance.* This balance is figured by deducting payments and credits made during the billing cycle from the outstanding balance at the beginning of the billing cycle.

(4) *Previous balance.* This balance is the outstanding balance at the beginning of the billing cycle.

§ 226.5b   Requirements for home equity plans

The requirements of this section apply to open-end credit plans secured by the consumer's dwelling. For purposes of this section, an annual percentage rate is the annual percentage rate corresponding to the periodic rate as determined under § 226.14(b).

(a) *Form of disclosures*—(1) *General.* The disclosures required by paragraph (d) of this section shall be made clearly and conspicuously and shall be grouped together and segregated from all unrelated information. The disclosures may be provided on the application form or on a separate form. The disclosure described in paragraph (d)(4)(iii), the itemization of third-party fees described in paragraph (d)(8), and the variable-rate information described in paragraph (d)(12) of this section may be provided separately from the other required disclosures.

(2) *Precedence of certain disclosures.* The disclosures described in paragraph (d)(1) through (4)(ii) of this section shall precede the other required disclosures.

(3) For an application that is accessed by the consumer in electronic form, the disclosures required under this section may be provided to the consumer in electronic form on or with the application.

(b) *Time of disclosures.* The disclosures and brochure required by paragraphs (d) and (e) of this section shall be provided at the time an application is provided to the consumer.[10a]

(c) *Duties of third parties.* Persons other than the creditor who provide applications to consumers for home equity plans must provide the brochure required under paragraph (e) of this section at the time an application is provided. If such persons have the disclosures required under paragraph (d) of this section for a creditor's home equity plan, they also shall provide the disclosures at such time.[10a]

(d) *Content of disclosures.* The creditor shall provide the following disclosures, as applicable:

(1) *Retention of information.* A statement that the consumer should make or otherwise retain a copy of the disclosures.

(2) *Conditions for disclosed terms.*

(i) A statement of the time by which the consumer must submit an application to obtain specific terms disclosed and an identification of any disclosed term that is subject to change prior to opening the plan.

(ii) A statement that, if a disclosed term changes (other than a change due to fluctuations in the index in a variable-rate plan) prior to opening the plan and the consumer therefore elects not to open the

---

10a. The disclosures and the brochure may be delivered or placed in the mail not later than three business days following receipt of a consumer's application in the case of applications contained in magazines or other publications, or when the application is received by telephone or through an intermediary agent or broker.

plan, the consumer may receive a refund of all fees paid in connection with the application.

(3) *Security interest and risk to home.* A statement that the creditor will acquire a security interest in the consumer's dwelling and that loss of the dwelling may occur in the event of default.

(4) *Possible actions by creditor.*

(i) A statement that, under certain conditions, the creditor may terminate the plan and require payment of the outstanding balance in full in a single payment and impose fees upon termination; prohibit additional extensions of credit or reduce the credit limit; and, as specified in the initial agreement, implement certain changes in the plan.

(ii) A statement that the consumer may receive, upon request, information about the conditions under which such actions may occur.

(iii) In lieu of the disclosure required under paragraph (d)(4)(ii) of this section, a statement of such conditions.

(5) *Payment terms.* The payment terms of the plan, including:

(i) The length of the draw period and any repayment period.

(ii) An explanation of how the minimum periodic payment will be determined and the timing of the payments. If paying only the minimum periodic payments may not repay any of the principal or may repay less than the outstanding balance, a statement of this fact, as well as a statement that a balloon payment may result.[10b]

(iii) An example, based on a $10,000 outstanding balance and a recent annual percentage rate,[10c] showing the minimum periodic payment, any balloon payment, and the time it would take to repay the $10,000 outstanding balance if the consumer made only those payments and obtained no additional extensions of credit.

If different payment terms may apply to the draw and any repayment period, or if different payment terms may apply within either period, the disclosures shall reflect the different payment terms.

(6) *Annual percentage rate.* For fixed-rate plans, a recent annual percentage rate[10c] imposed under the plan and a statement that the rate does not include costs other than interest.

10b. A balloon payment results if paying the minimum periodic payments does not fully amortize the outstanding balance by a specified date or time, and the consumer must repay the entire outstanding balance at such time.

10c. For fixed-rate plans, a recent annual percentage rate is a rate that has been in effect under the plan within the twelve months preceding the date the disclosures are provided to the consumer. For variable-rate plans, a recent annual percentage rate is the most recent rate provided in the historical example described in paragraph (d)(12)(xi) of this section or a rate that has been in effect under the plan since the date of the most recent rate in the table.

(7) *Fees imposed by creditor.* An itemization of any fees imposed by the creditor to open, use, or maintain the plan, stated as a dollar amount or percentage, and when such fees are payable.

(8) *Fees imposed by third parties to open a plan.* A good faith estimate, stated as a single dollar amount or range, of any fees that may be imposed by persons other than the creditor to open the plan, as well as a statement that the consumer may receive, upon request, a good faith itemization of such fees. In lieu of the statement, the itemization of such fees may be provided.

(9) *Negative amortization.* A statement that negative amortization may occur and that negative amortization increases the principal balance and reduces the consumer's equity in the dwelling.

(10) *Transaction requirements.* Any limitations on the number of extensions of credit and the amount of credit that may be obtained during any time period, as well as any minimum outstanding balance and minimum draw requirements, stated as dollar amounts or percentages.

(11) *Tax implications.* A statement that the consumer should consult a tax advisor regarding the deductibility of interest and charges under the plan.

(12) *Disclosures for variable-rate plans.* For a plan in which the annual percentage rate is variable, the following disclosures, as applicable:

(i) The fact that the annual percentage rate, payment, or term may change due to the variable-rate feature.

(ii) A statement that the annual percentage rate does not include costs other than interest.

(iii) The index used in making rate adjustments and a source of information about the index.

(iv) An explanation of how the annual percentage rate will be determined, including an explanation of how the index is adjusted, such as by the addition of a margin.

(v) A statement that the consumer should ask about the current index value, margin, discount or premium, and annual percentage rate.

(vi) A statement that the initial annual percentage rate is not based on the index and margin used to make later rate adjustments, and the period of time such initial rate will be in effect.

(vii) The frequency of changes in the annual percentage rate.

(viii) Any rules relating to changes in the index value and the annual percentage rate and resulting changes in the payment amount, including, for example, an explanation of payment limitations and rate carryover.

(ix) A statement of any annual or more frequent periodic limitations on changes in the annual percentage rate (or a statement that no annual limitation exists), as well as a statement of the maximum annual percentage rate that may be imposed under each payment option.

(x) The minimum periodic payment required when the maximum annual percentage rate for each payment option is in effect for a $10,000 outstanding balance, and a statement of the earliest date or time the maximum rate may be imposed.

(xi) An historical example, based on a $10,000 extension of credit, illustrating how annual percentage rates and payments would have been affected by index value changes implemented according to the terms of the plan. The historical example shall be based on the most recent 15 years of index values (selected for the same time period each year) and shall reflect all significant plan terms, such as negative amortization, rate carryover, rate discounts, and rate and payment limitations, that would have been affected by the index movement during the period.

(xii) A statement that rate information will be provided on or with each periodic statement.

(e) *Brochure*. The home equity brochure published by the Board or a suitable substitute shall be provided.

(f) *Limitations on home equity plans*. No creditor may, by contract or otherwise:

(1) Change the annual percentage rate unless:

(i) Such change is based on an index that is not under the creditor's control; and

(ii) Such index is available to the general public.

(2) Terminate a plan and demand repayment of the entire outstanding balance in advance of the original term (except for reverse mortgage transactions that are subject to paragraph (f)(4) of this section) unless:

(i) There is fraud or material misrepresentation by the consumer in connection with the plan;

(ii) The consumer fails to meet the repayment terms of the agreement for any outstanding balance;

(iii) Any action or inaction by the consumer adversely affects the creditor's security for the plan, or any right of the creditor in such security; or

(iv) Federal law dealing with credit extended by a depository institution to its executive officers specifically requires that as a condition of the plan the credit shall become due and payable on demand, provided that the creditor includes such a provision in the initial agreement.

(3) Change any term, except that a creditor may:

(i) Provide in the initial agreement that it may prohibit additional extensions of credit or reduce the credit limit during any period in which the maximum annual percentage rate is reached. A creditor also may provide in the initial agreement that specified changes will occur if a specified event takes place (for example, that the annual percentage rate will increase a specified amount if the consumer leaves the creditor's employment).

(ii) Change the index and margin used under the plan if the original index is no longer available, the new index has an historical movement substantially similar to that of the original index, and the new index and margin would have resulted in an annual percentage rate substantially similar to the rate in effect at the time the original index became unavailable.

(iii) Make a specified change if the consumer specifically agrees to it in writing at that time.

(iv) Make a change that will unequivocally benefit the consumer throughout the remainder of the plan.

(v) Make an insignificant change to terms.

(vi) Prohibit additional extensions of credit or reduce the credit limit applicable to an agreement during any period in which:

(A) The value of the dwelling that secures the plan declines significantly below the dwelling's appraised value for purposes of the plan;

(B) The creditor reasonably believes that the consumer will be unable to fulfill the repayment obligations under the plan because of a material change in the consumer's financial circumstances;

(C) The consumer is in default of any material obligation under the agreement;

(D) The creditor is precluded by government action from imposing the annual percentage rate provided for in the agreement;

(E) The priority of the creditor's security interest is adversely affected by government action to the extent that the value of the security interest is less than 120 percent of the credit line; or

(F) The creditor is notified by its regulatory agency that continued advances constitute an unsafe and unsound practice.

(4) For reverse mortgage transactions that are subject to § 226.33, terminate a plan and demand repayment of the entire outstanding balance in advance of the original term except:

(i) In the case of default;

(ii) If the consumer transfers title to the property securing the note;

(iii) If the consumer ceases using the property securing the note as the primary dwelling; or

(iv) Upon the consumer's death.

(g) *Refund of fees.* A creditor shall refund all fees paid by the consumer to anyone in connection with an application if any term required to be disclosed under paragraph (d) of this section changes (other than a change due to fluctuations in the index in a variable-rate plan) before the plan is opened and, as a result, the consumer elects not to open the plan.

(h) *Imposition of nonrefundable fees.* Neither a creditor nor any other person may impose a nonrefundable fee in connection with an application until three business days after the consumer receives the disclosures and brochure required under this section.[10d]

§ 226.6 Initial disclosure statement

The creditor shall disclose to the consumer, in terminology consistent with that to be used on the periodic statement, each of the following items, to the extent applicable:

(a) *Finance charge.* The circumstances under which a finance charge will be imposed and an explanation of how it will be determined, as follows:

(1) A statement of when finance charges begin to accrue, including an explanation of whether or not any time period exists within which any credit extended may be repaid without incurring a finance charge. If such a time period is provided, a creditor may, at its option and without disclosure, impose no finance charge when payment is received after the time period's expiration.

(2) A disclosure of each periodic rate that may be used to compute the finance charge, the range of balances to which it is applicable,[11] and the corresponding annual percentage rate.[12] When different periodic rates apply to different types of transactions, the types of transactions to which the periodic rates apply shall also be disclosed.

(3) An explanation of the method used to determine the balance on which the finance charge may be computed.

(4) An explanation of how the amount of any finance charge will be determined,[13] including a description of how any finance charge other than the periodic rate will be determined.

10d. If the disclosures and brochure are mailed to the consumer, the consumer is considered to have received them three business days after they are mailed.

11. A creditor is not required to adjust the range of balances disclosure to reflect the balance below which only a minimum charge applies.

12. If a creditor is offering a variable rate plan, the creditor shall also disclose: (1) the circumstances under which the rate(s) may increase; (2) any limitations on the increase; and (3) the effect(s) of an increase.

13. If no finance charge is imposed when the outstanding balance is less than a certain amount, no disclosure is required of that fact or of the balance below which no finance charge will be imposed.

(b) *Other charges*. The amount of any charge other than a finance charge that may be imposed as part of the plan, or an explanation of how the charge will be determined.

(c) *Security interests*. The fact that the creditor has or will acquire a security interest in the property purchased under the plan, or in other property identified by item or type.

(d) *Statement of billing rights*. A statement that outlines the consumer's rights and the creditor's responsibilities under § 226.12(c) and § 226.13 and that is substantially similar to the statement found in Appendix G.

(e) *Home equity plan information*. The following disclosures described in § 226.5b(d), as applicable:

(1) A statement of the conditions under which the creditor may take certain action, as described in § 226.5b(d)(4)(i), such as terminating the plan or changing the terms.

(2) The payment information described in § 226.5b(d)(5)(i) and (ii) for both the draw period and any repayment period.

(3) A statement that negative amortization may occur as described in § 226.5b(d)(9).

(4) A statement of any transaction requirements as described in § 226.5b(d)(10).

(5) A statement regarding the tax implications as described in § 226.5b(d)(11).

(6) A statement that the annual percentage rate imposed under the plan does not include costs other than interest as described in §§ 226.5b(d)(6) and § 226.5b(d)(12)(ii).

(7) The variable-rate disclosures described in § 226.5b(d)(12)(viii), (x), (xi), and (xii), as well as the disclosure described in § 226.5b(d)(5)(iii), unless the disclosures provided with the application were in a form the consumer could keep and included a representative payment example for the category of payment option chosen by the consumer.

§ 226.7 Periodic statement

The creditor shall furnish the consumer with a periodic statement that discloses the following items, to the extent applicable:

(a) *Previous balance*. The account balance outstanding at the beginning of the billing cycle.

(b) *Identification of transactions*. An identification of each credit transaction in accordance with § 226.8.

(c) *Credits*. Any credit to the account during the billing cycle, including the amount and the date of crediting. The date need not be provided if a delay in crediting does not result in any finance or other charge.

(d) *Periodic rates*. Each periodic rate that may be used to compute the finance charge, the range of balances to which it is applicable,[14] and the corresponding annual percentage rate.[15] If different periodic rates apply to different types of transactions, the types of transactions to which the periodic rates apply shall also be disclosed.

If no finance charge is imposed when the outstanding balance is less than a certain amount, no disclosure is required of that fact or of the balance below which no finance charge will be imposed.

(e) *Balance on which finance charge computed*. The amount of the balance to which a periodic rate was applied and an explanation of how that balance was determined. When a balance is determined without first deducting all credits and payments made during the billing cycle, that fact and the amount of the credits and payments shall be disclosed.

(f) *Amount of finance charge*. The amount of any finance charge debited or added to the account during the billing cycle, using the term *finance charge*. The components of the finance charge shall be individually itemized and identified to show the amount(s) due to the application of any periodic rates and the amount(s) of any other type of finance charge. If there is more than one periodic rate, the amount of the finance charge attributable to each rate need not be separately itemized and identified.

(g) *Annual percentage rate*. When a finance charge is imposed during the billing cycle, the annual percentage rate(s) determined under § 226.14, using the term *annual percentage rate*.

(h) *Other charges*. The amounts, itemized and identified by type, of any charges other than finance charges debited to the account during the billing cycle.

(i) *Closing date of billing cycle; new balance*. The closing date of the billing cycle and the account balance outstanding on that date.

(j) *Free-ride period*. The date by which or the time period within which the new balance or any portion of the new balance must be paid to avoid additional finance charges. If such a time period is provided, a creditor may, at its option and without disclosure, impose no finance charge when payment is received after the time period's expiration.

(k) *Address for notice of billing errors*. The address to be used for notice of billing errors. Alternatively, the address may be provided on the billing rights statement permitted by § 226.9(a)(2).

---

14. A creditor is not required to adjust the range of balances disclosure to reflect the balance below which only a minimum charge applies.

15. If a variable rate plan is involved, the creditor shall disclose the fact that the periodic rate(s) may vary.

§ 226.8   Identification of transactions

The creditor shall identify credit transactions on or with the first periodic statement that reflects the transaction by furnishing the following information, as applicable.[16]

(a) *Sale credit.* For each credit transaction involving the sale of property or services, the following rules shall apply:

(1) *Copy of credit document provided.* When an actual copy of the receipt or other credit document is provided with the first periodic statement reflecting the transaction, the transaction is sufficiently identified if the amount of the transaction and either the date of the transaction or the date of debiting the transaction to the consumer's account are disclosed on the copy or on the periodic statement.

(2) *Copy of credit document not provided—creditor and seller same or related person(s).* When the creditor and the seller are the same person or related persons, and an actual copy of the receipt or other credit document is not provided with the periodic statement, the creditor shall disclose the amount and date of the transaction, and a brief identification[17] of the property or services purchased.[18]

(3) *Copy of credit document not provided—creditor and seller not same or related person(s).* When the creditor and seller are not the same person or related persons, and an actual copy of the receipt or other credit document is not provided with the periodic statement, the creditor shall disclose the amount and date of the transaction; the seller's name; and the city, and state or foreign country where the transaction took place.[19]

(b) *Nonsale credit.* A nonsale credit transaction is sufficiently identified if the first periodic statement reflecting the transaction discloses a

---

16. Failure to disclose the information required by this section shall not be deemed a failure to comply with the regulation if: (1) the creditor maintains procedures reasonably adapted to obtain and provide the information; and (2) the creditor treats an inquiry for clarification or documentation as a notice of a billing error, including correcting the account in accordance with § 226.13(e). This applies to transactions that take place outside a state, as defined in § 226.2(a), whether or not the creditor maintains procedures reasonably adopted to obtain the required information.

17. As an alternative to the brief identification, the creditor may disclose a number or symbol that also appears on the receipt or other credit document given to the consumer, if the number or symbol reasonably identifies that transaction with that creditor, and if the creditor treats an inquiry for clarification or documentation as a notice of a billing error,

including correcting the account in accordance with § 226.13(e).

18. An identification of property or services may be replaced by the seller's name and location of the transaction when: (1) the creditor and the seller are the same person; (2) the creditor's open-end plan has fewer than 15,000 accounts; (3) the creditor provides the consumer with point-of-sale documentation for that transaction; and (4) the creditor treats an inquiry for clarification or documentation as a notice of a billing error, including correcting the account in accordance with § 226.13(e).

19. The creditor may omit the address or provide any suitable designation that helps the consumer to identify the transaction when the transaction (1) took place at a location that is not fixed; (2) took place in the consumer's home; or (3) was a mail or telephone order.

brief identification of the transaction;[20] the amount of the transaction; and at least one of the following dates: the date of the transaction, the date of debiting the transaction to the consumer's account, or, if the consumer signed the credit document, the date appearing on the document. If an actual copy of the receipt or other credit document is provided and that copy shows the amount and at least one of the specified dates, the brief identification may be omitted.

§ 226.9 Subsequent disclosure requirements

(a) *Furnishing statement of billing rights.* (1) *Annual statement.* The creditor shall mail or deliver the billing rights statement required by § 226.6(d) at least once per calendar year, at intervals of not less than 6 months nor more than 18 months, either to all consumers or to each consumer entitled to receive a periodic statement under § 226.5(b)(2) for any one billing cycle.

(2) *Alternative summary statement.* As an alternative to paragraph (a)(1) of this section, the creditor may mail or deliver, on or with each periodic statement, a statement substantially similar to that in Appendix G.

(b) *Disclosures for supplemental credit devices and additional features*—(1) If a creditor, within 30 days after mailing or delivering the initial disclosures under § 226.6(a), adds a credit feature to the consumer's account or mails or delivers to the consumer a credit device for which the finance charge terms are the same as those previously disclosed, no additional disclosures are necessary. After 30 days, if the creditor adds a credit feature or furnishes a credit device (other than as a renewal, resupply, or the original issuance of a credit card) on the same finance charge terms, the creditor shall disclose, before the consumer uses the feature or device for the first time, that it is for use in obtaining credit under the terms previously disclosed.

(2) Whenever a credit future is added or a credit device is mailed or delivered, and the finance charge terms for the feature or device differ from disclosures previously given, the disclosures required by § 226.6(a) that are applicable to the added feature or device shall be given before the consumer uses the feature or device for the first time.

(c) *Change in terms*—(1) *Written notice required.* Whenever any term required to be disclosed under § 226.6 is changed or the required minimum periodic payment is increased, the creditor shall mail or deliver written notice of the change to each consumer who may be affected. The notice shall be mailed or delivered at least 15 days prior to the effective date of the change. The 15–day timing requirement does not apply if the change

---

20. As an alternative to the brief identification, the creditor may disclose a number or symbol that also appears on the receipt or other credit document given to the consumer, if the number or symbol reasonably identifies that transaction with that creditor, and if the creditor treats an inquiry for clarification or documentation as a notice of a billing error, including correcting the account in accordance with § 226.13(e).

has been agreed to by the consumer, or if a periodic rate or other finance charge is increased because of the consumer's delinquency or default; the notice shall be given, however, before the effective date of the change.

(2) *Notice not required.* No notice under this section is required when the change involves late payment charges, charges for documentary evidence, or over-the-limit charges; a reduction of any component of a finance or other charge; suspension of future credit privileges or termination of an account or plan; or when the change results from an agreement involving a court proceeding, or from the consumer's default or delinquency (other than an increase in the periodic rate or other finance charge).

(3) *Notice for home equity plans.* If a creditor prohibits additional extensions of credit or reduces the credit limit applicable to a home equity plan pursuant to § 226.5b(f)(3)(i) or § 226.5b(f)(3)(vi), the creditor shall mail or deliver written notice of the action to each consumer who will be affected. The notice must be provided not later than three business days after the action is taken and shall contain specific reasons for the action. If the creditor requires the consumer to request reinstatement of credit privileges, the notice also shall state that fact.

(d) *Finance charge imposed at time of transaction.* (1) Any person, other than the card issuer, who imposes a finance charge at the time of honoring a consumer's credit card, shall disclose the amount of that finance charge prior to its imposition.

(2) The card issuer, if other than the person honoring the consumer's credit card, shall have no responsibility for the disclosure required by paragraph (d)(1) of this section, and shall not consider any such charge for purposes of §§ 226.5a, 226.6 and 226.7.

(e) *Disclosures upon renewal of credit or charge card—(1) Notice prior to renewal.* Except as provided in paragraph (e)(2) of this section, a card issuer that imposes any annual or other periodic fee to renew a credit or charge card account of the type subject to § 226.5a, including any fee based on account activity or inactivity, shall mail or deliver written notice of the renewal to the cardholder. The notice shall be provided at least 30 days or one billing cycle, whichever is less, before the mailing or the delivery of the periodic statement on which the renewal fee is initially charged to the account. The notice shall contain the following information:

(i) The disclosures contained in § 226.5a(b)(1) through (7) that would apply if the account were renewed;[20a] and

(ii) How and when the cardholder may terminate credit availability under the account to avoid paying the renewal fee.

(2) *Delayed notice.* The disclosures required by paragraph (e)(1) of this section may be provided later than the time in paragraph (e)(1) of this

---

20a. These disclosures need not be provided in tabular format or in a prominent location.

section, but no later than the mailing or the delivery of the periodic statement on which the renewal fee is initially charged to the account, if the card issuer also discloses at that time that:

(i) The cardholder has 30 days from the time the periodic statement is mailed or delivered to avoid paying the fee or to have the fee recredited if the cardholder terminates credit availability under the account; and

(ii) The cardholder may use the card during the interim period without having to pay the fee.

(3) *Notification on periodic statements.* The disclosures required by this paragraph may be made on or with a periodic statement. If any of the disclosures are provided on the back of a periodic statement, the card issuer shall include a reference to those disclosures on the front of the statement.

(f) *Change in credit card account insurance provided*—(1) *Notice prior to change.* If a credit card issuer plans to change the provider of insurance for repayment of all or part of the outstanding balance of an open-end credit card account of the type subject to § 226.5a, the card issuer shall mail or deliver the cardholder written notice of the change not less than 30 days before the change in providers occurs. The notice shall also include the following items, to the extent applicable:

(i) Any increase in the rate that will result from the change;

(ii) Any substantial decrease in coverage that will result from the change; and

(iii) A statement that the cardholder may discontinue the insurance.

(2) *Notice when change in provider occurs.* If a change described in paragraph (f)(1) of this section occurs, the card issuer shall provide the cardholder with a written notice no later than 30 days after the change, including the following items, to the extent applicable:

(i) The name and address of the new insurance provider;

(ii) A copy of the new policy or group certificate containing the basic terms of the insurance, including the rate to be charged; and

(iii) A statement that the cardholder may discontinue the insurance.

(3) *Substantial decrease in coverage.* For purposes of this paragraph, a substantial decrease in coverage is a decrease in a significant term of coverage that might reasonably be expected to affect the cardholder's decision to continue the insurance. Significant terms of coverage include, for example, the following:

(i) Type of coverage provided;

(ii) Age at which coverage terminates or becomes more restrictive;

(iii) Maximum insurable loan balance, maximum periodic benefit payment, maximum number of payments, or other term affecting the dollar amount of coverage or benefits provided;

(iv) Eligibility requirements and number and identity of persons covered;

(v) Definition of a key term of coverage such as disability;

(vi) Exclusions from or limitations on coverage; and

(vii) Waiting periods and whether coverage is retroactive.

(4) *Combined notification.* The notices required by paragraph (f)(1) and (2) of this section may be combined provided the timing requirement of paragraph (f)(1) of this section is met. The notices may be provided on or with a periodic statement.

§ 226.10   Prompt crediting of payments

(a) *General rule.* A creditor shall credit a payment to the consumer's account as of the date of receipt, except when a delay in crediting does not result in a finance or other charge or except as provided in paragraph (b) of this section.

(b) *Specific requirements for payments.* If a creditor specifies, on or with the periodic statement, requirements for the consumer to follow in making payments, but accepts a payment that does not conform to the requirements, the creditor shall credit the payment within 5 days of receipt.

(c) *Adjustment of account.* If a creditor fails to credit a payment, as required by paragraphs (a) and (b) of this section, in time to avoid the imposition of finance or other charges, the creditor shall adjust the consumer's account so that the charges imposed are credited to the consumer's account during the next billing cycle.

§ 226.11   Treatment of credit balances

When a credit balance in excess of $1 is created on a credit account (through transmittal of funds to a creditor in excess of the total balance due on an account, through rebates of unearned finance charges or insurance premiums, or through amounts otherwise owed to or held for the benefit of a consumer), the creditor shall:

(a) Credit the amount of the credit balance to the consumer's account;

(b) Refund any part of the remaining credit balance within 7 business days from receipt of a written request from the consumer; and

(c) Make a good faith effort to refund to the consumer by cash, check, or money order, or credit to a deposit account of the consumer, any part of the credit balance remaining in the account for more than 6 months. No further action is required if the consumer's current location is not known to the creditor and cannot be traced through the consumer's last known address or telephone number.

§ 226.12   Special credit card provisions

(a) *Issuance of credit cards*. Regardless of the purpose for which a credit card is to be used, including business, commercial, or agricultural use, no credit card shall be issued to any person except:

(1) In response to an oral or written request or application for the card; or

(2) As a renewal of, or substitute for, an accepted credit card.[21]

(b) *Liability of cardholder for unauthorized use*—(1) *Limitation on amount*. The liability of a cardholder for unauthorized use[22] of a credit card shall not exceed the lesser of $50 or the amount of money, property, labor, or services obtained by the unauthorized use before notification to the card issuer under paragraph (b)(3) of this section.

(2) *Conditions of liability*. A cardholder shall be liable for unauthorized use of a credit card only if:

(i) The credit card is an accepted credit card;

(ii) The card issuer has provided adequate notice[23] of the cardholder's maximum potential liability and of means by which the card issuer may be notified of loss or theft of the card. The notice shall state that the cardholder's liability shall not exceed $50 (or any lesser amount) and that the cardholder may give oral or written notification, and shall describe a means of notification (for example, a telephone number, an address, or both); and

(iii) The card issuer has provided a means to identify the cardholder on the account or the authorized user of the card.

(3) *Notification to card issuer*. Notification to a card issuer is given when steps have been taken as may be reasonably required in the ordinary course of business to provide the card issuer with the pertinent information about the loss, theft, or possible unauthorized use of a credit card, regardless of whether any particular officer, employee, or agent of the card issuer does, in fact, receive the information. Notification may be given, at the

---

21. For purposes of this section, *accepted credit card* means any credit card that a cardholder has requested or applied for and received, or has signed, used, or authorized another person to use to obtain credit. Any credit card issued as a renewal or substitute in accordance with this paragraph becomes an accepted credit card when received by the cardholder.

22. *Unauthorized use* means the use of a credit card by a person, other than the cardholder, who does not have actual, im-

plied, or apparent authority for such use, and from which the cardholder receives no benefit.

23. *Adequate notice* means a printed notice to a cardholder that sets forth clearly the pertinent facts so that the cardholder may reasonably be expected to have noticed it and understood its meaning. The notice may be given by any means reasonably assuring receipt by the cardholder.

option of the person giving it, in person, by telephone, or in writing. Notification in writing is considered given at the time of receipt or, whether or not received, at the expiration of the time ordinarily required for transmission, whichever is earlier.

(4) *Effect of other applicable law or agreement.* If state law or an agreement between a cardholder and the card issuer imposes lesser liability than that provided in this paragraph, the lesser liability shall govern.

(5) *Business use of credit cards.* If 10 or more credit cards are issued by one card issuer for use by the employees of an organization, this section does not prohibit the card issuer and the organization from agreeing to liability for unauthorized use without regard to this section. However, liability for unauthorized use may be imposed on an employee of the organization, by either the card issuer or the organization, only in accordance with this section.

(c) *Right of cardholder to assert claims or defenses against card issuer*[24]—(1) *General rule.* When a person who honors a credit card fails to resolve satisfactorily a dispute as to property or services purchased with the credit card in a consumer credit transaction, the cardholder may assert against the card issuer all claims (other than tort claims) and defenses arising out of the transaction and relating to the failure to resolve the dispute. The cardholder may withhold payment up to the amount of credit outstanding for the property or services that gave rise to the dispute and any finance or other charges imposed on that amount.[25]

(2) *Adverse credit reports prohibited.* If, in accordance with paragraph (c)(1) of this section, the cardholder withholds payment of the amount of credit outstanding for the disputed transaction, the card issuer shall not report that amount as delinquent until the dispute is settled or judgment is rendered.

(3) *Limitations.* The rights stated in paragraphs (c)(1) and (2) of this section apply only if:

(i) The cardholder has made a good faith attempt to resolve the dispute with the person honoring the credit card; and

(ii) The amount of credit extended to obtain the property or services that result in the assertion of the claim or defense by the

24. This paragraph does not apply to the use of a check guarantee card or a debit card in connection with an overdraft credit plan, or to a check guarantee card used in connection with cash advance checks.

25. The amount of the claim or defense that the cardholder may assert shall not exceed the amount of credit outstanding for the disputed transaction at the time the cardholder first notifies the card issuer or the person honoring the credit card of the existence of the claim or defense. To determine the amount of credit outstanding for purposes of this section, payments and other credits shall be applied to: (1) late charges in the order of entry to the account; then to (2) finance charges in the order of entry to the account; and then to (3) any other debits in the order of entry to the account. If more than one item is included in a single extension of credit, credits are to be distributed pro rata according to prices and applicable taxes.

cardholder exceeds $50, and the disputed transaction occurred in the same state as the cardholder's current designated address or, if not within the same state, within 100 miles from that address.[26]

(d) *Offsets by card issuer prohibited.* (1) A card issuer may not take any action, either before or after termination of credit card privileges, to offset a cardholder's indebtedness arising from a consumer credit transaction under the relevant credit card plan against funds of the cardholder held on deposit with the card issuer.

(2) This paragraph does not alter or affect the right of a card issuer acting under state or federal law to do any of the following with regard to funds of a cardholder held on deposit with the card issuer if the same procedure is constitutionally available to creditors generally: obtain or enforce a consensual security interest in the funds; attach or otherwise levy upon the funds; or obtain or enforce a court order relating to the funds.

(3) This paragraph does not prohibit a plan, if authorized in writing by the cardholder, under which the card issuer may periodically deduct all or part of the cardholder's credit card debt from a deposit account held with the card issuer (subject to the limitations in § 226.13(d)(1)).

(e) *Prompt notification of returns and crediting of refunds.* (1) When a creditor other than the card issuer accepts the return of property or forgives a debt for services that is to be reflected as a credit to the consumer's credit card account, that creditor shall, within 7 business days from accepting the return or forgiving the debt, transmit a credit statement to the card issuer through the card issuer's normal channels for credit statements.

(2) The card issuer shall, within 3 business days from receipt of a credit statement, credit the consumer's account with the amount of the refund.

(3) If a creditor other than a card issuer routinely gives cash refunds to consumers paying in cash, the creditor shall also give credit or cash refunds to consumers using credit cards, unless it discloses at the time the transaction is consummated that credit or cash refunds for returns are not given. This section does not require refunds for returns nor does it prohibit refunds in kind.

(f) *Discounts; tie-in arrangements.* No card issuer may, by contract or otherwise:

(1) Prohibit any person who honors a credit card from offering a discount to a consumer to induce the consumer to pay by cash, check, or

---

26. The limitations stated in paragraph (c)(3)(ii) of this section shall not apply when the person honoring the credit card: (1) is the same person as the card issuer; (2) is controlled by the card issuer directly or indirectly; (3) is under the direct or indirect control of a third person that also directly or indirectly controls the card issuer; (4) controls the card issuer directly or indirectly; (5) is a franchised dealer in the card issuer's products or services; or (6) has obtained the order for the disputed transaction through a mail solicitation made or participated in by the card issuer.

similar means rather than by use of a credit card or its underlying account for the purchase of property or services; or

(2) Require any person who honors the card issuer's credit card to open or maintain any account or obtain any other service not essential to the operation of the credit card plan from the card issuer or any other person, as a condition of participation in a credit card plan. If maintenance of an account for clearing purposes is determined to be essential to the operation of the credit card plan, it may be required only if no service charges or minimum balance requirements are imposed.

(g) *Relation to Electronic Fund Transfer Act and Regulation E.* For guidance on whether Regulation Z or Regulation E applies in instances involving both credit and electronic fund transfer aspects, refer to Regulation E, 12 CFR 205.12(a) regarding issuance and liability for unauthorized use. On matters other than issuance and liability, this section applies to the credit aspects of combined credit/electronic fund transfer transactions, as applicable.

§ 226.13   Billing error resolution[27]

(a) *Definition of billing error.* For purposes of this section, the term *billing error* means:

(1) A reflection on or with a periodic statement of an extension of credit that is not made to the consumer or to a person who has actual, implied, or apparent authority to use the consumer's credit card or open-end credit plan.

(2) A reflection on or with a periodic statement of an extension of credit that is not identified in accordance with the requirements of §§ 226.7(b) and 226.8.

(3) A reflection on or with a periodic statement of an extension of credit for property or services not accepted by the consumer or the consumer's designee, or not delivered to the consumer or the consumer's designee as agreed.

(4) A reflection on a periodic statement of the creditor's failure to credit properly a payment or other credit issued to the consumer's account.

(5) A reflection on a periodic statement of a computational or similar error of an accounting nature that is made by the creditor.

(6) A reflection on a periodic statement of an extension of credit for which the consumer requests additional clarification, including documentary evidence.

---

27. A creditor shall not accelerate any part of the consumer's indebtedness or restrict or close a consumer's account solely because the consumer has exercised in good faith rights provided by this section. A credi-tor may be subject to the forfeiture penalty under § 161(e) of the act for failure to comply with any of the requirements of this section.

(7) The creditor's failure to mail or deliver a periodic statement to the consumer's last known address if that address was received by the creditor, in writing, at least 20 days before the end of the billing cycle for which the statement was required.

(b) *Billing error notice.*[28] A billing error notice is a written notice[29] from a consumer that:

(1) Is received by a creditor at the address disclosed under 226.7(k) no later than 60 days after the creditor transmitted the first periodic statement that reflects the alleged billing error;

(2) Enables the creditor to identify the consumer's name and account number; and

(3) To the extent possible, indicates the consumer's belief and the reasons for the belief that a billing error exists, and the type, date, and amount of the error.

(c) *Time for resolution; general procedures.* (1) The creditor shall mail or deliver written acknowledgment to the consumer within 30 days of receiving a billing error notice, unless the creditor has complied with the appropriate resolution procedures of paragraphs (e) and (f) of this section, as applicable, within the 30–day period; and

(2) The creditor shall comply with the appropriate resolution procedures of paragraphs (e) and (f) of this section, as applicable, within 2 complete billing cycles (but in no event later than 90 days) after receiving a billing error notice.

(d) *Rules pending resolution.* Until a billing error is resolved under paragraphs (e) or (f) of this section, the following rules apply:

(1) *Consumer's right to withhold disputed amount; collection action prohibited.* The consumer need not pay (and the creditor may not try to collect) any portion of any required payment that the consumer believes is related to the disputed amount (including related finance or other charges).[30] If the cardholder maintains a deposit account with the card issuer and has agreed to pay the credit card indebtedness by periodic deductions from the cardholder's deposit account, the card issuer shall not deduct any part of the disputed amount or related finance or other charges

---

28. The creditor need not comply with the requirements of paragraphs (c) through (g) of this section if the consumer concludes that no billing error occurred and voluntarily withdraws the billing error notice

29. The creditor may require that the written notice not be made on the payment medium or other material accompanying the periodic statement if the creditor so stipulates in the billing rights statement required by §§ 226.6(d) and 226.9(a).

30. A creditor is not prohibited from taking action to collect any undisputed por-

tion of the item or bill; from deducting any disputed amount and related finance or other charges from the consumer's credit limit on the account; or from reflecting a disputed amount and related finance or other charges on a periodic statement, provided that the creditor indicates on or with the periodic statement that payment of any disputed amount and related finance or other charges is not required pending the creditor's compliance with this section.

if a billing error notice is received any time up to 3 business days before the scheduled payment date.

(2) *Adverse credit reports prohibited.* The creditor or its agent shall not (directly or indirectly) make or threaten to make an adverse report to any person about the consumer's credit standing, or report that an amount or account is delinquent, because the consumer failed to pay the disputed amount or related finance or other charges.

(e) *Procedures if billing error occurred as asserted.* If a creditor determines that a billing error occurred as asserted, it shall within the time limits in paragraph (c)(2) of this section:

(1) Correct the billing error and credit the consumer's account with any disputed amount and related finance or other charges, as applicable; and

(2) Mail or deliver a correction notice to the consumer.

(f) *Procedures if different billing error or no billing error occurred.* If, after conducting a reasonable investigation,[31] a creditor determines that no billing error occurred or that a different billing error occurred from that asserted, the creditor shall within the time limits in paragraph (c)(2) of this section:

(1) Mail or deliver to the consumer an explanation that sets forth the reasons for the creditor's belief that the billing error alleged by the consumer is incorrect in whole or in part;

(2) Furnish copies of documentary evidence of the consumer's indebtedness, if the consumer so requests; and

(3) If a different billing error occurred, correct the billing error and credit the consumer's account with any disputed amount and related finance or other charges, as applicable.

(g) *Creditor's rights and duties after resolution.* If a creditor, after complying with all of the requirements of this section, determines that a consumer owes all or part of the disputed amount and related finance or other charges, the creditor:

(1) Shall promptly notify the consumer in writing of the time when payment is due and the portion of the disputed amount and related finance or other charges that the consumer still owes;

(2) Shall allow any time period disclosed under §§ 226.6(a)(1) and 226.7(j), during which the consumer can pay the amount due under

---

31. If a consumer submits a billing error notice alleging either the nondelivery of property or services under paragraph (a)(3) of this section or that information appearing on a periodic statement is incorrect because a person honoring the consumer's credit card has made an incorrect report to the card issuer, the creditor shall not deny the assertion unless it conducts a reasonable investigation and determines that the property or services were actually delivered, mailed, or sent as agreed or that the information was correct.

paragraph (g)(1) of this section without incurring additional finance or other charges;

(3) May report an account or amount as delinquent because the amount due under paragraph (g)(1) of this section remains unpaid after the creditor has allowed any time period disclosed under §§ 226.6(a)(1) and 266.7(j) or 10 days (whichever is longer) during which the consumer can pay the amount; but

(4) May not report that an amount or account is delinquent because the amount due under paragraph (g)(1) of the section remains unpaid, if the creditor receives (within the time allowed for payment in paragraph (g)(3) of this section) further written notice from the consumer that any portion of the billing error is still in dispute, unless the creditor also:

(i) Promptly reports that the amount or account is in dispute;

(ii) Mails or delivers to the consumer (at the same time the report is made) a written notice of the name and address of each person to whom the creditor makes a report; and

(iii) Promptly reports any subsequent resolution of the reported delinquency to all persons to whom the creditor has made a report.

(h) *Reassertion of billing error.* A creditor that has fully complied with the requirements of this section has no further responsibilities under this section (other than as provided in paragraph (g)(4) of this section) if a consumer reasserts substantially the same billing error.

(i) *Relation to Electronic Fund Transfer Act and Regulation E.* If an extension of credit is incident to an electronic fund transfer, under an agreement between a consumer and a financial institution to extend credit when the consumer's account is overdrawn or to maintain a specified minimum balance in the consumer's account, the creditor shall comply with the requirements of Regulation E, 12 CFR 205.11 governing error resolution rather than those of paragraphs (a), (b), (c), (e), (f), and (h) of this section.

§ 226.14 Determination of annual percentage rate

(a) *General rule.* The annual percentage rate is a measure of the cost of credit, expressed as a yearly rate. An annual percentage rate shall be considered accurate if it is not more than 1/8 of 1 percentage point above or below the annual percentage rate determined in accordance with this section.[31a]

(b) *Annual percentage rate for sections §§ 226.5a and 226.5b disclosures, for initial disclosures and for advertising purposes.* Where one or

---

31a. An error in disclosure of the annual percentage rate or finance charge shall not, in itself, be considered a violation of this regulation if: (1) The error resulted from a corresponding error in a calculation tool used in good faith by the creditor; and (2) upon discovery of the error, the creditor promptly discontinues use of that calculation tool for disclosure purposes, and notifies the Board in writing of the error in the calculation tool.

more periodic rates may be used to compute the finance charge, the annual percentage rate(s) to be disclosed for purposes of §§ 226.5a, 226.5b, 226.6, and 226.16 shall be computed by multiplying each periodic rate by the number of periods in a year.

(c) *Annual percentage rate for periodic statements.* The annual percentage rate(s) to be disclosed for purposes of § 226.7(d) shall be computed by multiplying each periodic rate by the number of periods in a year and, for purposes of § 226.7(g), shall be determined as follows:

(1) If the finance charge is determined solely by applying one or more periodic rates, at the creditor's option, either:

(i) By multiplying each periodic rate by the number of periods in a year; or

(ii) By dividing the total finance charge for the billing cycle by the sum of the balances to which the periodic rates were applied and multiplying the quotient (expressed as a percentage) by the number of billing cycles in a year.

(2) If the finance charge imposed during the billing cycle is or includes a minimum, fixed, or other charge not due to the application of a periodic rate, other than a charge with respect to any specific transaction during the billing cycle, by dividing the total finance charge for the billing cycle by the amount of the balance(s) to which it is applicable[32] and multiplying the quotient (expressed as a percentage) by the number of billing cycles in a year.[33]

(3) If the finance charge imposed during the billing cycle is or includes a charge relating to a specific transaction during the billing cycle (even if the total finance charge also includes any other minimum, fixed, or other charge not due to the application of a periodic rate), by dividing the total finance charge imposed during the billing cycle by the total of all balances and other amounts on which a finance charge was imposed during the billing cycle without duplication, and multiplying the quotient (expressed as a percentage) by the number of billing cycles in a year,[34] except that the annual percentage rate shall not be less than the largest rate determined by multiplying each periodic rate imposed during the billing cycle by the number of periods in a year.[35]

---

32. If there is no balance to which the finance charge is applicable, an annual percentage rate cannot be determined under this section.

33. Where the finance charge imposed during the billing cycle is or includes a loan fee, points, or similar charges that relates to the opening of the account, the amount of such charge shall not be included in the calculation of the annual percentage rate.

34. See Appendix F regarding determination of the denominator of the fraction under this paragraph.

35. Where the finance charge imposed during the billing cycle is or includes a loan fee, points, or similar charges that relates to the opening of the account, the amount of such charge shall not be included in the calculation of the annual percentage rate.

(4) If the finance charge imposed during the billing cycle is or includes a minimum, fixed, or other charge not due to the application of a periodic rate and the total finance charge imposed during the billing cycle does not exceed 50 cents for a monthly or longer billing cycle, or the pro rata part of 50 cents for a billing cycle shorter than monthly, at the creditor's option, by multiplying each applicable periodic rate by the number of periods in a year, notwithstanding the provisions of paragraphs (c)(2) and (3) of this section.

(d) *Calculations where daily periodic rate applied.* If the provisions of paragraph (c)(1)(ii) or (2) of this section apply and all or a portion of the finance charge is determined by the application of one or more daily periodic rates, the annual percentage rate may be determined either:

(1) By dividing the total finance charge by the average of the daily balances and multiplying the quotient by the number of billing cycles in a year; or

(2) By dividing the total finance charge by the sum of the daily balances and multiplying the quotient by 365.

§ 226.15   Right of rescission

(a) *Consumer's right to rescind.* (1)(i) Except as provided in paragraph (a)(1)(ii) of this section, in a credit plan in which a security interest is or will be retained or acquired in a consumer's principal dwelling, each consumer whose ownership interest is or will be subject to the security interest shall have the right to rescind: each credit extension made under the plan; the plan when the plan is opened; a security interest when added or increased to secure an existing plan; and the increase when a credit limit on the plan is increased.

(ii) As provided in section 125(e) of the act, the consumer does not have the right to rescind each credit extension made under the plan if such extension is made in accordance with a previously established credit limit for the plan.

(2) To exercise the right to rescind, the consumer shall notify the creditor of the rescission by mail, telegram, or other means of written communication. Notice is considered given when mailed, or when filed for telegraphic transmission, or, if sent by other means, when delivered to the creditor's designated place of business.

(3) The consumer may exercise the right to rescind until midnight of the third business day following the occurrence described in paragraph (a)(1) of this section that gave rise to the right of rescission, delivery of the notice required by paragraph (b) of this section, or delivery of all material disclosures,[36] whichever occurs last. If the required notice and material

---

36. The term "material disclosures" means the information that must be provided to satisfy the requirements in section 226.6 with regard to the method of determining the finance charge and the balance upon which a finance charge will be imposed, the annual

disclosures are not delivered, the right to rescind shall expire 3 years after the occurrence giving rise to the right of rescission, or upon transfer of all of the consumer's interest in the property, or upon sale of the property, whichever occurs first. In the case of certain administrative proceedings, the rescission period shall be extended in accordance with section 125(f) of the act.

(4) When more than one consumer has the right to rescind, the exercise of the right by one consumer shall be effective as to all consumers.

(b) *Notice of right to rescind.* In any transaction or occurrence subject to rescission, a creditor shall deliver two copies of the notice of the right to rescind to each consumer entitled to rescind (one copy to each if the notice is delivered in electronic form in accordance with the consumer consent and other applicable provisions of the E–Sign Act). The notice shall identify the transaction or occurrence and clearly and conspicuously disclose the following:

(1) The retention or acquisition of a security interest in the consumer's principal dwelling.

(2) The consumer's right to rescind, as described in paragraph (a)(1) of this section.

(3) How to exercise the right to rescind, with a form for that purpose, designating the address of the creditor's place of business.

(4) The effects of rescission, as described in paragraph (d) of this section.

(5) The date the rescission period expires.

(c) *Delay of creditor's performance.* Unless a consumer waives the right to rescind under paragraph (e) of this section, no money shall be disbursed other than in escrow, no services shall be performed, and no materials delivered until after the rescission period has expired and the creditor is reasonably satisfied that the consumer has not rescinded. A creditor does not violate this section if a third party with no knowledge of the event activating the rescission right does not delay in providing materials or services, as long as the debt incurred for those materials or services is not secured by the property subject to rescission.

(d) *Effects of rescission.* (1) When a consumer rescinds a transaction, the security interest giving rise to the right of rescission becomes void, and the consumer shall not be liable for any amount, including any finance charge.

(2) Within 20 calendar days after receipt of a notice of rescission, the creditor shall return any money or property that has been given to anyone

percentage rate, the amount or method of determining the amount of any membership or participation fee that may be imposed as part of the plan, and the payment information described in § 226.5b(d)(5)(i) and (ii) that is required under § 226.6(e)(2).

in connection with the transaction and shall take any action necessary to reflect the termination of the security interest.

(3) If the creditor has delivered any money or property, the consumer may retain possession until the creditor has met its obligation under paragraph (d)(2) of this section. When the creditor has complied with that paragraph, the consumer shall tender the money or property to the creditor or, where the latter would be impracticable or inequitable, tender its reasonable value. At the consumer's option, tender of property may be made at the location of the property or at the consumer's residence. Tender of money must be made at the creditor's designated place of business. If the creditor does not take possession of the money or property within 20 calendar days after the consumer's tender, the consumer may keep it without further obligation.

(4) The procedures outlined in paragraphs (d)(2) and (3) of this section may be modified by court order.

(e) *Consumer's waiver of right to rescind.* (1) The consumer may modify or waive the right to rescind if the consumer determines that the extension of credit is needed to meet a bona fide personal financial emergency. To modify or waive the right, the consumer shall give the creditor a dated written statement that describes the emergency, specifically modifies or waives the right to rescind, and bears the signature of all the consumers entitled to rescind. Printed forms for this purpose are prohibited, except as provided in paragraph (e)(2) of this section.

(2) The need of the consumer to obtain funds immediately shall be regarded as a bona fide personal financial emergency provided that the dwelling securing the extension of credit is located in an area declared during June through September 1993, pursuant to 42 U.S.C. 5170, to be a major disaster area because of severe storms and flooding in the Midwest. In this instance, creditors may use printed forms for the consumer to waive the right to rescind. This exemption to paragraph (e)(1) of this section shall expire one year from the date an area was declared a major disaster.

(3) The consumer's need to obtain funds immediately shall be regarded as a bona fide personal financial emergency provided that the dwelling securing the extension of credit is located in area declared during June through September 1994 to be a major disaster area, pursuant to 42 U.S.C. 5170, because of severe storms and flooding in the South. In this instance, creditors may use printed forms for the consumer to waive the right to rescind. This exemption to paragraph (e)(1) of this section shall expire one year from the date an area was declared a major disaster.

(4) The consumer's need to obtain funds immediately shall be regarded as a bona fide personal financial emergency provided that the dwelling securing the extension of credit is located in an area declared during October 1994 to be a major disaster area, pursuant to 42 U.S.C. 5170, because of severe storms and flooding in Texas. In this instance, creditors may use printed forms for the consumer to waive the right to rescind. This

exemption to paragraph (e)(1) of this section shall expire one year from the date an area was declared a major disaster.

(f) *Exempt transactions.* The right to rescind does not apply to the following:

(1) A residential mortgage transaction.

(2) A credit plan in which a state agency is a creditor.

§ 226.16   Advertising

(a) *Actually available terms.* If an advertisement for credit states specific credit terms, it shall state only those terms that actually are or will be arranged or offered by the creditor.

(b) *Advertisement of terms that require additional disclosures.* If any of the terms required to be disclosed under § 226.6 is set forth in an advertisement, the advertisement shall also clearly and conspicuously set forth the following:[36d]

(1) Any minimum, fixed, transaction, activity or similar charge that could be imposed.

(2) Any periodic rate that may be applied expressed as an annual percentage rate as determined under § 226.14(b). If the plan provides for a variable periodic rate, that fact shall be disclosed.

(3) Any membership or participation fee that could be imposed.

(c) *Catalogs or other multiple-page advertisements; electronic advertisements.* (1) If a catalog or other multiple-page advertisement, or an electronic advertisement (such as an advertisement appearing on an Internet Web site), gives information in a table or schedule in sufficient detail to permit determination of the disclosures required by paragraph (b) of this section, it shall be considered a single advertisement if:

(i) The table or schedule is clearly and conspicuously set forth; and

(ii) Any statement of terms set forth in § 226.6 appearing anywhere else in the catalog or advertisement clearly refers to the page or location where the table or schedule begins.

(2) A catalog or other multiple-page advertisement or an electronic advertisement (such as an advertisement appearing on an Internet Web site) complies with this paragraph if the table or schedule of terms includes all appropriate disclosures for a representative scale of amounts up to the level of the more commonly sold higher-priced property or services offered.

(d) *Additional requirements for home equity plans—(1) Advertisement of terms that require additional disclosures.* If any of the terms required to be disclosed under § 226.6(a) or (b) or the payment terms of the plan are

---

36d. The disclosures given in accordance with § 226.5a do not constitute advertising terms for purposes of the requirements of this section.

set forth, affirmatively or negatively, in an advertisement for a home equity plan subject to the requirements of § 226.5b, the advertisement also shall clearly and conspicuously set forth the following:

(i) Any loan fee that is a percentage of the credit limit under the plan and an estimate of any other fees imposed for opening the plan, stated as a single dollar amount or a reasonable range.

(ii) Any periodic rate used to compute the finance charge, expressed as an annual percentage rate as determined under section 226.14(b).

(iii) The maximum annual percentage rate that may be imposed in a variable-rate plan.

(2) *Discounted and premium rates.* If an advertisement states an initial annual percentage rate that is not based on the index and margin used to make later rate adjustments in a variable-rate plan, the advertisement also shall state with equal prominence and in close proximity to the initial rate:

(i) The period of time such initial rate will be in effect; and

(ii) A reasonably current annual percentage rate that would have been in effect using the index and margin.

(3) *Balloon payment.* If an advertisement contains a statement of any minimum periodic payment and a balloon payment may result if only the minimum periodic payments are made, even if such a payment is uncertain or unlikely, the advertisement also shall state with equal prominence and in close proximity to the minimum periodic payment statement that a balloon payment may result, if applicable.[36e] A balloon payment results if paying the minimum periodic payments does not fully amortize the outstanding balance by a specified date or time, and the consumer is required to repay the entire outstanding balance at such time. If a balloon payment will occur when the consumer makes only the minimum payments required under the plan, an advertisement for such a program which contains any statement of any minimum periodic payment shall also state with equal prominence and in close proximity to the minimum periodic payment statement:

(i) That a balloon payment will result; and

(ii) The amount and timing of the balloon payment that will result if the consumer makes only the minimum payments for the maximum period of time that the consumer is permitted to make such payments.

(4) *Tax implications.* An advertisement that states that any interest expense incurred under the home-equity plan is or may be tax deductible may not be misleading in this regard. If an advertisement distributed in paper form or through the Internet (rather than by radio or television) is for a home-equity plan secured by the consumer's principal dwelling, and

---

36e. [Reserved]

the advertisement states that the advertised extension of credit may exceed the fair market value of the dwelling, the advertisement shall clearly and conspicuously state that:

(i) The interest on the portion of the credit extension that is greater than the fair market value of the dwelling is not tax deductible for Federal income tax purposes; and

(ii) The consumer should consult a tax adviser for further information regarding the deductibility of interest and charges.

(5) *Misleading terms.* An advertisement may not refer to a home equity plan as "free money" or contain a similarly misleading term.

(6) *Promotional rates and payments*—(i) *Definitions.* The following definitions apply for purposes of paragraph (d)(6) of this section:

(A) *Promotional rate.* The term "promotional rate" means, in a variable-rate plan, any annual percentage rate that is not based on the index and margin that will be used to make rate adjustments under the plan, if that rate is less than a reasonably current annual percentage rate that would be in effect under the index and margin that will be used to make rate adjustments under the plan.

(B) *Promotional payment.* The term "promotional payment" means—

(1) For a variable-rate plan, any minimum payment applicable for a promotional period that:

(i) Is not derived by applying the index and margin to the outstanding balance when such index and margin will be used to determine other minimum payments under the plan; and

(ii) Is less than other minimum payments under the plan derived by applying a reasonably current index and margin that will be used to determine the amount of such payments, given an assumed balance.

(2) For a plan other than a variable-rate plan, any minimum payment applicable for a promotional period if that payment is less than other payments required under the plan given an assumed balance.

(C) *Promotional period.* A "promotional period" means a period of time, less than the full term of the loan, that the promotional rate or promotional payment may be applicable.

(ii) *Stating the promotional period and post-promotional rate or payments.* If any annual percentage rate that may be applied to a plan is a promotional rate, or if any payment applicable to a plan is a promotional payment, the following must be disclosed in any advertisement, other than television or radio advertisements, in a clear and conspicuous manner with equal prominence and in close proximity to each listing of the promotional rate or payment:

(A) The period of time during which the promotional rate or promotional payment will apply;

(B) In the case of a promotional rate, any annual percentage rate that will apply under the plan. If such rate is variable, the annual percentage rate must be disclosed in accordance with the accuracy standards in §§ 226.5b, or 226.16(b)(1)(ii) as applicable; and

(C) In the case of a promotional payment, the amounts and time periods of any payments that will apply under the plan. In variable-rate transactions, payments that will be determined based on application of an index and margin shall be disclosed based on a reasonably current index and margin.

(iii) *Envelope excluded.* The requirements in paragraph (d)(6)(ii) of this section do not apply to an envelope in which an application or solicitation is mailed, or to a banner advertisement or pop-up advertisement linked to an application or solicitation provided electronically.

(e) *Alternative disclosures—television or radio advertisements.* An advertisement for a home-equity plan subject to the requirements of § 226.5b made through television or radio stating any of the terms requiring additional disclosures under paragraph (b) or (d)(1) of this section may alternatively comply with paragraph (b) or (d)(1) of this section by stating the information required by paragraph (b)(2) of this section or paragraph (d)(1)(ii) of this section, as applicable, and listing a toll-free telephone number, or any telephone number that allows a consumer to reverse the phone charges when calling for information, along with a reference that such number may be used by consumers to obtain additional cost information.

SUBPART C.   CLOSED–END CREDIT

§ 226.17   **General disclosure requirements**

(a) *Form of disclosures.* (1) The creditor shall make the disclosures required by this subpart clearly and conspicuously in writing, in a form that the consumer may keep. The disclosures required by this subpart may be provided to the consumer in electronic form, subject to compliance with the consumer consent and other applicable provisions of the Electronic

Signatures in Global and National Commerce Act (E–Sign Act) (15 U.S.C. § 7001 et seq.). The disclosures required by §§ 226.17(g), 226.19(b), and 226.24 may be provided to the consumer in electronic form without regard to the consumer consent or other provisions of the E–Sign Act in the circumstances set forth in those sections. The disclosures shall be grouped together, shall be segregated from everything else, and shall not contain any information not directly related[37] to the disclosures required under § 226.18.[38] The itemization of the amount financed under § 226.18(c)(1) must be separate from the other disclosures under that section.

(2) The terms *finance charge* and *annual percentage rate*, when required to be disclosed under § 226.18(d) and (e) together with a corresponding amount or percentage rate, shall be more conspicuous than any other disclosure, except the creditor's identity under § 226.18(a).

(b) *Time of disclosures.* The creditor shall make disclosures before consummation of the transaction. In certain mortgage transactions, special timing requirements are set forth in § 226.19(a). In certain variable-rate transactions, special timing requirements for variable-rate disclosures are set forth in § 226.19(b) and § 226.20(c). In certain transactions involving mail or telephone orders or a series of sales, the timing of disclosures may be delayed in accordance with paragraphs (g) and (h) of this section.

(c) *Basis of disclosures and use of estimates.* (1) The disclosures shall reflect the terms of the legal obligation between the parties.

(2)(i) If any information necessary for an accurate disclosure is unknown to the creditor, the creditor shall make the disclosure based on the best information reasonably available at the time the disclosure is provided to the consumer, and shall state clearly that the disclosure is an estimate.

(ii) For a transaction in which a portion of the interest is determined on a per-diem basis and collected at consummation, any disclosure affected by the per-diem interest shall be considered accurate if the disclosure is based on the information known to the creditor at the time that the disclosure documents are prepared for consummation of the transaction.

(3) The creditor may disregard the effects of the following in making calculations and disclosures.

(i) That payments must be collected in whole cents.

(ii) That dates of scheduled payments and advances may be changed because the scheduled date is not a business day.

(iii) That months have different numbers of days.

---

37. The disclosures may include an acknowledgment of receipt, the date of the transaction, and the consumer's name, address, and account number.

38. The following disclosures may be made together with or separately from other required disclosures: the creditor's identity under § 226.18(a), the variable rate example under § 226.18(f)(1)(iv), insurance or debt cancellation under § 226.18(n), and certain security interest charges under § 226.18(*o*).

(iv) The occurrence of leap year.

(4) In making calculations and disclosures, the creditor may disregard any irregularity in the first period that falls within the limits described below and any payment schedule irregularity that results from the irregular first period.

(i) For transactions in which the term is less than 1 year, a first period not more than 6 days shorter or 13 days longer than a regular period;

(ii) For transactions in which the term is at least 1 year and less than 10 years, a first period not more than 11 days shorter or 21 days longer than a regular period; and

(iii) For transactions in which the term is at least 10 years, a first period shorter than or not more than 32 days longer than a regular period.

(5) If an obligation is payable on demand, the creditor shall make the disclosures based on an assumed maturity of 1 year. If an alternate maturity date is stated in the legal obligation between the parties, the disclosures shall be based on that date.

(6)(i) A series of advances under an agreement to extend credit up to a certain amount may be considered as one transaction.

(ii) When a multiple-advance loan to finance the construction of a dwelling may be permanently financed by the same creditor, the construction phase and the permanent phase may be treated as either one transaction or more than one transaction.

(d) *Multiple creditors; multiple consumers.* If a transaction involves more than one creditor, only one set of disclosures shall be given and the creditors shall agree among themselves which creditor must comply with the requirements that this regulation imposes on any or all of them. If there is more than one consumer, the disclosures may be made to any consumer who is primarily liable on the obligation. If the transaction is rescindable under § 226.23, however, the disclosures shall be made to each consumer who has the right to rescind.

(e) *Effect of subsequent events.* If a disclosure becomes inaccurate because of an event that occurs after the creditor delivers the required disclosures, the inaccuracy is not a violation of this regulation, although new disclosures may be required under paragraph (f) of this section, § 226.19, or § 226.20.

(f) *Early disclosures.* If disclosures required by this subpart are given before the date of consummation of a transaction and a subsequent event makes them inaccurate, the creditor shall disclose before consummation (except that, for certain mortgage transactions, § 226.19(a)(2) permits redisclosure no later than consummation or settlement, whichever is later).[39]

(g) *Mail or telephone orders—delay in disclosures.* If a creditor receives a purchase order or a request for an extension of credit by mail, telephone, or facsimile machine without face-to-face or direct telephone solicitation, the creditor may delay the disclosures until the due date of the first payment, if the following information for representative amounts or ranges of credit is made available in written form or in electronic form to the consumer or to the public before the actual purchase order or request:

(1) The cash price or the principal loan amount.

(2) The total sale price.

(3) The finance charge.

(4) The annual percentage rate, and if the rate may increase after consummation, the following disclosures:

(i) The circumstances under which the rate may increase.

(ii) Any limitations on the increase.

(iii) The effect of an increase.

(5) The terms of repayment.

(h) *Series of sales—delay in disclosures.* If a credit sale is one of a series made under an agreement providing that subsequent sales may be added to an outstanding balance, the creditor may delay the required disclosures until the due date of the first payment for the current sale, if the following two conditions are met:

(1) The consumer has approved in writing the annual percentage rate or rates, the range of balances to which they apply, and the method of treating any unearned finance charge on an existing balance.

(2) The creditor retains no security interest in any property after the creditor has received payments equal to the cash price and any finance charge attributable to the sale of that property. For purposes of this provision, in the case of items purchased on different dates, the first purchased is deemed the first item paid for; in the case of items purchased on the same date, the lowest priced is deemed the first item paid for.

(*i*) *Interim student credit extensions.* For each transaction involving an interim credit extension under a student credit program, the creditor need not make the following disclosures: the finance charge under § 226.18(d), the payment schedule under § 226.18(g), the total of payments under § 226.18(h), or the total sale price under § 226.18(j).

§ 226.18   Content of disclosures

For each transaction, the creditor shall disclose the following information as applicable:

39.   [Reserved]

(a) *Creditor.* The identity of the creditor making the disclosures.

(b) *Amount financed.* The *amount financed,* using that term, and a brief description such as "the amount of credit provided to you or on your behalf." The amount financed is calculated by:

(1) Determining the principal loan amount or the cash price (subtracting any downpayment);

(2) Adding any other amounts that are financed by the creditor and are not part of the finance charge; and

(3) Subtracting any prepaid finance charge.

(c) *Itemization of amount financed.* (1) A separate written itemization of the amount financed, including:[40]

(i) The amount of any proceeds distributed directly to the consumer.

(ii) The amount credited to the consumer's account with the creditor.

(iii) Any amounts paid to other persons by the creditor on the consumer's behalf. The creditor shall identify those persons.[41]

(iv) The prepaid finance charge.

(2) The creditor need not comply with paragraph (c)(1) of this section if the creditor provides a statement that the consumer has the right to receive a written itemization of the amount financed, together with a space for the consumer to indicate whether it is desired, and the consumer does not request it.

(d) *Finance charge.* The *finance charge,* using that term, and a brief description such as "the dollar amount the credit will cost you."

(1) *Mortgage loans.* In a transaction secured by real property or a dwelling, the disclosed finance charge and other disclosures affected by the disclosed finance charge (including the amount financed and the annual percentage rate) shall be treated as accurate if the amount disclosed as the finance charge:

(i) is understated by no more than $100; or

(ii) is greater than the amount required to be disclosed.

(2) *Other credit.* In any other transaction, the amount disclosed as the finance charge shall be treated as accurate if, in a transaction involving an amount financed of $1,000 or less, it is not more than $5 above or below the amount required to be disclosed; or, in a transaction involving an

---

40. Good faith estimates of settlement costs provided for transactions subject to the Real Estate Settlement Procedures Act (12 U.S.C. 2601 et seq.) may be substituted for the disclosures required by paragraph (c) of this section.

41. The following payees may be described using generic or other general terms and need not be further identified: public officials or government agencies, credit reporting agencies, appraisers, and insurance companies.

amount financed of more than $1,000, it is not more than $10 above or below the amount required to be disclosed.

(e) *Annual percentage rate.* The *annual percentage rate*, using that term, and a brief description such as "the cost of your credit as a yearly rate."[42]

(f) *Variable rate.* (1) If the annual percentage rate may increase after consummation in a transaction not secured by the consumer's principal dwelling or in a transaction secured by the consumer's principal dwelling with a term of one year or less, the following disclosures:[43]

   (i) The circumstances under which the rate may increase.

   (ii) Any limitations on the increase.

   (iii) The effect of an increase.

   (iv) An example of the payment terms that would result from an increase.

(2) If the annual percentage rate may increase after consummation in a transaction secured by the consumer's principal dwelling with a term greater than one year, the following disclosures:

   (i) The fact that the transaction contains a variable-rate feature.

   (ii) A statement that variable-rate disclosures have been provided earlier.

(g) *Payment schedule.* The number, amounts, and timing of payments scheduled to repay the obligation.

(1) In a demand obligation with no alternate maturity date, the creditor may comply with this paragraph by disclosing the due dates or payment periods of any scheduled interest payments for the first year.

(2) In a transaction in which a series of payments varies because a finance charge is applied to the unpaid principal balance, the creditor may comply with this paragraph by disclosing the following information:

   (i) The dollar amounts of the largest and smallest payments in the series.

   (ii) A reference to the variations in the other payments in the series.

(h) *Total of payments.* The *total of payments*, using that term, and a descriptive explanation such as "the amount you will have paid when you have made all scheduled payments."[44]

---

42. For any transaction involving a finance charge of $5 or less on an amount financed of $75 or less, or a finance charge of $7.50 or less on an amount financed of more than $75, the creditor need not disclose the annual percentage rate.

43. Information provided in accordance with §§ 226.18(f)(2) and 226.19(b) may be substituted for the disclosures required by paragraph (f)(1) of this section.

44. In any transaction involving a single payment, the creditor need not disclose the total of payments.

(*i*) *Demand feature.* If the obligation has a demand feature, that fact shall be disclosed. When the disclosures are based on an assumed maturity of 1 year as provided in § 226.17(c)(5), that fact shall also be disclosed.

(j) *Total sale price.* In a credit sale, the *total sale price*, using that term, and a descriptive explanation (including the amount of any downpayment) such as "the total price of your purchase on credit, including your downpayment of $___." The total sale price is the sum of the cash price, the items described in paragraph (b)(2), and the finance charge disclosed under paragraph (d) of this section.

(k) *Prepayment.* (1) When an obligation includes a finance charge computed from time to time by application of a rate to the unpaid principal balance, a statement indicating whether or not a penalty may be imposed if the obligation is prepaid in full.

(2) When an obligation includes a finance charge other than the finance charge described in paragraph (k)(1) of this section, a statement indicating whether or not the consumer is entitled to a rebate of any finance charge if the obligation is prepaid in full.

(*l*) *Late payment.* Any dollar or percentage charge that may be imposed before maturity due to a late payment, other than a deferral or extension charge.

(m) *Security interest.* The fact that the creditor has or will acquire a security interest in the property purchased as part of the transaction, or in other property identified by item or type.

(n) *Insurance and debt cancellation.* The items required by § 226.4(d) in order to exclude certain insurance premiums and debt cancellation fees from the finance charge.

(o) *Certain security interest charges.* The disclosures required by § 226.4(e) in order to exclude from the finance charge certain fees prescribed by law or certain premiums for insurance in lieu of perfecting a security interest.

(p) *Contract reference.* A statement that the consumer should refer to the appropriate contract document for information about nonpayment, default, the right to accelerate the maturity of the obligation, and prepayment rebates and penalties. At the creditor's option, the statement may also include a reference to the contract for further information about security interests and, in a residential mortgage transaction, about the creditor's policy regarding assumption of the obligation.

(q) *Assumption policy.* In a residential mortgage transaction, a statement whether or not a subsequent purchaser of the dwelling from the consumer may be permitted to assume the remaining obligation on its original terms.

(r) *Required deposit.* If the creditor requires the consumer to maintain a deposit as a condition of the specific transaction, a statement that the annual percentage rate does not reflect the effect of the required deposit.[45]

§ 226.19 Certain residential mortgage and variable-rate transactions

(a) *Mortgage transactions subject to RESPA*—(1)(i) *Time of disclosures.* In a mortgage transaction subject to the Real Estate Settlement Procedures Act (12 U.S.C. § 2601 et seq.) that is secured by the consumer's principal dwelling, other than a home equity line of credit subject to § 226.5b, the creditor shall make good faith estimates of the disclosures required by § 226.18 before consummation, or shall deliver or place them in the mail not later than three business days after the creditor receives the consumer's written application, whichever is earlier.

(ii) *Imposition of fees.* Except as provided in paragraph (a)(1)(iii) of this section, neither a creditor nor any other person may impose a fee on the consumer in connection with the consumer's application for a mortgage transaction subject to paragraph (a)(1)(i) of this section before the consumer has received the disclosures required by paragraph (a)(1)(i) of this section. If the disclosures are mailed to the consumer, the consumer is considered to have received them three business days after they are mailed.

(iii) *Exception to fee restriction.* A creditor or other person may impose a fee for obtaining the consumer's credit history before the consumer has received the disclosures required by paragraph (a)(1)(i) of this section, provided the fee is bona fide and reasonable in amount.

(2) *Redisclosure required.* If the annual percentage rate at the time of consummation varies from the annual percentage rate disclosed earlier by more than 1/8 of 1 percentage point in a regular transaction or more than 1/4 of 1 percentage point in an irregular transaction, as defined in § 226.22, the creditor shall disclose all the changed terms no later than consummation or settlement.

(b) *Certain variable-rate transactions.*[45a] If the annual percentage rate may increase after consummation in a transaction secured by the consumer's principal dwelling with a term greater than one year, the following disclosures must be provided at the time an application for is provided or before the consumer pays a nonrefundable fee, whichever is earlier:[45b]

---

45. A required deposit need not include, for example: (1) an escrow account for items such as taxes, insurance or repairs; (2) a deposit that earns not less than 5 percent per year; or (3) payments under a Morris Plan.

45a. Information provided in accordance with variable-rate regulations of other federal agencies may be substituted for the disclosures required by paragraph (b) of this section.

45b. Disclosures may be delivered or placed in the mail not later than three business days following receipt of a consumer's application when the application reaches the creditor by telephone, or through an intermediary agent or broker.

(1) The booklet titled *Consumer Handbook on Adjustable Rate Mortgages* published by the Board and the Federal Home Loan Bank Board, or a suitable substitute.

(2) A loan program disclosure for each variable-rate program in which the consumer expresses an interest. The following disclosures, as applicable, shall be provided:

(i) The fact that the interest rate, payment, or term of the loan can change.

(ii) The index or formula used in making adjustments, and a source of information about the index or formula.

(iii) An explanation of how the interest rate and payment will be determined, including an explanation of how the index is adjusted, such as by the addition of a margin.

(iv) A statement that the consumer should ask about the current margin value and current interest rate.

(v) The fact that the interest rate will be discounted, and a statement that the consumer should ask about the amount of the interest rate discount.

(vi) The frequency of interest rate and payment changes.

(vii) Any rules relating to changes in the index, interest rate, payment amount, and outstanding loan balance including, for example, an explanation of interest rate or payment limitations, negative amortization, and interest rate carryover.

(viii) At the option of the creditor, either of the following:

(A) A historical example, based on a $10,000 loan amount, illustrating how payments and the loan balance would have been affected by interest rate changes implemented according to the terms of the loan program disclosure. The example shall reflect the most recent 15 years of index values. The example shall reflect all significant loan program terms, such as negative amortization, interest rate carryover, interest rate discounts, and interest rate and payment limitations, that would have been affected by the index movement during the period.

(B) The maximum interest rate and payment for a $10,000 loan originated at the initial interest rate (index value plus margin, adjusted by the amount of any discount or premium) in effect as of an identified month and year for the loan program disclosure assuming the maximum periodic increases in rates and payments under the program; and the initial interest rate and payment for that loan and a statement that the periodic payment may increase or decrease substantially depending on changes in the rate.

(ix) An explanation of how the consumer may calculate the payments for the loan amount to be borrowed based on either:

(A) The most recent payment shown in the historical example in paragraph (b)(2)(viii)(A) of this section; or

(B) The initial interest rate used to calculate the maximum interest rate and payment in paragraph (b)(2)(viii)(B) of this section.

(x) The fact that the loan program contains a demand feature.

(xi) The type of information that will be provided in notices of adjustments and the timing of such notices.

(xii) A statement that disclosure forms are available for the creditor's other variable-rate loan programs.

(c) *Electronic disclosures.* For an application that is accessed by the consumer in electronic form, the disclosures required by paragraph (b) of this section may be provided to the consumer in electronic form on or with the application.

§ 226.20   Subsequent disclosure requirements

(a) *Refinancings.* A refinancing occurs when an existing obligation that was subject to this subpart is satisfied and replaced by a new obligation undertaken by the same consumer. A refinancing is a new transaction requiring new disclosures to the consumer. The new finance charge shall include any unearned portion of the old finance charge that is not credited to the existing obligation. The following shall not be treated as a refinancing:

(1) A renewal of a single payment obligation with no change in the original terms.

(2) A reduction in the annual percentage rate with a corresponding change in the payment schedule.

(3) An agreement involving a court proceeding.

(4) A change in the payment schedule or a change in collateral requirements as a result of the consumer's default or delinquency, unless the rate is increased, or the new amount financed exceeds the unpaid balance plus earned finance charge and premiums for continuation of insurance of the types described in § 226.4(d).

(5) The renewal of optional insurance purchased by the consumer and added to an existing transaction, if disclosures relating to the initial purchase were provided as required by this subpart.

(b) *Assumptions.* An assumption occurs when a creditor expressly agrees in writing with a subsequent consumer to accept that consumer as a primary obligor on an existing residential mortgage transaction. Before the assumption occurs, the creditor shall make new disclosures to the subsequent consumer, based on the remaining obligation. If the finance charge originally imposed on the existing obligation was an add-on or discount finance charge, the creditor need only disclose:

(1) The unpaid balance of the obligation assumed.

(2) The total charges imposed by the creditor in connection with the assumption.

(3) The information required to be disclosed under § 226.18(k), (*l*), (m), and (n)

(4) The annual percentage rate originally imposed on the obligation.

(5) The payment schedule under § 226.18(g) and the total of payments under § 226.18(h) based on the remaining obligation.

(c) *Variable-rate adjustments.*[45c] An adjustment to the interest rate with or without a corresponding adjustment to the payment in a variable-rate transaction subject to § 226.19(b) is an event requiring new disclosures to the consumer. At least once each year during which an interest rate adjustment is implemented without an accompanying payment change, and at least 25, but no more than 120, calendar days before a payment at a new level is due, the following disclosures, as applicable, must be delivered or placed in the mail:

(1) The current and prior interest rates.

(2) The index values upon which the current and prior interest rates are based.

(3) The extent to which the creditor has foregone any increase in the interest rate.

(4) The contractual effects of the adjustment, including the payment due after the adjustment is made, and a statement of the loan balance.

(5) The payment, if different from that referred to in paragraph (c)(4) of this section, that would be required to fully amortize the loan at the new interest rate over the remainder of the loan term.

§ 226.21   Treatment of credit balances

When a credit balance in excess of $1 is created in connection with a transaction (through transmittal of funds to a creditor in excess of the total balance due on an account, through rebates of unearned finance charges or insurance premiums, or through amounts otherwise owed to or held for the benefit of a consumer), the creditor shall:

(a) Credit the amount of the credit balance to the consumer's account;

(b) Refund any part of the remaining credit balance, upon the written request of the consumer; and

(c) Make a good faith effort to refund to the consumer by cash, check, or money order, or credit to a deposit account of the consumer, any part of the credit balance remaining in the account for more than 6 months, except

---

45c. Information provided in accordance with variable-rate subsequent disclosure regulations of other federal agencies may be substituted for the disclosure required by paragraph (c) of this section.

that no further action is required if the consumer's current location is not known to the creditor and cannot be traced through the consumer's last known address or telephone number.

§ 226.22   Determination of annual percentage rate

(a) *Accuracy of annual percentage rate.* (1) The annual percentage rate is a measure of the cost of credit, expressed as a yearly rate, that relates the amount and timing of value received by the consumer to the amount and timing of payments made. The annual percentage rate shall be determined in accordance with either the actuarial method or the United States Rule method. Explanations, equations and instructions for determining the annual percentage rate in accordance with the actuarial method are set forth in Appendix J to this regulation.[45d]

(2) As a general rule, the annual percentage rate shall be considered accurate if it is not more than 1/8 of 1 percentage point above or below the annual percentage rate determined in accordance with paragraph (a)(1) of this section.

(3) In an irregular transaction, the annual percentage rate shall be considered accurate if it is not more than 1/4 of 1 percentage point above or below the annual percentage rate determined in accordance with paragraph (a)(1) of this section.[46]

(4) *Mortgage loans.* If the annual percentage rate disclosed in a transaction secured by real property or a dwelling varies from the actual rate determined in accordance with paragraph (a)(1) of this section, in addition to the tolerances applicable under paragraphs (a)(2) and (3) of this section, the disclosed annual percentage rate shall also be considered accurate if:

(i) The rate results from the disclosed finance charge; and

(ii)(A) The disclosed finance charge would be considered accurate under § 226.18(d)(1); or

(B) For purposes of rescission, if the disclosed finance charge would be considered accurate under § 226.23(g) or (h), whichever applies.

(5) *Additional tolerance for mortgage loans.* In a transaction secured by real property or a dwelling, in addition to the tolerances applicable under paragraphs (a)(2) and (3) of this section, if the disclosed finance

---

45d. An error in disclosure of the annual percentage rate or finance charge shall not, in itself, to considered a violation of this regulation if: (1) The error resulted from a corresponding error in a calculation tool used in good faith by the creditor; and (2) upon discovery of the error, the creditor promptly discontinues use of that calculation tool for disclosure purposes and notifies the Board in writing of the error in the calculation tool.

46. For purposes of paragraph (a)(3) of this section, an irregular transaction is one that includes one or more of the following features: multiple advances, irregular payment periods, or irregular payment amounts (other than an irregular first period or an irregular first or final payment).

charge is calculated incorrectly but is considered accurate under § 226.18(d)(1) or § 226.23(g) or (h), the disclosed annual percentage rate shall be considered accurate:

(i) If the disclosed finance charge is understated, and the disclosed annual percentage rate is also understated but it is closer to the actual annual percentage rate than the rate that would be considered accurate under paragraph (a)(4) of this section;

(ii) If the disclosed finance charge is overstated, and the disclosed annual percentage rate is also overstated but it is closer to the actual annual percentage rate than the rate that would be considered accurate under paragraph (a)(4) of this section.

(b) *Computation tools.* (1) The Regulation Z Annual Percentage Rate Tables produced by the Board may be used to determine the annual percentage rate, and any rate determined from those tables in accordance with the accompanying instructions complies with the requirements of this section. Volume I of the tables applies to single advance transactions involving up to 480 monthly payments or 104 weekly payments. It may be used for regular transactions and for transactions with any of the following irregularities: an irregular first period, an irregular first payment, and an irregular final payment. Volume II of the tables applies to transactions involving multiple advances and any type of payment or period irregularity.

(2) Creditors may use any other computation tool in determining the annual percentage rate if the rate so determined equals the rate determined in accordance with Appendix J, within the degree of accuracy set forth in paragraph (a) of this section.

(c) *Single add-on rate transactions.* If a single add-on rate is applied to all transactions with maturities up to 60 months and if all payments are equal in amount and period, a single annual percentage rate may be disclosed for all those transactions, so long as it is the highest annual percentage rate for any such transaction.

(d) *Certain transactions involving ranges of balances.* For purposes of disclosing the annual percentage rate referred to in § 226.17(g)(4) (Mail or telephone orders—delay in disclosures) and (h) (Series of sales—delay in disclosures), if the same finance charge is imposed on all balances within a specified range of balances, the annual percentage rate computed for the median balance may be disclosed for all the balances. However, if the annual percentage rate computed for the median balance understates the annual percentage rate computed for the lowest balance by more than 8 percent of the latter rate, the annual percentage rate shall be computed on whatever lower balance will produce an annual percentage rate that does not result in an understatement of more than 8 percent of the rate determined on the lowest balance.

§ 226.23   Right of rescission

(a) *Consumer's right to rescind.* (1) In a credit transaction in which a security interest is or will be retained or acquired in a consumer's principal dwelling, each consumer whose ownership interest is or will be subject to the security interest shall have the right to rescind the transaction, except for transactions described in paragraph (f) of this section.[47]

(2) To exercise the right to rescind, the consumer shall notify the creditor of the rescission by mail, telegram or other means of written communication. Notice is considered given when mailed, when filed for telegraphic transmission or, if sent by other means, when delivered to the creditor's designated place of business.

(3) The consumer may exercise the right to rescind until midnight of the third business day following consummation, delivery of the notice required by paragraph (b) of this section, or delivery of all material disclosures,[48] whichever occurs last. If the required notice or material disclosures are not delivered, the right to rescind shall expire 3 years after consummation, upon transfer of all of the consumer's interest in the property, upon sale of the property, whichever occurs first. In the case of certain administrative proceedings, the rescission period shall be extended in accordance with section 125(f) of the act.

(4) When more than one consumer in a transaction has the right to rescind, the exercise of the right by one consumer shall be effective as to all consumers.

(b)(1) *Notice of right to rescind.* In a transaction subject to rescission, a creditor shall deliver two copies of the notice of the right to rescind to each consumer entitled to rescind (one copy to each if the notice is delivered in electronic form in accordance with the consumer consent and other applicable provisions of the E–Sign Act). The notice shall be on a separate document that identifies the transaction and shall clearly and conspicuously disclose the following:

(i) The retention or acquisition of a security interest in the consumer's principal dwelling.

(ii) The consumer's right to rescind the transaction.

(iii) How to exercise the right to rescind, with a form for that purpose, designating the address of the creditor's place of business.

(iv) The effects of rescission, as described in paragraph (d) of this section.

(v) The date the rescission period expires.

---

47. For purposes of this section, the addition to an existing obligation of a security interest in a consumer's principal dwelling is a transaction. The right of rescission applies only to the addition of the security interest and not the existing obligation. The creditor shall deliver the notice required by paragraph (b) of this section but need not deliver new material disclosures. Delivery of the required notice shall begin the rescission period.

48. The term "material disclosures" means the required disclosures of the annual percentage rate, the finance charge, the amount financed, the total payments, the payment schedule, and the disclosures and limitations referred to in § 226.32(c) and (d).

(2) *Proper form of notice.* To satisfy the disclosure requirements of paragraph (b)(1) of this section, the creditor shall provide the appropriate model form in Appendix H of this part or a substantially similar notice.

(c) *Delay of creditor's performance.* Unless a consumer waives the right of rescission under paragraph (e) of this section, no money shall be disbursed other than in escrow, no services shall be performed and no materials delivered until the rescission period has expired and the creditor is reasonably satisfied that the consumer has not rescinded.

(d) *Effects of rescission.* (1) When a consumer rescinds a transaction, the security interest giving rise to the right of rescission becomes void and the consumer shall not be liable for any amount, including any finance charge.

(2) Within 20 calendar days after receipt of a notice of rescission, the creditor shall return any money or property that has been given to anyone in connection with the transaction and shall take any action necessary to reflect the termination of the security interest.

(3) If the creditor has delivered any money or property, the consumer may retain possession until the creditor has met its obligation under paragraph (d)(2) of this section. When the creditor has complied with that paragraph, the consumer shall tender the money or property to the creditor or, where the latter would be impracticable or inequitable, tender its reasonable value. At the consumer's option, tender of property may be made at the location of the property or at the consumer's residence. Tender of money must be made at the creditor's designated place of business. If the creditor does not take possession of the money or property within 20 calendar days after the consumer's tender, the consumer may keep it without further obligation.

(4) The procedures outlined in paragraphs (d)(2) and (3) of this section may be modified by court order.

(e) *Consumer's waiver of right to rescind.* (1) The consumer may modify or waive the right to rescind if the consumer determines that the extension of credit is needed to meet a bona fide personal financial emergency. To modify or waive the right, the consumer shall give the creditor a dated written statement that describes the emergency, specifically modifies or waives the right to rescind, and bears the signature of all the consumers entitled to rescind. Printed forms for this purpose are prohibited, except as provided in paragraph (e)(2) of this section.

(2) The need of the consumer to obtain funds immediately shall be regarded as a bona fide personal financial emergency provided that the dwelling securing the extension of credit is located in an area declared during June through September 1993, pursuant to 42 U.S.C. 5170, to be a major disaster area because of severe storms and flooding in the Midwest. In this instance, creditors may use printed forms for the consumer to waive the right to rescind. This exemption to paragraph (e)(1) of this section shall expire one year from the date an area was declared a major disaster.

(3) The consumer's need to obtain funds immediately shall be regarded as a bona fide personal financial emergency provided that the dwelling securing the extension of credit is located in an area declared during June through September 1994 to be a major disaster area, pursuant to 42 U.S.C. 5170, because of severe storms and flooding in the South. In this instance, creditors may use printed forms for the consumer to waive the right to rescind. This exemption to paragraph (e)(1) of this section shall expire one year from the date an area was declared a major disaster.

(4) The consumer's need to obtain funds immediately shall be regarded as a bona fide personal financial emergency provided that the dwelling securing the extension of credit is located in an area declared during October 1994 to be a major disaster area, pursuant to 42 U.S.C. 5170, because of severe storms and flooding in Texas. In this instance, creditors may use printed forms for the consumer to waive the right to rescind. This exemption to paragraph (e)(1) of this section shall expire one year from the date an area was declared a major disaster.

(f) *Exempt transactions.* The right to rescind does not apply to the following:

(1) A residential mortgage transaction.

(2) A refinancing or consolidation by the same creditor of an extension of credit already secured by the consumer's principal dwelling. The right of rescission shall apply, however, to the extent the new amount financed exceeds the unpaid principal balance, any earned unpaid finance charge on the existing debt, and amounts attributed solely to the costs of the refinancing or consolidation.

(3) A transaction in which a state agency is a creditor.

(4) An advance, other than an initial advance, in a series of advances or in a series of single-payment obligations that is treated as a single transaction under § 226.17(c)(6), if the notice required by paragraph (b) of this section and all material disclosures have been given to the consumer.

(5) A renewal of optional insurance premiums that is not considered a refinancing under § 226.20(a)(5).

(g) *Tolerances for accuracy—*(1) *One-half of 1 percent tolerance.* Except as provided in paragraphs (g)(2) and (h)(2) of this section, the finance charge and other disclosures affected by the finance charge (such as the amount financed and the annual percentage rate) shall be considered accurate for purposes of this section if the disclosed finance charge:

(i) is understated by no more than 1/2 of 1 percent of the face amount of the note or $100, whichever is greater; or

(ii) is greater than the amount required to be disclosed.

(2) *One percent tolerance.* In a refinancing of a residential mortgage transaction with a new creditor (other than a transaction covered by § 226.32), if there is no new advance and no consolidation of existing loans, the finance charge and other disclosures affected by the finance charge

(such as the amount financed and the annual percentage rate) shall be considered accurate for purposes of this section if the disclosed finance charge:

    (i) is understated by no more than 1 percent of the face amount of the note or $100, whichever is greater; or

    (ii) is greater than the amount required to be disclosed.

(h) *Special rules for foreclosures*—(1) *Right to rescind.* After the initiation of foreclosure on the consumer's principal dwelling that secures the credit obligation, the consumer shall have the right to rescind the transaction if:

    (i) A mortgage broker fee that should have been included in the finance charge was not included; or

    (ii) The creditor did not provide the properly completed appropriate model form in Appendix H of this part, or a substantially similar notice of rescission.

(2) *Tolerance for disclosures.* After the initiation of foreclosure on the consumer's principal dwelling that secures the credit obligation, the finance charge and other disclosures affected by the finance charge (such as the amount financed and the annual percentage rate) shall be considered accurate for purposes of this section if the disclosed finance charge:

    (i) is understated by no more than $35; or

    (ii) is greater than the amount required to be disclosed.

§ 226.24 Advertising

(a) *Actually available terms.* If an advertisement for credit states specific credit terms, it shall state only those terms that actually are or will be arranged or offered by the creditor.

(b) *Clear and conspicuous standard.* Disclosures required by this section shall be made clearly and conspicuously.

(c) *Advertisement of rate of finance charge.* If an advertisement states a rate of finance charge, it shall state the rate as an "annual percentage rate," using that term. If the annual percentage rate may be increased after consummation, the advertisement shall state that fact. If an advertisement is for credit not secured by a dwelling, the advertisement shall not state any other rate, except that a simple annual rate or periodic rate that is applied to an unpaid balance may be stated in conjunction with, but not more conspicuously than, the annual percentage rate. If an advertisement is for credit secured by a dwelling, the advertisement shall not state any other rate, except that a simple annual rate that is applied to an unpaid balance may be stated in conjunction with, but not more conspicuously than, the annual percentage rate.

(d) *Advertisement of terms that require additional disclosures.* (1) *Triggering terms.* If any of the following terms is set forth in an advertisement, the advertisement shall meet the requirements of paragraph (d)(2) of this section:

(i) The amount or percentage of any downpayment.

(ii) The number of payments or period of repayment.

(iii) The amount of any payment.

(iv) The amount of any finance charge.

(2) *Additional terms.* An advertisement stating any of the terms in paragraph (d)(1) of this section shall state the following terms,[49] as applicable (an example of one or more typical extensions of credit with a statement of all the terms applicable to each may be used):

(i) The amount or percentage of the downpayment.

(ii) The terms of repayment.

(iii) The *annual percentage rate*, using that term, and, if the rate may be increased after consummation, that fact.

(e) *Catalogs and multiple-page advertisements; electronic advertisements.* (1) If a catalog or other multiple-page advertisement, or an electronic advertisement (such as an advertisement appearing on an Internet Web site), gives information in a table or schedule in sufficient detail to permit determination of the disclosures required by paragraph (d)(2) of this section, it shall be considered a single advertisement if:

(i) The table or schedule is clearly and conspicuously set forth; and

(ii) Any statement of the credit terms in paragraph (d)(1) of this section appearing anywhere else in the catalog or advertisement clearly refers to the page or location on which the table or schedule begins.

(2) A catalog or multiple-page advertisement or an electronic advertisement (such as an advertisement appearing on an Internet Web site) complies with paragraph (d)(2) of this section if the table or schedule of terms includes all appropriate disclosures for a representative scale of amounts up to the level of the more commonly sold higher-priced property or services offered.

(f) *Disclosure of rates and payments in advertisements for credit secured by a dwelling*

(1) *Scope.* The requirements of this paragraph apply to any advertisement for credit secured by a dwelling, other than television or radio advertisements, including promotional materials accompanying applications.

(2) *Disclosure of rates*—(i) *In general.* If an advertisement for credit secured by a dwelling states a simple annual rate of interest and more than

---

49. [Reserved]

one simple annual rate of interest will apply over the term of the advertised loan, the advertisement shall disclose in a clear and conspicuous manner:

(A) Each simple annual rate of interest that will apply. In variable-rate transactions, a rate determined by adding an index and margin shall be disclosed based on a reasonably current index and margin;

(B) The period of time during which each simple annual rate of interest will apply; and

(C) The annual percentage rate for the loan. If such rate is variable, the annual percentage rate shall comply with the accuracy standards in §§ 226.17(c) and 226.22.

(ii) *Clear and conspicuous requirement.* For purposes of paragraph (f)(2)(i) of this section, clearly and conspicuously disclosed means that the required information in paragraphs (f)(2)(i)(A) through (C) shall be disclosed with equal prominence and in close proximity to any advertised rate that triggered the required disclosures. The required information in paragraph (f)(2)(i)(C) may be disclosed with greater prominence than the other information.

(3) *Disclosure of payments*—(i) *In general.* In addition to the requirements of paragraph (c) of this section, if an advertisement for credit secured by a dwelling states the amount of any payment, the advertisement shall disclose in a clear and conspicuous manner:

(A) The amount of each payment that will apply over the term of the loan, including any balloon payment. In variable-rate transactions, payments that will be determined based on the application of the sum of an index and margin shall be disclosed based on a reasonably current index and margin;

(B) The period of time during which each payment will apply; and

(C) In an advertisement for credit secured by a first lien on a dwelling, the fact that the payments do not include amounts for taxes and insurance premiums, if applicable, and that the actual payment obligation will be greater.

(ii) Clear and conspicuous requirement. For purposes of paragraph (f)(3)(i) of this section, a clear and conspicuous disclosure means that the required information in paragraphs (f)(3)(i)(A) and (B) shall be disclosed with equal prominence and in close proximity to any advertised payment that triggered the required disclosures, and that the required information in paragraph (f)(3)(i)(C) shall be disclosed with prominence and in close proximity to the advertised payments.

(4) *Envelope excluded.* The requirements in paragraphs (f)(2) and (f)(3) of this section do not apply to an envelope in which an application or solicitation is mailed, or to a banner advertisement or pop-up advertisement linked to an application or solicitation provided electronically.

(g) *Alternative disclosures—television or radio advertisements.* An advertisement made through television or radio stating any of the terms requiring additional disclosures under paragraph (d)(2) of this section may comply with paragraph (d)(2) of this section either by:

(1) Stating clearly and conspicuously each of the additional disclosures required under paragraph (d)(2) of this section; or

(2) Stating clearly and conspicuously the information required by paragraph (d)(2)(iii) of this section and listing a toll-free telephone number, or any telephone number that allows a consumer to reverse the phone charges when calling for information, along with a reference that such number may be used by consumers to obtain additional cost information.

(h) *Tax implications.* If an advertisement distributed in paper form or through the Internet (rather than by radio or television) is for a loan secured by the consumer's principal dwelling, and the advertisement states that the advertised extension of credit may exceed the fair market value of the dwelling, the advertisement shall clearly and conspicuously state that:

(1) The interest on the portion of the credit extension that is greater than the fair market value of the dwelling is not tax deductible for Federal income tax purposes; and

(2) The consumer should consult a tax adviser for further information regarding the deductibility of interest and charges.

(i) *Prohibited acts or practices in advertisements for credit secured by a dwelling.* The following acts or practices are prohibited in advertisements for credit secured by a dwelling:

(1) *Misleading advertising of "fixed" rates and payments.* Using the word "fixed" to refer to rates, payments, or the credit transaction in an advertisement for variable-rate transactions or other transactions where the payment will increase, unless:

(i) In the case of an advertisement solely for one or more variable-rate transactions,

(A) The phrase "Adjustable–Rate Mortgage," "Variable–Rate Mortgage," or "ARM" appears in the advertisement before the first use of the word "fixed" and is at least as conspicuous as any use of the word "fixed" in the advertisement; and

(B) Each use of the word "fixed" to refer to a rate or payment is accompanied by an equally prominent and closely proximate statement of the time period for which the rate or payment is fixed, and the fact that the rate may vary or the payment may increase after that period;

(ii) In the case of an advertisement solely for non-variable-rate transactions where the payment will increase (e.g., a stepped-rate mortgage transaction with an initial lower payment), each use of the word "fixed" to refer to the payment is accompanied by an equally prominent and closely proximate statement of the time period for which the payment is fixed, and the fact that the payment will increase after that period; or

(iii) In the case of an advertisement for both variable-rate transactions and non-variable-rate transactions,

(A) The phrase "Adjustable–Rate Mortgage," "Variable–Rate Mortgage," or "ARM" appears in the advertisement with equal prominence as any use of the term "fixed," "Fixed Rate Mortgage," or similar terms; and

(B) Each use of the word "fixed" to refer to a rate, payment, or the credit transaction either refers solely to the transactions for which rates are fixed and complies with paragraph (i)(1)(ii) of this section, if applicable, or, if it refers to the variable-rate transactions, is accompanied by an equally prominent and closely proximate statement of the time period for which the rate or payment is fixed, and the fact that the rate may vary or the payment may increase after that period.

(2) *Misleading comparisons in advertisements.* Making any comparison in an advertisement between actual or hypothetical credit payments or rates and any payment or simple annual rate that will be available under the advertised product for a period less than the full term of the loan, unless:

(i) *In general.* The advertisement includes a clear and conspicuous comparison to the information required to be disclosed under sections 226.24(f)(2) and (3); and

(ii) *Application to variable-rate transactions.* If the advertisement is for a variable-rate transaction, and the advertised payment or simple annual rate is based on the index and margin that will be used to make subsequent rate or payment adjustments over the term of the loan, the advertisement includes an equally prominent statement in close proximity to the payment or rate that the payment or rate is subject to adjustment and the time period when the first adjustment will occur.

(3) *Misrepresentations about government endorsement.* Making any statement in an advertisement that the product offered is a "government loan program," "government-supported loan," or is otherwise endorsed or sponsored by any federal, state, or local government entity, unless the advertisement is for an FHA loan, VA loan, or similar loan program that is, in fact, endorsed or sponsored by a federal, state, or local government entity.

(4) *Misleading use of the current lender's name.* Using the name of the consumer's current lender in an advertisement that is not sent by or on behalf of the consumer's current lender, unless the advertisement:

(i) Discloses with equal prominence the name of the person or creditor making the advertisement; and

(ii) Includes a clear and conspicuous statement that the person making the advertisement is not associated with, or acting on behalf of, the consumer's current lender.

(5) *Misleading claims of debt elimination.* Making any misleading claim in an advertisement that the mortgage product offered will eliminate debt or result in a waiver or forgiveness of a consumer's existing loan terms with, or obligations to, another creditor.

(6) *Misleading use of the term "counselor."* Using the term "counselor" in an advertisement to refer to a for-profit mortgage broker or mortgage creditor, its employees, or persons working for the broker or creditor that are involved in offering, originating or selling mortgages.

(7) *Misleading foreign-language advertisements.* Providing information about some trigger terms or required disclosures, such as an initial rate or payment, only in a foreign language in an advertisement, but providing information about other trigger terms or required disclosures, such as information about the fully-indexed rate or fully amortizing payment, only in English in the same advertisement.

SUBPART D.   MISCELLANEOUS

§ 226.25   Record retention

(a) *General rule.* A creditor shall retain evidence of compliance with this regulation (other than advertising requirements under §§ 226.16 and 226.24) for 2 years after the date disclosures are required to be made or action is required to be taken. The administrative agencies responsible for enforcing the regulation may require creditors under their jurisdictions to retain records for a longer period if necessary to carry out their enforcement responsibilities under section 108 of the act.

(b) *Inspection of records.* A creditor shall permit the agency responsible for enforcing this regulation with respect to that creditor to inspect its relevant records for compliance.

§ 226.26   Use of annual percentage rate in oral disclosures

(a) *Open-end credit.* In an oral response to a consumer's inquiry about the cost of open-end credit, only the annual percentage rate or rates shall be stated, except that the periodic rate or rates also may be stated. If the annual percentage rate cannot be determined in advance because there are finance charges other than a periodic rate, the corresponding annual percentage rate shall be stated, and other cost information may be given.

(b) *Closed-end credit.* In an oral response to a consumer's inquiry about the cost of closed-end credit, only the annual percentage rate shall be stated, except that a simple annual rate or periodic rate also may be stated if it is applied to an unpaid balance. If the annual percentage rate cannot be determined in advance, the annual percentage rate for a sample transaction shall be stated, and other cost information for the consumer's specific transaction may be given.

§ 226.27   Language of disclosures

Disclosures required by this regulation may be made in a language other than English, provided that the disclosures are made available in English upon the consumer's request. This requirement for providing English disclosures on request does not apply to advertisements subject to §§ 226.16 and 226.24.

§ 226.28   Effect on State laws

(a) *Inconsistent disclosure requirements.* (1) Except as provided in paragraph (d) of this section, state law requirements that are inconsistent with the requirements contained in chapter 1 (General Provisions), chapter 2 (Credit Transactions), or chapter 3 (Credit Advertising) of the act and the implementing provisions of this regulation are preempted to the extent of the inconsistency. A state law is inconsistent if it requires a creditor to make disclosures or take actions that contradict the requirements of the federal law. A state law is contradictory if it requires the use of the same term to represent a different amount or a different meaning than the federal law, or if it requires the use of a term different from that required in the federal law to describe the same item. A creditor, state, or other interested party may request the Board to determine whether a state law requirement is inconsistent. After the Board determines that a state law is inconsistent, a creditor may not make disclosures using the inconsistent term or form.

(2)(i) State law requirements are inconsistent with the requirements contained in sections 161 (Correction of billing errors) or 162 (Regulation of credit reports) of the act and the implementing provisions of this regulation and are preempted if they provide rights, responsibilities, or procedures for consumers or creditors that are different from those required by the federal law. However, a state law that allows a consumer to inquire about an open-end credit account and imposes on the creditor an obligation to respond to such inquiry after the time allowed in the federal law for the consumer to submit written notice of a billing error shall not be preempted in any situation where the time period for making written notice under this regulation has expired. If a creditor gives written notice of a consumer's rights under such state law, the notice shall state that reliance on the longer time period available under state law may result in the loss of important rights that could be preserved by acting more promptly under federal law; it shall also explain that the state law provisions apply only after expiration of the time period for submitting a proper written notice of a billing error under the federal law. If the state disclosures are made on the same side of a page as the required federal disclosures, the state disclosures shall appear under a demarcation line below the federal disclosures, and the federal disclosures shall be identified by a heading indicating that they are made in compliance with federal law.

(ii) State law requirements are inconsistent with the requirements contained in chapter 4 (Credit billing) of the act (other than section

161 or 162) and the implementing provisions of this regulation and are preempted if the creditor cannot comply with state law without violating federal law.

(iii) A state may request the Board to determine whether its law is inconsistent with chapter 4 of the act and its implementing provisions.

(b) *Equivalent disclosure requirements.* If the Board determines that a disclosure required by state law (other than a requirement relating to the finance charge, annual percentage rate, or the disclosures required under § 226.32) is substantially the same in meaning as a disclosure required under the act or this regulation, creditors in that state may make the state disclosure in lieu of the federal disclosure. A creditor, state, or other interested party may request the Board to determine whether a state disclosure is substantially the same in meaning as a federal disclosure.

(c) *Request for determination.* The procedures under which a request for a determination may be made under this section are set forth in Appendix A.

(d) *Special rule for credit and charge cards.* State law requirements relating to the disclosure of credit information in any credit or charge card application or solicitation that is subject to the requirements of section 127(c) of chapter 2 of the act (§ 226.5a of the regulation) or in any renewal notice for a credit or charge card that is subject to the requirements of section 127(d) of chapter 2 of the act (§ 226.9(e) of the regulation) are preempted. State laws relating to the enforcement of section 127 (c) and (d) of the act are not preempted.

§ 226.29   State exemptions

(a) *General rule.* Any state may apply to the Board to exempt a class of transactions within the state from the requirements of chapter 2 (Credit transactions) or chapter 4 (Credit billing) of the act and the corresponding provisions of this regulation. The Board shall grant an exemption if it determines that:

(1) The state law is substantially similar to the federal law or, in the case of chapter 4, affords the consumer greater protection than the federal law; and

(2) There is adequate provision for enforcement.

(b) *Civil liability.* (1) No exemptions granted under this section shall extend to the civil liability provisions of section 130 and 131 of the act.

(2) If an exemption has been granted, the disclosures required by the applicable state law (except any additional requirements not imposed by federal law) shall constitute the disclosures required by this act.

(c) *Applications.* The procedures under which a state may apply for an exemption under this section are set forth in Appendix B.

§ 226.30   Limitation on rates

A creditor shall include in any consumer credit contract secured by a dwelling and subject to the act and this regulation the maximum interest rate that may be imposed during the term of the obligation[50] when:

(a) In the case of closed-end credit, the annual percentage rate may increase after consummation, or

(b) In the case of open-end credit, the annual percentage rate may increase during the plan.

SUBPART E.   SPECIAL RULES FOR CERTAIN HOME MORTGAGE TRANSACTIONS

§ 226.31   General rules

(a) *Relation to other subparts in this part.* The requirements and limitations of this subpart are in addition to and not in lieu of those contained in other subparts of this part.

(b) *Form of disclosures.* The creditor shall make the disclosures required by this subpart clearly and conspicuously in writing, in a form that the consumer may keep. The disclosures required by this subpart may be provided to the consumer in electronic form, subject to compliance with the consumer consent and other applicable provisions of the Electronic Signatures in Global and National Commerce Act (E–Sign Act) (15 U.S.C. § 7001 et seq.)

(c) *Timing of disclosure*—(1) *Disclosures for certain closed-end home mortgages.* The creditor shall furnish the disclosures required by § 226.32 at least three business days prior to consummation of a mortgage transaction covered by § 226.32.

(i) *Change in terms.* After complying with paragraph (c)(1) of this section and prior to consummation, if the creditor changes any term that makes the disclosures inaccurate, new disclosures shall be provided in accordance with the requirements of this subpart.

(ii) *Telephone disclosures.* A creditor may provide new disclosures by telephone if the consumer initiates the change and if, at consummation:

(A) The creditor provides new written disclosures; and

(B) The consumer and creditor sign a statement that the new disclosures were provided by telephone at least three days prior to consummation.

(iii) *Consumer's waiver of waiting period before consummation.* The consumer may, after receiving the disclosures required by para-

---

50. Compliance with this section will constitute compliance with the disclosure requirements on limitations on increases in footnote 12 to §§ 226.6(a)(2) and 226.18(f)(2) until October 1, 1988.

graph (c)(1) of this section, modify or waive the three-day waiting period between delivery of those disclosures and consummation if the consumer determines that the extension of credit is needed to meet a bona fide personal financial emergency. To modify or waive the right, the consumer shall give the creditor a dated written statement that describes the emergency, specifically modifies or waives the waiting period, and bears the signature of all the consumers entitled to the waiting period. Printed forms for this purpose are prohibited, except when creditors are permitted to use printed forms pursuant to § 226.23(e)(2).

(2) *Disclosures for reverse mortgages.* The creditor shall furnish the disclosures required by § 226.33 at least three business days prior to:

(i) Consummation of a closed-end credit transaction; or

(ii) The first transaction under an open-end credit plan.

(d) *Basis of disclosures and use of estimates.*—(1) *Legal Obligation.* Disclosures shall reflect the terms of the legal obligation between the parties.

(2) *Estimates.* If any information necessary for an accurate disclosure is unknown to the creditor, the creditor shall make the disclosure based on the best information reasonably available at the time the disclosure is provided, and shall state clearly that the disclosure is an estimate.

(3) *Per-diem interest.* For a transaction in which a portion of the interest is determined on a per-diem basis and collected at consummation, any disclosure affected by the per-diem interest shall be considered accurate if the disclosure is based on the information known to the creditor at the time that the disclosure documents are prepared.

(e) *Multiple creditors; multiple consumers.* If a transaction involves more than one creditor, only one set of disclosures shall be given and the creditors shall agree among themselves which creditor must comply with the requirements that this part imposes on any or all of them. If there is more than one consumer, the disclosures may be made to any consumer who is primarily liable on the obligation. If the transaction is rescindable under § 226.15 or § 226.23, however, the disclosures shall be made to each consumer who has the right to rescind.

(f) *Effect of subsequent events.* If a disclosure becomes inaccurate because of an event that occurs after the creditor delivers the required disclosures, the inaccuracy is not a violation of Regulation Z (12 CFR part 226), although new disclosures may be required for mortgages covered by § 226.32 under paragraph (c) of this section, § 226.9(c), § 226.19, or § 226.20.

(g) *Accuracy of annual percentage rate.* For purposes of § 226.32, the annual percentage rate shall be considered accurate, and may be used in determining whether a transaction is covered by § 226.32, if it is accurate according to the requirements and within the tolerances under § 226.22.

The finance charge tolerances for rescission under § 226.23(g) or (h) shall not apply for this purpose.

§ 226.32 Requirements for certain closed-end home mortgages

(a) *Coverage.* (1) Except as provided in paragraph (a)(2) of this section, the requirements of this section apply to a consumer credit transaction that is secured by the consumer's principal dwelling, and in which either:

(i) The annual percentage rate at consummation will exceed by more than 8 percentage points for first-lien loans, or by more than 10 percentage points for subordinate-lien loans, the yield on Treasury securities having comparable periods of maturity to the loan maturity as of the fifteenth day of the month immediately preceding the month in which the application for the extension of credit is received by the creditor; or

(ii) The total points and fees payable by the consumer at or before loan closing will exceed the greater of 8 percent of the total loan amount, or $400; the $400 figure shall be adjusted annually on January 1 by the annual percentage change in the Consumer Price Index that was reported on the preceding June 1.

(2) This section does not apply to the following:

(i) A residential mortgage transaction.

(ii) A reverse mortgage transaction subject to § 226.33.

(iii) An open-end credit plan subject to subpart B of this part.

(b) *Definitions.* For purposes of this subpart, the following definitions apply:

(1) For purposes of paragraph (a)(1)(ii) of this section, points and fees means:

(i) All items required to be disclosed under §§ 226.4(a) and 226.4(b), except interest or the time-price differential;

(ii) All compensation paid to mortgage brokers;

(iii) All items listed in § 226.4(c)(7) (other than amounts held for future payment of taxes) unless the charge is reasonable, the creditor receives no direct or indirect compensation in connection with the charge, and the charge is not paid to an affiliate of the creditor; and

(iv) Premiums or other charges for credit life, accident, health, or loss-of-income insurance, or debt-cancellation coverage (whether or not the debt-cancellation coverage is insurance under applicable law) that provides for cancellation of all or part of the consumer's liability in the event of the loss of life, health, or income or in the case of accident, written in connection with the credit transaction.

(2) *Affiliate* means any company that controls, is controlled by, or is under common control with another company, as set forth in the Bank Holding Company Act of 1956 (12 U.S.C. § 1841 et seq.).

(c) *Disclosures.* In addition to other disclosures required by this part, in a mortgage subject to this section, the creditor shall disclose the following in conspicuous type size:

(1) *Notices.* The following statement: "You are not required to complete this agreement merely because you have received these disclosures or have signed a loan application. If you obtain this loan, the lender will have a mortgage on your home. You could lose your home, and any money you have put into it, if you do not meet your obligations under the loan."

(2) *Annual percentage rate.* The annual percentage rate.

(3) *Regular payment; balloon payment.* The amount of the regular monthly (or other periodic) payment and the amount of any balloon payment. The regular payment disclosed under this paragraph shall be treated as accurate if it is based on an amount borrowed that is deemed accurate and is disclosed under paragraph (c)(5) of this section.

(4) *Variable-rate.* For variable-rate transactions, a statement that the interest rate and monthly payment may increase, and the amount of the single maximum monthly payment, based on the maximum interest rate required to be disclosed under § 226.30.

(5) *Amount borrowed.* For a mortgage refinancing, the total amount the consumer will borrow, as reflected by the face amount of the note; and where the amount borrowed includes premiums or other charges for optional credit insurance or debt-cancellation coverage, that fact shall be stated, grouped together with the disclosure of the amount borrowed. The disclosure of the amount borrowed shall be treated as accurate if it is not more than $100 above or below the amount required to be disclosed.

(d) *Limitations.* A mortgage transaction subject to this section shall not provide for the following terms:

(1)(i) *Balloon payment.* For a loan with a term of less than five years, a payment schedule with regular periodic payments that when aggregated do not fully amortize the outstanding principal balance.

(ii) *Exception.* The limitations in paragraph (d)(1)(i) of this section do not apply to loans with maturities of less than one year, if the purpose of the loan is a "bridge" loan connected with the acquisition or construction of a dwelling intended to become the consumer's principal dwelling.

(2) *Negative amortization.* A payment schedule with regular periodic payments that cause the principal balance to increase.

(3) *Advance payments.* A payment schedule that consolidates more than two periodic payments and pays them in advance from the proceeds.

(4) *Increased interest rate.* An increase in the interest rate after default.

(5) *Rebates.* A refund calculated by a method less favorable than the actuarial method (as defined by section 933(d) of the Housing and Commu-

nity Development Act of 1992, 15 U.S.C. 1615(d)), for rebates of interest arising from a loan acceleration due to default.

(6) *Prepayment penalties.* Except as allowed under paragraph (d)(7) of this section, a penalty for paying all or part of the principal before the date on which the principal is due. A prepayment penalty includes computing a refund of unearned interest by a method that is less favorable to the consumer than the actuarial method, as defined by section 933(d) of the Housing and Community Development Act of 1992, 15 U.S.C. § 1615(d).

(7) *Prepayment penalty exception.* A mortgage transaction subject to this section may provide for a prepayment penalty (including a refund calculated according to the rule of 78s) otherwise permitted by law if, under the terms of the loan:

(i) The penalty will not apply after the two-year period following consummation;

(ii) The penalty will not apply if the source of the prepayment funds is a refinancing by the creditor or an affiliate of the creditor;

(iii) At consummation, the consumer's total monthly debt payments (including amounts owed under the mortgage) do not exceed 50 percent of the consumer's monthly gross income, as verified in accordance with § 226.34(a)(4)(ii); and

(iv) The amount of the periodic payment of principal or interest or both may not change during the four-year period following consummation.

(8) *Due-on-demand clause.* A demand feature that permits the creditor to terminate the loan in advance of the original maturity date and to demand repayment of the entire outstanding balance, except in the following circumstances:

(i) There is fraud or material misrepresentation by the consumer in connection with the loan;

(ii) The consumer fails to meet the repayment terms of the agreement for any outstanding balance; or

(iii) There is any action or inaction by the consumer that adversely affects the creditor's security for the loan, or any right of the creditor in such security.

(e) *Prohibited acts and practices.* A creditor extending mortgage credit subject to this section may not:

(1) *Repayment ability.* Engage in a pattern or practice of extending such credit to a consumer based on the consumer's collateral if, considering the consumer's current and expected income, current obligations, and employment status, the consumer will be unable to make the scheduled payments to repay the obligation.

(2) *Home improvement contracts.* Pay a contractor under a home improvement contract from the proceeds of a mortgage covered by this section, other than:

(i) By an instrument payable to the consumer or jointly to the consumer and the contractor; or

(ii) At the election of the consumer, through a third-party escrow agent in accordance with terms established in a written agreement signed by the consumer, the creditor, and the contractor prior to the disbursement.

(3) *Notice to assignee.* Sell or otherwise assign a mortgage subject to this section without furnishing the following statement to the purchaser or assignee: "Notice: This is a mortgage subject to special rules under the federal Truth in Lending Act. Purchasers or assignees of this mortgage could be liable for all claims and defenses with respect to the mortgage that the borrower could assert against the creditor."

§ 226.33   Requirements for reverse mortgages

(a) *Definition.* For purposes of this subpart, *reverse mortgage transaction* means a nonrecourse consumer credit obligation in which:

(1) A mortgage, deed of trust, or equivalent consensual security interest securing one or more advances is created in the consumer's principal dwelling; and

(2) Any principal, interest, or shared appreciation or equity is due and payable (other than in the case of default) only after:

(i) The consumer dies;

(ii) The dwelling is transferred; or

(iii) The consumer ceases to occupy the dwelling as a principal dwelling.

(b) *Content of disclosures.* In addition to other disclosures required by this part, in a reverse mortgage transaction the creditor shall provide the following disclosures in a form substantially similar to the model form found in paragraph (d) of Appendix K of this part:

(1) *Notice.* A statement that the consumer is not obligated to complete the reverse mortgage transaction merely because the consumer has received the disclosures required by this section or has signed an application for a reverse mortgage loan.

(2) *Total annual loan cost rates.* A good-faith projection of the total cost of the credit, determined in accordance with paragraph (c) of this section and expressed as a table of "total annual loan cost rates," using that term, in accordance with Appendix K of this part.

(3) *Itemization of pertinent information.* An itemization of loan terms, charges, the age of the youngest borrower and the appraised property value.

(4) *Explanation of table.* An explanation of the table of total annual loan cost rates as provided in the model form found in paragraph (d) of Appendix K of this part.

(c) *Projected total cost of credit.* The projected total cost of credit shall reflect the following factors, as applicable:

(1) *Costs to consumer.* All costs and charges to the consumer, including the costs of any annuity the consumer purchases as part of the reverse mortgage transaction.

(2) *Payments to consumer.* All advances to and for the benefit of the consumer, including annuity payments that the consumer will receive from an annuity that the consumer purchases as part of the reverse mortgage transaction.

(3) *Additional creditor compensation.* Any shared appreciation or equity in the dwelling that the creditor is entitled by contract to receive.

(4) *Limitations on consumer liability.* Any limitation on the consumer's liability (such as nonrecourse limits and equity conservation agreements).

(5) *Assumed annual appreciation rates.* Each of the following assumed annual appreciation rates for the dwelling:

(i) 0 percent.

(ii) 4 percent.

(iii) 8 percent.

(6) *Assumed loan period.* (i) Each of the following assumed loan periods, as provided in Appendix L of this part:

(A) Two years.

(B) The actuarial life expectancy of the consumer to become obligated on the reverse mortgage transaction (as of that consumer's most recent birthday). In the case of multiple consumers, the period shall be the actuarial life expectancy of the youngest consumer (as of that consumer's most recent birthday).

(C) The actuarial life expectancy specified by paragraph (c)(6)(i)(B) of this section, multiplied by a factor of 1.4 and rounded to the nearest full year.

(ii) At the creditor's option, the actuarial life expectancy specified by paragraph (c)(6)(i)(B) of this section, multiplied by a factor of .5 and rounded to the nearest full year.

§ 226.34 Prohibited acts or practices in connection with credit subject to § 226.32

(a) *Prohibited acts or practices for loans subject to § 226.32.* A creditor extending mortgage credit subject to § 226.32 shall not—

(1) *Home improvement contracts.* Pay a contractor under a home improvement contract from the proceeds of a mortgage covered by § 226.32, other than:

(i) By an instrument payable to the consumer or jointly to the consumer and the contractor; or

(ii) At the election of the consumer, through a third-party escrow agent in accordance with terms established in a written agreement signed by the consumer, the creditor, and the contractor prior to the disbursement.

(2) *Notice to assignee.* Sell or otherwise assign a mortgage subject to § 226.32 without furnishing the following statement to the purchaser or assignee: "Notice: This is a mortgage subject to special rules under the federal Truth in Lending Act. Purchasers or assignees of this mortgage could be liable for all claims and defenses with respect to the mortgage that the borrower could assert against the creditor."

(3) *Refinancings within one-year period.* Within one year of having extended credit subject to § 226.32, refinance any loan subject to § 226.32 to the same borrower into another loan subject to § 226.32, unless the refinancing is in the borrower's interest. An assignee holding or servicing an extension of mortgage credit subject to § 226.32, shall not, for the remainder of the one-year period following the date of origination of the credit, refinance any loan subject to § 226.32 to the same borrower into another loan subject to § 226.32, unless the refinancing is in the borrower's interest. A creditor (or assignee) is prohibited from engaging in acts or practices to evade this provision, including a pattern or practice of arranging for the refinancing of its own loans by affiliated or unaffiliated creditors, or modifying a loan agreement (whether or not the existing loan is satisfied and replaced by the new loan) and charging a fee.

(4) *Repayment ability.* Extend credit subject to § 226.32 to a consumer based on the value of the consumer's collateral without regard to the consumer's repayment ability as of consummation, including the consumer's current and reasonably expected income, employment, assets other than the collateral, current obligations, and mortgage-related obligations.

(i) *Mortgage-related obligations.* For purposes of this paragraph (a)(4), mortgage-related obligations are expected property taxes, premiums for mortgage-related insurance required by the creditor as set forth in § 226.35(b)(3)(i), and similar expenses.

(ii) *Verification of repayment ability.* Under this paragraph (a)(4) a creditor must verify the consumer's repayment ability as follows:

(A) A creditor must verify amounts of income or assets that it relies on to determine repayment ability, including expected income or assets, by the consumer's Internal Revenue Service Form W–2, tax returns, payroll receipts, financial institution records, or other third-party documents that provide reasonably reliable evidence of the consumer's income or assets.

(B) Notwithstanding paragraph (a)(4)(ii)(A), a creditor has not violated paragraph (a)(4)(ii) if the amounts of income and assets that the creditor relied upon in determining repayment ability are not materially greater than the amounts of the consumer's income or assets that the creditor could have verified pursuant to paragraph (a)(4)(ii)(A) at the time the loan was consummated.

(C) A creditor must verify the consumer's current obligations.

(iii) *Presumption of compliance.* A creditor is presumed to have complied with this paragraph (a)(4) with respect to a transaction if the creditor:

(A) Verifies the consumer's repayment ability as provided in paragraph (a)(4)(ii);

(B) Determines the consumer's repayment ability using the largest payment of principal and interest scheduled in the first seven years following consummation and taking into account current obligations and mortgage-related obligations as defined in paragraph (a)(4)(i); and

(C) Assesses the consumer's repayment ability taking into account at least one of the following: The ratio of total debt obligations to income, or the income the consumer will have after paying debt obligations.

(iv) *Exclusions from presumption of compliance.* Notwithstanding the previous paragraph, no presumption of compliance is available for a transaction for which:

(A) The regular periodic payments for the first seven years would cause the principal balance to increase; or

(B) The term of the loan is less than seven years and the regular periodic payments when aggregated do not fully amortize the outstanding principal balance.

(v) *Exemption.* This paragraph (a)(4) does not apply to temporary or "bridge" loans with terms of twelve months or less, such as a loan to purchase a new dwelling where the consumer plans to sell a current dwelling within twelve months.

(b) *Prohibited acts or practices for dwelling-secured loans; open-end credit.* In connection with credit secured by the consumer's dwelling that does not meet the definition in § 226.2(a)(20), a creditor shall not structure a home-secured loan as an open-end plan to evade the requirements of § 226.32.

§ 226.35   Prohibited acts or practices in connection with higher-priced mortgage loans

(a) *Higher-priced mortgage loans*—(1) For purposes of this section, a higher-priced mortgage loan is a consumer credit transaction secured by the consumer's principal dwelling with an annual percentage rate that exceeds the average prime offer rate for a comparable transaction as of the date the interest rate is set by 1.5 or more percentage points for loans secured by a first lien on a dwelling, or by 3.5 or more percentage points for loans secured by a subordinate lien on a dwelling.

(2) "Average prime offer rate" means an annual percentage rate that is derived from average interest rates, points, and other loan pricing terms currently offered to consumers by a representative sample of creditors for mortgage transactions that have low-risk pricing characteristics. The Board publishes average prime offer rates for a broad range of types of transactions in a table updated at least weekly as well as the methodology the Board uses to derive these rates.

(3) Notwithstanding paragraph (a)(1) of this section, the term "higher-priced mortgage loan" does not include a transaction to finance the initial construction of a dwelling, a temporary or "bridge" loan with a term of twelve months or less, such as a loan to purchase a new dwelling where the consumer plans to sell a current dwelling within twelve months, a reverse-mortgage transaction subject to § 226.33, or a home equity line of credit subject to § 226.5b.

(b) *Rules for higher-priced mortgage loans.* Higher-priced mortgage loans are subject to the following restrictions:

(1) *Repayment ability.* A creditor shall not extend credit based on the value of the consumer's collateral without regard to the consumer's repayment ability as of consummation as provided in § 226.34(a)(4).

(2) *Prepayment penalties.* A loan may not include a penalty described by § 226.32(d)(6) unless:

(i) The penalty is otherwise permitted by law, including § 226.32(d)(7) if the loan is a mortgage transaction described in § 226.32(a); and

(ii) Under the terms of the loan—

(A) The penalty will not apply after the two-year period following consummation;

(B) The penalty will not apply if the source of the prepayment funds is a refinancing by the creditor or an affiliate of the creditor; and

(C) The amount of the periodic payment of principal or interest or both may not change during the four-year period following consummation.

(3) *Escrows—*(i) *Failure to escrow for property taxes and insurance.* Except as provided in paragraph (b)(3)(ii) of this section, a creditor may not extend a loan secured by a first lien on a principal dwelling unless an escrow account is established before consummation for payment of property taxes and premiums for mortgage-related insurance required by the creditor, such as insurance against loss of or damage to property, or against liability arising out of the ownership or use of the property, or insurance protecting the creditor against the consumer's default or other credit loss.

(ii) *Exemptions for loans secured by shares in a cooperative and for certain condominium units*—(A) Escrow accounts need not be established for loans secured by shares in a cooperative; and

(B) Insurance premiums described in paragraph (b)(3)(i) of this section need not be included in escrow accounts for loans secured by condominium units, where the condominium association has an obligation to the condominium unit owners to maintain a master policy insuring condominium units.

(iii) *Cancellation.* A creditor or servicer may permit a consumer to cancel the escrow account required in paragraph (b)(3)(i) of this section only in response to a consumer's dated written request to cancel the escrow account that is received no earlier than 365 days after consummation.

(iv) *Definition of escrow account.* For purposes of this section, "escrow account" shall have the same meaning as in 24 CFR 3500.17(b) as amended.

(4) *Evasion; open-end credit.* In connection with credit secured by a consumer's principal dwelling that does not meet the definition of open-end credit in § 226.2(a)(20), a creditor shall not structure a home-secured loan as an open-end plan to evade the requirements of this section.

§ 226.36 Prohibited acts or practices in connection with credit secured by a consumer's principal dwelling

(a) *Mortgage broker defined.* For purposes of this section, the term "mortgage broker" means a person, other than an employee of a creditor, who for compensation or other monetary gain, or in expectation of compensation or other monetary gain, arranges, negotiates, or otherwise obtains an extension of consumer credit for another person. The term includes a person meeting this definition, even if the consumer credit obligation is initially payable to such person, unless the person provides the funds for the transaction at consummation out of the person's own resources, out of deposits held by the person, or by drawing on a bona fide warehouse line of credit.

(b) *Misrepresentation of value of consumer's dwelling*—(1) *Coercion of appraiser.* In connection with a consumer credit transaction secured by a consumer's principal dwelling, no creditor or mortgage broker, and no affiliate of a creditor or mortgage broker shall directly or indirectly coerce, influence, or otherwise encourage an appraiser to misstate or misrepresent the value of such dwelling.

(i) Examples of actions that violate this paragraph (b)(1) include:

(A) Implying to an appraiser that current or future retention of the appraiser depends on the amount at which the appraiser values a consumer's principal dwelling;

(B) Excluding an appraiser from consideration for future engagement because the appraiser reports a value of a consumer's principal dwelling that does not meet or exceed a minimum threshold;

(C) Telling an appraiser a minimum reported value of a consumer's principal dwelling that is needed to approve the loan;

(D) Failing to compensate an appraiser because the appraiser does not value a consumer's principal dwelling at or above a certain amount; and

(E) Conditioning an appraiser's compensation on loan consummation.

(ii) Examples of actions that do not violate this paragraph (b)(1) include:

(A) Asking an appraiser to consider additional information about a consumer's principal dwelling or about comparable properties;

(B) Requesting that an appraiser provide additional information about the basis for a valuation;

(C) Requesting that an appraiser correct factual errors in a valuation;

(D) Obtaining multiple appraisals of a consumer's principal dwelling, so long as the creditor adheres to a policy of selecting the most reliable appraisal, rather than the appraisal that states the highest value;

(E) Withholding compensation from an appraiser for breach of contract or substandard performance of services as provided by contract; and

(F) Taking action permitted or required by applicable federal or state statute, regulation, or agency guidance.

(2) *When extension of credit prohibited.* In connection with a consumer credit transaction secured by a consumer's principal dwelling, a creditor who knows, at or before loan consummation, of a violation of paragraph (b)(1) of this section in connection with an appraisal shall not extend credit based on such appraisal unless the creditor documents that it has acted with reasonable diligence to determine that the appraisal does not materially misstate or misrepresent the value of such dwelling.

(3) *Appraiser defined.* As used in this paragraph (b), an appraiser is a person who engages in the business of providing assessments of the value of dwellings. The term "appraiser" includes persons that employ, refer, or manage appraisers and affiliates of such persons.

(c) *Servicing practices.* (1) In connection with a consumer credit transaction secured by a consumer's principal dwelling, no servicer shall—

(i) Fail to credit a payment to the consumer's loan account as of the date of receipt, except when a delay in crediting does not result in any charge to the consumer or in the reporting of negative information to a consumer reporting agency, or except as provided in paragraph (c)(2) of this section;

(ii) Impose on the consumer any late fee or delinquency charge in connection with a payment, when the only delinquency is attributable to late fees or delinquency charges assessed on an earlier payment, and the payment is otherwise a full payment for the applicable period and is paid on its due date or within any applicable grace period; or

(iii) Fail to provide, within a reasonable time after receiving a request from the consumer or any person acting on behalf of the consumer, an accurate statement of the total outstanding balance that would be required to satisfy the consumer's obligation in full as of a specified date.

(2) If a servicer specifies in writing requirements for the consumer to follow in making payments, but accepts a payment that does not conform to the requirements, the servicer shall credit the payment as of 5 days after receipt.

(3) For purposes of this paragraph (c), the terms "servicer" and "servicing" have the same meanings as provided in 24 CFR 3500.2(b), as amended.

(d) This section does not apply to a home equity line of credit subject to § 226.5b.

APPENDIX F.   Annual Percentage Rate Computations for Certain Open–End Credit Plans

In determining the denominator of the fraction under § 226.14(c)(3), no amount will be used more than once when adding the sum of the balances[51] subject to periodic rates to the sum of the amounts subject to specific transaction charges. In every case, the full amount of transactions subject to specific transaction charges shall be included in the denominator. Other balances or parts of balances shall be included according to the manner of determining the balance subject to a periodic rate, as illustrated in the following examples of accounts on monthly billing cycles:

1.   Previous balance—None.

A specific transaction of $100 occurs on the first day of the billing cycle. The average daily balance is $100. A specific transaction charge of 3% is applicable to the specific transaction. The periodic rate is 1½% applicable to the average daily balance. The numerator is the amount of the finance charge, which is $4.50. The denominator is the amount of the transaction (which is $100), plus the amount by which the balance subject to the periodic rate exceeds the amount of the specific transactions (such excess in this case is 0), totaling $100.

---

51. Where a portion of the finance charge is determined by application of one or more daily periodic rates, the phrase "sum of the balances" shall also mean the "average of daily balances."

The annual percentage rate is the quotient (which is 4 ½) multiplied by 12 (the number of months in a year), i.e., 54%.

2. Previous balance—$100.

A specific transaction of $100 occurs at the midpoint of the billing cycle. The average daily balance is $150. A specific transaction charge of 3% is applicable to the specific transaction. The periodic rate is 1½% applicable to the average daily balance. The numerator is the amount of the finance charge which is $5.25. The denominator is the amount of the transaction (which is $100), plus the amount by which the balance subject to the periodic rate exceeds the amount of the specific transaction (such excess in this case is $50), totaling $150. As explained in example 1, the annual percentage rate is 3½% x 12 = 42%.

3. If, in example 2, the periodic rate applies only to the previous balance, the numerator is $4.50 and the denominator is $200 (the amount of the transaction, $100, plus the balance subject only to the periodic rate, the $100 previous balance). As explained in example 1, the annual percentage rate is 2¼% x 12 = 27%.

4. If, in example 2, the periodic rate applies only to an adjusted balance (previous balance less payments and credits) and the consumer made a payment of $50 at the midpoint of the billing cycle, the numerator is $3.75 and the denominator is $150 (the amount of the transaction, $100, plus the balance subject to the periodic rate, the $50 adjusted balance). As explained in example 1, the annual percentage rate is 2½% x 12 = 30%.

5. Previous balance—$100.

A specific transaction (check) of $100 occurs at the midpoint of the billing cycle. The average daily balance is $150. The specific transaction charge is $.25 per check. The periodic rate is 1½% applied to the average daily balance. The numerator is the amount of the finance charge, which is $2.50 and includes the $.25 check charge and the $2.25 resulting from the application of the periodic rate. The denominator is the full amount of the specific transaction (which is $100) plus the amount by which the average daily balance exceeds the amount of the specific transaction (which in this case is $50), totaling $150. As explained in example 1, the annual percentage rate would be 1⅔% x 12 = 20%.

6. Previous balance—none.

A specific transaction of $100 occurs at the midpoint of the billing cycle. The average daily balance is $50. The specific transaction charge is 3% of the transaction amount or $3.00. The periodic rate is 1½% per month applied to the average daily balance. The numerator is the amount of the finance charge, which is $3.75, including the $3.00 transaction charge and $.75 resulting from application of the periodic rate. The denominator is the full amount of the specific transaction ($100) plus the amount by which the balance subject to the periodic rate exceeds the amount of the transaction

($0). Where the specific transaction amount exceeds the balance subject to the periodic rate, the resulting number is considered to be zero rather than a negative number ($50 – $100 = –$50). The denominator, in this case, is $100. As explained in example 1, the annual percentage rate is 3¾% x 12 = 45%.

APPENDIX G.   Open–End Model Forms and Clauses

G–1.   Balance Computation Methods Model Clauses

(a) Adjusted balance method

We figure [a portion of] the finance charge on your account by applying the periodic rate to the "adjusted balance" of your account. We get the "adjusted balance" by taking the balance you owed at the end of the previous billing cycle and subtracting [any unpaid finance charges and] any payments and credits received during the present billing cycle.

(b) Previous balance method

We figure [a portion of] the finance charge on your account by applying the periodic rate to the amount you owe at the beginning of each billing cycle [minus any unpaid finance charges.] We do not subtract any payments or credits received during the billing cycle. [The amount of payments and credits to your account this billing cycle was $____.]

(c) Average daily balance method (excluding current transactions)

We figure [a portion of] the finance charge on your account by applying the periodic rate to the "average daily balance" of your account (excluding current transactions). To get the "average daily balance" we take the beginning balance of your account each day and subtract any payments or credits [and any unpaid finance charges]. We do not add in any new [purchases/advances/loans]. This gives us the daily balance. Then, we add all the daily balances for the billing cycle together and divide the total by the number of days in the billing cycle. This gives us the "average daily balance."

(d) Average daily balance method (including current transactions)

We figure [a portion of] the finance charge on your account by applying the periodic rate to the "average daily balance" of your account (including current transactions). To get the "average daily balance" we take the beginning balance of your account each day, add any new [purchases/advances/loans], and subtract any payments or credits, [and unpaid finance charges]. This gives us the daily balance. Then, we add up all the daily balances for the billing cycle and divide the total by the number of days in the billing cycle. This gives us the "average daily balance."

(e) Ending balance method

We figure [a portion of] the finance charge on your account by applying the periodic rate to the amount you owe at the end of each cycle (including new purchases and deducting payments and credits made during the billing cycle).

G–2. Liability for Unauthorized Use Model Clause

You may be liable for the unauthorized use of your credit card [or other term that describes the credit card]. You will not be liable for unauthorized use that occurs after you notify [name of card issuer or its designee] at [address], orally or in writing, of the loss, theft, or possible unauthorized use. In any case, your liability will not exceed [insert $50 or any lesser amount under agreement with the cardholder.]

G–3. Long Form Billing Error Rights Model Form

YOUR BILLING RIGHTS KEEP THIS NOTICE FOR FUTURE USE

This notice contains important information about your rights and our responsibilities under the Fair Credit Billing Act.

Notify Us In Case of Errors or Questions About Your Bill

If you think your bill is wrong, or if you need more information about a transaction on your bill, write us [on a separate sheet] at [address] [the address listed on your bill]. Write to us as soon as possible. We must hear from you no later than 60 days after we sent you the first bill on which the error or problem appeared. You can telephone us, but doing so will not preserve your rights.

In your letter, give us the following information:

- Your name and account number.
- The dollar amount of the suspected error.
- Describe the error and explain, if you can, why you believe there is an error. If you need more information, describe the item you are not sure about.

If you have authorized us to pay your credit card bill automatically from your savings or checking account, you can stop the payment on any amount you think is wrong. To stop the payment your letter must reach us three business days before the automatic payment is scheduled to occur.

Your Rights and Our Responsibilities After We Receive Your Written Notice

We must acknowledge your letter within 30 days, unless we have corrected the error by then. Within 90 days, we must either correct the error or explain why we believe the bill was correct.

After we receive your letter, we cannot try to collect any amount you question, or report you as delinquent. We can continue to bill you for the amount you question, including finance charges, and we can apply any unpaid amount against your credit limit. You do not have to pay any questioned amount while we are investigating, but you are still obligated to pay the parts of your bill that are not in question.

If we find that we made a mistake on your bill, you will not have to pay any finance charges related to any questioned amount. If we didn't make a mistake, you may have to pay finance charges, and you will have to make up any missed payments on the questioned amount. In either case, we will send you a statement of the amount you owe and the date that it is due.

If you fail to pay the amount that we think you owe, we may report you as delinquent. However, if our explanation does not satisfy you and you write to us within ten days telling us that you still refuse to pay, we must tell anyone we report you to that you have a question about your bill. And, we must tell you the name of anyone we reported you to. We must tell anyone we report you to that the matter has been settled between us when it finally is.

If we don't follow these rules, we can't collect the first $50 of the questioned amount, even if your bill was correct.

Special Rule for Credit Card Purchases

If you have a problem with the quality of property or services that you purchased with a credit card, and you have tried in good faith to correct the problem with the merchant, you may have the right not to pay the remaining amount due on the property or services. There are two limitations on this right:

(a) You must have made the purchase in your home state or, if not within your home state, within 100 miles of your current mailing address; and

(b) The purchase price must have been more than $50.

These limitations do not apply if we own or operate the merchant, or if we mailed you the advertisement for the property or services.

G–4.   Alternative Billing Error Rights Model Form

BILLING RIGHTS SUMMARY

In Case of Errors or Questions About Your Bill

If you think your bill is wrong, or if you need more information about a transaction on your bill, write us [on a separate sheet] at [address] [the address shown on your bill] as soon as possible. We must hear from you no later than 60 days after we sent you the first bill on which the error or problem appeared. You can telephone us, but doing so will not preserve your rights.

In your letter, give us the following information:

- Your name and account number.
- The dollar amount of the suspected error.
- Describe the error and explain, if you can, why you believe there is an error. If you need more information, describe the item you are unsure about.

You do not have to pay any amount in question while we are investigating, but you are still obligated to pay the parts of your bill that are not in question. While we investigate your question, we cannot report you as delinquent or take any action to collect the amount you question.

Special Rule for Credit Card Purchases

If you have a problem with the quality of goods or services that you purchased with a credit card, and you have tried in good faith to correct the problem with the merchant, you may not have to pay the remaining amount due on the goods or services. You have this protection only when the purchase price was more than $50 and the purchase was made in your home state or within 100 miles of your mailing address. (If we own or operate the merchant, or if we mailed you the advertisement for the property or services, all purchases are covered regardless of amount or location of purchase.)

G–5.   Rescission Model Form (When Opening An Account)

NOTICE OF RIGHT TO CANCEL

1.   Your Right to Cancel.

We have agreed to establish an open-end credit account for you, and you have agreed to give us a [mortgage/lien/security interest] [on/in] your home as security for the account. You have a legal right under federal law to cancel the account, without cost, within three business days after the latest of the following events:

(1) the opening date of your account which is _____; or

(2) the date you received your Truth-in-Lending disclosures; or

(3) the date you received this notice of your right to cancel the account.

If you cancel the account, the [mortgage/lien/security interest] [on/in] your home is also cancelled. Within 20 days of receiving your notice, we must take the necessary steps to reflect the fact that the [mortgage/lien/security interest] [on/in] your home has been cancelled. We must return to you any money or property you have given to us or to anyone else in connection with the account.

You may keep any money or property we have given you until we have done the things mentioned above, but you must then offer to return the money or property. If it is impractical or unfair for you to return the property, you must offer its reasonable value. You may offer to return the property at your home or at the location of the property. Money must be returned to the address shown below. If we do not take possession of the money or property within 20 calendar days of your offer, you may keep it without further obligation.

2. How to Cancel.

If you decide to cancel the account, you may do so by notifying us, in writing, at

(creditor's name and business address).

You may use any written statement that is signed and dated by you and states your intention to cancel, or you may use this notice by dating and signing below. Keep one copy of this notice no matter how you notify us because it contains important information about your rights.

If you cancel by mail or telegram, you must send the notice no later than midnight of _____(date)

(or midnight of the third business day following the latest of the three events listed above). If you send or deliver your written notice to cancel some other way, it must be delivered to the above address no later than that time.

I WISH TO CANCEL.

_____   _____

Consumer's Signature   Date

G–6.   Rescission Model Form (For Each Transaction)

NOTICE OF RIGHT TO CANCEL

1.   Your Right to Cancel.

We have extended credit to you under your open-end credit account. This extension of credit will increase the amount you owe on your account. We already have a [mortgage/lien/security interest] [on/in] your home as security for your account. You have a legal right under federal law to cancel the extension of credit, without cost, within three business days after the latest of the following events:

(1) the date of the additional extension of credit which is _____; or

(2) the date you received your Truth-in-Lending disclosures; or

(3) the date you received this notice of your right to cancel the additional extension of credit.

If you cancel the additional extension of credit, your cancellation will only apply to the additional amount and to any increase in the [mortgage/lien/security interest] that resulted because of the additional amount. It will not affect the amount you presently owe, and it will not affect the [mortgage/lien/security interest] we already have [on/in] your home. Within 20 calendar days after we receive your notice of cancellation, we must take the necessary steps to reflect the fact that any increase in the [mortgage/lien/security interest] [on/in] your home has been cancelled. We must also return to you any money or property you have given to us or to anyone else in connection with this extension of credit.

You may keep any money or property we have given you until we have done the things mentioned above, but you must then offer to return the money or property. If it is impractical or unfair for you to return the property, you must offer its reasonable value. You may offer to return the property at your home or at the location of the property. Money must be returned to the address shown below. If we do not take possession of the money or property within 20 calendar days of your offer, you may keep it without further obligation.

2.   How to Cancel.

If you decide to cancel the additional extension of credit, you may do so by notifying us, in writing, at

(creditor's name and business address).

You may use any written statement that is signed and dated by you and states your intention to cancel, or you may use this notice by dating and signing below. Keep one copy of this notice no matter how you notify us because it contains important information about your rights.

If you cancel by mail or telegram, you must send the notice no later than midnight of _____(date) (or midnight of the third business day following the latest of the three events listed above). If you send or deliver your written notice to cancel some other way, it must be delivered to the above address no later than that time.

I WISH TO CANCEL.

_____   _____

Consumer's Signature   Date

G–10(A). Applications and Solicitations
Model Form (Credit Cards)

Annual percentage rate (APR) for purchases	_____% until (expiration date), after that, _____ %
Other APRs	Balance transfer APR: _____% Cash advance APR: _____% Penalty APR: _____% See explanation below*
Variable-rate information	Your APR may vary. The rate for [purchases] [cash advances][balance transfers] is determined by (explanation). See explanation below**
Grace period for repayment of balances for purchases	[__ days] [until ____] [not less than __ days] [between __ and __days] [__ days on average] [You have no grace period in which to repay your balance for purchases before a finance charge will be imposed.]
Method of computing the balance for purchases	
Annual fees	[Annual] [Membership] fee: $ _____ per year] [(type of fee): $ _____ per year] [(type of fee): $ _____]
Minimum finance charge	$ _____
Transaction fee for purchases	[$ _____] [____ % of ____]
Transaction fee for cash advances: [$ ____] [____% of _____] **Balance transfer fee:** [$____] [___% of ____] **Late-payment fee:** [$ ____] [___ % of ____] **Over-the-credit-limit fee:** $ ___	

     * Explanation of penalty.
     **Explanation of variable rate.

G–10(B). Applications and Solicitations
Model Form (Credit Cards)

Annual percentage rate for purchases	Variable-rate information	Grace period for repayment of the balance for purchases	Method of computing the balance for purchases	Annual fees	Minimum finance charge	Transaction fee for purchases
____%	Your annual percentage rate may vary. The rate is determined by (explanation).	[____ days] [Until ____] [Not less than ____ days] [Between ____ and ____ days] [____ days on average] [None]		[Annual fee: $____ per year] [Membership fee: $____ per year] [(type of fee): $____ per year] [(type of fee): $____]	$____	[$____] [____% of ____]

Transaction fee for cash advances: [$____] [____ % of ____]   Late-payment fee: [$____] [____ % of ____]

Over-the-credit-limit fee: $____

G–10(C). Applications and Solicitations
Model Form (Charge Cards)

Annual fees	Transaction fee for purchases	Transaction fee for cash advances, and fees for paying late or exceeding the credit limit
[Annual fee: $____ per year] [Membership fee: $____ per year] [(type of fee): $____ per year] [(type of fee): $____]	[$____] [____ % of ____]	Transaction fee for cash advance: [$____] [____% of ____] Late payment fee: [$____] [____% of ____] Over-the-credit-limit fee: $____
All charges made on this charge card are due and payable when you receive your periodic statement.		

G–11. Applications and Solicitations Made Available
to General Public Model Clauses

(a) Disclosure of Required Credit Information

The information about the costs of the card described in this [application] [solicitation] is accurate as of (month/year). This information may have changed after that date. To find out what may have changed, [call us at (telephone number)][write to us at (address)].

(b) Disclosure With Account Opening Statement

To find out about changes in the information in this [application] [solicitation], [call us at (telephone number)] [write to us at (address)].

(c) No Disclosure of Credit Information

There are costs associated with the use of this card. To obtain information about these costs, call us at (telephone number) or write to us at (address).

G–12. Charge Card Model Clause (When Access to Plan Offered by Another)

This charge card may allow you to access credit offered by another creditor. Our decision about issuing you a charge card will be independent of the other creditor's decision about allowing you access to a line of credit. Therefore, approval by us to issue you a card does not constitute approval by the other creditor to grant you credit privileges. If we issue you a charge card, you may receive it before the other creditor decides whether or not to grant you credit privileges.

G–13(A). Change in Insurance Provider Model Form (Combined Notice)

The credit card account you have with us is insured. This is to notify you that we plan to replace your current coverage with insurance coverage from a different insurer.

If we obtain insurance for your account from a different insurer, you may cancel the insurance.

[Your premium rate will increase to $_____ per _____.]

[Your coverage will be affected by the following:

[ ] The elimination of a type of coverage previously provided to you. [(explanation)] [See _____ of the attached policy for details.]

[ ] A lowering of the age at which your coverage will terminate or will become more restrictive. [(explanation)] [See _____ of the attached policy or certificate for details.]

[ ] A decrease in your maximum insurable loan balance, maximum periodic benefit payment, maximum number of payments, or any other decrease in the dollar amount of your coverage or benefits. [(explanation)] [See _____ of the attached policy or certificate for details.]

[ ] A restriction on the eligibility for benefits for you or others. [(explanation)] [See _____ of the attached policy or certificate for details.]

[ ] A restriction in the definition of "disability" or other key term of coverage. [(explanation)] [See _____ of the attached policy or certificate for details.]

[ ] The addition of exclusions or limitations that are broader or other than those under the current coverage. [(explanation)] [See _____ of the attached policy or certificate for details.]

[ ] An increase in the elimination (waiting) period or a change to nonretroactive coverage. [(explanation)] [See _____ of the attached policy or certificate for details).]]

[The name and mailing address of the new insurer providing the coverage for your account is (name and address).]

G–13(B). Change in Insurance Provider Model Form

We have changed the insurer providing the coverage for your account. The new insurer's name and address are (name and address). A copy of the new policy or certificate is attached.

You may cancel the insurance for your account.

G–14A Home Equity Sample

Important Terms of our Home Equity Line of Credit

This disclosure contains important information about our Home Equity Line of Credit. You should read it carefully and keep a copy for your records.

Availability of Terms: To obtain the terms described below, you must submit your application before January 1, 1990.

If these terms change (other than the annual percentage rate) and you decide, as a result, not to enter into an agreement with us, you are entitled to a refund of any fees that you have paid to us or anyone else in connection with your application.

Security Interest: We will take a mortgage on your home. You could lose your home if you do not meet the obligations in your agreement with us.

Possible Actions: Under certain circumstances, we can (1) terminate your line, require you to pay us the entire outstanding balance in one payment, and charge you certain fees; (2) refuse to make additional extensions of credit; and (3) reduce your credit limit.

If you ask, we will give you more specific information concerning when we can take these actions.

Minimum Payment Requirements: You can obtain advances of credit for 10 years (the "draw period"). During the draw period, payments will be due monthly. Your minimum monthly payment will equal the greater of $100 or 1/360 of the outstanding balance plus the finance charges that have accrued on the outstanding balance.

After the draw period ends, you will no longer be able to obtain credit advances and must pay the outstanding balance over 5 years (the "repayment period"). During the repayment period, payments will be due monthly. Your minimum monthly payment will equal 1/60 of the balance that was outstanding at the end of the draw period plus the finance charges that have accrued on the remaining balance.

Minimum Payment Example: If you made only the minimum monthly payments and took no other credit advances, it would take 15 years to pay off a credit advance of $10,000 at an ANNUAL PERCENTAGE RATE of 12%. During that period, you would make 120 monthly payments varying between $127.78 and $100.00 followed by 60 monthly payments varying between $187.06 and $118.08.

Fees and Charges: To open and maintain a line of credit, you must pay the following fees to us:

- Application fee: $150 (due at application)
- Points: 1% of credit limit (due when account opened)
- Annual maintenance fee: $75 (due each year)

You also must pay certain fees to third parties to open a line. These fees generally total between $500 and $900. If you ask, we will give you an itemization of the fees you will have to pay to third parties.

Minimum Draw and Balance Requirements: The minimum credit advance you can receive is $500. You must maintain an outstanding balance of at least $100.

Tax Deductibility: You should consult a tax advisor regarding the deductibility of interest and charges for the line.

Variable-Rate Information: The line has a variable-rate feature, and the annual percentage rate (corresponding to the periodic rate) and the minimum payment can change as a result.

The annual percentage rate includes only interest and not other costs.

The annual percentage rate is based on the value of an index. The index is the monthly average prime rate charged by banks and is published in the Federal Reserve Bulletin. To determine the annual percentage rate that will apply to your line, we add a margin to the value of the index.

Ask us for the current index value, margin and annual percentage rate. After you open a credit line, rate information will be provided on periodic statements that we will send you.

Rate Changes: The annual percentage rate can change each month. The maximum ANNUAL PERCENTAGE RATE that can apply is 18%. Except for this 18% "cap," there is no limit on the amount by which the rate can change during any one-year period.

Maximum Rate and Payment Examples: If you had an outstanding balance of $10,000 during the draw period, the minimum monthly payment at the maximum ANNUAL PERCENTAGE RATE of 18% would be $177.78. This annual percentage rate could be reached during the first month of the draw period.

If you had an outstanding balance of $10,000 at the beginning of the repayment period, the minimum monthly payment at the maximum ANNUAL PERCENTAGE RATE of 18% would be $316.67. This annual percentage rate could be reached during the first month of the repayment period.

Historical Example: The following table shows how the annual percentage rate and the minimum monthly payments for a single $10,000 credit advance would have changed based on changes in the index over the past 15 years. The index values are from September of each year. While

509

only one payment amount per year is shown, payments would have varied during each year.

The table assumes that no additional credit advances were taken, that only the minimum payments were made each month, and that the rate remained constant during each year. It does not necessarily indicate how the index or your payments will change in the future.

Year	Index	Margin*		Annual Percentage Rate	Minimum Monthly Payment
	(%)	(%)		(%)	($)
1974	12.00	2		14.00	144.44
1975	7.88	2		9.88	106.50
1976	7.00	2		9.00	100.00
1977	7.13	2		9.13	100.00
1978	9.41	2	*Draw Period*	11.41	105.47
1979	12.90	2		14.90	126.16
1980	12.23	2		14.23	117.53
1981	20.08	2		18.00**	138.07
1982	13.50	2		15.50	117.89
1983	11.00	2		13.00	100.00
1984	12.97	2		14.97	203.81
1985	9.50	2		11.50	170.18
1986	7.50	2	*Repayment Period*	9.50	149.78
1987	8.70	2		10.70	141.50
1988	10.00	2		12.00	130.55

*This is a margin we have used recently.

**This rate reflects the 18% rate cap.

G–14B. Home Equity Sample

Important Terms of our Home Equity Line of Credit

This disclosure contains important information about our Home Equity Line of Credit. You should read it carefully and keep a copy for your records.

Availability of Terms: All of the terms described below are subject to change.

If these terms change (other than the annual percentage rate) and you decide, as a result, not to enter into an agreement with us, you are entitled to a refund of any fees you paid to us or anyone else in connection with your application.

Security Interest: We will take a mortgage on your home. You could lose your home if you do not meet the obligations in your agreement with us.

Possible Actions: We can terminate your line, require you to pay us the entire outstanding balance in one payment, and charge you certain fees if:

You engage in fraud or material misrepresentation in connection with the line.

- You do not meet the repayment terms.

- Your action or inaction adversely affects the collateral or our rights in the collateral.

- We can refuse to make additional extensions of credit or reduce your credit limit if:

- The value of the dwelling securing the line declines significantly below its appraised value for purposes of the line.

- We reasonably believe you will not be able to meet the repayment requirements due to a material change in your financial circumstances.

- You are in default of a material obligation in the agreement.

- Government action prevents us from imposing the annual percentage rate provided for or impairs our security interest such that the value of the interest is less than 120 percent of the credit line.

- A regulatory agency has notified us that continued advances would constitute an unsafe and unsound practice.

- The maximum annual percentage rate is reached.

The initial agreement permits us to make certain changes to the terms of the agreement at specified times or upon the occurrence of specified events.

Minimum Payment Requirements: You can obtain advances of credit for 10 years (the "draw period"). You can choose one of three payment options for the draw period:

- *Monthly interest-only payments.* Under this option, your payments will be due monthly and will equal the finance charges that accrued on the outstanding balance during the preceding month.

- *Quarterly interest-only payments.* Under this option, your payments will be due quarterly and will equal the finance charges that accrued on the outstanding balance during the preceding quarter.

- *2% of the balance.* Under this option, your payments will be due monthly and will equal 2% of the outstanding balance on your line plus finance charges that accrued on the outstanding balance during the preceding month.

If the payment determined under any option is less than $50, the minimum payment will equal $50 or the outstanding balance on your line, whichever is less.

Under both the monthly and quarterly interest-only payment options, the minimum payment will not reduce the principal that is outstanding on your line.

After the draw period ends, you will no longer be able to obtain credit advances and must repay the outstanding balance (the "repayment period"). The length of the repayment period will depend on the balance outstanding at the beginning of it. During the repayment period, payments will be due monthly and will equal 3% of the outstanding balance on your line plus finance charges that accrued on the outstanding balance or $50, whichever is greater.

Minimum Payment Examples: If you took a single $10,000 advance and the ANNUAL PERCENTAGE RATE was 9.52%:

• Under the monthly interest-only payment option, it would take 18 years and 1 month to pay off the advance if you made only the minimum payments. During that period, you would make 120 payments of $79.33, followed by 96 payments varying between $379.33 and $50 and one final payment of $10.75.

• Under the 2% of the balance payment option, it would take 10 years and 8 months to pay off the advance if you made only the minimum payments. During that period, you would make 120 payments varying between $279.33 and $50, followed by 7 payments of $50 and one final payment of $21.53.

Fees and Charges: To open and maintain a line of credit, you must pay us the following fees:

• Application fee: $100 (due at application)

• Points: 1% of credit limit (due when account opened)

• Annual maintenance fee: $50 during the first 3 years, $75 thereafter (due each year)

You also must pay certain fees to third parties to open a line. These fees generally total between $500 and $900. If you ask, we will give you an itemization of the fees you will have to pay to third parties.

Minimum Draw Requirement: The minimum credit advance that you can receive is $200.

Tax Deductibility: You should consult a tax advisor regarding the deductibility of interest and charges for the line.

Variable-Rate Feature: The line has a variable-rate feature, and the annual percentage rage (corresponding to the periodic rate) and the minimum monthly payment can change as a result.

The annual percentage rate includes only interest and not other costs.

The annual percentage rate is based on the value of an index. During the draw period, the index is the monthly average prime rate charged by banks. During the repayment period, the index is the weekly average yield on U.S. Treasury securities adjusted to a constant maturity of one year. Information on these indices is published in the Federal Reserve Bulletin. To determine the annual percentage rate that will apply to your line, we add a margin to the value of the index.

The initial annual percentage rate is "discounted"—it is not based on the index and margin used for later rate adjustments. The initial rate will be in effect for the first year your credit line is open.

Ask us for the current index values, margin, discount and annual percentage rate. After you open a credit line, rate information will be provided on periodic statements that we send you.

Rate Changes: The annual percentage rate can change monthly. The maximum ANNUAL PERCENTAGE RATE that can apply is 18%. Apart from this rate "cap," there is no limit on the amount by which the rate can change during any one-year period.

Maximum Rate and Payment Examples: If the ANNUAL PERCENTAGE RATE during the draw period equaled the 18% maximum and you had an outstanding balance of $10,000:

• Under the monthly interest-only payment option, the minimum monthly payment would be $150.

• Under the 2% of the balance payment option, the minimum monthly payment would be $350.

This annual percentage rate could be reached during the first month of the draw period.

If you had an outstanding balance of $10,000 during the repayment period, the minimum monthly payment at the maximum ANNUAL PERCENTAGE RATE of 18% would be $450. This annual percentage rate could be reached during the first month of the repayment period.

Historical Example: The following table shows how the annual percentage rate and the monthly payments for a single $10,000 credit advance would have changed based on changes in the indices over the past 15 years. For the draw period, the index values for the prime rate are from September of each year. For the repayment period, the index values for the yield on U.S. Treasury securities are from the first week ending in July. While only one payment amount per year is shown, payments under the 2% of the balance payment option and during the repayment period would have varied during each year.

The table assumes that no additional credit advances were taken, that only the minimum payments were made, and that the rate remained constant during each year. It does not necessarily indicate how the indices or your payments will change in the future.

	Year	Index	Margin*	ANNUAL PERCENTAGE RATE	Monthly Interest-Only Payments	Monthly 2% of Balance Payments
		%	%	%	($)	($)
	1974	12.00	2	10.00**	83.33	283.33
	1975	7.88	2	9.88	82.33	221.55
	1976	7.00	2	9.00	75.00	169.34
	1977	7.13	2	9.13	76.08	133.41
Draw	1978	9.41	2	11.41	95.08	111.89
Period	1979	12.90	2	14.90	124.17	96.46
	1980	12.23	2	14.23	118.58	74.39
	1981	20.08	2	18.00***	150.00	64.13
	1982	13.50	2	15.50	129.17	50.00
	1983	11.00	2	13.00	108.33	50.00
	1984	12.17	2	14.17	418.08	50.00
Repayment	1985	7.66	2	9.66	264.01	
Period	1986	6.36	2	8.36	177.96	
	1987	6.71	2	8.71	124.45	
	1988	7.52	2	9.52	87.92	

*This is a margin we have used recently.

**This rate reflects a 4% "discount" we have used recently.

***This rate reflects the 18% rate cap.

G–15.   Home Equity Model Clauses

(a) Retention of Information: This disclosure contains important information about hour Home Equity Line of Credit. You should read it carefully and keep a copy for your records.

(b) Availability of Terms: To obtain the terms described below, you must submit your application before (date). However the (description of terms) are subject to change.

or

All of the terms described below are subject to change.

If these terms change [(other than the annual percentage rate)] and you decide, as a result, not to enter into an agreement with us, you are entitled to a refund of any fees you paid to us or anyone else in connection with your application.

(c) Security Interest: We will take a [security interest in/mortgage on] your home. You could lose your home if you do not meet the obligations in your agreement with us.

(d) Possible Actions: Under certain circumstances, we can (1) terminate your line, require you to pay us the entire outstanding balance in one payment [, and charge you certain fees]; (2) refuse to make additional extensions of credit; (3) reduce your credit limit [; and (4) make specific changes that are set forth in your agreement with us].

If you ask, we will give you more specific information about when we can take these actions.

or

Possible Actions: We can terminate your account, require you to pay us the entire outstanding balance in one payment [, and charge your certain fees] if:

• You engage in fraud or material misrepresentation in connection with the line.

• You do not meet the repayment terms.

• Your action or inaction adversely affects the collateral or our rights in the collateral.

• We can refuse to make additional extensions of credit or reduce your credit limit if:

• The value of the dwelling securing the line declines significantly below its appraised value for purposes of the line.

• We reasonably believe you will not be able to meet the repayment requirements due to a material change in your financial circumstances.

• You are in default of a material obligation in the agreement.

• Government action prevents us from imposing the annual percentage rate provided for or impairs our security interest such that the value of the interest is less than 120 percent of the credit line.

• A regulatory agency has notified us that continued advances would constitute an unsafe and unsound practice.

• The maximum annual percentage rate is reached.

[The initial agreement permits us to make certain changes to the terms of the agreement at specified times or upon the occurrence of specified events.]

(e) Minimum Payment Requirements: The length of the [draw period/repayment period] is (length). Payments will be due (frequency). Your minimum payment will equal (how payment determined).

[The minimum payment will not reduce the principal that is outstanding on your line./The minimum payment will not fully repay the principal that is outstanding on your line.] You will then be required to pay the entire balance in a single "balloon" payment.

(f) Minimum Payment Example: If you made only the minimum payments and took no other credit advance, it would take (length of time) to pay off a credit advance of $10,000 at an ANNUAL PERCENTAGE RATE of (recent rate). During that period, you would make (number) (frequency) payments of $_____.

(g) Fees and Charges: To open and maintain a line of credit, you must pay the following fees to us:

(Description of fee) [$_____/_____% of _____] (When payable)

(Description of fee) [$_____/_____% of _____] (When payable)

You also must pay certain fees to third parties. These fees generally total [$_____/_____% of _____/between $_____ and $_____]. If you ask, we will give you an itemization of the fees you will have to pay to third parties.

(h) Minimum Draw and Balance Requirements: The minimum credit advance you can receive is $_____. You must maintain an outstanding balance of at least $_____.

(*i*) Negative Amortization: Under some circumstances, your payments will not cover the finance charges that accrue and "negative amortization" will occur. Negative amortization will increase the amount that you owe us and reduce your equity in your home.

(j) Tax Deductibility: You should consult a tax advisor regarding the deductibility of interest and charges for the line.

(k) Other Products: If you ask, we will provide you with information on our other available home equity lines.

(*l*) Variable–Rate Feature: The plan has a variable-rate feature and the annual percentage rate (corresponding to the periodic rate) and the [minimum payment/term of the line] can change as a result.

The annual percentage rate includes only interest and not other costs.

The annual percentage rate is based on the value of an index. The index is the (identification of index) and is [published in/available from] (source of information). To determine the annual percentage rate that will apply to your line, we add a margin to the value of the index.

[The initial annual percentage rate is "discounted"—it is not based on the index and margin used for later rate adjustments. The initial rate will be in effect for (period).]

Ask us for the current index value, margin, [discount,] and annual percentage rate. After you open a credit line, rate information will be provided on periodic statements that we send you.

(m) Rate Changes: The annual percentage rate can change (frequency). [The rate cannot increase by more than _____ percentage points in any one year period./There is no limit on the amount by which the rate can change in any one year period.] [The maximum ANNUAL PERCENTAGE RATE that can apply is _____%. [The ANNUAL PERCENTAGE RATE cannot increase by more than _____ percentage points above the initial rate.] [Ask us for the specific rate limitations that will apply to your credit line.]

(n) Maximum Rate and Payment Examples: If you had an outstanding balance of $10,000, the minimum payment at the maximum ANNUAL PERCENTAGE RATE of _____% would be $_____. This annual percentage rate could be reached (when maximum rate could be reached).

(o) Historical Example: The following table shows how the annual percentage rate and the minimum payments for a single $10,000 credit advance would have changed based on changes in the index over the past 15 years. The index values are from (when values are measured). [While only one payment amount per year is shown, payments would have varied during each year.]

The table assumes that no additional credit advances were taken, that only the minimum payments were made, and that the rate remained constant during each year. It does not necessarily indicate how the index or your payments will change in the future. [Table omitted.]

APPENDIX H.   Closed-end Model Forms and Clauses

H–1.   Credit Sale Model Form (§ 226.18).

H–2.   Loan Model Form (§ 226.18).

H–3.   Amount Financed Itemization Model Form (§ 226.18(c)).

H–4(A).   Variable–Rate Model Clauses (§ 226.18(f)(1)).

H–4(B).   Variable–Rate Model Clauses (§ 226.18(f)(2)).

H–4(C).   Variable–Rate Model Clauses (§ 226.19(b)).

H–4(D).   Variable–Rate Model Clauses (§ 226.20(c)).

H–5.   Demand Feature Model Clauses (§ 226.18(i)).

H–6.   Assumption Policy Model Clause (§ 226.18(q)).

H–7.   Required Deposit Model Clause (§ 226.18(r)).

H–8.   Rescission Model Form (General) (§ 226.23).

H–9.   Rescission Model Form (Refinancing With Original Creditor) (§ 226.23) [Omitted].

H–10.   Credit Sale Sample [Omitted].

H–11.   Installment Loan Sample [Omitted].

H–12.   Refinancing Sample [Omitted].

H–13.   Mortgage with Demand Feature Sample [Omitted].

H–14.   Variable–Rate Mortgage Sample (§ 226.19(b)) [Omitted].

H–15.   Graduated Payment Mortgage Sample [Omitted].

H–16.   Mortgage Sample (§ 226.32) [Omitted].

H–1. Credit Sale Model Form

ANNUAL PERCENTAGE RATE The cost of your credit as a yearly rate.	FINANCE CHARGE The dollar amount the credit will cost you.	Amount Financed The amount of credit provided to you or on your behalf.	Total of Payments The amount you will have paid after you have made all payments as scheduled.	Total Sale Price The total cost of your purchase on credit, including you downpayment of $ _____
%	$	$	$	$

You have the right to receive at this time an itemization of the Amount Financed.

☐ I want an itemization.   ☐ I do not want an itemization.

Your payment schedule will be:

Number of Payments	Amount of Payments	When Payments Are Due

Insurance

Credit life insurance and credit disability insurance are not required to obtain credit, and will not be provided unless you sign and agree to pay the additional cost.

Type	Premium	Signature
Credit Life		I want credit life insurance. ___ Signature
Credit Disability		I want credit disability insurance. ___ Signature
Credit Life and Disability		I want credit life and disability insurance. ___ Signature

You may obtain property insurance from anyone you want that is acceptable to (creditor). If you get the insurance from (creditor). you will pay $ _____

Security: You are giving a security interest in:

☐ the goods or property being purchased.

☐ (brief description of other property).

Filing fees $ _____   Non-filing insurance $ _____

Late Charge: If a payment is late, you will be charged $ _____ / _____ % of the payment.

Prepayment: If you pay off early, you

☐ may ☐ will not have to pay a penalty.

☐ may ☐ will not be entitled to a refund of part of the finance charge.

See your contract documents for any additional information about nonpayment, default, any required repayment in full before the scheduled date, and prepayment refunds and penalties.

___

e means an estimate

[E4061]

519

H–2. Loan Model Form

ANNUAL PERCENTAGE RATE The cost of your credit as a yearly rate.	FINANCE CHARGE The dollar amount the credit will cost you.	Amount Financed The amount of credit provided to you or on your behalf.	Total of Payments The amount you will have paid after you have made all payments as scheduled.
%	$	$	$

You have the right to receive at this time an itemization of the Amount Financed.

☐ I want an itemization.   ☐ I do not want an itemization.

Your payment schedule will be:

Number of Payments	Amount of Payments	When Payments Are Due

Insurance
Credit life insurance and credit disability insurance are not required to obtain credit, and will not be provided unless you sign and agree to pay the additional cost.

Type	Premium	Signature
Credit Life		I want credit life insurance. _____ Signature
Credit Disability		I want credit disability insurance. _____ Signature
Credit Life and Disability		I want credit life and disability insurance. _____ Signature

You may obtain property insurance from anyone you want that is acceptable to   (creditor).   If you get the insurance from   (creditor).   you will pay $ _____

Security: You are giving a security interest in:

☐ the goods or property being purchased.

☐ (brief description of other property).

Filing fees $ _____   Non-filing insurance $ _____

Late Charge: If a payment is late, you will be charged $ _____ / _____ % of the payment.

Prepayment: If you pay off early, you

☐ may   ☐ will not   have to pay a penalty.

☐ may   ☐ will not   be entitled to a refund of part of the finance charge.

See your contract documents for any additional information about nonpayment, default, any required repayment in full before the scheduled date, and prepayment refunds and penalties.

_____

e means an estimate

[E4060]

H–3. Amount Financed Itemization Model Form

Itemization of the Amount Financed of $ _____

$ _____ Amount given to you directly

$ _____ Amount paid on your account

Amount paid to others on your behalf

$_____ to [public officials] [credit bureau] [appraiser] [insurance company]

$_____ to (name of another creditor)

$_____ to (other)

$_____ Prepaid finance charge

H–4(A).   Variable–Rate Model Clauses

The annual percentage rate may increase during the term of this transaction if:

[the prime interest rate of (creditor) increases.]

[the balance in your deposit account falls below $_____.]

[you terminate your employment with (employer).]

[The interest rate will not increase above _____%.]

[The maximum interest rate increase at one time will be _____%.]

[The rate will not increase more than once every (time period).]

Any increase will take the form of:

[higher payment amounts.]

[more payments of the same amount.]

[a larger amount due at maturity.]

Example based on the specific transaction

[If the interest rate increases by _____% in (time period),

[your regular payments will increase to $_____.]

[you will have to make _____ additional payments.]

[your final payment will increase to $_____.]]

Example based on a typical transaction

[If your loan were for $_____ at _____% for (term) and the rate increased to _____% in (time period),

[your regular payments would increase by $_____.]

[you would have to make _____ additional payments.]

[your final payment would increase by $_____.]]

H–4(B).   Variable–Rate Model Clauses

Your loan contains a variable-rate feature. Disclosures about the variable-rate feature have been provided to you earlier.

H–4(C).   Variable–Rate Model Clauses

This disclosure describes the features of the adjustable-rate mortgage (ARM) program you are considering. Information on other ARM programs is available upon request.

How Your Interest Rate and Payment Are Determined

- Your interest rate will be based on [an index plus a margin] [a formula].

- Your payment will be based on the interest rate, loan balance, and loan term.

   — [The interest rate will be based on (identification of index) plus our margin. Ask for our current interest rate and margin.]

   — [The interest rate will be based on (identification of formula). Ask us for our current interest rate.]

   — Information about the index [formula for rate adjustments] is published [can be found] _____.

   — [The initial interest rate is not based on the (index) (formula) used to make later adjustments. Ask us for the amount of current interest rate discounts.]

How Your Interest Rate Can Change

- Your interest rate can change (frequency).

- [Your interest rate cannot increase or decrease more than ___ percentage points at each adjustment.]

- Your interest rate cannot increase [or decrease] more than ___ percentage points over the term of the loan.

How Your Payment Can Change

- Your payment can change (frequency) based on changes in the interest rate.

- [Your payment cannot increase more than (amount or percentage) at each adjustment.]

- You will be notified in writing _____ days before the due date of a payment at a new level. This notice will contain information about your interest rates, payment amount, and loan balance.

- [You will be notified once each year during which interest rate adjustments, but no payment adjustments, have been made to your loan. This notice will contain information about your interest rates, payment amount, and loan balance.]

- [For example, on a $10,000 [term] loan with an initial interest rate of _____ [(the rate shown in the interest rate column below for the year 19__)] [(in effect (month) (year)], the maximum amount that the interest rate can rise under this program is _____ percentage points, to _____%, and the monthly payment can rise from a first-year payment of $_____ to a maximum of $_____ in the _____ year. To see what your payments would be, divide your mortgage amount by $10,000; then multiply the monthly payment by that amount. (For example, the monthly payment for a mortgage amount of $60,000 would be: $60,000 + $10,000 = 6; 6 x ___ = $_____ per month.)]

Example

The example below shows how your payments would have changed under this ARM program based on actual changes in the index from 1982 to 1996. This does not necessarily indicate how your index will change in the future. [Omitted.]

H–4(D).   Variable–Rate Model Clauses

Your new interest rate will be _____%, which is based on an index value of _____%.

Your previous interest rate was _____%, which was based on an index value of _____%.

The new interest rate does not reflect a change of _____ percentage point in the index value which was not added because of _____.]

[The new payment will be $_____.]

[Your new loan balance is $_____.]

[Your (new) (existing) payment will not be sufficient to cover the interest due and the difference will be added to the loan amount. The payment amount needed to pay your loan in full by the end of the term at the new interest rate is $_____.]

[The following interest rate adjustments have been implemented this year without changing your payment: _____.

These interest rates were based on the following index values: _____.]

H–5.   Demand Feature Model Clauses

This obligation [is payable on demand.]

[has a demand feature.]

[All disclosures are based on an assumed maturity of one year.]

H–6.   Assumption Policy Model Clause

Assumption: Someone buying your house [may, subject to conditions, be allowed to] [cannot] assume the remainder of the mortgage on the original terms.

H–7.   Required Deposit Model Clause

The annual percentage rate does not take into account your required deposit.

H–8. Rescission Model Form (General)

NOTICE OF RIGHT TO CANCEL

Your Right to Cancel

You are entering into a transaction that will result in a

[mortgage/lien/security interest] [on/in] your home. You have a legal right under federal law to cancel this transaction, without cost, within three business days from whichever of the following events occurs last:

(1) the date of the transaction, which is _____; or

(2) the date you received your Truth in Lending disclosures; or

(3) the date you received this notice of your right to cancel.

If you cancel the transaction, the [mortgage/lien/security interest] is also cancelled. Within 20 calendar days after we receive your notice, we must take the steps necessary to reflect the fact that the [mortgage/lien/security interest] [on/in] your home has been cancelled, and we must return to you any money or property you have given to us or to anyone else in connection with this transaction.

You may keep any money or property we have given you until we have done the things mentioned above, but you must then offer to return the money or property. If it is impractical or unfair for you to return the property, you must offer its reasonable value. You may offer to return the property at your home or at the location of the property. Money must be returned to the address below. If we do not take possession of the money or property within 20 calendar days of your offer, you may keep it without further obligation.

How to Cancel

If you decide to cancel this transaction, you may do so by notifying us in writing, at

(creditor's name and business address).

You may use any written statement that is signed and dated by you and states your intention to cancel, or you may use this notice by dating and signing below. Keep one copy of this notice because it contains important information about your rights.

If you cancel by mail or telegram, you must send the notice no later than midnight of

(date)

(or midnight of the third business day following the latest of the three events listed above.) If you send or deliver your written notice to cancel some other way, it must be delivered to the above address no later than that time.

I WISH TO CANCEL.

_____   _____

Consumer's Signature   Date

APPENDIX J. Annual Percentage Rate Computations for Closed–End Credit Transactions

(A) INTRODUCTION

(1) Section 226.22(a) of Regulation Z provides that the annual percentage rate for other than open end credit transactions shall be determined in accordance with either the actuarial method or the United States Rule method. This appendix contains an explanation of the actuarial method as well as equations, instructions and examples of how this method applies to single advance and multiple advance transactions.

(2) Under the actuarial method, at the end of each unit-period (or fractional unit-period) the unpaid balance of the amount financed is increased by the finance charge earned during that period and is decreased by the total payment (if any) made at the end of that period. The determination of unit-periods and fractional unit-periods shall be consistent with the definitions and rules in paragraphs (b)(3), (4) and (5) of this section and the general equation in paragraph (b)(8) of this section.

(3) In contrast, under the United States Rule method, at the end of each payment period, the unpaid balance of the amount financed is increased by the finance charge earned during that payment period and is decreased by the payment made at the end of that payment period. If the payment is less than the finance charge earned, the adjustment of the unpaid balance of the amount financed is postponed until the end of the next payment period. If at that time the sum of the two payments is still less than the total earned finance charge for the two payment periods, the adjustment of the unpaid balance of the amount financed is postponed still another payment period, and so forth.

(B) INSTRUCTIONS AND EQUATIONS FOR THE ACTUARIAL METHOD

(1) *General rule*

The annual percentage rate shall be the nominal annual percentage rate determined by multiplying the unit-period rate by the number of unit-periods in a year.

(2) *Term of the transaction*

The term of the transaction begins on the date of its consummation, except that if the finance charge or any portion of it is earned beginning on a later date, the term begins on the later date. The term ends on the date the last payment is due, except that if an advance is scheduled after that date, the term ends on the later date. For computation purposes, the length of the term shall be equal to the time interval between any point in time on the beginning date to the same point in time on the ending date.

(3) *Definitions of time intervals*

(i) A period is the interval of time between advances or between payments and includes the interval of time between the date the finance charge begins to be earned and the date of the first advance thereafter or the date of the first payment thereafter, as applicable.

(ii) A common period is any period that occurs more than once in a transaction.

(iii) A standard interval of time is a day, week, semi-month, month, or a multiple of a week or a month up to, but not exceeding, 1 year.

(iv) All months shall be considered equal. Full months shall be measured from any point in time on a given date of a given month to the same point in time on the same date of another month. If a series of payments (or advances) is scheduled for the last day of each month, months shall be measured from the last day of the given month to the last day of another month. If payments (or advances) are scheduled for the 29th or 30th of each month, the last day of February shall be used when applicable.

(4) *Unit-period*

(i) In all transactions other than a single advance, single payment transaction, the unit-period shall be that common period, not to exceed 1 year, that occurs most frequently in the transaction, except that

(A) If 2 or more common periods occur with equal frequency, the smaller of such common periods shall be the unit-period; or

(B) If there is no common period in the transaction, the unit-period shall be that period which is the average of all periods rounded to the nearest whole standard interval of time. If the average is equally near 2 standard intervals of time, the lower shall be the unit-period.

(ii) In a single advance, single payment transaction, the unit-period shall be the term of the transaction, but shall not exceed 1 year.

(5) *Number of unit-periods between 2 given dates*

(i) The number of days between 2 dates shall be the number of 24–hour intervals between any point in time on the first date to the same point in time on the second date.

(ii) If the unit-period is a month, the number of full unit-periods between 2 dates shall be the number of months measured back from the later date. The remaining fraction of a unit-period shall be the number of days measured forward from the earlier date to the beginning of the first full unit-period, divided by 30. If the unit-period is a month, there are 12 unit-periods per year.

(iii) If the unit-period is a semi-month or a multiple of a month not exceeding 11 months, the number of days between 2 dates shall be 30 times the number of full months measured back from the later date, plus the number of remaining days. The number of full unit-periods and the remaining fraction of a unit-period shall be determined by dividing such number of days by 15 in the case of a semimonthly unit-period or by the appropriate multiple of 30 in the case of a multi-monthly unit-period. If the unit-period is a semi-month, the number of unit-periods per year shall be 24. If the number of unit-periods is a multiple of a month, the number of unit-periods per year shall be 12 divided by the number of months per unit-period.

(iv) If the unit-period is a day, a week, or a multiple of a week, the number of full unit-periods and the remaining fractions of a unit-period shall be determined by dividing the number of days between the 2 given dates by the number of days per unit-period. If the unit-period is a day, the number of unit-periods per year shall be 365. If the unit-period is a week or a multiple of a week, the number of unit-periods per year shall be 52 divided by the number of weeks per unit-period.

(v) If the unit-period is a year, the number of full unit-periods between 2 dates shall be the number of full years (each equal to 12 months) measured back from the later date. The remaining fraction of a unit-period shall be

(A) The remaining number of months divided by 12 if the remaining interval is equal to a whole number of months, or

(B) The remaining number of days divided by 365 if the remaining interval is not equal to a whole number of months.

(vi) In a single advance, single payment transaction in which the term is less than a year and is equal to a whole number of months, the number of unit-periods in the term shall be 1, and the number of unit-periods per year shall be 12 divided by the number of months in the term or 365 divided by the number of days in the term.

(vii) In a single advance, single payment transaction in which the term is less than a year and is not equal to a whole number of months, the number of unit-periods in the term shall be 1, and the number of unit-periods per year shall be 365 divided by the number of days in the term.

(6) *Percentage rate for a fraction of a unit-period*

The percentage rate of finance charge for a fraction (less than 1) of a unit-period shall be equal to such fraction multiplied by the percentage rate of finance charge per unit-period.

(7) *Symbols*

The symbols used to express the terms of a transaction in the equation set forth in paragraph (b)(8) of this section are defined as follows:

A_k = The amount of the kth advance.

q_k = The number of full unit periods from the beginning of the term of the transaction to the kth advance.

e_k = The fraction of a unit period in the time interval from the beginning of the term of the transaction to the kth advance.

m = The number of advances.

P_j = The amount of the jth payment.

t_j = The number of full unit periods from the beginning of the term of the transaction to the jth payment.

f_j = The fraction of a unit period in the time interval from the beginning of the term of the transaction to the jth payment.

n = The number of payments.

i = The percentage rate of finance charge per unit period, expressed as a decimal equivalent.

Symbols used in the examples shown in this appendix are defined as follows:

$\ddot{a}_{\overline{x}|}$ = The present value of 1 per unit period for x unit periods, first payment due immediately.

$$= 1 + \frac{1}{(1 + i)} + \frac{1}{(1 + i)^2} +$$

$$\cdots\cdots + \frac{1}{(1 + i)^{x-1}}$$

w = The number of unit periods per year.

$I = wi \times 100 =$ The nominal annual percentage rate.

(8) *General equation*

The following equation sets forth the relationship among the terms of a transaction:

$$\frac{A_1}{(1 + e_1 i)(1 + i)^{q_1}} + \frac{A_2}{(1 + e_2 i)(1 + i)^{q_2}} +$$

$$\cdots + \frac{A_m}{(1 + e_m i)(1 + i)^{q_m}} =$$

$$\frac{P_1}{(1 + f_1 i)(1 + i)^{t_1}} + \frac{P_2}{(1 + f_2 i)(1 + i)^{t_2}} +$$

$$\cdots + \frac{P_n}{(1 + f_n i)(1 + i)^{t_n}}$$

(9) *Solution of general equation by iteration process*

(i) The general equation in paragraph (b)(8) of this section, when applied to a simple transaction in which a loan of $1000 is repaid by 36 monthly payments of $33.61 each, takes the special form:

$$A = \frac{33.61\ \ddot{a}_{\overline{36|}}}{(1 + i)}$$

Step 1:

Let I_1 = estimated annual percentage rate =	12.50%
Evaluate expression for A, letting $i = I_1/(100w) =$	.010416667
Result (referred to as A') =	1004.674391

Step 2:

Let $I_2 = I_1 + .1 =$	12.60%
Evaluate expression for A, letting $i = I_2/(100w) =$	.010500000
Result (referred to as A") =	1003.235366

Step 3:

Interpolate for I (annual percentage rate):

$$I = I_1 + .1 \left[\frac{(A - A')}{(A'' - A')} \right] = 12.50 +$$

$$.1 \left[\frac{(1000.000000 - 1004.674391)}{(1003.235366 - 1004.674391)} \right]$$

$$= 12.82483042\%$$

Step 4:

First iteration, let I_1 = 12.82483042% and repeat Steps 1, 2, and 3 obtaining a new I =	12.82557859%
Second iteration, let I_1 = 12.82557859% and repeat Steps 1, 2, and 3 obtaining a new I =	12.82557529%

In this case, no further iterations are required to obtain the annual percentage rate correct to two decimal places, 12.83%.

(ii) When the iteration approach is used, it is expected that calculators or computers will be programmed to carry all available decimals throughout the calculation and that enough iterations will be performed to make virtually certain that the annual percentage rate obtained, when rounded to two decimals, is correct. Annual percentage rates in the examples below were obtained by using a 10–digit programmable calculator and the iteration procedure described above.

(c) *Examples for the actuarial method. (1) Single advance transaction, with or without an odd first period, and otherwise regular.* The general equation in paragraph (b)(8) of this section can be put in the following special form for this type of transaction:

$$A = \frac{1}{(1 + fi)(1 + i)^t} \left[P\ddot{a}_{\overline{n}|} \right]$$

Example (i): Monthly payments (regular first period)

    Amount advanced (A) = $5000. Payment (P) = $230.

    Number of payments (n) = 24.

    Unit-period = 1 month. Unit-periods per year (w) = 12.

    Advance, 1–10–78. First payment, 2–10–78.

    From 1–10–78 through 2–10–78 = 1 unit-period. (t = 1; f=0)

    Annual percentage rate (I) = wi = .0969 = 9.69%

Example (ii): Monthly payments (long first period)

    Amount advanced (A) = $6000. Payment (P) = $200.

    Number of payments (n) = 36.

    Unit-period = 1 month. Unit-periods per year (w) = 12.

    Advance, 2–10–78. First payment, 4–1–78.

    From 3–1–78 through 4–1–78 = 1 unit-period. (t = 1)

    From 2–10–78 through 3–1–78 = 19 days. (f = 19/30)

    Annual percentage rate (I) = wi = .1182 = 11.82%

Example (iii): Semimonthly payments (short first period)

    Amount advanced (A) = $5000. Payment (P) = $219.17.

    Number of payments (n) = 24.

    Unit-period = 1/2 month. Unit-periods per year (w) = 24.

    Advance, 2–23–78. First payment, 3–1–78. Payments made on 1st and 16th of each month.

    From 2–23–78 through 3–1–78 = 6 days. (t = 0; f = 6/15)

    Annual percentage rate (I) = wi = .1034 = 10.34 %

Example (iv): Quarterly payments (long first period)

    Amount advanced (A) = $10,000. Payment (P) = $385.

    Number of payments (n) = 40.

    Unit-period = 3 months. Unit-periods per year (w) = 4.

    Advance, 5–23–78. First payment, 10–1–78.

    From 7–1–78 through 10–1–78 = 1 unit-period. (t = 1)

531

From 6–1–78 through 7–1–78 = 1 month = 30 days. From 5–23–78 through 6–1–78 = 9 days. (f = 39/90)

Annual percentage rate (I) = wi = .0897 = 8.97 %

Example (v): Weekly payments (long first period)

Amount advanced (A) = $500. Payment (P) = $17.60.

Number of payments (n) = 30.

Unit-period = 1 week. Unit-periods per year (w) = 52.

Advance, 3–20–78. First payment, 4–21–78.

From 3–24–78 through 4–21–78 = 4 unit-periods. (t = 4)

From 3–20–78 through 3–24–78 = 4 days. (f = 4/7)

Annual percentage rate (I) = wi = .1496 = 14.96 %

(2) *Single advance transaction, with an odd first payment, with or without an odd first period, and otherwise regular*. [Omitted]

(3) *Single advance transaction, with an odd final payment, with or without an odd first period, and otherwise regular*. [Omitted]

(4) *Single advance transaction, with an odd first payment, odd final payment, with or without an odd first period, and otherwise regular*. [Omitted]

(5) *Single advance, single payment transaction*. The general equation in paragraph (b)(8) of this section can be put in the special forms below for single advance, single payment transactions. Forms 1 through 3 are for the direct determination of the annual percentage rate under special conditions. Form 4 requires the use of the iteration procedure of paragraph (b)(9) of this section and can be used for all single advance, single payment transactions regardless of term.

$$I = 100w \left[\frac{P}{A} - 1 \right]$$

Form 2—Term more than one year but less than two years:

$$I = \frac{50}{f} \left\{ \left[(1 + f)^2 + 4f \left(\frac{P}{A} - 1 \right) \right]^{1/2} - (1 + f) \right\}$$

Form 3—Term equal to exactly a year or exact multiple of a year:

$$I = 100 \left[\left(\frac{P}{A} \right)^{1/t} - 1 \right]$$

Form 4—Special form for iteration procedure (no restriction on term):

$$A = \frac{P}{(1 + fi)(1 + i)^t}$$

Example (i): Single advance, single payment (term of less than 1 year, measured in days)

Amount advanced (A) = $1000. Payment (P) = $1080.

Unit-period = 255 days. Unit-periods per year (w) = 3 65/255.

Advance, 1–3–78. Payment, 9–15–78.

From 1–3–78 through 9–15–78 = 255 days. (t = 1; f = 0)

Annual percentage rate (I) = wi = .1145 = 11.45%. (Use Form 1 or 4.)

Example (ii): Single advance, single payment (term of less than 1 year, measured in exact calendar months)

Amount advanced (A) = $1000. Payment (P) = $1044.

Unit-period = 6 months. Unit-periods per year (w) = 2.

Advance, 7–15–78. Payment, 1–15–79.

From 7–15–78 through 1–15–79 = 6 mos. (t = 1; f = 0)

Annual percentage rate (I) = wi = .0880 = 8.80%. (Use Form 1 or 4.)

Example (iii): Single advance, single payment (term of more than 1 year but less than 2 years, fraction measured in exact months)

Amount advanced (A) = $1000. Payment (P) = $1135.19.

Unit-period = 1 year. Unit-periods per year (w) = 1.

Advance, 7–17–78. Payment, 1–17–80.

From 1–17–79 through 1–17–80 = 1 unit-period. (t = 1)

From 7–17–78 through 1–17–79 = 6 mos. (f = 6/12)

Annual percentage rate (I) = wi = .0876 = 8.76%. (Use Form 2 or 4.)

Example (iv): Single advance, single payment (term of exactly 2 years)

Amount advanced (A) = $1000. Payment (P) = $1240.

Unit-period = 1 year. Unit-periods per year (w) = 1.

Advance, 1–3–78. Payment, 1–3–80.

From 1–3–78 through 1–3–79 = 1 unit-period. (t = 2; f = 0)

Annual percentage rate (I) = wi = .1136 = 11.36%. (Use Form 3 or 4.)

(6) *Complex single advance transaction*. [Omitted]

FEDERAL RESERVE BOARD, REGULATION M, CONSUMER LEASING

12 C.F.R. Part 213

Table of Sections

---

§ 213.1 Authority, scope, purpose, and enforcement

(a) *Authority.* The regulation in this part, known as Regulation M, is issued by the Board of Governors of the Federal Reserve System to implement the consumer leasing provisions of the Truth in Lending Act, which is Title I of the Consumer Credit Protection Act, as amended (15 U.S.C. § 1601 et seq.). Information collection requirements contained in this regulation have been approved by the Office of Management and Budget under the provisions of 44 U.S.C. 3501 et seq. and have been assigned OMB control number 7100–0202.

(b) *Scope and purpose.* This part applies to all persons that are lessors of personal property under consumer leases as those terms are defined in § 213.2(e)(1) and (h). The purpose of this part is:

(1) To ensure that lessees of personal property receive meaningful disclosures that enable them to compare lease terms with other leases and, where appropriate, with credit transactions;

(2) To limit the amount of balloon payments in consumer lease transactions; and

(3) To provide for the accurate disclosure of lease terms in advertising.

(c) *Enforcement and liability.* Section 108 of the act contains the administrative enforcement provisions. Sections 112, 130, 131, and 185 of the act contain the liability provisions for failing to comply with the requirements of the act and this part.

§ 213.2   Definitions

For the purposes of this part the following definitions apply:

(a) *Act* means the Truth in Lending Act (15 U.S.C. § 1601 et seq.) and the Consumer Leasing Act is chapter 5 of the Truth in Lending Act.

(b) *Advertisement* means a commercial message in any medium that directly or indirectly promotes a consumer lease transaction.

(c) *Board* refers to the Board of Governors of the Federal Reserve System.

(d) *Closed-end lease* means a consumer lease other than an open-end lease as defined in this section.

(e)(1) *Consumer lease* means a contract in the form of a bailment or lease for the use of personal property by a natural person primarily for personal, family, or household purposes, for a period exceeding four months and for a total contractual obligation not exceeding $25,000, whether or not the lessee has the option to purchase or otherwise become the owner of the property at the expiration of the lease. Unless the context indicates otherwise, in this part "lease" means "consumer lease."

(2) The term does not include a lease that meets the definition of a credit sale in Regulation Z (12 CFR 226.2(a)). It also does not include a lease for agricultural, business, or commercial purposes or a lease made to an organization.

(3) This part does not apply to a lease transaction of personal property which is incident to the lease of real property and which provides that:

(i) The lessee has no liability for the value of the personal property at the end of the lease term except for abnormal wear and tear; and

(ii) The lessee has no option to purchase the leased property.

(f) *Gross capitalized cost* means the amount agreed upon by the lessor and the lessee as the value of the leased property and any items that are capitalized or amortized during the lease term, including but not limited to taxes, insurance, service agreements, and any outstanding prior credit or lease balance. Capitalized cost reduction means the total amount of any rebate, cash payment, net trade-in allowance, and noncash credit that reduces the gross capitalized cost. The adjusted capitalized cost equals the gross capitalized cost less the capitalized cost reduction, and is the amount used by the lessor in calculating the base periodic payment.

(g) *Lessee* means a natural person who enters into or is offered a consumer lease.

(h) *Lessor* means a person who regularly leases, offers to lease, or arranges for the lease of personal property under a consumer lease. A person who has leased, offered, or arranged to lease personal property more than five times in the preceding calendar year or more than five times in the current calendar year is subject to the act and this part.

(*i*) *Open-end lease* means a consumer lease in which the lessee's liability at the end of the lease term is based on the difference between the residual value of the leased property and its realized value.

(j) *Organization* means a corporation, trust, estate, partnership, cooperative, association, or government entity or instrumentality.

(k) *Person* means a natural person or an organization.

(*l*) *Personal property* means any property that is not real property under the law of the state where the property is located at the time it is offered or made available for lease.

(m) *Realized value* means:

(1) The price received by the lessor for the leased property at disposition;

(2) The highest offer for disposition of the leased property; or

(3) The fair market value of the leased property at the end of the lease term.

(n) *Residual value* means the value of the leased property at the end of the lease term, as estimated or assigned at consummation by the lessor, used in calculating the base periodic payment.

(o) *Security interest and security* mean any interest in property that secures the payment or performance of an obligation.

(p) *State* means any state, the District of Columbia, the Commonwealth of Puerto Rico, and any territory or possession of the United States.

§ 213.3   General disclosure requirements

(a) *General requirements.* A lessor shall make the disclosures required by § 213.4, as applicable. The disclosures shall be made clearly and conspicuously in writing in a form the consumer may keep, in accordance with this section. The disclosures required by this part may be provided to the lessee in electronic form, subject to compliance with the consumer consent and other applicable provisions of the Electronic Signatures in Global and National Commerce Act (E–Sign Act) (15 U.S.C. § 7001 *et seq.*). For an advertisement accessed by the consumer in electronic form, the disclosures required by § 213.7 may be provided to the consumer in electronic form in the advertisement, without regard to the consumer consent or other provisions of the E–Sign Act.

(1) *Form of disclosures.* The disclosures required by § 213.4 shall be given to the lessee together in a dated statement that identifies the lessor and the lessee; the disclosures may be made either in a separate statement that identifies the consumer lease transaction or in the contract or other document evidencing the lease. Alternatively, the disclosures required to be segregated from other information under paragraph (a)(2) of this section may be provided in a separate dated statement that identifies the lease, and the other required disclosures may be provided in the lease contract or

other document evidencing the lease. In a lease of multiple items, the property description required by § 213.4(a) may be given in a separate statement that is incorporated by reference in the disclosure statement required by this paragraph.

(2) *Segregation of certain disclosures.* The following disclosures shall be segregated from other information and shall contain only directly related information: §§ 213.4(b) through (f), (g)(2), (h)(3), (i)(1), (j), and (m)(1). The headings, content, and format for the disclosures referred to in this paragraph (a)(2) shall be provided in a manner substantially similar to the applicable model form in appendix A of this part.

(3) *Timing of disclosures.* A lessor shall provide the disclosures to the lessee prior to the consummation of a consumer lease.

(4) *Language of disclosures.* The disclosures required by § 213.4 may be made in a language other than English provided that they are made available in English upon the lessee's request.

(b) *Additional information; nonsegregated disclosures.* Additional information may be provided with any disclosure not listed in paragraph (a)(2) of this section, but it shall not be stated, used, or placed so as to mislead or confuse the lessee or contradict, obscure, or detract attention from any disclosure required by this part.

(c) *Multiple lessors or lessees.* When a transaction involves more than one lessor, the disclosures required by this part may be made by one lessor on behalf of all the lessors. When a lease involves more than one lessee, the lessor may provide the disclosures to any lessee who is primarily liable on the lease.

(d) *Use of estimates.* If an amount or other item needed to comply with a required disclosure is unknown or unavailable after reasonable efforts have been made to ascertain the information, the lessor may use a reasonable estimate that is based on the best information available to the lessor, is clearly identified as an estimate, and is not used to circumvent or evade any disclosures required by this part.

(e) *Effect of subsequent occurrence.* If a required disclosure becomes inaccurate because of an event occurring after consummation, the inaccuracy is not a violation of this part.

(f) *Minor variations.* A lessor may disregard the effects of the following in making disclosures:

(1) That payments must be collected in whole cents;

(2) That dates of scheduled payments may be different because a scheduled date is not a business day;

(3) That months have different numbers of days; and

(4) That February 29 occurs in a leap year.

§ 213.4   Content of disclosures

For any consumer lease subject to this part, the lessor shall disclose the following information, as applicable:

(a) *Description of property.* A brief description of the leased property sufficient to identify the property to the lessee and lessor.

(b) *Amount due at lease signing or delivery.* The total amount to be paid prior to or at consummation or by delivery, if delivery occurs after consummation, using the term "amount due at lease signing or delivery." The lessor shall itemize each component by type and amount, including any refundable security deposit, advance monthly or other periodic payment, and capitalized cost reduction; and in motor-vehicle leases, shall itemize how the amount due will be paid, by type and amount, including any net trade-in allowance, rebates, noncash credits, and cash payments in a format substantially similar to the model forms in appendix A of this part.

(c) *Payment schedule and total amount of periodic payments.* The number, amount, and due dates or periods of payments scheduled under the lease, and the total amount of the periodic payments.

(d) *Other charges.* The total amount of other charges payable to the lessor, itemized by type and amount, that are not included in the periodic payments. Such charges include the amount of any liability the lease imposes upon the lessee at the end of the lease term; the potential difference between the residual and realized values referred to in paragraph (k) of this section is excluded.

(e) *Total of payments.* The total of payments, with a description such as "the amount you will have paid by the end of the lease." This amount is the sum of the amount due at lease signing (less any refundable amounts), the total amount of periodic payments (less any portion of the periodic payment paid at lease signing), and other charges under paragraphs (b), (c), and (d) of this section. In an open-end lease, a description such as "you will owe an additional amount if the actual value of the vehicle is less than the residual value" shall accompany the disclosure.

(f) *Payment calculation.* In a motor-vehicle lease, a mathematical progression of how the scheduled periodic payment is derived, in a format substantially similar to the applicable model form in appendix A of this part, which shall contain the following:

(1) *Gross capitalized cost.* The gross capitalized cost, including a disclosure of the agreed upon value of the vehicle, a description such as "the agreed upon value of the vehicle [state the amount] and any items you pay for over the lease term (such as service contracts, insurance, and any outstanding prior credit or lease balance)," and a statement of the lessee's option to receive a separate written itemization of the gross capitalized cost. If requested by the lessee, the itemization shall be provided before consummation.

(2) *Capitalized cost reduction.* The capitalized cost reduction, with a description such as "the amount of any net trade-in allowance, rebate, noncash credit, or cash you pay that reduces the gross capitalized cost."

(3) *Adjusted capitalized cost.* The adjusted capitalized cost, with a description such as "the amount used in calculating your base [periodic] payment."

(4) *Residual value.* The residual value, with a description such as "the value of the vehicle at the end of the lease used in calculating your base [periodic] payment."

(5) *Depreciation and any amortized amounts.* The depreciation and any amortized amounts, which is the difference between the adjusted capitalized cost and the residual value, with a description such as "the amount charged for the vehicle's decline in value through normal use and for any other items paid over the lease term."

(6) *Rent charge.* The rent charge, with a description such as "the amount charged in addition to the depreciation and any amortized amounts." This amount is the difference between the total of the base periodic payments over the lease term minus the depreciation and any amortized amounts.

(7) *Total of base periodic payments.* The total of base periodic payments with a description such as "depreciation and any amortized amounts plus the rent charge."

(8) *Lease term.* The lease payments with a description such as "the number of payments in your lease."

(9) *Base periodic payment.* The total of the base periodic payments divided by the number of payment periods in the lease.

(10) *Itemization of other charges.* An itemization of any other charges that are part of the periodic payment.

(11) *Total periodic payment.* The sum of the base periodic payment and any other charges that are part of the periodic payment.

(g) *Early termination—*(1) *Conditions and disclosure of charges.* A statement of the conditions under which the lessee or lessor may terminate the lease prior to the end of the lease term; and the amount or a description of the method for determining the amount of any penalty or other charge for early termination, which must be reasonable.

(2) *Early-termination notice.* In a motor-vehicle lease, a notice substantially similar to the following: "Early Termination. You may have to pay a substantial charge if you end this lease early. The charge may be up to several thousand dollars. The actual charge will depend on when the lease is terminated. The earlier you end the lease, the greater this charge is likely to be."

(h) *Maintenance responsibilities.* The following provisions are required:

(1) *Statement of responsibilities.* A statement specifying whether the lessor or the lessee is responsible for maintaining or servicing the leased property, together with a brief description of the responsibility;

(2) *Wear and use standard.* A statement of the lessor's standards for wear and use (if any), which must be reasonable; and

(3) *Notice of wear and use standard.* In a motor-vehicle lease, a notice regarding wear and use substantially similar to the following: "Excessive Wear and Use. You may be charged for excessive wear based on our standards for normal use." The notice shall also specify the amount or method for determining any charge for excess mileage.

(*i*) *Purchase option.* A statement of whether or not the lessee has the option to purchase the leased property, and:

(1) *End of lease term.* If at the end of the lease term, the purchase price; and

(2) *During lease term.* If prior to the end of the lease term, the purchase price or the method for determining the price and when the lessee may exercise this option.

(j) *Statement referencing nonsegregated disclosures.* A statement that the lessee should refer to the lease documents for additional information on early termination, purchase options and maintenance responsibilities, warranties, late and default charges, insurance, and any security interests, if applicable.

(k) *Liability between residual and realized values.* A statement of the lessee's liability, if any, at early termination or at the end of the lease term for the difference between the residual value of the leased property and its realized value.

(*l*) *Right of appraisal.* If the lessee's liability at early termination or at the end of the lease term is based on the realized value of the leased property, a statement that the lessee may obtain, at the lessee's expense, a professional appraisal by an independent third party (agreed to by the lessee and the lessor) of the value that could be realized at sale of the leased property. The appraisal shall be final and binding on the parties.

(m) *Liability at end of lease term based on residual value.* If the lessee is liable at the end of the lease term for the difference between the residual value of the leased property and its realized value:

(1) *Rent and other charges.* The rent and other charges, paid by the lessee and required by the lessor as an incident to the lease transaction, with a description such as "the total amount of rent and other charges imposed in connection with your lease [state the amount]."

(2) *Excess liability.* A statement about a rebuttable presumption that, at the end of the lease term, the residual value of the leased property is unreasonable and not in good faith to the extent that the residual value exceeds the realized value by more than three times the base monthly payment (or more than three times the average payment allocable to a

monthly period, if the lease calls for periodic payments other than monthly); and that the lessor cannot collect the excess amount unless the lessor brings a successful court action and pays the lessee's reasonable attorney's fees, or unless the excess of the residual value over the realized value is due to unreasonable or excessive wear or use of the leased property (in which case the rebuttable presumption does not apply).

(3) *Mutually agreeable final adjustment.* A statement that the lessee and lessor are permitted, after termination of the lease, to make any mutually agreeable final adjustment regarding excess liability.

(n) *Fees and taxes.* The total dollar amount for all official and license fees, registration, title, or taxes required to be paid in connection with the lease.

(o) *Insurance.* A brief identification of insurance in connection with the lease including:

(1) *Through the lessor.* If the insurance is provided by or paid through the lessor, the types and amounts of coverage and the cost to the lessee; or

(2) *Through a third party.* If the lessee must obtain the insurance, the types and amounts of coverage required of the lessee.

(p) *Warranties or guarantees.* A statement identifying all express warranties and guarantees from the manufacturer or lessor with respect to the leased property that apply to the lessee.

(q) *Penalties and other charges for delinquency.* The amount or the method of determining the amount of any penalty or other charge for delinquency, default, or late payments, which must be reasonable.

(r) *Security interest.* A description of any security interest, other than a security deposit disclosed under paragraph (b) of this section, held or to be retained by the lessor; and a clear identification of the property to which the security interest relates.

(s) *Limitations on rate information.* If a lessor provides a percentage rate in an advertisement or in documents evidencing the lease transaction, a notice stating that "this percentage may not measure the overall cost of financing this lease" shall accompany the rate disclosure. The lessor shall not use the term "annual percentage rate," "annual lease rate," or any equivalent term.

(t) *Non-motor vehicle open-end leases.* Non-motor vehicle open-end leases remain subject to section 182(10) of the act regarding end of term liability.

§ 213.5   Renegotiations, extensions, and assumptions

(a) *Renegotiation.* A renegotiation occurs when a consumer lease subject to this part is satisfied and replaced by a new lease undertaken by the same consumer. A renegotiation requires new disclosures, except as provided in paragraph (d) of this section.

(b) *Extension*. An extension is a continuation, agreed to by the lessor and the lessee, of an existing consumer lease beyond the originally scheduled end of the lease term, except when the continuation is the result of a renegotiation. An extension that exceeds six months requires new disclosures, except as provided in paragraph (d) of this section.

(c) *Assumption*. New disclosures are not required when a consumer lease is assumed by another person, whether or not the lessor charges an assumption fee.

(d) *Exceptions*. New disclosures are not required for the following, even if they meet the definition of a renegotiation or an extension:

(1) A reduction in the rent charge;

(2) The deferment of one or more payments, whether or not a fee is charged;

(3) The extension of a lease for not more than six months on a month-to-month basis or otherwise;

(4) A substitution of leased property with property that has a substantially equivalent or greater economic value, provided no other lease terms are changed;

(5) The addition, deletion, or substitution of leased property in a multiple-item lease, provided the average periodic payment does not change by more than 25 percent; or

(6) An agreement resulting from a court proceeding.

§ 213.6   [Reserved]

§ 213.7   Advertising

(a) *General rule*. An advertisement for a consumer lease may state that a specific lease of property at specific amounts or terms is available only if the lessor usually and customarily leases or will lease the property at those amounts or terms.

(b) *Clear and conspicuous standard*. Disclosures required by this section shall be made clearly and conspicuously.

(1) *Amount due at lease signing or delivery*. Except for the statement of a periodic payment, any affirmative or negative reference to a charge that is a part of the disclosure required under paragraph (d)(2)(ii) of this section shall not be more prominent than that disclosure.

(2) *Advertisement of a lease rate*. If a lessor provides a percentage rate in an advertisement, the rate shall not be more prominent than any of the disclosures in § 213.4, with the exception of the notice in § 213.4(s) required to accompany the rate; and the lessor shall not use the term "annual percentage rate," "annual lease rate," or equivalent term.

(c) *Catalogs and multipage advertisements*. A catalog or other multipage advertisement, or an electronic advertisement (such as an advertisement appearing on an Internet Web site), that provides a table or schedule of the required disclosures shall be considered a single advertisement if, for lease terms that appear without all the required disclosures, the advertisement refers to the page or pages on which the table or schedule appears.

(d) *Advertisement of terms that require additional disclosure*   (1) *Triggering terms*. An advertisement that states any of the following items shall contain the disclosures required by paragraph (d)(2) of this section, except as provided in paragraphs (e) and (f) of this section:

(i) The amount of any payment; or

(ii) A statement of any capitalized cost reduction or other payment (or that no payment is required) prior to or at consummation or by delivery, if delivery occurs after consummation.

(2) *Additional terms*. An advertisement stating any item listed in paragraph (d)(1) of this section shall also state the following items:

(i) That the transaction advertised is a lease;

(ii) The total amount due prior to or at consummation or by delivery, if delivery occurs after consummation;

(iii) The number, amounts, and due dates or periods of scheduled payments under the lease;

(iv) A statement of whether or not a security deposit is required; and

(v) A statement that an extra charge may be imposed at the end of the lease term where the lessee's liability (if any) is based on the difference between the residual value of the leased property and its realized value at the end of the lease term.

(e) *Alternative disclosures—merchandise tags*. A merchandise tag stating any item listed in paragraph (d)(1) of this section may comply with paragraph (d)(2) of this section by referring to a sign or display prominently posted in the lessor's place of business that contains a table or schedule of the required disclosures.

(f) *Alternative disclosures—television or radio advertisements.*—(1) *Toll-free number or print advertisement*. An advertisement made through television or radio stating any item listed in paragraph (d)(1) of this section complies with paragraph (d)(2) of this section if the advertisement states the items listed in paragraphs (d)(2)(i) through (iii) of this section, and:

(i) Lists a toll-free telephone number along with a reference that such number may be used by consumers to obtain the information required by paragraph (d)(2) of this section; or

(ii) Directs the consumer to a written advertisement in a publication of general circulation in the community served by the media station, including the name and the date of the publication, with a statement that information required by paragraph (d)(2) of this section is included in the advertisement. The written advertisement shall be published beginning at least three days before and ending at least ten days after the broadcast.

(2) *Establishment of toll-free number.* (i) The toll-free telephone number shall be available for no fewer than ten days, beginning on the date of the broadcast.

(ii) The lessor shall provide the information required by paragraph (d)(2) of this section orally, or in writing upon request.

§ 213.8　Record retention

A lessor shall retain evidence of compliance with the requirements imposed by this part, other than the advertising requirements under § 213.7, for a period of not less than two years after the date the disclosures are required to be made or an action is required to be taken.

§ 213.9　Relation to state laws

(a) *Inconsistent state law.* A state law that is inconsistent with the requirements of the act and this part is preempted to the extent of the inconsistency. If a lessor cannot comply with a state law without violating a provision of this part, the state law is inconsistent within the meaning of section 186(a) of the act and is preempted, unless the state law gives greater protection and benefit to the consumer. A state, through an official having primary enforcement or interpretative responsibilities for the state consumer leasing law, may apply to the Board for a preemption determination.

(b) *Exemptions.*—(1) *Application.* A state may apply to the Board for an exemption from the requirements of the act and this part for any class of lease transactions within the state. The Board will grant such an exemption if the Board determines that:

(i) The class of leasing transactions is subject to state law requirements substantially similar to the act and this part or that lessees are afforded greater protection under state law; and

(ii) There is adequate provision for state enforcement.

(2) *Enforcement and liability.* After an exemption has been granted, the requirements of the applicable state law (except for additional requirements not imposed by federal law) will constitute the requirements of the act and this part. No exemption will extend to the civil liability provisions of sections 130, 131, and 185 of the act.

Appendix A.　Model Forms

A–1.　Model Open–End or Finance Vehicle Lease Disclosures
A–2.　Model Closed–End or Net Vehicle Lease Disclosures
A–3.　Model Furniture Lease Disclosures

A–1. Model Open–End or Finance Vehicle Lease Disclosures

Date _____

Lessor(s) _____   Lessee(s) _____

Amount Due at Lease Signing or Delivery (Itemized below)* $ _____	Monthly Payments Your first monthly payment of $ _____ is due on _____, followed by _____ payments of $ _____ due on the _____ of each month. The total of your monthly payments is $ _____.	Other Charges (not part of your monthly payment) Disposition fee (if you do not purchase the vehicle) $ _____ _____ _____ Total $ _____	Total of Payments (The amount you will have paid by the end of the lease) $ _____ You will owe an additional amount if the actual value of the vehicle is less than the residual value.

* Itemization of Amount Due at Lease Signing or Delivery

Amount Due At Lease Signing or Delivery:	How the Amount Due at Lease Signing or Delivery will be paid:
Capitalized cost reduction $ _____ First monthly payment _____ Refundable security deposit _____ Title fees _____ Registration fees _____ _____ Total $ _____	Net trade-in allowance $ _____ Rebates and noncash credits _____ Amount to be paid in cash _____ _____ _____ Total $ _____

Your monthly payment is determined as shown below:

Gross capitalized cost. The agreed upon value of the vehicle ($ _____) and any items you pay over the lease term (such as service contracts, insurance, and any outstanding prior credit or lease balance) .... $ _____

If you want an itemization of this amount, please check this box. ☐

Capitalized cost reduction. The amount of any net trade-in allowance, rebate, noncash credit, or cash you pay that reduces the gross capitalized cost .... – _____

Adjusted capitalized cost. The amount used in calculating your base monthly payment .... = _____

Residual value. The value of the vehicle at the end of the lease used in calculating your base monthly payment .... – _____

Depreciation and any amortized amounts. The amount charged for the vehicle's decline in value through normal use and for other items paid over the lease term .... = _____

Rent charge. The amount charged in addition to the depreciation and any amortized amounts .... + _____

Total of base monthly payments. The depreciation and any amortized amounts plus the rent charge .... = _____

Lease payments. The number of payments in your lease .... ÷ _____

Base monthly payment .... = _____

Monthly sales/use tax .... + _____

_____ .... + _____

Total monthly payment .... = $ _____

Rent and other charges. The total amount of rent and other charges imposed in connection with your lease $ _____ .

Early Termination. You may have to pay a substantial charge if you end this lease early. <u>The charge may be up to several thousand dollars.</u> The actual charge will depend on when the lease is terminated. The earlier you end the lease, the greater this charge is likely to be.

Excessive Wear and Use. You may be charged for excessive wear based on our standards for normal use [and for mileage in excess of _____ miles per year at the rate of _____ per mile].

Purchase Option at End of Lease Term. [You have an option to purchase the vehicle at the end of the lease term for $ _____ [and a purchase option fee of $ _____].] [You do not have an option to purchase the vehicle at the end of the lease term.]

Other Important Terms. See your lease documents for additional information on early termination, purchase options and maintenance responsibilities, warranties, late and default charges, insurance, and any security interest, if applicable.

[The following provisions are the nonsegregated disclosures required under Regulation M.]

Description of Leased Property				
Year	Make	Model	Body Style	Vehicle ID #

Official Fees and Taxes. The total amount you will pay for official and license fees, registration, title, and taxes over the term of your lease, whether included with your monthly payments or assessed otherwise: $ _____ .

Insurance. The following types and amounts of insurance will be acquired in connection with this lease:

_____ .

_____ We (lessor) will provide the insurance coverage quoted above for a total premium cost of $ _____ .

_____ You (lessee) agree to provide insurance coverage in the amount and types indicated above.

End of Term Liability. (a) The residual value ($ _____) of the vehicle is based on a reasonable, good faith estimate of the value of the vehicle at the end of the lease term. If the actual value of the vehicle at that time is greater than the residual value, you will have no further liability under this lease, except for other charges already incurred [and are entitled to a credit or refund of any surplus.] If the actual value of the vehicle is less than the residual value, you will be liable for any difference up to $ _____ (3 times the monthly payment). For any difference in excess of that amount, you will be liable only if:
1. Excessive use or damage [as described in paragraph ____] [representing more than normal wear and use] resulted in an unusually low value at the end of the term.
2. The matter is not otherwise resolved and we win a lawsuit against you seeking a higher payment.
3. You voluntarily agree with us after the end of the lease term to make a higher payment.
Should we bring a lawsuit against you, we must prove that our original estimate of the value of the leased property at the end of the lease term was reasonable and was made in good faith. For example, we might prove that the actual value was less than the original estimated value, although the original estimate was reasonable, because of an unanticipated decline in value for that type of vehicle. We must also pay your attorney's fees.
(b) If you disagree with the value we assign to the vehicle, you may obtain, at your own expense, from an independent third party agreeable to both of us, a professional appraisal of the _____ value of the leased vehicle which could be realized at sale. The appraised value shall then be used as the actual value.

Standards for Wear and Use. The following standards are applicable for determining unreasonable or excess wear and use of the leased vehicle:

_____ .

Maintenance.
[You are responsible for the following maintenance and servicing of the leased vehicle:

_____].

[We are responsible for the following maintenance and servicing of the leased vehicle:

_____].

Warranties. The leased vehicle is subject to the following express warranties:

_____ .

Early Termination and Default. (a) You may terminate this lease before the end of the lease term under the following conditions:

_____ .

The charge for such early termination is:

_____ .

(b) We may terminate this lease before the end of the lease term under the following conditions:

_____ .

Upon such termination we shall be entitled to the following charge(s) for:

_____ .

(c) To the extent these charges take into account the value of the vehicle at termination, if you disagree with the value we assign to the vehicle, you may obtain, at your own expense, from an independent third party agreeable to both of us, a professional appraisal of the _____ value of the leased vehicle which could be realized at sale. The appraised value shall then be used as the actual value.

Security Interest. We reserve a security interest of the following type in the property listed below to secure performance of your obligations under this lease:

_____ .

Late Payments. The charge for late payments is: _____ .

Option to Purchase Leased Property Prior to the End of the Lease. [You have an option to purchase the leased vehicle prior to the end of the term. The price will be [$ _____ /[the method of determining the price].] [You do not have an option to purchase the leased vehicle.]

A–2. Model Closed–End or Net Vehicle Lease Disclosures

Date _____

Lessor(s) _____   Lessee(s) _____

Amount Due at Lease Signing or Delivery (Itemized below)* $ _____	Monthly Payments Your first monthly payment of $ _____ is due on _____, followed by _____ payments of $ _____ due on the _____ of each month. The total of your monthly payments is $ _____.	Other Charges (not part of your monthly payment) Disposition fee (if you do not purchase the vehicle) $_____ _____ _____ Total $_____	Total of Payments (The amount you will have paid by the end of the lease) $ _____

* Itemization of Amount Due at Lease Signing or Delivery

Amount Due at Lease Signing or Delivery:

Capitalized cost reduction $ _____
First monthly payment   _____
Refundable security deposit   _____
Title fees   _____
Registration fees   _____
_____
                              Total $ _____

How the Amount Due at Lease Signing or Delivery will be paid:

Net trade-in allowance $ _____
Rebates and noncash credits   _____
Amount to be paid in cash   _____
_____
                    Total $ _____

Your monthly payment is determined as shown below:

Gross capitalized cost. The agreed upon value of the vehicle ($ _____) and any items you pay over the lease term (such as service contracts, insurance, and any outstanding prior credit or lease balance) .... $ _____

If you want an itemization of this amount, please check this box. ☐

Capitalized cost reduction. The amount of any net trade-in allowance, rebate, noncash credit, or cash you pay that reduces the gross capitalized cost .... − _____

Adjusted capitalized cost. The amount used in calculating your base monthly payment .... = _____

Residual value. The value of the vehicle at the end of the lease used in calculating your base monthly payment .... − _____

Depreciation and any amortized amounts. The amount charged for the vehicle's decline in value through normal use and for other items paid over the lease term .... = _____

Rent charge. The amount charged in addition to the depreciation and any amortized amounts .... + _____

Total of base monthly payments. The depreciation and any amortized amounts plus the rent charge .... = _____

Lease payments. The number of payments in your lease .... ÷ _____

Base monthly payment .... = _____

Monthly sales/use tax .... + _____

_____ .... + _____

Total monthly payment .... = $ _____

Early Termination. You may have to pay a substantial charge if you end this lease early. The charge may be up to several thousand dollars. The actual charge will depend on when the lease is terminated. The earlier you end the lease, the greater this charge is likely to be.

Excessive Wear and Use. You may be charged for excessive wear based on our standards for normal use [and for mileage in excess of _____ miles per year at the rate of _____ per mile].

Purchase Option at End of Lease Term. [You have an option to purchase the vehicle at the end of the lease term for $ _____ [and a purchase option fee of $ _____].] [You do not have an option to purchase the vehicle at the end of the lease term.]

Other Important Terms. See your lease documents for additional information on early termination, purchase options and maintenance responsibilities, warranties, late and default charges, insurance, and any security interest, if applicable.

[The following provisions are the nonsegregated disclosures required under Regulation M.]

Description of Leased Property				
Year	Make	Model	Body Style	Vehicle ID #

Official Fees and Taxes. The total amount you will pay for official and license fees, registration, title, and taxes over the term of your lease, whether included with your monthly payments or assessed otherwise: $ _____ .

Insurance. The following types and amounts of insurance will be acquired in connection with this lease:
_____ .

_____ We (lessor) will provide the insurance coverage quoted above for a total premium cost of $ _____ .

_____ You (lessee) agree to provide insurance coverage in the amount and types indicated above.

Standards for Wear and Use. The following standards are applicable for determining unreasonable or excess wear and use of the leased vehicle:
_____

Maintenance.
[You are responsible for the following maintenance and servicing of the leased vehicle:
_____];

[We are responsible for the following maintenance and servicing of the leased vehicle:
_____].

Warranties. The leased vehicle is subject to the following express warranties:
_____ .

Early Termination and Default. (a) You may terminate this lease before the end of the lease term under the following conditions:
_____ .

The charge for such early termination is:
_____ .

(b) We may terminate this lease before the end of the lease term under the following conditions:
_____ .

Upon such termination we shall be entitled to the following charge(s) for:
_____ .

(c) To the extent these charges take into account the value of the vehicle at termination, if you disagree with the value we assign to the vehicle, you may obtain, at your own expense, from an independent third party agreeable to both of us, a professional appraisal of the _____ value of the leased vehicle which could be realized at sale. The appraised value shall then be used as the actual value.

Security Interest. We reserve a security interest of the following type in the property listed below to secure performance of your obligations under this lease:
_____ .

Late Payments. The charge for late payments is: _____ .

Option to Purchase Leased Property Prior to the End of the Lease. [You have an option to purchase the leased vehicle prior to the end of the term. The price will be [$ _____ /[the method of determining the price].] [You do not have an option to purchase the leased vehicle.]

A–3. Model Furniture Lease Disclosures

Date _____

Lessor(s) _____   Lessee(s) _____

Description of Leased Property				
Item	Color	Stock #	Mfg.	Quantity

Amount Due at Lease Signing or Delivery	Monthly Payments	Other Charges (not part of your monthly payment)	Total of Payments (The amount you will have paid by the end of the lease)
First monthly payment $ _____ Refundable security deposit $ _____ Delivery/Installation fee $ _____ _____ $ _____ Total $ _____	Your first monthly payment of $ _____ is due on _____, followed by _____ payments of $ _____ due on the _____ of each month. The total of your monthly payments is $ _____.	Pick-up fee $ _____ _____ $ _____ Total $ _____	$ _____

Purchase Option at End of Lease Term. [You have an option to purchase the leased property at the end of the lease term for $ _____ [and a purchase option fee of $ _____].] [You do not have an option to purchase the leased property at the end of the lease term.]

Other Important Terms. See your lease documents for additional information on early termination, purchase options and maintenance responsibilities, warranties, late and default charges, insurance, and any security interest, if applicable.

[The following provisions are the nonsegregated disclosures required under Regulation M.]

Official Fees and Taxes. The total amount you will pay for official fees, and taxes over the term of your lease, whether included with your monthly payments or assessed otherwise: $ _____ .

Insurance. The following types and amounts of insurance will be acquired in connection with this lease: _____
_____ .

_____ We (lessor) will provide the insurance coverage quoted above for a total premium cost of $ _____ .

_____ You (lessee) agree to provide insurance coverage in the amount and types indicated above.

Standards for Wear and Use. The following standards are applicable for determining unreasonable or excess wear and use of the leased property: _____

Maintenance.
   [You are responsible for the following maintenance and servicing of the leased property: _____ .]

   [We are responsible for the following maintenance and servicing of the leased property: _____ .]

Warranties. The leased property is subject to the following express warranties: _____ .

Early Termination and Default. (a) You may terminate this lease before the end of the lease term under the following conditions: _____ .

   The charge for such early termination is: _____ .

   (b) We may terminate this lease before the end of the lease term under the following conditions: _____ .

   Upon such termination we shall be entitled to the following charge(s) for: _____ .

   (c) To the extent these charges take into account the value of the leased property at termination, if you disagree with the value we assign to the property, you may obtain, at your own expense, from an independent third party agreeable to both of us, a professional appraisal of the _____ value of the property which could be realized at sale. The appraised value shall then be used as the actual value.

Security Interest. We reserve a security interest of the following type in the property listed below to secure performance of your obligations under this lease: _____

Late Payments. The charge for late payments is: _____ .

Purchase Option Prior to the End of the Lease Term.

   [You have an option to purchase the leased property prior to the end of the term. The price will be [$ _____]/the method of determining the price].]

   [You do not have an option to purchase the leased property.]

COMMENTARY ON THE FAIR CREDIT REPORTING ACT*

16 C.F.R. PART 600 APPENDIX

INTRODUCTION

1. *Official status.* This Commentary contains interpretations of the Federal Trade Commission (Commission) of the Fair Credit Reporting Act (FCRA). It is a guideline intended to clarify how the Commission will construe the FCRA in light of Congressional intent as reflected in the statute and its legislative history. The Commentary does not have the force or effect of regulations or statutory provisions, and its contents may be revised and updated as the Commission considers necessary or appropriate.

2. *Status of previous interpretations.* The Commentary . . . is intended to supersede all prior formal Commission interpretations, informal staff opinion letters, and the staff manual. . . .

3. *Statutory references.* Reference to several different provisions of the FCRA is frequently required in order to make a complete analysis of an issue. For various sections and subsections of the FCRA, the Commentary discusses the most important and common overlapping references under the heading "Relation to other (sub)sections."

4. *Issuance of staff interpretations.* The Commission will revise and update the Commentary as it deems necessary, based on the staff's experience in responding to public inquiries about, and enforcing, the FCRA. The Commission welcomes input from interested industry and consumer groups and other public parties on the Commentary and on issues discussed in it. Staff will continue to respond to requests for informal staff interpretations. . . .

. . .

Section 603—Definitions and Rules of Construction

(b) *"Person"*

1. *Relation to Other Sections.* Certain "persons" must comply with the Act. The term "consumer reporting agency" is defined in section 603(f) to include certain "persons." Section 619 subjects any "person" who knowingly and willfully obtains information from a consumer reporting agency on a consumer under false pretenses to criminal sanctions. Requirements relating to report users apply to "persons." Section 606 imposes disclosure obligations on "persons" who obtain investigative reports or cause them to be prepared. Section 615(c) uses the term "person" to denote those subject to disclosure obligations under sections 615(a) and 615(b).

---

* Repetition of the statutory language and paraphrases of that language have been omitted without ellipses.—Ed.

2. *Examples.* The term "person" includes universities, creditors, collection agencies, insurance companies, private investigators, and employers.

(c) *"Consumer"*

1. *Relation to Other Sections.* The term "consumer" denotes an individual entitled to the Act's protections. Consumer reports, as defined in section 603(d), are reports about consumers. A "consumer" is entitled to obtain disclosures under section 609 from consumer reporting agencies and to take certain steps that require such agencies to follow procedures in section 611, concerning disputes about the completeness or accuracy of items of information in the consumer's file. Disclosures required under section 606 by one procuring an investigative report must be made to the "consumer" on whom the report is sought. Notifications required by section 615 must be provided to "consumers." A "consumer" is the party entitled to sue for willful noncompliance (section 616) or negligent noncompliance (section 617) with the Act's requirements.

2. *General.* The definition includes only a natural person. It does not include artificial entities (e.g., partnerships, corporations, trusts, estates, cooperatives, associations) or entities created by statute (e.g., governments, governmental subdivisions or agencies).

(d) *"Consumer Report"*

1. *Relation to "Consumer Reporting Agency."* To be a "consumer report," the information must be furnished by a "consumer reporting agency" as that term is defined in section 603(f). Conversely, the term "consumer reporting agency" is restricted to persons that regularly engage in assembling or evaluating consumer credit information or other information on consumers for the purpose of furnishing "consumer reports" to third parties. In other words, the terms "consumer reporting agency" in section 603(f) and "consumer report" in section 603 (d) are mutually dependent and must therefore be construed together. For example, information is not a "consumer report" if the person furnishing the information is clearly not a "consumer reporting agency" (e.g., if the person furnishing the information does not regularly furnish such information for monetary fees or on a cooperative nonprofit basis).

2. *Relation to the Applicability of the Act.* If a report is not a "consumer report," then the Act does not usually apply to it.[1] For example, because a commercial credit report is not a report on a consumer, it is not a "consumer report." Therefore, the user need not notify the subject of the name and address of the credit bureau when taking adverse action, and the provider need not omit "obsolete" information, as would be required if the FCRA applied.

---

1. However, a creditor denying a consumer's application based on a report from a "third party" must give the disclosure required by section 615(b).

3. *Report Concerning a "Consumer's" Attributes and History.*

A. *General.* A "consumer report" is a report on a "consumer" to be used for certain purposes involving that "consumer."

B. *Artificial entities.* Reports about corporations, associations, and other collective entities are not consumer reports, and the Act does not apply to them.

C. *Reports on businesses for business purposes.* Reports used to determine the eligibility of a business, rather than a consumer, for certain purposes, are not consumer reports and the FCRA does not apply to them, even if they contain information on individuals, because Congress did not intend for the FCRA to apply to reports used for commercial purposes (see 116 Cong. Rec. 36572 (1970) (Conf. Report on H.R. 15073)).

4. *"(C)redit Worthiness, Credit Standing, Credit Capacity, Character, General Reputation, Personal Characteristics, or Mode of Living* * *"*

A. *General.* To be a "consumer report," the information must bear on at least one of the seven characteristics listed in this definition.

B. *Credit guides.* Credit guides are listings, furnished by credit bureaus to credit grantors, that rate how well consumers pay their bills. Such guides are a series of "consumer reports," because they contain information which is used for the purpose of serving as a factor in establishing the consumers' eligibility for credit. However, if they are coded (by identification such as social security number, driver's license number, or bank account number) so that the consumer's identity is not disclosed, they are not "consumer reports" until decoded. (See discussion of uncoded credit guides under section 604(3)(A), item 8 infra.)

C. *Motor vehicle reports.* Motor vehicle reports are distributed by state motor vehicle departments, generally to insurance companies upon request, and usually reveal a consumer's entire driving record, including arrests for driving offenses. Such reports are consumer reports when they are sold by a Department of Motor Vehicles for insurance underwriting purposes and contain information bearing on the consumer's "personal characteristics," such as arrest information. The Act's legislative history indicates Congress intended the Act to cover mutually beneficial exchanges of information between commercial enterprises rather than between governmental entities. Accordingly, these reports are not consumer reports when provided to other governmental authorities involved in licensing or law enforcement activities. (See discussion titled "State Departments of Motor Vehicles," under section 603(f), item 10 infra.)

D. *Consumer lists.* A list of the names of creditworthy individuals, or of individuals on whom credit bureaus have derogatory information, is a series of "consumer reports" because the information bears on credit worthiness.

E. *Public record information.* A report solely of public record information is not a "consumer report" unless that information is provided by a consumer reporting agency, is collected or used for the purposes identified in section 603(d), and bears on at least one of the seven characteristics listed in the definition. Public record information relating to records of arrest, or the institution or disposition of civil or criminal proceedings, bears on one or more of these characteristics.

F. *Name and address.* A report limited solely to the consumer's name and address alone, with no connotations as to credit worthiness or other characteristics, does not constitute a "consumer report," if it does not bear on any of the seven factors.

G. *Rental characteristics.* Reports about rental characteristics (e.g., consumers' evictions, rental payment histories, treatment of premises) are consumer reports, because they relate to character, general reputation, personal characteristics, or mode of living.

5. *"(U)sed or Expected to Be Used or Collected in Whole or in Part for the Purpose of Serving as a Factor in Establishing the Consumer's Eligibility* * * *"*

A. *Law enforcement bulletins.* Bulletins that are limited to a series of descriptions, sometimes accompanied by photographs, of individuals who are being sought by law enforcement authorities for alleged crimes are not a series of "consumer reports" because they have not been collected for use in evaluating consumers for credit, insurance, employment or other consumer purposes, and it cannot reasonably be anticipated they will be used for such purposes.

B. *Directories.* Telephone directories and city directories, to the extent they only provide information regarding name, address and phone number, marital status, home ownership, and number of children, are not "consumer reports," because the information is not used or expected to be used in evaluating consumers for credit, insurance, employment or other purposes and does not reflect on credit standing, credit worthiness, or any of the other factors. A list of names of individuals with checking accounts is not a series of consumer reports because the information does not bear on credit worthiness or any of the other factors. A trade directory, such as a list of all insurance agents licensed to do business in a state, is not a series of consumer reports because it is commercial information that would be used for commercial purposes.

C. *Use of prior consumer report in preparation.* A report that would not otherwise be a consumer report may be a consumer report, notwithstanding the purpose for which it is furnished, if it includes a prior consumer report or information from consumer report files, because it would contain some information "collected in whole or in part" for consumer reporting purposes. For example, an insurance claims report would be a consumer report if a consumer report (or information from a consumer report) were used to prepare it. (See discussion, infra, in item 6–C under this subsection.)

D. *Use of reports for purposes not anticipated by the reporting party.* The question arises whether a report that is not otherwise a consumer report is subject to the FCRA because the recipient subsequently uses the report for a permissible purpose. If the reporting party's procedures are such that it neither knows of nor should reasonably anticipate such use, the report is not a consumer report. If a reporting party has taken reasonable steps to insure that the report is not used for such a purpose, and if it neither knows of, nor can reasonably anticipate such use, the report should not be deemed a consumer report by virtue of uses beyond the reporting party's control. A reporting party might establish that it does not reasonably anticipate such use of the report by requiring the recipient to certify that the report will not be used for one of the purposes listed in section 604. (Such procedure may be compared to the requirement in section 607(a), discussed infra, that consumer reporting agencies furnishing consumer reports require that prospective users certify the purposes for which the information is sought and certify that the information will be used for no other purpose.) For example, a claims reporting service could use such a certification to avoid having its insurance claims reports deemed "consumer reports" if the report recipient/insurer were to use the report later for "underwriting purposes" under section 604(3)(C), such as terminating insurance coverage or raising the premium.

6. *"(E)stablishing the Consumer's Eligibility for (1) Credit or Insurance to Be Used Primarily for Personal, Family or Household Purposes, or (2) Employment Purposes, or (3) Other Purposes Authorized Under Section 604"*

A. *Relation to section 604*. Because section 603(d)(3) refers to "purposes authorized under section 604" (often described as "permissible purposes" of consumer reports), some of which overlap purposes enumerated in section 603 (e.g., 603(d)(1) and 603(d)(2)), sections 603 and 604 must be construed together, to determine what are "consumer reports" and "permissible purposes" under the two sections. See discussion infra, under section 604.

B. *Commercial credit or insurance*. A report on a consumer for credit or insurance in connection with a business operated by the consumer is not a "consumer report," and the Act does not apply to it.

C. *Insurance claims reports*. (It is assumed that information in prior consumer reports is not used in claims reports. See discussion, supra, in item 5–C under this subsection.) Reports provided to insurers by claims investigation services solely to determine the validity of insurance claims are not consumer reports, because section 604(3)(C) specifically sets forth only underwriting (not claims) as an insurance-related purpose, and section 603(d)(1) deals specifically with eligibility for insurance and no other insurance-related purposes. To construe section 604(3)(E) as including reports furnished in connection with insurance claims would be to disregard the specific language of sections 604(3)(C) and 603(d)(1).

D. *Scope of employment purpose*. A report that is used or is expected to be used or collected in whole or in part in connection with establishing an employee's eligibility for "promotion, reassignment or retention," as well as to evaluate a job applicant, is a consumer report because sections

603(d)(2) and 604(3)(B) use the term "employment purposes," which section 603(h) defines to include these situations.

E. *Bad check lists.* A report indicating that an individual has issued bad checks, provided by printed list or otherwise, to a business for use in determining whether to accept consumers' checks tendered in transactions primarily for personal, family or household purposes, is a consumer report. The information furnished bears on consumers' character, general reputation and personal characteristics, and it is used or expected to be used in connection with business transactions involving consumers.

F. *Tenant screening reports.* A report used to determine whether to rent a residence to a consumer is a consumer report, because it is used for a business transaction that the consumer wishes to enter into for personal, family or household purposes.

7. *Exclusions From the Definition of "Consumer Report"*

A. *"(Any) reports containing information solely as to transactions or experiences between the consumer and the person making the report;"—*

(1) *Examples of Sources.* The exemption applies to reports limited to transactions or experiences between the consumer and the entity making the report (e.g., retail stores, hospitals, present or former employers, banks, mortgage servicing companies, credit unions, or universities).

(2) *Information beyond the reporting entity's own transactions or experiences with the consumer.* The exemption does not apply to reports by these entities of information beyond their own transactions or experiences with the consumer. An example is a creditor's or an insurance company's report of the reasons it cancelled credit or insurance, based on information from an outside source.

(3) *Opinions Concerning Transactions or Experiences.* The exemption applies to reports that are not limited to the facts, but also include opinions (e.g., use of the term "slow pay" to describe a consumer's transactions with a creditor), as long as the facts underlying the opinions involve only transactions or experiences between the consumer and the reporting entity.

B. *"(A)ny authorization or approval of a specific extension of credit directly or indirectly by the issuer of a credit card or similar device;"—*

(1) *General.* The exemption applies to a credit or debit card issuer's written, oral, or electronic communication of its decision whether or not to authorize a charge, in response to a request from a merchant or other party that the consumer has asked to honor the card.

C. *"(A)ny report in which a person who has been requested by a third party to make a specific extension of credit directly or indirectly to the consumer conveys his decision with respect to such request, if the third party advises the consumer of the name and address of the person to whom the request was made and such person makes the disclosures to the consumer required under section 615.''—*

(1) *General.* The exemption covers retailers' attempts to obtain credit for their individual customers from an outside source (such as a bank or a finance company). The communication by the financial institution of its decision whether to extend credit is not a "consumer report" if the retailer informs the customer of the name and address of the financial institution to which the application or contract is offered and the financial institution makes the disclosures required by section 615 of the Act. Such disclosures must be made only when there is a denial of, or increase in the charge for, credit or insurance. (See discussion of section 615, item 10, infra.)

(2) *Information included in the exemption.* The exemption is not limited to a simple "yes" or "no" response, but includes the information constituting the basis for the credit denial, because it applies to "any report."

(3) *How third party creditors can insure that the exemption applies.* Creditors, who are requested by dealers or merchants to make such specific extensions of credit, can assure that communication of their decision to the dealer or merchant will be exempt under this section from the term "consumer report," by having written agreements that require such parties to inform the consumer of the creditor's name and address and by complying with any applicable provisions of section 615.

(e) *"Investigative Consumer Report"*

1. *Relation to Other Sections.* The term "investigative consumer report" denotes a subset of "consumer report" for which the Act imposes additional requirements on recipients and consumer reporting agencies. Persons procuring "investigative consumer reports" must make certain disclosures to the consumers who are the subjects of the reports, as required by section 606. Consumer reporting agencies must comply with section 614, when furnishing "investigative consumer reports" containing adverse information that is not a matter of public record. Consumer reporting agencies making disclosure to consumers pursuant to section 609 are not required to disclose "sources of information acquired solely for use in preparing an investigative consumer report and actually used for no other purpose."

2. *General.* An "investigative consumer report" is a type of "consumer report" that contains information that is both related to a consumer's character, general reputation, personal characteristics or mode of living and obtained by personal interviews with the consumer's neighbors, friends, associates or others.

3. *Types of Sources Interviewed.* A report consisting of information from any third party concerning the subject's character (reputation, etc.) may be an investigative consumer report because the phrase "obtained

through personal interviews* * *with others" includes any source that is a third party interviewee. A report containing interview information obtained solely from the subject is not an "investigative consumer report."

4. *Telephone Interviews.* A consumer report that contains information on a consumer's "character, general reputation, personal characteristics or mode of living" obtained through telephone interviews with third parties is an "investigative consumer report," because "personal interviews" includes interviews conducted by telephone as well as in person.

5. *Identity of Interviewer.* A consumer report is an "investigative consumer report" if personal interviews are used to obtain information reported on a consumer's "character, general reputation, personal characteristics or mode of living," regardless of who conducted the interview.

6. *Noninvestigative Information in "Investigative Consumer Reports."* An "investigative consumer report" may also contain noninvestigative information, because the definition includes reports, a "portion" of which are investigative reports.

7. *Exclusions From "Investigative Consumer Reports."* A report that consists solely of information gathered from observation by one who drives by the consumer's residence is not an "investigative consumer report," because it contains no information from "personal interviews."

(f) *"Consumer Reporting Agency"*

1. *Relation to Other Sections.*

A. *Duties imposed on "consumer reporting agencies."* The Act imposes a number of duties on "consumer reporting agencies." They must have permissible purposes to furnish consumer reports (section 604), avoid furnishing obsolete adverse information in certain consumer reports (sections 605, 607(a)), adopt reasonable procedures to assure privacy (sections 604, 607(a)), and accuracy (section 607(b)) of consumer reports, provide only limited disclosures to governmental agencies (section 608), provide consumers certain disclosures upon request (sections 609 and 610) at no cost or for a reasonable charge (section 612), follow certain procedures if a consumer disputes the completeness or accuracy of any item of information contained in his file (section 611), and follow certain procedures in reporting public record information for employment purposes or when reporting adverse information other than public record information in investigative consumer reports (sections 613, 614).

B. *Relation to "consumer reports."* The term "consumer reporting agency," as defined in section 603(f), includes certain persons who assemble or evaluate information on individuals for the purpose of furnishing "consumer reports" to third parties. Conversely, section 603(d) defines the term "consumer report" to mean the communication of certain information by a "consumer reporting agency." In other words, the terms "consumer report" in section 603(d) and "consumer reporting agency" as defined in section 603(f) are defined in a mutually dependent manner and must therefore be construed together. For example, a party is not a "consumer reporting agency" if it provides only information that is excepted from the definition of "consumer report" under section 603(d), such as reports limited to the party's own transactions or experiences with a consumer, or credit information on organizations.

2. *Isolated Reports.* Parties that do not "regularly" engage in assembling or evaluating information for the purpose of furnishing consumer reports to third parties are not consumer reporting agencies. For example, a creditor that furnished information on a consumer to a governmental entity in connection with one of its investigations, would not "regularly" be making such disclosure for a fee or on a cooperative nonprofit basis, and therefore would not become a consumer reporting agency, even if the information exceeded the creditor's transactions or experiences with the consumer.

3. *Provision of Credit Report to Report Subject.* A consumer report user does not become a consumer reporting agency by regularly giving a copy of the report, or otherwise disclosing it, to the consumer who is the subject of the report, because it is not disclosing the information to a "third party."

4. *Employment Agency.* An employment agency that routinely obtains information on job applicants from their former employers and furnishes the information to prospective employers is a consumer reporting agency.

5. *Information Compiled for Insurance Underwriting.* A business that compiles claim payment histories on individuals from insurers and furnishes them to insurance companies for use in underwriting decisions concerning those individuals is a consumer reporting agency.

6. *Private Investigators and Detective Agencies.* Private investigators and detective agencies that regularly obtain consumer reports and furnish them to clients may thereby become consumer reporting agencies.

7. *Collection Agencies and Creditors.* Collection agencies and creditors become consumer reporting agencies if they regularly furnish information beyond their transactions or experiences with consumers to third parties for use in connection with consumers' transactions.

8. *Joint Users of Consumer Reports.* Entities that share consumer reports with others that are jointly involved in decisions for which there are permissible purposes to obtain the reports may be "joint users" rather than consumer reporting agencies. For example, if a lender forwards consumer reports to governmental agencies administering loan guarantee programs (or to other prospective loan insurers or guarantors), or to other parties whose approval is needed before it grants credit, or to another creditor for use in considering a consumer's loan application at the consumer's request, the lender does not become a consumer reporting agency by virtue of such action. An agent or employee that obtains consumer reports does not become a consumer reporting agency by sharing such reports with its principal or employer in connection with the purposes for which the reports were initially obtained.

9. *Loan Exchanges.* Loan exchanges, which are generally owned and operated on a cooperative basis by consumer finance companies, constitute a mechanism whereby each member furnishes the exchange information concerning the full identity and loan amount of each of its borrowers, and receives information from the exchange concerning the number and types of outstanding loans for each of its applicants. A loan exchange or any other exchange that regularly collects information bearing on decisions to grant consumers credit or insurance for personal, family or household purposes, or employment, is a "consumer reporting agency."

10. *State Departments of Motor Vehicles.* State motor vehicle departments are "consumer reporting agencies" if they regularly furnish motor vehicle reports containing information bearing on the consumer's "personal characteristics," such as arrest information, to insurance companies for insurance underwriting purposes. (See discussion of motor vehicle reports under section 603(d), item 4–C supra.)

11. *Federal Agencies.* The Office of Personnel Management collects and files data concerning current and potential employees of the Federal Government and transmits that information to other government agencies for employment purposes. Because Congress did not intend that the FCRA apply to the Office of Personnel Management and similar federal agencies (see 116 Cong. Rec. 36576 (1970) (remarks of Rep. Brown)), no such agency is a "consumer reporting agency."

12. *Credit Application Information.* A creditor that provides information from a consumer's application to a credit bureau, for verification as part of the creditor's evaluation process that includes obtaining a report on the consumer from that credit bureau, does not thereby become a "consumer reporting agency," because the creditor does not provide the information for "fees, dues, or on a cooperative nonprofit basis," but rather pays the bureau to verify the information when it provides a consumer report on the applicant.

(g) *"File"*

1. Consumer reporting agencies are required to make disclosures of all information in their "files" to consumers upon request (section 609) and to follow reinvestigation procedures if the consumer disputes the completeness or accuracy of any item of information contained in his "file" (section 611).

2. The term "file" denotes all information on the consumer that is recorded and retained by a consumer reporting agency that might be furnished, or has been furnished, in a consumer report on that consumer.

3. *Audit Trail.* The term "file" does not include an "audit trail" (a list of changes made by a consumer reporting agency to a consumer's credit history record, maintained to detect fraudulent changes to that record), because such information is not furnished in consumer reports or used as a basis for preparing them.

4. *Other Information.* The term "file" does not include information in billing records or in the consumer relations folder that a consumer reporting agency opens on a consumer who obtains disclosures or files a dispute, if the information has not been used in a consumer report and would not be used in preparing one.

(h) *"Employment Purposes"*

1. *Relation to Other Sections.* The term "employment purposes" is used as part of the definition of "consumer reports" (section 603(d)(2)) and as a permissible purpose for the furnishing of consumer reports (section 604(3)(B)). Where an investigative consumer report is to be used for "employment purposes" for which a consumer has not specifically applied, section 606(a)(2) provides that the notice otherwise required by section 606(a)(1) need not be sent. When a consumer reporting agency furnishes public record information in reports "for employment purposes," it must follow the procedure set out in section 613.

2. *Security Clearances.* A report in connection with security clearances of a government contractor's employees would be for "employment purposes" under this section.

(*i*) *"Medical Information"*

1. *Relation to Other Sections.* Under section 609(a)(1), a consumer reporting agency must, upon the consumer's request and proper identification, disclose the nature and substance of all information in its files on the consumer, except "medical information."

2. *Information from Non-medical Sources.* Information from non-medical sources such as employers, is not "medical information."

Section 604—Permissible Purposes of Reports

1. *Relation to Section 603.* Sections 603(d)(3) and 604 must be construed together to determine what are "permissible purposes," because section 603(d)(3) refers to "purposes authorized under section 604" (often described as "permissible purposes" of consumer reports), and some purposes are enumerated in section 603 (e.g., sections 603(d)(1) and 603(d)(2)). Subsections of sections 603 and 604 that specifically set forth "permissible purposes" relating to credit, insurance and employment, are the only subsections that cover "permissible purposes" relating to those three areas. Section 604(3)(E), a general subsection, is limited to purposes not otherwise addressed in section 604(3)(A)–(D).

A. *Credit.* Sections 603(d)(1)—which defines "consumer report" to include certain reports for the purpose of serving as a factor in establishing the consumer's eligibility for credit or insurance primarily for personal, family, or household purposes—and 604(3)(A) must be read together as fully describing permissible purposes involving credit for obtaining consumer reports. Accordingly, section 604(3)(A) permits the furnishing of a consumer report for use in connection with a credit transaction involving the consumer, primarily for personal, family or household purposes, and involving the extension of credit to, or review or collection of an account of, the consumer.

B. *Insurance*. Sections 603(d)(1) and 604(3)(C) must be read together as describing the only permissible insurance purposes for obtaining consumer reports. Accordingly, section 604(3)(C) permits the furnishing of a consumer report, provided it is for use in connection with the underwriting of insurance involving the consumer, primarily for personal, family, or household purposes.

C. *Employment*. Employment is covered exclusively by sections 603(d)(2) and 604(3)(B), and by section 603(h) (which defines "employment purposes"). Therefore, "permissible purposes" relating to employment include reports used for evaluating a consumer "for employment, promotion, reassignment or retention as an employee."

D. *Other purposes*. "Other purposes" are referred to in section 603(d)(3) and covered by section 604(3)(E), as well as sections 604(1), 604(2) and 604(3)(D) (which contain specific purposes not involving credit, insurance, employment). Permissible purposes relating to section 604(3)(E) are limited to transactions that consumers enter into primarily for personal, family or household purposes (excluding credit, insurance or employment, which are specifically covered by other subsections discussed above). The FCRA does not cover reports furnished for transactions that consumers enter into primarily in connection with businesses they operate (e.g., a consumer's rental of equipment for use in his retail store).

2. *Relation to Other Sections*.

A. *Section 607(a)*. Section 607(a) requires consumer reporting agencies to keep information confidential by furnishing consumer reports only for purposes listed under section 604, and to follow specified, reasonable procedures to achieve this end. Section 619 provides criminal sanctions against any person who knowingly and willfully obtains information on a consumer from a consumer reporting agency under false pretenses.

B *Section 608*. Section 608 allows "consumer reporting agencies" to furnish governmental agencies specified identifying information concerning consumers, notwithstanding the limitations of section 604.

Section 604(1)

1. *Subpoena*. A subpoena, including a grand jury subpoena, is not an "order of a court" unless signed by a judge.

2. *Internal Revenue Service Summons*. An I.R.S. summons is an exception to the requirement that an order be signed by a judge before it constitutes an "order of a court" under this section, because a 1976 revision to Federal statutes (26 U.S.C. 7609) specifically requires a consumer reporting agency to furnish a consumer report in response to an I.R.S. summons upon receipt of the designated I.R.S. certificate that the consumer has not filed a timely motion to quash the summons.

Section 604(2)

1. *No Other Permissible Purpose Needed.* If the report subject furnishes written authorization for a report, that creates a permissible purpose for furnishing the report.

2. *Refusal to Furnish Report.* The consumer reporting agency may refuse to furnish the report because the statute is permissive, not mandatory. (Requirements that consumer reporting agencies make disclosure to consumers (as contrasted with furnishing reports to users) are discussed under sections 609 and 610, infra.)

Section 604(3)(A)

1. *Reports Sought in Connection with the "Review or Collection of an Account."*

A. *Reports for collection.* A collection agency has a permissible purpose under this section to receive a consumer report on a consumer for use in attempting to collect that consumer's debt, regardless of whether that debt is assigned or referred for collection. Similarly, a detective agency or private investigator, attempting to collect a debt owed by a consumer, would have a permissible purpose to obtain a consumer report on that individual for use in collecting that debt. An attorney may obtain a consumer report under this section on a consumer for use in connection with a decision whether to sue that individual to collect a credit account.

B. *Unsolicited reports.* A consumer reporting agency may not send an unsolicited consumer report to the recipient of a previous report on the same consumer, because the recipient will not necessarily have a permissible purpose to receive the unsolicited report.[2] For example, the recipient may have rejected the consumer's application or ceased to do business with the consumer. (See also discussion in section 607, item 2–G, *infra.*)

2. *Judgment Creditors.* A judgment creditor has a permissible purpose to receive a consumer report on the judgment debtor for use in connection with collection of the judgment debt, because it is in the same position as any creditor attempting to collect a debt from a consumer who is the subject of a consumer report.

3. *Child Support Debts.* A district attorney's office or other child support agency may obtain a consumer report in connection with enforcement of the report subject's child support obligation, established by court (or quasi-judicial administrative) orders, since the agency is acting as or on behalf of the judgment creditor, and is, in effect, collecting a debt. However, a consumer reporting agency may not furnish consumer reports to child support agencies seeking to *establish* paternity or the duty to pay child support.

2. Of course a consumer reporting agency must furnish notifications required by section 611(d), upon the consumer's requests, to prior recipients of reports containing disputed information that is deleted or that is the subject of a dispute statement under section 611(b).

4. *Tax Obligations.* A tax collection agency has no general permissible purpose to obtain a consumer report to collect delinquent tax accounts, because this subsection applies only to collection of "credit" accounts. However, if a tax collection agency acquired a tax lien having the same effect as a judgment or obtained a judgment, it would be a judgment creditor and would have a permissible purpose for obtaining a consumer report on the consumer who owed the tax. Similarly, if a consumer taxpayer entered an agreement with a tax collection agency to pay taxes according to some timetable, that agreement would create a debtor-creditor relationship, thereby giving the agency a permissible purpose to obtain a consumer report on that consumer.

5. *Information on an Applicant's Spouse.*

A. *Permissible purpose.* A creditor may request any information concerning an applicant's spouse if that spouse will be permitted to use the account or will be contractually liable upon the account, or the applicant is relying on the spouse's income as a basis for repayment of the credit requested. A creditor may request any information concerning an applicant's spouse if (1) the state law doctrine of necessaries applies to the transaction, or (2) the applicant resides in a community property state, or (3) the property upon which the applicant is relying as a basis for repayment of the credit requested is located in such a state, or (4) the applicant is acting as the agent of the nonapplicant spouse.

B. *Lack of permissible purpose.* If the creditor receives information clearly indicating that the applicant is not acting as the agent of the nonapplicant spouse, and that the applicant is relying only on separate property to repay the credit extended, and that the state law doctrine of necessaries does not apply to the transaction and that the applicant does not reside in a community property state, the creditor does not have a permissible purpose for obtaining a report on a nonapplicant spouse. A permissible purpose for making a consumer report on a nonapplicant spouse can never exist under the FCRA, where Regulation B, issued under the Equal Credit Opportunity Act (12 CFR 202), prohibits the creditor from requesting information on such spouse. There is no permissible purpose to obtain a consumer report on a nonapplicant former spouse or on a nonapplicant spouse who has legally separated or otherwise indicated an intent to legally disassociate with the marriage. (This does not preclude reporting a prior joint credit account of former spouses for which the spouse that is the subject of the report is still contractually liable. See discussion in section 607, item 3–D *infra*.)

6. *Prescreening.* "Prescreening" means the process whereby a consumer reporting agency compiles or edits a list of consumers who meet specific criteria and provides this list to the client or a third party (such as a mailing service) on behalf of the client for use in soliciting these consumers for the client's products or services. The process may also include demographic or other analysis of the consumers on the list (e.g., use of census tract data reflecting real estate values) by the consumer reporting

agency or by a third party employed for that purpose (by either the agency or its client) before the list is provided to the consumer reporting agency's client. In such situations, the client's creditworthiness criteria may be provided only to the consumer reporting agency and not to the third party performing the demographic analysis. The consumer reporting agency that performs a "prescreening" service may furnish a client with several different lists of consumers who meet different sets of creditworthiness criteria supplied by the client, who intends to make different credit offers (e.g., various credit limits) to consumers who meet the different criteria.

A prescreened list constitutes a series of consumer reports, because the list conveys the information that each consumer named meets certain criteria for creditworthiness. Prescreening is permissible under the FCRA if the client agrees in advance that each consumer whose name is on the list after prescreening will receive an offer of credit. In these circumstances, a permissible purpose for the prescreening service exists under this section, because of the client's present intent to grant credit to all consumers on the final list, with the result that the information is used "in connection with a credit transaction involving the consumer on whom the information is to be furnished and involving the extension of credit to * * * the consumer."

7. *Seller of Property Extending Credit.* A seller of property has a permissible purpose under this subsection to obtain a consumer report on a prospective purchaser to whom he is planning to extend credit.

8. *Uncoded Credit Guides.* A consumer reporting agency may not furnish an uncoded credit guide, because the recipient does not have a permissible purpose to obtain a consumer report on each consumer listed. (As discussed under section 603(d), item 4 *supra*, credit guides are listings that credit bureaus furnish to credit grantors, rating how consumers pay their bills. Such guides are a series of "consumer reports" on the "consumers" listed therein, unless coded so that the consumer's identity is not disclosed.)

9. *Liability for Bad Checks.* A party attempting to recover the amount due on a bad check is attempting to collect a debt and, therefore, has a permissible purpose to obtain a consumer report on the consumer who wrote it, and on any other consumer who is liable for the amount of that check under applicable state law.

Section 604(3)(B)

1. *Current Employees.* An employer may obtain a consumer report on a current employee in connection with an investigation of the disappearance of money from employment premises, because "retention as an employee" is included in the definition of "employment purposes" (section 603(h)).

2. *Consumer Reports on Applicants and Non-applicants.* An employer may obtain a consumer report for use in evaluating the subject's applica-

tion for employment but may not obtain a consumer report to evaluate the application of a consumer who is not the subject of the report.

3. *Grand Jurors.* The fact that grand jurors are usually paid a stipend for their service does not provide a district attorney's office a permissible purpose for obtaining consumer reports on them, because such service is a duty, not "employment."

Section 604(3)(C)

1. *Underwriting.* An insurer may obtain a consumer report to decide whether or not to issue a policy to the consumer, the amount and terms of coverage, the duration of the policy, the rates or fees charged, or whether or not to renew or cancel a policy, because these are all "underwriting" decisions.

2. *Claims.* An insurer may not obtain a consumer report for the purpose of evaluating a claim (to ascertain its validity or otherwise determine what action should be taken), because permissible purposes relating to insurance are limited by this section to "underwriting" purposes.

Section 604(3)(D)

1. *Appropriate recipient.* Any party charged by law (including a rule or regulation having the force of law) with responsibility for assessing the consumer's eligibility for the benefit (not only the agency directly responsible for administering the benefit) has a permissible purpose to receive a consumer report. For example, a district attorney's office or social services bureau, required by law to consider a consumer's financial status in determining whether that consumer qualifies for welfare benefits, has a permissible purpose to obtain a report on the consumer for that purpose. Similarly, consumer reporting agencies may furnish consumer reports to townships on consumers whose financial status the townships are required by law to consider in determining the consumers' eligibility for assistance, or to professional boards (e.g., bar examiners) required by law to consider such information on applicants for admission to practice.

2. *Inappropriate Recipient.* Parties not charged with the responsibility of determining a consumer's eligibility for a license or other benefit, for example, a party competing for an FCC radio station construction permit, would not have a permissible purpose to obtain a consumer report on that consumer.

3. *Initial or Continuing Benefit.* The permissible purpose includes the determination of a consumer's continuing eligibility for a benefit, as well as the evaluation of a consumer's initial application for a benefit. If the governmental body has reason to believe a particular consumer's eligibility is in doubt, or wishes to conduct random checks to confirm eligibility, it has a permissible purpose to receive a consumer report.

Section 604(3)(E)

1. *Relation to Other Subsections of Section 604(3).* The issue of whether credit, employment, or insurance provides a permissible purpose is determined exclusively by reference to subsection (A), (B), or (C), respectively.

2. *Commercial Transactions.* The term "business transaction" in this section means a business transaction with a consumer primarily for personal, family, or household purposes. Business transactions that involve purely commercial purposes are not covered by the FCRA.

3. *"Legitimate Business Need."* Under this subsection, a party has a permissible purpose to obtain a consumer report on a consumer for use in connection with some action the consumer takes from which he or she might expect to receive a benefit that is not more specifically covered by subsections (A), (B), or (C). For example, a consumer report may be obtained on a consumer who applies to rent an apartment, offers to pay for goods with a check, applies for a checking account or similar service, seeks to be included in a computer dating service, or who has sought and received over-payments of government benefits that he has refused to return.

4. *Litigation.* The possibility that a party may be involved in litigation involving a consumer does not provide a permissible purpose for that party to receive a consumer report on such consumer under this subsection, because litigation is not a "business transaction" involving the consumer. Therefore, potential plaintiffs may not always obtain reports on potential defendants to determine whether they are worth suing. The transaction that gives rise to the litigation may or may not provide a permissible purpose. A party seeking to sue on a *credit* account would have a permissible purpose under section 604(3)(A). (That section also permits judgment creditors and lien creditors to obtain consumer reports on judgment debtors or individuals whose property is subject to the lien creditor's lien.) If that transaction is a business transaction involving the consumer, there is a permissible purpose. If the litigation arises from a tort, there is no permissible purpose. Similarly, a consumer report may not be obtained solely for use in discrediting a witness at trial or for locating a witness. This section does not permit consumer reporting agencies to furnish consumer reports for the purpose of locating a person suspected of committing a crime. (As stated in the discussion of section 608 *infra* (item 2), section 608 permits the furnishing of specified, limited identifying information to governmental agencies, notwithstanding the provisions of section 604.)

5. *Impermissible Purposes.* A consumer reporting agency may not furnish a consumer report to satisfy a requester's curiosity, or for use by a news reporter in preparing a newspaper or magazine article.

6. *Agents.*

A. *General.* An agent[3] of a party with a "permissible purpose" may obtain a consumer report on behalf of his principal, where he is involved in the decision that gives rise to the permissible purpose. Such involvement may include the agent's making a decision (or taking action) for the principal, or assisting the principal in making the decision (e.g., by evaluating information). In these circumstances, the agent is acting on behalf of the principal. In some cases, the agent and principal are referred to as "joint users." See discussion in section 603(f), *supra* (item 8).

B. *Real estate agent.* A real estate agent may obtain a consumer report on behalf of a seller, to evaluate the eligibility as a prospective purchaser of a subject who has expressed an interest in purchasing property from the seller.

C. *Private detective agency.* A private detective agency may obtain a consumer report as agent for its client while investigating a report subject that is a client's prospective employee, or in connection with advising a client concerning a business transaction with the report subject or in attempting to collect a debt owed its client by the subject of the report. In these circumstances, the detective agency is acting on behalf of its client.

D. *Rental clearance agency.* A rental clearance agency that obtains consumer reports to assist owners of residential properties in screening consumers as tenants, has a permissible purpose to obtain the reports, if it uses them in applying the landlord's criteria to approve or disapprove the subjects as tenant applicants. Similarly, an apartment manager investigating applicants for apartment rentals by a landlord may obtain consumer reports on these applicants.

E. *Attorney.* An attorney collecting a debt for a creditor client, including a party suing on a debt or collecting on behalf of a judgment creditor or lien creditor, has a permissible purpose to obtain a consumer report on the debtor to the same extent as the client.

Section 604—General

1. *Furnishing of Consumer Reports to Other Consumer Reporting Agencies.* A consumer reporting agency may furnish a consumer report to another consumer reporting agency for it to furnish pursuant to a subscriber's request. In these circumstances, one consumer reporting agency is acting on behalf of another.

2. *Consumer's Permission Not Needed.* When permissible purposes exist, parties may obtain, and consumer reporting agencies may furnish, consumer reports without the consumers' permission or over their objection. Similarly, parties may furnish information concerning their transactions with consumers to consumer reporting agencies and others, and consumer reporting agencies may gather information, without consumers' permission.

---

3. Of course agents and principals are bound by the Act.

3. *User's Disclosure of Report to Subject Consumer.* The FCRA does not prohibit a consumer report user from giving a copy of the report, or otherwise disclosing it, to the consumer who is the subject of the report.

Section 605—Obsolete Information

1. *General.* Section 605(a) provides that most adverse information more than seven years old may not be reported, except in certain circumstances set out in section 605(b). With respect to delinquent accounts, accounts placed for collection, and accounts charged to profit and loss, there are many dates that could be deemed to commence seven year reporting periods. The discussion in subsections (a)(2), (a)(4), and (a)(6) is intended to set forth a clear, workable rule that effectuates Congressional intent.

2. *Favorable Information.* The Act imposes no time restriction on reporting of information that is not adverse.

3. *Retention of Information in Files.* Consumer reporting agencies may retain obsolete adverse information and furnish it in reports for purposes that are exempt under subsection (b) (e.g., credit for a principal amount of $50,000 or more).

4. *Use of Shorter Periods.* The section does not require consumer reporting agencies to report adverse information for the time periods set forth, but only prohibits them from reporting adverse items beyond those time periods.

5. *Inapplicability to Users.* The section does not limit creditors or others from using adverse information that would be "obsolete" under its terms, because it applies only to reporting by consumer reporting agencies. Similarly, this section does not bar a creditor's reporting such adverse obsolete information concerning its transactions or experiences with a consumer, because the report would not constitute a consumer report.

6. *Indicating the Existence of Nonspecified, Obsolete Information.* A consumer reporting agency may not furnish a consumer report indicating the existence of obsolete adverse information, even if no specific item is reported. For example, a consumer reporting agency may not communicate the existence of a debt older than seven years by reporting that a credit grantor cannot locate a debtor whose debt was charged off ten years ago.

7. *Operative Dates.* The times or dates set forth in this section, which relate to the occurrence of events involving adverse information, determine whether the item is obsolete. The date that the consumer reporting agency acquired the adverse information is irrelevant to how long that information may be reported.

Section 605(a)(1)

1. *Relation to Other Subsections.* The reporting of suits and judgments is governed by subsection (a)(2), the reporting of accounts placed for collection or charged to profit and loss is governed by subsection (a)(4), and

the reporting of other delinquent accounts is governed by subsection (a)(6). Any such item, even if discharged in bankruptcy, may be reported separately for the applicable seven year period, while the existence of the bankruptcy filing may be reported for ten years.

2. *Wage Earner Plans.* Wage earner plans may be reported for ten years, because they are covered by Title 11 of the United States Code.

3. *Date for Filing.* A voluntary bankruptcy petition may be reported for ten years from the date that it is filed, because the filing of the petition constitutes the entry of an "order for relief" under this subsection, just like a filing under the Bankruptcy Act (11 U.S.C. 301).

Section 605(a)(2)

1. *Operative Date.* For a suit, the term "date of entry" means the date the suit was initiated. A protracted suit may be reported for more than seven years from the date it was entered, if the governing statute of limitations has not expired. For a judgment, the term "date of entry" means the date the judgment was rendered.

2. *Paid Judgments.* Paid judgments cannot be reported for more than seven years after the judgment was entered, because payment of the judgment eliminates any "governing statute of limitations" under this subsection that might otherwise lengthen the period.

Section 605(a)(3)

1. *Unpaid Liens.* If a tax lien (or other lien) remains unsatisfied, it may be reported as long as it remains filed against the consumer, without limitation, because this subsection addresses only paid tax liens.

Section 605(a)(4)

1. *Placement for Collection.* The term "placed for collection" means internal collection activity by the creditor, as well as placement with an outside collector, whichever occurs first. Sending of the initial past due notices does not constitute placement for collection. Placement for collection occurs when dunning notices or other collection efforts are initiated. The reporting period is not extended by assignment to another entity for further collection, or by a partial or full payment of the account. However, where a borrower brings his delinquent account to date and returns to his regular payment schedule, and later defaults again, a consumer reporting agency may disregard any collection activity with respect to the first delinquency and measure the reporting period from the date the account was placed for collection as a result of the borrower's ultimate default. A consumer's repayment agreement with a collection agency can be treated as a new account that has its own seven year period.

2. *Charge to Profit and Loss.* The term "charged to profit and loss" means action taken by the creditor to write off the account, and the applicable time period is measured from that event. If an account that was

charged off is later paid in part or paid in full by the consumer, the reporting period of seven years from the charge-off is not extended by this subsequent payment.

3. *Reporting of a Delinquent Account That is Later Placed for Collection or Charged to Profit and Loss.* The fact that an account has been placed for collection or charged to profit and loss may be reported for seven years from the date that either of those events occurs, regardless of the date the account became delinquent. The fact of delinquency may also be reported for seven years from the date the account became delinquent.

Section 605(a)(5)

1. *Records.* The term "records" means any information a consumer reporting agency has in its files relating to arrest, indictment or conviction of a crime.

2. *Computation of Time Period.* The seven year reporting period runs from the date of disposition, release or parole, as applicable. For example, if charges are dismissed at or before trial, or the consumer is acquitted, the date of such dismissal or acquittal is the date of disposition. If the consumer is convicted of a crime and sentenced to confinement, the date of release or placement on parole controls. (Confinement, whether continuing or resulting from revocation of parole, may be reported until seven years after the confinement is terminated.) The sentencing date controls for a convicted consumer whose sentence does not include confinement. The fact that information concerning the arrest, indictment, or conviction of crime is obtained by the reporting agency at a later date from a more recent source (such as a newspaper or interview) does not serve to extend this reporting period.

Section 605(a)(6)

1. *Relation to Other Subsections.* This section applies to all adverse information that is not covered by section 605(a)(1)–(5). For example, a delinquent account that has neither been placed for collection, nor charged to profit and loss, may be reported for seven years from the date of the last regularly scheduled payment. (Accounts placed for collection or charged to profit and loss may be reported for the time periods stated in section 605(a)(4).)

2. *Non Tax Liens.* Liens (other than paid tax liens) may be reported as long as they remain filed against the consumer or the consumer's property, and remain effective (under any applicable statute of limitations). (See discussion under section 605(a)(3), *supra*.)

Section 606—Disclosure of Investigative Consumer Reports

1. *Relation to Other Sections.* The term "investigative consumer report" is defined at section 603(e) to mean a consumer report, all or a portion of which contains information obtained through personal interviews (in person or by telephone) with persons other than the subject,

which information relates to the subject's character, general reputation, personal characteristics or mode of living.

2. *Inapplicability to Consumer Reporting Agencies.* The section applies only to report users, not consumer reporting agencies. The FCRA does not require consumer reporting agencies to inform consumers that information will be gathered or that reports will be furnished concerning them.

3. *Inapplicability to Noninvestigative Consumer Reports.* The section does not apply to noninvestigative reports.

4. *Exemptions.* An employer who orders investigative consumer reports on a current employee who has not applied for a job change need not notify the employee, because the term "employment purposes" is defined to include "promotion, reassignment or retention" and subsection (b) provides that the disclosure requirements do not apply to "employment purposes for which the consumer has not specifically applied."

5. *Form and Delivery of Notice.* The notice must be in writing and delivered to the consumer. The user may include the disclosure in an application for employment, insurance, or credit, if it is clear and conspicuous and not obscured by other language. A user may send the required notice via first class mail. The notice must be mailed or otherwise delivered to the consumer not later than three days after the report was first requested.

6. *Content of Notice of Right to Disclosure.* The notice must clearly and accurately disclose that an "investigative consumer report" including information as to the consumer's character, general reputation, personal characteristics and mode of living (whichever are applicable), may be made. The disclosure must also state that an investigative consumer report involves personal interviews with sources such as neighbors, friends, or associates. The notice may include any additional, accurate information about the report, such as the types of interviews that will be conducted. The notice must include a statement informing the consumer of the right to request complete and accurate disclosure of the nature and scope of the investigation.

7. *Content of Disclosure of Report.* When the consumer requests disclosure of the "nature and scope" of the investigation, such disclosure must include a complete and accurate description of the types of questions asked, the number and types of persons interviewed, and the name and address of the investigating agency. The user need not disclose the names of sources of information, nor must it provide the consumer with a copy of the report. A report user that provides the consumer with a blank copy of the standardized form used to transmit the report from the agency to the user complies with the requirement that it disclose the "nature" of the investigation.

571

Section 607—Compliance Procedures

1. *Procedures to Avoid Reporting Obsolete Information.*

A. *General.* A consumer reporting agency should establish procedures with its sources of adverse information that will avoid the risk of reporting obsolete information. For example, the agency should either require a creditor to supply the date an account was placed for collection or charged off, or the agency should use a conservative date for such placement or charge off (such as the date of the last regularly scheduled payment), to be sure of complying with the statute.

B. *Retention of obsolete information for reporting in excepted circumstances.* If a consumer reporting agency retains adverse information in its files that is "obsolete" under section 605(a) (e.g., information about a satisfied judgment that is more than seven years old), so that it may be reported for use in transactions described by section 605(b) (i.e., applications for credit or life insurance for $50,000 or more, or employment at an annual salary of $20,000 or more), it must have procedural safeguards to avoid reporting the information except in those situations. The procedure should require that such obsolete information be released only after an internal decision that its release will not violate section 605.

2. *Procedures to Avoid Reporting for Impermissible Purposes.*

A. *Verification.* A consumer reporting agency should have a system to verify that it is dealing with a legitimate business having a "permissible purpose" for the information reported. What constitutes adequate verification will vary with the circumstances. If the consumer reporting agency is not familiar with the user, appropriate procedures might require an on-site visit to the user's place of business, or a check of the user's references.

B. *Required certification by user.* A consumer reporting agency should adopt procedures that require prospective report users to identify themselves, certify the purpose for which the information is sought, and certify that the information will be used for no other purpose. A consumer reporting agency should determine initially that users have permissible purposes and ascertain what those purposes are. It should obtain a specific, written certification that the recipient will obtain reports for those purposes and no others. The user's certification that the report will be used for no other purposes should expressly prohibit the user from sharing the report or providing it to anyone else, other than the subject of the report or to a joint user having the same purpose. A consumer reporting agency should refuse to provide reports to those refusing to provide such certification.

C. *Blanket or individual certification.* Once the consumer reporting agency obtains a certification from a user (e.g., a creditor) that typically has a permissible purpose for receiving a consumer report, stating that it will use those reports only for specified permissible purposes (e.g., for credit or employment purposes), a certification of purpose need not be furnished for each individual report obtained, provided there is no reason to believe the user may be violating its certification. However, in furnishing reports to users that typically could have both permissible and impermissible purposes for ordering consumer reports (e.g., attorneys and detective agencies), the consumer reporting agency must require the user to provide a separate certification each time it requests a consumer report.

D. *Procedures to avoid recipients' abuse of certification.* When doubt arises concerning any user's compliance with its contractual certification, a consumer reporting agency must take steps to insure compliance, such as requiring a separate, advance certification for each report it furnishes that user, or auditing that user to verify that it is obtaining reports only for permissible purposes. A consumer reporting agency must cease furnishing consumer reports to users who repeatedly request consumer reports for impermissible purposes.

E. *Unauthorized access.* A consumer reporting agency should take several other steps when doubt arises concerning whether a user is obtaining reports for a permissible purpose from a computerized system. If it appears that a third party, not a subscriber, has obtained unauthorized access to the system, the consumer reporting agency should take appropriate steps such as altering authorized users' means of access, such as codes and passwords, and making random checks to ensure that future reports are obtained only for permissible purposes. If a subscriber has inadvertently sought reports for impermissible purposes or its employee has obtained reports without a permissible purpose, it would be appropriate for the consumer reporting agency to alter the subscriber's means of access, and require an individual written certification of the permissible purpose for each report requested or randomly verify such purposes. A consumer reporting agency should refuse to furnish any further reports to a user that repeatedly violates certifications.

F. *Use of computerized systems.* A consumer reporting agency may furnish consumer reports to users via terminals, provided the consumer reporting agency has taken the necessary steps to ensure that the users have a permissible purpose to receive the reports. (The agency would have to record the identity of consumer report recipients for each consumer, to be able to make any disclosures required under section 609(a)(3) or section 611(d)).

G. *Activity reports.* If a consumer reporting agency provides "activity reports" on all customers who have open-end accounts with a credit grantor, it must make certain that the credit grantor always notifies the agency when accounts are closed and paid in full, to avoid furnishing reports on former customers or other customers for whom the credit grantor lacks a permissible purpose. (See also discussion in section 604(3)(A), item 1, *supra*.)

3. *Reasonable Procedures to Assure Maximum Possible Accuracy.*

A. *General.* The section does not require error free consumer reports. If a consumer reporting agency accurately transcribes, stores and communicates consumer information received from a source that it reasonably believes to be reputable, and which is credible on its face, the agency does not violate this section simply by reporting an item of information that turns out to be inaccurate. However, when a consumer reporting agency learns or should reasonably be aware of errors in its reports that may indicate systematic problems (by virtue of information from consumers, report users, from periodic review of its reporting system, or otherwise) it must review its procedures for assuring accuracy. Examples of errors that would require such review are the issuance of a consumer report pertaining entirely to a consumer other than the one on whom a report was requested, and the issuance of a consumer report containing information on two or more consumers (e.g., information that was mixed in the file) in response to a request for a report on only one of those consumers.

B. *Required steps to improve accuracy.* If the agency's review of its procedures reveals, or the agency should reasonably be aware of, steps it can take to improve the accuracy of its reports at a reasonable cost, it must take any such steps. It should correct inaccuracies that come to its attention. A consumer reporting agency must also adopt reasonable procedures to eliminate systematic errors that it knows about, or should reasonably be aware of, resulting from procedures followed by its sources of information. For example, if a particular credit grantor has often furnished a significant amount of erroneous consumer account information, the agency must require the creditor to revise its procedures to correct whatever problems cause the errors or stop reporting information from that creditor.

C. *Use of automatic data processing equipment.* Consumer reporting agencies that use automatic data processing equipment (particularly for long distance transmission of information) should have reasonable procedures to assure that the data is accurately converted into a machine-readable format and not distorted by machine malfunction or transmission failure. Reasonable security procedures must be adopted to minimize the possibility that computerized consumer information will be stolen or altered by either authorized or unauthorized users of the information system.

D. Reliability of sources. Whether a consumer reporting agency may rely on the accuracy of information from a source depends on the circumstances. This section does not hold a consumer reporting agency responsible where an item of information that it receives from a source that it reasonably believes to be reputable appears credible on its face, and is transcribed, stored and communicated as provided by that source. Requirements are more stringent where the information furnished appears implausible or inconsistent, or where procedures for furnishing it seem likely to result in inaccuracies, or where the consumer reporting agency has had numerous problems regarding information from a particular source.

E. *Undesignated information in credit transactions.* "Undesignated information" means all credit history information in a married (or formerly married) consumer's file, which was not reported to the consumer reporting agency with a designation indicating that the information relates to either the consumer's joint or individual credit experience. The question arises what is meant by reasonable procedures under this section for treatment of credit history in the file of only one (present or former) spouse (usually the husband) that has not been designated by the procedure in Regulation B, 12 CFR 202.10, which implements the Equal Credit Opportunity Act. (This situation exists only for certain credit history file information compiled before June 1, 1077, and certain accounts opened before that date.) A consumer reporting agency may report information solely in the file of spouse A, when spouse B applies for a separate extension of credit, only if such information relates to accounts for which spouse B was either a user or was contractually liable, or the report recipient has a permissible purpose for a report on spouse A. A consumer reporting agency may not supply all undesignated information from the file of a consumer's spouse in response to a request for a report on the consumer, because some or all of that information may not relate to both spouses. Consumer reporting agencies must honor without charge the request of a married or formerly married individual that undesignated information (that appears only in the files of the individual's present or former spouse) be segregated-*i.e.*, placed in a separate file that is accessible under that individual's name. This procedure insures greater accuracy and protection of the privacy of spouses than does the automatic reporting of undesignated information.

F. *Reporting of credit obligation—*

(1) *Past due accounts.* A consumer reporting agency must employ reasonable procedures to keep its file current on past due accounts (e.g., by requiring its creditors to notify the credit bureau when a previously past due account has been paid or discharged in bankruptcy), but its failure to show such activity in particular instances, despite the maintenance of reasonable procedures to keep files current, does not violate this section. For example, a consumer reporting agency that reports accurately in 1985 that as of 1983 the consumer owed a retail store money, without mentioning that the consumer eventually paid the debt, does not violate this section if it was not informed by the store or the consumer of the later payment.

(2) *Significant, verified information.* A consumer reporting agency must report significant, verified information it possesses about an item. For instance, a consumer reporting agency may continue to report a paid account that was previously delinquent, but should also report that the account has been paid. Similarly, a consumer reporting agency may include delinquencies on debts discharged in bankruptcy in consumer reports, but must accurately note the status of the debt (e.g., discharged, voluntarily repaid). Finally, if a reported bankruptcy has been dismissed, that fact should be reported.

(3) *Guarantor obligations.* Personal guarantees for obligations incurred by others (including a corporation) may be included in a consumer report on the individual who is the guarantor. The report should accurately reflect the individual's involvement (e.g., as guarantor of the corporate debt).

4. *Effect of Criminal Sanctions*. Notwithstanding the fact that section 619 provides criminal sanctions against persons who knowingly and willfully obtain information on a consumer from a consumer reporting agency under false pretenses, a consumer reporting agency must follow reasonable procedures to limit the furnishing of reports to those with permissible purposes.

5. *Disclosure of Credit Denial*. When reporting that a consumer was denied a benefit (such as credit), a consumer reporting agency need not report the reasons for the denial.

6. *Content of Report*. A consumer report need not be tailored to the user's needs. It may contain any information that is complete, accurate, and not obsolete on the consumer who is the subject of the report. A consumer report may include an account that was discharged in bankruptcy (as well as the bankruptcy itself), as long as it reports a zero balance due to reflect the fact that the consumer is no longer liable for the discharged debt. A consumer report may include a list of recipients of reports on the consumer who is the subject of the report.

7. *Completeness of Reports*. Consumer reporting agencies are not required to include all existing derogatory or favorable information about a consumer in their reports. (See, however, discussion in section 611, item 14, *infra*, concerning conveying consumer dispute statements.) However, a consumer reporting agency may not mislead its subscribers as to the completeness of its reports by deleting nonderogatory information and not disclosing its policy of making such deletions.

8. *User Notice of Adverse Action Based on a Consumer Report*. A consumer reporting agency need not require users of its consumer reports to provide any notice to consumers against whom adverse action is taken based on a consumer report. The FCRA imposes such notice requirements directly on users, under the circumstances set out in section 615.

Section 608—Disclosures to Governmental Agencies

1. *Permissible Purpose Necessary for Additional Information*. A consumer reporting agency may furnish limited identifying information concerning a consumer to a governmental agency (e.g., an agency seeking a fugitive from justice) even if that agency does not have a "permissible purpose" under section 604 to receive a consumer report. However, a governmental agency must have a permissible purpose in order to obtain information beyond what is authorized by this section.

2. *Entities Covered by Section*. The term "governmental agency" includes federal, state, county and municipal agencies, and grand juries. Only governmental agencies may obtain disclosures of identifying information under this section.

Section 609—Disclosures to Consumers

1. *Relation to Other Sections*. This section states what consumer reporting agencies must disclose to consumers, upon request and proper

identification. Section 610 sets forth the conditions under which those disclosures must be made, and section 612 sets forth the circumstances under which consumer reporting agencies may charge for making such disclosures. The term "file" as used in section 609(a)(1) is defined in section 603(g). The term "investigative consumer report," which is used in section 609(a)(2), is defined in section 603(e). The term "medical information," which is used in section 609(a)(1), is defined in section 603(i).

2. *Proper Identification.* A consumer reporting agency must take reasonable steps to verify the identity of an individual seeking disclosure under this section.

3. *Manner of "Proper Identification."* If a consumer provides sufficient identifying information, the consumer reporting agency cannot insist that the consumer execute a "request for interview" form, or provide the items listed on it, as a prerequisite to disclosure. However, the agency may use a form to identify consumers requesting disclosure if it does not use the form to inhibit disclosure, or to obtain any waiver of the consumers' rights. A consumer reporting agency may provide disclosure by telephone without a written request, if the consumer is properly identified, but may insist on a written request before providing such disclosure.

4. *Power of Attorney.* A consumer reporting agency may disclose a consumer's file to a third party authorized by the consumer's written power of attorney to obtain the disclosure, if the third party presents adequate identification and fulfills other applicable conditions of disclosure. However, the agency may also disclose the information directly to the consumer.

5. *Nature of Disclosure Required.* A consumer reporting agency must disclose the nature and substance of all items in the consumer's file, no matter how or where they are stored (e.g., in other offices of the consumer reporting agency). The consumer reporting agency must have personnel trained to explain to the consumer any information furnished in accordance with the Act. Particularly when the file includes coded information that would be meaningless to the consumer, the agency's personnel must assist the consumer to understand the disclosures. Any summary must not mischaracterize the nature of any item of information in the file. The consumer reporting agency is not required to provide a copy of the file, or any other written disclosure, or to read the file verbatim to the consumer or to permit the consumer to examine any information in its files. A consumer reporting agency may choose to usually comply with the FCRA in writing, by providing a copy of the file to the consumer or otherwise.

6. *Medical Information.* Medical information includes information obtained with the consumer's consent from physicians and medical facilities, but does not include comments on a consumer's health by non-medical personnel. A consumer reporting agency is not required to disclose medical information in its files to consumers, but may do so. Alternatively, a consumer reporting agency may inform consumers that there is medical information in the files concerning them and supply the name of the doctor

or other source of the information. Consumer reporting agencies may also disclose such information to a physician of the consumer's choice, upon the consumer's written instructions pursuant to section 604(2).

7. *Ancillary Information.* A consumer reporting agency is not required to disclose information consisting of an audit trail of changes it makes in the consumer's file, billing records, or the contents of a consumer relations folder, if the information is not from consumer reports and will not be used in preparing future consumer reports. Such data is not included in the term "information in the files" which must be disclosed to the consumer pursuant to this section. A consumer reporting agency must disclose claims report information only if it has appeared in consumer reports.

8. *Information on Other Consumers.* The consumer has no right to information in the consumer reporting agency's files on other individuals, because the disclosure must be limited to information "on the consumer." However, all information in the files of the consumer making the request must be disclosed, including information about another individual that relates to the consumer (e.g., concerning that individual's dealings with the subject of the consumer report).

9. *Disclosure of Sources of Information.* Consumer reporting agencies must disclose the sources of information, except for sources of information acquired solely for use in preparing an investigative consumer report and actually used for no other purpose. When it has used information from another consumer reporting agency, the other agency should be reported as a source.

10. *Disclosure of Recipients of Consumer Reports.* Consumer reporting agencies must maintain records of recipients of prior consumer reports sufficient to enable them to meet the FCRA's requirements that they disclose the identity of recipients of prior consumer reports. A consumer reporting agency that furnishes a consumer report directly to a report user at the request of another consumer reporting agency must disclose the identity of the user that was the ultimate recipient of the report, not the other agency that acted as an intermediary in procuring the report.

11. *Disclosure of Recipients of Prescreened Lists.* A consumer reporting agency must furnish to a consumer requesting file disclosure the identity of recipients of any prescreened lists that contained the consumer's name when submitted to creditors (or other users) by the consumer reporting agency.

12. *Risk Scores.* A consumer reporting agency is not required to disclose a risk score (or other numerical evaluation, however named) that is provided to the agency's client (based on an analysis of data on the consumer) but not retained by the agency. Such a score is not information "in (the agency's) files at the time of the request" by the consumer for file disclosure.

Section 610—Conditions of Disclosure

1. *Time of Disclosure.* A consumer reporting agency must make disclosures during normal business hours, upon reasonable notice. However, the consumer reporting agency may waive reasonable notice, and the consumer may agree to disclosure outside of normal business hours. A consumer reporting agency may make in-person disclosure to consumers who have made appointments ahead of other consumers, because the disclosures are only required to be made "on reasonable notice."

2. *Extra Conditions Prohibited.* A consumer reporting agency may not add conditions not set out in the FCRA as a prerequisite to the required disclosure.

3. *Manner of Disclosure.* A consumer reporting agency may, with the consumer's actual or implied consent, meet its disclosure obligations by mail, in lieu of the in-person or telephone disclosures specified in the statute.

4. *Disclosure in the Presence of Third Parties.* When the consumer requests disclosure in a third party's presence, the consumer reporting agency may require that a consumer sign an authorization before such disclosure is made. The consumer may choose the third party to accompany him or her for the disclosure.

5. *Expense of Telephone Calls.* A consumer reporting agency is not required to pay the telephone charge for a telephone interview with a consumer obtaining disclosure.

6. *Qualified Defamation Privilege.* The privilege extended by subsection 610(e) does not apply to an action brought by a consumer if the action is based on information not disclosed pursuant to sections 609, 610 or 615. A disclosure to a consumer's representative (e.g., based on the consumer's power of attorney) constitutes "information disclosed pursuant to section 609" and is thus covered by this privilege.

Section 611—Procedure in Case of Disputed Accuracy

1. *Relation to Other Sections.* This section sets forth procedures consumer reporting agencies must follow if a consumer conveys a dispute of the completeness or accuracy of any item of information in the consumer's file to the consumer reporting agency. Section 609 provides for disclosures by consumer reporting agencies to consumers, and section 610 sets forth conditions of disclosure. Section 612 permits a consumer reporting agency to impose charges for certain disclosures, including the furnishing of certain information to recipients of prior reports, as provided by section 611(d).

2. *Proper Reinvestigation.* A consumer reporting agency conducting a reinvestigation must make a good faith effort to determine the accuracy of the disputed item or items. At a minimum, it must check with the original sources or other reliable sources of the disputed information and inform them of the nature of the consumer's dispute. In reinvestigating and

attempting to verify a disputed credit transaction, a consumer reporting agency may rely on the accuracy of a creditor's ledger sheets and need not require the creditor to produce documentation such as the actual signed sales slips. Depending on the nature of the dispute, reinvestigation and verification may require more than asking the original source of the disputed information the same question and receiving the same answer. If the original source is contacted for reinvestigation, the consumer reporting agency should at least explain to the source that the original statement has been disputed, state the consumer's position, and then ask whether the source would confirm the information, qualify it, or accept the consumer's explanation.

3. *Complaint of Insufficient File, or Lack of File.* The FCRA does not require a consumer reporting agency to add new items of information to its file. A consumer reporting agency is not required to create new files on consumers for whom it has no file, nor is it required to add new lines of information about new accounts not reflected in an existing file, because the section permits the consumer to dispute only the completeness or accuracy of particular items of information in the file. If a consumer reporting agency chooses to add lines of information at the consumer's request, it may charge a fee for doing so.

4. *Explanation of Extenuating Circumstances.* A consumer reporting agency has no duty to reinvestigate, or take any other action under this section, if a consumer merely provides a reason for a failure to pay a debt (e.g., sudden illness or layoff), and does not challenge the accuracy or completeness of the item of information in the file relating to a debt. Most creditors are aware that a variety of circumstances may render consumers unable to repay credit obligations. though a consumer reporting agency is not required to accept a consumer dispute statement that does not challenge the accuracy or completeness of an item in the consumer's file, it may accept such a statement and may charge a fee for doing so.

5. *Reinvestigation of a Debt.* A consumer reporting agency must reinvestigate if a consumer conveys to it a dispute concerning the validity or status of a debt, such as whether the debt was owed by the consumer, or whether the debt had subsequently been paid. For example, if a consumer alleges that a judgment reflected in the file as unpaid has been satisfied, or notifies a consumer reporting agency that a past due obligation reflected in the file as unpaid was subsequently paid, the consumer reporting agency must reinvestigate the matter. If a file reflects a debt discharged in bankruptcy without reflecting subsequent reaffirmation and payment of that debt, a consumer may require that the item be reinvestigated.

6. *Status of a Debt.* The consumer reporting agency must, upon reinvestigation, "record the current status" of the disputed item. This requires inclusion of any information relating to a change in status of an ongoing matter (e.g., that a credit account had been closed, that a debt shown as past due had subsequently been paid or discharged in bankrupt-

cy, or that a debt shown as discharged in bankruptcy was later reaffirmed and/or paid).

7. *Dispute Conveyed to Party Other Than the Consumer Reporting Agency.* A consumer reporting agency is required to take action under this section only if the consumer directly communicates a dispute to it. It is not required to respond to a dispute of information that the consumer merely conveys to others (e.g., to a source of information). (But see, however, discussion in section 607, item 3–A, of consumer reporting agencies' duties to correct errors that come to their attention.)

8. *Dispute Conveyed to the Consumer Reporting Agency by a Party Other Than the Consumer.* A consumer reporting agency need not reinvestigate a dispute about a consumer's file raised by any third party, because the obligation under the section arises only where an "item of information in his file is disputed by the consumer."

9. *Consumer Disclosures and Adverse Action Not Prerequisites to Reinvestigation Duty.* A consumer reporting agency's obligation to reinvestigate disputed items is not contingent upon the consumer's having been denied a benefit or having asserted any rights under the FCRA other than disputing items of information.

10. *Reasonable Period of Time.* A consumer reporting agency is required to reinvestigate and record the current status of disputed information within a reasonable period of time after the consumer conveys the dispute to it. Although consumer reporting agencies are able to reinvestigate most disputes within 30 days, a "reasonable time" for a particular reinvestigation may be shorter or longer depending on the circumstances of the dispute. For example, where the consumer provides documentary evidence (e.g., a certified copy of a court record to show that a judgment has been paid) when submitting the dispute, the creditor may require a shorter time to reinvestigate. On the other hand, where the dispute is more complicated than normal (e.g., the consumer alleges in good faith that a creditor has falsified its report of the consumer's account history because of a personal grudge), the "reasonable time" needed to conduct the reinvestigation may be longer.

11. *Frivolous or Irrelevant.* The mere presence of contradictory information in the file does not provide the consumer reporting agency "reasonable grounds to believe that the dispute by the consumer is frivolous or irrelevant." A consumer reporting agency must assume a consumer's dispute is bona fide, unless there is evidence to the contrary. Such evidence may constitute receipt of letters from consumers disputing all information in their files without providing any allegations concerning the specific items in the files, or of several letters in similar format that indicate that a particular third party (e.g., a "credit repair" operator) is counselling consumers to dispute all items in their files, regardless of whether the information is known to be accurate. The agency is not required to repeat a reinvestigation that it has previously conducted simply because the consumer reiterates a dispute about the same item of information, unless the

consumer provides additional evidence that the item is inaccurate or incomplete, or alleges changed circumstances.

12. *Deletion of Accurate Information That has not Been Disputed.* The consumer reporting agency is not required to delete accurate information that could not be verified upon reinvestigation, if it has not been "disputed by a consumer." For example, if a creditor deletes adverse information from its files with the result that information could not be reverified if disputed, it is still permissible for a consumer reporting agency to report it (subject to the obsolescence provisions of section 605) until it is disputed.

13. *Consumer Dispute Statements on Multiple Items.* A consumer who disputes multiple items of information in his file may submit a one hundred word statement as to each disputed item.

14. *Conveying Dispute Statements to Recipients of Subsequent Reports.* A consumer reporting agency may not merely tell the recipient of a subsequent report containing disputed information that the consumer's statement is on file but will be provided only if requested, because subsection (c) requires the agency to provide either the statement or "a clear and accurate codification or summary thereof."

Section 612—Charges for Certain Disclosures

1. *Irrelevance of Subsequent Grant of Credit or Reason For Denial.* A consumer denied credit because of a consumer report from a consumer reporting agency has the right to a free disclosure from that agency within 30 days of receipt of the section 615(a) notice, even if credit was subsequently granted or the basis of the denial was that the references supplied by the consumer are too few or too new to appear in the credit file.

2. *Charge for Reinvestigation Prohibited.* This section does not permit consumer reporting agencies to charge for making the reinvestigation or following other procedures required by section 611(a)–(c).

3. *Permissible Charges for Services Requested by Consumers.* A consumer reporting agency may charge fees for creating files on consumers at their request, or for other services not required by the FCRA that are requested by consumers.

Section 613—Public Record Information for Employment Purposes

1. *Relation to Other Sections.* A consumer reporting agency that complies with section 613(1) must also follow reasonable procedures to assure maximum possible accuracy, as required by section 607(b).

2. *Alternate Methods of Compliance.* A consumer reporting agency that furnishes public record information for employment purposes must comply with either subsection (1) or (2), but need not comply with both.

3. *Information From Another Consumer Reporting Agency.* If a consumer reporting agency uses information or reports from other consumer reporting agencies in a report for employment purposes, it must comply with this section.

4. *Method of Providing Notice.* A consumer reporting agency may use first class mail to provide the notice required by subsection (1).

5. *Waiver.* The procedures required by this section cannot be waived by the consumer to whom the report relates.

Section 615—Requirements on Users of Consumer Reports

1. *Relation to Other Sections and Regulation B.* Sections 606 and 615 are the only two sections that require users of reports to make disclosures to consumers. Section 606 applies only to users of "investigative consumer reports." Creditors should not confuse compliance with section 615(a), which only requires disclosure of the name and address of the consumer reporting agency, and compliance with the Equal Credit Opportunity Act, 15 U.S.C. 1691 *et seq.* and Regulation B, 12 C.F.R. 202, which require disclosure of the *reasons* for adverse action. Compliance with section 615(a), therefore, does not constitute compliance with Regulation B.

2. *Limited Scope of Requirements.* The section does not require that creditors disclose their credit criteria or standards or that employees furnish copies of personnel files to former employees. The section does not require that the user provide any kind of advance notification to consumers before a consumer report is obtained. (See section 606 regarding notice of investigative consumer reports.)

3. *Method of Disclosure.* The disclosures required by this section need not be made in writing. However, users will have evidence that they have taken reasonable steps to comply with this section if they provide written disclosures and retain copies for at least two years, the applicable statute of limitations for most civil liability actions under the FCRA.

4. *Adverse Action Based on Direct Information.* This section does not require that a user send any notice to a consumer concerning adverse action regarding that consumer that is based neither on information from a consumer reporting agency nor on information from a third party. For example, no disclosures are required concerning adverse action based on information provided by the consumer in an application or based on past experience in direct transactions with the consumer.

5. *Creditors Using "Prescreened" Mailing Lists.* A creditor is not required to provide notices regarding consumer reporting agencies that prepare mailing lists by "prescreening" because they do not involve consumer requests for credit and credit has not been denied to consumers whose names are deleted from a list furnished to the agency for use in this procedure. See discussion of "prescreening," under section 604(3)(A), item 6, *supra.*

6. *Applicability to Users of Motor Vehicle Reports.* An insurer that refuses to issue a policy, or charges a higher than normal premium, based on a motor vehicle report is required to comply with subsection(a).

7. *Securities and Insurance Transactions.* A consumer report user that denies credit to a consumer in connection with a securities transaction

must provide the required notice, because the denial is of "credit * * * for personal purposes," unless the consumer engages in such transactions as a business.

8. *Denial of Employment.* An employer must provide the notice required by subsection (a) to an individual who has applied for employment and has been rejected based on a consumer report. However, an employer is not required to send a notice when it decides not to offer a position to an individual who has not applied for it, because in this case employment is not "denied." (See discussion in section 606, item 4, *supra.*)

9. *Adverse Action Involving Credit.* A creditor must provide the required notice when it denies the consumer's request for credit (including a rejection based on a scoring system, where a credit report received less than the maximum number of points possible and caused the application to receive an insufficient score), denies the consumer's request for increased credit, grants credit in an amount less than the consumer requested, or raises the charge for credit.

10. *Adverse Action Not Involving Credit, Insurance or Employment.* The Act does not require that a report user provide any notice to consumers when taking adverse action not relating to credit, insurance or employment. For example, a landlord who refuses to rent an apartment to a consumer based on credit or other information in a consumer report need not provide the notice. Similarly, a party that uses credit or other information in a consumer report as a basis for refusing to accept payment by check need not comply with this section. Checks have historically been treated as cash items, and thus such refusal does not involve a denial of credit, insurance or employment.

11. *Adverse Action Based on Non-derogatory Adverse Information.* A party taking adverse action concerning credit or insurance or denying employment, "wholly or partly because of information contained in a consumer report," must provide the required notice, even if the information is not derogatory. For example, the user must give the notice if the denial is based wholly or partly on the absence of a file or on the fact that the file contained insufficient references.

12. *Name and Address of the Consumer Reporting Agency.* The "section 615(a)" notice must include the consumer reporting agency's street address, not just a post office box address.

13. *Agency to Be Identified.* The consumer report user should provide the name and address of the consumer reporting agency from which it obtained the consumer report, even if that agency obtained all or part of the report from another agency.

14. *Denial Based Partly on a Consumer Report.* A "section 615(a)" notice must be sent even if the adverse action is based only partly on a consumer report.

15. *Denial of Credit Based on Information From "Third Parties."* Subsection (b) imposes requirements on a creditor when it denies (or

increases the charge for) credit for personal, family or household purposes involving a consumer, based on information from a "third party" source, which means a source *other* than the consumer reporting agency, the creditor's own files, or the consumer's application (e.g., creditor, employer, landlord, or the public record). Where a creditor denies a consumer's application based on information obtained directly from another lender, even if the lender's name was furnished to the creditor by a consumer reporting agency, the creditor must give a "third party" disclosure.

16. *Substance of Required "Third Party" Disclosures.* When the adverse action is communicated to the consumer, the creditor must clearly and accurately disclose to the consumer his or her right to make a written request for the disclosure of the nature of the third party information that led to the adverse action. Upon timely receipt of such a request, however, the creditor need disclose only the nature of the information that led to the adverse action (e.g., history of late rent payments or bad checks); it need not identify the source that provided the information or the criteria that led to the adverse action. A creditor may comply with subsection (b) by providing a statement of the nature of the third party information that led to the denial when it notifies the consumer of the denial. A statement of principal, specific reasons for adverse action based on third party information that is sufficient to comply with the requirements of the Equal Credit Opportunity Act (e.g., "unable to verify employment") is sufficient to constitute disclosure of the "nature of the information" under subsection (b).

Section 619—Obtaining Information Under False Pretense

1. *Relation to Other Sections.* The presence of this provision does not excuse a consumer reporting agency's failure to follow reasonable procedures, as required by section 607(a), to limit the furnishing of consumer reports to the purposes listed under section 604.

Section 621—Administrative Enforcement

1. *General.* The Commission can use its cease-and-desist power and other procedural, investigative and enforcement powers which it has under the FTC Act to secure compliance, irrespective of commerce or any other jurisdictional tests in the FTC Act.

2. *Geographic Coverage.* The Commission's authority encompasses the United States, the District of Columbia, the Commonwealth of Puerto Rico, and all United States territories but does not extend to activities outside those areas.

3. *Status of Commission Commentary and Staff Interpretations.* The FCRA does not give any Federal agency authority to promulgate rules having the force and effect, of statutory provisions. The Commission has issued this Commentary, superseding the eight formal Interpretations of the Act (16 CFR 600.1–600.8), previously issued pursuant to § 1.73 of the Commission's Rules, 16 CFR 1.73. The Commentary does not constitute

substantive rules and does not have the force or effect of statutory provisions. It constitutes guidelines to clarify the Act that are advisory in nature and represent the Commission's views as to what particular provisions of the Act mean. Staff opinion letters constitute staff interpretations of the Act's provisions, but do not have the force or effect of statutory provisions and, as provided in § 1.72 of the Commission's Rules, 16 CFR 1.72, do not bind the Commission.

Section 622—Relation to State Laws

1. *Basic Rule.* State law is pre-empted by the FCRA only when compliance with inconsistent state law would result in violation of the FCRA.

2. *Examples of Statutes that Are Not Pre-empted.* A state law requirement that an employer provide notice to a consumer before ordering a consumer report, or that a consumer reporting agency must provide the consumer with a written copy of his file, would not be pre-empted, because a party that complies with such provisions would not violate the FCRA.

3. *Examples of Statutes that Are Pre-empted.* A state law authorizing grand juries to compel consumer reporting agencies to provide consumer reports, by means of subpoenas signed by a court clerk, is pre-empted by the FCRA's requirement that such reports be furnished only pursuant to an "order of the court" signed by a judge (section 604(1)), or furnished for other purposes not applicable to grand jury subpoenas (section 604(2)–(3)), and by section 607(a). A state statute requiring automatic disclosure of a deletion or dispute statement to every person who has previously received a consumer report containing the disputed information, regardless of whether the consumer designates such persons to receive this disclosure, is pre-empted by section 604 of the FCRA, which permits disclosure only for specified, permissible purposes and by section 607(a), which requires consumer reporting agencies to limit the furnishing of consumer reports to purposes listed under section 604. Absent a specific designation by the consumer, the consumer reporting agency has no reason to believe all past recipients would have a present, permissible purpose to receive the reports.

4. *Statute Providing Access for Enforcement Purposes.* A state "little FCRA" that permits state officials access to a consumer reporting agency's files for the purpose of enforcing that statute just as Federal agencies are permitted access to such files under the FCRA, is not pre-empted by the FCRA.

FTC REGULATIONS UNDER THE FAIR CREDIT REPORTING ACT

Table of Sections

PART 603—DEFINITIONS

§ 603.1 Terms defined in the Fair Credit Reporting Act

Any term used in any part in this subchapter, if defined in the Fair Credit Reporting Act (FCRA) and not otherwise defined in that rule, has the same meaning provided by the FCRA.

§ 603.2 Identity theft

(a) The term "identity theft" means a fraud committed or attempted using the identifying information of another person without authority.

(b) The term "identifying information" means any name or number that may be used, alone or in conjunction with any other information, to identify a specific person, including any—

(1) Name, social security number, date of birth, official State or government issued driver's license or identification number, alien registration number, government passport number, employer or taxpayer identification number;

(2) Unique biometric data, such as fingerprint, voice print, retina or iris image, or other unique physical representation;

(3) Unique electronic identification number, address, or routing code; or

(4) Telecommunication identifying information or access device (as defined in 18 U.S.C. § 1029(e)).

§ 603.3   Identity theft report

(a) The term "identity theft report" means a report—

(1) That alleges identity theft with as much specificity as the consumer can provide;

(2) That is a copy of an official, valid report filed by the consumer with a Federal, State, or local law enforcement agency, including the United States Postal Inspection Service, the filing of which subjects the person filing the report to criminal penalties relating to the filing of false information, if, in fact, the information in the report is false; and

(3) That may include additional information or documentation that an information furnisher or consumer reporting agency reasonably requests for the purpose of determining the validity of the alleged identity theft, provided that the information furnisher or consumer reporting agency:

(i) Makes such request not later than fifteen days after the date of receipt of the copy of the report form identified in paragraph (a)(2) of this section or the request by the consumer for the particular service, whichever shall be the later;

(ii) Makes any supplemental requests for information or documentation and final determination on the acceptance of the identity theft report within another fifteen days after its initial request for information or documentation; and

(iii) Shall have five days to make a final determination on the acceptance of the identity theft report, in the event that the consumer reporting agency or information furnisher receives any such additional information or documentation on the eleventh day or later within the fifteen day period set forth in paragraph (a)(3)(ii) of this section.

(b) Examples of the specificity referenced in paragraph (a)(1) of this section are provided for illustrative purposes only, as follows:

(1) Specific dates relating to the identity theft such as when the loss or theft of personal information occurred or when the fraud(s) using the personal information occurred, and how the consumer discovered or otherwise learned of the theft.

(2) Identification information or any other information about the perpetrator, if known.

(3) Name(s) of information furnisher(s), account numbers, or other relevant account information related to the identity theft.

(4) Any other information known to the consumer about the identity theft.

(c) Examples of when it would or would not be reasonable to request additional information or documentation referenced in paragraph (a)(3) of this section are provided for illustrative purposes only, as follows:

(1) A law enforcement report containing detailed information about the identity theft and the signature, badge number or other identification information of the individual law enforcement official taking the report should be sufficient on its face to support a victim's request. In this case, without an identifiable concern, such as an indication that the report was fraudulent, it would not be reasonable for an information furnisher or consumer reporting agency to request additional information or documentation.

(2) A consumer might provide a law enforcement report similar to the report in paragraph (c)(1) of this section but certain important information such as the consumer's date of birth or Social Security number may be missing because the consumer chose not to provide it. The information furnisher or consumer reporting agency could accept this report, but it would be reasonable to require that the consumer provide the missing information.

(3) A consumer might provide a law enforcement report generated by an automated system with a simple allegation that an identity theft occurred to support a request for a tradeline block or cessation of information furnishing. In such a case, it would be reasonable for an information furnisher or consumer reporting agency to ask that the consumer fill out and have notarized the Commission's ID Theft Affidavit or a similar form and provide some form of identification documentation.

(4) A consumer might provide a law enforcement report generated by an automated system with a simple allegation that an identity theft occurred to support a request for an extended fraud alert. In this case, it would not be reasonable for a consumer reporting agency to require additional documentation or information, such as a notarized affidavit.

PART 681—IDENTITY THEFT RULES

§ 681.1 Duties of users of consumer reports regarding address discrepancies

(a) *Scope.* This section applies to users of consumer reports that are subject to administrative enforcement of the FCRA by the Federal Trade Commission pursuant to [FCRA § 621,] 15 U.S.C. § 1681s(a)(1) (users).

(b) *Definition.* For purposes of this section, a *notice of address discrepancy* means a notice sent to a user by a consumer reporting agency pursuant to [FCRA § 605(h)(1),] 15 U.S.C. § 1681c(h)(1), that informs the user of a substantial difference between the address for the consumer that the user provided to request the consumer report and the address(es) in the agency's file for the consumer.

(c) *Reasonable belief.*—(1) *Requirement to form a reasonable belief.* A user must develop and implement reasonable policies and procedures designed to enable the user to form a reasonable belief that a consumer report relates to the consumer about whom it has requested the report, when the user receives a notice of address discrepancy.

(2) *Examples of reasonable policies and procedures.* (i) Comparing the information in the consumer report provided by the consumer reporting agency with information the user:

(A) Obtains and uses to verify the consumer's identity in accordance with the requirements of the Customer Information Program (CIP) rules implementing 31 U.S.C. § 5318(*l*) (31 CFR 103.121);

(B) Maintains in its own records, such as applications, change of address notifications, other customer account records, or retained CIP documentation; or

(C) Obtains from third-party sources; or

(ii) Verifying the information in the consumer report provided by the consumer reporting agency with the consumer.

(d) *Consumer's address.*—(1) *Requirement to furnish consumer's address to a consumer reporting agency.* A user must develop and implement reasonable policies and procedures for furnishing an address for the consumer that the user has reasonably confirmed is accurate to the consumer reporting agency from whom it received the notice of address discrepancy when the user:

(i) Can form a reasonable belief that the consumer report relates to the consumer about whom the user requested the report;

(ii) Establishes a continuing relationship with the consumer; and

(iii) Regularly and in the ordinary course of business furnishes information to the consumer reporting agency from which the notice of address discrepancy relating to the consumer was obtained.

(2) *Examples of confirmation methods.* The user may reasonably confirm an address is accurate by:

(i) Verifying the address with the consumer about whom it has requested the report;

(ii) Reviewing its own records to verify the address of the consumer;

(iii) Verifying the address through third-party sources; or

(iv) Using other reasonable means.

(3) *Timing.* The policies and procedures developed in accordance with paragraph (d)(1) of this section must provide that the user will furnish the consumer's address that the user has reasonably confirmed is accurate to the consumer reporting agency as part of the information it regularly furnishes for the reporting period in which it establishes a relationship with the consumer.

§ 681.2 Duties regarding the detection, prevention, and mitigation of identity theft

(a) *Scope.* This section applies to financial institutions and creditors that are subject to administrative enforcement of the FCRA by the Federal Trade Commission pursuant to [FCRA § 621(a)(1),] 15 U.S.C. § 1681s(a)(1).

(b) *Definitions.* For purposes of this section, and appendix A, the following definitions apply:

(1) *Account* means a continuing relationship established by a person with a financial institution or creditor to obtain a product or service for personal, family, household or business purposes. Account includes:

(i) An extension of credit, such as the purchase of property or services involving a deferred payment; and

(ii) A deposit account.

(2) The term *board of directors* includes:

(i) In the case of a branch or agency of a foreign bank, the managing official in charge of the branch or agency; and

(ii) In the case of any other creditor that does not have a board of directors, a designated employee at the level of senior management.

(3) *Covered account* means:

(i) An account that a financial institution or creditor offers or maintains, primarily for personal, family, or household purposes, that involves or is designed to permit multiple payments or transactions, such as a credit card account, mortgage loan, automobile loan, margin account, cell phone account, utility account, checking account, or savings account; and

(ii) Any other account that the financial institution or creditor offers or maintains for which there is a reasonably foreseeable risk to customers or to the safety and soundness of the financial institution or creditor from identity theft, including financial, operational, compliance, reputation, or litigation risks.

(4) *Credit* has the same meaning as in [FCRA § 603(r)(5),] 15 U.S.C. § 1681a(r)(5).

(5) *Creditor* has the same meaning as [FCRA § 603(r)(5),] in 15 U.S.C. § 1681a(r)(5), and includes lenders such as banks, finance

companies, automobile dealers, mortgage brokers, utility companies, and telecommunications companies.

(6) *Customer* means a person that has a covered account with a financial institution or creditor.

(7) *Financial institution* has the same meaning as in [FCRA § 603(t),] 15 U.S.C. § 1681a(t).

(8) *Identity theft* has the same meaning as in 16 CFR 603.2(a).

(9) *Red Flag* means a pattern, practice, or specific activity that indicates the possible existence of identity theft.

(10) *Service provider* means a person that provides a service directly to the financial institution or creditor.

(c) *Periodic Identification of Covered Accounts.* Each financial institution or creditor must periodically determine whether it offers or maintains covered accounts. As a part of this determination, a financial institution or creditor must conduct a risk assessment to determine whether it offers or maintains covered accounts described in paragraph (b)(3)(ii) of this section, taking into consideration:

(1) The methods it provides to open its accounts;

(2) The methods it provides to access its accounts; and

(3) Its previous experiences with identity theft.

(d) *Establishment of an Identity Theft Prevention Program.*—(1) *Program requirement.* Each financial institution or creditor that offers or maintains one or more covered accounts must develop and implement a written Identity Theft Prevention Program (Program) that is designed to detect, prevent, and mitigate identity theft in connection with the opening of a covered account or any existing covered account. The Program must be appropriate to the size and complexity of the financial institution or creditor and the nature and scope of its activities.

(2) *Elements of the Program.* The Program must include reasonable policies and procedures to:

(i) Identify relevant Red Flags for the covered accounts that the financial institution or creditor offers or maintains, and incorporate those Red Flags into its Program;

(ii) Detect Red Flags that have been incorporated into the Program of the financial institution or creditor;

(iii) Respond appropriately to any Red Flags that are detected pursuant to paragraph (d)(2)(ii) of this section to prevent and mitigate identity theft; and

(iv) Ensure the Program (including the Red Flags determined to be relevant) is updated periodically, to reflect changes in risks to customers and to the safety and soundness of the financial institution or creditor from identity theft.

(e) *Administration of the Program.* Each financial institution or creditor that is required to implement a Program must provide for the continued administration of the Program and must:

(1) Obtain approval of the initial written Program from either its board of directors or an appropriate committee of the board of directors;

(2) Involve the board of directors, an appropriate committee thereof, or a designated employee at the level of senior management in the oversight, development, implementation and administration of the Program;

(3) Train staff, as necessary, to effectively implement the Program; and

(4) Exercise appropriate and effective oversight of service provider arrangements.

(f) *Guidelines.* Each financial institution or creditor that is required to implement a Program must consider the guidelines in appendix A of this part and include in its Program those guidelines that are appropriate.

§ 681.3 Duties of card issuers regarding changes of address

(a) *Scope.* This section applies to a person described in § 681.2(a) that issues a debit or credit card (card issuer).

(b) *Definitions.* For purposes of this section:

(1) *Cardholder* means a consumer who has been issued a credit or debit card.

(2) *Clear and conspicuous* means reasonably understandable and designed to call attention to the nature and significance of the information presented.

(c) *Address validation requirements.* A card issuer must establish and implement reasonable policies and procedures to assess the validity of a change of address if it receives notification of a change of address for a consumer's debit or credit card account and, within a short period of time afterwards (during at least the first 30 days after it receives such notification), the card issuer receives a request for an additional or replacement card for the same account. Under these circumstances, the card issuer may not issue an additional or replacement card, until, in accordance with its reasonable policies and procedures and for the purpose of assessing the validity of the change of address, the card issuer:

(1)(i) Notifies the cardholder of the request:

(A) At the cardholder's former address; or

(B) By any other means of communication that the card issuer and the cardholder have previously agreed to use; and

(ii) Provides to the cardholder a reasonable means of promptly reporting incorrect address changes; or

(2) Otherwise assesses the validity of the change of address in accordance with the policies and procedures the card issuer has established pursuant to § 681.2 of this part.

(d) *Alternative timing of address validation.* A card issuer may satisfy the requirements of paragraph (c) of this section if it validates an address pursuant to the methods in paragraph (c)(1) or (c)(2) of this section when it receives an address change notification, before it receives a request for an additional or replacement card.

(e) *Form of notice.* Any written or electronic notice that the card issuer provides under this paragraph must be clear and conspicuous and provided separately from its regular correspondence with the cardholder.

FEDERAL RESERVE BOARD, REGULATION B, EQUAL CREDIT OPPORTUNITY

12 C.F.R. Part 202

Table of Sections

---

§ 202.1 Authority, scope and purpose

(a) *Authority and scope.* This regulation is issued by the Board of Governors of the Federal Reserve System pursuant to title VII (Equal Credit Opportunity Act) of the Consumer Credit Protection Act, as amended (15 U.S.C. 1601 *et seq.*). Except as otherwise provided herein, this regulation applies to all persons who are creditors, as defined in § 202.2(1). Information collection requirements contained in this regulation have been approved by the Office of Management and Budget under the provisions of 44 U.S.C. 3501 *et seq.* and have been assigned OMB No. 7100–0201.

(b) *Purpose.* The purpose of this regulation is to promote the availability of credit to all creditworthy applicants without regard to race, color, religion, national origin, sex, marital status, or age (provided the applicant has the capacity to contract); to the fact that all or part of the applicant's income derives from a public assistance program; or to the fact that the applicant has in good faith exercised any right under the Consumer Credit Protection Act. The regulation prohibits creditor practices that discrimi-

595

nate on the basis of any of these factors. The regulation also requires creditors to notify applicants of action taken on their applications; to report credit history in the names of both spouses on an account; to retain records of credit applications; to collect information about the applicant's race and other personal characteristics in applications for certain dwelling-related loans; and to provide applicants with copies of appraisal reports used in connection with credit transactions.

§ 202.2 Definitions

For the purposes of this regulation, unless the context indicates otherwise, the following definitions apply.

(a) *Account* means an extension of credit. When employed in relation to an account, the word use refers only to open-end credit.

(b) *Act* means the Equal Credit Opportunity Act (title VII of the Consumer Credit Protection Act).

(c) *Adverse action.* (1) The term means:

(i) A refusal to grant credit in substantially the amount or on substantially the terms requested in an application unless the creditor makes a counteroffer (to grant credit in a different amount or on other terms) and the applicant uses or expressly accepts the credit offered;

(ii) A termination of an account or an unfavorable change in the terms of an account that does not affect all or substantially all of a class of the creditor's accounts; or

(iii) A refusal to increase the amount of credit available to an applicant who has made an application for an increase.

(2) The term does not include:

(i) A change in the terms of an account expressly agreed to by an applicant.

(ii) Any action or forbearance relating to an account taken in connection with inactivity, default, or delinquency as to that account;

(iii) A refusal or failure to authorize an account transaction at point of sale or loan, except when the refusal is a termination or an unfavorable change in the terms of an account that does not affect all or substantially all of a class of the creditor's accounts, or when the refusal is a denial of an application for an increase in the amount of credit available under the account;

(iv) A refusal to extend credit because applicable law prohibits the creditor from extending the credit requested; or

(v) A refusal to extend credit because the creditor does not offer the type of credit or credit plan requested.

(3) An action that falls within the definition of both paragraphs (c)(1) and (c)(2) of this section is governed by paragraph (c)(2) of this section.

(d) *Age* refers only to the age of natural persons and means the number of fully elapsed years from the date of an applicant's birth.

(e) *Applicant* means any person who requests or who has received an extension of credit from a creditor, and includes any person who is or may become contractually liable regarding an extension of credit. For purposes of § 202.7(d), the term includes guarantors, sureties, endorsers, and similar parties.

(f) *Application* means an oral or written request for an extension of credit that is made in accordance with procedures used by a creditor for the type of credit requested. The term application does not include the use of an account or line of credit to obtain an amount of credit that is within a previously established credit limit. A *completed application* means an application in connection with which a creditor has received all the information that the creditor regularly obtains and considers in evaluating applications for the amount and type of credit requested (including, but not limited to, credit reports, any additional information requested from the applicant, and any approvals or reports by governmental agencies or other persons that are necessary to guarantee, insure, or provide security for the credit or collateral). The creditor shall exercise reasonable diligence in obtaining such information.

(g) *Business credit* refers to extensions of credit primarily for business or commercial (including agricultural) purposes, but excluding extensions of credit of the types described in § 202.3(a)–(d).

(h) *Consumer credit* means credit extended to a natural person primarily for personal, family, or household purposes.

(*i*) *Contractually liable* means expressly obligated to repay all debts arising on an account by reason of an agreement to that effect.

(j) *Credit* means the right granted by a creditor to an applicant to defer payment of a debt, incur debt and defer its payment, or purchase property or services and defer payment therefor.

(k) *Credit card* means any card, plate, coupon book, or other single credit device that may be used from time to time to obtain money, property, or services on credit.

(*l*) *Creditor* means a person who, in the ordinary course of business, regularly participates in a credit decision, including setting the terms of the credit. The term creditor includes a creditor's assignee, transferee, or subrogee who so participates. For purposes of § 202.4(a) and (b), the term creditor also includes a person who, in the ordinary course of business, regularly refers applicants or prospective applicants to creditors, or selects or offers to select creditors to whom requests for credit may be made. A person is not a creditor regarding any violation of the Act or this regulation committed by another creditor unless the person knew or had reasonable notice of the act, policy, or practice that constituted the violation before becoming involved in the credit transaction. The term does not include a person whose only participation in a credit transaction involves honoring a credit card.

(m) *Credit transaction* means every aspect of an applicant's dealings with a creditor regarding an application for credit or an existing extension of credit (including, but not limited to, information requirements; investigation procedures; standards of creditworthiness; terms of credit; furnishing of credit information; revocation, alteration, or termination of credit; and collection procedures).

(n) *Discriminate against an applicant* means to treat an applicant less favorably than other applicants.

(o) *Elderly* means age 62 or older.

(p) *Empirically derived and other credit scoring systems*—(1) *A credit scoring system* is a system that evaluates an applicant's creditworthiness mechanically, based on key attributes of the applicant and aspects of the transaction, and that determines, alone or in conjunction with an evaluation of additional information about the applicant, whether an applicant is deemed creditworthy. To qualify as an *empirically derived, demonstrably and statistically sound, credit scoring system,* the system must be:

(i) Based on data that are derived from an empirical comparison of sample groups or the population of creditworthy and noncreditworthy applicants who applied for credit within a reasonable preceding period of time;

(ii) Developed for the purpose of evaluating the creditworthiness of applicants with respect to the legitimate business interests of the creditor utilizing the system (including, but not limited to, minimizing bad debt losses and operating expenses in accordance with the creditor's business judgment);

(iii) Developed and validated using accepted statistical principles and methodology; and

(iv) Periodically revalidated by the use of appropriate statistical principles and methodology and adjusted as necessary to maintain predictive ability.

(2) A creditor may use an empirically derived, demonstrably and statistically sound, credit scoring system obtained from another person or may obtain credit experience from which to develop such a system. Any such system must satisfy the criteria set forth in paragraph (p)(1)(i) through (iv) of this section; if the creditor is unable during the development process to validate the system based on its own credit experience in accordance with paragraph (p)(1) of this section, the system must be validated when sufficient credit experience becomes available. A system that fails this validity test is no longer an empirically derived, demonstrably and statistically sound, credit scoring system for that creditor.

(q) *Extend credit* and *extension of credit* mean the granting of credit in any form (including, but not limited to, credit granted in addition to any existing credit or credit limit; credit granted pursuant to an open-end credit plan; the refinancing or other renewal of credit, including the issuance of a new credit card in place of an expiring credit card or in substitution for an existing credit card; the consolidation of two or more obligations; or the continuance of existing credit without any special effort to collect at or after maturity).

(r) *Good faith* means honesty in fact in the conduct or transaction.

(s) *Inadvertent error* means a mechanical, electronic, or clerical error that a creditor demonstrates was not intentional and occurred notwithstanding the maintenance of procedures reasonably adapted to avoid such errors.

(t) *Judgmental system of evaluating applicants* means any system for evaluating the creditworthiness of an applicant other than an empirically derived, demonstrably and statistically sound, credit scoring system.

(u) *Marital status* means the state of being unmarried, married, or separated, as defined by applicable state law. The term "unmarried" includes persons who are single, divorced, or widowed.

(v) *Negative factor or value,* in relation to the age of elderly applicants, means utilizing a factor, value, or weight that is less favorable regarding elderly applicants than the creditor's experience warrants or is less favorable than the factor, value, or weight assigned to the class of applicants that are not classified as elderly and are most favored by a creditor on the basis of age.

(w) *Open-end credit* means credit extended under a plan in which a creditor may permit an applicant to make purchases or obtain loans from time to time directly from the creditor or indirectly by use of a credit card, check, or other device.

(x) *Person* means a natural person, corporation, government or governmental subdivision or agency, trust, estate, partnership, cooperative, or association.

(y) *Pertinent element of creditworthiness,* in relation to a judgmental system of evaluating applicants, means any information about applicants that a creditor obtains and considers and that has a demonstrable relationship to a determination of creditworthiness.

(z) *Prohibited basis* means race, color, religion, national origin, sex, marital status, or age (provided that the applicant has the capacity to enter into a binding contract); the fact that all or part of the applicant's income derives from any public assistance program; or the fact that the applicant has in good faith exercised any right under the Consumer Credit Protection Act or any state law upon which an exemption has been granted by the Board.

(aa) *State* means any state, the District of Columbia, the Commonwealth of Puerto Rico, or any territory or possession of the United States.

§ 202.3   Limited exceptions for certain classes of transactions.

(a) *Public utilities credit*—(1) *Definition.* Public utilities credit refers to extensions of credit that involve public utility services provided through pipe, wire, or other connected facilities, or radio or similar transmission (including extensions of such facilities), if the charges for service, delayed payment, and any discount for prompt payment are filed with or regulated by a government unit.

(2) *Exceptions.* The following provisions of this regulation do not apply to public utilities credit:

(i) Section 202.5(d)(1) concerning information about marital status; and

(ii) Section 202.12(b) relating to record retention.

(b) *Securities credit*—(1) *Definition.* Securities credit refers to extensions of credit subject to regulation under section 7 of the Securities Exchange Act of 1934 or extensions of credit by a broker or dealer subject to regulation as a broker or dealer under the Securities Exchange Act of 1934.

(2) *Exceptions.* The following provisions of this regulation do not apply to securities credit:

(i) Section 202.5(b) concerning information about the sex of an applicant;

(ii) Section 202.5(c) concerning information about a spouse or former spouse;

(iii) Section 202.5(d)(1) concerning information about marital status;

(iv) Section 202.7(b) relating to designation of name to the extent necessary to comply with rules regarding an account in which a broker or dealer has an interest, or rules regarding the aggregation of accounts of spouses to determine controlling interests, beneficial interests, beneficial ownership, or purchase limitations and restrictions;

(v) Section 202.7(c) relating to action concerning open-end accounts, to the extent the action taken is on the basis of a change of name or marital status;

(vi) Section 202.7(d) relating to the signature of a spouse or other person;

(vii) Section 202.10 relating to furnishing of credit information; and

(viii) Section 202.12(b) relating to record retention.

(c) *Incidental credit*—(1) *Definition.* Incidental credit refers to extensions of consumer credit other than the types described in paragraphs (a) and (b) of this section:

(i) That are not made pursuant to the terms of a credit card account;

(ii) That are not subject to a finance charge (as defined in Regulation Z, 12 CFR 226.4); and

(iii) That are not payable by agreement in more than four installments.

(2) *Exceptions.* The following provisions of this regulation do not apply to incidental credit:

(i) Section 202.5(b) concerning information about the sex of an applicant, but only to the extent necessary for medical records or similar purposes;

(ii) Section 202.5(c) concerning information about a spouse or former spouse;

(iii) Section 202.5(d)(1) concerning information about marital status;

(iv) Section 202.5(d)(2) concerning information about income derived from alimony, child support, or separate maintenance payments;

(v) Section 202.7(d) relating to the signature of a spouse or other person;

(vi) Section 202.9 relating to notifications;

(vii) Section 202.10 relating to furnishing of credit information; and

(viii) Section 202.12(b) relating to record retention.

(d) *Government credit*—(1) *Definition.* Government credit refers to extensions of credit made to governments or governmental subdivisions, agencies, or instrumentalities.

(2) *Applicability of regulation.* Except for § 202.4(a), the general rule against discrimination on a prohibited basis, the requirements of this regulation do not apply to government credit.

§ 202.4   General rules

(a) *Discrimination.* A creditor shall not discriminate against an applicant on a prohibited basis regarding any aspect of a credit transaction.

(b) *Discouragement.* A creditor shall not make any oral or written statement, in advertising or otherwise, to applicants or prospective applicants that would discourage on a prohibited basis a reasonable person from making or pursuing an application.

(c) *Written applications.* A creditor shall take written applications for the dwelling-related types of credit covered by § 202.13(a).

(d) *Form of disclosures*—(1) *General rule.* A creditor that provides in writing any disclosures or information required by this regulation must provide the disclosures in a clear and conspicuous manner and, except for the disclosures required by §§ 202.5 and 202.13, in a form the applicant may retain.

(2) *Disclosures in electronic form.* The disclosures required by this part that are required to be given in writing may be provided to the applicant in electronic form, subject to compliance with the consumer consent and other applicable provisions of the Electronic Signatures in Global and National Commerce Act (E–Sign Act) (15 U.S.C. 7001 *et seq.*). Where the disclosures under §§ 202.5(b)(1), 202.5(b)(2), 202.5(d)(1), 202.5(d)(2), 202.13, and 202.14(a)(2)(i) accompany an application accessed by the applicant in electronic form, these disclosures may be provided to the applicant in electronic form on or with the application form, without regard to the consumer consent or other provisions of the E–Sign Act.

(e) *Foreign-language disclosures.* Disclosures may be made in languages other than English, provided they are available in English upon request.

§ 202.5   Rules concerning requests for information

(a) *General rules*—(1) *Requests for information.* Except as provided in paragraphs (b) through (d) of this section, a creditor may request any information in connection with a credit transaction.[1]

(2) *Required collection of information.* Notwithstanding paragraphs (b) through (d) of this section, a creditor shall request information for monitoring purposes as required by § 202.13 for credit secured by the applicant's dwelling. In addition, a creditor may obtain information required by a regulation, order, or agreement issued by, or entered into with, a court or an enforcement agency (including the Attorney General of the United States or a similar state official) to monitor or enforce compliance with the Act, this regulation, or other federal or state statutes or regulations.

(3) *Special-purpose credit.* A creditor may obtain information that is otherwise restricted to determine eligibility for a special purpose credit program, as provided in § 202.8(b), (c), and (d).

(b) *Limitation on information about race, color, religion, national origin, or sex.* A creditor shall not inquire about the race, color, religion, national origin, or sex of an applicant or any other person in connection with a credit transaction, except as provided in paragraphs (b)(1) and (b)(2) of this section.

(1) *Self-test.* A creditor may inquire about the race, color, religion, national origin, or sex of an applicant or any other person in connection with a credit transaction for the purpose of conducting a self-test that meets the requirements of § 202.15. A creditor that makes such an inquiry

---

1. This paragraph does not limit or abrogate any Federal or State law regarding privacy, privileged information, credit reporting limitations, or similar restrictions on obtainable information.

shall disclose orally or in writing, at the time the information is requested, that:

(i) The applicant will not be required to provide the information;

(ii) The creditor is requesting the information to monitor its compliance with the federal Equal Credit Opportunity Act;

(iii) Federal law prohibits the creditor from discriminating on the basis of this information, or on the basis of an applicant's decision not to furnish the information; and

(iv) If applicable, certain information will be collected based on visual observation or surname if not provided by the applicant or other person.

(2) *Sex.* An applicant may be requested to designate a title on an application form (such as Ms., Miss, Mr., or Mrs.) if the form discloses that the designation of a title is optional. An application form shall otherwise use only terms that are neutral as to sex.

(c) *Information about a spouse or former spouse—*(1) *General rule.* Except as permitted in this paragraph, a creditor may not request any information concerning the spouse or former spouse of an applicant.

(2) *Permissible inquiries.* A creditor may request any information concerning an applicant's spouse (or former spouse under paragraph (c)(2)(v) of this section) that may be requested about the applicant if:

(i) The spouse will be permitted to use the account;

(ii) The spouse will be contractually liable on the account;

(iii) The applicant is relying on the spouse's income as a basis for repayment of the credit requested;

(iv) The applicant resides in a community property state or is relying on property located in such a state as a basis for repayment of the credit requested; or

(v) The applicant is relying on alimony, child support, or separate maintenance payments from a spouse or former spouse as a basis for repayment of the credit requested.

(3) *Other accounts of the applicant.* A creditor may request that an applicant list any account on which the applicant is contractually liable and to provide the name and address of the person in whose name the account is held. A creditor may also ask an applicant to list the names in which the applicant has previously received credit.

(d) *Other limitations on information requests—*(1) *Marital status.* If an applicant applies for individual unsecured credit, a creditor shall not inquire about the applicant's marital status unless the applicant resides in a community property state or is relying on property located in such a state as a basis for repayment of the credit requested. If an application is for other than individual unsecured credit, a creditor may inquire about the applicant's marital status, but shall use only the terms *married, unmar-*

ried, and *separated.* A creditor may explain that the category *unmarried* includes single, divorced, and widowed persons.

(2) *Disclosure about income from alimony, child support, or separate maintenance.* A creditor shall not inquire whether income stated in an application is derived from alimony, child support, or separate maintenance payments unless the creditor discloses to the applicant that such income need not be revealed if the applicant does not want the creditor to consider it in determining the applicant's creditworthiness.

(3) *Childbearing, childrearing.* A creditor shall not inquire about birth control practices, intentions concerning the bearing or rearing of children, or capability to bear children. A creditor may inquire about the number and ages of an applicant's dependents or about dependent-related financial obligations or expenditures, provided such information is requested without regard to sex, marital status, or any other prohibited basis.

(e) *Permanent residency and immigration status.* A creditor may inquire about the permanent residency and immigration status of an applicant or any other person in connection with a credit transaction.

§ 202.6   Rules concerning evaluation of applications

(a) *General rule concerning use of information.* Except as otherwise provided in the Act and this regulation, a creditor may consider any information obtained, so long as the information is not used to discriminate against an applicant on a prohibited basis.[2]

(b) *Specific rules concerning use of information*—(1) Except as provided in the Act and this regulation, a creditor shall not take a prohibited basis into account in any system of evaluating the creditworthiness of applicants.

(2) *Age, receipt of public assistance.* (i) Except as permitted in this paragraph, a creditor shall not take into account an applicant's age (provided that the applicant has the capacity to enter into a binding contract) or whether an applicant's income derives from any public assistance program.

(ii) In an empirically derived, demonstrably and statistically sound, credit scoring system, a creditor may use an applicant's age as a predictive variable, provided that the age of an elderly applicant is not assigned a negative factor or value.

(iii) In a judgmental system of evaluating creditworthiness, a creditor may consider an applicant's age or whether an applicant's income derives from any public assistance program only for the purpose of determining a pertinent element of creditworthiness.

2. The legislative history of the Act indicates that the Congress intended an "effects test" concept, as outlined in the employment field by the Supreme Court in the cases of *Griggs* v. *Duke Power Co.,* 401 U.S. 424 (1971), and *Albemarle Paper Co.* v. *Moody,* 422 U.S. 405 (1975), to be applicable to a creditor's determination of creditworthiness.

(iv) In any system of evaluating creditworthiness, a creditor may consider the age of an elderly applicant when such age is used to favor the elderly applicant in extending credit.

(3) *Childbearing, childrearing.* In evaluating creditworthiness, a creditor shall not make assumptions or use aggregate statistics relating to the likelihood that any category of persons will bear or rear children or will, for that reason, receive diminished or interrupted income in the future.

(4) *Telephone listing.* A creditor shall not take into account whether there is a telephone listing in the name of an applicant for consumer credit but may take into account whether there is a telephone in the applicant's residence.

(5) *Income.* A creditor shall not discount or exclude from consideration the income of an applicant or the spouse of an applicant because of a prohibited basis or because the income is derived from part-time employment or is an annuity, pension, or other retirement benefit; a creditor may consider the amount and probable continuance of any income in evaluating an applicant's creditworthiness. When an applicant relies on alimony, child support, or separate maintenance payments in applying for credit, the creditor shall consider such payments as income to the extent that they are likely to be consistently made.

(6) *Credit history.* To the extent that a creditor considers credit history in evaluating the creditworthiness of similarly qualified applicants for a similar type and amount of credit, in evaluating an applicant's creditworthiness a creditor shall consider:

(i) The credit history, when available, of accounts designated as accounts that the applicant and the applicant's spouse are permitted to use or for which both are contractually liable;

(ii) On the applicant's request, any information the applicant may present that tends to indicate the credit history being considered by the creditor does not accurately reflect the applicant's creditworthiness; and

(iii) On the applicant's request, the credit history, when available, of any account reported in the name of the applicant's spouse or former spouse that the applicant can demonstrate accurately reflects the applicant's creditworthiness.

(7) *Immigration status.* A creditor may consider the applicant's immigration status or status as a permanent resident of the United States, and any additional information that may be necessary to ascertain the creditor's rights and remedies regarding repayment.

(8) *Marital status.* Except as otherwise permitted or required by law, a creditor shall evaluate married and unmarried applicants by the same standards; and in evaluating joint applicants, a creditor shall not treat applicants differently based on the existence, absence, or likelihood of a marital relationship between the parties.

(9) *Race, color, religion, national origin, sex.* Except as otherwise permitted or required by law, a creditor shall not consider race, color, religion, national origin, or sex (or an applicant's or other person's decision not to provide the information) in any aspect of a credit transaction.

(c) *State property laws.* A creditor's consideration or application of state property laws directly or indirectly affecting creditworthiness does not constitute unlawful discrimination for the purposes of the Act or this regulation.

§ 202.7   Rules concerning extensions of credit

(a) *Individual accounts.* A creditor shall not refuse to grant an individual account to a creditworthy applicant on the basis of sex, marital status, or any other prohibited basis.

(b) *Designation of name.* A creditor shall not refuse to allow an applicant to open or maintain an account in a birth-given first name and a surname that is the applicant's birth-given surname, the spouse's surname, or a combined surname.

(c) *Action concerning existing open-end accounts*—(1) *Limitations.* In the absence of evidence of the applicant's inability or unwillingness to repay, a creditor shall not take any of the following actions regarding an applicant who is contractually liable on an existing open-end account on the basis of the applicant's reaching a certain age or retiring or on the basis of a change in the applicant's name or marital status:

(i) Require a reapplication, except as provided in paragraph (c)(2) of this section;

(ii) Change the terms of the account; or

(iii) Terminate the account.

(2) *Requiring reapplication.* A creditor may require a reapplication for an open-end account on the basis of a change in the marital status of an applicant who is contractually liable if the credit granted was based in whole or in part on income of the applicant's spouse and if information available to the creditor indicates that the applicant's income may not support the amount of credit currently available.

(d) *Signature of spouse or other person*—(1) *Rule for qualified applicant.* Except as provided in this paragraph, a creditor shall not require the signature of an applicant's spouse or other person, other than a joint applicant, on any credit instrument if the applicant qualifies under the creditor's standards of creditworthiness for the amount and terms of the credit requested. A creditor shall not deem the submission of a joint financial statement or other evidence of jointly held assets as an application for joint credit.

(2) *Unsecured credit.* If an applicant requests unsecured credit and relies in part upon property that the applicant owns jointly with another person to satisfy the creditor's standards of creditworthiness, the creditor

may require the signature of the other person only on the instrument(s) necessary, or reasonably believed by the creditor to be necessary, under the law of the state in which the property is located, to enable the creditor to reach the property being relied upon in the event of the death or default of the applicant.

(3) *Unsecured credit—community property states.* If a married applicant requests unsecured credit and resides in a community property state, or if the applicant is relying on property located in such a state, a creditor may require the signature of the spouse on any instrument necessary, or reasonably believed by the creditor to be necessary, under applicable state law to make the community property available to satisfy the debt in the event of default if:

(i) Applicable state law denies the applicant power to manage or control sufficient community property to qualify for the credit requested under the creditor's standards of creditworthiness; and

(ii) The applicant does not have sufficient separate property to qualify for the credit requested without regard to community property.

(4) *Secured credit.* If an applicant requests secured credit, a creditor may require the signature of the applicant's spouse or other person on any instrument necessary, or reasonably believed by the creditor to be necessary, under applicable state law to make the property being offered as security available to satisfy the debt in the event of default, for example, an instrument to create a valid lien, pass clear title, waive inchoate rights, or assign earnings.

(5) *Additional parties.* If, under a creditor's standards of creditworthiness, the personal liability of an additional party is necessary to support the credit requested, a creditor may request a cosigner, guarantor, endorser, or similar party. The applicant's spouse may serve as an additional party, but the creditor shall not require that the spouse be the additional party.

(6) *Rights of additional parties.* A creditor shall not impose requirements upon an additional party that the creditor is prohibited from imposing upon an applicant under this section.

(e) *Insurance.* A creditor shall not refuse to extend credit and shall not terminate an account because credit life, health, accident, disability, or other credit-related insurance is not available on the basis of the applicant's age.

§ 202.8   Special purpose credit programs

(a) *Standards for programs.* Subject to the provisions of paragraph (b) of this section, the Act and this regulation permit a creditor to extend special purpose credit to applicants who meet eligibility requirements under the following types of credit programs:

(1) Any credit assistance program expressly authorized by federal or state law for the benefit of an economically disadvantaged class of persons;

(2) Any credit assistance program offered by a not-for-profit organization, as defined under section 501(c) of the Internal Revenue Code of 1954, as amended, for the benefit of its members or for the benefit of an economically disadvantaged class of persons; or

(3) Any special purpose credit program offered by a for-profit organization, or in which such an organization participates to meet special social needs, if:

(i) The program is established and administered pursuant to a written plan that identifies the class of persons that the program is designed to benefit and sets forth the procedures and standards for extending credit pursuant to the program; and

(ii) The program is established and administered to extend credit to a class of persons who, under the organization's customary standards of creditworthiness, probably would not receive such credit or would receive it on less favorable terms than are ordinarily available to other applicants applying to the organization for a similar type and amount of credit.

(b) *Rules in other sections*—(1) *General applicability.* All the provisions of this regulation apply to each of the special purpose credit programs described in paragraph (a) of this section except as modified by this section.

(2) *Common characteristics.* A program described in paragraph (a)(2) or (a)(3) of this section qualifies as a special purpose credit program only if it was established and is administered so as not to discriminate against an applicant on any prohibited basis; however, all program participants may be required to share one or more common characteristics (for example, race, national origin, or sex) so long as the program was not established and is not administered with the purpose of evading the requirements of the Act or this regulation.

(c) *Special rule concerning requests and use of information.* If participants in a special purpose credit program described in paragraph (a) of this section are required to possess one or more common characteristics (for example, race, national origin, or sex) and if the program otherwise satisfies the requirements of paragraph (a) of this section, a creditor may request and consider information regarding the common characteristic(s) in determining the applicant's eligibility for the program.

(d) *Special rule in the case of financial need.* If financial need is one of the criteria under a special purpose credit program described in paragraph (a) of this section, the creditor may request and consider, in determining an applicant's eligibility for the program, information regarding the applicant's marital status; alimony, child support, and separate maintenance income; and the spouse's financial resources. In addition, a creditor may obtain the signature of an applicant's spouse or other person on an application or credit instrument relating to a special purpose credit program if the signature is required by federal or state law.

§ 202.9   Notifications

(a) *Notification of action taken, ECOA notice, and statement of specific reasons*—(1) *When notification is required.* A creditor shall notify an applicant of action taken within:

(i) 30 days after receiving a completed application concerning the creditor's approval of, counteroffer to, or adverse action on the application;

(ii) 30 days after taking adverse action on an incomplete application, unless notice is provided in accordance with paragraph (c) of this section;

(iii) 30 days after taking adverse action on an existing account; or

(iv) 90 days after notifying the applicant of a counteroffer if the applicant does not expressly accept or use the credit offered.

(2) *Content of notification when adverse action is taken.* A notification given to an applicant when adverse action is taken shall be in writing and shall contain a statement of the action taken; the name and address of the creditor; a statement of the provisions of § 701(a) of the Act; the name and address of the federal agency that administers compliance with respect to the creditor; and either:

(i) A statement of specific reasons for the action taken; or

(ii) A disclosure of the applicant's right to a statement of specific reasons within 30 days, if the statement is requested within 60 days of the creditor's notification. The disclosure shall include the name, address, and telephone number of the person or office from which the statement of reasons can be obtained. If the creditor chooses to provide the reasons orally, the creditor shall also disclose the applicant's right to have them confirmed in writing within 30 days of receiving the applicant's written request for confirmation.

(3) *Notification to business credit applicants.* For business credit, a creditor shall comply with the notification requirements of this section in the following manner:

(i) With regard to a business that had gross revenues of $1 million or less in its preceding fiscal year (other than an extension of trade credit, credit incident to a factoring agreement, or other similar types of business credit), a creditor shall comply with paragraphs (a)(1) and (2) of this section, except that:

(A) The statement of the action taken may be given orally or in writing, when adverse action is taken;

(B) Disclosure of an applicant's right to a statement of reasons may be given at the time of application, instead of when adverse action is taken, provided the disclosure contains the information required by paragraph (a)(2)(ii) of this section and the ECOA notice specified in paragraph (b)(1) of this section;

(C) For an application made entirely by telephone, a creditor satisfies the requirements of paragraph (a)(3)(i) of this section by an oral statement of the action taken and of the applicant's right to a statement of reasons for adverse action.

(ii) With regard to a business that had gross revenues in excess of $1 million in its preceding fiscal year or an extension of trade credit, credit incident to a factoring agreement, or other similar types of business credit, a creditor shall:

(A) Notify the applicant, within a reasonable time, orally or in writing, of the action taken; and

(B) Provide a written statement of the reasons for adverse action and the ECOA notice specified in paragraph (b)(1) of this section if the applicant makes a written request for the reasons within 60 days of the creditor's notification.

(b) *Form of ECOA notice and statement of specific reasons*—(1) *ECOA notice.* To satisfy the disclosure requirements of paragraph (a)(2) of this section regarding section 701(a) of the Act, the creditor shall provide a notice that is substantially similar to the following: The federal Equal Credit Opportunity Act prohibits creditors from discriminating against credit applicants on the basis of race, color, religion, national origin, sex, marital status, age (provided the applicant has the capacity to enter into a binding contract); because all or part of the applicant's income derives from any public assistance program; or because the applicant has in good faith exercised any right under the Consumer Credit Protection Act. The federal agency that administers compliance with this law concerning this creditor is [name and address as specified by the appropriate agency listed in appendix A of this regulation].

(2) *Statement of specific reasons.* The statement of reasons for adverse action required by paragraph (a)(2)(i) of this section must be specific and indicate the principal reason(s) for the adverse action. Statements that the adverse action was based on the creditor's internal standards or policies or that the applicant, joint applicant, or similar party failed to achieve a qualifying score on the creditor's credit scoring system are insufficient.

(c) *Incomplete applications*—(1) *Notice alternatives.* Within 30 days after receiving an application that is incomplete regarding matters that an applicant can complete, the creditor shall notify the applicant either:

(i) Of action taken, in accordance with paragraph (a) of this section; or

(ii) Of the incompleteness, in accordance with paragraph (c)(2) of this section.

(2) *Notice of incompleteness.* If additional information is needed from an applicant, the creditor shall send a written notice to the applicant specifying the information needed, designating a reasonable period of time for the applicant to provide the information, and informing the applicant that failure to provide the information requested will result in no further consideration being given to the application. The creditor shall have no further obligation under this section if the applicant fails to respond within the designated time period. If the applicant supplies the requested information within the designated time period, the creditor shall take action on the application and notify the applicant in accordance with paragraph (a) of this section.

(3) *Oral request for information.* At its option, a creditor may inform the applicant orally of the need for additional information. If the application remains incomplete the creditor shall send a notice in accordance with paragraph (c)(1) of this section.

(d) *Oral notifications by small-volume creditors.* In the case of a creditor that did not receive more than 150 applications during the preceding calendar year, the requirements of this section (including statements of specific reasons) are satisfied by oral notifications.

(e) *Withdrawal of approved application.* When an applicant submits an application and the parties contemplate that the applicant will inquire about its status, if the creditor approves the application and the applicant has not inquired within 30 days after applying, the creditor may treat the application as withdrawn and need not comply with paragraph (a)(1) of this section.

(f) *Multiple applicants.* When an application involves more than one applicant, notification need only be given to one of them but must be given to the primary applicant where one is readily apparent.

(g) *Applications submitted through a third party.* When an application is made on behalf of an applicant to more than one creditor and the applicant expressly accepts or uses credit offered by one of the creditors, notification of action taken by any of the other creditors is not required. If no credit is offered or if the applicant does not expressly accept or use the credit offered, each creditor taking adverse action must comply with this section, directly or through a third party. A notice given by a third party shall disclose the identity of each creditor on whose behalf the notice is given.

§ 202.10   Furnishing of credit information

(a) *Designation of accounts.* A creditor that furnishes credit information shall designate:

(1) Any new account to reflect the participation of both spouses if the applicant's spouse is permitted to use or is contractually liable on the account (other than as a guarantor, surety, endorser, or similar party); and

(2) Any existing account to reflect such participation, within 90 days after receiving a written request to do so from one of the spouses.

(b) *Routine reports to consumer reporting agency.* If a creditor furnishes credit information to a consumer reporting agency concerning an account designated to reflect the participation of both spouses, the creditor shall furnish the information in a manner that will enable the agency to provide access to the information in the name of each spouse.

(c) *Reporting in response to inquiry.* If a creditor furnishes credit information in response to an inquiry, concerning an account designated to reflect the participation of both spouses, the creditor shall furnish the information in the name of the spouse about whom the information is requested.

§ 202.11   Relation to state law

(a) *Inconsistent state laws.* Except as otherwise provided in this section, this regulation alters, affects, or preempts only those state laws that are inconsistent with the Act and this regulation and then only to the extent of the inconsistency. A state law is not inconsistent if it is more protective of an applicant.

(b) *Preempted provisions of state law.* (1) A state law is deemed to be inconsistent with the requirements of the Act and this regulation and less protective of an applicant within the meaning of section 705(f) of the Act to the extent that the law:

(i) Requires or permits a practice or act prohibited by the Act or this regulation;

(ii) Prohibits the individual extension of consumer credit to both parties to a marriage if each spouse individually and voluntarily applies for such credit;

(iii) Prohibits inquiries or collection of data required to comply with the Act or this regulation;

(iv) Prohibits asking about or considering age in an empirically derived, demonstrably and statistically sound, credit scoring system to determine a pertinent element of creditworthiness, or to favor an elderly applicant; or

(v) Prohibits inquiries necessary to establish or administer a special purpose credit program as defined by § 202.8.

(2) A creditor, state, or other interested party may request that the Board determine whether a state law is inconsistent with the requirements of the Act and this regulation.

(c) *Laws on finance charges, loan ceilings.* If married applicants voluntarily apply for and obtain individual accounts with the same creditor, the accounts shall not be aggregated or otherwise combined for purposes of determining permissible finance charges or loan ceilings under any federal or state law. Permissible loan ceiling laws shall be construed to permit each spouse to become individually liable up to the amount of the loan ceilings, less the amount for which the applicant is jointly liable.

(d) *State and federal laws not affected.* This section does not alter or annul any provision of state property laws, laws relating to the disposition of decedents' estates, or federal or state banking regulations directed only toward insuring the solvency of financial institutions.

(e) *Exemption for state-regulated transactions—*(1) *Applications.* A state may apply to the Board for an exemption from the requirements of the Act and this regulation for any class of credit transactions within the state. The Board will grant such an exemption if the Board determines that:

(i) The class of credit transactions is subject to state law requirements substantially similar to those of the Act and this regulation or that applicants are afforded greater protection under state law; and

(ii) There is adequate provision for state enforcement.

(2) *Liability and enforcement.* (i) No exemption will extend to the civil liability provisions of section 706 of the Act or the administrative enforcement provisions of section 704 of the Act.

(ii) After an exemption has been granted, the requirements of the applicable state law (except for additional requirements not imposed by federal law) will constitute the requirements of the Act and this regulation.

§ 202.12   Record retention

(a) *Retention of prohibited information.* A creditor may retain in its files information that is prohibited by the Act or this regulation for use in evaluating applications, without violating the Act or this regulation, if the information was obtained:

(1) From any source prior to March 23, 1977;

(2) From consumer reporting agencies, an applicant, or others without the specific request of the creditor; or

(3) As required to monitor compliance with the Act and this regulation or other federal or state statutes or regulations.

(b) *Preservation of records—*(1) *Applications.* For 25 months (12 months for business credit, except as provided in paragraph (b)(5) of this section) after the date that a creditor notifies an applicant of action taken on an application or of incompleteness, the creditor shall retain in original form or a copy thereof:

(i) Any application that it receives, any information required to be obtained concerning characteristics of the applicant to monitor compliance with the Act and this regulation or other similar law, and any other written or recorded information used in evaluating the application and not returned to the applicant at the applicant's request;

(ii) A copy of the following documents if furnished to the applicant in written form (or, if furnished orally, any notation or memorandum made by the creditor):

(A) The notification of action taken; and

(B) The statement of specific reasons for adverse action; and

(iii) Any written statement submitted by the applicant alleging a violation of the Act or this regulation.

(2) *Existing accounts.* For 25 months (12 months for business credit, except as provided in paragraph (b)(5) of this section) after the date that a creditor notifies an applicant of adverse action regarding an existing account, the creditor shall retain as to that account, in original form or a copy thereof:

(i) Any written or recorded information concerning the adverse action; and

(ii) Any written statement submitted by the applicant alleging a violation of the Act or this regulation.

(3) *Other applications.* For 25 months (12 months for business credit, except as provided in paragraph (b)(5) of this section) after the date that a creditor receives an application for which the creditor is not required to comply with the notification requirements of § 202.9, the creditor shall retain all written or recorded information in its possession concerning the applicant, including any notation of action taken.

(4) *Enforcement proceedings and investigations.* A creditor shall retain the information beyond 25 months (12 months for business credit, except as provided in paragraph (b)(5) of this section) if the creditor has actual notice that it is under investigation or is subject to an enforcement proceeding for an alleged violation of the Act or this regulation, by the Attorney General of the United States or by an enforcement agency charged with monitoring that creditor's compliance with the Act and this regulation, or if it has been served with notice of an action filed pursuant to section 706 of the Act and § 202.17 of this regulation. The creditor shall retain the information until final disposition of the matter, unless an earlier time is allowed by order of the agency or court.

(5) *Special rule for certain business credit applications.* With regard to a business that had gross revenues in excess of $1 million in its preceding fiscal year, or an extension of trade credit, credit incident to a factoring agreement, or other similar types of business credit, the creditor shall retain records for at least 60 days after notifying the applicant of the action taken. If within that time period the applicant requests in writing the reasons for adverse action or that records be retained, the creditor shall retain records for 12 months.

(6) *Self-tests.* For 25 months after a self-test (as defined in § 202.15) has been completed, the creditor shall retain all written or recorded information about the self-test. A creditor shall retain information beyond

25 months if it has actual notice that it is under investigation or is subject to an enforcement proceeding for an alleged violation, or if it has been served with notice of a civil action. In such cases, the creditor shall retain the information until final disposition of the matter, unless an earlier time is allowed by the appropriate agency or court order.

(7) *Prescreened solicitations.* For 25 months after the date on which an offer of credit is made to potential customers (12 months for business credit, except as provided in paragraph (b)(5) of this section), the creditor shall retain in original form or a copy thereof:

(i) The text of any prescreened solicitation;

(ii) The list of criteria the creditor used to select potential recipients of the solicitation; and

(iii) Any correspondence related to complaints (formal or informal) about the solicitation.

§ 202.13   Information for monitoring purposes

(a) *Information to be requested.* (1) A creditor that receives an application for credit primarily for the purchase or refinancing of a dwelling occupied or to be occupied by the applicant as a principal residence, where the extension of credit will be secured by the dwelling, shall request as part of the application the following information regarding the applicant(s):

(i) Ethnicity, using the categories Hispanic or Latino, and not Hispanic or Latino; and race, using the categories American Indian or Alaska Native, Asian, Black or African American, Native Hawaiian or Other Pacific Islander, and White;

(ii) Sex;

(iii) Marital status, using the categories married, unmarried, and separated; and

(iv) Age.

(2) *Dwelling* means a residential structure that contains one to four units, whether or not that structure is attached to real property. The term includes, but is not limited to, an individual condominium or cooperative unit and a mobile or other manufactured home.

(b) *Obtaining information.* Questions regarding ethnicity, race, sex, marital status, and age may be listed, at the creditor's option, on the application form or on a separate form that refers to the application. The applicant(s) shall be asked but not required to supply the requested information. If the applicant(s) chooses not to provide the information or any part of it, that fact shall be noted on the form. The creditor shall then also note on the form, to the extent possible, the ethnicity, race, and sex of the applicant(s) on the basis of visual observation or surname.

(c) *Disclosure to applicant(s).* The creditor shall inform the applicant(s) that the information regarding ethnicity, race, sex, marital status, and age is being requested by the federal government for the purpose of monitoring compliance with federal statutes that prohibit creditors from discriminating against applicants on those bases. The creditor shall also inform the applicant(s) that if the applicant(s) chooses not to provide the information, the creditor is required to note the ethnicity, race and sex on the basis of visual observation or surname.

(d) *Substitute monitoring program.* A monitoring program required by an agency charged with administrative enforcement under section 704 of the Act may be substituted for the requirements contained in paragraphs (a), (b), and (c) of this section.

§ 202.14   Rules on providing appraisal reports

(a) *Providing appraisals.* A creditor shall provide a copy of an appraisal report used in connection with an application for credit that is to be secured by a lien on a dwelling. A creditor shall comply with either paragraph (a)(1) or (a)(2) of this section.

(1) *Routine delivery.* A creditor may routinely provide a copy of an appraisal report to an applicant (whether credit is granted or denied or the application is withdrawn).

(2) *Upon request.* A creditor that does not routinely provide appraisal reports shall provide a copy upon an applicant's written request.

(i) *Notice.* A creditor that provides appraisal reports only upon request shall notify an applicant in writing of the right to receive a copy of an appraisal report. The notice may be given at any time during the application process but no later than when the creditor provides notice of action taken under § 202.9 of this regulation. The notice shall specify that the applicant's request must be in writing, give the creditor's mailing address, and state the time for making the request as provided in paragraph (a)(2)(ii) of this section.

(ii) *Delivery.* A creditor shall mail or deliver a copy of the appraisal report promptly (generally within 30 days) after the creditor receives an applicant's request, receives the report, or receives reimbursement from the applicant for the report, whichever is last to occur. A creditor need not provide a copy when the applicant's request is received more than 90 days after the creditor has provided notice of action taken on the application under § 202.9 of this regulation or 90 days after the application is withdrawn.

(b) *Credit unions.* A creditor that is subject to the regulations of the National Credit Union Administration on making copies of appraisal reports available is not subject to this section.

(c) *Definitions.* For purposes of paragraph (a) of this section, the term dwelling means a residential structure that contains one to four units whether or not that structure is attached to real property. The term includes, but is not limited to, an individual condominium or cooperative unit, and a mobile or other manufactured home. The term *appraisal report* means the document(s) relied upon by a creditor in evaluating the value of the dwelling.

§ 202.15   Incentives for self-testing and self-correction

(a) *General rules*—(1) *Voluntary self-testing and correction.* The report or results of a self-test that a creditor voluntarily conducts (or authorizes) are privileged as provided in this section. Data collection required by law or by any governmental authority is not a voluntary self-test.

(2) *Corrective action required.* The privilege in this section applies only if the creditor has taken or is taking appropriate corrective action.

(3) *Other privileges.* The privilege created by this section does not preclude the assertion of any other privilege that may also apply.

(b) *Self-test defined*—(1) *Definition.* A self-test is any program, practice, or study that:

(i) Is designed and used specifically to determine the extent or effectiveness of a creditor's compliance with the Act or this regulation; and

(ii) Creates data or factual information that is not available and cannot be derived from loan or application files or other records related to credit transactions.

(2) *Types of information privileged.* The privilege under this section applies to the report or results of the self-test, data or factual information created by the self-test, and any analysis, opinions, and conclusions pertaining to the self-test report or results. The privilege covers workpapers or draft documents as well as final documents.

(3) *Types of information not privileged.* The privilege under this section does not apply to:

(i) Information about whether a creditor conducted a self-test, the methodology used or the scope of the self-test, the time period covered by the self-test, or the dates it was conducted; or

(ii) Loan and application files or other business records related to credit transactions, and information derived from such files and records, even if the information has been aggregated, summarized, or reorganized to facilitate analysis.

(c) *Appropriate corrective action*—(1) *General requirement.* For the privilege in this section to apply, appropriate corrective action is required when the self-test shows that it is more likely than not that a violation occurred, even though no violation has been formally adjudicated.

(2) *Determining the scope of appropriate corrective action.* A creditor must take corrective action that is reasonably likely to remedy the cause and effect of a likely violation by:

(i) Identifying the policies or practices that are the likely cause of the violation; and

(ii) Assessing the extent and scope of any violation.

(3) *Types of relief.* Appropriate corrective action may include both prospective and remedial relief, except that to establish a privilege under this section:

(i) A creditor is not required to provide remedial relief to a tester used in a self-test;

(ii) A creditor is only required to provide remedial relief to an applicant identified by the self-test as one whose rights were more likely than not violated; and

(iii) A creditor is not required to provide remedial relief to a particular applicant if the statute of limitations applicable to the violation expired before the creditor obtained the results of the self-test or the applicant is otherwise ineligible for such relief.

(4) *No admission of violation.* Taking corrective action is not an admission that a violation occurred.

(d) *Scope of privilege*—(1) *General rule.* The report or results of a privileged self-test may not be obtained or used:

(i) By a government agency in any examination or investigation relating to compliance with the Act or this regulation; or

(ii) By a government agency or an applicant (including a prospective applicant who alleges a violation of § 202.4(b)) in any proceeding or civil action in which a violation of the Act or this regulation is alleged.

(2) *Loss of privilege.* The report or results of a self-test are not privileged under paragraph (d)(1) of this section if the creditor or a person with lawful access to the report or results:

(i) Voluntarily discloses any part of the report or results, or any other information privileged under this section, to an applicant or government agency or to the public;

(ii) Discloses any part of the report or results, or any other information privileged under this section, as a defense to charges that the creditor has violated the Act or regulation; or

(iii) Fails or is unable to produce written or recorded information about the self-test that is required to be retained under § 202.12(b)(6) when the information is needed to determine whether the privilege applies. This paragraph does not limit any other penalty or remedy that may be available for a violation of § 202.12.

(3) *Limited use of privileged information.* Notwithstanding paragraph (d)(1) of this section, the self-test report or results and any other information privileged under this section may be obtained and used by an applicant or government agency solely to determine a penalty or remedy after a violation of the Act or this regulation has been adjudicated or admitted. Disclosures for this limited purpose may be used only for the particular

proceeding in which the adjudication or admission was made. Information disclosed under this paragraph (d)(3) remains privileged under paragraph (d)(1) of this section.

§ 202.16   Enforcement, penalties and liabilities

(a) *Administrative enforcement.* (1) As set forth more fully in section 704 of the Act, administrative enforcement of the Act and this regulation regarding certain creditors is assigned to the Comptroller of the Currency, Board of Governors of the Federal Reserve System, Board of Directors of the Federal Deposit Insurance Corporation, Office of Thrift Supervision, National Credit Union Administration, Surface Transportation Board, Secretary of Agriculture, Farm Credit Administration, Securities and Exchange Commission, Small Business Administration, and Secretary of Transportation.

(2) Except to the extent that administrative enforcement is specifically assigned to other authorities, compliance with the requirements imposed under the Act and this regulation is enforced by the Federal Trade Commission.

(b) *Penalties and liabilities.* (1) Sections 702(g) and 706(a) and (b) of the Act provide that any creditor that fails to comply with a requirement imposed by the Act or this regulation is subject to civil liability for actual and punitive damages in individual or class actions. Pursuant to sections 702(g) and 704(b), (c), and (d) of the Act, violations of the Act or this regulation also constitute violations of other federal laws. Liability for punitive damages can apply only to nongovernmental entities and is limited to $10,000 in individual actions and the lesser of $500,000 or 1 percent of the creditor's net worth in class actions. Section 706(c) provides for equitable and declaratory relief and section 706(d) authorizes the awarding of costs and reasonable attorney's fees to an aggrieved applicant in a successful action.

(2) As provided in section 706(f), a civil action under the Act or this regulation may be brought in the appropriate United States district court without regard to the amount in controversy or in any other court of competent jurisdiction within two years after the date of the occurrence of the violation, or within one year after the commencement of an administrative enforcement proceeding or of a civil action brought by the Attorney General of the United States within two years after the alleged violation.

(3) If an agency responsible for administrative enforcement is unable to obtain compliance with the Act or this regulation, it may refer the matter to the Attorney General of the United States. If the Board, the Comptroller of the Currency, the Federal Deposit Insurance Corporation, the Office of Thrift Supervision, or the National Credit Union Administration has reason to believe that one or more creditors have engaged in a pattern or practice of discouraging or denying applications in violation of the Act or this regulation, the agency shall refer the matter to the Attorney General. If the agency has reason to believe that one or more creditors

violated section 701(a) of the Act, the agency may refer a matter to the Attorney General.

(4) On referral, or whenever the Attorney General has reason to believe that one or more creditors have engaged in a pattern or practice in violation of the Act or this regulation, the Attorney General may bring a civil action for such relief as may be appropriate, including actual and punitive damages and injunctive relief.

(5) If the Board, the Comptroller of the Currency, the Federal Deposit Insurance Corporation, the Office of Thrift Supervision, or the National Credit Union Administration has reason to believe (as a result of a consumer complaint, a consumer compliance examination, or some other basis) that a violation of the Act or this regulation has occurred which is also a violation of the Fair Housing Act, and the matter is not referred to the Attorney General, the agency shall:

(i) Notify the Secretary of Housing and Urban Development; and

(ii) Inform the applicant that the Secretary of Housing and Urban Development has been notified and that remedies may be available under the Fair Housing Act.

(c) *Failure of compliance.* A creditor's failure to comply with §§ 202.6(b)(6), 202.9, 202.10, 202.12 or 202.13 is not a violation if it results from an inadvertent error. On discovering an error under §§ 202.9 and 202.10, the creditor shall correct it as soon as possible. If a creditor inadvertently obtains the monitoring information regarding the ethnicity, race, and sex of the applicant in a dwelling-related transaction not covered by § 202.13, the creditor may retain information and act on the application without violating the regulation.

APPENDIX C TO PART 202—SAMPLE NOTIFICATION FORMS

1. This appendix contains ten sample notification forms. Forms C–1 through C–4 are intended for use in notifying an applicant that adverse action has been taken on an application or account under §§ 202.9(a)(1) and (2)(i) of this regulation. Form C–5 is a notice of disclosure of the right to request specific reasons for adverse action under §§ 202.9(a)(1) and (2)(ii). Form C–6 is designed for use in notifying an applicant, under § 202.9(c)(2), that an application is incomplete. Forms C–7 and C–8 are intended for use in connection with applications for business credit under § 202.9(a)(3). Form C–9 is designed for use in notifying an applicant of the right to receive a copy of an appraisal under § 202.14. Form C–10 is designed for use in notifying an applicant for nonmortgage credit that the creditor is requesting applicant characteristic information.

2. Form C–1 contains the Fair Credit Reporting Act disclosure as required by sections 615(a) and (b) of that act. Forms C–2 through C–5 contain only the section 615(a) disclosure (that a creditor obtained information from a consumer reporting agency that played a part in the credit decision). A creditor must provide the section 615(a) disclosure when adverse action is taken against a consumer based on information from a

consumer reporting agency. A creditor must provide the section 615(b) disclosure when adverse action is taken based on information from an outside source other than a consumer reporting agency. In addition, a creditor must provide the section 615(b) disclosure if the creditor obtained information from an affiliate other than information in a consumer report or other than information concerning the affiliate's own transactions or experiences with the consumer. Creditors may comply with the disclosure requirements for adverse action based on information in a consumer report obtained from an affiliate by providing *either* the section 615(a) or section 615(b) disclosure.

3. The sample forms are illustrative and may not be appropriate for all creditors. They were designed to include some of the factors that creditors most commonly consider. If a creditor chooses to use the checklist of reasons provided in one of the sample forms in this appendix and if reasons commonly used by the creditor are not provided on the form, the creditor should modify the checklist by substituting or adding other reasons. For example, if "inadequate down payment" or "no deposit relationship with us" are common reasons for taking adverse action on an application, the creditor ought to add or substitute such reasons for those presently contained on the sample forms.

4. If the reasons listed on the forms are not the factors actually used, a creditor will not satisfy the notice requirement by simply checking the closest identifiable factor listed. For example, some creditors consider only references from banks or other depository institutions and disregard finance company references altogether; their statement of reasons should disclose "insufficient bank references," not "insufficient credit references." Similarly, a creditor that considers bank references and other credit references as distinct factors should treat the two factors separately and disclose them as appropriate. The creditor should either add such other factors to the form or check "other" and include the appropriate explanation. The creditor need not, however, describe how or why a factor adversely affected the application. For example, the notice may say "length of residence" rather than "too short a period of residence."

5. A creditor may design its own notification forms or use all or a portion of the forms contained in this appendix. Proper use of Forms C–1 through C–4 will satisfy the requirement of § 202.9(a)(2)(i). Proper use of Forms C–5 and C–6 constitutes full compliance with §§ 202.9(a)(2)(ii) and 202.9(c)(2), respectively. Proper use of Forms C–7 and C–8 will satisfy the requirements of § 202.9(a)(2)(i) and (ii), respectively, for applications for business credit. Proper use of Form C–9 will satisfy the requirements of § 202.14 of this part. Proper use of Form C–10 will satisfy the requirements of § 202.5(b)(1).

FORM C–1—SAMPLE NOTICE OF ACTION TAKEN AND STATEMENT OF REASONS

Statement of Credit Denial, Termination or Change

Date: _____

Applicant's Name: _____

Applicant's Address: _____

Description of Account, Transaction, or Requested Credit: _____
_____

Description of Action Taken: _____
_____

Part I—Principal Reason(s) for Credit Denial, Termination, or Other Action Taken Concerning Credit

This section must be completed in all instances.

____ Credit application incomplete

____ Insufficient number of credit references provided

____ Unacceptable type of credit references provided

____ Unable to verify credit references

____ Temporary or irregular employment

____ Unable to verify employment

____ Length of employment

____ Income insufficient for amount of credit requested

____ Excessive obligations in relation to income

____ Unable to verify income

____ Length of residence

____ Temporary residence

____ Unable to verify residence

____ No credit file

____ Limited credit experience

____ Poor credit performance with us

____ Delinquent past or present credit obligations with others

____ Collection action or judgment

____ Garnishment or attachment

____ Foreclosure or repossession

____ Bankruptcy

____ Number of recent inquiries on credit bureau report

____ Value or type of collateral not sufficient

____ Other, specify: _____

Part II—Disclosure of Use of Information Obtained From an Outside Source

This section should be completed if the credit decision was based in whole or in part on information that has been obtained from an outside source.

____ Our credit decision was based in whole or in part on information obtained in a report from the consumer reporting agency listed below. You have a right under the Fair Credit Reporting Act to know the information contained in your credit file at the consumer reporting agency. The reporting agency played no part in our decision and is unable to supply specific reasons why we have denied credit to you. You also have a right to a free copy of your report from the reporting agency, if you request it no later than 60 days after you receive this notice. In addition, if you find that any information contained in the report you receive is inaccurate or incomplete, you have the right to dispute the matter with the reporting agency.

Name: _____

Address: _____

[Toll-free] Telephone number: _____

____ Our credit decision was based in whole or in part on information obtained from an affiliate or from an outside source other than a consumer reporting agency. Under the Fair Credit Reporting Act, you have the right to make a written request, no later than 60 days after you receive this notice, for disclosure of the nature of this information.

If you have any questions regarding this notice, you should contact:

Creditor's name: _____
Creditor's address: _____
Creditor's telephone number:
_____

Notice: The federal Equal Credit Opportunity Act prohibits creditors from discriminating against credit applicants on the basis of race, color, religion, national origin, sex, marital status, age (provided the applicant has the capacity to enter into a binding contract); because all or part of the applicant's income derives from any public assistance program; or because the applicant has in good faith exercised any right under the Consumer Credit Protection Act. The federal agency that administers compliance with this law concerning this creditor is (name and address as specified by the appropriate agency listed in appendix A).

FORM C–2—SAMPLE NOTICE OF ACTION TAKEN AND STATEMENT OF REASONS

Date

Dear Applicant: Thank you for your recent application. Your request for [a loan/a credit card/an increase in your credit limit] was carefully considered, and we regret that we are unable to approve your application at this time, for the following reason(s):

Your Income:

___ is below our minimum requirement.

___ is insufficient to sustain payments on the amount of credit requested.

___ could not be verified.

Your Employment:

___ is not of sufficient length to qualify.

___ could not be verified.

Your Credit History:

___ of making payments on time was not satisfactory.

___ could not be verified.

Your Application:

___ lacks a sufficient number of credit references.

___ lacks acceptable types of credit references.

___ reveals that current obligations are excessive in relation to income.

Other: _____

The consumer reporting agency contacted that provided information that influenced our decision in whole or in part was [name, address and [toll-free] telephone number of the reporting agency]. The reporting agency played no part in our decision and is unable to supply specific reasons why we have denied credit to you. You have a right under the Fair Credit Reporting Act to know the information contained in your credit file at the consumer reporting agency. You also have a right to a free copy of your report from the reporting agency, if you request it no later than 60 days after you receive this notice. In addition, if you find that any information contained in the report you receive is inaccurate or incomplete, you have the right to dispute the matter with the reporting agency. Any questions regarding such information should be directed to [consumer reporting agency]. If you have any questions regarding this letter, you should contact us at [creditor's name, address and telephone number].

Notice: The federal Equal Credit Opportunity Act prohibits creditors from discriminating against credit applicants on the basis of race, color, religion, national origin, sex, marital status, age (provided the applicant has the capacity to enter into a binding contract); because all or part of the applicant's income derives from any public assistance program; or because the applicant has in good faith exercised any right under the Consumer Credit Protection Act. The federal agency that administers compliance with this law concerning this creditor is (name and address as specified by the appropriate agency listed in appendix A).

FORM C–3—SAMPLE NOTICE OF ACTION TAKEN AND STATE-MENT OF REASONS (CREDIT SCORING)

Date

Dear Applicant: Thank you for your recent application for _____. We regret that we are unable to approve your request.

Your application was processed by a credit scoring system that assigns a numerical value to the various items of information we consider in evaluating an application. These numerical values are based upon the results of analyses of repayment histories of large numbers of customers.

The information you provided in your application did not score a sufficient number of points for approval of the application. The reasons you did not score well compared with other applicants were:

- Insufficient bank references
- Type of occupation
- Insufficient credit experience
- Number of recent inquiries on credit bureau report

In evaluating your application the consumer reporting agency listed below provided us with information that in whole or in part influenced our decision. The consumer reporting agency played no part in our decision and is unable to supply specific reasons why we have denied credit to you. You have a right under the Fair Credit Reporting Act to know the information contained in your credit file at the consumer reporting agency. It can be obtained by contacting: [name, address, and [toll-free] telephone number of the consumer reporting agency]. You also have a right to a free copy of your report from the reporting agency, if you request it no later than 60 days after you receive this notice. In addition, if you find that any information contained in the report you receive is inaccurate or incomplete, you have the right to dispute the matter with the reporting agency.

If you have any questions regarding this letter, you should contact us at

Creditor's Name: _____
Address: _____
_____
Telephone: _____
Sincerely,

Notice: The federal Equal Credit Opportunity Act prohibits creditors from discriminating against credit applicants on the basis of race, color, religion, national origin, sex, marital status, age (with certain limited exceptions); because all or part of the applicant's income derives from any public assistance program; or because the applicant has in good faith exercised any right under the Consumer Credit Protection Act. The federal agency that administers compliance with this law concerning this creditor is (name and address as specified by the appropriate agency listed in appendix A).

FORM C-4—SAMPLE NOTICE OF ACTION TAKEN, STATEMENT OF REASONS AND COUNTEROFFER

Date

Dear Applicant: Thank you for your application for _____.
We are unable to offer you credit on the terms that you requested for the following reason(s): _____

_____

We can, however, offer you credit on the following terms: _____

_____

If this offer is acceptable to you, please notify us within [amount of time] at the following address: _____

_____

Our credit decision on your application was based in whole or in part on information obtained in a report from [name, address and [toll-free] telephone number of the consumer reporting agency]. You have a right under the Fair Credit Reporting Act to know the information contained in your credit file at the consumer reporting agency. The reporting agency played no part in our decision and is unable to supply specific reasons why we have denied credit to you. You also have a right to a free copy of your report from the reporting agency, if you request it no later than 60 days after you receive this notice. In addition, if you find that any information contained in the report you receive is inaccurate or incomplete, you have the right to dispute the matter with the reporting agency.

You should know that the federal Equal Credit Opportunity Act prohibits creditors, such as ourselves, from discriminating against credit applicants on the basis of their race, color, religion, national origin, sex, marital status, age (provided the applicant has the capacity to enter into a binding contract), because they receive income from a public assistance program, or because they may have exercised their rights under the Consumer Credit Protection Act. If you believe there has been discrimination in handling your application you should contact the [name and address of the appropriate federal enforcement agency listed in appendix A].

Sincerely,

FORM C–5—SAMPLE DISCLOSURE OF RIGHT TO REQUEST SPECIFIC REASONS FOR CREDIT DENIAL

Date

Dear Applicant: Thank you for applying to us for _____.

After carefully reviewing your application, we are sorry to advise you that we cannot [open an account for you/grant a loan to you/increase your credit limit] at this time. If you would like a statement of specific reasons why your application was denied, please contact [our credit service manager] shown below within 60 days of the date of this letter. We will provide you with the statement of reasons within 30 days after receiving your request.

> Creditor's Name
>
> Address
>
> Telephone Number

If we obtained information from a consumer reporting agency as part of our consideration of your application, its name, address, and [toll-free] telephone number is shown below. The reporting agency played no part in our decision and is unable to supply specific reasons why we have denied credit to you. [You have a right under the Fair Credit Reporting Act to know the information contained in your credit file at the consumer reporting agency.] You have a right to a free copy of your report from the reporting agency, if you request it no later than 60 days after you receive this notice. In addition, if you find that any information contained in the report you received is inaccurate or incomplete, you have the right to dispute the matter with the reporting agency. You can find out about the information contained in your file (if one was used) by contacting:

> Consumer reporting agency's name
>
> Address
>
> [Toll-free] Telephone number

> Sincerely,

Notice: The federal Equal Credit Opportunity Act prohibits creditors from discriminating against credit applicants on the basis of race, color, religion, national origin, sex, marital status, age (provided the applicant has the capacity to enter into a binding contract); because all or part of the applicant's income derives from any public assistance program; or because the applicant has in good faith exercised any right under the Consumer Credit Protection Act. The federal agency that administers compliance with this law concerning this creditor is (name and address as specified by the appropriate agency listed in appendix A).

FORM C–6—SAMPLE NOTICE OF INCOMPLETE APPLICATION AND REQUEST FOR ADDITIONAL INFORMATION

Creditor's name

Address

Telephone number

Date

Dear Applicant: Thank you for your application for credit. The following information is needed to make a decision on your application: _____

We need to receive this information by _____ (date). If we do not receive it by that date, we will regrettably be unable to give further consideration to your credit request.

Sincerely,

FORM C–7—SAMPLE NOTICE OF ACTION TAKEN AND STATEMENT OF REASONS (BUSINESS CREDIT)

Creditor's Name

Creditor's address

Date

Dear Applicant: Thank you for applying to us for credit. We have given your request careful consideration, and regret that we are unable to extend credit to you at this time for the following reasons:

(Insert appropriate reason, such as: Value or type of collateral not sufficient; Lack of established earnings record; Slow or past due in trade or loan payments)

Sincerely,

Notice: The federal Equal Credit Opportunity Act prohibits creditors from discriminating against credit applicants on the basis of race, color, religion, national origin, sex, marital status, age (provided the applicant has the capacity to enter into a binding contract); because all or part of the applicant's income derives from any public assistance program; or because the applicant has in good faith exercised any right under the Consumer Credit Protection Act. The federal agency that administers compliance with this law concerning this creditor is [name and address as specified by the appropriate agency listed in appendix A].

FORM C–8—SAMPLE DISCLOSURE OF RIGHT TO REQUEST SPECIFIC REASONS FOR CREDIT DENIAL GIVEN AT TIME OF APPLICATION (BUSINESS CREDIT)

Creditor's name

Creditor's address

If your application for business credit is denied, you have the right to a written statement of the specific reasons for the denial. To obtain the statement, please contact [name, address and telephone number of the person or office from which the statement of reasons can be obtained] within 60 days from the date you are notified of our decision. We will send you a written statement of reasons for the denial within 30 days of receiving your request for the statement.

Notice: The federal Equal Credit Opportunity Act prohibits creditors from discriminating against credit applicants on the basis of race, color, religion, national origin, sex, marital status, age (provided the applicant has the capacity to enter into a binding contract); because all or part of the applicant's income derives from any public assistance program; or because the applicant has in good faith exercised any right under the Consumer Credit Protection Act. The federal agency that administers compliance with this law concerning this creditor is [name and address as specified by the appropriate agency listed in appendix A].

FORM C-9—SAMPLE DISCLOSURE OF RIGHT TO RECEIVE A COPY OF AN APPRAISAL

You have the right to a copy of the appraisal report used in connection with your application for credit. If you wish a copy, please write to us at the mailing address we have provided. We must hear from you no later than 90 days after we notify you about the action taken on your credit application or you withdraw your application.

[In your letter, give us the following information:]

FORM C-10—SAMPLE DISCLOSURE ABOUT VOLUNTARY DATA NOTATION

We are requesting the following information to monitor our compliance with the federal Equal Credit Opportunity Act, which prohibits unlawful discrimination. You are not required to provide this information. We will not take this information (or your decision not to provide this information) into account in connection with your application or credit transaction. The law provides that a creditor may not discriminate based on this information, or based on whether or not you choose to provide it. [If you choose not to provide the information, we will note it by visual observation or surname].

SUPPLEMENT I TO PART 202—OFFICIAL STAFF INTERPRETATIONS

Following is an official staff interpretation of Regulation B (12 CFR part 202) issued under authority delegated by the Federal Reserve Board to officials in the Division of Consumer and Community Affairs. References are to sections of the regulation or the Equal Credit Opportunity Act (15 U.S.C. 1601 *et seq.*).

Introduction

1. *Official status.* Section 706(e) of the Equal Credit Opportunity Act protects a creditor from civil liability for any act done or omitted in good faith in conformity with an interpretation issued by a duly authorized official of the Federal Reserve Board. This commentary is the means by which the Division of Consumer and Community Affairs of the Federal Reserve Board issues official staff interpretations of Regulation B. Good-faith compliance with this commentary affords a creditor protection under section 706(e) of the Act.

2. *Issuance of interpretations.* Under Appendix D to the regulation, any person may request an official staff interpretation. Interpretations will be issued at the discretion of designated officials and incorporated in this commentary following publication for comment in the Federal Register. Except in unusual circumstances, official staff interpretations will be issued only by means of this commentary.

3. *Status of previous interpretations.* Interpretations of Regulation B previously issued by the Federal Reserve Board and its staff have been incorporated into this commentary as appropriate. All other previous Board and staff interpretations, official and unofficial, are superseded by this commentary.

4. *Footnotes.* Footnotes in the regulation have the same legal effect as the text of the regulation, whether they are explanatory or illustrative in nature.

5. *Comment designations.* The comments are designated with as much specificity as possible according to the particular regulatory provision addressed. Each comment in the commentary is identified by a number and the regulatory section or paragraph that it interprets. For example, comments to § 202.2(c) are further divided by subparagraph, such as comment 2(c)(1)(ii)–1 and comment 2(c)(2)(ii)–1.

§ 202.1 Authority, Scope, and Purpose

1(a) *Authority and scope.*

1. *Scope.* The Equal Credit Opportunity Act and Regulation B apply to all credit—commercial as well as personal—without regard to the nature or type of the credit or the creditor. If a transaction provides for the deferral of the payment of a debt, it is credit covered by Regulation B even though it may not be a credit transaction covered by Regulation Z (Truth in Lending) (12 CFR part 226). Further, the definition of creditor is not restricted to the party or person to whom the obligation is initially payable, as is the case under Regulation Z. Moreover, the Act and regulation apply to all methods of credit evaluation, whether performed judgmentally or by use of a credit scoring system.

2. *Foreign applicability.* Regulation B generally does not apply to lending activities that occur outside the United States. The regulation does apply to lending activities that take place within the United States (as well as the Commonwealth of Puerto Rico and any territory or possession of the United States), whether or not the applicant is a citizen.

3. *Board.* The term *Board,* as used in this regulation, means the Board of Governors of the Federal Reserve System.

§ 202.2 Definitions

2(c) *Adverse action.*

Paragraph 2(c)(1)(i)

1. *Application for credit.* If the applicant applied in accordance with the creditor's procedures, a refusal to refinance or extend the term of a business or other loan is adverse action.

Paragraph 2(c)(1)(ii)

1. *Move from service area.* If a credit card issuer terminates the open-end account of a customer because the customer has moved out of the card issuer's service area, the termination is adverse action unless termination on this ground was explicitly provided for in the credit agreement between the parties. In cases where termination is adverse action, notification is required under § 202.9.

2. *Termination based on credit limit.* If a creditor terminates credit accounts that have low credit limits (for example, under $400) but keeps open accounts with higher credit limits, the termination is adverse action and notification is required under § 202.9.

Paragraph 2(c)(2)(ii)

1. *Default—exercise of due-on-sale clause.* If a mortgagor sells or transfers mortgaged property without the consent of the mortgagee, and the mortgagee exercises its contractual right to accelerate the mortgage loan, the mortgagee may treat the mortgagor as being in default. An adverse action notice need not be given to the mortgagor or the transferee. (See comment 2(e)–1 for treatment of a purchaser who requests to assume the loan.)

2. *Current delinquency or default.* The term adverse action does not include a creditor's termination of an account when the accountholder is currently in default or delinquent on that account. Notification in accordance with § 202.9 of the regulation generally is required, however, if the creditor's action is based on a past delinquency or default on the account.

Paragraph 2(c)(2)(iii)

1. *Point-of-sale transactions.* Denial of credit at point of sale is not adverse action except under those circumstances specified in the regulation. For example, denial at point of sale is not adverse action in the following situations:

    i. A credit cardholder presents an expired card or a card that has been reported to the card issuer as lost or stolen.

    ii. The amount of a transaction exceeds a cash advance or credit limit.

iii. The circumstances (such as excessive use of a credit card in a short period of time) suggest that fraud is involved.

iv. The authorization facilities are not functioning.

v. Billing statements have been returned to the creditor for lack of a forwarding address.

2. *Application for increase in available credit.* A refusal or failure to authorize an account transaction at the point of sale or loan is not adverse action except when the refusal is a denial of an application, submitted in accordance with the creditor's procedures, for an increase in the amount of credit.

Paragraph 2(c)(2)(v)

1. *Terms of credit versus type of credit offered.* When an applicant applies for credit and the creditor does not offer the credit terms requested by the applicant (for example, the interest rate, length of maturity, collateral, or amount of downpayment), a denial of the application for that reason is adverse action (unless the creditor makes a counteroffer that is accepted by the applicant) and the applicant is entitled to notification under § 202.9.

2(e) *Applicant.*

1. *Request to assume loan.* If a mortgagor sells or transfers the mortgaged property and the buyer makes an application to the creditor to assume the mortgage loan, the mortgagee must treat the buyer as an applicant unless its policy is not to permit assumptions.

2(f) *Application.*

1. *General.* A creditor has the latitude under the regulation to establish its own application process and to decide the type and amount of information it will require from credit applicants.

2. *Procedures used.* The term "procedures" refers to the actual practices followed by a creditor for making credit decisions as well as its stated application procedures. For example, if a creditor's stated policy is to require all applications to be in writing on the creditor's application form, but the creditor also makes credit decisions based on oral requests, the creditor's procedures are to accept both oral and written applications.

3. *When an inquiry or prequalification request becomes an application.* A creditor is encouraged to provide consumers with information about loan terms. However, if in giving information to the consumer the creditor also evaluates information about the consumer, decides to decline the request, and communicates this to the consumer, the creditor has treated the inquiry or prequalification request as an application and must then comply with the notification requirements under § 202.9. Whether the inquiry or prequalification request becomes an application depends on how the creditor responds to the consumer, not on what the consumer says or asks. (See comment 9–5 for further discussion of prequalification requests; see comment 2(f)–5 for a discussion of preapproval requests.)

4. *Examples of inquiries that are not applications.* The following examples illustrate situations in which only an inquiry has taken place:

i. A consumer calls to ask about loan terms and an employee explains the creditor's basic loan terms, such as interest rates, loan-to-value ratio, and debt-to-income ratio.

ii. A consumer calls to ask about interest rates for car loans, and, in order to quote the appropriate rate, the loan officer asks for the make and sales price of the car and the amount of the downpayment, then gives the consumer the rate.

iii. A consumer asks about terms for a loan to purchase a home and tells the loan officer her income and intended downpayment, but the loan officer only explains the creditor's loan-to-value ratio policy and other basic lending policies, without telling the consumer whether she qualifies for the loan.

iv. A consumer calls to ask about terms for a loan to purchase vacant land and states his income and the sales price of the property to be financed, and asks whether he qualifies for a loan; the employee responds by describing the general lending policies, explaining that he would need to look at all of the consumer's qualifications before making a decision, and offering to send an application form to the consumer.

5. *Examples of an application.* An application for credit includes the following situations:

i. A person asks a financial institution to "preapprove" her for a loan (for example, to finance a house or a vehicle she plans to buy) and the institution reviews the request under a program in which the institution, after a comprehensive analysis of her creditworthiness, issues a written commitment valid for a designated period of time to extend a loan up to a specified amount. The written commitment may not be subject to conditions other than conditions that require the identification of adequate collateral, conditions that require no material change in the applicant's financial condition or creditworthiness prior to funding the loan, and limited conditions that are not related to the financial condition or creditworthiness of the applicant that the lender ordinarily attaches to a traditional application (such as certification of a clear termite inspection for a home purchase loan, or a maximum mileage requirement for a used car loan). But if the creditor's program does not provide for giving written commitments, requests for preapprovals are treated as prequalification requests for purposes of the regulation.

ii. Under the same facts as above, the financial institution evaluates the person's creditworthiness and determines that she does not qualify for a preapproval.

6. *Completed application—diligence requirement.* The regulation defines a completed application in terms that give a creditor the latitude to establish its own information requirements. Nevertheless, the creditor must act with reasonable diligence to collect information needed to com-

plete the application. For example, the creditor should request information from third parties, such as a credit report, promptly after receiving the application. If additional information is needed from the applicant, such as an address or a telephone number to verify employment, the creditor should contact the applicant promptly. (But see comment 9(a)(1)–3, which discusses the creditor's option to deny an application on the basis of incompleteness.)

2(g) *Business credit.*

1. *Definition.* The test for deciding whether a transaction qualifies as business credit is one of primary purpose. For example, an open-end credit account used for both personal and business purposes is not business credit unless the primary purpose of the account is business-related. A creditor may rely on an applicant's statement of the purpose for the credit requested.

2(j) *Credit.*

1. *General.* Regulation B covers a wider range of credit transactions than Regulation Z (Truth in Lending). Under Regulation B, a transaction is credit if there is a right to defer payment of a debt—regardless of whether the credit is for personal or commercial purposes, the number of installments required for repayment, or whether the transaction is subject to a finance charge.

2(l) *Creditor.*

1. *Assignees.* The term creditor includes all persons participating in the credit decision. This may include an assignee or a potential purchaser of the obligation who influences the credit decision by indicating whether or not it will purchase the obligation if the transaction is consummated.

2. *Referrals to creditors.* For certain purposes, the term creditor includes persons such as real estate brokers, automobile dealers, home builders, and home-improvement contractors who do not participate in credit decisions but who only accept applications and refer applicants to creditors, or select or offer to select creditors to whom credit requests can be made. These persons must comply with § 202.4(a), the general rule prohibiting discrimination, and with § 202.4(b), the general rule against discouraging applications.

2(p) *Empirically derived and other credit scoring systems.*

1. *Purpose of definition.* The definition under § 202.2(p)(1)(i) through (iv) sets the criteria that a credit system must meet in order to use age as a predictive factor. Credit systems that do not meet these criteria are judgmental systems and may consider age only for the purpose of determining a "pertinent element of creditworthiness." (Both types of systems may favor an elderly applicant. See § 202.6(b)(2).)

2. *Periodic revalidation.* The regulation does not specify how often credit scoring systems must be revalidated. The credit scoring system must be revalidated frequently enough to ensure that it continues to meet

recognized professional statistical standards for statistical soundness. To ensure that predictive ability is being maintained, the creditor must period-ically review the performance of the system. This could be done, for example, by analyzing the loan portfolio to determine the delinquency rate for each score interval, or by analyzing population stability over time to detect deviations of recent applications from the applicant population used to validate the system. If this analysis indicates that the system no longer predicts risk with statistical soundness, the system must be adjusted as necessary to reestablish its predictive ability. A creditor is responsible for ensuring its system is validated and revalidated based on the creditor's own data.

3. *Pooled data scoring systems.* A scoring system or the data from which to develop such a system may be obtained from either a single credit grantor or multiple credit grantors. The resulting system will qualify as an empirically derived, demonstrably and statistically sound, credit scoring system provided the criteria set forth in paragraph (p)(1)(i) through (iv) of this section are met. A creditor is responsible for ensuring its system is validated and revalidated based on the creditor's own data when it becomes available.

4. *Effects test and disparate treatment.* An empirically derived, demon-strably and statistically sound, credit scoring system may include age as a predictive factor (provided that the age of an elderly applicant is not assigned a negative factor or value). Besides age, no other prohibited basis may be used as a variable. Generally, credit scoring systems treat all applicants objectively and thus avoid problems of disparate treatment. In cases where a credit scoring system is used in conjunction with individual discretion, disparate treatment could conceivably occur in the evaluation process. In addition, neutral factors used in credit scoring systems could nonetheless be subject to challenge under the effects test. (See comment 6(a)–2 for a discussion of the effects test).

2(w) *Open-end credit.*

1. *Open-end real estate mortgages.* The term "open-end credit" does not include negotiated advances under an open-end real estate mortgage or a letter of credit.

2(z) *Prohibited basis.*

1. *Persons associated with applicant.* As used in this regulation, prohibited basis refers not only to characteristics—the race, color, religion, national origin, sex, marital status, or age—of an applicant (or officers of an applicant in the case of a corporation) but also to the characteristics of individuals with whom an applicant is affiliated or with whom the applicant associates. This means, for example, that under the general rule stated in § 202.4(a), a creditor may not discriminate against an applicant because of that person's personal or business dealings with members of a certain religion, because of the national origin of any persons associated with the extension of credit (such as the tenants in the apartment complex being

financed), or because of the race of other residents in the neighborhood where the property offered as collateral is located.

2. *National origin.* A creditor may not refuse to grant credit because an applicant comes from a particular country but may take the applicant's immigration status into account. A creditor may also take into account any applicable law, regulation, or executive order restricting dealings with citizens (or the government) of a particular country or imposing limitations regarding credit extended for their use.

3. *Public assistance program.* Any federal, state, or local governmental assistance program that provides a continuing, periodic income supplement, whether premised on entitlement or need, is "public assistance" for purposes of the regulation. The term includes (but is not limited to) Temporary Aid to Needy Families, food stamps, rent and mortgage supplement or assistance programs, social security and supplemental security income, and unemployment compensation. Only physicians, hospitals, and others to whom the benefits are payable need consider Medicare and Medicaid as public assistance.

§ 202.3   Limited Exceptions for Certain Classes of Transactions

1. *Scope.* Under this section, procedural requirements of the regulation do not apply to certain types of credit. All classes of transactions remain subject to § 202.4(a), the general rule barring discrimination on a prohibited basis, and to any other provision not specifically excepted.

3(a) *Public-utilities credit.*

1. *Definition.* This definition applies only to credit for the purchase of a utility service, such as electricity, gas, or telephone service. Credit provided or offered by a public utility for some other purpose—such as for financing the purchase of a gas dryer, telephone equipment, or other durable goods, or for insulation or other home improvements—is not excepted.

2. *Security deposits.* A utility company is a creditor when it supplies utility service and bills the user after the service has been provided. Thus, any credit term (such as a requirement for a security deposit) is subject to the regulation's bar against discrimination on a prohibited basis.

3. *Telephone companies.* A telephone company's credit transactions qualify for the exceptions provided in § 202.3(a)(2) only if the company is regulated by a government unit or files the charges for service, delayed payment, or any discount for prompt payment with a government unit.

3(c) *Incidental credit.*

1. *Examples.* If a service provider (such as a hospital, doctor, lawyer, or merchant) allows the client or customer to defer the payment of a bill, this deferral of debt is credit for purposes of the regulation, even though there is no finance charge and no agreement for payment in installments.

Because of the exceptions provided by this section, however, these particular credit extensions are excepted from compliance with certain procedural requirements as specified in § 202.3(c).

3(d) *Government credit.*

1. *Credit to governments.* The exception relates to credit extended to (not by) governmental entities. For example, credit extended to a local government is covered by this exception, but credit extended to consumers by a federal or state housing agency does not qualify for special treatment under this category.

§ 202.4   General Rules

Paragraph 4(a)

1. *Scope of rule.* The general rule stated in § 202.4(a) covers all dealings, without exception, between an applicant and a creditor, whether or not addressed by other provisions of the regulation. Other provisions of the regulation identify specific practices that the Board has decided are impermissible because they could result in credit discrimination on a basis prohibited by the Act. The general rule covers, for example, application procedures, criteria used to evaluate creditworthiness, administration of accounts, and treatment of delinquent or slow accounts. Thus, whether or not specifically prohibited elsewhere in the regulation, a credit practice that treats applicants differently on a prohibited basis violates the law because it violates the general rule. Disparate treatment on a prohibited basis is illegal whether or not it results from a conscious intent to discriminate.

2. *Examples.*

i. Disparate treatment would exist, for example, in the following situations:

A.   A creditor provides information only on "subprime" and similar products to minority applicants who request information about the creditor's mortgage products, but provides information on a wider variety of mortgage products to similarly situated nonminority applicants.

B.   A creditor provides more comprehensive information to men than to similarly situated women.

C.   A creditor requires a minority applicant to provide greater documentation to obtain a loan than a similarly situated nonminority applicant.

D.   A creditor waives or relaxes credit standards for a nonminority applicant but not for a similarly situated minority applicant.

ii. Treating applicants differently on a prohibited basis is unlawful if the creditor lacks a legitimate nondiscriminatory reason for its action, or if the asserted reason is found to be a pretext for discrimination.

Paragraph 4(b)

1. *Prospective applicants.* Generally, the regulation's protections apply only to persons who have requested or received an extension of credit. In keeping with the purpose of the Act—to promote the availability of credit on a nondiscriminatory basis—§ 202.4(b) covers acts or practices directed at prospective applicants that could discourage a reasonable person, on a prohibited basis, from applying for credit. Practices prohibited by this section include:

i. A statement that the applicant should not bother to apply, after the applicant states that he is retired.

ii. The use of words, symbols, models or other forms of communication in advertising that express, imply, or suggest a discriminatory preference or a policy of exclusion in violation of the Act.

iii. The use of interview scripts that discourage applications on a prohibited basis.

2. *Affirmative advertising.* A creditor may affirmatively solicit or encourage members of traditionally disadvantaged groups to apply for credit, especially groups that might not normally seek credit from that creditor.

Paragraph 4(c)

1. *Requirement for written applications.* Model application forms are provided in Appendix B to the regulation, although use of a printed form is not required. A creditor will satisfy the requirement by writing down the information that it normally considers in making a credit decision. The creditor may complete an application on behalf of an applicant and need not require the applicant to sign the application.

2. *Telephone applications.* A creditor that accepts applications by telephone for dwelling-related credit covered by § 202.13 can meet the requirement for written applications by writing down pertinent information that is provided by the applicant.

3. *Computerized entry.* Information entered directly into and retained by a computerized system qualifies as a written application under this paragraph. (See the commentary to § 202.13(b), *Applications through electronic media* and *Applications through video.*)

Paragraph 4(d)

1. *Clear and conspicuous.* This standard requires that disclosures be presented in a reasonably understandable format in a way that does not obscure the required information. No minimum type size is mandated, but the disclosures must be legible, whether typewritten, handwritten, or printed by computer.

2. *Form of disclosures.* Whether the disclosures required to be on or with an application must be in electronic form depends upon the following:

i. If an applicant accesses a credit application electronically (other than as described under ii below), such as online at a home computer, the creditor must provide the disclosures in electronic form (such as with the application form on its website) in order to meet the requirement to provide disclosures in a timely manner on or with the application. If the creditor instead mailed paper disclosures to the applicant, this requirement would not be met.

ii. In contrast, if an applicant is physically present in the creditor's office, and accesses a credit application electronically, such as via a terminal or kiosk (or if the applicant uses a terminal or kiosk located on the premises of an affiliate or third party that has arranged with the creditor to provide applications to consumers), the creditor may provide disclosures in either electronic or paper form, provided the creditor complies with the timing, delivery, and retainability requirements of the regulation.

§ 202.5 Rules Concerning Requests for Information

5(a) *General rules.*

Paragraph 5(a)(1)

1. *Requests for information.* This section governs the types of information that a creditor may gather. Section 202.6 governs how information may be used.

Paragraph 5(a)(2)

1. *Local laws.* Information that a creditor is allowed to collect pursuant to a "state" statute or regulation includes information required by a local statute, regulation, or ordinance.

2. *Information required by Regulation C.* Regulation C generally requires creditors covered by the Home Mortgage Disclosure Act (HMDA) to collect and report information about the race, ethnicity, and sex of applicants for home-improvement loans and home-purchase loans, including some types of loans not covered by § 202.13.

3. *Collecting information on behalf of creditors.* Persons such as loan brokers and correspondents do not violate the ECOA or Regulation B if they collect information that they are otherwise prohibited from collecting, where the purpose of collecting the information is to provide it to a creditor that is subject to the Home Mortgage Disclosure Act or another federal or state statute or regulation requiring data collection.

5(d) *Other limitations on information requests.*

Paragraph 5(d)(1)

1. *Indirect disclosure of prohibited information.* The fact that certain credit-related information may indirectly disclose marital status does not bar a creditor from seeking such information. For example, the creditor may ask about:

i. The applicant's obligation to pay alimony, child support, or separate maintenance income.

ii. The source of income to be used as the basis for repaying the credit requested, which could disclose that it is the income of a spouse.

iii. Whether any obligation disclosed by the applicant has a co-obligor, which could disclose that the co-obligor is a spouse or former spouse.

iv. The ownership of assets, which could disclose the interest of a spouse.

Paragraph 5(d)(2)

1. *Disclosure about income.* The sample application forms in appendix B to the regulation illustrate how a creditor may inform an applicant of the right not to disclose alimony, child support, or separate maintenance income.

2. *General inquiry about source of income.* Since a general inquiry about the source of income may lead an applicant to disclose alimony, child support, or separate maintenance income, a creditor making such an inquiry on an application form should preface the request with the disclosure required by this paragraph.

3. *Specific inquiry about sources of income.* A creditor need not give the disclosure if the inquiry about income is specific and worded in a way that is unlikely to lead the applicant to disclose the fact that income is derived from alimony, child support, or separate maintenance payments. For example, an application form that asks about specific types of income such as salary, wages, or investment income need not include the disclosure.

§ 202.6   Rules Concerning Evaluation of Applications

6(a) *General rule concerning use of information.*

1. *General.* When evaluating an application for credit, a creditor generally may consider any information obtained. However, a creditor may not consider in its evaluation of creditworthiness any information that it is barred by § 202.5 from obtaining or from using for any purpose other than to conduct a self-test under § 202.15.

2. *Effects test.* The effects test is a judicial doctrine that was developed in a series of employment cases decided by the U.S. Supreme Court under Title VII of the Civil Rights Act of 1964 (42 U.S.C. 2000e *et seq.*), and the burdens of proof for such employment cases were codified by Congress in the Civil Rights Act of 1991 (42 U.S.C. 2000e–2). Congressional intent that this doctrine apply to the credit area is documented in the Senate Report that accompanied H.R. 6516, No. 94–589, pp. 4–5; and in the House Report that accompanied H.R. 6516, No. 94–210, p.5. The Act and regulation may prohibit a creditor practice that is discriminatory in effect because it has a disproportionately negative impact on a prohibited basis, even

though the creditor has no intent to discriminate and the practice appears neutral on its face, unless the creditor practice meets a legitimate business need that cannot reasonably be achieved as well by means that are less disparate in their impact. For example, requiring that applicants have income in excess of a certain amount to qualify for an overdraft line of credit could mean that women and minority applicants will be rejected at a higher rate than men and nonminority applicants. If there is a demonstrable relationship between the income requirement and creditworthiness for the level of credit involved, however, use of the income standard would likely be permissible.

6(b) *Specific rules concerning use of information.*

Paragraph 6(b)(1)

1. *Prohibited basis—special purpose credit.* In a special purpose credit program, a creditor may consider a prohibited basis to determine whether the applicant possesses a characteristic needed for eligibility. (See § 202.8.)

Paragraph 6(b)(2)

1. *Favoring the elderly.* Any system of evaluating creditworthiness may favor a credit applicant who is age 62 or older. A credit program that offers more favorable credit terms to applicants age 62 or older is also permissible; a program that offers more favorable credit terms to applicants at an age lower than 62 is permissible only if it meets the special-purpose credit requirements of § 202.8.

2. *Consideration of age in a credit scoring system.* Age may be taken directly into account in a credit scoring system that is "demonstrably and statistically sound," as defined in § 202.2(p), with one limitation: applicants age 62 years or older must be treated at least as favorably as applicants who are under age 62. If age is scored by assigning points to an applicant's age category, elderly applicants must receive the same or a greater number of points as the most favored class of nonelderly applicants.

i. *Age-split scorecards.* Some credit systems segment the population and use different scorecards based on the age of an applicant. In such a system, one card may cover a narrow age range (for example, applicants in their twenties or younger) who are evaluated under attributes predictive for that age group. A second card may cover all other applicants, who are evaluated under the attributes predictive for that broader class. When a system uses a card covering a wide age range that encompasses elderly applicants, the credit scoring system is not deemed to score age. Thus, the system does not raise the issue of assigning a negative factor or value to the age of elderly applicants. But if a system segments the population by age into multiple scorecards, and includes elderly applicants in a narrower age range, the credit scoring system does score age. To comply with the Act and regulation in such a case, the creditor must ensure that the system does not assign a negative factor or value to the age of elderly applicants as a class.

3. *Consideration of age in a judgmental system.* In a judgmental system, defined in § 202.2(t), a creditor may not decide whether to extend credit or set the terms and conditions of credit based on age or information related exclusively to age. Age or age-related information may be considered only in evaluating other "pertinent elements of creditworthiness" that are drawn from the particular facts and circumstances concerning the applicant. For example, a creditor may not reject an application or terminate an account because the applicant is 60 years old. But a creditor that uses a judgmental system may relate the applicant's age to other information about the applicant that the creditor considers in evaluating creditworthiness. As the following examples illustrate, the evaluation must be made in an individualized, case-by-case manner:

     i.   A creditor may consider the applicant's occupation and length of time to retirement to ascertain whether the applicant's income (including retirement income) will support the extension of credit to its maturity.

     ii. A creditor may consider the adequacy of any security offered when the term of the credit extension exceeds the life expectancy of the applicant and the cost of realizing on the collateral could exceed the applicant's equity. An elderly applicant might not qualify for a 5 percent down, 30–year mortgage loan but might qualify with a larger downpayment or a shorter loan maturity.

     iii. A creditor may consider the applicant's age to assess the significance of length of employment (a young applicant may have just entered the job market) or length of time at an address (an elderly applicant may recently have retired and moved from a long-term residence).

4. *Consideration of age in a reverse mortgage.* A reverse mortgage is a home-secured loan in which the borrower receives payments from the creditor, and does not become obligated to repay these amounts (other than in the case of default) until the borrower dies, moves permanently from the home, or transfers title to the home, or upon a specified maturity date. Disbursements to the borrower under a reverse mortgage typically are determined by considering the value of the borrower's home, the current interest rate, and the borrower's life expectancy. A reverse mortgage program that requires borrowers to be age 62 or older is permissible under § 202.6(b)(2)(iv). In addition, under § 202.6(b)(2)(iii), a creditor may consider a borrower's age to evaluate a pertinent element of creditworthiness, such as the amount of the credit or monthly payments that the borrower will receive, or the estimated repayment date.

5. *Consideration of age in a combined system.* A creditor using a credit scoring system that qualifies as "empirically derived" under § 202.2(p) may consider other factors (such as a credit report or the applicant's cash flow) on a judgmental basis. Doing so will not negate the classification of the credit scoring component of the combined system as "demonstrably and statistically sound." While age could be used in the

credit scoring portion, however, in the judgmental portion age may not be considered directly. It may be used only for the purpose of determining a "pertinent element of creditworthiness." (See comment 6(b)(2)–3.)

6. *Consideration of public assistance.* When considering income derived from a public assistance program, a creditor may take into account, for example:

i. The length of time an applicant will likely remain eligible to receive such income.

ii. Whether the applicant will continue to qualify for benefits based on the status of the applicant's dependents (as in the case of Temporary Aid to Needy Families, or social security payments to a minor).

iii. Whether the creditor can attach or garnish the income to assure payment of the debt in the event of default.

Paragraph 6(b)(5)

1. *Consideration of an individual applicant.* A creditor must evaluate income derived from part-time employment, alimony, child support, separate maintenance payments, retirement benefits, or public assistance on an individual basis, not on the basis of aggregate statistics; and must assess its reliability or unreliability by analyzing the applicant's actual circumstances, not by analyzing statistical measures derived from a group.

2. *Payments consistently made.* In determining the likelihood of consistent payments of alimony, child support, or separate maintenance, a creditor may consider factors such as whether payments are received pursuant to a written agreement or court decree; the length of time that the payments have been received; whether the payments are regularly received by the applicant; the availability of court or other procedures to compel payment; and the creditworthiness of the payor, including the credit history of the payor when it is available to the creditor.

3. *Consideration of income.*

i. A creditor need not consider income at all in evaluating creditworthiness. If a creditor does consider income, there are several acceptable methods, whether in a credit scoring or a judgmental system:

A. A creditor may score or take into account the total sum of all income stated by the applicant without taking steps to evaluate the income for reliability.

B. A creditor may evaluate each component of the applicant's income, and then score or take into account income determined to be reliable separately from other income; or the creditor may disregard that portion of income that is not reliable when it aggregates reliable income.

C. A creditor that does not evaluate all income components for reliability must treat as reliable any component of protected income that is not evaluated.

ii. In considering the separate components of an applicant's income, the creditor may not automatically discount or exclude from consideration any protected income. Any discounting or exclusion must be based on the applicant's actual circumstances.

4. *Part-time employment, sources of income.* A creditor may score or take into account the fact that an applicant has more than one source of earned income—a full-time and a part-time job or two part-time jobs. A creditor may also score or treat earned income from a secondary source differently than earned income from a primary source. The creditor may not, however, score or otherwise take into account the number of sources for income such as retirement income, social security, supplemental security income, and alimony. Nor may the creditor treat negatively the fact that an applicant's only earned income is derived from, for example, a part-time job.

Paragraph 6(b)(6)

1. *Types of credit references.* A creditor may restrict the types of credit history and credit references that it will consider, provided that the restrictions are applied to all credit applicants without regard to sex, marital status, or any other prohibited basis. On the applicant's request, however, a creditor must consider credit information not reported through a credit bureau when the information relates to the same types of credit references and history that the creditor would consider if reported through a credit bureau.

Paragraph 6(b)(7)

1. *National origin—immigration status.* The applicant's immigration status and ties to the community (such as employment and continued residence in the area) could have a bearing on a creditor's ability to obtain repayment. Accordingly, the creditor may consider immigration status and differentiate, for example, between a noncitizen who is a long-time resident with permanent resident status and a noncitizen who is temporarily in this country on a student visa.

2. *National origin—citizenship.* A denial of credit on the ground that an applicant is not a United States citizen is not per se discrimination based on national origin.

Paragraph 6(b)(8)

1. *Prohibited basis—marital status.* A creditor may consider the marital status of an applicant or joint applicant for the purpose of ascertaining the creditor's rights and remedies applicable to the particular extension of credit. For example, in a secured transaction involving real property, a creditor could take into account whether state law gives the applicant's spouse an interest in the property being offered as collateral.

§ 202.7   Rules Concerning Extensions of Credit

7(a) *Individual accounts.*

1. *Open-end credit—authorized user.* A creditor may not require a creditworthy applicant seeking an individual credit account to provide

additional signatures. But the creditor may condition the designation of an authorized user by the account holder on the authorized user's becoming contractually liable for the account, as long as the creditor does not differentiate on any prohibited basis in imposing this requirement.

2. *Open-end credit—choice of authorized user.* A creditor that permits an account holder to designate an authorized user may not restrict this designation on a prohibited basis. For example, if the creditor allows the designation of spouses as authorized users, the creditor may not refuse to accept a nonspouse as an authorized user.

3. *Overdraft authority on transaction accounts.* If a transaction account (such as a checking account or NOW account) includes an overdraft line of credit, the creditor may require that all persons authorized to draw on the transaction account assume liability for any overdraft.

7(b) *Designation of name.*

1. *Single name on account.* A creditor may require that joint applicants on an account designate a single name for purposes of administering the account and that a single name be embossed on any credit cards issued on the account. But the creditor may not require that the name be the husband's name. (See § 202.10 for rules governing the furnishing of credit history on accounts held by spouses.)

7(c) *Action concerning existing open-end accounts.*

Paragraph 7(c)(1)

1. *Termination coincidental with marital status change.* When an account holder's marital status changes, a creditor generally may not terminate the account unless it has evidence that the account holder is now unable or unwilling to repay. But the creditor may terminate an account on which both spouses are jointly liable, even if the action coincides with a change in marital status, when one or both spouses:

    i. Repudiate responsibility for future charges on the joint account.

    ii. Request separate accounts in their own names.

    iii. Request that the joint account be closed.

2. *Updating information.* A creditor may periodically request updated information from applicants but may not use events related to a prohibited basis—such as an applicant's retirement or reaching a particular age, or a change in name or marital status—to trigger such a request.

Paragraph 7(c)(2)

1. *Procedure pending reapplication.* A creditor may require a reapplication from an account holder, even when there is no evidence of unwillingness or inability to repay, if (1) the credit was based on the qualifications of a person who is no longer available to support the credit and (2) the creditor has information indicating that the account holder's income may be insufficient to support the credit. While a reapplication is pending, the

creditor must allow the account holder full access to the account under the existing contract terms. The creditor may specify a reasonable time period within which the account holder must submit the required information.

7(d) *Signature of spouse or other person.*

1. *Qualified applicant.* The signature rules ensure that qualified applicants are able to obtain credit in their own names. Thus, when an applicant requests individual credit, a creditor generally may not require the signature of another person unless the creditor has first determined that the applicant alone does not qualify for the credit requested.

2. *Unqualified applicant.* When an applicant requests individual credit but does not meet a creditor's standards, the creditor may require a cosigner, guarantor, endorser, or similar party—but cannot require that it be the spouse. (See commentary to § 202.7(d)(5) and (6).)

Paragraph 7(d)(1)

1. *Signature of another person.* It is impermissible for a creditor to require an applicant who is individually creditworthy to provide a cosigner—even if the creditor applies the requirement without regard to sex, marital status, or any other prohibited basis. (But see comment 7(d)(6)–1 concerning guarantors of closely held corporations.)

2. *Joint applicant.* The term "joint applicant" refers to someone who applies contemporaneously with the applicant for shared or joint credit. It does not refer to someone whose signature is required by the creditor as a condition for granting the credit requested.

3. *Evidence of joint application.* A person's intent to be a joint applicant must be evidenced at the time of application. Signatures on a promissory note may not be used to show intent to apply for joint credit. On the other hand, signatures or initials on a credit application affirming applicants' intent to apply for joint credit may be used to establish intent to apply for joint credit. (See Appendix B). The method used to establish intent must be distinct from the means used by individuals to affirm the accuracy of information. For example, signatures on a joint financial statement affirming the veracity of information are not sufficient to establish intent to apply for joint credit.

Paragraph 7(d)(2)

1. *Jointly owned property.* If an applicant requests unsecured credit, does not own sufficient separate property, and relies on joint property to establish creditworthiness, the creditor must value the applicant's interest in the jointly owned property. A creditor may not request that a nonapplicant joint owner sign any instrument as a condition of the credit extension unless the applicant's interest does not support the amount and terms of the credit sought.

i. *Valuation of applicant's interest.* In determining the value of an applicant's interest in jointly owned property, a creditor may consider factors such as the form of ownership and the property's susceptibility to attachment, execution, severance, or partition; the value of the applicant's interest after such action; and the cost associated with the action. This determination must be based on the existing form of ownership, and not on the possibility of a subsequent change. For example, in determining whether a married applicant's interest in jointly owned property is sufficient to satisfy the creditor's standards of creditworthiness for individual credit, a creditor may not consider that the applicant's separate property could be transferred into tenancy by the entirety after consummation. Similarly, a creditor may not consider the possibility that the couple may divorce. Accordingly, a creditor may not require the signature of the nonapplicant spouse in these or similar circumstances.

ii. *Other options to support credit.* If the applicant's interest in jointly owned property does not support the amount and terms of credit sought, the creditor may offer the applicant other options to qualify for the extension of credit. For example:

A. Providing a co-signer or other party (§ 202.7(d)(5));

B. Requesting that the credit be granted on a secured basis (§ 202.7(d)(4)); or

C. Providing the signature of the joint owner on an instrument that ensures access to the property in the event of the applicant's death or default, but does not impose personal liability unless necessary under state law (such as a limited guarantee). A creditor may not routinely require, however, that a joint owner sign an instrument (such as a quitclaim deed) that would result in the forfeiture of the joint owner's interest in the property.

2. *Need for signature—reasonable belief.* A creditor's reasonable belief as to what instruments need to be signed by a person other than the applicant should be supported by a thorough review of pertinent statutory and decisional law or an opinion of the state attorney general.

Paragraph 7(d)(3)

1. *Residency.* In assessing the creditworthiness of a person who applies for credit in a community property state, a creditor may assume that the applicant is a resident of the state unless the applicant indicates otherwise.

Paragraph 7(d)(4)

1. *Creation of enforceable lien.* Some state laws require that both spouses join in executing any instrument by which real property is encumbered. If an applicant offers such property as security for credit, a creditor may require the applicant's spouse to sign the instruments necessary to create a valid security interest in the property. The creditor may not require the spouse to sign the note evidencing the credit obligation if signing only the mortgage or other security agreement is sufficient to make the property available to satisfy the debt in the event of default. However,

if under state law both spouses must sign the note to create an enforceable lien, the creditor may require the signatures.

2. *Need for signature—reasonable belief.* Generally, a signature to make the secured property available will only be needed on a security agreement. A creditor's reasonable belief that, to ensure access to the property, the spouse's signature is needed on an instrument that imposes personal liability should be supported by a thorough review of pertinent statutory and decisional law or an opinion of the state attorney general.

3. *Integrated instruments.* When a creditor uses an integrated instrument that combines the note and the security agreement, the spouse cannot be asked to sign the integrated instrument if the signature is only needed to grant a security interest. But the spouse could be asked to sign an integrated instrument that makes clear—for example, by a legend placed next to the spouse's signature—that the spouse's signature is only to grant a security interest and that signing the instrument does not impose personal liability.

Paragraph 7(d)(5)

1. *Qualifications of additional parties.* In establishing guidelines for eligibility of guarantors, cosigners, or similar additional parties, a creditor may restrict the applicant's choice of additional parties but may not discriminate on the basis of sex, marital status, or any other prohibited basis. For example, the creditor could require that the additional party live in the creditor's market area.

2. *Reliance on income of another person—individual credit.* An applicant who requests individual credit relying on the income of another person (including a spouse in a non-community property state) may be required to provide the signature of the other person to make the income available to pay the debt. In community property states, the signature of a spouse may be required if the applicant relies on the spouse's separate income. If the applicant relies on the spouse's future earnings that as a matter of state law cannot be characterized as community property until earned, the creditor may require the spouse's signature, but need not do so—even if it is the creditor's practice to require the signature when an applicant relies on the future earnings of a person other than a spouse. (See § 202.6(c) on consideration of state property laws.)

3. *Renewals.* If the borrower's creditworthiness is reevaluated when a credit obligation is renewed, the creditor must determine whether an additional party is still warranted and, if not warranted, release the additional party.

Paragraph 7(d)(6)

1. *Guarantees.* A guarantee on an extension of credit is part of a credit transaction and therefore subject to the regulation. A creditor may require the personal guarantee of the partners, directors, or officers of a business, and the shareholders of a closely held corporation, even if the business or corporation is creditworthy. The requirement must be based on

the guarantor's relationship with the business or corporation, however, and not on a prohibited basis. For example, a creditor may not require guarantees only for women-owned or minority-owned businesses. Similarly, a creditor may not require guarantees only of the married officers of a business or the married shareholders of a closely held corporation.

2. *Spousal guarantees.* The rules in § 202.7(d) bar a creditor from requiring the signature of a guarantor's spouse just as they bar the creditor from requiring the signature of an applicant's spouse. For example, although a creditor may require all officers of a closely held corporation to personally guarantee a corporate loan, the creditor may not automatically require that spouses of married officers also sign the guarantee. If an evaluation of the financial circumstances of an officer indicates that an additional signature is necessary, however, the creditor may require the signature of another person in appropriate circumstances in accordance with § 202.7(d)(2).

7(e) *Insurance.*

1. *Differences in terms.* Differences in the availability, rates, and other terms on which credit-related casualty insurance or credit life, health, accident, or disability insurance is offered or provided to an applicant does not violate Regulation B.

2. *Insurance information.* A creditor may obtain information about an applicant's age, sex, or marital status for insurance purposes. The information may only be used for determining eligibility and premium rates for insurance, however, and not in making the credit decision.

§ 202.8   Special Purpose Credit Programs

8(a) *Standards for programs.*

1. *Determining qualified programs.* The Board does not determine whether individual programs qualify for special purpose credit status, or whether a particular program benefits an "economically disadvantaged class of persons." The agency or creditor administering or offering the loan program must make these decisions regarding the status of its program.

2. *Compliance with a program authorized by federal or state law.* A creditor does not violate Regulation B when it complies in good faith with a regulation promulgated by a government agency implementing a special purpose credit program under § 202.8(a)(1). It is the agency's responsibility to promulgate a regulation that is consistent with federal and state law.

3. *Expressly authorized.* Credit programs authorized by federal or state law include programs offered pursuant to federal, state, or local statute, regulation or ordinance, or pursuant to judicial or administrative order.

4. *Creditor liability.* A refusal to grant credit to an applicant is not a violation of the Act or regulation if the applicant does not meet the eligibility requirements under a special purpose credit program.

5. *Determining need.* In designing a special purpose credit program under § 202.8(a), a, for-profit organization must determine that the program will benefit a class of people who would otherwise be denied credit or would receive it on less favorable terms. This determination can be based on a broad analysis using the organization's own research or data from outside sources, including governmental reports and studies. For example, a creditor might design new products to reach consumers who would not meet, or have not met, its traditional standards of creditworthiness due to such factors as credit inexperience or the use of credit sources that may not report to consumer reporting agencies. Or, a bank could review Home Mortgage Disclosure Act data along with demographic data for its assessment area and conclude that there is a need for a special purpose credit program for low-income minority borrowers.

6. *Elements of the program.* The written plan must contain information that supports the need for the particular program. The plan also must either state a specific period of time for which the program will last, or contain a statement regarding when the program will be reevaluated to determine if there is a continuing need for it.

8(b) *Rules in other sections.*

1. *Applicability of rules.* A creditor that rejects an application because the applicant does not meet the eligibility requirements (common characteristic or financial need, for example) must nevertheless notify the applicant of action taken as required by § 202.9.

8(c) *Special rule concerning requests and use of information.*

1. *Request of prohibited basis information.* This section permits a creditor to request and consider certain information that would otherwise be prohibited by §§ 202.5 and 202.6 to determine an applicant's eligibility for a particular program.

2. *Examples.* Examples of programs under which the creditor can ask for and consider information about a prohibited basis are:

   i. Energy conservation programs to assist the elderly, for which the creditor must consider the applicant's age.

   ii. Programs under a Minority Enterprise Small Business Investment Corporation, for which a creditor must consider the applicant's minority status.

8(d) *Special rule in the case of financial need.*

1. *Request of prohibited basis information.* This section permits a creditor to request and consider certain information that would otherwise be prohibited by §§ 202.5 and 202.6, and to require signatures that would otherwise be prohibited by § 202.7(d).

2. *Examples.* Examples of programs in which financial need is a criterion are:

i. Subsidized housing programs for low-to moderate-income households, for which a creditor may have to consider the applicant's receipt of alimony or child support, the spouse's or parents' income, etc.

ii. Student loan programs based on the family's financial need, for which a creditor may have to consider the spouse's or parents' financial resources.

3. *Student loans.* In a guaranteed student loan program, a creditor may obtain the signature of a parent as a guarantor when required by federal or state law or agency regulation, or when the student does not meet the creditor's standards of creditworthiness. (See § 202.7(d)(1) and (5).) The creditor may not require an additional signature when a student has a work or credit history that satisfies the creditor's standards.

§ 202.9 Notifications

1. *Use of the term adverse action.* The regulation does not require that a creditor use the term adverse action in communicating to an applicant that a request for an extension of credit has not been approved. In notifying an applicant of adverse action as defined by § 202.2(c)(1), a creditor may use any words or phrases that describe the action taken on the application.

2. *Expressly withdrawn applications.* When an applicant expressly withdraws a credit application, the creditor is not required to comply with the notification requirements under § 202.9. (The creditor must comply, however, with the record retention requirements of the regulation. See § 202.12(b)(3).)

3. *When notification occurs.* Notification occurs when a creditor delivers or mails a notice to the applicant's last known address or, in the case of an oral notification, when the creditor communicates the credit decision to the applicant.

4. *Location of notice.* The notifications required under § 202.9 may appear on either or both sides of a form or letter.

5. *Prequalification requests.* Whether a creditor must provide a notice of action taken for a prequalification request depends on the creditor's response to the request, as discussed in comment 2(f)-3. For instance, a creditor may treat the request as an inquiry if the creditor evaluates specific information about the consumer and tells the consumer the loan amount, rate, and other terms of credit the consumer could qualify for under various loan programs, explaining the process the consumer must follow to submit a mortgage application and the information the creditor will analyze in reaching a credit decision. On the other hand, a creditor has treated a request as an application, and is subject to the adverse action notice requirements of § 202.9 if, after evaluating information, the creditor decides that it will not approve the request and communicates that decision to the consumer. For example, if the creditor tells the consumer that it

would not approve an application for a mortgage because of a bankruptcy in the consumer's record, the creditor has denied an application for credit.

9(a) *Notification of action taken, ECOA notice, and statement of specific reasons.*

Paragraph 9(a)(1)

1. *Timing of notice—when an application is complete.* Once a creditor has obtained all the information it normally considers in making a credit decision, the application is complete and the creditor has 30 days in which to notify the applicant of the credit decision. (See also comment 2(f)–6.)

2. *Notification of approval.* Notification of approval may be express or by implication. For example, the creditor will satisfy the notification requirement when it gives the applicant the credit card, money, property, or services requested.

3. *Incomplete application—denial for incompleteness.* When an application is incomplete regarding information that the applicant can provide and the creditor lacks sufficient data for a credit decision, the creditor may deny the application giving as the reason for denial that the application is incomplete. The creditor has the option, alternatively, of providing a notice of incompleteness under § 202.9(c).

4. *Incomplete application—denial for reasons other than incompleteness.* When an application is missing information but provides sufficient data for a credit decision, the creditor may evaluate the application, make its credit decision, and notify the applicant accordingly. If credit is denied, the applicant must be given the specific reasons for the credit denial (or notice of the right to receive the reasons); in this instance missing information or "incomplete application" cannot be given as the reason for the denial.

5. *Length of counteroffer.* Section 202.9(a)(1)(iv) does not require a creditor to hold a counteroffer open for 90 days or any other particular length of time.

6. *Counteroffer combined with adverse action notice.* A creditor that gives the applicant a combined counteroffer and adverse action notice that complies with § 202.9(a)(2) need not send a second adverse action notice if the applicant does not accept the counteroffer. A sample of a combined notice is contained in form C–4 of Appendix C to the regulation.

7. *Denial of a telephone application.* When an application is made by telephone and adverse action is taken, the creditor must request the applicant's name and address in order to provide written notification under this section. If the applicant declines to provide that information, then the creditor has no further notification responsibility.

Paragraph 9(a)(3)

1. *Coverage.* In determining which rules in this paragraph apply to a given business credit application, a creditor may rely on the applicant's assertion about the revenue size of the business. (Applications to start a

business are governed by the rules in § 202.9(a)(3)(i).) If an applicant applies for credit as a sole proprietor, the revenues of the sole proprietorship will determine which rules govern the application. However, if an applicant applies for business credit as an individual, the rules in § 202.9(a)(3)(i) apply unless the application is for trade or similar credit.

2. *Trade credit.* The term trade credit generally is limited to a financing arrangement that involves a buyer and a seller—such as a supplier who finances the sale of equipment, supplies, or inventory; it does not apply to an extension of credit by a bank or other financial institution for the financing of such items.

3. *Factoring.* Factoring refers to a purchase of accounts receivable, and thus is not subject to the Act or regulation. If there is a credit extension incident to the factoring arrangement, the notification rules in § 202.9(a)(3)(ii) apply, as do other relevant sections of the Act and regulation.

4. *Manner of compliance.* In complying with the notice provisions of the Act and regulation, creditors offering business credit may follow the rules governing consumer credit. Similarly, creditors may elect to treat all business credit the same (irrespective of revenue size) by providing notice in accordance with § 202.9(a)(3)(i).

5. *Timing of notification.* A creditor subject to § 202.9(a)(3)(ii)(A) is required to notify a business credit applicant, orally or in writing, of action taken on an application within a reasonable time of receiving a completed application. Notice provided in accordance with the timing requirements of § 202.9(a)(1) is deemed reasonable in all instances.

9(b) *Form of ECOA notice and statement of specific reasons.*

Paragraph 9(b)(1)

1. *Substantially similar notice.* The ECOA notice sent with a notification of a credit denial or other adverse action will comply with the regulation if it is "substantially similar" to the notice contained in § 202.9(b)(1). For example, a creditor may add a reference to the fact that the ECOA permits age to be considered in certain credit scoring systems, or add a reference to a similar state statute or regulation and to a state enforcement agency.

Paragraph 9(b)(2)

1. *Number of specific reasons.* A creditor must disclose the principal reasons for denying an application or taking other adverse action. The regulation does not mandate that a specific number of reasons be disclosed, but disclosure of more than four reasons is not likely to be helpful to the applicant.

2. *Source of specific reasons.* The specific reasons disclosed under §§ 202.9(a)(2) and (b)(2) must relate to and accurately describe the factors actually considered or scored by a creditor.

3. *Description of reasons.* A creditor need not describe how or why a factor adversely affected an applicant. For example, the notice may say "length of residence" rather than "too short a period of residence."

4. *Credit scoring system.* If a creditor bases the denial or other adverse action on a credit scoring system, the reasons disclosed must relate only to those factors actually scored in the system. Moreover, no factor that was a principal reason for adverse action may be excluded from disclosure. The creditor must disclose the actual reasons for denial (for example, "age of automobile") even if the relationship of that factor to predicting creditworthiness may not be clear to the applicant.

5. *Credit scoring—method for selecting reasons.* The regulation does not require that any one method be used for selecting reasons for a credit denial or other adverse action that is based on a credit scoring system. Various methods will meet the requirements of the regulation. One method is to identify the factors for which the applicant's score fell furthest below the average score for each of those factors achieved by applicants whose total score was at or slightly above the minimum passing score. Another method is to identify the factors for which the applicant's score fell furthest below the average score for each of those factors achieved by all applicants. These average scores could be calculated during the development or use of the system. Any other method that produces results substantially similar to either of these methods is also acceptable under the regulation.

6. *Judgmental system.* If a creditor uses a judgmental system, the reasons for the denial or other adverse action must relate to those factors in the applicant's record actually reviewed by the person making the decision.

7. *Combined credit scoring and judgmental system.* If a creditor denies an application based on a credit evaluation system that employs both credit scoring and judgmental components, the reasons for the denial must come from the component of the system that the applicant failed. For example, if a creditor initially credit scores an application and denies the credit request as a result of that scoring, the reasons disclosed to the applicant must relate to the factors scored in the system. If the application passes the credit scoring stage but the creditor then denies the credit request based on a judgmental assessment of the applicant's record, the reasons disclosed must relate to the factors reviewed judgmentally, even if the factors were also considered in the credit scoring component. If the application is not approved or denied as a result of the credit scoring, but falls into a gray band, and the creditor performs a judgmental assessment and denies the credit after that assessment, the reasons disclosed must come from both components of the system. The same result applies where a judgmental assessment is the first component of the combined system. As provided in comment 9(b)(2)–1, disclosure of more than a combined total of four reasons is not likely to be helpful to the applicant.

8. *Automatic denial.* Some credit decision methods contain features that call for automatic denial because of one or more negative factors in the

applicant's record (such as the applicant's previous bad credit history with that creditor, the applicant's declaration of bankruptcy, or the fact that the applicant is a minor). When a creditor denies the credit request because of an automatic-denial factor, the creditor must disclose that specific factor.

9 *Combined ECOA–FCRA disclosures.* The ECOA requires disclosure of the principal reasons for denying or taking other adverse action on an application for an extension of credit. The Fair Credit Reporting Act (FCRA) requires a creditor to disclose when it has based its decision in whole or in part on information from a source other than the applicant or its own files. Disclosing that a credit report was obtained and used in the denial of the application, as the FCRA requires, does not satisfy the ECOA requirement to disclose specific reasons. For example, if the applicant's credit history reveals delinquent credit obligations and the application is denied for that reason, to satisfy § 202.9(b)(2) the creditor must disclose that the application was denied because of the applicant's delinquent credit obligations. To satisfy the FCRA requirement, the creditor must also disclose that a credit report was obtained and used in the denial of the application. Sample forms C–1 through C–5 of Appendix C of the regulation provide for the two disclosures.

9(c) *Incomplete applications.*

Paragraph 9(c)(1)

1. *Exception for preapprovals.* The requirement to provide a notice of incompleteness does not apply to preapprovals that constitute applications under § 202.2(f).

Paragraph 9(c)(2)

1. *Reapplication.* If information requested by a creditor is submitted by an applicant after the expiration of the time period designated by the creditor, the creditor may require the applicant to make a new application.

Paragraph 9(c)(3)

1. *Oral inquiries for additional information.* If an applicant fails to provide the information in response to an oral request, a creditor must send a written notice to the applicant within the 30–day period specified in § 202.9(c)(1) and (2). If the applicant provides the information, the creditor must take action on the application and notify the applicant in accordance with § 202.9(a).

9(g) *Applications submitted through a third party.*

1. *Third parties.* The notification of adverse action may be given by one of the creditors to whom an application was submitted, or by a noncreditor third party. If one notification is provided on behalf of multiple creditors, the notice must contain the name and address of each creditor. The notice must either disclose the applicant's right to a statement of specific reasons within 30 days, or give the primary reasons each creditor relied upon in taking the adverse action—clearly indicating which reasons relate to which creditor.

2. *Third party notice—enforcement agency.* If a single adverse action notice is being provided to an applicant on behalf of several creditors and they are under the jurisdiction of different federal enforcement agencies, the notice need not name each agency; disclosure of any one of them will suffice.

3. *Third-party notice—liability.* When a notice is to be provided through a third party, a creditor is not liable for an act or omission of the third party that constitutes a violation of the regulation if the creditor accurately and in a timely manner provided the third party with the information necessary for the notification and maintains reasonable procedures adapted to prevent such violations.

§ 202.10   Furnishing of Credit Information

1. *Scope.* The requirements of § 202.10 for designating and reporting credit information apply only to consumer credit transactions. Moreover, they apply only to creditors that opt to furnish credit information to credit bureaus or to other creditors; there is no requirement that a creditor furnish credit information on its accounts.

2. *Reporting on all accounts.* The requirements of § 202.10 apply only to accounts held or used by spouses. However, a creditor has the option to designate all joint accounts (or all accounts with an authorized user) to reflect the participation of both parties, whether or not the accounts are held by persons married to each other.

3. *Designating accounts.* In designating accounts and reporting credit information, a creditor need not distinguish between accounts on which the spouse is an authorized user and accounts on which the spouse is a contractually liable party.

4. *File and index systems.* The regulation does not require the creation or maintenance of separate files in the name of each participant on a joint or user account, or require any other particular system of recordkeeping or indexing. It requires only that a creditor be able to report information in the name of each spouse on accounts covered by § 202.10. Thus, if a creditor receives a credit inquiry about the wife, it should be able to locate her credit file without asking the husband's name.

10(a)   *Designation of accounts.*

1. *New parties.* When new parties who are spouses undertake a legal obligation on an account, as in the case of a mortgage loan assumption, the creditor must change the designation on the account to reflect the new parties and must furnish subsequent credit information on the account in the new names.

2. *Request to change designation of account.* A request to change the manner in which information concerning an account is furnished does not alter the legal liability of either spouse on the account and does not require a creditor to change the name in which the account is maintained.

§ 202.11   Relation to State Law

11(a)   Inconsistent state laws.

1. *Preemption determination—New York.* The Board has determined that the following provisions in the state law of New York are preempted by the federal law, effective November 11, 1988:

   i. Article 15, section 296a(1)(b)—Unlawful discriminatory practices in relation to credit on the basis of race, creed, color, national origin, age, sex, marital status, or disability. This provision is preempted to the extent that it bars taking a prohibited basis into account when establishing eligibility for certain special-purpose credit programs.

   ii. Article 15, section 296a(1)(c)'Unlawful discriminatory practice to make any record or inquiry based on race, creed, color, national origin, age, sex, marital status, or disability. This provision is preempted to the extent that it bars a creditor from requesting and considering information regarding the particular characteristics (for example, race, national origin, or sex) required for eligibility for special-purpose credit programs.

2. *Preemption determination—Ohio.* The Board has determined that the following provision in the state law of Ohio is preempted by the federal law, effective July 23, 1990:

   i. Section 4112.021(B)(1)—Unlawful discriminatory practices in credit transactions. This provision is preempted to the extent that it bars asking or favorably considering the age of an elderly applicant; prohibits the consideration of age in a credit scoring system; permits without limitation the consideration of age in real estate transactions; and limits the consideration of age in special-purpose credit programs to certain government-sponsored programs identified in the state law.

§ 202.12   Record Retention

12(a) *Retention of prohibited information.*

1. *Receipt of prohibited information.* Unless the creditor specifically requested such information, a creditor does not violate this section when it receives prohibited information from a consumer reporting agency.

2. *Use of retained information.* Although a creditor may keep in its files prohibited information as provided in § 202.12(a), the creditor may use the information in evaluating credit applications only if permitted to do so by § 202.6.

12(b) *Preservation of records.*

1. *Copies.* Copies of the original record include carbon copies, photocopies, microfilm or microfiche copies, or copies produced by any other accurate retrieval system, such as documents stored and reproduced by computer. A creditor that uses a computerized or mechanized system need not keep a paper copy of a document (for example, of an adverse action

notice) if it can regenerate all pertinent information in a timely manner for examination or other purposes.

2. *Computerized decisions.* A creditor that enters information items from a written application into a computerized or mechanized system and makes the credit decision mechanically, based only on the items of information entered into the system, may comply with § 202.12(b) by retaining the information actually entered. It is not required to store the complete written application, nor is it required to enter the remaining items of information into the system. If the transaction is subject to § 202.13, however, the creditor is required to enter and retain the data on personal characteristics in order to comply with the requirements of that section.

Paragraph 12(b)(3)

1. *Withdrawn and brokered applications.* In most cases, the 25–month retention period for applications runs from the date a notification is sent to the applicant granting or denying the credit requested. In certain transactions, a creditor is not obligated to provide a notice of the action taken. (See, for example, comment 9–2.) In such cases, the 25–month requirement runs from the date of application, as when:

   i.   An application is withdrawn by the applicant.

   ii. An application is submitted to more than one creditor on behalf of the applicant, and the application is approved by one of the other creditors.

12(b)(6) *Self-tests*

1. The rule requires all written or recorded information about a self-test to be retained for 25 months after a self-test has been completed. For this purpose, a self-test is completed after the creditor has obtained the results and made a determination about what corrective action, if any, is appropriate. Creditors are required to retain information about the scope of the self-test, the methodology used and time period covered by the self-test, the report or results of the self-test including any analysis or conclusions, and any corrective action taken in response to the self-test.

12(b)(7) *Preapplication marketing information.*

1. *Prescreened credit solicitations.* The rule requires creditors to retain copies of prescreened credit solicitations. For purposes of this regulation, a prescreened solicitation is an "offer of credit" as described in 15 U.S.C. 1681a(1) of the Fair Credit Reporting Act. A creditor complies with this rule if it retains a copy of each solicitation mailing that contains different terms, such as the amount of credit offered, annual percentage rate, or annual fee.

2. *List of criteria.* A creditor must retain the list of criteria used to select potential recipients. This includes the criteria used by the creditor both to determine the potential recipients of the particular solicitation and to determine who will actually be offered credit.

3. *Correspondence.* A creditor may retain correspondence relating to consumers' complaints about prescreened solicitations in any manner that is reasonably accessible and is understandable to examiners. There is no requirement to establish a separate database or set of files for such correspondence, or to match consumer complaints with specific solicitation programs.

§ 202.13   Information for Monitoring Purposes

13(a) *Information to be requested.*

1. *Natural person.* Section 202.13 applies only to applications from natural persons.

2. *Principal residence.* The requirements of § 202.13 apply only if an application relates to a dwelling that is or will be occupied by the applicant as the principal residence. A credit application related to a vacation home or a rental unit is not covered. In the case of a two-to four-unit dwelling, the application is covered if the applicant intends to occupy one of the units as a principal residence.

3. *Temporary financing.* An application for temporary financing to construct a dwelling is not subject to § 202.13. But an application for both a temporary loan to finance construction of a dwelling and a permanent mortgage loan to take effect upon the completion of construction is subject to § 202.13.

4. *New principal residence.* A person can have only one principal residence at a time. However, if a person buys or builds a new dwelling that will become that person's principal residence within a year or upon completion of construction, the new dwelling is considered the principal residence for purposes of § 202.13.

5. *Transactions not covered.* The information-collection requirements of this section apply to applications for credit primarily for the purchase or refinancing of a dwelling that is or will become the applicant's principal residence. Therefore, applications for credit secured by the applicant's principal residence but made primarily for a purpose other than the purchase or refinancing of the principal residence (such as loans for home improvement and debt consolidation) are not subject to the information-collection requirements. An application for an open-end home equity line of credit is not subject to this section unless it is readily apparent to the creditor when the application is taken that the primary purpose of the line is for the purchase or refinancing of a principal dwelling.

6. *Refinancings.* A refinancing occurs when an existing obligation is satisfied and replaced by a new obligation undertaken by the same borrower. A creditor that receives an application to refinance an existing extension of credit made by that creditor for the purchase of the applicant's dwelling may request the monitoring information again but is not required to do so if it was obtained in the earlier transaction.

7. *Data collection under Regulation C.* See comment 5(a)(2)–2.

13(b) *Obtaining of information.*

1. *Forms for collecting data.* A creditor may collect the information specified in § 202.13(a) either on an application form or on a separate form referring to the application. The applicant must be offered the option to select more than one racial designation.

2. *Written applications.* The regulation requires written applications for the types of credit covered by § 202.13. A creditor can satisfy this requirement by recording on paper or by means of computer the information that the applicant provides orally and that the creditor normally considers in a credit decision.

3. *Telephone, mail applications.*

i. A creditor that accepts an application by telephone or mail must request the monitoring information.

ii. A creditor that accepts an application by mail need not make a special request for the monitoring information if the applicant has failed to provide it on the application form returned to the creditor.

iii. If it is not evident on the face of an application that it was received by mail, telephone, or via an electronic medium, the creditor should indicate on the form or other application record how the application was received.

4. *Video and other electronic-application processes.*

i. If a creditor takes an application through an electronic medium that allows the creditor to see the applicant, the creditor must treat the application as taken in person. The creditor must note the monitoring information on the basis of visual observation or surname, if the applicant chooses not to provide the information.

ii. If an applicant applies through an electronic medium without video capability, the creditor treats the application as if it were received by mail.

5. *Applications through loan-shopping services.* When a creditor receives an application through an unaffiliated loan-shopping service, it does not have to request the monitoring information for purposes of the ECOA or Regulation B. Creditors subject to the Home Mortgage Disclosure Act should be aware, however, that data collection may be called for under Regulation C (12 CFR part 203), which generally requires creditors to report, among other things, the sex and race of an applicant on brokered applications or applications received through a correspondent.

6. *Inadvertent notation.* If a creditor inadvertently obtains the monitoring information in a dwelling-related transaction not covered by § 202.13, the creditor may process and retain the application without violating the regulation.

13(c) *Disclosure to applicants.*

1. *Procedures for providing disclosures.* The disclosure to an applicant regarding the monitoring information may be provided in writing. Appen-

dix B contains a sample disclosure. A creditor may devise its own disclosure so long as it is substantially similar. The creditor need not orally request the monitoring information if it is requested in writing.

13(d) *Substitute monitoring program.*

1. *Substitute program.* An enforcement agency may adopt, under its established rulemaking or enforcement procedures, a program requiring creditors under its jurisdiction to collect information in addition to information required by this section.

§ 202.14 Rules on Providing Appraisal Reports

14(a) *Providing appraisals.*

1. *Coverage.* This section covers applications for credit to be secured by a lien on a dwelling, as that term is defined in § 202.14(c), whether the credit is for a business purpose (for example, a loan to start a business) or a consumer purpose (for example, a loan to finance a child's education).

2. *Renewals.* This section applies when an applicant requests the renewal of an existing extension of credit and the creditor obtains a new appraisal report. This section does not apply when a creditor uses the appraisal report previously obtained to evaluate the renewal request.

14(a)(2)(i) *Notice.*

1. *Multiple applicants.* When an application that is subject to this section involves more than one applicant, the notice about the appraisal report need only be given to one applicant, but it must be given to the primary applicant where one is readily apparent.

14(a)(2)(ii) *Delivery.*

1. *Reimbursement.* Creditors may charge for photocopy and postage costs incurred in providing a copy of the appraisal report, unless prohibited by state or other law. If the consumer has already paid for the report—for example, as part of an application fee—the creditor may not require additional fees for the appraisal (other than photocopy and postage costs).

14(c) *Definitions.*

1. *Appraisal reports.* Examples of appraisal reports are:

   i. A report prepared by an appraiser (whether or not licensed or certified), including written comments and other documents submitted to the creditor in support of the appraiser's estimate or opinion of the property's value.

   ii. A document prepared by the creditor's staff that assigns value to the property, if a third-party appraisal report has not been used.

   iii. An internal review document reflecting that the creditor's valuation is different from a valuation in a third party's appraisal report (or different from valuations that are publicly available or valuations such as manufacturers' invoices for mobile homes).

2. *Other reports.* The term "appraisal report" does not cover all documents relating to the value of the applicant's property. Examples of reports not covered are:

i.   Internal documents, if a third-party appraisal report was used to establish the value of the property.

ii. Governmental agency statements of appraised value.

iii. Valuations lists that are publicly available (such as published sales prices or mortgage amounts, tax assessments, and retail price ranges) and valuations such as manufacturers' invoices for mobile homes.

§ 202.15   Incentives for Self–Testing and Self–Correction

15(a) *General rules.*

15(a)(1) *Voluntary self-testing and correction.*

1. Activities required by any governmental authority are not voluntary self-tests. A governmental authority includes both administrative and judicial authorities for federal, state, and local governments.

15(a)(2) *Corrective action required.*

1. To qualify for the privilege, appropriate corrective action is required when the results of a self-test show that it is more likely than not that there has been a violation of the ECOA or this regulation. A self-test is also privileged when it identifies no violations.

2. In some cases, the issue of whether certain information is privileged may arise before the self-test is complete or corrective actions are fully under way. This would not necessarily prevent a creditor from asserting the privilege. In situations where the self-test is not complete, for the privilege to apply the lender must satisfy the regulation's requirements within a reasonable period of time. To assert the privilege where the self-test shows a likely violation, the rule requires, at a minimum, that the creditor establish a plan for corrective action and a method to demonstrate progress in implementing the plan. Creditors must take appropriate corrective action on a timely basis after the results of the self-test are known.

3. A creditor's determination about the type of corrective action needed, or a finding that no corrective action is required, is not conclusive in determining whether the requirements of this paragraph have been satisfied. If a creditor's claim of privilege is challenged, an assessment of the need for corrective action or the type of corrective action that is appropriate must be based on a review of the self-testing results, which may require an *in camera* inspection of the privileged documents.

15(a)(3) *Other privileges.*

1. A creditor may assert the privilege established under this section in addition to asserting any other privilege that may apply, such as the attorney-client privilege or the work-product privilege. Self-testing data

may be privileged under this section whether or not the creditor's assertion of another privilege is upheld.

15(b) *Self-test defined.*

15(b)(1) *Definition.*

Paragraph 15(b)(1)(i)

1. To qualify for the privilege, a self-test must be sufficient to constitute a determination of the extent or effectiveness of the creditor's compliance with the Act and Regulation B. Accordingly, a self-test is only privileged if it was designed and used for that purpose. A self-test that is designed or used to determine compliance with other laws or regulations or for other purposes is not privileged under this rule. For example, a self-test designed to evaluate employee efficiency or customers' satisfaction with the level of service provided by the creditor is not privileged even if evidence of discrimination is uncovered incidentally. If a self-test is designed for multiple purposes, only the portion designed to determine compliance with the ECOA is eligible for the privilege.

Paragraph 15(b)(1)(ii)

1. The principal attribute of self-testing is that it constitutes a voluntary undertaking by the creditor to produce new data or factual information that otherwise would not be available and could not be derived from loan or application files or other records related to credit transactions. Self-testing includes, but is not limited to, the practice of using fictitious applicants for credit (testers), either with or without the use of matched pairs. A creditor may elect to test a defined segment of its business, for example, loan applications processed by a specific branch or loan officer, or applications made for a particular type of credit or loan program. A creditor also may use other methods of generating information that is not available in loan and application files, such as surveying mortgage loan applicants. To the extent permitted by law, creditors might also develop new methods that go beyond traditional pre-application testing, such as hiring testers to submit fictitious loan applications for processing.

2. The privilege does not protect a creditor's analysis performed as part of processing or underwriting a credit application. A creditor's evaluation or analysis of its loan files, Home Mortgage Disclosure Act data, or similar types of records (such as broker or loan officer compensation records) does not produce new information about a creditor's compliance and is not a self-test for purposes of this section. Similarly, a statistical analysis of data derived from existing loan files is not privileged.

15(b)(3) *Types of information not privileged.*

Paragraph 15(b)(3)(i)

1. The information listed in this paragraph is not privileged and may be used to determine whether the prerequisites for the privilege have been satisfied. Accordingly, a creditor might be asked to identify the self-testing method, for example, whether preapplication testers were used or data

were compiled by surveying loan applicants. Information about the scope of the self-test (such as the types of credit transactions examined, or the geographic area covered by the test) also is not privileged.

Paragraph 15(b)(3)(ii)

1. Property appraisal reports, minutes of loan committee meetings or other documents reflecting the basis for a decision to approve or deny an application, loan policies or procedures, underwriting standards, and broker compensation records are examples of the types of records that are not privileged. If a creditor arranges for testers to submit loan applications for processing, the records are not related to actual credit transactions for purposes of this paragraph and may be privileged self-testing records.

15(c) *Appropriate corrective action.*

1. The rule only addresses the corrective actions required for a creditor to take advantage of the privilege in this section. A creditor may be required to take other actions or provide additional relief if a formal finding of discrimination is made.

15(c)(1) *General requirement.*

1. Appropriate corrective action is required even though no violation has been formally adjudicated or admitted by the creditor. In determining whether it is more likely than not that a violation occurred, a creditor must treat testers as if they are actual applicants for credit. A creditor may not refuse to take appropriate corrective action under this section because the self-test used fictitious loan applicants. The fact that a tester's agreement with the creditor waives the tester's legal right to assert a violation does not eliminate the requirement for the creditor to take corrective action, although no remedial relief for the tester is required under paragraph 15(c)(3).

15(c)(2) *Determining the scope of appropriate corrective action.*

1. Whether a creditor has taken or is taking corrective action that is appropriate will be determined on a case-by-case basis. Generally, the scope of the corrective action that is needed to preserve the privilege is governed by the scope of the self-test. For example, a creditor that self-tests mortgage loans and discovers evidence of discrimination may focus its corrective actions on mortgage loans, and is not required to expand its testing to other types of loans.

2. In identifying the policies or practices that are a likely cause of the violation, a creditor might identify inadequate or improper lending policies, failure to implement established policies, employee conduct, or other causes. The extent and scope of a likely violation may be assessed by determining which areas of operations are likely to be affected by those policies and practices, for example, by determining the types of loans and stages of the application process involved and the branches or offices where the violations may have occurred.

3. Depending on the method and scope of the self-test and the results of the test, appropriate corrective action may include one or more of the following:

i. If the self-test identifies individuals whose applications were inappropriately processed, offering to extend credit if the application was improperly denied and compensating such persons for out-of-pocket costs and other compensatory damages;

ii. Correcting institutional policies or procedures that may have contributed to the likely violation, and adopting new policies as appropriate;

iii. Identifying and then training and/or disciplining the employees involved;

iv. Developing outreach programs, marketing strategies, or loan products to serve more effectively segments of the lender's markets that may have been affected by the likely discrimination; and

v. Improving audit and oversight systems to avoid a recurrence of the likely violations.

15(c)(3) *Types of relief.*

Paragraph 15(c)(3)(ii)

1. The use of pre-application testers to identify policies and practices that illegally discriminate does not require creditors to review existing loan files for the purpose of identifying and compensating applicants who might have been adversely affected.

2. If a self-test identifies a specific applicant who was discriminated against on a prohibited basis, to qualify for the privilege in this section the creditor must provide appropriate remedial relief to that applicant; the creditor is not required to identify other applicants who might also have been adversely affected.

Paragraph 15(c)(3)(iii)

1. A creditor is not required to provide remedial relief to an applicant that would not be available by law. An applicant might also be ineligible for certain types of relief due to changed circumstances. For example, a creditor is not required to offer credit to a denied applicant if the applicant no longer qualifies for the credit due to a change in financial circumstances, although some other type of relief might be appropriate.

15(d)(1) *Scope of privilege.*

1. The privilege applies with respect to any examination, investigation or proceeding by federal, state, or local government agencies relating to compliance with the Act or this regulation. Accordingly, in a case brought under the ECOA, the privilege established under this section preempts any inconsistent laws or court rules to the extent they might require disclosure of privileged self-testing data. The privilege does not apply in other cases (such as in litigation filed solely under a state's fair lending statute). In such cases, if a court orders a creditor to disclose self-test results, the disclosure is not a voluntary disclosure or waiver of the privilege for purposes of paragraph 15(d)(2); a creditor may protect the information by seeking a protective order to limit availability and use of the

self-testing data and prevent dissemination beyond what is necessary in that case. Paragraph 15(d)(1) precludes a party who has obtained privileged information from using it in a case brought under the ECOA, provided the creditor has not lost the privilege through voluntary disclosure under paragraph 15(d)(2).

15(d)(2) *Loss of privilege.*

Paragraph 15(d)(2)(i)

1. A creditor's corrective action, by itself, is not considered a voluntary disclosure of the self-test report or results. For example, a creditor does not disclose the results of a self-test merely by offering to extend credit to a denied applicant or by inviting the applicant to reapply for credit. Voluntary disclosure could occur under this paragraph, however, if the creditor disclosed the self-test results in connection with a new offer of credit.

2. The disclosure of self-testing results to an independent contractor acting as an auditor or consultant for the creditor on compliance matters does not result in loss of the privilege.

Paragraph 15(d)(2)(ii)

1. The privilege is lost if the creditor discloses privileged information, such as the results of the self-test. The privilege is not lost if the creditor merely reveals or refers to the existence of the self-test.

Paragraph 15(d)(2)(iii)

1. A creditor's claim of privilege may be challenged in a court or administrative law proceeding with appropriate jurisdiction. In resolving the issue, the presiding officer may require the creditor to produce privileged information about the self-test.

Paragraph 15(d)(3) *Limited use of privileged information*

1. A creditor may be required to produce privileged documents for the purpose of determining a penalty or remedy after a violation of the ECOA or Regulation B has been formally adjudicated or admitted. A creditor's compliance with such a requirement does not evidence the creditor's intent to forfeit the privilege.

§ 202.16   Enforcement, Penalties, and Liabilities

17(c) *Failure of compliance.*

1. *Inadvertent errors.* Inadvertent errors include, but are not limited to, clerical mistake, calculation error, computer malfunction, and printing error. An error of legal judgment is not an inadvertent error under the regulation.

2. *Correction of error.* For inadvertent errors that occur under §§ 202.12 and 202.13, this section requires that they be corrected prospectively.

Appendix B—Model Application Forms [Omitted]

Appendix C—Sample Notification Forms [Omitted]

ELECTRONIC FUND TRANSFERS
REGULATION E

12 CFR 205

Table of Sections

---

§ 205.1   Authority and purpose

(a) *Authority.* The regulation in this part, known as Regulation E, is issued by the Board of Governors of the Federal Reserve System pursuant to the Electronic Fund Transfer Act (15 U.S.C. 1693 et seq.). The information-collection requirements have been approved by the Office of Management and Budget under 44 U.S.C. 3501 et seq. and have been assigned OMB No. 7100–0200.

(b) *Purpose.* This part carries out the purposes of the Electronic Fund Transfer Act, which establishes the basic rights, liabilities, and responsibilities of consumers who use electronic fund transfer services and of financial institutions that offer these services. The primary objective of the act and this part is the protection of individual consumers engaging in electronic fund transfers.

§ 205.2   Definitions

For purposes of this part, the following definitions apply:

(a)(1) *Access device* means a card, code, or other means of access to a consumer's account, or any combination thereof, that may be used by the consumer to initiate electronic fund transfers.

(2) An access device becomes an *accepted access device* when the consumer:

(i) Requests and receives, or signs, or uses (or authorizes another to use) the access device to transfer money between accounts or to obtain money, property, or services;

(ii) Requests validation of an access device issued on an unsolicited basis; or

(iii) Receives an access device in renewal of, or in substitution for, an accepted access device from either the financial institution that initially issued the device or a successor.

(b)(1) *Account* means a demand deposit (checking), savings, or other consumer asset account (other than an occasional or incidental credit balance in a credit plan) held directly or indirectly by a financial institution and established primarily for personal, family, or household purposes.

(2) The term includes a "payroll card account" which is an account that is directly or indirectly established through an employer and to which electronic fund transfers of the consumer's wages, salary, or other employee compensation (such as commissions), are made on a recurring basis, whether the account is operated or managed by the employer, a third-party payroll processor, a depository institution or any other person. For rules governing payroll card accounts, see § 205.18.

(c) *Act* means the Electronic Fund Transfer Act (title IX of the Consumer Credit Protection Act, 15 U.S.C. 1693 et seq.).

(d) *Business day* means any day on which the offices of the consumer's financial institution are open to the public for carrying on substantially all business functions.

(e) *Consumer* means a natural person.

(f) *Credit* means the right granted by a financial institution to a consumer to defer payment of debt, incur debt and defer its payment, or purchase property or services and defer payment therefor.

(g) *Electronic fund transfer* is defined in § 205.3.

(h) *Electronic terminal* means an electronic device, other than a telephone operated by a consumer, through which a consumer may initiate an electronic fund transfer. The term includes, but is not limited to, point-of-sale terminals, automated teller machines, and cash dispensing machines.

(*i*) *Financial institution* means a bank, savings association, credit union, or any other person that directly or indirectly holds an account belonging to a consumer, or that issues an access device and agrees with a consumer to provide electronic fund transfer services.

(j) *Person* means a natural person or an organization, including a corporation, government agency, estate, trust, partnership, proprietorship, cooperative, or association.

(k) *Preauthorized electronic fund transfer* means an electronic fund transfer authorized in advance to recur at substantially regular intervals.

(*l*) *State* means any state, territory, or possession of the United States; the District of Columbia; the Commonwealth of Puerto Rico; or any political subdivision of the above in this paragraph (*l*).

(m) *Unauthorized electronic fund transfer* means an electronic fund transfer from a consumer's account initiated by a person other than the consumer without actual authority to initiate the transfer and from which the consumer receives no benefit. The term does not include an electronic fund transfer initiated:

(1) By a person who was furnished the access device to the consumer's account by the consumer, unless the consumer has notified the financial institution that transfers by that person are no longer authorized;

(2) With fraudulent intent by the consumer or any person acting in concert with the consumer; or

(3) By the financial institution or its employee.

§ 205.3 Coverage

(a) *General.* This part applies to any electronic fund transfer that authorizes a financial institution to debit or credit a consumer's account. Generally, this part applies to financial institutions. For purposes of §§ 205.3(b)(2) and (b)(3), 205.10 (b), (d), and (e), and 205.13, this part applies to any person.

(b) *Electronic fund transfer*—(i) *Definition.* The term *electronic fund transfer* means any transfer of funds that is initiated through an electronic terminal, telephone, computer, or magnetic tape for the purpose of ordering, instructing, or authorizing a financial institution to debit or credit an account. The term includes, but is not limited to:

(1) Point-of-sale transfers;

(2) Automated teller machine transfers;

(3) Direct deposits or withdrawals of funds;

(4) Transfers initiated by telephone; and

(5) Transfers resulting from debit card transactions, whether or not initiated through an electronic terminal.

(2) *Electronic fund transfer using information from a check.* (i) This part applies where a check, draft, or similar paper instrument is used as a source of information to initiate a one-time electronic fund transfer from a consumer's account. The consumer must authorize the transfer.

(ii) The person initiating an electronic fund transfer using the consumer's check as a source of information for the transfer must provide a notice that the transaction will or may be processed as an EFT, and obtain a consumer's authorization for each transfer. A consumer authorizes a one-time electronic fund transfer (in providing a check to a merchant or other payee for the MICR encoding, that is, the routing number of the financial institution, the consumer's account number and the serial number) when the consumer receives notice and goes forward with the underlying transaction. For point-of-sale transfers, the notice must be posted in a prominent and conspicuous location, and a copy thereof, or a substantially similar notice, must be provided to the consumer at the time of the transaction.

(iii) The person that initiates an electronic fund transfer using the consumer's check as a source of information for the transfer shall also provide a notice to the consumer at the same time it provides the notice required under paragraph (b)(2)(ii) that when a check is used to initiate an electronic fund transfer, funds may be debited from the consumer's account as soon as the same day payment is received, and, as applicable, that the consumer's check will not be returned by the financial institution holding the consumer's account. For point-of-sale transfers, the person initiating the transfer may post the notice required in this paragraph (b)(2)(iii) in a prominent and conspicuous location and need not include this notice on the copy of the notice given to the consumer under paragraph (b)(2)(ii). The requirements in this paragraph (b)(2)(iii) shall remain in effect until December 31, 2009.

(iv) A person may provide notices that are substantially similar to those set forth in Appendix A–6 to comply with the requirements of this paragraph (b)(2).

(3) *Collection of returned item fees via electronic fund transfer.* (i) *General.* The person initiating an electronic fund transfer to collect a fee for the return of an electronic fund transfer or a check that is unpaid, including due to insufficient or uncollected funds in the consumer's account, must obtain the consumer's authorization for each transfer. A consumer authorizes a one-time electronic fund transfer from his or her account to pay the fee for the returned item or transfer if the person collecting the fee provides notice to the consumer stating that the person may electronically collect the fee, and the consumer goes forward with the underlying transaction. The notice must state that the fee will be collected by means of an electronic fund transfer from the consumer's account if the payment is returned unpaid and must disclose the dollar amount of the fee. If the fee may vary due to the amount of the transaction or due to other factors, then, except as otherwise provided in paragraph (b)(3)(ii) of this section, the person collecting the fee may disclose, in place of the dollar amount of the fee, an explanation of how the fee will be determined.

(ii) *Point-of-sale transactions.* If a fee for an electronic fund transfer or check returned unpaid may be collected electronically in connection with a point-of-sale transaction, the person initiating an electronic fund transfer to collect the fee must post the notice described in paragraph (b)(3)(i) of this section in a prominent and conspicuous location. The person also must either provide the consumer with a copy of the posted notice (or a substantially similar notice) at the time of the transaction, or mail the copy (or a substantially similar notice) to the consumer's address as soon as reasonably practicable after the person initiates the electronic fund transfer to collect the fee. If the amount of the fee may vary due to the amount of the transaction or due to other factors, the posted notice may explain how the fee will be determined, but the notice provided to the consumer must state the dollar amount of the fee if the amount can be calculated at the time the notice is provided or mailed to the consumer.

(iii) *Delayed compliance date for fee disclosure.* Through December 31, 2007, the notice required to be provided to consumers under paragraph (b)(3)(ii) of this section in connection with a point-of-sale transaction, whether given to the consumer at the time of the transaction or subsequently mailed to the consumer, need not include either the dollar amount of any fee collected electronically for a check or electronic fund transfer returned unpaid or an explanation of how the amount of the fee will be determined.

(c) *Exclusions from coverage.* The term electronic fund transfer does not include:

(1) *Checks.* Any transfer of funds originated by check, draft, or similar paper instrument; or any payment made by check, draft, or similar paper instrument at an electronic terminal.

(2) *Check guarantee or authorization.* Any transfer of funds that guarantees payment or authorizes acceptance of a check, draft, or similar paper instrument but that does not directly result in a debit or credit to a consumer's account.

(3) *Wire or other similar transfers.* Any transfer of funds through Fedwire or through a similar wire transfer system that is used primarily for transfers between financial institutions or between businesses.

(4) *Securities and commodities transfers.* Any transfer of funds the primary purpose of which is the purchase or sale of a security or commodity, if the security or commodity is:

(i) Regulated by the Securities and Exchange Commission or the Commodity Futures Trading Commission;

(ii) Purchased or sold through a broker-dealer regulated by the Securities and Exchange Commission or through a futures commission merchant regulated by the Commodity Futures Trading Commission; or

(iii) Held in book-entry form by a Federal Reserve Bank or federal agency.

(5) *Automatic transfers by account-holding institution.* Any transfer of funds under an agreement between a consumer and a financial institution which provides that the institution will initiate individual transfers without a specific request from the consumer:

(i) Between a consumer's accounts within the financial institution;

(ii) From a consumer's account to an account of a member of the consumer's family held in the same financial institution; or

(iii) Between a consumer's account and an account of the financial institution, except that these transfers remain subject to § 205.10(e) regarding compulsory use and sections 915 and 916 of the act regarding civil and criminal liability.

(6) *Telephone-initiated transfers.* Any transfer of funds that:

(i) Is initiated by a telephone communication between a consumer and a financial institution making the transfer; and

(ii) Does not take place under a telephone bill-payment or other written plan in which periodic or recurring transfers are contemplated.

(7) *Small institutions.* Any preauthorized transfer to or from an account if the assets of the account-holding financial institution were $100 million or less on the preceding December 31. If assets of the account-holding institution subsequently exceed $100 million, the institution's exemption for preauthorized transfers terminates one year from the end of the calendar year in which the assets exceed $100 million. Preauthorized transfers exempt under this paragraph (c)(7) remain subject to § 205.10(e) regarding compulsory use and sections 915 and 916 of the act regarding civil and criminal liability.

§ 205.4   General disclosure requirements; jointly offered services

(a)(1) *Form of disclosures.* Disclosures required under this part shall be clear and readily understandable, in writing, and in a form the consumer may keep. The disclosures required by this part may be provided to the consumer in electronic form, subject to compliance with the consumer consent and other applicable provisions of the Electronic Signatures in Global and National Commerce Act (E–Sign Act) (15 U.S.C. 7001 *et seq.*). A financial institution may use commonly accepted or readily understandable abbreviations in complying with the disclosure requirements of this part.

(2) *Foreign language disclosures.* Disclosures required under this part may be made in a language other than English, provided that the disclosures are made available in English upon the consumer's request.

(b) *Additional information; disclosures required by other laws.* A financial institution may include additional information and may combine disclosures required by other laws (such as the Truth in Lending Act (15 U.S.C. 1601 et seq.) or the Truth in Savings Act (12 U.S.C. 4301 et seq.)) with the disclosures required by this part.

(c) *Multiple accounts and account holders—(1) Multiple accounts.* A financial institution may combine the required disclosures into a single statement for a consumer who holds more than one account at the institution.

(2) *Multiple account holders.* For joint accounts held by two or more consumers, a financial institution need provide only one set of the required disclosures and may provide them to any of the account holders.

(d) *Services offered jointly.* Financial institutions that provide electronic fund transfer services jointly may contract among themselves to comply with the requirements that this part imposes on any or all of them. An institution need make only the disclosures required by §§ 205.7 and 205.8 that are within its knowledge and within the purview of its relationship with the consumer for whom it holds an account.

§ 205.5   Issuance of access devices

(a) *Solicited issuance.* Except as provided in paragraph (b) of this section, a financial institution may issue an access device to a consumer only:

(1) In response to an oral or written request for the device; or

(2) As a renewal of, or in substitution for, an accepted access device whether issued by the institution or a successor.

(b) *Unsolicited issuance.* A financial institution may distribute an access device to a consumer on an unsolicited basis if the access device is:

(1) Not validated, meaning that the institution has not yet performed all the procedures that would enable a consumer to initiate an electronic fund transfer using the access device;

(2) Accompanied by a clear explanation that the access device is not validated and how the consumer may dispose of it if validation is not desired;

(3) Accompanied by the disclosures required by § 205.7, of the consumer's rights and liabilities that will apply if the access device is validated; and

(4) Validated only in response to the consumer's oral or written request for validation, after the institution has verified the consumer's identity by a reasonable means.

§ 205.6   Liability of consumer for unauthorized transfers

(a) *Conditions for liability.* A consumer may be held liable, within the limitations described in paragraph (b) of this section, for an unauthorized electronic fund transfer involving the consumer's account only if the financial institution has provided the disclosures required by § 205.7(b)(1), (2), and (3). If the unauthorized transfer involved an access device, it must be an accepted access device and the financial institution must have provided a means to identify the consumer to whom it was issued.

(b) *Limitations on amount of liability.* A consumer's liability for an unauthorized electronic fund transfer or a series of related unauthorized transfers shall be determined as follows:

673

(1) *Timely notice given.* If the consumer notifies the financial institution within two business days after learning of the loss or theft of the access device, the consumer's liability shall not exceed the lesser of $50 or the amount of unauthorized transfers that occur before notice to the financial institution.

(2) *Timely notice not given.* If the consumer fails to notify the financial institution within two business days after learning of the loss or theft of the access device, the consumer's liability shall not exceed the lesser of $500 or the sum of:

(i) $50 or the amount of unauthorized transfers that occur within the two business days, whichever is less; and

(ii) The amount of unauthorized transfers that occur after the close of two business days and before notice to the institution, provided the institution establishes that these transfers would not have occurred had the consumer notified the institution within that two-day period.

(3) *Periodic statement; timely notice not given.* A consumer must report an unauthorized electronic fund transfer that appears on a periodic statement within 60 days of the financial institution's transmittal of the statement to avoid liability for subsequent transfers. If the consumer fails to do so, the consumer's liability shall not exceed the amount of the unauthorized transfers that occur after the close of the 60 days and before notice to the institution, and that the institution establishes would not have occurred had the consumer notified the institution within the 60–day period. When an access device is involved in the unauthorized transfer, the consumer may be liable for other amounts set forth in paragraphs (b)(1) or (b)(2) of this section, as applicable.

(4) *Extension of time limits.* If the consumer's delay in notifying the financial institution was due to extenuating circumstances, the institution shall extend the times specified above to a reasonable period.

(5) *Notice to financial institution.* (i) Notice to a financial institution is given when a consumer takes steps reasonably necessary to provide the institution with the pertinent information, whether or not a particular employee or agent of the institution actually receives the information.

(ii) The consumer may notify the institution in person, by telephone, or in writing.

(iii) Written notice is considered given at the time the consumer mails the notice or delivers it for transmission to the institution by any other usual means. Notice may be considered constructively given when the institution becomes aware of circumstances leading to the reasonable belief that an unauthorized transfer to or from the consumer's account has been or may be made.

(6) *Liability under state law or agreement.* If state law or an agreement between the consumer and the financial institution imposes less liability

than is provided by this section, the consumer's liability shall not exceed the amount imposed under the state law or agreement.

§ 205.7   Initial disclosures

(a) *Timing of disclosures.* A financial institution shall make the disclosures required by this section at the time a consumer contracts for an electronic fund transfer service or before the first electronic fund transfer is made involving the consumer's account.

(b) *Content of disclosures.* A financial institution shall provide the following disclosures, as applicable:

(1) *Liability of consumer.* A summary of the consumer's liability, under § 205.6 or under state or other applicable law or agreement, for unauthorized electronic fund transfers.

(2) *Telephone number and address.* The telephone number and address of the person or office to be notified when the consumer believes that an unauthorized electronic fund transfer has been or may be made.

(3) *Business days.* The financial institution's business days.

(4) *Types of transfers; limitations.* The type of electronic fund transfers that the consumer may make and any limitations on the frequency and dollar amount of transfers. Details of the limitations need not be disclosed if confidentiality is essential to maintain the security of the electronic fund transfer system.

(5) *Fees.* Any fees imposed by the financial institution for electronic fund transfers or for the right to make transfers.

(6) *Documentation.* A summary of the consumer's right to receipts and periodic statements, as provided in § 205.9, and notices regarding preauthorized transfers as provided in §§ 205.10(a) and 205.10(d).

(7) *Stop payment.* A summary of the consumer's right to stop payment of a preauthorized electronic fund transfer and the procedure for placing a stop-payment order, as provided in § 205.10(c).

(8) *Liability of institution.* A summary of the financial institution's liability to the consumer under section 910 of the act for failure to make or to stop certain transfers.

(9) *Confidentiality.* The circumstances under which, in the ordinary course of business, the financial institution may provide information concerning the consumer's account to third parties.

(10) *Error resolution.* A notice that is substantially similar to Model Form A–3 as set out in Appendix A of this part concerning error resolution.

(11) ATM fees. A notice that a fee may be imposed by an automated teller machine operator as defined in § 205.16(a)(1), when the consumer initiates an electronic fund transfer or makes a balance inquiry, and by any network used to complete the transaction.

(c) *Addition of electronic fund transfer services.* If an electronic fund transfer service is added to a consumer's account and is subject to terms and conditions different from those described in the initial disclosures, disclosures for the new service are required.

§ 205.8   Change in terms notice; error resolution notice

(a) *Change in terms notice—*(1) *Prior notice required.* A financial institution shall mail or deliver a written notice to the consumer, at least 21 days before the effective date, of any change in a term or condition required to be disclosed under § 205.7(b) if the change would result in:

(i) Increased fees for the consumer;

(ii) Increased liability for the consumer;

(iii) Fewer types of available electronic fund transfers; or

(iv) Stricter limitations on the frequency or dollar amount of transfers.

(2) *Prior notice exception.* A financial institution need not give prior notice if an immediate change in terms or conditions is necessary to maintain or restore the security of an account or an electronic fund transfer system. If the institution makes such a change permanent and disclosure would not jeopardize the security of the account or system, the institution shall notify the consumer in writing on or with the next regularly scheduled periodic statement or within 30 days of making the change permanent.

(b) *Error resolution notice.* For accounts to or from which electronic fund transfers can be made, a financial institution shall mail or deliver to the consumer, at least once each calendar year, an error resolution notice substantially similar to the model form set forth in Appendix A of this part (Model Form A–3). Alternatively, an institution may include an abbreviated notice substantially similar to the model form error resolution notice set forth in Appendix A of this part (Model Form A–3), on or with each periodic statement required by § 205.9(b).

§ 205.9   Receipts at electronic terminals; periodic statements

(a) *Receipts at electronic terminals.* A financial institution shall make a receipt available to a consumer at the time the consumer initiates an electronic fund transfer at an electronic terminal. The receipt shall set forth the following information, as applicable:

(1) *Amount.* The amount of the transfer. A transaction fee may be included in this amount, provided the amount of the fee is disclosed on the receipt and displayed on or at the terminal.

(2) *Date.* The date the consumer initiates the transfer.

(3) *Type.* The type of transfer and the type of the consumer's account(s) to or from which funds are transferred. The type of account may be omitted if the access device used is able to access only one account at that terminal.

(4) *Identification*. A number or code that identifies the consumer's account or accounts, or the access device used to initiate the transfer. The number or code need not exceed four digits or letters to comply with the requirements of this paragraph (a)(4).

(5) *Terminal location*. The location of the terminal where the transfer is initiated, or an identification such as a code or terminal number. Except in limited circumstances where all terminals are located in the same city or state, if the location is disclosed, it shall include the city and state or foreign country and one of the following:

(i) The street address; or

(ii) A generally accepted name for the specific location; or

(iii) The name of the owner or operator of the terminal if other than the account-holding institution.

(6) *Third party transfer*. The name of any third party to or from whom funds are transferred.

(b) *Periodic statements*. For an account to or from which electronic fund transfers can be made, a financial institution shall send a periodic statement for each monthly cycle in which an electronic fund transfer has occurred; and shall send a periodic statement at least quarterly if no transfer has occurred. The statement shall set forth the following information, as applicable:

(1) *Transaction information*. For each electronic fund transfer occurring during the cycle:

(i) The amount of the transfer;

(ii) The date the transfer was credited or debited to the consumer's account;

(iii) The type of transfer and type of account to or from which funds were transferred;

(iv) For a transfer initiated by the consumer at an electronic terminal (except for a deposit of cash or a check, draft, or similar paper instrument), the terminal location described in paragraph (a)(5) of this section; and

(v) The name of any third party to or from whom funds were transferred.

(2) *Account number*. The number of the account.

(3) *Fees*. The amount of any fees assessed against the account during the statement period for electronic fund transfers, for the right to make transfers, or for account maintenance.

(4) *Account balances*. The balance in the account at the beginning and at the close of the statement period.

(5) *Address and telephone number for inquiries*. The address and telephone number to be used for inquiries or notice of errors, preceded by

"Direct inquiries to" or similar language. The address and telephone number provided on an error resolution notice under § 205.8(b) given on or with the statement satisfies this requirement.

(6) *Telephone number for preauthorized transfers.* A telephone number the consumer may call to ascertain whether preauthorized transfers to the consumer's account have occurred, if the financial institution uses the telephone-notice option under § 205.10(a)(1)(iii).

(c) *Exceptions to the periodic statement requirement for certain accounts*—(1) *Preauthorized transfers to accounts.* For accounts that may be accessed only by preauthorized transfers to the account the following rules apply:

(i) *Passbook accounts.* For passbook accounts, the financial institution need not provide a periodic statement if the institution updates the passbook upon presentation or enters on a separate document the amount and date of each electronic fund transfer since the passbook was last presented.

(ii) *Other accounts.* For accounts other than passbook accounts, the financial institution must send a periodic statement at least quarterly.

(2) *Intra-institutional transfers.* For an electronic fund transfer initiated by the consumer between two accounts of the consumer in the same institution, documenting the transfer on a periodic statement for one of the two accounts satisfies the periodic statement requirement.

(3) *Relationship between paragraphs (c)(1) and (c)(2) of this section.* An account that is accessed by preauthorized transfers to the account described in paragraph (c)(1) of this section and by intra-institutional transfers described in paragraph (c)(2) of this section, but by no other type of electronic fund transfers, qualifies for the exceptions provided by paragraph (c)(1) of this section.

(d) *Documentation for foreign-initiated transfers.* The failure by a financial institution to provide a terminal receipt for an electronic fund transfer or to document the transfer on a periodic statement does not violate this part if:

(1) The transfer is not initiated within a state; and

(2) The financial institution treats an inquiry for clarification or documentation as a notice of error in accordance with § 205.11.

(e) *Exception for receipts in small-value transfers.* A financial institution is not subject to the requirement to make available a receipt under paragraph (a) of this section if the amount of the transfer is $15 or less.

§ 205.10   Preauthorized transfers

(a) *Preauthorized transfers to consumer's account*—(1) *Notice by financial institution.* When a person initiates preauthorized electronic fund transfers to a consumer's account at least once every 60 days, the account-holding financial institution shall provide notice to the consumer by:

(i) *Positive notice.* Providing oral or written notice of the transfer within two business days after the transfer occurs; or

(ii) *Negative notice.* Providing oral or written notice, within two business days after the date on which the transfer was scheduled to occur, that the transfer did not occur; or

(iii) *Readily-available telephone line.* Providing a readily available telephone line that the consumer may call to determine whether the transfer occurred and disclosing the telephone number on the initial disclosure of account terms and on each periodic statement.

(2) *Notice by payor.* A financial institution need not provide notice of a transfer if the payor gives the consumer positive notice that the transfer has been initiated.

(3) *Crediting.* A financial institution that receives a preauthorized transfer of the type described in paragraph (a)(1) of this section shall credit the amount of the transfer as of the date the funds for the transfer are received.

(b) *Written authorization for preauthorized transfers from consumer's account.* Preauthorized electronic fund transfers from a consumer's account may be authorized only by a writing signed or similarly authenticated by the consumer. The person that obtains the authorization shall provide a copy to the consumer.

(c) *Consumer's right to stop payment*—(1) *Notice.* A consumer may stop payment of a preauthorized electronic fund transfer from the consumer's account by notifying the financial institution orally or in writing at least three business days before the scheduled date of the transfer.

(2) *Written confirmation.* The financial institution may require the consumer to give written confirmation of a stop-payment order within 14 days of an oral notification. An institution that requires written confirmation shall inform the consumer of the requirement and provide the address where confirmation must be sent when the consumer gives the oral notification. An oral stop-payment order ceases to be binding after 14 days if the consumer fails to provide the required written confirmation.

(d) *Notice of transfers varying in amount*— (1) *Notice.* When a preauthorized electronic fund transfer from the consumer's account will vary in amount from the previous transfer under the same authorization or from the preauthorized amount, the designated payee or the financial institution shall send the consumer written notice of the amount and date of the transfer at least 10 days before the scheduled date of transfer.

(2) *Range.* The designated payee or the institution shall inform the consumer of the right to receive notice of all varying transfers, but may give the consumer the option of receiving notice only when a transfer falls

outside a specified range of amounts or only when a transfer differs from the most recent transfer by more than an agreed-upon amount.

(e) *Compulsory use*—(1) *Credit.* No financial institution or other person may condition an extension of credit to a consumer on the consumer's repayment by preauthorized electronic fund transfers, except for credit extended under an overdraft credit plan or extended to maintain a specified minimum balance in the consumer's account.

(2) *Employment or government benefit.* No financial institution or other person may require a consumer to establish an account for receipt of electronic fund transfers with a particular institution as a condition of employment or receipt of a government benefit.

§ 205.11   Procedures for resolving errors

(a) *Definition of error*—(1) *Types of transfers or inquiries covered.* The term error means:

(i) An unauthorized electronic fund transfer;

(ii) An incorrect electronic fund transfer to or from the consumer's account;

(iii) The omission of an electronic fund transfer from a periodic statement;

(iv) A computational or bookkeeping error made by the financial institution relating to an electronic fund transfer;

(v) The consumer's receipt of an incorrect amount of money from an electronic terminal;

(vi) An electronic fund transfer not identified in accordance with §§ 205.9 or 205.10(a); or

(vii) The consumer's request for documentation required by §§ 205.9 or 205.10(a) or for additional information or clarification concerning an electronic fund transfer, including a request the consumer makes to determine whether an error exists under paragraphs (a)(1)(i) through (vi) of this section.

(2) *Types of inquiries not covered.* The term error does not include:

(i) A routine inquiry about the consumer's account balance;

(ii) A request for information for tax or other recordkeeping purposes; or

(iii) A request for duplicate copies of documentation.

(b) *Notice of error from consumer*—(1) *Timing; contents.* A financial institution shall comply with the requirements of this section with respect to any oral or written notice of error from the consumer that:

(i) Is received by the institution no later than 60 days after the institution sends the periodic statement or provides the passbook documentation, required by § 205.9, on which the alleged error is first reflected;

(ii) Enables the institution to identify the consumer's name and account number; and

(iii) Indicates why the consumer believes an error exists and includes to the extent possible the type, date, and amount of the error, except for requests described in paragraph (a)(1)(vii) of this section.

(2) *Written confirmation.* A financial institution may require the consumer to give written confirmation of an error within 10 business days of an oral notice. An institution that requires written confirmation shall inform the consumer of the requirement and provide the address where confirmation must be sent when the consumer gives the oral notification.

(3) *Request for documentation or clarifications.* When a notice of error is based on documentation or clarification that the consumer requested under paragraph (a)(1)(vii) of this section, the consumer's notice of error is timely if received by the financial institution no later than 60 days after the institution sends the information requested.

(c) *Time limits and extent of investigation*—(1) *Ten-day period.* A financial institution shall investigate promptly and, except as otherwise provided in this paragraph (c), shall determine whether an error occurred within 10 business days of receiving a notice of error. The institution shall report the results to the consumer within three business days after completing its investigation. The institution shall correct the error within one business day after determining that an error occurred.

(2) *Forty-five day period.* If the financial institution is unable to complete its investigation within 10 business days, the institution may take up to 45 days from receipt of a notice of error to investigate and determine whether an error occurred, provided the institution does the following:

(i) Provisionally credits the consumer's account in the amount of the alleged error (including interest where applicable) within 10 business days of receiving the error notice. If the financial institution has a reasonable basis for believing that an unauthorized electronic fund transfer has occurred and the institution has satisfied the requirements of § 205.6(a), the institution may withhold a maximum of $50 from the amount credited. An institution need not provisionally credit the consumer's account if:

(A) The institution requires but does not receive written confirmation within 10 business days of an oral notice of error; or

(B) The alleged error involves an account that is subject to Regulation T (Securities Credit by Brokers and Dealers, 12 CFR Part 220);

(ii) Informs the consumer, within two business days after the provisional crediting, of the amount and date of the provisional crediting and gives the consumer full use of the funds during the investigation;

(iii) Corrects the error, if any, within one business day after determining that an error occurred; and

(iv) Reports the results to the consumer within three business days after completing its investigation (including, if applicable, notice that a provisional credit has been made final).

(3) *Extension of time periods.* The time periods in paragraphs (c)(1) and (c)(2) of this section are extended as follows:

(i) The applicable time is 20 business days in place of 10 business days under paragraphs (c)(1) and (c)(2) of this section if the notice of error involves an electronic fund transfer to or from the account within 30 days after the first deposit to the account was made.

(ii) The applicable time is 90 days in place of 45 days under paragraph (c)(2) of this section, for completing an investigation, if a notice of error involves an electronic fund transfer that:

(A) Was not initiated within a state;

(B) Resulted from a point-of-sale debit card transaction; or

(C) Occurred within 30 days after the first deposit to the account was made.

(4) *Investigation.* With the exception of transfers covered by § 205.14, a financial institution's review of its own records regarding an alleged error satisfies the requirements of this section if:

(i) The alleged error concerns a transfer to or from a third party; and

(ii) There is no agreement between the institution and the third party for the type of electronic fund transfer involved.

(d) *Procedures if financial institution determines no error or different error occurred.* In addition to following the procedures specified in paragraph (c) of this section, the financial institution shall follow the procedures set forth in this paragraph (d) if it determines that no error occurred or that an error occurred in a manner or amount different from that described by the consumer:

(1) *Written explanation.* The institution's report of the results of its investigation shall include a written explanation of the institution's findings and shall note the consumer's right to request the documents that the institution relied on in making its determination. Upon request, the institution shall promptly provide copies of the documents.

(2) *Debiting provisional credit.* Upon debiting a provisionally credited amount, the financial institution shall:

(i) Notify the consumer of the date and amount of the debiting;

(ii) Notify the consumer that the institution will honor checks, drafts, or similar instruments payable to third parties and preauthorized transfers from the consumer's account (without charge to the consumer as a result of an overdraft) for five business days after the notification. The institution shall honor items as specified in the notice, but need honor only items that it would have paid if the provisionally credited funds had not been debited.

(e) *Reassertion of error.* A financial institution that has fully complied with the error resolution requirements has no further responsibilities under this section should the consumer later reassert the same error, except in the case of an error asserted by the consumer following receipt of information provided under paragraph (a)(1)(vii) of this section.

§ 205.12   Relation to other laws

(a) *Relation to Truth in Lending.* (1) The Electronic Fund Transfer Act and this part govern:

(i) The addition to an accepted credit card, as defined in Regulation Z (12 CFR 226.12(a)(2), footnote 21), of the capability to initiate electronic fund transfers;

(ii) The issuance of an access device that permits credit extensions (under a preexisting agreement between a consumer and a financial institution) only when the consumer's account is overdrawn or to maintain a specified minimum balance in the consumer's account; and

(iii) A consumer's liability for an unauthorized electronic fund transfer and the investigation of errors involving an extension of credit that occurs under an agreement between the consumer and a financial institution to extend credit when the consumer's account is overdrawn or to maintain a specified minimum balance in the consumer's account.

(2) The Truth in Lending Act and Regulation Z (12 CFR Part 226), which prohibit the unsolicited issuance of credit cards, govern:

(i) The addition of a credit feature to an accepted access device; and

(ii) Except as provided in paragraph (a)(1)(ii) of this section, the issuance of a credit card that is also an access device.

(b) *Preemption of inconsistent state laws—(1) Inconsistent requirements.* The Board shall determine, upon its own motion or upon the request of a state, financial institution, or other interested party, whether the act and this part preempt state law relating to electronic fund transfers. Only state laws that are inconsistent with the act and this part are preempted and then only to the extent of the inconsistency. A state law is not inconsistent with the act and this part if it is more protective of consumers.

(2) *Standards for determination.* State law is inconsistent with the requirements of the act and this part if it:

(i) Requires or permits a practice or act prohibited by the federal law;

(ii) Provides for consumer liability for unauthorized electronic fund transfers that exceeds the limits imposed by the federal law;

(iii) Allows longer time periods than the federal law for investigating and correcting alleged errors, or does not require the financial institution to credit the consumer's account during an error investigation in accordance with § 205.11(c)(2)(i); or

(iv) Requires initial disclosures, periodic statements, or receipts that are different in content from those required by the federal law except to the extent that the disclosures relate to consumer rights granted by the state law and not by the federal law.

(c) *State exemptions*—(1) *General rule.* Any state may apply for an exemption from the requirements of the act or this part for any class of electronic fund transfers within the state. The Board shall grant an exemption if it determines that:

(i) Under state law the class of electronic fund transfers is subject to requirements substantially similar to those imposed by the federal law; and

(ii) There is adequate provision for state enforcement.

(2) *Exception.* To assure that the federal and state courts continue to have concurrent jurisdiction, and to aid in implementing the act:

(i) No exemption shall extend to the civil liability provisions of section 915 of the act; and

(ii) When the Board grants an exemption, the state law requirements shall constitute the requirements of the federal law for purposes of section 915 of the act, except for state law requirements not imposed by the federal law.

§ 205.13   Administrative enforcement; record retention

(a) *Enforcement by federal agencies.* Compliance with this part is enforced by the agencies listed in Appendix B of this part.

(b) *Record retention.* (1) Any person subject to the act and this part shall retain evidence of compliance with the requirements imposed by the act and this part for a period of not less than two years from the date disclosures are required to be made or action is required to be taken.

(2) Any person subject to the act and this part having actual notice that it is the subject of an investigation or an enforcement proceeding by its enforcement agency, or having been served with notice of an action filed under sections 910, 915, or 916(a) of the act, shall retain the records that pertain to the investigation, action, or proceeding until final disposition of the matter unless an earlier time is allowed by court or agency order.

§ 205.14   Electronic fund transfer service provider not holding consumer's account

(a) *Provider of electronic fund transfer service.* A person that provides an electronic fund transfer service to a consumer but that does not hold the consumer's account is subject to all requirements of this part if the person:

(1) Issues a debit card (or other access device) that the consumer can use to access the consumer's account held by a financial institution; and

(2) Has no agreement with the account-holding institution regarding such access.

(b) *Compliance by service provider.* In addition to the requirements generally applicable under this part, the service provider shall comply with the following special rules:

(1) *Disclosures and documentation.* The service provider shall give the disclosures and documentation required by §§ 205.7, 205.8, and 205.9 that are within the purview of its relationship with the consumer. The service provider need not furnish the periodic statement required by § 205.9(b) if the following conditions are met:

(i) The debit card (or other access device) issued to the consumer bears the service provider's name and an address or telephone number for making inquiries or giving notice of error;

(ii) The consumer receives a notice concerning use of the debit card that is substantially similar to the notice contained in Appendix A of this part;

(iii) The consumer receives, on or with the receipts required § 205.9(a), the address and telephone number to be used for an inquiry, to give notice of an error, or to report the loss or theft of the debit card;

(iv) The service provider transmits to the account-holding institution the information specified in § 205.9(b)(1), in the format prescribed by the automated clearinghouse system used to clear the fund transfers;

(v) The service provider extends the time period for notice of loss or theft of a debit card, set forth in § 205.6(b)(1) and (2), from two business days to four business days after the consumer learns of the loss or theft; and extends the time periods for reporting unauthorized transfers or errors, set forth in §§ 205.6(b)(3) and 205.11(b)(1)(i), from 60 days to 90 days following the transmittal of a periodic statement by the account-holding institution.

(2) *Error resolution.* (i) The service provider shall extend by a reasonable time the period in which notice of an error must be received, specified in § 205.11(b)(1)(i), if a delay resulted from an initial attempt by the consumer to notify the account-holding institution.

(ii) The service provider shall disclose to the consumer the date on which it initiates a transfer to effect a provisional credit in accordance with § 205.11(c)(2)(ii).

(iii) If the service provider determines an error occurred, it shall transfer funds to or from the consumer's account, in the appropriate amount and within the applicable time period, in accordance with § 205.11(c)(2)(i).

(iv) If funds were provisionally credited and the service provider determines no error occurred, it may reverse the credit. The service provider shall notify the account-holding institution of the period during which the account-holding institution must honor debits to the account in accordance with § 205.11(d)(2)(ii). If an overdraft results, the service provider shall promptly reimburse the account-holding institution in the amount of the overdraft.

(c) *Compliance by account-holding institution.* The account-holding institution need not comply with the requirements of the act and this part with respect to electronic fund transfers initiated through the service provider except as follows:

(1) *Documentation.* The account-holding institution shall provide a periodic statement that describes each electronic fund transfer initiated by the consumer with the access device issued by the service provider. The account-holding institution has no liability for the failure to comply with this requirement if the service provider did not provide the necessary information; and

(2) *Error resolution.* Upon request, the account-holding institution shall provide information or copies of documents needed by the service provider to investigate errors or to furnish copies of documents to the consumer. The account-holding institution shall also honor debits to the account in accordance with § 205.11(d)(2)(ii).

§ 205.15   Electronic fund transfer of government benefits

(a) *Government agency subject to regulation.* (1) A government agency is deemed to be a financial institution for purposes of the act and this part if directly or indirectly it issues an access device to a consumer for use in initiating an electronic fund transfer of government benefits from an account, other than needs-tested benefits in a program established under state or local law or administered by a state or local agency. The agency shall comply with all applicable requirements of the act and this part, except as provided in this section.

(2) For purposes of this section, the term *account* means an account established by a government agency for distributing government benefits to a consumer electronically, such as through automated teller machines or point-of-sale terminals, but does not include an account for distributing needs-tested benefits in a program established under state or local law or administered by a state or local agency.

(b) *Issuance of access devices.* For purposes of this section, a consumer is deemed to request an access device when the consumer applies for government benefits that the agency disburses or will disburse by means of an electronic fund transfer. The agency shall verify the identity of the consumer receiving the device by reasonable means before the device is activated.

(c) *Alternative to periodic statement.* A government agency need not furnish the periodic statement required by § 205.9(b) if the agency makes available to the consumer:

(1) The consumer's account balance, through a readily available telephone line and at a terminal (such as by providing balance information at a balance-inquiry terminal or providing it, routinely or upon request, on a terminal receipt at the time of an electronic fund transfer); and

(2) A written history of the consumer's account transactions that is provided promptly in response to an oral or written request and that covers at least 60 days preceding the date of a request by the consumer.

(d) *Modified requirements.* A government agency that does not furnish periodic statements, in accordance with paragraph (c) of this section, shall comply with the following special rules:

(1) *Initial disclosures.* The agency shall modify the disclosures under § 205.7(b) by disclosing:

(i) *Account balance.* The means by which the consumer may obtain information concerning the account balance, including a telephone number. The agency provides a notice substantially similar to the notice contained in paragraph A–5 in Appendix A of this part.

(ii) *Written account history.* A summary of the consumer's right to receive a written account history upon request, in place of the periodic statement required by § 205.7(b)(6), and the telephone number to call to request an account history. This disclosure may be made by providing a notice substantially similar to the notice contained in paragraph A–5 in Appendix A of this part.

(iii) *Error resolution.* A notice concerning error resolution that is substantially similar to the notice contained in paragraph A–5 in Appendix A of this part, in place of the notice required by § 205.7(b)(10).

(2) *Annual error resolution notice.* The agency shall provide an annual notice concerning error resolution that is substantially similar to the notice contained in paragraph A–5 in appendix A, in place of the notice required by § 205.8(b).

(3) *Limitations on liability.* For purposes of § 205.6(b)(3), regarding a 60–day period for reporting any unauthorized transfer that appears on a periodic statement, the 60–day period shall begin with transmittal of a written account history or other account information provided to the consumer under paragraph (c) of this section.

(4) *Error resolution.* The agency shall comply with the requirements of § 205.11 in response to an oral or written notice of an error from the consumer that is received no later than 60 days after the consumer obtains the written account history or other account information, under paragraph (c) of this section, in which the error is first reflected.

§ 205.16   Disclosures at automated teller machines

(a) *Definition.* Automated teller machine operator means any person that operates an automated teller machine at which a consumer initiates an electronic fund transfer or a balance inquiry and that does not hold the account to or from which the transfer is made, or about which an inquiry is made.

(b) *General.* An automated teller machine operator that imposes a fee on a consumer for initiating an electronic fund transfer or a balance inquiry shall:

(1) Provide notice that a fee will be imposed for providing electronic fund transfer services or a balance inquiry; and

(2) Disclose the amount of the fee.

(c) *Notice requirement.* To meet the requirements of paragraph (b) of this section, an automated teller machine operator must comply with the following:

(1) *On the machine.* Post in a prominent and conspicuous location on or at the automated teller machine a notice that:

(i) A fee will be imposed for providing electronic fund transfer services or for a balance inquiry; or

(ii) A fee may be imposed for providing electronic fund transfer services or for a balance inquiry, but the notice in this paragraph (c)(1)(ii) may be substituted for the notice in paragraph (c)(1)(i) only if there are circumstances under which a fee will not be imposed for such services; and

(2) *Screen or paper notice.* Provide the notice required by paragraphs (b)(1) and (b)(2) of this section either by showing it on the screen of the automated teller machine or by providing it on paper, before the consumer is committed to paying a fee.

(d) *Temporary exemption.* Through December 31, 2004, the notice requirement in paragraph (c)(2) of this section does not apply to any automated teller machine that lacks the technical capability to provide such information.

(e) *Imposition of fee.* An automated teller machine operator may impose a fee on a consumer for initiating an electronic fund transfer or a balance inquiry only if

(1) The consumer is provided the notices required under paragraph (c) of this section, and

(2) The consumer elects to continue the transaction or inquiry after receiving such notices.

§ 205.17   [Reserved]

§ 205.18   Requirements for Financial Institutions Offering Payroll Card Accounts

(a) *Coverage.* A financial institution shall comply with all applicable requirements of the act and this part with respect to payroll card accounts except as provided in this section.

(b) *Alternative to periodic statements.*

(1) A financial institution need not furnish periodic statements required by § 205.9(b) if the institution makes available to the consumer—

(i) The consumer's account balance, through a readily available telephone line;

(ii) An electronic history of the consumer's account transactions, such as through an Internet Web site, that covers at least 60 days preceding the date the consumer electronically accesses the account; and

(iii) A written history of the consumer's account transactions that is provided promptly in response to an oral or written request and that covers at least 60 days preceding the date the financial institution receives the consumer's request.

(2) The history of account transactions provided under paragraphs (b)(1)(ii) and (iii) of this section must include the information set forth in § 205.9(b).

(c) *Modified requirements.* A financial institution that provides information under paragraph (b) of this section, shall comply with the following:

(1) *Initial disclosures.* The financial institution shall modify the disclosures under § 205.7(b) by disclosing—

(i) *Account information.* A telephone number that the consumer may call to obtain the account balance, the means by which the consumer can obtain an electronic account history, such as the address of an Internet Web site, and a summary of the consumer's right to receive a written account history upon request (in place of the summary of the right to receive a periodic statement required by § 205.7(b)(6)), including a telephone number to call to request a history. The disclosure required by this paragraph (c)(1)(i) may be made by providing a notice substantially similar to the notice contained in paragraph A–7(a) in appendix A of this part.

(ii) *Error resolution.* A notice concerning error resolution that is substantially similar to the notice contained in paragraph A–7(b) in appendix A of this part, in place of the notice required by § 205.7(b)(10).

(2) *Annual error resolution notice.* The financial institution shall provide an annual notice concerning error resolution that is substantially similar to the notice contained in paragraph A–7(b) in appendix A of this part, in place of the notice required by § 205.8(b). Alternatively, a financial institution may include on or with each electronic and written history provided in accordance with § 205.18(b)(1), a notice substantially similar to the abbreviated notice for periodic statements contained in paragraph A–3(b) in appendix A of this part, modified as necessary to reflect the error resolution provisions set forth in this section.

(3) *Limitations on liability.* (i) For purposes of § 205.6(b)(3), the 60–day period for reporting any unauthorized transfer shall begin on the earlier of:

(A) The date the consumer electronically accesses the consumer's account under paragraph (b)(1)(ii) of this section, provided that the electronic history made available to the consumer reflects the transfer; or

(B) The date the financial institution sends a written history of the consumer's account transactions requested by the consumer under paragraph (b)(1)(iii) of this section in which the unauthorized transfer is first reflected.

(ii) A financial institution may comply with paragraph (c)(3)(i) of this section by limiting the consumer's liability for an unauthorized transfer as provided under § 205.6(b)(3) for any transfer reported by the consumer within 120 days after the transfer was credited or debited to the consumer's account.

(4) *Error resolution.* (i) The financial institution shall comply with the requirements of § 205.11 in response to an oral or written notice of an error from the consumer that is received by the earlier of—

(A) Sixty days after the date the consumer electronically accesses the consumer's account under paragraph (b)(1)(ii) of this section, provided that the electronic history made available to the consumer reflects the alleged error; or

(B) Sixty days after the date the financial institution sends a written history of the consumer's account transactions requested by the consumer under paragraph (b)(1)(iii) of this section in which the alleged error is first reflected.

(ii) In lieu of following the procedures in paragraph (c)(4)(i) of this section, a financial institution complies with the requirements for resolving errors in § 205.11 if it investigates any oral or written notice of an error from the consumer that is received by the institution within 120 days after the transfer allegedly in error was credited or debited to the consumer's account.

MAGNUSON–MOSS WARRANTY ACT

15 U.S.C. §§ 2301–2312

Table of Sections

---

§ 101. Definitions [15 U.S.C. § 2301]

For the purposes of this title:

(1) The term "consumer product" means any tangible personal property which is distributed in commerce and which is normally used for personal, family, or household purposes (including any such property intended to be attached to or installed in any real property without regard to whether it is so attached or installed).

(2) The term "Commission" means the Federal Trade Commission.

(3) The term "consumer" means a buyer (other than for purposes of resale) of any consumer product, any person to whom such product is transferred during the duration of an implied or written warranty (or service contract) applicable to the product, and any other person who is entitled by the terms of such warranty (or service contract) or under applicable State law to enforce against the warrantor (or service contractor) the obligations of the warranty (or service contract).

(4) The term "supplier" means any person engaged in the business of making a consumer product directly or indirectly available to consumers.

(5) The term "warrantor" means any supplier or other person who gives or offers to give a written warranty or who is or may be obligated under an implied warranty.

(6) The term "written warranty" means—

(A) any written affirmation of fact or written promise made in connection with the sale of a consumer product by a supplier to a buyer which relates to the nature of the material or workmanship and affirms or promises that such material or workmanship is defect free or will meet a specified level of performance over a specified period of time, or

(B) any undertaking in writing in connection with the sale by a supplier of a consumer product to refund, repair, replace, or take other remedial action with respect to such product in the event that such product fails to meet the specifications set forth in the undertaking,

which written affirmation, promise, or undertaking becomes part of the basis of the bargain between a supplier and a buyer for purposes other than resale of such product.

(7) The term "implied warranty" means an implied warranty arising under State law (as modified by sections 108 and 104(a)) in connection with the sale by a supplier of a consumer product.

(8) The term "service contract" means a contract in writing to perform, over a fixed period of time or for a specified duration, services relating to the maintenance or repair (or both) of a consumer product.

(9) The term "reasonable and necessary maintenance" consists of those operations (A) which the consumer reasonably can be expected to perform or have performed and (B) which are necessary to keep any consumer product performing its intended function and operating at a reasonable level of performance.

(10) The term "remedy" means whichever of the following actions the warrantor elects:

(A) repair,

(B) replacement, or

(C) refund;

except that the warrantor may not elect refund unless (i) the warrantor is unable to provide replacement and repair is not commercially practicable or cannot be timely made, or (ii) the consumer is willing to accept such refund.

(11) The term "replacement" means furnishing a new consumer product which is identical or reasonably equivalent to the warranted consumer product.

(12) The term "refund" means refunding the actual purchase price (less reasonable depreciation based on actual use where permitted by rules of the Commission).

(13) The term "distributed in commerce" means sold in commerce, introduced or delivered for introduction into commerce, or held for sale or distribution after introduction into commerce.

(14) The term "commerce" means trade, traffic, commerce, or transportation—

    (A) between a place in a State and any place outside thereof, or

    (B) which affects trade, traffic, commerce, or transportation described in subparagraph (A).

(15) The term "State" means a State, the District of Columbia, the Commonwealth of Puerto Rico, the Virgin Islands, Guam, the Canal Zone, or American Samoa. The term "State law" includes a law of the United States applicable only to the District of Columbia or only to a territory or possession of the United States; and the term "Federal law" excludes any State law.

§ 102. Rules governing contents of warranties [15 U.S.C. § 2302]

(a) Full and conspicuous disclosure of terms and conditions; additional requirements for contents

In order to improve the adequacy of information available to consumers, prevent deception, and improve competition in the marketing of consumer products, any warrantor warranting a consumer product to a consumer by means of a written warranty shall, to the extent required by rules of the Commission, fully and conspicuously disclose in simple and readily understood language the terms and conditions of such warranty. Such rules may require inclusion in the written warranty of any of the following items among others:

(1) The clear identification of the names and addresses of the warrantors.

(2) The identity of the party or parties to whom the warranty is extended.

(3) The products or parts covered.

(4) A statement of what the warrantor will do in the event of a defect, malfunction, or failure to conform with such written warranty—at whose expense—and for what period of time.

(5) A statement of what the consumer must do and expenses he must bear.

(6) Exceptions and exclusions from the terms of the warranty.

(7) The step-by-step procedure which the consumer should take in order to obtain performance of any obligation under the warranty, including the identification of any person or class of persons authorized to perform the obligations set forth in the warranty.

(8) Information respecting the availability of any informal dispute settlement procedure offered by the warrantor and a recital, where the warranty so provides, that the purchaser may be required to resort to such procedure before pursuing any legal remedies in the courts.

(9) A brief, general description of the legal remedies available to the consumer.

(10) The time at which the warrantor will perform any obligations under the warranty.

(11) The period of time within which, after notice of a defect, malfunction, or failure to conform with the warranty, the warrantor will perform any obligations under the warranty.

(12) The characteristics or properties of the products, or parts thereof, that are not covered by the warranty.

(13) The elements of the warranty in words or phrases which would not mislead a reasonable, average consumer as to the nature or scope of the warranty.

(b) Availability of terms to consumer; manner and form for presentation and display of information; duration; extension of period for written warranty or service contract

(1)(A) The Commission shall prescribe rules requiring that the terms of any written warranty on a consumer product be made available to the consumer (or prospective consumer) prior to the sale of the product to him.

(B) The Commission may prescribe rules for determining the manner and form in which information with respect to any written warranty of a consumer product shall be clearly and conspicuously presented or displayed so as not to mislead the reasonable, average consumer, when such information is contained in advertising, labeling, point-of-sale material, or other representations in writing.

(2) Nothing in this [Act] (other than paragraph (3) of this subsection) shall be deemed to authorize the Commission to prescribe the duration of written warranties given or to require that a consumer product or any of its components be warranted.

(3) The Commission may prescribe rules for extending the period of time a written warranty or service contract is in effect to correspond with any period of time in excess of a reasonable period (not less than 10 days) during which the consumer is deprived of the use of such consumer product by reason of failure of the product to conform with the written warranty or by reason of the failure of the warrantor (or service contractor) to carry out such warranty (or service contract) within the period specified in the warranty (or service contract).

(c) Prohibitions on conditions for written or implied warranty; waiver by Commission

No warrantor of a consumer product may condition his written or implied warranty of such product on the consumer's using, in connection with such product, any article or service (other than article or service provided without charge under the terms of the warranty) which is identified by brand, trade, or corporate name; except that the prohibition of this subsection may be waived by the Commission if—

(1) the warrantor satisfies the Commission that the warranted product will function properly only if the article or service so identified is used in connection with the warranted product, and

(2) the Commission finds that such a waiver is in the public interest.

The Commission shall identify in the Federal Register, and permit public comment on, all applications for waiver of the prohibition of this subsection, and shall publish in the Federal Register its disposition of any such application, including the reasons therefor.

(d) Incorporation by reference of detailed substantive warranty provisions

The Commission may by rule devise detailed substantive warranty provisions which warrantors may incorporate by reference in their warranties.

(e) Applicability to consumer products costing more than $5

The provisions of this section apply only to warranties which pertain to consumer products actually costing the consumer more than $5.

§ 103. Designation of warranties [15 U.S.C. § 2303]

(a) Full (statement of duration) or limited warranty

Any warrantor warranting a consumer product by means of a written warranty shall clearly and conspicuously designate such warranty in the following manner, unless exempted from doing so by the Commission pursuant to subsection (c) of this section:

(1) If the written warranty meets the Federal minimum standards for warranty set forth in section 104 of this Act, then it shall be conspicuously designated a "full (statement of duration) warranty."

(2) If the written warranty does not meet the Federal minimum standards for warranty set forth in section 104 of this Act, then it shall be conspicuously designated a "limited warranty."

(b) Applicability of requirements, standards, etc., to representations or statements of customer satisfaction

Sections 102, 103 and 104 shall not apply to statements or representations which are similar to expressions of general policy concerning customer satisfaction and which are not subject to any specific limitations.

(c) Exemptions by Commission

In addition to exercising the authority pertaining to disclosure granted in section 102 of this Act, the Commission may by rule determine when a written warranty does not have to be designated either "full (statement of duration)" or "limited" in accordance with this section.

(d) Applicability to consumer products costing more than $10 and not designated as full warranties

The provisions of subsections (a) and (c) of this section apply only to warranties which pertain to consumer products actually costing the consumer more than $10 and which are not designated "full (statement of duration) warranties."

§ 104. Federal minimum standards for warranty [15 U.S.C. § 2304]

(a) Remedies under written warranty; duration of implied warranty; exclusion or limitation on consequential damages for breach of written or implied warranty; election of refund or replacement

In order for a warrantor warranting a consumer product by means of a written warranty to meet the Federal minimum standards for warranty—

(1) such warrantor must as a minimum remedy such consumer product within a reasonable time and without charge, in the case of a defect, malfunction, or failure to conform with such written warranty;

(2) notwithstanding section 108(b), such warrantor may not impose any limitation on the duration of any implied warranty on the product;

(3) such warrantor may not exclude or limit consequential damages for breach of any written or implied warranty on such product, unless such exclusion or limitation conspicuously appears on the face of the warranty; and

(4) if the product (or a component part thereof) contains a defect or malfunction after a reasonable number of attempts by the warrantor to remedy defects or malfunctions in such product, such warrantor must permit the consumer to elect either a refund for, or replacement without charge of, such product or part (as the case may be). The Commission may by rule specify for purposes of this paragraph, what constitutes a reasonable number of attempts to remedy particular kinds of defects or malfunctions under different circumstances. If the warrantor replaces a component part of a consumer product, such replacement shall include installing the part in the product without charge.

(b) Duties and conditions imposed on consumer by warrantor

(1) In fulfilling the duties under subsection (a) of this section respecting a written warranty, the warrantor shall not impose any duty other than notification upon any consumer as a condition of securing remedy of any consumer product which malfunctions, is defective, or does not conform to the written warranty unless the warrantor has demonstrated in a rulemaking proceeding, or can demonstrate in an administrative or judicial enforcement proceeding (including private enforcement), or in an informal dispute settlement proceeding, that such a duty is reasonable.

(2) Notwithstanding paragraph (1), a warrantor may require, as a condition to replacement of, or refund for, any consumer product under subsection (a) of this section, that such consumer product shall be made available to the warrantor free and clear of liens, and other encumbrances, except as otherwise provided by rule or order of the Commission in cases in which such a requirement would not be practicable.

(3) The Commission may, by rule define in detail the duties set forth in subsection (a) of this section and the applicability of such duties to warrantors of different categories of consumer products with "full (statement of duration)" warranties.

(4) The duties under subsection (a) of this section extend from the warrantor to each person who is a consumer with respect to the consumer product.

(c) Waiver of standards

The performance of the duties under subsection (a) of this section shall not be required of the warrantor if he can show that the defect, malfunction, or failure of any warranted consumer product to conform with a written warranty, was caused by damage (not resulting from defect or malfunction) while in the possession of the consumer, or unreasonable use (including failure to provide reasonable and necessary maintenance).

(d) Remedy without charge

For purposes of this section and of section 102(c), the term "without charge" means that the warrantor may not assess the consumer for any costs the warrantor or his representatives incur in connection with the required remedy of a warranted consumer product. An obligation under subsection (a)(1)(A) of this section to remedy without charge does not necessarily require the warrantor to compensate the consumer for incidental expenses; however, if any incidental expenses are incurred because the remedy is not made within a reasonable time or because the warrantor imposed an unreasonable duty upon the consumer as a condition of securing remedy, then the consumer shall be entitled to recover reasonable incidental expenses which are so incurred in any action against the warrantor.

(e) Incorporation of standards to products designated with full warranty for purposes of judicial actions

If a supplier designates a warranty applicable to a consumer product as a "full (statement of duration)" warranty, then the warranty on such product shall, for purposes of any action under section 110(d) or under any State law, be deemed to incorporate at least the minimum requirements of this section and rules prescribed under this section.

§ 105. Full and limited warranting of a consumer product [15 U.S.C. § 2305]

Nothing in this [Act] shall prohibit the selling of a consumer product which has both full and limited warranties if such warranties are clearly and conspicuously differentiated.

§ 106. Service contracts; rules for full, clear and conspicuous disclosure of terms and conditions; addition to or in lieu of written warranty [15 U.S.C. § 2306]

(a) The Commission may prescribe by rule the manner and form in which the terms and conditions of service contracts shall be fully, clearly, and conspicuously disclosed.

(b) Nothing in this [Act] shall be construed to prevent a supplier or warrantor from entering into a service contract with the consumer in addition to or in lieu of a written warranty if such contract fully, clearly, and conspicuously discloses its terms and conditions in simple and readily understood language.

§ 107. Designation of representatives by warrantor to perform duties under written or implied warranty [15 U.S.C. § 2307]

Nothing in this [Act] shall be construed to prevent any warrantor from designating representatives to perform duties under the written or implied warranty: *Provided,* That such warrantor shall make reasonable arrangements for compensation of such designated representatives, but no such designation shall relieve the warrantor of his direct responsibilities to the consumer or make the representative a co-warrantor.

§ 108. Implied warranties [15 U.S.C. § 2308]

(a) Restrictions on disclaimers or modifications

No supplier may disclaim or modify (except as provided in subsection (b) of this section) any implied warranty to a consumer with respect to such consumer product if (1) such supplier makes any written warranty to the consumer with respect to such consumer product, or (2) at the time of sale, or within 90 days thereafter, such supplier enters into a service contract with the consumer which applies to such consumer product.

(b) Limitation on duration

For purposes of this [Act] (other than section 104(a)(2)), implied warranties may be limited in duration to the duration of a written warranty of reasonable duration, if such limitation is conscionable and is set forth in clear and unmistakable language and prominently displayed on the face of the warranty.

(c) Effectiveness of disclaimers, modifications, or limitations

A disclaimer, modification, or limitation made in violation of this section shall be ineffective for purposes of this [Act] and State law.

§ 109. Procedures applicable to promulgation of rules by Commission [15 U.S.C. § 2309]

(a) Oral presentation

Any rule prescribed under this [Act] shall be prescribed in accordance with section 553 of Title 5; except that the Commission shall give interested persons an opportunity for oral presentations of data, views, and arguments, in addition to written submissions. A transcript shall be kept of any oral presentation. Any such rule shall be subject to judicial review under section 18(e) of the Federal Trade Commission Act in the same manner as rules prescribed under section 18(a)(1)(B) of such Act, except that section 18(e)(3)(B) of such Act shall not apply.

(b) Warranties and warranty practices involved in sale of used motor vehicles

The Commission shall initiate within one year after January 4, 1975, a rulemaking proceeding dealing with warranties and warranty practices in connection with the sale of used motor vehicles; and, to the extent necessary to supplement the protections offered the consumer by this [Act] shall prescribe rules dealing with such warranties and practices. In prescribing rules under this subsection, the Commission may exercise any authority it may have under this [Act], or other law, and in addition it may require disclosure that a used motor vehicle is sold without any warranty and specify the form and content of such disclosure.

§ 110. Remedies in consumer disputes [15 U.S.C. § 2310]

(a) Informal dispute settlement procedures; establishment; rules setting forth minimum requirements; effect of compliance by warrantor; review of informal procedures or implementation by Commission; application to existing informal procedures

(1) Congress hereby declares it to be its policy to encourage warrantors to establish procedures whereby consumer disputes are fairly and expeditiously settled through informal dispute settlement mechanisms.

(2) The Commission shall prescribe rules setting forth minimum requirements for any informal dispute settlement procedure which is incorporated into the terms of a written warranty to which any provision of this [Act] applies. Such rules shall provide for participation in such procedure by independent or governmental entities.

(3) One or more warrantors may establish an informal dispute settlement procedure which meets the requirements of the Commission's rules under paragraph (2). If—

(A) a warrantor establishes such a procedure,

(B) such procedure, and its implementation, meets the requirements of such rules, and

(C) he incorporates in a written warranty a requirement that the consumer resort to such procedure before pursuing any legal remedy under this section respecting such warranty,

then (i) the consumer may not commence a civil action (other than a class action) under subsection (d) of this section unless he initially resorts to such procedure; and (ii) a class of consumers may not proceed in a class action under subsection (d) of this section except to the extent the court determines necessary to establish the representative capacity of the named plaintiffs, unless the named plaintiffs (upon notifying the defendant that they are named plaintiffs in a class action with respect to a warranty obligation) initially resort to such procedure. In the case of such a class action which is brought in a district court of the United States, the representative capacity of the named plaintiffs shall be established in the application of rule 23 of the Federal Rules of Civil Procedure. In any civil action arising out of a warranty obligation and relating to a matter considered in such a procedure, any decision in such procedure shall be admissible in evidence.

(4) The Commission on its own initiative may, or upon written complaint filed by any interested person shall, review the bona fide operation of any dispute settlement procedure resort to which is stated in a written warranty to be a prerequisite to pursuing a legal remedy under this section. If the Commission finds that such procedure or its implementation fails to comply with the requirements of the rules under paragraph (2), the Commission may take appropriate remedial action under any authority it may have under this chapter or any other provision of law.

(5) Until rules under paragraph (2) take effect, this subsection shall not affect the validity of any informal dispute settlement procedure respecting consumer warranties, but in any action under subsection (d) of this section, the court may invalidate any such procedure if it finds that such procedure is unfair.

(b) Prohibited acts

It shall be a violation of section 5(a)(1) of the Federal Trade Commission Act for any person to fail to comply with any requirement imposed on such person by this [Act] (or a rule thereunder) or to violate any prohibition contained in this [Act] (or a rule thereunder).

(c) Injunction proceedings by Attorney General or Commission for deceptive warranty, noncompliance with requirements, or violating prohibitions; procedures; definitions

(1) The district courts of the United States shall have jurisdiction of any action brought by the Attorney General (in his capacity as such), or by the Commission by any of its attorneys designated by it for such purpose, to restrain (A) any warrantor from making a deceptive warranty with respect to a consumer product, or (B) any person from failing to comply with any requirement imposed on such person by or pursuant to this [Act] or from violating any prohibition contained in this [Act]. Upon proper showing that, weighing the equities and considering the Commission's or Attorney General's likelihood of ultimate success, such action would be in the public interest and after notice to the defendant, a temporary restraining order or preliminary injunction may be granted without bond. In the case of an action brought by the Commission, if a complaint under section 5 of the Federal Trade Commission Act is not filed within such period (not exceeding 10 days) as may be specified by the court after the issuance of

the temporary restraining order or preliminary injunction, the order or injunction shall be dissolved by the court and be of no further force and effect. Any suit shall be brought in the district in which such person resides or transacts business. Whenever it appears to the court that the ends of justice require that other persons should be parties in the action, the court may cause them to be summoned whether or not they reside in the district in which the court is held, and to that end process may be served in any district.

(2) For the purposes of this subsection, the term "deceptive warranty" means (A) a written warranty which (i) contains an affirmation, promise, description, or representation which is either false or fraudulent, or which, in light of all of the circumstances, would mislead a reasonable individual exercising due care; or (ii) fails to contain information which is necessary in light of all of the circumstances, to make the warranty not misleading to a reasonable individual exercising due care; or (B) a written warranty created by the use of such terms as "guaranty" or "warranty", if the terms and conditions of such warranty so limit its scope and application as to deceive a reasonable individual.

(d) Civil action by consumer for damages, etc.; jurisdiction; recovery of costs and expenses; cognizable claims

(1) Subject to subsections (a)(3) and (e) of this section, a consumer who is damaged by the failure of a supplier, warrantor, or service contractor to comply with any obligation under this [Act], or under a written warranty, implied warranty, or service contract, may bring suit for damages and other legal and equitable relief—

(A) in any court of competent jurisdiction in any State or the District of Columbia; or

(B) in an appropriate district court of the United States, subject to paragraph (3) of this subsection.

(2) If a consumer finally prevails in any action brought under paragraph (1) of this subsection, he may be allowed by the court to recover as part of the judgment a sum equal to the aggregate amount of cost and expenses (including attorneys' fees based on actual time expended) determined by the court to have been reasonably incurred by the plaintiff for or in connection with the commencement and prosecution of such action, unless the court in its discretion shall determine that such an award of attorneys' fees would be inappropriate.

(3) No claim shall be cognizable in a suit brought under paragraph (1)(B) of this subsection—

(A) if the amount in controversy of any individual claim is less than the sum or value of $25;

(B) if the amount in controversy is less than the sum or value of $50,000 (exclusive of interest and costs) computed on the basis of all claims to be determined in this suit; or

(C) if the action is brought as a class action, and the number of named plaintiffs is less than one hundred.

(e) Class actions; conditions; procedures applicable

No action (other than a class action or an action respecting a warranty to which subsection (a)(3) of this section applies) may be brought under subsection (d) of this section for failure to comply with any obligation under any written or implied warranty or service contract, and a class of consumers may not proceed in a class action under such subsection with respect to such a failure except to the extent the court determines necessary to establish the representative capacity of the named plaintiffs, unless the person obligated under the warranty or service contract is afforded a reasonable opportunity to cure such failure to comply. In the case of such a class action (other than a class action respecting a warranty to which subsection (a)(3) of this section applies) brought under subsection (d) of this section for breach of any written or implied warranty or service contract, such reasonable opportunity will be afforded by the named plaintiffs and they shall at that time notify the defendant that they are acting on behalf of the class. In the case of such a class action which is brought in a district court of the United States, the representative capacity of the named plaintiffs shall be established in the application of rule 23 of the Federal Rules of Civil Procedure.

(f) Warrantors subject to enforcement of remedies

For purposes of this section, only the warrantor actually making a written affirmation of fact, promise, or undertaking shall be deemed to have created a written warranty, and any rights arising thereunder may be enforced under this section only against such warrantor and no other person.

§ 111. Applicability to other laws [15 U.S.C. § 2311]

(a) Federal Trade Commission Act and Federal Seed Act

(1) Nothing contained in this [Act] shall be construed to repeal, invalidate, or supersede the Federal Trade Commission Act or any statute defined therein as an Antitrust Act.

(2) Nothing in this [Act] shall be construed to repeal, invalidate, or supersede the Federal Seed Act and nothing in this [Act] shall apply to seed for planting.

(b) Rights, remedies, and liabilities

(1) Nothing in this [Act] shall invalidate or restrict any right or remedy of any consumer under State law or any other Federal law.

(2) Nothing in this [Act] (other than sections 108 and 104(a)(2) and (4)) shall (A) affect the liability of, or impose liability on, any person for personal injury, or (B) supersede any provision of State law regarding consequential damages for injury to the person or other injury.

(c) State warranty laws

(1) Except as provided in subsection (b) of this section and in paragraph (2) of this subsection, a State requirement—

    (A) which relates to labeling or disclosure with respect to written warranties or performance thereunder;

    (B) which is within the scope of an applicable requirement of sections 102, 103, and 104 (and rules implementing such sections), and

    (C) which is not identical to a requirement of section 102, 103, or 104 (or a rule thereunder),

shall not be applicable to written warranties complying with such sections (or rules thereunder).

(2) If, upon application of an appropriate State agency, the Commission determines (pursuant to rules issued in accordance with section 109) that any requirement of such State covering any transaction to which this [Act] applies (A) affords protection to consumers greater than the requirements of this [Act] and (B) does not unduly burden interstate commerce, then such State requirement shall be applicable (notwithstanding the provisions of paragraph (1) of this subsection) to the extent specified in such determination for so long as the State administers and enforces effectively any such greater requirement.

(d) Other Federal warranty laws

This chapter (other than section 102(c)) shall be inapplicable to any written warranty the making or content of which is otherwise governed by Federal law. If only a portion of a written warranty is so governed by Federal law, the remaining portion shall be subject to this [Act].

FEDERAL TRADE COMMISSION RULES, REGULATIONS, STATEMENTS AND INTERPRETATIONS UNDER THE MAGNUSON–MOSS WARRANTY ACT

16 C.F.R. Parts 700–703

PART 700. INTERPRETATIONS OF MAGNUSON–MOSS WARRANTY ACT

Table of Sections

---

§ 700.1 Products Covered

(a) The Act applies to written warranties on tangible personal property which is normally used for personal, family, or household purposes. This definition includes property which is intended to be attached to or installed in any real property without regard to whether it is so attached or installed. This means that a product is a "consumer product" if the use of that type of product is not uncommon. The percentage of sales or the use to which a product is put by any individual buyer is not determinative. For example, products such as automobiles and typewriters which are used for both personal and commercial purposes come within the definition of consumer product. Where it is unclear whether a particular product is covered under the definition of consumer product, any ambiguity will be resolved in favor of coverage.

(b) Agricultural products such as farm machinery, structures and implements used in the business or occupation of farming are not covered by the Act where their personal, family, or household use is uncommon. However, those agricultural products normally used for personal or household gardening (for example, to produce goods for personal consumption, and not for resale) are consumer products under the Act.

(c) The definition of "Consumer product" limits the applicability of the Act to personal property, "including any such property intended to be attached to or installed in any real property without regard to whether it is so attached or installed." This provision brings under the Act separate items of equipment attached to real property, such as air conditioners, furnaces, and water heaters.

(d) The coverage of separate items of equipment attached to real property includes, but is not limited to, appliances and other thermal, mechanical, and electrical equipment. (It does not extend to the wiring, plumbing, ducts, and other items which are integral component parts of the structure.) State law would classify many such products as fixtures to, and therefore a part of, realty. The statutory definition is designed to bring such products under the Act regardless of whether they may be considered fixtures under state law.

(e) The coverage of building materials which are not separate items of equipment is based on the nature of the purchase transaction. An analysis of the transaction will determine whether the goods are real or personal property. The numerous products which go into the construction of a consumer dwelling are all consumer products when sold "over the counter," as by hardware and building supply retailers. This is also true where a consumer contracts for the purchase of such materials in connection with the improvement, repair, or modification of a home (for example, paneling, dropped ceilings, siding, roofing, storm windows, remodeling). However, where such products are at the time of sale integrated into the structure of a dwelling they are not consumer products as they cannot be practically distinguished from realty. Thus, for example, the beams, wallboard, wiring, plumbing, windows, roofing, and other structural components of a dwelling are not consumer products when they are sold as part of real estate covered by a written warranty.

(f) In the case where a consumer contracts with a builder to construct a home, a substantial addition to a home, or other realty (such as a garage or an in-ground swimming pool) the building materials to be used are not consumer products. Although the materials are separately identifiable at the time the contract is made, it is the intention of the parties to contract for the construction of realty which will integrate the component materials. Of course, as noted above, any separate items of equipment to be attached to such realty are consumer products under the Act.

(g) Certain provisions of the Act apply only to products actually costing the consumer more than a specified amount. Section 103 applies to consumer products actually costing the consumer more than $10, excluding tax. The $10 minimum will be interpreted to include multiple-packaged items which may individually sell for less than $10, but which have been packaged in a manner that does not permit breaking the package to purchase an item or items at a price less than $10. Thus, a written warranty on a dozen items packaged and priced for sale at $12 must be designated, even though identical items may be offered in smaller quantities at under $10. This interpretation applies in the same manner to the minimum dollar limits in section 102 and rules promulgated under that section.

(h) Warranties on replacement parts and components used to repair consumer products are covered; warranties on services are not covered. Therefore, warranties which apply solely to a repairer's workmanship in performing repairs are not subject to the Act. Where a written agreement warrants both the parts provided to effect a repair and the workmanship in making that repair, the warranty must comply with the Act and the rules thereunder.

(i) The Act covers written warranties on consumer products "distributed in commerce" as that term is defined in section 101(3). Thus, by its terms the Act arguably applies to products exported to foreign jurisdictions. However, the public interest would not be served by the use of Commission resources to enforce the Act with respect to such products. Moreover, the legislative intent to apply the requirements of the Act to such products is not sufficiently clear to justify such an extraordinary result. The Commission does not contemplate the enforcement of the Act with respect to consumer products exported to foreign jurisdictions. Products exported for sale at military post exchanges remain subject to the same enforcement standards as products sold within the United States, its territories and possessions.

§ 700.2   Date of Manufacture

Section 112 of the Act provides that the Act shall apply only to those consumer products manufactured after July 4, 1975. When a consumer purchases repair of a consumer product the date of manufacture of any replacement parts used is the measuring date for determining coverage under the Act. The date of manufacture of the consumer product being repaired is in this instance not relevant. Where a consumer purchases or obtains on an exchange basis a rebuilt consumer product, the date that the rebuilding process is completed determines the Act's applicability.

§ 700.3   Written Warranty

(a) The Act imposes specific duties and liabilities on suppliers who offer written warranties on consumer products. Certain representations, such as energy efficiency ratings for electrical appliances, care labeling of wearing apparel, and other product information disclosures may be express warranties under the Uniform Commercial Code. However, these disclosures alone are not written warranties under this Act. Section 101(6) provides that a written affirmation of fact or a written promise of a specified level of performance must relate to a specified period of time in order to be considered a "written warranty."[1] A product information

---

1. A "written warranty" is also created by a written affirmation of fact or a written promise that the product is defect free, or by a written undertaking of remedial action within the meaning of section 101(6)(B).

disclosure without a specified time period to which the disclosure relates is therefore not a written warranty. In addition, section 111(d) exempts from the Act (except section 102(c)) any written warranty the making or content of which is required by federal law. The Commission encourages the disclosure of product information which is not deceptive and which may benefit consumers, and will not construe the Act to impede information disclosure in product advertising or labeling.

(b) Certain terms, or conditions, of sale of a consumer product may not be "written warranties" as that term is defined in section 101(6), and should not be offered or described in a manner that may deceive consumers as to their enforceability under the Act. For example, a seller of consumer products may give consumers an unconditional right to revoke acceptance of goods within a certain number of days after delivery without regard to defects or failure to meet a specified level of performance. Or a seller may permit consumers to return products for any reason for credit toward purchase of another item. Such terms of sale taken alone are not written warranties under the Act. Therefore, suppliers should avoid any characterization of such terms of sale as warranties. The use of such terms as "free trial period" and "trade-in credit policy" in this regard would be appropriate. Furthermore, such terms of sale should be stated separately from any written warranty. Of course, the offering and performance of such terms of sale remain subject to section 5 of the Federal Trade Commission Act, 15 U.S.C. 45.

(c) The Magnuson–Moss Warranty Act generally applies to written warranties covering consumer products. Many consumer products are covered by warranties which are neither intended for, nor enforceable by, consumers. A common example is a warranty given by a component supplier to a manufacturer of consumer products. (The manufacturer may, in turn, warrant these components to consumers.) The component supplier's warranty is generally given solely to the product manufacturer, and is neither intended to be conveyed to the consumer nor brought to the consumer's attention in connection with the sale. Such warranties are not subject to the Act, since a written warranty under section 101(6) of the Act must become "part of the basis of the bargain between a supplier and a buyer for purposes other than resale." However, the Act applies to a component supplier's warranty in writing which is given to the consumer. An example is a supplier's written warranty to the consumer covering a refrigerator that is sold installed in a boat or recreational vehicle. The supplier of the refrigerator relies on the boat or vehicle assembler to convey the written agreement to the consumer. In this case, the supplier's written warranty is to a consumer, and is covered by the Act.

§ 700.4 Parties "Actually Making" a Written Warranty

Section 110(f) of the Act provides that only the supplier "actually making" a written warranty is liable for purposes of FTC and private enforcement of the Act.   A supplier who does no more than distribute or sell a consumer product covered by a written warranty offered by another person or business and which identifies that person or business as the warrantor is not liable for failure of the written warranty to comply with the Act or rules thereunder.   However, other actions and written and oral representations of such a supplier in connection with the offer or sale of a warranted product may obligate that supplier under the Act.   If under state law the supplier is deemed to have "adopted" the written affirmation of fact, promise, or undertaking, the supplier is also obligated under the Act.   Suppliers are advised to consult state law to determine those actions and representations which may make them co-warrantors, and therefore obligated under the warranty of the other person or business.

§ 700.5   Expressions of General Policy

(a) Under section 103(b), statements or representations of general policy concerning customer satisfaction which are not subject to any specific limitation need not be designated as full or limited warranties, and are exempt from the requirements of sections 102, 103, and 104 of the Act and rules thereunder.   However, such statements remain subject to the enforcement provisions of section 110 of the Act, and to section 5 of the Federal Trade Commission Act, 15 U.S.C. 45.

(b) The section 103(b) exemption applies only to general policies, not to those which are limited to specific consumer products manufactured or sold by the supplier offering such a policy.   In addition, to qualify for an exemption under section 103(b) such policies may not be subject to any specific limitations.   For example, policies which have an express limitation of duration or a limitation of the amount to be refunded are not exempted. This does not preclude the imposition of reasonable limitations based on the circumstances in each instance a consumer seeks to invoke such an agreement.   For instance, a warrantor may refuse to honor such an expression of policy where a consumer has used a product for 10 years without previously expressing any dissatisfaction with the product.   Such a refusal would not be a specific limitation under this provision.

§ 700.6   Designation of Warranties

(a) Section 103 of the Act provides that written warranties on consumer products manufactured after July 4, 1975, and actually costing the consumer more than $10, excluding tax, must be designated either "Full (statement of duration) Warranty" or "Limited Warranty." Warrantors may include a statement of duration in a limited warranty designation. The designation or designations should appear clearly and conspicuously as a caption, or prominent title, clearly separated from the text of the warranty.   The full (statement of duration) warranty and limited warranty are the exclusive designations permitted under the Act, unless a specific exception is created by rule.

(b) Section 104(b)(4) states that "the duties under subsection (a) (of section 104) extend from the warrantor to each person who is a consumer with respect to the consumer product." Section 101(3) defines a consumer as "a buyer (other than for purposes of resale) of any consumer product, any person to whom such product is transferred during the duration of an implied or written warranty (or service contract) applicable to the product...." Therefore, a full warranty may not expressly restrict the warranty rights of a transferee during its stated duration. However, where the duration of a full warranty is defined solely in terms of first purchaser ownership there can be no violation of section 104(b)(4), since the duration of the warranty expires, by definition, at the time of transfer. No rights of a subsequent transferee are cut off as there is no transfer of ownership "during the duration of (any) warranty." Thus, these provisions do not preclude the offering of a full warranty with its duration determined exclusively by the period during which the first purchaser owns the product, or uses it in conjunction with another product. For example, an automotive battery or muffler warranty may be designated as "full warranty for as long as you own your car." Because this type of warranty leads the consumer to believe that proof of purchase is not needed so long as he or she owns the product a duty to furnish documentary proof may not be reasonably imposed on the consumer under this type of warranty. The burden is on the warrantor to prove that a particular claimant under this type of warranty is not the original purchaser or owner of the product. Warrantors or their designated agents may, however, ask consumers to state or affirm that they are the first purchaser of the product.

§ 700.7 Use of Warranty Registration Cards

(a) Under section 104(b)(1) of the Act a warrantor offering a full warranty may not impose on consumers any duty other than notification of a defect as a condition of securing remedy of the defect or malfunction, unless such additional duty can be demonstrated by the warrantor to be reasonable. Warrantors have in the past stipulated the return of a "warranty registration" or similar card. By "warranty registration card" the Commission means a card which must be returned by the consumer shortly after purchase of the product and which is stipulated or implied in the warranty to be a condition precedent to warranty coverage and performance.

(b) A requirement that the consumer return a warranty registration card or a similar notice as a condition of performance under a full warranty is an unreasonable duty. Thus, a provision such as, "This warranty is void unless the warranty registration card is returned to the warrantor" is not permissible in a full warranty, nor is it permissible to imply such a condition in a full warranty.

(c) This does not prohibit the use of such registration cards where a warrantor suggests use of the card as one possible means of proof of the date the product was purchased. For example, it is permissible to provide in a full warranty that a consumer may fill out and return a card to place on file proof of the date the product was purchased. Any such suggestion to the consumer must include notice that failure to return the card will not affect rights under the warranty, so long as the consumer can show in a reasonable manner the date the product was purchased.   Nor does this interpretation prohibit a seller from obtaining from purchasers at the time of sale information requested by the warrantor.

§ 700.8   Warrantor's Decision as Final

A warrantor shall not indicate in any written warranty or service contract either directly or indirectly that the decision of the warrantor, service contractor, or any designated third party is final or binding in any dispute concerning the warranty or service contract.   Nor shall a warrantor or service contractor state that it alone shall determine what is a defect under the agreement.   Such statements are deceptive since section 110(d) of the Act gives state and federal courts jurisdiction over suits for breach of warranty and service contract.

§ 700.9   Duty to Install Under a Full Warranty

Under section 104(a)(1) of the Act, the remedy under a full warranty must be provided to the consumer without charge.   If the warranted product has utility only when installed, a full warranty must provide such installation without charge regardless of whether or not the consumer originally paid for installation by the warrantor or his agent.   However, this does not preclude the warrantor from imposing on the consumer a duty to remove, return, or reinstall where such duty can be demonstrated by the warrantor to meet the standard of reasonableness under section 104(b)(1).

§ 700.10   Section 102(c)

(a) Section 102(c) prohibits tying arrangements that condition coverage under a written warranty on the consumer's use of an article or service identified by brand, trade, or corporate name unless that article or service is provided without charge to the consumer.

(b) Under a limited warranty that provides only for replacement of defective parts and no portion of labor charges, section 102(c) prohibits a condition that the consumer use only service (labor) identified by the warrantor to install the replacement parts.   A warrantor or his designated representative may not provide parts under the warranty in a manner which impedes or precludes the choice by the consumer of the person or business to perform necessary labor to install such parts.

(c) No warrantor may condition the continued validity of a warranty on the use of only authorized repair service and/or authorized replacement parts for non-warranty service and maintenance.   For example, provisions such as, "this warranty is void if service is performed by anyone other than an authorized 'ABC' dealer and all replacement parts must be genuine 'ABC' parts, and the like, are prohibited where the service or parts are not covered by the warranty.   These provisions violate the Act in two ways. First, they violate the section 102(c) ban against tying arrangements.

Second, such provisions are deceptive under section 110 of the Act, because a warrantor cannot, as a matter of law, avoid liability under a written warranty where a defect is unrelated to the use by a consumer of 'unauthorized' articles or service. This does not preclude a warrantor from expressly excluding liability for defects or damage caused by such 'unauthorized' articles or service; nor does it preclude the warrantor from denying liability where the warrantor can demonstrate that the defect or damage was so caused.''

§ 700.11 Written Warranty, Service Contract, and Insurance Distinguished for Purposes of Compliance Under the Act

(a) The Act recognizes two types of agreements which may provide similar coverage of consumer products, the written warranty, and the service contract. In addition, other agreements may meet the statutory definitions of either "written warranty" or "service contract," but are sold and regulated under state law as contracts of insurance. One example is the automobile breakdown insurance policies sold in many jurisdictions and regulated by the state as a form of casualty insurance. The McCarran–Ferguson Act, 15 U.S.C. 1011 et seq., precludes jurisdiction under federal law over "the business of insurance" to the extent an agreement is regulated by state law as insurance. Thus, such agreements are subject to the Magnuson–Moss Warranty Act only to the extent they are not regulated in a particular state as the business of insurance.

(b) "Written warranty" and "service contract" are defined in sections 101(6) and 101(8) of the Act, respectively. A written warranty must be "part of the basis of the bargain." This means that it must be conveyed at the time of sale of the consumer product and the consumer must not give any consideration beyond the purchase price of the consumer product in order to benefit from the agreement. It is not a requirement of the Act that an agreement obligate a supplier of the consumer product to a written warranty, but merely that it be part of the basis of the bargain between a supplier and a consumer. This contemplates written warranties by third-party non-suppliers.

(c) A service contract under the Act must meet the definitions of section 101(8). An agreement which would meet the definition of written warranty in section 101(6)(A) or (B) but for its failure to satisfy the basis of the bargain test is a service contract. For example, an agreement which calls for some consideration in addition to the purchase price of the consumer product, or which is entered into at some date after the purchase of the consumer product to which it applies, is a service contract. An agreement which relates only to the performance of maintenance and/or inspection services and which is not an undertaking, promise, or affirmation with respect to a specified level of performance, or that the product is free of defects in materials or workmanship, is a service contract. An agreement to perform periodic cleaning and inspection of a product over a specified period of time, even when offered at the time of sale and without charge to the consumer, is an example of such a service contract.

PART 701. DISCLOSURE OF WRITTEN CONSUMER PRODUCT WARRANTY TERMS AND CONDITIONS

Table of Sections

---

§ 701.1 Definitions

(a) "The Act" means the Magnuson-Moss Warranty Federal Trade Commission Improvement Act, 15 U.S.C. 2301, et seq.

(b) "Consumer product" means any tangible personal property which is distributed in commerce and which is normally used for personal, family, or household purposes (including any such property intended to be attached to or installed in any real property without regard to whether it is so attached or installed). Products which are purchased solely for commercial or industrial use are excluded solely for purposes of this Part.

(c) "Written warranty" means:

(1) Any written affirmation of fact or written promise made in connection with the sale of a consumer product by a supplier to a buyer which relates to the nature of the material or workmanship and affirms or promises that such material or workmanship is defect free or will meet a specified level of performance over a specified period of time, or

(2) Any undertaking in writing in connection with the sale by a supplier of a consumer product to refund, repair, replace, or take other remedial action with respect to such product in the event that such product fails to meet the specifications set forth in the undertaking, which written affirmation, promise or undertaking becomes part of the basis of the bargain between a supplier and a buyer for purposes other than resale of such product.

(d) "Implied warranty" means an implied warranty arising under State law (as modified by secs. 104(a) and 108 of the Act) in connection with the sale by a supplier of a consumer product.

(e) "Remedy" means whichever of the following actions the warrantor elects:

(1) Repair,

(2) Replacement, or

712

(3) Refund; except that the warrantor may not elect refund unless: (i) The warrantor is unable to provide replacement and repair is not commercially practicable or cannot be timely made, or

(ii) The consumer is willing to accept such refund.

(f) "Supplier" means any person engaged in the business of making a consumer product directly or indirectly available to consumers.

(g) "Warrantor" means any supplier or other person who gives or offers to give a written warranty.

(h) "Consumer" means a buyer (other than for purposes of resale or use in the ordinary course of the buyer's business) of any consumer product, any person to whom such product is transferred during the duration of an implied or written warranty applicable to the product, and any other such person who is entitled by the terms of such warranty or under applicable State law to enforce against the warrantor the obligations of the warranty.

(i) "On the face of the warranty" means:

(1) Where the warranty is a single sheet with printing on both sides of the sheet or where the warranty is comprised of more than one sheet, the page on which the warranty text begins;

(2) Where the warranty is included as part of a larger document, such as a use and care manual, the page in such document on which the warranty text begins.

§ 701.2   Scope

The regulations in this part establish requirements for warrantors for disclosing the terms and conditions of written warranties on consumer products actually costing the consumer more than $15.00.

§ 701.3   Written Warranty Terms

(a) Any warrantor warranting to a consumer by means of a written warranty a consumer product actually costing the consumer more than $15.00 shall clearly and conspicuously disclose in a single document in simple and readily understood language, the following items of information:

(1) The identity of the party or parties to whom the written warranty is extended, if the enforceability of the written warranty is limited to the original consumer purchaser or is otherwise limited to persons other than every consumer owner during the term of the warranty;

(2) A clear description and identification of products, or parts, or characteristics, or components or properties covered by and where necessary for clarification, excluded from the warranty;

(3) A statement of what the warrantor will do in the event of a defect, malfunction or failure to conform with the written warranty, including the items or services the warrantor will pay for or provide, and, where

necessary for clarification, those which the warrantor will not pay for or provide;

(4) The point in time or event on which the warranty term commences, if different from the purchase date, and the time period or other measurement of warranty duration;

(5) A step-by-step explanation of the procedure which the consumer should follow in order to obtain performance of any warranty obligation, including the persons or class of persons authorized to perform warranty obligations. This includes the name(s) of the warrantor(s), together with: The mailing address(es) of the warrantor(s), and/or the name or title and the address of any employee or department of the warrantor responsible for the performance of warranty obligations, and/or a telephone number which consumers may use without charge to obtain information on warranty performance;

(6) Information respecting the availability of any informal dispute settlement mechanism elected by the warrantor in compliance with Part 703 of this subchapter;

(7) Any limitations on the duration of implied warranties, disclosed on the face of the warranty as provided in Section 108 of the Act, accompanied by the following statement:

Some states do not allow limitations on how long an implied warranty lasts, so the above limitation may not apply to you.

(8) Any exclusions of or limitations on relief such as incidental or consequential damages, accompanied by the following statement, which may be combined with the statement required in paragraph (a)(7) of this section:

Some states do not allow the exclusion or limitation of incidental or consequential damages, so the above limitation or exclusion may not apply to you.

(9) A statement in the following language:

This warranty gives you specific legal rights, and you may also have other rights which vary from state to state.

(b) Paragraphs (a)(1) through (9) of this section shall not be applicable with respect to statements of general policy on emblems, seals or insignias issued by third parties promising replacement or refund if a consumer product is defective, which statements contain no representation or assurance of the quality or performance characteristics of the product; provided that (1) the disclosures required by paragraphs (a)(1) through (9) of this section are published by such third parties in each issue of a publication with a general circulation, and (2) such disclosures are provided free of charge to any consumer upon written request.

§ 701.4 Owner Registration Cards

When a warrantor employs any card such as an owner's registration card, a warranty registration card, or the like, and the return of such card is a condition precedent to warranty coverage and performance, the warrantor shall disclose this fact in the warranty. If the return of such card reasonably appears to be a condition precedent to warranty coverage and performance, but is not such a condition, that fact shall be disclosed in the warranty.

PART 702. PRE–SALE AVAILABILITY OF WRITTEN WARRANTY TERMS

Table of Sections

---

§ 702.1 Definitions

(a) "The Act" means the Magnuson-Moss Warranty Federal Trade Commission Improvement Act, 15 U.S.C. 2301, et seq.

(b) "Consumer product" means any tangible personal property which is distributed in commerce and which is normally used for personal, family, or household purposes (including any such property intended to be attached to or installed in any real property without regard to whether it is so attached or installed). Products which are purchased solely for commercial or industrial use are excluded solely for purposes of this part.

(c) "Written warranty" means:

(1) Any written affirmation of fact or written promise made in connection with the sale of a consumer product by a supplier to a buyer which relates to the nature of the material or workmanship and affirms or promises that such material or workmanship is defect free or will meet a specified level of performance over a specified period of time, or

(2) Any undertaking in writing in connection with the sale by a supplier of a consumer product to refund, repair, replace, or take other remedial action with respect to such product in the event that such product fails to meet the specifications set forth in the undertaking, which written affirmation, promise or undertaking becomes part of the basis of the bargain between a supplier and a buyer for purposes other than resale of such product.

(d) "Warrantor" means any supplier or other person who gives or offers to give a written warranty.

(e) "Seller" means any person who sells or offers for sale for purposes other than resale or use in the ordinary course of the buyer's business any consumer product.

(f) "Supplier" means any person engaged in the business of making a consumer product directly or indirectly available to consumers.

§ 702.2 Scope

The regulations in this part establish requirements for sellers and warrantors for making the terms of any written warranty on a consumer product available to the consumer prior to sale.

§ 702.3   Pre-sale Availability of Written Warranty Terms

The following requirements apply to consumer products actually costing the consumer more than $15.00:

(a) *Duties of the seller.* Except as provided in paragraphs (c) through (d) of this section, the seller of a consumer product with a written warranty shall make a text of the warranty readily available for examination by the prospective buyer by:

(1) Displaying it in close proximity to the warranted product, or

(2) Furnishing it upon request prior to sale and placing signs reasonably calculated to elicit the prospective buyer's attention in prominent locations in the store or department advising such prospective buyers of the availability of warranties upon request.

(b) *Duties of the warrantor.* (1) A warrantor who gives a written warranty warranting to a consumer a consumer product actually costing the consumer more than $15.00 shall:

(i) Provide sellers with warranty materials necessary for such sellers to comply with the requirements set forth in paragraph (a) of this section, by the use of one or more of the following means:

(A) Providing a copy of the written warranty with every warranted consumer product; and/or

(B) Providing a tag, sign, sticker, label, decal or other attachment to the product, which contains the full text of the written warranty; and/or

(C) Printing on or otherwise attaching the text of the written warranty to the package, carton, or other container if that package, carton or other container is normally used for display purposes. If the warrantor elects this option a copy of the written warranty must also accompany the warranted product; and/or

(D) Providing a notice, sign, or poster disclosing the text of a consumer product warranty. If the warrantor elects this option, a copy of the written warranty must also accompany each warranted product.

(ii) Provide catalog, mail order, and door-to-door sellers with copies of written warranties necessary for such sellers to comply with the requirements set forth in paragraphs (c) and (d) of this section.

(2) Paragraph (a)(1) of this section shall not be applicable with respect to statements of general policy on emblems, seals or insignias issued by third parties promising replacement or refund if a consumer product is defective, which statements contain no representation or assurance of the quality or performance characteristics of the product; provided that

(i) The disclosures required by § 701.3(a)(1) through (9) of this part are published by such third parties in each issue of a publication with a general circulation, and

(ii) Such disclosures are provided free of charge to any consumer upon written request.

(c) *Catalog and mail order sales.* (1) For purposes of this paragraph:

(i) "Catalog or mail order sales" means any offer for sale, or any solicitation for an order for a consumer product with a written warranty, which includes instructions for ordering the product which do not require a personal visit to the seller's establishment.

(ii) "Close conjunction" means on the page containing the description of the warranted product, or on the page facing that page.

(2) Any seller who offers for sale to consumers consumer products with written warranties by means of a catalog or mail order solicitation shall:

(i) Clearly and conspicuously disclose in such catalog or solicitation in close conjunction to the description of the warranted product, or in an information section of the catalog or solicitation clearly referenced, including a page number, in close conjunction to the description of the warranted product, either:

(A) The full text of the written warranty; or

(B) That the written warranty can be obtained free upon specific written request, and the address where such warranty can be obtained. If this option is elected, such seller shall promptly provide a copy of any written warranty requested by the consumer.

(d) *Door-to-door sales.* (1) For purposes of this paragraph:

(i) "Door-to-door sale" means a sale of consumer products in which the seller or his representative personally solicits the sale, including those in response to or following an invitation by a buyer, and the buyer's agreement or offer to purchase is made at a place other than the place of business of the seller.

(ii) "Prospective buyer" means an individual solicited by a door-to-door seller to buy a consumer product who indicates sufficient interest in that consumer product or maintains sufficient contact with the seller for the seller reasonably to conclude that the person solicited is considering purchasing the product.

(2) Any seller who offers for sale to consumers consumer products with written warranties by means of door-to-door sales shall, prior to the consummation of the sale, disclose the fact that the sales representative has copies of the warranties for the warranted products being offered for sale, which may be inspected by the prospective buyer at any time during the sales presentation. Such disclosure shall be made orally and shall be included in any written materials shown to prospective buyers.

PART 703. INFORMAL DISPUTE SETTLEMENT PROCEDURES

Table of Sections

---

§ 703.1 Definitions

(a) "The Act" means the Magnuson-Moss Warranty—Federal Trade Commission Improvement Act, 15 U.S.C. 2301, et seq.

(b) "Consumer product" means any tangible personal property which is distributed in commerce and which is normally used for personal, family, or household purposes (including any such property intended to be attached to or installed in any real property without regard to whether it is so attached or installed).

(c) "Written warranty" means:

(1) Any written affirmation of fact or written promise made in connection with the sale of a consumer product by a supplier to a buyer which relates to the nature of the material or workmanship and affirms or promises that such material or workmanship is defect free or will meet a specified level of performance over a specified period of time, or

(2) Any undertaking in writing in connection with the sale by a supplier of a consumer product to refund, repair, replace, or take other remedial action with respect to such product in the event that such product fails to meet the specifications set forth in the undertaking, which written affirmation, promise or undertaking becomes part of the basis of the bargain between a supplier and a buyer for purposes other than resale of such product.

(d) "Warrantor" means any person who gives or offers to give a written warranty which incorporates an informal dispute settlement mechanism.

(e) "Mechanism" means an informal dispute settlement procedure which is incorporated into the terms of a written warranty to which any provision of Title I of the Act applies, as provided in Section 110 of the Act.

719

(f) "Members" means the person or persons within a Mechanism actually deciding disputes.

(g) "Consumer" means a buyer (other than for purposes of resale) of any consumer product, any person to whom such product is transferred during the duration of a written warranty applicable to the product, and any other person who is entitled by the terms of such warranty or under applicable state law to enforce against the warrantor the obligations of the warranty.

(h) "On the face of the warranty" means:

(1) If the warranty is a single sheet with printing on both sides of the sheet, or if the warranty is comprised of more than one sheet, the page on which the warranty text begins;

(2) If the warranty is included as part of a longer document, such as a use and care manual, the page in such document on which the warranty text begins.

§ 703.2   Duties of Warrantor

(a) The warrantor shall not incorporate into the terms of a written warranty a Mechanism that fails to comply with the requirements contained in §§ 703.3–703.8 of this part. This paragraph shall not prohibit a warrantor from incorporating into the terms of a written warranty the step-by-step procedure which the consumer should take in order to obtain performance of any obligation under the warranty as described in section 102(a)(7) of the Act and required by Part 701 of this subchapter.

(b) The warrantor shall disclose clearly and conspicuously at least the following information on the face of the written warranty:

(1) A statement of the availability of the informal dispute settlement mechanism;

(2) The name and address of the Mechanism, or the name and a telephone number of the Mechanism which consumers may use without charge;

(3) A statement of any requirement that the consumer resort to the Mechanism before exercising rights or seeking remedies created by Title I of the Act; together with the disclosure that if a consumer chooses to seek redress by pursuing rights and remedies not created by Title I of the Act, resort to the Mechanism would not be required by any provision of the Act; and

(4) A statement, if applicable, indicating where further information on the Mechanism can be found in materials accompanying the product, as provided in § 703.2(c) of this section.

(c) The warrantor shall include in the written warranty or in a separate section of materials accompanying the product, the following information:

(1) Either (i) a form addressed to the Mechanism containing spaces requesting the information which the Mechanism may require for prompt resolution of warranty disputes; or (ii) a telephone number of the Mechanism which consumers may use without charge;

(2) The name and address of the Mechanism;

(3) A brief description of Mechanism procedures;

(4) The time limits adhered to by the Mechanism; and

(5) The types of information which the Mechanism may require for prompt resolution of warranty disputes.

(d) The warrantor shall take steps reasonably calculated to make consumers aware of the Mechanism's existence at the time consumers experience warranty disputes. Nothing contained in paragraphs (b), (c), or (d) of this section shall limit the warrantor's option to encourage consumers to seek redress directly from the warrantor as long as the warrantor does not expressly require consumers to seek redress directly from the warrantor. The warrantor shall proceed fairly and expeditiously to attempt to resolve all disputes submitted directly to the warrantor.

(e) Whenever a dispute is submitted directly to the warrantor, the warrantor shall, within a reasonable time, decide whether, and to what extent, it will satisfy the consumer, and inform the consumer of its decision. In its notification to the consumer of its decision, the warrantor shall include the information required in § 703.2(b) and (c) of this section.

(f) The warrantor shall: (1) Respond fully and promptly to reasonable requests by the Mechanism for information relating to disputes;

(2) Upon notification of any decision of the Mechanism that would require action on the part of the warrantor, immediately notify the Mechanism whether, and to what extent, warrantor will abide by the decision; and

(3) Perform any obligations it has agreed to.

(g) The warrantor shall act in good faith in determining whether, and to what extent, it will abide by a Mechanism decision.

(h) The warrantor shall comply with any reasonable requirements imposed by the Mechanism to fairly and expeditiously resolve warranty disputes.

MINIMUM REQUIREMENTS OF THE MECHANISM

§ 703.3 Mechanism Organization

(a) The Mechanism shall be funded and competently staffed at a level sufficient to ensure fair and expeditious resolution of all disputes, and shall not charge consumers any fee for use of the Mechanism.

(b) The warrantor and the sponsor of the Mechanism (if other than the warrantor) shall take all steps necessary to ensure that the Mechanism, and its members and staff, are sufficiently insulated from the warrantor and the sponsor, so that the decisions of the members and the performance of the staff are not influenced by either the warrantor or the sponsor. Necessary steps shall include, at a minimum, committing funds in advance, basing personnel decisions solely on merit, and not assigning conflicting warrantor or sponsor duties to Mechanism staff persons.

(c) The Mechanism shall impose any other reasonable requirements necessary to ensure that the members and staff act fairly and expeditiously in each dispute.

§ 703.4   Qualification of Members

(a) No member deciding a dispute shall be: (1) A party to the dispute, or an employee or agent of a party other than for purposes of deciding disputes; or

(2) A person who is or may become a party in any legal action, including but not limited to class actions, relating to the product or complaint in dispute, or an employee or agent of such person other than for purposes of deciding disputes. For purposes of this paragraph (a) a person shall not be considered a "party" solely because he or she acquires or owns an interest in a party solely for investment, and the acquisition or ownership of an interest which is offered to the general public shall be prima facie evidence of its acquisition or ownership solely for investment.

(b) When one or two members are deciding a dispute, all shall be persons having no direct involvement in the manufacture, distribution, sale or service of any product. When three or more members are deciding a dispute, at least two-thirds shall be persons having no direct involvement in the manufacture, distribution, sale or service of any product. "Direct involvement" shall not include acquiring or owning an interest solely for investment, and the acquisition or ownership of an interest which is offered to the general public shall be prima facie evidence of its acquisition or ownership solely for investment. Nothing contained in this section shall prevent the members from consulting with any persons knowledgeable in the technical, commercial or other areas relating to the product which is the subject of the dispute.

(c) Members shall be persons interested in the fair and expeditious settlement of consumer disputes.

§ 703.5   Operation of the Mechanism

(a) The Mechanism shall establish written operating procedures which shall include at least those items specified in paragraphs (b) through (j) of this section. Copies of the written procedures shall be made available to any person upon request.

(b) Upon notification of a dispute, the Mechanism shall immediately inform both the warrantor and the consumer of receipt of the dispute.

(c) The Mechanism shall investigate, gather and organize all information necessary for a fair and expeditious decision in each dispute. When any evidence gathered by or submitted to the Mechanism raises issues relating to the number of repair attempts, the length of repair periods, the possibility of unreasonable use of the product, or any other issues relevant in light of Title I of the Act (or rules thereunder), including issues relating to consequential damages, or any other remedy under the Act (or rules thereunder), the Mechanism shall investigate these issues. When information which will or may be used in the decision, submitted by one party, or a consultant under § 703.4(b) of this part, or any other source tends to contradict facts submitted by the other party, the Mechanism shall clearly, accurately, and completely disclose to both parties the contradictory information (and its source) and shall provide both parties an opportunity to explain or rebut the information and to submit additional materials. The Mechanism shall not require any information not reasonably necessary to decide the dispute.

(d) If the dispute has not been settled, the Mechanism shall, as expeditiously as possible but at least within 40 days of notification of the dispute, except as provided in paragraph (e) of this section:

(1) Render a fair decision based on the information gathered as described in paragraph (c) of this section, and on any information submitted at an oral presentation which conforms to the requirements of paragraph (f) of this section (A decision shall include any remedies appropriate under the circumstances, including repair, replacement, refund, reimbursement for expenses, compensation for damages, and any other remedies available under the written warranty or the Act (or rules thereunder); and a decision shall state a specified reasonable time for performance);

(2) Disclose to the warrantor its decision and the reasons therefor;

(3) If the decision would require action on the part of the warrantor, determine whether, and to what extent, warrantor will abide by its decision; and

(4) Disclose to the consumer its decision, the reasons therefor, warrantor's intended actions (if the decision would require action on the part of the warrantor), and the information described in paragraph (g) of this section. For purposes of this paragraph (d) a dispute shall be deemed settled when the Mechanism has ascertained from the consumer that:

(i) The dispute has been settled to the consumer's satisfaction; and (ii) the settlement contains a specified reasonable time for performance.

(e) The Mechanism may delay the performance of its duties under paragraph (d) of this section beyond the 40 day time limit:

(1) Where the period of delay is due solely to failure of a consumer to provide promptly his or her name and address, brand name and model number of the product involved, and a statement as to the nature of the defect or other complaint; or

(2) For a 7 day period in those cases where the consumer has made no attempt to seek redress directly from the warrantor.

(f) The Mechanism may allow an oral presentation by a party to a dispute (or a party's representative) only if:

(1) Both warrantor and consumer expressly agree to the presentation;

(2) Prior to agreement the Mechanism fully discloses to the consumer the following information:

(i) That the presentation by either party will take place only if both parties so agree, but that if they agree, and one party fails to appear at the agreed upon time and place, the presentation by the other party may still be allowed;

(ii) That the members will decide the dispute whether or not an oral presentation is made;

(iii) The proposed date, time and place for the presentation; and

(iv) A brief description of what will occur at the presentation including, if applicable, parties' rights to bring witnesses and/or counsel; and

(3) Each party has the right to be present during the other party's oral presentation. Nothing contained in this paragraph (b) of this section shall preclude the Mechanism from allowing an oral presentation by one party, if the other party fails to appear at the agreed upon time and place, as long as all of the requirements of this paragraph have been satisfied.

(g) The Mechanism shall inform the consumer, at the time of disclosure required in paragraph (d) of this section that:

(1) If he or she is dissatisfied with its decision or warrantor's intended actions, or eventual performance, legal remedies, including use of small claims court, may be pursued;

(2) The Mechanism's decision is admissible in evidence as provided in section 110(a)(3) of the Act; and

(3) The consumer may obtain, at reasonable cost, copies of all Mechanism records relating to the consumer's dispute.

(h) If the warrantor has agreed to perform any obligations, either as part of a settlement agreed to after notification to the Mechanism of the dispute or as a result of a decision under paragraph (d) of this section, the Mechanism shall ascertain from the consumer within 10 working days of the date for performance whether performance has occurred.

(i) A requirement that a consumer resort to the Mechanism prior to commencement of an action under section 110(d) of the Act shall be satisfied 40 days after notification to the Mechanism of the dispute or when the Mechanism completes all of its duties under paragraph (d) of this section, whichever occurs sooner. Except that, if the Mechanism delays performance of its paragraph (d) of this section duties as allowed by paragraph (e) of this section, the requirement that the consumer initially resort to the Mechanism shall not be satisfied until the period of delay allowed by paragraph (e) of this section has ended.

(j) Decisions of the Mechanism shall not be legally binding on any person. However, the warrantor shall act in good faith, as provided in § 703.2(g) of this part. In any civil action arising out of a warranty obligation and relating to a matter considered by the Mechanism, any decision of the Mechanism shall be admissible in evidence, as provided in section 110(a)(3) of the Act.

§ 703.6   Recordkeeping

(a) The Mechanism shall maintain records on each dispute referred to it which shall include:

(1) Name, address and telephone number of the consumer;

(2) Name, address, telephone number and contact person of the warrantor;

(3) Brand name and model number of the product involved;

(4) The date of receipt of the dispute and the date of disclosure to the consumer of the decision;

(5) All letters or other written documents submitted by either party;

(6) All other evidence collected by the Mechanism relating to the dispute, including summaries of relevant and material portions of telephone calls and meetings between the Mechanism and any other person (including consultants described in § 703.4(b) of this part);

(7) A summary of any relevant and material information presented by either party at an oral presentation;

(8) The decision of the members including information as to date, time and place of meeting, and the identity of members voting; or information on any other resolution;

(9) A copy of the disclosure to the parties of the decision;

(10) A statement of the warrantor's intended action(s);

(11) Copies of follow-up letters (or summaries of relevant and material portions of follow-up telephone calls) to the consumer, and responses thereto; and

(12) Any other documents and communications (or summaries of relevant and material portions of oral communications) relating to the dispute.

(b) The Mechanism shall maintain an index of each warrantor's disputes grouped under brand name and subgrouped under product model.

(c) The Mechanism shall maintain an index for each warrantor as will show:

(1) All disputes in which the warrantor has promised some performance (either by settlement or in response to a Mechanism decision) and has failed to comply; and

(2) All disputes in which the warrantor has refused to abide by a Mechanism decision.

(d) The Mechanism shall maintain an index as will show all disputes delayed beyond 40 days.

(e) The Mechanism shall compile semi-annually and maintain statistics which show the number and percent of disputes in each of the following categories:

(1) Resolved by staff of the Mechanism and warrantor has complied;

(2) Resolved by staff of the Mechanism, time for compliance has occurred, and warrantor has not complied;

(3) Resolved by staff of the Mechanism and time for compliance has not yet occurred;

(4) Decided by members and warrantor has complied;

(5) Decided by members, time for compliance has occurred, and warrantor has not complied;

(6) Decided by members and time for compliance has not yet occurred;

(7) Decided by members adverse to the consumer;

(8) No jurisdiction;

(9) Decision delayed beyond 40 days under § 703.5(e)(1) of this part;

(10) Decision delayed beyond 40 days under § 703.5(e)(2) of this part;

(11) Decision delayed beyond 40 days for any other reason; and

(12) Pending decision.

(f) The Mechanism shall retain all records specified in paragraphs (a) through (e) of this section for at least 4 years after final disposition of the dispute.

§ 703.7 Audits

(a) The Mechanism shall have an audit conducted at least annually, to determine whether the Mechanism and its implementation are in compliance with this part. All records of the Mechanism required to be kept under § 703.6 of this part shall be available for audit.

(b) Each audit provided for in paragraph (a) of this section shall include at a minimum the following:

(1) Evaluation of warrantors' efforts to make consumers aware of the Mechanism's existence as required in § 703.2(d) of this part;

(2) Review of the indexes maintained pursuant to § 703.6(b), (c), and (d) of this part; and

(3) Analysis of a random sample of disputes handled by the Mechanism to determine the following:

(i) Adequacy of the Mechanism's complaint and other forms, investigation, mediation and follow-up efforts, and other aspects of complaint handling; and

(ii) Accuracy of the Mechanism's statistical compilations under § 703.6(e) of this part. (For purposes of this subparagraph "analysis" shall include oral or written contact with the consumers involved in each of the disputes in the random sample.)

(c) A report of each audit under this section shall be submitted to the Federal Trade Commission, and shall be made available to any person at reasonable cost. The Mechanism may direct its auditor to delete names of parties to disputes, and identity of products involved, from the audit report.

(d) Auditors shall be selected by the Mechanism. No auditor may be involved with the Mechanism as a warrantor, sponsor or member, or employee or agent thereof, other than for purposes of the audit.

§ 703.8   Openness of Records and Proceedings

(a) The statistical summaries specified in § 703.6(e) of this part shall be available to any person for inspection and copying.

(b) Except as provided under paragraphs (a) and (e) of this section, and paragraph (c) of § 703.7 of this part, all records of the Mechanism may be kept confidential, or made available only on such terms and conditions, or in such form, as the Mechanism shall permit.

(c) The policy of the Mechanism with respect to records made available at the Mechanism's option shall be set out in the procedures under § 703.5(a) of this part; the policy shall be applied uniformly to all requests for access to or copies of such records.

(d) Meetings of the members to hear and decide disputes shall be open to observers on reasonable and nondiscriminatory terms. The identity of the parties and products involved in disputes need not be disclosed at meetings.

(e) Upon request the Mechanism shall provide to either party to a dispute:

(1) Access to all records relating to the dispute; and

(2) Copies of any records relating to the dispute, at reasonable cost.

(f) The Mechanism shall make available to any person upon request, information relating to the qualifications of Mechanism staff and members.

PART TWO.   STATE STATUTES

DECEPTIVE PRACTICES STATUTES (LITTLE–FTC ACTS)

Massachusetts (Mass.Gen.Laws Ann. ch. 93A)
New Jersey (N.J.Stat.Ann. tit. 58, ch. 8)
Oregon (Ore.Rev.Stat. § 646.605 et seq.)
Uniform Consumer Sales Practices Act

MASSACHUSETTS

Mass.Gen.Laws Ann. ch. 93A

REGULATION OF BUSINESS PRACTICES FOR CONSUMER'S PROTECTION

Table of Sections

---

§ 1. Definitions

The following words, as used in this chapter unless the text otherwise requires or a different meaning is specifically required, shall mean:—

(a) "Person" shall include, where applicable, natural persons, corporations, trusts, partnerships, incorporated or unincorporated associations, and any other legal entity.

(b) "Trade" and "commerce" shall include the advertising, the offering for sale, rent or lease, the sale, rent, lease or distribution of any services and any property, tangible or intangible, real, personal or mixed, any security as defined in subparagraph (k) of section four hundred and one of chapter one hundred and ten A and any contract of sale of a commodity for future delivery, and any other article, commodity, or thing of value wherever situate, and shall include any trade or commerce directly or indirectly affecting the people of this commonwealth.

(c) "Documentary material" shall include the original or a copy of any book, record, report, memorandum, paper, communication, tabulation, map, chart, photograph, mechanical transcription, or other tangible document or recording, wherever situate.

(d) "Examination of documentary material", the inspection, study, or copying of any such material, and the taking of testimony under oath or acknowledgment in respect of any such documentary material.

§ 2. Unfair practices; legislative intent; rules and regulations

(a) Unfair methods of competition and unfair or deceptive acts or practices in the conduct of any trade or commerce are hereby declared unlawful.

(b) It is the intent of the legislature that in construing paragraph (a) of this section in actions brought under sections four, nine and eleven, the courts will be guided by the interpretations given by the Federal Trade Commission and the Federal Courts to section 5(a)(1) of the Federal Trade Commission Act (15 U.S.C. 45(a)(1)), as from time to time amended.

(c) The attorney general may make rules and regulations interpreting the provisions of subsection 2(a) of this chapter. Such rules and regulations shall not be inconsistent with the rules, regulations and decisions of the Federal Trade Commission and the Federal Courts interpreting the provisions of 15 U.S.C. 45(a)(1) (The Federal Trade Commission Act), as from time to time amended.

§ 3. Exempted transactions

Nothing in this chapter shall apply to transactions or actions otherwise permitted under laws as administered by any regulatory board or officer acting under statutory authority of the commonwealth or of the United States.

For the purpose of this section, the burden of proving exemptions from the provisions of this chapter shall be upon the person claiming the exemptions.

§ 4. Actions by attorney general; notice; venue; injunctions

Whenever the attorney general has reason to believe that any person is using or is about to use any method, act, or practice declared by section two to be unlawful, and that proceedings would be in the public interest, he may bring an action in the name of the commonwealth against such person to restrain by temporary restraining order or preliminary or permanent injunction the use of such method, act or practice.... Said court may issue temporary restraining orders or preliminary or permanent injunctions and make such other orders or judgments as may be necessary to restore to any person who has suffered any ascertainable loss by reason of the use or employment of such unlawful method, act or practice any moneys or property, real or personal, which may have been acquired by means of such method, act, or practice. If the court finds that a person has employed any method, act or practice which he knew or should have known to be in violation of said section two, the court may require such person to pay to the commonwealth a civil penalty of not more than five thousand dollars for each such violation and also may require the said person to pay the reasonable costs of investigation and litigation of such violation, including reasonable attorneys' fees. If the court finds any method, act, or practice unlawful with regard to any security or any contract of sale of a commodity for future delivery as defined in section two, the court may issue such orders or judgments as may be necessary to restore any person who has suffered any ascertainable loss of any moneys or property, real or personal, or up to three but not less than two times that amount if the court finds that the use of the act or practice was a willful violation of said section two, a civil penalty to be paid to the commonwealth of not more than five thousand dollars for each such violation, and also may require said person to pay the reasonable costs of investigation and litigation of such violation, including reasonable attorneys fees.

.   .   .

§ 9. Civil actions and remedies; class action; demand for relief; damages; costs; exhausting administrative remedies

(1) Any person, other than a person entitled to bring action under section eleven of this chapter, who has been injured by another person's use or employment of any method, act or practice declared to be unlawful by section two or any rule or regulation issued thereunder or any person whose rights are affected by another person violating the provisions of clause (9) of section three of chapter one hundred and seventy-six D may bring an action in the superior court, or in the housing court as provided in section three of chapter one hundred and eighty-five C whether by way of original complaint, counterclaim, cross-claim or third party action, for damages and such equitable relief, including an injunction, as the court deems to be necessary and proper.

(2) Any persons entitled to bring such action may, if the use or employment of the unfair or deceptive act or practice has caused similar injury to numerous other persons similarly situated and if the court finds in a preliminary hearing that he adequately and fairly represents such other persons, bring the action on behalf of himself and such other similarly injured and situated persons; the court shall require that notice of such action be given to unnamed petitioners in the most effective practicable manner. Such action shall not be dismissed, settled or compromised without the approval of the court, and notice of any proposed dismissal,

settlement or compromise shall be given to all members of the class of petitioners in such manner as the court directs.

(3) At least thirty days prior to the filing of any such action, a written demand for relief, identifying the claimant and reasonably describing the unfair or deceptive act or practice relied upon and the injury suffered, shall be mailed or delivered to any prospective respondent. Any person receiving such a demand for relief who, within thirty days of the mailing or delivery of the demand for relief, makes a written tender of settlement which is rejected by the claimant may, in any subsequent action, file the written tender and an affidavit concerning its rejection and thereby limit any recovery to the relief tendered if the court finds that the relief tendered was reasonable in relation to the injury actually suffered by the petitioner. In all other cases, if the court finds for the petitioner, recovery shall be in the amount of actual damages or twenty-five dollars, whichever is greater; or up to three but not less than two times such amount if the court finds that the use or employment of the act or practice was a willful or knowing violation of said section two or that the refusal to grant relief upon demand was made in bad faith with knowledge or reason to know that the act or practice complained of violated said section two. For the purposes of this chapter, the amount of actual damages to be multiplied by the court shall be the amount of the judgment on all claims arising out of the same and underlying transaction or occurrence, regardless of the existence or nonexistence of insurance coverage available in payment of the claim. In addition, the court shall award such other equitable relief, including an injunction, as it deems to be necessary and proper. The demand requirements of this paragraph shall not apply if the claim is asserted by way of counterclaim or cross-claim, or if the prospective respondent does not maintain a place of business or does not keep assets within the commonwealth, but such respondent may otherwise employ the provisions of this section by making a written offer of relief and paying the rejected tender into court as soon as practicable after receiving notice of an action commenced under this section. Notwithstanding any other provision to the contrary, if the court finds any method, act or practice unlawful with regard to any security or any contract of sale of a commodity for future delivery as defined in section two, and if the court finds for the petitioner, recovery shall be in the amount of actual damages.

(3A) A person may assert a claim under this section in a district court, whether by way of original complaint, counterclaim, cross-claim or third-party action, for money damages only. Said damages may include double or treble damages, attorneys' fees and costs, as herein provided. The demand requirements and provision for tender of offer of settlement provided in paragraph (3) shall also be applicable under this paragraph, except that no rights to equitable relief shall be created under this paragraph, nor shall a person asserting a claim hereunder be able to assert any claim on behalf of other similarly insured and situated persons as provided in paragraph (2).

(4) If the court finds in any action commenced hereunder that there has been a violation of section two, the petitioner shall, in addition to other relief provided for by this section and irrespective of the amount in controversy, be awarded reasonable attorney's fees and costs incurred in connection with said action; provided, however, the court shall deny recovery of attorney's fees and costs which are incurred after the rejection of a reasonable written offer of settlement made within thirty days of the mailing or delivery of the written demand for relief required by this section.

(5) Deleted. . . .

(6) Any person entitled to bring an action under this section shall not be required to initiate, pursue or exhaust any remedy established by any regulation, administrative procedure, local, state or federal law or statute or the common law in order to bring an action under this section or to obtain injunctive relief or recover damages or attorney's fees or costs or other relief as provided in this section. Failure to exhaust administrative remedies shall not be a defense to any proceeding under this section, except as provided in paragraph seven.

(7) The court may upon motion by the respondent before the time for answering and after a hearing suspend proceedings brought under this section to permit the respondent to initiate action in which the petitioner shall be named a party before any appropriate regulatory board or officer providing adjudicatory hearings to complainants if the respondent's evidence indicates that:

(a) there is a substantial likelihood that final action by the court favorable to the petitioner would require of the respondent conduct or practices that would disrupt or be inconsistent with a regulatory scheme that regulates or covers the actions or transactions complained of by the petitioner established and administered under law by any state or federal regulatory board or officer acting under statutory authority of the commonwealth or of the United States; or

(b) that said regulatory board or officer has a substantial interest in reviewing said transactions or actions prior to judicial action under this chapter and that the said regulatory board or officer has the power to provide substantially the relief sought by the petitioner and the class, if any, which the petitioner represents, under this section.

. . .

§ 11. Persons engaged in business; actions for unfair trade practices; class actions; damages; injunction; costs

Any person who engages in the conduct of any trade or commerce and who suffers any loss of money or property, real or personal, as a result of the use or employment by another person who engages in any trade or commerce of an unfair method of competition or an unfair or deceptive act or practice declared unlawful by section two or by any rule or regulation issued under paragraph (c) of section two may, as hereinafter provided, bring an action in the superior court, or in the housing court as provided in section three of chapter one hundred and eighty-five C, whether by way of original complaint, counterclaim, cross-claim or third-party action for damages and such equitable relief, including an injunction, as the court deems to be necessary and proper.

Such person, if he has not suffered any loss of money or property may obtain such an injunction if it can be shown that the aforementioned unfair method of competition, act or practice may have the effect of causing such loss of money or property.

Any persons entitled to bring such action may, if the use or employment of the unfair method of competition or the unfair or deceptive act or practice has caused similar injury to numerous other persons similarly situated and if the court finds in a preliminary hearing that he adequately and fairly represents such other persons, bring the action on behalf of himself and such other similarly injured and situated persons; the court shall require that notice of such action be given to unnamed petitioners in the most effective, practicable manner. Such action shall not be dismissed, settled or compromised without the approval of the court, and notice of any proposed dismissal, settlement or compromise shall be given to all members of the class of petitioners in such a manner as the court directs.

A person may assert a claim under this section in a district court, whether by way of original complaint, counterclaim, cross-claim or third-party action, for money damages only. Said damages may include double or treble damages, attorneys' fees and costs, as hereinafter provided, with provision for tendering by the person against whom the claim is asserted of a written offer of settlement for single damages, also as hereinafter provided. No rights to equitable relief shall be created under this paragraph, nor shall a person asserting such claim be able to assert any claim on behalf of other similarly injured and situated persons as provided in the preceding paragraph. The provisions of sections ninety-five to one hundred and ten, inclusive, of chapter two hundred and thirty-one, where applicable, shall apply to a claim under this section, except that the provisions for remand, removal and transfer shall be controlled by the amount of single damages claimed hereunder.

If the court finds for the petitioner, recovery shall be in the amount of actual damages; or up to three, but not less than two, times such amount if the court finds that the use or employment of the method of competition or the act or practice was a willful or knowing violation of said section two. For the purposes of this chapter, the amount of actual damages to be multiplied by the court shall be the amount of the judgment on all claims arising out of the same and underlying transaction or occurrence regardless of the existence or nonexistence of insurance coverage available in payment of the claim. In addition, the court shall award such other equitable relief, including an injunction, as it deems to be necessary and proper. The respondent may tender with his answer in any such action a written offer of settlement for single damages. If such tender or settlement is rejected by the petitioner, and if the court finds that the relief tendered was reasonable in relation to the injury actually suffered by the petitioner, then the court shall not award more than single damages.

If the court finds in any action commenced hereunder, that there has been a violation of section two, the petitioner shall, in addition to other relief provided for by this section and irrespective of the amount in controversy, be awarded reasonable attorneys' fees and costs incurred in said action.

In any action brought under this section, in addition to the provisions of paragraph (b) of section two, the court shall also be guided in its interpretation of unfair methods of competition by those provisions of chapter ninety-three known as the Massachusetts Antitrust Act.

No action shall be brought or maintained under this section unless the actions and transactions constituting the alleged unfair method of competition or the unfair or deceptive act or practice occurred primarily and substantially within the commonwealth. For the purposes of this paragraph, the burden of proof shall be upon the person claiming that such transactions and actions did not occur primarily and substantially within the commonwealth.

NEW JERSEY

N.J.Stat.Ann. tit. 56, ch. 8

FRAUDS, ETC., IN SALES OR ADVERTISEMENTS OF MERCHANDISE

Table of Selected Sections

§ 56:8–1. Definitions

(a) The term "advertisement" shall include the attempt directly or indirectly by publication, dissemination, solicitation, indorsement or circulation or in any other way to induce directly or indirectly any person to enter or not enter into any obligation or acquire any title or interest in any merchandise or to increase the consumption thereof or to make any loan;

(b) The term "Attorney General" shall mean the Attorney General of the State of New Jersey or any person acting on his behalf;

(c) The term "merchandise" shall include any objects, wares, goods, commodities, services or anything offered, directly or indirectly to the public for sale;

(d) The term "person" as used in this act shall include any natural person or his legal representative, partnership, corporation, company, trust, business entity or association, and any agent, employee, salesman, partner, officer, director, member, stockholder, associate, trustee or cestuis que trustent thereof;

(e) The term "sale" shall include any sale, rental or distribution, offer for sale, rental or distribution or attempt directly or indirectly to sell, rent or distribute.

(f) The term "senior citizen" means a natural person 60 years of age or older.

§ 56:8–2. Fraud, etc., in Connection with Sale or Advertisement of Merchandise or Real Estate as Unlawful Practice

The act, use or employment by any person of any unconscionable commercial practice, deception, fraud, false pretense, false promise, misrepresentation, or the knowing concealment, suppression, or omission of any material fact with intent that others rely upon such concealment, suppression or omission, in connection with the sale or advertisement of any merchandise or real estate, or with the subsequent performance of such person as aforesaid, whether or not any person has in fact been misled, deceived or damaged thereby, is declared to be an unlawful practice; provided, however, that nothing herein contained shall apply to the owner or publisher of newspapers, magazines, publications or printed matter wherein such advertisement appears, or to the owner or operator of a radio or television station which disseminates such advertisement when the owner, publisher, or operator has no knowledge of the intent, design or purpose of the advertiser.

§ 56:8–2.13. Cumulation of Rights and Remedies; Construction of Act

The rights, remedies and prohibitions accorded by the provisions of this act are hereby declared to be in addition to and cumulative of any other right, remedy or prohibition accorded by the common law or statutes of this State, and nothing contained herein shall be construed to deny, abrogate or impair any such common law or statutory right, remedy or prohibition.

§ 56:8–3. Investigation by Attorney General; Powers and Duties

When it shall appear to the Attorney General that a person has engaged in, is engaging in, or is about to engage in any practice declared to be unlawful by this act, or when he believes it to be in the public interest that an investigation should be made to ascertain whether a person in fact has engaged in, is engaging in or is about to engage in, any such practice, he may:

(a) Require such person to file on such forms as are prescribed a statement or report in writing under oath or otherwise, as to all the facts and circumstances concerning the sale or advertisement of merchandise by such person, and such other data and information as he may deem necessary;

(b) Examine under oath any person in connection with the sale or advertisement of any merchandise;

(c) Examine any merchandise or sample thereof, record, book, document, account or paper as he may deem necessary; and

(d) Pursuant to an order of the Superior Court impound any record, book, document, account, paper, or sample of merchandise that is produced in accordance with this act, and retain the same in his possession until the completion of all proceedings in connection with which the same are produced.

§ 56:8–3.1. Violations; Penalty

Upon receiving evidence of any violation of the provisions of chapter 39 of the laws of 1960, the Attorney General, or his designee, is empowered to hold hearings upon said violation and upon finding the violation to have been committed, to assess a penalty against the person alleged to have committed such violation in such amount within the limits of chapter 39 of the laws of 1966 as the Attorney General deems proper under the circumstances. Any such amounts collected by the Attorney General shall be paid forthwith into the State Treasury for the general purposes of the State.

§ 56:8–4. Additional Powers

To accomplish the objectives and to carry out the duties prescribed by this act, the Attorney General, in addition to other powers conferred upon him by this act, may issue subpoenas to any person, administer an oath or affirmation to any person, conduct hearings in aid of any investigation or inquiry, promulgate such rules and regulations, and prescribe such forms as may be necessary, which shall have the force of law.

§ 56:8–8. Injunction Against Unlawful Practices; Appointment of Receiver; Additional Penalties

Whenever it shall appear to the Attorney General that a person has engaged in, is engaging in or is about to engage in any practice declared to be unlawful by this act he may seek and obtain in a summary action in the Superior Court an injunction prohibiting such person from continuing such practices or engaging therein or doing any acts in furtherance thereof or an order appointing a receiver, or both. In addition to any other remedy authorized herein the court may enjoin an individual from managing or owning any business organization within this State, and from serving as an officer, director, trustee, member of any executive board or similar governing body, principal, manager, stockholder owning 10% or more of the aggregate outstanding capital stock of all classes of any corporation doing business in this State, vacate or annul the charter of a corporation created by or under the laws of this State, revoke the certificate of authority to do business in this State of a foreign corporation, and revoke any other licenses, permits or certificates issued pursuant to law to such person whenever such management, ownership, activity, charter authority license, permit or certificate have been or may be used to further such unlawful practice. The court may make such orders or judgments as may be necessary to prevent the use or employment by a person of any prohibited practices, or which may be necessary to restore to any person in interest any moneys or property, real or personal which may have been acquired by means of any practice herein declared to be unlawful.

§ 56:8–13. Penalties

Any person who violates any of the provisions of the act to which this act is a supplement shall, in addition to any other penalty provided by law, be liable to a penalty of not more than $10,000.00 for the first offense and not more than $20,000.00 for the second and each subsequent offense. The penalty shall be exclusive of and in addition to any moneys or property ordered to be paid or restored to any person in interest pursuant to section 56:8–14 or section 56:8–15.

§ 56:8–14. Enforcement of Penalty; Process

.   .   .

In any action brought pursuant to this section to enforce any order of the Attorney General or his designee the court may, without regard to jurisdictional limitations, restore to any person in interest any moneys or property, real or personal, which have been acquired by any means declared to be unlawful under this act, except that the court shall restore to any senior citizen twice the amount or value, as the case may be, of any moneys or property, real or personal, which have been acquired by any means declared to be unlawful under [§ 56:8–1 et seq.].

.   .   .

A person who fails to restore any moneys or property, real or personal, found to have been acquired unlawfully from a senior citizen shall be subject to punishment for criminal contempt pursuant to N.J.S. 2C:29–9, which is a crime of the fourth degree.

§ 56:8–15. Restoration of Moneys or Property Unlawfully Acquired; Order

In addition to the assessment of civil penalties, the Attorney General or his designee may, after a hearing as provided in [§ 56:8–3.1], and upon a finding of an unlawful practice under this act and the act hereby amended and supplemented, order that any moneys or property, real or personal, which have been acquired by means of such unlawful practice be restored to any person in interest, except that if any moneys or property, real or personal, have been acquired by means of an unlawful practice perpetrated against a senior citizen, the amount of moneys or property, real or personal, ordered restored shall be twice the amount acquired.

§ 56:8–18. Cease and Desist Order; Violations; Penalty

Where the Attorney General or his designee, after a hearing as provided in [§ 56:8–3.1], finds that an unlawful practice has been or may be committed, he may order the person committing such unlawful practice to cease and desist or refrain from committing said practice in the future. When it shall appear to the Attorney General that a person against whom a cease and desist order has been entered has violated said order, the Attorney General may initiate a summary proceeding in the Superior Court for the violation thereof. Any person found to have violated a cease and desist order shall pay to the State of New Jersey civil penalties in the amount of not more than $25,000.00 for each violation of said order. In the event that any person fails to pay a civil penalty assessed by the court for violation of a cease and desist order, the court assessing the unpaid penalty is authorized, upon application of the Attorney General, to grant any relief which may be obtained under any statute or court rule governing the collection and enforcement of penalties.

§ 56:8–19. Action, Counterclaim by Injured Person; Recovery of Damages, Costs

Any person who suffers any ascertainable loss of moneys or property, real or personal, as a result of the use or employment by another person of any method, act, or practice declared unlawful under this act or the act hereby amended and supplemented may bring an action or assert a counterclaim therefor in any court of competent jurisdiction. In any action under this section the court shall, in addition to any other appropriate legal or equitable relief, award threefold the damages sustained by any person in interest. In all actions under this section, including those brought by the Attorney General, the court shall also award reasonable attorneys' fees, filing fees and reasonable costs of suit.

§ 56:8–19.1. Exemption from Consumer Fraud Law, Certain Real Estate Licensees, Circumstances

Notwithstanding any provision of [§ 56:8–1 et seq.] to the contrary, there shall be no right of recovery of punitive damages, attorney fees, or both, under [§ 56:8–19], against a real estate broker, broker-salesperson or salesperson licensed under R.S.45:15–1 et seq. for the communication of any false, misleading or deceptive information provided to the real estate broker, broker-salesperson or salesperson, by or on behalf of the seller of real estate located in New Jersey, if the real estate broker, broker-salesperson or salesperson demonstrates that he:

a. Had no actual knowledge of the false, misleading or deceptive character of the information; and

b. Made a reasonable and diligent inquiry to ascertain whether the information is of a false, misleading or deceptive character. For purposes of this section, communications by a real estate broker, broker-salesperson or salesperson which shall be deemed to satisfy the requirements of a "reasonable and diligent inquiry" include, but shall not be limited to, communications which disclose information:

(1) provided in a report or upon a representation by a person, licensed or certified by the State of New Jersey, including, but not limited to, an appraiser, home inspector, plumber or electrical contractor, or an unlicensed home inspector until December 30, 2005, of a particular physical condition pertaining to the real estate derived from inspection of the real estate by that person;

(2) provided in a report or upon a representation by any governmental official or employee, if the particular information of a physical condition is likely to be within the knowledge of that governmental official or employee; or

(3) that the real estate broker, broker-salesperson or salesperson obtained from the seller in a property condition disclosure statement, which form shall comply with regulations promulgated by the director in consultation with the New Jersey Real Estate Commission, provided

that the real estate broker, broker-salesperson or salesperson informed the buyer that the seller is the source of the information and that, prior to making that communication to the buyer, the real estate broker, broker-salesperson or salesperson visually inspected the property with reasonable diligence to ascertain the accuracy of the information disclosed by the seller.

Nothing in this section shall be interpreted to affect the obligations of a real estate broker, broker-salesperson or salesperson pursuant to the "New Residential Construction Off–Site Conditions Disclosure Act," [§ 46:3C–1 et seq.], or any other law or regulation.

§ 56:8–20. Notice to Attorney General of Action or Defense by Injured Person; Intervention

Any party to an action asserting a claim, counterclaim or defense based upon violation of this act or the act hereby amended or supplemented shall mail a copy of the initial or responsive pleading containing the claim, counterclaim or defense to the Attorney General within 10 days after the filing of such pleading with the court. Upon application to the court wherein the matter is pending, the Attorney General shall be permitted to intervene or to appear in any status appropriate to the matter.

OREGON

Ore.Rev.Stat. §§ 646.605 et seq.

UNLAWFUL TRADE PRACTICES

Table of Sections

---

§ 646.605 Definitions for ORS 646.605 to 646.652

As used in ORS 646.605 to 646.652:

. . .

(6) "Real estate, goods or services" means those that are or may be obtained primarily for personal, family or household purposes, or that are or may be obtained for any purposes as a result of a telephone solicitation, and includes franchises, distributorships and other similar business opportunities, but does not include insurance. Real estate does not cover conduct covered by ORS chapter 90.

(7) "Telephone solicitation" means a solicitation where a person, in the course of the person's business, vocation or occupation, uses a telephone or an automatic dialing-announcing device to initiate telephonic contact with a potential customer and the person is not one of the following:

(a) A person who is a broker-dealer or salesperson licensed under ORS 59.175, or a mortgage banker or mortgage broker licensed under ORS 59.850 when the solicitation is for a security qualified for sale pursuant to ORS 59.055;

(b) A real estate licensee or a person who is otherwise authorized to engage in professional real estate activity pursuant to ORS chapter 696, when the solicitation involves professional real estate activity;

(c) A person licensed or exempt from licensure as a builder pursuant to ORS chapter 701, when the solicitation involves the construction, alteration, repair, improvement or demolition of a structure;

(d) A person licensed or otherwise authorized to sell insurance as an agent pursuant to ORS chapter 744, when the solicitation involves insurance;

(e) A person soliciting the sale of a newspaper of general circulation, a magazine or membership in a book or record club who complies with ORS 646.611, when the solicitation involves newspapers, magazines or membership in a book or record club;

(f) A person soliciting without the intent to complete and who does not complete the sales presentation during the telephone solicitation and who only completes the sales presentation at a later face-to-face meeting between the solicitor and the prospective purchaser;

(g) A supervised financial institution or parent, subsidiary or affiliate thereof. As used in this paragraph, "supervised financial institution" means any financial institution or trust company, as those terms are defined in ORS 706.008, or any personal property broker, consumer finance lender, commercial finance lender or insurer that is subject to regulation by an official or agency of this state or of the United States;

(h) A person who is authorized to conduct prearrangement or preconstruction funeral or cemetery sales, pursuant to ORS chapter 692, when the solicitation involves prearrangement or preconstruction funeral or cemetery plans;

(i) A person who solicits the services provided by a cable television system licensed or franchised pursuant to state, local or federal law, when the solicitation involves cable television services;

(j) A person or affiliate of a person whose business is regulated by the Public Utility Commission of Oregon;

(k) A person who sells farm products as defined by ORS 576.006 if the solicitation neither intends to nor actually results in a sale that costs the purchaser in excess of $100;

(l) An issuer or subsidiary of an issuer that has a class of securities that is subject to section 12 of the Securities Exchange Act of 1934 and that is either registered or exempt from registration under paragraph (A), (B), (C), (E), (F), (G) or (H) or subsection (g) of that section;

(m) A person soliciting exclusively the sale of telephone answering services to be provided by that person or that person's employer when the solicitation involves answering services; or

(n) A telecommunications utility with access lines of 15,000 or less or a cooperative telephone association when the solicitation involves regulated goods or services.

(8) "Trade" and "commerce" mean advertising, offering or distributing, whether by sale, rental or otherwise, any real estate, goods or services, and include any trade or commerce directly or indirectly affecting the people of this state.

(9) "Unconscionable tactics" include, but are not limited to, actions by which a person:

(a) Knowingly takes advantage of a customer's physical infirmity, ignorance, illiteracy or inability to understand the language of the agreement;

(b) Knowingly permits a customer to enter into a transaction from which the customer will derive no material benefit; or

(c) Permits a customer to enter into a transaction with knowledge that there is no reasonable probability of payment of the attendant financial obligation in full by the customer when due.

(10) A willful violation occurs when the person committing the violation knew or should have known that the conduct of the person was a violation.

(11) A loan is made "in close connection with the sale of a manufactured dwelling" if:

(a) The lender directly or indirectly controls, is controlled by or is under common control with the seller, unless the relationship is remote and is not a factor in the transaction;

(b) The lender gives a commission, rebate or credit in any form to a seller who refers the borrower to the lender, other than payment of the proceeds of the loan jointly to the seller and the borrower;

(c) The lender is related to the seller by blood or marriage;

(d) The seller directly and materially assists the borrower in obtaining the loan;

(e) The seller prepares documents that are given to the lender and used in connection with the loan; or

(f) The lender supplies documents to the seller used by the borrower in obtaining the loan.

§ 646.607 Unconscionable Tactic or Failure to Deliver, or to Refund Payment for Undelivered Real Estate, Goods, or Services as Unlawful Practice

A person engages in an unlawful practice when in the course of the person's business, vocation or occupation the person:

(1) Employs any unconscionable tactic in connection with sale, rental or other disposition of real estate, goods or services, or collection or enforcement of an obligation; or

(2) Fails to deliver all or any portion of real estate, goods or services as promised, and upon request of the customer, fails to refund any money that has been received from the customer that was for the purchase of the undelivered real estate, goods or services and that is not retained by the seller pursuant to any right, claim or defense asserted in good faith. This subsection does not create a warranty obligation and does not apply to a dispute over the quality of real estate, goods or services delivered to a customer.

(3) Violates ORS 401.107(1) to (4).

§ 646.608 Unlawful Business, Trade Practices; Proof; Attorney General's Rules

(1) A person engages in an unlawful practice when in the course of the person's business, vocation or occupation the person does any of the following:

(a) Passes off real estate, goods or services as those of another.

(b) Causes likelihood of confusion or of misunderstanding as to the source, sponsorship, approval, or certification of real estate, goods or services.

(c) Causes likelihood of confusion or of misunderstanding as to affiliation, connection, or association with, or certification by, another.

(d) Uses deceptive representations or designations of geographic origin in connection with real estate, goods or services.

(e) Represents that real estate, goods or services have sponsorship, approval, characteristics, ingredients, uses, benefits, quantities or qualities that they do not have or that a person has a sponsorship, approval, status, qualification, affiliation, or connection that the person does not have.

(f) Represents that real estate or goods are original or new if they are deteriorated, altered, reconditioned, reclaimed, used or second-hand.

(g) Represents that real estate, goods or services are of a particular standard, quality, or grade, or that real estate or goods are of a particular style or model, if they are of another.

(h) Disparages the real estate, goods, services, property or business of a customer or another by false or misleading representations of fact.

(*i*) Advertises real estate, goods or services with intent not to provide them as advertised, or with intent not to supply reasonably expectable public demand, unless the advertisement discloses a limitation of quantity.

(j) Makes false or misleading representations of fact concerning the reasons for, existence of, or amounts of price reductions.

(k) Makes false or misleading representations concerning credit availability or the nature of the transaction or obligation incurred.

(*l*) Makes false or misleading representations relating to commissions or other compensation to be paid in exchange for permitting real estate, goods or services to be used for model or demonstration purposes or in exchange for submitting names of potential customers.

(m) Performs service on or dismantles any goods or real estate when not authorized by the owner or apparent owner thereof.

(n) Solicits potential customers by telephone or door to door as a seller unless the person provides the information required under ORS 646.611.

(*o*) In a sale, rental or other disposition of real estate, goods or services, gives or offers to give a rebate or discount or otherwise pays or offers to pay value to the customer in consideration of the customer giving to the person the names of prospective purchasers, lessees, or borrowers, or otherwise aiding the person in making a sale, lease, or loan to another person, if earning the rebate, discount or other value is contingent upon occurrence of an event subsequent to the time the customer enters into the transaction.

(p) Makes any false or misleading statement about a prize, contest or promotion used to publicize a product, business or service.

(q) Promises to deliver real estate, goods or services within a certain period of time with intent not to deliver them as promised.

(r) Organizes or induces or attempts to induce membership in a pyramid club.

(s) Makes false or misleading representations of fact concerning the offering price of, or the person's cost for real estate, goods or services.

(t) Concurrent with tender or delivery of any real estate, goods or services fails to disclose any known material defect or material nonconformity.

(u) Engages in any other unfair or deceptive conduct in trade or commerce.

(v) Violates any of the provisions relating to auction sales, auctioneers or auction marts under ORS 698.640, whether in a commercial or noncommercial situation.

(w) Manufactures mercury fever thermometers.

(x) Sells or supplies mercury fever thermometers unless the thermometer is required by federal law, or is:

(A) Prescribed by a person licensed under ORS chapter 677; and

(B) Supplied with instructions on the careful handling of the thermometer to avoid breakage and on the proper cleanup of mercury should breakage occur.

(y) Sells a thermostat that contains mercury unless the thermostat is labeled in a manner to inform the purchaser that mercury is present in the thermostat and that the thermostat may not be disposed of until the mercury is removed, reused, recycled or otherwise managed to ensure that the mercury does not become part of the solid waste stream or wastewater. For purposes of this paragraph, "thermostat" means a device commonly used to sense and, through electrical communication with heating, cooling or ventilation equipment, control room temperature.

(z) Sells or offers for sale a motor vehicle manufactured after January 1, 2006, that contains mercury light switches.

(aa) Violates the provisions of ORS 803.375, 803.385 or 815.410 to 815.430 [regulating motor vehicle registration and disclosure of odometer readings].

(bb) Violates ORS 646A.070(1) [regulating sales of telephone equipment].

(cc) Violates any requirement of ORS 646A.030 to 646A.040 [regulating health spa contracts].

(dd) Violates the provisions of ORS 128.801 to 128.898 [regulating professional fund raisers].

(ee) Violates ORS 646.883 or 646.885 [regulating comparative price advertising].

(ff) Violates any provision of ORS 646A.020 [regulating certain travel associations].

(gg) Violates ORS 646.569 [regulating telephone solicitation].

(hh) Violates the provisions of ORS 646A.142 [requiring certain disclosures in connection with automobile rentals].

(*ii*) Violates ORS 646A.360 [prohibiting the sending of unsolicited advertising over facsimile machines].

(jj) Violates ORS 646.553 or 646.557 or any rule adopted pursuant thereto [regulating telemarketers].

(kk) Violates ORS 646.563 [prohibiting certain telephone solicitation].

(*ll*) Violates ORS 759.690 or any rule adopted pursuant thereto [regulating telephone operator services].

(mm) Violates the provisions of ORS 759.705, 759.710 and 759.720 or any rule adopted pursuant thereto [regulating pay-per-call services]

(nn) Violates ORS 646A.210 or 646A.214 [prohibiting merchants from requiring personal information in connection with check or credit card transactions].

(*oo*) Violates any provision of ORS 646A.124 to 646A.134 [regulating rent-to-own transactions].

(pp) Violates ORS 646A.254 [regulating credit-repair organizations].

. . .

(2) A representation under subsection (1) of this section or ORS 646.607 may be any manifestation of any assertion by words or conduct, including, but not limited to, a failure to disclose a fact.

(3) In order to prevail in an action or suit under ORS 646.605 to 646.652, a prosecuting attorney need not prove competition between the parties or actual confusion or misunderstanding.

(4) An action or suit may not be brought under subsection (1)(u) of this section unless the Attorney General has first established a rule in

accordance with the provisions of ORS chapter 183 declaring the conduct to be unfair or deceptive in trade or commerce.

(5). . .

§ 646.612 Application of ORS 646.607 and 646.608

ORS 646.607 and 646.608 do not apply to:

(1) Conduct in compliance with the orders or rules of, or a statute administered by a federal, state or local governmental agency.

(2) Acts done by the publisher, owner, agent or employe of a newspaper, periodical or radio or television station in the publication or dissemination of an advertisement, when the publisher, owner, agent or employe did not have knowledge of the false, misleading or deceptive character of the advertisement.

§ 646.632 Enjoining Unlawful Trade Practices; Notice to Defendant; Voluntary Compliance; Voluntary Compliance Agreement as Judgment

(1) A prosecuting attorney who has probable cause to believe that a person is engaging in, has engaged in, or is about to engage in an unlawful trade practice may bring suit in the name of the State of Oregon in the appropriate court to restrain such person from engaging in the alleged unlawful trade practice.

. . .

§ 646.636 Remedial Power of Court

The court may make such additional orders or judgments as may be necessary to restore to any person in interest any moneys or property, real or personal, of which the person was deprived by means of any practice declared to be unlawful in ORS 646.607 or 646.608, or as may be necessary to insure cessation of unlawful trade practices.

§ 646.638 Civil Action by Private Party; Damages; Attorney Fees; Effect of Prior Injunction; Time for Commencing Action; Counterclaim

(1) Except as provided in subsection (8) of this section, any person who suffers any ascertainable loss of money or property, real or personal, as a result of wilful use or employment by another person of a method, act or practice declared unlawful by ORS 646.608, may bring an individual action in an appropriate court to recover actual damages or $200, whichever is greater. The court or the jury, as the case may be, may award punitive

damages and the court may provide such equitable relief as it deems necessary or proper.

(2) Upon commencement of any action brought under subsection (1) of this section the party bringing the action shall mail a copy of the complaint or other initial pleading to the Attorney General and, upon entry of any judgment or decree in the action, shall mail a copy of such judgment or decree to the Attorney General. Failure to mail a copy of the complaint shall not be a jurisdictional defect, but a court may not enter judgment for the plaintiff until proof of mailing is filed with the court. Proof of mailing may be by affidavit or by return receipt of mailing.

(3) Except as provided in subsection (4) of this section, the court may award reasonable attorney fees to the prevailing party in an action under this section.

(4) The court may not award attorney fees to a prevailing defendant under the provisions of subsection (3) of this section if the action under this section is maintained as a class action pursuant to ORCP 32.

(5) Any permanent injunction or final judgment or order of the court made under ORS 646.632 or 646.636 shall be prima facie evidence in an action brought under this section that the respondent used or employed a method, act or practice declared unlawful by ORS 646.608, but an assurance of voluntary compliance, whether or not approved by the court, shall not be evidence of such violation.

(6) Actions brought under this section shall be commenced within one year from the discovery of the unlawful method, act or practice. However, whenever any complaint is filed by a prosecuting attorney to prevent, restrain or punish violations of ORS 646.608, running of the statute of limitations with respect to every private right of action under this section and based in whole or in part on any matter complained of in said proceeding shall be suspended during the pendency thereof.

(7) Notwithstanding subsection (6) of this section, in any action brought by a seller or lessor against a purchaser or lessee of real estate, goods or services, such purchaser or lessee may assert any counterclaim the purchaser or lessee has arising out of a violation of ORS 646.605 to 646.652.

(8) This section does not apply to any method, act or practice described in ORS 646.608(1)(aa). Actions for violation of laws relating to odometers are provided under ORS 815.410 and 815.415.

§ 646.642 Civil Penalties

(1) Any person who wilfully violates the terms of an injunction issued under ORS 646.632 shall forfeit and pay to the state a civil penalty to be set by the court of not more than $25,000 per violation. For the purposes of this section, the court issuing the injunction shall retain jurisdiction and the cause shall be continued, and in such cases the prosecuting attorney acting in the name of the state may petition for recovery of civil penalties.

(2) Any person who wilfully violates any provision of an assurance of voluntary compliance approved and filed with an appropriate court under ORS 646.632 shall forfeit and pay to the state a civil penalty to be set by the court of not more than $25,000 per violation. Any prosecuting attorney may apply to an appropriate court for recovery of such civil penalty. In any action brought by a prosecuting attorney under this section, and in any contempt action brought by a prosecuting attorney pursuant to ORS 646.632(4), the court may award to the prevailing attorney, in addition to any other relief provided by law, reasonable attorney fees and costs at trial and on appeal.

(3) In any suit brought under ORS 646.632, if the court finds that a person is wilfully using or has wilfully used a method, act or practice declared unlawful by ORS 646.607 or 646.608, the prosecuting attorney, upon petition to the court, may recover, on behalf of the state, a civil penalty to be set by the court of not exceeding $25,000 per violation.

§ 646.648   Unlawful Practice by Manufactured Dwelling Dealer

(1) As used in this section:

(a) "Buyer" means a person who buys or agrees to buy a manufactured dwelling from a manufactured dwelling dealer.

(b) "Cash sale price" means the price for which a manufactured dwelling dealer would sell to a buyer, and the buyer would buy from a dealer, a manufactured dwelling that is covered by a purchase agreement, if the sale were a sale for cash instead of a retail installment sale.

(c) "Manufactured dwelling" has the meaning given that term in ORS 446.003.

(d) "Manufactured dwelling dealer" means a person licensed under ORS 446.691 or 446.696 or a temporary manufactured structure dealer licensee under ORS 646.701.

(e) "Retail installment sale" has the meaning given that term in ORS 83.510.

(2) A manufactured dwelling dealer engages in an unlawful practice when, in a sale of a manufactured dwelling, the dealer does any of the following:

(a) Misrepresents to a buyer that, as a condition of financing, the buyer must purchase:

(A) Credit life insurance;

(B) Credit disability insurance;

(C) Credit unemployment insurance;

(D) Credit property insurance;

(E) Health insurance;

(F) Life insurance; or

(G) An extended warranty.

(b) In close connection with the sale, misrepresents to a lender:

(A) The cash sale price;

(B) The amount of the buyer's down payment; or

(C) The buyer's credit or employment history.

§ 646.656   Remedies Supplementary to Existing Statutory or Common-law Remedies

The remedies provided in ORS 646.605 to 646.652 are in addition to all other remedies, civil or criminal, existing at common law or under the laws of this state.

UNIFORM CONSUMER SALES PRACTICES ACT

Table of Sections

---

§ 1. [Purposes, Rules of Construction]

This Act shall be construed liberally to promote the following policies:

(1) to simplify, clarify, and modernize the law governing consumer sales practices;

(2) to protect consumers from suppliers who commit deceptive and unconscionable sales practices;

(3) to encourage the development of fair consumer sales practices;

(4) to make state regulation of consumer sales practices not inconsistent with the policies of the Federal Trade Commission Act relating to consumer protection; and

(5) to make uniform the law, including the administrative rules, with respect to the subject of this Act among those states which enact it.

§ 2. [Definitions]

As used in this Act:

(1) "consumer transaction" means a sale, lease, assignment, award by chance, or other disposition of an item of goods, a service, or an intangible [except securities] to an individual for purposes that are primarily personal, family, or household, or that relate to a business opportunity that requires both his expenditure of money or property and his personal services on a continuing basis and in which he has not been previously engaged, or a solicitation by a supplier with respect to any of these dispositions;

(2) "Enforcing Authority" means [appropriate official or officials];

(3) "final judgment" means a judgment, including any supporting opinion, that determines the rights of the parties and concerning which appellate remedies have been exhausted or the time for appeal has expired;

(4) "person" means an individual, corporation, government, governmental subdivision or agency, business trust, estate, trust, partnership, association, cooperative, or any other legal entity;

(5) "supplier" means a seller, lessor, assignor, or other person who regularly solicits, engages in, or enforces consumer transactions, whether or not he deals directly with the consumer.

§ 3. [Deceptive Consumer Sales Practices]

(a) A deceptive act or practice by a supplier in connection with a consumer transaction violates this Act whether it occurs before, during, or after the transaction.

(b) Without limiting the scope of subsection (a), the act or practice of a supplier in indicating any of the following is deceptive:

(1) that the subject of a consumer transaction has sponsorship, approval, performance characteristics, accessories, uses, or benefits it does not have;

(2) that the subject of a consumer transaction is of a particular standard, quality, grade, style, or model, if it is not;

(3) that the subject of a consumer transaction is new, or unused, if it is not, or that the subject of a consumer transaction has been used to an extent that is materially different from the fact;

(4) that the subject of a consumer transaction is available to the consumer for a reason that does not exist;

(5) that the subject of a consumer transaction has been supplied in accordance with a previous representation, if it has not;

(6) that the subject of a consumer transaction will be supplied in greater quantity than the supplier intends;

(7) that replacement or repair is needed, if it is not;

(8) that a specific price advantage exists, if it does not;

(9) that the supplier has a sponsorship, approval, or affiliation he does not have;

(10) that a consumer transaction involves or does not involve a warranty, a disclaimer of warranties, particular warranty terms, or other rights, remedies, or obligations if the indication is false; or

(11) that the consumer will receive a rebate, discount, or other benefit as an inducement for entering into a consumer transaction in return for giving the supplier the names of prospective consumers or otherwise helping the supplier to enter into other consumer transactions, if receipt of the benefit is contingent on an event occurring after the consumer enters into the transaction.

§ 4. [Unconscionable Consumer Sales Practices]

(a) An unconscionable act or practice by a supplier in connection with a consumer transaction violates this Act whether it occurs before, during, or after the transaction.

(b) The unconscionability of an act or practice is a question of law for the court. If it is claimed or appears to the court that an act or practice may be unconscionable, the parties shall be given a reasonable opportunity to present evidence as to its setting, purpose and effect to aid the court in making its determination.

(c) In determining whether an act or practice is unconscionable, the court shall consider circumstances such as the following of which the supplier knew or had reason to know:

(1) that he took advantage of the inability of the consumer reasonably to protect his interests because of his physical infirmity, ignorance, illiteracy, inability to understand the language of an agreement, or similar factors;

(2) that when the consumer transaction was entered into the price grossly exceeded the price at which similar property or services were readily obtainable in similar transactions by like consumers;

(3) that when the consumer transaction was entered into the consumer was unable to receive a substantial benefit from the subject of the transaction;

(4) that when the consumer transaction was entered into there was no reasonable probability of payment of the obligation in full by the consumer;

(5) that the transaction he induced the consumer to enter into was excessively one-sided in favor of the supplier; or

(6) that he made a misleading statement of opinion on which the consumer was likely to rely to his detriment.

Commissioners' Comment

[Subsecs. (a) and (b)]. These subsections forbid unconscionable advertising techniques, unconscionable contract terms, and unconscionable debt collection practices. As under Uniform Commercial Code § 2–302 (1962 Official Text with Comments), unconscionability is a question of law for the court. Unconscionability typically involves conduct by which a supplier seeks to induce or to require a consumer to assume risks which materially exceed the benefits to him of a related consumer transaction.

[Subsec. (c)]. "Knowledge or reason to know" often will be established by a supplier's course of conduct. Although probative, this scienter is not invariably required in order to establish unconscionability under § 4(a).

[Subsec. (c)(1)]. This subsection includes such conduct as selling an English-language encyclopedia set for personal use to a Spanish–American bachelor laborer who does not read English, or using legal verbiage in a manner which can not be readily comprehended by a low-income consumer who both reads and speaks English.

[Subsec. (c)(2)]. This subsection includes such conduct as a home solicitation sale of a set of cookware to a housewife for $375 in an area where a set of comparable quality is readily available to such a housewife for $125 or less.

[Subsec. (c)(3)]. This subsection includes such conduct as the sale of two expensive vacuum cleaners to two poor families whom the salesman knows, or has reason to know, share the same apartment and the same rug.

[Subsec. (c)(4)]. This subsection includes such conduct as the sale of goods, services, or intangibles to a low-income consumer whom the salesman knows, or has reason to know, does not have sufficient income to make the stipulated payments.

[Subsec. (c)(5)]. This subsection includes such conduct as requiring a consumer to sign a one-sided adhesion contract which contains a penalty clause, an acceleration clause, a confession-of-judgment clause, a disclaimer of all warranties, and a clause permitting the supplier, but not the consumer, to cancel the contract at will. As indicated by this illustration, this subsection applies to contract terms which result in an excessively one-sided consumer transaction even though some or all of the contract terms are lawful in and of themselves. The exemption from the Act by subsection 14(a)(1) of acts or practices required or specifically permitted by or under federal or state law should accordingly be reconciled with this subsection by exempting only required or specifically permitted aggregations of contract terms and required or specifically permitted contract terms.

[Subsec. (c)(6)]. This subsection applies to misleading subjective expressions of opinion on which a supplier should reasonably expect a consumer to rely to his detriment. For example, a violation of this subsection would occur if a prospective purchaser asked a supplier what the useful life of a paint job was and the supplier, with reason to know that repainting would be necessary within two years, responded, "in my opinion the paint will wear like iron." Overt factual misstatements expressed in the form of opinion are dealt with by § 3's proscription of deceptive consumer sales practices. For example, a violation of § 3 would occur if a prospective purchaser asked a supplier what the useful life of a two-year paint job was and the supplier responded, "in my opinion repainting will not be necessary for five years."

§ 4A.   [Jurisdiction and Service of Process]

[(a) The [_____] court of this state [may exercise] [has] jurisdiction over any supplier as to any act or practice in this State governed by this Act or as to any claim arising from a consumer transaction subject to this Act.]

[(b) In addition to any other method provided by [rule or] statute, personal jurisdiction over a supplier may be acquired in a civil action or proceeding instituted in the [_____] court by the service of process in the following manner. If a supplier engages in any act or practice in this State governed by this Act, or engages in a consumer transaction subject to this Act, he may designate an agent upon whom service of process may be made in this State. The agent must be a resident of or a corporation authorized to do business in this State. The designation must be in writing and filed with the [Secretary of State]. If no designation is made and filed, or if process cannot be served in this State upon the designated agent, whether or not the supplier is a resident of this State or is authorized to do business in this State, process may be served upon the [Secretary of State], but service upon him is not effective unless the plaintiff promptly mails a copy of the process and pleadings by registered or certified mail to the defendant at his last reasonably ascertainable address. An affidavit of compliance with this section must be filed with the clerk of the court on or before the return day of the process, if any, or within any future time the court allows.]

Commissioners' Comment

[Subsec. (a)]. This optional subsection grants the courts of an enacting state jurisdiction with respect to violations of the Act. It may be omitted in states where an express statutory grant of judicial jurisdiction is unnecessary.

[Subsec. (b)]. This optional subsection provides a method for obtaining personal jurisdiction over out-of-state suppliers who have violated the Act. It may be omitted in states with comparable "long-arm" statutes.

§ 5. [Duties of the Enforcing Authority]

(A) The Enforcing Authority shall:

(1) enforce this Act throughout the State;

(2) cooperate with state and local officials, officials of other states, and officials of the Federal government in the administration of comparable statutes;

(3) inform consumers and suppliers on a continuing basis of the provisions of this Act and of acts or practices that violate this Act, including mailing information concerning final judgments to persons who request it, for which he may charge a reasonable fee to cover the expense;

(4) receive and act on complaints;

(5) maintain a public file of (i) final judgments rendered under this Act that have been either reported officially or made available for public dissemination under Section 5(a)(3), (ii) final consent judgments, and (iii), to the extent the Enforcing Authority considers appropriate, assurances of voluntary compliance; and

(6) report [annually on or before January 1] to the [Governor and Legislature] on the operations of his office and on the acts or practices occurring in this State that violate this Act.

(b) The Enforcing Authority's report shall include a statement of the investigatory and enforcement procedures and policies of his office, of the number of investigations and enforcement proceedings instituted and of their disposition, and of the other activities of his office and of other persons to carry out the purposes of this Act.

(c) In carrying out his duties, the Enforcing Authority may not publicly disclose the identity of a person investigated unless his identity has become a matter of public record in an enforcement proceeding or he has consented to public disclosure.

§ 6.　[General Powers of the Enforcing Authority]

(a) The Enforcing Authority may conduct research, hold public hearings, make inquiries, and publish studies relating to consumer sales acts or practices.

(b) The Enforcing Authority shall adopt substantive rules that prohibit with specificity acts or practices that violate Section 3 and appropriate procedural rules.

§ 7.　[Rule-making Requirements]

Alternative A

[The [State Administrative Procedure Act] applies to administrative action taken by the Enforcing Authority under this Act.]

Alternative B

[(a) In addition to complying with other rule-making requirements imposed by this Act, the Enforcing Authority shall:

(1) adopt as a rule a description of the organization of his office, stating the general course and method of operation of his office and methods whereby the public may obtain information or make submissions or requests;

(2) adopt rules of practice setting forth the nature and requirements of all formal and informal procedures available, including a description of the forms and instructions used by the Enforcing Authority or his office; and

(3) make available for public inspection all rules, written statements of policy, and interpretations formulated, adopted, or used by the Enforcing Authority in discharging his functions.

(b) A rule of the Enforcing Authority is invalid, and may not be invoked by the Enforcing Authority for any purpose, until it has been made available for public inspection under subsection (a). This provision does not apply to a person who has knowledge of a rule before engaging in an act or practice that violates this Act.]

Commissioners' Comment

Alternative A may be enacted in states that have administrative procedure acts. If a state does not have an administrative procedure act, Alternative B should be selected. The provisions in Alternative B and the accompanying optional §§ 7A–7E are derived from Uniform Consumer Credit Code §§ 6.403–408 (1969 Official Text with Comments).

§ 8. [Investigatory Powers of the Enforcing Authority]

(a) If, by his own inquiries or as a result of complaints, the Enforcing Authority has reason to believe that a person has engaged in, is engaging in, or is about to engage in an act or practice that violates this Act, he may administer oaths and affirmations, subpoena witnesses or matter, and collect evidence.

(b) If matter that the Enforcing Authority subpoenas is located outside this State, the person subpoenaed may either make it available to the Enforcing Authority at a convenient location within the State or pay the reasonable and necessary expenses for the Enforcing Authority or his representative to examine the matter at the place where it is located. The Enforcing Authority may designate representatives, including officials of the state in which the matter is located, to inspect the matter on his behalf, and he may respond to similar requests from officials of other states.

(c) Upon failure of a person without lawful excuse to obey a subpoena and upon reasonable notice to all persons affected, the Enforcing Authority may apply to the [_____] court for an order compelling compliance.

(d) [After consultation with the Attorney General,] the Enforcing Authority may request that an individual who refuses to comply with a subpoena on the ground that testimony or matter may incriminate him be ordered by the court to provide the testimony or matter. Except in a prosecution for [perjury] [false swearing], an individual who complies with a court order to provide testimony or matter after asserting a privilege against self-incrimination to which he is entitled by law, may not be subjected to a criminal proceeding or to a civil penalty with respect to the transaction concerning which he is required to testify or produce relevant matter. This subsection does not apply to damages recoverable under Section 11(b) or to civil sanctions imposed under Section 9(a)(2).

§ 9. [Remedies of the Enforcing Authority]

(a) The Enforcing Authority may bring an action:

(1) to obtain a declaratory judgment that an act or practice violates this Act; or

(2) to enjoin, in accordance with the principles of equity, a supplier who has violated, is violating, or is otherwise likely to violate this Act;

(3) to recover actual damages, or obtain relief under subsection (b)(2), on behalf of consumers who complained to the Enforcing Authority before he instituted enforcement proceedings under this Act.

(b)(1) The Enforcing Authority may bring a class action on behalf of consumers for the actual damages caused by an act or practice specified as violating this Act in a rule adopted by the Enforcing Authority under Section 6(b) before the consumer transactions on which the action is based, or declared to violate Section 3 or 4 by final judgment of [insert the appropriate court or courts of general jurisdiction and appellate courts] of this State that was either reported officially or made available for public dissemination under Section 5(a)(3) by the Enforcing Authority [10] days before the consumer transactions on which the action is based, or, with respect to a supplier who agreed to it, was prohibited specifically by the terms of a consent judgment that became final before the consumer transactions on which the action is based.

(2) On motion of the Enforcing Authority and without bond in an action under this subsection, the court may make appropriate orders, including appointment of a master or receiver or sequestration of assets, to reimburse consumers found to have been damaged, or to carry out a transaction in accordance with consumers' reasonable expectations, or to strike or limit the application of unconscionable clauses of contracts to avoid an unconscionable result, or to grant other appropriate relief. The court may assess the expenses of a master or receiver against a supplier.

(3) If a supplier shows by a preponderance of the evidence that a violation of this Act resulted from a bona fide error notwithstanding the maintenance of procedures reasonably adapted to avoid the error, recovery under Section 9(b) is limited to the amount, if any, by which the supplier was unjustly enriched by the violation.

(4) If an act or practice that violates this Act unjustly enriches a supplier and damages can be computed with reasonable certainty, damages recoverable on behalf of consumers who cannot be located with due diligence [shall escheat to the State] [shall be allocated under the Uniform Disposition of Unclaimed Property Act].

(5) No action may be brought by the Enforcing Authority under this subsection more than 2 years after the occurrence of a violation of this Act, or more than one year after the last payment in a consumer transaction involved in a violation of this Act, whichever is later.

(c) The Enforcing Authority may terminate an investigation or an action other than a class action upon acceptance of a supplier's written assurance of voluntary compliance with this Act. Acceptance of an assurance may be conditioned on a commitment to reimburse consumers or take other appropriate corrective action. An assurance is not evidence of a prior violation of this Act. However, unless an assurance has been rescinded by agreement of the parties or voided by a court for good cause, subsequent failure to comply with the terms of an assurance is prima facie evidence of a violation of this Act.

§ 10. [Coordination with Other Supervision]

(a) If the Enforcing Authority receives a complaint or other information relating to noncompliance with this Act by a supplier who is subject to other supervision in this State, the Enforcing Authority shall inform the official or agency having that supervision. The Enforcing Authority may request information about such suppliers from the official or agency.

(b) The Enforcing Authority and any other official or agency in this State having supervisory authority over a supplier shall consult and assist each other in maintaining compliance with this Act. Within the scope of their authority, they may jointly or separately make investigations, prosecute suits, and take other official action they consider appropriate.

§ 11. [Private Remedies]

(a) Whether he seeks or is entitled to damages or has an adequate remedy at law, a consumer may bring an action to:

(1) obtain a declaratory judgment that an act or practice violates this Act; or

(2) enjoin, in accordance with the principles of equity, a supplier who has violated, is violating, or is otherwise likely to violate this Act.

(b) Except in a class action, a consumer who suffers loss as a result of a violation of this Act may recover actual damages or [$100], whichever is greater.

(c) Whether a consumer seeks or is entitled to recover damages or has an adequate remedy at law, he may bring a class action for declaratory judgment, an injunction, and appropriate ancillary relief, except damages, against an act or practice that violates this Act.

(d)(1) A consumer who suffers loss as a result of a violation of this Act may bring a class action for the actual damages caused by an act or practice (i) specified as violating this Act in a rule adopted by the Enforcing Authority under Section 6(b) before the consumer transactions on which the action is based, or (ii) declared to violate Section 3 or 4 by a final judgment of [insert the appropriate court or courts of general jurisdiction and appellate courts] of this State that was either reported officially or made available for public dissemination under Section 5(a)(3) by the Enforcing Authority [10] days before the consumer transaction on which the action is based, or (iii) with respect to a supplier who agreed to it, was prohibited specifically by the terms of a consent judgment which became final before the consumer transactions on which the action is based.

(2) If a supplier shows by a preponderance of the evidence that a violation of this Act resulted from a bona fide error notwithstanding the maintenance of procedures reasonably adapted to avoid the error, recovery under this section is limited to the amount, if any, by which the supplier was unjustly enriched by the violation.

(3) If an act or practice that violates this Act unjustly enriches a supplier and the damages can be computed with reasonable certainty, damages recoverable on behalf of consumers who cannot be located with due diligence [shall escheat to the State] [shall be allocated under the Uniform Disposition of Unclaimed Property Act].

(e) Except for services performed by the Enforcing Authority, the court may award to the prevailing party a reasonable attorney's fee limited to the work reasonably performed if:

(1) the consumer complaining of the act or practice that violates this Act has brought or maintained an action he knew to be groundless; or a supplier has committed an act or practice that violates this Act; and

(2) an action under this section has been terminated by a judgment or required by the court to be settled under Section 13(a).

(f) Except for consent judgments entered before testimony is taken, a final judgment in favor of the Enforcing Authority under Section 9 is admissible as prima facie evidence of the facts on which it is based in later proceedings under this section against the same person or a person in privity with him.

(g) When a judgment under this section becomes final, the prevailing party shall mail a copy to the Enforcing Authority for inclusion in the public file maintained under Section 5(a)(5).

(h) An action under this section must be brought within 2 years after occurrence of a violation of this Act, within one year after the last payment in a consumer transaction involved in a violation of this Act, or within one year after the termination of proceedings by the Enforcing Authority with respect to a violation of this Act, whichever is later. However, when a supplier sues a consumer, he may assert as a counterclaim any claim under this Act arising out of the transaction on which suit is brought.

§ 12. [Class Actions]

(a) An action may be maintained as a class action under this Act only if:

(1) the class is so numerous that joinder of all members is impracticable;

(2) there are questions of law or fact common to the class;

(3) the claims or defenses of the representative parties are typical of the claims or defenses of the class;

(4) the representative parties will fairly and adequately protect the interests of the class; and

(5) either:

(A) the prosecution of separate actions by or against individual members of the class would create a risk of:

(i) inconsistent or varying adjudications with respect to individual members of the class which would establish incompatible standards of conduct for the party opposing the class; or

(ii) adjudications with respect to individual members of the class which would as a practical matter be dispositive of the interests of the other members not parties to the adjudications or substantially impair or impede their ability to protect their interests; or

(B) the party opposing the class has acted or refused to act on grounds generally applicable to the class, thereby making appropriate final injunctive relief or corresponding declaratory relief with respect to the class as a whole; or

(C) the court finds that the questions of law or fact common to the members of the class predominate over any questions affecting only individual members, and that a class action is superior to other available methods for the fair and efficient adjudication of the controversy.

(b) The matters pertinent to the findings under subsection (a)(5)(C) include:

(1) the interest of members of the class in individually controlling the prosecution or defense of separate actions;

(2) the extent and nature of any litigation concerning the controversy already commenced by or against members of the class;

(3) the desirability or undesirability of concentrating the litigation of the claims in the particular forum; and

(4) the difficulties likely to be encountered in the management of a class action.

(c) As soon as practicable after the commencement of an action brought as a class action, the court shall determine by order whether it is to be so maintained. An order under this subsection may be conditional, and may be amended before the decision on the merits.

(d) In a class action maintained under subsection (a)(5)(C) the court may direct to the members of the class the best notice practicable under the circumstances, including individual notice to all members who can be identified through reasonable effort. The notice shall advise each member that:

(1) the court will exclude him from the class, if he so requests by a specified date;

(2) the judgment, whether favorable or not, will include all members who do not request exclusion; and

(3) any member who does not request exclusion may, if he desires, enter an appearance through his counsel.

(e) When appropriate, an action may be brought or maintained as a class action with respect to particular issues, or a class may be divided into subclasses and each subclass treated as a class.

(f) In the conduct of a class action the court may make appropriate orders:

(1) determining the course of proceedings or prescribing measures to prevent undue repetition or complication in the presentation of evidence or argument;

(2) requiring, for the protection of the members of the class or otherwise for the fair conduct of the action, that notice be given in the manner the court directs to some or all of the members or to the Enforcing Authority of any step in the action, or of the proposed extent of the judgment, or of the opportunity of members to signify whether they consider the representation fair and adequate, to intervene and present claims or defenses, or otherwise to come into the action;

(3) imposing conditions on the representative parties or on intervenors;

(4) requiring that the pleadings be amended to eliminate allegations as to representation of absent persons, and that the action proceed accordingly; or

(5) dealing with similar procedural matters.

(g) A class action shall not be dismissed or compromised without approval of the court. Notice of the proposed dismissal or compromise shall be given to all members of the class in such manner as the court directs.

(h) The judgment in an action maintained as a class action under subsection (a)(5)(A) or (B), whether or not favorable to the class, shall describe those whom the court finds to be members of the class. The judgment in a class action maintained under subsection (a)(5)(C), whether or not favorable to the class, shall specify or describe those to whom the notice provided in subsection (d) was directed, and who have not requested exclusion, and whom the court finds to be members of the class.

Commissioners' Comment

In order to facilitate its administration, this section is modeled closely on Federal Rule of Civil Procedure 23. The principal substantive deviation from the federal approach appears in § 12(d). Unlike its federal counterpart, § 12(d) allows a court discretion with respect to providing class members notice of an opportunity to exclude themselves from class actions based on the existence of common questions of law or fact. On the other hand, like the federal rule, § 12 permits actions against a class of defendants as well as actions on behalf of a plaintiff-class.

§ 13. [Special Provisions Relating to Class Actions]

(a)(1) A defendant in a class action may file a written offer of settlement. If it is not accepted within a reasonable time by a plaintiff class representative, the defendant may file an affidavit reciting the rejection. The court may determine that the offer has enough merit to present to the members of the class. If is so determines, it shall order a hearing to determine whether the offer should be approved. It shall give the best notice of the hearing that is practicable under the circumstances, including notice to each member who can be identified through reasonable effort. The notice shall specify the terms of the offer and a reasonable period within which members of the class who request it are entitled to be excluded from the class. The statute of limitations for those who are excluded pursuant to this subsection is tolled for the period the class action has been pending, plus an additional year.

(2) If a member who has previously lost an opportunity to be excluded from the class is excluded at his request in response to notice of the offer of settlement during the period specified under paragraph (1), he may not thereafter participate in a class action respecting the same consumer transaction, unless the court later disapproves the offer of settlement or approves a settlement materially different from that proposed in the original offer of settlement. After the expiration of the period specified under paragraph (1), a member of the class is not entitled to be excluded from it.

(3) If the court later approves the offer of settlement, including changes, if any, required by the court in the interest of a just settlement of the action, it shall enter a judgment, which is binding on all persons who are then members of the class. If the court disapproves the offer or approves a settlement materially different from that proposed in the original offer, notice shall be given to a person who was excluded from the action at his request in response to notice of the offer under paragraph (1) that he is entitled to rejoin the class, and, in the case of approval, participate in the settlement.

(b) On the commencement of a class action under Section 11, the class representative shall mail by certified mail with return receipt requested or personally serve a copy of the complaint on the Enforcing Authority. Within 30 days after the receipt of a copy of the complaint, but not thereafter, the Enforcing Authority may intervene in the class action.

Commissioners' Comment

This section permits a court in its discretion to require settlement of actions that have been brought on behalf of a plaintiff-class. In order to do so, the court must notify individual class members of an opportunity to exclude themselves from the settlement proceedings. As long as they have not had a prior opportunity to exclude themselves from a class action under § 12, persons who exclude themselves from a class action under § 13(a) thereafter can maintain either class or individual actions with respect to the same consumer transaction. However, with the two exceptions noted in § 13(a)(2) and (3), persons who have had a prior opportunity to exclude themselves under § 12 and later exclude themselves under § 13(a) thereafter can maintain only individual actions with respect to the same consumer transaction. If the court determines that a supplier has avoided a finding that he violated this Act by resort to § 13, the court may award a reasonable attorney's fee to the representative of the consumer class, § 11(e).

.   .   .

§ 14. [Application]

(a) This Act does not apply to:

(1) an act or practice required or specifically permitted by or under Federal law, or by or under State law;

(2) a publisher, broadcaster, printer, or other person engaged in the dissemination of information or the reproduction of printed or pictorial matter insofar as the information or matter has been disseminated or reproduced on behalf of others without actual knowledge that it violated this Act;

(3) a claim for personal injury or death or a claim for damage to property other than the property that is the subject of the consumer transaction; or

(4) the credit terms of a transaction otherwise subject to this Act.

(b) A person alleged to have violated this Act has the burden of showing the applicability of this Section.

Commissioners' Comment

.   .   .

[Subsec. (a)(3)].   This subsection has primary application to product liability claims. To the extent that joinder is appropriate, it does not bar the joinder of a product liability claim with a related claim for violation of this Act, § 15.

[Subsec. (a)(4)].   This subsection exempts only the credit terms of a consumer transaction. For example, advertising and contractual provisions with respect to the finance charge in a consumer transaction would be exempt, but advertising and contractual provisions with respect to the nature or quality of the subject of a consumer transaction would not be exempt.

.   .   .

§ 15. [Effect on Other Remedies]

The remedies of this Act are in addition to remedies otherwise available for the same conduct under state or local law, except that a class action relating to a transaction governed by this Act may be brought only as prescribed by this Act.

LEMON LAWS

Missouri (Vernon's Ann.Mo.Stat. §§ 407.560–407.569)
New York (N.Y.Gen.Bus.Law §§ 198–a, 198–b (McKinney))

NEW MOTOR VEHICLE WARRANTIES ACT

Vernon's Ann.Mo.Stat. §§ 407.560–407.579

Table of Sections

---

§ 407.560 Definitions

As used in sections 407.560 to 407.579, the following terms mean:

(1) "Collateral charges," those additional charges to a consumer not directly attributable to a manufacturer's suggested retail price label for the new motor vehicle. For the purposes of sections 407.560 to 407.579, "collateral charges" includes all sales tax, license fees, registration fees, title fees and motor vehicle inspections;

(2) "Comparable motor vehicle," an identical or reasonably equivalent motor vehicle;

(3) "Consumer," the purchaser, other than for the purposes of resale, of a new motor vehicle, primarily used for personal, family, or household purposes, and any person to whom such new motor vehicle is transferred for the same purposes during the duration of an express warranty applicable to such new motor vehicle, and any other person entitled by the terms of such warranty to enforce the obligations of the warranty;

(4) "Express warranty," any written affirmation of the fact or promise made by a manufacturer to a consumer in connection with the sale of new

765

motor vehicles which relates to the nature of the material or workmanship or will meet a specified level of performance over a specified period of time;

(5) "Manufacturer," any person engaged in the manufacturing or assembling of new motor vehicles as a regular business;

(6) "New motor vehicle," any vehicle being transferred for the first time from a manufacturer, distributor or new vehicle dealer, which has not been registered or titled in this state or any other state and which is offered for sale, barter or exchange by a dealer who is franchised to sell, barter or exchange that particular make of new motor vehicle. The term "new motor vehicle" shall include only those vehicles propelled by power other than muscular power, but the term shall not include vehicles used as a commercial motor vehicle, off-road vehicles, mopeds, motorcycles or recreational motor vehicles as defined in section 301.010, RSMo, except for the chassis, engine, powertrain and component parts of recreational motor vehicles. The term "new motor vehicle" shall also include demonstrators or lease-purchase vehicles as long as a manufacturer's warranty was issued as a condition of sale.

§ 407.563   Law Applicable to Breach of New Motor Vehicles Warranties

The provisions of sections 400.2–602 to 400.2–609, RSMo [§§ 2–602 to 2–609 of the UCC—Ed.], shall not apply to sales of new motor vehicles and such sales shall be governed by the provisions of sections 407.560 to 407.579.

§ 407.565   Report of Nonconformity Required, When—Repairs, Duty of Manufacturer or Agent, When

For the purposes of sections 407.560 to 407.579, if a new motor vehicle does not conform to all applicable express warranties, and the consumer reports the nonconformity to the manufacturer, or its agent, during the term of such express warranties, or during the period of one year following the date of original delivery of the new motor vehicle to the consumer, whichever period expires earlier, the manufacturer, or its agent, shall make such repairs as are necessary to conform the new vehicle to such express warranties, notwithstanding the fact that such repairs are made after the expiration of such term or such one-year period.

§ 407.567   Replacement of Motor Vehicle or Refund of Purchase Price, When—Allowance Deducted for Consumer's Use

1. If the manufacturer, through its authorized dealer or its agent, cannot conform the new motor vehicle to any applicable express warranty by repairing or correcting any default or condition which impairs the use, market value, or safety of the new motor vehicle to the consumer after a reasonable number of attempts, the manufacturer shall, at its option, either replace the new motor vehicle with a comparable new vehicle

acceptable to the consumer, or take title of the vehicle from the consumer and refund to the consumer the full purchase price, including all reasonably incurred collateral charges, less a reasonable allowance for the consumer's use of the vehicle. The subtraction of a reasonable allowance for use shall apply when either a replacement or refund of the new motor vehicle occurs.

2. Refunds shall be made to the consumer and lienholder of record, if any, as their interests may appear.

§ 407.569. Affirmative Defenses

It shall be an affirmative defense to any claim under sections 407.560 to 407.579 that:

(1) An alleged nonconformity does not substantially impair the use, market value, or safety of the motor vehicle;

(2) A nonconformity is the result of abuse, neglect, or unauthorized modifications or alterations of a motor vehicle;

(3) A claim by a consumer was not filed in good faith; or

(4) Any other affirmative defense allowed by law.

§ 407.571 Presumptions of Nonconformity—Exception

It shall be presumed that a reasonable number of attempts have been undertaken to conform a new motor vehicle to the applicable express warranties if within the terms, conditions, or limitations of the express warranty, or during the period of one year following the date of original delivery of the new motor vehicle to a consumer, whichever expires earlier, either:

(1) The same nonconformity has been subject to repair four or more times by the manufacturer, or its agents, and such nonconformity continues to exist; or

(2) The new vehicle is out of service by reason of repair of the nonconformity by the manufacturer, through its authorized dealer or its agents, for a cumulative total of thirty or more working days, exclusive of down time for routine maintenance as prescribed by the manufacturer, since delivery of the new vehicle to the consumer. The thirty-day period may be extended by a period of time during which repair services are not available to the consumer because of conditions beyond the control of the manufacturer or its agents.

§ 407.573 Warranty Extension, When—Complaint Remedies Information to Be Furnished—Notice to Manufacturer Required—Manufacturer's Duties, Time Limitation

1. The terms, conditions, or limitations of the express warranty or the period of one year following the date of original delivery of the new motor vehicle to a consumer, whichever expires earlier, may be extended if the

new motor vehicle warranty problem has been reported but has not been repaired by the manufacturer, or its agent, by the expiration of the applicable time period.

2.   The manufacturer shall provide information for consumer complaint remedies with each new motor vehicle. It shall be the responsibility of the consumer, or his representative, prior to availing himself of the provisions of sections 407.560 to 407.579, to give written notification to the manufacturer of the need for the repair of the nonconformity, in order to allow the manufacturer an opportunity to cure the alleged defect. The manufacturer shall immediately notify the consumer of a reasonably accessible repair facility of a franchised new vehicle dealer to conform the new vehicle to the express warranty. After delivery of the new vehicle to an authorized repair facility by the consumer, the manufacturer shall have ten calendar days to conform the new motor vehicle to the express warranty. Upon notification from the consumer that the new vehicle has not been conformed to the express warranty, the manufacturer shall inform the consumer if an informal dispute settlement procedure has been established by the manufacturer in accordance with section 407.575. However, if prior notice by the manufacturer of an informal dispute settlement procedure has been given, no further notice is required.

3.   Any action brought under sections 407.560 to 407.579 shall be commenced within six months following expiration of the terms, conditions, or limitations of the express warranty, or within eighteen months following the date of original delivery of the new motor vehicle to a consumer, whichever is earlier, or, in the event that a consumer resorts to an informal dispute settlement procedure as provided in sections 407.560 to 407.579, within ninety days following the final action of any panel established pursuant to such procedure.

§ 407.575   Manufacturer with Approved Settlement Procedure, Consumer's Duty

If a manufacturer has established an informal dispute settlement procedure which complies in all respects with the provisions of the code of Federal Regulations, 16 C.F.R. 703, provisions of sections 407.560 to 407.579 concerning refunds or replacements shall not apply to any consumer who has not first resorted to such procedure.

§ 407.577   Court Action by Consumer, Costs, Expenses, Attorney's Fees, How Paid

1.   If a consumer undertakes a court action after complying with the provisions of sections 407.560 to 407.579 and finally prevails in that action, he shall be allowed by the court to recover as part of the judgment a sum equal to the aggregate amount of costs and expenses, including attorney's fees based on actual time expended, determined by the court to have been reasonably incurred by the plaintiff for or in connection with the commencement and prosecution of such action.

2.   If any claim by a consumer under sections 407.560 to 407.579 is found by a court to have been filed in bad faith, or solely for the purpose of harassment, or in the absence of a substantial justiciable issue of either law or fact raised by the consumer, or for which the final recovery is not at least ten percent greater than any settlement offer made by the manufacturer prior to the commencement of the court action, then the consumer shall be liable for all costs and reasonable attorney's fees incurred by the manufacturer, or its agent, as a direct result of the bad faith claim.

§ 407.579 Consumer's Right to Other Remedies—Law to Apply, When

1.   Except as provided in subdivision (1) of section 407.560, nothing in sections 407.560 to 407.579 shall in any way limit the rights or remedies which are otherwise available to a consumer at law or in equity.

2.   Sections 407.560 to 407.579 shall apply to any new motor vehicle sold after January 1, 1985.

NEW MOTOR VEHICLE WARRANTIES

N.Y.Gen.Bus.Law § 198–a (McKinney)

§ 198–a. Warranties

(a) As used in this section:

(1) "Consumer" means the purchaser, lessee or transferee, other than for purposes of resale, of a motor vehicle which is used primarily for personal, family or household purposes and any other person entitled by the terms of the manufacturer's warranty to enforce the obligations of such warranty;

(2) "Motor vehicle" means a motor vehicle excluding motorcycles and off-road vehicles, which was subject to a manufacturer's express warranty at the time of original delivery and either (i) was purchased, leased or transferred in this state within either the first eighteen thousand miles of operation or two years from the date of original delivery, whichever is earlier, or (ii) is registered in this state;

(3) "Manufacturer's express warranty" or "warranty" means the written warranty, so labeled, of the manufacturer of a new motor vehicle, including any terms or conditions precedent to the enforcement of obligations under that warranty.

(4) "Mileage deduction formula" means the mileage which is in excess of twelve thousand miles times the purchase price, or the lease price if applicable, of the vehicle divided by one hundred thousand miles.

(5) "Lessee" means any consumer who leases a motor vehicle pursuant to a written lease agreement which provides that the lessee is responsible for repairs to such motor vehicle.

(6) "Lease price" means the aggregate of:

(i) the lessor's actual purchase cost;

(ii) the freight cost, if applicable;

(iii) the cost for accessories, if applicable;

(iv) any fee paid to another to obtain the lease; and

(v) an amount equal to five percent of the lessor's actual purchase cost as prescribed in subparagraph (i) of this paragraph.

(7) "Service fees" means the portion of a lease payment attributable to:

(i) an amount for earned interest calculated on the rental payments previously paid to the lessor for the leased vehicle at an annual rate equal to two points above the prime rate in effect on the date of the execution of the lease; and

(ii) any insurance or other costs expended by the lessor for the benefit of the lessee.

(8) "Capitalized cost" means the aggregate deposit and rental payments previously paid to the lessor for the leased vehicle less service fees.

(b)(1) If a new motor vehicle which is sold and registered in this state does not conform to all express warranties during the first eighteen thousand miles of operation or during the period of two years following the date of original delivery of the motor vehicle to such consumer, whichever is the earlier date, the consumer shall during such period report the nonconformity, defect or condition to the manufacturer, its agent or its authorized dealer. If the notification is received by the manufacturer's agent or authorized dealer, the agent or dealer shall within seven days forward written notice thereof to the manufacturer by certified mail, return receipt requested, and shall include in such notice a statement indicating whether or not such repairs have been undertaken. The manufacturer, its agent or its authorized dealer shall correct said nonconformity, defect or condition at no charge to the consumer, notwithstanding the fact that such repairs are made after the expiration of such period of operation or such two year period.

(2) If a manufacturer's agent or authorized dealer refuses to undertake repairs within seven days of receipt of the notice by a consumer of a nonconformity, defect or condition pursuant to paragraph one of this subdivision, the consumer may immediately forward written notice of such refusal to the manufacturer by certified mail, return receipt requested. The manufacturer or its authorized agent shall have twenty days from receipt of such notice of refusal to commence such repairs. If within such twenty day period, the manufacturer or its authorized agent fails to commence such repairs, the manufacturer, at the option of the consumer, shall replace the motor vehicle with a comparable motor vehicle, or accept return of the vehicle from the consumer and refund to the consumer the full purchase price or, if applicable, the lease price and any trade-in allowance plus fees and charges. Such fees and charges shall include but

not be limited to all license fees, registration fees and any similar governmental charges, less an allowance for the consumer's use of the vehicle in excess of the first twelve thousand miles of operation pursuant to the mileage deduction formula defined in paragraph four of subdivision (a) of this section, and a reasonable allowance for any damage not attributable to normal wear or improvements.

(c)(1) If, within the period specified in subdivision (b) of this section, the manufacturer or its agents or authorized dealers are unable to repair or correct any defect or condition which substantially impairs the value of the motor vehicle to the consumer after a reasonable number of attempts, the manufacturer, at the option of the consumer, shall replace the motor vehicle with a comparable motor vehicle, or accept return of the vehicle from the consumer and refund to the consumer the full purchase price or, if applicable, the lease price and any trade-in allowance plus fees and charges. Any return of a motor vehicle may, at the option of the consumer, be made to the dealer or other authorized agent of the manufacturer who sold such vehicle to the consumer or to the dealer or other authorized agent who attempted to repair or correct the defect or condition which necessitated the return and shall not be subject to any further shipping charges. Such fees and charges shall include but not be limited to all license fees, registration fees and any similar governmental charges, less an allowance for the consumer's use of the vehicle in excess of the first twelve thousand miles of operation pursuant to the mileage deduction formula defined in paragraph four of subdivision (a) of this section, and a reasonable allowance for any damage not attributable to normal wear or improvements.

(2) A manufacturer which accepts return of the motor vehicle because the motor vehicle does not conform to its warranty shall notify the commissioner of the department of motor vehicles that the motor vehicle was returned to the manufacturer for nonconformity to its warranty and shall disclose, in accordance with the provisions of section four hundred seventeen-a of the vehicle and traffic law prior to resale either at wholesale or retail, that it was previously returned to the manufacturer for nonconformity to its warranty. Refunds shall be made to the consumer and lienholder, if any, as their interests may appear on the records of ownership kept by the department of motor vehicles. Refunds shall be accompanied by the proper application for credit or refund of state and local sales taxes as published by the department of taxation and finance and by a notice that the sales tax paid on the purchase price, lease price or portion thereof being refunded is refundable by the commissioner of taxation and finance in accordance with the provisions of subdivision (f) of section eleven hundred thirty-nine of the tax law. If applicable, refunds shall be made to the lessor and lessee as their interests may appear on the records of ownership kept by the department of motor vehicles, as follows: the lessee shall receive the capitalized cost and the lessor shall receive the lease price less the aggregate deposit and rental payments previously paid to the lessor for the leased vehicle. The terms of the lease shall be deemed terminated contemporaneously with the date of the arbitrator's decision and award and no

penalty for early termination shall be assessed as a result thereof. Refunds shall be accompanied by the proper application form for credit or refund of state and local sales tax as published by the department of taxation and finance and a notice that the sales tax paid on the lease price or portion thereof being refunded is refundable by the commissioner of taxation and finance in accordance with the provisions of subdivision (f) of section eleven hundred thirty-nine of the tax law.

(3) It shall be an affirmative defense to any claim under this section that:

(i) the nonconformity, defect or condition does not substantially impair such value; or

(ii) the nonconformity, defect or condition is the result of abuse, neglect or unauthorized modifications or alterations of the motor vehicle.

(d) It shall be presumed that a reasonable number of attempts have been undertaken to conform a motor vehicle to the applicable express warranties, if:

(1) the same nonconformity, defect or condition has been subject to repair four or more times by the manufacturer or its agents or authorized dealers within the first eighteen thousand miles of operation or during the period of two years following the date of original delivery of the motor vehicle to a consumer, whichever is the earlier date, but such nonconformity, defect or condition continues to exist; or

(2) the vehicle is out of service by reason of repair of one or more nonconformities, defects or conditions for a cumulative total of thirty or more calendar days during either period, whichever is the earlier date.

(e) The term of an express warranty, the two year warranty period and the thirty day out of service period shall be extended by any time during which repair services are not available to the consumer because of a war, invasion or strike, fire, flood or other natural disaster.

(f) Nothing in this section shall in any way limit the rights or remedies which are otherwise available to a consumer under any other law.

(g) If a manufacturer has established an informal dispute settlement mechanism, such mechanism shall comply in all respects with the provisions of this section and the provisions of subdivision (c) of this section concerning refunds or replacement shall not apply to any consumer who has not first resorted to such mechanism. In the event that an arbitrator in such an informal dispute mechanism awards a refund or replacement vehicle, he or she shall not reduce the award to an amount less than the full purchase price or the lease price, if applicable, or a vehicle of equal value, plus all fees and charges except to the extent such reductions are specifically permitted under subdivision (c) of this section.

(h) A manufacturer shall have up to thirty days from the date the consumer notifies the manufacturer of his or her acceptance of the arbitrator's decision to comply with the terms of that decision. Failure to comply with the thirty day limitation shall also entitle the consumer to recover a fee of twenty-five dollars for each business day of noncompliance up to five hundred dollars. Provided, however, that nothing contained in this subdivision shall impose any liability on a manufacturer where a delay beyond the thirty day period is attributable to a consumer who has requested a replacement vehicle built to order or with options that are not comparable to the vehicle being replaced or otherwise made compliance impossible within said period. In no event shall a consumer who has resorted to an informal dispute settlement mechanism be precluded from seeking the rights or remedies available by law.

(*i*) Any agreement entered into by a consumer for the purchase of a new motor vehicle which waives, limits or disclaims the rights set forth in this section shall be void as contrary to public policy. Said rights shall inure to a subsequent transferee of such motor vehicle.

Any provision of any agreement entered into by a consumer for the purchase of a new motor vehicle which includes as an additional cost for such motor vehicle an expense identified as being for the purpose of affording such consumer his or her rights under this section, shall be void as contrary to public policy.

(j) Any action brought pursuant to this section shall be commenced within four years of the date of original delivery of the motor vehicle to the consumer.

(k) Each consumer shall have the option of submitting any dispute arising under this section upon the payment of a prescribed filing fee to an alternate arbitration mechanism established pursuant to regulations promulgated hereunder by the New York state attorney general. Upon application of the consumer and payment of the filing fee, all manufacturers shall submit to such alternate arbitration.

Such alternate arbitration shall be conducted by a professional arbitrator or arbitration firm appointed by and under regulations established by the New York state attorney general. Such mechanism shall insure the personal objectivity of its arbitrators and the right of each party to present its case, to be in attendance during any presentation made by the other party and to rebut or refute such presentation. In all other respects, such alternate arbitration mechanism shall be governed by article seventy-five of the civil practice law and rules; provided, however, that notwithstanding paragraph (i) of subdivision (a) of section seventy-five hundred two of the civil practice law and rules, special proceedings brought before a court pursuant to such article seventy-five in relation to an arbitration hereunder shall be brought only in the county where the consumer resides or where the arbitration was held or is pending.

(*l*) A court may award reasonable attorney's fees to a prevailing plaintiff or to a consumer who prevails in any judicial action or proceeding arising out of an arbitration proceeding held pursuant to subdivision (k) of this section. In the event a prevailing plaintiff is required to retain the services of an attorney to enforce collection of an award granted pursuant to this section, the court may assess against the manufacturer reasonable attorney's fees for services rendered to enforce collection of said award.

(m)(1) Each manufacturer shall require that each informal dispute settlement mechanism used by it provide, at a minimum, the following:

(i) that the arbitrators participating in such mechanism are trained in arbitration and familiar with the provisions of this section, that the arbitrators and consumers who request arbitration are provided with a written copy of the provisions of this section, together with the notice set forth below entitled "NEW CAR LEMON LAW BILL OF RIGHTS," and that consumers, upon request, are given an opportunity to make an oral presentation to the arbitrator;

(ii) that the rights and procedures used in the mechanism comply with federal regulations promulgated by the federal trade commission relating to informal dispute settlement mechanisms; and

(iii) that the remedies set forth under subdivision (c) of this section are awarded if, after a reasonable number of attempts have been undertaken under subdivision (d) of this section to conform the vehicle to the express warranties, the defect or nonconformity still exists.

(2) The following notice shall be provided to consumers and arbitrators and shall be printed in conspicuous ten point bold face type:

NEW CAR LEMON LAW BILL OF RIGHTS

(1) IN ADDITION TO ANY WARRANTIES OFFERED BY THE MANUFACTURER, YOUR NEW CAR, IF PURCHASED AND REGISTERED IN NEW YORK STATE, IS WARRANTED AGAINST ALL MATERIAL DEFECTS FOR EIGHTEEN THOUSAND MILES OR TWO YEARS, WHICHEVER COMES FIRST.

(2) YOU MUST REPORT ANY PROBLEMS TO THE MANUFACTURER, ITS AGENT, OR AUTHORIZED DEALER.

(3) UPON NOTIFICATION, THE PROBLEM MUST BE CORRECTED FREE OF CHARGE.

(4) IF THE SAME PROBLEM CANNOT BE REPAIRED AFTER FOUR OR MORE ATTEMPTS; OR IF YOUR CAR IS OUT OF SERVICE TO REPAIR A PROBLEM FOR A TOTAL OF THIRTY DAYS DURING THE WARRANTY PERIOD; OR IF THE MANUFACTURER OR ITS AGENT REFUSES TO REPAIR A SUBSTANTIAL DEFECT OR CONDITION WITHIN TWENTY DAYS OF RECEIPT OF NOTICE SENT BY YOU TO THE MANUFACTURER BY CERTIFIED MAIL, RETURN RECEIPT REQUESTED; THEN YOU MAY BE ENTITLED TO EITHER A COMPARABLE CAR OR A REFUND OF YOUR PURCHASE PRICE, PLUS LICENSE AND REGISTRATION FEES, MINUS A MILEAGE ALLOWANCE ONLY IF THE VEHICLE HAS BEEN DRIVEN MORE THAN

12,000 MILES. SPECIAL NOTIFICATION REQUIREMENTS MAY APPLY TO MOTOR HOMES.

(5) A MANUFACTURER MAY DENY LIABILITY IF THE PROBLEM IS CAUSED BY ABUSE, NEGLECT, OR UNAUTHORIZED MODIFICATIONS OF THE CAR.

(6) A MANUFACTURER MAY REFUSE TO EXCHANGE A COMPARABLE CAR OR REFUND YOUR PURCHASE PRICE IF THE PROBLEM DOES NOT SUBSTANTIALLY IMPAIR THE VALUE OF YOUR CAR.

(7) IF A MANUFACTURER HAS ESTABLISHED AN ARBITRATION PROCEDURE, THE MANUFACTURER MAY REFUSE TO EXCHANGE A COMPARABLE CAR OR REFUND YOUR PURCHASE PRICE UNTIL YOU FIRST RESORT TO THE PROCEDURE.

(8) IF THE MANUFACTURER DOES NOT HAVE AN ARBITRATION PROCEDURE, YOU MAY RESORT TO ANY REMEDY BY LAW AND MAY BE ENTITLED TO YOUR ATTORNEY'S FEES IF YOU PREVAIL.

(9) NO CONTRACT OR AGREEMENT CAN VOID ANY OF THESE RIGHTS.

(10) AS AN ALTERNATIVE TO THE ARBITRATION PROCEDURE MADE AVAILABLE THROUGH THE MANUFACTURER, YOU MAY INSTEAD CHOOSE TO SUBMIT YOUR CLAIM TO AN INDEPENDENT ARBITRATOR, APPROVED BY THE ATTORNEY GENERAL. YOU MAY HAVE TO PAY A FEE FOR SUCH AN ARBITRATION. CONTACT YOUR LOCAL CONSUMER OFFICE OR ATTORNEY GENERAL'S OFFICE TO FIND OUT HOW TO ARRANGE FOR INDEPENDENT ARBITRATION.

(3) All informal dispute settlement mechanisms shall maintain the following records:

(i) the number of purchase price and lease price refunds and vehicle replacements requested, the number of each awarded in arbitration, the amount of each award and the number of awards that were compiled with in a timely manner;

(ii) the number of awards where additional repairs or a warranty extension was the most prominent remedy, the amount or value of each award, and the number of such awards that were compiled with in a timely manner;

(iii) the number and total dollar amount of awards where some form of reimbursement for expenses or compensation for losses was the most prominent remedy, the amount or value of each award and the number of such awards that were complied with in a timely manner; and

(iv) the average number of days from the date of a consumer's initial request to arbitrate until the date of the final arbitrator's decision and the average number of days from the date of the final arbitrator's decision to the date on which performance was satisfactorily carried out.

(n) Special provisions applicable to motor homes:

(1) To the extent that the provisions of this subdivision are inconsistent with the other provisions of this section, the provisions of this subdivision shall apply.

(2) For purposes of this section, the manufacturer of a motor home is any person, partnership, corporation, factory branch, or other entity engaged in the business of manufacturing or assembling new motor homes for sale in this state.

(3) This section does not apply to the living facilities of motor homes, which are the portions thereof designed, used or maintained primarily as living quarters and shall include, but not be limited to the flooring, plumbing system and fixtures, roof air conditioner, furnace, generator, electrical systems other than automotive circuits, the side entrance door, exterior compartments, and windows other than the windshield and driver and front passenger windows.

(4) If, within the first eighteen thousand miles of operation or during the period of two years following the date of original delivery of the motor vehicle to such consumer, whichever is the earlier date, the manufacturer of a motor home or its agents or its authorized dealers or repair shops to which they refer a consumer are unable to repair or correct any covered defect or condition which substantially impairs the value of the motor home to the consumer after a reasonable number of attempts, the motor home manufacturer, at the option of the consumer, shall replace the motor home with a comparable motor home, or accept return of the motor home from the consumer and refund to the consumer the full purchase price or, if applicable, the lease price and any trade-in allowance plus fees and charges as well as the other fees and charges set forth in paragraph one of subdivision (c) of this section.

(5) If an agent or authorized dealer of a motor home manufacturer or a repair shop to which they refer a consumer refuses to undertake repairs within seven days of receipt of notice by a consumer of a nonconformity, defect or condition within the first eighteen thousand miles of operation or during the period of two years following the date of original delivery of the motor home to such consumer, whichever is the earlier date, the consumer may immediately forward written notice of such refusal to the motor home manufacturer by certified mail, return receipt requested. The motor home manufacturer or its authorized agent or a repair shop to which they refer a consumer shall have twenty days from receipt of such notice of refusal to commence such repairs. If within such twenty day period, the motor home manufacturer or its authorized agent or repair shop to which they refer a consumer, fails to commence such repairs, the motor home manufacturer, at the option of the consumer, shall replace the motor home with a comparable motor home, or accept return of the motor home from the consumer and refund to the consumer the full purchase price or, if applicable, the lease price, and any trade-in allowance or other charges, fees, or allowances. Such fees and charges shall include but not be limited

to all license fees, registration fees, and any similar governmental charges, less an allowance for the consumer's use of the vehicle in excess of the first twelve thousand miles of operation pursuant to the mileage deduction formula defined in paragraph four of subdivision (a) of this section, and a reasonable allowance for any damage not attributable to normal wear or improvements.

(6) If within the first eighteen thousand miles of operation or during the period of two years following the date of original delivery of the motor home to such consumer, whichever is the earlier date, the same covered nonconformity, defect or condition in a motor home has been subject to repair two times or a motor home has been out of service by reason of repair for twenty-one days, whichever occurs first, the consumer must have reported this to the motor home manufacturer or its authorized dealer by certified mail, return receipt requested, and may institute any proceeding or other action pursuant to this section if the motor home has been out of service by reason of three repair attempts or for at least thirty days. The special notification requirements of this paragraph shall only apply if the manufacturer or its authorized dealer provides a prior written copy of the requirements of this paragraph to the consumer and receipt of the notice is acknowledged by the consumer in writing. If the consumer who has received notice from the manufacturer fails to comply with the special notification requirements of this paragraph, additional repair attempts or days out of service by reason of repair shall not be taken into account in determining whether the consumer is entitled to a remedy provided in paragraph four of this subdivision. However, additional repair attempts or days out of service by reason of repair that occur after the consumer complies with such special notification requirements shall be taken into account in making that determination. It shall not count as a repair attempt if the repair facility is not authorized by the applicable motor home manufacturer to perform warranty work on the identified nonconformity. It shall count as only one repair attempt for a motor home if the same nonconformity is being addressed a second time due to the consumer's decision to continue traveling and to seek the repair of the same nonconformity at another repair facility rather than wait for the initial repair to be completed.

(7) Nothing in this section shall in any way limit any rights, remedies or causes of action that a consumer or motor home manufacturer may otherwise have against the manufacturer of the motor home's chassis, or its propulsion and other components.

(8)(A) Each manufacturer shall require that each informal dispute settlement mechanism used by it provide, at a minimum, the following:

    (i) that the arbitrators participating in such mechanism are trained in arbitration and familiar with the provisions of this section, that the arbitrators and consumers who request arbitration are provided with a written copy of the provisions of this section, together with the notice set forth below entitled "NEW MOTOR HOME LEMON

LAW BILL OF RIGHTS,'' and that consumers, upon request, are given an opportunity to make an oral presentation to the arbitrator;

(ii) that the rights and procedures used in the mechanism comply with federal regulations promulgated by the federal trade commission relating to informal dispute settlement mechanisms; and

(iii) that the remedies set forth under subdivision (c) of this section are awarded if, after a reasonable number of attempts have been undertaken under subdivision (d) of this section to conform the vehicle to the express warranties, the defect or nonconformity still exists.

(B) Notwithstanding the provisions of paragraph two of subdivision (m) of this section, the following provision shall apply for purposes of this subdivision:

The following notice shall be provided to consumers and arbitrators and shall be printed in conspicuous ten point bold face type:

NEW MOTOR HOME LEMON LAW BILL OF RIGHTS

(1) IN ADDITION TO ANY WARRANTIES OFFERED BY THE MANUFACTURER, YOUR NEW MOTOR HOME, IF PURCHASED AND REGISTERED IN NEW YORK STATE, IS WARRANTED AGAINST ALL MATERIAL DEFECTS FOR EIGHTEEN THOUSAND MILES OR TWO YEARS, WHICHEVER COMES FIRST. HOWEVER, THIS ADDITIONAL WARRANTY DOES NOT APPLY TO THE LIVING FACILITIES OF MOTOR HOMES, WHICH ARE THE PORTIONS THEREOF DESIGNED, USED OR MAINTAINED PRIMARILY AS LIVING QUARTERS AND SHALL INCLUDE, BUT NOT BE LIMITED TO THE FLOORING, PLUMBING SYSTEM AND FIXTURES, ROOF AIR CONDITIONER, FURNACE, GENERATOR, ELECTRICAL SYSTEMS OTHER THAN AUTOMOTIVE CIRCUITS, THE SIDE ENTRANCE DOOR, EXTERIOR COMPARTMENTS, AND WINDOWS OTHER THAN THE WINDSHIELD AND DRIVER AND FRONT PASSENGER WINDOWS.

(2) YOU MUST REPORT ANY PROBLEMS TO THE MANUFACTURER, ITS AGENT, OR AUTHORIZED DEALER.

(3) UPON NOTIFICATION, THE PROBLEM MUST BE CORRECTED FREE OF CHARGE.

(4) IF, WITHIN THE FIRST EIGHTEEN THOUSAND MILES OF OPERATION OR DURING THE PERIOD OF TWO YEARS FOLLOWING THE DATE OF ORIGINAL DELIVERY OF THE MOTOR VEHICLE TO SUCH CONSUMER, WHICHEVER IS THE EARLIER DATE THE MANUFACTURER OF A MOTOR HOME OR ITS AGENTS OR ITS AUTHORIZED DEALERS OR REPAIR SHOPS TO WHICH THEY REFER A CONSUMER ARE UNABLE TO REPAIR OR CORRECT ANY COVERED DEFECT OR CONDITION WHICH SUBSTANTIALLY IMPAIRS THE VALUE OF THE MOTOR HOME TO THE CONSUMER AFTER A REASONABLE NUMBER OF ATTEMPTS, THE MOTOR HOME MANUFAC-

TURER, AT THE OPTION OF THE CONSUMER, SHALL REPLACE THE MOTOR HOME WITH A COMPARABLE MOTOR HOME, OR ACCEPT RETURN OF THE MOTOR HOME FROM THE CONSUMER AND REFUND TO THE CONSUMER THE FULL PURCHASE PRICE OR, IF APPLICABLE, THE LEASE PRICE AND ANY TRADE–IN ALLOWANCE, PLUS FEES AND CHARGES, AS WELL AS THE OTHER FEES AND CHARGES, INCLUDING BUT NOT LIMITED TO ALL LICENSE FEES, REGISTRATION FEES, AND ANY SIMILAR GOVERNMENTAL CHARGES, LESS AN ALLOWANCE FOR THE CONSUMER'S USE OF THE VEHICLE IN EXCESS OF TWELVE THOUSAND MILES TIMES THE PURCHASE PRICE, OR THE LEASE PRICE IF APPLICABLE, OF THE VEHICLE DIVIDED BY ONE HUNDRED THOUSAND MILES, AND A REASONABLE ALLOWANCE FOR ANY DAMAGE NOT ATTRIBUTABLE TO NORMAL WEAR OR IMPROVEMENTS.

(5) SPECIAL NOTICE PROVISION: IF WITHIN EIGHTEEN THOUSAND MILES OR TWO YEARS, WHICHEVER COMES FIRST, THE SAME COVERED NONCONFORMITY, DEFECT OR CONDITION IN YOUR MOTOR HOME HAS BEEN SUBJECT TO REPAIR TWO TIMES OR YOUR MOTOR HOME HAS BEEN OUT OF SERVICE BY REASON OF REPAIR FOR TWENTY–ONE DAYS, WHICHEVER COMES FIRST, YOU MUST HAVE REPORTED THIS TO THE MOTOR HOME MANUFACTURER OR ITS AUTHORIZED DEALER BY CERTIFIED MAIL, RETURN RECEIPT REQUESTED, AND YOU MAY INSTITUTE ANY PROCEEDING OR OTHER ACTION PURSUANT TO THE LEMON LAW IF THE MOTOR HOME HAS BEEN OUT OF SERVICE BY REASON OF THREE REPAIR ATTEMPTS OR FOR AT LEAST THIRTY DAYS. THIS SPECIAL NOTICE REQUIREMENT SHALL ONLY APPLY IF THE MANUFACTURER OR ITS AUTHORIZED DEALER PROVIDES WRITTEN COPY OF THE REQUIREMENTS OF THIS PARAGRAPH TO YOU AND RECEIPT OF NOTICE IS ACKNOWLEDGED BY YOU IN WRITING. IF YOU FAIL TO COMPLY WITH THE SPECIAL NOTIFICATION REQUIREMENTS OF THIS PARAGRAPH, ADDITIONAL REPAIR ATTEMPTS OR DAYS OUT OF SERVICE BY REASON OF REPAIR SHALL NOT BE TAKEN INTO ACCOUNT IN DETERMINING WHETHER YOU ARE ENTITLED TO A REMEDY PROVIDED IN PARAGRAPH FOUR. HOWEVER, ADDITIONAL REPAIR ATTEMPTS OR DAYS OUT OF SERVICE BY REASON OF REPAIR THAT OCCUR AFTER YOU COMPLY WITH SUCH SPECIAL NOTIFICATION REQUIREMENTS SHALL BE TAKEN INTO ACCOUNT IN MAKING THAT DETERMINATION. NOTICE TO THE MANUFACTURER SHOULD BE SENT TO THE FOLLOWING: _____ NOTICE TO THE DEALER SHOULD BE SENT TO THE FOLLOWING: _____.

(6) A MANUFACTURER MAY DENY LIABILITY IF THE PROBLEM IS CAUSED BY ABUSE, NEGLECT, OR UNAUTHORIZED MODIFICATIONS OF THE MOTOR HOME.

(7) A MANUFACTURER MAY REFUSE TO EXCHANGE A COMPARABLE MOTOR HOME OR REFUND YOUR PURCHASE PRICE IF THE PROBLEM IS NOT COVERED BY THE LEMON LAW OR DOES NOT SUBSTANTIALLY IMPAIR THE VALUE OF YOUR MOTOR HOME.

(8) IF A MANUFACTURER HAS ESTABLISHED AN ARBITRATION PROCEDURE, THE MANUFACTURER MAY REFUSE TO EXCHANGE A COMPARABLE MOTOR HOME OR REFUND YOUR PURCHASE PRICE UNTIL YOU FIRST RESORT TO THE PROCEDURE.

(9) IF THE MANUFACTURER DOES NOT HAVE AN ARBITRATION PROCEDURE, YOU MAY RESORT TO ANY REMEDY BY LAW AND MAY BE ENTITLED TO YOUR ATTORNEY'S FEES IF YOU PREVAIL.

(10) NO CONTRACT OR AGREEMENT CAN VOID ANY OF THESE RIGHTS.

(11) AS AN ALTERNATIVE TO THE ARBITRATION PROCEDURE MADE AVAILABLE THROUGH THE MANUFACTURER, YOU MAY INSTEAD CHOOSE TO SUBMIT YOUR CLAIM TO AN INDEPENDENT ARBITRATOR, APPROVED BY THE ATTORNEY GENERAL. YOU MAY HAVE TO PAY A FEE FOR SUCH ARBITRATION. CONTACT YOUR LOCAL CONSUMER OFFICE OR ATTORNEY GENERAL'S OFFICE TO FIND OUT HOW TO ARRANGE FOR INDEPENDENT ARBITRATION.

(o) At the time of purchase or lease of a motor vehicle from an authorized dealer in this state, the manufacturer shall provide to the dealer or leaseholder, and the dealer or leaseholder shall provide to the consumer a notice, printed in not less than eight point bold face type, entitled "New Car Lemon Law Bill of Rights." The text of such notice shall be identical with the notice required by paragraph two of subdivision (m) of this section.

USED MOTOR VEHICLE WARRANTIES

N.Y.Gen.Bus.Law § 198–b (McKinney)

§ 198–b.   Sale or lease of used motor vehicles

a.   Definitions. As used in this section, the following words shall have the following meanings:

1. "Consumer" means the purchaser, or lessee, other than for purposes of resale, of a used motor vehicle primarily used for personal, family, or household purposes and subject to a warranty, and the spouse or child of the purchaser or the lessee if either such motor vehicle or the lease of such motor vehicle is transferred to the spouse or child during the duration of any warranty applicable to such motor vehicle, and any other person entitled by the terms of such warranty to enforce the obligations of the warranty;

2. "Used motor vehicle" means a motor vehicle, excluding motor homes and off-road vehicles, which has been purchased, leased, or transferred either after eighteen thousand miles of operation or two years from the date of original delivery, whichever is earlier;

3. "Dealer" means any person or business which sells, offers for sale, leases or offers for lease a used vehicle after selling, offering for sale, leasing or offering for lease three or more used vehicles in the previous twelve month period, but does not include:

(a) a bank or financial institution except in the case of a lease of a used motor vehicle,

(b) a business selling a used vehicle to an employee of that business,

(c) a regulated public utility which sells at public auction vehicles used in the ordinary course of its operations, provided that any advertisements of such sales conspicuously disclose the "as is" nature of the sale,

(d) the sale of a leased vehicle to that vehicle's lessee, a family member of the lessee, or an employee of the lessee, or

(e) the state, its agencies, bureaus, boards, commissions and authorities, and all of the political subdivisions of the state, including the agencies and authorities of such subdivisions;

4. "Warranty" means any undertaking in connection with the sale or lease by a dealer of a used motor vehicle to refund, repair, replace, maintain or take other action with respect to such used motor vehicle and provided at no extra charge beyond the price of the used motor vehicle;

5. "Service contract" means a contract in writing for any period of time or any specific mileage to refund, repair, replace, maintain or take other action with respect to a used motor vehicle and provided at an extra charge beyond the price of the used motor vehicle or of the lease contract for the used motor vehicle;

6. "Repair insurance" means a contract in writing for any period of time or any specific mileage to refund, repair, replace, maintain or take other action with respect to a used motor vehicle and which is regulated by the insurance department.

b. Written warranty required; terms. 1. No dealer shall sell or lease a used motor vehicle to a consumer without giving the consumer a written warranty which shall at minimum apply for the following terms:

(a) If the used motor vehicle has thirty-six thousand miles or less, the warranty shall be at minimum ninety days or four thousand miles, whichever comes first.

(b) If the used motor vehicle has more than thirty-six thousand miles, but less than eighty thousand miles, the warranty shall be at minimum sixty days or three thousand miles, whichever comes first.

(c) If the used motor vehicle has eighty thousand miles or more but no more than one hundred thousand miles, the warranty shall be at a minimum thirty days or one thousand miles, whichever comes first.

2.   The written warranty shall require the dealer or his agent to repair or, at the election of the dealer, reimburse the consumer for the reasonable cost of repairing the failure of a covered part. Covered parts shall at least include the following items:

(a) Engine. All lubricated parts, water pump, fuel pump, manifolds, engine block, cylinder head, rotary engine housings and flywheel.

(b) Transmission. The transmission case, internal parts, and the torque converter.

(c) Drive axle. Front and rear drive axle housings and internal parts, axle shafts, propeller shafts and universal joints.

(d) Brakes. Master cylinder, vacuum assist booster, wheel cylinders, hydraulic lines and fittings and disc brake calipers.

(e) Radiator.

(f) Steering. The steering gear housing and all internal parts, power steering pump, valve body, piston and rack.

(g) Alternator, generator, starter, ignition system excluding the battery.

3.   Such repair or reimbursement shall be made by the dealer notwithstanding the fact that the warranty period has expired, provided the consumer notifies the dealer of the failure of a covered part within the specified warranty period.

4.   The written warranty may contain additional language excluding coverage:

(a) for a failure of a covered part caused by a lack of customary maintenance;

(b) for a failure of a covered part caused by collision, abuse, negligence, theft, vandalism, fire or other casualty and damage from the environment (windstorm, lightning, road hazards, etc.);

(c) if the odometer has been stopped or altered such that the vehicle's actual mileage cannot be readily determined or if any covered part has been altered such that a covered part was thereby caused to fail;

(d) for maintenance services and the parts used in connection with such services such as seals, gaskets, oil or grease unless required in connection with the repair of a covered part;

(e) for a motor tuneup;

(f) for a failure resulting from racing or other competition;

(g) for a failure caused by towing a trailer or another vehicle unless the used motor vehicle is equipped for this as recommended by the manufacturer;

(h) if the used motor vehicle is used to carry passengers for hire;

(*i*) if the used motor vehicle is rented to someone other than the consumer as defined in paragraph one of subdivision a of this section;

(j) for repair of valves and/or rings to correct low compression and/or oil consumption which are considered normal wear;

(k) to the extent otherwise permitted by law, for property damage arising or allegedly arising out of the failure of a covered part; and

(*l*) to the extent otherwise permitted by law, for loss of the use of the used motor vehicle, loss of time, inconvenience, commercial loss or consequential damages.

c. Failure to honor warranty. 1. If the dealer or his agent fails to correct a malfunction or defect as required by the warranty specified in this section which substantially impairs the value of the used motor vehicle to the consumer after a reasonable period of time, the dealer shall accept return of the used motor vehicle from the consumer and refund to the consumer the full purchase price, or in the case of a lease contract all payments made under the contract, including sales or compensating use tax, less a reasonable allowance for any damage not attributable to normal wear or usage, and adjustment for any modifications which either increase or decrease the market value of the vehicle or of the lease contract, and in the case of a lease contract, shall cancel all further payments due from the consumer under the lease contract. In determining the purchase price to be refunded or in determining all payments made under a lease contract to be refunded, the purchase price, or all payments made under a lease contract, shall be deemed equal to the sum of the actual cash difference paid for the used motor vehicle, or for the lease contract, plus, if the dealer elects to not return any vehicles traded-in by the consumer, the wholesale value of any such traded-in vehicles as listed in the National Auto Dealers Association Used Car Guide, or such other guide as may be specified in regulations promulgated by the commissioner of motor vehicles, as adjusted for mileage, improvements, and any major physical or mechanical defects in the traded-in vehicle at the time of trade-in. The dealer selling or leasing the used motor vehicle shall deliver to the consumer a written notice including conspicuous language indicating that if the consumer should be entitled to a refund pursuant to this section, the value of any vehicle traded-in by the consumer, if the dealer elects to not return it to the consumer, for purposes of determining the amount of such refund will be determined by reference to the National Auto Dealers Association Used Car Guide wholesale value, or such other guide as may be approved by the commissioner of motor vehicles, as adjusted for mileage, improvements, and any major physical or mechanical defects, rather than the value listed in the sales contract. Refunds shall be made to the consumer and lienholder, if any, as their interests may appear on the records of ownership kept by the department of motor vehicles. If the amount to be refunded to the lienholder will be insufficient to discharge the lien, the dealer shall notify the consumer in writing by registered or certified mail that the consumer has thirty days to pay the lienholder the amount which, together with the amount to be refunded by the dealer, will be sufficient to discharge the lien. The notice to the consumer shall contain conspicuous language warning the consumer that failure to pay such funds to the lienholder within thirty days will terminate the dealer's obligation to provide a refund. If the consumer fails to make such payment within thirty days, the dealer shall have no further responsibility to provide a refund under this section. Alternatively, the dealer may elect to offer to replace the used motor vehicle with a comparably priced vehicle, with such adjustment in price as the parties may agree to. The consumer shall not be obligated to accept a replacement vehicle, but may instead elect to receive the refund provided under this section. It shall be an affirmative defense to any claim under this section that:

(a) The malfunction or defect does not substantially impair such value; or

(b) The malfunction or defect is the result of abuse, neglect or unreasonable modifications or alterations of the used motor vehicle.

2. It shall be presumed that a dealer has had a reasonable opportunity to correct a malfunction or defect in a used motor vehicle, if:

(a) The same malfunction or defect has been subject to repair three or more times by the selling or leasing dealer or his agent within the warranty period, but such malfunction or defect continues to exist; or

(b) The vehicle is out of service by reason of repair or malfunction or defect for a cumulative total of fifteen or more days during the warranty period. Said period shall not include days when the dealer is unable to complete the repair because of the unavailability of necessary repair parts. The dealer shall be required to exercise due diligence in attempting to obtain necessary repair parts. Provided, however, that if a vehicle has been out of service for a cumulative total of forty-five days, even if a portion of that time is attributable to the unavailability of replacement parts, the consumer shall be entitled to the replacement or refund remedies provided in this section.

3. The term of any warranty, service contract or repair insurance shall be extended by any time period during which the used motor vehicle is in the possession of the dealer or his duly authorized agent for the purpose of repairing the used motor vehicle under the terms and obligations of said warranty, service contract or repair insurance.

4. The term of any warranty, service contract or repair insurance, and the fifteen day out-of-service period, shall be extended by any time during which repair services are not available to the consumer because of a war, invasion or strike, fire, flood or other natural disaster.

d. Waiver void. 1. Any agreement entered into by a consumer for the purchase or lease of a used motor vehicle which waives, limits or disclaims the rights set forth in this article shall be void as contrary to public policy. Further, if a dealer fails to give the written warranty required by this article, the dealer nevertheless shall be deemed to have given said warranty as a matter of law.

2. Nothing in this section shall in any way limit the rights or remedies which are otherwise available to a consumer under any other law.

3. Notwithstanding paragraph one of this subdivision, this article shall not apply to used motor vehicles sold for, or in the case of a lease where the value of the used motor vehicle as agreed to by the consumer and the dealer which vehicle is the subject of the contract is, less than one thousand five hundred dollars, or to used motor vehicles with over one hundred thousand miles at the time of sale or lease if said mileage is indicated in writing at the time of sale or lease. Further, this article shall not apply to the sale or lease of historical motor vehicles as defined in section four hundred one of the vehicle and traffic law.

e. Time of delivery, location of warranty and notice. The written warranty provided for in subdivision b of this section and the written notice provided for in subdivision c of this section shall be delivered to the consumer at or before the time the consumer signs the sales or lease contract for the used motor vehicle. The warranty and the notice may be set forth on one sheet or on separate sheets. They may be separate from, attached to, or a part of the sales or lease contract. If they are part of the sales or lease contract, they shall be separated from the other contract provisions and each headed by a conspicuous title.

f. Arbitration and enforcement. 1. If a dealer has established or participates in an informal dispute settlement procedure which complies in all respects with the provisions of part seven hundred three of title sixteen of the code of federal regulations the provisions of this article concerning refunds or replacement shall not apply to any consumer who has not first resorted to such procedure. Dealers utilizing informal dispute settlement procedures pursuant to this subdivision shall insure that arbitrators participating in such informal dispute settlement procedures are familiar with the provisions of this section and shall provide to arbitrators and consumers who seek arbitration a copy of the provisions of this section together with the following notice in conspicuous ten point bold face type:

USED CAR LEMON LAW BILL OF RIGHTS

1. If you purchase a used car for more than one thousand five hundred dollars, or lease a used car where you and the dealer have agreed that the car's value is more than one thousand five hundred dollars, from anyone selling or leasing three or more used cars a year, you must be given a written warranty.

2. If your used car has 18,000 miles or less, you may be protected by the new car lemon law.

3. (a) If your used car has more than 18,000 miles and up to and including 36,000 miles, a warranty must be provided for at least 90 days or 4,000 miles, whichever comes first.

(b) If your used car has more than 36,000 miles but less than 80,000 miles, a warranty must be provided for at least 60 days or 3,000 miles, whichever comes first.

(c) If your used car has 80,000 miles or more but no more than 100,000 miles, a warranty must be provided for at least 30 days or 1,000 miles, whichever comes first. Cars with over 100,000 miles are not covered.

4. If your engine, transmission, drive axle, brakes, radiator, steering, alternator, generator, starter, or ignition system (excluding the battery) are defective, the dealer or his agent must repair or, if he so chooses, reimburse you for the reasonable cost of repair.

5. If the same problem cannot be repaired after three or more attempts, you are entitled to return the car and receive a refund of your purchase price or of all payments made under your lease contract, and of sales tax and fees, minus a reasonable allowance for any damage not attributable to normal usage or wear, and, in the case of a lease contract, a cancellation of all further payments you are otherwise required to make under the lease contract.

6. If your car is out of service to repair a problem for a total of fifteen days or more during the warranty period you are entitled to return the car and receive a refund of your purchase price or of all payments made under your lease contract, and of sales tax and fees, minus a reasonable allowance for any damage not attributable to normal usage or wear, and, in the case of a lease contract, a cancellation of all further payments you are otherwise required to make under the lease contract.

7. A dealer may put into the written warranty certain provisions which will prohibit your recovery under certain conditions; however, the dealer may not cause you to waive any rights under this law.

8. A dealer may refuse to refund your purchase price, or the payments made under your lease contract, if the problem does not substantially impair the value of your car, or if the problem is caused by abuse, neglect, or unreasonable modification.

9. If a dealer has established an arbitration procedure, the dealer may refuse to refund your purchase price until you first resort to the procedure. If the dealer does not have an arbitration procedure, you may resort to any remedy provided by law and may be entitled to your attorney's fees if you prevail.

10. As an alternative to the arbitration procedure made available through the dealer you may instead choose to submit your claim to an independent arbitrator, approved by the attorney general. You may have to pay a fee for such an arbitration. Contact your local consumer office or attorney general's office to find out how to arrange for independent arbitration.

11. If any dealer refuses to honor your rights or you are not satisfied by the informal dispute settlement procedure, complain to the New York State Attorney General, Executive Office, Capitol, Albany, N.Y. 12224.

2. A dealer shall have up to thirty days from the date of notice by the consumer that the arbitrator's decision has been accepted to comply with the terms of such decision. Provided, however, that nothing contained in this subdivision shall impose any liability on a dealer where a delay beyond the thirty day period is attributable to a consumer who has requested a particular replacement vehicle or otherwise made compliance impossible within said period.

3. Upon the payment of a prescribed filing fee, a consumer shall have the option of submitting any dispute arising under this section to an alternate arbitration mechanism established pursuant to regulations promulgated hereunder by the attorney general. Upon application of the consumer and payment of the filing fee, the dealer shall submit to such alternate arbitration.

Such alternate arbitration shall be conducted by a professional arbitrator or arbitration firm appointed by and under regulations established by the attorney general. Such mechanism shall ensure the personal objectivity of its arbitrators and the right of each party to present its case, to be in attendance during any presentation made by the other party and to rebut or refute such presentation. In all other respects, such alternate arbitration mechanism shall be governed by article seventy-five of the civil practice law and rules.

The notice required by paragraph one of this subdivision, entitled Used Car Lemon Law Bill of Rights, shall be provided to arbitrators and consumers who seek arbitration under this subdivision.

A dealer shall have thirty days from the date of mailing of a copy of the arbitrator's decision to such dealer to comply with the terms of such decision. Failure to comply within the thirty day period shall entitle the consumer to recover, in addition to any other recovery to which he may be entitled, a fee of twenty-five dollars for each business day beyond thirty days up to five hundred dollars; provided however, that nothing in this subdivision shall impose any liability on a dealer where a delay beyond the thirty day period is attributable to a consumer who has requested a particular replacement vehicle or otherwise made compliance impossible within said period.

The commissioner of motor vehicles or any person deputized by him may deny the application of any person for registration under section four hundred fifteen of the vehicle and traffic law and suspend or revoke a registration under such section or refuse to issue a renewal thereof if he or such deputy determines that such applicant or registrant or any officer, director, stockholder, or partner, or any other person directly or indirectly interested in the business has deliberately failed to pay an arbitration award, which has not been stayed or appealed, rendered in an arbitration proceeding pursuant to this paragraph for sixty days after the date of mailing of a copy of the award to the registrant. Any action taken by the commissioner of motor vehicles pursuant to this paragraph shall be governed by the procedures set forth in subdivision nine of section four hundred fifteen of the vehicle and traffic law.

4. In no event shall a consumer who has resorted to an informal dispute settlement procedure be precluded from seeking the rights or remedies available by law.

5. In an action brought to enforce the provisions of this article, the court may award reasonable attorney's fees to a prevailing plaintiff or to a consumer who prevails in any judicial action or proceeding arising out of an arbitration proceeding held pursuant to paragraph three of this subdivision. In the event a prevailing plaintiff is required to retain the services of an attorney to enforce collection of an award granted pursuant to this section, the court may assess against the dealer reasonable attorney's fees for services rendered to enforce collection of said award.

6. Any action brought pursuant to this article shall be commenced within four years of the date of original delivery of the used motor vehicle to the consumer.

g. **Notice of consumer rights**. At the time of purchase or lease of a used motor vehicle from a dealer in this state, the dealer shall provide to the consumer a notice, printed in not less than eight point bold face type, entitled "Used Car Lemon Law Bill of Rights." The text of such notice shall be identical with the notice required by paragraph one of subdivision f of this section.

RETAIL INSTALLMENT SALES ACT

N.J.Stat.Ann. §§ 17:16C–1 to 16C–61

Table of Sections

§ 17:16C–1. Definitions

In this act, unless the context otherwise requires, the following words and terms shall have the following meanings:

(a) "Goods" means all chattels personal which are primarily for personal, family or household purposes, including merchandise certificates and coupons to be exchanged for goods or services, having a cash price of $10,000.00 or less, but not including money or other choses in action. Goods shall not include chattels personal sold for commercial or business use.

(b) "Retail installment contract" means any contract, other than a retail charge account or an instrument reflecting a sale pursuant thereto, entered into in this State between a retail seller and a retail buyer evidencing an agreement to pay the retail purchase price of goods or services, which are primarily for personal, family or household purposes, or any part thereof, in two or more installments over a period of time. This term includes a security agreement, chattel mortgage, conditional sales contract, or other similar instrument and any contract for the bailment or leasing of goods by which the bailee or lessee agrees to pay as compensation a sum substantially equivalent to or in excess of the value of the goods, and by which it is agreed that the bailee or lessee is bound to become, or has the option of becoming, the owner of such goods upon full compliance with the terms of such retail installment contract.

(c) "Retail seller" means a person who sells or agrees to sell goods or services under a retail installment contract or a retail charge account to a retail buyer, and shall include a motor vehicle installment seller.

(d) "Retail buyer" means a person who buys or agrees to buy goods or services from a retail seller, not for the purpose of resale, pursuant to a retail installment contract or a retail charge account.

(e) "Person" means an individual, partnership, firm, corporation, banking institution, association or any other group of individuals however organized.

791

(f) "Sales finance company" means and includes any person engaging in this State in the business of acquiring or arranging for the acquisition of retail installment contracts or obligations incurred pursuant to retail charge accounts by purchase, discount, pledge or otherwise from a retail seller which is not wholly owned by or does not wholly own such person, and any person engaging, directly or indirectly, in the business of soliciting the purchase of retail installment contracts or obligations incurred pursuant to retail charge accounts from a retail seller which is not wholly owned by or does not wholly own such person, or in the business of aiding the retail seller in selling, assigning or arranging for the sale or assignment of retail installment contracts or obligations incurred pursuant to retail charge accounts, and any person other than a retail seller who enters into a retail charge account with a retail buyer.

(g) "Motor vehicle" includes all vehicles used for transportation upon a highway propelled otherwise than by muscular power, excepting such vehicles as run only upon rails or tracks.

(h) "Motor vehicle installment seller" means a dealer in motor vehicles, who is required to be licensed under chapter 10 of Title 39 of the Revised Statutes and who sells or offers to sell a motor vehicle to a retail buyer under a retail installment contract.

(i) "Cash price" means the minimum price for which the goods or services subject to a retail installment contract or a retail charge account or other goods or services of like kind and quality may be purchased for cash from the seller by the buyer, as stated in the retail installment contract, the retail charge account or an instrument reflecting a sale pursuant thereto.

(j) "Down payment" means all payments made in cash or in goods or partly in cash and partly in goods, received by the retail seller prior to or substantially contemporaneous with either the execution of the retail installment contract or the delivery of the goods, whichever occurs later.

(k) "Official fees" means the filing or other fees required by law to be paid to a public officer to perfect an interest or lien, on the goods, retained or taken by a retail seller under a retail installment contract and motor vehicle license and transfer fees paid to the State.

(l) "Time price differential" means the amount or amounts, however denominated or computed, in addition to the cash price or prices, to be paid by the retail buyer for the privilege of purchasing goods or services pursuant to a retail installment contract or a retail charge account. The term does not include the amount, if a separate charge is made therefor, for insurance and official fees.

(m) "Holder" means any person, including a retail seller, who is entitled to the rights of a retail seller under a retail installment contract or retail charge account.

(n) "Banking institution" means any bank, national banking association, savings bank, or Federally chartered savings bank authorized to do business in this State, and for the purposes of this act only, an association as defined in section 5 of the "Savings and Loan Act (1963)" P.L.1963, c. 144 (C. 17:12B–5).

(o) "Commissioner" means the Commissioner of Banking of New Jersey and includes his deputies or any salaried employee of the Department of Banking named or appointed by the said commissioner to perform any function in the administration or enforcement of this act.

(p) "Payment-period" means the period of time scheduled by a retail installment contract to elapse between the days upon which installment payments are scheduled to be made on such contract; except that, when installment payments are scheduled to be omitted, pursuant to section 26, "payment-period" means the period of time scheduled by the contract to elapse between the days upon which installment payments are scheduled to be made during that portion of the contract period in which no installment payment is scheduled to be omitted.

(q) "Contract period" means the period beginning on the date of a retail installment contract and ending on the date scheduled by the contract for the payment of the final installment.

(r) "Retail charge account" means any account, other than a retail installment contract or a home repair contract which is subject to the "Home Repair Financing Act" (P.L.1960, c. 41; C. 17:16C–62 et seq.), established by an agreement which prescribes the terms under which a retail buyer may from time to time purchase or lease goods or services which are primarily for personal, family or household purposes, and under which the unpaid balance thereunder, whenever incurred, is payable in one or more installments and under which a time price differential may be added in each billing period as provided herein. Retail charge account also includes all accounts arising out of the utilization by the holder of a credit card, letter of credit or other credit identification issued by a sales finance company, giving the holder the privilege of using the credit card, letter of credit or other credit identification to become a retail buyer in transactions out of which debt arises: (1) by the sales finance company's payment or agreement to pay the retail buyer's obligations; or (2) by the sales finance company's purchase from the retail seller of the obligations of the user of the credit card, letter of credit or other credit identification as a retail buyer.

(s) "Services" means and includes work, labor and services, professional and otherwise which are primarily for personal, family or household purposes but does not include services which are subject to the "Home Repair Financing Act," and insurance premiums financing which is subject to the "Insurance Premium Finance Company Act" (P.L.1968, c. 221; C. 17:16D–1 et seq.).

(t) "Billing period" means the time interval between regular periodic billing statement dates. In the case of monthly billing periods, such intervals shall be considered equal intervals of time if the billing date of a billing period does not vary more than 4 days from the billing date of the immediately preceding billing period. In the case of billing periods which are not monthly, the permissible variation in billing dates shall be that proportion of 4 days (adjusted to the nearest whole number) which the number of days in the billing period bears to 30.

(u) "Professional services" means services rendered or performed by a person authorized by law to practice a recognized profession whose practice is regulated by law and the performance of which services requires knowledge of an advanced type in a field of learning acquired by a prolonged formal course of specialized instruction and study as distinguished from general academic instruction or apprenticeship and training.

§ 17:16C-2. Necessity of License

No person shall hereafter engage in or continue to engage in the business of a sales finance company or in the business of a motor vehicle installment seller in this State without first obtaining a license from the commissioner as provided for in this act; provided, however, that no sales finance company shall be required to obtain a license to engage in the business of a motor vehicle installment seller for the purpose of disposing of any goods to which it has obtained title as a result of legal or contract right under any retail installment contract; and provided, further, that any banking institution authorized to do business in this State shall be authorized to transact business as a sales finance company, subject to all of the provisions of this act, except that it shall not be required to obtain a license or pay a license fee hereunder.

§ 17:16C-4. Issuance or Refusal of License

Within 60 days after the filing of the application and the payment of the fees hereinafter set forth the commissioner shall either:

(a) Issue and deliver to the applicant a license to engage in the business of a sales finance company or a motor vehicle installment seller in accordance with the provisions of this act at the location specified in the said application; or

(b) Refuse to issue the license for any reason for which he may suspend, revoke or refuse to renew any license under section 10 of this act.

§ 17:16C-10. Refusal to Issue, Revocation, Suspension, and Refusal to Renew License; Notice and Hearing; Grounds; Motor Vehicle Installment Seller License

(a) The commissioner may refuse to issue and may revoke, suspend or refuse to renew a license or impose a penalty pursuant to this act if the commissioner finds, after notice and an opportunity for a hearing in accordance with the "Administrative Procedure Act," P.L.1968, c. 410 (C.

52:14B–1 et seq.) and any rules adopted thereunder, that any person, applicant for or holder of the license has:

(1) Violated any of the provisions of P.L.1960, c. 40 (C.17:16C–1 et seq.) or any order, rule or regulation made or issued pursuant to that act;

(2) Withheld information or made a material misstatement in the application for the license;

(3) Been convicted of an offense involving breach of trust, moral turpitude or fraudulent or dishonest dealing, or had a final judgment entered against him in a civil action upon grounds of fraud, misrepresentation or deceit;

(4) Become insolvent, or failed to attain or maintain the required net worth;

(5) Demonstrated unworthiness, incompetence, bad faith or dishonesty in the transacting of business as a licensee; or

(6) Engaged in any other conduct which would be deemed by the commissioner to be the cause for denial of the license.

(b) A license of a corporation, partnership, association or other entity may be suspended or revoked if any officer, director or member of the licensee has committed any act which would be cause for suspending or revoking a license to him as an individual.

(c) No license issued under this act to a motor vehicle installment seller shall be valid unless such seller is the holder of a valid and subsisting license issued pursuant to chapter 10 of Title 39 of the Revised Statutes.

§ 17:16C–11. Suspension, Revocation or Refusal to Renew Particular License or All Licenses Issued to Licensee

The commissioner may suspend, revoke or refuse to renew the particular license with respect to which grounds for revocation, suspension or refusal to renew may occur or exist, or, if he finds that such grounds for suspension or revocation are of general application to all offices, or more than 1 office, operated by the licensee, he may revoke, suspend or refuse to renew all of the licenses issued to the licensee or such number of licenses as such grounds apply to, as the case may be.

§ 17:16C–15. Investigations by Commissioner

The commissioner, if he has reasonable cause to believe that any licensee, or any other person, has violated any of the provisions of this act or of any other law relating to retail installment sales or contracts, shall have the power to make such investigations as he shall deem necessary, and may examine the books, accounts, records and files of such licensee or any other such person believed to have violated this act or any other law relating to retail installment sales or contracts.

§ 17:16C–16. Subpoenas; Oaths and Affirmations, Power to Administer

The commissioner shall have power to issue subpoenas to compel the attendance of witnesses and the production of documents, papers, books, records and other evidence before him in any matter over which he has jurisdiction, control or supervision pertaining to this act. The commissioner shall have the power to administer oaths and affirmations to any person whose testimony is required.

§ 17:16C–18. Maintenance of Books, Accounts and Records

Every retail seller, sales finance company, motor vehicle installment seller and holder shall maintain at its place or places of business in this State such books, accounts and records relating to all transactions within this act as will enable the commissioner to enforce full compliance with the provisions of this act.

§ 17:16C–20. Information to Be Shown in Books, Accounts and Records

The commissioner is hereby authorized to prescribe the minimum information to be shown in such books, accounts and records of the licensee so that such records will enable the commissioner to determine compliance with the provisions of this act.

§ 17:16C–21. Retail Installment Contract; Writing Required; Agreements Between Retail Buyer and Seller; Signatures

Every retail installment contract shall be in writing and shall contain all of the agreements between the retail buyer and retail seller relating to the installment sale of the goods purchased and shall be signed both by the retail buyer and the retail seller.

§ 17:16C–22. Contents of Retail Installment Contract; Blank Spaces

Every retail installment contract shall state the names and addresses of all parties thereto, the date when signed by the retail buyer, and shall contain a description of the goods sold which shall be sufficient for identification. No retail installment contract shall be signed by any party thereto when such contract contains blank spaces to be filled in after such contract has been signed; however, this provision shall not apply to serial numbers or other identifying marks which are not available for the description of the goods at the time of the execution of the contract.

§ 17:16C–23. Copy of Contract to Be Furnished to Buyer

A copy of the retail installment contract shall be furnished by the retail seller to the retail buyer at the time the retail buyer signs the contract except that such copy need not contain the signature of the retail seller. Such copy shall be furnished the retail buyer without charge.

§ 17:16C–24. Notice to Buyer in Retail Installment Contract

Every retail installment contract shall contain the following notice printed prominently, in the form herein indicated, in 10–point bold type or larger, directly above the notice required by section 25:

"NOTICE TO RETAIL BUYER

Do not sign this contract in blank.

You are entitled to a copy of the contract at the time you sign.

Keep it to protect your legal rights."

§ 17:16C–25. Acknowledgment by Buyer of Receipt of Copy of Contract

Any acknowledgment by the retail buyer of receipt of a copy of the contract shall be printed or written in a size equal to at least 10–point bold type and, if contained in the contract, shall appear directly above the space provided in the contract form for the signature of the retail buyer.

§ 17:16C–26. Payment of Time Balance in Substantially Equal Amounts on Dates Separated by Substantially Equal Payment-periods; Exceptions

Every retail installment contract shall provide for the payment of the time balance in substantially equal amounts on dates separated by substantially equal payment-periods; except that the retail seller may defer the initial installment for any period of time up to one year from the date of execution of the retail installment contract; and, provided, further, that when appropriate for the purpose of facilitating payment, in accordance with a retail buyer's intermittent income, a contract may provide for payment on a schedule which reduces or omits payments over a period or periods not in excess of 93 days in any 12–month period or a contract may provide an installment schedule which reduces or omits payments over any period or periods of time during which period or periods the retail buyer's income is reduced or suspended. When a retail installment contract provides for unequal or irregular installments, the time price differential shall not exceed the effective rate provided in section 41 of P.L.1960, c.40 (C.17:16C–41), having due regard for the schedule of installments. When in any retail installment contract the purchase of goods is combined with the purchase of food, the time balance on which is stated as one amount, that part of the time balance on the sale of goods shall be subject to the provisions of this section, but that part of the time balance on the purchase of food may be payable in a shorter time and added to the equal payment installment on goods.

§ 17:16C–27. Separate Items to Be Set Forth in Retail Installment Contract

Every retail installment contract shall set forth the following separate items:

(a) The cash price of the goods which are the subject matter of the retail installment contract;

(b) The down payment made by the retail buyer, indicating whether made in cash or in goods or partly in cash and partly in goods. The amount of the payment in cash and in goods shall be shown separately. A description of the goods, if any, sufficient for identification, shall be shown;

(c) The unpaid cash balance which shall be the difference between the cash price (subsection (a)) and the down payment (subsection (b));

(d) The amount, if any, if a separate charge is made therefor, included for insurance and other benefits, specifying the coverages and benefits;

(e) The amount of official fees;

(f) The principal balance, which is the sum of subsections (c), (d) and (e);

(g) The amount of the time price differential;

(h) The time balance, which is the sum of subsections (f) and (g), owed by the retail buyer to the retail seller, the number of installments required, the amount of each installment expressed in dollars and the due date or period thereof;

(i) The time sales price, which is the sum of subsections (b) and (h).

§ 17:16C–28. Inclusion in Retail Installment Contract of Additional Goods Purchased After Original Agreement; Additional Statements

Whenever a retail installment contract by its terms permits the inclusion of additional goods purchased after the original agreement, and such goods are so purchased and the amount due on the new purchase is combined with an unpaid balance on any prior purchase so as to permit the retail seller to retain title to or reserve a lien upon all goods under the combined agreement, the retail seller shall, at the time of the additional purchase, deliver to the retail buyer and attach to the original agreement:

(a) A statement containing all the information with respect to the additional purchase required to be included in a retail installment contract; and

(b) A statement showing the amount due on the agreement immediately previous to the new purchase, the amount due after the new purchase, the payments agreed to be made thereafter, and the number of additional months required to complete the payments.

§ 17:16C–29.   Allocation of Payment on Continuing Agreement After Addition of Additional Purchases; Prepayment; Redemption of Separate Purchases

Whenever a payment is made on such a continuing agreement after additional purchases have been added, the payment shall be considered as allocated among each of the separate purchases included, in full to the purchase made earliest in time, and the retail seller before repossessing or attempting to repossess any goods under any such agreement shall actually allocate in such manner all such payments made to him by the retail buyer. When the amount owing on any separate purchase has been fully paid, the goods so paid for shall become the absolute property of the retail buyer and shall not be subject to repossession for any subsequent default on the agreement. The retail buyer under any such agreement may at any time prepay the amount due on any of the separate purchases and in case of repossession may redeem any of such separate purchases by payment of the amount due on such purchase alone.

§ 17:16C–30.   Insurance at Retail Buyer's Expense; Dual Protection

Where title to or a lien upon goods sold by the retail seller is retained or taken by the retail seller the retail buyer may be required to insure the goods at the retail buyer's expense for the protection of the retail seller or subsequent holder which insurance may be purchased by the holder. Such insurance shall be written for the dual protection of the retail buyer and the retail seller or subsequent holder to the extent of his interest in the goods and shall be limited to insurance against substantial risk of damage, destruction, or theft of such goods and shall be upon terms and conditions, which are reasonable and appropriate, considering the type and conditions of such goods. When the retail buyer fails or is unable to acquire insurance or the retail seller or subsequent holder is unable to purchase insurance covering the dual protection of the retail buyer and retail seller or subsequent holder, the retail seller or holder may purchase a single interest insurance policy on the goods and may collect the premium therefor from the retail buyer.

§ 17:16C–31.   Selection of Insurer Acceptable to Retail Seller; Inclusion of Premium in Contract; Cancellation of Insurance by Holder After Repossession and Sale

The retail buyer shall have the privilege of supplying insurance on the goods through an agent or broker of his own selection and selecting an insurance company acceptable to the retail seller; provided, however, the inclusion of the premium for such insurance in the retail installment contract, when the retail buyer selects the company, agent or broker, shall be optional with the retail seller. The amount, if any, included for such insurance shall not exceed the premiums chargeable in accordance with the applicable rates filed with the commissioner for such insurance. The retail seller or holder, if the premium for dual insurance on the goods is included in a retail installment contract, shall within 25 days after the execution of the retail installment contract send or cause to be sent to the retail buyer a policy or policies or certificate of insurance, written by an insurance company authorized to do business in this State, clearly setting forth the amount of the premium, the kind or kinds of insurance and the scope of the coverage and all the terms, exceptions, limitations, restrictions and conditions of the contract or contracts of insurance. The holder of a retail installment contract shall, if the goods described therein have been repossessed and sold, cancel any insurance on the goods and any other insurance or other benefits then in force and shall credit the amount of the return premium thereon to the unpaid balance outstanding on the retail installment contract.

§ 17:16C–32. Notice That Policy Required in Sale of Motor Vehicle Includes No Liability or Property Damage Coverage

Whenever, in the sale of a motor vehicle, the retail buyer is required, under the provisions of this act, to provide a policy of insurance and such policy of insurance does not contain the liability insurance required by section 1 of P.L.1972, c. 197 (C. 39:6B–1), the retail installment contract shall contain, immediately following the statement therein concerning insurance, the following notice printed prominently, in the form herein indicated or in such other form as may be approved by the commissioner, in 10–point type or larger:

"THIS DOES NOT INCLUDE INSURANCE ON YOUR LIABILITY FOR BODILY INJURY OR PROPERTY DAMAGE. WITHOUT SUCH INSURANCE, YOU MAY NOT OPERATE THIS VEHICLE ON PUBLIC HIGHWAYS."

§ 17:16C–33. Additional Insurance; Cancellation Rights

In addition to insurance on the goods, by agreement with the retail buyer, the retail seller may purchase such other insurance and other benefits as the retail buyer shall contract for; provided, however, that the retail buyer may cancel such additional insurance and other benefits, other than credit life and credit accident and health insurance, at any time prior to the expiration of such insurance contracts or benefits.

§ 17:16C–34. Cancellation of Insurance Policies; Crediting Next Maturing Installment of Contract with Refund

If any policy or policies or certificates of insurance or other benefits are canceled, or the premiums thereon adjusted, the unearned insurance premium refund or refund on other benefits received by the retail seller or subsequent holder of the retail installment contract shall be credited to the next maturing installments of the retail installment contract, except to the extent applied toward payment for similar insurance protecting the interest of the buyer and the retail seller or holder of the contract or any of them; provided that in the case of credit life or credit accident and health insurance, the refund to the buyer shall be made in accordance with chapter 169 of the laws of 1958 [§ 17:38A–1 et seq.], and provided further that if the amount of such refund is less than the minimum prescribed by the commissioner, no refund need be made.

§ 17:16C–34.1 Retail Charge Account; Terms; Regulations; Effective Date of Accounts

(a) A retail charge account may be entered into between a retail buyer and a retail seller or a person wholly owned by or which wholly owns a retail seller or between a retail buyer and a sales finance company on its own behalf or on behalf of one or more retail sellers from whom the sales finance company may purchase or acquire the obligations of the retail buyer incurred pursuant to a retail charge account.

(b) A retail charge account shall be subject to such provisions not inconsistent with this act or otherwise prohibited by law which may be agreed upon, but shall be subject to the requirements for open end credit accounts as prescribed by regulations of the Board of Governors of the Federal Reserve System issued pursuant to Title I of the Consumer Credit Protection Act, referred to in this act as the "Truth in Lending Act and Regulations."

(c) A retail charge account shall become effective when an agreement is signed by the retail buyer or when the retail buyer or someone authorized by the retail buyer makes a purchase pursuant to the terms of the account.

§ 17:16C–35. Prohibited Contract Provisions; Acceleration Clause

No retail installment contract or retail charge account or separate instruments executed in connection therewith shall contain any acceleration clause under which any part or all of the balance, not yet matured, may be declared immediately due and payable because the retail seller or holder deems himself to be insecure and any such provision shall be void and unenforceable.

§ 17:16C–36. Waiver of Right of Action by Retail Buyer Against Seller, Holder, etc.

No retail installment contract or retail charge account or separate instruments executed in connection therewith shall contain any provisions whereby the retail buyer waives any right of action or defense against the retail seller, sales finance company, holder or other person acting on his or her behalf for any illegal act committed in the collection of the payments under the contract or account or in the repossession of the goods, the subject of the retail installment contract or retail charge account and any such provision shall be void and unenforceable.

§ 17:16C–37.   Power of Attorney to Confess Judgment;   Other Powers of Attorney

No retail installment contract or retail charge account or separate instruments executed in connection therewith shall contain any power of attorney to confess judgment or any other power of attorney and any such provision shall be void and unenforceable.

§ 17:16C–38.   Relief of Retail Seller from Liability Under Contract

No retail installment contract or retail charge account or separate instruments executed in connection therewith shall contain any provision relieving the retail seller from liability for any legal remedies which the retail buyer may have against the retail seller under the contract or account and any such provision shall be void and unenforceable.

§ 17:16C–38.1   Remedy of Buyer Against Seller; Provision Relieving Holder or Other Assignee from Liability; Prohibition

No retail installment contract shall contain any provision relieving the holder, or other assignee, from liability for any civil remedy sounding in contract which the retail buyer may have against the retail seller under the retail installment contract or under any separate instrument executed in connection therewith.

§ 17:16C–38.2   Imprint of Words "Consumer Note" on Face of Note; Note Not a Negotiable Instrument or Security Interest; Subjection of Subsequent Holder to Claims and Defenses of Buyer

No retail installment contract shall require or entail the execution of any note unless such note shall have printed the words "CONSUMER NOTE" in 10–point bold type or larger on the face thereof. Such a note with the words "CONSUMER NOTE" printed thereon shall be subject to the terms and conditions of the retail installment contract and shall not be a negotiable instrument within the meaning of chapter 3 (Negotiable Instruments) N.J.S. 12A:3–101 et seq., or a security interest within the meaning of chapter 9 (Secured Transactions) N.J.S. 12A:9–101 et seq. of the Uniform Commercial Code. Any subsequent holder of a consumer note shall be subject to all claims and defenses of the retail buyer against the retail seller arising out of the transaction but no such claim or defense may be asserted against such holder in excess of the time sales price under the retail installment contract for any sale, except that, in the case of the sale of a new motor vehicle, as defined in R.S. 39:10–2, no claim or defense may be asserted against such holder in excess of the time balance under the retail installment contract. No claim or defense which the retail buyer may have against the retail seller arising otherwise than out of the retail installment contract or any separate instrument executed in connection therewith shall be asserted against any subsequent holder.

§ 17:16C–38.3 Violations; Penalty

Any person who procures the execution of a note in violation of this act shall be liable to a penalty of not more than $500.00 for each offense.

§ 17:16C–38.4 Execution of Note in Violation of Act; Disallowance of Finance, Collection, etc., Charges

In the event that a note is executed in connection with a retail installment contract in violation of this act, no finance, delinquency, collection, repossession or refinancing charges may be recovered in any action or proceeding based on the contract or the consumer note.

§ 17:16C–39. Assignment of Salary, Wages, Commissions or Other Compensation for Services

No retail seller, sales finance company or holder shall at any time take in a retail installment contract, a retail charge account or in a separate instrument, any assignment of or order for the payment of any salary, wages, commissions, or other compensation for services, or any part thereof, earned or to be earned and any such provision shall be void and unenforceable.

§ 17:16C–39.1 Real Property Mortgage as Additional Security; Prohibition

No retail installment contract, retail charge account or separate instrument executed in connection therewith shall contain any provision whereby the retail seller, sales finance company or holder takes a real property mortgage as additional security in connection with a retail sale. Any such provision shall be void and unenforceable.

§ 17:16C–40. Loan of Money or Advance of Credit to Retail Buyer; Rate of Interest

No retail seller, sales finance company or holder shall make any loan of money or advance of credit to a retail buyer on or in connection with any retail installment contract or retail charge account and charge, contract for or receive thereon a greater rate of interest than he would otherwise be permitted by law to charge except in accordance with the provisions of this act; provided, however, that nothing contained in this section shall prohibit a banking institution from making any loan which it otherwise is permitted by law to make.

§ 17:16C–40.1 Loan Secured by Purchase Money Security Interest to Finance Purchase of Motor Vehicle

A sales finance company licensed under the provisions of [this Act] or any act replacing or succeeding thereto which regulates "retail installment sales," may loan to any one person any sum of money up to a maximum of $10,000.00 secured by a purchase money security interest to finance the purchase of a passenger motor vehicle not intended to be used for the transportation of passengers for hire or upon a contract basis. The principal amount of such loan may be repaid in not more than 48 substantially equal monthly installments. Notwithstanding the provisions of R.S. 31:1–1 or any other law to the contrary, the sales finance company may charge interest at a rate or rates agreed to by the sales finance company and the borrower. Such interest shall be computed on the full amount of such loan for the period from the making of the loan to the date of maturity of the final installment, and shall be added to the principal amount of the loan. For the purpose of this act, a purchase money security interest is hereby defined to be a security interest taken by a sales finance company, pursuant to the provisions of chapter 9 of Title 12A of the New Jersey Statutes, in connection with and as security for an advance of money on behalf of a retail buyer of a motor vehicle of the motor vehicle dealer in payment of the unpaid balance of the cash price.

Effective on the first day of the twelfth month following the effective date of this act, when the unpaid balance owing upon a precomputed loan is repaid in full or the maturity of the unpaid balance of such loan is accelerated before the date scheduled for the payment of the final installment, the association shall allow a credit on account of the precomputed interest, calculated according to the actuarial refund method, as if all payments were made as scheduled, or if deferred, as deferred; provided, however, that if the loan is prepaid within 12 months after the first payment is due, an association may charge a prepayment penalty of not more than (a) $20.00 on any loan up to and including $2,000.00; (b) an amount equal to 1% of the loan on any loan greater than $2,000.00 and up to and including $5,000.00; and (c) $100.00 on any loan exceeding $5,000.00.

§ 17:16C–40.2   Violation of Provisions; Revocation or Suspension of License

A violation of any provision of this act shall be cause for the revocation or suspension of the license of the sales finance company by the commissioner upon notice and opportunity to be heard in accordance with the provisions of P.L.1958, chapter 68 [§ 17:1–8.5 et seq.].

§ 17:16C–41.   Time Price Differential; Rates; Computation

A retail seller and a motor vehicle installment seller, under the provisions of this act, shall have authority to charge, contract for, receive or collect a time price differential as defined in this act, on any retail installment contract evidencing the sale of goods or services in an amount or amounts as agreed to by the retail seller or motor vehicle installment seller and the buyer on motor vehicles and on all other goods or services.

The retail installment contract may provide for an increase, or may provide for a decrease, or both, in the time price differential applicable to the contract. No increase during the entire loan term shall result in an interest rate of more than 6% per annum over the rate applicable initially, nor shall the rate be raised more than 3% per annum during any 12–month period. The lender shall not be obligated to decrease the interest rate more than 6% over the term of the loan, nor more than 3% per annum during any 12–month period. If a rate increase is applied to the loan, the lender shall also be obligated to adopt and implement uniform standards for decreasing the rate. If the contract provides for the possibility of an increase or decrease, or both, in the rate, that fact shall be clearly described in plain language, in at least 8–point bold face type on the face of the contract. No rate increase shall take effect during the first 3 years of the term of the contract, or thereafter, (a) unless at least 90 days prior to the effective date of the first such increase, or 30 days prior to the effective date of any subsequent increase, a written notice has been mailed or delivered to the retail buyer that clearly and conspicuously describes such increase, and (b) unless at least 365 days have elapsed without any increase. No increase during the entire contract term shall result in an interest rate of more than 6% per annum over the rate applicable initially, nor shall the rate be raised more than 3% per annum during any 12–month period.

If the retail installment contract does provide that the time price differential may be increased then, notwithstanding the provisions of section 43 of P.L.1960, c. 40 (C. 17:16C–43), when the unpaid balance owing upon a contract is paid in full or the maturity of the unpaid balance of such contract is accelerated before the date scheduled for the payment of the final installment, the holder of the contract shall allow a credit on account of the precomputed time price differential calculated according to the actuarial refund method, as if all payments were made as scheduled, or if deferred, as deferred; provided, however, that if the contract is prepaid within 12 months after the first payment is due, a holder may charge a prepayment penalty of not more than (a) $20.00 on any contract up to and including $2,000.00; (b) an amount equal to 1% of the loan on any contract greater than $2,000.00 and up to and including $5,000.00; and (c) $100.00 on any contract exceeding $5,000.00. Effective on the first day of the twelfth month following the effective date of this act, if the retail installment contract does provide for a time price differential, then, notwithstanding the provisions of section 43 of P.L.1960, c. 40 (C. 17:16C–43), when the unpaid balance owing upon a contract is paid in full or the maturity of the unpaid balance of such contract is accelerated before the date scheduled for the payment of the final installment, the holder of the contract shall allow a credit on account of the precomputed time price differential calculated according to the actuarial refund method, as if all payments were made as scheduled, or if deferred, as deferred; provided, however, that if the contract is prepaid within 12 months after the first payment is due, a holder may charge a prepayment penalty of not more than (a) $20.00 on any contract up to and including $2,000.00; (b) an amount equal to 1% of the loan on any contract greater than $2,000.00 and up to and including $5,000.00; and (c) $100.00 on any contract exceeding $5,000.00.

The time price differential shall be computed on the amount of the principal balance as determined in section 27(f), from the date of the contract to the due date of the final installment, notwithstanding the fact that the contract is to be repaid in installments.

If the time price differential so computed is less than $12.00, and if the due date of the last installment of the contract is more than 8 months after the date of the contract, a charge of not more than $12.00 may be made in lieu of the time price differential. If the time price differential so computed is less than $10.00, and if the due date of the last installment of the contract is 8 months or less after the date of contract, a charge of not more than $10.00 may be made in lieu of the time price differential.

§ 17:16C–42. Delinquency or Collection Charge for Default in Payment; Attorney's Fees

(a) The holder of any retail installment contract may collect a delinquency or collection charge for default in the payment of any such contract or any installment thereof, if provided for in the contract when such default shall have continued for a period of 10 days, such charge not to exceed $10. Such charge may be collected by the holder of the retail installment contract or charged to the buyer's retail installment contract account. If charged to the buyer's retail installment contract account, such charge shall be made within 35 days from the date of such default and then a written notification that such charge has been made shall be mailed to the retail buyer within 5 days from the date when such charge was made.

(b) The holder of any retail charge account may collect a delinquency or collection charge in an amount not to exceed $10, if provided for in the retail charge account agreement, on any minimum payment which has not been paid in full for a period of 10 days after its due date, as originally scheduled.

(c) A delinquency or collection charge under this section may be collected only once on each minimum payment due however long it remains in default. A delinquency charge may be collected at the time it accrues or at any time afterward.

(d) The retail installment contract or retail charge account may provide for the payment of attorney's fees not exceeding 20% of the first $500.00 and 10% on any excess of the amount due and payable under such contract or account when referred to an attorney, not a salaried employee of the holder of the contract or account, for collection.

(e) The retail installment contract or retail charge account may provide for a return check fee not to exceed $20 which the holder of the contract may charge the buyer if a check of the buyer is returned to the holder uncollected due to insufficient funds in the buyer's account.

§ 17:16C-43. Prepayment; Credit on Account

When the balance owing on a retail installment contract is repaid in full at any time before the end of the contract period, the holder of the contract shall allow a credit on account of the time price differential, the amount of which shall be determined by the application of the formula $C = AN \div D$, in which "C" represents the amount of the credit to be given; "A" represents the amount of the time price differential, less an acquisition cost of $15.00; "D" represents an amount determined as follows: there shall be ascribed to each payment-period included in the contract period, beginning with the first payment-period scheduled by the contract, the cardinal number descriptive of the number of payment-periods scheduled by the contract to elapse from the beginning of each such payment-period to the end of the contract period, and the sum of all such cardinal numbers shall constitute the quantity "D"; and "N" represents the difference between the quantity "D" and the sum of all the cardinal numbers ascribed to the payment-periods which have elapsed, in whole or in part, from the date of the contract to the date upon which such repayment is made. This section shall not apply when the amount of the credit is less than $1.00.

§ 17:16C-44. Extension of Scheduled Due Date; Reduction of Amount of Installments; Additional Charge; Options

The holder of a retail installment contract may extend the scheduled due date of any retail installment contract and defer the scheduled due date of any or all installment payments, or reduce the amount of any or all installments and may, as a consideration therefor, make a total additional charge not to exceed the amount ascertained under either of the following methods of computation at the respective rates indicated by the following options:

Option 1. The additional charge shall be computed on the amount of the scheduled installment on installments extended, deferred or reduced for the period or periods for which each installment or part thereof is extended, deferred or reduced at the following rates on contracts originally in the respective classifications set forth in section 41 of this act:

Class I. 1% per month;

Class II. 1½% per month;

Class III. 2% per month;

Class IV. 2% per month.

Option 2. The holder of a retail installment contract by written agreement may renew the entire unpaid balance on any retail installment contract and may make a charge therefor at the rates charged in the original contract from the date of renewal to the maturity of the final installment. The amount of the balance to be renewed shall be obtained by adding to the existing unpaid balance on the original contract, the cost of any insurance or other benefits for the period of the extension and any accrued default charges and refunding the unearned portion of the time price differential charged according to the formula provided in section 43 of this act; provided, however, that in computing the unearned time price differential charge no allowance shall be taken for the amount of the acquisition cost permitted therein.

§ 17:16C–44.1   Retail Charge Account;   Time Price Differential;   Rate;   Computation

(a) Notwithstanding any other law to the contrary, a retail seller, sales finance company, banking institution or other holder may charge, receive and collect a time price differential in each billing period on obligations incurred pursuant to any retail charge account, which shall be determined as specified in the terms of the account, subject to the limitations provided herein. Such time price differential for each monthly billing period shall not exceed the amount resulting from applying the periodic rates provided herein to the greater of the following amounts (including unpaid time price differentials):

(i) The average daily balance of the account for such billing period, or

(ii) The balance of the account at the beginning or end of such billing period.

The periodic rate or rates shall not exceed an amount agreed to by the retail seller, sales finance company, banking institution, or other holder and the retail buyer.

The terms of the retail charge account may provide that the time price differential may be increased or may be decreased or both from time to time provided, however, that no increase shall be effective unless: (1) at least 90 days prior to the effective date of the first such increase, or 30 days prior to the effective date of any subsequent increase, a written notice has been mailed or delivered to the retail buyer that clearly and conspicuously describes such change and the indebtedness to which it applies and states that the incurrence by the retail buyer or another person authorized by him of any further indebtedness under the plan to which the agreement relates on or after the effective date of the increase specified in the notice shall constitute acceptance of the increase and (b) either the retail buyer agrees in writing to the increase or the retail buyer or another person authorized by him incurs such further indebtedness on or after the effective date of the increase stated in the notice. The provisions of this paragraph permitting an increase in the time price differential shall not apply in the case of an agreement which expressly prohibits changing of the time price differential or which provides limitations on changing of the time price differential which are more restrictive than the requirements of this paragraph. If the terms of the retail charge account provide for the possibility of an increase or decrease, or both, in the time price differential, that fact shall be clearly described in plain language, in at least 8–point bold face type on the face of the written notice.

Notwithstanding the foregoing limitation, if the terms of the account so provide, the time price differential may be computed on the median amount within a specified range. Such time price differential for each monthly billing period shall not exceed the amount resulting from applying the respective periodic rates specified above to the median amount within the specified range in which the greater of the amounts specified in (i) and (ii) is included; provided, subject to the classifications and differentiations as may reasonably be established by the retail seller, sales finance company, banking institution or other holder, the same time price differential is charged on all balances within the specified range and provided further that the time price differential determined by applying the respective periodic rates specified above to the median amount within the range does not exceed by more than 8% the amount of the time price differential determined by applying the respective periodic rates specified above to the lowest amount in the range.

(b) If the billing period is not monthly, the maximum periodic rate shall be that rate which bears the same relation to the respective periodic rates per month specified above as the number of days in the billing period bears to 30.

(c) Notwithstanding the limitation provided in (a) above, for any monthly billing period in which a time price differential may be charged pursuant to the terms of the account a minimum time price differential of not more than $0.50 may be charged; if the billing period is not monthly, a minimum time price differential may be charged in such amount which bears the same relation to $0.50 as the number of days in the billing period bears to 30.

§ 17:16C–45.   Limitation on Sale, Transfer or Assignment of Obligation or Evidence of Indebtedness by Retail Seller

No retail seller under a retail installment contract, executed in this State, shall sell, transfer or assign the obligation represented by such contract or any evidence of indebtedness thereunder to any person who is not authorized as a sales finance company pursuant to the provisions of this act, except that such obligation or evidence of indebtedness may be sold, transferred or assigned to a State or national bank outside of this State if the retail installment contract is retained by the retail seller or sales finance company and collection of payments thereon is made to the retail seller or sales finance company.

§ 17:16C–46.   Sale, Transfer or Assignment Without Notice to Retail Buyer; Payment or Tender to Last Known Holder

If a retail installment contract is lawfully sold, transferred or assigned, pursuant to the provisions of this act, and a written notice of such sale, transfer or assignment setting forth the name and address of the new holder and of the person authorized to receive future payments on such contract is not given to the retail buyer, any payment or tender of payment made to and any service of notice on the last known holder by the retail buyer shall be binding upon any subsequent holder.

§ 17:16C–47. Assignment of Aggregation of Retail Installment Contracts as Collateral Security for Bona Fide Commercial Loan

The provisions of section 45 shall not apply to any assignment of an aggregation of retail installment contracts, which is executed by a retail seller or sales finance company as collateral security only for a bona fide commercial loan, and under which, in the absence of default or other bona fide breach of the contract, ownership of the assigned retail installment contracts remains vested in the retail seller or sales finance company, and collection of payments on such assigned contracts is made by the retail seller or sales finance company; and provided such assignment of contracts is not made for the purpose of evading or circumventing the provisions of this act.

§ 17:16C–47.1 Purchases of Retail Installment Contract or Retail Charge Account by Sales Finance Company; Terms, Conditions and Price

A sales finance company may purchase a retail installment contract or obligations incurred pursuant to a retail charge account from a retail seller or sales finance company on such terms and conditions and for such price as may be mutually agreed upon.

§ 17:16C–48. Furnishing Statement of Retail Buyer's Account

Upon written request from the retail buyer, the retail seller or holder of the retail installment contract shall give or forward to the retail buyer within 10 days from receipt of the written request a written statement of the retail buyer's account, showing the dates and amounts of all payments made or credited to the account and the total amount, if any, unpaid under such contract. No more than 2 such statements shall be required from a holder in any 12–month period.

§ 17:16C–49. Receipt for Payment; Contents

Whenever payment is made on account of any retail installment contract in cash, the person receiving such payment shall, at the time of receiving such payment, furnish to the retail buyer, or the person making such payment on behalf of the retail buyer, a complete written receipt therefor, showing the date, identification of the account and the amount paid.

§ 17:16C–50.   Additional Charges Prohibited; Exceptions

No retail seller, sales finance company, or holder shall charge, contract for, collect or receive from any retail buyer, directly or indirectly, any further or other amount for costs, charges, insurance premiums, examination, appraisal service, brokerage, commission, expense, interest, discount, fees, fines, penalties or other things of value in connection with retail installment contracts or retail charge accounts other than the charges permitted by this act, except court costs, attorney fees and the expenses of retaking and storing repossessed goods which are authorized by law.

§ 17:16C–51.   Collection of Charges if Sale Not Made Prohibited; Status of Deposit on Contemplated Purchase of Goods

No retail seller shall collect or retain any amount whatsoever in connection with the contemplated sale of goods under a retail installment sales contract, if such sale is not made; provided, however, that nothing contained herein shall affect the legal status of a deposit paid by a prospective retail buyer to a retail seller as a binder on the contemplated purchase of goods.

§ 17:16C–52.   Duties of Holder upon Payment in Full

Upon payment in full by the retail buyer of the time balance and other amounts lawfully due under a retail installment contract, the holder shall:

(a) Return to the retail buyer either the original instruments evidencing indebtedness or constituting security under a retail installment contract, which were signed by the retail buyer or his sureties or guarantors in conjunction with such contract or a copy thereof, excepting such instruments as are filed or recorded with a public official and retained in the files of such official;

(b) Release all security interest in the goods or in any collateral security to the obligation of the retail buyer under such contract;

(c) Deliver to the retail buyer such good and sufficient assignments and certificates of title as may be necessary to vest the retail buyer with complete evidence of title.

§ 17:16C–54.   Unauthorized Costs and Charges

Whenever, in any retail installment contract or retail charge account under this act, the retail seller, sales finance company or holder has knowingly charged, contracted for or received from the retail buyer any costs or charges not authorized by this act, all costs and charges in connection with such contract or account, other than for insurance authorized by this act, shall be void and unenforceable, and any such costs or charges other than for insurance authorized by this act shall be applied to the unpaid balance or, if the account has been fully paid, remitted to the retail buyer, and the retail buyer shall be entitled to recover all such costs or charges.

§ 17:16C–56. Violations of Act; Penalty; Enforcement by Summary Proceedings

(a) Any person conducting business under this act and any director, officer, partner, member, employee, agent, or representative thereof who shall knowingly violate any provision of this act or shall directly or indirectly counsel, aid or abet such violation shall be liable to a penalty of not more than $500.00 for each offense.

(b) The penalties provided for by this act shall be sued for and recovered by and in the name of the commissioner and shall be collected and enforced by summary proceedings pursuant to the Penalty Enforcement Law (N.J.S. 2A:58–1 et seq.).

SMALL LOAN ACT

Code of Ala. tit. 5, ch. 18

Tables of Sections

---

§ 5–18–1.   Short title

This chapter shall be known and may be cited as the Alabama Small Loan Act.

§ 5–18–2.   Legislative findings of fact and declaration of intent

(a) The legislature finds as facts and determines that:

(1) There exists among citizens of this state a widespread demand for small loans. The scope and intensity of this demand have been increased progressively by many social and economic forces;

(2) The expense of making and collecting small loans, which are usually made on comparatively unsubstantial security to wage earners, salaried employees and other persons of relatively low incomes, is necessarily high in relation to the amounts lent;

(3) Such loans cannot be made profitably under the limitations imposed by existing laws relating to interest and usury. These limitations have tended to exclude lawful enterprises from the small loan field. Since the demand for small loans cannot be legislated out of existence, many small borrowers have been left to the mercy of those willing to bear the opprobrium and risk the penalties of usury for a large profit;

(4) Interest charges are often disguised by the use of subterfuges to evade the usury law. These subterfuges are so complicated and technical that the usual borrower of small sums is defenseless even if he is aware of the usurious nature of the transaction and of his legal rights;

(5) As a result, borrowers of small sums are being exploited to the injury of the borrower, his dependents and the general public. Charges are generally exorbitant in relation to those necessary to the conduct of a legitimate small loan business, trickery and fraud are common and oppressive collection practices are prevalent; and

(6) These evils characterize and distinguish loans of $749.00 or less. Legislation to control this class of loans is necessary to protect the public welfare.

(b) It is the intent of the legislature in enacting this law to bring under public supervision those engaged in the business of making such loans, to eliminate practices that facilitate abuse of borrowers, to establish a system of regulation for the purpose of insuring honest and efficient small loan service and of stimulating competitive reductions in charges, to allow lenders who meet the conditions of this chapter a rate of charge sufficiently high to permit a business profit and to provide the administrative machinery necessary for effective enforcement.

§ 5–18–3. Definitions

The following terms, when used in this chapter, shall have the following meanings, unless the context clearly requires a different meaning. The meaning ascribed to the singular form shall apply also to the plural.

(1) Person. Such term shall include individuals, copartnerships, associations, trusts, corporations and any other legal entities.

(2) License. A license, issued under the authority of this chapter, to make loans in accordance with the provisions of this chapter at a single place of business.

(3) Licensee. A person to whom one or more licenses have been issued.

(4) Supervisor. The supervisor of the bureau of loans of the state banking department.

(5) Bureau. The bureau of loans of the state banking department.

(6) Cash advance. The amount of cash or its equivalent that the borrower actually receives or is paid at his direction or on his behalf.

§ 5–18–4. License—Required; exemptions; penalties for violation of section.

(a) *License required.*—No person shall engage in the business of lending in amounts of less than one thousand dollars ($1,000) and contract for, exact or receive, directly or indirectly, on or in connection with any such loan, any charges whether for interest, insurance, compensation, consideration or expense, which in the aggregate are greater than the interest that the lender would be permitted by law to charge for a loan of money if he were not a licensee under this chapter, except as provided in and authorized by this chapter and without first having obtained a license from the supervisor. For the purpose of this section, a loan shall be deemed to be in the amount of less than one thousand dollars ($1,000) if the net amount or value advanced to or on behalf of the borrower, after deducting all payments for interest, expenses and charges of any nature taken substantially contemporaneously with the making of the loan, is less than one thousand dollars ($1,000).

(b) *Exemptions.*—This chapter shall not apply to any person doing business under the authority of, and as permitted by, any law of this state or of the United States relating to banks, trust companies, savings or building and loan associations, credit unions as defined by law nor to any lawful, bona fide pawnbroking business, nor shall this chapter apply to any person making loans to their tenants engaged in agriculture, nor to loans by agricultural suppliers to persons whose principal business is farming, nor shall it apply to agricultural credit corporations or associations organized under an act of the congress of the United States, nor shall it apply to the business of financing the purchase of motor vehicles, refrigerators or other personal property, nor shall it apply to loans insured or guaranteed by the United States or any of its agencies.

(c) *Evasions.*—The provisions of subsection (a) of this section shall apply to any person who seeks to evade its application by any device, subterfuge or pretense whatsoever including, but not thereby limiting the generality of the foregoing: the loan, forbearance, use or sale of credit (as guarantor, surety, endorser, comaker or otherwise), money, insurance, goods or things in action; the use of collateral or related sales or purchases of goods or services or agreements to sell or purchase, whether real or pretended; and, receiving or charging compensation for goods or services, whether or not sold, delivered or provided and the real or pretended negotiation, arrangement or procurement of a loan through any use of activity of a third person, whether real or fictitious.

(d) *Penalties.*—Whoever violates or participates in the violation of any provision of this section shall be guilty of a misdemeanor and, upon conviction thereof, shall be punishable by a fine of not more than five hundred dollars ($500) nor less than one hundred dollars ($100), or by imprisonment for not more than six months, or by both such fine and imprisonment in the discretion of the court. Any contract of loan in the making or collection of which any act shall have been done which violates this section shall be void, and the lender shall have no right to collect, receive or retain any principal, interest or charges whatsoever.

§ 5–18–5. License—Application; fees; disposition of fees

Application for a license shall be in writing, under oath and in the form prescribed by the supervisor. The application shall give the approximate location where the business is to be conducted and shall contain such further relevant information as the supervisor may require, including the names and addresses of the partners, officers, directors or trustees and of such of the principal owners or members as will provide the basis for the investigations and findings contemplated by Section 5–18–6. At the time of making such application, the applicant shall pay to the supervisor the sum of one hundred dollars ($100) as a fee for investigating the application. All licensees under this chapter shall pay an annual license fee of five hundred dollars ($500) for each office, branch or place of business of the licensee, which shall be due on October 1 of each year and shall be for a one-year period ending September 30 following and shall be delinquent on November 1 of each year, and there shall be a penalty of 10 percent for each month or portion thereof added to such license fee upon delinquency and collected by the bureau. Two hundred dollars ($200) of each such license fee collected shall be paid into the special fund provided by Section 5–2A–20 and used in the supervision and examination of such licensees; provided further that in fiscal year 1986, two hundred fifty dollars ($250) of each such license fee collected shall be paid into the special fund provided in Section 5–2A–20 and used in the supervision and examination of such licensees; provided further that in fiscal year 1987, three hundred dollars ($300) of each such license fee collected shall be paid into the special fund provided by Section 5–2A–20 and used in the supervision and examination of such licensees; provided further that in fiscal year 1988, three hundred fifty dollars ($350) of each such license fee collected shall be paid into the special fund provided in Section 5–2A–20 and used in the supervision and examination of such licensees; and provided further that in fiscal year 1989 and thereafter, all such license fees collected shall be paid into the special fund provided by Section 5–2A–20 and used in the supervision and examination of such licensees. If any applicant licensed under this chapter for the first time shall commence business after April 1 in any year, the amount of the license fee shall be one half the amount of a full year's license fee. The amount of the license fee and penalties, if any, shall be paid to the Supervisor of the Bureau of Loans, who shall remit the same to the Treasurer of the State of Alabama as provided by law. The license provided for in this chapter shall be in addition to all other licenses now or hereafter provided for by law and shall be in addition to the tax provided for by Chapter 16 of Title 40; and the amount of the license fee levied by this section shall not be credited upon or deducted from, in whole or in part, the tax levied by said Chapter 16 as to the current state tax year or as to any prior or subsequent state tax year. No refunds for the current or any prior or subsequent state tax year or any portion of the tax levied by said Chapter 16 shall be made on the ground that the license fee levied by this section was not credited upon or deducted from the tax levied by said Chapter 16, and no civil action shall lie to enforce any claim for such refund.

§ 5–18–6. License—Investigation of application; issuance or denial of license

(a) *Investigation of application.*—Upon the filing of such application and the payment of such fees, the supervisor shall investigate the facts concerning the application and the requirements provided for in subsection (b) of this section. The supervisor shall grant or deny such application for a license within 90 days from the filing thereof with the required information and fees unless the period is extended by written agreement between the applicant and the supervisor.

(b) *Issuance of license.*—If the supervisor shall find that the liquid assets, financial responsibility, experience, character and the general fitness of the applicant are such as to warrant the belief that the business will be operated lawfully, honestly, fairly and efficiently, within the purposes of this chapter, and that allowing such applicant to engage in the business would promote the convenience and advantage of the community in which the business of the applicant is to be conducted, he shall thereupon enter an order granting such application and file his findings with the bureau and forthwith issue and deliver a license to the applicant.

(c) *Denial of license.*—If the supervisor shall not so find, he shall notify the applicant in writing who may request a hearing on the application. The request for a hearing must be within 30 days of the rejection, with the hearing to be held within 30 days of the date of the request. After such hearing or if no hearing is demanded, the supervisor may deny such application by written order accompanied by his findings of fact and shall deliver a copy of such order and findings to the applicant. The investigation fee shall be retained by the supervisor while the license fee shall be returned to the applicant.

§ 5–18–7. License—Contents; posting; continuing effect

(a) *Contents of license; posting.*—Each license shall state the address at which the business is to be conducted and shall state fully the name of the licensee and, if the licensee is a copartnership or association, the names of the members thereof and, if a corporation, the date and place of its incorporation. Each license shall be kept conspicuously posted in the licensed place of business and shall not be transferable or assignable.

(b) *Continuing effect of license.*—Each license shall remain in full force and effect until surrendered, revoked or suspended as provided in this chapter.

§ 5–18–8. License—Place of business of licensee

(a) *Separate license for each place of business.*—Not more than one place of business shall be maintained under the same license, but the supervisor may issue additional licenses to the same licensee upon his compliance with all the provisions of this chapter governing the issuance of the first or original license.

(b) *Removal.*—No change in the place of business of a licensee to a location outside of the original municipality shall be permitted under the same license. When a licensee wishes to change his place of business within the same municipality, he shall give written notice thereof to the supervisor who shall investigate the facts and, if he shall find the proposed location is reasonably accessible to borrowers under existing loan contracts, shall enter an order permitting the change and shall amend the license accordingly. If the supervisor shall not so find, he shall enter an order denying the licensee such permission in the manner specified in and subject to the provisions of subsection (c) of section 5–18–6.

(c) *Residence of borrower.*—Nothing in this chapter shall be construed to restrict the loans of any licensee to residents of the community in which the licensed place of business is situated.

§ 5–18–9. License—Revocation, suspension, etc.; investigation of complaints

(a) *Revocation of license.*—The supervisor shall, upon 10 days' written notice to the licensee stating the contemplated action and in general the grounds therefor and upon reasonable opportunity to be heard, revoke any license issued under this chapter if he finds that:

(1) The licensee has failed to pay the annual license fee;

(2) The licensee, either knowingly or without the exercise of due care to prevent the same, has violated any provisions of this chapter or any regulation or order lawfully made pursuant to and within the authority of this chapter;

(3) Any fact or condition exists which, if it had existed or had been known to exist at the time of the original application for such license, clearly would have justified the supervisor in refusing originally to issue such license; except, that the license shall not be revoked because of convenience and advantage; or

(4) The licensee is guilty of using unreasonable collection tactics.

(b) *Suspension of license.*—If the supervisor finds that probable cause for revocation of any license exists and that enforcement of the chapter requires immediate suspension of such license pending investigation, he may, upon three days' written notice and a hearing, enter an order suspending such license for a period not exceeding 30 days.

(c) *Records and notice.*—Whenever the supervisor shall revoke or suspend a license issued pursuant to this chapter, he shall enter an order to that effect and forthwith notify the licensee of the revocation or suspension. Within five days after the entry of such an order he shall file with the bureau his findings and a summary of the evidence supporting them, and he shall forthwith deliver a copy thereof to the licensee.

(d) *Surrender of license.* Any licensee may surrender any license by delivering it to the supervisor with written notice of its surrender, but such surrender shall not affect his civil or criminal liability for acts committed prior thereto.

(e) *Preexisting contracts.*—No revocation, suspension or surrender of any license shall impair or affect the obligation of any preexisting contract between the licensee and any borrower.

(f) *Reinstatement of license.*—The supervisor may reinstate suspended licenses or issue new licenses to a person whose license or licenses have been revoked if no fact or condition then exists which clearly would have justified the supervisor in refusing originally to issue such license under this chapter.

(g) *Complaints of violation investigated.*—The supervisor shall, upon sworn complaint of any borrower, investigate or cause to be investigated any alleged violation of this chapter.

§ 5–18–10. Examinations of licensees; investigations; enforcement powers of supervisor

(a) *Annual examinations of licensees.*—At least once each year and at such other time as may be deemed necessary by the supervisor of the bureau of loans, an examination shall be made of the place of business of each licensee and of the loans, transactions, books, papers and records of such licensee so far as they pertain to the business licensed under this chapter. As cost of examination, the licensee shall pay to the bureau of loans the actual cost of each examination, the amount of which shall be reasonably prescribed under rules and regulations promulgated by the superintendent of banks; provided, however, the cost for each day of examination by each examiner shall not exceed eight times the average hourly rate for auditing purposes as charged by three recognized certified public accountancy firms in the city of Montgomery, Alabama. In addition thereto, the licensee shall pay as per diem the amount authorized by law for state employees traveling inside the state in the service of the state. All such fees shall be paid into the special fund set up by the state treasury pursuant to section 5–2A–20, and used in the supervision and examination of licensees.

(b) *Investigations.*—For the purpose of discovering violations of this chapter or of securing information lawfully required hereunder, the supervisor or his duly authorized representatives may at any time investigate the business and examine the books, accounts, papers and records used therein of (1) any licensee, (2) any other person engaged in the business described in subsection (a) of section 5–18–4 or participating in the business as principal, agent, broker or otherwise and (3) any person who the supervisor has reasonable cause to believe is violating or is about to violate any provisions of this chapter, whether or not the person shall claim to be within the authority or beyond the scope of this chapter. For purposes of this section, any person who shall advertise for, solicit or hold himself out as willing to make loan transactions in the amount or of the value of less than one thousand dollars ($1,000) shall be presumed to be engaged in the business described in subsection (a) of section 5–18–4.

(c) *Access to records; witnesses.*—For the purposes of this section, the supervisor or his duly authorized representatives shall have and be given free access to the offices and places of business, files, safes and vaults of all such persons and shall have authority to require the attendance of any person and to examine him under oath relative to such loans or such business or to the subject matter of any examination, investigation or hearing.

(d) *Cease and desist orders; injunctions; receivers.*—Whenever the supervisor has reasonable cause to believe that any person is violating or is threatening to or intends to violate any provision of this chapter, he may in addition to all actions provided for in this chapter and in addition to all other remedies that he may have at law and without prejudice thereto enter an order requiring such person to desist or to refrain from such violation, and an action may be brought on the relation of the attorney general or the supervisor to enjoin the person from engaging in or continuing the violation or from doing any act or acts in furtherance thereof. In any such action, an order or judgment may be entered awarding the preliminary or final injunction as may be deemed proper. In addition to all other means provided by law for the enforcement of a restraining order or injunction, the court in which the action is brought shall have power and jurisdiction to impound and to appoint a receiver for the property and business of the defendant, including books, papers, documents and records pertaining thereto or so much thereof as the court may deem reasonably necessary to prevent violations of this chapter through or by means of the use of said property and business. The receiver, when appointed and qualified, shall have such powers and duties as to custody, collection, administration, winding up and liquidation of the property and business as shall from time to time be conferred upon him by the court.

(e) Reports of examinations and investigations of the supervisor, and the books and records of licensees are to be held strictly confidential, and may not be produced, reproduced, or otherwise made available by the State Banking Department to any persons other than those within the State Banking Department unless pursuant to a lawfully issued subpoena. This subsection does not apply to disclosures in proceedings brought by the supervisor pursuant to this chapter.

§ 5–18–11. Books, accounts and records of licensees; annual report

(a) *Books and records.*—Each licensee shall keep and use in his business such books, accounts and records as will enable the supervisor to determine whether such licensee is complying with the provisions of this chapter and with the orders and regulations lawfully made by the supervisor hereunder. Each licensee shall preserve such books, accounts and records for at least two years after making the final entry on any loan recorded therein.

(b) *Annual report.*

(1) Each licensee shall annually, on or before May 1, file a report with the supervisor as to each licensed place of business under this chapter, covering the preceding calendar year. This report shall include the following information, all reported in accordance with sound and generally accepted accounting practice:

a. Balance sheets at the beginning and end of the period;

b. A statement of income and expenses for the period;

c. A reconciliation of surplus or net earnings with the balance sheets;

d. A schedule of assets used and useful in the business;

e. An analysis of charges, sizes of loans and types of security on loans and an analysis of delinquent accounts;

f. An analysis of suits, repossessions and sales of chattels; and

g. The type of business organization and, if the licensee is a corporation, the principal officers and the resident agent, the partners if the licensee is a partnership or the owner if a sole proprietorship.

(2) If the licensee conducts other businesses or is affiliated with other licensees under this chapter, or if any other situation exists under which allocations are necessary, the licensee shall make such allocation according to appropriate and reasonable methods.

(3) If the licensee is affiliated with other licensees under this chapter, a composite report may be filed on behalf of all affiliated licensees within the state of Alabama, but such composite report shall not be required by the supervisor.

(4) Such report shall be made under oath and shall be in the form prescribed by the supervisor who shall make and publish annually an analysis and recapitulation of such reports.

§ 5–18–12. Promulgation of rules, regulations and orders by supervisor; furnishing of certified copies of licenses, regulations or orders

(a) *Rules, regulations and orders.*—The supervisor shall have authority to make reasonable rules, regulations and orders for the administration and enforcement of this chapter, in addition hereto and not inconsistent herewith. The regulation or order shall be referenced to the section or sections of the chapter which set forth the legislative standard which it interprets or to which it applies. Every regulation shall be promulgated by an order, and any ruling, demand, requirement or similar administrative act may be promulgated by an order. Every order shall be in writing, shall state its effective date and the date of its promulgation and shall be entered in an indexed permanent book which shall be a public record. A copy of every order promulgating a regulation and of every other order containing a requirement of general application shall be mailed to each licensee at least 10 days before the effective date thereof. The failure of a licensee to receive a copy of the regulations shall not exempt him from the duty of compliance with the valid regulations lawfully issued.

(b) *Certified copies of official documents.*—On application of any person and payment of the costs thereof, the supervisor shall furnish, under his seal and signed by him or his deputy a certified copy of any license, regulation or order. In any court or proceeding, such copy shall be prima facie evidence of the fact of the issuance of the license, regulation or order.

(c) As set forth in Section 5–19–21, the supervisor may promulgate reasonable rules and regulations, consistent with the laws of this state, as may be necessary to carry out the provisions of this chapter, and issue written interpretations of consumer finance laws and regulations. The courts of this state shall apply each regulation that becomes effective and each written interpretation that is issued under this subsection, unless the regulation or interpretation is found to be arbitrary and capricious, outside the supervisor's statutory authority, or violative of the Constitution of Alabama of 1901. Any licensee whose practices are consistent with any regulation or written interpretation shall not be liable for any violation of this chapter, even though the rule of interpretation thereof, is ruled invalid for any reason by a court of competent jurisdiction.

§ 5–18–13. Advertising—Schedule of charges

(a) *Advertising, etc.*—No licensee or other person subject to this chapter shall advertise, display, distribute or broadcast or cause to permit to be advertised, displayed, distributed or broadcast in any manner whatsoever any false, misleading or deceptive statement or representation with regard to the rates, terms or conditions for loans in the amount or of the value of less than one thousand dollars ($1,000). The supervisor may require that charges or rates of charge, if stated by a licensee, be stated fully and clearly in such manner as he or she may deem necessary to prevent misunderstanding thereof by prospective borrowers. The supervisor may permit or require licensees to refer in their advertising to the fact that their business is under state supervision, subject to conditions imposed by him or her to prevent an erroneous impression as to the scope or degree of protections provided by this chapter.

(b) *Schedule of charges.*—Each licensee shall prominently display in each licensed place of business a full and accurate schedule of the rates of charge upon all classes of loans currently to be made by him or her.

§ 5–18–14. Conduct of other business in office of licensee; loan business confined to licensed offices; acceptance of liens on real estate as security for loans

(a) *Other business in same office.*—No licensee shall conduct the business of making loans under this chapter within any office, suite, room or place of business in which any other business is solicited or engaged in or in association or conjunction with any other business until three days' written notice of an intention so to do has been given the supervisor. Upon receipt of written notification, the supervisor may investigate the facts and, if he finds that the character of the licensee and the nature of the other business warrant belief that such conduct of business would conceal violation or evasion of this chapter or of regulations lawfully made hereunder, he shall enter an order directing the licensee to discontinue said other business. The order shall be entered in the manner specified in and subject to the provisions of subsection (c) of section 5–18–6.

(b) *Business confined to licensed office.*—No licensee shall conduct the business of making loans provided for by this chapter under any name or at any place of business within this state other than that stated in the license. Nothing in this section shall prevent the making of loans by mail nor prohibit accommodations to individual borrowers when necessitated by sickness or other emergency situations.

(c) *Liens on real estate.*—No licensee shall take a lien upon real estate as security for any loan made under this chapter, except such lien as is created by law through the entry or recording of a judgment.

§ 5–18–15. Interest rates, charges, and fees

(a) *Maximum rates of interest and charge.* Every licensee under this chapter may contract for and receive as interest on any loan of money less than one thousand dollars ($1,000) an amount at a rate not exceeding three percent a month on that part of the unpaid principal balance not in excess of two hundred dollars ($200), two percent a month on that part of the unpaid principal balance in excess of two hundred dollars ($200) but less than one thousand dollars ($1,000).

(b) *Account maintenance fee.* In addition to the maximum rate of interest and charges pursuant to subsection (a), a licensee may enter into a contract of loan under this chapter in which the borrower agrees to pay an account maintenance fee of not more than three dollars ($3) for each month of the scheduled period of repayment of the loan provided that the scheduled monthly payments are equal to or greater than thirty dollars ($30). Such account maintenance fee shall be determined at the date of the loan, but may not be prepaid. Such fee as so determined shall not bear interest and shall constitute a part of the finance charge.

(c) *Method of computing charges.* (1) Interest or charges under this chapter shall not be paid, deducted, discounted, or received in advance or compounded, but the rate of charge authorized by subsections (a) and (b) of this section may be precomputed as provided in subdivision (2) of this subsection. For the purpose of this section, one month shall be that period of time from any date in a month to a corresponding date in the next month and, if there is not a corresponding date, then to the next day of the next month, and a day shall be considered one thirtieth of a month when computation is made for a fraction of a month.

(2) When the loan contract requires repayment in substantially equal and consecutive monthly installments of principal and charges or interest combined, the charges or interest may be precomputed at the agreed monthly or periodic rate not in excess of that provided for in subsection (a) and (b) of this section on scheduled unpaid principal balances according to the terms of the contract and added to the principal of the loan. Every payment may be applied to the combined total of principal and precomputed charge until the contract is fully paid. The acceptance or payment of charges on loans made under the provisions of this subsection shall not be deemed to constitute payment, deduction or receipt thereof in advance nor compounding under subdivision (1) above.

(d) *Refunds.* (1) When any loan contract is paid in full by cash, a new loan, renewal, or otherwise one month or more before the final installment date, the licensee shall refund or credit the borrower with that portion of the total charges which shall be due the borrower as determined by schedules prepared under the rule of seventy-eighths or sum of the digits principle as follows: The amount of the refund or credit shall be as great a proportion of the total charges originally contracted for as the sum of the periodic time balances of the contract scheduled to follow the date of prepayment bears to the sum of all the periodic time balances of the contract, both sums to be determined according to the payment schedule originally contracted for.

(2) If the loan contract, with charges precomputed under subsections (a) and (b) of this section, is not prepaid in full but becomes partially prepaid in an amount equal to three or more installments, the licensee shall reduce the balance due by the amount that would be required to be refunded for prepayment in full on the date of the partial prepayment and compute charges as payments are made thereafter in the manner prescribed in subdivision (1) of subsection (c) of this section, or the licensee may with the consent of the borrower reschedule the remaining installments and precompute charges as prescribed in subdivision (2) of subsection (c) of this section.

(e) *Default or extension charges.* If the contract so provides, when a scheduled payment is in default or delinquent for 10 or more days, the licensee may charge and collect an additional late charge not to exceed the greater of ten dollars ($10) or five percent of the amount of the scheduled payment in default. Each of the late charges permitted under this subsection may be collected only once on any scheduled payment, regardless of the period during which the payment remains in default or is delinquent. It is the intent of this subsection that if the payment date of all wholly unpaid installments is deferred or extended one or more full months and the contract so provides, the licensee may charge and collect a deferment or default charge only on the installment which is delinquent at the date the contract is extended or deferred.

(f) *Rules and regulations.* In the addition to the general authority granted to him or her by subsection (a) of Section 5–18–12, the supervisor may make such rules and regulations as he or she may deem necessary or advisable to insure that rebates, default charges, and deferment charges are so computed, paid to or collected from borrowers that the total charges collected by licensees under this section are substantially equivalent to charges authorized to be collected by licensees under this section.

(g) *Recording fees.* The licensee may collect from the borrower the actual fees paid a public official or agency of the state for filing, recording, or releasing any instrument securing the loan.

(h) *Further charges; splitting of contracts.* No further or other charges shall be directly or indirectly contracted for or received by any licensee, including insurance premiums of any kind, except those specifically authorized by this chapter or by Chapter 8 of Title 8. No licensee shall divide into separate parts any contract made for the purpose of or with the effect of obtaining charges in excess of those authorized by this section. All balances due to a licensee from any person as a borrower, or as an endorser, guarantor or surety for any borrower or otherwise, shall be considered a part of any loan being made by a licensee to the person for the purpose of computing charges.

(i) *Installment payments; contract period.* No licensee shall enter into any contract of loan under this chapter in which the borrower agrees to make any scheduled repayment of the cash advance more than 25 calendar months from the date of making the contract of loan. Every loan contract shall require payment of the cash advance and charges in installments which shall be payable at approximately equal periodic intervals; except, that payment dates may be omitted to accommodate borrowers with seasonal incomes. No installment contracted for shall be substantially larger than any preceding installment.

(j) *Interest after due date of final installment.* Interest as provided in this section shall not accrue or be recovered or charged on any loan made under this chapter for any longer than six months after the due date of the final installment of principal or interest. After the expiration of said six-month period, interest may be charged at a rate not to exceed eight percent per annum.

(k) *Inducing borrower to become obligated under more than one contract.* No licensee shall induce or permit any person or any husband and wife, jointly or severally, to become obligated directly or contingently or both under more than one contract of loan at the same time for the purpose of obtaining a higher rate of charge than would otherwise be permitted by this section. It shall be unlawful for any licensee to evade or attempt to evade this section by inducing a customer to borrow from another loan company in which he or she has a pecuniary interest or with whom he or she has an arrangement for exchange of customers.

(*l*) *Liabilities of licensees making excess charges.* Any licensee making any charge in excess of the amount authorized herein, except as the result of a deliberate violation of or reckless disregard for this chapter, shall refund to the borrower the total amount of the actual economic damages which at the licensee's option may be done by payment to the borrower, or by reducing the amount of the borrower's principal obligation. If the borrower is entitled to a refund and the licensee refuses to refund within 60 days after written demand, including the filing of a legal action, the licensee shall forfeit, in addition to the actual economic damages his or her right to any finance charge. If the licensee has made an excess charge in deliberate violation of or in reckless disregard for this chapter, the licensee and the several members, officers, directors, agents, and employees thereof who shall have participated in a deliberate violation of or reckless disregard for this chapter, shall be guilty of a misdemeanor which, upon conviction, shall be punishable by a fine of not more than five hundred dollars ($500) and not less than one hundred dollars ($100) or by imprisonment of not more than six months, or by both fine and imprisonment in the direction of the court. The remedies provided herein shall be the remedy of the borrower under this chapter as the result of this violation. No action under this section may be brought more than 18 months after the due date of the last scheduled payment of the agreement pursuant to which the charge was made.

(m) *Alternative rates of charge.* (1) As an alternative to the interest rates and charges permitted to be charged by a licensee pursuant to subsections (a) and (b) of this section, on loans of less than one thousand dollars ($1,000), a licensee may charge an acquisition charge for making the loan in an amount not in excess of 10 percent of the amount of the principal, and an installment account handling charge in an amount no greater than the following:

a.   Twelve dollars ($12) per month on any loan of an amount of one hundred dollars ($100) or more up to and including the amount of three hundred dollars ($300).

b.   Fourteen dollars ($14) per month on any loan of an amount in excess of three hundred dollars ($300), but not more than four hundred dollars ($400).

c.   Sixteen dollars ($16) per month on any loan of an amount in excess of four hundred dollars ($400), but not more than five hundred dollars ($500).

d.   Seventeen dollars ($17) per month on any loan of an amount in excess of five hundred dollars ($500), but not more than eight hundred dollars ($800).

e.   Twenty dollars ($20) per month on any loan of an amount in excess of eight hundred dollars, but less than one thousand dollars ($1,000).

Provided, however, that the scheduled payments are in amounts equal to or greater than forty dollars ($40) per month, inclusive of the installment account handling charge. The acquisition charge and the installment account handling charge may be calculated for the term of the contract and added to the amount of the principal. The acceptance or payment of charges on loans made under this subsection shall not be deemed to constitute payment, deduction, or receipt thereof in advance nor compounding under this subsection.

(2) The maximum term of any loan made under this subsection is 12 months.

(3) Upon the prepayment in full of any loan under this subsection, the installment account handling charge is subject to the provisions of subsection (d), as it relates to refunds. The acquisition charge shall not be subject to refund.

(4) No insurance charge under Section 5–18–17, no interest surcharge under Section 8–8–14, nor any other charge of any nature whatsoever, is permitted for loans made pursuant to the rate structure of this subsection, except for acquisition charges and installment account handling charges as provided under this subsection, default charges under subsection (e), recording fees under subsection (g), bad check charges under Section 8–8–15, and assessed court costs.

(5) The loan charges allowed under this subsection may not be imposed on a loan to a borrower who has more than one loan outstanding with the licensee and upon which loan charges were imposed under this subsection.

(6) No licensee shall file a claim against a decedent borrower's estate for any unpaid indebtedness for a loan whose charges include an acquisition charge or an installment account handling charge under this subsection.

§ 5–18–15.1. Additional late charge

Notwithstanding the provisions of subsection (e) of Section 5–18–15, Code of Alabama 1975, for contracts entered into after June 7, 2007, the additional late charge a licensee licensed under this chapter [the Alabama Small Loan Act] may charge when a scheduled payment is in default or delinquent for 10 or more days is hereby increased from a charge not to exceed the greater of ten dollars ($10) or five percent of the scheduled payment in default to a charge not to exceed the greater of eighteen dollars ($18) or five percent of the scheduled payment in default.

§ 5–18–16. Duties of licensees as to making and payment of loans

(a) *Copy of contract or statement; receipts; payment in advance; release of obligation and security.*—Every licensee shall:

(1) At the time a loan is made deliver to the borrower or, if there are two or more borrowers, to one of them a copy of the loan contract, executed by the borrower, in the English language showing in clear and distinct terms:

a.   The name and address of the lender and one of the primary obligors on the loan.

b.   The date of the loan contract.

c.   Schedule of installments or description thereof.

d.   The cash advance.

e.   The face amount of the note evidencing the loan.

f.   The amount collected or paid for insurance, if any.

g.   The amount collected or paid for filing or other fees allowed by this chapter.

h.   The collateral or security for the loan.

(2) Give to the person making any cash payment on account of any loan a receipt at the time the payment is made which receipt need only show the total amount of the cash payment. No receipt shall be required in the case of payments made by the borrower's check or money order, and the use of a coupon book system shall be deemed in compliance with this section.

(3) Permit the payment to be made in advance in any amount on any contract of loan at any time during a licensee's regular business hours.

(4) Upon repayment of the loan in full, mark plainly every obligation and security signed by any obligor with the word "Paid" or "Cancelled," and release any mortgage, restore any pledge, and cancel and return any note and any assignment given to the licensee.

(b) *Confessions of judgment; incomplete instruments.*—No licensee shall:

(1) Take any confession of judgment or any power of attorney running to himself or herself or to any third person to confess judgment or to appear for the borrower in a judicial proceeding; nor

(2) Take any note or promise to pay that does not disclose the total amount to be repaid, a schedule of payments or a description thereof and the agreed rate or aggregate amount of charge, nor any instrument in which blanks are left to be filled in after execution.

(c) *Installments.*—Every loan contract shall provide for repayment of principal and charges at approximately equal periodic intervals of time, which shall be so arranged that no installment is substantially greater in amount than any preceding installment.

(d) *Confidential relationship or fiduciary duty not created by loan transaction.*—Absent other factors, a loan transaction does not create a confidential relationship between the borrower and the licensee nor does it give rise to or create a fiduciary duty on the part of the licensee.

§ 5–18–17. Insurance in connection with credit transaction

(a) With respect to any insurance written in connection with any credit transaction under this chapter, the creditor shall be subject to the same restrictions, prohibitions, powers and allowances as any creditor bank, retail establishment, sales finance company, licensee or any other creditor under section 5–19–20; and shall be subject to the same rates and regulations promulgated pursuant to that section.

(b) Insurance sold by a licensee or its agents shall be regulated by the Supervisor of the Bureau of Loans. All insurance shall be written by a company authorized to conduct business in the state of Alabama.

§ 5–18–18. Charges, rates, etc., as to certain loans

Licensees may charge to a borrower the rates permitted by this chapter only on principal loan balances less than one thousand dollars ($1,000). No licensee shall induce or permit any person, jointly or severally, to become obligated directly or contingently, or both, on more than one loan made pursuant to this chapter at the same time for the purpose of obtaining a higher finance charge than would otherwise be permitted by Section 5–18–15. If a licensee makes a loan of one thousand dollars ($1,000) or more, the charges authorized by this chapter shall not apply to any part of the loan. The rates on the entire amount of a loan of one thousand dollars ($1,000) or more shall be governed by the applicable provisions of Chapter 8 of Title 8 or Chapter 19 of this title.

The supervisor may suspend or revoke the license of any licensee who violates this section in the manner prescribed by Section 5–18–9, and the penalties provided for in subsection (l) of Section 5–18–15 shall apply to any person, firm or corporation violating this section.

§ 5–18–19. Collection of loans made outside state

Any loans made outside this state in accordance with the law applicable to such loan in the state in which the loan was made may be collected in this state.

§ 5–18–20. Review of orders, etc., of supervisor

In addition to any other remedy he may have, any licensee and any person considering himself aggrieved by any act or order of the supervisor under this chapter may, within 30 days from the entry of the order complained of, or within 60 days of the act complained of if there is no order, petition the circuit court of Montgomery county for review of such act or order; provided, that such petition shall be docketed, heard and tried in the same manner as other extraordinary writs issued by the court and a copy of the petition and order setting the same for hearing shall be served on the supervisor, giving him such notice of the time and place of the hearing as may be directed by the court.

§ 5–18–21.   Enforceability of provisions and agreements which violate chapter; liability of licensee for actual damage

Except where other specific remedies are provided in this chapter for violations, in which event those remedies shall apply, any provision of a loan contract which violates this chapter shall not be enforceable by the licensee to the extent, but only to the extent, of the violation, and the other remaining provisions and agreements shall be enforceable and shall not be void and shall not be affected by the violation. Except as set forth in subsection (*l*) of Section 5–18–15, any licensee who fails to comply with any requirement imposed under this chapter with respect to any person is liable to the person for the actual damage sustained by the person as the result of the failure.

§ 5–18–22.   Modification, amendment or repeal of chapter

This chapter or any part thereof may be modified, amended or repealed so as to effect a cancellation or alteration of any license or right of a licensee hereunder; provided, that such cancellation or alteration shall not impair or affect the obligation of any preexisting lawful contract between any licensee and any borrower.

§ 5–18–23.   Maintenance of listing of licensees doing business in state; public access to reports, etc.

(a) The supervisor shall cause to be kept on file in the bureau of loans, open to public inspection during business hours, an alphabetical listing of all licensees doing business in Alabama, and such list shall reveal the true ownership of the licensee companies. If the company is a corporation, the list shall indicate the name of the corporation, the address of the home office and the names and addresses of its officers and directors.

(b) Except as provided in subsection (a) of this section, all applications, reports and other papers and documents submitted by licensees to the supervisor or to the bureau shall be open to public inspection only upon approval of the supervisor, but the supervisor shall not deny any person access to such records when the disclosure thereof to such person is in the public interest.

§ 5–18–24.   Penalties for violation of provisions of chapter. Repealed.

CREDIT INSURANCE ACT

MODEL BILL TO PROVIDE FOR THE REGULATION OF CREDIT LIFE INSURANCE AND CREDIT ACCIDENT AND HEALTH INSURANCE

Promulgated by the National Association of Insurance Commissioners (1977)

Table of Sections

---

§ 1. Purpose

The purpose of this Act is to promote the public welfare by regulating credit life insurance and credit accident and health insurance. Nothing in this Act is intended to prohibit or discourage reasonable competition. The provisions of this Act shall be liberally construed.

§ 2. Scope and Definitions

A. Citation and Scope

(1) This Act may be cited as "The Model Act for the Regulation of Credit Life Insurance and Credit Accident and Health Insurance."

(2) All life insurance and all accident and health insurance in connection with loans or other credit transactions shall be subject to the provisions of this Act, except such insurance in connection with a loan or other credit transaction of more than ten years duration; nor shall insurance be

subject to the provisions of this Act where the issuance of such insurance is an isolated transaction on the part of the insurer not related to an agreement or a plan for insuring debtors of the creditor.

B. Definitions

For the purpose of this Act:

(1) "Credit life insurance" means insurance on the life of a debtor pursuant to or in connection with a specific loan or other credit transaction;

(2) "Credit accident and health insurance" means insurance on a debtor to provide indemnity for payments becoming due on a specific loan or other credit transaction while the debtor is disabled as defined in the policy;

(3) "Creditor" means the lender of money or vendor or lessor of goods, services, or property, rights or privileges, for which payment is arranged through a credit transaction, or any successor to the right, title or interest of any such lender, vendor, or lessor, and an affiliate, associate or subsidiary of any of them or any director, officer or employee of any of them or any other person in any way associated with any of them;

(4) "Debtor" means a borrower of money or a purchaser or lessee of goods, services, property, rights or privileges for which payment is arranged through a credit transaction;

(5) "Indebtedness" means the total amount payable by a debtor to a creditor in connection with a loan or other credit transaction;

(6) "Commissioner" means (Insurance Supervisory Authority of the State).

§ 3. Forms of Credit Life Insurance and Credit Accident and Health Insurance

Credit life insurance and credit accident and health insurance shall be issued only in the following forms:

A. Individual policies of life insurance issued to debtors on the term plan;

B. Individual policies of accident and health insurance issued to debtors on a term plan or disability benefit provisions in individual policies of credit life insurance;

C. Group policies of life insurance issued to creditors providing insurance upon the lives of debtors on the term plan;

D. Group policies of accident and health insurance issued to creditors on a term plan insuring debtors or disability benefit provisions in group credit life insurance policies to provide such coverage.

§ 4. Amount of Credit Life Insurance and Credit Accident and Health Insurance

A.   Credit Life Insurance

(1) The initial amount of credit life insurance shall not exceed the total amount repayable under the contract of indebtedness and, where an indebtedness is repayable in substantially equal installments, the amount of insurance shall at no time exceed the scheduled or actual amount of unpaid indebtedness, whichever is greater.

Note: If desired the following provisions may be added as subsections (2) and (3).

(2) Notwithstanding the provisions of the above paragraph, insurance on agricultural credit transaction commitments, not exceeding one year in duration may be written up to the amount of the loan commitment, on a non-decreasing or level term plan.

(3) Notwithstanding the provisions of paragraph A(1) of this or any other subsection, insurance on educational credit transaction commitments may be written for the amount of the portion of such commitment that has not been advanced by the creditor.

B.   Credit Accident and Health Insurance

The total amount of periodic indemnity payable by credit accident and health insurance in the event of disability, as defined in the policy, shall not exceed the aggregate of the periodic scheduled unpaid installments of the indebtedness; and the amount of each periodic indemnity payment shall not exceed the original indebtedness divided by the number of periodic installments.

§ 5. Term of Credit Life Insurance and Credit Accident and Health Insurance

The term of any credit life insurance or credit accident and health insurance shall, subject to acceptance by the insurer, commence on the date when the debtor becomes obligated to the creditor, except that, where a group policy provides coverage with respect to existing obligations, the insurance on a debtor with respect to such indebtedness shall commence on the effective date of the policy.   Where evidence of insurability is required and such evidence is furnished more than thirty (30) days after the date when the debtor becomes obligated to the creditor, the term of the insurance may commence on the date on which the insurance company determines the evidence to be satisfactory, and in such event there shall be an appropriate refund or adjustment of any charge to the debtor for insurance.   The term of such insurance shall not extend more than fifteen days beyond the scheduled maturity date of the indebtedness except when extended without additional cost to the debtor.   If the indebtedness is discharged due to renewal or refinancing prior to the scheduled maturity date, the insurance in force shall be terminated before any new insurance may be issued in connection with the renewed or refinanced indebtedness.

In all cases of termination prior to scheduled maturity, a refund shall be paid or credited as provided in Section 8.

§ 6. Provisions of Policies and Certificates of Insurance: Disclosure to Debtors

A. All credit life insurance and credit accident and health insurance shall be evidenced by an individual policy, or in the case of group insurance by a certificate of insurance, which individual policy or group certificate of insurance shall be delivered to the debtor.

B. Each individual policy or group certificate of credit life insurance, and/or credit accident and health insurance shall, in addition to other requirements of law, set forth the name and home office address of the insurer, the name or names of the debtor or in the case of a certificate under a group policy, the identity by name or otherwise of the debtor, the premium or amount of payment, if any, by the debtor separately for credit life insurance and credit accident and health insurance, a description of the coverage including the amount and term thereof, and any exceptions, limitations and restrictions, and shall state that the benefits shall be paid to the creditor to reduce or extinguish the unpaid indebtedness and, wherever the amount of insurance may exceed the unpaid indebtedness, that any such excess shall be payable to a beneficiary, other than the creditor, named by the debtor or to his estate.

C. Said individual policy or group certificate of insurance shall be delivered to the insured debtor at the time the indebtedness is incurred except as hereinafter provided.

D. If said individual policy or group certificate of insurance is not delivered to the debtor at the time the indebtedness is incurred, a copy of the application for such policy or a notice of proposed insurance, signed by the debtor and setting forth the name and home office address of the insurer, the name or names of the debtor, the premium or amount of payment by the debtor, if any, separately for credit life insurance and credit accident and health insurance, the amount, term and a brief description of the coverage provided, shall be delivered to the debtor at the time such indebtedness is incurred. The copy of the application for, or notice of proposed insurance, shall also refer exclusively to insurance coverage, and shall be separate and apart from the loan, sale or other credit statement of account, instrument or agreement, unless the information required by this subsection is prominently set forth therein. Upon acceptance of the insurance by the insurer and within thirty (30) days of the date upon which the indebtedness is incurred, the insurer shall cause the individual policy or group certificates of insurance to be delivered to the debtor. Said application or notice of proposed insurance shall state that upon acceptance by the insurer, the insurance shall become effective as provided in Section 5.

E. If the named insurer does not accept the risk, then and in such event the debtor shall receive a policy or certificate of insurance setting forth the name and home office address of the substituted insurer and the amount of the premium to be charged, and if the amount of premium is less than that set forth in the notice of proposed insurance an appropriate refund shall be made.

§ 7. Filing, Approval and Withdrawal of Forms

A. All policies, certificates of insurance, notices of proposed insurance, applications for insurance, endorsements and riders delivered or issued for delivery in this State and the schedules of premium rates pertaining thereto shall be filed with the Commissioner.

B. The Commissioner shall within thirty (30) days after the filing of any such policies, certificates of insurance, notices of proposed insurance, applications for insurance, endorsements and riders, disapprove any such form if the benefits provided therein are not reasonable in relation to the premium charge, or if it contains provisions which are unjust, unfair, inequitable, misleading, deceptive or encourage misrepresentation of the coverage, or are contrary to any provision of the Insurance Code or of any rule or regulation promulgated thereunder.

C. If the Commissioner notifies the insurer that the form is disapproved, it is unlawful thereafter for such insurer to issue or use such form. In such notice, the Commissioner shall specify the reason for his disapproval and state that a hearing will be granted within twenty (20) days after request in writing by the insurer. No such policy, certificate of insurance, notice of proposed insurance, nor any application, endorsement or rider, shall be issued or used until the expiration of thirty (30) days after it has been so filed, unless the Commissioner shall give his prior written approval thereto.

D. The Commissioner may, at any time after a hearing held not less than twenty (20) days after written notice to the insurer, withdraw his approval of any such form on any ground set forth in subsection B above. The written notice of such hearing shall state the reason for the proposed withdrawal.

E. It is not lawful for the insurer to issue such forms or use them after the effective date of such withdrawal.

F. If a group policy of credit life insurance or credit accident and health insurance

(i) has been delivered in this State before the effective date of this Act, or

(ii) has been or is delivered in another State before or after the effective date of this Act,

the insurer shall be required to file only the group certificate and notice of proposed insurance delivered or issued for delivery in this State as specified in subsections B and D of Section 6 of this Act and such forms shall be approved by the Commissioner if they conform with the requirements specified in said subsections and if the schedules of premium rates applicable to the insurance evidenced by such certificate or notice are not in excess of the insurer's schedules of premium rates filed with the Commissioner; provided, however, the premium rate in effect on existing group policies may be continued until the first policy anniversary date following the date this Act becomes operative as provided in Section 12.

G. Any order or final determination of the Commissioner under the provisions of this section shall be subject to judicial review.

§ 8. Premiums and Refunds

A. Any insurer may revise its schedules of premium rates from time to time, and shall file such revised schedules with the Commissioner. No insurer shall issue any credit life insurance policy or credit accident and health insurance policy for which the premium rate exceeds that determined by the schedules of such insurer as then on file with the Commissioner.

B. Each individual policy, or group certificate shall provide that in the event of termination of the insurance prior to the scheduled maturity date of the indebtedness, any refund of an amount paid by the debtor for insurance shall be paid or credited promptly to the person entitled thereto; provided, however, that the Commissioner shall prescribe a minimum refund and no refund which would be less than such minimum need be made. The formula to be used in computing such refund shall be filed with and approved by the Commissioner.

C. If a creditor requires a debtor to make any payment for credit life insurance or credit accident and health insurance and an individual policy or group certificate of insurance is not issued, the creditor shall immediately give written notice to such debtor and shall promptly make an appropriate credit to the account.

D. The amount charged to a debtor for any credit life or credit health and accident insurance shall not exceed the premiums charged by the insurer, as computed at the time the charge to the debtor is determined.

Note: Where a state prohibits payments for insurance by the debtor in connection with credit transactions, the following paragraph may be included.

E. Nothing in this Act shall be construed to authorize any payments for insurance now prohibited under any statute, or rule thereunder, governing credit transactions.

§ 9. Issuance of Policies

All policies of credit life insurance and credit accident and health insurance shall be delivered or issued for delivery in this state only by an insurer authorized to do an insurance business therein, and shall be issued only through holders of licenses or authorizations issued by the Commissioner.

§ 10.   Claims

A.   All claims shall be promptly reported to the insurer or its designated claim representative, and the insurer shall maintain adequate claim files. All claims shall be settled as soon as possible and in accordance with the terms of the insurance contract.

B.   All claims shall be paid either by draft drawn upon the insurer or by check of the insurer to the order of the claimant to whom payment of the claim is due pursuant to the policy provisions, or upon direction of such claimant to one specified.

C.   No plan or arrangement shall be used whereby any person, firm or corporation other than the insurer or its designated claim representative shall be authorized to settle or adjust claims. The creditor shall not be designated as claim representative for the insurer in adjusting claims; provided, that a group policyholder may, by arrangement with the group insurer, draw drafts or checks in payment of claims due to the group policyholder subject to audit and review by the insurer.

§ 11.   Existing Insurance—Choice of Insurer

When credit life insurance or credit accident and health insurance is required as additional security for any indebtedness, the debtor shall, upon request to the creditor, have the option of furnishing the required amount of insurance through existing policies of insurance owned or controlled by him or of procuring and furnishing the required coverage through any insurer authorized to transact an insurance business within this state.

§ 12.   Enforcement

The Commissioner may, after notice and hearing, issue such rules and regulations as he deems appropriate for the supervision of this Act. Whenever the Commissioner finds that there has been a violation of this Act or any rules or regulations issued pursuant thereto, and after written notice thereof and hearing given to the insurer or other person authorized or licensed by the Commissioner, he shall set forth the details of his findings together with an order for compliance by a specified date. Such order shall be binding on the insurer and other person authorized or licensed by the Commissioner on the date specified unless sooner withdrawn by the Commissioner or a stay thereof has been ordered by a court of competent jurisdiction. The provisions of Sections 5, 6, 7 and 8 of this Act shall not be operative until ninety (90) days after the effective date of this Act, and the Commissioner in his discretion may extend by not more than an additional ninety (90) days the initial period within which the provisions of said sections shall not be operative.

§ 13.   Judicial Review

Any party to the proceeding affected by an order of the Commissioner shall be entitled to judicial review by following the procedure set forth in (insert applicable section).

§ 14. Penalties

In addition to any other penalty provided by law, any person, firm or corporation which violates an order of the Commissioner after it has become final, and while such order is in effect, shall, upon proof thereof to the satisfaction of the court, forfeit and pay to the State of (insert state) a sum not to exceed $250.00 which may be recovered in a civil action, except that if such violation is found to be willful, the amount of such penalty shall be a sum not to exceed $1,000.00. The Commissioner, in his discretion, may revoke or suspend the license or certificate of authority of the person, firm or corporation guilty of such violation. Such order for suspension or revocation shall be upon notice and hearing, and shall be subject to judicial review as provided in Section 13 of this Act.

§ 15. Separability Provision

If any provision of this Act, or the application of such provision to any person or circumstances, shall be held invalid, the remainder of the Act, and the application of such provision to any person or circumstances other than those as to which it is held invalid, shall not be affected thereby.

UNIFORM COMMERCIAL CODE*

Table of Sections

ARTICLE 1. GENERAL PROVISIONS [1978 Text]

PART 1. SHORT TITLE, CONSTRUCTION, APPLICATION AND SUBJECT MATTER OF THE ACT

PART 2. GENERAL DEFINITIONS AND PRINCIPLES OF INTERPRETATION

ARTICLE 1. GENERAL PROVISIONS [2002 Text]

PART 1. GENERAL PROVISIONS

840

Sec.

PART 3. GENERAL OBLIGATION AND CONSTRUCTION OF CONTRACT

843

853

ARTICLE 10.   EFFECTIVE DATE AND REPEALER [Omitted]

ARTICLE 11.   EFFECTIVE DATE AND TRANSITION PROVISIONS [Omitted]

ARTICLE 1.   GENERAL PROVISIONS [1978 Text]

PART 1.   SHORT TITLE, CONSTRUCTION, APPLICATION AND SUBJECT MATTER OF THE ACT

§ 1–101.   Short Title

This Act shall be known and may be cited as Uniform Commercial Code.

§ 1–102.   Purposes; Rules of Construction; Variation by Agreement

(1) This Act shall be liberally construed and applied to promote its underlying purposes and policies.

(2) Underlying purposes and policies of this Act are

(a) to simplify, clarify and modernize the law governing commercial transactions;

(b) to permit the continued expansion of commercial practices through custom, usage and agreement of the parties;

(c) to make uniform the law among the various jurisdictions.

(3) The effect of provisions of this Act may be varied by agreement, except as otherwise provided in this Act and except that the obligations of good faith, diligence, reasonableness and care prescribed by this Act may not be disclaimed by agreement but the parties may by agreement determine the standards by which the performance of such obligations is to be measured if such standards are not manifestly unreasonable.

(4) The presence in certain provisions of this Act of the words "unless otherwise agreed" or words of similar import does not imply that the effect of other provisions may not be varied by agreement under subsection (3).

(5) In this Act unless the context otherwise requires

(a) words in the singular number include the plural, and in the plural include the singular;

(b) words of the masculine gender include the feminine and the neuter, and when the sense so indicates words of the neuter gender may refer to any gender.

§ 1–103. Supplementary General Principles of Law Applicable

Unless displaced by the particular provisions of this Act, the principles of law and equity, including the law merchant and the law relative to capacity to contract, principal and agent, estoppel, fraud, misrepresentation, duress, coercion, mistake, bankruptcy, or other validating or invalidating cause shall supplement its provisions.

§ 1–104. Construction Against Implicit Repeal

This Act being a general act intended as a unified coverage of its subject matter, no part of it shall be deemed to be impliedly repealed by subsequent legislation if such construction can reasonably be avoided.

§ 1–105. Territorial Application of the Act; Parties' Power to Choose Applicable Law

(1) Except as provided hereafter in this section, when a transaction bears a reasonable relation to this state and also to another state or nation the parties may agree that the law either of this state or of such other state or nation shall govern their rights and duties. Failing such agreement this Act applies to transactions bearing an appropriate relation to this state.

.   .   .

§ 1–106. Remedies to Be Liberally Administered

(1) The remedies provided by this Act shall be liberally administered to the end that the aggrieved party may be put in as good a position as if the other party had fully performed but neither consequential or special nor penal damages may be had except as specifically provided in this Act or by other rule of law.

(2) Any right or obligation declared by this Act is enforceable by action unless the provision declaring it specifies a different and limited effect.

PART 2. GENERAL DEFINITIONS AND PRINCIPLES OF INTERPRETATION

§ 1–201. General Definitions

Subject to additional definitions contained in the subsequent Articles of this Act which are applicable to specific Articles or Parts thereof, and unless the context otherwise requires, in this Act:

(1) "Action" in the sense of a judicial proceeding includes recoupment, counterclaim, set-off, suit in equity and any other proceedings in which rights are determined.

(2) "Aggrieved party" means a party entitled to resort to a remedy.

(3) "Agreement" means the bargain of the parties in fact as found in their language or by implication from other circumstances including course of dealing or usage of trade or course of performance as provided in this Act (Sections 1–205 and 2–208). Whether an agreement has legal consequences is determined by the provisions of this Act, if applicable; otherwise by the law of contracts (Section 1–103). (Compare "Contract.")

(4) "Bank" means any person engaged in the business of banking.

(5) "Bearer" means the person in possession of an instrument, document of title, or certificated security payable to bearer or indorsed in blank.

(6) "Bill of lading" means a document evidencing the receipt of goods for shipment issued by a person engaged in the business of transporting or forwarding goods, and includes an airbill. "Airbill" means a document serving for air transportation as a bill of lading does for marine or rail transportation, and includes an air consignment note or air waybill.

(7) "Branch" includes a separately incorporated foreign branch of a bank.

(8) "Burden of establishing" a fact means the burden of persuading the triers of fact that the existence of the fact is more probable than its non-existence.

(9) "Buyer in ordinary course of business" means a person who in good faith and without knowledge that the sale to him is in violation of the ownership rights or security interest of a third party in the goods buys in ordinary course from a person in the business of selling goods of that kind

but does not include a pawnbroker. All persons who sell minerals or the like (including oil and gas) at wellhead or minehead shall be deemed to be persons in the business of selling goods of that kind. "Buying" may be for cash or by exchange of other property or on secured or unsecured credit and includes receiving goods or documents of title under a pre-existing contract for sale but does not include a transfer in bulk or as security for or in total or partial satisfaction of a money debt.

(10) "Conspicuous": A term or clause is conspicuous when it is so written that a reasonable person against whom it is to operate ought to have noticed it. A printed heading in capitals (as: NON-NEGOTIABLE BILL OF LADING) is conspicuous. Language in the body of a form is "conspicuous" if it is in larger or other contrasting type or color. But in a telegram any stated term is "conspicuous." Whether a term or clause is "conspicuous" or not is for decision by the court.

(11) "Contract" means the total legal obligation which results from the parties' agreement as affected by this Act and any other applicable rules of law. (Compare "Agreement.")

(12) "Creditor" includes a general creditor, a secured creditor, a lien creditor and any representative of creditors, including an assignee for the benefit of creditors, a trustee in bankruptcy, a receiver in equity and an executor or administrator of an insolvent debtor's or assignor's estate.

(13) "Defendant" includes a person in the position of defendant in a cross-action or counterclaim.

(14) "Delivery" with respect to instruments, documents of title, chattel paper, or certificated securities means voluntary transfer of possession.

(15) "Document of title" includes bill of lading, dock warrant, dock receipt, warehouse receipt or order for the delivery of goods, and also any other document which in the regular course of business or financing is treated as adequately evidencing that the person in possession of it is entitled to receive, hold and dispose of the document and the goods it covers. To be a document of title a document must purport to be issued by or addressed to a bailee and purport to cover goods in the bailee's possession which are either identified or are fungible portions of an identified mass.

(16) "Fault" means wrongful act, omission or breach.

(17) "Fungible" with respect to goods or securities means goods or securities of which any unit is, by nature or usage of trade, the equivalent of any other like unit. Goods which are not fungible shall be deemed fungible for the purposes of this Act to the extent that under a particular agreement or document unlike units are treated as equivalents.

(18) "Genuine" means free of forgery or counterfeiting.

(19) "Good faith" means honesty in fact in the conduct or transaction concerned.

857

(20) "Holder," with respect to a negotiable instrument, means the person in possession if the instrument is payable to bearer or, in the case of an instrument payable to an identified person, if the identified person is in possession. "Holder" with respect to a document of title means the person in possession if the goods are deliverable to bearer or to the order of the person in possession.

(21) To "honor" is to pay or to accept and pay, or where a credit so engages to purchase or discount a draft complying with the terms of the credit.

(22) "Insolvency proceedings" includes any assignment for the benefit of creditors or other proceedings intended to liquidate or rehabilitate the estate of the person involved.

(23) A person is "insolvent" who either has ceased to pay his debts in the ordinary course of business or cannot pay his debts as they become due or is insolvent within the meaning of the federal bankruptcy law.

(24) "Money" means a medium of exchange authorized or adopted by a domestic or foreign government as a part of its currency.

(25) A person has "notice" of a fact when

(a) he has actual knowledge of it; or

(b) he has received a notice or notification of it; or

(c) from all the facts and circumstances known to him at the time in question he has reason to know that it exists.

A person "knows" or has "knowledge" of a fact when he has actual knowledge of it. "Discover" or "learn" or a word or phrase of similar import refers to knowledge rather than to reason to know. The time and circumstances under which a notice or notification may cease to be effective are not determined by this Act.

(26) A person "notifies" or "gives" a notice or notification to another by taking such steps as may be reasonably required to inform the other in ordinary course whether or not such other actually comes to know of it. A person "receives" a notice or notification when

(a) it comes to his attention; or

(b) it is duly delivered at the place of business through which the contract was made or at any other place held out by him as the place for receipt of such communications.

(27) Notice, knowledge or a notice or notification received by an organization is effective for a particular transaction from the time when it is brought to the attention of the individual conducting that transaction, and in any event from the time when it would have been brought to his attention if the organization had exercised due diligence. An organization exercises due diligence if it maintains reasonable routines for communicating significant information to the person conducting the transaction and there is reasonable compliance with the routines. Due diligence does not

require an individual acting for the organization to communicate information unless such communication is part of his regular duties or unless he has reason to know of the transaction and that the transaction would be materially affected by the information.

(28) "Organization" includes a corporation, government or governmental subdivision or agency, business trust, estate, trust, partnership or association, two or more persons having a joint or common interest, or any other legal or commercial entity.

(29) "Party," as distinct from "third party", means a person who has engaged in a transaction or made an agreement within this Act.

(30) "Person" includes an individual or an organization (See Section 1-102).

(31) "Presumption" or "presumed" means that the trier of fact must find the existence of the fact presumed unless and until evidence is introduced which would support a finding of its non-existence.

(32) "Purchase" includes taking by sale, discount, negotiation, mortgage, pledge, lien, issue or re-issue, gift or any other voluntary transaction creating an interest in property.

(33) "Purchaser" means a person who takes by purchase.

(34) "Remedy" means any remedial right to which an aggrieved party is entitled with or without resort to a tribunal.

(35) "Representative" includes an agent, an officer of a corporation or association, and a trustee, executor or administrator of an estate, or any other person empowered to act for another.

(36) "Rights" includes remedies.

(37) [1978 version] "Security interest" means an interest in personal property or fixtures which secures payment or performance of an obligation. The retention or reservation of title by a seller of goods notwithstanding shipment or delivery to the buyer (Section 2-401) is limited in effect to a reservation of a "security interest." The term also includes any interest of a buyer of accounts or chattel paper which is subject to Article 9. The special property interest of a buyer of goods on identification of such goods to a contract for sale under Section 2-401 is not a "security interest," but a buyer may also acquire a "security interest" by complying with Article 9. Unless a lease or consignment is intended as security, reservation of title thereunder is not a "security interest," but a consignment is in any event subject to the provisions on consignment sales (Section 2-326). Whether a lease is intended as security is to be determined by the facts of each case; however, (a) the inclusion of an option to purchase does not of itself make the lease one intended for security, and (b) an agreement that upon compliance with the terms of the lease the lessee shall become or has the option to become the owner of the property for no additional consideration or for a nominal consideration does make the lease one intended for security.

(37) [1987 version] "Security interest" means an interest in personal property or fixtures which secures payment or performance of an obligation. The retention or reservation of title by a seller of goods notwithstanding shipment or delivery to the buyer (Section 2–401) is limited in effect to a reservation of a "security interest." The term also includes any interest of a buyer of accounts or chattel paper which is subject to Article 9. The special property interest of a buyer of goods on identification of those goods to a contract for sale under Section 2–401 is not a "security interest," but a buyer may also acquire a "security interest" by complying with Article 9. Unless a consignment is intended as security, reservation of title thereunder is not a "security interest," but a consignment in any event is subject to the provisions on consignment sales (Section 2–326).

Whether a transaction creates a lease or security interest is determined by the facts of each case; however, a transaction creates a security interest if the consideration the lessee is to pay the lessor for the right to possession and use of the goods is an obligation for the term of the lease not subject to termination by the lessee, and

(a) the original term of the lease is equal to or greater than the remaining economic life of the goods,

(b) the lessee is bound to renew the lease for the remaining economic life of the goods or is bound to become the owner of the goods,

(c) the lessee has an option to renew the lease for the remaining economic life of the goods for no additional consideration or nominal additional consideration upon compliance with the lease agreement, or

(d) the lessee has an option to become the owner of the goods for no additional consideration or nominal additional consideration upon compliance with the lease agreement.

A transaction does not create a security interest merely because it provides that

(a) the present value of the consideration the lessee is obligated to pay the lessor for the right to possession and use of the goods is substantially equal to or is greater than the fair market value of the goods at the time the lease is entered into,

(b) the lessee assumes risk of loss of the goods, or agrees to pay taxes, insurance, filing, recording, or registration fees, or service or maintenance costs with respect to the goods,

(c) the lessee has an option to renew the lease or to become the owner of the goods,

(d) the lessee has an option to renew the lease for a fixed rent that is equal to or greater than the reasonably predictable fair market rent for the use of the goods for the term of the renewal at the time the option is to be performed, or

(e) the lessee has an option to become the owner of the goods for a fixed price that is equal to or greater than the reasonably predictable fair market value of the goods at the time the option is to be performed.

For purposes of this subsection (37):

(x) Additional consideration is not nominal if (i) when the option to renew the lease is granted to the lessee the rent is stated to be the fair market rent for the use of the goods for the term of the renewal determined at the time the option is to be performed, or (ii) when the option to become the owner of the goods is granted to the lessee the price is stated to be the fair market value of the goods determined at the time the option is to be performed. Additional consideration is nominal if it is less than the lessee's reasonably predictable cost of performing under the lease agreement if the option is not exercised;

(y) "Reasonably predictable" and "remaining economic life of the goods" are to be determined with reference to the facts and circumstances at the time the transaction is entered into; and

(z) "Present value" means the amount as of a date certain of one or more sums payable in the future, discounted to the date certain. The discount is determined by the interest rate specified by the parties if the rate is not manifestly unreasonable at the time the transaction is entered into; otherwise, the discount is determined by a commercially reasonable rate that takes into account the facts and circumstances of each case at the time the transaction was entered into.

(38) "Send" in connection with any writing or notice means to deposit in the mail or deliver for transmission by any other usual means of communication with postage or cost of transmission provided for and properly addressed and in the case of an instrument to an address specified thereon or otherwise agreed, or if there be none to any address reasonable under the circumstances. The receipt of any writing or notice within the time at which it would have arrived if properly sent has the effect of a proper sending.

(39) "Signed" includes any symbol executed or adopted by a party with present intention to authenticate a writing.

(40) "Surety" includes guarantor.

(41) "Telegram" includes a message transmitted by radio, teletype, cable, any mechanical method of transmission, or the like.

(42) "Term" means that portion of an agreement which relates to a particular matter.

(43) "Unauthorized" signature or indorsement means one made without actual, implied or apparent authority and includes a forgery.

(44) "Value." Except as otherwise provided with respect to negotiable instruments and bank collections (Sections 3–303, 4–208 and 4–209) a person gives "value" for rights if he acquires them

(a) in return for a binding commitment to extend credit or for the extension of immediately available credit whether or not drawn upon and whether or not a chargeback is provided for in the event of difficulties in collection; or

(b) as security for or in total or partial satisfaction of a pre-existing claim; or

(c) by accepting delivery pursuant to a pre-existing contract for purchase; or

(d) generally, in return for any consideration sufficient to support a simple contract.

(45) "Warehouse receipt" means a receipt issued by a person engaged in the business of storing goods for hire.

(46) "Written" or "writing" includes printing, typewriting or any other intentional reduction to tangible form.

§ 1-203. Obligation of Good Faith

Every contract or duty within this Act imposes an obligation of good faith in its performance or enforcement.

Official Comment

Purposes:

This section sets forth a basic principle running throughout this Act. The principle involved is that in commercial transactions good faith is required in the performance and enforcement of all agreements or duties. Particular applications of this general principle appear in specific provisions of the Act such as the option to accelerate at will (Section 1–208), the right to cure a defective delivery of goods (Section 2–508), the duty of a merchant buyer who has rejected goods to effect salvage operations (Section 2–603), substituted performance (Section 2–614), and failure of presupposed conditions (Section 2–615). The concept, however, is broader than any of these illustrations and applies generally, as stated in this section, to the performance or enforcement of every contract or duty within this Act. It is further implemented by Section 1–205 on course of dealing and usage of trade. This section does not support an independent cause of action for failure to perform or enforce in good faith. Rather, this section means that a failure to perform or enforce, in good faith, a specific duty or obligation under the contract, constitutes a breach of that contract or makes unavailable, under the particular circumstances, a remedial right or power. This distinction makes it clear that the doctrine or good faith merely directs a court towards interpreting contracts within the commercial context in which they are created, performed, and enforced, and does not create a separate duty of fairness and reasonableness which can be independently breached. . . .

It is to be noted that under the Sales Article definition of good faith (Section 2–103), contracts made by a merchant have incorporated in them the explicit standard not only of honesty in fact (Section 1–201), but also of observance by the merchant of reasonable commercial standards of fair dealing in the trade.

§ 1–205. Course of Dealing and Usage of Trade

(1) A course of dealing is a sequence of previous conduct between the parties to a particular transaction which is fairly to be regarded as establishing a common basis of understanding for interpreting their expressions and other conduct.

(2) A usage of trade is any practice or method of dealing having such regularity of observance in a place, vocation or trade as to justify an expectation that it will be observed with respect to the transaction in question. The existence and scope of such a usage are to be proved as facts. If it is established that such a usage is embodied in a written trade code or similar writing the interpretation of the writing is for the court.

(3) A course of dealing between parties and any usage of trade in the vocation or trade in which they are engaged or of which they are or should be aware give particular meaning to and supplement or qualify terms of an agreement.

(4) The express terms of an agreement and an applicable course of dealing or usage of trade shall be construed wherever reasonable as consistent with each other; but when such construction is unreasonable express terms control both course of dealing and usage of trade and course of dealing controls usage of trade.

(5) An applicable usage of trade in the place where any part of performance is to occur shall be used in interpreting the agreement as to that part of the performance.

(6) Evidence of a relevant usage of trade offered by one party is not admissible unless and until he has given the other party such notice as the court finds sufficient to prevent unfair surprise to the latter.

§ 1–207. Performance or Acceptance Under Reservation of Rights

(1) A party who with explicit reservation of rights performs or promises performance or assents to performance in a manner demanded or offered by the other party does not thereby prejudice the rights reserved. Such words as "without prejudice," "under protest" or the like are sufficient.

(2) Subsection (1) does not apply to an accord and satisfaction.

§ 1–208. Option to Accelerate at Will

A term providing that one party or his successor in interest may accelerate payment or performance or require collateral or additional collateral "at will" or "when he deems himself insecure" or in words of similar import shall be construed to mean that he shall have power to do so only if he in good faith believes that the prospect of payment or performance is impaired. The burden of establishing lack of good faith is on the party against whom the power has been exercised.

Official Comment

Purposes:

The increased use of acceleration clauses either in the case of sales on credit or in time paper or in security transactions has led to some confusion in the cases as to the effect to be given to a clause which seemingly grants the power of an acceleration at the whim and caprice of one party. This Section is intended to make clear that despite language which can be so construed and which further might be held to make the agreement void as against public policy or to make the contract illusory or too indefinite for enforcement, the clause means that the option is to be exercised only in the good faith belief that the prospect of payment or performance is impaired.

Obviously this section has no application to demand instruments or obligations whose very nature permits call at any time with or without reason. This section applies only to an agreement or to paper which in the first instance is payable at a future date.

ARTICLE 1. GENERAL PROVISIONS [2002 Text]

PART 1. GENERAL PROVISIONS

§ 1–101. Short Titles

(a) This [Act] may be cited as the Uniform Commercial Code.

(b) This article may be cited as Uniform Commercial Code–General Provisions.

§ 1–102. Scope of Article

This article applies to a transaction to the extent that it is governed by another article of [the Uniform Commercial Code].

§ 1–103. Construction of [Uniform Commercial Code] to Promote its Purposes and Policies; Applicability of Supplemental Principles of Law

(a) [The Uniform Commercial Code] must be liberally construed and applied to promote its underlying purposes and policies, which are:

  (1) to simplify, clarify, and modernize the law governing commercial transactions;

  (2) to permit the continued expansion of commercial practices through custom, usage, and agreement of the parties; and

  (3) to make uniform the law among the various jurisdictions.

(b) Unless displaced by the particular provisions of [the Uniform Commercial Code], the principles of law and equity, including the law merchant and the law relative to capacity to contract, principal and agent, estoppel, fraud, misrepresentation, duress, coercion, mistake, bankruptcy, and other validating or invalidating cause supplement its provisions.

Official Comment

Source: Former Section 1–102(1)–(2); Former Section 1–103.

Changes from former law: This section is derived from subsections (1) and (2) of former Section 1–102 and from former Section 1–103. Subsection (a) of this section combines subsections (1) and (2) of former Section 1–102. Except for changing the form of reference to the Uniform Commercial Code and minor stylistic changes, its language is the same as subsections (1) and (2) of former Section 1–102. Except for changing the form of reference to the Uniform Commercial Code and minor stylistic changes, subsection (b) of this section is identical to former Section 1–103. The provisions have been combined in this section to reflect the interrelationship between them.

1. The Uniform Commercial Code is drawn to provide flexibility so that, since it is intended to be a semi-permanent and infrequently-amended piece of legislation, it will provide its own machinery for expansion of commercial practices. It is intended to make it possible for the law embodied in the Uniform Commercial Code to be applied by the courts in the light of unforeseen and new circumstances and practices. The proper construction of the Uniform Commercial Code requires, of course, that its interpretation and application be limited to its reason.

Even prior to the enactment of the Uniform Commercial Code, courts were careful to keep broad acts from being hampered in their effects by later acts of limited scope. See *Pacific Wool Growers v. Draper & Co.*, 158 Or. 1, 73 P.2d 1391 (1937), and compare Section 1–104. The courts have often recognized that the policies embodied in an act are applicable in reason to subject-matter that was not expressly included in the language of the act, *Commercial Nat. Bank of New Orleans v. Canal–Louisiana Bank & Trust Co.*, 239 U.S. 520, 36 S.Ct. 194, 60 L.Ed. 417 (1916) (bona fide purchase policy of Uniform Warehouse Receipts Act extended to case not covered but of equivalent nature), and did the same where reason and policy so required, even where the subject-matter had been intentionally excluded from the act in general. *Agar v. Orda*, 264 N.Y. 248, 190 N.E. 479 (1934) (Uniform Sales Act change in seller's remedies applied to contract for sale of choses in action even though the general coverage of that Act was intentionally limited to goods "other than things in action.") They implemented a statutory policy with liberal and useful remedies not provided in the statutory text. They disregarded a statutory limitation of remedy where the reason of the limitation did not apply. *Fiterman v. J. N. Johnson & Co.*, 156 Minn. 201, 194 N.W. 399 (1923) (requirement of return of the goods as a condition to rescission for breach of warranty; also, partial rescission allowed). Nothing in the Uniform Commercial Code stands in the way of the continuance of such action by the courts.

The Uniform Commercial Code should be construed in accordance with its underlying purposes and policies. The text of each section should be read in the light of the purpose and policy of the rule or principle in question, as also of the Uniform Commercial Code as a whole, and the application of the language should be construed narrowly or broadly, as the case may be, in conformity with the purposes and policies involved.

2. *Applicability of supplemental principles of law.* Subsection (b) states the basic relationship of the Uniform Commercial Code to supplemental bodies of law. The Uniform Commercial Code was drafted against the backdrop of existing bodies of law, including the common law and equity, and relies on those bodies of law to supplement it provisions in many important ways. At the same time, the Uniform Commercial Code is the primary source of commercial law rules in areas that it governs, and its rules represent choices made by its drafters and the enacting legislatures about the appropriate policies to be furthered in the transactions it covers. Therefore, while principles of common law and equity may *supplement* provisions of the Uniform Commercial Code, they may not be used to *supplant* its provisions, or the purposes and policies those provisions reflect, unless a specific provision of the Uniform Commercial Code provides otherwise. In the absence of such a provision, the Uniform Commercial Code preempts principles of common law and equity that are inconsistent with either its provisions or its purposes and policies.

The language of subsection (b) is intended to reflect both the concept of supplementation and the concept of preemption. Some courts, however, had difficulty in applying the identical language of former Section 1–103 to determine when other law appropriately may be applied to supplement the Uniform Commercial Code, and when that law has been displaced by the Code. Some decisions applied other law in situations in which that application, while not inconsistent with the text of any particular provision of the Uniform Commercial Code, clearly was inconsistent with the underlying purposes and policies reflected in the relevant provisions of the Code. *See, e.g., Sheerbonnet, Ltd. v. American Express Bank, Ltd.,* 951 F. Supp. 403 (S.D.N.Y. 1995). In part, this difficulty arose from Comment 1 to former Section 1–103, which stated that "this section indicates the continued applicability to commercial contracts of all supplemental bodies of law except insofar as they are explicitly displaced by this Act." The "explicitly displaced" language of that Comment did not accurately reflect the proper scope of Uniform Commercial Code preemption, which extends to displacement of other law that is inconsistent with the purposes and policies of the Uniform Commercial Code, as well as with its text.

3. *Application of subsection (b) to statutes.* The primary focus of Section 1–103 is on the relationship between the Uniform Commercial Code and principles of common law and equity as developed by the courts. State law, however, increasingly is statutory. Not only are there a growing number of state statutes addressing specific issues that come within the scope of the Uniform Com-

mercial Code, but in some States many general principles of common law and equity have been codified. When the other law relating to a matter within the scope of the Uniform Commercial Code is a statute, the principles of subsection (b) remain relevant to the court's analysis of the relationship between that statute and the Uniform Commercial Code, but other principles of statutory interpretation that specifically address the interrelationship between statutes will be relevant as well. In some situations, the principles of subsection (b) still will be determinative. For example, the mere fact that an equitable principle is stated in statutory form rather than in judicial decisions should not change the court's analysis of whether the principle can be used to supplement the Uniform Commercial Code–under subsection (b), equitable principles may supplement provisions of the Uniform Commercial Code only if they are consistent with the purposes and policies of the Uniform Commercial Code as well as its text. In other situations, however, other interpretive principles addressing the interrelationship between statutes may lead the court to conclude that the other statute is controlling, even though it conflicts with the Uniform Commercial Code. This, for example, would be the result in a situation where the other statute was specifically intended to provide additional protection to a class of individuals engaging in transactions covered by the Uniform Commercial Code.

4. *Listing not exclusive.* The list of sources of supplemental law in subsection (b) is intended to be merely illustrative of the other law that may supplement the Uniform Commercial Code, and is not exclusive. No listing could be exhaustive. Further, the fact that a particular section of the Uniform Commercial Code makes express reference to other law is not intended to suggest the negation of the general application of the principles of subsection (b). Note also that the word "bankruptcy" in subsection (b), continuing the use of that word from former Section 1–103, should be understood not as a specific reference to federal bankruptcy law but, rather as a reference to general principles of insolvency, whether under federal or state law.

§ 1–104. Construction Against Implied Repeal

[The Uniform Commercial Code] being a general act intended as a unified coverage of its subject matter, no part of it shall be deemed to be impliedly repealed by subsequent legislation if such construction can reasonably be avoided.

§ 1–105. Severability

If any provision or clause of [the Uniform Commercial Code] or its application to any person or circumstance is held invalid, the invalidity does not affect other provisions or applications of [the Uniform Commercial Code] which can be given effect without the invalid provision or application, and to this end the provisions of [the Uniform Commercial Code] are severable.

PART 2.   GENERAL DEFINITIONS AND
PRINCIPLES OF INTERPRETATION

§ 1–201.   General Definitions

(a) Unless the context otherwise requires, words or phrases defined in this section, or in the additional definitions contained in other articles of [the Uniform Commercial Code] that apply to particular articles or parts thereof, have the meanings stated.

(b) Subject to definitions contained in other articles of [the Uniform Commercial Code] that apply to particular articles or parts thereof:

(1) "Action," in the sense of a judicial proceeding, includes recoupment, counterclaim, set-off, suit in equity, and any other proceeding in which rights are determined.

(2) "Aggrieved party" means a party entitled to pursue a remedy.

(3) "Agreement," as distinguished from "contract," means the bargain of the parties in fact, as found in their language or inferred from other circumstances, including course of performance, course of dealing, or usage of trade as provided in Section 1–303.

(4) "Bank" means a person engaged in the business of banking and includes a savings bank, savings and loan association, credit union, and trust company.

(5) "Bearer" means a person in possession of a negotiable instrument, document of title, or certificated security that is payable to bearer or indorsed in blank.

(6) "Bill of lading" means a document evidencing the receipt of goods for shipment issued by a person engaged in the business of transporting or forwarding goods.

(7) "Branch" includes a separately incorporated foreign branch of a bank.

(8) "Burden of establishing" a fact means the burden of persuading the trier of fact that the existence of the fact is more probable than its nonexistence.

(9) "Buyer in ordinary course of business" means a person that buys goods in good faith, without knowledge that the sale violates the rights of another person in the goods, and in the ordinary course from a person, other than a pawnbroker, in the business of selling goods of that kind. A person buys goods in the ordinary course if the sale to the person comports with the usual or customary practices in the kind of business in which the seller is engaged or with the seller's own usual or customary practices. A person that sells oil, gas, or other minerals at the wellhead or minehead is a person in the business of selling goods of that kind. A buyer in ordinary course of business may buy for cash, by

exchange of other property, or on secured or unsecured credit, and may acquire goods or documents of title under a preexisting contract for sale. Only a buyer that takes possession of the goods or has a right to recover the goods from the seller under Article 2 may be a buyer in ordinary course of business. "Buyer in ordinary course of business" does not include a person that acquires goods in a transfer in bulk or as security for or in total or partial satisfaction of a money debt.

(10) "Conspicuous," with reference to a term, means so written, displayed, or presented that a reasonable person against which it is to operate ought to have noticed it. Whether a term is "conspicuous" or not is a decision for the court. Conspicuous terms include the following:

 (A) a heading in capitals equal to or greater in size than the surrounding text, or in contrasting type, font, or color to the surrounding text of the same or lesser size; and

 (B) language in the body of a record or display in larger type than the surrounding text, or in contrasting type, font, or color to the surrounding text of the same size, or set off from surrounding text of the same size by symbols or other marks that call attention to the language.

(11) "Consumer" means an individual who enters into a transaction primarily for personal, family, or household purposes.

(12) "Contract," as distinguished from "agreement," means the total legal obligation that results from the parties' agreement as determined by [the Uniform Commercial Code] as supplemented by any other applicable laws.

(13) "Creditor" includes a general creditor, a secured creditor, a lien creditor, and any representative of creditors, including an assignee for the benefit of creditors, a trustee in bankruptcy, a receiver in equity, and an executor or administrator of an insolvent debtor's or assignor's estate.

(14) "Defendant" includes a person in the position of defendant in a counterclaim, cross-claim, or third-party claim.

(15) "Delivery," with respect to an instrument, document of title, or chattel paper, means voluntary transfer of possession.

(16) "Document of title" includes bill of lading, dock warrant, dock receipt, warehouse receipt or order for the delivery of goods, and also any other document which in the regular course of business or financing is treated as adequately evidencing that the person in possession of it is entitled to receive, hold, and dispose of the document and the goods it covers. To be a document of title, a document must purport to be issued by or addressed to a bailee and purport to cover goods in the bailee's possession which are either identified or are fungible portions of an identified mass.

(17) "Fault" means a default, breach, or wrongful act or omission.

(18) "Fungible goods" means:

(A) goods of which any unit, by nature or usage of trade, is the equivalent of any other like unit; or

(B) goods that by agreement are treated as equivalent.

(19) "Genuine" means free of forgery or counterfeiting.

(20) "Good faith," except as otherwise provided in Article 5, means honesty in fact and the observance of reasonable commercial standards of fair dealing.

(21) "Holder" means:

(A) the person in possession of a negotiable instrument that is payable either to bearer or to an identified person that is the person in possession; or

(B) the person in possession of a document of title if the goods are deliverable either to bearer or to the order of the person in possession.

(22) "Insolvency proceeding" includes an assignment for the benefit of creditors or other proceeding intended to liquidate or rehabilitate the estate of the person involved.

(23) "Insolvent" means:

(A) having generally ceased to pay debts in the ordinary course of business other than as a result of bona fide dispute;

(B) being unable to pay debts as they become due; or

(C) being insolvent within the meaning of federal bankruptcy law.

(24) "Money" means a medium of exchange currently authorized or adopted by a domestic or foreign government. The term includes a monetary unit of account established by an intergovernmental organization or by agreement between two or more countries.

(25) "Organization" means a person other than an individual.

(26) "Party," as distinguished from "third party," means a person that has engaged in a transaction or made an agreement subject to [the Uniform Commercial Code].

(27) "Person" means an individual, corporation, business trust, estate, trust, partnership, limited liability company, association, joint venture, government, governmental subdivision, agency, or instrumentality, public corporation, or any other legal or commercial entity.

(28) "Present value" means the amount as of a date certain of one or more sums payable in the future, discounted to the date certain by use of either an interest rate specified by the parties if that rate is not manifestly unreasonable at the time the transaction is entered into or,

if an interest rate is not so specified, a commercially reasonable rate that takes into account the facts and circumstances at the time the transaction is entered into.

(29) "Purchase" means taking by sale, lease, discount, negotiation, mortgage, pledge, lien, security interest, issue or reissue, gift, or any other voluntary transaction creating an interest in property.

(30) "Purchaser" means a person that takes by purchase.

(31) "Record" means information that is inscribed on a tangible medium or that is stored in an electronic or other medium and is retrievable in perceivable form.

(32) "Remedy" means any remedial right to which an aggrieved party is entitled with or without resort to a tribunal.

(33) "Representative" means a person empowered to act for another, including an agent, an officer of a corporation or association, and a trustee, executor, or administrator of an estate.

(34) "Right" includes remedy.

(35) "Security interest" means an interest in personal property or fixtures which secures payment or performance of an obligation. "Security interest" includes any interest of a consignor and a buyer of accounts, chattel paper, a payment intangible, or a promissory note in a transaction that is subject to Article 9. "Security interest" does not include the special property interest of a buyer of goods on identification of those goods to a contract for sale under Section 2–401, but a buyer may also acquire a "security interest" by complying with Article 9. Except as otherwise provided in Section 2–505, the right of a seller or lessor of goods under Article 2 or 2A to retain or acquire possession of the goods is not a "security interest", but a seller or lessor may also acquire a "security interest" by complying with Article 9. The retention or reservation of title by a seller of goods notwithstanding shipment or delivery to the buyer under Section 2–401 is limited in effect to a reservation of a "security interest." Whether a transaction in the form of a lease creates a "security interest" is determined pursuant to Section 1–203.

(36) "Send" in connection with a writing, record, or notice means:

(A) to deposit in the mail or deliver for transmission by any other usual means of communication with postage or cost of transmission provided for and properly addressed and, in the case of an instrument, to an address specified thereon or otherwise agreed, or if there be none to any address reasonable under the circumstances; or

(B) in any other way to cause to be received any record or notice within the time it would have arrived if properly sent.

(37) "Signed" includes using any symbol executed or adopted with present intention to adopt or accept a writing.

(38) "State" means a State of the United States, the District of Columbia, Puerto Rico, the United States Virgin Islands, or any territory or insular possession subject to the jurisdiction of the United States.

(39) "Surety" includes a guarantor or other secondary obligor.

(40) "Term" means a portion of an agreement that relates to a particular matter.

(41) "Unauthorized signature" means a signature made without actual, implied, or apparent authority. The term includes a forgery.

(42) "Warehouse receipt" means a receipt issued by a person engaged in the business of storing goods for hire.

(43) "Writing" includes printing, typewriting, or any other intentional reduction to tangible form. "Written" has a corresponding meaning.

Official Comment

. . .

3. "Agreement." Derived from former Section 1–201. As used in the Uniform Commercial Code the word is intended to include full recognition of usage of trade, course of dealing, course of performance and the surrounding circumstances as effective parts thereof, and of any agreement permitted under the provisions of the Uniform Commercial Code to displace a stated rule of law. Whether an agreement has legal consequences is determined by applicable provisions of the Uniform Commercial Code and, to the extent provided in Section 1–103, by the law of contracts.

. . .

10. "Conspicuous." Derived from former Section 1–201(10). This definition states the general standard that to be conspicuous a term ought to be noticed by a reasonable person. Whether a term is conspicuous is an issue for the court. Subparagraphs (A) and (B) set out several methods for making a term conspicuous. Requiring that a term be conspicuous blends a notice function (the term ought to be noticed) and a planning function (giving guidance to the party relying on the term regarding how that result can be achieved). Al-

though these paragraphs indicate some of the methods for making a term attention-calling, the test is whether attention can reasonably be expected to be called to it. The statutory language should not be construed to permit a result that is inconsistent with that test.

. . .

20. "Good faith." Former Section 1–201(19) defined "good faith" simply as honesty in fact; the definition contained no element of commercial reasonableness. Initially, that definition applied throughout the Code with only one exception. Former Section 2–103(1)(b) provided that "in this Article ... good faith in the case of a merchant means honesty in fact and the observance of reasonable commercial standards of fair dealing in the trade." This alternative definition was limited in applicability in three ways. First, it applied only to transactions within the scope of Article 2. Second, it applied only to merchants. Third, strictly construed it applied only to uses of the phrase "good faith" in Article 2; thus, so construed it would not define "good faith" for its most important use–the obligation of good faith imposed by former Section 1–203.

Over time, however, amendments to the Uniform Commercial Code brought the Article 2 merchant concept of good faith (subjective honesty and objective commercial reasonableness) into other Articles. First, Article 2A explicitly incorporated the Article 2 standard. See Section 2A–103(7). Then, other Articles broadened the applicability of that standard by adopting it for all parties rather than just for merchants. *See, e.g.*, Sections 3–103(a)(4), 4A–105(a)(6), 8–102(a)(10), and 9–102(a)(43). All of these definitions are comprised of two elements–honesty in fact *and* the observance of reasonable commercial standards of fair dealing. Only revised Article 5 defines "good faith" solely in terms of subjective honesty, and only Article 6 and Article 7 are without definitions of good faith. (It should be noted that, while revised Article 6 did not define good faith, Comment 2 to revised Section 6–102 states that "this Article adopts the definition of 'good faith' in Article 1 in all cases, even when the buyer is a merchant.") Given these developments, it is appropriate to move the broader definition of "good faith" to Article 1. Of course, this definition is subject to the applicability of the narrower definition in revised Article 5.

. . .

§ 1–202. Notice; Knowledge

(a) Subject to subsection (f), a person has "notice" of a fact if the person:

(1) has actual knowledge of it;

(2) has received a notice or notification of it; or

(3) from all the facts and circumstances known to the person at the time in question, has reason to know that it exists.

(b) "Knowledge" means actual knowledge. "Knows" has a corresponding meaning.

(c) "Discover," "learn," or words of similar import refer to knowledge rather than to reason to know.

(d) A person "notifies" or "gives" a notice or notification to another person by taking such steps as may be reasonably required to inform the other person in ordinary course, whether or not the other person actually comes to know of it.

(e) Subject to subsection (f), a person "receives" a notice or notification when:

(1) it comes to that person's attention; or

(2) it is duly delivered in a form reasonable under the circumstances at the place of business through which the contract was made or at another location held out by that person as the place for receipt of such communications.

(f) Notice, knowledge, or a notice or notification received by an organization is effective for a particular transaction from the time it is brought to the attention of the individual conducting that transaction and, in any event, from the time it would have been brought to the individual's attention if the organization had exercised due diligence. An organization exercises due diligence if it maintains reasonable routines for communicating significant information to the person conducting the transaction and there is reasonable compliance with the routines. Due diligence does not require an individual acting for the organization to communicate information unless the communication is part of the individual's regular duties or the individual has reason to know of the transaction and that the transaction would be materially affected by the information.

PART 3.   TERRITORIAL APPLICABILITY AND GENERAL RULES

§ 1–301.   Territorial Applicability; Parties' Power to Choose Applicable Law

(a) In this section:

(1) "Domestic transaction" means a transaction other than an international transaction.

(2) "International transaction" means a transaction that bears a reasonable relation to a country other than the United States.

(b) This section applies to a transaction to the extent that it is governed by another article of the [Uniform Commercial Code].

(c) Except as otherwise provided in this section:

(1) an agreement by parties to a domestic transaction that any or all of their rights and obligations are to be determined by the law of this State or of another State is effective, whether or not the transaction bears a relation to the State designated; and

(2) an agreement by parties to an international transaction that any or all of their rights and obligations are to be determined by the law of this State or of another State or country is effective, whether or not the transaction bears a relation to the State or country designated.

(d) In the absence of an agreement effective under subsection (c), and except as provided in subsections (e) and (g), the rights and obligations of the parties are determined by the law that would be selected by application of this State's conflict of laws principles.

(e) If one of the parties to a transaction is a consumer, the following rules apply:

(1) An agreement referred to in subsection (c) is not effective unless the transaction bears a reasonable relation to the State or country designated.

(2) Application of the law of the State or country determined pursuant to subsection (c) or (d) may not deprive the consumer of the protection of any rule of law governing a matter within the scope of this section, which both is protective of consumers and may not be varied by agreement:

(A) of the State or country in which the consumer principally resides, unless subparagraph (B) applies; or

(B) if the transaction is a sale of goods, of the State or country in which the consumer both makes the contract and takes delivery of those goods, if such State or country is not the State or country in which the consumer principally resides.

(f) An agreement otherwise effective under subsection (c) is not effective to the extent that application of the law of the State or country designated would be contrary to a fundamental policy of the State or country whose law would govern in the absence of agreement under subsection (d).

(g) To the extent that [the Uniform Commercial Code] governs a transaction, if one of the following provisions of [the Uniform Commercial Code] specifies the applicable law, that provision governs and a contrary agreement is effective only to the extent permitted by the law so specified:

(1) Section 2–402;

(2) Sections 2A–105 and 2A–106;

(3) Section 4–102;

(4) Section 4A–507;

(5) Section 5–116;

[(6) Section 6–103;]

(7) Section 8–110;

(8) Sections 9–301 through 9–307.

Official Comment

. . .

Summary of changes from former law: . . .

Section 1–301 addresses contractual designation of governing law somewhat differently than does former Section 1–105. Former law allowed the parties to any transaction to designate a jurisdiction whose law governs if the transaction bears a "reasonable relation" to that jurisdiction. Section 1–301 deviates from this approach by providing different rules for transactions involving a consumer than for non-consumer transactions, such as "business to business" transactions.

In the context of consumer transactions, the language of Section 1–301, unlike that of former Section 1–105, protects consumers against the possibility of losing the protection of consumer protection rules applicable to the aspects of the transaction governed by the Uniform Commercial Code. In most situations, the relevant consumer protection rules will be those of the consumer's home jurisdiction. A special rule, however, is provided for certain face-to-face sales transactions. (See Comment 3.)

. . .

3. *Consumer transactions.* If one of the parties is a consumer (as defined in Section 1–201(b)(11)), subsection (e) provides the parties less autonomy to designate the State or country whose law will govern.

First, in the case of a consumer transaction, subsection (e)(1) provides that the transaction must bear a reasonable relation to the State or country designated. Thus, the rules of subsection (c) allowing the parties to choose the law of a jurisdiction to which the transaction bears no relation do not apply to consumer transactions.

875

Second, subsection (e)(2) provides that application of the law of the State or country determined by the rules of this section (whether or not that State or country was designated by the parties) cannot deprive the consumer of the protection of rules of law which govern matters within the scope of Section 1–301, are protective of consumers, and are not variable by agreement. The phrase "rule of law" is intended to refer to case law as well as statutes and administrative regulations. The requirement that the rule of law be one "governing a matter within the scope of this section" means that, consistent with the scope of Section 1–301, which governs choice of law only with regard to the aspects of a transaction governed by the Uniform Commercial Code, the relevant consumer rules are those that govern those aspects of the transaction. Such rules may be found in the Uniform Commercial Code itself, as are the consumer-protective rules in Part 6 of Article 9, or in other law if that other law governs the UCC aspects of the transaction. See, for example, the rule in Section 2.403 of the Uniform Consumer Credit Code which prohibits certain sellers and lessors from taking negotiable instruments other than checks and provides that a holder is not in good faith if the holder takes a negotiable instrument with notice that it is issued in violation of that section.

With one exception (explained in the next paragraph), the rules of law the protection of which the consumer may not be deprived are those of the jurisdiction in which the consumer principally resides. The jurisdiction in which the consumer principally resides is determined at the time relevant to the particular issue involved. Thus, for example, if the issue is one related to formation of a contract, the relevant consumer protective rules are rules of the jurisdiction in which the consumer principally resided at the time the facts relevant to contract formation occurred, even if the consumer no longer principally resides in that jurisdiction at the time the dispute arises or is litigated. If, on the other hand, the issue is one relating to enforcement of obligations, then the relevant consumer protective rules are those of the jurisdiction in which the consumer principally resides at the time enforcement is sought, even if the consumer did not principally reside in that jurisdiction at the time the transaction was entered into.

In the case of a sale of goods to a consumer, in which the consumer both makes the contract and takes possession of the goods in the same jurisdiction and that jurisdiction is not the consumer's principal residence, the rule in subsection (e)(2)(B) applies. In that situation, the relevant consumer protective rules, the protection of which the consumer may not be deprived by the choice of law rules of subsections (c) and (d), are those of the State or country in which both the contract is made and the consumer takes delivery of the goods. This rule, adapted from Section 2A–106 and Article 5 of the EC Convention on the Law Applicable to Contractual Obligations, enables a seller of goods engaging in face-to-face transactions to ascertain the consumer protection rules to which those sales are subject, without the necessity of determining the principal residence of each buyer. The reference in subsection (e)(2)(B) to the State or country in which the consumer makes the contract should not be read to incorporate formalistic concepts of where the last event necessary to conclude the contract took place; rather, the intent is to identify the state in which all material steps necessary to enter into the contract were taken by the consumer.

The following examples illustrate the application of Section 1–301(e)(2) in the context of a contractual choice of law provision:

Example 3: Seller, located in State A, agrees to sell goods to Consumer, whose principal residence is in State B. The parties agree that the law of State A would govern this transaction. Seller ships the goods to Consumer in State B. An issue related to contract formation subsequently arises. Under the law of State A, that issue is governed by State A's uniform version of Article 2. Under the law of State B, that issue is governed by a non-uniform rule, protective of consumers and not variable by agreement, that brings about a different result than would occur under the uniform version of Article 2. Under Section 1–301(e)(2)(A), the parties' agreement that the law of State A would govern their transaction cannot deprive Consumer of the protection of State B's consumer protective rule. This is the case whether State B's rule is codified in Article 2 of its Uniform Commercial Code or is found elsewhere in the law of State B.

Example 4: Same facts as Example 3, except that (i) Consumer takes all material steps necessary to enter into the agreement to purchase the goods from Seller, and takes delivery of those goods, while on vacation in State A and (ii) the parties agree that the law of State C (in which Seller's chief executive office is located) would govern their transaction. Under subsections (c)(1) and (e)(1), the designation of the law of State C as governing will be effective so long as the transaction is found to bear a reasonable relation to State C (assuming that the relevant law of State C is not contrary to a fundamental policy of the State whose law would govern in the absence of agreement), but that designation cannot deprive Consumer of the protection of any rule of State A that is within the scope of this section and is both protective of consumers and not variable by agreement. State B's consumer protective rule is not relevant because, under Section 1–301(e)(2)(B), the relevant consumer protective rules are those of the jurisdiction in which the consumer both made the contract and took delivery of the goods–here, State A–rather than those of the jurisdiction in which the consumer principally resides.

It is important to note that subsection (e)(2) applies to all determinations of applicable law in transactions in which one party is a consumer, whether that determination is made under subsection (c) (in cases in which the parties have designated the governing law in their agreement) or subsection (d) (in cases in which the parties have not made such a designation). In the latter situation, application of the otherwise-applicable conflict of laws principles of the forum might lead to application of the laws of a State or country other than that of the consumer's principal residence. In such a case, however, subsection (e)(2) applies to preserve the applicability of consumer protection rules for the benefit of the consumer as described above.

· · ·

6. *Fundamental policy.* Subsection (f) provides that an agreement designating the governing law will not be given effect to the extent that application of the designated law would be contrary to a fundamental policy of the State or country whose law would otherwise govern. This rule provides a narrow exception to the broad autonomy afforded to parties in subsection (c). One of the prime objectives of contract law is to protect the justified expectations of the parties and to make it possible for them to foretell with accuracy what will be their rights and liabilities under the contract. In this way, certainty and predictability of result are most likely to be

secured. See Restatement (Second) Conflict of Laws, Section 187, comment *e.*

Under the fundamental policy doctrine, a court should not refrain from applying the designated law merely because application of that law would lead to a result different than would be obtained under the local law of the State or country whose law would otherwise govern. Rather, the difference must be contrary to a public policy of that jurisdiction that is so substantial that it justifies overriding the concerns for certainty and predictability underlying modern commercial law as well as concerns for judicial economy generally. Thus, application of the designated law will rarely be found to be contrary to a fundamental policy of the State or country whose law would otherwise govern when the difference between the two concerns a requirement, such as a statute of frauds, that relates to formalities, or general rules of contract law, such as those concerned with the need for consideration.

. . .

Application of the designated law may be contrary to a fundamental policy of the State or country whose law would otherwise govern either (i) because the substance of the designated law violates a fundamental principle of justice of that State or country or (ii) because it differs from a rule of that State or country that is "mandatory" in that it *must* be applied in the courts of that State or country without regard to otherwise-applicable choice of law rules of that State or country and without regard to whether the designated law is otherwise offensive. The mandatory rules concept appears in international conventions in this field, *e.g.*, EC Convention on the Law Applicable to Contractual Obligations, although in some cases the concept is applied to authorize the *forum* state to apply *its* mandatory rules, rather than those of the State or country whose law would otherwise govern. The latter situation is not addressed by this section. (See Comment 9.)

It is obvious that a rule that is freely changeable by agreement of the parties under the law of the State or country whose law would otherwise govern cannot be construed as a mandatory rule of that State or country. This does not mean, however, that rules that cannot be changed by agreement under that law are, for that reason alone, mandatory rules. Otherwise, contractual choice of law in the context of the Uniform Commercial Code would be illusory and redundant; the parties would be able to accomplish by choice of law no more than can be accomplished under Section 1–302, which allows variation of otherwise applicable rules by agreement. (Under Section 1–302, the parties could agree to vary the rules that would otherwise govern their transaction by substituting for those rules the rules that would apply if the transaction were governed by the law of the designated State or country without designation of governing law.) Indeed, other than cases in which a mandatory choice of law rule is established by statute (see, *e.g.*, Sections 9–301 through 9–307, explicitly preserved in subsection (g)), cases in which courts have declined to follow the designated law solely because a rule of the State or country whose law would otherwise govern is mandatory are rare.

. . .

§ 1–302. Variation by Agreement

(a) Except as otherwise provided in subsection (b) or elsewhere in [the Uniform Commercial Code], the effect of provisions of [the Uniform Commercial Code] may be varied by agreement.

(b) The obligations of good faith, diligence, reasonableness, and care prescribed by [the Uniform Commercial Code] may not be disclaimed by agreement. The parties, by agreement, may determine the standards by which the performance of those obligations is to be measured if those standards are not manifestly unreasonable. Whenever [the Uniform Commercial Code] requires an action to be taken within a reasonable time, a time that is not manifestly unreasonable may be fixed by agreement.

(c) The presence in certain provisions of [the Uniform Commercial Code] of the phrase "unless otherwise agreed," or words of similar import, does not imply that the effect of other provisions may not be varied by agreement under this section.

§ 1–303. Course of Performance, Course of Dealing, and Usage of Trade

(a) A "course of performance" is a sequence of conduct between the parties to a particular transaction that exists if:

(1) the agreement of the parties with respect to the transaction involves repeated occasions for performance by a party; and

(2) the other party, with knowledge of the nature of the performance and opportunity for objection to it, accepts the performance or acquiesces in it without objection.

(b) A "course of dealing" is a sequence of conduct concerning previous transactions between the parties to a particular transaction that is fairly to be regarded as establishing a common basis of understanding for interpreting their expressions and other conduct.

(c) A "usage of trade" is any practice or method of dealing having such regularity of observance in a place, vocation, or trade as to justify an expectation that it will be observed with respect to the transaction in question. The existence and scope of such a usage must be proved as facts. If it is established that such a usage is embodied in a trade code or similar record, the interpretation of the record is a question of law.

(d) A course of performance or course of dealing between the parties or usage of trade in the vocation or trade in which they are engaged or of which they are or should be aware is relevant in ascertaining the meaning of the parties' agreement, may give particular meaning to specific terms of the agreement, and may supplement or qualify the terms of the agreement. A usage of trade applicable in the place in which part of the performance under the agreement is to occur may be so utilized as to that part of the performance.

(e) Except as otherwise provided in subsection (f), the express terms of an agreement and any applicable course of performance, course of dealing, or usage of trade must be construed whenever reasonable as consistent with each other. If such a construction is unreasonable:

(1) express terms prevail over course of performance, course of dealing, and usage of trade;

879

(2) course of performance prevails over course of dealing and usage of trade; and

(3) course of dealing prevails over usage of trade.

(f) Subject to Section 2–209, a course of performance is relevant to show a waiver or modification of any term inconsistent with the course of performance.

(g) Evidence of a relevant usage of trade offered by one party is not admissible unless that party has given the other party notice that the court finds sufficient to prevent unfair surprise to the other party.

§ 1–304. Obligation of Good Faith

Every contract or duty within [the Uniform Commercial Code] imposes an obligation of good faith in its performance and enforcement.

Official Comment

Source: Former Section 1–203.

Changes from former law: Except for changing the form of reference to the Uniform Commercial Code, this section is identical to former Section 1–203.

1. This section sets forth a basic principle running throughout the Uniform Commercial Code. The principle is that in commercial transactions good faith is required in the performance and enforcement of all agreements or duties. While this duty is explicitly stated in some provisions of the Uniform Commercial Code, the applicability of the duty is broader than merely these situations and applies generally, as stated in this section, to the performance or enforcement of every contract or duty within this Act. It is further implemented by Section 1–303 on course of dealing, course of performance, and usage of trade. This section does not support an independent cause of action for failure to perform or enforce in good faith. Rather, this section means that a failure to perform or enforce, in good faith, a specific duty or obligation under the contract, constitutes a breach of that contract or makes unavailable, under the particular circumstances, a remedial right or power. This distinction makes it clear that the doctrine of good faith merely directs a court towards interpreting contracts within the commercial context in which they are created, performed, and enforced, and does not create a separate duty of fairness and reasonableness which can be independently breached.

2. "Performance and enforcement" of contracts and duties within the Uniform Commercial Code include the exercise of rights created by the Uniform Commercial Code.

§ 1–305. Remedies to be Liberally Administered

(a) The remedies provided by [the Uniform Commercial Code] must be liberally administered to the end that the aggrieved party may be put in as good a position as if the other party had fully performed but neither consequential or special damages nor penal damages may be had except as specifically provided in [the Uniform Commercial Code] or by other rule of law.

(b) Any right or obligation declared by [the Uniform Commercial Code] is enforceable by action unless the provision declaring it specifies a different and limited effect.

§ 1–308. Performance or Acceptance Under Reservation of Rights

(a) A party that with explicit reservation of rights performs or promises performance or assents to performance in a manner demanded or offered by the other party does not thereby prejudice the rights reserved. Such words as "without prejudice," "under protest," or the like are sufficient.

(b) Subsection (a) does not apply to an accord and satisfaction.

§ 1–309. Option to Accelerate at Will

A term providing that one party or that party's successor in interest may accelerate payment or performance or require collateral or additional collateral "at will" or when the party "deems itself insecure," or words of similar import, means that the party has power to do so only if that party in good faith believes that the prospect of payment or performance is impaired. The burden of establishing lack of good faith is on the party against which the power has been exercised.

Official Comment

Source: Former Section 1–208.

Changes from former law: Except for minor stylistic changes, this section is identical to former Section 1–208.

1. The common use of acceleration clauses in many transactions governed by the Uniform Commercial Code, including sales of goods on credit, notes payable at a definite time, and secured transactions, raises an issue as to the effect to be given to a clause that seemingly grants the power to accelerate at the whim and caprice of one party. This section is intended to make clear that despite language that might be so construed and which further might be held to make the agreement void as against public policy or to make the contract illusory or too indefinite for enforcement, the option is to be exercised only in the good faith belief that the prospect of payment or performance is impaired.

Obviously this section has no application to demand instruments or obligations whose very nature permits call at any time with or without reason. This section applies only to an obligation of payment or performance which in the first instance is due at a future date.

ARTICLE 2.   SALES [1978 Text]

PART 1.   SHORT TITLE, GENERAL CONSTRUCTION AND SUBJECT MATTER

§ 2–102.   Scope; Certain Security and Other Transactions Excluded from This Article

Unless the context otherwise requires, this Article applies to transactions in goods; it does not apply to any transaction which although in the form of an unconditional contract to sell or present sale is intended to operate only as a security transaction nor does this Article impair or repeal any statute regulating sales to consumers, farmers or other specified classes of buyers.

§ 2–103.   Definitions and Index of Definitions

(1) In this Article unless the context otherwise requires

   (a) "Buyer" means a person who buys or contracts to buy goods.

   (b) "Good faith" in the case of a merchant means honesty in fact and the observance of reasonable commercial standards of fair dealing in the trade.

   (c) "Receipt" of goods means taking physical possession of them.

   (d) "Seller" means a person who sells or contracts to sell goods.

   .   .   .

(4) In addition Article 1 contains general definitions and principles of construction and interpretation applicable throughout this Article.

§ 2–104.   Definitions: "Merchant"; "Between Merchants"; "Financing Agency"

(1) "Merchant" means a person who deals in goods of the kind or otherwise by his occupation holds himself out as having knowledge or skill peculiar to the practices or goods involved in the transaction or to whom such knowledge or skill may be attributed by his employment of an agent or broker or other intermediary who by his occupation holds himself out as having such knowledge or skill.

(2) "Financing agency" means a bank, finance company or other person who in the ordinary course of business makes advances against goods or documents of title or who by arrangement with either the seller or the buyer intervenes in ordinary course to make or collect payment due or claimed under the contract for sale, as by purchasing or paying the seller's draft or making advances against it or by merely taking it for collection whether or not documents of title accompany the draft. "Financing agen-

882

cy" includes also a bank or other person who similarly intervenes between persons who are in the position of seller and buyer in respect to the goods (Section 2–707).

(3) "Between merchants" means in any transaction with respect to which both parties are chargeable with the knowledge or skill of merchants.

Official Comment

Purposes:

1. This Article assumes that transactions between professionals in a given field require special and clear rules which may not apply to a casual or inexperienced seller or buyer. It thus adopts a policy of expressly stating rules applicable "between merchants" and "as against a merchant," wherever they are needed instead of making them depend upon the circumstances of each case. . . . This section lays the foundation of this policy by defining those who are to be regarded as professionals or "merchants" and by stating when a transaction is deemed to be "between merchants."

2. The term "merchant" as defined here roots in the "law merchant" concept of a professional in business. The professional status under the definition may be based upon specialized knowledge as to the goods, specialized knowledge as to business practices, or specialized knowledge as to both and which kind of specialized knowledge may be sufficient to establish the merchant status is indicated by the nature of the provisions.

The special provisions as to merchants appear only in this Article and they are of three kinds. Sections 2–201(2), 2–205, 2–207 and 2–209 dealing with the statute of frauds, firm offers, confirmatory memoranda and modification rest on normal business practices which are or ought to be typical of and familiar to any person in business. For purposes of these sections almost every person in business would, therefore, be deemed to be a "merchant" under the language "who . . . by his occupation holds himself out as having knowledge or skill peculiar to the practices . . . involved in the transaction . . . ." since the practices involved in the transaction are non-specialized business practices such as answering mail. In this type of provision, banks or even universities, for example, well may be "merchants." But even these sections only apply to a merchant in his mercantile capacity; a lawyer or bank president buying fishing tackle for his own use is not a merchant.

On the other hand, in Section 2–314 on the warranty of merchantability, such warranty is implied only "if the seller is a merchant with respect to goods of that kind." Obviously this qualification restricts the implied warranty to a much smaller group than everyone who is engaged in business and requires a professional status as to particular kinds of goods. . . .

A third group of sections includes 2–103(1)(b), which provides that in the case of a merchant "good faith" includes observance of reasonable commercial standards of fair dealing in the trade; . . . .

3. The "or to whom such knowledge or skill may be attributed by his employment of an agent or broker . . ." clause of the definition of merchant means that even persons such as universities, for example, can come within the definition of merchant if they have regular purchasing departments or business personnel who are familiar with business practices and who are equipped to take any action required.

§ 2-106. Definitions: "Contract"; "Agreement"; "Contract for Sale"; "Sale"; "Present Sale"; "Conforming" to Contract; "Termination"; "Cancellation"

(1) In this Article unless the context otherwise requires "contract" and "agreement" are limited to those relating to the present or future sale of goods. "Contract for sale" includes both a present sale of goods and a contract to sell goods at a future time. A "sale" consists in the passing of title from the seller to the buyer for a price (Section 2-401). A "present sale" means a sale which is accomplished by the making of the contract.

(2) Goods or conduct including any part of a performance are "conforming" or conform to the contract when they are in accordance with the obligations under the contract.

(3) "Termination" occurs when either party pursuant to a power created by agreement or law puts an end to the contract otherwise than for its breach. On "termination" all obligations which are still executory on both sides are discharged but any right based on prior breach or performance survives.

(4) "Cancellation" occurs when either party puts an end to the contract for breach by the other and its effect is the same as that of "termination" except that the cancelling party also retains any remedy for breach of the whole contract or any unperformed balance.

PART 2.   FORM, FORMATION AND READJUSTMENT OF CONTRACT

§ 2-202.   Final Written Expression: Parol or Extrinsic Evidence

Terms with respect to which the confirmatory memoranda of the parties agree or which are otherwise set forth in a writing intended by the parties as a final expression of their agreement with respect to such terms as are included therein may not be contradicted by evidence of any prior agreement or of a contemporaneous oral agreement but may be explained or supplemented

(a) by course of dealing or usage of trade (Section 1-205) or by course of performance (Section 2-208); and

(b) by evidence of consistent additional terms unless the court finds the writing to have been intended also as a complete and exclusive statement of the terms of the agreement.

Official Comment

Purposes:

1.   This section definitely rejects:

(a) Any assumption that because a writing has been worked out which is final on some matters, it is to be taken as including all the matters agreed upon;

(b) The premise that the language used has the meaning attributable to such language by rules of construction existing in the law rather than the meaning which arises out of the commercial context in which it was used; and

(c) The requirement that a condition precedent to the admissibility of the type of evidence specified in paragraph (a) is an original determination by the court that the language used is ambiguous.

2. Paragraph (a) makes admissible evidence of course of dealing, usage of trade and course of performance to explain or supplement the terms of any writing stating the agreement of the parties in order that the true understanding of the parties as to the agreement may be reached. Such writings are to be read on the assumption that the course of prior dealings between the parties and the usages of trade were taken for granted when the document was phrased. Unless carefully negated they have become an element of the meaning of the words used. Similarly, the course of actual performance by the parties is considered the best indication of what they intended the writing to mean.

3. Under paragraph (b) consistent additional terms, not reduced to writing, may be proved unless the court finds that the writing was intended by both parties as a complete and exclusive statement of all the terms. If the additional terms are such that, if agreed upon, they would certainly have been included in the document in the view of the court, then evidence of their alleged making must be kept from the trier of fact.

§ 2–208. Course of Performance or Practical Construction

(1) Where the contract for sale involves repeated occasions for performance by either party with knowledge of the nature of the performance and opportunity for objection to it by the other, any course of performance accepted or acquiesced in without objection shall be relevant to determine the meaning of the agreement.

(2) The express terms of the agreement and any such course of performance, as well as any course of dealing and usage of trade, shall be construed whenever reasonable as consistent with each other; but when such construction is unreasonable, express terms shall control course of performance and course of performance shall control both course of dealing and usage of trade (Section 1–205).

(3) Subject to the provisions of the next section on modification and waiver, such course of performance shall be relevant to show a waiver or modification of any term inconsistent with such course of performance.

§ 2–209. Modification, Rescission and Waiver

(1) An agreement modifying a contract within this Article needs no consideration to be binding.

(2) A signed agreement which excludes modification or rescission except by a signed writing cannot be otherwise modified or rescinded, but except as between merchants such a requirement on a form supplied by the merchant must be separately signed by the other party.

(3) The requirements of the statute of frauds section of this Article (Section 2–201) must be satisfied if the contract as modified is within its provisions.

(4) Although an attempt at modification or rescission does not satisfy the requirements of subsection (2) or (3) it can operate as a waiver.

(5) A party who has made a waiver affecting an executory portion of the contract may retract the waiver by reasonable notification received by the other party that strict performance will be required of any term waived, unless the retraction would be unjust in view of a material change of position in reliance on the waiver.

§ 2–210. Delegation of Performance; Assignment of Rights

(1) A party may perform his duty through a delegate unless otherwise agreed or unless the other party has a substantial interest in having his original promisor perform or control the acts required by the contract. No delegation of performance relieves the party delegating of any duty to perform or any liability for breach.

(2) Unless otherwise agreed all rights of either seller or buyer can be assigned except where the assignment would materially change the duty of the other party, or increase materially the burden or risk imposed on him by his contract, or impair materially his chance of obtaining return performance. A right to damages for breach of the whole contract or a right arising out of the assignor's due performance of his entire obligation can be assigned despite agreement otherwise.

(3) Unless the circumstances indicate the contrary a prohibition of assignment of "the contract" is to be construed as barring only the delegation to the assignee of the assignor's performance.

(4) An assignment of "the contract" or of "all my rights under the contract" or an assignment in similar general terms is an assignment of rights and unless the language or the circumstances (as in an assignment for security) indicate the contrary, it is a delegation of performance of the duties of the assignor and its acceptance by the assignee constitutes a promise by him to perform those duties. This promise is enforceable by either the assignor or the other party to the original contract.

(5) The other party may treat any assignment which delegates performance as creating reasonable grounds for insecurity and may without prejudice to his rights against the assignor demand assurances from the assignee (Section 2–609).

PART 3.   GENERAL OBLIGATION AND CONSTRUCTION OF CONTRACT

§ 2–301. General Obligations of Parties

The obligation of the seller is to transfer and deliver and that of the buyer is to accept and pay in accordance with the contract.

§ 2–302. Unconscionable Contract or Clause

(1) If the court as a matter of law finds the contract or any clause of the contract to have been unconscionable at the time it was made the court

may refuse to enforce the contract, or it may enforce the remainder of the contract without the unconscionable clause, or it may so limit the application of any unconscionable clause as to avoid any unconscionable result.

(2) When it is claimed or appears to the court that the contract or any clause thereof may be unconscionable the parties shall be afforded a reasonable opportunity to present evidence as to its commercial setting, purpose and effect to aid the court in making the determination.

Official Comment

Purposes:

1. This section is intended to make it possible for the courts to police explicitly against the contracts or clauses which they find to be unconscionable. In the past such policing has been accomplished by adverse construction of language, by manipulation of the rules of offer and acceptance or by determinations that the clause is contrary to public policy or to the dominant purpose of the contract. This section is intended to allow the court to pass directly on the unconscionability of the contract or particular clause therein and to make a conclusion of law as to its unconscionability. The basic test is whether, in the light of the general commercial background and the commercial needs of the particular trade or case, the clauses involved are so one-sided as to be unconscionable under the circumstances existing at the time of the making of the contract. Subsection (2) makes it clear that it is proper for the court to hear evidence upon these questions. The principle is one of the prevention of oppression and unfair surprise (Cf. Campbell Soup Co. v. Wentz, 172 F.2d 80, 3d Cir. 1948) and not of disturbance of allocation of risks because of superior bargaining power. The underlying basis of this section is illustrated by the results in cases such as the following:

Kansas City Wholesale Grocery Co. v. Weber Packing Corporation, 93 Utah 414, 73 P.2d 1272 (1937), where a clause limiting time for complaints was held inapplicable to latent defects in a shipment of catsup which could be discovered only by microscopic analysis; Hardy v. General Motors Acceptance Corporation, 38 Ga.App. 463, 144 S.E. 327 (1928), holding that a disclaimer of warranty clause applied only to express warranties, thus letting in a fair implied warranty; Andrews Bros. v. Singer & Co. (1934 CA) 1 K.B. 17, holding that where a car with substantial mileage was delivered instead of a "new" car, a disclaimer of warranties, including those "implied," left unaffected an "express obligation" on the description, even though the Sale of Goods Act called such an implied warranty; New Prague Flouring Mill Co. v. G. A. Spears, 194 Iowa 417, 189 N.W. 815 (1922), holding that a clause permitting the seller, upon the buyer's failure to supply shipping instructions, to cancel, ship, or allow delivery date to be indefinitely postponed 30 days at a time by the inaction, does not indefinitely postpone the date of measuring damages for the buyer's breach, to the seller's advantage; and Kansas Flour Mills Co. v. Dirks, 100 Kan. 376, 164 P. 273 (1917), where under a similar clause in a rising market the court permitted the buyer to measure his damages for non-delivery at the end of only one 30 day postponement; Green v. Arcos, Ltd. (1931 CA) 47 T.L.R. 336, where a blanket clause prohibiting rejection of shipments by the buyer was restricted to apply to shipments where discrepancies represented merely mercantile variations; Meyer v. Packard Cleveland Motor Co., 106 Ohio St. 328, 140 N.E. 118 (1922), in which the court held that a "waiver" of all agreements not specified did not preclude implied warranty of fitness of a rebuilt dump truck for ordinary use as a dump truck; Austin Co. v. J. H. Tillman Co., 104 Or. 541, 209 P. 131 (1922), where a clause limiting the buyer's remedy to return was held to be applicable only if the seller had delivered a machine needed for a construction job which reasonably met the contract description; Bekkevold v. Potts, 173 Minn. 87, 216 N.W. 790, 59 A.L.R. 1164 (1927), refusing to allow warranty of fitness for purpose imposed by law to be negated by clause excluding all warranties "made" by the seller; Robert A. Munroe & Co. v. Meyer (1930) 2 K.B. 312, holding that the warranty of description overrides a clause reading "with all faults and defects" where adulterated meat not up to the contract description was delivered.

2. Under this section the court, in its discretion, may refuse to enforce the contract as a whole if it is permeated by the unconscionability, or it may strike any single clause or group of clauses which are so tainted or which are contrary to the essential purpose of the agreement, or it may simply limit unconscionable clauses so as to avoid unconscionable results.

3. The present section is addressed to the court, and the decision is to be made by it. The commercial evidence referred to in subsection (2) is for the court's consideration, not the jury's. Only the agreement which results from the court's action on these matters is to be submitted to the general triers of the facts.

§ 2–312. Warranty of Title and Against Infringement; Buyer's Obligation Against Infringement

(1) Subject to subsection (2) there is in a contract for sale a warranty by the seller that

(a) the title conveyed shall be good, and its transfer rightful; and

(b) the goods shall be delivered free from any security interest or other lien or encumbrance of which the buyer at the time of contracting has no knowledge.

(2) A warranty under subsection (1) will be excluded or modified only by specific language or by circumstances which give the buyer reason to know that the person selling does not claim title in himself or that he is purporting to sell only such right or title as he or a third person may have.

(3) Unless otherwise agreed a seller who is a merchant regularly dealing in goods of the kind warrants that the goods shall be delivered free of the rightful claim of any third person by way of infringement or the like but a buyer who furnishes specifications to the seller must hold the seller harmless against any such claim which arises out of compliance with the specifications.

§ 2–313. Express Warranties by Affirmation, Promise, Description, Sample

(1) Express warranties by the seller are created as follows:

(a) Any affirmation of fact or promise made by the seller to the buyer which relates to the goods and becomes part of the basis of the bargain creates an express warranty that the goods shall conform to the affirmation or promise.

(b) Any description of the goods which is made part of the basis of the bargain creates an express warranty that the goods shall conform to the description.

(c) Any sample or model which is made part of the basis of the bargain creates an express warranty that the whole of the goods shall conform to the sample or model.

(2) It is not necessary to the creation of an express warranty that the seller use formal words such as "warrant" or "guarantee" or that he have a specific intention to make a warranty, but an affirmation merely of the value of the goods or a statement purporting to be merely the seller's opinion or commendation of the goods does not create a warranty.

Official Comment

Purposes of Changes: To consolidate and systematize basic principles with the result that:

1. "Express" warranties rest on "dickered" aspects of the individual bargain, and go so clearly to the essence of that bargain that words of disclaimer in a form are repugnant to the basic dickered terms. "Implied" warranties rest so clearly on a common factual situation or set of conditions that no particular language or action is necessary to evidence them and they will arise in such a situation unless unmistakably negated.

This section reverts to the older case law insofar as the warranties of description and sample are designated "express" rather than "implied."

2. Although this section is limited in its scope and direct purpose to warranties made by the seller to the buyer as part of a contract for sale, the warranty sections of this Article are not designed in any way to disturb those lines of case law growth which have recognized that warranties need not be confined either to sales contracts or to the direct parties to such a contract. They may arise in other appropriate circumstances such as in the case of bailments for hire, whether such bailment is itself the main contract or is merely a supplying of containers under a contract for the sale of their contents. The provisions of Section 2–318 on third party beneficiaries expressly recognize this

case law development within one particular area. Beyond that, the matter is left to the case law with the intention that the policies of this Act may offer useful guidance in dealing with further cases as they arise.

3. The present section deals with affirmations of fact by the seller, descriptions of the goods or exhibitions of samples, exactly as any other part of a negotiation which ends in a contract is dealt with. No specific intention to make a warranty is necessary if any of these factors is made part of the basis of the bargain. In actual practice affirmations of fact made by the seller about the goods during a bargain are regarded as part of the description of those goods; hence no particular reliance on such statements need be shown in order to weave them into the fabric of the agreement. Rather, any fact which is to take such affirmations, once made, out of the agreement requires clear affirmative proof. The issue normally is one of fact.

4. In view of the principle that the whole purpose of the law of warranty is to determine what it is that the seller has in essence agreed to sell, the policy is adopted of those cases which refuse except in unusual circumstances to recognize a material deletion of the seller's obligation. Thus, a contract is normally a contract for a sale of something describable and described. A clause generally disclaiming "all warranties, express or implied" cannot reduce the seller's

889

obligation with respect to such description and therefore cannot be given literal effect under Section 2–316.

This is not intended to mean that the parties, if they consciously desire, cannot make their own bargain as they wish. But in determining what they have agreed upon good faith is a factor and consideration should be given to the fact that the probability is small that a real price is intended to be exchanged for a pseudo-obligation.

5. Paragraph (1)(b) makes specific some of the principles set forth above when a description of the goods is given by the seller.

A description need not be by words. Technical specifications, blueprints and the like can afford more exact description than mere language and if made part of the basis of the bargain goods must conform with them. Past deliveries may set the description of quality, either expressly or impliedly by course of dealing. Of course, all descriptions by merchants must be read against the applicable trade usages with the general rules as to merchantability resolving any doubts.

6. The basic situation as to statements affecting the true essence of the bargain is no different when a sample or model is involved in the transaction. This section includes both a "sample" actually drawn from the bulk of goods which is the subject matter of the sale, and a "model" which is offered for inspection when the subject matter is not at hand and which has not been drawn from the bulk of the goods.

Although the underlying principles are unchanged, the facts are often ambiguous when something is shown as illustrative, rather than as a straight sample. In general, the presumption is that any sample or model just as any affirmation of fact is intended to become a basis of the bargain. But there is no escape from the question of fact. When the seller exhibits a sample purporting to be drawn from an existing bulk, good faith of course requires that the sample be fairly drawn. But in mercantile experience the mere exhibition of a "sample" does not of itself show whether it is merely intended to "suggest" or to "be" the character of the subject-matter of the contract. The question is whether the seller has so acted with reference to the sample as to make him responsible that the whole shall have at least the values shown by it. The circumstances aid in answering this question. If the sample has been drawn from an existing bulk, it must be regarded as describing values of the goods contracted for unless it is accompanied by an unmistakable denial of such responsibility. If, on the other hand, a model of merchandise not on hand is offered, the mercantile presumption that it has become a literal description of the subject matter is not so strong, and particularly so if modification on the buyer's initiative impairs any feature of the model.

7. The precise time when words of description or affirmation are made or samples are shown is not material. The sole question is whether the language or samples or models are fairly to be regarded as part of the contract. If language is used after the closing of the deal (as when the buyer when taking delivery asks and receives an additional assurance), the warranty becomes a modification, and need not be supported by consideration if it is otherwise reasonable and in order (Section 2–209).

8. Concerning affirmations of value or a seller's opinion or commendation under subsection (2), the basic question remains the same: What statements of the seller have in the circumstances and in objective judgment become part of the basis of the bargain? As indicated above, all of the statements of the seller do so unless good reason is shown to the contrary. The provisions of subsection (2) are included, however, since common experience discloses that some statements

or predictions cannot fairly be viewed as entering into the bargain. Even as to false statements of value, however, the possibility is left open that a remedy may be provided by the law relating to fraud or misrepresentation.

§ 2–314. Implied Warranty: Merchantability; Usage of Trade

(1) Unless excluded or modified (Section 2–316), a warranty that the goods shall be merchantable is implied in a contract for their sale if the seller is a merchant with respect to goods of that kind. Under this section the serving for value of food or drink to be consumed either on the premises or elsewhere is a sale.

(2) Goods to be merchantable must be at least such as

(a) pass without objection in the trade under the contract description; and

(b) in the case of fungible goods, are of fair average quality within the description; and

(c) are fit for the ordinary purposes for which such goods are used; and

(d) run, within the variations permitted by the agreement, of even kind, quality and quantity within each unit and among all units involved; and

(e) are adequately contained, packaged, and labeled as the agreement may require; and

(f) conform to the promises or affirmations of fact made on the container or label if any.

(3) Unless excluded or modified (Section 2–316) other implied warranties may arise from course of dealing or usage of trade.

Official Comment

Purposes of Changes: This section, drawn in view of the steadily developing case law on the subject, is intended to make it clear that:

1. The seller's obligation applies to present sales as well as to contracts to sell subject to the effects of any examination of specific goods. (Subsection (2) of Section 2–316). Also, the warranty of merchantability applies to sales for use as well as to sales for resale.

2. The question when the warranty is imposed turns basically on the meaning of the terms of the agreement as recognized in the trade. Goods delivered under an agreement made by a merchant in a given line of trade must be of a quality comparable to that gener-ally acceptable in that line of trade under the description or other designation of the goods used in the agreement. The responsibility imposed rests on any mer-chant-seller, and the absence of the words "grower or manufacturer or not" which appeared in Section 15(2) of the Uniform Sales Act does not restrict the applicability of this section.

3. A specific designation of goods by the buyer does not exclude the sell-er's obligation that they be fit for the general purposes appropriate to such goods. A contract for the sale of second-hand goods, however, involves only such obligation as is appropriate to such goods for that is their contract descrip-tion. A person making an isolated sale of goods is not a "merchant" within the

meaning of the full scope of this section and, thus, no warranty of merchantability would apply. His knowledge of any defects not apparent on inspection would, however, without need for express agreement and in keeping with the underlying reason of the present section and the provisions on good faith, impose an obligation that known material but hidden defects be fully disclosed.

4. Although a seller may not be a "merchant" as to the goods in question, if he states generally that they are "guaranteed" the provisions of this section may furnish a guide to the content of the resulting express warranty. This has particular significance in the case of second-hand sales, and has further significance in limiting the effect of fine-print disclaimer clauses where their effect would be inconsistent with large-print assertions of "guarantee."

. . .

6. Subsection (2) does not purport to exhaust the meaning of "merchantable" nor to negate any of its attributes not specifically mentioned in the text of the statute, but arising by usage of trade or through case law. The language used is "must be at least such as . . . ," and the intention is to leave open other possible attributes of merchantability.

7. Paragraphs (a) and (b) of subsection (2) are to be read together. Both refer, as indicated above, to the standards of that line of the trade which fits the transaction and the seller's business. "Fair average" is a term directly appropriate to agricultural bulk products and means goods centering around the middle belt of quality, not the least or the worst that can be understood in the particular trade by the designation, but such as can pass "without objection." Of course a fair percentage of the least is permissible but the goods are not "fair average" if they are all of the least or worst quality possible under the description. In cases of doubt as to what quality is intended, the price at which a merchant closes a contract is an excellent index of the nature and scope of his obligation under the present section.

8. Fitness for the ordinary purposes for which goods of the type are used is a fundamental concept of the present section and is covered in paragraph (c). As stated above, merchantability is also a part of the obligation owing to the purchaser for use. Correspondingly, protection, under this aspect of the warranty, of the person buying for resale to the ultimate consumer is equally necessary, and merchantable goods must therefore be "honestly" resalable in the normal course of business because they are what they purport to be.

9. Paragraph (d) on evenness of kind, quality and quantity follows case law. But precautionary language has been added as a remainder of the frequent usages of trade which permit substantial variations both with and without an allowance or an obligation to replace the varying units.

10. Paragraph (e) applies only where the nature of the goods and of the transaction require a certain type of container, package or label. Paragraph (f) applies, on the other hand, wherever there is a label or container on which representations are made, even though the original contract, either by express terms or usage of trade, may not have required either the labelling or the representation. This follows from the general obligation of good faith which requires that a buyer should not be placed in the position of reselling or using goods delivered under false representations appearing on the package or container. No problem of extra consideration arises in this connection since, under this Article, an obligation is imposed by the original contract not to deliver mislabeled articles, and the obligation is imposed where mercantile good faith so requires and without reference to the doctrine of consideration.

11. Exclusion or modification of the warranty of merchantability, or of any part of it, is dealt with in the section to which the text of the present section makes explicit precautionary reference. That section must be read with particular reference to its subsection (4) on limitation of remedies. The warranty of merchantability, wherever it is normal, is so commonly taken for granted that its exclusion from the contract is a matter threatening surprise and therefore requiring special precaution.

12. Subsection (3) is to make explicit that usage of trade and course of dealing can create warranties and that they are implied rather than express warranties and thus subject to exclusion or modification under Section 2–316. A typical instance would be the obligation to provide pedigree papers to evidence conformity of the animal to the contract in the case of a pedigreed dog or blooded bull.

13. In an action based on breach of warranty, it is of course necessary to show not only the existence of the warranty but the fact that the warranty was broken and that the breach of the warranty was the proximate cause of the loss sustained. In such an action an affirmative showing by the seller that the loss resulted from some action or event following his own delivery of the goods can operate as a defense. Equally, evidence indicating that the seller exercised care in the manufacture, processing or selection of the goods is relevant to the issue of whether the warranty was in fact broken. Action by the buyer following an examination of the goods which ought to have indicated the defect complained of can be shown as matter bearing on whether the breach itself was the cause of the injury.

§ 2–315. Implied Warranty: Fitness for Particular Purpose

Where the seller at the time of contracting has reason to know any particular purpose for which the goods are required and that the buyer is relying on the seller's skill or judgment to select or furnish suitable goods, there is unless excluded or modified under the next section an implied warranty that the goods shall be fit for such purpose.

Official Comment

Purposes of Changes:

1. Whether or not this warranty arises in any individual case is basically a question of fact to be determined by the circumstances of the contracting. Under this section the buyer need not bring home to the seller actual knowledge of the particular purpose for which the goods are intended or of his reliance on the seller's skill and judgment, if the circumstances are such that the seller has reason to realize the purpose intended or that the reliance exists. The buyer, of course, must actually be relying on the seller.

2. A "particular purpose" differs from the ordinary purpose for which the goods are used in that it envisages a specific use by the buyer which is peculiar to the nature of his business whereas the ordinary purposes for which goods are used are those envisaged in the concept of merchantability and go to uses which are customarily made of the goods in question. For example, shoes are generally used for the purpose of walking upon ordinary ground, but a seller may know that a particular pair was selected to be used for climbing mountains.

A contract may of course include both a warranty of merchantability and one of fitness for a particular purpose.

The provisions of this Article on the cumulation and conflict of express and implied warranties must be considered on the question of inconsistency between or among warranties. In such a case any question of fact as to which warranty was intended by the parties to apply must be resolved in favor of the warranty of fitness for particular purpose as against all other warranties except where the buyer has taken upon himself the responsibility of furnishing the technical specifications.

3. In connection with the warranty of fitness for a particular purpose the provisions of this Article on the allocation or division of risks are particularly applicable in any transaction in which the purpose for which the goods are to be used combines requirements both as to the quality of the goods themselves and compliance with certain laws or regulations. How the risks are divided is a question of fact to be determined, where not expressly contained in the agreement, from the circumstances of contracting, usage of trade, course of performance and the like, matters which may constitute the "otherwise agreement" of the parties by which they may divide the risk or burden.

4. . . . Although normally the warranty will arise only where the seller is a merchant with the appropriate "skill or judgment," it can arise as to non-merchants where this is justified by the particular circumstances.

5. The elimination of the "patent or other trade name" exception constitutes the major extension of the warranty of fitness which has been made by the cases and continued in this Article. Under the present section the existence of a patent or other trade name and the designation of the article by that name, or indeed in any other definite manner, is only one of the facts to be considered on the question of whether the buyer actually relied on the seller, but it is not of itself decisive of the issue. If the buyer himself is insisting on a particular brand he is not relying on the seller's skill and judgment and so no warranty results. But the mere fact that the article purchased has a particular patent or trade name is not sufficient to indicate nonreliance if the article has been recommended by the seller as adequate for the buyer's purposes.

. . .

§ 2–316. **Exclusion or Modification of Warranties**

(1) Words or conduct relevant to the creation of an express warranty and words or conduct tending to negate or limit warranty shall be construed wherever reasonable as consistent with each other; but subject to the provisions of this Article on parol or extrinsic evidence (Section 2–202) negation or limitation is inoperative to the extent that such construction is unreasonable.

(2) Subject to subsection (3), to exclude or modify the implied warranty of merchantability or any part of it the language must mention merchantability and in case of a writing must be conspicuous, and to exclude or modify any implied warranty of fitness the exclusion must be by a writing and conspicuous. Language to exclude all implied warranties of fitness is sufficient if it states, for example, that "There are no warranties which extend beyond the description on the face hereof."

(3) Notwithstanding subsection (2)

(a) unless the circumstances indicate otherwise, all implied warranties are excluded by expressions like "as is," "with all faults" or other language which in common understanding calls the buyer's attention to the exclusion of warranties and makes plain that there is no implied warranty; and

(b) when the buyer before entering into the contract has examined the goods or the sample or model as fully as he desired or has refused to examine the goods there is no implied warranty with regard to defects which an examination ought in the circumstances to have revealed to him; and

(c) an implied warranty can also be excluded or modified by course of dealing or course of performance or usage of trade.

(4) Remedies for breach of warranty can be limited in accordance with the provisions of this Article on liquidation or limitation of damages and on contractual modification of remedy (Sections 2–718 and 2–719).

Official Comment

Purposes:

1. This section is designed principally to deal with those frequent clauses in sales contracts which seek to exclude "all warranties, express or implied." It seeks to protect a buyer from unexpected and unbargained language of disclaimer by denying effect to such language when inconsistent with language of express warranty and permitting the exclusion of implied warranties only by conspicuous language or other circumstances which protect the buyer from surprise.

2. The seller is protected under this Article against false allegations of oral warranties by its provisions on parol and extrinsic evidence and against unauthorized representations by the customary "lack of authority" clauses. This Article treats the limitation or avoidance of consequential damages as a matter of limiting remedies for breach, separate from the matter of creation of liability under a warranty. If no warranty exists, there is of course no problem of limiting remedies for breach of warranty. Under subsection (4) the question of limitation of remedy is governed by the sections referred to rather than by this section.

3. Disclaimer of the implied warranty of merchantability is permitted under subsection (2), but with the safeguard that such disclaimers must mention merchantability and in case of a writing must be conspicuous.

4. Unlike the implied warranty of merchantability, implied warranties of fitness for a particular purpose may be excluded by general language, but only if it is in writing and conspicuous.

5. Subsection (2) presupposes that the implied warranty in question exists unless excluded or modified. Whether or not language of disclaimer satisfies the requirements of this section, such language may be relevant under other sections to the question whether the warranty was ever in fact created. Thus, unless the provisions of this Article on parol and extrinsic evidence prevent, oral language of disclaimer may raise issues of fact as to whether reliance by the buyer occurred and whether the seller had "reason to know" under the section on implied warranty of fitness for a particular purpose.

6. The exceptions to the general rule set forth in paragraphs (a), (b) and (c) of subsection (3) are common factual situations in which the circumstances surrounding the transaction are in themselves sufficient to call the buyer's attention to the fact that no implied warranties are made or that a certain implied warranty is being excluded.

7. Paragraph (a) of subsection (3) deals with general terms such as "as

is," "as they stand," "with all faults," and the like. Such terms in ordinary commercial usage are understood to mean that the buyer takes the entire risk as to the quality of the goods involved. The terms covered by paragraph (a) are in fact merely a particularization of paragraph (c) which provides for exclusion or modification of implied warranties by usage of trade.

8. Under paragraph (b) of subsection (3) warranties may be excluded or modified by the circumstances where the buyer examines the goods or a sample or model of them before entering into the contract. "Examination" as used in this paragraph is not synonymous with inspection before acceptance or at any other time after the contract has been made. It goes rather to the nature of the responsibility assumed by the seller at the time of the making of the contract. Of course if the buyer discovers the defect and uses the goods anyway, or if he unreasonably fails to examine the goods before he uses them, resulting injuries may be found to result from his own action rather than proximately from a breach of warranty. See Sections 2–314 and 2–715 and comments thereto.

In order to bring the transaction within the scope of "refused to examine" in paragraph (b), it is not sufficient that the goods are available for inspection. There must in addition be a demand by the seller that the buyer examine the goods fully. The seller by the demand puts the buyer on notice that he is assuming the risk of defects which the examination ought to reveal. The language "refused to examine" in this paragraph is intended to make clear the necessity for such demand.

Application of the doctrine of "caveat emptor" in all cases where the buyer examines the goods regardless of statements made by the seller is, however, rejected by this Article. Thus, if the offer of examination is accompanied by words as to their merchantability or specific attributes and the buyer indicates clearly that he is relying on those words rather than on his examination, they give rise to an "express" warranty. In such cases the question is one of fact as to whether a warranty of merchantability has been expressly incorporated in the agreement. Disclaimer of such an express warranty is governed by subsection (1) of the present section.

The particular buyer's skill and the normal method of examining goods in the circumstances determine what defects are excluded by the examination. A failure to notice defects which are obvious cannot excuse the buyer. However, an examination under circumstances which do not permit chemical or other testing of the goods would not exclude defects which could be ascertained only by such testing. Nor can latent defects be excluded by a simple examination. A professional buyer examining a product in his field will be held to have assumed the risk as to all defects which a professional in the field ought to observe, while a nonprofessional buyer will be held to have assumed the risk only for such defects as a layman might be expected to observe.

. . .

§ 2–317. Cumulation and Conflict of Warranties Express or Implied

Warranties whether express or implied shall be construed as consistent with each other and as cumulative, but if such construction is unreasonable the intention of the parties shall determine which warranty is dominant. In ascertaining that intention the following rules apply:

(a) Exact or technical specifications displace an inconsistent sample or model or general language of description.

(b) A sample from an existing bulk displaces inconsistent general language of description.

(c) Express warranties displace inconsistent implied warranties other than an implied warranty of fitness for a particular purpose.

Official Comment

Purposes of Changes:

. . .

2. The rules of this section are designed to aid in determining the intention of the parties as to which of inconsistent warranties which have arisen from the circumstances of their transaction shall prevail. These rules of intention are to be applied only where factors making for an equitable estoppel of the seller do not exist and where he has in perfect good faith made warranties which later turn out to be inconsistent. To the extent that the seller has led the buyer to believe that all of the warranties can be performed, he is estopped from setting up any essential inconsistency as a defense.

. . .

§ 2–318. Third Party Beneficiaries of Warranties Express or Implied

Alternative A

A seller's warranty whether express or implied extends to any natural person who is in the family or household of his buyer or who is a guest in his home if it is reasonable to expect that such person may use, consume or be affected by the goods and who is injured in person by breach of the warranty. A seller may not exclude or limit the operation of this section.

Alternative B

A seller's warranty whether express or implied extends to any natural person who may reasonably be expected to use, consume or be affected by the goods and who is injured in person by breach of the warranty. A seller may not exclude or limit the operation of this section.

Alternative C

A seller's warranty whether express or implied extends to any person who may reasonably be expected to use, consume or be affected by the goods and who is injured by breach of the warranty. A seller may not exclude or limit the operation of this section with respect to injury to the person of an individual to whom the warranty extends.

Official Comment

Purposes:

1. The last sentence of this section does not mean that a seller is precluded from excluding or disclaiming a warranty which might otherwise arise in connection with the sale provided such exclusion or modification is permitted by Section 2–316. Nor does that sentence preclude the seller from limiting the remedies of his own buyer and of any beneficiaries, in any manner provided in Sections 2–718 or 2–719. To the extent that the contract of sale contains provisions under which warranties are excluded or modified, or remedies for breach are limited, such provisions are

897

equally operative against beneficiaries of warranties under this section. What this last sentence forbids is exclusion of liability by the seller to the persons to whom the warranties which he has made to his buyer would extend under this section.

2. The purpose of this section is to give certain beneficiaries the benefit of the same warranty which the buyer received in the contract of sale, thereby freeing any such beneficiaries from any technical rules as to "privity." It seeks to accomplish this purpose without any derogation of any right or remedy resting on negligence. It rests primarily upon the merchant-seller's warranty under this Article that the goods sold are merchantable and fit for the ordinary purposes for which such goods are used rather than the warranty of fitness for a particular purpose. Implicit in the section is that any beneficiary of a warranty may bring a direct action for breach of warranty against the seller whose warranty extends to him [As amended in 1966].

3. The first alternative expressly includes as beneficiaries within its provisions the family, household and guests of the purchaser. Beyond this, the section in this form is neutral and is not intended to enlarge or restrict the developing case law on whether the seller's warranties, given to his buyer who resells, extend to other persons in the distributive chain. The second alternative is designed for states where the case law has already developed further and for those that desire to expand the class of beneficiaries. The third alternative goes further, following the trend of modern decisions as indicated by Restatement of Torts 2d § 402A . . . in extending the rule beyond injuries to the person.

PART 5.   PERFORMANCE

§ 2–507.   Effect of Seller's Tender; Delivery on Condition

(1) Tender of delivery is a condition to the buyer's duty to accept the goods and, unless otherwise agreed, to his duty to pay for them. Tender entitles the seller to acceptance of the goods and to payment according to the contract.

(2) Where payment is due and demanded on the delivery to the buyer of goods or documents of title, his right as against the seller to retain or dispose of them is conditional upon his making the payment due.

§ 2–508.   Cure by Seller of Improper Tender or Delivery; Replacement

(1) Where any tender or delivery by the seller is rejected because nonconforming and the time for performance has not yet expired, the seller may seasonably notify the buyer of his intention to cure and may then within the contract time make a conforming delivery.

(2) Where the buyer rejects a non-conforming tender which the seller had reasonable grounds to believe would be acceptable with or without money allowance the seller may if he seasonably notifies the buyer have a further reasonable time to substitute a conforming tender.

Official Comment

Purposes:

1. Subsection (1) permits a seller who has made a non-conforming tender in any case to make a conforming delivery within the contract time upon seasonable notification to the buyer. It applies even where the seller has taken back the non-conforming goods and refunded the purchase price. He may still make a good tender within the contract period. The closer, however, it is to the contract date, the greater is the necessity for extreme promptness on the seller's part in notifying of his intention to cure, if such notification is to be "seasonable" under this subsection.

The rule of this subsection, moreover, is qualified by its underlying reasons. Thus if, after contracting for June delivery, a buyer later makes known to the seller his need for shipment early in the month and the seller ships accordingly, the "contract time" has been cut down by the supervening modification and the time for cure of tender must be referred to this modified time term.

2. Subsection (2) seeks to avoid injustice to the seller by reason of a surprise rejection by the buyer. However, the seller is not protected unless he had "reasonable grounds to believe" that the tender would be acceptable. Such reasonable grounds can lie in prior course of dealing, course of performance or usage of trade as well as in the particular circumstances surrounding the making of the contract. The seller is charged with commercial knowledge of any factors in a particular sales situation which require him to comply strictly with his obligations under the contract as, for example, strict conformity of documents in an overseas shipment or the sale of precision parts or chemicals for use in manufacture. Further, if the buyer gives notice either implicitly, as by a prior course of dealing involving rigorous inspections, or expressly, as by the deliberate inclusion of a "no replacement" clause in the contract, the seller is to be held to rigid compliance. If the clause appears in a "form" contract evidence that it is out of line with trade usage or the prior course of dealing and was not called to the seller's attention may be sufficient to show that the seller had reasonable grounds to believe that the tender would be acceptable.

3. The words "a further reasonable time to substitute a conforming tender" are intended as words of limitation to protect the buyer. What is a "reasonable time" depends upon the attending circumstances. Compare Section 2–511 on the comparable case of a seller's surprise demand for legal tender.

. . .

PART 6. BREACH, REPUDIATION AND EXCUSE

§ 2–601. Buyer's Rights on Improper Delivery

Subject to the provisions of this Article on breach in installment contracts (Section 2–612) and unless otherwise agreed under the sections on contractual limitations of remedy (Sections 2–718 and 2–719), if the goods or the tender of delivery fail in any respect to conform to the contract, the buyer may

(a) reject the whole; or

(b) accept the whole; or

(c) accept any commercial unit or units and reject the rest.

§ 2–602. Manner and Effect of Rightful Rejection

(1) Rejection of goods must be within a reasonable time after their delivery or tender. It is ineffective unless the buyer seasonably notifies the seller.

(2) Subject to the provisions of the two following sections on rejected goods (Sections 2–603 and 2–604),

> (a) after rejection any exercise of ownership by the buyer with respect to any commercial unit is wrongful as against the seller; and

> (b) if the buyer has before rejection taken physical possession of goods in which he does not have a security interest under the provisions of this Article (subsection (3) of Section 2–711), he is under a duty after rejection to hold them with reasonable care at the seller's disposition for a time sufficient to permit the seller to remove them; but

> (c) the buyer has no further obligations with regard to goods rightfully rejected.

(3) The seller's rights with respect to goods wrongfully rejected are governed by the provisions of this Article on Seller's remedies in general (Section 2–703).

Official Comment

Purposes of Changes: To make it clear that:

1. A tender or delivery of goods made pursuant to a contract of sale, even though wholly non-conforming, requires affirmative action by the buyer to avoid acceptance. Under subsection (1), therefore, the buyer is given a reasonable time to notify the seller of his rejection, but without such seasonable notification his rejection is ineffective. The sections of this Article dealing with inspection of goods must be read in connection with the buyer's reasonable time for action under this subsection. Contract provisions limiting the time for rejection fall within the rule of the section on "Time" and are effective if the time set gives the buyer a reasonable time for discovery of defects. What con-stitutes a due "notifying" of rejection by the buyer to the seller is defined in Section 1–201.

. . .

3. The present section applies only to rightful rejection by the buyer. If the seller has made a tender which in all respects conforms to the contract, the buyer has a positive duty to accept and his failure to do so constitutes a "wrongful rejection" which gives the seller immediate remedies for breach. Subsection (3) is included here to emphasize the sharp distinction between the rejection of an improper tender and the non-acceptance which is a breach by the buyer.

4. The provisions of this section are to be appropriately limited or modified when a negotiation is in process.

§ 2–605. Waiver of Buyer's Objections by Failure to Particularize

(1) The buyer's failure to state in connection with rejection a particular defect which is ascertainable by reasonable inspection precludes him from relying on the unstated defect to justify rejection or to establish breach

(a) where the seller could have cured it if stated seasonably; or

(b) between merchants when the seller has after rejection made a request in writing for a full and final written statement of all defects on which the buyer proposes to rely.

(2) Payment against documents made without reservation of rights precludes recovery of the payment for defects apparent on the face of the documents.

Official Comment

Purposes:

. . .

2. Where the defect in a tender is one which could have been cured by the seller, a buyer who merely rejects the delivery without stating his objections to it is probably acting in commercial bad faith and seeking to get out of a deal which has become unprofitable. Subsection (1)(a), following the general policy of this Article which looks to preserving the deal wherever possible, therefore insists that the seller's right to correct his tender in such circumstances be protected.

. . .

§ 2–606. What Constitutes Acceptance of Goods

(1) Acceptance of goods occurs when the buyer

(a) after a reasonable opportunity to inspect the goods signifies to the seller that the goods are conforming or that he will take or retain them in spite of their non-conformity; or

(b) fails to make an effective rejection (subsection (1) of Section 2–602), but such acceptance does not occur until the buyer has had a reasonable opportunity to inspect them; or

(c) does any act inconsistent with the seller's ownership; but if such act is wrongful as against the seller it is an acceptance only if ratified by him.

(2) Acceptance of a part of any commercial unit is acceptance of that entire unit.

§ 2–607. Effect of Acceptance; Notice of Breach; Burden of Establishing Breach After Acceptance; Notice of Claim or Litigation to Person Answerable Over

(1) The buyer must pay at the contract rate for any goods accepted.

(2) Acceptance of goods by the buyer precludes rejection of the goods accepted and if made with knowledge of a non-conformity cannot be revoked because of it unless the acceptance was on the reasonable assumption that the non-conformity would be seasonably cured but acceptance does not of itself impair any other remedy provided by this Article for non-conformity.

(3) Where a tender has been accepted

(a) the buyer must within a reasonable time after he discovers or should have discovered any breach notify the seller of breach or be barred from any remedy; and

(b) if the claim is one for infringement or the like (subsection (3) of Section 2–312) and the buyer is sued as a result of such a breach he must so notify the seller within a reasonable time after he receives notice of the litigation or be barred from any remedy over for liability established by the litigation.

(4) The burden is on the buyer to establish any breach with respect to the goods accepted.

(5) Where the buyer is sued for breach of a warranty or other obligation for which his seller is answerable over

(a) he may give his seller written notice of the litigation. If the notice states that the seller may come in and defend and that if the seller does not do so he will be bound in any action against him by his buyer by any determination of fact common to the two litigations, then unless the seller after seasonable receipt of the notice does come in and defend he is so bound.

(b) if the claim is one for infringement or the like (subsection (3) of Section 2–312) the original seller may demand in writing that his buyer turn over to him control of the litigation including settlement or else be barred from any remedy over and if he also agrees to bear all expense and to satisfy any adverse judgment, then unless the buyer after seasonable receipt of the demand does turn over control the buyer is so barred.

(6) The provisions of subsections (3), (4) and (5) apply to any obligation of a buyer to hold the seller harmless against infringement or the like (subsection (3) of Section 2–312).

Official Comment

Purposes of Changes: To continue the prior basic policies with respect to acceptance of goods while making a number of minor though material changes in the interest of simplicity and commercial convenience so that:

. . .

4. The time of notification is to be determined by applying commercial standards to a merchant buyer. "A reasonable time" for notification from a retail consumer is to be judged by different standards so that in his case it will be extended, for the rule of requiring notification is designed to defeat commercial bad faith, not to deprive a good faith consumer of his remedy.

The content of the notification need merely be sufficient to let the seller know that the transaction is still troublesome and must be watched. There is no reason to require that the notification which saves the buyer's rights under this section must include a clear statement of all the objections that will be relied on by the buyer, as under the section covering statements of defects upon rejection (Section 2–605). Nor is there reason for requiring the notification to be a claim for damages or of any threatened litigation or other resort to a remedy. The notification which saves the buyer's rights under this Article need only be such as informs the seller that the transaction is claimed to involve a breach, and thus opens the way for normal settlement through negotiation.

5. Under this Article various beneficiaries are given rights for injuries sustained by them because of the seller's breach of warranty. Such a beneficiary does not fall within the reason of the present section in regard to discovery of defects and the giving of notice within a reasonable time after acceptance, since he has nothing to do with acceptance. However, the reason of this section does extend to requiring the beneficiary to notify the seller that an injury has occurred. What is said above, with regard to the extended time for reasonable notification from the lay consumer after the injury is also applicable here; but even a beneficiary can be properly held to the use of good faith in notifying, once he has had time to become aware of the legal situation.

.   .   .

§ 2–608. Revocation of Acceptance in Whole or in Part

(1) The buyer may revoke his acceptance of a lot or commercial unit whose non-conformity substantially impairs its value to him if he has accepted it

(a) on the reasonable assumption that its non-conformity would be cured and it has not been seasonably cured; or

(b) without discovery of such non-conformity if his acceptance was reasonably induced either by the difficulty of discovery before acceptance or by the seller's assurances.

(2) Revocation of acceptance must occur within a reasonable time after the buyer discovers or should have discovered the ground for it and before any substantial change in condition of the goods which is not caused by their own defects. It is not effective until the buyer notifies the seller of it.

(3) A buyer who so revokes has the same rights and duties with regard to the goods involved as if he had rejected them.

Official Comment

Purposes of Changes: To make it clear that:

1. Although the prior basic policy is continued, the buyer is no longer required to elect between revocation of acceptance and recovery of damages for breach. Both are now available to him. The non-alternative character of the two remedies is stressed by the terms used in the present section. The section no longer speaks of "rescission," a term capable of ambiguous application either to transfer of title to the goods or to the contract of sale and susceptible also of confusion with cancellation for cause of an executed or executory portion of the contract. The remedy under this section is instead referred to simply as "revocation of acceptance" of goods tendered under a contract for sale and involves no suggestion of "election" of any sort.

2. Revocation of acceptance is possible only where the non-conformity substantially impairs the value of the goods to the buyer. For this purpose the test is not what the seller had reason to know at the time of contracting; the question is whether the non-conformity is such as will in fact cause a substantial impairment of value to the buyer though the seller had no advance knowledge as to the buyer's particular circumstances.

3. "Assurances" by the seller under paragraph (b) of subsection (1) can

rest as well in the circumstances or in the contract as in explicit language used at the time of delivery. The reason for recognizing such assurances is that they induce the buyer to delay discovery. These are the only assurances involved in paragraph (b). Explicit assurances may be made either in good faith or bad faith. In either case any remedy accorded by this Article is available to the buyer under the section on remedies for fraud.

4. Subsection (2) requires notification of revocation of acceptance within a reasonable time after discovery of the grounds for such revocation. Since this remedy will be generally resorted to only after attempts at adjustment have failed, the reasonable time period should extend in most cases beyond the time in which notification of breach must be given, beyond the time for discovery of non-conformity after acceptance and beyond the time for rejection after tender. The parties may by their agreement limit the time for notification under this section, but the same sanctions and considerations apply to such agreements as are discussed in the comment on manner and effect of rightful rejection.

5. The content of the notice under subsection (2) is to be determined in this case as in others by considerations of good faith, prevention of surprise, and reasonable adjustment. More will generally be necessary than the mere notification of breach required under the preceding section. On the other hand the requirements of the section on waiver of buyer's objections do not apply here. The fact that quick notification of trouble is desirable affords good ground for being slow to bind a buyer by his first statement. Following the general policy of this Article, the requirements of the content of notification are less stringent in the case of a non-merchant buyer.

6. Under subsection (2) the prior policy is continued of seeking substantial justice in regard to the condition of goods restored to the seller. Thus the buyer may not revoke his acceptance if the goods have materially deteriorated except by reason of their own defects. Worthless goods, however, need not be offered back and minor defects in the articles reoffered are to be disregarded.

7. The policy of the section allowing partial acceptance is carried over into the present section and the buyer may revoke his acceptance, in appropriate cases, as to the entire lot or any commercial unit thereof.

§ 2–609. Right to Adequate Assurance of Performance

(1) A contract for sale imposes an obligation on each party that the other's expectation of receiving due performance will not be impaired. When reasonable grounds for insecurity arise with respect to the performance of either party the other may in writing demand adequate assurance of due performance and until he receives such assurance may if commercially reasonable suspend any performance for which he has not already received the agreed return.

(2) Between merchants the reasonableness of grounds for insecurity and the adequacy of any assurance offered shall be determined according to commercial standards.

(3) Acceptance of any improper delivery or payment does not prejudice the aggrieved party's right to demand adequate assurance of future performance.

(4) After receipt of a justified demand failure to provide within a reasonable time not exceeding thirty days such assurance of due perform-

ance as is adequate under the circumstances of the particular case is a repudiation of the contract.

Official Comment

Purposes:

1. The section rests on the recognition of the fact that the essential purpose of a contract between commercial men is actual performance and they do not bargain merely for a promise, or for a promise plus the right to win a lawsuit and that a continuing sense of reliance and security that the promised performance will be forthcoming when due, is an important feature of the bargain. If either the willingness or the ability of a party to perform declines materially between the time of contracting and the time for performance, the other party is threatened with the loss of a substantial part of what he has bargained for. A seller needs protection not merely against having to deliver on credit to a shaky buyer, but also against having to procure and manufacture the goods, perhaps turning down other customers. Once he has been given reason to believe that the buyer's performance has become uncertain, it is an undue hardship to force him to continue his own performance. Similarly, a buyer who believes that the seller's deliveries have become uncertain cannot safely wait for the due date of performance when he has been buying to assure himself of materials for his current manufacturing or to replenish his stock of merchandise.

2. Three measures have been adopted to meet the needs of commercial men in such situations. First, the aggrieved party is permitted to suspend his own performance and any preparation therefor, with excuse for any resulting necessary delay, until the situation has been clarified. "Suspend performance" under this section means to hold up performance pending the outcome of the demand, and includes also the holding up of any preparatory action. This is the same principle which governs the ancient law of stoppage and seller's lien, and also of excuse of a buyer from prepayment if the seller's actions manifest that he cannot or will not perform. (Original Act, Section 63(2).)

Secondly, the aggrieved party is given the right to require adequate assurance that the other party's performance will be duly forthcoming. This principle is reflected in the familiar clauses permitting the seller to curtail deliveries if the buyer's credit becomes impaired, which when held within the limits of reasonableness and good faith actually express no more than the fair business meaning of any commercial contract.

Third, and finally, this section provides the means by which the aggrieved party may treat the contract as broken if his reasonable grounds for insecurity are not cleared up within a reasonable time. This is the principle underlying the law of anticipatory breach, whether by way of defective part performance or by repudiation. The present section merges these three principles of law and commercial practice into a single theory of general application to all sales agreements looking to future performance.

3. Subsection (2) of the present section requires that "reasonable" grounds and "adequate" assurance as used in subsection (1) be defined by commercial rather than legal standards. The express reference to commercial standards carries no connotation that the obligation of good faith is not equally applicable here.

Under commercial standards and in accord with commercial practice, a ground for insecurity need not arise from or be directly related to the contract in question. The law as to "dependence" or "independence" of promises within a single contract does not control the application of the present section.

. . .

4. What constitutes "adequate" assurance of due performance is subject to the same test of factual conditions. For example, where the buyer can make use of a defective delivery, a mere promise by a seller of good repute that he is giving the matter his attention and that the defect will not be repeated, is normally sufficient. Under the same circumstances, however, a similar statement by a known corner-cutter might well be considered insufficient without the posting of a guaranty or, if so demanded by the buyer, a speedy replacement of the delivery involved. By the same token where a delivery has defects, even though easily curable, which interfere with easy use by the buyer, no verbal assurance can be deemed adequate which is not accompanied by replacement, repair, money-allowance, or other commercially reasonable cure.

. . .

The adequacy of the assurance given is not measured as in the type of "satisfaction" situation affected with intangibles, such as in personal service cases, cases involving a third party's judgment as final, or cases in which the whole contract is dependent on one party's satisfaction, as in a sale on approval. Here, the seller must exercise good faith and observe commercial standards. . . .

The entire foregoing discussion as to adequacy of assurance by way of explanation is subject to qualification when repeated occasions for the application of this section arise. This Act recognizes that repeated delinquencies must be viewed as cumulative. On the other hand, commercial sense also requires that if repeated claims for assurance are made under this section, the basis for these claims must be increasingly obvious.

. . .

PART 7. REMEDIES

§ 2–703. Seller's Remedies in General

Where the buyer wrongfully rejects or revokes acceptance of goods or fails to make a payment due on or before delivery or repudiates with respect to a part or the whole, then with respect to any goods directly affected and, if the breach is of the whole contract (Section 2–612), then also with respect to the whole undelivered balance, the aggrieved seller may

(a) withhold delivery of such goods;

(b) stop delivery by any bailee as hereafter provided (Section 2–705);

(c) proceed under the next section respecting goods still unidentified to the contract;

(d) resell and recover damages as hereafter provided (Section 2–706);

(e) recover damages for non-acceptance (Section 2–708) or in a proper case the price (Section 2–709);

(f) cancel.

Official Comment

Purposes:

1. This section is an index section which gathers together in one convenient place all of the various remedies open to a seller for any breach by the buyer. This Article rejects any doctrine of election of remedy as a fundamental policy and thus the remedies are essentially cumulative in nature and include all of the available remedies for breach. Whether the pursuit of one remedy bars another depends entirely on the facts of the individual case.

. . .

§ 2–706. Seller's Resale Including Contract for Resale

(1) Under the conditions stated in Section 2–703 on seller's remedies, the seller may resell the goods concerned or the undelivered balance thereof. Where the resale is made in good faith and in a commercially reasonable manner the seller may recover the difference between the resale price and the contract price together with any incidental damages allowed under the provisions of this Article (Section 2–710), but less expenses saved in consequence of the buyer's breach.

(2) Except as otherwise provided in subsection (3) or unless otherwise agreed resale may be at public or private sale including sale by way of one or more contracts to sell or of identification to an existing contract of the seller. Sale may be as a unit or in parcels and at any time and place and on any terms but every aspect of the sale including the method, manner, time, place and terms must be commercially reasonable. The resale must be reasonably identified as referring to the broken contract, but it is not necessary that the goods be in existence or that any or all of them have been identified to the contract before the breach.

(3) Where the resale is at private sale the seller must give the buyer reasonable notification of his intention to resell.

(4) Where the resale is at public sale

(a) only identified goods can be sold except where there is a recognized market for a public sale of futures in goods of the kind; and

(b) it must be made at a usual place or market for public sale if one is reasonably available and except in the case of goods which are perishable or threaten to decline in value speedily the seller must give the buyer reasonable notice of the time and place of the resale; and

(c) if the goods are not to be within the view of those attending the sale the notification of sale must state the place where the goods are located and provide for their reasonable inspection by prospective bidders; and

(d) the seller may buy.

(5) A purchaser who buys in good faith at a resale takes the goods free of any rights of the original buyer even though the seller fails to comply with one or more of the requirements of this section.

(6) The seller is not accountable to the buyer for any profit made on any resale. A person in the position of a seller (Section 2–707) or a buyer who has rightfully rejected or justifiably revoked acceptance must account for any excess over the amount of his security interest, as hereinafter defined (subsection (3) of Section 2–711).

Official Comment

Purposes of Changes: To simplify the prior statutory provision and to make it clear that:

1. The only condition precedent to the seller's right of resale under subsection (1) is a breach by the buyer within the section on the seller's remedies in general or insolvency. . . .

2. In order to recover the damages prescribed in subsection (1) the seller must act "in good faith and in a commercially reasonable manner" in making the resale. This standard is intended to be more comprehensive than that of "reasonable care and judgment" established by the prior uniform statutory provision. Failure to act properly under this section deprives the seller of the measure of damages here provided and relegates him to that provided in Section 2–708.

. . .

4. Subsection (2) frees the remedy of resale from legalistic restrictions and enables the seller to resell in accordance with reasonable commercial practices so as to realize as high a price as possible in the circumstances. By "public" sale is meant a sale by auction. A "private" sale may be effected by solicitation and negotiation conducted either directly or through a broker. In choosing between a public and private sale the character of the goods must be considered and relevant trade practices and usages must be observed.

§ 2–708. Seller's Damages for Non-acceptance or Repudiation

(1) Subject to subsection (2) and to the provisions of this Article with respect to proof of market price (Section 2–723), the measure of damages for non-acceptance or repudiation by the buyer is the difference between the market price at the time and place for tender and the unpaid contract price together with any incidental damages provided in this Article (Section 2–710), but less expenses saved in consequence of the buyer's breach.

(2) If the measure of damages provided in subsection (1) is inadequate to put the seller in as good a position as performance would have done then the measure of damages is the profit (including reasonable overhead) which the seller would have made from full performance by the buyer, together with any incidental damages provided in this Article (Section 2–710), due allowance for costs reasonably incurred and due credit for payments or proceeds of resale.

Official Comment

Purposes of Changes: To make it clear that:

. . .

2. The provision of this section permitting recovery of expected profit including reasonable overhead where the standard measure of damages is inadequate, together with the new requirement that price actions may be sustained only where resale is impractical, are designed to eliminate the unfair and economically wasteful results arising under the older law when fixed price articles were involved. This section per-

mits the recovery of lost profits in all appropriate cases, which would include all standard priced goods. The normal measure there would be list price less cost to the dealer or list price less manufacturing cost to the manufacturer. It is not necessary to a recovery of "profit" to show a history of earnings, especially if a new venture is involved.

3. In all cases the seller may recover incidental damages

§ 2–709. Action for the Price

(1) When the buyer fails to pay the price as it becomes due the seller may recover, together with any incidental damages under the next section, the price

(a) of goods accepted or of conforming goods lost or damaged within a commercially reasonable time after risk of their loss has passed to the buyer; and

(b) of goods identified to the contract if the seller is unable after reasonable effort to resell them at a reasonable price or the circumstances reasonably indicate that such effort will be unavailing.

(2) Where the seller sues for the price he must hold for the buyer any goods which have been identified to the contract and are still in his control except that if resale becomes possible he may resell them at any time prior to the collection of the judgment. The net proceeds of any such resale must be credited to the buyer and payment of the judgment entitles him to any goods not resold.

(3) After the buyer has wrongfully rejected or revoked acceptance of the goods or has failed to make a payment due or has repudiated (Section 2–610), a seller who is held not entitled to the price under this section shall nevertheless be awarded damages for non-acceptance under the preceding section.

§ 2–710. Seller's Incidental Damages

Incidental damages to an aggrieved seller include any commercially reasonable charges, expenses or commissions incurred in stopping delivery, in the transportation, care and custody of goods after the buyer's breach, in connection with return or resale of the goods or otherwise resulting from the breach.

§ 2–711. Buyer's Remedies in General; Buyer's Security Interest in Rejected Goods

(1) Where the seller fails to make delivery or repudiates or the buyer rightfully rejects or justifiably revokes acceptance then with respect to any goods involved, and with respect to the whole if the breach goes to the whole contract (Section 2–612), the buyer may cancel and whether or not he has done so may in addition to recovering so much of the price as has been paid

(a) "cover" and have damages under the next section as to all the goods affected whether or not they have been identified to the contract; or

(b) recover damages for non-delivery as provided in this Article (Section 2–713).

(2) Where the seller fails to deliver or repudiates the buyer may also

(a) if the goods have been identified recover them as provided in this Article (Section 2–502); or

(b) in a proper case obtain specific performance or replevy the goods as provided in this Article (Section 2–716).

(3) On rightful rejection or justifiable revocation of acceptance a buyer has a security interest in goods in his possession or control for any payments made on their price and any expenses reasonably incurred in their inspection, receipt, transportation, care and custody and may hold such goods and resell them in like manner as an aggrieved seller (Section 2–706).

§ 2–712. "Cover"; Buyer's Procurement of Substitute Goods

(1) After a breach within the preceding section the buyer may "cover" by making in good faith and without unreasonable delay any reasonable purchase of or contract to purchase goods in substitution for those due from the seller.

(2) The buyer may recover from the seller as damages the difference between the cost of cover and the contract price together with any incidental or consequential damages as hereinafter defined (Section 2–715), but less expenses saved in consequence of the seller's breach.

(3) Failure of the buyer to effect cover within this section does not bar him from any other remedy.

§ 2–713. Buyer's Damages for Non-delivery or Repudiation

(1) Subject to the provisions of this Article with respect to proof of market price (Section 2–723), the measure of damages for non-delivery or repudiation by the seller is the difference between the market price at the time when the buyer learned of the breach and the contract price together with any incidental and consequential damages provided in this Article (Section 2–715), but less expenses saved in consequence of the seller's breach.

(2) Market price is to be determined as of the place for tender or, in cases of rejection after arrival or revocation of acceptance, as of the place of arrival.

§ 2–714. Buyer's Damages for Breach in Regard to Accepted Goods

(1) Where the buyer has accepted goods and given notification (subsection (3) of Section 2–607) he may recover as damages for any non-

conformity of tender the loss resulting in the ordinary course of events from the seller's breach as determined in any manner which is reasonable.

(2) The measure of damages for breach of warranty is the difference at the time and place of acceptance between the value of the goods accepted and the value they would have had if they had been as warranted, unless special circumstances show proximate damages of a different amount.

(3) In a proper case any incidental and consequential damages under the next section may also be recovered.

§ 2–715. Buyer's Incidental and Consequential Damages

(1) Incidental damages resulting from the seller's breach include expenses reasonably incurred in inspection, receipt, transportation and care and custody of goods rightfully rejected, any commercially reasonable charges, expenses or commissions in connection with effecting cover and any other reasonable expense incident to the delay or other breach.

(2) Consequential damages resulting from the seller's breach include

(a) any loss resulting from general or particular requirements and needs of which the seller at the time of contracting had reason to know and which could not reasonably be prevented by cover or otherwise; and

(b) injury to person or property proximately resulting from any breach of warranty.

§ 2–716. Buyer's Right to Specific Performance or Replevin

(1) Specific performance may be decreed where the goods are unique or in other proper circumstances.

(2) The decree for specific performance may include such terms and conditions as to payment of the price, damages, or other relief as the court may deem just.

(3) The buyer has a right of replevin for goods identified to the contract if after reasonable effort he is unable to effect cover for such goods or the circumstances reasonably indicate that such effort will be unavailing or if the goods have been shipped under reservation and satisfaction of the security interest in them has been made or tendered.

§ 2–717. Deduction of Damages from the Price

The buyer on notifying the seller of his intention to do so may deduct all or any part of the damages resulting from any breach of the contract from any part of the price still due under the same contract.

§ 2–718. Liquidation or Limitation of Damages; Deposits

(1) Damages for breach by either party may be liquidated in the agreement but only at an amount which is reasonable in the light of the anticipated or actual harm caused by the breach, the difficulties of proof of

loss, and the inconvenience or nonfeasibility of otherwise obtaining an adequate remedy. A term fixing unreasonably large liquidated damages is void as a penalty.

(2) Where the seller justifiably withholds delivery of goods because of the buyer's breach, the buyer is entitled to restitution of any amount by which the sum of his payments exceeds

(a) the amount to which the seller is entitled by virtue of terms liquidating the seller's damages in accordance with subsection (1), or

(b) in the absence of such terms, twenty per cent of the value of the total performance for which the buyer is obligated under the contract or $500, whichever is smaller.

(3) The buyer's right to restitution under subsection (2) is subject to offset to the extent that the seller establishes

(a) a right to recover damages under the provisions of this Article other than subsection (1), and

(b) the amount or value of any benefits received by the buyer directly or indirectly by reason of the contract.

(4) Where a seller has received payment in goods their reasonable value or the proceeds of their resale shall be treated as payments for the purposes of subsection (2); but if the seller has notice of the buyer's breach before reselling goods received in part performance, his resale is subject to the conditions laid down in this Article on resale by an aggrieved seller (Section 2–706).

§ 2–719. Contractual Modification or Limitation of Remedy

(1) Subject to the provisions of subsections (2) and (3) of this section and of the preceding section on liquidation and limitation of damages,

(a) the agreement may provide for remedies in addition to or in substitution for those provided in this Article and may limit or alter the measure of damages recoverable under this Article, as by limiting the buyer's remedies to return of the goods and repayment of the price or to repair and replacement of non-conforming goods or parts; and

(b) resort to a remedy as provided is optional unless the remedy is expressly agreed to be exclusive, in which case it is the sole remedy.

(2) Where circumstances cause an exclusive or limited remedy to fail of its essential purpose, remedy may be had as provided in this Act.

(3) Consequential damages may be limited or excluded unless the limitation or exclusion is unconscionable. Limitation of consequential damages for injury to the person in the case of consumer goods is prima facie unconscionable but limitation of damages where the loss is commercial is not.

Official Comment

Purposes:

1. Under this section parties are left free to shape their remedies to their particular requirements and reasonable agreements limiting or modifying remedies are to be given effect.

However, it is of the very essence of a sales contract that at least minimum adequate remedies be available. If the parties intend to conclude a contract for sale within this Article they must accept the legal consequence that there be at least a fair quantum of remedy for breach of the obligations or duties outlined in the contract. Thus any clause purporting to modify or limit the remedial provisions of this Article in an unconscionable manner is subject to deletion and in that event the remedies made available by this Article are applicable as if the stricken clause had never existed. Similarly, under subsection (2), where an apparently fair and reasonable clause because of circumstances fails in its purpose or operates to deprive either party of the substantial value of the bargain, it must give way to the general remedy provisions of this Article.

2. Subsection (1)(b) creates a presumption that clauses prescribing remedies are cumulative rather than exclusive. If the parties intend the term to describe the sole remedy under the contract, this must be clearly expressed.

3. Subsection (3) recognizes the validity of clauses limiting or excluding consequential damages but makes it clear that they may not operate in an unconscionable manner. Actually such terms are merely an allocation of unknown or undeterminable risks. The seller in all cases is free to disclaim warranties in the manner provided in Section 2–316.

§ 2–721. Remedies for Fraud

Remedies for material misrepresentation or fraud include all remedies available under this Article for non-fraudulent breach. Neither rescission or a claim for rescission of the contract for sale nor rejection or return of the goods shall bar or be deemed inconsistent with a claim for damages or other remedy.

Official Comment

Purposes: To correct the situation by which remedies for fraud have been more circumscribed than the more modern and mercantile remedies for breach of warranty. Thus the remedies for fraud are extended by this section to coincide in scope with those for non-fraudulent breach. This section thus makes it clear that neither rescission of the contract for fraud nor rejection of the goods bars other remedies unless the circumstances of the case make the remedies incompatible.

§ 2–725. Statute of Limitations in Contracts for Sale

(1) An action for breach of any contract for sale must be commenced within four years after the cause of action has accrued. By the original agreement the parties may reduce the period of limitation to not less than one year but may not extend it.

(2) A cause of action accrues when the breach occurs, regardless of the aggrieved party's lack of knowledge of the breach. A breach of warranty occurs when tender of delivery is made, except that where a warranty explicitly extends to future performance of the goods and discovery of the breach must await the time of such performance the cause of action accrues when the breach is or should have been discovered.

(3) Where an action commenced within the time limited by subsection (1) is so terminated as to leave available a remedy by another action for the same breach such other action may be commenced after the expiration of the time limited and within six months after the termination of the first action unless the termination resulted from voluntary discontinuance or from dismissal for failure or neglect to prosecute.

(4) This section does not alter the law on tolling of the statute of limitations nor does it apply to causes of action which have accrued before this Act becomes effective.

ARTICLE 2. SALES [2003 Amendments]

PART 1. SHORT TITLE, GENERAL CONSTRUCTION AND SUBJECT MATTER

§ 2–103. Definitions and Index of Definitions

(1) In this article unless the context otherwise requires

. . .

(n) "Remedial promise" means a promise by the seller to repair or replace the goods or to refund all or part of the price upon the happening of a specified event.

. . .

Preliminary Official Comment

A "remedial promise" is a promise by the seller to take remedial action upon the happening of a specified event. The types of remedies contemplated by this term as used in this Article are specified in the definition B repair or replacement of the goods, or refund of all or part of the price. No other promise by a seller qualifies as a remedial promise. Further, the seller is entitled to specify precisely the event that will trigger its obligation. Typical examples include a commitment to repair any parts that prove to be defective, or a commitment to refund the purchase price if the goods fail to perform in a certain manner. A post-sale promise to correct a problem with the goods that the seller is not obligated to correct that is made to placate a dissatisfied customer is not within the definition of remedial promise.

It is irrelevant whether the promised remedy is exclusive under Section 2–719(1) or additional to the remedies otherwise provided to the buyer under this Article. Whether the promised remedy is exclusive, and if so whether it has failed its essential purpose, is determined under Section 2–719.

The distinction between a remedial promise and a warranty that is made in this Article resolves a statute-of-limitations problem. Under original Section 2–725, a right of action for breach of an express warranty accrued at the time of tender unless the warranty explicitly extended to the future performance of the goods, in which case a time of discovery rule applied. By contrast, a right of action for breach of an ordinary (non-warranty) promise accrued when the promise was breached. A number of courts held that commitments by sellers to take remedial action in the event the goods proved to be defective during a specified period of time constituted warranties and applied the time-of-tender rule; other courts used strained reasoning that allowed them to apply the discovery rule even though the promise at issue referred to the future performance of the seller, not the goods.

Under this Article, a promise by the seller to take remedial action is not a warranty at all and therefore is not subject to either the time-of-tender or time-of-discovery rule. Section 2–725(2)(c) separately addresses the accrual of a right of action for a remedial promise.

For a further explanation, *see* Official Comment 2 to Section 2–725.

.   .   .

PART 2.   FORM, FORMATION, TERMS AND READJUSTMENT OF CONTRACT; ELECTRONIC CONTRACTING
PART 3.   GENERAL OBLIGATION AND CONSTRUCTION OF CONTRACT

§ 2–313.   Express Warranties by Affirmation, Promise, Description, Sample; Remedial Promise.

(1) In this section, "immediate buyer" means a buyer that enters into a contract with the seller.

(2) Express warranties by the seller to the immediate buyer are created as follows:

(a) Any affirmation of fact or promise made by the seller which relates to the goods and becomes part of the basis of the bargain creates an express warranty that the goods shall conform to the affirmation or promise.

(b) Any description of the goods which is made part of the basis of the bargain creates an express warranty that the goods shall conform to the description.

(c) Any sample or model which is made part of the basis of the bargain creates an express warranty that the whole of the goods shall conform to the sample or model.

(3) It is not necessary to the creation of an express warranty that the seller use formal words such as "warrant" or "guarantee" or that the seller have a specific intention to make a warranty, but an affirmation merely of the value of the goods or a statement purporting to be merely the seller's opinion or commendation of the goods does not create a warranty.

(4) Any remedial promise made by the seller to the immediate buyer creates an obligation that the promise will be performed upon the happening of the specified event.

Preliminary Official Comment

1. Subsections (2) and (3) are identical to original Article 2 except that the term "immediate buyer" is used to make clear that the section is limited to express warranties and remedial promises made by a seller to a buyer with which the seller has a contractual relationship. Sections 2–313A and 2–313B address obligations that run directly from a seller to a remote purchaser.

2. Subsection (4) introduces the term "remedial promise," which was not used in original Article 2. This section deals with remedial promises to immediate buyers; sections 2–313A and 2–313B deal with remedial promises running directly from a seller to a remote purchaser. Remedial promise is defined in Section 2–103(1)(n).

3. "Express" warranties rest on "dickered" aspects of the individual bar-

gain, and go so clearly to the essence of that bargain that words of disclaimer in a form are repugnant to the basic dickered terms. "Implied" warranties rest so clearly on a common factual situation or set of conditions that no particular language or action is necessary to evidence them and they will arise in such a situation unless unmistakably negated. As with original Article 2, warranties of description and sample are designated "express" rather than "implied."

4. This section is limited in its scope and direct purpose to express warranties and remedial promises made by the seller to the immediate buyer as part of a contract for sale. It is not designed in any way to disturb those lines of case law growth which have recognized that warranties need not be confined to contracts within the scope of this Article.

Section 2–313B recognizes that a seller may incur an obligation to a remote purchaser through a medium for communication to the public, such as advertising. An express warranty to an immediate buyer may also arise through a medium for communication to the public if the elements of this section are satisfied.

The fact that a buyer has rights against an immediate seller under this section does not preclude the buyer from also asserting rights against a remote seller under Section 2–313A or 2–313B.

5. The present section deals with affirmations of fact or promises made by the seller, descriptions of the goods, or exhibitions of samples or models, exactly as any other part of a negotiation which ends in a contract is dealt with. No specific intention to make a warranty is necessary if any of these factors is made part of the basis of the bargain. In actual practice affirmations of fact and promises made by the seller about the goods during a bargain are regarded as part of the description of those goods; hence no particular reliance on these statements need be shown in order to weave them into the fabric of the agreement. Rather, any fact which is to take these affirmations or promises, once made, out of the agreement requires clear affirmative proof. The issue normally is one of fact.

6. In view of the principle that the whole purpose of the law of warranty is to determine what it is that the seller has in essence agreed to sell, the policy is adopted of those cases which refuse except in unusual circumstances to recognize a material deletion of the seller's obligation. Thus, a contract is normally a contract for a sale of something describable and described. A clause generally disclaiming "all warranties, express or implied" cannot reduce the seller's obligation for the description and therefore cannot be given literal effect under Section 2–316(1).

This is not intended to mean that the parties, if they consciously desire, cannot make their own bargain as they wish. But in determining what they have agreed upon good faith is a factor and consideration should be given to the fact that the probability is small that a real price is intended to be exchanged for a pseudo-obligation.

7. Subsection (2)(b) makes specific some of the principles set forth above when a description of the goods is given by the seller.

A description need not be by words. Technical specifications, blueprints and the like can afford more exact description than mere language and if made part of the basis of the bargain goods must conform with them. Past deliveries may set the description of quality, either expressly or impliedly by course of dealing. Of course, all descriptions by merchants must be read against the applicable trade usages with the general rules as to merchantability resolving any doubts.

8. The basic situation as to statements affecting the true essence of the bargain is no different when a sample or model is involved in the transaction. This section includes both a "sample" actually drawn from the bulk of goods which is the subject matter of the sale, and a "model" which is offered for inspection when the subject matter is not at hand and which has not been drawn from the bulk of the goods.

Although the underlying principles are unchanged, the facts are often ambiguous when something is shown as illustrative, rather than as a straight sample. In general, the presumption is that any sample or model, just as any affirmation of fact, is intended to become a basis of the bargain. But there is no escape from the question of fact. When the seller exhibits a sample purporting to be drawn from an existing bulk, good faith of course requires that the sample be fairly drawn. But in mercantile experience the mere exhibition of a "sample" does not of itself show whether it is merely intended to "suggest" or to "be" the character of the subject-matter of the contract. The question is whether the seller has so acted with reference to the sample as to become responsible that the whole shall have at least the values shown by it. The circumstances aid in answering this question. If the sample has been drawn from an existing bulk, it must be regarded as describing values of the goods contracted for unless it is accompanied by an unmistakable denial of responsibility. If, on the other hand, a model of merchandise not on hand is offered, the mercantile presumption that it has become a literal description of the subject matter is not so strong, and particularly so if modification on the buyer's initiative impairs any feature of the model.

9. The precise time when words of description or affirmation are made or samples are shown is not material. The sole question is whether the language or samples or models are fairly to be regarded as part of the contract. If language that would otherwise create an obligation under this section is used after the closing of the deal (as when the buyer when taking delivery asks and receives an additional assurance), an obligation will arise if the requirements for a modification are satisfied. *See* Downie v. Abex Corp., 741 F.2d 1235 (10th Cir. 1984).

10. Concerning affirmations of value or a seller's opinion or commendation under subsection (3), the basic question remains the same: What statements of the seller have in the circumstances and in objective judgment become part of the basis of the bargain? As indicated above, all of the statements of the seller do so unless good reason is shown to the contrary. The provisions of subsection (3) are included, however, since common experience discloses that some statements or predictions cannot fairly be viewed as entering into the bargain. Even as to false statements of value, however, the possibility is left open that a remedy may be provided by the law relating to fraud or misrepresentation.

There are a number of factors relevant to determining whether an expression creates a warranty under this section or is merely puffing. For example, the relevant factors may include whether the seller's representations taken in context, (1) were general rather than specific, (2) related to the consequences of buying rather than the goods themselves, (3) were "hedged" in some way, (4) were related to experimental rather than standard goods, (5) were concerned with some aspects of the goods but not a hidden or unexpected non-conformity, (6) were informal statements made in a formal contracting process, (7) were phrased in terms of opinion rather than fact, or (8) were not capable of objective measurement.

11. The use of the word "promise" in subsection (2)(a) is unusual in that it refers to statements about the quality or

performance characteristics of the goods. For example, a seller might make an affirmation of fact to the buyer that the goods are of a certain quality, or may promise that the goods when delivered will be of a certain quality, or may promise that the goods will perform in a certain manner after delivery. In normal usage, "promise" refers to a what a person, not goods, will do; that is, a promise is a commitment to act, or refrain from acting, in a certain manner in the future. A promise about the quality or performance characteristics of the goods creates an express warranty if the other elements of a warranty are present whereas a promise by which the seller commits itself to take remedial action upon the happening of a specified event is a remedial promise. The distinction has meaning in the context of the statute of limitations. A right of action for breach of an express warranty accrues when the goods are tendered to the immediate buyer (Section 2–725(3)(a)) unless the warranty consists of a promise that explicitly extends to the future performance of the goods and discovery must await the time for performance, in which case accrual occurs when the immediate buyer discovers or should have discovered the breach (Section 2–725(3)(d)). Section 2–725(2)(c) separately addresses the accrual of a right of action for breach of a remedial promise.

Remedial promise is dealt with in a separate subsection to make clear that it is a concept separate and apart from express warranty and that the elements of an express warranty, such as basis of the bargain, are not applicable.

§ 2–313A. Obligation to Remote Purchaser Created by Record Packaged With or Accompanying Goods

(1) This section applies only to new goods and goods sold or leased as new goods in a transaction of purchase in the normal chain of distribution. In this section:

(a) "Immediate buyer" means a buyer that enters into a contract with the seller.

(b) "Remote purchaser" means a person that buys or leases goods from an immediate buyer or other person in the normal chain of distribution.

(2) If a seller in a record packaged with or accompanying the goods makes an affirmation of fact or promise that relates to the goods, provides a description that relates to the goods, or makes a remedial promise, and the seller reasonably expects the record to be, and the record is, furnished to the remote purchaser, the seller has an obligation to the remote purchaser that:

(a) the goods will conform to the affirmation of fact, promise or description unless a reasonable person in the position of the remote purchaser would not believe that the affirmation of fact, promise or description created an obligation; and

(b) the seller will perform the remedial promise.

(3) It is not necessary to the creation of an obligation under this section that the seller use formal words such as "warrant" or "guarantee" or that the seller have a specific intention to undertake an obligation, but an affirmation merely of the value of the goods or a statement purporting

to be merely the seller's opinion or commendation of the goods does not create an obligation.

(4) The following rules apply to the remedies for breach of an obligation created under this section:

(a) The seller may modify or limit the remedies available to the remote purchaser if the modification or limitation is furnished to the remote purchaser no later than the time of purchase or if the modification or limitation is contained in the record that contains the affirmation of fact, promise or description.

(b) Subject to a modification or limitation of remedy, a seller in breach is liable for incidental or consequential damages under Section 2–715, but the seller is not liable for lost profits.

(c) The remote purchaser may recover as damages for breach of a seller's obligation arising under subsection (2) the loss resulting in the ordinary course of events as determined in any manner that is reasonable.

(5) An obligation that is not a remedial promise is breached if the goods did not conform to the affirmation of fact, promise or description creating the obligation when the goods left the seller's control.

Preliminary Official Comment

1. Sections 2–313A and 2–313B are new, and they follow case law and practice in extending a seller's obligations regarding new goods to remote purchasers. This section deals with what are commonly called "pass-through warranties." In the paradigm situation, a manufacturer will sell goods in a package to a retailer and include in the package a record that sets forth the obligations that the manufacturer is willing to undertake in favor of the ultimate party in the distributive chain, the person that buys or leases the goods from the retailer. If the manufacturer had sold the goods directly to the ultimate party the statements in the record might amount to an express warranty or remedial promise under Section 2–313.

No direct contract exists between the seller and the remote purchaser, and thus the seller's obligation under this section is not referred to as an "express warranty." Use of "obligation" rather than "express warranty" avoids any inference that the basis of the bargain test is applicable here. The test for whether an obligation other than a remedial promise arises is similar in some respects to the basis of the bargain test, but the test set forth in this section is exclusive. Because "remedial promise" in Section 2–313 is not subject to the basis of the bargain test, that term is used in this section.

2. The party to which an obligation runs under this section may either buy or lease the goods, and thus the term "remote purchaser" is used. The term is more limited than "purchaser" in Article 1, however, and does not include a donee or any voluntary transferee who is not a buyer or lessee. Moreover, the remote purchaser must be part of the normal chain of distribution for the particular product. That chain will by definition include at least three parties and may well include more B for example, the manufacturer might sell first to a wholesaler, that would then resell the goods to a retailer for sale or lease to the public. A buyer or lessee from the retailer would qualify as a remote purchaser and could invoke

this section against either the manufacturer or the wholesaler (if the wholesaler provided a record to the retailer to be furnished to the ultimate party), but no subsequent transferee, such as a used-goods buyer or sublessee, could qualify. The law governing assignment and third-party beneficiary, including Section 2–318, must be consulted to determine whether a party other than the remote purchaser can enforce an obligation created under this section.

3. The application of this section is limited to new goods and goods sold or leased as new goods within the normal chain of distribution. It does not apply to goods that are sold outside the normal chain, such as "gray" goods or salvaged goods, nor does it apply if the goods are unused but sold as seconds. The concept is flexible, and determining whether goods have been sold or leased in the normal chain of distribution requires consideration of the seller's expectations with regard to the manner in which its goods will reach the remote purchaser. For example, a car manufacturer may be aware that certain of its dealers transfer cars among themselves, and under the particular circumstances of the case a court might find that a new car sold initially to one dealer but leased to the remote purchaser by another dealer was leased in the normal chain of distribution. The concept may also include such practices as door-to-door sales and distribution through a non-profit organization (*e.g.,* Girl Scout cookies).

The phrase "goods sold or leased as new goods" refers to goods that in the normal course of business would be considered new. There are many instances in which goods might be used for a limited purpose yet be sold or leased in the normal chain of distribution as new goods. For example, goods that have been returned to a dealer by a purchaser and placed back into the dealer's inventory might be sold or leased as new goods in the normal chain of distribu-

tion. Other examples might include goods that have been used for the purpose of inspection (*e.g.,* a car that has been test-driven) and goods that have been returned by a sale-or-return buyer (Section 2–326).

4. This section applies only to obligations set forth in a record that is packaged with the goods or otherwise accompanies them (subsection (2)). Examples include a label affixed to the outside of a container, a card inside a container, or a booklet handed to the remote purchaser at the time of purchase. In addition, the seller must be able to anticipate that the remote purchaser will acquire the record, and therefore this section is limited to records that the seller reasonably expects to be furnished, and that are in fact furnished, to the remote purchaser.

Neither this section nor Section 2–313B are intended to overrule cases that impose liability on facts outside the direct scope of one of the sections. For example, the sections are not intended to overrule a decision imposing liability on a seller that distributes a sample to a remote purchaser.

5. Obligations other than remedial promises created under this section are analogous to express warranties and are subject to a test that is akin to the basis of the bargain test of Section 2–313(2). The seller is entitled to shape the scope of the obligation, and the seller's language tending to create an obligation must be considered in context. If a reasonable person in the position of the remote purchaser, reading the seller's language in its entirety, would not believe that an affirmation of fact, promise or description created an obligation, there is no liability under this section.

6. There is no difference between remedial promise as used in this section (and Section 2–313B) and the same term as used in Section 2–313.

7. Subsection (4)(a) makes clear that the seller may employ the provisions of Section 2–719 to modify or limit the remedies available to the remote purchaser for breach of the seller's obligation hereunder. The modification or limitation may appear on the same record as the one which creates the obligation, or it may be provided to the remote purchaser separately, but in no event may it be furnished to the remote purchaser any later than the time of purchase.

The requirements and limitations set forth in Section 2–719, such as the requirement of an express statement of exclusivity and the tests for failure of essential purpose (Section 2–719(2)) and unconscionability (Section 2–719(3)) are applicable to a modification or limitation of remedy under this section.

8. As with express warranties, no specific language or intention is necessary to create an obligation, and whether an obligation exists is normally an issue of fact. Subsection (3) is virtually identical to Section 2–313(3), and the tests developed under the common law and under that section to determine whether a statement creates an obligation or is mere puffing are directly applicable to this section.

Just as a seller can limit the extent to which its language creates an express warranty under Section 2–313 by placing that language in a broader context, so too can a seller under this section or Section 2–313B limit the extent of its liability to a remote purchaser (subsection(4)(a)). In other words, the seller, in undertaking an obligation under these sections, can spell out the scope and limits of that obligation.

9. As a rule, a remote purchaser may recover monetary damages measured in the same manner as in the case of an aggrieved buyer under Section 2–714, including incidental and consequential damages to the extent they would be available to an aggrieved buyer. Subsection (4)(c) parallels Section 2–714(1) in allowing the buyer to recover for loss resulting in the ordinary course of events as determined in any manner which is reasonable. In the case of an obligation that is not a remedial promise, the normal measure of damages would be the difference between the value of the goods if they had conformed to the seller's statements and their actual value, and the normal measure of damages for breach of a remedial promise would be the difference between the value of the promised remedial performance and the value of the actual performance received.

Subsection (4)(b) precludes a remote purchaser from recovering consequential damages that take the form of lost profits.

§ 2–313B. Obligation to Remote Purchaser Created by Communication to the Public.

(1) This section applies only to new goods and goods sold or leased as new goods in a transaction of purchase in the normal chain of distribution. In this section:

(a) "Immediate buyer" means a buyer that enters into a contract with the seller.

(b) "Remote purchaser" means a person that buys or leases goods from an immediate buyer or other person in the normal chain of distribution.

(2) If a seller in advertising or a similar communication to the public makes an affirmation of fact or promise that relates to the goods, provides

a description that relates to the goods, or makes a remedial promise, and the remote purchaser enters into a transaction of purchase with knowledge of and with the expectation that the goods will conform to the affirmation of fact, promise, or description, or that the seller will perform the remedial promise, the seller has an obligation to the remote purchaser that:

(a) the goods will conform to the affirmation of fact, promise or description unless a reasonable person in the position of the remote purchaser would not believe that the affirmation of fact, promise or description created an obligation; and

(b) the seller will perform the remedial promise.

(3) It is not necessary to the creation of an obligation under this section that the seller use formal words such as "warrant" or "guarantee" or that the seller have a specific intention to undertake an obligation, but an affirmation merely of the value of the goods or a statement purporting to be merely the seller's opinion or commendation of the goods does not create an obligation.

(4) The following rules apply to the remedies for breach of an obligation created under this section:

(a) The seller may modify or limit the remedies available to the remote purchaser if the modification or limitation is furnished to the remote purchaser no later than the time of purchase. The modification or limitation may be furnished as part of the communication that contains the affirmation of fact, promise or description.

(b) Subject to a modification or limitation of remedy, a seller in breach is liable for incidental or consequential damages under Section 2–715, but the seller is not liable for lost profits.

(c) The remote purchaser may recover as damages for breach of a seller's obligation arising under subsection (2) the loss resulting in the ordinary course of events as determined in any manner that is reasonable.

(5) An obligation that is not a remedial promise is breached if the goods did not conform to the affirmation of fact, promise or description creating the obligation when the goods left the seller's control.

Preliminary Official Comment

1. Sections 2–313B and 2–313A are new, and they follow case law and practice in extending a seller's obligations regarding new goods to remote purchasers. This section deals with obligations to a remote purchaser created by advertising or a similar communication to the public. In the paradigm situation, a manufacturer will engage in an advertising campaign directed towards all or part of the market for its product and will make statements that if made to an immediate buyer would amount to an express warranty or remedial promise under Section 2–313. The goods, however, are sold to someone other than the recipient of the advertising and are then resold or leased to the recipient. By imposing liability on the seller, this section adopts the approach of cases such as *Randy Knitwear, Inc. v. American*

Cyanamid Co., 11 N.Y.2d 5, 226 N.Y.S.2d 363, 181 N.E.2d 399 (Ct. App. 1962).

If the seller's advertisement is made to an immediate buyer, whether the seller incurs liability is determined by Section 2–313 and this section is inapplicable.

2.   This section parallels Section 2–313A in most respects, and the Official Comments to that section should be consulted. In particular, the reasoning of Comment 1 (scope and terminology), Comment 2 (definition of remote purchaser), Comment 3 (new goods and goods sold as new goods in the normal chain of distribution), Comment 4 (reasonable person in the position of the remote purchaser), Comment 6 (modification or limitation of remedy), Comment 7 (puffing and limitations on extent of obligation) and Comment 8 (damages) is adopted here.

3.   This section provides an additional test for enforceability not found in Section 2–313A. In order to be held liable, the remote purchaser must, at the time of purchase, have knowledge of the affirmation of fact, promise, description or remedial promise and must also have an expectation that the goods will conform or that the seller will comply. This test is entirely subjective, while the reasonable person test in subsection (2)(a) is objective in nature.

Put another way, the seller will incur no liability to the remote purchaser if: i) the purchaser did not have knowledge of the seller's statement at the time of purchase; ii) the remote purchaser knew of the seller's statement at the time of purchase but did not expect the goods to conform or the seller to comply; iii) a reasonable person in the position of the remote purchaser would not believe that the seller's statement created an obligation (this test does not apply to remedial promises), or iv) the seller's statement is puffing.

In determining whether the tests set forth in this section are satisfied, a court should consider the temporal relationship between the communication and the purchase. For example, the remote purchaser may acquire the goods years after the seller's advertising campaign. In this circumstance, it would be highly unusual for the advertisement to have created the level of expectation in the remote purchaser or belief in the reasonable person in the position of the remote person necessary for the creation of an obligation under this section.

5.   In determining whether an obligation arises under this Section, all information known to the remote purchaser at the time of contracting must be considered. For example, a news release by a manufacturer limiting the statements made in its advertising and known by the remote purchaser, or a communication to the remote purchaser by the immediate seller limiting the statements made in the manufacturer's advertising must be considered in determining whether the expectation test applicable to the remote purchaser and the belief test applicable to the reasonable person in the position of the remote purchaser are satisfied.

6.   The remedies for breach of an obligation arising under this section may be modified or limited as set forth in Section 2–719. The modification or limitation may be contained in the advertisement that creates the obligation, or it may be separately furnished to the remote purchaser no later than the time of purchase.

7.   Section 2–318 deals with the extension of obligations to certain third-party beneficiaries. Of course, no extension is necessary if the goods are purchased by an agent. In this case, the knowledge and expectation of the principal, not the agent, are relevant in determining whether an obligation arises under this section. Nothing in this Act precludes a court from determining that a household operates as a buying unit under the law of agency.

§ 2–314.   Implied Warranty: Merchantability; Usage of Trade

(1) Unless excluded or modified (Section 2–316), a warranty that the goods shall be merchantable is implied in a contract for their sale if the seller is a merchant with respect to goods of that kind. Under this section the serving for value of food or drink to be consumed either on the premises or elsewhere is a sale.

(2) Goods to be merchantable must be at least such as

(a) pass without objection in the trade under the contract description; and

(b) in the case of fungible goods, are of fair average quality within the description; and

(c) are fit for the ordinary purposes for which goods of that description are used; and

(d) run, within the variations permitted by the agreement, of even kind, quality and quantity within each unit and among all units involved; and

(e) are adequately contained, packaged, and labeled as the agreement may require; and

(f) conform to the promise or affirmations of fact made on the container or label if any.

(3) Unless excluded or modified (Section 2–316) other implied warranties may arise from course of dealing or usage of trade.

Preliminary Official Comment

1. The phrase "goods of that description" rather than "for which such goods are used" is used in subsection (2)(c). This emphasizes the importance of the agreed description in determining fitness for ordinary purposes.

2. The seller's obligation applies to present sales as well as to contracts to sell subject to the effects of any examination of specific goods. *See* Section 2–316(5). Also, the warranty of merchantability applies to sales for use as well as to sales for resale.

3. The question when the warranty is imposed turns basically on the meaning of the terms of the agreement as recognized in the trade. Goods delivered under an agreement made by a merchant in a given line of trade must be of a quality comparable to that generally acceptable in that line of trade under the description or other designation of the goods used in the agreement. The responsibility imposed rests on any merchant-seller.

4. A specific designation of goods by the buyer does not exclude the seller's obligation that they be fit for the general purposes appropriate to the goods. A contract for the sale of second-hand goods, however, involves only an obligation as is appropriate to the goods for that is their contract description. A person making an isolated sale of goods is not a "merchant" within the meaning of the full scope of this section and, thus, no warranty of merchantability would apply. The seller's knowledge of any defects not apparent on inspection

would, however, without need for express agreement and in keeping with the underlying reason of the present section and the provisions on good faith, impose an obligation that known material but hidden defects be fully disclosed.

5. Although a seller may not be a "merchant" as to the goods in question, if the seller states generally that the goods are "guaranteed" the provisions of this section may furnish a guide to the content of the resulting express warranty. This has particular significance in the case of second-hand sales, and has further significance in limiting the effect of fine-print disclaimer clauses where their effect would be inconsistent with large-print assertions of "guarantee."

6. The second sentence of subsection (1) covers the warranty with respect to food and drink. The serving for value of food or drink for consumption on the premises or elsewhere is treated as a sale. Thus, both the patron in a restaurant and a buyer of "take out" food are protected by the implied warranty of merchantability.

7. Suppose that an unmerchantable lawn mower causes personal injury to the buyer, who is operating the mower. Without more, the buyer can sue the seller for breach of the implied warranty of merchantability and recover for injury to person "proximately resulting" from the breach. Section 2–715(2)(b).

This opportunity does not resolve the tension between warranty law and tort law where goods cause personal injury or property damage. The primary source of that tension arises from disagreement over whether the concept of defect in tort and the concept of merchantability in Article 2 are coextensive where personal injuries are involved, *i.e.,* if goods are merchantable under warranty law can they still be defective under tort law, and if goods are not defective under tort law can they be unmerchantable under warranty law? The answer to both questions should be

no, and the tension between merchantability in warranty and defect in tort where personal injury or property damage is involved should be resolved as follows:

> When recovery is sought for injury to person or property, whether goods are merchantable is to be determined by applicable state products liability law. When, however, a claim for injury to person or property is based on an implied warranty of fitness under Section 2–315 or an express warranty under Section 2–313 or an obligation arising under Section 2–313A or 2–313B, this Article determines whether an implied warranty of fitness or an express warranty was made and breached, as well as what damages are recoverable under Section 2–715.

To illustrate, suppose that the seller makes a representation about the safety of a lawn mower that becomes part of the basis of the buyer's bargain. The buyer is injured when the gas tank cracks and a fire breaks out. If the lawnmower without the representation is not defective under applicable tort law, it is not unmerchantable under this section. On the other hand, if the lawnmower did not conform to the representation about safety, the seller made and breached an express warranty and the buyer may sue under Article 2.

8. Subsection (2) does not purport to exhaust the meaning of "merchantable" nor to negate any of its attributes not specifically mentioned in the text of the statute, but arising by usage of trade or through case law. The language used is "must be at least such as . . . ," and the intention is to leave open other possible attributes of merchantability.

9. Paragraphs (a) and (b) of subsection (2) are to be read together. Both refer, as indicated above, to the standards of that line of the trade which fits the transaction and the seller's business. "Fair average" is a term directly

appropriate to agricultural bulk products and means goods centering around the middle belt of quality, not the least or the worst that can be understood in the particular trade by the designation, but such as can pass "without objection." Of course a fair percentage of the least is permissible but the goods are not "fair average" if they are all of the least or worst quality possible under the description. In cases of doubt as to what quality is intended, the price at which a merchant closes a contract is an excellent indication of the nature and scope of the merchant's obligation under the present section.

10.　Fitness for the ordinary purposes for which goods of the type are used is a fundamental concept of the present section and is covered in paragraph (2)(c). As stated above, merchantability is also a part of the obligation owing to the buyer for use. Correspondingly, protection, under this aspect of the warranty, of the person buying for resale to the ultimate consumer is equally necessary, and merchantable goods must therefore be "honestly" resaleable in the normal course of business because they are what they purport to be.

11.　Paragraph (2)(d) on evenness of kind, quality and quantity follows case law. But precautionary language has been added as a remainder of the frequent usages of trade which permit substantial variations both with and without an allowance or an obligation to replace the varying units.

12.　Paragraph (2)(e) applies only where the nature of the goods and of the transaction require a certain type of container, package or label. Paragraph (2)(f) applies, on the other hand, wherever there is a label or container on which representations are made, even though the original contract, either by express terms or usage of trade, may not have required either the labeling or the representation. This follows from the general obligation of good faith which requires that a buyer should not be placed in the position of reselling or using goods delivered under false representations appearing on the package or container. No problem of extra consideration arises in this connection since, under this Article, an obligation is imposed by the original contract not to deliver mislabeled articles, and the obligation is imposed where mercantile good faith so requires and without reference to the doctrine of consideration.

13.　Exclusion or modification of the warranty of merchantability, or of any part of it, is dealt with in Section 2–316. That section must be read with particular reference to its subsection (6) on limitation of remedies. The warranty of merchantability, wherever it is normal, is so commonly taken for granted that its exclusion from the contract is a matter threatening surprise and therefore requiring special precaution.

14.　Subsection (3) is to make explicit that usage of trade and course of dealing can create warranties and that they are implied rather than express warranties and thus subject to exclusion or modification under Section 2–316. A typical instance would be the obligation to provide pedigree papers to evidence conformity of the animal to the contract in the case of a pedigreed dog or blooded bull.

15.　In an action based on breach of warranty, it is of course necessary to show not only the existence of the warranty but the fact that the warranty was broken and that the breach of the warranty was the proximate cause of the loss sustained. In such an action an affirmative showing by the seller that the loss resulted from some action or event following the seller's delivery of the goods can operate as a defense. Equally, evidence indicating that the seller exercised care in the manufacture, processing or selection of the goods is relevant to the issue of whether the warranty was in fact broken. Action by the buyer following an examination of the goods which ought to have indicated the defect complained of can be shown as matter bearing on whether the breach itself was the cause of the injury.

[§ 2–315. Implied Warranty: Fitness for Particular Purpose. See § 2–315 of the 1978 Text.]

§ 2–316. Exclusion or Modification of Warranties

(1) Words or conduct relevant to the creation of an express warranty and words or conduct tending to negate or limit warranty shall be construed wherever reasonable as consistent with each other; but subject to the provisions of this Article on parol or extrinsic evidence (Section 2–202) negation or limitation is inoperative to the extent that such construction is unreasonable.

(2) Subject to subsection (3), to exclude or modify the implied warranty of merchantability or any part of it in a consumer contract the language must be in a record, be conspicuous and state "The seller undertakes no responsibility for the quality of the goods except as otherwise provided in this contract," and in any other contract the language must mention merchantability and in case of a record must be conspicuous. Subject to subsection (3), to exclude or modify the implied warranty of fitness the exclusion must be in a record and be conspicuous. Language to exclude all implied warranties of fitness in a consumer contract must state "The seller assumes no responsibility that the goods will be fit for any particular purpose for which you may be buying these goods, except as otherwise provided in the contract," and in any other contract the language is sufficient if it states, for example, that "There are no warranties which extend beyond the description on the face hereof." Language that satisfies the requirements of this subsection for the exclusion and modification of a warranty in a consumer contract also satisfies the requirements for any other contract.

(3) Notwithstanding subsection (2):

(a) unless the circumstances indicate otherwise, all implied warranties are excluded by expressions like "as is," "with all faults" or other language which in common understanding calls the buyer's attention to the exclusion of warranties, makes plain that there is no implied warranty, and in a consumer contract evidenced by a record is set forth conspicuously in the record; and

(b) when the buyer before entering into the contract has examined the goods or the sample or model as fully as desired or has refused to examine the goods after a demand by the seller there is no implied warranty with regard to defects which an examination ought in the circumstances to have revealed to the buyer; and

(c) an implied warranty can also be excluded or modified by course of dealing or course of performance or usage of trade.

(4) Remedies for breach of warranty can be limited in accordance with the provisions of this article on liquidation or limitation of damages and on contractual modification of remedy (Sections 2–718 and 2–719).

Preliminary Official Comment

1. **Changes.** This section contains the following changes from original Section 2–316:

(a) Subsection (2) sets forth new and more informative language for disclaimers of the implied warranty of merchantability and the implied warranty of fitness in consumer contracts. In both instances the language must be in a record and must be conspicuous. Use of this new language satisfies the requirements of this subsection for nonconsumer contracts.

(b) If a consumer contract is set forth in a record, subsection (3) cannot be satisfied unless the language is in a record and is conspicuous.

(c) Subsection (3)(b) now explicitly requires that there can be no refusal by a buyer unless there is a demand by the seller. Formerly, this requirement was found only in the comments.

2. Subsection (1) is designed principally to deal with those frequent clauses in sales contracts which seek to exclude "all warranties, express or implied." It seeks to protect a buyer from unexpected and unbargained language of disclaimer by denying effect to this language when inconsistent with language of express warranty and permitting the exclusion of implied warranties only by language or other circumstances which protect the buyer from surprise.

The seller is protected against false allegations of oral warranties by this Article's provisions on parol and extrinsic evidence and against unauthorized representations by the customary "lack of authority" clauses. This Article treats the limitation or avoidance of consequential damages as a matter of limiting remedies for breach, separate from the matter of creation of liability under a warranty. If no warranty exists, there is of course no problem of limiting remedies for breach of warranty. Under subsection (4), the question of limitation of remedy is governed by the sections referred to rather than by this section.

3. The organizational structure of this section has not been changed. The general test for disclaimers of implied warranties remains in subsection (3)(a), and the more specific tests remain in subsection (2). A disclaimer that satisfies the requirements of subsection (3)(a) need not also satisfy any of the requirements of subsection (2).

4. Subsection (2) now distinguishes between commercial and consumer contracts. In a commercial contract, language within the contemplation of the subsection disclaiming the implied warranty of merchantability need not be in a record, but if it is in a record it must be conspicuous. Under this subsection, both record and conspicuousness are required to disclaim the implied warranty of merchantability in a consumer contract and to disclaim the implied warranty of fitness in any contract. Use of the language required by this subsection for consumer contracts satisfies the subsections language requirements for other contracts.

5. Subsection (3)(a) deals with general terms such as "as is," "as they stand," "with all faults," and the like. These terms in ordinary commercial usage are understood to mean that the buyer takes the entire risk as to the quality of the goods involved. The terms covered by the subsection are in fact merely a particularization of subsection (3)(c), which provides for exclusion or modification of implied warranties by usage of trade. Nothing in subsection (3)(a) prevents a term such as "there

are no implied warranties" from being effective in appropriate circumstances, as when the term is a negotiated term between commercial parties.

Satisfaction of subsection (3)(a) does not require that the language be set forth in a record, but if there is a record the language must be conspicuous if the contract is a consumer contract.

6. Subsection (2) presupposes that the implied warranty in question exists unless excluded or modified. Whether or not language of disclaimer satisfies the requirements of this section, the language may be relevant under other sections to the question whether the warranty was ever in fact created. Thus, unless the provisions of this Article on parol and extrinsic evidence prevent, oral language of disclaimer may raise issues of fact as to whether reliance by the buyer occurred and whether the seller had "reason to know" under the section on implied warranty of fitness for a particular purpose.

7. The exceptions to the general rule set forth in subsections (3)(b) and (3)(c) are common factual situations in which the circumstances surrounding the transaction are in themselves sufficient to call the buyer's attention to the fact that no implied warranties are made or that a certain implied warranty is being excluded.

Under subsection (3)(b), warranties may be excluded or modified by the circumstances where the buyer examines the goods or a sample or model of them before entering into the contract. "Examination" as used in this paragraph is not synonymous with inspection before acceptance or at any other time after the contract has been made. It goes rather to the nature of the responsibility assumed by the seller at the time of the making of the contract. Of course if the buyer discovers the defect and uses the goods anyway, or if the buyer unreasonably fails to examine the goods before

using them, resulting injuries may be found to result from the buyer's own action rather than proximately from a breach of warranty. *See* Sections 2–314 and 2–715.

To bring the transaction within the scope of "refused to examine" in subsection (3)(a), it is not sufficient that the goods are available for inspection. There must in addition be an actual examination by the buyer or a demand by the seller that the buyer examine the goods fully. The seller's demand must place the buyer on notice that the buyer is assuming the risk of defects which the examination ought to reveal.

Application of the doctrine of "caveat emptor" in all cases where the buyer examines the goods regardless of statements made by the seller is, however, rejected by this Article. Thus, if the offer of examination is accompanied by words as to their merchantability or specific attributes and the buyer indicates clearly a reliance on those words rather than on the buyer's examination, they give rise to an "express" warranty. In these cases the question is one of fact as to whether a warranty of merchantability has been expressly incorporated in the agreement.

The particular buyer's skill and the normal method of examining goods in the circumstances determine what defects are excluded by the examination. A failure to notice defects which are obvious cannot excuse the buyer. However, an examination under circumstances which do not permit chemical or other testing of the goods would not exclude defects which could be ascertained only by testing. Nor can latent defects be excluded by a simple examination. A professional buyer examining a product in the buyer's field will be held to have assumed the risk as to all defects which a professional in the field ought to observe, while a nonprofessional buyer will be held to have assumed the risk only for the defects as a layperson might be expected to observe.

8. The situation in which the buyer gives precise and complete specifications to the seller is not explicitly covered in this section, but this is a frequent circumstance by which the implied warranties may be excluded. The warranty of fitness for a particular purpose would not normally arise since in this situation there is usually no reliance on the seller by the buyer. The warranty of merchantability in a transaction of this type, however, must be considered in connection with the next section on the cumulation and conflict of warranties. Under paragraph (c) of that section in case of an inconsistency the implied warranty of merchantability is displaced by the express warranty that the goods will comply with the specifications. Thus, where the buyer gives detailed specifications as to the goods, neither of the implied warranties as to quality will normally apply to the transaction unless consistent with the specifications.

[§ 2–317. Cumulation and Conflict of Warranties Express or Implied. See § 2–317 of the 1978 Text.]

§ 2–318. Third Party Beneficiaries of Warranties Express or Implied.

(1) In this section:

(a) "Immediate buyer" means a buyer that enters into a contract with the seller.

(b) "Remote purchaser" means a person that buys or leases goods from an immediate buyer or other person in the normal chain of distribution.

Alternative A to subsection (2)

(2) A seller's warranty whether express or implied to an immediate buyer, a seller's remedial promise to an immediate buyer, or a seller's obligation to a remote purchaser under Section 2–313A or 2–313B extends to any natural person who is in the family or household of the immediate buyer or the remote purchaser or who is a guest in the home of either if it is reasonable to expect that the person may use, consume or be affected by the goods and who is injured in person by breach of the warranty, remedial promise or obligation. A seller may not exclude or limit the operation of this section.

Alternative B to subsection (2)

(2) A seller's warranty whether express or implied to an immediate buyer, a seller's remedial promise to an immediate buyer, or a seller's obligation to a remote purchaser under Section 2–313A or 2–313B extends to any natural person who may reasonably be expected to use, consume or be affected by the goods and who is injured in person by breach of the warranty, remedial promise or obligation. A seller may not exclude or limit the operation of this section.

Alternative C to subsection (2)

(2) A seller's warranty whether express or implied to an immediate buyer, a seller's remedial promise to an immediate buyer, or a seller's obligation to a remote purchaser under Section 2–313A or 2–313B extends to any person that may reasonably be expected to use, consume or be affected by the goods and that is injured by breach of the warranty, remedial promise or obligation. A seller may not exclude or limit the operation of this section with respect to injury to the person of an individual to whom the warranty, remedial promise or obligation extends.

Preliminary Official Comment

1. This section retains original Article 2's alternative approaches but expands each alternative to cover obligations arising under Sections 2–313A and 2–313B and remedial promises.

2. The last sentence of each alternative to subsection (2) is not meant to suggest that a seller is precluded from excluding or disclaiming a warranty which might otherwise arise in connection with the sale provided the exclusion or modification is permitted by Section 2–316. Nor is it intended to suggest that the seller is precluded from limiting the remedies of the immediate buyer or remote purchaser in any manner provided in Sections 2–718 or 2–719. *See also* Section 2–313A(4) and Section 2–313B(4). To the extent that the contract of sale contains provisions under which warranties are excluded or modified, or remedies for breach are limited, the provisions are equally operative against beneficiaries of warranties under this section. What this last sentence forbids is exclusion of liability by the seller to the persons to whom the warranties, obligations and remedial promises accruing to the immediate buyer or remote purchaser would extend under this section.

The last sentence of Alternative C permits a seller to reduce its obligations to third-party beneficiaries to a level commensurate with that imposed on the seller under Alternative B—that is, to eliminate liability to persons that are not individuals and to eliminate liability for damages other than personal injury.

3. As used in this section, the term "remote purchaser" refers to the party to whom an obligation initially runs under Section 2–313A or 2–313B. It does not refer to any subsequent purchaser of the goods.

4. As applied to warranties and remedial promises arising under Sections 2–313, 2–314 and 2–315, the purpose of this section is to give certain beneficiaries the benefit of the warranties and remedial promises which the immediate buyer received in the contract of sale, thereby freeing any beneficiaries from any technical rules as to "privity." It seeks to accomplish this purpose without any derogation of any right or remedy arising under the law of torts. Implicit in the section is that any beneficiary of a warranty may bring a direct action for breach of warranty against the seller whose warranty extends to the beneficiary.

Obligations and remedial promises under Sections 2–313A and 2–313B arise initially in a non-privity context but are extended under this section to the same extent as warranties and remedial promises running to a buyer in privity.

PART 5.   PERFORMANCE

§ 2–507.   Effect of Seller's Tender; Delivery on Condition

(1) Tender of delivery is a condition to the buyer's duty to accept the goods and, unless otherwise agreed, to the buyer's duty to pay for them. Tender entitles the seller to acceptance of the goods and to payment according to the contract.

(2) Where payment is due and demanded on the delivery to the buyer of goods or documents of title, the seller may reclaim the goods delivered upon a demand made within a reasonable time after the seller discovers or should have discovered that payment was not made.

(3) The seller's right to reclaim under subsection (2) is subject to the rights of a buyer in ordinary course or other good-faith purchaser for value under this Article (Section 2–403).

§ 2–508.   Cure by Seller of Improper Tender or Delivery; Replacement

(1) Where the buyer rejects goods or a tender of delivery under Section 2–601 or 2–612 or except in a consumer contract justifiably revokes acceptance under Section 2–608(1)(b) and the agreed time for performance has not expired, a seller that has performed in good faith, upon seasonable notice to the buyer and at the seller's own expense, may cure the breach of contract by making a conforming tender of delivery within the agreed time. The seller shall compensate the buyer for all of the buyer's reasonable expenses caused by the seller's breach of contract and subsequent cure.

(2) Where the buyer rejects goods or a tender of delivery under Section 2–601 or 2–612 or except in a consumer contract justifiably revokes acceptance under Section 2–608(1)(b) and the agreed time for performance has expired, a seller that has performed in good faith, upon seasonable notice to the buyer and at the seller's own expense, may cure the breach of contract, if the cure is appropriate and timely under the circumstances, by making a tender of conforming goods. The seller shall compensate the buyer for all of the buyer's reasonable expenses caused by the seller's breach of contract and subsequent cure.

Preliminary Official Comment

1. Subsection (1) permits a seller that has made a nonconforming tender in any case to make a conforming tender within the contract time upon seasonable notification to the buyer. It presumes that the buyer has rightfully rejected or justifiably revoked acceptance under Section 2–608(1)(b) through timely notification to the seller and has complied with any particularization requirements imposed by Section 2–605(1). The subsection applies even where the seller has taken back the nonconforming goods and refunded the purchase price. The seller may still make a good tender within the contract period. The closer, however, it is to the contract date, the

greater is the necessity for extreme promptness on the seller's part in notifying of the intention to cure, if the notification is to be "seasonable" under this subsection.

The rule of this subsection, moreover, is qualified by its underlying reasons. Thus if, after contracting for June delivery, a buyer later makes known to the seller a need for shipment early in the month and the seller ships accordingly, the "contract time" has been cut down by the supervening modification and the time for cure of tender must be referred to this modified time term.

2. Cure after a justifiable revocation of acceptance is not available as a matter of right in a consumer contract. Further, even in a nonconsumer contract no cure is available if the revocation is predicated on Section 2–608(1)(a). If the buyer is revoking because of a known defect that the seller has not been willing or able to cure, there is no justification for giving the seller a second chance to cure.

3. Subsection (2) expands the seller's right to cure after the time for performance has expired. As under subsection (1), the buyer's rightful rejection or in a nonconsumer contract justifiable revocation of acceptance under Section 2–608(1)(b) trigger the seller's right to cure. Original Section 2–508(2) was directed toward preventing surprise rejections by requiring the seller to have "reasonable grounds to believe" the nonconforming tender was acceptable. Although this test has been abandoned, the requirement that the initial tender be made in good faith prevents a seller from deliberately tendering goods that it knows the buyer cannot use in order to save its contract and then, upon rejection, insisting on a second bite at the apple. The good faith standard applies under both subsection (1) and subsection (2).

4. The seller's cure under both subsection (1) and subsection (2) must be of conforming goods. Conforming goods includes not only conformity to the contracted-for quality but also as to quantity or assortment or other similar obligations under the contract. Since the time for performance has expired in a case governed by subsection (2), however, the seller's tender of conforming goods required to effect a cure under this section could not conform to the contracted time for performance. Thus, subsection (1) requires that cure be tendered "within the agreed time" while subsection (2) requires that the tender be "appropriate and timely under the circumstances."

The requirement that the cure be "appropriate and timely under the circumstances" provides important protection for the buyer. If the buyer is acquiring inventory on a just-in-time basis and needs to procure substitute goods from another supplier in order to keep the buyer's process moving, the cure would not be timely. If the seller knows from the circumstances that strict compliance with the contract obligations is expected, the seller's cure would not be appropriate. If the seller attempts to cure by repair, the cure would not be appropriate if it resulted in goods that did not conform in every respect to the requirements of the contract. The standard for quality on the second tender is still governed by Section 2–601. Whether a cure is appropriate and timely should be tested based upon the circumstances and needs of the buyer. Seasonable notice to the buyer and timely cure incorporate the idea that the notice and offered cure would be untimely if the buyer has reasonably changed its position in good faith reliance on the nonconforming tender.

5. Cure is at the seller's expense, and the seller is obligated to compensate the buyer for all the buyer's reasonable expenses caused by the breach and the cure. The term "reasonable expenses" is not limited to expenses that would qualify as incidental damages.

PART 6. BREACH, REPUDIATION AND EXCUSE

§ 2–601. Buyer's Rights on Improper Delivery

Subject to the provisions of this Article on breach in installment contracts (Section 2–612) and on shipment by seller (Section 2–504), and unless otherwise agreed under the sections on contractual limitations of remedy (Sections 2–718 and 2–719), if the goods or the tender of delivery fail in any respect to conform to the contract, the buyer may

(a) reject the whole; or

(b) accept the whole; or

(c) accept any commercial unit or units and reject the rest.

§ 2–602. Manner and Effect of Rejection

(1) Rejection of goods must be within a reasonable time after their delivery or tender. It is ineffective unless the buyer seasonably notifies the seller.

(2) Subject to the provisions of the two following sections on rejected goods (Sections 2–603 and 2–604) and to Section 2–608(4),

(a) after rejection any exercise of ownership by the buyer with respect to any commercial unit is wrongful as against the seller; and

(b) if the buyer has before rejection taken physical possession of goods in which the buyer does not have a security interest under the provisions of this Article (subsection (3) of Section 2–711), the buyer is under a duty after rejection to hold them with reasonable care at the seller's disposition for a time sufficient to permit the seller to remove them; but

(c) the buyer has no further obligations with regard to goods rightfully rejected.

(3) The seller's rights with respect to goods wrongfully rejected are governed by the provisions of this Article on Seller's remedies in general (Section 2–703).

Preliminary Official Comment

1. Elimination of the word "rightful" in the title makes it clear that a buyer can effectively reject goods even though the rejection is wrongful and constitutes a breach. *See* Section 2–703(1). The word "rightful" has also been deleted from the titles to Section 2–603 and 2–604. *See* Official Comments to those sections.

2. Subsection (2) has been amended to make it subject to Section 2–608(4), which deals with the problem of post-rejection or post-revocation use of the goods. *See* Official Comment to Section 2–608.

[3. See also the Official Comments to Section 2–602 of the 1978 Text.—Ed.]

§ 2–606. What Constitutes Acceptance of Goods

(1) Acceptance of goods occurs when the buyer

(a) after a reasonable opportunity to inspect the goods signifies to the seller that the goods are conforming or that the buyer will take or retain them in spite of their non-conformity; or

(b) fails to make an effective rejection (subsection (1) of Section 2–602), but such acceptance does not occur until the buyer has had a reasonable opportunity to inspect them; or

(c) except as otherwise provided in Section 2–608(4), does any act inconsistent with the seller's ownership if the act is ratified by the seller.

(2) Acceptance of a part of any commercial unit is acceptance of that entire unit.

§ 2–607. Effect of Acceptance; Notice of Breach; Burden of Establishing Breach After Acceptance; Notice of Claim or Litigation to Person Answerable Over

(1) The buyer must pay at the contract rate for any goods accepted.

(2) Acceptance of goods by the buyer precludes rejection of the goods accepted and if made with knowledge of a non-conformity cannot be revoked because of it unless the acceptance was on the reasonable assumption that the non-conformity would be seasonably cured but acceptance does not of itself impair any other remedy provided by this Article for non-conformity.

(3) Where a tender has been accepted

(a) the buyer must within a reasonable time after the buyer discovers or should have discovered any breach notify the seller; however, failure to give timely notice bars the buyer from a remedy only to the extent that the seller is prejudiced by the failure and

(b) if the claim is one for infringement or the like (subsection (3) of Section 2–312) and the buyer is sued as a result of such a breach the buyer must so notify the seller within a reasonable time after the buyer receives notice of the litigation or be barred from any remedy over for liability established by the litigation.

(4) The burden is on the buyer to establish any breach with respect to the goods accepted.

(5) Where the buyer is sued for indemnity, breach of a warranty or other obligation for which another party is answerable over

(a) the buyer may give the other party notice of the litigation in a record. If the notice states that the other party may come in and defend and that if the other party does not do so the other party will be bound in any action against the other party by the buyer by any determination of fact common to the two litigations, then unless the other party after seasonable receipt of the notice does come in and defend the other party is so bound.

(b) if the claim is one for infringement or the like (subsection (3) of Section 2–312) the original seller may demand in a record that its buyer turn over to it control of the litigation including settlement or else be barred from any remedy over and if it also agrees to bear all expense and to satisfy any adverse judgment, then unless the buyer after seasonable receipt of the demand does turn over control the buyer is so barred.

(6) The provisions of subsections (3), (4) and (5) apply to any obligation of a buyer to hold the seller harmless against infringement or the like (subsection (3) of Section 2–312).

Preliminary Official Comment

1. Subsection (3)(a) provides that a failure to give notice to the seller bars the buyer from a remedy for breach of contract only if the seller suffers prejudice due to the failure to notify. *See* Restatement (Second) of Contracts § 229, excusing a condition where the failure is not material and implementation would result in disproportionate forfeiture.

· · ·

[2. See also the Official Comments to Section 2–607 of the 1978 Text.—Ed.]

§ 2–608.　Revocation of Acceptance in Whole or in Part

(1) The buyer may revoke acceptance of a lot or commercial unit whose non-conformity substantially impairs its value to the buyer if the buyer has accepted it

(a) on the reasonable assumption that its non-conformity would be cured and it has not been seasonably cured; or

(b) without discovery of such non-conformity if the buyer's acceptance was reasonably induced either by the difficulty of discovery before acceptance or by the seller's assurances.

(2) Revocation of acceptance must occur within a reasonable time after the buyer discovers or should have discovered the ground for it and before any substantial change in condition of the goods which is not caused by their own defects. The revocation is not effective until the buyer notifies the seller of it.

(3) A buyer that so revokes has the same rights and duties with regard to the goods involved as if the buyer had rejected them.

(4) If a buyer uses the goods after a rightful rejection or justifiable revocation of acceptance, the following rules apply:

(a) Any use by the buyer that is unreasonable under the circumstances is wrongful as against the seller and is an acceptance only if ratified by the seller.

(b) Any use of the goods that is reasonable under the circumstances is not wrongful as against the seller and is not an acceptance, but in an appropriate case the buyer shall be obligated to the seller for the value of the use to the buyer.

Preliminary Official Comment

Subsection (4), which is now, deals with the problem of post-rejection or revocation use of the goods. The courts have developed several alternative approaches. Under original Article 2, a buyer's post-rejection or revocation use of the goods could be treated as an acceptance, thus undoing the rejection or revocation, could be a violation of the buyer's obligation of reasonable care, or could be a reasonable use for which the buyer must compensate the seller. Subsection (4) adopts the third approach. If the buyer's use after an effective rejection or a justified revocation of acceptance is unreasonable under the circumstances, it is inconsistent with the rejection or revocation of acceptance and is wrongful as against the seller. This gives the seller the option of ratifying the use, thereby treating it as an acceptance, or pursuing a non-Code remedy for conversion.

If the buyer's use is reasonable under the circumstances, the buyer's actions cannot be treated as an acceptance. The buyer must compensate the seller for the value of the use of the goods to the buyer. Determining the appropriate level of compensation requires a consideration of the buyer's particular circumstances and should take into account the defective condition of the goods. There may be circumstances, such as where the use is solely for the purpose of protecting the buyer's security interest in the goods, where no compensation is due the seller. In other circumstances, the seller's right to compensation must be netted out against any right of the buyer to damages.

[See also the Official Comments to Section 2–608 of the 1978 Text.—Ed.]

§ 2–609.   Right to Adequate Assurance of Performance

(1) A contract for sale imposes an obligation on each party that the other's expectation of receiving due performance will not be impaired. When reasonable grounds for insecurity arise with respect to the performance of either party the other may demand in a record adequate assurance of due performance and until the party receives the assurance may if commercially reasonable suspend any performance for which it has not already received the agreed return.

(2) Between merchants the reasonableness of grounds for insecurity and the adequacy of any assurance offered shall be determined according to commercial standards.

(3) Acceptance of any improper delivery or payment does not prejudice the aggrieved party's right to demand adequate assurance of future performance.

(4) After receipt of a justified demand failure to provide within a reasonable time not exceeding thirty days such assurance of due performance as is adequate under the circumstances of the particular case is a repudiation of the contract.

Official Comments

[See the Official Comments to Section 2–609 of the 1978 Text.—Ed.]

PART 7.   REMEDIES

§ 2–703.   Seller's Remedies in General

(1) A breach of contract by the buyer includes the buyer's wrongful rejection or wrongful attempt to revoke acceptance of goods, wrongful failure to perform a contractual obligation, failure to make a payment when due, or repudiation.

(2) If the buyer is in breach of contract the seller may to the extent provided for by this Act or other law:

(a) withhold delivery of the goods;

(b) stop delivery of the goods under Section 2–705;

(c) proceed under Section 2–704 with respect to goods unidentified to the contract or unfinished;

(d) reclaim the goods under Section 2–507(2) or 2–702(2);

(e) require payment directly from the buyer under Section 2–325(c);

(f) cancel;

(g) resell and recover damages under Section 2–706;

(h) recover damages for nonacceptance or repudiation under Section 2–708(1);

(*i*) recover lost profits under Section 2–708(2);

(j) recover the price under Section 2–709;

(k) obtain specific performance under Section 2–716;

(*l*) recover liquidated damages under Section 2–718;

(m) in other cases, recover damages in any manner that is reasonable under the circumstances.

(3) If a buyer becomes insolvent, the seller may:

(a) withhold delivery under Section 2–702(1);

(b) stop delivery of the goods under Section 2–705;

(c) reclaim the goods under Section 2–702(2).

Preliminary Official Comment

1. This section is a list of the remedies of the seller available under this Article to remedy any breach by the buyer. It also lists the seller's statutory remedies in the event of buyer insolvency. The subsection does not address the extent to which other law provides additional remedies or supplements the statutory remedies in Article 2 (*see* Section 1–103).

In addition to the statutory remedies, it contemplates agreed upon remedies, *see* subsection (2)(*l*). It does not address remedies that become available upon demand for adequate assurance under Section 2–609.

This Article rejects any doctrine of election of remedy as a fundamental policy and thus the remedies are essentially cumulative in nature and include all of the available remedies for breach. Whether the pursuit of one remedy bars another depends entirely on the facts of the individual case.

.   .   .

§ 2-711. Buyer's Remedies in General; Buyer's Security Interest in Rejected Goods

(1) A breach of contract by the seller includes the seller's wrongful failure to deliver or to perform a contractual obligation, making of a nonconforming tender of delivery or performance, or repudiation.

(2) If the seller is in breach of contract under subsection (1) the buyer may to the extent provided for by this Act or other law:

(a) in the case of rightful cancellation, rightful rejection or justifiable revocation of acceptance recover so much of the price as has been paid;

(b) deduct damages from any part of the price still due under Section 2-717;

(c) cancel;

(d) cover and have damages under Section 2-712 as to all goods affected whether or not they have been identified to the contract;

(e) recover damages for non-delivery or repudiation under Section 2-713;

(f) recover damages for breach with regard to accepted goods or breach with regard to a remedial promise under Section 2-714;

(g) recover identified goods under Section 2-502;

(h) obtain specific performance or obtain the goods by replevin or the like under Section 2-716;

(*i*) recover liquidated damages under Section 2-718;

(j) in other cases, recover damages in any manner that is reasonable under the circumstances.

(3) On rightful rejection or justifiable revocation of acceptance a buyer has a security interest in goods in the buyer's possession or control for any payments made on their price and any expenses reasonably incurred in their inspection, receipt, transportation, care and custody and may hold such goods and resell them in like manner as an aggrieved seller (Section 2-706).

§ 2-712. "Cover"; Buyer's Procurement of Substitute Goods

(1) If the seller wrongfully fails to deliver or repudiates or the buyer rightfully rejects or justifiably revokes acceptance, the buyer may "cover" by making in good faith and without unreasonable delay any reasonable purchase of or contract to purchase goods in substitution for those due from the seller.

(2) The buyer may recover from the seller as damages the difference between the cost of cover and the contract price together with any inciden-

tal or consequential damages as hereinafter defined (Section 2–715), but less expenses saved in consequence of the seller's breach.

(3) Failure of the buyer to effect cover within this section does not bar the buyer from any other remedy.

§ 2–713. Buyer's Damages for Non–Delivery or Repudiation

(1) Subject to the provisions of this Article with respect to proof of market price (Section 2–723), if the seller wrongfully fails to deliver or repudiates or the buyer rightfully rejects or justifiably revokes acceptance

(a) the measure of damages in the case of wrongful failure to deliver by the seller or rightful rejection or justifiable revocation of acceptance by the buyer is the difference between the market price at the time for tender under the contract and the contract price together with any incidental or consequential damages provided in this Article (Section 2–715), but less expenses saved in consequence of the seller's breach; and

(b) the measure of damages for repudiation by the seller is the difference between the market price at the expiration of a commercially reasonable time after the buyer learned of the repudiation, but no later than the time stated in paragraph (a), and the contract price together with any incidental or consequential damages provided in this Article (Section 2–715), but less expenses saved in consequence of the seller's breach.

(2) Market price is to be determined as of the place for tender or, in cases of rejection after arrival or revocation of acceptance, as of the place of arrival.

§ 2–714. Buyer's Damages for Breach in Regard to Accepted Goods

(1) Where the buyer has accepted goods and given notification (subsection (3) of Section 2–607) the buyer may recover as damages for any nonconformity of tender the loss resulting in the ordinary course of events from the seller's breach as determined in any manner which is reasonable.

(2) The measure of damages for breach of warranty is the difference at the time and place of acceptance between the value of the goods accepted and the value they would have had if they had been as warranted, unless special circumstances show proximate damages of a different amount.

(3) In a proper case any incidental and consequential damages under the next section may also be recovered.

[§ 2–715. Buyer's Incidental and Consequential Damages. See § 2–715 of the 1978 Text.]

§ 2–716. Specific Performance; Buyer's Right Replevin

(1) Specific performance may be decreed where the goods are unique or in other proper circumstances. In a contract other than a consumer

contract, specific performance may be decreed if the parties have agreed to that remedy. However, even if the parties agree to specific performance, specific performance may not be decreed if the breaching party's sole remaining contractual obligation is the payment of money.

(2) The decree for specific performance may include such terms and conditions as to payment of the price, damages, or other relief as the court may deem just.

(3) The buyer has a right of replevin or the like for goods identified to the contract if after reasonable effort the buyer is unable to effect cover for such goods or the circumstances reasonably indicate that such effort will be unavailing or if the goods have been shipped under reservation and satisfaction of the security interest in them has been made or tendered.

(4) The buyer's right under subsection (3) vests upon acquisition of a special property, even if the seller had not then repudiated or failed to deliver.

§ 2–717. Deduction of Damages From the Price.

The buyer on notifying the seller of an intention to do so may deduct all or any part of the damages resulting from any breach of the contract from any part of the price still due under the same contract.

§ 2–718. Liquidation or Limitation of Damages; Deposits.

(1) Damages for breach by either party may be liquidated in the agreement but only at an amount which is reasonable in the light of the anticipated or actual harm caused by the breach and, in a consumer contract, the difficulties of proof of loss and the inconvenience or nonfeasibility of otherwise obtaining an adequate remedy. Section 2–719 determines the enforceability of a term that limits but does not liquidate damages.

(2) Where the seller justifiably withholds delivery of goods or stops performance because of the buyer's breach or insolvency, the buyer is entitled to restitution of any amount by which the sum of the buyer's payments exceeds the amount to which the seller is entitled by virtue of terms liquidating the seller's damages in accordance with subsection (1).

(3) The buyer's right to restitution under subsection (2) is subject to offset to the extent that the seller establishes

(a) a right to recover damages under the provisions of this Article other than subsection (1), and

(b) the amount or value of any benefits received by the buyer directly or indirectly by reason of the contract.

(4) Where a seller has received payment in goods their reasonable value or the proceeds of their resale shall be treated as payments for the purposes of subsection (2); but if the seller has notice of the buyer's breach before reselling goods received in part performance, the resale is subject to

the conditions laid down in this Article on resale by an aggrieved seller (Section 2–706).

[2–719. Contractual Modification or Limitation of Remedy. See § 2–719 of the 1978 Text.]

[2–721. Remedies for Fraud. See § 2–721 of the 1978 Text.]

§ 2–725. Statute of Limitations in Contracts for Sale.

(1) Except as otherwise provided in this section, an action for breach of any contract for sale must be commenced within the later of four years after the right of action has accrued under subsection (2) or (3) or one year after the breach was or should have been discovered, but no longer than five years after the right of action accrued. By the original agreement the parties may reduce the period of limitation to not less than one year but may not extend it; however, in a consumer contract, the period of limitation may not be reduced.

(2) Except as otherwise provided in subsection (3), the following rules apply:

(a) Except as otherwise provided in this subsection, a right of action for breach of a contract accrues when the breach occurs, even if the aggrieved party did not have knowledge of the breach.

(b) For breach of a contract by repudiation, a right of action accrues at the earlier of when the aggrieved party elects to treat the repudiation as a breach or when a commercially reasonable time for awaiting performance has expired.

(c) For breach of a remedial promise, a right of action accrues when the remedial promise is not performed when due.

(d) In an action by a buyer against a person that is answerable over to the buyer for a claim asserted against the buyer, the buyer's right of action against the person answerable over accrues at the time the claim was originally asserted against the buyer.

(3) If a breach of a warranty arising under Section 2–312, 2–313(2), 2–314, or 2–315, or a breach of an obligation other than a remedial promise arising under Section 2–313A or 2–313B, is claimed the following rules apply:

(a) Except as otherwise provided in paragraph (c), a right of action for breach of a warranty arising under Section 2–313(2), 2–314 or 2–315 accrues when the seller has tendered delivery to the immediate buyer, as defined in Section 2–313, and has completed performance of any agreed installation or assembly of the goods.

(b) Except as otherwise provided in paragraph (c), a right of action for breach of an obligation other than a remedial promise arising under Section 2–313A or 2–313B accrues when the remote purchaser, as defined in sections 2–313A and 2–313B, receives the goods.

(c) Where a warranty arising under Section 2–313(2) or an obligation other than a remedial promise arising under 2–313A or 2–313B explicitly extends to future performance of the goods and discovery of the breach must await the time for performance the right of action accrues when the immediate buyer as defined in Section 2–313 or the remote purchaser as defined in Sections 2–313A and 2–313B discovers or should have discovered the breach.

(d) A right of action for breach of warranty arising under Section 2–312 accrues when the aggrieved party discovers or should have discovered the breach. However, an action for breach of the warranty of non-infringement may not be commenced more than six years after tender of delivery of the goods to the aggrieved party.

(4) Where an action commenced within the time limited by subsection (1) is so terminated as to leave available a remedy by another action for the same breach such other action may be commenced after the expiration of the time limited and within six months after the termination of the first action unless the termination resulted from voluntary discontinuance or from dismissal for failure or neglect to prosecute.

(5) This section does not alter the law on tolling of the statute of limitations nor does it apply to causes of action which have accrued before this Act becomes effective.

ARTICLE 2A. LEASES [1990 Text]

PART 1. GENERAL PROVISIONS

§ 2A-102. Scope

This Article applies to any transaction, regardless of form, that creates a lease.

§ 2A-103. Definitions and Index of Definitions

(1) In this Article unless the context otherwise requires:

(a) "Buyer in ordinary course of business" means a person who in good faith and without knowledge that the sale to him [or her] is in violation of the ownership rights or security interest or leasehold interest of a third party in the goods buys in ordinary course from a person in the business of selling goods of that kind but does not include a pawnbroker. "Buying" may be for cash or by exchange of other property or on secured or unsecured credit and includes receiving goods or documents of title under a pre-existing contract for sale but does not include a transfer in bulk or as security for or in total or partial satisfaction of a money debt.

(b) "Cancellation" occurs when either party puts an end to the lease contract for default by the other party.

(c) "Commercial unit" means such a unit of goods as by commercial usage is a single whole for purposes of lease and division of which materially impairs its character or value on the market or in use. A commercial unit may be a single article, as a machine, or a set of articles, as a suite of furniture or a line of machinery, or a quantity, as a gross or carload, or any other unit treated in use or in the relevant market as a single whole.

(d) "Conforming" goods or performance under a lease contract means goods or performance that are in accordance with the obligations under the lease contract.

(e) "Consumer lease" means a lease that a lessor regularly engaged in the business of leasing or selling makes to a lessee, except an organization, who takes under the lease primarily for a personal, family, or household purpose, if the total payments to be made under the lease contract, excluding payments for options to renew or buy, do not exceed $25,000.

(f) "Fault" means wrongful act, omission, breach, or default.

(g) "Finance lease" means a lease in which (i) the lessor does not select, manufacture or supply the goods, (ii) the lessor acquires the goods or the right to possession and use of the goods in connection with the lease, and (iii) either the lessee receives a copy of the contract evidencing the lessor's purchase of the goods on or before signing the lease contract, or the lessee's approval of the contract evidencing the lessor's purchase of the goods is a condition to effectiveness of the lease contract.

(h) "Goods" means all things that are movable at the time of identification to the lease contract, or are fixtures (Section 2A–309), but the term does not include money, documents, instruments, accounts, chattel paper, general intangibles, or minerals or the like, including oil and gas, before extraction. The term also includes the unborn young of animals.

(*i*) "Installment lease contract" means a lease contract that authorizes or requires the delivery of goods in separate lots to be separately accepted, even though the lease contract contains a clause "each delivery is a separate lease" or its equivalent.

(j) "Lease" means a transfer of the right to possession and use of goods for a term in return for consideration, but a sale, including a sale on approval or a sale or return, or retention or creation of a security interest is not a lease. Unless the context clearly indicates otherwise, the term includes a sublease.

(k) "Lease agreement" means the bargain, with respect to the lease, of the lessor and the lessee in fact as found in their language or by implication from other circumstances including course of dealing or usage of trade or course of performance as provided in this Article. Unless the context clearly indicates otherwise, the term includes a sublease agreement.

(*l*) "Lease contract" means the total legal obligation that results from the lease agreement as affected by this Article and any other applicable rules of law. Unless the context clearly indicates otherwise, the term includes a sublease contract.

(m) "Leasehold interest" means the interest of the lessor or the lessee under a lease contract.

(n) "Lessee" means a person who acquires the right to possession and use of goods under a lease. Unless the context clearly indicates otherwise, the term includes a sublessee.

(*o*) "Lessee in ordinary course of business" means a person who in good faith and without knowledge that the lease to him [or her] is in violation of the ownership rights or security interest or leasehold interest of a third party in the goods, leases in ordinary course from a person in the business of selling or leasing goods of that kind but does not include a pawnbroker. "Leasing" may be for cash or by exchange of other property or on secured or unsecured credit and includes receiving goods or documents of title under a pre-existing lease contract but does not include a transfer in bulk or as security for or in total or partial satisfaction of a money debt.

(p) "Lessor" means a person who transfers the right to possession and use of goods under a lease. Unless the context clearly indicates otherwise, the term includes a sublessor.

(q) "Lessor's residual interest" means the lessor's interest in the goods after expiration, termination, or cancellation of the lease contract.

(r) "Lien" means a charge against or interest in goods to secure payment of a debt or performance of an obligation, but the term does not include a security interest.

(s) "Lot" means a parcel or a single article that is the subject matter of a separate lease or delivery, whether or not it is sufficient to perform the lease contract.

(t) "Merchant lessee" means a lessee that is a merchant with respect to goods of the kind subject to the lease.

(u) "Present value" means the amount as of a date certain of one or more sums payable in the future, discounted to the date certain. The discount is determined by the interest rate specified by the parties if the rate was not manifestly unreasonable at the time the transaction was entered into; otherwise, the discount is determined by a commercially reasonable rate that takes into account the facts and circumstances of each case at the time the transaction was entered into.

(v) "Purchase" includes taking by sale, lease, mortgage, security interest, pledge, gift, or any other voluntary transaction creating an interest in goods.

(w) "Sublease" means a lease of goods the right to possession and use of which was acquired by the lessor as a lessee under an existing lease.

(x) "Supplier" means a person from whom a lessor buys or leases goods to be leased under a finance lease.

(y) "Supply contract" means a contract under which a lessor buys or leases goods to be leased.

(z) "Termination" occurs when either party pursuant to a power created by agreement or law puts an end to the lease contract otherwise than for default.

.   .   .

§ 2A–104. Leases Subject to Other Statutes

(1) A lease, although subject to this Article, is also subject to any applicable:

(a) statute of the United States;

(b) certificate of title statute of this State: (list any certificate of title statutes covering automobiles, trailers, mobile homes, boats, farm tractors, and the like);

(c) certificate of title statute of another jurisdiction (Section 2A–105); or

(d) consumer protection statute of this State.

(2) In case of conflict between the provisions of this Article, other than Sections 2A–105, 2A–304(3) and 2A–305(3), and any statute referred to in subsection (1), the provisions of that statute control.

(3) Failure to comply with any applicable statute has only the effect specified therein.

§ 2A–106. Limitation on Power of Parties to Consumer Lease to Choose Applicable Law and Judicial Forum

(1) If the law chosen by the parties to a consumer lease is that of a jurisdiction other than a jurisdiction in which the lessee resides at the time the lease agreement becomes enforceable or within 30 days thereafter or in which the goods are to be used, the choice is not enforceable.

(2) If the judicial forum chosen by the parties to a consumer lease is a forum that would not otherwise have jurisdiction over the lessee, the choice is not enforceable.

§ 2A–108. Unconscionability

(1) If the court as a matter of law finds a lease contract or any clause of a lease contract to have been unconscionable at the time it was made the court may refuse to enforce the lease contract, or it may enforce the remainder of the lease contract without the unconscionable clause, or it may so limit the application of any unconscionable clause as to avoid any unconscionable result.

(2) With respect to a consumer lease, if the court as a matter of law finds that a lease contract or any clause of a lease contract has been induced by unconscionable conduct or that unconscionable conduct has occurred in the collection of a claim arising from a lease contract, the court may grant appropriate relief.

(3) Before making a finding of unconscionability under subsection (1) or (2), the court, on its own motion or that of a party, shall afford the parties a reasonable opportunity to present evidence as to the setting, purpose, and effect of the lease contract or clause thereof, or of the conduct.

(4) In an action in which the lessee claims unconscionability with respect to a consumer lease:

(a) If the court finds unconscionability under subsection (1) or (2), the court shall award reasonable attorney's fees to the lessee.

(b) If the court does not find unconscionability and the lessee claiming unconscionability has brought or maintained an action he [or she] knew to be groundless, the court shall award reasonable attorney's fees to the party against whom the claim is made.

(c) In determining attorney's fees, the amount of the recovery on behalf of the claimant under subsections (1) and (2) is not controlling.

§ 2A–109. Option to Accelerate at Will

(1) A term providing that one party or his [or her] successor in interest may accelerate payment or performance or require collateral or additional collateral "at will" or "when he [or she] deems himself [or herself] insecure" or in words of similar import must be construed to mean that he [or she] has power to do so only if he [or she] in good faith believes that the prospect of payment or performance is impaired.

(2) With respect to a consumer lease, the burden of establishing good faith under subsection (1) is on the party who exercised the power; otherwise the burden of establishing lack of good faith is on the party against whom the power has been exercised.

PART 2.   FORMATION AND CONSTRUCTION OF LEASE CONTRACT

§ 2A–209. Lessee Under Finance Lease as Beneficiary of Supply Contract

(1) The benefit of the supplier's promises to the lessor under the supply contract and of all warranties, whether express or implied, under the supply contract, extends to the lessee to the extent of the lessee's leasehold interest under a finance lease related to the supply contract, but subject to the terms of the supply contract and all of the supplier's defenses or claims arising therefrom.

(2) The extension of the benefit of the supplier's promises and warranties to the lessee (Section 2A–209(1)) does not: (a) modify the rights and obligations of the parties to the supply contract, whether arising therefrom or otherwise, or (b) impose any duty or liability under the supply contract on the lessee.

(3) Any modification or rescission of the supply contract by the supplier and the lessor is effective against the lessee unless, prior to the modification or rescission, the supplier has received notice that the lessee has entered into a finance lease related to the supply contract. If the supply contract is modified or rescinded after the lessee enters the finance lease, the lessee has a cause of action against the lessor, and against the supplier if the supplier has notice of the lessee's entering the finance lease when the supply contract is modified or rescinded. The lessee's recovery from such action shall put the lessee in as good a position as if the modification or rescission had not occurred.

§ 2A–210. Express Warranties

(1) Express warranties by the lessor are created as follows:

(a) Any affirmation of fact or promise made by the lessor to the lessee which relates to the goods and becomes part of the basis of the bargain creates an express warranty that the goods will conform to the affirmation or promise.

(b) Any description of the goods which is made part of the basis of the bargain creates an express warranty that the goods will conform to the description.

(c) Any sample or model that is made part of the basis of the bargain creates an express warranty that the whole of the goods will conform to the sample or model.

(2) It is not necessary to the creation of an express warranty that the lessor use formal words, such as "warrant" or "guarantee," or that the lessor have a specific intention to make a warranty, but an affirmation merely of the value of the goods or a statement purporting to be merely the lessor's opinion or commendation of the goods does not create a warranty.

§ 2A–212. Implied Warranty of Merchantability

(1) Except in a finance lease, a warranty that the goods will be merchantable is implied in a lease contract if the lessor is a merchant with respect to goods of that kind.

(2) Goods to be merchantable must be at least such as

(a) pass without objection in the trade under the description in the lease agreement;

(b) in the case of fungible goods, are of fair average quality within the description;

(c) are fit for the ordinary purposes for which goods of that type are used;

(d) run, within the variation permitted by the lease agreement, of even kind, quality, and quantity within each unit and among all units involved;

(e) are adequately contained, packaged, and labeled as the lease agreement may require; and

(f) conform to any promises or affirmations of fact made on the container or label.

(3) Other implied warranties may arise from course of dealing or usage of trade.

§ 2A–213. Implied Warranty of Fitness for Particular Purpose

Except in a finance lease, if the lessor at the time the lease contract is made has reason to know of any particular purpose for which the goods are required and that the lessee is relying on the lessor's skill or judgment to select or furnish suitable goods, there is in the lease contract an implied warranty that the goods will be fit for that purpose.

§ 2A–214. Exclusion or Modification of Warranties

(1) Words or conduct relevant to the creation of an express warranty and words or conduct tending to negate or limit a warranty must be construed wherever reasonable as consistent with each other; but, subject to the provisions of Section 2A–202 on parol or extrinsic evidence, negation or limitation is inoperative to the extent that the construction is unreasonable.

(2) Subject to subsection (3), to exclude or modify the implied warranty of merchantability or any part of it the language must mention "merchantability", be by a writing, and be conspicuous. Subject to subsection (3), to exclude or modify any implied warranty of fitness the exclusion must be by a writing and be conspicuous. Language to exclude all implied warranties of fitness is sufficient if it is in writing, is conspicuous and states, for example, "There is no warranty that the goods will be fit for a particular purpose".

(3) Notwithstanding subsection (2), but subject to subsection (4),

(a) unless the circumstances indicate otherwise, all implied warranties are excluded by expressions like "as is," or "with all faults," or by other language that in common understanding calls the lessee's attention to the exclusion of warranties and makes plain that there is no implied warranty, if in writing and conspicuous;

(b) if the lessee before entering into the lease contract has examined the goods or the sample or model as fully as desired or has refused to examine the goods, there is no implied warranty with regard to defects that an examination ought in the circumstances to have revealed; and

(c) an implied warranty may also be excluded or modified by course of dealing, course of performance, or usage of trade.

(4) To exclude or modify a warranty against interference or against infringement (Section 2A–211) or any part of it, the language must be specific, be by a writing, and be conspicuous, unless the circumstances, including course of performance, course of dealing, or usage of trade, give the lessee reason to know that the goods are being leased subject to a claim or interest of any person.

§ 2A–215. Cumulation and Conflict of Warranties Express or Implied

Warranties, whether express or implied, must be construed as consistent with each other and as cumulative, but if that construction is unreasonable, the intention of the parties determines which warranty is dominant. In ascertaining that intention the following rules apply:

(a) Exact or technical specifications displace an inconsistent sample or model or general language of description.

(b) A sample from an existing bulk displaces inconsistent general language of description.

(c) Express warranties displace inconsistent implied warranties other than an implied warranty of fitness for a particular purpose.

§ 2A–216. Third–Party Beneficiaries of Express and Implied Warranties

ALTERNATIVE A

A warranty to or for the benefit of a lessee under this Article, whether express or implied, extends to any natural person who is in the family or household of the lessee or who is a guest in the lessee's home if it is reasonable to expect that such person may use, consume, or be affected by the goods and who is injured in person by breach of the warranty. This section does not displace principles of law and equity that extend a warranty to or for the benefit of a lessee to other persons. The operation of this section may not be excluded, modified, or limited, but an exclusion, modification, or limitation of the warranty, including any with respect to rights and remedies, effective against the lessee is also effective against any beneficiary designated under this section.

ALTERNATIVE B

A warranty to or for the benefit of a lessee under this Article, whether express or implied, extends to any natural person who may reasonably be expected to use, consume, or be affected by the goods and who is injured in person by breach of the warranty. This section does not displace principles of law and equity that extend a warranty to or for the benefit of a lessee to other persons. The operation of this section may not be excluded, modified, or limited, but an exclusion, modification, or limitation of the warranty, including any with respect to rights and remedies, effective against the lessee is also effective against the beneficiary designated under this section.

ALTERNATIVE C

A warranty to or for the benefit of a lessee under this Article, whether express or implied, extends to any person who may reasonably be expected to use, consume, or be affected by the goods and who is injured by breach of the warranty. The operation of this section may not be excluded, modified, or limited with respect to injury to the person of an individual to whom the warranty extends, but an exclusion, modification, or limitation of the warranty, including any with respect to rights and remedies, effective against the lessee is also effective against the beneficiary designated under this section.

PART 3.   EFFECT OF LEASE CONTRACT

§ 2A–301. Enforceability of Lease Contract

Except as otherwise provided in this Article, a lease contract is effective and enforceable according to its terms between the parties, against purchasers of the goods and against creditors of the parties.

§ 2A–303. Alienability of Party's Interest Under Lease Contract or of Lessor's Residual Interest in Goods; Delegation of Performance; Assignment of Rights

(1) Any interest of a party under a lease contract and the lessor's residual interest in the goods may be transferred unless

(a) the transfer is voluntary and the lease contract prohibits the transfer; or

(b) the transfer materially changes the duty of or materially increases the burden or risk imposed on the other party to the lease contract, and within a reasonable time after notice of the transfer the other party demands that the transferee comply with subsection (2) and the transferee fails to comply.

(2) Within a reasonable time after demand pursuant to subsection (1)(b), the transferee shall:

(a) cure or provide adequate assurance that he [or she] will promptly cure any default other than one arising from the transfer;

(b) compensate or provide adequate assurance that he [or she] will promptly compensate the other party to the lease contract and any other person holding an interest in the lease contract, except the party whose interest is being transferred, for any loss to that party resulting from the transfer;

(c) provide adequate assurance of future due performance under the lease contract; and

(d) assume the lease contract.

(3) Demand pursuant to subsection (1)(b) is without prejudice to the other party's rights against the transferee and the party whose interest is transferred.

(4) An assignment of "the lease" or of "all my rights under the lease" or an assignment in similar general terms is a transfer of rights, and unless the language or the circumstances, as in an assignment for security, indicate the contrary, the assignment is a delegation of duties by the assignor to the assignee and acceptance by the assignee constitutes a promise by him [or her] to perform those duties. This promise is enforceable by either the assignor or the other party to the lease contract.

(5) Unless otherwise agreed by the lessor and the lessee, no delegation of performance relieves the assignor as against the other party of any duty to perform or any liability for default.

(6) A right to damages for default with respect to the whole lease contract or a right arising out of the assignor's due performance of his [or her] entire obligation can be assigned despite agreement otherwise.

(7) To prohibit the transfer of an interest of a party under a lease contract, the language of prohibition must be specific, by a writing, and conspicuous.

PART 4.   PERFORMANCE OF LEASE CONTRACT: REPUDIATED, SUBSTITUTED AND EXCUSED

§ 2A-401.   Insecurity: Adequate Assurance of Performance

(1) A lease contract imposes an obligation on each party that the other's expectation of receiving due performance will not be impaired.

(2) If reasonable grounds for insecurity arise with respect to the performance of either party, the insecure party may demand in writing adequate assurance of due performance. Until the insecure party receives that assurance, if commercially reasonable the insecure party may suspend any performance for which he [or she] has not already received the agreed return.

(3) A repudiation of the lease contract occurs if assurance of due performance adequate under the circumstances of the particular case is not provided to the insecure party within a reasonable time, not to exceed 30 days after receipt of a demand by the other party.

(4) Between merchants, the reasonableness of grounds for insecurity and the adequacy of any assurance offered must be determined according to commercial standards.

(5) Acceptance of any nonconforming delivery or payment does not prejudice the aggrieved party's right to demand adequate assurance of future performance.

§ 2A-402.   Anticipatory Repudiation

If either party repudiates a lease contract with respect to a performance not yet due under the lease contract, the loss of which performance will substantially impair the value of the lease contract to the other, the aggrieved party may:

> (a) for a commercially reasonable time, await retraction of repudiation and performance by the repudiating party;

> (b) make demand pursuant to Section 2A-401 and await assurance of future performance adequate under the circumstances of the particular case; or

(c) resort to any right or remedy upon default under the lease contract or this Article, even though the aggrieved party has notified the repudiating party that the aggrieved party would await the repudiating party's performance and assurance and has urged retraction. In addition, whether or not the aggrieved party is pursuing one of the foregoing remedies, the aggrieved party may suspend performance or, if the aggrieved party is the lessor, proceed in accordance with the provisions of this Article on the lessor's right to identify goods to the lease contract notwithstanding default or to salvage unfinished goods (Section 2A–524).

PART 5.   DEFAULT

A.   IN GENERAL

§ 2A–501.   Default: Procedure

(1) Whether the lessor or the lessee is in default under a lease contract is determined by the lease agreement and this Article.

(2) If the lessor or the lessee is in default under the lease contract, the party seeking enforcement has rights and remedies as provided in this Article and, except as limited by this Article, as provided in the lease agreement.

(3) If the lessor or the lessee is in default under the lease contract, the party seeking enforcement may reduce the party's claim to judgment, or otherwise enforce the lease contract by self-help or any available judicial procedure or nonjudicial procedure, including administrative proceeding, arbitration, or the like, in accordance with this Article.

(4) Except as otherwise provided in this Article or the lease agreement, the rights and remedies referred to in subsections (2) and (3) are cumulative.

(5) If the lease agreement covers both real property and goods, the party seeking enforcement may proceed under this Part as to the goods, or under other applicable law as to both the real property and the goods in accordance with his [or her] rights and remedies in respect of the real property, in which case this Part does not apply.

§ 2A–502.   Notice After Default

Except as otherwise provided in this Article or the lease agreement, the lessor or lessee in default under the lease contract is not entitled to notice of default or notice of enforcement from the other party to the lease agreement.

§ 2A–503.   Modification or Impairment of Rights and Remedies

(1) Except as otherwise provided in this Article, the lease agreement may include rights and remedies for default in addition to or in substitu-

tion for those provided in this Article and may limit or alter the measure of damages recoverable under this Article.

(2) Resort to a remedy provided under this Article or in the lease agreement is optional unless the remedy is expressly agreed to be exclusive. If circumstances cause an exclusive or limited remedy to fail of its essential purpose, or provision for an exclusive remedy is unconscionable, remedy may be had as provided in this Article.

(3) Consequential damages may be liquidated under Section 2A–504, or may otherwise be limited, altered, or excluded unless the limitation, alteration, or exclusion is unconscionable. Limitation of consequential damages for injury to the person in the case of consumer goods is prima facie unconscionable but limitation of damages where the loss is commercial is not.

(4) Rights and remedies on default by the lessor or the lessee with respect to any obligation or promise collateral or ancillary to the lease contract are not impaired by this Article.

§ 2A–504. Liquidation of Damages

(1) Damages payable by either party for default, or any other act or omission, including indemnity for loss or diminution of anticipated tax benefits or loss or damage to lessor's residual interest, may be liquidated in the lease agreement but only at an amount or by a formula that is reasonable in light of the then anticipated harm caused by the default or other act or omission.

(2) If the lease agreement provides for liquidation of damages, and such provision does not comply with subsection (1), or such provision is an exclusive or limited remedy that circumstances cause to fail of its essential purpose, remedy may be had as provided in this Article.

(3) If the lessor justifiably withholds or stops delivery of goods because of the lessee's default or insolvency (Section 2A–525 or 2A–526), the lessee is entitled to restitution of any amount by which the sum of his [or her] payments exceeds:

(a) the amount to which the lessor is entitled by virtue of terms liquidating the lessor's damages in accordance with subsection (1); or

(b) in the absence of those terms, 20 percent of the then present value of the total rent the lessee was obligated to pay for the balance of the lease term, or, in the case of a consumer lease, the lesser of such amount or $500.

(4) A lessee's right to restitution under subsection (3) is subject to offset to the extent the lessor establishes:

(a) a right to recover damages under the provisions of this Article other than subsection (1); and

(b) the amount or value of any benefits received by the lessee directly or indirectly by reason of the lease contract.

§ 2A–505.   Cancellation and Termination and Effect of Cancellation, Termination, Rescission, or Fraud on Rights and Remedies

(1) On cancellation of the lease contract, all obligations that are still executory on both sides are discharged, but any right based on prior default or performance survives, and the cancelling party also retains any remedy for default of the whole lease contract or any unperformed balance.

(2) On termination of the lease contract, all obligations that are still executory on both sides are discharged but any right based on prior default or performance survives.

(3) Unless the contrary intention clearly appears, expressions of "cancellation," "rescission," or the like of the lease contract may not be construed as a renunciation or discharge of any claim in damages for an antecedent default.

(4) Rights and remedies for material misrepresentation or fraud include all rights and remedies available under this Article for default.

(5) Neither rescission nor a claim for rescission of the lease contract nor rejection or return of the goods may bar or be deemed inconsistent with a claim for damages or other right or remedy.

B.   DEFAULT BY LESSOR

§ 2A–508.   Lessee's Remedies

(1) If a lessor fails to deliver the goods in conformity to the lease contract (Section 2A–509) or repudiates the lease contract (Section 2A–402), or a lessee rightfully rejects the goods (Section 2A–509) or justifiably revokes acceptance of the goods (Section 2A–517), then with respect to any goods involved, and with respect to all of the goods if under an installment lease contract the value of the whole lease contract is substantially impaired (Section 2A–510), the lessor is in default under the lease contract and the lessee may:

(a) cancel the lease contract (Section 2A–505(1));

(b) recover so much of the rent and security as has been paid, but in the case of an installment lease contract the recovery is that which is just under the circumstances;

(c) cover and recover damages as to all goods affected whether or not they have been identified to the lease contract (Sections 2A–518 and 2A–520), or recover damages for nondelivery (Sections 2A–519 and 2A–520).

(2) If a lessor fails to deliver the goods in conformity to the lease contract or repudiates the lease contract, the lessee may also:

(a) if the goods have been identified, recover them (Section 2A–522); or

(b) in a proper case, obtain specific performance or replevy the goods (Section 2A–521).

(3) If a lessor is otherwise in default under a lease contract, the lessee may exercise the rights and remedies provided in the lease contract and this Article.

(4) If a lessor has breached a warranty, whether express or implied, the lessee may recover damages (Section 2A–519(4)).

(5) On rightful rejection or justifiable revocation of acceptance, a lessee has a security interest in goods in the lessee's possession or control for any rent and security that has been paid and any expenses reasonably incurred in their inspection, receipt, transportation, and care and custody and may hold those goods and dispose of them in good faith and in a commercially reasonable manner, subject to the provisions of Section 2A–527(5).

(6) Subject to the provisions of Section 2A–407, a lessee, on notifying the lessor of the lessee's intention to do so, may deduct all or any part of the damages resulting from any default under the lease contract from any part of the rent still due under the same lease contract.

§ 2A–509. Lessee's Rights on Improper Delivery; Rightful Rejection

(1) Subject to the provisions of Section 2A–510 on default in installment lease contracts, if the goods or the tender or delivery fail in any respect to conform to the lease contract, the lessee may reject or accept the goods or accept any commercial unit or units and reject the rest of the goods.

(2) Rejection of goods is ineffective unless it is within a reasonable time after tender or delivery of the goods and the lessee seasonably notifies the lessor.

§ 2A–513. Cure by Lessor of Improper Tender or Delivery; Replacement

(1) If any tender or delivery by the lessor or the supplier is rejected because nonconforming and the time for performance has not yet expired, the lessor or the supplier may seasonably notify the lessee of the lessor's or the supplier's intention to cure and may then make a conforming delivery within the time provided in the lease contract.

(2) If the lessee rejects a nonconforming tender that the lessor or the supplier had reasonable grounds to believe would be acceptable with or without money allowance, the lessor or the supplier may have a further reasonable time to substitute a conforming tender if he [or she] seasonably notifies the lessee.

§ 2A–516. Effect of Acceptance of Goods; Notice of Default; Burden of Establishing Default After Acceptance; Notice of Claim or Litigation to Person Answerable Over

(1) A lessee must pay rent for any goods accepted in accordance with the lease contract, with due allowance for goods rightfully rejected or not delivered.

(2) A lessee's acceptance of goods precludes rejection of the goods accepted. In the case of a finance lease, if made with knowledge of a nonconformity, acceptance cannot be revoked because of it. In any other case, if made with knowledge of a nonconformity, acceptance cannot be revoked because of it unless the acceptance was on the reasonable assumption that the nonconformity would be seasonably cured. Acceptance does not of itself impair any other remedy provided by this Article or the lease agreement for nonconformity.

(3) If a tender has been accepted:

(a) within a reasonable time after the lessee discovers or should have discovered any default, the lessee shall notify the lessor and the supplier, or be barred from any remedy;

(b) except in the case of a consumer lease, within a reasonable time after the lessee receives notice of litigation for infringement or the like (Section 2A–211) the lessee shall notify the lessor or be barred from any remedy over for liability established by the litigation; and

(c) the burden is on the lessee to establish any default.

(4) If a lessee is sued for breach of a warranty or other obligation for which a lessor or a supplier is answerable over:

(a) The lessee may give the lessor or the supplier written notice of the litigation. If the notice states that the lessor or the supplier may come in and defend and that if the lessor or the supplier does not do so he [or she] will be bound in any action against him [or her] by the lessee by any determination of fact common to the two litigations, then unless the lessor or the supplier after seasonable receipt of the notice does come in and defend he [or she] is so bound.

(b) The lessor or the supplier may demand in writing that the lessee turn over control of the litigation including settlement if the claim is one for infringement or the like (Section 2A–211) or else be barred from any remedy over. If the demand states that the lessor or the supplier agrees to bear all expense and to satisfy any adverse judgment, then unless the lessee after seasonable receipt of the demand does turn over control the lessee is so barred.

(5) The provisions of subsections (3) and (4) apply to any obligation of a lessee to hold the lessor or the supplier harmless against infringement or the like (Section 2A–211).

§ 2A–517.   Revocation of Acceptance of Goods

(1) A lessee may revoke acceptance of a lot or commercial unit whose nonconformity substantially impairs its value to the lessee if he [or she] has accepted it:

(a) oxoopt in the case of a finance lease, on the reasonable assumption that its nonconformity would be cured and it has not been seasonably cured; or

(b) without discovery of the nonconformity if the lessee's acceptance was reasonably induced either by the lessor's assurances or, except in the case of a finance lease, by the difficulty of discovery before acceptance.

(2) Revocation of acceptance must occur within a reasonable time after the lessee discovers or should have discovered the ground for it and before any substantial change in condition of the goods which is not caused by the nonconformity. Revocation is not effective until the lessee notifies the lessor.

(3) A lessee who so revokes has the same rights and duties with regard to the goods involved as if the lessee had rejected them.

§ 2A–518.   Cover; Substitute Goods

(1) After default by a lessor under the lease contract (Section 2A–508(1)), the lessee may cover by making any purchase or lease of or contract to purchase or lease goods in substitution for those due from the lessor.

(2) Except as otherwise provided with respect to damages liquidated in the lease agreement (Section 2A–504) or determined by agreement of the parties (Section 1–102(3)), if a lessee's cover is by lease agreement substantially similar to the original lease agreement and the lease agreement is made in good faith and in a commercially reasonable manner, the lessee may recover from the lessor as damages (a) the present value, as of the date of default, of the difference between the total rent for the lease term of the new lease agreement and the total rent for the remaining lease term of the original lease agreement and (b) any incidental or consequential damages less expenses saved in consequence of the lessor's default.

(3) If a lessee's cover is by lease agreement that for any reason does not qualify for treatment under subsection (2), or is by purchase or otherwise, the lessee may recover from the lessor as if the lessee had elected not to cover and Section 2A–519 governs.

§ 2A–519.   Lessee's Damages for Non-delivery, Repudiation, Default and Breach of Warranty in Regard to Accepted Goods

(1) Except as otherwise provided with respect to damages liquidated in the lease agreement (Section 2A–504) or determined by agreement of the

parties (Section 1–102(3)), if a lessee elects not to cover or a lessee elects to cover and the cover is by lease agreement that for any reason does not qualify for treatment under Section 2A–518(2), or is by purchase or otherwise, the measure of damages for non-delivery or repudiation by the lessor or for rejection or revocation of acceptance by the lessee is the present value as of the date of the default of the difference between the then market rent and the original rent, computed for the remaining lease term of the original lease agreement together with incidental and consequential damages, less expenses saved in consequence of the lessor's default.

(2) Market rent is to be determined as of the place for tender or, in cases of rejection after arrival or revocation of acceptance, as of the place of arrival.

(3) If the lessee has accepted goods and given notification (Section 2A–516(3)), the measure of damages for non-conforming tender or delivery by a lessor is the loss resulting in the ordinary course of events from the lessor's default as determined in any manner that is reasonable together with incidental and consequential damages, less expenses saved in consequence of the lessor's default.

(4) The measure of damages for breach of warranty is the present value at the time and place of acceptance of the difference between the value of the use of the goods accepted and the value if they had been as warranted for the lease term, unless special circumstances show proximate damages of a different amount, together with incidental and consequential damages, less expenses saved in consequence of the lessor's default or breach of warranty.

§ 2A–520.   Lessee's Incidental and Consequential Damages

(1) Incidental damages resulting from a lessor's default include expenses reasonably incurred in inspection, receipt, transportation, and care and custody of goods rightfully rejected or goods the acceptance of which is justifiably revoked, any commercially reasonable charges, expenses or commissions in connection with effecting cover, and any other reasonable expense incident to the default.

(2) Consequential damages resulting from a lessor's default include:

(a) any loss resulting from general or particular requirements and needs of which the lessor at the time of contracting had reason to know and which could not reasonably be prevented by cover or otherwise; and

(b) injury to person or property proximately resulting from any breach of warranty.

C.   DEFAULT BY LESSEE

§ 2A–523.   Lessor's Remedies

(1) If a lessee wrongfully rejects or revokes acceptance of goods or fails to make a payment when due or repudiates with respect to a part or the

whole, then, with respect to any goods involved, and with respect to all of the goods if under an installment lease contract the value of the whole lease contract is substantially impaired (Section 2A–510), the lessee is in default under the lease contract and the lessor may:

(a) cancel the lease contract (Section 2A–505(1)),

(b) proceed respecting goods not identified to the lease contract (Section 2A–524);

(c) withhold delivery of the goods and take possession of goods previously delivered (Section 2A–525);

(d) stop delivery of the goods by any bailee (Section 2A–526);

(e) dispose of the goods and recover damages (Section 2A–527), or retain the goods and recover damages (Section 2A–528), or in a proper case recover rent (Section 2A–529).

(2) If a lessee is otherwise in default under a lease contract, the lessor may exercise the rights and remedies provided in the lease contract and this Article.

§ 2A–525. Lessor's Right to Possession of Goods

(1) If a lessor discovers the lessee to be insolvent, the lessor may refuse to deliver the goods.

(2) The lessor has on default by the lessee under the lease contract the right to take possession of the goods. If the lease contract so provides, the lessor may require the lessee to assemble the goods and make them available to the lessor at a place to be designated by the lessor which is reasonably convenient to both parties. Without removal, the lessor may render unusable any goods employed in trade or business, and may dispose of goods on the lessee's premises (Section 2A–527).

(3) The lessor may proceed under subsection (2) without judicial process if that can be done without breach of the peace or the lessor may proceed by action.

§ 2A–527. Lessor's Rights to Dispose of Goods

(1) After a default by a lessee under the lease contract (Section 2A–523(1)) or after the lessor refuses to deliver or takes possession of goods (Section 2A–525 or 2A–526), the lessor may dispose of the goods concerned or the undelivered balance thereof by lease, sale or otherwise.

(2) Except as otherwise provided with respect to damages liquidated in the lease agreement (Section 2A–504) or determined by agreement of the parties (Section 1–102(3)), if the disposition is by lease agreement substantially similar to the original lease agreement and the lease agreement is made in good faith and in a commercially reasonable manner, the lessor may recover from the lessee as damages (a) accrued and unpaid rent as of the date of default, (b) the present value as of the date of default of the difference between the total rent for the remaining lease term of the

original lease agreement and the total rent for the lease term of the new lease agreement, and (c) any incidental damages allowed under Section 2A–530, less expenses saved in consequence of the lessee's default.

(3) If the lessor's disposition is by lease agreement that for any reason does not qualify for treatment under subsection (2), or is by sale or otherwise, the lessor may recover from the lessee as if the lessor had elected not to dispose of the goods and Section 2A–528 governs.

(4) A subsequent buyer or lessee who buys or leases from the lessor in good faith for value as a result of a disposition under this section takes the goods free of the original lease contract and any rights of the original lessee even though the lessor fails to comply with one or more of the requirements of this Article.

(5) The lessor is not accountable to the lessee for any profit made on any disposition. A lessee who has rightfully rejected or justifiably revoked acceptance shall account to the lessor for any excess over the amount of the lessee's security interest (Section 2A–508(5)).

§ 2A–528. Lessor's Damages for Non–Acceptance or Repudiation

(1) Except as otherwise provided with respect to damages liquidated in the lease agreement (Section 2A–504) or determined by agreement of the parties (Section 1–102(3)), if a lessor elects to retain the goods or a lessor elects to dispose of the goods and disposition is by lease agreement that for any reason does not qualify for treatment under Section 2A–527(2), or is by sale or otherwise, the lessor may recover from the lessee as damages for non-acceptance or repudiation by the lessee (a) accrued and unpaid rent as of the date of default, (b) the present value as of the date of default of the difference between the total rent for the remaining lease term of the original lease agreement and the market rent at the time and place for tender computed for the same lease term, and (c) any incidental damages allowed under Section 2A–530, less expenses saved in consequence of the lessee's default.

(2) If the measure of damages provided in subsection (1) is inadequate to put a lessor in as good a position as performance would have, the measure of damages is the profit, including reasonable overhead, the lessor would have made from full performance by the lessee, together with any incidental damages allowed under Section 2A–530, due allowance for costs reasonably incurred and due credit for payments or proceeds of disposition.

§ 2A–529. Lessor's Action for the Rent

(1) After default by the lessee under the lease contract (Section 2A–523(1)), if the lessor complies with subsection (2), the lessor may recover from the lessee as damages:

(a) for goods accepted by the lessee and for conforming goods lost or damaged within a commercially reasonable time after risk of loss passes to the lessee (Section 2A–219), (i) accrued and unpaid rent as of the date of default, (ii) the present value as of the date of default of the rent for the remaining lease term of the lease agreement, and (iii) any incidental damages allowed under Section 2A–530, less expenses saved in consequence of the lessee's default; and

(b) for goods identified to the lease contract if the lessor is unable after reasonable effort to dispose of them at a reasonable price or the circumstances reasonably indicate that effort will be unavailing, (i) accrued and unpaid rent as of the date of default, (ii) the present value as of the date of default of the rent for the remaining lease term of the lease agreement, and (iii) any incidental damages allowed under Section 2A–530, less expenses saved in consequence of the lessee's default.

(2) Except as provided in subsection (3), the lessor shall hold for the lessee for the remaining lease term of the lease agreement any goods that have been identified to the lease contract and are in the lessor's control.

(3) The lessor may dispose of the goods at any time before collection of the judgment for damages obtained pursuant to subsection (1). If the disposition is before the end of the remaining lease term of the lease agreement, the lessor's recovery against the lessee for damages will be governed by Section 2A–527 or Section 2A–528.

(4) Payment of the judgment for damages obtained pursuant to subsection (1) entitles the lessee to use and possession of the goods not then disposed of for the remaining lease term of the lease agreement.

(5) After a lessee has wrongfully rejected or revoked acceptance of goods, has failed to pay rent then due, or has repudiated (Section 2A–402), a lessor who is held not entitled to rent under this section must nevertheless be awarded damages for non-acceptance under Sections 2A–527 and 2A–528.

§ 2A–530. Lessor's Incidental Damages

Incidental damages to an aggrieved lessor include any commercially reasonable charges, expenses, or commissions incurred in stopping delivery, in the transportation, care and custody of goods after the lessee's default, in connection with return or disposition of the goods, or otherwise resulting from the default.

ARTICLE 3. NEGOTIABLE INSTRUMENTS
[1990 TEXT]

[As Amended 2002]

PART 1. GENERAL PROVISIONS AND DEFINITIONS

§ 3–104. Negotiable Instrument

(a) Except as provided in subsections (c) and (d), "negotiable instruments" means an unconditional promise or order to pay a fixed amount of money, with or without interest or other charges described in the promise or order, if it:

(1) is payable to bearer or to order at the time it is issued or first comes into possession of a holder;

(2) is payable on demand or at a definite time; and

(3) does not state any other undertaking or instruction by the person promising or ordering payment to do any act in addition to the payment of money, but the promise or order may contain (i) an undertaking or power to give, maintain, or protect collateral to secure payment, (ii) an authorization or power to the holder to confess judgment or realize on or dispose of collateral, or (iii) a waiver of the benefit of any law intended for the advantage or protection of an obligor.

(b) "Instrument" means a negotiable instrument.

(c) An order that meets all of the requirements of subsection (a), except paragraph (1), and otherwise falls within the definition of "check" in subsection (f) is a negotiable instrument and a check.

(d) A promise or order other than a check is not an instrument if, at the time it is issued or first comes into possession of a holder, it contains a conspicuous statement, however expressed, to the effect that the promise or order is not negotiable or is not an instrument governed by this Article.

(e) An instrument is a "note" if it is a promise and is a "draft" if it is an order. If an instrument falls within the definition of both "note" and "draft," a person entitled to enforce the instrument may treat it as either.

(f) "Check" means (i) a draft, other than a documentary draft, payable on demand and drawn on a bank or (ii) a cashier's check or teller's check. An instrument may be a check even though it is described on its face by another term, such as "money order."

. . .

§ 3–106. Unconditional Promise or Order

(a) Except as provided in this section, for the purposes of Section 3–104(a), a promise or order is unconditional unless it states (i) an express condition to payment, (ii) that the promise or order is subject to or governed by another record, or (iii) that rights or obligations with respect to the promise or order are stated in another record. A reference to another record does not itself make the promise or order conditional.

(b) A promise or order is not made conditional (i) by a reference to another record for a statement of rights with respect to collateral, prepayment, or acceleration, or (ii) because payment is limited to resort to a particular fund or source.

(c) If a promise or order requires, as condition to payment, a countersignature by a person whose specimen signature appears on the promise or order, the condition does not make the promise or order conditional for the purposes of Section 3–104(a). If the person whose specimen signature appears on an instrument fails to countersign the instrument, the failure to countersign is a defense to the obligation of the issuer, but the failure does not prevent a transferee of the instrument from becoming a holder of the instrument.

(d) If a promise or order at the time it is issued or first comes into possession of a holder contains a statement, required by applicable statutory or administrative law, to the effect that the rights of a holder or transferee are subject to claims or defenses that the issuer could assert against the original payee, the promise or order is not thereby made conditional for the purposes of Section 3–104(a); but if the promise or order is an instrument, there cannot be a holder in due course of the instrument.

Official Comment

. . .

3. Subsection (d) concerns the effect of a statement to the effect that the rights of a holder or transferee are subject to claims and defense that the issuer could assert against the original payee. The subsection applies only if the statement is required by statutory or administrative law. The prime example is the Federal Trade Commission Rule (16 C.F.R. Part 433) preserving consumers' claims and defenses in consumer credit sales. The intent of the FTC rule is to make it impossible for there to be a holder in due course of a note bearing the FTC legend and undoubtedly that is the result. But, under former Article 3, the legend may also have had the unintended effect of making the note conditional, thus excluding the note from former Article 3 altogether. Subsection (d) is designed to make it possible to preclude the possibility of a holder in due course without excluding the instrument from Article 3. Most of the provisions of Article 3 are not affected by the holder-in-due-course doctrine and there is no reason why Article 3 should not apply to a note bearing the FTC legend if holder-in-due-course rights are not involved. Under subsection (d) the statement does not make the note conditional. If the note otherwise meets the requirements of Section 3–104(a) it is a negotiable instrument for all purposes except that there cannot be a holder in due course of the note. No particular form of legend or statement is required by subsection (d). The form of a particular legend or statement may be determined by the other statute or administrative law. For example, the FTC legend required in a note taken by the seller in a consumer sale of goods or services is tailored to that particular transaction and therefore uses language that is somewhat dif-

ferent from that stated in subsection (d), but the difference in expression does not affect the essential similarity of the message conveyed. The effect of the FTC legend is to make the rights of a holder or transferee subject to claims or defenses that the issuer could assert against the original payee of the note.

§ 3–108. Payable on Demand or at Definite Time

(a) A promise or order is "payable on demand" if it (i) states that it is payable on demand or at sight, or otherwise indicates that it is payable at the will of the holder, or (ii) does not state any time of payment.

(b) A promise or order is "payable at a definite time" if it is payable on elapse of a definite period of time after sight or acceptance or at a fixed date or dates or at a time or times readily ascertainable at the time the promise or order is issued, subject to rights of (i) prepayment, (ii) acceleration, (iii) extension at the option of the holder, or (iv) extension to a further definite time at the option of the maker or acceptor or automatically upon or after a specified act or event.

(c) If an instrument, payable at a fixed date, is also payable upon demand made before the fixed date, the instrument is payable on demand until the fixed date and, if demand for payment is not made before that date, becomes payable at a definite time on the fixed date.

§ 3–109. Payable to Bearer or to Order

(a) A promise or order is payable to bearer if it:

(1) states that it is payable to bearer or to the order of bearer or otherwise indicates that the person in possession of the promise or order is entitled to payment;

(2) does not state a payee; or

(3) states that it is payable to or to the order of cash or otherwise indicates that it is not payable to an identified person.

(b) A promise or order that is not payable to bearer is payable to order if it is payable (i) to the order of an identified person or (ii) to an identified person or order. A promise or order that is payable to order is payable to the identified person.

(c) An instrument payable to bearer may become payable to an identified person if it is specially endorsed pursuant to Section 3–205(a). An instrument payable to an identified person may become payable to bearer if it is endorsed in blank pursuant to Section 3–205(b).

§ 3–117. Other Agreements Affecting Instrument

Subject to applicable law regarding exclusion of proof of contemporaneous or previous agreements, the obligation of a party to an instrument to pay the instrument may be modified, supplemented, or nullified by a separate agreement of the obligor and a person entitled to enforce the instrument, if the instrument is issued or the obligation is incurred in reliance on the agreement or as part of the same transaction giving rise to the agreement. To the extent an obligation is modified, supplemented, or nullified by an agreement under this section, the agreement is a defense to the obligation.

Official Comment

1. The separate agreement might be a security agreement or mortgage or it might be an agreement that contradicts the terms of the instrument. For example, a person may be induced to sign an instrument under an agreement that the signer will not be liable on the instrument unless certain conditions are met. Suppose X requested credit from Creditor who is willing to give the credit only if an acceptable accommodation party will sign the note of X as co-maker. Y agrees to sign as co-maker on the condition that Creditor also obtain the signature of Z as co-maker. Creditor agrees and Y signs as co-maker with X. Creditor fails to obtain the signature of Z on the note. Under Sections 3–412 and 3–419(b), Y is obliged to pay the note, but Section 3–117 applies. In this case, the agreement modifies the terms of the note by stating a condition to the obligation of Y to pay the note. The case is essentially similar to a case in which a maker of a note is induced to sign the note by fraud of the holder. Although the agreement that Y not be liable on the note unless Z also signs may not have been fraudulently made, a subsequent attempt by Creditor to require Y to pay the note in violation of the agreement is a bad faith act. Section 3–117, in treating the agreement as a defense, allows Y to assert the agreement against Creditor, but the defense would not be good against a subsequent holder in due course of the note that took it without notice of the agreement. If there cannot be a holder in due course because of Section 3–106(d), a subsequent holder that took the note in good faith, for value and without knowledge of the agreement would not be able to enforce the liability of Y. This result is consistent with the risk that a holder not in due course takes with respect to fraud in inducing issuance of an instrument.

2. The effect of merger or integration clauses to the effect that a writing is intended to be the complete and exclusive statement of the terms of the agreement or that the agreement is not subject to conditions is left to the supplementary law of the jurisdiction pursuant to Section 1–103. Thus, in the case discussed in Comment 1, whether Y is permitted to prove the condition to Y's obligation to pay the note is determined by that law. Moreover, nothing in this section is intended to validate an agreement which is fraudulent or void as against public policy, as in the case of a note given to deceive a bank examiner.

PART 2.   NEGOTIATION, TRANSFER, AND INDORSEMENT

§ 3–201.   Negotiation

(a) "Negotiation" means a transfer of possession, whether voluntary or involuntary, of an instrument by a person other than the issuer to a person who thereby becomes its holder.

(b) Except for negotiation by a remitter, if an instrument is payable to an identified person, negotiation requires transfer of possession of the instrument and its indorsement by the holder. If an instrument is payable to bearer, it may be negotiated by transfer of possession alone.

§ 3–203. Transfer of Instrument; Rights Acquired by Transfer

(a) An instrument is transferred when it is delivered by a person other than its issuer for the purpose of giving to the person receiving delivery the right to enforce the instrument.

(b) Transfer of an instrument, whether or not the transfer is a negotiation, vests in the transferee any right of the transferor to enforce the instrument, including any right as a holder in due course, but the transferee cannot acquire rights of a holder in due course by a transfer, directly or indirectly, from a holder in due course if the transferee engaged in fraud or illegality affecting the instrument.

.   .   .

PART 3.   ENFORCEMENT OF INSTRUMENTS

§ 3–302. Holder in Due Course

(a) Subject to subsection (c) and Section 3–106(d), "holder in due course" means the holder of an instrument if:

(1) the instrument when issued or negotiated to the holder does not bear such apparent evidence of forgery or alteration or is not otherwise so irregular or incomplete as to call into question its authenticity; and

(2) the holder took the instrument (i) for value, (ii) in good faith, (iii) without notice that the instrument is overdue or has been dishonored or that there is an uncured default with respect to payment of another instrument issued as part of the same series, (iv) without notice that the instrument contains an unauthorized signature or has been altered, (v) without notice of any claim to the instrument described in Section 3–306, and (vi) without notice that any party has a defense or claim in recoupment described in Section 3–305(a).

(b) Notice of discharge of a party, other than discharge in an insolvency proceeding, is not notice of a defense under subsection (a), but discharge is effective against a person who became a holder in due course with notice of the discharge. Public filing or recording of a document does not of itself constitute notice of a defense, claim in recoupment, or claim to the instrument.

(c) Except to the extent a transferor or predecessor in interest has rights as a holder in due course, a person does not acquire rights of a holder in due course of an instrument taken (i) by legal process or by purchase in an execution, bankruptcy, or creditor's sale or similar proceeding, (ii) by purchase as part of a bulk transaction not in ordinary course of business of the transferor, or (iii) as the successor in interest to an estate or other organization.

(d) If, under Section 3–303(a)(1), the promise of performance that is the consideration for an instrument has been partially performed, the holder may assert rights as a holder in due course of the instrument only to the fraction of the amount payable under the instrument equal to the value of the partial performance divided by the value of the promised performance.

(e) If (i) the person entitled to enforce an instrument has only a security interest in the instrument and (ii) the person obliged to pay the instrument has a defense, claim in recoupment, or claim to the instrument that may be asserted against the person who granted the security interest, the person entitled to enforce the instrument may assert rights as a holder in due course only to an amount payable under the instrument which, at the time of enforcement of the instrument, does not exceed the amount of the unpaid obligation secured.

(f) To be effective, notice must be received at a time and in a manner that gives a reasonable opportunity to act on it.

(g) This section is subject to any law limiting status as a holder in due course in particular classes of transactions.

§ 3–303. Value and Consideration

(a) An instrument is issued or transferred for value if:

(1) the instrument is issued or transferred for a promise of performance, to the extent the promise has been performed;

(2) the transferee acquires a security interest or other lien in the instrument other than a lien obtained by judicial proceeding;

(3) the instrument is issued or transferred as payment of, or as security for, an antecedent claim against any person, whether or not the claim is due;

(4) the instrument is issued or transferred in exchange for a negotiable instrument; or

(5) the instrument is issued or transferred in exchange for the incurring of an irrevocable obligation to a third party by the person taking the instrument.

(b) "Consideration" means any consideration sufficient to support a simple contract. The drawer or maker of an instrument has a defense if the instrument is issued without consideration. If an instrument is issued for a promise of performance, the issuer has a defense to the extent performance of the promise is due and the promise has not been performed. If an instrument is issued for value as stated in subsection (a), the instrument is also issued for consideration.

§ 3–305. Defenses and Claims in Recoupment

(a) Except as stated in subsection (b), the right to enforce the obligation of a party to pay an instrument is subject to the following:

(1) a defense of the obligor based on (i) infancy of the obligor to the extent it is a defense to a simple contract, (ii) duress, lack of legal capacity, or illegality of the transaction which, under other law, nullifies the obligation of the obligor, (iii) fraud that induced the obligor to sign the instrument with neither knowledge nor reasonable opportunity to learn of its character or its essential terms, or (iv) discharge of the obligor in insolvency proceedings;

(2) a defense of the obligor stated in another section of this Article or a defense of the obligor that would be available if the person entitled to enforce the instrument were enforcing a right to payment under a simple contract; and

(3) a claim in recoupment of the obligor against the original payee of the instrument if the claim arose from the transaction that gave rise to the instrument; but the claim of the obligor may be asserted against a transferee of the instrument only to reduce the amount owing on the instrument at the time the action is brought.

(b) The right of a holder in due course to enforce the obligation of a party to pay the instrument is subject to defenses of the obligor stated in subsection (a)(1), but is not subject to defenses of the obligor stated in subsection (a)(2) or claims in recoupment stated in subsection (a)(3) against a person other than the holder.

(c) Except as stated in subsection (d), in an action to enforce the obligation of a party to pay the instrument, the obligor may not assert against the person entitled to enforce the instrument a defense, claim in recoupment, or claim to the instrument (Section 3–306) of another person, but the other person's claim to the instrument may be asserted by the obligor if the other person is joined in the action and personally asserts the claim against the person entitled to enforce the instrument. An obligor is not obliged to pay the instrument if the person seeking enforcement of the instrument does not have rights of a holder in due course and the obligor proves that the instrument is a lost or stolen instrument.

(d) In an action to enforce the obligation of an accommodation party to pay an instrument, the accommodation party may assert against the person entitled to enforce the instrument any defense or claim in recoupment under subsection (a) that the accommodated party could assert against the person entitled to enforce the instrument, except the defenses of discharge in insolvency proceedings, infancy, and lack of legal capacity.

(e) In a consumer transaction, if law other than this Article requires that an instrument include a statement to the effect that the rights of a holder or transferee are subject to a claim or defense that the issuer could assert against the original payee and the instrument does not include such a statement:

(1) the instrument has the same effect as if the instrument included such a statement;

(2) the issuer may assert against the holder or transferee all claims and defenses that would have been available if the instrument included such a statement; and

(3) the extent to which claims may be asserted against the holder or transferee is determined as if the instrument included such a statement.

(f) This section is subject to law other than this Article which establishes a different rule for consumer transactions.

[2002 Amendments added subsections (e) and (f)]

Official Comments

1. Subsection (a) states the defenses to the obligation of a party to pay the instrument. Subsection (a)(1) states the "real defenses" that may be asserted against any person entitled to enforce the instrument.

Subsection (a)(1)(i) allows assertion of the defense of infancy against a holder in due course, even though the effect of the defense is to render the instrument voidable but not void. The policy is one of protection of the infant even at the expense of occasional loss to an innocent purchaser. No attempt is made to state when infancy is available as a defense or the conditions under which it may be asserted. In some jurisdictions it is held that an infant cannot rescind the transaction or set up the defense unless the holder is restored to the position held before the instrument was taken which, in the case of a holder in due course, is normally impossible. In other states an infant who has misrepresented age may be estopped to assert infancy. Such questions are left to other law, as an integral part of the policy of each state as to the protection of infants.

Subsection (a)(1)(ii) covers mental incompetence guardianship, ultra vires acts or lack of corporate capacity to do business, or any other incapacity apart from infancy. Such incapacity is largely statutory. Its existence and effect is left to the law of each state. If under the state law the effect is to render the obligation of the instrument entirely null and void, the defense may be asserted against a holder in due course. If the effect is merely to render the obligation voidable at the election of the obligor, the defense is cut off.

Duress, which is also covered by subsection (a)(1)(ii), is a matter of degree. An instrument signed at the point of a gun is void, even in the hands of a holder in due course. One signed under threat to prosecute the son of the maker for theft may be merely voidable, so that the defense is cut off. Illegality is most frequently a matter of gambling or usury, but may arise in other forms under a variety of statutes. The statutes differ in their provisions and the interpretations given them. They are primarily a matter of local concern and local policy. All such matters are therefore left to the local law. If under that law the effect of the duress or the illegality is to make the obligation entirely null and void, the defense may be asserted against a holder in due course. Otherwise it is cut off.

Subsection (a)(1)(iii) refers to "real" or "essential" fraud, sometimes called fraud in the essence or fraud in the factum, as effective against a holder in due course. The common illustration is that of the maker who is tricked into signing a note in the belief that it is merely a receipt or some other document. The theory of the defense is that the signature on the instrument is ineffective because the signer did not intend to sign such an instrument at all. Under this provision the defense extends to an instrument signed with knowledge that it is a negotiable instrument, but with-

971

out knowledge of its essential terms. The test of the defense is that of excusable ignorance of the contents of the writing signed. The party must not only have been in ignorance, but must also have had no reasonable opportunity to obtain knowledge. In determining what is a reasonable opportunity all relevant factors are to be taken into account, including the intelligence, education, business experience, and ability to read or understand English of the signer. Also relevant is the nature of the representations that were made, whether the signer had good reason to rely on the representations or to have confidence in the person making them, the presence or absence of any third person who might read or explain the instrument to the signer, or any other possibility of obtaining independent information, and the apparent necessity, or lack of it, for acting without delay. Unless the misrepresentation meets this test, the defense is cut off by a holder in due course.

Subsection (a)(1)(iv) states specifically that the defense of discharge in insolvency proceedings is not cut off when the instrument is purchased by a holder in due course. "Insolvency proceedings" is defined in Section 1–201(22) and it includes bankruptcy whether or not the debtor is insolvent. Subsection (2)(e) of former Section 3–305 is omitted. The substance of that provision is stated in Section 3–601(b).

. . .

3. Subsection (a)(3) is concerned with claims in recoupment which can be illustrated by the following example. Buyer issues a note to the order of Seller in exchange for a promise of Seller to deliver specified equipment. If Seller fails to deliver the equipment or delivers equipment that is rightfully rejected, Buyer has a defense to the note because the performance that was the consideration for the note was not rendered. Section 3–303(b). This defense is included in Section 3–305(a)(2). That defense

can always be asserted against Seller. This result is the same as that reached under former Section 3–408.

But suppose Seller delivered the promised equipment and it was accepted by Buyer. The equipment, however, was defective. Buyer retained the equipment and incurred expenses with respect to its repair. In this case, Buyer does not have a defense under Section 3–303(b). Seller delivered the equipment and the equipment was accepted. Under Article 2, Buyer is obliged to pay the price of the equipment which is represented by the note. But Buyer may have a claim against Seller for breach of warranty. If Buyer has a warranty claim, the claim may be asserted against Seller as a counterclaim or as a claim in recoupment to reduce the amount owing on the note. It is not relevant whether Seller is or is not a holder in due course of the note or whether Seller knew or had notice that Buyer had the warranty claim. It is obvious that holder-in-due-course doctrine cannot be used to allow Seller to cut off a warranty claim that Buyer has against Seller. Subsection (b) specifically covers this point by stating that a holder in due course is not subject to a "claim in recoupment * * * against a person other than the holder."

Suppose Seller negotiates the note to Holder. If Holder had notice of Buyer's warranty claim at the time the note was negotiated to Holder, Holder is not a holder in due course (Section 3–302(a)(2)(iv)) and Buyer may assert the claim against Holder (Section 3–305(a)(3)) but only as a claim in recoupment, i.e. to reduce the amount owed on the note. If the warranty claim is $1,000 and the unpaid note is $10,000, Buyer owes $9,000 to Holder. If the warranty claim is more than the unpaid amount of the note, Buyer owes nothing to Holder, but Buyer cannot recover the unpaid amount of the warranty claim from Holder. If Buyer had already partially paid the note, Buyer is not entitled to recover the amounts paid. The claim can be used only as an offset to amounts owing on the note. If Holder had no notice of Buyer's claim and otherwise qualifies as a holder in due course, Buyer may not assert the claim against Holder. Section 3–305(b).

The result under Section 3–305 is consistent with the result reached under former Article 3, but the rules for reaching the result are stated differently. Under former Article 3 Buyer could assert rights against Holder only if Holder was not a holder in due course, and Holder's status depended upon whether Holder had notice of a defense by Buyer. Courts have held that Holder had that notice if Holder had notice of Buyer's warranty claim. The rationale under former Article 3 was "failure of consideration." This rationale does not distinguish between cases in which the seller fails to perform and those in which the buyer accepts the performance of seller but makes a claim against the seller because the performance is faulty. The term "failure of consideration" is subject to varying interpretations and is not used in Article 3. The use of the term "claim in recoupment" in Section 3–305(a)(3) is a more precise statement of the nature of Buyer's right against Holder. The use of the term does not change the law because the treatment of a defense under subsection (a)(2) and a claim in recoupment under subsection (a)(3) is essentially the same.

Under former Article 3 case law was divided on the issue of the extent to which an obligor on a note could assert against a transferee who is not a holder in due course a debt or other claim that the obligor had against the original payee of the instrument. Some courts limited claims to those that arose in the transaction that gave rise to the note. This is the approach taken in Section 3–305(a)(3). Other courts allowed the obligor on the note to use any debt or other claim, no matter how unrelated to the note, to offset the amount owed on the

note. Under current judicial authority and non-UCC statutory law, there will be many cases in which a transferee of a note arising from a sale transaction will not qualify as a holder in due course. For example, applicable law may require the use of a note to which there cannot be a holder in due course. See Section 3–106(d) and Comment 3 to Section 3–106. It is reasonable to provide that the buyer should not be denied the right to assert claims arising out of the sale transaction. Subsection (a)(3) is based on the belief that it is not reasonable to require the transferee to bear the risk that wholly unrelated claims may also be asserted. The determination of whether a claim arose from the transaction that gave rise to the instrument is determined by law other than this Article and thus may vary as local law varies.

. . .

[2002 Amendments added Official Comments 6 and 7:]

6. Subsection (e) is added to clarify the treatment of an instrument that omits the notice currently required by the Federal Trade Commission Rule related to certain consumer credit sales and consumer purchase money loans (16 C.F.R. Part 433). This subsection adopts the view that the instrument should be treated as if the language required by the FTC Rule were present. It is based on the language describing that rule in Section 3–106(d) and the analogous provision in Section 9–404(d).

7. Subsection (f) is modeled on Sections 9–403(e) and 9–404(c). It ensures that Section 3–305 is interpreted to accommodate relevant consumer-protection laws. The absence of such a provision from other sections in Article 3 should not justify any inference about the meaning of those sections.

. . .

§ 3–311. Accord and Satisfaction by Use of Instrument

(a) If a person against whom a claim is asserted proves that (i) that person in good faith tendered an instrument to the claimant as full satisfaction of the claim, (ii) the amount of the claim was unliquidated or subject to a bona fide dispute, and (iii) the claimant obtained payment of the instrument, the following subsections apply.

(b) Unless subsection (c) applies, the claim is discharged if the person against whom the claim is asserted proves that the instrument or an accompanying written communication contained a conspicuous statement to the effect that the instrument was tendered as full satisfaction of the claim.

(c) Subject to subsection (d), a claim is not discharged under subsection (b) if either of the following applies:

(1) The claimant, if an organization, proves that (i) within a reasonable time before the tender, the claimant sent a conspicuous statement to the person against whom the claim is asserted that communications concerning disputed debts, including an instrument tendered as full satisfaction of a debt, are to be sent to a designated person, office, or place, and (ii) the instrument or accompanying communication was not received by that designated person, office, or place.

(2) The claimant, whether or not an organization, proves that within 90 days after payment of the instrument, the claimant tendered repayment of the amount of the instrument to the person against whom the claim is asserted. This paragraph does not apply if the claimant is an organization that sent a statement complying with paragraph (1)(i).

(d) A claim is discharged if the person against whom the claim is asserted proves that within a reasonable time before collection of the instrument was initiated, the claimant, or an agent of the claimant having direct responsibility with respect to the disputed obligation, knew that the instrument was tendered in full satisfaction of the claim.

ARTICLE 3. COMMERCIAL PAPER [1972 TEXT]

PART 1. SHORT TITLE, FORM AND INTERPRETATION

§ 3–104. Form Of Negotiable Instruments; "Draft"; "Check", "Certificate Of Deposit"; "Note"

(1) Any writing to be a negotiable instrument within this Article must

    (a) be signed by the maker or drawer; and

    (b) contain an unconditional promise or order to pay a sum certain in money and no other promise, order, obligation or power given by the maker or drawer except as authorized by this Article; and

    (c) be payable on demand or at a definite time; and

    (d) be payable to order or to bearer.

(2) A writing which complies with the requirements of this section is

    (a) a "draft" ("bill of exchange") if it is an order;

    (b) a "check" if it is a draft drawn on a bank and payable on demand;

    (c) a "certificate of deposit" if it is an acknowledgment by a bank of receipt of money with an engagement to repay it;

    (d) a "note" if it is a promise other than a certificate of deposit.

   . . .

§ 3–105. When Promise Or Order Unconditional

(1) A promise or order otherwise unconditional is not made conditional by the fact that the instrument

    (a) is subject to implied or constructive conditions; or

    (b) states its consideration, whether performed or promised, or the transaction which gave rise to the instrument, or that the promise or order is made or the instrument matures in accordance with or "as per" such transaction; or

    (c) refers to or states that it arises out of a separate agreement or refers to a separate agreement for rights as to prepayment or acceleration; or

    (d) states that it is drawn under a letter of credit; or

    (e) states that it is secured, whether by mortgage, reservation of title or otherwise; or

    (f) indicates a particular account to be debited or any other fund or source from which reimbursement is expected; or

975

(g) is limited to payment out of a particular fund or the proceeds of a particular source, if the instrument is issued by a government or governmental agency or unit; or

(h) is limited to payment out of the entire assets of a partnership, unincorporated association, trust or estate by or on behalf of which the instrument is issued.

(2) A promise or order is not unconditional if the instrument

(a) states that it is subject to or governed by any other agreement; or

(b) states that it is to be paid only out of a particular fund or source except as provided in this section.

§ 3–106.   Sum Certain

(1) The sum payable is a sum certain even though it is to be paid

(a) with stated interest or by stated installments; or

(b) with stated different rates of interest before and after default or a specified date; or

(c) with a stated discount or addition if paid before or after the date fixed for payment; or

(d) with exchange or less exchange, whether at a fixed rate or at the current rate; or

(e) with costs of collection or an attorney's fee or both upon default.

(2) Nothing in this section shall validate any term which is otherwise illegal.

§ 3–108.   Payable On Demand

Instruments payable on demand include those payable at sight or on presentation and those in which no time for payment is stated.

§ 3–109.   Definite Time

(1) An instrument is payable at a definite time if by its terms it is payable

(a) on or before a stated date or at a fixed period after a stated date; or

(b) at a fixed period after sight; or

(c) at a definite time subject to any acceleration; or

(d) at a definite time subject to extension at the option of the holder, or to extension to a further definite time at the option of the maker or acceptor or automatically upon or after a specified act or event.

(2) An instrument which by its terms is otherwise payable only upon an act or event uncertain as to time of occurrence is not payable at a definite time even though the act or event has occurred.

§ 3–110. Payable to Order

(1) An instrument is payable to order when by its terms it is payable to the order or assigns of any person therein specified with reasonable certainty, or to him or his order, or when it is conspicuously designated on its face as "exchange" or the like and names a payee. It may be payable to the order of

(a) the maker or drawer; or

(b) the drawee; or

(c) a payee who is not maker, drawer or drawee; or

(d) two or more payees together or in the alternative; or

(e) an estate, trust or fund, in which case it is payable to the order of the representative of such estate, trust or fund or his successors; or

(f) an office, or an officer by his title as such in which case it is payable to the principal but the incumbent of the office or his successors may act as if he or they were the holder; or

(g) a partnership or unincorporated association, in which case it is payable to the partnership or association and may be indorsed or transferred by any person thereto authorized.

. . .

§ 3–111. Payable to Bearer

An instrument is payable to bearer when by its terms it is payable to

(a) bearer or the order of bearer; or

(b) a specified person or bearer; or

(c) "cash" or the order of "cash," or any other indication which does not purport to designate a specific payee.

§ 3–112. Terms and Omissions Not Affecting Negotiability

(1) The negotiability of an instrument is not affected by

(a) the omission of a statement of any consideration or of the place where the instrument is drawn or payable; or

(b) a statement that collateral has been given to secure obligations either on the instrument or otherwise of an obligor on the instrument or that in case of default on those obligations the holder may realize on or dispose of the collateral; or

(c) a promise or power to maintain or protect collateral or to give additional collateral; or

(d) a term authorizing a confession of judgment on the instrument if it is not paid when due; or

(e) a term purporting to waive the benefit of any law intended for the advantage or protection of any obligor; or

(f) a term in a draft providing that the payee by indorsing or cashing it acknowledges full satisfaction of an obligation of the drawer; or

(g) a statement in a draft drawn in a set of parts (Section 3–801) to the effect that the order is effective only if no other part has been honored.

(2) Nothing in this section shall validate any term which is otherwise illegal.

§ 3–119.   Other Writings Affecting Instrument

(1) As between the obligor and his immediate obligee or any transferee the terms of an instrument may be modified or affected by any other written agreement executed as a part of the same transaction, except that a holder in due course is not affected by any limitation of his rights arising out of the separate written agreement if he had no notice of the limitation when he took the instrument.

(2) A separate agreement does not affect the negotiability of an instrument.

Official Comment

Purposes: This section is new. It is intended to resolve conflicts as to the effect of a separate writing upon a negotiable instrument.

. . .

3. The section applies to negotiable instruments the ordinary rule that writings executed as a part of the same transaction are to be read together as a single agreement. As between the immediate parties a negotiable instrument is merely a contract, and is no exception to the principle that the courts will look to the entire contract in writing. Accordingly a note may be affected by an acceleration clause, a clause providing for discharge under certain conditions, or any other relevant term in the separate writing. "May be modified or affected" does not mean that the separate agreement must necessarily be given effect. There is still room for construction of the writing as not intended to affect the instrument at all, or as intended to affect it only for a limited purpose such as foreclosure or other realization of collateral. If there is outright contradiction between the two, as where the note is for $1,000 but the accompanying mortgage recites that it is for $2,000, the note may be held to stand on its own feet and not to be affected by the contradiction.

4. Under this Article a purchaser of the instrument may become a holder in due course although he takes it with knowledge that it was accompanied by a separate agreement, if he has no notice of any defense or claim arising from the terms of the agreement. If any limitation in the separate writing in itself amounts to a defense or claim, as in the case of an agreement that the note is a sham and cannot be enforced, a purchaser with notice of it cannot be a holder in due course. The section also

covers limitations which do not in themselves give notice of any present defense or claim, such as conditions providing that under certain conditions the note shall be extended for one year. A purchaser with notice of such limitations may be a holder in due course, but he takes the instrument subject to the limitation. If he is without such notice, he is not affected by such a limiting clause in the separate writing.

. . .

PART 2. TRANSFER AND NEGOTIATION

§ 3–201. Transfer: Right to Indorsement

(1) Transfer of an instrument vests in the transferee such rights as the transferor has therein, except that a transferee who has himself been a party to any fraud or illegality affecting the instrument or who as a prior holder had notice of a defense or claim against it cannot improve his position by taking from a later holder in due course.

(2) A transfer of a security interest in an instrument vests the foregoing rights in the transferee to the extent of the interest transferred.

. . .

§ 3–202. Negotiation

(1) Negotiation is the transfer of an instrument in such form that the transferee becomes a holder. If the instrument is payable to order it is negotiated by delivery with any necessary indorsement; if payable to bearer it is negotiated by delivery.

(2) An indorsement must be written by or on behalf of the holder and on the instrument or on a paper so firmly affixed thereto as to become a part thereof.

. . .

PART 3. RIGHTS OF A HOLDER

§ 3–301. Rights of a Holder

The holder of an instrument whether or not he is the owner may transfer or negotiate it and, except as otherwise provided in Section 3–603 on payment or satisfaction, discharge it or enforce payment in his own name.

§ 3–302. Holder in Due Course

(1) A holder in due course is a holder who takes the instrument

(a) for value; and

(b) in good faith; and

(c) without notice that it is overdue or has been dishonored or of any defense against or claim to it on the part of any person.

(2) A payee may be a holder in due course.

(3) A holder does not become a holder in due course of an instrument:

(a) by purchase of it at judicial sale or by taking it under legal process; or

(b) by acquiring it in taking over an estate; or

(c) by purchasing it as part of a bulk transaction not in regular course of business of the transferor.

(4) A purchaser of a limited interest can be a holder in due course only to the extent of the interest purchased.

§ 3–303. Taking for Value

A holder takes the instrument for value

(a) to the extent that the agreed consideration has been performed or that he acquires a security interest in or a lien on the instrument otherwise than by legal process; or

(b) when he takes the instrument in payment of or as security for an antecedent claim against any person whether or not the claim is due; or

(c) when he gives a negotiable instrument for it or makes an irrevocable commitment to a third person.

§ 3–304. Notice to Purchaser

(1) The purchaser has notice of a claim or defense if

(a) the instrument is so incomplete, bears such visible evidence of forgery or alteration, or is otherwise so irregular as to call into question its validity, terms or ownership or to create an ambiguity as to the party to pay; or

(b) the purchaser has notice that the obligation of any party is voidable in whole or in part, or that all parties have been discharged.

(2) The purchaser has notice of a claim against the instrument when he has knowledge that a fiduciary has negotiated the instrument in payment of or as security for his own debt or in any transaction for his own benefit or otherwise in breach of duty.

(3) The purchaser has notice that an instrument is overdue if he has reason to know

(a) that any part of the principal amount is overdue or that there is an uncured default in payment of another instrument of the same series; or

(b) that acceleration of the instrument has been made; or

(c) that he is taking a demand instrument after demand has been made or more than a reasonable length of time after its issue. A reasonable time for a check drawn and payable within the states and territories of the United States and the District of Columbia is presumed to be thirty days.

(4) Knowledge of the following facts does not of itself give the purchaser notice of a defense or claim

(a) that the instrument is antedated or postdated;

(b) that it was issued or negotiated in return for an executory promise or accompanied by a separate agreement, unless the purchaser has notice that a defense or claim has arisen from the terms thereof;

(c) that any party has signed for accommodation;

(d) that an incomplete instrument has been completed, unless the purchaser has notice of any improper completion;

(e) that any person negotiating the instrument is or was a fiduciary;

(f) that there has been default in payment of interest on the instrument or in payment of any other instrument, except one of the same series.

(5) The filing or recording of a document does not of itself constitute notice within the provisions of this Article to a person who would otherwise be a holder in due course.

(6) To be effective notice must be received at such time and in such manner as to give a reasonable opportunity to act on it.

§ 3–305. Rights of a Holder in Due Course

To the extent that a holder is a holder in due course he takes the instrument free from

(1) all claims to it on the part of any person; and

(2) all defenses of any party to the instrument with whom the holder has not dealt except

(a) infancy, to the extent that it is a defense to a simple contract; and

(b) such other incapacity, or duress, or illegality of the transaction, as renders the obligation of the party a nullity; and

(c) such misrepresentation as has induced the party to sign the instrument with neither knowledge nor reasonable opportunity to obtain knowledge of its character or its essential terms; and

(d) discharge in insolvency proceedings; and

(e) any other discharge of which the holder has notice when he takes the instrument.

Official Comment

Purposes of Changes and New Matter:

. . .

4. Paragraph (a) of subsection (2) is new. It follows the decisions under the original Act in providing that the defense of infancy may be asserted against a holder in due course, even though its effect is to render the instrument voidable but not void. The policy is one of protection of the infant against those who take advantage of him, even at the expense of occasional loss to an innocent purchaser. No attempt is made to state when infancy is available as a defense or the conditions under which it may be asserted. In some jurisdictions it is held that an infant cannot rescind the transaction or set up the defense unless he restores the holder to his former position, which in the case of a holder in due course is normally impossible. In other states an infant who has misrepresented his age may be estopped to assert his infancy. Such questions are left to the local law, as an integral part of the policy of each state as to the protection of infants.

5. Paragraph (b) of subsection (2) is new. It covers mental incompetence, guardianship, ultra vires acts or lack of corporate capacity to do business, any remaining incapacity of married women, or any other incapacity apart from infancy. Such incapacity is largely statutory. Its existence and effect is left to the law of each state. If under the local law the effect is to render the obligation of the instrument entirely null and void, the defense may be asserted against a holder in due course. If the effect is merely to render the obligation voidable at the election of the obligor, the defense is cut off.

6. Duress is a matter of degree. An instrument signed at the point of a gun is void, even in the hands of a holder in due course. One signed under threat to prosecute the son of the maker for theft may be merely voidable, so that the defense is cut off. Illegality is most frequently a matter of gambling or usury, but may arise in many other forms under a great variety of statutes. The statutes differ greatly in their provisions and the interpretations given them. They are primarily a matter of local concern and local policy. All such matters are therefore left to the local law. If under that law the effect of the duress or the illegality is to make the obligation entirely null and void, the defense may be asserted against a holder in due course. Otherwise it is cut off.

7. Paragraph (c) of subsection (2) is new. It follows the great majority of the decisions under the original Act in recognizing the defense of "real" or "essential" fraud, sometimes called fraud in the essence or fraud in the factum, as effective against a holder in due course. The common illustration is that of the maker who is tricked into signing a note in the belief that it is merely a receipt or some other document. The theory of the defense is that his signature on the instrument is ineffective because he did not intend to sign such an instrument at all. Under this provision the defense extends to an instrument signed with knowledge that it is a negotiable instrument, but without knowledge of its essential terms.

The test of the defense here stated is that of excusable ignorance of the contents of the writing signed. The party must not only have been in ignorance, but must also have had no reasonable opportunity to obtain knowledge. In determining what is a reasonable opportunity all relevant factors are to be taken into account, including the age and sex of the party, his intelligence, education and business experience; his ability to read or to understand English, the representations made to him and his reason to rely on them or to have confidence in the person making them; the presence or absence of any third person who might read or explain the instrument to him, or any other possibility of obtaining independent information; and the apparent necessity, or lack of it, for acting without delay.

Unless the misrepresentation meets this test, the defense is cut off by a holder in due course.

8. Paragraph (d) is also new. It is inserted to make it clear that any discharge in bankruptcy or other insolvency proceedings, as defined in this Article, is not cut off when the instrument is purchased by a holder in due course.

· · ·

§ 3–306. Rights of One Not Holder in Due Course

Unless he has the rights of a holder in due course any person takes the instrument subject to

(a) all valid claims to it on the part of any person; and

(b) all defenses of any party which would be available in an action on a simple contract; and

(c) the defenses of want or failure of consideration, non-performance of any condition precedent, non-delivery, or delivery for a special purpose (Section 3–408); and

(d) the defense that he or a person through whom he holds the instrument acquired it by theft, or that payment or satisfaction to such holder would be inconsistent with the terms of a restrictive indorsement. The claim of any third person to the instrument is not otherwise available as a defense to any party liable thereon unless the third person himself defends the action for such party.

ARTICLE 7. WAREHOUSE RECEIPTS, BILLS OF LADING AND OTHER DOCUMENTS OF TITLE

PART 2. WAREHOUSE RECEIPTS: SPECIAL PROVISIONS

§ 7–209. Lien of Warehouse

(a) A warehouse has a lien against the bailor on the goods covered by a warehouse receipt or storage agreement or on the proceeds thereof in its possession for charges for storage or transportation, including demurrage and terminal charges, insurance, labor, or other charges, present or future, in relation to the goods, and for expenses necessary for preservation of the goods or reasonably incurred in their sale pursuant to law....

. . .

(e) A warehouse loses its lien on any goods that it voluntarily delivers or unjustifiably refuses to deliver.

§ 7–210. Enforcement of Warehouse's Lien

(a) Except as otherwise provided in subsection (b), a warehouse's lien may be enforced by public or private sale of the goods, in bulk or in packages, at any time or place and on any terms that are commercially reasonable, after notifying all persons known to claim an interest in the goods. The notification must include a statement of the amount due, the nature of the proposed sale, and the time and place of any public sale. The fact that a better price could have been obtained by a sale at a different time or in a different method from that selected by the warehouse is not of itself sufficient to establish that the sale was not made in a commercially reasonable manner. The warehouse has sold in a commercially reasonable manner if the warehouse sells the goods in the usual manner in any recognized market therefor, sells at the price current in that market at the time of the sale, or has otherwise sold in conformity with commercially reasonable practices among dealers in the type of goods sold. A sale of more goods than apparently necessary to be offered to ensure satisfaction of the obligation is not commercially reasonable, except in cases covered by the preceding sentence.

(b) A warehouse's lien on goods, other than goods stored by a merchant in the course of its business, may be enforced only if the following requirements are satisfied:

(1) All persons known to claim an interest in the goods must be notified.

(2) The notification must include an itemized statement of the claim, a description of the goods subject to the lien, a demand for payment within a specified time not less than 10 days after receipt of the notification, and a conspicuous statement that unless the claim is

paid within that time the goods will be advertised for sale and sold by auction at a specified time and place.

(3) The sale must conform to the terms of the notification.

(4) The sale must be held at the nearest suitable place to where the goods are held or stored.

(5) After the expiration of the time given in the notification, an advertisement of the sale must be published once a week for two weeks consecutively in a newspaper of general circulation where the sale is to be held. The advertisement must include a description of the goods, the name of the person on whose account the goods are being held, and the time and place of the sale. The sale must take place at least 15 days after the first publication. If there is no newspaper of general circulation where the sale is to be held, the advertisement must be posted at least 10 days before the sale in not less than six conspicuous places in the neighborhood of the proposed sale.

(c) Before any sale pursuant to this section, any person claiming a right in the goods may pay the amount necessary to satisfy the lien and the reasonable expenses incurred in complying with this section. In that event, the goods may not be sold but must be retained by the warehouse subject to the terms of the receipt and this article.

(d) A warehouse may buy at any public sale held pursuant to this section.

(e) A purchaser in good faith of goods sold to enforce a warehouse's lien takes the goods free of any rights of persons against which the lien was valid, despite the warehouse's noncompliance with this section.

(f) A warehouse may satisfy its lien from the proceeds of any sale pursuant to this section but shall hold the balance, if any, for delivery on demand to any person to which the warehouse would have been bound to deliver the goods.

(g) The rights provided by this section are in addition to all other rights allowed by law to a creditor against a debtor.

(h) If a lien is on goods stored by a merchant in the course of its business, the lien may be enforced in accordance with subsection (a) or (b).

(*i*) A warehouse is liable for damages caused by failure to comply with the requirements for sale under this section and, in case of willful violation, is liable for conversion.

ARTICLE 9. SECURED TRANSACTIONS

PART 1. GENERAL PROVISIONS

[SUBPART 1. SHORT TITLE, DEFINITIONS, AND GENERAL CONCEPTS]

§ 9–101. Short Title. This Article May Be Cited As Uniform Commercial Code–Secured Transactions.

Official Comment

1. **Source.** This Article . . . provides a comprehensive scheme for the regulation of security interests in personal property and fixtures. For the most part this Article follows the general approach and retains much of the terminology of former Article 9. . . . Unlike the Comments to former Article 9, however, these Comments dwell very little on the pre-UCC state of the law. For that reason, the Comments to former Article 9 will remain of substantial historical value and interest. They also will remain useful in understanding the background and general conceptual approach of this Article.

. . .

This Article also includes headings for the subsections as an aid to readers. Unlike section captions, which are part of the UCC, see Section 1–109, subsection headings are not a part of the official text itself and have not been approved by the sponsors.

. . .

§ 9–102. Definitions and Index of Definitions

(a) **[Article 9 definitions.]** In this article:

. . .

(3) "Account debtor" means a person obligated on an account, chattel paper, or general intangible. The term does not include persons obligated to pay a negotiable instrument, even if the instrument constitutes part of chattel paper.

(4) "Accounting", except as used in "accounting for", means a record:

(A) authenticated by a secured party;

(B) indicating the aggregate unpaid secured obligations as of a date not more than 35 days earlier or 35 days later than the date of the record; and

(C) identifying the components of the obligations in reasonable detail.

. . .

(7) "Authenticate" means:

(A) to sign; or

(B) to execute or otherwise adopt a symbol, or encrypt or similarly process a record in whole or in part, with the present intent of the authenticating person to identify the person and adopt or accept a record.

.   .   .

(11) "Chattel paper" means a record or records that evidence both a monetary obligation and a security interest in specific goods, a security interest in specific goods and software used in the goods, a security interest in specific goods and license of software used in the goods, a lease of specific goods, or a lease of specific goods and license of software used in the goods. In this paragraph, "monetary obligation" means a monetary obligation secured by the goods or owed under a lease of the goods and includes a monetary obligation with respect to software used in the goods.   .   .   .

(12) "Collateral" means the property subject to a security interest or agricultural lien. The term includes:

(A) proceeds to which a security interest attaches;

(B) accounts, chattel paper, payment intangibles, and promissory notes that have been sold; and

(C) goods that are the subject of a consignment.

.   .   .

(18) "Communicate" means:

(A) to send a written or other tangible record;

(B) to transmit a record by any means agreed upon by the persons sending and receiving the record; or

(C) in the case of transmission of a record to or by a filing office, to transmit a record by any means prescribed by filing-office rule.

(19) "Consignee" means a merchant to which goods are delivered in a consignment.

(20) "Consignment" means a transaction, regardless of its form, in which a person delivers goods to a merchant for the purpose of sale and:

(A) the merchant:

(i) deals in goods of that kind under a name other than the name of the person making delivery;

(ii) is not an auctioneer; and

(iii) is not generally known by its creditors to be substantially engaged in selling the goods of others;

(B) with respect to each delivery, the aggregate value of the goods is $1,000 or more at the time of delivery;

(C) the goods are not consumer goods immediately before delivery; and

(D) the transaction does not create a security interest that secures an obligation.

(21) "Consignor" means a person that delivers goods to a consignee in a consignment.

(22) "Consumer debtor" means a debtor in a consumer transaction.

(23) "Consumer goods" means goods that are used or bought for use primarily for personal, family, or household purposes.

(24) "Consumer-goods transaction" means a consumer transaction in which:

(A) an individual incurs an obligation primarily for personal, family, or household purposes; and

(B) a security interest in consumer goods secures the obligation.

(25) "Consumer obligor" means an obligor who is an individual and who incurred the obligation as part of a transaction entered into primarily for personal, family, or household purposes.

(26) "Consumer transaction" means a transaction in which (i) an individual incurs an obligation primarily for personal, family, or household purposes, (ii) a security interest secures the obligation, and (iii) the collateral is held or acquired primarily for personal, family, or household purposes. The term includes consumer-goods transactions.

.   .   .

(28) "Debtor" means:

(A) a person having an interest, other than a security interest or other lien, in the collateral, whether or not the person is an obligor;

(B) a seller of accounts, chattel paper, payment intangibles, or promissory notes; or

(C) a consignee.

.   .   .

(33) "Equipment" means goods other than inventory, farm products, or consumer goods.

.   .   .

(41) "Fixtures" means goods that have become so related to particular real property that an interest in them arises under real property law.

(42) "General intangible" means any personal property, including things in action, other than accounts, chattel paper, commercial tort claims, deposit accounts, documents, goods, instruments, investment property, letter-of-credit rights, letters of credit, money, and oil, gas, or

other minerals before extraction. The term includes payment intangibles and software.

(43) "Good faith" means honesty in fact and the observance of reasonable commercial standards of fair dealing.

(44) "Goods" means all things that are movable when a security interest attaches. The term includes (i) fixtures, ... and (v) manufactured homes. The term also includes a computer program embedded in goods and any supporting information provided in connection with a transaction relating to the program if (i) the program is associated with the goods in such a manner that it customarily is considered part of the goods, or (ii) by becoming the owner of the goods, a person acquires a right to use the program in connection with the goods. The term does not include a computer program embedded in goods that consist solely of the medium in which the program is embedded. . . .

. . .

(47) "Instrument" means a negotiable instrument or any other writing that evidences a right to the payment of a monetary obligation, is not itself a security agreement or lease, and is of a type that in ordinary course of business is transferred by delivery with any necessary indorsement or assignment. The term does not include (i) investment property, (ii) letters of credit, or (iii) writings that evidence a right to payment arising out of the use of a credit or charge card or information contained on or for use with the card.

(48) "Inventory" means goods, other than farm products, which:

(A) are leased by a person as lessor;

(B) are held by a person for sale or lease or to be furnished under a contract of service;

(C) are furnished by a person under a contract of service; or

(D) consist of raw materials, work in process, or materials used or consumed in a business.

. . .

(59) "Obligor" means a person that, with respect to an obligation secured by a security interest in or an agricultural lien on the collateral, (i) owes payment or other performance of the obligation, (ii) has provided property other than the collateral to secure payment or other performance of the obligation, or (iii) is otherwise accountable in whole or in part for payment or other performance of the obligation. The term does not include issuers or nominated persons under a letter of credit.

(60) "Original debtor", except as used in Section 9–310(c), means a person that, as debtor, entered into a security agreement to which a new debtor has become bound under Section 9–203(d).

. . .

(62) "Person related to," with respect to an individual, means:

(A) the spouse of the individual;

(B) a brother, brother-in-law, sister, or sister-in-law of the individual;

(C) an ancestor or lineal descendant of the individual or the individual's spouse; or

(D) any other relative, by blood or marriage, of the individual or the individual's spouse who shares the same home with the individual.

(63) "Person related to," with respect to an organization, means:

(A) a person directly or indirectly controlling, controlled by, or under common control with the organization;

(B) an officer or director of, or a person performing similar functions with respect to, the organization;

(C) an officer or director of, or a person performing similar functions with respect to, a person described in subparagraph (A);

(D) the spouse of an individual described in subparagraph (A), (B), or (C); or

(E) an individual who is related by blood or marriage to an individual described in subparagraph (A), (B), (C), or (D) and shares the same home with the individual.

(64) "Proceeds," except as used in Section 9–609(b), means the following property:

(A) whatever is acquired upon the sale, lease, license, exchange, or other disposition of collateral;

(B) whatever is collected on, or distributed on account of, collateral;

(C) rights arising out of collateral;

(D) to the extent of the value of collateral, claims arising out of the loss, nonconformity, or interference with the use of, defects or infringement of rights in, or damage to, the collateral; or

(E) to the extent of the value of collateral and to the extent payable to the debtor or the secured party, insurance payable by reason of the loss or nonconformity of, defects or infringement of rights in, or damage to, the collateral.

(65) "Promissory note" means an instrument that evidences a promise to pay a monetary obligation, does not evidence an order to pay, and does not contain an acknowledgment by a bank that the bank has received for deposit a sum of money or funds.

(66) "Proposal" means a record authenticated by a secured party which includes the terms on which the secured party is willing to

accept collateral in full or partial satisfaction of the obligation it secures pursuant to Sections 9–620, 9–621, and 9–622.

. . .

(69) "Record," except as used in "for record," "of record," "record or legal title," and "record owner," means information that is inscribed on a tangible medium or which is stored in an electronic or other medium and is retrievable in perceivable form.

. . .

(71) "Secondary obligor" means an obligor to the extent that:

(A) the obligor's obligation is secondary; or

(B) the obligor has a right of recourse with respect to an obligation secured by collateral against the debtor, another obligor, or property of either.

(72) "Secured party" means:

(A) a person in whose favor a security interest is created or provided for under a security agreement, whether or not any obligation to be secured is outstanding;

(B) a person that holds an agricultural lien;

(C) a consignor;

(D) a person to which accounts, chattel paper, payment intangibles, or promissory notes have been sold;

(E) a trustee, indenture trustee, agent, collateral agent, or other representative in whose favor a security interest or agricultural lien is created or provided for; or

(F) a person that holds a security interest arising under Section 2–401, 2–505, 2–711(3), 2A–508(5), 4–210, or 5–118.

(73) "Security agreement" means an agreement that creates or provides for a security interest.

(74) "Send," in connection with a record or notification, means:

(A) to deposit in the mail, deliver for transmission, or transmit by any other usual means of communication, with postage or cost of transmission provided for, addressed to any address reasonable under the circumstances; or

(B) to cause the record or notification to be received within the time that it would have been received if properly sent under subparagraph (A).

(75) "Software" means a computer program and any supporting information provided in connection with a transaction relating to the program. The term does not include a computer program that is included in the definition of goods.

(76) "State" means a State of the United States, the District of Columbia, Puerto Rico, the United States Virgin Islands, or any territory or insular possession subject to the jurisdiction of the United States.

. . .

(78) "Tangible chattel paper" means chattel paper evidenced by a record or records consisting of information that is inscribed on a tangible medium.

. . .

(b) **[Definitions in other articles.]** The following definitions in other articles apply to this article:

. . .

"Contract for sale"	Section 2–106.
. . .	
"Holder in due course"	Section 3–302.
. . .	
"Lease"	Section 2A–103.
"Lease agreement"	Section 2A–103.
"Lease contract"	Section 2A–103.
"Leasehold interest"	Section 2A–103.
"Lessee"	Section 2A–103.
"Lessee in ordinary course of business"	Section 2A–103.
"Lessor"	Section 2A–103.
"Lessor's residual interest"	Section 2A–103.
. . .	
"Merchant"	Section 2–104.
"Negotiable instrument"	Section 3–104.
. . .	
"Note"	Section 3–104.
. . .	
"Sale"	Section 2–106.

. . .

(c) **[Article 1 definitions and principles.]** Article 1 contains general definitions and principles of construction and interpretation applicable throughout this article.

Official Comment

. . .

7. **Consumer-Related Definitions: "Consumer Debtor"; "Consumer Goods"; "Consumer-goods transaction"; "Consumer Obligor"; "Consumer Transaction."** . . .

"Consumer-goods transaction" is a subset of "consumer transaction." Under each definition, both the obligation secured and the collateral must have a personal, family, or household purpose. However, "mixed" business and personal transactions also may be characterized as a consumer-goods transaction or consumer transaction. Subparagraph (A) of the definition of consumer-goods transactions and clause (i) of the definition of consumer transaction are primary purposes tests. Under these tests, it is necessary to determine the primary purpose of the obligation or obligations secured. Subparagraph (B) and clause (iii) of these definitions are satisfied if any of the collateral is consumer goods, in the case of a consumer-goods transaction, or "is held or acquired primarily for personal, family, or household purposes," in the case of a consumer transaction. The fact that some of the obli-gations secured or some of the collateral for the obligation does not satisfy the tests (e.g., some of the collateral is acquired for a business purpose) does not prevent a transaction from being a "consumer transaction" or "consumer-goods transaction."

.   .   .

§ 9–103. Purchase–Money Security Interest; Application of Payments; Burden of Establishing.

(a) **[Definitions.]** In this section:

(1) "purchase-money collateral" means goods or software that secures a purchase-money obligation incurred with respect to that collateral; and

(2) "purchase-money obligation" means an obligation of an obligor incurred as all or part of the price of the collateral or for value given to enable the debtor to acquire rights in or the use of the collateral if the value is in fact so used.

(b) **[Purchase-money security interest in goods.]** A security interest in goods is a purchase-money security interest:

(1) to the extent that the goods are purchase-money collateral with respect to that security interest;

(2) if the security interest is in inventory that is or was purchase-money collateral, also to the extent that the security interest secures a purchase-money obligation incurred with respect to other inventory in which the secured party holds or held a purchase-money security interest; and

(3) also to the extent that the security interest secures a purchase-money obligation incurred with respect to software in which the secured party holds or held a purchase-money security interest.

(c) **[Purchase-money security interest in software.]** A security interest in software is a purchase-money security interest to the extent that the security interest also secures a purchase-money obligation incurred with respect to goods in which the secured party holds or held a purchase-money security interest if:

(1) the debtor acquired its interest in the software in an integrated transaction in which it acquired an interest in the goods; and

(2) the debtor acquired its interest in the software for the principal purpose of using the software in the goods.

(d) **[Consignor's inventory purchase-money security interest.]** The security interest of a consignor in goods that are the subject of a consignment is a purchase-money security interest in inventory.

(e) **[Application of payment in non-consumer-goods transaction.]** In a transaction other than a consumer-goods transaction, if the extent to which a security interest is a purchase-money security interest depends on the application of a payment to a particular obligation, the payment must be applied:

(1) in accordance with any reasonable method of application to which the parties agree;

(2) in the absence of the parties' agreement to a reasonable method, in accordance with any intention of the obligor manifested at or before the time of payment; or

(3) in the absence of an agreement to a reasonable method and a timely manifestation of the obligor's intention, in the following order:

(A) to obligations that are not secured; and

(B) if more than one obligation is secured, to obligations secured by purchase-money security interests in the order in which those obligations were incurred.

(f) **[No loss of status of purchase-money security interest in non-consumer-goods transaction.]** In a transaction other than a consumer-goods transaction, a purchase-money security interest does not lose its status as such, even if:

(1) the purchase-money collateral also secures an obligation that is not a purchase-money obligation;

(2) collateral that is not purchase-money collateral also secures the purchase-money obligation; or

(3) the purchase-money obligation has been renewed, refinanced, consolidated, or restructured.

(g) **[Burden of proof in non-consumer-goods transaction.]** In a transaction other than a consumer-goods transaction, a secured party claiming a purchase-money security interest has the burden of establishing the extent to which the security interest is a purchase-money security interest.

(h) **[Non-consumer-goods transactions; no inference.]** The limitation of the rules in subsections (e), (f), and (g) to transactions other than consumer-goods transactions is intended to leave to the court the determination of the proper rules in consumer-goods transactions. The court may not infer from that limitation the nature of the proper rule in consumer-goods transactions and may continue to apply established approaches.

§ 9–108. Sufficiency of Description

(a) **[Sufficiency of description.]** Except as otherwise provided in subsections (c), (d), and (e), a description of personal or real property is sufficient, whether or not it is specific, if it reasonably identifies what is described.

. . .

(c) **[Supergeneric description not sufficient.]** A description of collateral as "all the debtor's assets" or "all the debtor's personal property" or using words of similar import does not reasonably identify the collateral.

. . .

(e) **[When description by type insufficient.]** A description only by type of collateral defined in [the Uniform Commercial Code] is an insufficient description of:

(1) a commercial tort claim; or

(2) in a consumer transaction, consumer goods, a security entitlement, a securities account, or a commodity account.

Official Comment

. . .

5. **Consumer Investment Property; Commercial Tort Claims.** Subsection (e) requires greater specificity of description in order to prevent debtors from inadvertently encumbering certain property. Subsection (e) requires that a description by defined "type" of collateral alone of a commercial tort claim or, in a consumer transaction, of a security entitlement, securities account, or commodity account, is not sufficient. For example, "all existing and after-acquired investment property" or "all existing and after-acquired security entitle- ments," without more, would be insufficient in a consumer transaction to describe a security entitlement, securities account, or commodity account. The reference to "*only* by type" in subsection (e) means that a description is sufficient if it satisfies subsection (a) and contains a descriptive component beyond the "type" alone. Moreover, if the collateral consists of a securities account or commodity account, a description of the account is sufficient to cover all existing and future security entitlements or commodity contracts carried in the account. See Section 9–203(h), (i).

. . .

[SUBPART 2. APPLICABILITY OF ARTICLE]

§ 9–109. Scope

(a) **[General scope of article.]** Except as otherwise provided in subsections (c) and (d), this article applies to:

(1) a transaction, regardless of its form, that creates a security interest in personal property or fixtures by contract;

(2) an agricultural lien;

(3) a sale of accounts, chattel paper, payment intangibles, or promissory notes;

(4) a consignment;

(5) a security interest arising under Section 2–401, 2–505, 2–711(3), or 2A–508(5), as provided in Section 9–110; and

(6) a security interest arising under Section 4–210 or 5–118.

. . .

(d) **[Inapplicability of article.]** This article does not apply to:

(1) a landlord's lien, other than an agricultural lien;

(2) a lien, other than an agricultural lien, given by statute or other rule of law for services or materials, but Section 9–333 applies with respect to priority of the lien;

(3) an assignment of a claim for wages, salary, or other compensation of an employee;

.　.　.

(12) an assignment of a claim arising in tort, other than a commercial tort claim, but Sections 9–315 and 9–322 apply with respect to proceeds and priorities in proceeds; or

(13) an assignment of a deposit account in a consumer transaction, but Sections 9–315 and 9–322 apply with respect to proceeds and priorities in proceeds.

§ 9–110.　Security Interests Arising Under Article 2 or 2a.

A security interest arising under Section 2–401, 2–505, 2–711(3), or 2A–508(5) is subject to this article. However, until the debtor obtains possession of the goods:

(1) the security interest is enforceable, even if Section 9–203(b)(3) has not been satisfied;

(2) filing is not required to perfect the security interest;

(3) the rights of the secured party after default by the debtor are governed by Article 2 or 2A; and

(4) the security interest has priority over a conflicting security interest created by the debtor.

Official Comments

.　.　.

4. **Priority.** This section adds to former Section 9–113 a priority rule. Until the debtor obtains possession of the goods, a security interest arising under one of the specified sections of Article 2 or 2A has priority over conflicting security interests created by the debtor. Thus, . . . a security interest under Section 2–711(3) or 2A–508(5) has priority over security interests claimed by the seller's or lessor's secured lender. This result is appropriate, inasmuch as the payments giving rise to the debt secured by the Article 2 or 2A security interest are likely to be included among the lender's proceeds.

.　.　.

PART 2. EFFECTIVENESS OF SECURITY AGREEMENT;
ATTACHMENT OF SECURITY INTEREST; RIGHTS
OF PARTIES TO SECURITY AGREEMENT

[SUBPART 1. EFFECTIVENESS AND ATTACHMENT]

§ 9–201. General Effectiveness of Security Agreement

(a) **[General effectiveness.]** Except as otherwise provided in [the Uniform Commercial Code], a security agreement is effective according to its terms between the parties, against purchasers of the collateral, and against creditors.

(b) **[Applicable consumer laws and other law.]** A transaction subject to this article is subject to any applicable rule of law which establishes a different rule for consumers and [insert reference to (i) any other statute or regulation that regulates the rates, charges, agreements, and practices for loans, credit sales, or other extensions of credit and (ii) any consumer-protection statute or regulation].

(c) **[Other applicable law controls.]** In case of conflict between this article and a rule of law, statute, or regulation described in subsection (b), the rule of law, statute, or regulation controls. Failure to comply with a statute or regulation described in subsection (b) has only the effect the statute or regulation specifies.

(d) **[Further deference to other applicable law.]** This article does not:

(1) validate any rate, charge, agreement, or practice that violates a rule of law, statute, or regulation described in subsection (b); or

(2) extend the application of the rule of law, statute, or regulation to a transaction not otherwise subject to it.

§ 9–203. Attachment and Enforceability of Security Interest; Proceeds; Supporting Obligations; Formal Requisites

(a) **[Attachment.]** A security interest attaches to collateral when it becomes enforceable against the debtor with respect to the collateral, unless an agreement expressly postpones the time of attachment.

(b) **[Enforceability.]** Except as otherwise provided in subsections (c) through (i), a security interest is enforceable against the debtor and third parties with respect to the collateral only if:

(1) value has been given;

(2) the debtor has rights in the collateral or the power to transfer rights in the collateral to a secured party; and

(3) one of the following conditions is met:

(A) the debtor has authenticated a security agreement that provides a description of the collateral   .   .   .   .

.   .   .

997

§ 9–204. After–Acquired Property; Future Advances

(a) **[After-acquired collateral.]** Except as otherwise provided in subsection (b), a security agreement may create or provide for a security interest in after-acquired collateral.

(b) **[When after-acquired property clause not effective.]** A security interest does not attach under a term constituting an after-acquired property clause to:

(1) consumer goods, other than an accession when given as additional security, unless the debtor acquires rights in them within 10 days after the secured party gives value; or

(2) a commercial tort claim.

. . .

[SUBPART 2. RIGHTS AND DUTIES]

§ 9–207. Rights and Duties of Secured Party Having Possession or Control of Collateral

(a) **[Duty of care when secured party in possession.]** Except as otherwise provided in subsection (d), a secured party shall use reasonable care in the custody and preservation of collateral in the secured party's possession. In the case of chattel paper or an instrument, reasonable care includes taking necessary steps to preserve rights against prior parties unless otherwise agreed.

(b) **[Expenses, risks, duties, and rights when secured party in possession.]** Except as otherwise provided in subsection (d), if a secured party has possession of collateral:

(1) reasonable expenses, including the cost of insurance and payment of taxes or other charges, incurred in the custody, preservation, use, or operation of the collateral are chargeable to the debtor and are secured by the collateral;

(2) the risk of accidental loss or damage is on the debtor to the extent of a deficiency in any effective insurance coverage;

(3) the secured party shall keep the collateral identifiable, but fungible collateral may be commingled; and

(4) the secured party may use or operate the collateral:

(A) for the purpose of preserving the collateral or its value;

(B) as permitted by an order of a court having competent jurisdiction; or

(C) except in the case of consumer goods, in the manner and to the extent agreed by the debtor.

. . .

Official Comment

. . .

4. **Applicability Following Default.** This section applies when the secured party has possession of collateral either before or after default. See Sections 9–601(b), 9–609. Subsection (b)(4)(C) limits agreements concerning the use or operation of collateral to collateral other than consumer goods. Under Section 9–602(1), a debtor cannot waive or vary that limitation.

. . .

§ 9–210. Request for Accounting; Request Regarding List of Collateral or Statement of Account

(a) **[Definitions.]** In this section:

(1) "Request" means a record of a type described in paragraph (2), (3), or (4).

(2) "Request for an accounting" means a record authenticated by a debtor requesting that the recipient provide an accounting of the unpaid obligations secured by collateral and reasonably identifying the transaction or relationship that is the subject of the request.

(3) "Request regarding a list of collateral" means a record authenticated by a debtor requesting that the recipient approve or correct a list of what the debtor believes to be the collateral securing an obligation and reasonably identifying the transaction or relationship that is the subject of the request.

(4) "Request regarding a statement of account" means a record authenticated by a debtor requesting that the recipient approve or correct a statement indicating what the debtor believes to be the aggregate amount of unpaid obligations secured by collateral as of a specified date and reasonably identifying the transaction or relationship that is the subject of the request.

(b) **[Duty to respond to requests.]** Subject to subsections (c), (d), (e), and (f), a secured party, other than a buyer of accounts, chattel paper, payment intangibles, or promissory notes or a consignor, shall comply with a request within 14 days after receipt:

(1) in the case of a request for an accounting, by authenticating and sending to the debtor an accounting; and

(2) in the case of a request regarding a list of collateral or a request regarding a statement of account, by authenticating and sending to the debtor an approval or correction.

. . .

(f) **[Charges for responses.]** A debtor is entitled without charge to one response to a request under this section during any six-month period.

The secured party may require payment of a charge not exceeding $25 for each additional response.

PART 3.   PERFECTION AND PRIORITY

[SUBPART 2.   PERFECTION]

§ 9–309.   Security Interest Perfected Upon Attachment.

The following security interests are perfected when they attach:

(1) a purchase-money security interest in consumer goods, except as otherwise provided in Section 9–311(b) with respect to consumer goods that are subject to a statute or treaty described in Section 9–311(a);

. . .

(3) a sale of a payment intangible;

(4) a sale of a promissory note;

. . .

(6) a security interest arising under Section 2–401, 2–505, 2–711(3), or 2A–508(5), until the debtor obtains possession of the collateral;

. . .

Official Comment

. . .

3. **Purchase-Money Security Interest in Consumer Goods.** Former Section 9–302(1)(d) has been revised and appears here as paragraph (1). No filing or other step is required to perfect a purchase-money security interest in consumer goods, other than goods, such as automobiles, that are subject to a statute or treaty described in Section 9–311(a). However, filing is required to perfect a non-purchase-money security interest in consumer goods and is necessary to prevent a buyer of consumer goods from taking free of a security interest under Section 9–320(b). A fixture filing is required for priority over conflicting interests in fixtures to the extent provided in Section 9–334.

. . .

§ 9–310.   When Filing Required to Perfect Security Interest or Agricultural Lien; Security Interests and Agricultural Liens to Which Filing Provisions Do Not Apply

(a) **[General rule: perfection by filing.]** Except as otherwise provided in subsection (b) and Section 9–312(b), a financing statement must be filed to perfect all security interests and agricultural liens.

(b) **[Exceptions: filing not necessary.]** The filing of a financing statement is not necessary to perfect a security interest:

. . .

(2) that is perfected under Section 9–309 when it attaches;

. . .

(6) in collateral in the secured party's possession under Section 9–313;

.   .   .

§ 9–313. When Possession By or Delivery to Secured Party Perfects Security Interest Without Filing

(a) **[Perfection by possession or delivery.]** Except as otherwise provided in subsection (b), a secured party may perfect a security interest in negotiable documents, goods, instruments, money, or tangible chattel paper by taking possession of the collateral. .   .   .

.   .   .

(d) **[Time of perfection by possession; continuation of perfection.]** If perfection of a security interest depends upon possession of the collateral by a secured party, perfection occurs no earlier than the time the secured party takes possession and continues only while the secured party retains possession.

.   .   .

[SUBPART 3.   PRIORITY]

§ 9–320. Buyer of Goods

(a) **[Buyer in ordinary course of business.]** Except as otherwise provided in subsection (e), a buyer in ordinary course of business, other than a person buying farm products from a person engaged in farming operations, takes free of a security interest created by the buyer's seller, even if the security interest is perfected and the buyer knows of its existence.

(b) **[Buyer of consumer goods.]** Except as otherwise provided in subsection (e), a buyer of goods from a person who used or bought the goods for use primarily for personal, family, or household purposes takes free of a security interest, even if perfected, if the buyer buys:

(1) without knowledge of the security interest;

(2) for value;

(3) primarily for the buyer's personal, family, or household purposes; and

(4) before the filing of a financing statement covering the goods.

.   .   .

Official Comment

.   .   .

5. **Buyers of Consumer Goods.** Subsection (b), which derives from former Section 9–307(2), deals with buyers of collateral that the debtor-seller holds as "consumer goods" (defined in Section 9–102). Under Section 9–309(1), a pur-

chase-money interest in consumer goods, except goods that are subject to a statute or treaty described in Section 9–311(a) (such as automobiles that are subject to a certificate-of-title statute), is perfected automatically upon attachment. There is no need to file to perfect. Under subsection (b) a buyer of consumer goods takes free of a security interest, even though perfected, if the buyer buys (1) without knowledge of the security interest, (2) for value, (3) primarily for the buyer's own personal, family, or household purposes, and (4) before a financing statement is filed.

As to purchase money-security interests which are perfected without filing under Section 9–309(1): A secured party may file a financing statement, although filing is not required for perfection. If the secured party does file, all buyers take subject to the security interest. If the secured party does not file, a buyer who meets the qualifications stated in the preceding paragraph takes free of the security interest.

. . .

§ 9–321.　Licensee of General Intangible and Lessee of Goods in Ordinary Course of Business

. . .

(c) [**Rights of lessee in ordinary course of business.**] A lessee in ordinary course of business takes its leasehold interest free of a security interest in the goods created by the lessor, even if the security interest is perfected and the lessee knows of its existence.

PART 4.　RIGHTS OF THIRD PARTIES

§ 9–403.　Agreement Not to Assert Defenses Against Assignee

(a) [**"Value."**] In this section, "value" has the meaning provided in Section 3–303(a).

(b) [**Agreement not to assert claim or defense.**] Except as otherwise provided in this section, an agreement between an account debtor and an assignor not to assert against an assignee any claim or defense that the account debtor may have against the assignor is enforceable by an assignee that takes an assignment:

(1) for value;

(2) in good faith;

(3) without notice of a claim of a property or possessory right to the property assigned; and

(4) without notice of a defense or claim in recoupment of the type that may be asserted against a person entitled to enforce a negotiable instrument under Section 3–305(a).

(c) [**When subsection (b) not applicable.**] Subsection (b) does not apply to defenses of a type that may be asserted against a holder in due course of a negotiable instrument under Section 3–305(b).

(d) [**Omission of required statement in consumer transaction.**] In a consumer transaction, if a record evidences the account debtor's obligation, law other than this article requires that the record include a statement to the effect that the rights of an assignee are subject to claims or defenses that the account debtor could assert against the original obligee, and the record does not include such a statement:

(1) the record has the same effect as if the record included such a statement; and

(2) the account debtor may assert against an assignee those claims and defenses that would have been available if the record included such a statement.

(e) **[Rule for individual under other law.]** This section is subject to law other than this article which establishes a different rule for an account debtor who is an individual and who incurred the obligation primarily for personal, family, or household purposes.

(f) **[Other law not displaced.]** Except as otherwise provided in subsection (d), this section does not displace law other than this article which gives effect to an agreement by an account debtor not to assert a claim or defense against an assignee.

Official Comment

. . .

2. **Scope and Purpose.** Subsection (b) . . . generally validates an agreement between an account debtor and an assignor that the account debtor will not assert against an assignee claims and defenses that it may have against the assignor. These agreements are typical in installment sale agreements and leases. . . . This section applies only to the obligations of an "account debtor," as defined in Section 9–102. Thus, it does not determine the circumstances under which and the extent to which a person who is obligated on a negotiable instrument is disabled from asserting claims and defenses. Rather, Article 3 must be consulted. See, e.g., Sections 3–305, 3–306. Article 3 governs even when the negotiable instrument constitutes part of chattel paper. See Section 9–102 (an obligor on a negotiable instrument constituting part of chattel paper is not an "account debtor").

3. **Conditions of Validation; Relationship to Article 3.** Subsection (b) validates an account debtor's agreement only if the assignee takes an assignment for value, in good faith, and without notice of conflicting claims to the property assigned or of certain claims or defenses of the account debtor . . . . [T]his section is designed to put the assignee in a position that is no better and no worse than that of a holder in due course of a negotiable instrument under Article 3. . . .

5. **Relationship to Federal Trade Commission Rule.** Subsection (d) is new. It applies to rights evidenced by a record that is required to contain, but does not contain, the notice set forth in Federal Trade Commission Rule 433, 16 C.F.R. Part 433 (the "Holder-in-Due–Course Regulations"). Under this subsection, an assignee of such a record takes subject to the consumer account debtor's claims and defenses to the same extent as it would have if the writing had contained the required notice. Thus, subsection (d) effectively renders waiver-of-defense clauses ineffective in the transactions with consumers to which it applies.

6. **Relationship to Other Law.** Like former Section 9–206(1), this section takes no position on the enforceability of waivers of claims and defenses by consumer account debtors, leaving that question to other law. However, the reference to "law other than this article" in subsection (e) encompasses ad-

ministrative rules and regulations; the
reference in former Section 9–206(1)
that it replaces ("statute or decision")
arguably did not.

. . .

§ 9–404. Rights Acquired By Assignee; Claims and Defenses Against Assignee

(a) **[Assignee's rights subject to terms, claims, and defenses; exceptions.]** Unless an account debtor has made an enforceable agreement not to assert defenses or claims, and subject to subsections (b) through (e), the rights of an assignee are subject to:

(1) all terms of the agreement between the account debtor and assignor and any defense or claim in recoupment arising from the transaction that gave rise to the contract; and

(2) any other defense or claim of the account debtor against the assignor which accrues before the account debtor receives a notification of the assignment authenticated by the assignor or the assignee.

(b) **[Account debtor's claim reduces amount owed to assignee.]** Subject to subsection (c) and except as otherwise provided in subsection (d), the claim of an account debtor against an assignor may be asserted against an assignee under subsection (a) only to reduce the amount the account debtor owes.

(c) **[Rule for individual under other law.]** This section is subject to law other than this article which establishes a different rule for an account debtor who is an individual and who incurred the obligation primarily for personal, family, or household purposes.

(d) **[Omission of required statement in consumer transaction.]** In a consumer transaction, if a record evidences the account debtor's obligation, law other than this article requires that the record include a statement to the effect that the account debtor's recovery against an assignee with respect to claims and defenses against the assignor may not exceed amounts paid by the account debtor under the record, and the record does not include such a statement, the extent to which a claim of an account debtor against the assignor may be asserted against an assignee is determined as if the record included such a statement.

(e) **[Inapplicability to health-care-insurance receivable.]** This section does not apply to an assignment of a health-care-insurance receivable.

Official Comment

. . .

3. **Limitation on Affirmative Claims.** Subsection (b) is new [and] ... generally does not afford the account debtor the right to an affirmative recovery from an assignee.

4. **Consumer Account Debtors; Relationship to Federal Trade Commission Rule.** Subsections (c) and (d) also are new. Subsection (c) makes clear that the rules of this section are subject to other law establishing special rules for consumer account debtors. An "ac-

count debtor who is an individual" as used in subsection (c) includes individuals who are jointly or jointly and severally obligated. Subsection (d) applies to rights evidenced by a record that is required to contain, but does not contain, the notice set forth in Federal Trade Commission Rule 433, 16 C.F.R. Part 433 (the "Holder-in-Due–Course Regulations"). Under subsection (d), a consumer account debtor has the same right to an affirmative recovery from an assignee of such a record as the consumer would have had against the assignee had the record contained the required notice.

.   .   .

PART 6.   DEFAULT

[SUBPART 1.   DEFAULT AND ENFORCEMENT OF SECURITY INTEREST]

§ 9–601.   Rights After Default; Judicial Enforcement; Consignor or Buyer of Accounts, Chattel Paper, Payment Intangibles, or Promissory Notes

(a) **[Rights of secured party after default.]** After default, a secured party has the rights provided in this part and, except as otherwise provided In Section 9–602, those provided by agreement of the parties. A secured party:

(1) may reduce a claim to judgment, foreclose, or otherwise enforce the claim, security interest, or agricultural lien by any available judicial procedure; and

(2) if the collateral is documents, may proceed either as to the documents or as to the goods they cover.

(b) **[Rights and duties of secured party in possession or control.]** A secured party in possession of collateral or control of collateral under Section 9–104, 9–105, 9–106, or 9–107 has the rights and duties provided in Section 9–207.

(c) **[Rights cumulative; simultaneous exercise.]** The rights under subsections (a) and (b) are cumulative and may be exercised simultaneously.

(d) **[Rights of debtor and obligor.]** Except as otherwise provided in subsection (g) and Section 9–605, after default, a debtor and an obligor have the rights provided in this part and by agreement of the parties.

(e) **[Lien of levy after judgment.]** If a secured party has reduced its claim to judgment, the lien of any levy that may be made upon the collateral by virtue of an execution based upon the judgment relates back to the earliest of:

(1) the date of perfection of the security interest or agricultural lien in the collateral;

(2) the date of filing a financing statement covering the collateral; or

(3) any date specified in a statute under which the agricultural lien was created.

(f) **[Execution sale.]** A sale pursuant to an execution is a foreclosure of the security interest or agricultural lien by judicial procedure within the meaning of this section. A secured party may purchase at the sale and thereafter hold the collateral free of any other requirements of this article.

(g) **[Consignor or buyer of certain rights to payment.]** Except as otherwise provided in Section 9–607(c), this part imposes no duties upon a secured party that is a consignor or is a buyer of accounts, chattel paper, payment intangibles, or promissory notes.

Official Comment

1. **Source.** Former Section 9–501(1), (2), (5).

2. **Enforcement: In General.** The rights of a secured party to enforce its security interest in collateral after the debtor's default are an important feature of a secured transaction. (Note that the term "rights," as defined in Section 1–201, includes "remedies.") This Part provides those rights as well as certain limitations on their exercise for the protection of the defaulting debtor, other creditors, and other affected persons. However, subsections (a) and (d) make clear that the rights provided in this Part do not exclude other rights provided by agreement.

3. **When Remedies Arise.** Under subsection (a) the secured party's rights arise "[a]fter default." . . . [T]his Article leaves to the agreement of the parties the circumstances giving rise to a default. This Article does not determine whether a secured party's post-default conduct can constitute a waiver of default in the face of an agreement stating that such conduct shall not constitute a waiver. Rather, it continues to leave to the parties' agreement, as supplemented by law other than this Article, the determination whether a default has occurred or has been waived. See Section 1–103.

. . .

5. **Cumulative Remedies.** Former Section 9–501(1) provided that the secured party's remedies were cumulative, but it did not explicitly provide whether the remedies could be exercised simultaneously. Subsection (c) permits the simultaneous exercise of remedies if the secured party acts in good faith. The liability scheme of Subpart 2 affords redress to an aggrieved debtor or obligor. Moreover, permitting the simultaneous exercise of remedies under subsection (c) does not override any non-UCC law, including the law of tort and statutes regulating collection of debts, under which the simultaneous exercise of remedies in a particular case constitutes abusive behavior or harassment giving rise to liability.

. . .

§ 9–602. Waiver and Variance of Rights and Duties.

Except as otherwise provided in Section 9–624, to the extent that they give rights to a debtor or obligor and impose duties on a secured party, the debtor or obligor may not waive or vary the rules stated in the following listed sections:

(1) Section 9–207(b)(4)(C), which deals with use and operation of the collateral by the secured party;

(2) Section 9–210, which deals with requests for an accounting and requests concerning a list of collateral and statement of account;

(3) Section 9–607(c), which deals with collection and enforcement of collateral;

(4) Sections 9–608(a) and 9–615(c) to the extent that they deal with application or payment of noncash proceeds of collection, enforcement, or disposition;

(5) Sections 9–608(a) and 9–615(d) to the extent that they require accounting for or payment of surplus proceeds of collateral;

(6) Section 9–609 to the extent that it imposes upon a secured party that takes possession of collateral without judicial process the duty to do so without breach of the peace;

(7) Sections 9–610(b), 9–611, 9–613, and 9–614, which deal with disposition of collateral;

(8) Section 9–615(f), which deals with calculation of a deficiency or surplus when a disposition is made to the secured party, a person related to the secured party, or a secondary obligor;

(9) Section 9–616, which deals with explanation of the calculation of a surplus or deficiency;

(10) Sections 9–620, 9–621, and 9–622, which deal with acceptance of collateral in satisfaction of obligation;

(11) Section 9–623, which deals with redemption of collateral;

(12) Section 9–624, which deals with permissible waivers; and

(13) Sections 9–625 and 9–626, which deal with the secured party's liability for failure to comply with this article.

Official Comment

1. **Source.** Former Section 9–501(3).

2. **Waiver: In General.** Section 1–102(3) addresses which provisions of the UCC are mandatory and which may be varied by agreement. With exceptions relating to good faith, diligence, reasonableness, and care, immediate parties, as between themselves, may vary its provisions by agreement. However, in the context of rights and duties after default, our legal system traditionally has looked with suspicion on agreements that limit the debtor's rights and free the secured party of its duties.... The context of default offers great opportunity for overreaching. The suspicious attitudes of the courts have been grounded in common sense. This section

... codifies this long-standing and deeply rooted attitude. The specified rights of the debtor and duties of the secured party may not be waived or varied except as stated. Provisions that are not specified in this section are subject to the general rules in Section 1–102(3)

3. **Nonwaivable Rights and Duties.** . . .

This section provides generally that the specified rights and duties "may not be waived or varied." However, it does not restrict the ability of parties to agree to settle, compromise, or renounce claims for past conduct that may have constituted a violation or breach of those rights and duties, even if the settlement involves an express "waiver."

. . .

§ 9–603.　Agreement on Standards Concerning Rights and Duties.

(a) **[Agreed standards.]** The parties may determine by agreement the standards measuring the fulfillment of the rights of a debtor or obligor and the duties of a secured party under a rule stated in Section 9–602 if the standards are not manifestly unreasonable.

(b) **[Agreed standards inapplicable to breach of peace.]** Subsection (a) does not apply to the duty under Section 9–609 to refrain from breaching the peace.

§ 9–609.　Secured Party's Right to Take Possession After Default.

(a) **[Possession; rendering equipment unusable; disposition on debtor's premises.]** After default, a secured party:

(1) may take possession of the collateral; and

(2) without removal, may render equipment unusable and dispose of collateral on a debtor's premises under Section 9–610.

(b) **[Judicial and nonjudicial process.]** A secured party may proceed under subsection (a)

(1) pursuant to judicial process; or

(2) without judicial process, if it proceeds without breach of the peace.

(c) **[Assembly of collateral.]** If so agreed, and in any event after default, a secured party may require the debtor to assemble the collateral and make it available to the secured party at a place to be designated by the secured party which is reasonably convenient to both parties.

Official Comment

3. **Judicial Process; Breach of Peace.** Subsection (b) permits a secured party to proceed under this section without judicial process if it does so "without breach of the peace." ... [T]his section does not define or explain the conduct that will constitute a breach of the peace, leaving that matter for continuing development by the courts. In considering whether a secured party has engaged in a breach of the peace, however, courts should hold the secured party responsible for the actions of others taken on the secured party's behalf, including independent contractors engaged by the secured party to take possession of collateral.

This section does not authorize a secured party who repossesses without judicial process to utilize the assistance of a law-enforcement officer. A number of cases have held that a repossessing secured party's use of a law-enforcement officer without benefit of judicial process constituted a failure to comply with former Section 9–503.

4. **Damages for Breach of Peace.** Concerning damages that may be recovered based on a secured party's breach of the peace in connection with taking possession of collateral, see Section 9–625, Comment 3.

. . .

§ 9–610.　Disposition of Collateral After Default

(a) **[Disposition after default.]** After default, a secured party may sell, lease, license, or otherwise dispose of any or all of the collateral in its present condition or following any commercially reasonable preparation or processing.

(b) **[Commercially reasonable disposition.]** Every aspect of a disposition of collateral, including the method, manner, time, place, and other terms, must be commercially reasonable. If commercially reasonable, a secured party may dispose of collateral by public or private proceedings, by one or more contracts, as a unit or in parcels, and at any time and place and on any terms.

(c) **[Purchase by secured party.]** A secured party may purchase collateral:

(1) at a public disposition; or

(2) at a private disposition only if the collateral is of a kind that is customarily sold on a recognized market or the subject of widely distributed standard price quotations.

(d) **[Warranties on disposition.]** A contract for sale, lease, license, or other disposition includes the warranties relating to title, possession, quiet enjoyment, and the like which by operation of law accompany a voluntary disposition of property of the kind subject to the contract.

(e) **[Disclaimer of warranties.]** A secured party may disclaim or modify warranties under subsection (d):

(1) in a manner that would be effective to disclaim or modify the warranties in a voluntary disposition of property of the kind subject to the contract of disposition; or

(2) by communicating to the purchaser a record evidencing the contract for disposition and including an express disclaimer or modification of the warranties.

(f) **[Record sufficient to disclaim warranties.]** A record is sufficient to disclaim warranties under subsection (e) if it indicates "There is no warranty relating to title, possession, quiet enjoyment, or the like in this disposition" or uses words of similar import.

Official Comment

1. **Source.** Former Section 9–504(1), (3).

2. **Commercially Reasonable Dispositions.** . . . Although subsection (b) permits both public and private dispositions, "every aspect of a disposition . . . must be commercially reasonable." This section encourages private dispositions on the assumption that they frequently will result in higher realization on collateral for the benefit of all concerned. Subsection (a) does not restrict dispositions to sales; collateral may be sold, leased, licensed, or otherwise disposed. Section 9–627 provides guidance for determining the circumstances under which a disposition is "commercially reasonable."

3. **Time of Disposition.** This Article does not specify a period within which a secured party must dispose of collateral. This is consistent with this Article's policy to encourage private dispositions through regular commercial channels. It may, for example, be prudent not to dispose of goods when the market has collapsed. Or, it might be

more appropriate to sell a large inventory in parcels over a period of time instead of in bulk. Of course, under subsection (b) every aspect of a disposition of collateral must be commercially reasonable. This requirement explicitly includes the "method, manner, time, place and other terms." For example, if a secured party does not proceed under Section 9–620 and holds collateral for a long period of time without disposing of it, and if there is no good reason for not making a prompt disposition, the secured party may be determined not to have acted in a "commercially reasonable" manner. See also Section 1–203 (general obligation of good faith).

4. Pre-Disposition Preparation and Processing. Former Section 9–504(1) appeared to give the secured party the choice of disposing of collateral either "in its then condition or following any commercially reasonable preparation or processing." Some courts held that the "commercially reasonable" standard of former Section 9–504(3) nevertheless could impose an affirmative duty on the secured party to process or prepare the collateral prior to disposition. Subsection (a) retains the substance of the quoted language. Although courts should not be quick to impose a duty of preparation or processing on the secured party, subsection (a) does not grant the secured party the right to dispose of the collateral "in its then condition" under *all* circumstances. A secured party may not dispose of collateral "in its then condition" when, taking into account the costs and probable benefits of preparation or processing and the fact that the secured party would be advancing the costs at its risk, it would be commercially unreasonable to dispose of the collateral in that condition.

7. Public vs. Private Dispositions. This Part maintains two distinctions between "public" and other dispositions: (i) the secured party may buy at the former, but normally not at the latter

(Section 9–610(c)), and (ii) the debtor is entitled to notification of "the time and place of a public disposition" and notification of "the time after which" a private disposition or other intended disposition is to be made (Section 9–613(1)(E)). . . . Although the term is not defined, as used in this Article, a "public disposition" is one at which the price is determined after the public has had a meaningful opportunity for competitive bidding. "Meaningful opportunity" is meant to imply that some form of advertisement or public notice must precede the sale (or other disposition) and that the public must have access to the sale (disposition)

. . .

9. "Recognized Market." A "recognized market," as used in subsection (c) and Section 9–611(d), is one in which the items sold are fungible and prices are not subject to individual negotiation. For example, the New York Stock Exchange is a recognized market. A market in which prices are individually negotiated or the items are not fungible is not a recognized market, even if the items are the subject of widely disseminated price guides or are disposed of through dealer auctions.

10. Relevance of Price. While not itself sufficient to establish a violation of this Part, a low price suggests that a court should scrutinize carefully all aspects of a disposition to ensure that each aspect was commercially reasonable. Note also that even if the disposition is commercially reasonable, Section 9–615(f) provides a special method for calculating a deficiency or surplus if (i) the transferee in the disposition is the secured party, a person related to the secured party, or a secondary obligor, and (ii) the amount of proceeds of the disposition is significantly below the range of proceeds that a complying disposition to a person other than the secured party, a person related to the secured party, or a secondary obligor would have brought.

§ 9–611. Notification Before Disposition of Collateral

(a) **["Notification date."]** In this section, "notification date" means the earlier of the date on which:

(1) a secured party sends to the debtor and any secondary obligor an authenticated notification of disposition; or

(2) the debtor and any secondary obligor waive the right to notification.

(b) **[Notification of disposition required.]** Except as otherwise provided in subsection (d), a secured party that disposes of collateral under Section 9–610 shall send to the persons specified in subsection (c) a reasonable authenticated notification of disposition.

(c) **[Persons to be notified.]** To comply with subsection (b), the secured party shall send an authenticated notification of disposition to:

(1) the debtor;

(2) any secondary obligor; and

(3) if the collateral is other than consumer goods:

(A) any other person from which the secured party has received, before the notification date, an authenticated notification of a claim of an interest in the collateral;

(B) any other secured party or lienholder that, 10 days before the notification date, held a security interest in or other lien on the collateral perfected by the filing of a financing statement that:

(i) identified the collateral;

(ii) was indexed under the debtor's name as of that date; and

(iii) was filed in the office in which to file a financing statement against the debtor covering the collateral as of that date; and

(C) any other secured party that, 10 days before the notification date, held a security interest in the collateral perfected by compliance with a statute, regulation, or treaty described in Section 9–311(a).

(d) **[Subsection (b) inapplicable: perishable collateral; recognized market.]** Subsection (b) does not apply if the collateral is perishable or threatens to decline speedily in value or is of a type customarily sold on a recognized market.

(e) **[Compliance with subsection (c)(3)(B).]** A secured party complies with the requirement for notification prescribed by subsection (c)(3)(B) if:

(1) not later than 20 days or earlier than 30 days before the notification date, the secured party requests, in a commercially reasonable manner, information concerning financing statements indexed under the debtor's name in the office indicated in subsection (c)(3)(B); and

(2) before the notification date, the secured party:

(A) did not receive a response to the request for information; or

(B) received a response to the request for information and sent an authenticated notification of disposition to each secured party or other lienholder named in that response whose financing statement covered the collateral.

Official Comment

. . .

3. **Notification to Debtors and Secondary Obligors.** This section imposes a duty to send notification of a disposition not only to the debtor but also to any secondary obligor. Subsections (b) and (c) resolve an uncertainty under former Article 9 by providing that secondary obligors (sureties) are entitled to receive notification of an intended disposition of collateral regardless of who created the security interest in the collateral. If the surety created the security interest, it would be the debtor. If it did not, it would be a secondary obligor. (This Article also resolves the question of the secondary obliger's ability to waive, pre-default, the right to notification—waiver generally is not permitted. See Section 9–602.) Section 9–605 relieves a secured party from any duty to send notification to a debtor or secondary obligor unknown to the secured party.

Under subsection (b), the principal obligor (borrower) is not always entitled to notification of disposition.

Example: Behnfeldt borrows on an unsecured basis, and Bruno grants a security interest in her car to secure the debt. Behnfeldt is a primary obligor, not a secondary obligor. As such, she is not entitled to

notification of disposition under this section.

. . .

6. **Second Try.** This Article leaves to judicial resolution, based upon the facts of each case, the question whether the requirement of "reasonable notification" requires a "second try," i.e., whether a secured party who sends notification and learns that the debtor did not receive it must attempt to locate the debtor and send another notification.

. . .

8. **Failure to Conduct Notified Disposition.** Nothing in this Article prevents a secured party from electing not to conduct a disposition after sending a notification. Nor does this Article prevent a secured party from electing to send a revised notification if its plans for disposition change. This assumes, however, that the secured party acts in good faith, the revised notification is reasonable, and the revised plan for disposition and any attendant delay are commercially reasonable.

9. **Waiver.** A debtor or secondary obligor may waive the right to notification under this section only by a post-default authenticated agreement. See Section 9–624(a).

§ 9–612. Timeliness of Notification Before Disposition of Collateral

(a) **[Reasonable time is question of fact.]** Except as otherwise provided in subsection (b), whether a notification is sent within a reasonable time is a question of fact.

(b) **[10–day period sufficient in non-consumer transaction.]** In a transaction other than a consumer transaction, a notification of disposition sent after default and 10 days or more before the earliest time of disposition set forth in the notification is sent within a reasonable time before the disposition.

Official Comment

. . .

2. **Reasonable Notification.** ... A notification that is sent so near to the disposition date that a notified person could not be expected to act on or take account of the notification would be unreasonable.

3. **Timeliness of Notification: Safe Harbor.** The 10–day notice period in subsection (b) is intended to be a "safe harbor" and not a minimum requirement. To qualify for the "safe harbor" the notification must be sent after default. A notification also must be sent in a commercially reasonable manner. See Section 9–611(b) ("reasonable authenticated notification"). These requirements prevent a secured party from taking advantage of the "safe harbor" by, for example, giving the debtor a notification at the time of the original extension of credit or sending the notice by surface mail to a debtor overseas.

§ 9–613. Contents and Form of Notification Before Disposition of Collateral: General.

Except in a consumer-goods transaction, the following rules apply:

(1) The contents of a notification of disposition are sufficient if the notification:

(A) describes the debtor and the secured party;

(B) describes the collateral that is the subject of the intended disposition;

(C) states the method of intended disposition;

(D) states that the debtor is entitled to an accounting of the unpaid indebtedness and states the charge, if any, for an accounting; and

(E) states the time and place of a public disposition or the time after which any other disposition is to be made.

(2) Whether the contents of a notification that lacks any of the information specified in paragraph (1) are nevertheless sufficient is a question of fact.

(3) The contents of a notification providing substantially the information specified in paragraph (1) are sufficient, even if the notification includes:

(A) information not specified by that paragraph; or

(B) minor errors that are not seriously misleading.

(4) A particular phrasing of the notification is not required.

(5) The following form of notification and the form appearing in Section 9–614(3), when completed, each provides sufficient information:

NOTIFICATION OF DISPOSITION OF COLLATERAL

To: _____ [*Name of debtor, obligor, or other person to which the notification is sent*]

From: _____ [*Name, address, and telephone number of secured party*]

Name of Debtor(s): _____ [*Include only if debtor(s) are not an addressee*]

[*For a public disposition:*]

We will sell [or lease or license, *as applicable*] the _____ [*describe collateral*] _____ [to the highest qualified bidder] in public as follows:

Day and Date: _____

Time: _____

Place: _____

[*For a private disposition:*]

We will sell [or lease or license, *as applicable*] the _____ [*describe collateral*] _____ privately sometime after _____ [*day and date*] _____.

You are entitled to an accounting of the unpaid indebtedness secured by the property that we intend to sell [or lease or license, *as applicable*] [for a charge of $___]. You may request an accounting by calling us at _____ [*telephone number*] _____.

[End of Form]

§ 9–614. Contents and Form of Notification Before Disposition of Collateral: Consumer–Goods Transaction.

In a consumer-goods transaction, the following rules apply:

(1) A notification of disposition must provide the following information:

(A) the information specified in Section 9–613(a)(1)

(B) a description of any liability for a deficiency of the person to which the notification is sent;

(C) a telephone number from which the amount that must be paid to the secured party to redeem the collateral under Section 9–623 is available; and

(D) a telephone number or mailing address from which additional information concerning the disposition and the obligation secured is available.

(2) A particular phrasing of the notification is not required.

(3) The following form of notification, when completed, provides sufficient information:

_____ [*Name and address of secured party*]

_____ [*Date*]

NOTICE OF OUR PLAN TO SELL PROPERTY

_____ [*Name and address of any obligor who is also a debtor*]

Subject: _____ [*Identification of Transaction*]

We have your _____ [*describe collateral*] _____, because you broke promises in our agreement.

[*For a public disposition:*]

We will sell _____ [*describe collateral*] _____ at public sale. A sale could include a lease or license. The sale will be held as follows:

Date: _____

Time: _____

Place: _____

You may attend the sale and bring bidders if you want.

[*For a private disposition:*]

We will sell _____ [*describe collateral*] _____ at private sale sometime after [*date*] _____. A sale could include a lease or license.

The money that we get from the sale (after paying our costs) will reduce the amount you owe. If we get less money than you owe, you [*will or will not, as applicable*] _____ still owe us the difference. If we get more money than you owe, you will get the extra money, unless we must pay it to someone else.

You can get the property back at any time before we sell it by paying us the full amount you owe (not just the past due payments), including our expenses. To learn the exact amount you must pay, call us at _____ [*telephone number*] _____.

If you want us to explain to you in writing how we have figured the amount that you owe us, you may call us at _____ [*telephone number*] _____ or write us at _____ [*secured party's address*] _____ and request a written explanation. [We will charge you $__ for the explanation if we sent you another written explanation of the amount you owe us within the last six months.]

If you need more information about the sale call us at _____ [*telephone number*] _____ or write us at _____ [*secured party's address*] _____.

We are sending this notice to the following other people who have an interest in _____ [*describe collateral*] _____ or who owe money under your agreement:

_____ [*Names of all other debtors and obligors, if any*]

[End of Form]

(4) A notification in the form of paragraph (3) is sufficient, even if additional information appears at the end of the form.

(5) A notification in the form of paragraph (3) is sufficient, even if it includes errors in information not required by paragraph (1), unless the error is misleading with respect to rights arising under this article.

(6) If a notification under this section is not in the form of paragraph (3), law other than this article determines the effect of including information not required by paragraph (1)

Official Comment

. . .

2. **Notification in Consumer-Goods Transactions.** Paragraph (1) sets forth the information required for a reasonable notification in a consumer-goods transaction. A notification that lacks any of the information set forth in paragraph (1) is insufficient as a matter of law. Compare Section 9–613(2), under which the trier of fact may find a notification to be sufficient even if it lacks some information listed in paragraph (1) of that section.

3. **Safe-Harbor Form of Notification; Errors in Information.** Although paragraph (2) provides that a particular phrasing of a notification is not required, paragraph (3) specifies a safe-harbor form that, when properly completed, satisfies paragraph (1). Paragraphs (4), (5), and (6) contain special rules applicable to erroneous and additional information. Under paragraph (4), a notification in the safe-harbor form specified in paragraph (3) is not rendered insufficient if it contains additional information at the end of the form. Paragraph (5) provides that non-misleading errors in information contained in a notification are permitted if the safe-harbor form is used *and if the errors are in information not required by paragraph (1)*. Finally, if a notification is in a form other than the paragraph (3) safe-harbor form, other law determines the effect of including in the notification information other than that required by paragraph (1).

§ 9–615. Application of Proceeds of Disposition; Liability for Deficiency and Right to Surplus

(a) **[Application of proceeds.]** A secured party shall apply or pay over for application the cash proceeds of disposition under Section 9–610 in the following order to:

(1) the reasonable expenses of retaking, holding, preparing for disposition, processing, and disposing, and, to the extent provided for by agreement and not prohibited by law, reasonable attorney's fees and legal expenses incurred by the secured party;

(2) the satisfaction of obligations secured by the security interest or agricultural lien under which the disposition is made;

(3) the satisfaction of obligations secured by any subordinate security interest in or other subordinate lien on the collateral if:

(A) the secured party receives from the holder of the subordinate security interest or other lien an authenticated demand for proceeds before distribution of the proceeds is completed; and

(B) in a case in which a consignor has an interest in the collateral, the subordinate security interest or other lien is senior to the interest of the consignor; and

(4) a secured party that is a consignor of the collateral if the secured party receives from the consignor an authenticated demand for proceeds before distribution of the proceeds is completed.

(b) **[Proof of subordinate interest.]** If requested by a secured party, a holder of a subordinate security interest or other lien shall furnish reasonable proof of the interest or lien within a reasonable time. Unless the holder does so, the secured party need not comply with the holder's demand under subsection (a)(3).

(c) **[Application of noncash proceeds.]** A secured party need not apply or pay over for application noncash proceeds of disposition under Section 9–610 unless the failure to do so would be commercially unreasonable. A secured party that applies or pays over for application noncash proceeds shall do so in a commercially reasonable manner.

(d) **[Surplus or deficiency if obligation secured.]** If the security interest under which a disposition is made secures payment or performance of an obligation, after making the payments and applications required by subsection (a) and permitted by subsection (c):

(1) unless subsection (a)(4) requires the secured party to apply or pay over cash proceeds to a consignor, the secured party shall account to and pay a debtor for any surplus; and

(2) the obligor is liable for any deficiency.

(e) **[No surplus or deficiency in sales of certain rights to payment.]** If the underlying transaction is a sale of accounts, chattel paper, payment intangibles, or promissory notes:

(1) the debtor is not entitled to any surplus; and

(2) the obligor is not liable for any deficiency.

(f) **[Calculation of surplus or deficiency in disposition to person related to secured party.]** The surplus or deficiency following a disposition is calculated based on the amount of proceeds that would have been realized in a disposition complying with this part to a transferee other than the secured party, a person related to the secured party, or a secondary obligor if:

(1) the transferee in the disposition is the secured party, a person related to the secured party, or a secondary obligor; and

(2) the amount of proceeds of the disposition is significantly below the range of proceeds that a complying disposition to a person other than the secured party, a person related to the secured party, or a secondary obligor would have brought.

(g) **[Cash proceeds received by junior secured party.]** A secured party that receives cash proceeds of a disposition in good faith and without knowledge that the receipt violates the rights of the holder of a security interest or other lien that is not subordinate to the security interest or agricultural lien under which the disposition is made:

(1) takes the cash proceeds free of the security interest or other lien;

(2) is not obligated to apply the proceeds of the of the disposition to the satisfaction of obligations secured by the security interest or other lien; and

(3) is not obligated to account to or pay the holder of the security interest or other lien for any surplus.

Official Comment

3. **Noncash Proceeds.** Subsection (c) addresses the application of noncash proceeds of a disposition, such as a note or lease. . . .

Example: A secured party in the business of selling or financing automobiles takes possession of collateral (an automobile) following its debtor's default. The secured party decided to sell the automobile in a private disposition under Section 9–610 and sends appropriate notification under Section 9–611. After undertaking its normal credit investigation and in accordance with its normal credit policies, the secured party sells the automobile on credit, on terms typical of the credit terms normally extended by the secured party in the ordinary course of its business. The automobile stands as collateral for the remaining balance of the price. The noncash proceeds received by the secured party are chattel paper. The secured party may wish to credit its debtor (the assignor) with the principal amount of the chattel paper or may wish to credit the debtor only as and when the payments are made on the chattel paper by the buyer.

Under subsection (c), the secured party is under no duty to apply the noncash proceeds (here, the chattel paper) or their value to the secured obligation unless its failure to do so would be commercially unreasonable. If a se-cured party elects to apply the chattel paper to the outstanding obligation, however, it must do so in a commercially reasonable manner. The facts in the example indicate that it would be commercially unreasonable for the secured party to fail to apply the value of the chattel paper to the original debtor's secured obligation. . . . [T]he noncash proceeds received in this example are of the type that the secured party regularly generates in the ordinary course of its financing business in non-foreclosure transactions. The original debtor should not be exposed to delay or uncertainty in this situation. . . .

. . .

6. **Certain "Low–Price" Dispositions.** Subsection (f) provides a special method for calculating a deficiency or surplus when the secured party, a person related to the secured party (defined in Section 9–102), or a secondary obligor acquires the collateral at a foreclosure disposition. It recognizes that when the foreclosing secured party or a related party is the transferee of the collateral, the secured party sometimes lacks the incentive to maximize the proceeds of disposition. As a consequence, the disposition may comply with the procedural requirements of this Article (e.g., it is conducted in a commercially reasonable manner following reasonable notice) but nevertheless fetch a low price.

Subsection (f) adjusts for this lack of incentive. If the proceeds of a disposition of collateral to a secured party, a person related to the secured party, or a secondary obligor are "significantly below the range of proceeds that a complying disposition to a person other than the secured party, a person related to the secured party, or a secondary obligor would have brought," then instead of calculating a deficiency (or surplus) based on the actual net proceeds, the calculation is based upon the amount that would have been received in a commercially reasonable disposition to a person other than the secured party, a person related to the secured party, or a secondary obligor. Subsection (f) thus rejects the view that the secured party's receipt of such a price necessarily constitutes noncompliance with Part 6. However, such a price may suggest the need for greater judicial scrutiny. See Section 9–610, Comment 10.

7. **"Person Related To."** Section 9–102 defines "person related to." That term is a key element of the system provided in subsection (f) for low-price dispositions. One part of the definition applies when the secured party is an individual, and the other applies when the secured party is an organization. The definition is patterned closely on the corresponding definition in Section 1.301(32) of the Uniform Consumer Credit Code.

§ 9–616. Explanation of Calculation of Surplus or Deficiency

(a) **[Definitions.]** In this section:

(1) "Explanation" means a writing that:

(A) states the amount of the surplus or deficiency;

(B) provides an explanation in accordance with subsection (c) of how the secured party calculated the surplus or deficiency;

(C) states, if applicable, that future debits, credits, charges, including additional credit service charges or interest, rebates, and expenses may affect the amount of the surplus or deficiency; and

(D) provides a telephone number or mailing address from which additional information concerning the transaction is available.

(2) "Request" means a record:

(A) authenticated by a debtor or consumer obligor;

(B) requesting that the recipient provide an explanation; and

(C) sent after disposition of the collateral under Section 9–610.

(b) **[Explanation of calculation.]** In a consumer-goods transaction in which the debtor is entitled to a surplus or a consumer obligor is liable for a deficiency under Section 9–615, the secured party shall:

(1) send an explanation to the debtor or consumer obligor, as applicable, after the disposition and:

(A) before or when the secured party accounts to the debtor and pays any surplus or first makes written demand on the consumer obligor after the disposition for payment of the deficiency; and

(B) within 14 days after receipt of a request; or

(2) in the case of a consumer obligor who is liable for a deficiency, within 14 days after receipt of a request, send to the consumer obligor a record waiving the secured party's right to a deficiency.

(c) **[Required information.]** To comply with subsection (a)(1)(B), a writing must provide the following information in the following order:

(1) the aggregate amount of obligations secured by the security interest under which the disposition was made, and, if the amount reflects a rebate of unearned interest or credit service charge, an indication of that fact, calculated as of a specified date:

(A) if the secured party takes or receives possession of the collateral after default, not more than 35 days before the secured party takes or receives possession; or

(B) if the secured party takes or receives possession of the collateral before default or does not take possession of the collateral, not more than 35 days before the disposition;

(2) the amount of proceeds of the disposition;

(3) the aggregate amount of the obligations after deducting the amount of proceeds;

(4) the amount, in the aggregate or by type, and types of expenses, including expenses of retaking, holding, preparing for disposition, processing, and disposing of the collateral, and attorney's fees secured by the collateral which are known to the secured party and relate to the current disposition;

(5) the amount, in the aggregate or by type, and types of credits, including rebates of interest or credit service charges, to which the obligor is known to be entitled and which are not reflected in the amount in paragraph (1); and

(6) the amount of the surplus or deficiency.

(d) **[Substantial compliance.]** A particular phrasing of the explanation is not required. An explanation complying substantially with the requirements of subsection (a) is sufficient, even if it includes minor errors that are not seriously misleading.

(e) **[Charges for responses.]** A debtor or consumer obligor is entitled without charge to one response to a request under this section during any six-month period in which the secured party did not send to the debtor or consumer obligor an explanation pursuant to subsection (b)(1). The secured party may require payment of a charge not exceeding $25 for each additional response.

Official Comment

1. **Source.** New.

2. **Duty to Send Information Concerning Surplus or Deficiency.**

This section reflects the view that, in every consumer-goods transaction, the debtor or obligor is entitled to know the amount of a surplus or deficiency and the basis upon which the surplus or deficiency was calculated. Under subsection (b)(1), a secured party is obligated to provide this information (an "explanation," defined in subsection (a)(1)) no later than the time that it accounts for and pays a surplus or the time of its first written attempt to collect the deficiency. The obligor need not make a request for an accounting in order to receive an explanation. A secured party who does not attempt to collect a deficiency in writing or account for and pay a surplus has no obligation to send an explanation under subsection (b)(1) and, consequently, cannot be liable for noncompliance.

A debtor or secondary obligor need not wait until the secured party commences written collection efforts in order to receive an explanation of how a deficiency or surplus was calculated. Subsection (b)(2) obliges the secured party to send an explanation within 14 days after it receives a "request" (defined in subsection (a)(2)).

3. **Explanation of Calculation of Surplus or Deficiency.** Subsection (c) contains the requirements for how a calculation of a surplus or deficiency must be explained in order to satisfy subsection (a)(1)(B). It gives a secured party some discretion concerning rebates of interest or credit service charges. The secured party may include these rebates in the aggregate amount of obligations secured, under subsection (c)(1), or may include them with other types of rebates and credits under subsection (c)(5). Rebates of interest or credit service charges are the only types of rebates for which this discretion is provided. If the secured party provides an explanation that includes rebates of pre-computed interest, its explanation must so indicate. The expenses and attorney's fees to be described pursuant to subsection (c)(4) are those relating to the most recent disposition, not those that may have been incurred in connection with earlier enforcement efforts and which have been resolved by the parties.

4. **Liability for Noncompliance.** A secured party who fails to comply with subsection (b)(2) is liable for any loss caused plus $500. See Section 9–625(b), (c), (e)(6). A secured party who fails to send an explanation under subsection (b)(1) is liable for any loss caused plus, if the noncompliance was "part of a pattern, or consistent with a practice of noncompliance," $500. See Section 9–625(b), (c), (e)(5). However, a secured party who fails to comply with this section is not liable for statutory minimum damages under Section 9–625(c)(2). See Section 9–628(d).

§ 9–617. Rights of Transferee of Collateral

(a) **[Effects of disposition.]** A secured party's disposition of collateral after default:

(1) transfers to a transferee for value all of the debtor's rights in the collateral;

(2) discharges the security interest under which the disposition is made; and

(3) discharges any subordinate security interest or other subordinate lien [other than liens created under [cite acts or statutes providing for liens, if any, that are not to be discharged]].

(b) **[Rights of good-faith transferee.]** A transferee that acts in good faith takes free of the rights and interests described in subsection (a), even if the secured party fails to comply with this article or the requirements of any judicial proceeding.

(c) **[Rights of other transferee.]** If a transferee does not take free of the rights and interests described in subsection (a), the transferee takes the collateral subject to:

(1) the debtor's rights in the collateral;

(2) the security interest or agricultural lien under which the disposition is made; and

(3) any other security interest or other lien.

§ 9–618. Rights and Duties of Certain Secondary Obligors

(a) **[Rights and duties of secondary obligor.]** A secondary obligor acquires the rights and becomes obligated to perform the duties of the secured party after the secondary obligor:

(1) receives an assignment of a secured obligation from the secured party;

(2) receives a transfer of collateral from the secured party and agrees to accept the rights and assume the duties of the secured party; or

(3) is subrogated to the rights of a secured party with respect to collateral.

(b) **[Effect of assignment, transfer, or subrogation.]** An assignment, transfer, or subrogation described in subsection (a):

(1) is not a disposition of collateral under Section 9–610; and

(2) relieves the secured party of further duties under this article.

Official Comment

1. **Source.** Former Section 9–504(5).

2. **Scope of This Section.** Under this section, assignments of secured obligations and other transactions (regardless of form) that function like assignments of secured obligations are not dispositions to which Part 6 applies. Rather, they constitute assignments of rights and (occasionally) delegations of duties. Application of this section may require an investigation into the agreement of the parties, which may not be reflected in the words of the repurchase agreement (e.g., when the agreement requires a recourse party to "purchase the collateral" but contemplates that the purchaser will then conduct an Article 9 foreclosure disposition).

This section, like former Section 9–504(5), does not constitute a general and comprehensive rule for allocating rights and duties upon assignment of a secured obligation. Rather, it applies only in situations involving a secondary obligor described in subsection (a). In other contexts, the agreement of the parties and applicable law other than Article 9 determine whether the assignment imposes upon the assignee any duty to the debtor and whether the assignor retains its duties to the debtor after the assignment.

Subsection (a)(1) applies when there has been an assignment of an obligation that is secured at the time it is assigned. Thus, if a secondary obligor acquires the collateral at a disposition under Section 9–610 and simultaneously or subsequently discharges the unsecured deficiency claim, subsection (a)(1) is not implicated. Similarly, subsection (a)(3) applies only when the secondary obligor is subrogated to the secured party's rights with respect to collateral. Thus, this subsection will not be implicated if a secondary obligor discharges the debtor's unsecured obligation for a post-disposition deficiency. Similarly, if the secured party disposes of some of the collateral and the secondary obligor thereafter discharges the remaining obligation, subsection (a) applies only with respect to rights and duties concerning the remaining collateral, and, under subsection (b), the subrogation is not a disposition *of the remaining collateral*.

As discussed more fully in Comment 3, a secondary obligor may receive a transfer of collateral in a disposition under Section 9–610 in exchange for a payment that is applied against the secured obligation. However, a secondary obligor who pays and receives a transfer of collateral does not necessarily become subrogated to the rights of the secured party as contemplated by subsection (a)(3). Only to the extent the secondary obligor makes a payment in satisfaction of its secondary obligation would it become subrogated. To the extent its payment constitutes the price of the collateral in a Section 9–610 disposition by the secured party, the secondary obligor would not be subrogated. Thus, if the amount paid by the secondary obligor for the collateral in a Section 9–610 disposition is itself insufficient to dis-

charge the secured obligation, but the secondary obligor makes an additional payment that satisfies the remaining balance, the secondary obligor would be subrogated to the secured party's deficiency claim. However, the duties of the secured party *as such* would have come to an end with respect to that collateral. In some situations the capacity in which the payment is made may be unclear. Accordingly, the parties should in their relationship provide clear evidence of the nature and circumstances of the payment by the secondary obligor.

3. **Transfer of Collateral to Secondary Obligor.** It is possible for a secured party to transfer collateral to a secondary obligor in a transaction that is a disposition under Section 9–610 and that establishes a surplus or deficiency under Section 9–615. Indeed, this Article includes a special rule, in Section 9–615(f), for establishing a deficiency in the case of some dispositions to, *inter alia*, secondary obligors. This Article rejects the view, which some may have ascribed to former Section 9–504(5), that a transfer of collateral to a recourse party can *never* constitute a disposition of collateral which discharges a security interest. Inasmuch as a secured party could itself buy collateral at its own public sale, it makes no sense to prohibit a recourse party ever from buying at the sale.

. . .

§ 9–619. Transfer of Record or Legal Title

(a) **["Transfer statement."]** In this section, "transfer statement" means a record authenticated by a secured party stating:

(1) that the debtor has defaulted in connection with an obligation secured by specified collateral;

(2) that the secured party has exercised its post-default remedies with respect to the collateral;

(3) that, by reason of the exercise, a transferee has acquired the rights of the debtor in the collateral; and

(4) the name and mailing address of the secured party, debtor, and transferee.

(b) **[Effect of transfer statement.]** A transfer statement entitles the transferee to the transfer of record of all rights of the debtor in the collateral specified in the statement in any official filing, recording, registration, or certificate-of-title system covering the collateral. If a transfer statement is presented with the applicable fee and request form to the official or office responsible for maintaining the system, the official or office shall:

(1) accept the transfer statement;

(2) promptly amend its records to reflect the transfer; and

(3) if applicable, issue a new appropriate certificate of title in the name of the transferee.

(c) **[Transfer not a disposition; no relief of secured party's duties.]** A transfer of the record or legal title to collateral to a secured party under subsection (b) or otherwise is not of itself a disposition of collateral under this article and does not of itself relieve the secured party of its duties under this article.

Official Comment

1. **Source.** New.

2. **Transfer of Record or Legal Title.** Potential buyers of collateral that is covered by a certificate of title (e.g., an automobile) or is subject to a registration system (e.g., a copyright) typically require as a condition of their purchase that the certificate or registry reflect their ownership. In many cases, this condition can be met only with the consent of the record owner. If the record owner is the debtor and, as may be the case after the default, the debtor refuses to cooperate, the secured party may have great difficulty disposing of the collateral.

Subsection (b) provides a simple mechanism for obtaining record or legal title, for use primarily when other law does not provide one. Of course, use of this mechanism will not be effective to clear title to the extent that subsection (b) is preempted by federal law. Subsection (b) contemplates a transfer of record or legal title to a third party, following a secured party's exercise of its disposition or acceptance remedies under this Part, as well as a transfer by a debtor to a secured party prior to the secured party's exercise of those remedies. Under subsection (c), a transfer of record or legal title (under subsection (b) or under other law) to a secured party prior to the exercise of those remedies merely puts the secured party in a position to pass legal or record title to a transferee at foreclosure. A secured party who has obtained record or legal title retains its duties with respect to enforcement of its security interest, and the debtor retains its rights as well.

. . .

§ 9–620. Acceptance of Collateral in Full or Partial Satisfaction of Obligation; Compulsory Disposition of Collateral

(a) **[Conditions to acceptance in satisfaction.]** Except as otherwise provided in subsection (g), a secured party may accept collateral in full or partial satisfaction of the obligation it secures only if:

(1) the debtor consents to the acceptance under subsection (c);

(2) the secured party does not receive, within the time set forth in subsection (d), a notification of objection to the proposal authenticated by:

    (A) a person to which the secured party was required to send a proposal under Section 9–621; or

    (B) any other person, other than the debtor, holding an interest in the collateral subordinate to the security interest that is the subject of the proposal;

(3) if the collateral is consumer goods, the collateral is not in the possession of the debtor when the debtor consents to the acceptance; and

(4) subsection (e) does not require the secured party to dispose of the collateral or the debtor waives the requirement pursuant to Section 9–624.

(b) **[Purported acceptance ineffective.]** A purported or apparent acceptance of collateral under this section is ineffective unless:

(1) the secured party consents to the acceptance in an authenticated record or sends a proposal to the debtor; and

(2) the conditions of subsection (a) are met.

(c) **[Debtor's consent.]** For purposes of this section:

(1) a debtor consents to an acceptance of collateral in partial satisfaction of the obligation it secures only if the debtor agrees to the terms of the acceptance in a record authenticated after default; and

(2) a debtor consents to an acceptance of collateral in full satisfaction of the obligation it secures only if the debtor agrees to the terms of the acceptance in a record authenticated after default or the secured party:

    (A) sends to the debtor after default a proposal that is unconditional or subject only to a condition that collateral not in the possession of the secured party be preserved or maintained;

    (B) in the proposal, proposes to accept collateral in full satisfaction of the obligation it secures; and

    (C) does not receive a notification of objection authenticated by the debtor within 20 days after the proposal is sent.

(d) **[Effectiveness of notification.]** To be effective under subsection (a)(2), a notification of objection must be received by the secured party:

(1) in the case of a person to which the proposal was sent pursuant to Section 9–621, within 20 days after notification was sent to that person; and

(2) in other cases:

    (A) within 20 days after the last notification was sent pursuant to Section 9–621; or

(B) if a notification was not sent, before the debtor consents to the acceptance under subsection (c).

(e) **[Mandatory disposition of consumer goods.]** A secured party that has taken possession of collateral shall dispose of the collateral pursuant to Section 9–610 within the time specified in subsection (f) if:

(1) 60 percent of the cash price has been paid in the case of a purchase-money security interest in consumer goods; or

(2) 60 percent of the principal amount of the obligation secured has been paid in the case of a non-purchase-money security interest in consumer goods.

(f) **[Compliance with mandatory disposition requirement.]** To comply with subsection (e), the secured party shall dispose of the collateral:

(1) within 90 days after taking possession; or

(2) within any longer period to which the debtor and all secondary obligors have agreed in an agreement to that effect entered into and authenticated after default.

(g) **[No partial satisfaction in consumer transaction.]** In a consumer transaction, a secured party may not accept collateral in partial satisfaction of the obligation it secures.

Official Comment

. . .

2. **Overview.** This section . . . reflects the belief that strict foreclosures should be encouraged and often will produce better results than a disposition for all concerned.

Subsection (a) sets forth the conditions necessary to an effective acceptance (formerly, retention) of collateral in full or partial satisfaction of the secured obligation. Section 9–621 requires in addition that a secured party who wishes to proceed under this section notify certain other persons who have or claim to have an interest in the collateral. Unlike the failure to meet the conditions in subsection (a), under Section 9–622(b) the failure to comply with the notification requirement of Section 9–621 does not render the acceptance of collateral ineffective. Rather, the acceptance can take effect notwithstanding the secured party's noncompliance. A person to whom the required notice was not sent has the right to recover damages under Section 9–625(b). Section 9–622(a) sets forth the effect of an acceptance of collateral.

3. **Conditions to Effective Acceptance.** Subsection (a) contains the conditions necessary to the effectiveness of an acceptance of collateral. Subsection (a)(1) requires the debtor's consent. Under subsections (c)(1) and (c)(2), the debtor may consent by agreeing to the acceptance in writing after default. Subsection (c)(2) contains an alternative method by which to satisfy the debtor's-consent condition in subsection (a)(1) . . .: The debtor consents if the secured party sends a proposal to the debtor and does not receive an objection within 20 days. Under subsection (c)(1), however, that silence is not deemed to be consent with respect to acceptances in partial satisfaction. Thus, a secured party who wishes to conduct a "partial strict foreclosure" must obtain the debtor's agreement in a record authenticated after default. In all other respects, the conditions necessary to an effective partial strict foreclosure are the same as

those governing acceptance of collateral in full satisfaction. (But see subsection (g), prohibiting partial strict foreclosure of a security interest in consumer transactions.)

. . .

Subsections (a)(3) and (a)(4) contain special rules for transactions in which consumers are involved. See Comment 12.

4. **Proposals.** Section 9–102 defines the term "proposal." It is necessary to send a "proposal" to the debtor only if the debtor does not agree to an acceptance in an authenticated record as described in subsection (c)(1) or (c)(2). Section 9–621(a) determines whether it is necessary to send a proposal to third parties. A proposal need not take any particular form as long as it sets forth the terms under which the secured party is willing to accept collateral in satisfaction. A proposal to accept collateral should specify the amount (or a means of calculating the amount, such as by including a per diem accrual figure) of the secured obligations to be satisfied, state the conditions (if any) under which the proposal may be revoked, and describe any other applicable conditions. Note, however, that a conditional proposal generally requires the debtor's agreement in order to take effect. See subsection (c).

5. **Secured Party's Agreement; No "Constructive" Strict Foreclosure.** The conditions of subsection (a) relate to actual or implied consent by the debtor and any secondary obligor or holder of a junior security interest or lien. To ensure that the debtor cannot unilaterally cause an acceptance of collateral, subsection (b) provides that compliance with these conditions is necessary but not sufficient to cause an acceptance of collateral. Rather, under subsection (b), acceptance does not occur unless, in addition, the secured party consents to the acceptance in an authenticated record or sends to the debtor a proposal. For this reason, a mere delay in collection or disposition of collateral does not constitute a "constructive" strict foreclosure. Instead, delay is a factor relating to whether the secured party acted in a commercially reasonable manner for purposes of Section 9–607 or 9–610. A debtor's voluntary surrender of collateral to a secured party and the secured party's acceptance of possession of the collateral does not, of itself, necessarily raise an implication that the secured party intends or is proposing to accept the collateral in satisfaction of the secured obligation under this section.

6. **When Acceptance Occurs.** This section does not impose any formalities or identify any steps that a secured party must take in order to accept collateral once the conditions of subsections (a) and (b) have been met. Absent facts or circumstances indicating a contrary intention, the fact that the conditions have been met provides a sufficient indication that the secured party has accepted the collateral on the terms to which the secured party has consented or proposed and the debtor has consented or failed to object. Following a proposal, acceptance of the collateral normally is automatic upon the secured party's becoming bound and the time for objection passing. As a matter of good business practice, an enforcing secured party may wish to memorialize its acceptance following a proposal, such as by notifying the debtor that the strict foreclosure is effective or by placing a written record to that effect in its files. The secured party's agreement to accept collateral is self-executing and cannot be breached. The secured party is bound by its agreement to accept collateral and by any proposal to which the debtor consents.

. . .

11. **Role of Good Faith.** Section 1–203 imposes an obligation of good faith on a secured party's enforcement

under this Article. This obligation may not be disclaimed by agreement. See Section 1–102. Thus, a proposal and acceptance made under this section in bad faith would not be effective. For example, a secured party's proposal to accept marketable securities worth $1,000 in full satisfaction of indebtedness in the amount of $100, made in the hopes that the debtor might inadvertently fail to object, would be made in bad faith. On the other hand, in the normal case proposals and acceptances should be not second-guessed on the basis of the "value" of the collateral involved. Disputes about valuation or even a clear excess of collateral value over the amount of obligations satisfied do not necessarily demonstrate the absence of good faith.

12. **Special Rules in Consumer Cases.** Subsection (e) imposes an obligation on the secured party to dispose of consumer goods under certain circumstances. Subsection (f) explains when a disposition that is required under subsection (e) is timely. An effective acceptance of collateral cannot occur if subsection (e) requires a disposition unless the debtor waives this requirement pursuant to Section 9–624(b). Moreover, a secured party who takes possession of collateral and unreasonably delays disposition violates subsection (e), if applicable, and may also violate Section 9–610 or other provisions of this Part. . . . Remedies available under other law, including conversion, remain available under this Article in appropriate cases. See Sections 1–103, 1–106.

Subsection (g) prohibits the secured party in consumer transactions from accepting collateral in partial satisfaction of the obligation it secures. If a secured party attempts an acceptance in partial satisfaction in a consumer transaction, the attempted acceptance is void.

§ 9–621. Notification of Proposal to Accept Collateral

(a) **[Persons to which proposal to be sent.]** A secured party that desires to accept collateral in full or partial satisfaction of the obligation it secures shall send its proposal to:

(1) any person from which the secured party has received, before the debtor consented to the acceptance, an authenticated notification of a claim of an interest in the collateral;

(2) any other secured party or lienholder that, 10 days before the debtor consented to the acceptance, held a security interest in or other lien on the collateral perfected by the filing of a financing statement that:

(A) identified the collateral;

(B) was indexed under the debtor's name as of that date; and

(C) was filed in the office or offices in which to file a financing statement against the debtor covering the collateral as of that date; and

(3) any other secured party that, 10 days before the debtor consented to the acceptance, held a security interest in the collateral perfected by compliance with a statute, regulation, or treaty described in Section 9–311(a).

(b) **[Proposal to be sent to secondary obligor in partial satisfaction.]** A secured party that desires to accept collateral in partial satisfaction of the obligation it secures shall send its proposal to any secondary obligor in addition to the persons described in subsection (a).

§ 9–622. Effect of Acceptance of Collateral

(a) **[Effect of acceptance.]** A secured party's acceptance of collateral in full or partial satisfaction of the obligation it secures:

(1) discharges the obligation to the extent consented to by the debtor;

(2) transfers to the secured party all of a debtor's rights in the collateral;

(3) discharges the security interest or agricultural lien that is the subject of the debtor's consent and any subordinate security interest or other subordinate lien; and

(4) terminates any other subordinate interest.

(b) **[Discharge of subordinate interest notwithstanding non-compliance.]** A subordinate interest is discharged or terminated under subsection (a), even if the secured party fails to comply with this article.

§ 9–623. Right to Redeem Collateral

(a) **[Persons that may redeem.]** A debtor, any secondary obligor, or any other secured party or lienholder may redeem collateral.

(b) **[Requirements for redemption.]** To redeem collateral, a person shall tender:

(1) fulfillment of all obligations secured by the collateral; and

(2) the reasonable expenses and attorney's fees described in Section 9–615(a)(1).

(c) **[When redemption may occur.]** A redemption may occur at any time before a secured party:

(1) has collected collateral under Section 9–607;

(2) has disposed of collateral or entered into a contract for its disposition under Section 9–610; or

(3) has accepted collateral in full or partial satisfaction of the obligation it secures under Section 9–622.

Official Comment

. . .

2. **Redemption Right.** . . . To redeem the collateral a person must tender fulfillment of all obligations secured, plus certain expenses. If the entire balance of a secured obligation has been accelerated, it would be necessary to tender the entire balance. A tender of fulfillment obviously means more than a new promise to perform an existing promise. It requires payment in full of all monetary obligations then due and performance in full of all other obligations then matured. If unmatured secured obligations remain, the security interest continues to secure them (i.e., as if there had been no default).

1029

. . .

§ 9–624.   Waiver

(a) **[Waiver of disposition notification.]** A debtor or secondary obligor may waive the right to notification of disposition of collateral under Section 9–611 only by an agreement to that effect entered into and authenticated after default.

(b) **[Waiver of mandatory disposition.]** A debtor may waive the right to require disposition of collateral under Section 9–620(e) only by an agreement to that effect entered into and authenticated after default.

(c) **[Waiver of redemption right.]** Except in a consumer-goods transaction, a debtor or secondary obligor may waive the right to redeem collateral under Section 9–623 only by an agreement to that effect entered into and authenticated after default.

[SUBPART 2.   NONCOMPLIANCE WITH ARTICLE]

§ 9–625.   Remedies for Secured Party's Failure to Comply With Article

(a) **[Judicial orders concerning noncompliance.]** If it is established that a secured party is not proceeding in accordance with this article, a court may order or restrain collection, enforcement, or disposition of collateral on appropriate terms and conditions.

(b) **[Damages for noncompliance.]** Subject to subsections (c), (d), and (f), a person is liable for damages in the amount of any loss caused by a failure to comply with this article. Loss caused by a failure to comply may include loss resulting from the debtor's inability to obtain, or increased costs of, alternative financing.

(c) **[Persons entitled to recover damages; statutory damages in consumer-goods transaction.]** Except as otherwise provided in Section 9–628:

(1) a person that, at the time of the failure, was a debtor, was an obligor, or held a security interest in or other lien on the collateral may recover damages under subsection (b) for its loss; and

(2) if the collateral is consumer goods, a person that was a debtor or a secondary obligor at the time a secured party failed to comply with this part may recover for that failure in any event an amount not less than the credit service charge plus 10 percent of the principal amount of the obligation or the time-price differential plus 10 percent of the cash price.

(d) **[Recovery when deficiency eliminated or reduced.]** A debtor whose deficiency is eliminated under Section 9–626 may recover damages for the loss of any surplus. However, a debtor or secondary obligor whose deficiency is eliminated or reduced under Section 9–626 may not otherwise recover under subsection (b) for noncompliance with the provisions of this part relating to collection, enforcement, disposition, or acceptance.

(e) **[Statutory damages: noncompliance with specified provisions.]** In addition to any damages recoverable under subsection (b), the debtor, consumer obligor, or person named as a debtor in a filed record, as applicable, may recover $500 in each case from a person that:

(1) fails to comply with Section 9–208;

(2) fails to comply with Section 9–209;

(3) files a record that the person is not entitled to file under Section 9–509(a);

(4) fails to cause the secured party of record to file or send a termination statement as required by Section 9–513(a) or (c);

(5) fails to comply with Section 9–616(b)(1) and whose failure is part of a pattern, or consistent with a practice, of noncompliance; or

(6) fails to comply with Section 9–616(b)(2).

(f) **[Statutory damages: noncompliance with Section 9–210.]** A debtor or consumer obligor may recover damages under subsection (b) and, in addition, $500 in each case from a person that, without reasonable cause, fails to comply with a request under Section 9–210. A recipient of a request under Section 9–210 which never claimed an interest in the collateral or obligations that are the subject of a request under that section has a reasonable excuse for failure to comply with the request within the meaning of this subsection.

(g) **[Limitation of security interest: noncompliance with Section 9–210.]** If a secured party fails to comply with a request regarding a list of collateral or a statement of account under Section 9–210, the secured party may claim a security interest only as shown in the list or statement included in the request as against a person that is reasonably misled by the failure.

Official Comment

. . .

2. **Remedies for Noncompliance; Scope.** Subsections (a) and (b) provide the basic remedies afforded to those aggrieved by a secured party's failure to comply with this Article. Like all provisions that create liability, they are subject to Section 9–628, which should be read in conjunction with Section 9–605. . . . Subsection (c)(2), which gives a minimum damage recovery in consumer-goods transactions, applies only to noncompliance with the provisions of this Part.

3. **Damages for Noncompliance with This Article.** Subsection (b) sets forth the basic remedy for failure to comply with the requirements of this Article: a damage recovery in the amount of loss caused by the noncompliance. Subsection (c) identifies who may recover under subsection (b). It affords a remedy to any aggrieved person who is a debtor or obligor. However, a principal obligor who is not a debtor may recover damages only for noncompliance with Section 9–616, inasmuch as none of the other rights and duties in this Article run in favor of such a principal obligor.

1031

Such a principal obligor could not suffer any loss or damage on account of non-compliance with rights or duties of which it is not a beneficiary. ... The last sentence of subsection (d) eliminates the possibility of double recovery or other over-compensation arising out of a reduction or elimination of a deficiency under Section 9–626, based on noncompliance with the provisions of this Part relating to collection, enforcement, disposition, or acceptance. Assuming no double recovery, a debtor whose deficiency is eliminated under Section 9–626 may pursue a claim for a surplus. Because Section 9–626 does not apply to consumer transactions, the statute is silent as to whether a double recovery or other over-compensation is possible in a consumer transaction.

Damages for violation of the requirements of this Article, including Section 9–609, are those reasonably calculated to put an eligible claimant in the position that it would have occupied had no violation occurred. See Section 1–106. Subsection (b) supports the recovery of actual damages for committing a breach of the peace in violation of Section 9–609, and principles of tort law supplement this subsection. See Section 1–103. However, to the extent that damages in tort compensate the debtor for the same loss dealt with by this Article, the debtor should be entitled to only one recovery.

4. **Minimum Damages in Consumer–Goods Transactions.** Subsection (c)(2) provides a minimum, statutory, damage recovery for a debtor and secondary obligor in a consumer-goods transaction. It ... is designed to ensure that every noncompliance with the requirements of Part 6 in a consumer-goods transaction results in liability, regardless of any injury that may have resulted. Subsection (c)(2) leaves the treatment of statutory damages as it was under former Article 9. A secured party is not liable for statutory damages under this subsection more than once with respect to any one secured obligation (see Section 9–628(e)), nor is a secured party liable under this subsection for failure to comply with Section 9–616 (see Section 9–628(d)).

Following former Section 9–507(1), this Article does not include a definition or explanation of the terms "credit service charge," "principal amount," "time-price differential," or "cash price," as used in subsection (c)(2). It leaves their construction and application to the court, taking into account the subsection's purpose of providing a minimum recovery in consumer-goods transactions.

. . .

§ 9–626. Action in Which Deficiency or Surplus Is in Issue

(a) **[Applicable rules if amount of deficiency or surplus in issue.]** In an action arising from a transaction, other than a consumer transaction, in which the amount of a deficiency or surplus is in issue, the following rules apply:

(1) A secured party need not prove compliance with the provisions of this part relating to collection, enforcement, disposition, or acceptance unless the debtor or a secondary obligor places the secured party's compliance in issue.

(2) If the secured party's compliance is placed in issue, the secured party has the burden of establishing that the collection, enforcement, disposition, or acceptance was conducted in accordance with this part.

(3) Except as otherwise provided in Section 9–628, if a secured party fails to prove that the collection, enforcement, disposition, or

acceptance was conducted in accordance with the provisions of this part relating to collection, enforcement, disposition, or acceptance, the liability of a debtor or a secondary obligor for a deficiency is limited to an amount by which the sum of the secured obligation, expenses, and attorney's fees exceeds the greater of:

(A) the proceeds of the collection, enforcement, disposition, or acceptance; or

(B) the amount of proceeds that would have been realized had the noncomplying secured party proceeded in accordance with the provisions of this part relating to collection, enforcement, disposition, or acceptance.

(4) For purposes of paragraph (3)(B), the amount of proceeds that would have been realized is equal to the sum of the secured obligation, expenses, and attorney's fees unless the secured party proves that the amount is less than that sum.

(5) If a deficiency or surplus is calculated under Section 9–615(f), the debtor or obligor has the burden of establishing that the amount of proceeds of the disposition is significantly below the range of prices that a complying disposition to a person other than the secured party, a person related to the secured party, or a secondary obligor would have brought.

(b) **[Non-consumer transactions; no inference.]** The limitation of the rules in subsection (a) to transactions other than consumer transactions is intended to leave to the court the determination of the proper rules in consumer transactions. The court may not infer from that limitation the nature of the proper rule in consumer transactions and may continue to apply established approaches.

Official Comment

1. **Source.** New.

2. **Scope.** The basic damage remedy under Section 9–625(b) is subject to the special rules in this section for transactions other than consumer transactions. This section addresses situations in which the amount of a deficiency or surplus is in issue, i.e., situations in which the secured party has collected, enforced, disposed of, or accepted the collateral. It contains special rules applicable to a determination of the amount of a deficiency or surplus. Because this section affects a person's liability for a deficiency, it is subject to Section 9–628, which should be read in conjunction with Section 9–605. The rules in this section apply only to noncompliance in

connection with the "collection, enforcement, disposition, or acceptance" under Part 6. For other types of noncompliance with Part 6, the general liability rule of Section 9–625(b)–recovery of actual damages–applies. Consider, for example, a repossession that does not comply with Section 9–609 for want of a default. The debtor's remedy is under Section 9–625(b). In a proper case, the secured party also may be liable for conversion under non-UCC law. If the secured party thereafter disposed of the collateral, however, it would violate Section 9–610 at that time, and this section would apply.

3. **Rebuttable Presumption Rule.** Subsection (a) establishes the rebuttable presumption rule for transac-

tions other than consumer transactions. Under paragraph (1), the secured party need not prove compliance with the relevant provisions of this Part as part of its prima facie case. If, however, the debtor or a secondary obligor raises the issue (in accordance with the forum's rules of pleading and practice), then the secured party bears the burden of proving that the collection, enforcement, disposition, or acceptance complied. In the event the secured party is unable to meet this burden, then paragraph (3) explains how to calculate the deficiency. Under this rebuttable presumption rule, the debtor or obligor is to be credited with the greater of the actual proceeds of the disposition or the proceeds that would have been realized had the secured party complied with the relevant provisions. If a deficiency remains, then the secured party is entitled to recover it. The references to "the secured obligation, expenses, and attorney's fees" in paragraphs (3) and (4) embrace the application rules in Sections 9–608(a) and 9–615(a).

Unless the secured party proves that compliance with the relevant provisions would have yielded a smaller amount, under paragraph (4) the amount that a complying collection, enforcement, or disposition would have yielded is deemed to be equal to the amount of the secured obligation, together with expenses and attorney's fees. Thus, the secured party may not recover any deficiency unless it meets this burden.

4. **Consumer Transactions.** Although subsection (a) adopts a version of the rebuttable presumption rule for transactions other than consumer transactions, with certain exceptions Part 6 does not specify the effect of a secured party's noncompliance in consumer transactions. (The exceptions are the provisions for the recovery of damages in Section 9–625.) Subsection (b) provides that the limitation of subsection (a) to transactions other than consumer transactions is intended to leave to the court the determination of the proper rules in consumer transactions. It also instructs the court not to draw any inference from the limitation as to the proper rules for consumer transactions and leaves the court free to continue to apply established approaches to those transactions.

Courts construing former Section 9–507 disagreed about the consequences of a secured party's failure to comply with the requirements of former Part 5. Three general approaches emerged. Some courts have held that a noncomplying secured party may not recover a deficiency (the "absolute bar" rule). A few courts held that the debtor can offset against a claim to a deficiency all damages recoverable under former Section 9–507 resulting from the secured party's noncompliance (the "offset" rule). A plurality of courts considering the issue held that the noncomplying secured party is barred from recovering a deficiency unless it overcomes a rebuttable presumption that compliance with former Part 5 would have yielded an amount sufficient to satisfy the secured debt. In addition to the nonuniformity resulting from court decisions, some States enacted special rules governing the availability of deficiencies.

5. **Burden of Proof When Section 9–615(f) Applies.** In a non-consumer transaction, subsection (a)(5) imposes upon a debtor or obligor the burden of proving that the proceeds of a disposition are so low that, under Section 9–615(f), the actual proceeds should not serve as the basis upon which a deficiency or surplus is calculated. Were the burden placed on the secured party, then debtors might be encouraged to challenge the price received in every disposition to the secured party, a person related to the secured party, or a secondary obligor.

6. **Delay in Applying This Section.** There is an inevitable delay be-

tween the time a secured party engages in a noncomplying collection, enforcement, disposition, or acceptance and the time of a subsequent judicial determination that the secured party did not comply with Part 6. During the interim, the secured party, believing that the secured obligation is larger than it ultimately is determined to be, may continue to enforce its security interest in collateral. If some or all of the secured indebtedness ultimately is discharged under this section, a reasonable application of this section would impose liability on the secured party for the amount of any excess, unwarranted recoveries but would not make the enforcement efforts wrongful.

§ 9–627. Determination of Whether Conduct Was Commercially Reasonable

(a) **[Greater amount obtainable under other circumstances; no preclusion of commercial reasonableness.]** The fact that a greater amount could have been obtained by a collection, enforcement, disposition, or acceptance at a different time or in a different method from that selected by the secured party is not of itself sufficient to preclude the secured party from establishing that the collection, enforcement, disposition, or acceptance was made in a commercially reasonable manner.

(b) **[Dispositions that are commercially reasonable.]** A disposition of collateral is made in a commercially reasonable manner if the disposition is made:

(1) in the usual manner on any recognized market;

(2) at the price current in any recognized market at the time of the disposition; or

(3) otherwise in conformity with reasonable commercial practices among dealers in the type of property that was the subject of the disposition.

(c) **[Approval by court or on behalf of creditors.]** A collection, enforcement, disposition, or acceptance is commercially reasonable if it has been approved:

(1) in a judicial proceeding;

(2) by a bona fide creditors' committee;

(3) by a representative of creditors; or

(4) by an assignee for the benefit of creditors.

(d) **[Approval under subsection (c) not necessary; absence of approval has no effect.]** Approval under subsection (c) need not be obtained, and lack of approval does not mean that the collection, enforcement, disposition, or acceptance is not commercially reasonable.

Official Comment

1. **Source.** Former Section 9–507(2).

2. **Relationship of Price to Commercial Reasonableness.** Some observers have found the notion contained in subsection (a) (derived from former Section 9–507(2)) (the fact that a

1035

better price could have been obtained does not establish lack of commercial reasonableness) to be inconsistent with that found in Section 9–610(b) derived from former Section 9–504(3) (every aspect of the disposition, including its terms, must be commercially reasonable). There is no such inconsistency. While not itself sufficient to establish a violation of this Part, a low price suggests that a court should scrutinize carefully all aspects of a disposition to ensure that each aspect was commercially reasonable.

The law long has grappled with the problem of dispositions of personal and real property which comply with applicable procedural requirements (e.g., advertising, notification to interested persons, etc.) but which yield a price that seems low. This Article addresses that issue in Section 9–615(f). That section applies only when the transferee is the secured party, a person related to the secured party, or a secondary obligor. It contains a special rule for calculating a deficiency or surplus in a complying disposition that yields a price that is "significantly below the range of proceeds that a complying disposition to a person other than the secured party, a person related to the secured party, or a secondary obligor would have brought."

. . .

§ 9–628. Nonliability and Limitation on Liability of Secured Party; Liability of Secondary Obligor.

(a) **[Limitation of liability of secured party for noncompliance with article.]** Unless a secured party knows that a person is a debtor or obligor, knows the identity of the person, and knows how to communicate with the person:

(1) the secured party is not liable to the person, or to a secured party or lienholder that has filed a financing statement against the person, for failure to comply with this article; and

(2) the secured party's failure to comply with this article does not affect the liability of the person for a deficiency.

(b) **[Limitation of liability based on status as secured party.]** A secured party is not liable because of its status as secured party:

(1) to a person that is a debtor or obligor, unless the secured party knows:

(A) that the person is a debtor or obligor;

(B) the identity of the person; and

(C) how to communicate with the person; or

(2) to a secured party or lienholder that has filed a financing statement against a person, unless the secured party knows:

(A) that the person is a debtor; and

(B) the identity of the person.

(c) **[Limitation of liability if reasonable belief that transaction not a consumer-goods transaction or consumer transaction.]** A secured party is not liable to any person, and a person's liability for a deficiency is not affected, because of any act or omission arising out of the secured party's reasonable belief that a transaction is not a consumer-goods transaction or a consumer transaction or that goods are not consumer goods, if the secured party's belief is based on its reasonable reliance on:

(1) a debtor's representation concerning the purpose for which collateral was to be used, acquired, or held; or

(2) an obligor's representation concerning the purpose for which a secured obligation was incurred.

(d) **[Limitation of liability for statutory damages.]** A secured party is not liable to any person under Section 9–625(c)(2) for its failure to comply with Section 9–616.

(e) **[Limitation of multiple liability for statutory damages.]** A secured party is not liable under Section 9–625(c)(2) more than once with respect to any one secured obligation.

UNIFORM CONSUMER CREDIT CODE
(1974 ACT)

Promulgated by the National Conference of Commissioners on Uniform State Laws (1974)

Table of Sections

ARTICLE 1. GENERAL PROVISIONS AND DEFINITIONS

PART 1. SHORT TITLE, CONSTRUCTION, GENERAL PROVISIONS

PART 2. SCOPE AND JURISDICTION

PART 3. DEFINITIONS

1039

ARTICLE 1. GENERAL PROVISIONS AND DEFINITIONS

PART 1. SHORT TITLE, CONSTRUCTION, GENERAL PROVISIONS

§ 1.102 [Purposes; Rules of Construction]

(1) This Act shall be liberally construed and applied to promote its underlying purposes and policies.

(2) The underlying purposes and policies of this Act are:

(a) to simplify, clarify, and modernize the law governing consumer credit and usury;

(b) to provide rate ceilings to assure an adequate supply of credit to consumers;

(c) to further consumer understanding of the terms of credit transactions and to foster competition among suppliers of consumer credit so that consumers may obtain credit at reasonable cost;

(d) to protect consumers against unfair practices by some suppliers of consumer credit, having due regard for the interests of legitimate and scrupulous creditors;

(e) to permit and encourage the development of fair and economically sound consumer credit practices;

(f) to conform the regulation of disclosure in consumer credit transactions to the Federal Truth in Lending Act; and

(g) to make uniform the law, including administrative rules, among the various jurisdictions.

(3) A reference to a requirement imposed by this Act includes reference to a related rule of the Administrator adopted pursuant to this Act.

§ 1.103 [Supplementary General Principles of Law Applicable]

Unless displaced by the particular provisions of this Act, the Uniform Commercial Code and the principles of law and equity, including the law relative to capacity to contract, principal and agent, estoppel, fraud, misrepresentation, duress, coercion, mistake, bankruptcy, or other validating or invalidating cause supplement its provisions. In the event of inconsistency between the Uniform Commercial Code and this Act the provisions of this Act control.

§ 1.106 [Adjustment of Dollar Amounts]

(1) From time to time the dollar amounts in this Act designated as subject to change shall change, as provided in this section, according to and to the extent of changes in the Consumer Price Index for Urban Wage

Earners and Clerical Workers: U.S. City Average, All Items, 1967 = 100, compiled by the Bureau of Labor Statistics, United States Department of Labor, and hereafter referred to as the Index. . . .

§ 1.107 [Waiver; Agreement to Forego Rights; Settlement of Claims]

(1) Except as otherwise permitted in this Act, a consumer may waive or agree to forego rights or benefits under this Act only in settlement of a bona fide dispute.

(2) A claim by a consumer against a creditor for an excess charge, any other violation of this Act, a civil penalty, or a claim against a consumer for a default or breach of a duty imposed by this Act, if disputed in good faith, may be settled by agreement.

(3) A claim against a consumer, whether or not disputed, may be settled for less value than the amount claimed.

(4) A settlement in which the consumer waives or agrees to forego rights or benefits under this Act is invalid if the court as a matter of law finds the settlement to have been unconscionable at the time it was made. The competence of the consumer, any deception or coercion practiced upon him, the nature and extent of the legal advice received by him, and the value of the consideration are relevant to the issue of unconscionability.

Comment

Unlike UCC Section 1–102(3) which broadly permits variation by agreement, this Act starts from the premise that a consumer may not in general waive or agree to forego rights or benefits under this Act. Compare UCC Section 9–501(3). If not specifically provided for in the Act, waiver or agreement to forego must be part of a settlement, and settlements are subject to review as provided for in this section.

§ 1.110 [Obligation of Good Faith]

(1) Every contract or duty within this Act imposes an obligation of good faith in its performance or enforcement.

(2) "Good faith" means honesty in fact in the conduct or transaction concerned.

PART 2. SCOPE AND JURISDICTION

§ 1.201 [Territorial Application]

(1) Except as otherwise provided in this section, this Act applies to a consumer credit transaction entered into in this State. For the purposes of this Act, a consumer credit transaction is entered into in this State if:

(a) pursuant to other than open-end credit, either a signed writing evidencing the obligation or offer of the consumer is received by the creditor in this State, or the creditor induces the consumer who is a resident of this State to enter into the transaction by face-to-face solicitation in this State; or

(b) pursuant to open-end credit, either the consumer's communication or his indication of intention to establish the open-end credit arrangement is received by the creditor in this State or, if no communication or indication of intention is given by the consumer before the first transaction, the creditor's communication notifying the consumer of the privilege of using the arrangement is mailed in this State.

(2) With respect to a consumer loan to which this Act does not otherwise apply, if a consumer who is a resident of this State, pursuant to solicitation in this State, sends a signed writing evidencing the obligation or offer of the consumer to a creditor in another state and receives the cash proceeds of the loan in this State:

(a) the creditor may not contract for or receive charges exceeding those permitted by the Article on Finance Charges and Related Provisions (Article 2); and

(b) the provisions on Powers and Functions of Administrator (Part 1) of the Article on Administration (Article 6) apply as though the loan were entered into in this State.

(3) The Part on Limitations on Creditors' Remedies (Part 1) of the Article on Remedies and Penalties (Article 5) applies to actions or other proceedings brought in this State to enforce rights arising from consumer credit transactions or extortionate extensions of credit, wherever entered into.

(4) Except as provided in subsection (2), a consumer credit transaction to which this Act does not apply entered into with a person who is a resident of this State at the time of the transaction is valid and enforceable in this State to the extent that it is valid and enforceable under the laws of another jurisdiction, but:

(a) a creditor may not collect through actions or other proceedings in this State an amount exceeding the total amount permitted if the Article on Finance Charges and Related Provisions (Article 2) were applicable; and

(b) a creditor may not enforce rights against the consumer in this State with respect to the provisions of agreements that violate the provisions on Limitations on Agreements and Practices (Part 3) and Limitations on Consumers' Liabilities (Part 4) of the Article on Regulation of Agreements and Practices (Article 3).

(5) Except as provided in subsections (2), (3), and (4), a consumer credit transaction entered into in another jurisdiction is valid and enforceable in this State according to its terms to the extent that it is valid and enforceable under the laws of the other jurisdiction.

(6) For the purposes of this Act, the residence of a consumer is the address given by him as his residence in a writing signed by him in

connection with a consumer credit transaction until he notifies the creditor of a different address as his residence, and is then the different address.

(7) Notwithstanding other provisions of this section:

(a) except as provided in subsection (3), this Act does not apply if the consumer is not a resident of this State at the time of a consumer credit transaction and the parties have agreed that the law of his residence applies; and

(b) this Act applies if the consumer is a resident of this State at the time of a consumer credit transaction and the parties have agreed that the law of his residence applies.

(8) Each of the following agreements or provisions of an agreement by a consumer who is a resident of this State at the time of a consumer credit transaction is invalid with respect to the transaction:

(a) that the law of another jurisdiction apply;

(b) that the consumer consents to be subject to the process of another jurisdiction;

(c) that the consumer appoints an agent to receive service of process;

(d) that fixes venue; and

(e) that the consumer consents to the jurisdiction of the court that does not otherwise have jurisdiction.

(9) The following provisions of this Act specify the applicable law governing certain cases:

(a) applicability (Section 6.102) of the Part on Powers and Functions of Administrator (Part 1) of the Article on Administration (Article 6); and

(b) applicability (Section 6.201) of the Part on Notification and Fees (Part 2) of the Article on Administration (Article 6).

Comment

1. This section enables the enacting State to apply this Act for the protection of its own consumer residents in multi-state transactions to the extent consistent with the need for workable operating procedures on the part of creditors. The territorial applicability of the Act varies with the kind of protection safeguard involved. The major substantive protective provisions in this Act are those on rate ceilings (Parts 2 and 4 of Article 2), disclosure (Part 2 of Article 3), limitations on agreements and practices (Part 3 of Article 3), home solicitation sales (Part 5 of Article 3), limitations on consumers' liabilities (Part 4 of Article 3), and limitations on creditors' remedies (Part 1 of Article 5). Except for the disclosure provisions, this section allows the enacting State to apply all of these protective provisions to its own consumer residents when enforcement actions are brought against them in the enacting State.

. . .

2. Subsection (1) serves as a general residual provision governing those matters not specifically treated elsewhere in the section and controls the applicability of the disclosure provisions. Under this subsection the creditor has a measure of

control over the applicability of the Act with respect to the disclosure requirements and can arrange his interstate operations in a manner which minimizes the operational difficulties arising from the variations in the disclosure requirements of the different state laws. This flexibility on the part of creditors with respect to the applicability of the disclosure provisions offers no threat to consumers because the Federal Consumer Credit Protection Act [15 U.S.C. § 1601 et seq.] assures consumers that disclosure requirements will be substantially similar in all states.

3. Creditors falling within the supervised lender category (Part 3 of Article 2) need be licensed only in the State where the loan is entered into, that is, where the debtor's writing is received [Subsection (1)]. However, in the case of a mail order loan to a consumer residing in an enacting State, even if the debtor's writing is received by the creditor in another State, the creditor may not exceed the rate ceilings of the enacting State and the Administrator may go into the creditor's State and investigate potential violations pursuant to Part 1 of Article 6 [Subsection (2)]. Of course, the general rule of subsection (1) that a transaction is entered into in the State where the consumer's writing is received yields whenever the creditor attempts to evade the Act by engaging in face-to-face solicitation in the State of the consumer's residence but contrives to have the consumer's writing sent the creditor in another State [Subsection (1)(a)].

. . .

§ 1.202   [Exclusions]

This Act does not apply to:

(1) extensions of credit to organizations;

(2) except as otherwise provided in the Article on Insurance (Article 4), the sale of insurance if the insured is not obligated to pay instalments of the premium and the insurance may terminate or be cancelled after non-payment of an instalment of the premium;

(3) transactions under public utility or common carrier tariffs if a subdivision or agency of this State or of the United States regulates the charges for the services involved, the charges for delayed payment, and any discount allowed for early payment;

(4) transactions in securities or commodities accounts with a broker-dealer registered with the Securities and Exchange Commission; [or]

(5) except with respect to the provisions on compliance with the Federal Truth in Lending Act (Section 3.201), [civil liability for violation of disclosure provisions (Section 5.203), criminal penalties for disclosure violations (Section 5.302)], and powers and functions of the Administrator with respect to disclosure violations (Part 1 of Article 6), pawnbrokers who are licensed and whose rates and charges are regulated under or pursuant to ordinances or other statutes[; or

(6) ceilings on rates or limits on loan maturities of credit extended by a credit union organized under the laws of this State or of the United States if these ceilings or limits are established by these laws or by applicable regulations].

PART 3. DEFINITIONS

§ 1.301 [General Definitions]

(1) "Actuarial method" means the method of allocating payments made on a debt between the amount financed and the finance charge pursuant to which a payment is applied first to the accumulated finance charge and any remainder is subtracted from, or any deficiency is added to, the unpaid balance of the amount financed. The Administrator may adopt rules not inconsistent with the Federal Truth in Lending Act further defining the term and prescribing its application.

(2) "Administrator" means the Administrator designated in the Article (Article 6) on Administration (Section 6.103).

(3) "Agreement" means the bargain of the parties in fact as found in their language or by implication from other circumstances including course of dealing, usage of trade, or course of performance.

(4) "Agricultural purpose" means a purpose relating to the production, harvest, exhibition, marketing, transportation, processing, or manufacture of agricultural products by a natural person who cultivates, plants, propagates, or nurtures the agricultural products. "Agricultural products" includes agricultural, horticultural, viticultural, and dairy products, livestock, wildlife, poultry, bees, forest products, fish and shellfish, and products thereof, including processed and manufactured products, and products raised or produced on farms and processed or manufactured products thereof.

(5) "Amount financed" means the total of the following items:

(a) in the case of a sale, the cash price of the goods, services, or interest in land, less the amount of any down payment made in cash or in property traded in, and the amount actually paid or to be paid by the seller pursuant to an agreement with the buyer to discharge a security interest in, a lien on, or a debt with respect to property traded in;

(b) in case of a loan, the net amount paid to, receivable by, or paid or payable for the account of the debtor, plus the amount of any discount excluded from the finance charge (paragraph (b)(iii) of subsection (20)); and

(c) in the case of a sale or loan, to the extent that payment is deferred and the amount is not otherwise included and is authorized and disclosed to the consumer as required by law:

(i) amounts actually paid or to be paid by the creditor for registration, certificate of title, or license fees, and

(ii) permitted additional charges (Section 2.501).

(6) "Billing cycle" means the time interval between periodic billing statement dates.

(7) "Card issuer" means a person who issues a credit card.

(8) "Cardholder" means a person to whom a credit card is issued or who has agreed with the card issuer to pay obligations arising from the issuance to or use of the card by another person.

(9) "Cash price" of goods, services, or an interest in land means the price at which they are offered for sale by the seller to cash buyers in the ordinary course of business and may include (1) the cash price of accessories or services related to the sale, such as delivery, installation, alterations, modifications, and improvements, and (b) taxes to the extent imposed on a cash sale of the goods, services, or interest in land. The cash price stated by the seller to the buyer in a disclosure statement required by law is presumed to be the cash price.

(10) "Conspicuous":

A term or clause is "conspicuous" when it is so written that a reasonable person against whom it is to operate ought to have noticed it. Whether or not a term or clause is conspicuous is for decision by the court.

(11) "Consumer" means the buyer, lessee, or debtor to whom credit is granted in a consumer credit transaction.

(12) "Consumer credit sale":

(a) Except as provided in paragraph (b), "consumer credit sale" means a sale of goods, services, or an interest in land in which:

(i) credit is granted either pursuant to a seller credit card or by a seller who regularly engages as a seller in credit transactions of the same kind;

(ii) the buyer is a person other than an organization;

(iii) the goods, services, or interest in land are purchased primarily for a personal, family, household, or agricultural purpose;

(iv) the debt is payable in instalments or a finance charge is made; and

(v) with respect to a sale of goods or services, the amount financed does not exceed $25,000.

(b) A "consumer credit sale" does not include:

(i) a sale in which the seller allows the buyer to purchase goods or services pursuant to a lender credit card, or

(ii) unless the sale is made subject to this Act by agreement (Section 1.109), a sale of an interest in land if the finance charge does not exceed 12 per cent per year calculated according to the actuarial method on the assumption that the debt will be paid according to the agreed terms and will not be paid before the end of the agreed term.

(c) The amount of $25,000 in paragraph (a)(v) is subject to change pursuant to the provisions on adjustment of dollar amounts (Section 1.106).

(13) "Consumer credit transaction" means a consumer credit sale or consumer loan or a refinancing or consolidation thereof, or a consumer lease.

(14) "Consumer lease":

(a) "Consumer lease" means a lease of goods:

(i) which a lessor regularly engaged in the business of leasing makes to a person, except an organization, who takes under the lease primarily for a personal, family, household, or agricultural purpose;

(ii) in which the amount payable under the lease does not exceed $25,000;

(iii) which is for a term exceeding four months; and

(iv) which is not made pursuant to a lender credit card.

(b) The amount of $25,000 in paragraph (a)(ii) is subject to change pursuant to the provisions on adjustment of dollar amounts (Section 1.106).

(15) "Consumer loan":

(a) Except as provided in paragraph (b), "consumer loan" means a loan made by a creditor regularly engaged in the business of making loans in which:

(i) the debtor is a person other than an organization;

(ii) the debt is incurred primarily for a personal, family, household, or agricultural purpose;

(iii) the debt is payable in instalments or a finance charge is made; and

(iv) the amount financed does not exceed $25,000 or the debt, other than one incurred primarily for an agricultural purpose, is secured by an interest in land.

(b) A "consumer loan" does not include:

(i) a sale or lease in which the seller or lessor allows the buyer or lessee to purchase or lease pursuant to a seller credit card, or

(ii) unless the loan is made subject to this Act by agreement (Section 1.109), a loan secured by an interest in land if the security interest is bona fide and not for the purpose of circumvention or evasion of this Act and the finance charge does not exceed 12 per cent per year calculated according to the actuarial method on the assumption that the debt will be paid according to the agreed terms and will not be paid before the end of the agreed term.

(c) A loan that would be a consumer loan if the lender were regularly engaged in the business of making loans is a consumer loan if the loan is arranged for a commission or other compensation by a person regularly engaged in the business of arranging those loans and the lender is not regularly engaged in the business of making loans. The arranger is deemed to be the creditor making the loan.

(d) The amount of $25,000 in paragraph (a)(iv) is subject to change pursuant to the provisions on adjustment of dollar amounts (Section 1.106).

(16) "Credit" means the right granted by a creditor to a consumer to defer payment of debt, to incur debt and defer its payment, or to purchase property or services and defer payment therefor.

(17) "Credit card" means a card or device issued under an arrangement pursuant to which a card issuer gives to a cardholder the privilege of obtaining credit from the card issuer or other person in purchasing or leasing property or services, obtaining loans, or otherwise. A transaction is "pursuant to a credit card" only if credit is obtained according to the terms of the arrangement by transmitting information contained on the card or device orally, in writing, by mechanical or electronic methods, or in any other manner. A transaction is not "pursuant to a credit card" if the card or device is used solely in that transaction to:

(a) identify the cardholder or evidence his credit-worthiness and credit is not obtained according to the terms of the arrangement;

(b) obtain a guarantee of payment from the cardholder's deposit account, whether or not the payment results in a credit extension to the cardholder by the card issuer; or

(c) effect an immediate transfer of funds from the cardholder's deposit account by electronic or other means, whether or not the transfer results in a credit extension to the cardholder by the card issuer.

(18) "Creditor" means the person who grants credit in a consumer credit transaction or, except as otherwise provided, an assignee of a creditor's right to payment, but use of the term does not in itself impose on an assignee any obligation of his assignor. In case of credit granted pursuant to a credit card, "creditor" means the card issuer and not another person honoring the credit card.

(19) "Earnings" means compensation paid or payable by an employer to an employee or for his account for personal services rendered or to be rendered by him, whether denominated as wages, salary, commission, bonus, or otherwise, and includes periodic payments pursuant to a pension, retirement, or disability program.

(20) "Finance charge":

(a) Except as provided in paragraph (b), "finance charge" means the sum of all charges payable directly or indirectly by the consumer and imposed directly or indirectly by the creditor as an incident to or as a condition of the extension of credit, including any of the following types of charges which are applicable:

(i) interest or any amount payable under a point, discount, or other system of charges, however denominated;

(ii) time-price differential, credit service, service, carrying, or other charge, however denominated;

(iii) premium or other charge for any guarantee or insurance protecting the creditor against the consumer's default or other credit loss; and

(iv) charges incurred for investigating the collateral or creditworthiness of the consumer or for commissions or brokerage for obtaining the credit, irrespective of the person to whom the charges are paid or payable, unless the creditor had no notice of the charges when the credit was granted.

(b) The term does not include:

(i) charges as a result of default or delinquency if made for actual unanticipated late payment, delinquency, default, or other like occurrence, unless the parties agree that these charges are finance charges; a charge is not made for actual unanticipated late payment, delinquency, default or other like occurrence if imposed on an account that is or may be debited from time to time for purchases or other debts and, under its terms, payment in full or of a specified amount is required when billed, and in the ordinary course of business the consumer is permitted to continue to have purchases or other debts debited to the account after imposition of the charge;

(ii) additional charges (Section 2.501) or deferral charges (Section 2.503); or

(iii) a discount, if a creditor purchases or satisfies obligations of a cardholder pursuant to a credit card and the purchase or satisfaction is made at less than the face amount of the obligation.

(21) "Goods" includes goods not in existence at the time the transaction is entered into and merchandise certificates, but excludes money, chattel paper, documents of title, and instruments.

(22) "Insurance premium loan" means a consumer loan that (a) is made for the sole purpose of financing the payment by or on behalf of an insured of the premium on one or more policies or contracts issued by or on behalf of an insurer, (b) is secured by an assignment by the insured to the lender of the unearned premium on the policy or contract, and (c) contains an authorization to cancel the policy or contract financed.

(23) Except as otherwise provided, "lender" includes an assignee of a lender's right to payment, but use of the term does not in itself impose on an assignee any obligation of the lender.

(24) "Lender credit card" means a credit card issued by a supervised lender.

(25) "Loan":

(a) Except as provided in paragraph (b), "loan" includes:

(i) the creation of debt by the lender's payment of or agreement to pay money to the debtor or to a third person for the account of the debtor;

(ii) the creation of debt pursuant to a lender credit card in any manner, including a cash advance or the card issuer's honoring a draft or similar order for the payment of money drawn or accepted by the debtor, paying or agreeing to pay the debtor's obligation, or purchasing or otherwise acquiring the debtor's obligation from the obligee or his assignees;

(iii) the creation of debt by a cash advance to a debtor pursuant to a seller credit card;

(iv) the creation of debt by a credit to an account with the lender upon which the debtor is entitled to draw immediately; and

(v) the forbearance of debt arising from a loan.

(b) "Loan" does not include:

(i) a card issuer's payment or agreement to pay money to a third person for the account of a debtor if the debt of the debtor arises from a sale or lease and results from use of a seller credit card; or

(ii) the forbearance of debt arising from a sale or lease.

(26) "Merchandise certificate" means a writing not redeemable in cash and usable in its face amount in lieu of cash in exchange for goods or services.

(27) "Official fees" means:

(a) fees and charges prescribed by law which actually are or will be paid to public officials for determining the existence of or for perfecting, releasing, terminating, or satisfying a security interest related to a consumer credit transaction; or

(b) premiums payable for insurance in lieu of perfecting a security interest otherwise required by the creditor in connection with the transaction, if the premium does not exceed the fees and charges described in paragraph (a) which would otherwise be payable.

(28) "Open-end credit" means an arrangement pursuant to which:

(a) a creditor may permit a consumer, from time to time, to purchase or lease on credit from the creditor or pursuant to a credit card, or to obtain loans from the creditor or pursuant to a credit card;

(b) the amounts financed and the finance and other appropriate charges are debited to an account;

(c) the finance charge, if made, is computed on the account periodically; and

(d) either the consumer has the privilege of paying in full or in instalments or the creditor periodically imposes charges computed on the account for delaying payment and permits the consumer to continue to purchase or lease on credit.

(29) "Organization" means a corporation, government or governmental subdivision or agency, trust, estate, partnership, cooperative, or association.

(30) "Payable in instalments" means that payment is required or permitted by agreement to be made in more than four periodic payments, excluding a downpayment. If any periodic payment other than the downpayment under an agreement requiring or permitting two or more periodic payments is more than twice the amount of any other periodic payment, excluding a downpayment, a consumer credit transaction is "payable in instalments."

(31) "Person" includes a natural person or an individual, and an organization.

(32) "Person related to" with respect to an individual means (a) the spouse of the individual, (b) a brother, brother-in-law, sister, sister-in-law of the individual, (c) an ancestor or lineal descendant of the individual or his spouse, and (d) any other relative, by blood or marriage, of the individual or his spouse who shares the same home with the individual. "Person related to" with respect to an organization means (a) a person directly or indirectly controlling, controlled by, or under common control with the organization, (b) an officer or director of the organization or a person performing similar functions with respect to the organization or to a person related to the organization, (c) the spouse of a person related to the organization, and (d) a relative by blood or marriage of a person related to the organization who shares the same home with him.

(33) "Precomputed consumer credit transaction" means a consumer credit transaction, other than a consumer lease, in which the debt is a sum comprising the amount financed and the amount of the finance charge computed in advance. A disclosure required by the Federal Truth in Lending Act does not in itself make a finance charge or transaction precomputed.

(34) "Presumed" or "presumption" means that the trier of fact must find the existence of the fact presumed unless and until evidence is introduced which would support a finding of its non-existence.

(35) "Sale of goods" includes an agreement in the form of a bailment or lease of goods if the bailee or lessee pays or agrees to pay as compensation for use a sum substantially equivalent to or in excess of the aggregate value of the goods involved and it is agreed that the bailee or lessee will become, or for no other or a nominal consideration has the option to become, the owner of the goods upon full compliance with the terms of the agreement.

(36) "Sale of an interest in land" includes a lease in which the lessee has an option to purchase the interest and all or a substantial part of the rental or other payments previously made by him are applied to the purchase price.

(37) "Sale of services" means furnishing or agreeing to furnish services and includes making arrangements to have services furnished by another.

(38) "Seller" includes, except as otherwise provided, an assignee of the seller's right to payment, but use of the term does not in itself impose on an assignee any obligation of the seller.

(39) "Seller credit card" means either:

(a) a credit card issued primarily for the purpose of giving the cardholder the privilege of using the card to purchase or lease property or services from the card issuer, persons related to the card issuer, or persons licensed or franchised to do business under the card issuer's business or trade name or designation, or both from any of these persons and from other persons; or

(b) a credit card issued by a person except a supervised lender primarily for the purpose of giving the cardholder the privilege of using the credit card to purchase or lease property or services from at least 100 persons not related to the card issuer.

(40) "Services" includes (a) work, labor, and other personal services, (b) privileges with respect to transportation, hotel and restaurant accommodations, education, entertainment, recreation, physical culture, hospital accommodations, funerals, cemetery accommodations, and the like, and (c) insurance.

(41) "Supervised financial organization" means a person, except an insurance company or other organization primarily engaged in an insurance business:

(a) organized, chartered, or holding an authorization certificate under laws of this State or of the United States that authorizes the person to make loans and to receive deposits, including a savings, share, certificate or deposit account, and

(b) subject to supervision by an official or agency of this State or of the United States.

(42) "Supervised lender" means a person authorized to make or take assignments of supervised loans, under a license issued by the Administrator (Section 2.301) or as a supervised financial organization (subsection (41)).

(43) "Supervised loan" means a consumer loan, including a loan made pursuant to open-end credit, in which the rate of the finance charge, calculated according to the actuarial method, exceeds 18 per cent per year.

Comment

Subsection (1):

This subsection is derived from CCPA Section 107(a)(1)(A), 15 U.S.C. § 1606(a)(1)(A), and from Supplement I to Regulation Z(a). The intent is that with respect to the meaning and application of the defined term the Administrator will maintain by rule consistency between this Act and the Federal Truth in Lending Act.

The assumption underlying the actuarial method is that a periodic payment is applied first to the accumulated unpaid finance charge. If the payment exceeds the unpaid accumulated finance charge, the remainder of the payment is applied to reduce the unpaid balance of the amount financed.

To illustrate the application of this method assume that the amount financed on a four-month contract is $500, and that the finance charge is $12.56. Four monthly payments of $128.14 are contemplated. Thus the amount financed ($500) plus the finance charge ($12.56) equals the original unpaid balance ($512.56), which is divided into four equal monthly payments, the first payment being one month from date of contract. The application of the actuarial method is demonstrated below:

(A) Unpaid balance of amount financed		(B) Monthly rate	(C) Finance charge	(D) Amount financed	(E) Total monthly payment (C) + (D)]
			Application of payment		
500.00	×	1%	5.00	123.14	128.14
376.86	×	1%	3.77	124.37	128.14
252.49	×	1%	2.52	125.62	128.14
126.87	×	1%	1.27	126.87	128.14
			12.56	500.00	512.56

Rate disclosure involves finding that rate which will generate the stated finance charge when applied to the unpaid balances of the amount financed according to the actuarial method. A monthly rate of 1% produces a finance charge of $12.56, the difference between the sum of the monthly payments and the amount financed. The annual percentage rate would be twelve times the monthly rate, or 12%. In mathematical literature this is generally referred to as the nominal annual rate.

Note the application of the actuarial method. In the first month the first $5 (1% × $500) of the monthly payment of $128.14 is applied to the finance charge, leaving a balance of $123.14. This remainder is then applied to reduce the unpaid balance of the amount financed from $500 to $376.86. The same process is repeated in subsequent months.

. . .

Subsection (5):

The term "amount financed" means the amount of credit extended to the consumer and includes not only the net price in sales and the net amount advanced in loans but also other amounts such as official fees, insurance charges, and other additional charges (Section 2.501) to the extent that payment is deferred. An advance payment of finance charge or a required compensating balance is deducted from the "net amount paid" under paragraph (b) of this subsection. The term is a key definition in Parts 2 (maximum finance charges, sales) and 4 (maximum finance charges, loans) of Article 2 for it determines the amount on which the finance charge is imposed. This definition is in harmony with Regulation Z Sections 226.2(d), 226.4(b), and 226.8(c)(7) and (d)(1).

The reference in paragraph (b) to Section 1.301(20)(b)(iii) relates to the practice of credit card issuers of paying sellers honoring credit cards less than the face amount of the cardholder's obligation. Paragraph (b) makes clear that this discount is a part of the amount financed even though the amount of the discount is not paid to the seller for the cardholder's account. Since the seller absorbs the discount in the price of his product, the amount of the discount redounds to the cardholder's benefit and is properly included in the amount financed. That is, the cardholder would pay the same price for the product purchased whether he pays cash or uses a credit card. However, if the goods are sold at one price pursuant to credit cards and at a lower price for cash, then the lower price would be the cash price pursuant to Section 1.301(9) and the differential would be a finance charge pursuant to Section 1.301(20) and not part of the amount financed. The discount problem need only be specially treated when use of the credit card results in a loan, as in the case of lender credit cards (Section 1.301(25)(a)(ii)), for in the case of sales pursuant to seller credit cards (Section 1.301(12)(a)(i)) the cash price of the property or services sold includes the discount, if any, which is thereby included in the amount financed.

. . .

Subsection (14):

Leasing has become a popular alternative to credit sales as a means of distributing goods to consumers and merits inclusion in a comprehensive consumer credit code. The four month term requirement in paragraph (a)(iii) excludes from the Act the innumerable hourly, daily, or weekly rental or hire agreements typically involving automobiles, trailers, home repair tools, sick room equipment, and the like. If the transaction, though in form a lease, is in substance a sale within the meaning of Section 1.301(35), it is treated as a sale for all purposes in this Act and the provisions on consumer leases are inapplicable. The Act requires disclosure of the elements of the consumer lease transaction (Section 3.202); places limits on advertising respecting consumer leases (Section 3.209); contains a number of limitations on agreements and practices applicable to consumer leases (Part 3 of Article 3) and on the lessee's liability (Part 4 of Article 3, notably Section 3.401); regulates insurance provided in relation to consumer lease transactions (Article 4); makes provisions for remedies and penalties in consumer lease transactions (Article 5); and gives the Administrator powers over consumer lease transactions (Article 6). Since a finance charge is not made in the usual consumer lease transaction, the rate ceiling provisions of the Act (Article 2) are inapplicable.

Subsection (15):

. . .

With respect to this Act's treatment of real property transactions, the 12% cutoff was chosen as a convenient line of demarcation between two dissimilar transactions—the home mortgage and the high rate, "small loan" type of real estate loan. The exclusion of the home mortgage was made because the problems of home financing are sufficiently different to justify separate statutory treatment. On the other hand, the high rate second mortgage transaction has been a major source of consumer complaint and merits full coverage by this Act. Since the Truth in Lending Act applies to real estate credit without regard to the rate of finance charge, the provision on compliance with Truth in Lending (Section 3.201) applies to all consumer real estate transactions without regard to the rate of the finance charge.

. . .

Subsection (17):

The meaning of "credit card" and "pursuant to a credit card" are broadly defined to allow for continuing technological developments in this area. The term "credit card" is defined to encompass the varied arrangements under which creditors equip consumers with some form of "card or device" that enables them to obtain credit from the issuing creditor or others. A "credit card" may be conceived of in its broadest sense as a repository of information, and a transaction is "pursuant to a credit card" when credit is obtained in accordance with the arrangement under which the card was issued by the transmission of some information on the card. Hence, a cardholder who telephones an airline and buys a ticket by giving the agent his credit card number or a cardholder who communicates the requisite information to a seller by using a device which gives off an electronic impulse is each engaging in a transaction "pursuant to a credit card" so long as they are acting within the terms of the arrangement. However, a creditor who himself extends credit to a consumer relying on the consumer's credit card issued by another creditor merely as an identification or verification of credit-worthiness of the consumer has not extended credit "pursuant to a credit card."

Moreover, use of a credit card to obtain a guarantee of payment or to effect an immediate transfer from the cardholder's deposit account is not "pursuant to a credit card" whether or not the payment or transfer results in a credit extension to the cardholder by the card issuer.

. . .

Subsection (20):

This definition, together with the provisions on "additional charges" (Section 2.501), is substantially similar to the concept of finance charge embodied in Regulation Z Section 226.4. In general, charges "incident to or as a condition of the extension of credit" are finance charges, whatever the parties call them, if imposed by the creditor on the consumer, unless the charge is excluded by paragraph (b) as a default or delinquency charge, an additional or deferral charge, or a credit card discount.

True default or delinquency charges are not finance charges and are separately regulated by Section 2.502. The test prescribed by Regulation Z Section 226.4(c) and Interpretation 226.401 is adopted in paragraph (b)(i) for determining when a charge is a true default or delinquency charge. In some instances this will leave the question of the applicability of the Act to depend on the factual determination whether a given charge is (1) a true late charge, which would make the Act inapplicable if there is no provision either for payment in instalments or a finance charge, or (2) a finance charge, which would make the Act applicable even though there is no provision for payment in instalments (Section 1.301(12)(a)(iv)). An example is the case in which an oil company extends 30–day credit with no right to defer payment further and imposes a charge for late payment but does not require surrender of the credit card if full payment is not made by the consumer when billed. . . .

Subsection (25):

The distinction between loans and sales is basic to the applicability of the rate ceiling provisions (Parts 2 and 4 of Article 2), the licensing provisions (Part 3 of Article 2), provisions relating to credit cards (Section 1.301(24) "lender credit card" and (39) "seller credit card"), and other provisions of the Act. The traditional concept of a loan as an advance of money or a commitment to advance money is continued in paragraph (a)(i) and (iv). The development of the credit card has blurred somewhat accepted boundaries between loans and sales and has necessitated a clarification of the rules in this regard. See the discussion of this matter in Comment to Section 1.301(39) "seller credit card." Use of a lender credit card, whether for purchases or cash advances, results in a loan.

The arrangement for the card issuer's payment to the person honoring the credit card may take different forms. It does not matter under paragraph (a)(ii) whether the arrangement calls for the third party to be the payee of a draft drawn by the cardholder on the card issuer, for the card issuer to take an assignment of the debt from the third party, or for the card issuer merely to pay to the third party the discounted amount of the cardholder's obligation. Each of these methods is sufficiently similar in function to be treated alike by this section.

Under this Act forbearance of debt is characterized on the basis of the nature of the original debt. Thus forbearance of debt arising from sales or leases is not a loan transaction within this Act (paragraph (b)(ii)). Sellers and lessors can enter into refinancings to meet the needs of consumers without having these transactions classified as loans resulting in the applicability of the licensing provisions and other provisions of the Act designed to regulate lenders.

Occasionally seller credit card issuers may allow their cardholders to obtain nominal cash advances pursuant to their credit card. An example is an automobile rental company which extends to its cardholders as a convenience the privilege of obtaining cash advances up to $40 in emergency situations. This is a loan transaction under paragraph (a)(iii), and if the finance charge exceeds 18% (Section 2.401(1)) the licensing provisions of Part 3 of Article 2 apply.

. . .

Subsection (28):

The problem arises how the Act applies to a transaction in which a seller credit card issuer allows a cardholder to make purchases and add them to an account payable at a fixed time after billing with no right to defer payment further and with a charge imposed for late payment. If the charge imposed is a "true" late payment under Section 1.301(20)(b)(i), the transaction is not a consumer credit sale because there is neither a finance charge nor the privilege of paying in instalments (Section 1.301(12)(a)(iv)). The Act's only coverage of such a case is a limit on the amount of the late charge (Section 2.601(2)). If the late charge is in fact a finance charge under the test set out in Section 1.301(20)(b)(i), the transaction is a consumer credit sale and the Act applies fully. The last "or" clause in paragraph (d) directs that such a transaction be treated as open-end credit. A similar result is reached by Regulation Z Section 226.2(r) and Interpretation 226.401.

Subsection (30):

Two guiding principles in determining the scope of the Act are: (1) The Act should not apply to the myriad credit transactions in which no finance charge is made and no substantial period of credit extension is involved. The old-fashioned 30–day department store charge account is an example. (2) The Act should apply to credit extended over a substantial period of time even though the creditor does not separately state a finance charge. The transactions of the credit jeweler who "buries" his finance charge and sells his merchandise for the same price on a 12–month instalment contract as for cash is an example. The drafting technique by which these ends are attained is the definition of consumer credit sales (Section 1.301(12)(a)(iv)) and consumer loans (Section 1.301(15)(a)(iii)) as transactions in which either a finance charge is made or which are payable in instalments.…

Subsection (33):

A credit transaction is precomputed whether the finance charge is "added-on" to the amount financed or, as is common in loan situations, the "discount" method is used and the finance charge is deducted from the face amount of the credit at the time of the credit extension. In both transactions the debt is expressed as a sum comprising the amount financed and the amount of the finance charge. If a loan transaction involves a principal of $2,000 repayable in 12 monthly instalments at an interest rate of 10% on the declining balance, the transaction is not precomputed even though the creditor must for purposes of the Federal Truth in Lending Act disclose a sum including both the $2,000 and the amount of the finance charge the debtor would pay if each instalment were paid on time.

. . .

Subsection (39):

Seller credit cards are issued primarily for the purpose of enabling cardholders to purchase property or services. Paragraph (a) applies to cards issued by card issuers who are themselves involved in the selling process either as retailers or as distributors who license or franchise retailers. So long as the card is issued for the purpose of purchasing from the issuer, a person related to the issuer, or a licensee or franchisee of the issuer, the card falls within paragraph (a) even though it may also be honored by sellers having no relation to the card issuer. For example, an oil distributor may issue a card for the purpose of allowing cardholders to buy petroleum products from independently owned franchisees of the issuer; the card falls within paragraph (a) even though it may also be honored by hotels, motels, and other service stations unrelated to the card issuer.

Paragraph (b) covers credit cards issued for the purpose of enabling cardholders to purchase from sellers unrelated to the card issuer. "Travel and entertainment" credit cards are the stereotype. The requirement that the card be honored by at least 100 unrelated retailers is designed to assure that this kind of card will be issued for bona fide sales purposes by entities large enough to be visible to the Administrator and will not be used as a subterfuge for masking unlicensed loans.

Although lender credit cards (Section 1.301(24)) are also used for purchasing property or services, they are increasingly utilized for cash loans. By classifying the use of credit cards issued by banks and licensed lenders as creating loans (Section 1.301(25)(a)(ii)), whether the card was used for purchases or cash advanced, the Act recognizes that credit card transactions are but one of many ways in which banks and other financial institutions extend credit and that it is not operationally desirable to introduce regulatory distinctions that would force these institutions to treat sales and loans pursuant to credit cards differently for purposes of maximum charges and other provisions of the Act.

Subsection (40):

The retail instalment sales acts often excluded from the definition of services those furnished by members of professions—physicians, dentists, and the like. This Act makes no such exclusion, but the definition of consumer credit sale in Section 1.301(12) excludes the usual arrangement that professional men use in selling their services in that they usually do not enter into instalment contracts with their patients or clients and do not impose finance charges. However, this Act does apply to the so-called "credit dentist" who sells his services on instalment contract with or without provision for a finance charge.

.   .   .

ARTICLE 2. FINANCE CHARGES AND RELATED PROVISIONS

PART 1. GENERAL PROVISIONS

§ 2.102 [Scope]

Part 2 of this Article applies to consumer credit sales. Parts 3 and 4 apply to consumer loans, including loans made by supervised lenders. Part 5 applies to other charges and modifications with respect to consumer credit transactions. Part 6 applies to other credit transactions.

PART 2. CONSUMER CREDIT SALES: MAXIMUM FINANCE CHARGES

§ 2.201 [Finance Charge for Consumer Credit Sales Not Pursuant to Open–End Credit]

(1) With respect to a consumer credit sale, except a sale pursuant to open-end credit, a creditor may contract for and receive a finance charge not exceeding that permitted in this section.

(2) The finance charge, calculated according to the actuarial method, may not exceed the equivalent of the greater of either of the following:

(a) the total of:

(i) 36 per cent per year on that part of the unpaid balances of the amount financed which is $300 or less;

(ii) 21 per cent per year on that part of the unpaid balances of the amount financed which exceeds $300 but does not exceed $1,000; and

(iii) 15 per cent per year on that part of the unpaid balances of the amount financed which exceeds $1,000; or

(b) 18 per cent per year on the unpaid balances of the amount financed.

(3) This section does not limit or restrict the manner of calculating the finance charge whether by way of add-on, discount, single annual percentage rate, or otherwise, so long as the rate of the finance charge does not exceed that permitted by this section. The finance charge may be contracted for and earned at the single annual percentage rate that would earn the same finance charge as the graduated rates when the debt is paid according to the agreed terms and the calculations are made according to the actuarial method. If the sale is a precomputed consumer credit transaction:

(a) the finance charge may be calculated on the assumption that all scheduled payments will be made when due, and

(b) the effect of prepayment is governed by the provisions on rebate upon prepayment (Section 2.510).

(4) For purposes of this section, the term of a sale agreement commences with the date the credit is granted or, if goods are delivered or services performed ten days or more after that date, with the date of commencement of delivery or performance. Any month may be counted as $\frac{1}{12}$th of a year, but a day is counted as $\frac{1}{365}$th of a year. Subject to classifications and differentiations the seller may reasonably establish, a part of a month in excess of 15 days may be treated as a full month if periods of 15 days or less are disregarded and that procedure is not consistently used to obtain a greater yield than would otherwise be permitted. The Administrator may adopt rules not inconsistent with the Federal Truth in Lending Act with respect to treating as regular other minor irregularities in amount or time.

(5) Subject to classifications and differentiations the seller may reasonably establish, he may make the same finance charge on all amounts financed within a specified range. A finance charge so made does not violate subsection (2) if:

(a) when applied to the median amount within each range, it does not exceed the maximum permitted by subsection (2), and

(b) when applied to the lowest amount within each range, it does not produce a rate of finance charge exceeding the rate calculated according to paragraph (a) by more than eight per cent of the rate calculated according to paragraph (a).

(6) Notwithstanding subsection (2), the seller may contract for and receive a minimum finance charge of not more than $5 when the amount financed does not exceed $75, or $7.50 when the amount financed exceeds $75.

(7) The amounts of $300 and $1,000 in subsection (2) are subject to change pursuant to the provisions on adjustment of dollar amounts (Section 1.106).

Comment

1. Purpose of rate ceilings provisions. The purpose of this section and subsection (2) of Section 2.401 (Finance Charge for Consumer Loans) is to set ceilings and not to fix rates. Even under present statutes, considerable rate competition exists. The intent of this Act is to provide even more effective competition. Therefore, while this section sets rate ceilings, several sections are designed to generate sufficient competition to set rates. In addition, other provisions have been omitted by design, because they would have tended to restrict competition. Other provisions related to this section include:

(1) Disclosure of the finance charge both in dollar amounts and as annual percentages, as required by the Federal Truth in Lending Act and Section 3.201, is designed to facilitate comparative shopping. This is the most effective means of limiting prices. For most goods and services offered for sale in competitive markets, disclosure of the price generally has been deemed sufficient to regulate prices.

(2) The absence of special rate ceilings according to the type of credit grantors, type of item financed, or the form of credit extension is by design. Segmentation of the market for credit by differentiated rate ceilings tends to reduce competition and introduce rigidities into the market that benefit a few suppliers at the expense of others and work to the disadvantage of consumers.

(3) Greater freedom of entry to the credit field is fostered by several provisions, as well as by several deliberate omissions. Open–end credit may be offered both in connection with consumer credit sales, consumer loans, and supervised loans. No type of credit grantor is limited by this Act in the amount of credit that may be extended. By design the license required to make supervised loans is made readily accessible to those showing financial responsibility, character, and fitness. Provisions for minimum financial assets and for a showing of convenience and advantage have been deliberately omitted, since their inclusion would tend to restrict competition and require establishment of rates, rather than ceilings.

Because of the different cost structures that will be developed as a result of this Act, comparison of these rate ceilings cannot be made to existing rate ceilings. In this respect, the rate ceilings in this section are intimately related to other parts of the Act which provide for limitations on agreements and practices (Article 3, Part 3), limitations on creditors' remedies (Article 5, Part 1), limitations on consumers' liabilities (Article 3, Part 4), and consumers' remedies (Article 5, Part 2). These provisions will tend to raise operating costs of credit grantors above current levels. Other things being equal, these provisions would require higher rate ceilings than now exist to assure the same availability of credit to consumers. If they were not provided, the least credit-worthy consumers now in the market would be relegated to the illegal market.

The rate ceiling declines with the amount of credit granted by design. There are substantial fixed costs in granting consumer instalment credit. Up to a point the relative amount of fixed costs declines as the amount of credit granted increases. The present rate structure is designed not to restrict the amount of credit granted in any size category. Consequently, any changes in the rate ceilings provided would require a complete re-evaluation of the gradation in the rate structure, as well as of the other provisions of this Act which are closely related in an economic sense to rate ceilings.

2. Explanation of operation of rate ceilings. This explanation of maximum rates applies equally to finance charges made under Section 2.201 (finance charge for consumer credit sales not pursuant to open-end credit) and under subsection (2) of Section 2.401 (finance charge for consumer loans).

(1) Other than precomputed transactions: With respect to other than precomputed transactions the graduated rates permitted are calculated on unpaid principal balances. For example, Table A below illustrates the calculation of the monthly finance charge at the graduated rates on unpaid principal balances of various dollar amounts up to $1,500.

(2) Precomputed transactions: With respect to precomputed transactions, the graduated rates permitted are calculated on the periodic declining unpaid balances. The provisions for graduated rates should not be construed as requiring simultaneous liquidation of different portions of the original unpaid balance. Thus, the 21% annual rate permitted on unpaid balances exceeding $300, but not exceeding $1,000 does not apply to the initial unpaid balance in that range for the scheduled maturity of the transaction, but only to the extent that periodic declining unpaid balances fall within the range from $300.01 to $1,000.

The operation of this principle with respect to a precomputed transaction involving a $1,500 principal amount to be repaid in twelve months is illustrated in Table A below. The table shows the total dollar charge, the monthly payments and the charge earned each month when the rates stated in Sections 2.201 and 2.401(2) are computed on the unpaid balance as of each scheduled payment date and each payment is applied first to the earned charge and then to principal. It also shows the unpaid balances which result from applying the rates stated in Sections 2.201 and 2.401(2) and the parts of each unpaid balance to which each rate applies each month. The total dollar charge so computed is $211.71, but three cents is waived rather than increase the final payment.

3. Explanation of subsection (5). With respect to Sections 2.201(5) and 2.401(5), the variation permitted is limited to 8% of the rate of the finance charge and does not permit an eight percentage point variation. For example, if a credit grantor were to levy an annual add-on finance charge of $10 per $100 of initial unpaid balance, under the provisions of this section he could establish the following maximum range for one-year contracts:

Amount Financed	Finance Charge
$92.45–$107.55	$10.00

The median amount financed is $100; that is, this amount is $7.55 from both the upper and lower limits of the specified range. Alternatively, it is just halfway between $92.45 and $107.55.

The specified range is limited by the 8% requirement. On one-year contracts the add-on finance charge results in an actuarial rate of 17.972%. Sections 2.201(5)(b) and 2.401(5)(b) specify that the yield on the lowest amount within the range may not be more than 8% higher than the yield provided on the median amount. Thus the yield on the lowest amount may not exceed 19.40% [17.972 + (.08 × 17.972) = 19.4098]. It follows that the lower amount must be such that the $10 credit service charge produces an annual rate not in excess of 19.40%. Interpolation from annuity tables shows that the lower amount must be about $92.45. Since the median is halfway between the upper and lower limits, the upper amount must be $107.55. These are close approximations; in actual practice precise limits can be determined.

To gain the convenience of using a single dollar amount of finance charge for a specified range of amounts financed the credit grantor must undercharge for amounts financed above the median. Thus the $10 finance charge is about $0.76 less than the $10.76 finance charge that could have been received by precise application of an add-on rate of $10 per $100 per annum on the initial unpaid balance. These results are summarized below for one-year monthly instalment contracts.

(A)	(B)	(C)	(D)	(E)
	Actual	Accurate	Dollar	Annual
Amount	finance	finance	difference	percentage
financed	charge	charge	(C) − (B)	rate
$107.55	$10.00	$10.755	− $0.755	16.74%
$100.00	$10.00	$10.00	0.00	17.97%
$ 92.45	$10.00	$ 9.245	+ $0.755	19.40%

The 8% variation is derived from Regulation Z Section 226.5(c).

TABLE A

Amortization Schedule for $1,500 to be paid in 12 equal and consecutive monthly instalments of Principal Amount and Finance Charge combined with the charge computed at maximum graduated rates authorized by Sections 2.201 and 2.401(2)—36% per year on that part of the unpaid balances not exceeding $300, plus 21% per year on that part of the unpaid balances exceeding $300 but not exceeding $1,000, plus 15% per year on that part of the unpaid balances exceeding $1,000, yields $211.68.

	Unpaid principal Balances Outstanding during Month				Application of $142.64 Monthly Payments	
Mo.	36%	21%	15%	Total	Charges	Principal
1	$300.00	$700.00	$500.00	$1500.00	$27.50	$115.14
2	300.00	700.00	384.86	1384.86	26.06	116.58
3	300.00	700.00	268.28	1268.28	24.60	118.04
4	300.00	700.00	150.24	1150.24	23.13	119.51
5	300.00	700.00	30.73	1030.73	21.63*	121.01
6	300.00	609.72	....	909.72	19.67	122.97
7	300.00	486.75	....	786.75	17.52	125.12
8	300.00	361.63	....	661.63	15.33	127.31
9	300.00	234.32	....	534.32	13.10	129.54
10	300.00	104.78	....	404.78	10.83	131.81
11	272.97	....		272.97	8.19	134.45
12	138.52	....	....	138.52	4.12**	138.52
	TOTALS				$211.68	$1500.00

*Finance Charge rates are applied to parts of Unpaid Principal Balances scheduled to be outstanding. For example, the Finance Charge on $1030.73 is computed as follows:

$$\frac{1}{12} \times 36\% \text{ on} \quad \$300.00 = \$\ 9.00$$
$$\frac{1}{12} \times 21\% \text{ on} \quad 700.00 = 12.25$$
$$\frac{1}{12} \times 15\% \text{ on} \quad \underline{\ \ 30.73} = \underline{\ \ \ .38}$$
$$\$1030.73 \quad \$21.63$$

**The charge earned the last month is $4.15, but three cents is waived and applied to principal to make the final payment equal to the others.

For purposes of disclosure under the Truth in Lending Act the credit grantor must determine the single annual percentage rate, which, when applied according to the actuarial method, earns the same dollar amount of finance charge that is produced by the graduated rates. Table B shows that an annual rate of 25.10% applied monthly to the periodic declining unpaid balances produces the same total dollar charge of $211.68 calculated by application of graduated rates in Table A.

TABLE B

Amortization Schedule for $1500 to be paid in 12 equal and consecutive monthly instalments of Principal Amount and Finance Charge combined showing that the Single Annual Percentage Rate of 25.10% computed by the Actuarial Method yields $211.68.

1067

	Unpaid Principal	Application of $142.64 Monthly Payments	
Mo.	Balances	Charges	Principal
1	$1500.00	$ 31.38	$ 111.26
2	1388.74	29.05	113.59
3	1275.15	26.67	115.97
4	1159.18	24.25	118.39
5	1040.79	21.77	120.87
6	919.92	19.24	123.40
7	796.52	16.66	125.98
8	670.54	14.03	128.61
9	541.93	11.34	131.30
10	410.63	8.59	134.05
11	276.58	5.79	136.85
12	139.73	2.91*	139.73
	TOTALS	$211.68	$1500.00

* The charge earned the last month is $2.92 but 1 cent is waived and applied to principal to make the final payment equal to the others.

This Act is intended to give creditors the following choice in making their charges under Sections 2.201 and 2.401(2).

(1) The contract may be precomputed to include the dollar finance charge for payment according to schedule. In the example shown, the dollar finance charge of $211.68 would be added to the original unpaid principal, making a total of $1,711.68 to be repaid in twelve monthly instalments of $142.64.

A precomputed transaction is subject to delinquency charges pursuant to Section 2.502 or deferral charges pursuant to Section 2.503 in case of delinquency or deferral and to rebate for prepayment pursuant to Section 2.510 in case of prepayment in full.

(2) The contract need not be precomputed, but may provide for: (a) the addition of finance charges, computed on unpaid balances of the principal amount, at the rates specified in Sections 2.201 and 2.401(2); in this case there is no rebate for prepayment in full because charges are collected only as earned, and there are no separate charges for default or deferment; or (b) not more than the maximum single annual percentage rate computed on actual unpaid balances for the actual time outstanding. The single annual percentage is the rate which yields the charge for payment according to schedule when the rate is computed according to the actuarial method. In the example, the rate is 25.10%. In this case there is no rebate for prepayment in full because the charges are collected only as earned, and there are no separate charges for default or deferment.

4. Explanation of Section 2.201(6). Subsection (6) of this section permits minimum charges equal to finance charges for which the CCPA (15 U.S.C. § 1601 et seq.) requires no annual percentage rate disclosure. The CCPA does not set limits on the amounts of minimum charges, but does require annual percentage rate disclosure when the minimum charges exceed those permitted by subsection (6). Subsection (6) also sets limits on the amounts of minimum charges.

5. Operation of 18% APR finance charge ceiling. According to tables furnished by Financial Publishing Company, the 18% APR finance charge ceiling rate on unpaid balances of the amount financed permitted by subsection (2)(b) yields a greater finance charge than the sliding scale ceiling rates of 36%, 21% and 15% when applied to unpaid balances of the amount financed on amounts equal to or exceeding the following for the respective following number of equal monthly instalments (the corresponding Total of Payments, Finance Charge and amount of equal monthly instalments is set out below):

No. of Monthly Instalments	Unpaid Balance of Amount to be Financed	Total of Payments	Finance Charge	Amount of Monthly Instalments
3	$5,190.00	$5,346.51	$156.51	$1,782.17
6	5,853.00	6,164.16	311.16	1,027.36
9	5,953.00	6,408.45	455.45	712.15
12	6,016.00	6,618.72	602.72	551.56
15	6,011.00	6,757.50	746.50	450.50
18	5,985.00	6,874.02	889.02	381.89
24	5,906.00	7,076.64	1170.64	294.86
30	5,800.00	7,245.60	1445.60	241.52
36	5,695.00	7,412.40	1717.40	205.90
42	5,594.00	7,581.00	1987.00	180.50
48	5,491.00	7,742.88	2251.88	161.31
54	5,393.00	7,907.76	2514.76	146.44
60	5,301.00	8,077.20	2776.20	134.62
66	5,209.00	8,242.74	3033.74	124.89
72	5,121.00	8,410.32	3289.32	116.81
78	5,041.00	8,587.02	3546.02	110.09
84	4,958.00	8,754.48	3796.48	104.22
90	4,882.00	8,929.80	4047.80	99.22
96	4,810.00	9,108.48	4298.48	94.88
102	4,741.00	9,289.14	4548.14	91.07
108	4,676.00	9,473.76	4797.76	87.72
114	4,615.00	9,662.64	5047.64	84.76
120	4,554.00	9,848.40	5294.40	82.07

§ 2.202 [Finance Charge for Consumer Credit Sales Pursuant to Open–End Credit]

(1) With respect to a consumer credit sale pursuant to open-end credit, a creditor may contract for and receive a finance charge not exceeding that permitted in this section.

(2) For each billing cycle a finance charge may be made which is a percentage of an amount not exceeding the greatest of:

(a) the average daily balance of the open-end account in the billing cycle for which the charge is made, which is the sum of the amount unpaid each day during that cycle, divided by the number of days in that cycle; the amount unpaid on a day is determined by adding to any balance unpaid as of the beginning of that day all purchases and other debits and deducting all payments and other credits made or received as of that day;

(b) the balance of the open-end account at the beginning of the first day of the billing cycle [after deducting all payments and credits made in the cycle except credits attributable to purchases charged to the account during the cycle]; or

(c) the median amount within a specified range including the balance of the open-end account not exceeding that permitted by paragraph (a) or (b); a finance charge may be made pursuant to this paragraph only if the creditor, subject to classifications and differentiations he may reasonably establish, makes the same charge on all balances within the specified range and if the percentage when applied to the median amount within the range does not produce a charge exceeding the charge resulting from applying that percentage to the lowest amount within the range by more than eight per cent of the charge on the median amount.

(3) If the billing cycle is monthly, the finance charge may not exceed an amount equal to two per cent of that part of the maximum amount pursuant to subsection (2) which is $500 or less and one and one-half per cent of that part of the maximum amount which is more than $500. If the billing cycle is not monthly, the maximum charge for the billing cycle shall bear the same relation to the applicable monthly maximum charge as the number of days in the billing cycle bears to 365 divided by 12. A billing cycle is monthly if the closing date of the cycle is the same date each month or does not vary by more than four days from the regular date. Without regard to the length of the billing cycle, the finance charge may be computed at a daily rate that does not exceed $\frac{1}{365}$ths of 12 times the monthly charge permitted by this section for a billing cycle that is monthly.

(4) If the finance charge determined pursuant to subsection (3) is less than 50 cents, a finance charge may be made which does not exceed 50 cents if the billing cycle is monthly or longer, or the pro rata part of 50 cents which bears the same relation to 50 cents as the number of days in the billing cycle bears to 365 divided by 12 if the billing cycle is shorter than monthly.

(5) The amounts of $500 in subsection (3) are subject to change pursuant to the provisions on adjustment of dollar amounts (Section 1.106).

Comment

1. See Comment 1 to Section 2.201 for an explanation of the theory of rate regulation adopted by the Act.

2. Subsection (2) allows the creditor an option with respect to the balance on which the finance charge is imposed. The Federal Truth in Lending Act requires the creditor to disclose the method of determining the balance on which the finance charge is imposed (Regulation Z Section 226.7(a)(2) and (b)(8)). The average daily balance method authorized by paragraph (a) of subsection (2) is that commonly utilized by creditors employing electronic data processing equipment. Paragraph (b) of subsection (2), read with the bracketed material included, states the adjusted balance method under which the balance at the beginning of the cycle is reduced by all payments and credits during the cycle. Although under this method the balance is adjusted downward by payments and credits during the cycle, it is not adjusted upward by new purchases made within the cycle. The except clause is necessary to prevent the beginning balance from being reduced by returns of merchandise attributable to purchases made within the cycle the amounts of which had not been included in that balance. Paragraph (b) of subsection (2), read without the bracketed material, states the previous or beginning balance method under which the opening balance is neither decreased by payments or credits during the billing cycle nor increased by new purchases made during that period. Either the previous

balance or the adjusted balance method is usable by a creditor with a manual system of entries. The brackets in paragraph (b) of subsection (2) acknowledge the as yet unresolved controversy in the Congress and the state legislatures about the comparative merit of the previous and adjusted balance methods.

. . .

PART 3.   CONSUMER LOANS: SUPERVISED LENDERS

§ 2.301   [Authority to Make Supervised Loans]

Unless a person is a supervised financial organization or has obtained a license from the Administrator authorizing him so to do, he may not engage in the business of:

(1) making supervised loans, or

(2) taking assignments of and undertaking direct collection of payments from or enforcement of rights against consumers arising from supervised loans, but he may collect and enforce for three months without a license if he promptly applies for a license and his application has not been denied.

§ 2.302   [License to Make Supervised Loans]

(1) The Administrator shall receive and act on all applications for licenses to make supervised loans under this Act. Applications shall be in the form and filed in the manner prescribed by the Administrator and contain or be accompanied by the information the Administrator requires by rule.

(2) The Administrator may not issue a license unless upon investigation he finds that the financial responsibility, character, and fitness of the applicant, and of the members thereof if the applicant is a partnership or association or of the officers and directors thereof if the applicant is a corporation, warrant belief that the business will be operated honestly and fairly within the purposes of this Act. In determining the financial responsibility of an applicant proposing to engage in making insurance premium loans, the Administrator shall consider the liabilities the lender may incur for erroneous cancellation of insurance.

(3) Upon written request, the applicant is entitled to a hearing on the question of his qualifications for a license if (a) the Administrator notifies the applicant in writing that his application has been denied, or (b) the Administrator does not issue a license within 60 days after the application for the license was filed. A request for a hearing may not be made more than 15 days after the Administrator mails a writing to the applicant notifying him that the application has been denied and stating in substance the Administrator's findings supporting denial of the application.

(4) The Administrator shall issue additional licenses to the same licensee upon compliance with all the provisions of this Act governing issuance of a single license. A separate license is required for each place of

business. Each license remains in full force and effect until surrendered, suspended, or revoked.

(5) A licensee may not change the location of any place of business without giving the Administrator at least 15 days prior written notice.

(6) A licensee may conduct the business of making supervised loans only at or from a place of business for which he holds a license and only under the name in the license. Credit granted pursuant to a lender credit card does not violate this subsection.

Comment

1. This section is intimately related to the provisions on maximum finance charges (Parts 2 and 4 of Article 2) and disclosure (Part 2 of Article 3). A major objective of this Act is to facilitate entry into the cash loan field so that the resultant rate competition fostered by disclosure will generally force rates below the permitted maximum charges. To this end this section adopts a test of "financial responsibility, character and fitness" rather than the test of "convenience and advantage" often used in prior small loan laws. Competition is further encouraged by the absence of licensing requirements in consumer credit sales (Section 2.201) and in consumer loans not made by supervised lenders (subsection (1) of Section 2.401).

2. A secondary purpose is to reduce the likelihood of establishing localized monopolies in the granting of cash credit. Such monopolies tend to push rates charged to maximum permitted levels and to establish conditions under which some share of the anticipated monopoly profits are devoted to direct or indirect pressures to obtain the license.

. . .

§ 2.303   [Revocation or Suspension of License]

(1) The Administrator may issue to a person licensed to make supervised loans an order to show cause why his license with respect to one or more specific places of business should not be suspended for a period not in excess of six months or be revoked. The order shall set a place for a hearing and a time therefor that is no less than ten days from the date of the order. After the hearing the Administrator shall revoke or suspend the license or, if there are mitigating circumstances, may accept an assurance of discontinuance (Section 6.109) and allow retention of the license, if he finds that:

(a) the licensee has repeatedly and intentionally violated this Act or any rule or order lawfully made pursuant to this Act, or has violated an assurance of discontinuance; or

(b) facts or conditions exist which clearly would have justified the Administrator in refusing to grant a license for that place or those places of business were these facts or conditions known to exist at the time the application for the license was made.

(2) A revocation or suspension of a license is not lawful unless the Administrator, before instituting proceedings, gives notice to the licensee of

the facts or conduct which warrant the intended action, and the licensee is afforded an opportunity to show compliance with all lawful requirements for retention of the license.

(3) If the Administrator finds that probable cause for revocation of a license exists and that enforcement of this Act requires immediate suspension of the license pending investigation, he, after a hearing upon five days' written notice, may enter an order suspending the license for not more than 30 days.

(4) Whenever the Administrator revokes or suspends a license, he shall enter an order to that effect and forthwith notify the licensee of the revocation or suspension. Within five days after entry of the order he shall deliver to the licensee a copy of the order and the findings supporting the order.

(5) A person holding a license to make supervised loans may relinquish the license by notifying the Administrator in writing of its relinquishment, but the relinquishment does not affect his liability for acts previously committed.

(6) Revocation, suspension, or relinquishment of a license does not impair or affect the obligation of any preexisting lawful contract between the licensee and any consumer.

(7) The administrator may reinstate a license, terminate a suspension, or grant a new license to a person whose license has been revoked or suspended if no fact or condition then exists which clearly would have justified the Administrator in refusing to grant a license.

§ 2.307   [Restrictions on Interest in Land As Security]

(1) A lender may contract for an interest in land as security, except to secure a supervised loan in which the amount financed is $1,000 or less. A security interest taken in violation of this section is unenforceable to the extent of that loan.

(2) The amount of $1,000 in subsection (1) is subject to change pursuant to the provisions on adjustment of dollar amounts (Section 1.106).

§ 2.308   [Regular Schedule of Payments; Maximum Loan Term]

(1) Supervised loans, not made pursuant to open-end credit and in which the amount financed is $1,000 or less, shall be scheduled to be payable in substantially equal instalments at substantially equal periodic intervals except to the extent that the schedule of payments is adjusted to the seasonal or irregular income of the debtor, and

(a) over a period not exceeding 37 months if the amount financed exceeds $300, or

(b) over a period not exceeding 25 months if the amount financed is $300 or less.

(2) The amounts of $300 and $1,000 in subsection (1) are subject to change pursuant to the provisions on adjustment of dollar amounts (Section 1.106).

§ 2.309 [No Other Business for Purpose of Evasion]

A supervised lender may not carry on other business for the purpose of evasion or violation of this Act at a location where he makes supervised loans.

PART 4. CONSUMER LOANS: MAXIMUM FINANCE CHARGES

§ 2.401 [Finance Charge for Consumer Loans]

(1) With respect to a consumer loan, including a loan pursuant to open-end credit, a lender who is not a supervised lender may contract for and receive a finance charge, calculated according to the actuarial method, not exceeding 18 per cent per year. With respect to a consumer loan made pursuant to open-end credit, the finance charge shall be deemed not to exceed 18 per cent per year if the finance charge contracted for and received does not exceed a charge for each monthly billing cycle which is one and one-half per cent of the average daily balance of the open-end account in the billing cycle for which the charge is made. The average daily balance of the open-end account is the sum of the amount unpaid each day during that cycle divided by the number of days in the cycle. The amount unpaid on a day is determined by adding to any balance unpaid as of the beginning of that day all purchases, loans, and other debits and deducting all payments and other credits made or received as of that day. If the billing cycle is not monthly, the finance charge shall be deemed not to exceed 18 per cent per year if the finance charge contracted for and received does not exceed a percentage which bears the same relation to one and one-half per cent as the number of days in the billing cycle bears to 365 divided by 12. A billing cycle is monthly if the closing date of the cycle is the same date each month or does not vary by more than four days from the regular date.

(2) With respect to a consumer loan, including a loan pursuant to open-end credit, a supervised lender may contract for and receive a finance charge, calculated according to the actuarial method, not exceeding the equivalent of the greater of either of the following:

(a) the total of:

(i) 36 per cent per year on that part of the unpaid balances of the amount financed which is $300 or less;

(ii) 21 per cent per year on that part of the unpaid balances of the amount financed which exceeds $300 but does not exceed $1,000; and

(iii) 15 per cent per year on that part of the unpaid balances of the amount financed which exceeds $1,000; or

(b) 18 per cent per year on the unpaid balances of the amount financed.

(3) This section does not limit or restrict the manner of calculating the finance charge, whether by way of add-on, discount, single annual percentage rate, or otherwise, so long as the rate of the finance charge does not exceed that permitted by this section. The finance charge may be contracted for and earned at the single annual percentage rate that would earn the same finance charge as the graduated rates when the debt is paid according to the agreed terms and the calculations are made according to the actuarial method. If the loan is a precomputed consumer credit transaction:

(a) the finance charge may be calculated on the assumption that all scheduled payments will be made when due, and

(b) the effect of prepayment is governed by the provisions on rebate upon prepayment (Section 2.510).

(4) Except as provided in subsection (6), the term of a loan for purposes of this section commences on the day the loan is made. Any month may be counted as $\frac{1}{12}$th of a year, but a day is counted as $\frac{1}{365}$th of a year. Subject to classifications and differentiations the lender may reasonably establish, a part of a month in excess of 15 days may be treated as a full month if periods of 15 days or less are disregarded and that procedure is not consistently used to obtain a greater yield than would otherwise be permitted. The Administrator may adopt rules not inconsistent with the Federal Truth in Lending Act with respect to treating as regular other minor irregularities in amount or time.

(5) Subject to classifications and differentiations the lender may reasonably establish, he may make the same finance charge on all amounts financed within a specified range. A finance charge so made does not violate subsection (1) or (2) if:

(a) when applied to the median amount within each range, it does not exceed the maximum permitted by the applicable subsection, and

(b) when applied to the lowest amount within each range, it does not produce a rate of finance charge exceeding the rate calculated according to paragraph (a) by more than eight per cent of the rate calculated according to paragraph (a).

(6) With respect to an insurance premium loan, the term of the loan commences on the earliest inception date of a policy or contract of insurance payment of the premium on which is financed by the loan.

(7) The amounts of $300 and $1,000 in subsection (2) are subject to change pursuant to the provisions on adjustment of dollar amounts (Section 1.106).

Comment

1. For an extensive explanation of the purposes and operation of the rate ceilings provisions of this Act, see the Comment to Section 2.201. Subsection (1)

sets the ceilings for all consumer loans not made by supervised lenders at 18% per annum, and this ceiling applies to open-end credit as well as to closed-end credit. The operation of open-end credit is such that a creditor cannot know whether he is exceeding a rate ceiling stated in terms of a rate calculated according to the actuarial method unless he calculates the rate on daily balances. In "deeming" that 1½% per month on the average daily balance is the equivalent of 18% per year, this subsection allows the creditor to use a somewhat simplified method of calculation.

2. The ceilings for loans by supervised lenders in subsection (2) also apply to open-end credit. This enables supervised lenders to serve the needs of higher risk consumers by the use of credit cards and other open-end credit plans.

Lenders are not required to use a graduated rate, but may find it more economical to use a single annual rate provided that it does not exceed the rate ceiling specified. Lenders may not levy delinquency charges (Section 2.502) and deferral charges (Section 2.503) on open-end credit accounts. By the same token a debtor is not entitled to rebates upon prepayment with respect to open-end accounts since at the time of his prepayment there will be no unearned prepaid finance charges on the open-end account.

.   .   .

PART 5.   CONSUMER CREDIT TRANSACTIONS: OTHER CHARGES AND MODIFICATIONS

§ 2.501   [Additional Charges]

(1) In addition to the finance charge permitted by the parts of this Article on maximum finance charges for consumer credit sales and consumer loans (Parts 2 and 4), a creditor may contract for and receive the following additional charges:

(a) official fees and taxes;

(b) charges for insurance as described in subsection (2);

(c) annual charges, payable in advance, for the privilege of using a credit card which entitles the cardholder to purchase or lease goods or services from at least 100 persons not related to the card issuer, under an arrangement pursuant to which the debts resulting from the purchases or leases are payable to the card issuer;

(d) with respect to a debt secured by an interest in land, the following "closing costs," if they are bona fide, reasonable in amount, and not for the purpose of circumvention or evasion of this Act:

(i) fees or premiums for title examination, abstract of title, title insurance, surveys, or similar purposes,

(ii) fees for preparation of a deed, settlement statement, or other documents, if not paid to the creditor or a person related to the creditor,

(iii) escrows for future payments of taxes, including assessments for improvements, insurance, and water, sewer and land rents, and

(iv) fees for notarizing deeds and other documents, if not paid to the creditor or a person related to the creditor; and

(e) charges for other benefits, including insurance, conferred on the consumer, if the benefits are of value to him and if the charges are reasonable in relation to the benefits, are of a type that is not for credit, and are authorized as permissible additional charges by rule adopted by the Administrator.

(2) An additional charge may be made for insurance written in connection with the transaction:

(a) with respect to insurance against loss of or damage to property, or against liability arising out of the ownership or use of property, if the creditor furnishes a clear, conspicuous, and specific statement in writing to the consumer setting forth the cost of the insurance if obtained from or through the creditor and stating that the consumer may choose the person through whom the insurance is to be obtained;

(b) with respect to consumer credit insurance providing life, accident, or health coverage, if the insurance coverage is not required by the creditor and this fact is clearly and conspicuously disclosed in writing to the consumer, and if, in order to obtain the insurance in connection with the extension of credit, the consumer gives specific, dated, and separately signed affirmative written indication of his desire to do so after written disclosure to him of the cost thereof; and

(c) with respect to vendor's single interest insurance, but only (i) to the extent that the insurer has no right of subrogation against the consumer, and (ii) to the extent that the insurance does not duplicate the coverage of other insurance under which loss is payable to the creditor as his interest may appear, against loss of or damage to property for which a separate charge is made to the consumer pursuant to paragraph (a), and (iii) if a clear, conspicuous, and specific statement in writing is furnished by the creditor to the consumer setting forth the cost of the insurance if obtained from or through the creditor and stating that the consumer may choose the person through whom the insurance is to be obtained.

Comment

1. The two categories of charges a creditor is permitted to make at the inception of a credit extension are finance charges (Section 1.301(20)) and additional charges as enumerated in this section. In general, the charges designated as additional charges fall roughly into three classes: (1) those that would likely have been incurred had there been no credit extension (e.g., closing costs); (2) those closely related to the extension of credit but providing valuable subsidiary benefits to the consumer (e.g., the front-end credit card charge; life, accident, health, and property insurance); and (3) those ultimately payable to third parties with no portion of the charge returnable to the creditor by commission or otherwise (e.g., taxes; official fees for perfecting security interests). These classes are nonexclusive; for instance property insurance would sometimes fall within class (1) and closing costs fit into class (3) as well as in (1). Paragraph (e) of subsection (1)

provides the Administrator with the flexibility needed to allow him to deal with new kinds of charges as new credit transactions evolve.

2.   Though this section coincides with Regulation Z Section 226.4(a) in excluding premiums for insurance from the finance charge under certain stated conditions, it varies from Regulation Z Section 226.4(e) in that it does not include appraisal fees and credit report charges as additional charges.   Section 1.301(20)(a)(iv) expressly designates these charges as part of the finance charge. Another variation from Truth in Lending is the treatment of vendor's single interest insurance (V.S.I.).   Federal Reserve Interpretation 226.404 allows exclusion of the premium for V.S.I. insurance from the finance charge.   Paragraph (c) of subsection (2) adopts a more sophisticated test and allows the premium to be treated as an additional charge in limited situations in which the vendor's single interest coverage does not duplicate the coverage of other insurance under which loss is payable to the creditor as his interest may appear, against loss of or damage to property for which a separate charge is made to the consumer.   In this case, the charge is sufficiently beneficial to the consumer to justify classifying the premium as an additional charge.

§ 2.502   [Delinquency Charges]

(1) With respect to a precomputed consumer credit transaction, the parties may contract for a delinquency charge on any instalment not paid in full within ten days after its due date, as originally scheduled or as deferred, in an amount, not exceeding $5, which is not more than five per cent of the unpaid amount of the instalment.

(2) A delinquency charge under subsection (1) may be collected only once on an instalment however long it remains in default.   No delinquency charge may be collected with respect to a deferred instalment unless the instalment is not paid in full within ten days after its deferred due date.   A delinquency charge may be collected at the time it accrues or at any time thereafter.

(3) A delinquency charge under subsection (1) may not be collected on an instalment paid in full within ten days after its scheduled or deferred instalment due date even though an earlier maturing instalment or a delinquency or deferral charge on an earlier instalment has not been paid in full.   For purposes of this subsection a payment is deemed to have been applied first to any instalment due in the computational period (paragraph (a) of subsection (1) of Section 2.503) in which it is received and then to delinquent instalments and charges.

(4) If two instalments or parts thereof of a precomputed consumer loan are in default for ten days or more, the lender may elect to convert the loan from a precomputed loan to one in which the finance charge is based on unpaid balances.   In this event he shall make a rebate pursuant to the provisions on rebate upon prepayment (Section 2.510) as if the date of prepayment were one day before the maturity date of a delinquent instalment, and thereafter may make a finance charge as authorized by the provisions on finance charge for consumer loans by lenders not supervised lenders (subsection (1) of Section 2.401) or finance charge for consumer

loans by supervised lenders (subsection (2) of Section 2.401), whichever is appropriate. The amount of the rebate shall not be reduced by the amount of any permitted minimum charge (Section 2.510). If the creditor proceeds under this subsection, any delinquency or deferral charges made with respect to instalments due at or after the maturity date of the first delinquent instalment shall be rebated, and no further delinquency or deferral charges shall be made.

(5) The amount of $5 in subsection (1) is subject to change pursuant to the provisions on adjustment of dollar amounts (Section 1.106).

Comment

1. If a consumer is late in making a payment under a precomputed credit transaction, the creditor would receive no income for the period of delay unless a delinquency charge were permitted. The alternative of not permitting delinquency charges is rejected because the result would be to enforce a lower effective ceiling on finance charge rates for delinquent consumers than for consumers who pay promptly. Delinquency charges are inapplicable to open-end credit plans under which the finance charge continues to accumulate through any period of delay thus compensating the creditor for this period.

. . .

§ 2.503 [Deferral Charges]

(1) In this section and in the provisions on rebate upon prepayment (Section 2.510) the following defined terms apply with respect to a precomputed consumer credit transaction:

(a) "Computational period" means (i) the interval between scheduled due dates of instalments under the transaction if the intervals are substantially equal or, (ii) if the intervals are not substantially equal, one month if the smallest interval between the scheduled due dates of instalments under the transaction is one month or more, and, otherwise, one week.

(b) "Deferral" means a postponement of the scheduled due date of an instalment as originally scheduled or as previously deferred.

(c) "Deferral period" means a period in which no instalment is scheduled to be paid by reason of a deferral.

(d) The "interval" between specified dates means the interval between them including one or the other but not both of them; if the interval between the date of a transaction and the due date of the first scheduled instalment does not exceed one month by more than 15 days when the computational period is one month, or does not exceed 11 days when the computational period is one week, the interval may be considered by the creditor as one computational period.

(e) "Periodic balance" means the amount scheduled to be outstanding on the last day of a computational period before deducting the instalment, if any, scheduled to be paid on that day.

(f) "Standard deferral" means a deferral with respect to a transaction made as of the due date of an instalment as scheduled before the deferral by which the due dates of that instalment and all subsequent instalments as scheduled before the deferral are deferred for a period equal to the deferral period. A standard deferral may be for one or more full computational periods or a portion of one computational period or a combination of any of these.

(g) "Sum of the balances method," also known as the "Rule of 78," means a method employed with respect to a transaction to determine the portion of the finance charge attributable to a period of time before the scheduled due date of the final instalment of the transaction. The amount so attributable is determined by multiplying the finance charge by a fraction the numerator of which is the sum of the periodic balances included within the period and the denominator of which is the sum of all periodic balances under the transaction. According to the sum of the balances method the portion of the finance charge attributable to a specified computational period is the difference between the portions of the finance charge attributable to the periods of time including and excluding, respectively, the computational period, both determined according to the sum of the balances method.

(h) "Transaction" means a precomputed consumer credit transaction unless the context otherwise requires.

(2) Before or after default in payment of a scheduled instalment of a transaction, the parties to the transaction may agree in writing to a deferral of all or part of one or more unpaid instalments and the creditor may make at the time of deferral and receive at that time or at any time thereafter a deferral charge not exceeding that provided in this section.

(3) A standard deferral may be made with respect to a transaction as of the due date, as originally scheduled or as deferred pursuant to a standard deferral, of an instalment with respect to which no delinquency charge (Section 2.502) has been made or, if made, is deducted from the deferral charge computed according to this subsection. The deferral charge for a standard deferral may equal but not exceed the portion of the finance charge attributable to the computational period immediately preceding the due date of the earliest maturing instalment deferred as determined according to the sum of the balances method multiplied by the whole or fractional number of computational periods in the deferral period, counting each day as $\frac{1}{30}$th of a month without regard to differences in lengths of months when the computational period is one month or as $\frac{1}{7}$th of a week when the computation period is one week. A deferral charge computed according to this subsection is earned pro rata during the deferral period and is fully earned on the last day of the deferral period.

(4) With respect to a transaction as to which a creditor elects not to make and does not make a standard deferral or a deferral charge for a standard deferral, a deferral charge computed according to this subsection may be made as of the due date, as scheduled originally or as deferred pursuant to either subsection (3) or this subsection, of an instalment with respect to which no delinquency charge (Section 2.502) has been made or, if made, is deducted from the deferral charge computed according to this subsection. A deferral charge pursuant to this subsection may equal but not exceed the rate of finance charge required to be disclosed to the consumer pursuant to law applied to each amount deferred for the period for which it is deferred computed without regard to differences in lengths of months, but proportionately for a part of a month, counting each day as ⅟₃₀th of a month or as ⅟₇th of a week. A deferral charge computed according to this subsection is earned pro rata with respect to each amount deferred during the period for which it is deferred.

(5) In addition to the deferral charge permitted by this section, a creditor may make and receive appropriate additional charges (Section 2.501), and any amount of these charges which is not paid may be added to the deferral charge computed according to subsection (3) or to the amount deferred for the purpose of computing the deferral charge computed according to subsection (4).

(6) The parties may agree in writing at the time of a transaction that, if an instalment is not paid within ten days after its due date, the creditor may unilaterally grant a deferral and make charges as provided in this section. A deferral charge may not be made for a period after the date that the creditor elects to accelerate the maturity of the transaction.

Comment

1. The definitions in subsection (1) apply to Section 2.510 as well. See subsection (3) of Section 2.510.

2. These definitions and the other provisions of this section can be illustrated more readily than explained.

Assume the loan transaction specified in the example in Comment 2 to Section 2.201, and that the loan is made on July 1, 1974. It is then a "precomputed consumer credit transaction" (subsections (13) and (33) of Section 1.301), e.g., a "consumer loan" (subsection (15) of Section 1.301), of which the "amount financed" (subsection (5) of Section 1.301) is $1500, the "finance charge" (subsection (20) of Section 1.301) is $211.68, computed at an annual percentage rate of 25.10%, and the "total of payments" is $1711.68 and is payable in 12 equal monthly instalments of $142.64 each beginning on Aug. 1, 1974, and ending on July 1, 1975.

The "computational period" (paragraph (a) of subsection (1) of this section) is one month. The "periodic balances" (paragraph (e) of subsection (1) of this section) of, and other calculations applicable to, the transaction are:

Col. 1	Col. 2 Inst. Due Date & Last Day of Each	Col. 3	Col. 4	Col. 5	Col. 6
Inst. No.	Comptnl. Period	Periodic Balances	Col. 3 ÷ by $11,125.92	Sum of Periodic Balances	Col. 5 ÷ by $11,125.92
1	Aug. 1, 1974	$ 1,711.68	12/78	$ 1,711.68	12/78
2	Sept. 1, 1974	1,569.04	11/78	3,280.72	23/78
3	Oct. 1, 1974	1,426.40	10/78	4,507.12	33/78
4	Nov. 1, 1974	1,283.76	9/78	5,990.88	42/78
5	Dec. 1, 1974	1,141.12	8/78	7,132.00	50/78
6	Jan. 1, 1975	998.48	7/78	8,130.48	57/78
7	Feb. 1, 1975	855.84	6/78	8,986.32	63/78
8	Mar. 1, 1975	713.20	5/78	9,699.52	68/78
9	Apr. 1, 1975	570.56	4/78	10,270.08	72/78
10	May 1, 1975	427.92	3/78	10,698.00	75/78
11	June 1, 1975	285.28	2/78	10,983.28	77/78
12	July 1, 1975	142.64	1/78	11,125.92	78/78
78		$11,125.92	78/78		

Col. 4 sets forth the fraction of the finance charge earned in each computational period as computed according to the "sum of the balances method" (paragraph (g) of subsection (1) of this section).

Col. 6 sets forth the fraction of the finance charge earned at the end of each computational period, also computed according to the sum of the balances method.

It will be noted that the fractions in Col. 4 and Col. 6, respectively, express more simply the fractions:

$$\frac{\text{Periodic balance}}{\text{Sum of all periodic balances under the transaction}}$$
and
$$\frac{\text{Sum of all periodic balances including computational period}}{\text{Sum of all periodic balances under the transaction}}$$

According to the "sum of the balances method" (paragraph (g) of subsection (1) of this section) the portion of the finance charge attributable to a period of time prior to the scheduled due date of the final instalment of the transaction is determined by multiplying the finance charge by a fraction the numerator of which is the sum of the periodic balances included within the period and the denominator is the total of all periodic balances under the transaction. Accordingly, in the assumed example, the portions of the total finance charge of $211.68 attributable to the periods ending, respectively, on Jan. 1, 1975, and Feb. 1, 1975, are $57/78$ths and $63/78$ths. Moreover, according to the "sum of the balances method" (the last sentence of paragraph (g) of subsection (1) of this section), the portion of the finance charge attributable to a specified computational period is the difference between the portions of the finance charge attributable to the periods of time including and excluding, respectively, that computational period; accordingly, in the assumed example the portion of the finance charge of $211.68 attributable to the computational period ending on Feb. 1, 1975, is $6/78$ths (i.e., $63/78$ths minus $57/78$ths) of $211.68, or $16.28.

3. Assume, further, that the consumer has paid the first 6 instalments, and that the parties have agreed to the deferral of the 7th instalment of $142.64 originally scheduled to be payable on Feb. 1, 1975, by 6 months until Aug. 1, 1975, or its equivalent, a deferral of the 7th and each of the five subsequent instalments of $142.64 each by one month each so that the 12th instalment originally scheduled for July, 1975 is payable on Aug. 1, 1975. The deferral is then a "standard deferral" (paragraph (f) of subsection (1) of this section) and the maximum deferral charge under subsection (3) of this section is $16.28, the finance charge so attributable to the computational period ending on Feb. 1, 1975, since the number of computational periods in the deferral period, the period in which no instalment is scheduled to be paid by reason of the deferral (paragraph (c) of subsection (1) of Section 2.503), is one.

The method of calculating deferral charges prescribed in subsection (3) of this section is that prescribed in the small loan laws of many States, e.g., New York Banking Law § 352(d)(4) computed by the application of the annual percentage rate of 25.10% (or 2.09⅙% per month) to each amount deferred for the period of its deferral, as provided in U3C (1968 Draft) Sections 2.204(1) and 3.204(1) or subsection (4) of this section, the deferral charge would be $142.64 × 6 × .0209 × ⅙ = $17.90, or $1.62 more than the deferral charge of $16.28 as calculated according to subsection (3) of this section.

. . .

§ 2.504 [Finance Charge on Refinancing]

With respect to a consumer credit transaction except a consumer lease, the creditor by agreement with the consumer may refinance the unpaid balance and contract for and receive a finance charge based on the amount financed resulting from the refinancing at a rate not exceeding that permitted by the provisions on finance charge for consumer credit sales other than open-end credit (Section 2.201) if a consumer credit sale is refinanced, or for consumer loans (subsection (1) or (2) of Section 2.401, whichever is appropriate) if a consumer loan is refinanced. For the purpose of determining the finance charge permitted, the amount financed resulting from the refinancing comprises the following:

(1) if the transaction was not precomputed, the total of the unpaid balance and the accrued charges on the date of the refinancing, or, if the transaction was precomputed, the amount which the consumer would have been required to pay upon prepayment pursuant to the provisions on rebate upon prepayment (Section 2.510) on the date of refinancing, but for the purpose of computing this amount no minimum charge is permitted; and

(2) appropriate additional charges (Section 2.501), payment of which is deferred.

§ 2.505 [Finance Charge on Consolidation]

(1) In this section, "consumer credit transaction" does not include a consumer lease.

(2) If a consumer owes an unpaid balance to a creditor with respect to a consumer credit transaction and becomes obligated on another consumer credit transaction with the same creditor, the parties may agree to a consolidation resulting in a single schedule of payments. If the previous

consumer credit transaction was not precomputed, the parties may agree to add the unpaid amount of the amount financed and accrued charges on the date of consolidation to the amount financed with respect to the subsequent consumer credit transaction. If the previous consumer credit transaction was precomputed, the parties may agree to refinance the unpaid balance pursuant to the provisions on refinancing (Section 2.504) and to consolidate the amount financed resulting from the refinancing by adding it to the amount financed with respect to the subsequent consumer credit transaction. In either case the creditor may contract for and receive a finance charge as provided in subsection (3) based on the aggregate amount financed resulting from the consolidation.

(3) If the debts consolidated arise exclusively from consumer credit sales, the transaction is a consolidation with respect to a consumer credit sale and the creditor may make a finance charge not exceeding that permitted by the provisions on finance charge for consumer credit sales other than open-end credit (Section 2.201). If the debts consolidated include a debt arising from a prior or contemporaneous consumer loan, the transaction is a consolidation with respect to a consumer loan and the creditor may make a finance charge not exceeding that permitted by the provisions on finance charge for consumer loans by lenders not supervised lenders (subsection (1) of Section 2.401) or consumer loans by supervised lenders (subsection (2) of Section 2.401), whichever is appropriate.

(4) If a consumer owes an unpaid balance to a creditor with respect to a consumer credit transaction arising out of a consumer credit sale, and becomes obligated on another consumer credit transaction arising out of another consumer credit sale by the same seller, the parties may agree to a consolidation resulting in a single schedule of payments either pursuant to subsection (2) or by adding together the unpaid balances with respect to the two sales.

§ 2.506   [Advances to Perform Covenants of Consumer]

(1) If the agreement with respect to a consumer credit transaction other than a consumer lease contains covenants by the consumer to perform certain duties pertaining to insuring or preserving collateral and the creditor pursuant to the agreement pays for performance of the duties on behalf of the consumer, he may add the amounts paid to the debt. Within a reasonable time after advancing any sums, he shall state to the consumer in writing the amount of sums advanced, any charges with respect to this amount, and any revised payment schedule and, if the duties of the consumer performed by the creditor pertain to insurance, a brief description of the insurance paid for by the creditor including the type and amount of coverages. Further information need not be given.

(2) A finance charge may be made for sums advanced pursuant to subsection (1) at a rate not exceeding the rate of finance charge required to be stated to the consumer pursuant to law in a disclosure statement, but with respect to open-end credit the amount of the advance may be added to the unpaid balance of the debt and the creditor may make a finance charge not exceeding that permitted by the appropriate provisions on finance charge for consumer credit sales pursuant to open-end credit (Section

2.202) or for consumer loans (subsection (1) or (2) of Section 2.401), whichever is appropriate.

Alternative A:

§ 2.507   [Attorney's Fees]

With respect to a consumer credit transaction, the agreement may not provide for payment by the consumer of attorney's fees. A provision in violation of this section is unenforceable.

Comment

. . . In providing that no charge may be made for attorney's fees, this section reflects a policy decision to follow some small loan acts in treating this expense, like other collection costs, as part of the creditor's cost of doing business, rather than as a charge to be imposed on the defaulting consumer. The provisions made in this Act for rate ceilings and additional charges are generous enough to justify this treatment of attorney's fees and collection costs as part of general overhead.

Alternative B:

§ 2.507   [Attorney's Fees]

(1) With respect to a consumer loan in which the finance charge calculated according to the actuarial method is more than 18 per cent per year, the agreement may not provide for payment by the consumer of attorney's fees:

(a) if the loan is not pursuant to open-end credit and the amount financed is $1,000 or less; or

(b) if the loan is pursuant to open-end credit and the balance of the account at the time of default is $1,000 or less.

A provision in violation of this subsection is unenforceable.

(2) With respect to any other consumer credit transaction, the agreement may provide for payment by the consumer of reasonable attorney's fees not in excess of 15 per cent of the unpaid debt after default and referral to an attorney not a salaried employee of the creditor. A provision in violation of this subsection is unenforceable.

(3) The amounts of $1,000 in subsection (1) are subject to change pursuant to the provisions on adjustment of dollar amounts (Section 1.106).

Comment

. . . In providing in subsection (1) that no charge may be made for attorney's fees in supervised loans of $1,000 or less this section follows some small loan acts in treating this expense, like other collection costs, as part of the creditor's cost of doing business, rather than as a charge to be imposed on the defaulting consumer. Subsection (2) reflects a policy decision in other consumer transactions of treating attorney's fees not as part of the creditor's general overhead to be indirectly borne by all of his customers but as a charge to be imposed, at least in part, on the defaulting consumer who gives rise to the expense.   This section allows the parties to agree that upon default and referral of the claim to an attorney a charge can be made. . . .

§ 2.509   [Right to Prepay]

Subject to the provisions on rebate upon prepayment (Section 2.510), the consumer may prepay in full the unpaid balance of a consumer credit transaction, except a consumer lease, at any time without penalty.

§ 2.510   [Rebate Upon Prepayment]

(1) Except as otherwise provided in this section, upon prepayment in full of a precomputed consumer credit transaction, the creditor shall rebate to the consumer an amount not less than the unearned portion of the finance charge computed according to this section.   If the rebate otherwise required is less than $1, no rebate need be made.

(2) Upon prepayment of a consumer credit transaction, whether or not precomputed, except a consumer lease or one pursuant to open-end credit, the creditor may collect or retain a minimum charge not exceeding $5 in a transaction which had an amount financed of $75 or less, or not exceeding $7.50 in a transaction which had an amount financed of more than $75, if the minimum charge was contracted for and the finance charge earned at the time of prepayment is less than the minimum charge contracted for.

(3) In the following subsections these terms have the meanings ascribed to them in subsection (1) of Section 2.503: computational period, deferral, deferral period, periodic balance, standard deferral, sum of the balances method, and transaction.

(4) If, with respect to a transaction payable according to its original terms in no more than [48] instalments, the creditor has made either:

(a) no deferral or deferral charge, the unearned portion of the finance charge is no less than the portion thereof attributable according to the sum of the balances method to the period from the first day of the computational period following that in which prepayment occurs to the scheduled due date of the final instalment of the transaction; or

(b) a standard deferral and a deferral charge pursuant to the provisions on a standard deferral, the unpaid balance of the transaction includes any unpaid portions of the deferral charge and any appropriate additional charges incident to the deferral, and the unearned portion of the finance charge is no less than the portion thereof attributable according to the sum of the balances method to the period from the first day of the computational period following that in which prepayment occurs except that the numerator of the fraction is the sum of the periodic balances, after rescheduling to give effect to any standard deferral, scheduled to follow the computational period in which prepayment occurs.   A separate rebate of the deferral charge is not required unless the unpaid balance of the transaction is paid in full during the deferral period, in which event the creditor shall also rebate the unearned portion of the deferral charge.

(5) In lieu of computing a rebate of the unearned portion of the finance charge as provided in subsection (4) of this section, the creditor:

(a) shall, with respect to a transaction payable according to its original terms in more than [48] instalments, and a transaction payable according to its original terms in no more than [48] instalments as to which the creditor has made a deferral other than a standard deferral, and

(b) may, in other cases,

recompute or redetermine the earned finance charge by applying, according to the actuarial method, the annual percentage rate of finance charge required to be disclosed to the consumer pursuant to law to the actual unpaid balances of the amount financed for the actual time that the unpaid balances were outstanding as of the date of prepayment, giving effect to each payment, including payments of any deferral and delinquency charges, as of the date of the payment. The Administrator shall adopt rules to simplify the calculation of the unearned portion of the finance charge, including allowance of the use of tables or other methods derived by application of a percentage rate which deviates by not more than one-half of one per cent from the rate of the finance charge required to be disclosed to the consumer pursuant to law, and based on the assumption that all payments were made as originally scheduled or as deferred.

(6) Except as otherwise provided in subsection (5), this section does not preclude the collection or retention by the creditor of delinquency charges (Section 2.502).

(7) If the maturity is accelerated for any reason and judgment is entered, the consumer is entitled to the same rebate as if payment had been made on the date judgment is entered.

(8) Upon prepayment in full of a precomputed consumer credit transaction by the proceeds of consumer credit insurance (Section 4.103), the consumer or his estate is entitled to the same rebate as though the consumer had prepaid the agreement on the date the proceeds of insurance are paid to the creditor, but no later than 20 business days after satisfactory proof of loss is furnished to the creditor.

Comment

. . .

4. Subsection (4) of this section prescribes a method for computing the unearned portion of the finance charge and hence the rebate upon prepayment of a transaction payable according to its original terms in no more than [48] instalments as to which the creditor has made either no deferral or a "standard deferral" and a deferral charge according to the provisions applying to a standard deferral.

Assume the transactions described in Comment 2 to Section 2.201 and in Comments 2 and 3 to Section 2.503. Assume, further, that the consumer has paid not only $855.84, the total of the first six monthly instalments payable before the deferral, but also the deferral charge of $16.28, calculated according to subsection (3) of Section 2.503, $285.28, the total of the 7th and 8th instalments of $142.64 each payable as deferred on Mar. 1 and Apr. 1, 1975, and has prepaid on Apr. 15, 1975, $570.56, the then unpaid balance of his "total of payments." His total payments then aggregate $1,727.96. Then:

(1) According to subsection (4) of this section, the fraction of the finance charge of $211.68 to be used to determine the rebate is the fraction of which the numerator is the sum of periodic balances as rescheduled pursuant to the deferral, viz., $1,426.40 (the total of $570.56, $427.92, $285.28, and $142.64 payable as deferred on the 1st days of May, June, July, and August, 1975 respectively) divided by $11,125.92 (the sum of all the periodic balances under the original transaction). The fraction then is $1,426.4%11,125.92, or dividing both numerator and denominator by $142.64 (the amount of each instalment), ^{10}/78. The rebate, the unearned portion of the total finance charge of $211.68, is $211.68 × ^{10}/78 = $27.14.

(2) Deducting $27.14 from $1,727.96, the total paid on the transaction by the consumer, produces $1,700.82 as its net cost to the consumer.

Make the same assumptions as above, except that the deferral charge has been computed according to U3C (1968 Draft) Sections 2.204(1) and 3.204(1) or according to subsection (4) of Section 2.503 of this Act. His total payments then aggregate $1,729.58, the total of $1,711.68 (12 payments of $142.64 each) and the deferral charge of $17.90 calculated according to subsection (4) of Section 2.503. Then were the unearned portions of the finance charge and the deferral charge to be computed separately as formerly required by U3C (1968 Text) Sections 2.210(6) and 3.210(6):

(1) The unearned portion of the finance charge would have been computed without regard to the deferral, i.e., as the fraction of which the numerator is $855.84 (the total of the four prepaid periodic balances of $427.92, $285.28, and $142.64, and $00., as originally scheduled) and the denominator is $11,125.92 (the total of the 12 periodic balances as originally scheduled), or $855.84/$11,125.92, or, dividing both the numerator and the denominator by $142.64 (the amount of each instalment), ^{6}/78. The rebate, the unearned portion of the finance charge of $211.68, is $211.68 × ^{6}/78 = $16.28.

(2) As noted in Comment 3 to Section 2.503, the deferral charge, calculated as provided in U3C (1968 Draft) Sections 2.204(1) and 3.204(1), was $17.90. The unearned portion of that deferral charge is the fraction of which the numerator is four (the number of instalments remaining to earn the deferral charge) and the denominator is six (the number of instalments deferred). The unearned portion of the deferral charge of $17.90 is $17.90 × ^{4}/6 = $11.93.

(3) Deducting $28.21, the total of (a) $16.28, the unearned portion of the finance charge, and (b) $11.93, the unearned portion of the deferral charge, from $1,729.58, the total paid by the consumer, produces $1,701.37 as the net cost of the transaction to the consumer.

Consequently, the methods of calculating deferral charges according to subsection (3) of Section 2.503 of this Act and rebate of unearned finance charge according to subsection (4) of this Section not only permit more simple calculations, but also produce a lower cost to the consumer than under the corresponding provisions of the 1968 Draft of the U3C, viz. under the illustrations above, $1,700.82 as compared to $1,701.37.

. . .

PART 6. OTHER CREDIT TRANSACTIONS

§ 2.601 [Charges for Other Credit Transactions]

(1) Except as provided in subsection (2), with respect to a credit transaction other than a consumer credit transaction, the parties may contract for payment by the debtor of any finance or other charge.

(2) With respect to a credit transaction which would be a consumer credit transaction if a finance charge were made, a charge for delinquency may not exceed amounts allowed for finance charges for consumer credit sales pursuant to open-end credit (Section 2.202).

Comment

1. An economic fundamental of this Act is that too low a rate ceiling prevents both consumer and commercial debtors who need credit from getting credit at reasonable rates from legitimate creditors. Because basic usury laws had that effect, the legislatures in almost all the States have enacted myriad exceptions to the usury statutes for consumer and commercial transactions such as small, industrial and instalment loan laws and prohibitions against a defense of usury by a corporation. The sale of goods, services, or interests in land on credit, whether in a consumer or commercial context, has been held by the courts of most of the States to be exempt from their usury laws under the time-price doctrine. That doctrine has been recognized and limited by the legislatures of most States which have enacted laws regulating consumer instalment sales.

This Act repeals the general usury statute as well as the exceptions to it, sets reasonable ceilings on all consumer credit rates, and in this section leaves the finance charge and other charges in transactions other than consumer credit transactions, such as:

    (a) A transaction by a seller or lender not regularly engaged in similar credit transactions,

    (b) A transaction over $25,000 in amount not involving real property,

    (c) A transaction in which an organization is the debtor, and

    (d) A transaction for a business purpose,

basically to the agreement of the parties. In all these types of transactions except the first, which is usually a family transaction or may be within subsection (15)(c) of Section 1.301, the debtors are usually sophisticated enough to take care of themselves in negotiating credit charges. It is difficult to impose an arbitrary rate ceiling for these transactions that will be high enough to allow for high risk business transactions without setting a limit that is so high as to be virtually meaningless. This Act contemplates the repeal of the general usury statute in any State which enacts it; hence the need for the time-price doctrine is eliminated in any such State. Given the basic philosophy of this Act, it should not be interpreted as rejecting the time-price doctrine in either its consumer or commercial context in any State which has not enacted the Act or which continues to have a general usury statute.

    . . .

ARTICLE 3.   REGULATION OF AGREEMENTS AND PRACTICES

PART 1.   GENERAL PROVISIONS

§ 3.102   [Scope]

Part 2 of this Article applies to disclosure with respect to consumer credit transactions. The provision on compliance with the Federal Truth in Lending Act (Section 3.201) applies to a sale of an interest in land or a loan secured by an interest in land, without regard to the rate of finance charge, if the sale or loan is otherwise a consumer credit sale or consumer loan. Parts 3 and 4 of this Article apply, respectively, to limitations on agreements and practices, and limitations on consumers' liabilities with respect to certain consumer credit transactions. Part 5 applies to home solicitation sales.

PART 2.   DISCLOSURE

§ 3.201   [Compliance With Federal Truth in Lending Act]

(1) A person upon whom the Federal Truth in Lending Act imposes duties or obligations shall make or give to the consumer the disclosures, information, and notices required of him by that Act and in all respects comply with that Act. To the extent the Federal Truth in Lending Act does not impose duties or obligations upon a person in a credit transaction, except a consumer lease, that is a consumer credit transaction under this Act, the person shall make or give to the consumer disclosures, information, and notices in accordance with the Federal Truth in Lending Act with respect to the credit transaction.

(2) The Federal Truth in Lending Act is deemed to apply to a credit transaction which is a consumer credit transaction under this Act, notwithstanding its inclusion in a class of transactions within this State which, by regulation of the Board of Governors of the Federal Reserve System, is exempt from the Federal Truth in Lending Act.

§ 3.202   [Consumer Leases]

(1) With respect to a consumer lease the lessor shall give to the lessee the following information:

(a) brief description or identification of the goods;

(b) amount of any payment required at the inception of the lease;

(c) amount paid or payable for official fees, registration, certificate of title, or license fees or taxes;

(d) amount of other charges not included in the periodic payments and a brief description of the charges;

1090

(e) brief description of insurance to be provided or paid for by the lessor, including the types and amounts of the coverages;

(f) number of periodic payments, the amount of each payment, the due date of the first payment, the due dates of subsequent payments or interval between payments, and the total amount payable by the lessee;

(g) statement of the conditions under which the lessee may terminate the lease before the end of the term; and

(h) statement of the liabilities the lease imposes upon the lessee at the end of the term.

(2) The disclosures required by this section:

(a) shall be made clearly and conspicuously in writing, a copy of which shall be delivered to the lessee;

(b) may be supplemented by additional information or explanations supplied by the lessor, but none shall be stated, utilized, or placed so as to mislead or confuse the lessee or contradict, obscure, or detract attention from the information required to be disclosed by this section;

(c) need be made only to the extent applicable;

(d) shall be made on the assumption that all scheduled payments will be made when due and will comply with this section although rendered inaccurate by an act, occurrence, or agreement after the required disclosure; and

(e) shall be made before the lease transaction is consummated, but may be made in the lease to be signed by the lessee.

§ 3.203 [Notice to Consumer]

The creditor shall give to the consumer a copy of any writing evidencing a consumer credit transaction, except one pursuant to open-end credit, if the writing requires or provides for the signature of the consumer. The writing evidencing the consumer's obligation to pay the debt shall contain a clear and conspicuous notice informing the consumer that he should not sign it before reading it, that he is entitled to a copy of it, and, except in case of a consumer lease, that he is entitled to prepay the unpaid balance at any time without penalty and may be entitled to receive a refund of unearned charges in accordance with law. The following notice if clear and conspicuous complies with this section:

NOTICE TO CONSUMER:
1. Do not sign this paper before you read it.
2. You are entitled to a copy of this paper.
3. You may prepay the unpaid balance at any time without penalty and may be entitled to receive a refund of unearned charges in accordance with law.

§ 3.204   [Notice of Assignment]

A consumer may pay the original creditor until he receives notification of assignment of rights to payment pursuant to a consumer credit transaction and that payment is to be made to the assignee. A notification which does not reasonably identify the rights assigned is ineffective. If requested by the consumer, the assignee shall seasonably furnish reasonable proof that the assignment has been made and unless he does so the consumer may pay the original creditor.

§ 3.205   [Change in Terms of Open–End Credit Accounts]

(1) Whether or not a change is authorized by prior agreement, a creditor may change the terms of an open-end credit account applying to any balance incurred before or after the effective date of the change. If the change increases the rate of the finance charge or of additional charges, alters the method of determining the balance upon which charges are made so that increased charges may result, or imposes or increases minimum charges, the change is effective with respect to a balance incurred before the effective date of the change only if the consumer after receiving disclosure of the change agrees to it in writing or the creditor delivers or mails to the consumer two written disclosures of the change, the first at least three months before the effective date of the change and the second at a later time before the effective date of the change.

(2) A disclosure provided for in subsection (1) is mailed to the consumer when mailed to him at his address used by the creditor for mailing him periodic billing statements.

(3) If a creditor attempts to change the terms of an open-end credit account as provided in subsection (1) without complying with this section, any additional cost or charge to the consumer resulting from the change is an excess charge and is subject to the remedies available to the consumer (Section 5.201) and to the Administrator (Section 6.113).

§ 3.208   [Notice to Co–Signers and Similar Parties]

(1) A natural person, other than the spouse of the consumer, is not obligated as a co-signer, co-maker, guarantor, indorser, surety, or similar party with respect to a consumer credit transaction, unless before or contemporaneously with signing any separate agreement of obligation or any writing setting forth the terms of the debtor's agreement, the person receives a separate written notice that contains a completed identification of the debt he may have to pay and reasonably informs him of his obligation with respect to it.

(2) A clear and conspicuous notice in substantially the following form complies with this section:

NOTICE

You agree to pay the debt identified below although you may not personally receive any property, services, or money. You may be sued for payment although the person who receives the property, services, or money is able to pay. This notice is not the contract that obligates you to pay the debt. Read the contract for the exact terms of your obligation.

IDENTIFICATION OF DEBT YOU MAY HAVE TO PAY

_____

(Name of Debtor)

_____

(Name of Creditor)

_____

(Date)

_____

(Kind of Debt)

I have received a copy of this notice.

_____

(Date)

_____

(Signed)

(3) The notice required by this section need not be given to a seller, lessor, or lender who is obligated to an assignee of his rights.

(4) A person entitled to notice under this section shall also be given a copy of any writing setting forth the terms of the debtor's agreement and of any separate agreement of obligation signed by the person entitled to the notice.

§ 3.209 [Advertising]

(1) A seller, lessor, or lender may not advertise, print, display, publish, distribute, broadcast, or cause to be advertised, printed, displayed, published, distributed, or broadcast in any manner any statement or representation with regard to the rates, terms, or conditions of credit with respect to a consumer credit transaction that is false, misleading, or deceptive.

(2) Advertising that complies with the Federal Truth in Lending Act does not violate this section.

(3) This section does not apply to the owner or personnel, as such, of any medium in which an advertisement appears or through which it is disseminated.

PART 3.   LIMITATIONS ON AGREEMENTS AND PRACTICES

§ 3.301   [Security in Sales and Leases]

(1) With respect to a consumer credit sale, a seller may take a security interest in the property sold. In addition, a seller may take a security interest in goods upon which services are performed or in which goods sold are installed or to which they are annexed, or in land to which the goods are affixed or which is maintained, repaired or improved as a result of the sale of the goods or services, if in the case of a security interest in land the debt secured is $1,000 or more, or, in the case of a security interest in goods the debt secured is $300 or more. The seller may also take a security interest in property to secure the debt arising from a consumer credit sale primarily for an agricultural purpose. Except as provided with respect to cross-collateral (Section 3.302) a seller may not otherwise take a security interest in property to secure the debt arising from a consumer credit sale.

(2) With respect to a consumer lease, except one primarily for an agricultural purpose, a lessor may not take a security interest in property to secure the debt arising from the lease. This subsection does not apply to a security deposit for a consumer lease.

(3) A security interest taken in violation of this section is void.

(4) The amounts of $1,000 and $300 in subsection (1) are subject to change pursuant to the provisions on adjustment of dollar amounts (Section 1.106).

§ 3.302   [Cross–Collateral]

(1) In addition to contracting for a security interest pursuant to the provisions on security in sales and leases (Section 3.301), a seller in a consumer credit sale may secure the debt arising from the sale by contracting for a security interest in other property if as a result of a prior sale the seller has an existing security interest in the other property. The seller may also contract for a security interest in the property sold in the subsequent sale as security for the previous debt.

(2) If the seller contracts for a security interest in other property pursuant to this section, the rate of finance charge thereafter on the aggregate unpaid balances so secured may not exceed that permitted if the balances so secured were consolidated pursuant to the provisions on finance charge on consolidation (subsection (2) of Section 2.505). The seller has a reasonable time after so contracting in which to make any adjustments required by this section.

Comment

. . .

2. Subsection (1) allows cross-collateral to be taken either for separate debts or for consolidated debts, but subsection (2) . . . prevents the seller from taking the

advantages of cross-collateral without also offering the buyer the lower rates that would have resulted had the debts been consolidated pursuant to Section 2.505(2).

§ 3.303 [Debt Secured By Cross–Collateral]

(1) If debts arising from two or more consumer credit sales, except sales primarily for an agricultural purpose or pursuant to open-end credit, are secured by cross-collateral (Section 3.302) or consolidated into one debt payable on a single schedule of payments, and the debt is secured by security interests taken with respect to one or more of the sales, payments received by the seller after the taking of cross-collateral or the consolidation are deemed, for the purpose of determining the amount of the debt secured by the various security interests, to have been applied first to the payment of the debts arising from the sales first made. To the extent debts are paid according to this section, security interests in items of property terminate as the debt originally incurred with respect to each item is paid.

(2) Payments received by the seller upon an open-end credit account are deemed, for the purpose of determining the amount of the debt secured by the various security interests, to have been applied first to the payment of finance charges in the order of their entry to the account and then to the payment of debts in the order in which the entries to the account showing the debts were made.

(3) If the debts consolidated arose from two or more sales made on the same day, payments received by the seller are deemed, for the purpose of determining the amount of the debt secured by the various security interests, to have been applied first to the payment of the smallest debt.

§ 3.304 [Use of Multiple Agreements]

(1) A creditor may not use multiple agreements with respect to a single consumer credit transaction with intent to obtain a higher finance charge than otherwise would be permitted by the provisions of the Article on Finance Charges and Related Provisions (Article 2).

(2) The excess amount of finance charge resulting from a violation of subsection (1) is an excess charge for the purposes of the provisions on rights of parties (Section 5.201) and the provisions on civil actions by Administrator (Section 6.113).

§ 3.305 [No Assignment of Earnings]

(1) A creditor may not take an assignment of earnings of the consumer for payment or as security for payment of a debt arising out of a consumer credit transaction. An assignment of earnings in violation of this section is unenforceable by the assignee of the earnings and revocable by the consumer. This section does not prohibit a consumer from authorizing deductions from his earnings in favor of his creditor if the authorization is revocable, the consumer is given a complete copy of the writing evidencing the

authorization at the time he signs it, and the writing contains on its face a conspicuous notice of the consumer's right to revoke the authorization.

(2) A sale of unpaid earnings made in consideration of the payment of money to or for the account of the seller of the earnings is deemed to be a loan to him secured by an assignment of earnings.

§ 3.306   [Authorization to Confess Judgment Prohibited]

A consumer may not authorize any person to confess judgment on a claim arising out of a consumer credit transaction. An authorization in violation of this section is void.

§ 3.307   [Certain Negotiable Instruments Prohibited]

With respect to a consumer credit sale or consumer lease, [except a sale or lease primarily for an agricultural purpose,] the creditor may not take a negotiable instrument other than a check dated not later than ten days after its issuance as evidence of the obligation of the consumer.

Comment

This section, together with Sections 3.403, 3.404 and 3.405, states a major tenet of this Act: that the holder in due course doctrine should be abrogated in consumer cases. Whatever beneficial effects this doctrine may have in promoting the currency of paper is greatly outweighed by the harshness of its consequences in denying consumers the right to raise valid defenses arising out of credit transactions. The first step in abolition of the doctrine is the prohibition found in this section of the use of negotiable instruments in consumer credit sales and consumer leases. The presence of the bracketed language recognizes the strong tradition of the use of negotiable instruments in agricultural transactions in some States.

§ 3.308   [Balloon Payments]

(1) Except as provided in subsection (2), if any scheduled payment of a consumer credit transaction is more than twice as large as the average of earlier scheduled payments, the consumer has the right to refinance, without penalty, the amount of that payment at the time it is due. The terms of the refinancing shall be no less favorable to the consumer than the terms of the original transaction.

(2) This section does not apply to:

(a) a consumer lease;

(b) a transaction pursuant to open-end credit;

(c) a transaction primarily for an agricultural purpose;

(d) a transaction to the extent that the payment schedule is adjusted to the seasonal or irregular income or scheduled payments or obligations of the consumer; or

(e) a transaction of a class defined by rule of the Administrator as not requiring for the protection of the consumer his right to refinance as provided in this section.

§ 3.309 [Referral Sales and Leases]

With respect to a consumer credit sale or consumer lease, the seller or lessor may not give or offer to give a rebate or discount or otherwise pay or offer to pay value to the consumer as an inducement for a sale or lease for the consumer giving to the seller or lessor the names of prospective buyers or lessees, or otherwise aiding the seller or lessor in making a sale or lease to another person, if the earning of the rebate, discount or other value is contingent upon the occurrence of an event after the time the consumer agrees to buy or lease. If a consumer is induced by a violation of this section to enter into a consumer credit sale or consumer lease, the agreement is unenforceable by the seller or lessor and the consumer, at his option, may rescind the agreement or retain the property delivered and the benefit of any services performed, without any obligation to pay for them. A sale or lease that would be a referral sale or lease if credit were extended by the seller or lessor is nonetheless so because the property or services are paid for in whole or in part by use of a credit card or by a consumer loan with respect to which the lender is subject to claims and defenses arising from the sale or lease (Section 3.405), and the consumer has the same rights against the card issuer or lender that he has against the seller or lessor under this section.

Comment

. . .

2. The evil this section is aimed at is the raising of expectations in a buyer of benefits to accrue to him from events which are to occur in the future. This provision has no effect on a seller's agreement to reduce at the time of the sale the price of an item in exchange for the buyer's giving the seller a list of prospective purchasers or assisting in other ways if the price reduction is not contingent on whether the purchasers do in fact buy or on whether other events occur in the future.

3. The misuse of the referral sale scheme has been so pervasive in some segments of vendor credit that this provision, in an effort to halt these practices, not only makes agreements in violation of this section unenforceable but also allows the buyer to retain the goods sold or the benefit of services rendered with no obligation to pay for them. Alternatively, the buyer may rescind the agreement, return the goods, and recover any payment. Use of a referral scheme subjects the offending seller or lessor to a penalty under Section 5.201. Creditors cannot evade this section by the use of credit cards or consumer loans.

PART 4. LIMITATIONS ON CONSUMERS' LIABILITIES

§ 3.401 [Restriction on Liability in Consumer Lease]

The obligation of a lessee upon expiration of a consumer lease [, except one primarily for an agricultural purpose,] may not exceed twice the average payment allocable to a monthly period under the lease. This limitation does not apply to charges for damages to the leased property or for other default.

Comment

This section is designed to protect consumer lessees against abuses associated with what are described in some areas of the country as "open-end" leases. Under such an agreement the parties contract that at the expiration of the lease the article leased, usually an automobile, will have a certain depreciated value and will be sold. If it brings less than the agreed depreciated value, the lessee is liable for the difference; if it brings more, the lessee is entitled to the surplus. Under such an agreement, the lessee will have no understanding of how much the lease might cost him unless he can accurately predict what the second hand market will be at the expiration of lease. Moreover, if the lessor sets an unrealistically high depreciated value the contingent liability of the lessee will increase accordingly, and the lessor can offer deceptively low rental payments to a gullible customer.

.   .   .

§ 3.402   [Limitation on Default Charges]

Except for reasonable expenses incurred in realizing on a security interest, the agreement with respect to a consumer credit transaction other than a consumer lease may not provide for any charges as a result of default by the consumer except those authorized by this Act. A provision in violation of this section is unenforceable.

§ 3.403   [Card Issuer Subject to Claims and Defenses]

(1) This section neither limits the liability of nor imposes liability on a card issuer as a manufacturer, supplier, seller, or lessor of property or services sold or leased pursuant to the credit card. This section may subject a card issuer to claims and defenses of a cardholder against a seller or lessor arising from sales or leases made pursuant to the credit card.

(2) A card issuer is subject to claims and defenses of a cardholder against the seller or lessor arising from the sale or lease of property or services by a seller or lessor licensed, franchised, or permitted by the card issuer or a person related to the card issuer to do business under the trade name or designation of the card issuer or a person related to the card issuer, to the extent of the original amount owing to the card issuer with respect to the sale or lease of the property or services as to which the claim or defense arose.

(3) Except as otherwise provided in this section, a card issuer, including a lender credit card issuer, is subject to all claims and defenses of a cardholder against the seller or lessor arising from the sale or lease of property or services pursuant to the credit card:

(a) if the original amount owing to the card issuer with respect to the sale or lease of the property or services as to which the claim or defense arose exceeds $50;

(b) if the residence of the cardholder and the place where the sale or lease occurred are [in the same state or] within 100 miles of each other;

(c) if the cardholder has made a good faith attempt to obtain satisfaction from the seller or lessor with respect to the claim or defense; and

(d) to the extent of the amount owing to the card issuer with respect to the sale or lease of the property or services as to which the claim or defense arose at the time the card issuer has notice of the claim or defense. Notice of the claim or defense may be given before the attempt specified in paragraph (c). Oral notice is effective unless the card issuer requests written confirmation when or promptly after oral notice is given and the cardholder fails to give the card issuer written confirmation within the period of time, not less than 14 days, stated to the cardholder when written confirmation is requested.

(4) For the purpose of determining the amount owing to the card issuer with respect to a sale or lease upon an open-end credit account, payments received for the account are deemed to have been applied first to the payment of finance charges in the order of their entry to the account and then to the payment of debts in the order in which the entries of the debts are made to the account.

(5) An agreement may not limit or waive the claims or defenses of a cardholder under this section.

§ 3.404   [Assignee Subject to Claims and Defenses]

(1) With respect to a consumer credit sale or consumer lease [, except one primarily for an agricultural purpose], an assignee of the rights of the seller or lessor is subject to all claims and defenses of the consumer against the seller or lessor arising from the sale or lease of property or services, notwithstanding that the assignee is a holder in due course of a negotiable instrument issued in violation of the provisions prohibiting certain negotiable instruments (Section 3.307).

(2) A claim or defense of a consumer specified in subsection (1) may be asserted against the assignee under this section only if the consumer has made a good faith attempt to obtain satisfaction from the seller or lessor with respect to the claim or defense and then only to the extent of the amount owing to the assignee with respect to the sale or lease of the property or services as to which the claim or defense arose at the time the assignee has notice of the claim or defense. Notice of the claim or defense may be given before the attempt specified in this subsection. Oral notice is effective unless the assignee requests written confirmation when or promptly after oral notice is given and the consumer fails to give the assignee written confirmation within the period of time, not less than 14 days, stated to the consumer when written confirmation is requested.

(3) For the purpose of determining the amount owing to the assignee with respect to the sale or lease:

(a) payments received by the assignee after the consolidation of two or more consumer credit sales, except pursuant to open-end credit, are deemed to have been applied first to the payment of the sales first made; if the sales consolidated arose from sales made on the same day, payments are deemed to have been applied first to the smallest sale; and

(b) payments received for an open-end credit account are deemed to have been applied first to the payment of finance charges in the order of their entry to the account and then to the payment of debts in the order in which the entries of the debts are made to the account.

(4) An agreement may not limit or waive the claims or defenses of a consumer under this section.

Comment

1. This section codifies a growing body of case law under UCC Section 9–206 to the effect that assignees take consumer paper subject to consumer claims and defenses.... The policy justifications for the section are to protect the consumer from the harshness of the holder in due course doctrine as well as to encourage financial institutions taking assignments of consumer paper to use discretion in dealing with sellers and lessors whose transactions give rise to an unusual percentage of consumer complaints. See Section 3.307.

2. The consumer, upon making a good faith attempt to obtain satisfaction from his seller or lessor, can assert his claim or defense against the assignee to the extent of the amount still owing to the assignee at the time the assignee learns of the claim or defense. If the assignee knows of the defense before any payments are made to him, the consumer can raise his claim or defense to the full amount of the assigned debt. Orderly procedures will necessitate some written record on the part of the assignee of the consumer's notification regarding his claim or defense, but the consumer ought to be able to rely on having given oral notification unless the assignee requests written confirmation. Hence, the assignee has the option of making his own written record upon receiving oral notice from the consumer or of requesting written notice from the consumer and allowing 14 days for the consumer to send his written confirmation. Subsection (3) uses the same tests for determining the amount owing on a debt as are used in Section 3.303.

§ 3.405 [Lender Subject to Claims and Defenses Arising From Sales and Leases]

(1) A lender, except the issuer of a lender credit card, who, with respect to a particular transaction, makes a consumer loan to enable a consumer to buy or lease from a particular seller or lessor property or services [, except primarily for an agricultural purpose,] is subject to all claims and defenses of the consumer against the seller or lessor arising from that sale or lease of the property or services if:

(a) the lender knows that the seller or lessor arranged for the extension of credit by the lender for a commission, brokerage, or referral fee;

(b) the lender is a person related to the seller or lessor, unless the relationship is remote or is not a factor in the transaction;

(c) the seller or lessor guarantees the loan or otherwise assumes the risk of loss by the lender upon the loan;

(d) the lender directly supplies the seller or lessor with the contract document used by the consumer to evidence the loan, and the seller or lessor has knowledge of the credit terms and participates in preparation of the document;

(e) the loan is conditioned upon the consumer's purchase or lease of the property or services from the particular seller or lessor, but the lender's payment of proceeds of the loan to the seller or lessor does not in itself establish that the loan was so conditioned; or

(f) the lender, before he makes the consumer loan, has knowledge or, from his course of dealing with the particular seller or lessor or his records, notice of substantial complaints by other buyers or lessees of the particular seller's or lessor's failure or refusal to perform his contracts with them and of the particular seller's or lessor's failure to remedy his defaults within a reasonable time after notice to him of the complaints.

(2) A claim or defense of a consumer specified in subsection (1) may be asserted against the lender under this section only if the consumer has made a good faith attempt to obtain satisfaction from the seller or lessor with respect to the claim or defense and then only to the extent of the amount owing to the lender with respect to the sale or lease of the property or services as to which the claim or defense arose at the time the lender has notice of the claim or defense. Notice of the claim or defense may be given before the attempt specified in this subsection. Oral notice is effective unless the lender requests written confirmation when or promptly after oral notice is given and the consumer fails to give the lender written confirmation within the period of time, not less than 14 days, stated to the consumer when written confirmation is requested.

(3) For the purpose of determining the amount owing to the lender with respect to the sale or lease:

(a) payments received by the lender after consolidation of two or more consumer loans, except pursuant to open-end credit, are deemed to have been applied first to the payment of the loans first made; if the loans consolidated arose from loans made on the same day, payments are deemed to have been applied first to the smallest loan; and

(b) payments received for an open-end credit account are deemed to have been applied first to the payment of finance charges in the order of their entry to the account and then to the payment of debts in the order in which the entries of the debts are made to the account.

(4) An agreement may not limit or waive the claims or defenses of a consumer under this section.

PART 5. HOME SOLICITATION SALES

§ 3.501 [Definition: "Home Solicitation Sale"]

"Home solicitation sale" means a consumer credit sale of goods or services, except primarily for an agricultural purpose, in which the seller or a person acting for him personally solicits the sale, and the buyer's agreement or offer to purchase is given to the seller or a person acting for him, at a residence. It does not include a sale made pursuant to a pre-existing open-end credit account with the seller or pursuant to prior negotiations between the parties at a business establishment at a fixed location where goods or services are offered or exhibited for sale, a transaction conducted and consummated entirely by mail or telephone, or a sale which is subject to the provisions of the Federal Truth in Lending Act on the consumer's right to rescind certain transactions. A sale that would be a home solicitation sale if credit were extended by the seller is nonetheless so because the goods or services are paid for in whole or in part by use of a credit card or by a consumer loan with respect to which the lender is subject to claims and defenses arising from the sale (Section 3.405), and the buyer has the same rights against the card issuer or lender that he has against the seller under this Part.

Comment

1. The Act singles out for special treatment consumer credit sales in which the buyer's order is given to the seller at a residence. An underlying consideration for Part 5 is the belief that in a significant proportion of such sales the consumer is induced to sign a sales contract by high pressure techniques. The Act recognizes that many buyers in such cases may be unwilling parties to the transaction and gives to them a limited right to cancel the sale. . . .

2. The definition of "home solicitation sales" differentiates between those types of transactions which have been the subject of particular abuse and those which have not. Although high pressure salesmanship can be practiced anywhere, the underlying theory of Section 3.501 is that the sale in the home is particularly susceptible to such methods. Two elements are required to bring a transaction within the definition. First, there must be personal solicitation at a residence. Second, the act of the buyer in binding himself by agreeing or offering to purchase, must also take place at a residence. The phrase "at a residence" rather than "in a residence" is used to prevent avoidance of the Act by the expedient of having the buyer sign the contract outside of, but in the immediate vicinity of, the home.

. . .

§ 3.502   [Buyer's Right to Cancel]

(1) Except as provided in subsection (5), in addition to any right otherwise to revoke an offer, the buyer may cancel a home solicitation sale until midnight of the third business day after the day on which the buyer signs an agreement or offer to purchase which complies with this Part.

(2) Cancellation occurs when the buyer gives written notice of cancellation to the seller at the address stated in the agreement or offer to purchase.

(3) Notice of cancellation, if given by mail, is given when it is properly addressed with postage prepaid and deposited in a mailbox.

(4) Notice of cancellation given by the buyer need not take a particular form and is sufficient if it indicates by any form of written expression the intention of the buyer not to be bound by the home solicitation sale.

(5) The buyer may not cancel a home solicitation sale if, by a separate dated and signed statement that is not as to its material provisions a printed form and describes an emergency requiring immediate remedy, the buyer requests the seller to provide goods or services without delay in order to safeguard the health, safety, or welfare of natural persons or to prevent damage to property the buyer owns or for which he is responsible, and

(a) the seller in good faith makes a substantial beginning of performance of the contract before the buyer gives notice of cancellation, and

(b) in the case of goods, they cannot be returned to the seller in substantially as good condition as when received by the buyer.

§ 3.503   [Form of Agreement or Offer;   Statement of Buyer's Rights]

(1) In a home solicitation sale, unless the buyer requests the seller to provide goods or services without delay in an emergency (subsection (5) of Section 3.502), the seller shall present to the buyer and obtain his signature to a written agreement or offer to purchase that designates as the date of the transaction the date on which the buyer actually signs and contains a statement of the buyer's rights that complies with subsection (2). A copy of any writing required by this subsection to be signed by the buyer, completed at least as to the date of the transaction and the name and mailing address of the seller, shall be given to the buyer at the time he signs the writing.

(2) The statement shall either:

(a) comply with any notice of cancellation or similar requirement of any trade regulation rule of the Federal Trade Commission which by its terms applies to the home solicitation sale; or

(b) appear under the conspicuous caption: "BUYER'S RIGHT TO CANCEL," and read as follows: "If you decide you do not want the goods or services, you may cancel this agreement by mailing a notice to the seller. The notice must say that you do not want the goods or services and must be mailed before midnight of the third business day after you sign this agreement. The notice must be mailed to:

_____

(insert name & mailing address of seller)."

(3) Until the seller has complied with this section the buyer may cancel the home solicitation sale by notifying the seller in any manner and by any means of his intention to cancel.

§ 3.504   [Restoration of Down Payment]

(1) Within ten days after a notice of cancellation has been received by the seller or an offer to purchase has been otherwise revoked, the seller

shall tender to the buyer any payments made by the buyer, any note or other evidence of indebtedness, and any goods traded in. A provision permitting the seller to keep all or any part of any goods traded in, payment, note, or evidence of indebtedness is in violation of this section and unenforceable.

(2) If the down payment includes goods traded in, the goods shall be tendered in substantially as good condition as when received by the seller. If the seller fails to tender the goods as provided by this section, the buyer may elect to recover an amount equal to the trade-in allowance stated in the agreement.

(3) Until the seller has complied with the obligations imposed by this section the buyer may retain possession of goods delivered to him by the seller and has a lien on the goods in his possession or control for any recovery to which he is entitled.

§ 3.505 [Duty of Buyer; No Compensation for Services Before Cancellation]

(1) Except as provided by the provisions on retention of goods by the buyer (subsection (3) of Section 3.504), and allowing for ordinary wear and tear or consumption of the goods contemplated by the transaction, within a reasonable time after a home solicitation sale has been cancelled or an offer to purchase revoked, the buyer upon demand shall tender to the seller any goods delivered by the seller pursuant to the sale, but he is not obligated to tender at any place other than his residence. If the seller fails to demand possession of goods within a reasonable time after cancellation or revocation, the goods become the property of the buyer without obligation to pay for them. For the purpose of this section, a reasonable time is presumed to be 40 days.

(2) The buyer shall take reasonable care of the goods in his possession before cancellation or revocation and for a reasonable time thereafter, during which time the goods are otherwise at the seller's risk.

(3) If a home solicitation sale is cancelled, the seller is not entitled to compensation for any services he performed pursuant to it.

ARTICLE 4. INSURANCE

PART 1. INSURANCE IN GENERAL

§ 4.102 [Scope [; Relation to Credit Insurance Act; Applicability to Parties]]

[(1)] This Article applies to insurance provided or to be provided in relation to a consumer credit transaction.

[(2) This Article supplements and does not repeal the Credit Insurance Act but to the extent of inconsistency between this Act and the Credit Insurance Act this Act controls. The provisions of this Act concerning administrative controls, liabilities, and penalties do not apply to persons acting as insurers, and the similar provisions of the Credit Insurance Act do not apply to creditors and debtors.]

Comment

. . .

The scope of this Article is broader than that of the NAIC Model Act.

. . .

§ 4.103 [Definition[s]: "Consumer Credit Insurance" [; "Credit Insurance Act"]]

In this Act:

[(1)] "Consumer credit insurance" means insurance, except insurance on property, by which the satisfaction of debt in whole or in part is a benefit provided, but does not include

(a) insurance provided in relation to a consumer credit transaction in which a payment is scheduled more than ten years after the extension of credit;

(b) insurance issued by an insurer as an isolated transaction not related to an agreement or plan for insuring consumers of or from the creditor; or

(c) insurance indemnifying the creditor against loss due to the consumer's default.

[(2) "Credit Insurance Act" means [NAIC Model Act, or any similar statute].]

§ 4.104 [Creditor's Provision of and Charge for Insurance; Excess Amount of Charge]

(1) Except as otherwise provided in this Article and subject to the provisions on additional charges (Section 2.501) and maximum finance charges (Parts 2 and 4 of Article 2), a creditor may agree to provide insurance, and may contract for and receive a charge for insurance separate

1105

from and in addition to other charges. A creditor need not make a separate charge for insurance provided or required by him. This Act does not authorize the issuance of the insurance prohibited under any statute, or rule thereunder, governing the business of insurance.

(2) The excess amount of a charge for insurance provided for in agreements in violation of this Article is an excess charge for purposes of the provisions of the Article on Remedies and Penalties (Article 5) as to effect of violations on rights of parties (Section 5.201) and of the provisions of the Article on Administration (Article 6) as to civil actions by the Administrator (Section 6.113).

§ 4.105   [Conditions Applying to Insurance to Be Provided by Creditor]

If a creditor agrees with a consumer to provide insurance:

(1) the insurance shall be evidenced by an individual policy or certificate of insurance delivered to the consumer, or mailed to him at his address as stated by him, within 30 days after the term of the insurance commences under the agreement between the creditor and consumer, or the creditor shall promptly notify the consumer of any failure or delay in providing the insurance; and

(2) the creditor shall pay to the consumer or his estate all proceeds of consumer credit or property insurance received by the creditor in excess of the amount to which the creditor is entitled within ten days after receipt by the creditor of the proceeds.

§ 4.106   [Unconscionability]

(1) In applying the provisions of this Act on unconscionability (Sections 5.108 and 6.111) to a separate charge for insurance, consideration shall be given, among other factors, to:

(a) potential benefits to the consumer including the satisfaction of his obligations;

(b) the creditor's need for the protection provided by the insurance; and

(c) the relation between the amount and terms of credit granted and the insurance benefits provided.

(2) If consumer credit insurance otherwise complies with this Article and other applicable law, neither the amount nor the term of the insurance nor the amount of a charge therefor is in itself unconscionable.

Comment

It may be shown that an agreement about insurance, like other terms of a consumer credit contract, is unconscionable, and the effects are those specified in Sections 5.108 and 6.111. However, it is the intent of this section that the issue be judged in relation to the particular risks insured. The section lists only some of the factors to be considered, and indicates that a balancing of benefits, needs, and costs is required. In general, the creditor's need for insurance protection and the consumer's potential benefit are more patent in connection with extensions of credit that are substantial as to amounts and periods; the expense of providing exceptional coverage is suspect in relation to relatively small extensions of credit. The relation between the credit terms and the insurance terms must be taken into account in applying this section.

§ 4.107 [Maximum Charge By Creditor for Insurance]

(1) Except as provided in subsection (2), if a creditor contracts for or receives a separate charge for insurance, the amount charged to the consumer for the insurance may not exceed the premium to be charged by the insurer, as computed at the time the charge to the consumer is determined, conforming to any rate filings required by law and made by the insurer with the [Commissioner] of Insurance.

(2) A creditor who provides consumer credit insurance in relation to open-end credit may calculate the charge to the consumer in each billing cycle by applying the current premium rate to the balance in the manner permitted with respect to finance charges by the provisions on finance charge for consumer credit sales pursuant to open-end credit (Section 2.202).

§ 4.108 [Refund Required; Amount]

(1) Upon prepayment in full of a consumer credit transaction other than a consumer lease by the proceeds of consumer credit insurance, the consumer or his estate is entitled to a refund of any portion of a separate charge for insurance which by reason of prepayment is retained by the creditor or returned to him by the insurer, unless the charge was computed from time to time on the basis of the balances of the consumer's account.

(2) This Article does not require a creditor to grant a refund to the consumer if all refunds due to him under this Article amount to less than $1 and, except as provided in subsection (1), does not require the creditor to account to the consumer for any portion of a separate charge for insurance because:

(a) the insurance is terminated by performance of the insurer's obligation;

(b) the creditor pays or accounts for premiums to the insurer in amounts and at times determined by the agreement between them; or

(c) the creditor receives directly or indirectly under any policy of insurance a gain or advantage not prohibited by law.

(3) Except as provided in subsection (2), the creditor shall promptly make or cause to be made an appropriate refund to the consumer with respect to any separate charge made to him for insurance if:

(a) the insurance is not provided or is provided for a shorter term than that for which the charge to the consumer for insurance was computed; or

(b) the insurance terminates before the end of the term for which it was written because of prepayment in full or otherwise.

(4) A refund required by subsection (3) is appropriate as to amount if it is computed according to a method prescribed or approved by the [Commissioner] of Insurance or a formula filed by the insurer with the [Commissioner] of Insurance at least 30 days before the consumer's right to a refund becomes determinable, unless the method or formula is employed after the [Commissioner] of Insurance notifies the insurer that he disapproves it.

Comment

1.   Subsection (1) concerns a premium for consumer credit insurance, or any part of it, that is not treated by the insurer as earned, even though the insurer has paid benefits for which the premium charge was made. If the premium was the subject of a separate charge to the consumer, a refund must be made. Making the refund is not practicable, however, and is not required, if the charge has been computed on the consumer's outstanding balances. Subsection (2)(a) recognizes that the insurer may, upon performance of its obligation, properly treat the premium as earned.

2.   Subsection (2)(c) permits a creditor to derive from consumer credit insurance gains and advantages not prohibited by law such as dividends and refunds resulting from favorable mortality or morbidity experience with respect to insured consumers, and is predicated on the following conclusions: (1) although the gains and advantages may be large to the creditor, they are relatively insignificant to each insured consumer and the calculating, clerical, and mailing costs of returning them to insured consumers would be unreasonably disproportionate to the amounts involved, and (2) the requirement of Article 4 that premiums for consumer credit insurance be reasonable in relation to benefits (Section 4.203), if properly enforced by the State Insurance [Commissioner], will preclude the possibility of the use of consumer credit insurance as a device by creditors for concealing hidden charges from consumers.

. . .

4.   A consumer is entitled to a refund rather than a credit in the event of a required rebate of any separate charge for insurance. This precludes a creditor from holding a rebate until the contract is sufficiently paid down to have it constitute a prepayment in full which, particularly in long term contracts such as to finance a mobile home, gives the creditor free use of the consumer's money for a substantial period of time.

§ 4.109   [Existing Insurance; Choice of Insurer]

If a creditor requires insurance, upon notice to him the consumer has the option of providing the required insurance through an existing policy of insurance owned or controlled by the consumer, or through a policy to be obtained and paid for by the consumer, but the creditor for reasonable cause may decline the insurance provided by the consumer.

§ 4.110   [Charge for Insurance in Connection With a Deferral, Refinancing, or Consolidation; Duplicate Charges]

(1) A creditor may not contract for or receive a separate charge for insurance in connection with a deferral (Section 2.503), a refinancing (Section 2.504), or a consolidation (Section 2.505), unless:

(a) the consumer agrees at or before the time of the deferral, refinancing, or consolidation that the charge may be made;

(b) the consumer is or is to be provided with insurance for an amount or a term, or insurance of a kind, in addition to that to which he would have been entitled had there been no deferral, refinancing, or consolidation;

(c) the consumer receives a refund or credit on account of any unexpired term of existing insurance in the amount required if the insurance were terminated (Section 4.108); and

(d) the charge does not exceed the amount permitted by this Article (Section 4.107).

(2) A creditor may not contract for or receive a separate charge for insurance which duplicates insurance with respect to which the creditor has previously contracted for or received a separate charge.

PART 2.   CONSUMER CREDIT INSURANCE

§ 4.201   [Term of Insurance]

(1) Consumer credit insurance provided by a creditor may be subject to the furnishing of evidence of insurability satisfactory to the insurer. Whether or not the evidence is required, the term of the insurance shall commence no later than when the consumer becomes obligated to the creditor or when the consumer applies for the insurance, whichever is later, except as follows:

(a) if any required evidence of insurability is not furnished until more than 30 days after the term otherwise would commence, the term may commence on the date the insurer determines the evidence to be satisfactory; or

(b) if the creditor provides insurance not previously provided covering debts previously created, the term may commence on the effective date of the policy.

(2) The originally scheduled term of consumer credit insurance shall extend at least until the due date of the last scheduled payment of the debt, except as follows:

(a) if the insurance relates to an open-end credit account, the term need extend only until payment of the debt under the account and may be sooner terminated after at least 30 days' notice to the consumer; or

(b) if the consumer is informed in writing that the insurance will be written for a specified shorter time, the term need extend only until the end of the specified time.

(3) The term of consumer credit insurance may not extend more than 15 days after the originally scheduled due date of the last scheduled payment of the debt, unless it is extended without additional cost to the consumer or as an incident to a deferral, refinancing, or consolidation.

§ 4.202   [Amount of Insurance]

(1) Except as provided in subsection (2):

(a) in the case of consumer credit insurance providing life coverage, the amount of insurance may not initially exceed the debt and, if the debt is payable in instalments, may not exceed at any time the greater of the scheduled or actual amount of the debt; or

(b) in the case of any other consumer credit insurance, the total amount of periodic benefits payable may not exceed the total of scheduled unpaid instalments of the debt, and the amount of any periodic benefit may not exceed the original amount of debt divided by the number of periodic instalments in which it is payable.

(2) If consumer credit insurance is provided in connection with an open-end credit account, the amounts payable as insurance benefits may be reasonably commensurate with the amount of debt as it exists from time to time. If consumer credit insurance is provided in connection with a commitment to grant credit in the future, the amounts payable as insurance benefits may be reasonably commensurate with the total from time to time of the amount of debt and the amount of the commitment. If the debt or the commitment is primarily for an agricultural purpose and there is no regular schedule of payments, the amounts payable as insurance benefits may equal the total of the initial amount of debt and the amount of the commitment.

Comment

. . .

3. Experience has demonstrated that limitations of these kinds are essential to the effectiveness of the requirement of Section 4.203(2) that premium rates be not unreasonable in relation to the benefits provided by consumer credit insurance.

§ 4.203   [Filing and Approval of Rates and Forms]

(1) A creditor may not use a form or a schedule of premium rates or charges, the filing of which is required by this section, if the [Commissioner] of Insurance has disapproved the form or schedule and has notified the insurer of his disapproval. A creditor may not use a form or schedule unless:

(a) the form or schedule has been on file with the [Commissioner] of Insurance for 30 days, or has earlier been approved by him; and

(b) the insurer has complied with this section with respect to the insurance.

(2) Except as provided in subsection (3), all policies, certificates of insurance, notices of proposed insurance, applications for insurance, endorsements, and riders relating to consumer credit insurance delivered or issued for delivery in this State, and the schedules of premium rates or charges pertaining thereto, shall be filed by the insurer with the [Commissioner] of Insurance. Within 30 days after the filing of any form or schedule, he shall disapprove it if the premium rates or charges are unreasonable in relation to the benefits provided under the form, or if the form contains provisions which are unjust, unfair, inequitable, or deceptive, encourage misrepresentation of the coverage, or are contrary to any provision of the [Insurance Code] or of any rule or regulation promulgated thereunder.

(3) If a group policy of consumer credit insurance has been delivered in another state, the forms to be filed by the insurer with the [Commissioner] of Insurance are the group certificates and notices of proposed insurance. He shall approve them if:

(a) they provide the information that would be required if the group policy were delivered in this State; and

(b) the applicable premium rates or charges do not exceed those established by his rules or regulations.

Comment

... Unlike the NAIC Model Act which is directed primarily to insurers, this section is directed to both creditors and insurers. Moreover, in its formulation as to the relationship of premium rates and charges to the benefits provided, subsection (2) follows New York Insurance Law Section 154.7. That provision, as construed by the New York Court of Appeals in Old Republic Life Insurance Company v. Wikler, 9 N.Y.2d 524, 215 N.Y.S.2d 481, 175 N.E.2d 147 (1961), gives the New York Superintendent of Insurance ample power as to premium rates for credit life and accident and health insurance. Doubt, whether reasonable or not, has been expressed whether equivalent power is conferred by the corresponding formulation of Section 7B of the NAIC Model Act.

. . .

PART 3. PROPERTY AND LIABILITY INSURANCE

§ 4.301 [Property Insurance]

(1) A creditor may not contract for or receive a separate charge for insurance against loss of or damage to property, unless:

(a) the insurance covers a substantial risk of loss of or damage to property related to the credit transaction;

(b) the amount, terms, and conditions of the insurance are reasonable in relation to the character and value of the property insured or to be insured; and

(c) the term of the insurance is reasonable in relation to the terms of credit.

(2) The term of the insurance is reasonable if it is customary and does not extend substantially beyond a scheduled maturity.

(3) With respect to a transaction, except pursuant to open-end credit, a creditor may not contract for or receive a separate charge for insurance against loss of or damage to property, unless the amount financed exclusive of charges for the insurance is $300 or more and the value of the property is $300 or more.

(4) With respect to a transaction pursuant to open-end credit, the Administrator may adopt rules consistent with the principles set out in subsections (1) and (2) prescribing whether, and the conditions under which, a creditor may contract for or receive a separate charge for insurance against loss of or damage to property.

(5) The amounts of $300 in subsection (3) are subject to change pursuant to the provisions on adjustment of dollar amounts (Section 1.106).

§ 4.302   [Insurance on Creditor's Interest Only]

If a creditor contracts for or receives a separate charge for insurance against loss of or damage to property, the risk of loss or damage not willfully caused by the consumer is on the consumer only to the extent of any deficiency in the effective coverage of the insurance, even though the insurance covers only the interest of the creditor.

§ 4.303   [Liability Insurance]

A creditor may not contract for or receive a separate charge for insurance against liability unless the insurance covers a substantial risk of liability arising out of the ownership or use of property related to the credit transaction.

ARTICLE 5.   REMEDIES AND PENALTIES

PART 1.   LIMITATIONS ON CREDITORS' REMEDIES

§ 5.102   [Scope]

This Part applies to actions or other proceedings to enforce rights arising from consumer credit transactions, to extortionate extensions of credit (Section 5.107), and to unconscionability (Section 5.108).

§ 5.103   [Restrictions on Deficiency Judgments]

(1) This section applies to a deficiency on a consumer credit sale of goods or services and on a consumer loan in which the lender is subject to claims and defenses arising from sales and leases (Section 3.405). A consumer is not liable for a deficiency unless the creditor had disposed of the goods in good faith and in a commercially reasonable manner.

(2) If the seller repossesses or voluntarily accepts surrender of goods that were the subject of the sale and in which he has a security interest, the consumer is not personally liable to the seller for the unpaid balance of the debt arising from the sale of a commercial unit of goods of which the cash sale price was $1,750 or less, and the seller is not obligated to resell the collateral unless the consumer has paid 60 per cent or more of the cash price and has not signed after default a statement renouncing his rights in the collateral.

(3) If the seller repossesses or voluntarily accepts surrender of goods that were not the subject of the sale but in which he has a security interest to secure a debt arising from a sale of goods or services or a combined sale of goods and services and the cash price of the sale was $1,750 or less, the consumer is not personally liable to the seller for the unpaid balance of the debt arising from the sale, and the seller's duty to dispose of the collateral is governed by the provisions on disposition of collateral (Part 5 of Article 9) of the Uniform Commercial Code.

(4) If the lender takes possession or voluntarily accepts surrender of goods in which he has a purchase money security interest to secure a debt arising from a consumer loan in which the lender is subject to claims and defenses arising from sales and leases (Section 3.405) and the net proceeds of the loan paid to or for the benefit of the consumer were $1,750 or less, the consumer is not personally liable to the lender for the unpaid balance of the debt arising from that loan and the lender's duty to dispose of the collateral is governed by the provisions on disposition of collateral (Part 5 of Article 9) of the Uniform Commercial Code.

(5) For the purpose of determining the unpaid balance of consolidated debts or debts pursuant to open-end credit, the allocation of payments to a debt shall be determined in the same manner as provided for determining the amount of debt secured by various security interests (Section 3.303).

(6) The consumer may be held liable in damages to the creditor if the consumer has wrongfully damaged the collateral or if, after default and demand, the consumer has wrongfully failed to make the collateral available to the creditor.

(7) If the creditor elects to bring an action against the consumer for a debt arising from a consumer credit sale of goods or services or from a consumer loan in which the lender is subject to claims and defenses arising from sales and leases (Section 3.405), when under this section he would not be entitled to a deficiency judgment if he took possession of the collateral, and obtains judgment:

(a) he may not take possession of the collateral, and

(b) the collateral is not subject to levy or sale on execution or similar proceedings pursuant to the judgment.

(8) The amounts of $1,750 in subsections (2), (3) and (4) are subject to change pursuant to the provisions on adjustment of dollar amounts (Section 1.106).

Comment

1.　Where there has been a default with respect to a secured consumer credit transaction, the rights of the creditor and consumer are controlled by Part 5 (Default) of UCC Article 9 [U.C.C. § 9–501 et seq.], except to the extent that such rights are changed by this Act....

2.　The provisions of the UCC ... are modified to some extent by this section with respect to proceedings to enforce rights arising from consumer credit sales and consumer loans in which the lender is subject to claims and defenses arising from sales and leases (Section 3.405). For both types of transactions, this section adopts the position of that line of cases under the UCC that directly or indirectly deny the creditor a deficiency if the creditor has not disposed of the collateral in good faith and in a commercially reasonable manner. See, e.g., Atlas Thrift Co. v. Horan, 27 Cal.App.3d 999, 104 Cal.Rptr. 315 (Cal.Ct.App.3d Dist.1972).

§ 5.104　[No Garnishment Before Judgment]

Before entry of judgment in an action against a consumer for debt arising from a consumer credit transaction, the creditor may not attach unpaid earnings of the consumer by garnishment or like proceedings.

§ 5.105　[Limitation on Garnishment]

(1) For purposes of this Part:

(a) "disposable earnings" means that part of the earnings of an individual remaining after the deduction from those earnings of amounts required by law to be withheld; and

(b) "garnishment" means any legal or equitable procedure through which earnings of an individual are required to be withheld for payment of a debt.

(2) The maximum part of the aggregate disposable earnings of an individual for any workweek which is subjected to garnishment to enforce payment of a judgment arising from a consumer credit transaction may not exceed the lesser of:

   (a) 25 per cent of his disposable earnings for that week, or

   (b) the amount by which his disposable earnings for that week exceed 40 times the Federal minimum hourly wage prescribed by Section 6(a)(1) of the Fair Labor Standards Act of 1938, U.S.C. tit. 29, § 206(a)(1), in effect at the time the earnings are payable.

In case of earnings for a pay period other than a week, the Administrator shall prescribe by rule a multiple of the Federal minimum hourly wage equivalent in effect to that set forth in paragraph (b).

(3) No court may make, execute, or enforce an order or process in violation of this section.

(4) At any time after entry of a judgment in favor of a creditor in an action against a consumer for debt arising from a consumer credit transaction, the consumer may file with the court his verified application for an order exempting from garnishment pursuant to that judgment, for an appropriate period of time, a greater portion or all of his aggregate disposable earnings for a workweek or other applicable pay period than is provided for in subsection (2). He shall designate in the application the portion of his earnings not exempt from garnishment under this section and other law, the period of time for which the additional exemption is sought, describe the judgment with respect to which the application is made, and state that the designated portion as well as his earnings that are exempt by law are necessary for the maintenance of him or a family supported wholly or partly by the earnings. Upon filing a sufficient application under this subsection, the court may issue any temporary order necessary under the circumstances to stay enforcement of the judgment by garnishment, shall set a hearing on the application not less than [five] nor more than [ten] days after the date of filing of the application, and shall cause notice of the application and the hearing date to be served on the judgment creditor or his attorney of record. At the hearing, if it appears to the court that all or any portion of the earnings sought to be additionally exempt are necessary for the maintenance of the consumer or a family supported wholly or partly by the earnings of the consumer for all or any part of the time requested in the application, the court shall issue an order granting the application to that extent; otherwise it shall deny the application. The order is subject to modification or vacation upon further application of any party to it upon a showing of changed circumstances after a hearing upon notice to all interested parties.

§ 5.106 [No Discharge From Employment for Garnishment]

An employer may not discharge an employee for the reason that a creditor of the employee has subjected or attempted to subject unpaid earnings of the employee to garnishment or like proceedings directed to the employer for the purpose of paying a judgment arising from a consumer credit transaction.

§ 5.107   [Extortionate Extensions of Credit]

(1) If it is the understanding of the creditor and the consumer at the time an extension of credit is made that delay in making repayment or failure to make repayment could result in the use of violence or other criminal means to cause harm to the person, reputation, or property of any person, the repayment of the extension of credit is unenforceable through civil judicial processes against the consumer.

(2) If it is shown that an extension of credit was made at an annual rate exceeding 45 per cent calculated according to the actuarial method and that the creditor then had a reputation for the use or threat of use of violence or other criminal means to cause harm to the person, reputation, or property of any person to collect extensions of credit or to punish the non-repayment thereof, there is prima facie evidence that the extension of credit was unenforceable under subsection (1).

§ 5.108   [Unconscionability; Inducement By Unconscionable Conduct; Unconscionable Debt Collection]

(1) With respect to a transaction that is, gives rise to, or leads the debtor to believe will give rise to, a consumer credit transaction, if the court as a matter of law finds:

(a) the agreement or transaction to have been unconscionable at the time it was made, or to have been induced by unconscionable conduct, the court may refuse to enforce the agreement; or

(b) any term or part of the agreement or transaction to have been unconscionable at the time it was made, the court may refuse to enforce the agreement, enforce the remainder of the agreement without the unconscionable term or part, or so limit the application of any unconscionable term or part as to avoid any unconscionable result.

(2) With respect to a consumer credit transaction, if the court as a matter of law finds that a person has engaged in, is engaging in, or is likely to engage in unconscionable conduct in collecting a debt arising from that transaction, the court may grant an injunction and award the consumer any actual damages he has sustained.

(3) If it is claimed or appears to the court that the agreement or transaction or any term or part thereof may be unconscionable, or that a person has engaged in, is engaging in, or is likely to engage in unconscionable conduct in collecting a debt, the parties shall be afforded a reasonable opportunity to present evidence as to the setting, purpose, and effect of the agreement or transaction or term or part thereof, or of the conduct, to aid the court in making the determination.

(4) In applying subsection (1), consideration shall be given to each of the following factors, among others, as applicable:

(a) belief by the seller, lessor, or lender at the time a transaction is entered into that there is no reasonable probability of payment in full of the obligation by the consumer or debtor;

(b) in the case of a consumer credit sale or consumer lease, knowledge by the seller or lessor at the time of the sale or lease of the inability of the consumer to receive substantial benefits from the property or services sold or leased;

(c) in the case of a consumer credit sale or consumer lease, gross disparity between the price of the property or services sold or leased and the value of the property or services measured by the price at which similar property or services are readily obtainable in credit transactions by like consumers;

(d) the fact that the creditor contracted for or received separate charges for insurance with respect to a consumer credit sale or consumer loan with the effect of making the sale or loan, considered as a whole, unconscionable; and

(e) the fact that the seller, lessor, or lender has knowingly taken advantage of the inability of the consumer or debtor reasonably to protect his interests by reason of physical or mental infirmities, ignorance, illiteracy, inability to understand the language of the agreement, or similar factors.

(5) In applying subsection (2), consideration shall be given to each of the following factors, among others, as applicable:

(a) using or threatening to use force, violence, or criminal prosecution against the consumer or members of his family;

(b) communicating with the consumer or a member of his family at frequent intervals or at unusual hours or under other circumstances so that it is a reasonable inference that the primary purpose of the communication was to harass the consumer;

(c) using fraudulent, deceptive, or misleading representations such as a communication which simulates legal process or which gives the appearance of being authorized, issued, or approved by a government, governmental agency, or attorney at law when it is not, or threatening or attempting to enforce a right with knowledge or reason to know that the right does not exist;

(d) causing or threatening to cause injury to the consumer's reputation or economic status by disclosing information affecting the consumer's reputation for credit-worthiness with knowledge or reason to know that the information is false; communicating with the consumer's employer before obtaining a final judgment against the consumer, except as permitted by statute or to verify the consumer's employment; disclosing to a person, with knowledge or reason to know that the person does not have a legitimate business need for the information, or in any way prohibited by statute, information affecting the consumer's credit or other reputation; or disclosing information concerning the existence of a debt known to be disputed by the consumer without disclosing that fact; and

(e) engaging in conduct with knowledge that like conduct has been restrained or enjoined by a court in a civil action by the Administrator against any person pursuant to the provisions on injunctions against fraudulent or unconscionable agreements or conduct (Section 6.111).

(6) If in an action in which unconscionability is claimed the court finds unconscionability pursuant to subsection (1) or (2), the court shall award reasonable fees to the attorney for the consumer or debtor. If the court does not find unconscionability and the consumer or debtor claiming unconscionability has brought or maintained an action he knew to be groundless, the court shall award reasonable fees to the attorney for the party against whom the claim is made. In determining attorney's fees, the amount of the recovery on behalf of the consumer is not controlling.

(7) The remedies of this section are in addition to remedies otherwise available for the same conduct under law other than this Act, but double recovery of actual damages may not be had.

(8) For the purpose of this section, a charge or practice expressly permitted by this Act is not in itself unconscionable.

Comment

1. Subsections (1) and (3) are derived in significant part from UCC Section 2–302. Subsection (1), as does UCC Section 2–302, provides that a court can refuse to enforce or can adjust an agreement or part of an agreement that was unconscionable on its face at the time it was made. However, many agreements are not in and of themselves unconscionable according to their terms, but they would never have been entered into by a consumer if unconscionable means had not been employed to induce the consumer to agree to the contract. It would be a frustration of the policy against unconscionable contracts for a creditor to be able to utilize unconscionable acts or practices to obtain an agreement. Consequently subsection (1) also gives to the court the power to refuse to enforce an agreement if it finds as a matter of law that it was induced by unconscionable conduct. Finally, subsection (1) includes provisions for court determination of unconscionability in a transaction that a consumer is led to believe will give rise to a consumer credit transaction so that, for example, a seller cannot bind the consumer to a short term sale contract payable in a lump sum on the assurance the seller will secure financing for the consumer, and then inform the consumer financing is unavailable and keep the downpayment or goods traded in as a penalty for non-payment.

In subsection (3) the omission of the adjective "commercial" found in UCC Section 2–302 from the provision concerning the presentation of evidence as to the conduct's or contract's "setting, purpose, and effect" is deliberate. Unlike the UCC, this section is concerned only with transactions involving consumers, and the relevant standard of conduct for purposes of this section is not that which might be acceptable as between knowledgeable merchants but rather that which measures acceptable conduct on the part of a businessman toward a consumer.

2. Subsection (2) provides a consumer remedy for unconscionable conduct in the collection of consumer credit debts. In recent years, there has been much legislative activity in this area. In subjecting this type of creditor conduct to the concept of unconscionability, this section provides a more flexible device for halting multifarious activities than the specific and somewhat rigid treatment contained in other legislation, and follows the lead of Section 6.111 of this Act which affords the Administrator the means to deal with this type of practice. Indeed this section considered as a whole confers on the consumer the ability to obtain relief in basically the same situations the Administrator is authorized to seek relief under Section 6.111, although not necessarily under the same conditions, e.g., no course of conduct is required. The section is not exclusive, however; subsection (7) stipulates that the remedies of this section are in addition to remedies otherwise available for the same conduct under law other than this Act so as to preserve, for example, the developing remedy for abusive debt collection in tort.

3. This section is intended to make it possible for the courts to police conduct which is, and contracts or clauses which are found to be unconscionable. The basic test is whether, in the light of the background and setting of the market, the needs of the particular trade or case, and the condition of the particular parties to the conduct or contract, the conduct involved is, or the contract or clauses involved are so one-sided as to be unconscionable under the circumstances existing at the time the conduct occurs or is threatened or at the time of the making of the contract. The principle is one of the prevention of oppression and unfair surprise and not the disturbance of reasonable allocation of risks or reasonable advantage because of superior bargaining power or position. The particular facts involved in each case are of utmost importance since certain conduct, contracts or contractual provisions may be unconscionable in some situations but not in others. . . .

4. Subsections (4) and (5) list a number of specific factors to be considered on the issue of unconscionability. It is impossible to anticipate all of the factors and considerations which may support a conclusion of unconscionability in a given instance so the listing is not exclusive. The following are illustrative of individual transactions which would entitle a consumer to relief under this section:

Under subsection (4)(a), a sale of goods to a low income consumer without expectation of payment but with the expectation of repossessing the goods sold and reselling them at a profit;

Under subsection (4)(b), a sale to a Spanish speaking laborer-bachelor of an English language encyclopedia set, or the sale of two expensive vacuum cleaners to two poor families sharing the same apartment and one rug;

Under subsection (4)(c), a home solicitation sale of a set of cookware or flatware to a housewife for $375 in an area where a set of comparable quality is readily available on credit in stores for $125 or less;

Under subsection (4)(e), a sale of goods on terms known by the seller to be disadvantageous to the consumer where the written agreement is in English, the consumer is literate only in Spanish, the transaction was negotiated orally in Spanish by the seller's salesman, and the written agreement was neither translated nor explained to the consumer, but the mere fact a consumer has little education and cannot read or write and must sign with an "X" is not itself determinative of unconscionability;

Under subsection (5)(a) and (c), threatening that the creditor will have the consumer thrown in jail and her welfare checks stopped if the debt is not paid.

5. Since the remedies of this section are non-monetary in nature except for the ability to recover actual damages for unconscionable debt collection, subsection (6) authorizes an award of reasonable attorneys fees to the successful consumer or debtor. However, to discourage litigation seeking exculpation from merely bad bargains, provision is also made for recovery by a creditor if the court does not find unconscionability and the consumer's or debtor's action was known by the consumer or debtor to be groundless.

6. Subsection (8) prohibits a finding that a charge or practice expressly permitted by this Act is in itself unconscionable. However, even though a practice or charge is authorized by this Act, the totality of a particular creditor's conduct may show that the practice or charge is part of unconscionable conduct. Therefore, in determining unconscionability, the creditor's total conduct, including that part of his conduct which is in accordance with the provisions of this Act, may be considered.

§ 5.109   [Default]

An agreement of the parties to a consumer credit transaction with respect to default on the part of the consumer is enforceable only to the extent that:

(1) the consumer fails to make a payment as required by agreement; or

(2) the prospect of payment, performance, or realization of collateral is significantly impaired; the burden of establishing the prospect of significant impairment is on the creditor.

§ 5.110   [Notice of Consumer's Right to Cure]

(1) With respect to a consumer credit transaction, after a consumer has been in default for ten days for failure to make a required payment and has not voluntarily surrendered possession of goods that are collateral, a creditor may give the consumer the notice described in this section. A creditor gives notice to the consumer under this section when he delivers the notice to the consumer or mails the notice to him at his residence (subsection (6) of Section 1.201).

(2) Except as provided in subsection (3), the notice shall be in writing and conspicuously state: the name, address, and telephone number of the creditor to whom payment is to be made, a brief identification of the credit transaction, the consumer's right to cure the default, and the amount of payment and date by which payment must be made to cure the default. A notice in substantially the following form complies with this subsection:

(name, address, and telephone number of creditor)

(account number, if any)

(brief identification of credit transaction)

(date)   is the LAST DAY FOR PAYMENT   (amount)   is the AMOUNT NOW DUE

You are late in making your payment(s). If you pay the AMOUNT NOW DUE (above) by the LAST DAY FOR PAYMENT (above), you may continue with the contract as though you were not late. If you do not pay by that date, we may exercise our rights under the law.

If you are late again in making your payments, we may exercise our rights without sending you another notice like this one. If you have questions, write or telephone the creditor promptly.

(3) If the consumer credit transaction is an insurance premium loan, the notice shall conform to the requirements of subsection (2) and a notice in substantially the form specified in that subsection complies with this subsection, except for the following:

(a) in lieu of a brief identification of the credit transaction, the notice shall identify the transaction as an insurance premium loan and each insurance policy or contract that may be cancelled;

(b) in lieu of the statement in the form of notice specified in subsection (2) that the creditor may exercise his rights under the law, the statement that each policy or contract identified in the notice may be cancelled; and

(c) the last paragraph of the form of notice specified in subsection (2) shall be omitted.

Comment

. . .

3. The forms of notice specified in this section are not mandatory. However, Section 5.111 provides that a default consisting of a failure to make a required payment may be cured by the consumer if he makes that payment before the expiration of the minimum period prescribed after written notice of his default and that prior to this time the creditor may not proceed against goods that are collateral or accelerate the maturity of the unpaid debt. This provision prevents the practice of some unscrupulous creditors who repossess collateral when a payment is only a day or two late. It also gives the average consumer the opportunity to rehabilitate his account, bring a billing error to the attention of or present a breach of warranty claim to the creditor, or negotiate a refinancing or deferral arrangement that may be required by a change in his financial circumstances.

. . .

§ 5.111 [Cure of Default]

(1) With respect to a consumer credit transaction, except as provided in subsection (2), after a default consisting only of the consumer's failure to make a required payment, a creditor, because of that default, may neither accelerate maturity of the unpaid balance of the obligation, nor take possession of or otherwise enforce a security interest in goods that are collateral until 20 days after a notice of the consumer's right to cure (Section 5.110) is given, nor, with respect to an insurance premium loan, give notice of cancellation as provided in subsection (4) until 13 days after a notice of the consumer's right to cure (Section 5.110) is given. Until expiration of the minimum applicable period after the notice is given, the

consumer may cure all defaults consisting of a failure to make the required payment by tendering the amount of all unpaid sums due at the time of the tender, without acceleration, plus any unpaid delinquency or deferral charges. Cure restores the consumer to his rights under the agreement as though the defaults had not occurred.

(2) With respect to defaults on the same obligation other than an insurance premium loan and subject to subsection (1), after a creditor has once given a notice of consumer's right to cure (Section 5.110), this section gives the consumer no right to cure and imposes no limitation on the creditor's right to proceed against the consumer or goods that are collateral. For the purpose of this section, in open-end credit, the obligation is the unpaid balance of the account and there is no right to cure and no limitation on the creditor's rights with respect to a default that occurs within 12 months after an earlier default as to which a creditor has given a notice of consumer's right to cure (Section 5.110).

(3) This section and the provisions on waiver, agreements to forego rights, and settlement of claims (Section 1.107) do not prohibit a consumer from voluntarily surrendering possession of goods which are collateral and the creditor from thereafter accelerating maturity of the obligation and enforcing the obligation and his security interest in the goods at any time after default.

(4) If a default on an insurance premium loan is not cured, the lender may give notice of cancellation of each insurance policy or contract to be cancelled. If given, the notice of cancellation shall be in writing and given to the insurer who issued the policy or contract and to the insured. The insurer, within two business days after receipt of the notice of cancellation together with a copy of the insurance premium loan agreement if not previously given to him, shall give any notice of cancellation required by the policy contract, or law and, within ten business days after the effective date of the cancellation, pay to the lender any premium unearned on the policy or contract as of that effective date. Within ten business days after receipt of the unearned premium, the lender shall pay to the consumer indebted upon the insurance premium loan any excess of the unearned premium received over the amount owing by the consumer upon the insurance premium loan.

§ 5.112 [Creditor's Right to Take Possession After Default]

Upon default by a consumer with respect to a consumer credit transaction, unless the consumer voluntarily surrenders possession of the collateral to the creditor, the creditor may take possession of the collateral without judicial process only if possession can be taken without entry into a dwelling and without the use of force or other breach of the peace.

Comment

1. Under Section 9–503 of the UCC a secured creditor has the right to take possession of collateral without resorting to legal process if he can do so without a

breach of the peace. This raises delicate problems when it comes to repossessing furniture or other property that is within a home or apartment. The disputes that result from such a situation are rarely the type that get to the appellate courts for resolution. It is necessary, therefore, to make it clear that dwellings cannot be entered absent the consent of the occupants except under the supervision of the court. . . .

§ 5.113   [Venue]

An action by a creditor against a consumer arising from a consumer credit transaction shall be brought in the [county] of the consumer's residence (subsection (6) of Section 1.201), unless an action is brought to enforce an interest in land securing the consumer's obligation, in which case the action may be brought in the [county] in which the land or a part thereof is located. If the [county] of the consumer's residence has changed, the consumer upon motion may have the action removed to the [county] of his current residence. If the residence of the consumer is not within this State, the action may be brought in the [county] in which the sale, lease, or loan was made. If the initial papers offered for filing in the action on their face show noncompliance with this section, the [clerk] shall not accept them.

§ 5.114   [Complaint; Proof]

(1) In an action brought by a creditor against a consumer arising from a consumer credit transaction, the complaint shall allege the facts of the consumer's default, the amount to which the creditor is entitled, and an indication of how that amount was determined.

(2) A default judgment may not be entered in the action in favor of the creditor unless the complaint is verified by the creditor or sworn testimony, by affidavit or otherwise, is adduced showing that the creditor is entitled to the relief demanded.

Comment

Studies that have been performed of consumers who have legal action brought against them show a high rate of judgments taken by default, in excess of 90 per cent in some urban areas. Modern rules of procedure that require a complaint to contain only the barest of facts contemplate contested litigation. In the event judgment is taken by default there is not enough information in the pleadings to enable the court to enter an accurate award. This section provides that the minimum amount of information necessary to compute the award shall be brought to the attention of the court.

§ 5.115   [Stay of Enforcement of or Relief From Default Judgment]

At any time after entry of a default judgment in favor of a creditor and against a consumer in an action arising from a consumer credit transaction, the court which rendered the judgment, for cause including lack of jurisdiction to render the judgment, and upon motion of a party or its own motion, with notice as the court may direct, may stay enforcement of or relieve the consumer from the judgment by order upon just and equitable conditions.

Comment

The high rate of judgments by default arising out of consumer credit transactions suggests a need for broad judicial discretion to open or void such judgments and re-examine the claims upon which they were rendered in appropriate cases where cause exists. Particularly, the systematic practice by some process servers (usually private process servers) of filing an affidavit of service on the consumer when, in fact, the summons has never been served but stuffed in a "sewer" or elsewhere, cannot furnish the basis for a judgment. However, such discretion is generally associated with courts of general jurisdiction and most actions arising from consumer credit transactions fall within the purview of limited jurisdiction courts. This section is intended to confer that discretion upon any court with jurisdiction to entertain actions arising from consumer credit transactions.

§ 5.116 [Limitation on Enforcement of Security for Supervised Loan]

(1) Except as to a purchase money security interest, this section applies to a security interest in an item of goods other than a motor vehicle which (a) is possessed by a consumer, (b) is being used by him or a member of a family wholly or partly supported by him, (c) is or may be claimed to be exempt from execution on a money judgment under the laws of this State, and (d) is collateral for a supervised loan.

(2) Unless the consumer, after written notice to him of his rights under this section, voluntarily surrenders to the lender possession of any item of goods to which this section applies, the lender, without an order or process of the [   ] court, may not take possession of the item or otherwise enforce the security interest according to its terms. The notice to the consumer shall conform to any rule adopted by the Administrator.

(3) The court may order or authorize process respecting an item of goods to which this section applies only after a hearing upon notice to the consumer of the hearing and his rights at it. The notice shall be as directed by the court. The order or authorization may prescribe appropriate conditions as to payments upon the debt secured or otherwise. The court may not order or authorize process respecting the item if it finds upon the hearing both that the consumer lacks the means to pay all or part of the debt secured and that continued possession and use of the item is necessary to avoid undue hardship for the consumer or a member of a family wholly or partly supported by him.

(4) The court, upon application of the lender or the consumer and notice to the other, and after a hearing and a finding of changed circumstances, may vacate or modify an order or authorization pursuant to this section.

Comment

1. This section responds to the recommendation of the National Commission on Consumer Finance that security interests in household goods should not be allowed in any loan or consolidation transaction if the goods were not acquired by the use of that credit because in the event of default the right to repossess or threat to repossess these goods have far too disruptive an impact on the family life of the debtor to be in the public interest. However, since the section more appropriately directs itself to a limitation on the right to enforce a security interest rather than to the right to contract for one, the purview of it extends beyond household goods to goods that this State has determined are entitled to exemption in accordance with the policy that a debtor should not be deprived of the necessities of life by his creditors if he is unable to pay his debts.

. . .

PART 2.   CONSUMERS' REMEDIES

§ 5.201   [Effect of Violations on Rights of Parties]

(1) If a creditor has violated any provision of this Act applying to collection of an excess charge or amount or enforcement of rights (subsections (2) and (4) of Section 1.201), authority to make supervised loans (Section 2.301), restrictions on interests in land as security (Section 2.307), limitations on the schedule of payments on loan terms for supervised loans (Section 2.308), attorney's fees (Section 2.507), charges for other credit transactions (Section 2.601), disclosure with respect to consumer leases (Section 3.202), notice to consumers (Section 3.203), receipts, statements of account, and evidences of payment (Section 3.206), form of insurance premium loan agreement (Section 3.207), notice to co-signers and similar parties (Section 3.208), security in sales and leases (Section 3.301), no assignments of earnings (Section 3.305), authorizations to confess judgment (Section 3.306), certain negotiable instruments prohibited (Section 3.307), referral sales and leases (Section 3.309), limitations on default charges (Section 3.402), card issuer subject to claims and defenses (subsection (5) of Section 3.403), assignees subject to claims and defenses (subsection (4) of Section 3.404), lenders subject to claims and defenses arising from sales and leases (subsection (4) of Section 3.405), limitation on enforcement of security for supervised loan (Section 5.116), or assurance of discontinuance (Section 6.109), the consumer has a [claim for relief] [cause of action] to recover actual damages and also a right in an action other than a class action, to recover from the person violating this Act a penalty in an amount determined by the court not less than $100 nor more than $1,000. With respect to violations arising from sales or loans made pursuant to open-end credit, no action pursuant to this subsection may be brought more than two years after the violations occurred. With respect to violations arising from other consumer credit transactions, no action pursuant to this subsection may be brought more than one year after the scheduled or accelerated maturity of the debt.

(2) A consumer is not obligated to pay a charge in excess of that allowed by this Act and has a right of refund of any excess charge paid. A refund may not be made by reducing the consumer's obligation by the amount of the excess charge, unless the creditor has notified the consumer that the consumer may request a refund and the consumer has not so requested within 30 days thereafter. If the consumer has paid an amount in excess of the lawful obligation under the agreement, the consumer may recover the excess amount from the person who made the excess charge or from an assignee of that person's rights who undertakes direct collection of payments from or enforcement of rights against consumers arising from the debt.

(3) If a creditor has contracted for or received a charge in excess of that allowed by this Act, or if a consumer is entitled to a refund and a person liable to the consumer refuses to make a refund within a reasonable time after demand, the consumer may recover from the creditor or the person liable in an action other than a class action a penalty in an amount determined by the court not less than $100 nor more than $1,000. With respect to excess charges arising from sales or loans made pursuant to open-end credit, no action pursuant to this subsection may be brought more than two years after the violation or passage of a reasonable time for refund occurs. With respect to excess charges arising from other consumer credit transactions no action pursuant to this subsection may be brought more than one year after the scheduled or accelerated maturity of the debt. For purposes of this subsection, a reasonable time is presumed to be 30 days.

(4) Except as otherwise provided, a violation of this Act does not impair rights on a debt.

(5) If an employer discharges an employee in violation of the provisions prohibiting discharge (Section 5.106), the employee within [ ] days may bring a civil action for recovery of wages lost as a result of the violation and for an order requiring reinstatement of the employee. Damages recoverable shall not exceed lost wages for six weeks.

(6) A creditor is not liable for a penalty under subsection (1) or (3) if he notifies the consumer of a violation before the creditor receives from the consumer written notice of the violation or the consumer has brought an action under this section, and the creditor corrects the violation within 45 days after notifying the consumer. If the violation consists of a prohibited agreement, giving the consumer a corrected copy of the writing containing the violation is sufficient notification and correction. If the violation consists of an excess charge, correction shall be made by an adjustment or refund. The Administrator and any official or agency of this State having supervisory authority over a supervised financial organization shall give prompt notice to a creditor of any violation discovered pursuant to an examination or investigation of the transaction, business, records, and acts of the creditor (Sections 2.305, 6.105 and 6.106).

(7) A creditor may not be held liable in an action brought under this section for a violation of this Act if the creditor shows by a preponderance of evidence that the violation was not intentional and resulted from a bona fide error notwithstanding the maintenance of procedures reasonably adapted to avoid the error.

(8) In an action in which it is found that a creditor has violated this Act, the court shall award to the consumer the costs of the action and to his attorneys their reasonable fees. In determining attorney's fees, the amount of the recovery on behalf of the consumer is not controlling.

Comment

1. Rights that are accompanied by inadequate remedies or no remedy at all and limitations on agreements and practices that do not provide for sufficient penalties or for any penalty at all are generally ineffective to accomplish the desired result. They become little more than exhortatory, easily ignored, and meaningless proclamations. In order to protect rights created and to deter provisions of agreements and practices proscribed by legislation, suitable remedies and penalties must exist. Since an aggrieved party is one of the persons best able to enforce violations of rights and limitations, this section sets forth a right of action in the consumer in the event of violation by the creditor of each section of this Act that does not include its own provision for infraction and better to deter such practices, even of some that do, as in the case of referral sales and leases (Section 3.309).

2. Subsection (1) lists 22 provisions of this Act for the contravention of which actual damages and a penalty could be recovered. The formula used for the penalty is derived from the CCPA (15 U.S.C. § 1601 et seq.) with a minimum and a maximum recovery. Within this range a court may apportion penalties according to the seriousness of the offense and the overall circumstances of each violation. The penalty is designed not only to provide a deterrent to potential violators but also an incentive to a consumer to bring an action when a violation has occurred. Consequently, penalties may not be recovered in a class action, although actual damages may be if the enacting State's rules of civil procedure permits.

3. Subsections (2) and (3) set forth the rights of the consumer with respect to excess charges by the creditor. A refund rather than a credit of an excess charge must be made if requested by the consumer to prevent the creditor from holding a refund due until the contract is sufficiently paid down to have it credited as a prepayment in full. Subsection (3) imposes the same penalty on those who make excess charges or refuse to make refunds to which a consumer is entitled as that for violators of provisions listed in subsection (1). This provision is necessary because if the only rights the consumer had were those provided in subsection (2), it would be worth the creditor's gamble to make excess charges. The only thing that could be lost would be the illegal charge itself, and even that would be unlikely in view of the small percentage of consumers who would seek recovery.

   . . .

5. Violations may occur for a variety of reasons, not all of them necessarily pernicious. Subsection (6) provides that if the creditor becomes aware of a violation, voluntarily notifies the consumer of the violation, and corrects the violation within 45 days after notification, he is not subject to a penalty. Such a provision encourages the autonomous correction of errors and violations. Voluntariness is considered to cease, however, either upon the commencement of an

action against the creditor or upon his receipt of written notification from the consumer of the violation. Consistent with the idea that many errors and violations will be rectified upon knowledge without resort to sanctions subsection (6) also provides that violations discovered pursuant to administrative examination or investigation shall promptly be brought to the attention of the creditor. Probably the most common type of creditor violation results from clerical mistake. No policy would be served in imposing liability for violations due to unintentional bona fide errors which occur notwithstanding the maintenance of procedures reasonably adapted to avoid them, and subsection (7) provides a creditor with an affirmative defense in such cases. Moreover, acts done or omitted in conformity with a rule, interpretation or declaratory ruling of the Administrator ought to result in no liability under this Act, except for refund of an excess charge. This Act so provides, as well as affording ample opportunity for creditor and consumer participation in the formulation and correction of rules. See Sections 6.104(4) and 6.107.

6. Subsection (8) directs the court to award to the consumer the costs of the action and to his attorney his reasonable fees in any action where it is found that a creditor has violated this Act. The direction to award attorney's fees should enable consumers to find attorneys to prosecute their cases, an essential element if the consumers' rights provided by this section are to be enforced, as an attorney is assured of adequate compensation. This is so whether or not the case goes to trial since any settlement offer will have to take the attorney's compensation into account.

PART 3.   CRIMINAL PENALTIES

§ 5.301   [Willful and Knowing Violations]

(1) A supervised lender who willfully and knowingly makes charges in excess of those permitted by the Article on Finance Charges and Related Provisions (Article 2) applying to supervised loans (Part 4) is guilty of a misdemeanor and upon conviction may be sentenced to pay a fine not exceeding $[_____], or to imprisonment not exceeding one year, or both.

(2) A person who, in violation of the provisions of this Act applying to authority to make supervised loans (Section 2.301), willfully and knowingly engages without a license in the business of making supervised loans, or of taking assignments of and undertaking direct collection of payments from and enforcement of rights against consumers arising from supervised loans, is guilty of a misdemeanor and upon conviction may be [sentenced to pay a fine not exceeding $[_____], or to imprisonment not exceeding one year, or both].

(3) A person who willfully and knowingly engages in the business of entering into consumer credit transactions, or of taking assignments of rights against consumers arising therefrom and undertaking direct collection of payments or enforcement of these rights, without complying with the provisions of this Act concerning notification (Section 6.202) or payment of fees (Section 6.203), is guilty of a misdemeanor and upon conviction may be [sentenced to pay a fine not exceeding $100].

ARTICLE 6.   ADMINISTRATION

PART 1.   POWERS AND FUNCTIONS OF ADMINISTRATOR

§ 6.104   [Powers of Administrator;   Reliance on Rules;   Duty to Report]

(1) In addition to other powers granted by this Act, the Administrator within the limitations provided by law may:

(a) receive and act on complaints, take action designed to obtain voluntary compliance with this Act, or commence proceedings on his own initiative;

(b) counsel persons and groups on their rights and duties under this Act;

(c) establish programs for the education of consumers with respect to credit practices and problems;

(d) make studies appropriate to effectuate the purposes and policies of this Act and make the results available to the public; [and]

(e) adopt, amend, and repeal rules to carry out the specific provisions of this Act, but not with respect to unconscionable agreements or fraudulent or unconscionable conduct [;

(f) maintain offices within this State; and]

[(g) appoint any necessary attorneys, hearing examiners, clerks, and other employees and agents and fix their compensation, and authorize attorneys appointed under this section to appear for and represent the Administrator in court].

(2) In addition to other powers granted by this Act, the Administrator shall enforce the Federal Truth in Lending Act, except to the extent otherwise provided by law.

(3) To keep the Administrator's rules in harmony with the rules of administrators in other jurisdictions that enact substantially the Uniform Consumer Credit Code, the Administrator, so far as is consistent with the purposes, policies, and provisions of this Act, shall:

(a) before adopting, amending, and repealing rules, advise and consult with administrators in other jurisdictions that enact substantially the Uniform Consumer Credit Code; and

(b) in adopting, amending, and repealing rules, take into consideration the rules of administrators in other jurisdictions that enact substantially the Uniform Consumer Credit Code.

(4) Except for refund of an excess charge, no liability is imposed under this Act for an act done or omitted in conformity with a rule, interpretation, or declaratory ruling of the Administrator, notwithstanding that after the act or omission the rule, interpretation, or ruling is amended or

repealed or is determined by judicial or other authority to be invalid for any reason.

(5) The Administrator shall report [annually on or before January 1] to the [Governor and Legislature] on the operation of his office, the use of consumer credit in this State, and the problems of persons of small means obtaining credit from persons regularly engaged in extending sales or loan credit. For the purpose of making the report, the Administrator may conduct research and make appropriate studies. The report shall include a description of the examination and investigation procedures and policies of his office, a statement of policies followed in deciding whether to investigate or examine the offices of credit suppliers subject to this Act, a statement of the number and percentages of offices which are periodically investigated or examined, a statement of the types of consumer credit problems of both creditors and consumers which have come to his attention through his examinations and investigations and the disposition of them under existing law, a statement of the extent to which rules of the Administrator pursuant to this Act are not in harmony with the rules of administrators in other jurisdictions that enact substantially the Uniform Consumer Credit Code and the reasons for these variations, and a general statement of the activities of his office and of others to promote the purposes of this Act. The report may not identify the creditors against whom action is taken by the Administrator.

§ 6.106   [Investigatory Powers]

(1) If the Administrator has cause to believe that a person has engaged in conduct or committed an act that is subject to action by the Administrator, he may make an investigation to determine whether the person has engaged in the conduct or committed the act. To the extent necessary for this purpose, he may administer oaths or affirmations, and, upon his own motion or upon request of any party, subpoena witnesses, compel their attendance, adduce evidence, and require the production of, or testimony as to, any matter relevant to the investigation, including the existence, description, nature, custody, condition, and location of any books, documents, or other tangible things and the identity and location of persons having knowledge of relevant facts, or any other matter reasonably calculated to lead to the discovery of admissible evidence.

(2) If the person's records are located outside this State, the person at his option shall make them available to the Administrator at a convenient location within this State or pay the reasonable and necessary expenses for the Administrator or his representative to examine them where they are located. The Administrator may designate representatives, including comparable officials of the State in which the records are located, to inspect them on his behalf.

(3) Upon application by the Administrator showing failure without lawful excuse to obey a subpoena or to give testimony, and upon reasonable

notice to all persons affected thereby, the [   ] court shall grant an order compelling compliance.

(4) The Administrator may not make public the name or identity of a person whose acts or conduct he investigates under this section or the facts disclosed in the investigation, but this subsection does not apply to disclosures in actions or enforcement proceedings pursuant to this Act.

§ 6.107 [Application of [Administrative Procedure Act] [Part on Administrative Procedure and Judicial Review]]

Except as otherwise provided, the [State Administrative Procedure Act] [Part on Administrative Procedure and Judicial Review (Part 4) of this Article] applies to and governs all administrative action taken by the Administrator pursuant to this Article.

Comment

If the enacting State has an adequate State administrative procedure act reference should be made to it in this section. Otherwise Part 4 of Article 6 [Section 6.401 et seq.] should be enacted and referred to here. Brackets and bracketed language in this section and its caption should be retained or deleted dependent upon which course is followed. . . .

§ 6.108 [Administrative Enforcement Orders]

(1) After notice and hearing the Administrator may order a creditor or a person acting in his behalf to cease and desist from violating this Act. A respondent aggrieved by an order of the Administrator may obtain judicial review of the order and the Administrator may obtain an order of the court for enforcement of his order in the [   ] court. The proceeding for review or enforcement is initiated by filing a petition in the court. Copies of the petition shall be served upon all parties of record.

(2) Within 30 days after service of the petition for review upon the Administrator, or within any further time the court allows, the Administrator shall transmit to the court the original or a certified copy of the entire record upon which the order is based, including any transcript of testimony, which need not be printed. By stipulation of all parties to the review proceeding, the record may be shortened. After hearing, the court may (a) reverse or modify the order if the findings of fact of the Administrator are clearly erroneous in view of the reliable, probative, and substantial evidence on the whole record, (b) grant any temporary relief or restraining order it deems just, and (c) enter an order enforcing, modifying, and enforcing as modified, or setting aside in whole or in part the order of the Administrator, or remanding the case to the Administrator for further proceedings.

(3) An objection not urged at the hearing shall not be considered by the court unless the failure to urge the objection is excused for good cause shown. A party may move the court to remand the case to the Administrator in the interest of justice for the purpose of adducing additional specified and material evidence and seeking findings thereon upon good cause shown for the failure to adduce this evidence before the Administrator.

(4) The jurisdiction of the court shall be exclusive and its final judgment or decree is subject to review by the [　] court in the same manner and form and with the same effect as in appeals from a final judgment or decree in a [special proceeding]. The Administrator's copy of the testimony shall be available at reasonable times to all parties for examination without cost.

(5) A proceeding for review under this section shall be initiated within 30 days after a copy of the order of the Administrator is received. If no proceeding is so initiated, the Administrator may obtain an order of the court for enforcement of his order upon showing that his order was issued in compliance with this section, that no proceeding for review was initiated within 30 days after a copy of the order was received, and that the respondent is subject to the jurisdiction of the court.

(6) With respect to unconscionable agreements or fraudulent or unconscionable conduct by the respondent, the Administrator may not issue an order pursuant to this section but may bring a civil action for an injunction (Section 6.111).

§ 6.109   [Assurance of Discontinuance]

If it is claimed that a person has engaged in conduct which could be subject to an order by the Administrator (Sections 2.303 and 6.108) or by a court (Sections 6.110, 6.111, and 6.112), the Administrator may accept an assurance in writing that the person will not engage in the same or similar conduct in the future. The assurance may include any of the following: stipulations for the voluntary payment by the creditor of the costs of investigation or of an amount to be held in escrow as restitution to debtors aggrieved by past or future conduct of the creditor or to cover costs of future investigation, or admissions of past specific acts by the creditor or that those acts violated this Act or other statutes. A violation of an assurance of discontinuance is a violation of this Act.

§ 6.110   [Injunctions Against Violations of Act]

The Administrator may bring a civil action to restrain any person from violating this Act and for other appropriate relief including but not limited to the following: to prevent a person from using or employing practices prohibited by this Act, to reform contracts to conform to this Act and to rescind contracts into which a creditor has induced a consumer to enter by conduct violating this Act, even though a consumer is not a party to the action. An action under this section may be joined with an action under the provisions on civil actions by Administrator (Section 6.113).

§ 6.111   [Injunctions Against Unconscionable Agreements and Fraudulent or Unconscionable Conduct Including Debt Collection]

(1) The Administrator may bring a civil action to restrain a person to whom this Part applies from engaging in a course of:

(a) making or enforcing unconscionable terms or provisions of consumer credit transactions;

(b) fraudulent or unconscionable conduct in inducing consumers to enter into consumer credit transactions;

(c) conduct of any of the types specified in paragraph (a) or (b) with respect to transactions that give rise to or that lead persons to believe will give rise to consumer credit transactions; or

(d) fraudulent or unconscionable conduct in the collection of debts arising from consumer credit transactions.

(2) In an action brought pursuant to this section the court may grant relief only if it finds:

(a) that the respondent has made unconscionable agreements or has engaged or is likely to engage in a course of fraudulent or unconscionable conduct;

(b) that the respondent's agreements have caused or are likely to cause or the conduct of the respondent has caused or is likely to cause injury to consumers or debtors; and

(c) that the respondent has been able to cause or will be able to cause the injury primarily because the transactions involved are credit transactions.

(3) In applying subsection (1)(a), (b), and (c), consideration shall be given to each of the factors specified in the provisions on unconscionability with respect to a transaction that is, gives rise to, or that a person leads the debtor to believe will give rise to, a consumer credit transaction (subsection (4) of Section 5.108), among others.

(4) In applying subsection (1)(d), consideration shall be given to each of the factors specified in the provisions on unconscionability with respect to the collection of debts arising from consumer credit transactions (subsection (5) of Section 5.108), among others.

(5) In an action brought pursuant to this section, a charge or practice expressly permitted by this Act is not in itself unconscionable.

Comment

. . .

2. One purpose of this section is to afford the Administrator a means of dealing with new patterns of fraudulent or unconscionable conduct unforeseen and, perhaps, unforeseeable at the writing of this Act. Another is to give him a more flexible remedy for halting reprehensible creditor practices that have been specifically and somewhat rigidly treated in previous consumer credit legislation. For instance, this Act has no specific prohibition against the creditor's allowing the consumer to sign a credit agreement containing blanks. In some situations there may be legitimate reasons for a contract to contain blanks at the time of signing. However, if the creditor deliberately leaves blanks to be filled in after the consum-

er's signature and without his consent, the Administrator may seek to restrain the practice as fraudulent or unconscionable conduct under this section.

.   .   .

§ 6.112   [Temporary Relief]

With respect to an action brought to enjoin violations of the Act (Section 6.110) or unconscionable agreements or fraudulent or unconscionable conduct (Section 6.111), the Administrator may apply to the court for appropriate temporary relief against a defendant, pending final determination of the action.   The court may grant appropriate temporary relief.

§ 6.113   [Civil Actions By Administrator]

(1) After demand, the Administrator may bring a civil action against a creditor to recover actual damages sustained and excess charges paid by one or more consumers who have a right to recover explicitly granted by this Act.   In a civil action under this subsection, penalties may not be recovered by the Administrator.   The court shall order amounts recovered under this subsection to be paid to each consumer or set off against his obligation.   A consumer's action, except a class action, takes precedence over a prior or subsequent action by the Administrator with respect to the claim of that consumer.   A consumer's class action takes precedence over a subsequent action by the Administrator with respect to claims common to both actions, but the Administrator may intervene.   An Administrator's action on behalf of a class of consumers takes precedence over a consumer's subsequent class action with respect to claims common to both actions. Whenever an action takes precedence over another action under this subsection, the latter action may be stayed to the extent appropriate while the precedent action is pending and dismissed if the precedent action is dismissed with prejudice or results in a final judgment granting or denying the claim asserted in the precedent action.   A defense available to a creditor in a civil action brought by a consumer is available to him in a civil action brought under this subsection.

(2) The Administrator may bring a civil action against a creditor or a person acting in his behalf to recover a civil penalty of no more than $5,000 for repeatedly and intentionally violating this Act.   A civil penalty pursuant to this subsection may not be imposed for a violation of this Act occurring more than two years before the action is brought or for making unconscionable agreements or engaging in a course of fraudulent or unconscionable conduct.

(3) The Administrator may bring a civil action against a creditor for failure to file notification in accordance with the provisions on notification (Section 6.202) or to pay fees in accordance with the provisions on fees (Section 6.203) to recover the fees the defendant has failed to pay and a civil penalty in an amount determined by the court not exceeding the greater of three times the amount of fees the defendant has failed to pay or $1,000.

§ 6.114 [Jury Trial]

The Administrator has no right to trial by jury in an action brought by him under this Act.

§ 6.115 [Consumer's Remedies Not Affected]

The grant of powers to the Administrator in this Article does not affect remedies available to consumers under this Act or under other principles of law or equity.

Comment

1. It is not the intention of the grant of powers to the Administrator or of any of the other provisions of this Act dealing with consumers' remedies to diminish in any way the availability of consumers' remedies under other principles of law or equity or to impede the development of judicially created law in this area. For example, the individual consumer has a cause of action under Section 5.201(2) and (3) to recover any charges in excess of those permitted in the Act and to recover a penalty in certain cases, and the Administrator may also bring an action under Section 6.113 to recover excess charges on behalf of consumers. Whether or not an action to recover excess charges by a class of private parties would lie depends upon the State law with respect to class actions. This Act does not specifically authorize such class actions nor does it preclude them. See also Section 5.105, Comment 7.

2. Various other consumers' remedies provided by other applicable law are not affected by this Act. Examples include the UCC provisions concerning the buyer's revocation of acceptance of goods delivered (UCC Section 2–608), the buyer's right to cancel the contract and to take a security interest in the goods delivered (UCC Section 2–711), the buyer's right to incidental and consequential damages (UCC Section 2–715), and the buyer's remedies for fraud (UCC Section 2–721). So, too, the limitations on contract provided for in the UCC in regard to penalties, liquidated damages, and limitation of remedies (UCC Sections 2–718 and 2–719) continue to apply to transactions governed by this Act.

†